Tourism

Tourism
The State of the Art

Edited by

A. V. Seaton
The Scottish Hotel School, University of Strathclyde, UK

JOHN WILEY & SONS

Chichester · New York · Brisbane · Toronto · Singapore

Other Wiley Editorial Offices

John Wiley & Sons, Inc., 605 Third Avenue,
New York, NY 10158-0012, USA

Jacaranda Wiley Ltd, 33 Park Road, Milton,
Queensland 4064, Australia

John Wiley & Sons (Canada) Ltd, 22 Worcester Road,
Rexdale, Ontario M9W 1L1, Canada

John Wiley & Sons (SEA) Pte Ltd, 37 Jalan Pemimpin #05-04,
Block B, Union Industrial Building, Singapore 2057

Library of Congress Cataloging-in-Publication Data

Tourism: the state of the art/edited by A. V. Seaton.
    p. cm.
Includes bibliographical references.
ISBN 0-471-95092-0
1. Tourist trade—Congresses. I. Seaton, A. V.
G154.9.T6915 1994
338.4′791—dc20   94-9552
                             CIP

British Library Cataloguing in Publication Data

A catalogue record for this book is available from the British Library

ISBN 0-471-95092-0

Typset in 10/11pt Times by Dobbie Typesetting Limited, Tavistock, Devon
Printed and bound in Great Britain by Bookcraft (Bath) Ltd

Contents

Part 2: The Tourism Industry

Part 3: Tourism Marketing and Research

Part 4: Tourism, the Public Sector and Scotland

Introduction Ronnie Smith and Brian Hay 470

Part 5: Tourism and Human Resource Management

Introduction Eddie Brogan and Roy C. Wood 550

Part 6: Tourism and the Environment

Introduction Hugh Somerville and Rory MacLellan 636

Part 7: Tourism and Society

Introduction A. V. Seaton 720

Contributors

G. Archdale ASW Consulting, The Old School House, Enmore Green, Shaftsbury SP7 8LP, UK

S. Baier Vorarlberg State Tourist Board, Postbox 302, Bregenz A-6901, Austria

S. Bakalis Department of Applied Economics, Victoria University of Technology, PO Box 14428, Melbourne Mail Centre, Melbourne 3000, Australia

T. Baum Buckingham University, Hunter Street, Buckingham MK18 1EG, UK

O. Bennett Greene Belfield-Smith Division, Touche Ross Management Consultants, 133 Fleet Street, London EC4A 2TR, UK

S. Berry University of Brighton, DSSM, 49 Dalrey Road, Eastbourne, East Sussex BN20 7UR, UK

S. Bleasdale School of Geography and Environmental Management, Faculty of Social Sciences and Education, Queensway, Enfield, Middlesex EN3 4SF, UK

E. Brogan Scottish Enterprise, 120 Bothwell Street, Glasgow G2 7JP, UK

G. Brown The Centre for Tourism, Southern Cross University, PO Box 157, Lismore, NSW 2480, Australia

M. Brown School of Food and Accommodation Management, Duncan of Jordanstone College of Art, University of Dundee, Perth Road, Dundee DD1 4HT, UK

D. Buhalis University of Surrey, Department of Management Studies for Tourism and Hotel Industries, Guildford GU2 5XH, UK

R. W. Butler Department of Geography, The University of Western Ontario, London, Ontario N6A 5C2, Canada

L. C. Cameron Monash University, Syme Business School, Gippsland Campus, Switchback Road, Churchill, Victoria 3842, Australia

C. Cooper University of Surrey, Department of MSTHI, Guildford, Surrey GU2 5XH, UK

G. M. S. Dann The University of the West Indies, Cave Hill Campus, PO Box 64, Bridgetown, Barbados, West Indies

R. Davidson 3 Rue Sainte-Anne, Montpellier 34000, France

P. Desinano Centro Italiano di studi superiori sul turismo e sulla promozione turistica, Universita di Perugia, Via S Francesco 197a (Palazzo Bernabei), Assisi 06081, Italy

P. U. C. Dieke University of Strathclyde, Scottish Hotel School, Curran Building, 94 Cathedral Street, Glasgow G4 0LG, UK

R. Doswell 26 Clarendon Way, Tunbridge Wells, Kent TN2 5LD, UK

A. J. Durie The Centre for Business History in Scotland, University Gardens, University of Glasgow, Glasgow G12 8QQ, UK

D. A. Edgar Department of Hospitality and Tourism, Napier University, 10 Colinton Road, Edinburgh EH10 5DT, UK

The main contact only for each chapter is listed.

G. Evans Centre for Leisure and Tourism Studies, University of North London, Stapleton House, 277–281 Holloway Road, London N7 8HN, UK

W. Faché Universiteit Gent, Henri Dunantlaan 2, B-9000 Gent, Belgium

M. Foley Glasgow Caledonian University, 1 Park Drive, Glasgow, UK

A. H. Forbes Bolton Business School, BIHE, Deane Campus, Deane Road, Bolton BL3 5AB, UK

L. France Department of Environment, University of Northumbria at Newcastle, Lipman Building, Newcastle NE1 8ST, UK

E. Frew Monash University, Syme School of Business, Monash University, Gippsland Campus, Switchback road, Churchill, Victoria 3842, Australia

F. Amor Garroset Institut Turistic Valencia, Aragon 30, Planta 8, Valencia 46021, Spain

D. A. C. Gee University of Strathclyde, The Scottish Hotel School, Curran Building, 94 Cathedral Street, Glasgow G4 0LG, UK

B. Goodall Tourism Research & Policy Unit, Department of Geography, University of Reading, Whiteknights, PO Box 227, Reading RG5 2AB, UK

J. Greenwood Project Manager, Dartmoor Area Tourism Initiative, c/o Spot Cottage, 3 Orchard Terrace, Buckfastleigh, South Devon TQ11 0AH, UK

C. A. Gunn Texas A & M University, Department of Recreation, Park and Tourism Sciences, 1602 Glade Street, College Station, Texas 77840, USA

M. Hart University of Las Palmas de Gran Canaria, C/Alfonso XIII, No. 2, Las Palmas 35003, Gran Canaria

R. Haylock RCI Europe Ltd, Kettering Parkway, Kettering, Northants NN15 6EY, UK

A. Holden University of North London, The Business School, Stapleton House, 277–281 Holloway Road, London N7 8HN, UK

H. L. Hughes Manchester Metropolitan University, Department of Hotel, Catering and Tourism, Old Hall Lane, Manchester M14 6HR, UK

E. Inskeep 6529 Caminito Catalan, La Jolla, California 92037, USA

C. L. Jenkins University of Strathclyde, The Scottish Hotel School, Curran Building, 94 Cathedral Street, Glasgow G4 0LG, UK

C. Jones Department of Organisation Studies, Lancashire Business School, University of Central Lancashire, Preston, Lancashire PR1 2HE, UK

B. M. Josiam Department of Hospitality and Tourism, University of Wisconsin-Stout, #442, School of Home Economics, Menomonie, Wisconsin 54751-0790, USA

B. King Department of Hospitality and Tourism Management, 299 York Street, S. Melbourne, Victoria 3205, Australia

P. Komilis The Centre of Planning and Economic Research, 22 Hippokratous Street, Athens, Greece

M. Korzay Bogosici University, Tourism Programme POB7, Bebek, Istanbul, Turkey

S. F. M. Li Hong Kong Polytechnic, Hung Hom, Kowloon, Hong Kong

Z.-H. Liu Faculty of Tourism & Hospitality, Cardiff Institute of Higher Education, Colchester Avenue, Cardiff CF3 7XR, UK

P. Long Centre for Travel and Tourism, New College Durham, Neville's Cross Centre, Durham DH1 4SY, UK

R. Lucas The Manchester Metropolitan University, Department of Hotel, Catering and Tourism Management, Hollings Faculty, Old Hall Lane, Manchester M14 5HR, UK

G. McBoyle Professor of Geography, University of Waterloo, Department of Geography, Waterloo, Ontario N2L 3G1, Canada

F. McMahon Dublin Institute of Technology, College of Catering, Cathal Brugha Street, Dublin 1, Ireland

V. M. Monfort The Valencian Tourist Board, Avda. Aragon 30-Planta 8, Valencia 46021, Spain

D. Munro Scot World Travel, 12 William Street, Edinburgh EH3 7NH, UK

R. M. Olesen The University of the Cariboo, 900 College Drive, Box 3010, Camloops V2C 5N3, British Columbia

S. J. Page Canterbury Christ Church College, Travel, Lifestyles and Health Project, Centre for Tourism Studies, Canterbury Christ Church College, Canterbury, Kent CT1 1QU, UK

A. Pedreño Fundación Cavanilles, University of Alicante, Rectorado, AP Correos 99, Alicante E-03080, Spain

A. Phelps Department of International Studies, The Nottingham Trent University, Clifton Lane, Nottingham NG11 8NS, UK

R. Prentice Queen Margaret College, Clerwood Terrace, Edinburgh EH12 8TS, UK

S. M. Pringle Department of Hospitality and Tourism, Napier University, 10 Colinton Road, Edinburgh EH10 5DT, UK

Y. Reisinger Faculty of Business, School of Tourism and Hotel Management, Griffith University, Gold Coast Campus, Parklands Drive, PMB 50 Gold Coast Mail Centre, Southport, Queensland 4217, Australia

G. Richards Tilburg University, Department of Leisure Studies, Tilburg University, Postbus 90153, Tilburg 5000 LE, The Netherlands

R. W. Riley Department of Health, Physical Education and Recreation, Illinois State University, 213 McCormick Hall, Normal, Illinois 61761, USA

D. W. Robinson Faculty of Natural Resources and Environmental Studies, University of Northern British Columbia, Outdoor Recreation and Tourism Programme, PO Bag 1950, Station A, Prince George BC V2L 5P2, Canada

W. S. Roehl Department of Tourism & Convention Administration, W F Harrah College of Hotel Administration, University of Nevada, Las Vegas, 4505 Maryland Parkway, Las Vegas, Nevada 89154-6023, USA

C. Ryan Department of Management Systems, Massey University, Private Bag 11222, Palmerston North, New Zealand

N. Saleem Sheffield Hallam University, School of Leisure and Food Management, Totley Hall Lane, Totley, Sheffield S17 4AB, UK

U. A. Schlentrich University of Strathclyde, The Scottish Hotel School, Curran Building, 94 Cathedral Street, Glasgow G4 0LG, UK

A. V. Seaton University of Strathclyde, The Scottish Hotel School, Curran Building, 94 Cathedral Street, Glasgow G4 0LG, UK

J. R. Seldon The University College of the Cariboo, 900 College Drive, Box 3010, Kamloops V2C 5N3, British Columbia

T. Selwyn Roehampton Institute, Southlands College, Wimbledon Parkside, London SW19 5NN, UK

H. Sezer Oxford Brookes School of Business, Wheatley Campus, Wheatley, Oxford OX33 1HX, UK

O. Sletvold Department of Tourism Studies, Finmark College, Follums Veg, Alta N-9500, Norway

E. Smeral Austrian Institute of Economic Research, PO Box 91, A-1103, Vienna A1103, Austria

R. Smith University of Strathclyde, The Scottish Hotel School, Curran Building, 94 Cathedral Street, Glasgow, G4 0LG, UK

T. Snaith Leisure and Environmental Management, The Buckinghamshire College, Queen Alexandra Road, High Wycombe, Bucks HP11 2JZ, UK

H. Somerville British Airways Environment Branch, S285 PO Box 10, Heathrow Airport, London TW6 2JA, UK

T. Stevens Faculty of Leisure, Tourism and Healthcare Studies, Swansea Institute of Higher Education, Mount Pleasant, Swansea SA1 6ED, Wales

D. Stewart-David University of Northumbria, Northumberland Building, Newcastle NE1 8JT, UK

J. Swarbrooke The Centre for Tourism, Sheffield Hallam University, City Campus, Pond Street, Sheffield S1 1WB, UK

J. S. Swift Staffordshire University, College Road, Stoke-on-Trent ST4 2DE, UK

J. Towner University of Northumbria, Department of Environment, University of Northumbria, Newcastle upon Tyne NE1 8ST, UK

A. S. Travis THR Consultancy, Phare Tourism Programme, Institute of Tourism, UL Merliniego 9A, Warsaw 02-511, Poland

C. S. Van Doren Texas A & M University, Department of Recreation, Park and Tourism Sciences, College Station TX 77843, USA

S. R. C. Wanhill School of Consumer Studies, Tourism and Hospitality Management, University of Wales, 65–67 Park Place, Cardiff CF1 3AS, UK

B. Wheeller The University of Birmingham, Edgbaston, Birmingham B15 2TT, UK

E. Wickens Oxford Brookes School of Business, Wheatley Campus, Wheatley, Oxford OX33 1HX, UK

P. C. Wight 9th Floor, Sterling Place, 9940-106 Street, Edmonton, Alberta T5X 2P6, Canada

P. F. Wilkinson, PhD York University, Faculty of Environmental Studies, 355 Lumbers Building, 4700 Keele Street, North York, Ontario M3J 1P3, Canada

A. P. Williams Hong Kong Polytechnic, Hung Hom, Kowloon, Hong Kong

D. Wilson Department of Social Anthropology, The Queen's University of Belfast, Belfast BT7 1NN, Northern Ireland

R. C. Wood University of Strathclyde, Scottish Hotel School, Curran Building, 94 Cathedral Street, Glasgow G4 0NG, UK

General Editor's Preface

This book attempts to provide an end of millennium overview of theory and practice within one of the newest and fastest growing fields of study, tourism planning. The book is an edited compilation of tourism articles originally delivered as papers at the international conference, 'Tourism—the state of the art', convened in Glasgow in 1994. The conference came about to mark the anniversaries of two of Scotland's major tourism institutions.

In 1994 the Scottish Hotel School at the University of Strathclyde celebrated its 50th anniversary, making it one of the oldest tourism and hospitality centres of higher education in the world. Opening its doors to students for the first time in October 1944, the School came into existence at a time of wartime crisis which had resulted in the damage or destruction of 24 000 hotels and licensed houses in Britain. A year earlier a government commission had commented on the 'almost complete unanimity among tourist and travel agencies that generally the standard of amenities in British hotels compares unfavourably with those in foreign countries' (Nicolson, 1947). The School was founded to improve the provision of tourism and hospitality education in Scotland (see Gee's short history of the Scottish Hotel School which follows this preface).

The second 1994 tourism anniversary was the 25th anniversary of the Scottish Tourist Board, established as Scotland's national tourism agency by Act of Parliament in 1969, along with the other UK national tourist boards. The 1969 legislation was the first time tourism had been recognised by Act of Parliament in Britain, putting public sector tourism support on the firmest footing it had achieved since an older institution, the British Travel Association, was founded by Lord Hacking in 1929.

The years constituting the histories of the Scottish Hotel School and the Scottish Tourist Board were ones in which tourism, as a specialist managerial and academic field, was effectively created in Britain. Though tourism had grown between and after the wars it had never been considered an industry worthy of systematic study or specialist managerial development. The first major British book on tourism was published in 1933 (Ogilvie, 1933) but until the late-1960s the main tourism publications were

historical, statistical or economic analyses, often of individual countries, rather than managerial texts. As late as 1975 one writer estimated that not more than half a dozen tourism texts had appeared in the English language in Britain or North America in the previous five years (Wahab, 1975). The journal situation was even worse with no periodical devoted to tourism except for AIEST's *Tourism Revue*, founded in 1946, and the occasional monographs assembled and disseminated from the Centre des Hautes Etudes Touristiques in Aix-en-Provence (which still flourishes today).

In the 1970s the situation began to change. The first general managerial texts on the tourism business began to appear (McIntosh, 1972; Burkhart and Medlik, 1974; Lundberg, 1974). Through the 1980s the literature mushroomed, fuelled by the increasing importance of tourism to post-industrial Western economies, and also by the perceived strategic role of tourism as a 'passport to growth' for developing countries which had no ready-made manufacturing base from which to take off. By the early 1990s there were seven refereed, international tourism journals (the *Journal of Travel and Tourism Marketing*, in addition to the six appraised by Van Doren, Koh and McCahill, Chapter 31 in this book), and the field had grown so much it had begun to split into specialisms (marketing, development, the environment, etc).

This rapid expansion in 25 years naturally provokes the question, 'So what is the state of the art in tourism today?' For two institutions which had been active throughout its period of major growth, convening a conference trying to answer that question seemed a useful way of marking their anniversaries. The decision was taken in 1991 to convene a major four-day conference in 1994 around the theme, 'Tourism—the state of the art'. The next step was to define what 'state of the art' meant. An attempt to do this was provided in a briefing sheet sent out to potential contributors expressing an interest in the conference. The brief specified four desiderata for papers:

● each article had to be on some substantial tourism topic/issue,

- each article had to include a definition/orientating discussion of the field,
- each article had to include a short history of the topic's development, referencing key contributors to knowledge and debate, and/or
- a report of a piece of significant, recent research in the chosen topic/issue area.

In vetting the abstracts and final papers, the conference committee occasionally extended these criteria when papers demonstrated merits in areas which were not explicitly specified, but were still deemed to constitute 'state of the art' qualities. The criteria were broadened to include: global case studies; best practice summaries; appraisals of new developments in tourism products, practices and technologies; papers which raised new issues or looked at old ones in an original light.

The accepted papers were grouped around seven principal workshop themes for conference purposes as follows:

- Tourism and Development
- The Tourism Industry
- Tourism Marketing and Research
- Tourism, the Public Sector and Scotland
- Tourism and Human Resource Management
- Tourism and the Environment
- Tourism and Society

These groupings have been retained as sectional divisions for the book.

The groupings clearly rang bells with industry as a number of sponsors from major public and private sector organisations came forward to support the individual workshops. In addition to our principal sponsor, the Scottish Tourist Board, the sponsors were: Scottish Enterprise, the Forte Organisation, John Wiley International, British Airways, Glasgow Development Agency and Glasgow City Council, as well as the University of Strathclyde itself.

By the time the deadline for accepted papers closed those tabled comprised contributions from America, Asia, Canada, Eastern and Western Europe, Australia and New Zealand. Their authors comprised a mix of established international tourism specialists and newcomers—a balance we had hoped to achieve. We believe that the book fully meets our original aim of providing a 'state of the art' tourism symposium that will retain its value into the new millennium.

February 1994
A. V. Seaton

References

Burkhart, C. and Medlik, R. (1974) *Tourism*, Heinemann, London.

Lundberg, Donald E. (1974) *The Tourism Business*, CBI, Massachusetts.

McIntosh, Robert (1972) *Tourism Principles, Practices, Philosophies*, Grid, Inc.

Nicolson, Nigel (1947) 'Come to Britain: the revival of the tourist industry', in Weidenfield, A. G. (Ed.), *The World Off Duty*, Contact, London, pp. 102–104.

Ogilvie, Sir Frederick (1933) *The Tourist Movement*, London.

Wahab, S. (1975) *Tourism Management*, Tourism International Press, Turin.

The Scottish Hotel School—the first fifty years

D. A. C. GEE

In the beginning ...

At noon on 6 June 1944, Winston Churchill announced to the House of Commons that the D-Day landings had begun and thus, with operation 'Overlord', the tide of victory in the war against Hitler was set in train. In Glasgow some four days earlier, the Director of The Glasgow and West of Scotland Commercial College, Dr T. Pettigrew Young, reported to the Governors that he had been approached by the Hotels and Restaurants Association, acting in consultation with the Scottish Education Department, to establish a School of Hotel Management within the college. So it was that two bold and imaginative schemes were set in motion one of which was to change the course of world history and the other which, in its own way, was to substantially influence the development of hotel and catering education in the United Kingdom.

Within about two weeks of its initial announcement, a draft scheme of work had been submitted and approved by the College authorities and immediate efforts made to recruit suitable candidates, which even involved radio publicity through the BBC. By the autumn of 1944, the liberation of Western Europe was well advanced and in Glasgow the first students took up their studies in hotel management.

Why a history?

In compiling a history of an institution, such as the Scottish Hotel School, one must attempt to explain those features responsible for its obvious success; in fifty years the Scottish Hotel School has many achievements to its credit. Fundamental to these achievements is people—staff, students and others—who have been responsible for initiating and shaping its development. Thus this brief history attempts to focus principally on people—their influence on academic and administrative developments— on visiting personalities, on staff and students and their publications, research and social activities, on former students, on personal reminiscences—and on the next fifty years . . .

From small beginnings ...

The Scottish Hotel School today owes its existence to a small group of businessmen: principally Etienne Vacher, then Supervisor of British Transport Hotels in Scotland, Arthur Towle, Chairman of the Scottish Division of the Hotels and Restaurants Association and second son of Sir William Towle, himself a leading force in the hotel industry, and Donald Grant, a Glasgow restaurateur, who first approached Tom Johnston of St Andrew's House in Edinburgh with a proposal to establish a School of Hotel Management. The Scottish Office immediately recognised the value of the group's proposal as the key to tourism development for Scotland. The speed and enthusiasm which Dr Pettigrew Young and the Governors of the Commercial College subsequently showed for the proposal is both a measure of the determined approach taken by the Hotel Association and the Scottish Office coupled with a desire by Dr Pettigrew Young in the closing year of the war to revive college activities, many of which had been eclipsed with the outbreak of war in 1939.

'The growing importance of Scotland as a tourist attraction, and as a stopping place between the countries of America and the continent of Europe has focussed public attention upon the provision of up-to-date hotel facilities and service throughout this country.' These opening remarks prefaced the first prospectuses for the Scottish School of Hotel Management when in 1944 courses of instruction extending over a period of two years were launched. During the first year (September to May) class instruction was given on four days per week at the Commercial College, Pitt Street, whilst the other two days were devoted to practical work in selected hotels (note the six-day working week at this time). Our founding businessmen felt that the excellence of the continental hotel industry owed much to professional schools then established on the continent, and thus they were determined to ensure that the future management in the Scottish hotel industry should not be 'at the mercy of hazardous practical experience alone'. Students were to receive instruction on 'Cashier's and Bill Office Routine; Hotel Control; Elements of General Book-keeping; Hotel Departments (kitchen, dining-room, bar, entrance hall, housekeeper's department); heating, lighting ventilation and refrigeration plant; general commercial practice; English and tourist geography of Great Britain'. In their second year, students would additionally receive instruction in 'accountancy, legal department and in management'.

In June 1945, Dr Pettigrew Young reported a successful conclusion to the first year of the course and on the placing of all students in hotels for summer vacation work each at a salary of £2 per week living in. By June 1946, 24 candidates had fulfilled the requirements of the first two-year course. Meanwhile the Scottish Education Department was anxious to establish a Chefs' Training Centre in the College. However, the College authorities resisted these proposals in spite of considerable persistence on the part of Mr MacDonald of the Scottish Education Department. This reluctance on the part of the Governors to have training kitchen facilities on college premises provided others with the impetus to secure alternative premises for the new school where space would permit such developments to take place. The decision to lease and subsequently acquire Ross Hall thus provided the School with a distinctive base which was to serve it well for the next 33 years.

As the fledgeling institution stretched its wings, the need for a specialist management structure became apparent. The close involvement of the hotel industry in the establishment of the School suggested a *Committee of Management* comprising nominees of the Hotel and Restaurant Association (Donald C. Grant; Major Charles Jarrett; Councillor John Smith of the Grosvenor Restaurant; John Walker of Eglington Hotels and Etienne J. Vacher representing British Transport Hotels) along with nominees of the Glasgow and West of Scotland Commercial College (Charles A. Oakley, Emeritus Professor Mellanby (chairman), Councillor Ernest (later Lord) Greenhill, William McLean and Robert Bowing). The Trades Union Council was represented by its Scottish Secretary, Baillie Charles Murdoch, whilst Dr Eric Thomson, who had now succeeded Dr Pettigrew Young as Director of the College, acted as Principal of the School. Reporting to the Committee of Management was an *Executive Committee* comprising six members. A *Visiting Committee* was also established and this included representatives from the hotel industry (G. A. Calazel JP of Peebles Hydro; Major Alastair D. Cameron MBE of the Bailie Nicol Jarvie Hotel, Aberfoyle; Joseph Dicken CA of Stirling Hotels, Frank G. Hole of the Euston Hotel, London; James Mercer of the Caledonian Hotel, Aberdeen; Alexander Miller of the North British Hotel, Edinburgh; R. Barlow More of More's Hotel, Glasgow; A. Morris of the Killin Hotel; John Nelson MBE of Glenburn Hydro, Rothesay; John Robertson of the Atholl Palace Hotel, Pitlochry; Arthur E. Towle CBE of British Transport Hotels; F. E. Walton of the Marine Hotel, Oban; with Eric Croft, Director of the Hotels and Restaurants Association of Great Britain, as a co-opted member). This management and advisory structure comprising many important and influential figures in the industry augured well for the new school.

With a move to more commodious premises imminent, the Management Committee decided on 22 April 1948 that the title for the School should be 'Scottish Hotel School' with the subtitle 'For Higher Education in Hotel-keeping'. It was decided that a Director should be appointed with responsibilities to the Principal of the Commercial College, and that courses in hotel management would be transferred to Ross Hall in October 1948. In the early summer of 1948 a small delegation representing the Management Committee went 'by air' to Paris, Zurich and Lausanne to inspect some of the Continental Hotel Schools and it was during this trip that contacts were made in Paris with a view to interviewing the Principal of the Hotel School at Grenoble, Monsieur Roger Dutron, who was subsequently appointed Director of the Scottish Hotel School. Other full-time and part-time appointments were made, including Robert Russell, one of the School's first alumni, René Miquel as Chef Instructor, and Ian Taylor, seconded from the parent institution in Pitt Street. With 19 academic, administrative and technical members of staff in place, the school was ready to begin the next phase of its development.

The School, with a French Director at the helm, initially found itself appreciated more on the continent of Europe than in the UK; his French influence established the highest standards of cuisine and food service. M. Dutron planned the enlargement of the kitchens, the acquisition of the latest equipment and an increase in the kitchen 'brigade'. A Board of Studies was established in 1953 and the scope and depth of the programme was increased, enabling the two-year course to expand to a three-year programme commencing in the autumn of 1957. Roger Dutron retired in 1955 and was succeeded for a four-year period by Hector Fabron, who laid the foundations for further physical developments at Ross Hall. The third Director, John Fuller, brought a fresh and reviving approach to hotel education. The curriculum was reshaped to include the latest thinking in management studies and expanded to include the appiication of scientific and technological aspects of hotel-keeping. By 1960, final diploma examinations were externally assessed and diploma holders exempted from the membership examinations of the Hotel and Catering Institute. The School attracted students from the USA, Canada, France, Spain, Hungary, Thailand, Turkey, South Africa, Rhodesia, India and the Irish Republic and at the same time a growing number of students undertook summer work experience abroad, principally in American, Canadian, Swiss, French, Belgian and Swedish hotels. Part-time courses were introduced in 1961 and management workshops were run in numerous locations away from home base. The 1962–63 Annual Report reported Intermediate and Final HCI Membership and City & Guilds awards made to part-time students.

The prospects of a British degree course in hotel administration might have been thin had it not been for the patient building of the full-time course whose diploma qualification by the late 1950s had begun to enjoy a status virtually equivalent to that of a degree. Thus, when the University of Strathclyde was established by Royal Charter in 1964, by the fusion of the Royal College of Science and Technology with the Scottish College of Commerce (of which the Scottish Hotel School was a part) the foundations for a full degree programme in hotel and catering management were already in place. Liaisons were established with hotel schools in other universities, notably with those in the universities of Michigan, Missouri and Cornell in North America—this last was also involved in a seminar run jointly with the Scottish Hotel School at Turnberry in January 1967.

The absorption of the Scottish Hotel School into the University of Strathclyde has been perhaps the most significant feature of the School's first 50 years. In 1965, the first students were enrolled into a newly developed Bachelor of Arts degree programme and for three years, degree and diploma courses ran in parallel. With a strong affiliation to the Schools of Business and Administration and of Social Studies (formed substantially from departments located at Pitt Street), the course comprised six specialist classes in Hotel Operations, Catering, Services Planning, Planning and Development and Catering Technology taken in combination with seven classes chosen from those offered by other departments. In the early years the 'hotel and institutional management' options were regarded as specialist classes with one subject selected from Accountancy, Administration or Business Economics taken throughout the three years as the principal area of study.

By 1968, the course had developed to the point where the school had its own principal subject with specialist options which included tourism. The degree was styled BA (Hotel and Catering Management). Whilst in 1968 the real world of tourism had not assumed the importance and scale of the 1990s, the Scottish Hotel School took the lead in the UK by recognising its importance as a growth activity and as a subject for academic study. That same year the Scottish Tourist Industry Consultancy Service was established in the School with financial support from the Scottish Tourist Board and the Highlands and Islands Development Board; this not only provided a valuable and timely service for industry as it sought to expand and develop new products and markets, but it also gave

pointers to areas where future research activity might be focused.

In 1972, with the undergraduate programme fully established, a one-year postgraduate programme in Tourism was launched leading to Diploma and Masters awards. In 1983, a similar initiative saw the introduction of a postgraduate Diploma and Masters course in Hotel Administration; ten years on, this course has developed a more international focus with an appropriately matching title.

Throughout the 1970s new classes were developed for the pass degree programme in international cuisine and in facilities planning. A fourth year was introduced enabling students to read for an Honours award when they could study new subject areas such as Manpower Planning, Systems Design and Property Management. The first two honours students graduated in 1979. As tourism began to assume greater economic, social and cultural importance in the 1970s and 1980s, the subject was made available for study by any student in the Strathclyde Business School first as a specialist subject in 1988, and then in 1989 as a principal subject to pass and joint honours level. Tourism can now be studied as a single honours subject in its own right, making the Scottish Hotel School the only department within the Strathclyde Business School to offer two principal subjects.

The present modular structure of degree programmes at Strathclyde now enables students from other departments and faculties of the University to study classes offered by the Scottish Hotel School. First-year Tourism classes attract growing numbers of 'external' students. This is beginning to translate into additional numbers 'majoring' in Tourism over the three- or four-year period of their course thus making themselves eligible to be counted as Hotel School alumni.

Current developments include a growth of student exchange programmes with universities overseas: two students are spending the 1993–94 session in institutions as different as the universities of Groningen in Holland and of Iowa in the USA. Future exchanges are planned with universities in Calgary, Purdue, Perugia and Innsbruck.

Since its inception in 1944, the Scottish Hotel School has pursued a path, the original aim of which is still followed today—students still 'aspire to responsible executive or managerial posts or to successful proprietorships'. As the business of hotels and hospitality has expanded and changed over 50 years, so courses at the Scottish Hotel School have been influenced by changes in management thinking, changes in consumer demand, changes in the varied applications of science and the advent of computer technology. The one-time cottage-industry type of business has now become highly competitive and the skills required of management have necessarily become more sharpened. Air travel has taken tourism from an activity of 'growing importance' to an international global industry of mega-proportions (who, in 1944, would have imagined that, 50 years on, Glasgow would be attracting 420 000 overseas tourist visitors per year—placing it third in the UK league table after London and Edinburgh?). Throughout this changing period, however, the underlying ethos of the Scottish Hotel School has been maintained by continuing to shape and influence the minds of men and women many of whom have made (and continue to make) a valuable contribution to the hotel, hospitality and tourism industry; indeed, as in the past, many will continue to be the catalysts of change for the future.

Of buildings . . .

Whilst the bulk of this history relates to people, one cannot ignore buildings. Again, Winston Churchill, speaking this time on the rebuilding of the House of Commons after bomb damage in 1943, mused 'we shape our dwellings and afterwards our dwellings shape us'. To well over two thousand staff and students, their days spent at Ross Hall will doubtless evoke nostalgia. Ross Hall enabled the School to become Britain's first and only residential hotel school; it added lustre to the School's reputation and it provided a unique and fine setting to engender the study of hotel and hospitality subjects. But it might not have been!

In 1946 the college authorities were pressed on numerous occasions by the Scottish Education Department to provide more appropriate and more extensive facilities for the School of Hotel Management—a suggestion was even put forward to house facilities in 'huts erected on vacant ground on the college site'—a proposal which fortunately failed to find favour with the Chairman's Committee of the College. This may have been the last straw for the advocates of change, but it did give the SED, with support from the Governors of the College, scope to discuss future plans directly with representatives of the Hotels and Restaurants Association. Events moved quickly, and when Ross Hall, a splendid Victorian mansion at Crookston and former residence of Sir Frederick Lobnitz Bt, came on the market, Donald Grant and other members of the Association were determined that it should be the home for the School. So much so, that the College Governors were 'informed' that on 5 June 1947 an offer to purchase the property had been accepted and that Don Grant had put up £17 000

of his own funds until the authorities had the necessary cash and permission to complete the purchase.

Meanwhile, the Parks Committee of Glasgow Corporation were anxious to acquire the gardens of Ross Hall which contained magnificent rockeries and a grotto laid out, it is said, by Taner. The Corporation thus agreed to purchase the estate from the Common Good Fund which did not require Treasury Consent, give the gardens to the Parks Department and lease the house to the Hotel School for a period of 60 years. The difficulties were far from over when the Corporation Housing Convenor learnt of the empty mansion and proposed to requisition the property to alleviate the city's serious housing problem. Friends of the Hotel School rallied yet again so that by the time the Corporation officials arrived to requisition the building, they were met with what appeared to be a furnished mansion complete with a dog lying on the doormat. The door was opened by a neatly dressed housekeeper and the party was able to see a nicely furnished hall, hats and coats on the stand and in a further room a table set for lunch and a cheery fire burning in the fireplace. The requisition party withdrew, doubtless much flustered, leaving the Hotel School free to move into its new premises—the 1948 session began on 12 October with 79 students.

Apart from alterations which were obviously required initially to change the use of the property from family mansion to a hotel school, a range of alterations and additions were to be made over the next 30 years. Temporary teaching accommodation was built, the kitchens enlarged and improved and other accommodation adapted to house residential students. The Hotel and Catering Association made significant contributions (both financial and 'in kind') towards the fulfilment of these plans. In June 1953 it was decided that female students should be housed in a separate residence and a property (named Mellanby Hall) was secured in Nithsdale Road for this purpose. In 1959 a new training restaurant and two new kitchens were built and in 1960 a reception training unit, library and science laboratory became operational. The following year, new classrooms above the training restaurant replaced the temporary classroom accommodation and a new housekeeping centre, improved bar and cellar unit and a hotel laundry completed developments to the existing house. With the implementation of such large-scale developments to a leased property, the college authorities were anxious to purchase the property from the Corporation. A sale was effected in 1962, at which point a five-storey residential block was built at the rear of the house to provide 83 study-bedrooms for male students. Women students were then reintegrated into Ross Hall from Mellanby Hall.

With its absorption into the University of Strathclyde, it was perhaps inevitable that the School would ultimately be brought back into the centre of the city. Starting with the 1982 session, the School made its third move to the Curran Building where it occupies purpose-built accommodation above the University Library on the University's John Anderson campus. Those with a nostalgia for Ross Hall will find the School's latest home very different; Ross Hall was indeed appropriate for its time; however, our present premises are perhaps just as appropriate for the present age. But, had it not been for some determined spirits in the early days, we may still (God forbid!) be labouring in huts in Pitt Street.

Of mice and men . . .

Mention has already been made of the key people responsible for establishing and developing the Scottish Hotel School, particularly in the early years. In a fifty-year span, very many people—some with a high profile and others contributing their bit behind the scenes—have devoted periods ranging from one or two years to almost entire careers to the work of the School.

Each change of Director (now styled Head of Department) has brought about changes in curriculum development, teaching and research emphasis. Since 1965 when funds were provided by the Rank Organisation, the School has had a professor at its head—John Fuller was appointed Rank Organisation Professor of Hotel Management in 1965. The Chair subsequently became fully established from 1971 when John Beavis was appointed. He was followed in 1983 by David Jeffries and in 1989 by the present Head of Department, Professor Kit Jenkins.

In the early years, academic leadership was provided by Ian Taylor (on secondment from Pitt Street) and Robert Russell, with René Miquel and Alec Currie holding centre stage in food production and service respectively. In 1948, other academic and technical support staff numbered seven.

As the years went by, staff came and went so that by 1967 the tally of academic staff was, for the record, as follows: Professor Fuller and Messrs Dan Boscoe, Tony Collyer, Alec Currie, David Gee, Walker Graham, Joe Houston, Charlie Jarvie, Eric Jolly, Hazel Jolly, Joyce Lloyd, John McKee, David Pattison, Edward Renold, Peter Shill and James Steel; the Scottish Tourist Industry Consultancy Service was directed by John Rice assisted by Douglas Callum; Roger Carter was a research assistant; Muriel Paterson and Mary Wyllie provided housekeeping expertise with James Simpson in the stores and cellar. Other cuisine staff included Ian Marshall,

Eddie Gould, and Gordon Sinclair. In departmental administration Elizabeth McArthur was succeeded by Morna Tindal. And that was not all! A wide range of visiting lecturers and consultants were involved, not least Bill Nicholson and D. G. Russell of the Scottish Tourist Board (whose involvement with the Scottish Hotel School goes back to 1950 and maybe even earlier), Professor Frank Fielden and Ian Ross (who lectured on hotel architecture and design) and Mary Andross (whose expertise was in food science).

Today in 1994, under the leadership of Kit Jenkins (Professor of International Tourism), academic staff include Marion Bennett, Jenny Cockill, Diane Creed, Peter Dieke, David Gee, Callein Gillespie, Alistair Goldsmith, Rory MacLellan, Alison Morrison, Raj Prasad, Tony Seaton, Ronnie Smith and Roy Wood. A Scottish Tourism Research Unit housed in the department is presided over by Tony Seaton and Visiting Professors include The Hon. Rocco Forte, Leonard Lickorish CBE, Graham Jeffrey (an alumnus of 1951/53) and Eddie Friel.

Visitors

The hotel and hospitality industry by its very nature expects to attract a wide range of visitors. The Scottish Hotel School has been no exception as it has played host to royalty, statesmen, industrialists and many others.

Whilst royalty may not have actually visited the Scottish Hotel School, the School in 1971 catered for HM The Queen, HRH The Duke of Edinburgh and HRH Princess Anne by preparing and serving lunch on the paddle steamer *Maid of the Loch* as she cruised the waters of Loch Lomond. In 1963 the School was involved in catering at the Palace of Holyroodhouse, Edinburgh, and subsequently at Auchencastle Hotel for the state visit of HM King Olaf of Norway, a service which was repeated in the Hotel School for his son, the then Crown Prince Harald, when he received an Honorary Degree from the University in October 1985.

Other visitors to the School (who may not have come solely for sustenance) included the President of Turkey in November 1967 as part of his State Visit, Helmut Schmidt, Chancellor of the former West Germany when he delivered the Hoover Address in July 1984, and Lord Snowdon, who in 1965 opened an exhibition and conference on Hotel Design promoted jointly by the School and the Council of Industrial Design. In January 1960, the Under-Secretary of State for Scotland, Niall MacPherson MP, visited the School, to be followed the next year in February by the Minister of State at the Scottish Office, Lord Craigton. Louis Darsonval, in his capacity as President of the Association Culinaire

Française, also visited in 1962 along with M. Charles Renner, the Consul-General of France in Scotland. Frank Hole (deputising for the indisposed British Railways Chairman, Sir Brian Robertson) opened the new training restaurant in 1962 and Lady Tweedsmuir MP, Under-Secretary of State of the Scottish Office, cut the ribbon to bring the new residence block into use in March 1964. When the School moved to its present location on the main University Campus, Reo Stakis (now Sir Reo Stakis) undertook the formal opening. Keynote speakers at conferences have included Professors Wanderstock, Meek, Eben Renolds and Bernatsky from Cornell and Lord Montagu of Beaulieu, and visiting lecturers have included The Hon. Rocco Forte, Tam Dalyell MP and George Robertson (then the Scottish Organiser of the General and Municipal Workers Union).

For over thirty years the School played host at least twice a year to the Scottish Society of Epicureans. The Society held its first dinner meeting at the Scottish Hotel School in March 1955 when the membership included a number of the School's governors. Etienne Vacher took an active interest in the planning of menus which provided students with experience in preparing and serving (and tasting behind the scenes) gourmet dishes and fine wines.

Some 'shining lights'

Since its foundation in 1944, some 3000 of the Scottish Hotel School's sons and daughters have gone out into the world and made their varied contributions to the professional and commercial life of this and many other countries of the world. It is in the nature of things that the majority have probably succeeded in pulling their weight without laying claim to distinction, but there have been some who have attained positions of some influence and others who have chosen to pursue careers away from the mainstream of hotel and hospitality management; perhaps it is apposite to make note of some of these achievements.

To date we have information on the whereabouts of just under half of the School's former students—and it is inevitable that some achievements, unknown to us at present, will go unrecorded. Equally, this account does not pretend to be anything other than a selective snapshot.

The School's first established *raison d'être* of providing people trained to lead the Scottish hotel scene has surely borne fruit and spilled over into other parts of the United Kingdom and even further afield. Of the early years, George Cameron, Nelson Vickers, Arthur Neil, James Clelland, Bruce Bannister, Graham Jeffrey, Harry Kruschandl, James MacLellan, David Levin, John Loughray and Morrison Grant have distinguished

themselves variously in hotel management; collectively they cover a geographic area which stretches from Glasgow to Washington DC, London to Los Angeles and Brussels to Benin. Some own and manage their own units whilst others are senior managers with international hotel corporations. A snapshot of those at the School in the 1970s produces a similar picture with Vinay Mehrotra, Ian Carswell, Taj Kassam, Tim Dawes, Christopher Brown, Diane Miller, Jonathan Love, Judith Davidson and Steve Wilkins being collectively spread between Kanpur and Vancouver, Windsor and Sydney NSW and pursuing careers in hotels, restaurant chains and contract catering at unit through to top executive level.

Many former students have gone into education—indeed eight of the present academic staff at the Hotel School are returnees of various vintages and the product of various SHS courses. Of those who have chosen to stay away from their Alma Mater, Mike McKechnie, Dolf Mogendorff, Robert Christie Mill, Alastair Morrison and David Leslie are in key positions and very many others are ploughing their furrow in academe. The Forces claimed Squadron Leader Tony Ball, Colonel Vince Cowley, Major Peter McCall, Flying Officer Ruth Punshon along with others. Bennett Brown, Paul Slattery, Ashley de Safrin, Jeremy Scroxton, Nigel Patterson, Arthur De Haast, Ian Stanton and Martin O'Grady are among those who provide consultancy services to the industry in Canada and the United States as well as within the UK.

James Kinniburgh, Mitch Fisher, Stuart Kerr, Joyce Carrell (now Johnston), Liam Donnelly, Lawrence MacFarlane, Rory Carlin, Robin Lim, Marilyn Lavers, John Heeley, Lawrence Watson and Robert Elliot can be found in occupations as diverse as an HMI, a legal adviser, a brewery brand manager, a management accountant, a demolition contractor, a managing director of a publishing company, a hospital hotel services manager, a group human resources manager, a director of tourism for a UK city and a managing director of a major food manufacturing business. In another sphere, Alan Lawson who captained the University Rugby Club in the 1968–69 session went on to play for Scotland.

To our knowledge, four alumni have honours—Tony Ball, Graham Ross and Roger Carter with OBEs, and John Fraser the MBE.

Whilst this section has only touched on the achievements of some former students following their departure from the relative safety of the Scottish Hotel School, it does demonstrate something of the diverse range of occupations our alumni pursue. And finally, it should be said that it is within the gift of a University to recognise others for achievements made during their career. The School is proud to record that the University conferred Honorary Degrees on two distinguished hoteliers: that of Doctor of Laws on Reo Stakis (now Sir Reo Stakis) in July 1986, and of Doctor of the University on Lord Forte in April 1992.

Of social activities . . .

Going to college or university presents the student with new knowledge and new skills; it should also enable the individual to grow in intellect, in judgement, in competence and in confidence. It also provides a wealth of new opportunities to meet new people from different backgrounds, from different parts of the world, many of whom have different approaches to life. Now, with 12 500 students, the University environment is one where there is something for everyone—cultural, sporting and a wide range of social activities. Students of the Scottish Hotel School, whilst now participating in the wider life of the University, have always organised a diverse range of in-house activities. Ross Hall in its day provided a unique sense of cohesion and a snapshot of the 1960s reveals the rich social life students enjoyed: away from Ross Hall, the Argosy could always be relied upon to revive flagging spirits whilst, back at base, badminton, rugby, ski, hockey, football and country dance clubs provided an outlet for physical exuberance. A Young Hoteliers Club blended fun with business and the Twenty-and-One Club enabled budding gourmets to indulge their passion for food and drink with choice after-dinner speakers—The Countess of Mar and Kellie launched the club in December 1963, and a dinner held in London the following month had HCI National President, D. G. S. Russell, as its principal guest. Some clubs and societies were short-lived—SUDS (a Hotel School Drama Group) got off the ground in 1965, but those who survived the session took themselves off to the University Drama Club the following year. Other regular activities just seemed to happen—like the Hotel School float and the Hotel School 'inspired' Café for the annual Charities Day appeal; like International evenings when overseas (as well as local) students produced their own brand of culinary delights; like the 'Going-Down Lunch' held in formal setting for those hoping to graduate (it was always held *before* the final exams for some reason!); like the Final Ball, where tradition demanded that the Director let slip those little (even intimate) secrets he knew about all those present. Those with journalistic tendencies produced *The Spatule* in the late 1950s (perhaps they just wanted to stir things up!), and this led to the magnificent annual production of a *Journal* (subsequently retitled the *Strathclyde Hotelier*) which survived in an unbroken run until 1989. Lyn Lavers and Roger Voss (both now in

journalism) cut their teeth with the 1965 and 1967 editions respectively. Whilst essentially a 'home-produced' journal, over the years many distinguished industrialists have contributed—including Derek Taylor (1989 and 1968), Alan Devereux (1987), Clement Freud (1978), Nat Abrahams (1972)—and a wealth of former students dispensing words of wisdom with almost every issue.

This rich social scene of the Scottish Hotel School continues today and it is perhaps to be expected—where students are training for a branch of the entertainment business.

And finally, in 1953 an official enquiry into disciplinary matters at the School noted 'familiarity between the sexes'—be that as it may, over the fifty years very many marriages between graduates have taken place, doubtless fostered by the unique atmosphere engendered by an institution such as ours. T. C. Smout, Professor of Scottish History at St Andrews University, and at present visiting Professor at Strathclyde, wrote of another place and of another time that he had 'happy memories—it was like crazy paving, and we flourished in the spaces between the stones'. For most that sentiment probably epitomises their time at the Scottish Hotel School.

Of scholarship . . .

In the context of university academe, 'scholarship' in the early years was perhaps measured by the outside world in terms of culinary achievements, principally at the 'Salon Culinaire de Londres'. George Potter won First Prize in the Coronation Menu Competition in 1953, Chris Ducatt also gained First Prize with the Gas Board's 'Plan a Kitchen' Competition in 1962. In the 1960s, Edward Renold led successive teams to Frankfurt and came away with Grands Prix and Gold Medals; Hotelympia successes also accrued to Hotel School teams. In 1970 Robert Christie Mill and in 1972 Alistair Morrison both won St Andrews Scholarships. In 1992, Neil Brownlee was named 'Student of the Year' in a Scottish Tourist Board sponsored award.

John Fuller was a prolific writer; his *Chef's Manual of Kitchen Management* must have remained high on college reading lists for many a long year. With other titles, both under his sole authorship and in collaboration with Alec Currie, David Gee and Edward Renold, the market for catering texts was substantially in the hands (not the pockets alas!) of Hotel School staff. James Steel, who also took a leading part in the 1967 Turnberry Seminar, found a best-seller with *Control in Catering*. Under John Beavis, the School published an annual survey of Inter-Hotel Financial Comparisons under the sponsorship of the National Economic Development Office.

In the 1990s, scholarship is perhaps regarded more seriously. Performance rating is now an important yardstick of credibility, but in this the Scottish Hotel School continues to sustain its lead position in hotel and hospitality education gaining a 'FIVE' rating in the latest research review—an exercise which was conducted throughout the UK university system and involved all subject areas. Authors in the department today who wield the pen (though now it is the word-processor) are Roy Wood with *Working in Hotels and Catering*, Professor Kit Jenkins, in collaboration with Visiting Professor Leonard Lickorish, with *Developing Tourism Destinations*, Tony Seaton, Peter Dieke and Marion Bennett with papers in *Annals of Tourism Research*, *Tourism Management* and other journals. Indeed all are currently involved in giving a new and up-to-date slant to hotel, hospitality and tourism knowledge.

Of awards . . .

The Scottish Hotel School has been fortunate in attracting sponsors and donors for prizes and awards. As early as 1949, William Younger provided a capital sum of £2500 from which Travelling Scholarships have been awarded every year since. In 1993 this Scholarship supported Alastair Hartley with a visit to Malaysia. Eglinton Hotels, Grand Metropolitan Hotels, Turnbull, BTHA and Fred Kobler awards have all been made over varying periods of years. Today, in addition to the Younger Award, the School is able to award an annual Savoy-Cornell Scholarship (made possible by the most generous support of the Savoy Educational Trust), the Lisa Morris Award (funded from a generous capital sum donated by Morris of Glasgow) and the John McKee Award (made possible from funds given in his memory). Though today inexpensive and fast air travel makes our world very much a global village, Francis Bacon's aphorism of 1625 that 'travel . . . is a part of education' is still true almost 400 years on—Hotel School students can thus still expand on their knowledge of international hotels, hotel-keeping and tourism through the availability of these awards.

'The best is yet'

So wrote John Fuller in the 1983 edition of the *Strathclyde Hotelier*. There is a certain cosy security in reviewing the past and, especially for those who participated in that past, elements of nostalgia inevitably creep in. The Scottish Hotel School can with pride say that it has consistently met recognisable student and employers needs; future generations of staff and students have a rich heritage on which to build, and each will have an important role to play in enabling the graduates of the future to enjoy useful and fulfilling lives and careers.

Acknowledgements

Whilst this brief history is not referenced in the true academic style, its compilation would not have been possible without access to archives held by the University, without letters, minutes of meetings and journals retained by various people over the years, and without the personal reminiscences of many whose lives have been touched and influenced by the Scottish Hotel School. If you, the reader, feel the story has missed out an important event or if your name has not (or indeed has) been mentioned, then I take full responsibility.

Part 1

TOURISM AND DEVELOPMENT

Tourism as a mass phenomenon developed in the 1950s. In that decade more people travelled for leisure and holiday purposes than ever before, and many for the first time travelled to foreign destinations. As the holiday and travel habit became part of the lifestyle of those living in the developed countries, travel agents and tour operators combined to broaden the travel horizon, bringing new and more distant destinations within the price range of tourists. Inevitably, for reasons of climate, culture and curiosity, many of the developing countries became tourist destinations. For some countries, e.g. Mexico, proximity to a wealthy tourist generating country such as the United States ensured that a visitor flow would develop over time to become one of the major sectors of Mexico's economy. For other more distant destinations, improvements in aircraft technology and the introduction of competitive price policies were important factors bringing them into the international tourist market.

Among the destinations more distant from the main tourist generating countries were those to be found in the Caribbean and Pacific regions, among the Pacific rim countries, and on the landmass of Asia. By the beginning of the 1990s very few countries had not yet experienced some tourism, whether it had been positively encouraged by government or not. Despite the growth of numbers of tourist arrivals and expenditures tourism as a development option attracted much debate and controversy.

Given the major economic expectations connected with tourism, as the sector developed it became apparent that it also brought economic disadvantages and often social, cultural, environmental and related problems. The fifteen papers in this Part of the book explore many of the salient features of tourism development.

The first four papers examine various issues of general importance to tourism. C. L. Jenkins discusses the topical issue of privatisation of tourism activity in the developing countries. There is now a groundswell of opinion, both governmental and associated with international lending agencies, which argues that government should play an essential supporting, but not necessarily an active, role in tourism. The paper explores what privatisation might mean in the context of the developing countries and examines some of the problems which may arise. Clare Gunn presents an overview of state-of-the-art planning for tourism, emphasising the 'concept of participatory goal setting and strategic planning as a process', and also gives consideration to the importance of involving communities in the planning process. Zhen-Hua Liu discusses the holistic nature of tourism development, emphasising the systems approach as the basis of our understanding of tourism growth dynamics. Oliver Bennett, from his experience as a tourism consultant, discusses many of the issues relating to sound funding proposals for tourism projects. He also looks at some of the problem areas and particularly suggests guidelines for the future.

The next seven papers are related to country-specific or area studies and many of them have been developed within a comparative framework. Paul Wilkinson examines resource management for tourism in small island economies where there are particular difficulties related to scale. Peter Dieke discusses the growth of tourism in sub-Saharan Africa and considers some of the issues which are of current concern in that region. Panajotis Komilis then considers the question of sustainable tourism development on a regional basis with particular reference to Greece. Haluk Sezer and Aileen Harrison continue this theme by looking at the development of tourism in Greece and Turkey, in particular looking at the economic aspects which might interest planners. This country emphasis is continued by Meral Korzay who looks in detail at the tourism development experience in Turkey. The next two country studies are based in the Caribbean with Sue Bleasdale and Sue Tapsell examining the efforts by the Government of Cuba to revitalise and restore its tourism industry. This perspective examines the way in which tourism has become a major possibility for growth in Cuba, given its isolation because of political events in the former Soviet Union and its estrangement from the United States. Kerry Woodcock and Lesley France then apply conventional development theories to the study of tourism in Jamaica with specific reference to the resort area of Ochos Rios.

In the last section there are four papers looking at the technical aspects of tourism development. Stephen Wanhill presents a thorough review of methods of appraisal of tourism projects relating these techniques to his wide experience as a tourism consultant. Egon Smeral examines the question of evaluating public resources used in tourism and proposes a method to do this. Sieghard Baier then looks at the question of the economic impact of travel and tourism in a mountain area by examining a case study in Austria. Naz Saleem explores the concept of destination capacity and suggests a way in which one might determine what the tourism carrying capacity is.

These papers focus on general and specific aspects of tourism in the development process. They provide specialist insights into an area which is both fascinating and controversial.

Professor C. L. Jenkins

1 Tourism in developing countries: the privatisation issue

C. L. JENKINS

Introduction

The conventional approach to tourism development in developing countries has usually been given a central role in both policy formulation and planning by government (Jenkins and Henry, 1982). This role is not surprising. In many, if not most, developing countries there is a scarcity of resources, a lack of expertise, and limited involvement in tourism by the private sector. For these reasons, government has often had to play a central role. Also, in the initial stages of tourism development, the government might be the only body which has resources to invest in the sector. It may also be the main guarantor for overseas investment. Government, in addition to providing the necessary infrastructure for tourism, has, in a number of countries, actually engaged as an entrepreneur in the tourism sector. This may have been done for political reasons or, usually, has reflected the absence of private investors with the capital, experience and willingness to invest in tourism.

However, over the last ten years, there has been growing concern that tourism has not delivered its expected benefits. To a large extent this might be a condition of the fact that tourism has given rise to expectations which were beyond its capacity to meet. There are many reasons for this, not least being the economic imperative which has long been associated with tourism.

For these reasons, it is now appropriate to reappraise the role of tourism in the development process and to ask whether a new approach is necessary? This reappraisal is something which is exercising the interests of politicians, planners and, not least, academics because of the growing importance of tourism in the global, regional and national economies. A further factor is that, as tourism has become more important in global economic activity, then not only governments, but also a very wide range of international agencies and interest groups are concerned with its future.

This paper considers these issues and examines what are the options for change and, in particular, examines whether a greater degree of private sector involvement in tourism policy formulation, planning, and implementation would be a major improvement on the current situation.

Definitions of policy

The multi-faceted nature of tourism does not permit it to be described as an industry in a technical sense: it has no single production characteristic, or defined operational parameters. Its economic dimension cannot occur without inputs of a social, cultural and environmental nature.

It is this wide-ranging and complex nature of tourism that requires careful analysis. Individual, ad hoc responses to tourism opportunities and problems do not constitute a policy for tourism. Such responses may merely provide short-term solutions to essentially long-term problems.

> There is no simple consensus of what is meant by the term policy. The Oxford Dictionary offers two definitions: 'prudent conduct' and 'a course of general plans of action'. What may be implied from both definitions is the notion of a reasoned consideration of alternative options. In tourism, with its many complexities and manifestations, it is often very difficult to define options let alone select a preferred course of action. Despite these difficulties, countries do require a policy or policy guidelines for the tourism sector. (Jenkins, 1991)

There is a strong linkage between policies, planning and implementation strategies. In many countries, particularly in the developing world, the formulation of policies and plans for the tourism sector have usually been undertaken by foreign consultants; implementation has been almost neglected with the host government being expected in most cases to undertake this for itself. Perhaps this is one of the fundamental weaknesses of tourism development where much emphasis has been placed on the technical coherence of the plans but where a lesser amount of attention is given to implementation. This weakness is probably one of the major reasons that tourism, in many countries, has been unable to match the high economic expectations which the sector has been accorded.

The traditional approach to tourism planning

There are a number of general characteristics which can be ascribed to the planning process for tourism in developing countries.

1. There has been a dominant role played by government. As noted in the introductory section, there are many good reasons why government has been given this role.
2. From its introduction as part of development strategy, there has always been a major emphasis on the economic benefits which tourism could generate (Checi and Co., 1969; H. S. Zinder Associates, 1969; Archer, 1973a, 1973b; Bryden, 1973; Erbes, 1973). This is not surprising given the need in many developing countries to create jobs and incomes, and to generate the necessary foreign exchange to help with the development effort. It was regarded very much as a 'growth point' activity.
3. The major expertise for undertaking planning and assisting with policy formulation for the tourism sector was usually, and still is provided and financed by international agencies. For this reason, tourism was developed very much as a by-product of the experience of the developed countries. As a consequence, development was usually guided and managed by foreign advisers, financed by foreign investors, and created what was, and is still regarded in some countries, as 'a foreigners' industry run by foreigners for foreigners'.
4. In addition to its traditional role of providing general infrastructure and also for the tourism sector, government sometimes had to undertake the role of entrepreneur to 'kick-start' the sector. There are many examples of tourism development investments wholly owned by governments which undertake what are operational and entrepreneurial roles. For example, the Indian Tourism Development Corporation invested extensively in hotels and airlines, and also provided travel agency and transport services. State ownership of airlines is common throughout the world.

As this scenario unfolded, and when the expected benefits from tourism were not achieved or only partly achieved, a more critical attitude towards the sector evolved. Governments and development agencies began to ask why tourism was not producing the volume of benefits which most of its adherents had promised. There was also a noticeable lack of investment in the tourism sector by the World Bank, the African Development Bank and the Asian Development Bank, all agencies which were strongly represented in regions of the world where tourism was a growing and major activity. In the case of the Asian Development Bank and the African Development Bank, direct investment in tourism, other than in general infrastructure, really did not occur until the late 1980s. The main institutional support for tourism was made by the United Nations Development Programme, particularly in providing technical assistance, usually through the World Tourism Organisation. The European Community has become arguably the principal support for tourism in the developing world, particularly facilitated by the LOME IV Convention. It currently has major tourism support initiatives in the South Pacific, the Caribbean and Asia.

Although there was widespread recognition of the potential of tourism to stimulate economic growth, there were apparent a number of problems which required analysis.

Problem areas

There are a number of general problems which can be associated with the history of tourism development.

As mentioned above, there has been general disappointment with the economic returns from the tourism sector. Perhaps this is not surprising. In the early 1970s the major emphasis on tourism as a development option was based on a very high expectation of its ability to generate economic advantages, usually related to foreign exchange earnings, to the creation of jobs, to the generation of both personal and government incomes, and to its acting as a stimulant to regional development. Strategic importance was placed on increasing the number of visitor arrivals, increasing the per visit spend, and increasing the length of stay. Priority was given to the gross volume of tourist expenditure. What was not considered in sufficient detail was the input necessary to retain a high proportion of that expenditure. It is well known that within developing countries leakages from the tourism sector are high, particularly in island economies (Wilkinson, 1987). The major criticism must be that tourism planners simply concentrated on creating more tourist expenditure without addressing the attendant issues of how to retain a higher proportion of that expenditure within the country. The net retention factor should have been the major economic target, but surprisingly this was not greatly addressed by planners. The growing volume of leakages out of the tourism sector often reflected the state of under-development of a particular country's economy and its inability to take advantage of inter-sectoral linkages to provide the inputs necessary to the tourism sector. To a large extent these problems are structural and can only be addressed over a long period of time. However, their accumulated effect was to create disappointment with the economic returns received from tourism.

This disappointment was exacerbated by insufficient knowledge of the market mix of international tourism. It is recognised that for most developing countries tourists are generated from the relatively wealthy advanced developed countries. The flow patterns have not greatly changed over the last fifty years or so and we find that the scale and type of development in third world countries is determined not by themselves, but by the market demands which are interpreted by the foreign tour operators. Cohen's term 'ecological bubble' (Cohen, 1972) has stood the test of time in the sense that it describes the expectations of tourists from developed countries travelling to developing countries. Without any doubt, these expectations are still maintained and therefore determine what should be provided in the developing countries for the foreign tourists. It causes a situation where within third world countries you often have first world facilities which are provided on an enclave basis for foreign visitors. This, of course, then gives rise to social and political discontent. Egypt, unfortunately, is a current example of this situation.

Although there is social and political discontent with tourism, we have to accept the reality that tourism is essentially an international industry and one which is market-driven. This means that what has to be supplied has to meet international standards and international demand; it is not sufficient to provide what a country wishes to offer without reference to expected standards. To a large extent, the problem has been that government has created facilities, aided by advisers, without realising that it is the market which determines acceptability and not government or planners.

This comment does not imply that the market for tourist destinations and level of services expected is homogeneous; it is not. Supplies of tourist amenities and services should identify those market segments which best match what the destination country has to offer and what it wants to offer. Demand is still driven by consumer preference, but that preference is linked to what a country perceives to be its desired form of development. Low-volume, market-specific tourism (eco-tourism) might be suitable for some destinations, e.g. the Maldives, but high-volume, general beach tourism could be more suited for others, e.g. Spain.

The inability of governments to react to market changes is not surprising. Government mainly provides infrastructure or limited revenue-generating facilities such as hotels, transport services, and travel agencies in some cases, which provide services to tourists. However, government with its bureaucratic structure is unable to react quickly to market changes and often lacks the flexibility in managerial approach and vision that allows a high-quality service to be developed. Government, for these reasons, is not a very useful or effective source of tourism management and this is one of the critical areas where much of the disappointment with tourism has to be focused.

Criticisms of the non-economic aspects of tourism have also increased. In the early 1970s, probably until the mid-decade, the major arguments for tourism were related to the economic benefits it could bring to the developing countries. Very little attention was given to the social, cultural and environmental impacts of tourism. These concerns certainly became more apparent in the late 1970s and 1980s, but to a very large extent the major thrust in development policy was on creating facilities which would attract foreign visitors and maximise economic impacts. A further consideration was that little attention was given to the host communities. Planning was essentially for foreign tourists and to meet the demands of the foreign markets.

There was also a growing political awareness that because of the nature of tourism and its reliance on the international market it was a sector over which the host country and governments could exercise only limited control. This gave rise to a feeling that it was an industry which had a great risk attached to its investments, because markets, that is tourists, could virtually disappear without any cause other than political or social instability. We see the effect that economic depression in the 1990s in the developed countries had on tourist flows to the developing world. Major political factors, e.g. the Gulf War, have had worldwide effects on tourism flow patterns. It is these unforeseen fluctuations, induced by events often outside the control and influence of the tourist-receiving countries, which have made many investors wary of the tourism sector.

The very low levels of development in certain tourist-receiving countries meant that indigenous people simply did not have the income to participate in tourism. The provision of facilities for tourists, very much in accordance with the 'ecological bubble' concept, meant that there was a tendency to create advanced enclaves within third world countries. Tourism, not surprisingly, was seen as a foreigners' industry creating facilities for a privileged elite which many indigenous people would never likely be able to afford. It is this type of image which has often caused problems for tourism, where many people argue that it is a demonstration of affluence in the midst of squalor. It is difficult to repudiate this argument except in economic terms. Investment in tourism should be justified on the basis of having a comparative advantage *vis-à-vis* other investment possibilities. The surplus generated from tourism investment then can, in part, be used for other development purposes. Too often, governments and national tourism organisations have failed to relay this message to local national populations; ignorance of tourism often breeds suspicion and misunderstanding.

Options for change

Given the circumstances described above, there appeared to be three scenarios for change which can be considered.

1. Status quo
   In this situation it is envisaged that the planning for tourism in developing countries will proceed as it has traditionally proceeded, that is, in giving a central focus to government and in trying to develop the sector based on maximum visitor flows. However, there is a modification to this scenario in that planners now are much more sensitive to the needs of the host community and are also recognising that not all types of tourism are necessarily beneficial. This means that a greater emphasis is being placed on the appropriate type and scale of tourism development in various countries.
2. Technical tinkering
   Technical tinkering reflects a situation where there is no intention to change the status quo described above except to try and improve the benefits from tourism by taking into account the economic structure of the country and ensuring that better linkages are achieved. This, if successful, would obviously have the effect of increasing the net retention of tourism earnings, but it would still envisage a planning scenario driven by a central role for government.
3. Radical change
   In this case the central role of government is diminished and a much greater emphasis is placed on the involvement, both at policy and planning levels and through implementation, of the private sector. It is this scenario which seems to be gaining support, particularly from the international agencies.

The new approach

In order to obtain enhanced benefits from investment in tourism, a new approach has become apparent in the last three or four years. This approach does not necessarily change the planning dimensions applied to tourism but rather re-orders the priorities and places greater emphasis on the indigenisation of ownership and operation within the tourism sector.

Some developing countries, e.g. India, the Bahamas and Kenya, have generated considerable expertise in tourism, but most countries still rely on the international agencies to fund initial development and to assist with the technical expertise required to develop the sector. The United Nations Development Programme is increasingly expecting countries either to become the executing agency for tourism projects or to carry out this task in conjunction with specialist agencies such as the World Tourism Organisation. A major change, therefore, is the increased determination to ensure that there is a transfer of knowledge and expertise from the consultants to their indigenous counterparts.

Second, there is a growing realisation that not all types of tourism are appropriate in certain countries or within regions of the countries. To a large extent this change in emphasis has been a product not only of developing expertise in tourism planning, but also of the growing number of interest groups who are now concerned about the scale, type and nature of tourism projects. The emergence of terms such as 'eco-tourism', 'green tourism', 'responsible tourism' reflects the fact that there is more interest now in the non-economic impacts (and benefits) arising from tourism than there were before. There is also a realisation that if tourism is to be sustainable in the long term, its sustainability is not based on economic criteria alone; it also has to be sustainable by becoming acceptable to the host communities. In countries where the tourist host community is essentially rural, then this usually means that rural people are the poorest people in the country and those with the lowest incomes. A growing concern, therefore, is that tourism should stimulate regional development and raise rural incomes and should do this in such a way that there is a growing indigenisation of ownership of tourism facilities and operations of those facilities by local people. The idea that tourism can simply be imposed on a country or a region has now been largely rejected in favour of a much more balanced approach to the needs of visitors and hosts.

The issue of indigenisation is important. One of the general grievances against tourism in developing countries is that much of the investment is owned by foreigners and managed by foreigners, and that the profits leak from the country. There are good reasons why this situation has prevailed but there are no good reasons why it should prevail indefinitely. Governments, by training and educational policies, must try to develop a management cadre and, eventually, an indigenous top managerial class. However, there is also a need to encourage indigenous investment in the tourism sector to ensure that benefits from tourism accrue to local people. As Richter (1991) has noted 'those who shape tourism policy must recognise its complexity and be more responsive to those who challenge sanguine assumptions about tourism benefits'.

In addition to this change of emphasis there has also been a change in attitudes towards how the benefits of tourism are best secured. As we see in the former Soviet Union, the political changes there have led to the emergence of the private sector and the market as the major determinants of economic growth. More tourism planners are accepting that flexibility is essential to take advantage of market opportunities and to react quickly to market changes. It is felt that this flexibility can only be obtained through an increased private sector involvement in tourism.

Privatisation—what does it mean?

Privatisation usually refers to an economic situation where the major developments in the economy are stimulated by private sector investors. This classically is the situation in most of the developed countries of the world. The argument is that market sensitivity is essential for sustainable development. Market sensitivity can only be acquired by those most involved in the market-place. This involvement is mainly the concern of the private sector firms which provide the services for tourists. As profit-driven organisations, they need to be providers of good service standards at acceptable prices in order to survive. It is very interesting to note that in most developing countries it is the government-owned services which usually are loss-making, most obviously in hotel and airline activities.

Market-sensitivity and the need for a greater involvement of the private sector diminishes the role of government in an operational but not in a control sense. Government still is responsible for the overall acceptability of the type of tourism that is developed. It also has a social responsibility to ensure that the benefits of tourism are not gained to the major detriment of social, cultural and environmental standards.

A movement from a centralised planning and operational system to one of complete privatisation has dangers. The current chaos in the states of the former Soviet Union indicates the perils of a rapid structural transformation. In this sense many of the developing countries are in no position to move towards a fully privatised tourism sector, but rather there is a movement towards more decentralisation and a greater attempt to operate government services at a more commercial standard. In China, for example, the new economic policies espoused by the government have designated certain zones where private enterprise is the dominant economic force. In tourism the Chinese authorities have also invested heavily, but the operation of most facilities has been left to the private sector.

Privatisation should not be regarded as a point of political dogma but rather as a pragmatic shift in policy which may have to be implemented in stages. Governments are under increasing pressure from the international lending agencies to move towards more market sensitive economies. If this movement is too rapid, as some structural adjustment programmes have been in African countries, then economic and political disturbances are likely. The tourism sector is perhaps only different in that it is, for most developing countries, an export sector where competitive standards and prices are determined by the international market. Most suppliers of tourism services in the developing countries are price-takers rather than price-makers. If tourism prices are subsidised, then this is not usually a deliberate policy of government but rather a consequence of the bargaining power of foreign tour operators.

Given these international pressures and the varying levels of economic development in third world countries, privatisation measures have to advance cautiously and selectively.

Limits to privatisation in tourism

For most developing countries the government will still have a major role to play in development strategy. This reflects the situation that in most of these countries the private sector is still embryonic, and in certain parts of the economy, may not be represented at all. This is not an argument for continuing centralisation of policy and operation of facilities. It may, at a point in time, simply reflect the situation as it is seen. Given this particular background then the first stage of privatisation is to move towards a more commercial aspect of development. This may be done through the setting up of parastatal companies which, although owned by government, will have the flexibility to operate in the private sector and to offer services at a commercial rate. This so-called commercialisation will make the operation of tourist facilities much more sensitive to market trends and forces than if these facilities were managed from a ministry. Over a period of time, a movement towards more privatised services can be made, either through the setting up of joint venture companies or by the privatisation of certain designated services, e.g. travel agency services, hotels, transport, etc.

The problem facing the development of tourism in the third world countries is that tourism often is most influenced by externalities. These externalities, such as the Gulf War or a serious downturn in the economies of major tourism-generating countries, can have dramatic and rapid effects in the tourist-receiving countries. It is for these reasons that governments often find it difficult to react to market changes. Private sector companies whose very existence relies on tourism will make such changes because of the need to ensure that business continues. It is the competitive nature of the market which suggests that the private sector is likely to best influence tourism development and can be proactive rather than simply reactive to market forces.

As a general concept it is difficult to know how far privatisation can extend. The considerations must be based on the levels of economic development, on tourism experience and on the political expectations of specific countries. An over-rapid movement towards privatisation will obviously cause as many problems as it produces benefits.

The way ahead

There is a growing body of opinion which suggests that the involvement of the private sector should not be limited to the provision of tourism services, but that the private sector should also be involved in tourism planning and policy formulation. This not only meets the general understanding that private sector companies are best able to read the market, but it also reflects the fact that governments have very limited budgets and therefore cannot invest in tourism or in any other sector of the economy without limitation. It is usually the case that government will be involved in creating and approving the international image that is projected for the country in the tourism market-place. International publicity and the servicing of the travel trade is very expensive. Most developing countries, even those with the most advanced tourism sectors, still find that international promotion and marketing is a heavy outlay in terms of foreign exchange. Increasingly, governments are attempting to involve the private sector companies in these activities. However, often the private sector companies feel that government does not have the market-based understanding or the flexibility to react to market demands. Private sector companies will not put funds into tourism promotion unless they have a major say in what is to be promoted, how promotion is to be done and where promotion is to be carried out. In Indonesia, for example, a joint government and private sector body, the Indonesian Tourism Promotion Board, has succeeded in almost quadrupling the amount of resources available for tourism marketing overseas. The government maintains its ultimate control over the sector and over general marketing policy, but decisions relating to the type, location and the extent of marketing are guided very much by the private sector through its majority membership of the Board.

There is a long experience of governments developing tourism facilities through tourism development corporations. These initiatives often were the means for governments' involvement in entrepreneurial activities, for example, not only building but also operating hotels and other facilities. They are vehicles on the road towards privatisation; through joint-participation with private companies, governments do become involved in commercial operations and have been so for many years. As the tourism sector develops and strategic objectives are met, the governments may choose to sell off their assets and re-invest in other tourism developments or in other sectors of the economy. Governments' intervention should be selective and specific.

Conclusions

There is no doubt that the role of government in tourism in the developing countries is changing. Government is seen as being a control agent and as guiding development through selective interventions. More pressure is being exerted on governments, particularly by the international agencies, to ensure that the private sector has a greater involvement in the development process, not just through the provision of services but also in contributing to the strategic development of the industry. There is no doubt that this trend will continue. It does not mean that government has no role to play in tourism. It is very much the 'hidden hand' which guides policy while ensuring that the services which, to a large extent make up the satisfaction for foreign tourists, are actually offered by those best able to provide them. If there is a concept which guides our understanding of future tourism development in the third world, it must be 'government should not do what the private sector is able and willing to do'.

References

Archer, B. H. (1973a) *The Impact of Domestic Tourism*, Economic Research Unit, University of Wales, Bangor.

Archer, B. H. (1973b) *The Gwynedd Multipliers*, Economic Research Unit, University of Wales, Bangor.

Bryden, J. (1973) *Tourism and Development*, Cambridge University Press, London.

Checi and Co. (1969) 'A plan for managing tourism in the Bahama Islands', Washington, DC.

Cohen, E. (1972) 'Towards a sociology of international tourism', *Social Research*, 39(1): 171.

Erbes, R. (1973) *International Tourism and the Economy of Developing Countries*, OECD, Paris.

Jenkins, C. L. (1991) *Developing Tourism Destinations: Policies and Perspectives*, Part II, *Development Strategies*, Longman, Harlow.

Jenkins, C. L. and Henry, B. M. (1982) 'Government involvement in tourism in developing countries', *Annals of Tourism Research*, 9: 499–521.

Richter, L. K. (1991) 'Political issues in tourism policy: a forecast', *World Travel and Tourism Review*, Vol. 1, CAB International, Oxford, p. 191.

Wilkinson, P. F. (1987) 'Tourism in small island nations: a fragile dependence', *Leisure Studies*, 6(2).

H. S. Zinder Associates (1969) 'The future of tourism in the eastern Caribbean', Washington, DC.

2 Emergence of effective tourism planning and development

C. A. GUNN

Introduction

The purpose of this paper is to describe the state of the art of planning for tourism development—to sketch the progress of planning concepts and applications for tourism with emphasis on recent changes. Although planning for specific sites, such as for resorts, has taken place for centuries, great changes have taken place in tourism planning concepts and applications in only the last few decades. As nations, provinces, cities, and investors now seek the rewards of tourism, these changes are opening up new opportunities. More areas are recognizing that better planning can prevent most negative environmental and social impacts at the same time that economic benefits can be enhanced. Even though much of the scope of this paper relates to the North American experience, many of the principles and ideas are applicable elsewhere.

Background

Because the topic of tourism planning is confused by ambiguity of the terms 'tourism' and 'planning', it is necessary at the outset to clarify meanings. For purposes here, tourism includes all travel (business and pleasure) except commuting from home to work. Included are the categories of visitor, tourist and excursionist as recommended by the World Tourism Organization. It encompasses all the physical development and management required to provide for the traveler's interests and needs. The term planning, however, is even more ambiguous. Within tourism, it popularly has many meanings: site and building planning, market forecasting, political planning, and market planning. The focus here is placed on physical planning, land use, and design.

In the context of state of the art, some forms of tourism planning and design have taken place for centuries. Even in ancient times, ships and coaches were designed for sea-going and land-based travelers who sought objectives of trade or mere curiosity. The brief travel history by Bridges (1959) cites the planning and building of travel services and facilities by ancient Romans and Egyptians. These plans and developments were created in response to travel market demand partly for commerce but also for health and to visit seaside resorts and major shrines, such as temples, statues and pyramids.

For centuries, the dominant form of tourism planning has been for facilities and services. This form continues to encompass individual building sites, travel routes and mechanisms for passenger transportation. Planning at a larger scale—community and region—seems to be a much more recent phenomenon. Even seaside and mountain resorts that emerged in the mid-nineteenth century tended to grow from individual site increments rather than from regional or area plans.

This site-scale emphasis was the logical outcome of the complex nature of tourism and the growth of specialization. It was logical for business enterprise to narrow its focus on only the site and its development for financial success. It was logical for governmental agencies, based upon their legal mandates and individual policies, to concern themselves primarily with tourism-related plans and developments within their own jurisdictions such as for parks and transportation. Equally specialized was the development of the planning and design professions. Probably the oldest was architecture, created primarily as a building design profession. Then, with Frederick Law Olmsted's land design work, especially for urban and natural resource parks, landscape architecture was created as a separate but related profession. Engineering developed with a strong focus on mechanical and structural design. Planning, as a profession, stemmed primarily in response to urban growth issues, land use, and allocation of public facilities. Educational institutions responded with the creation of distinct and autonomous professional programs. For reasons of public safety the professions of architecture, landscape architecture, engineering, and planning became legalized, requiring separate examination, licensing, and regulation. Related to tourism design has been the great growth of specialized educational programs in hotel, restaurant, travel agency, and park management.

These well-defined planning, design, and management disciplines have been utilized by many developers within all tourism sectors. Today, three sectors have become the major decision makers regarding investment, development and management of the many pieces that make up tourism. Worldwide, an important role in land ownership, development and management is performed by governmental agencies. Examples include transportation routes, airlines, parks, recreation areas, natural resource preserves, and basic infrastructure, such as water supply, waste disposal, police and fire protection. Throughout the world, the voluntary and nonprofit sector has become a major stakeholder in tourism. Lands, facilities and programs by nonprofit organizations offer many opportunities for tourism such as festivals, events, historic restoration and reuse, youth and adult camping, and religious pilgrimages. More conspicuous in developed nations is the profit-making private enterprise sector that plans, builds and operates hotels, motels, food services, travel agencies, airlines, resorts, tour companies, and theme parks. All three sectors have increased their interest in better tourism planning in the last few decades. Although nations vary in the balance of roles of these three sectors, all three can be found nearly everywhere.

This background is presented only to show that for a great many years the fields of design and planning have had—and for good reasons—a narrow and specialized focus rather than application to larger scales, such as the community, area or region. In spite of this background, significant changes in tourism design and planning have taken place in recent decades. These changes have not resulted from great inventions or startling research of planning. Instead, several factors have converged, resulting in a new paradigm.

Factors influencing planning

In only the last few decades, several new trends have dramatically influenced planning applications to tourism. The strong preoccupation with promotion by national, provincial, state and city tourism agencies is now being modified. Many of these tourism leaders are changing their budget balances to include new functions of research, education and planning. In the field of tourism planning, the following are among the leading factors fostering change.

New market understandings

For a long time, new tourism development was largely planned according to land and building patterns of the past and generalized assumptions regarding markets. New resorts were elaborations of past resorts; new motels like old motels; and new restaurants like former ones. More recently, this approach of supply-side imitation has been modified greatly in an attempt to meet new market needs.

Travel market research is revealing new classifications of travelers, demonstrating that not all market segments seek the same thing. Ritchie (1992) has pointed out that new market trends are creating new challenges—cultural and natural resource interests, better human relationships and desire for specialized travel products. Creative and innovative planning and design approaches are now changing in order to develop attractions, facilities, and services that are better reflections of segmented market needs. For example, new franchise food establishments such as McDonald's frequently modify a standard architectural design in an historic district to harmonize with historic buildings, meeting new cultural needs of travelers.

Hobbs (1992) has reported a stronger market demand for quality, now being reflected in the design and planning for all tourism development. The ordinary, hackneyed and commonplace no longer satisfy travel market demand.

Privatization

Throughout the world, democratic governments and market economies have been replacing command economies. Tourism-related businesses are growing in numbers. Airlines, hotels, resorts and attractions formerly developed and operated by governments are being opened up to private entrepreneurs. With increased demands upon governmental funds, many park and recreation services used by travelers are being turned over to private enterprise. Even in areas where governmental subsidy continues, private business directors are exercising greater control of planning and design of their facilities and services.

Advocates of a 'Quality/Value Managed' private tourism plan (Hallowell, 1992) cite market satisfaction rather than governmental control as a major opportunity before today's travel organizers. The US experience with deregulation of the airline industry has demonstrated improved service quality, safety and better fares (Morrison and Winston, 1992).

Decentralized private development is proving to be more responsive to changes in travel market needs and interests than centralized bureaucratic control. But, the new form of privatization includes many public–private cooperative ventures rather than pure *laissez-faire*.

Environmentalism

Universally, environmental concerns are stimulating greater interest in tourism planning and are expressed in two major ways.

First, tourism destinations are more aware today of environmental quality threats from all sources. Municipal and industrial waste continues to cause air, water, and land contamination. Depletion of forests, reduction of wildlife, air pollution and soil erosion continue to destroy resource potential for tourism. Gradually tourism proponents are beginning to recognize these threats and are expressing their concerns in political and physical plans.

Second, it is now well documented that tourism, if improperly planned and managed, can produce its own negative environmental impacts. A 2000-delegate five-day conference produces about 600 pounds of aluminum cans and paper waste equal to 170 trees (The 'Biodegradable Meeting', 1990). Beach resorts often were built too close to the water's edge and have been damaged by beach erosion. Many waterfront hotels have contaminated their own swimming, boating and fishing waters with untreated sewage. For example, a majority study of the Mediterranean region (Frenon and Batisse, 1989) emphasizes the lack of an overall environmental tourism policy with regulations needed to halt erosive trends. New resort, hotel and destination plans are reflecting the need for greater care in site selection, land use planning, and handling of potential environmental threats.

Many specialists and practitioners are now seeking planning and development processes within the ideology of 'sustainable development'. Nations, provinces and destinations are becoming more aware of the need to set sustainable development as a goal for tourism. Slater (1991) in a Canadian conference on tourism and sustainable development stated, 'All these initiatives—reducing and recycling waste, adopting energy efficient practices, providing complete and credible information, etc.—are all important steps to a more sustainable industry'.

Professionalism

Today's professional approach to tourism design and planning has broken dramatically from the past. Today a multifaceted planning-design team is replacing the individual specialty approach of the past. Such a team often includes architects, landscape architects, planners, and engineers. Some projects require additional specialists on the team such as historians, geologists, archeologists, wildlife specialists, and marine biologists.

Another major change is a new role for professional designers and planners—acting as a catalyst for new solutions. These professionals are moving from an elitist approach to greater involvement of all parties involved in and impacted by design decisions. This role that includes public involvement is more costly and takes more time but produces solutions that are more acceptable to all parties in both the short and long run. Such involvement is resolving many conflicts of the past. For example, planners resolved a twenty-year stalemate on a highway controversy in New Hampshire, USA. Plans for an Interstate Highway through a scenic mountain landmark area were stopped by environmentalists. This issue was finally resolved by means of planning leadership that brought opposing factions together. The solution: congressional action that allowed modified interstate standards (lower speed limit, narrow shoulders, narrow median) and protected scenic beauty. This catalytic action resulted in a plan that was agreeable to both highway engineers and public environmental groups (Rigterink, 1992).

Trend toward three scales

The traditional focus on site scale design and planning is now being modified by increased emphasis on the community/destination and regional scales. Even though many of the planning principles and processes are similar for all three scales, they are emerging as distinctive in their application (Gunn, 1993a).

Regional scale

Regional (national, provincial, state) tourism planning, although slow to develop, is now appearing more frequently. Preoccupation with promotion is now being modified by budgeting some resources for research and planning. As more research has revealed the social, economic and environmental impacts of tourism, the need for broad-scale planning has become more evident.

Among the earliest reported efforts for regional tourism planning were those by Gunn (1965), Kiemstedt (1967) and Lawson and Baud-Bovy (1977). Concepts by Gunn arose following several years of technical advisory work for tourist and resort businesses in the state of Michigan, beginning in 1945. (This work was sponsored by the Tourist and Resort Extension Service, Michigan State University.) After a few years of business counseling experience, it became clear that individual tourist business success was as dependent upon external as internal factors and that a broader-scale approach was needed. Study (Gunn, 1965) revealed the need for new concepts and processes for both environmental and economic goals.

Upper Michigan Project

Opportunity for an experimental application of these concepts came three decades ago with a project resulting in a seminal regional tourism plan, *Guidelines for Tourism-Recreation in Michigan's Upper Peninsula*, an area of 10 584 000 acres and a population of approximately 300 000 (Blank et al., 1966). Innovative was a planning process that involved a university, planning professionals, and local citizen committees for all fifteen counties of the region. The implementation of this process took about three years of interaction, study, and creative work. It involved three major steps: (1) study of resources, economic development, tourism sectors, and travel markets; (2) synthesis of study findings; and (3) derivation of conclusions and recommendations.

The project revealed several basic principles for regional tourism planning in addition to specific recommendations for growth in that region. These principles have proven their universal value in recent years and include the following:

- Economic impact comes first through service businesses —hotels, motels, restaurants, and shops. But these are facilitators, not total causes of tourism.
- Demand for these services results from visitors who travel to an area and take part in attractions—things to see and do (for business and pleasure). Attractions are the primary causes of travel.
- Attractions are owned, designed, built and managed land areas and structures that serve two functions: they have attracting power, drawing people to special locations, and they provide visitor satisfactions.
- Attractions depend greatly upon locations with abundant and high quality natural and cultural resources and access from nearby communities and market sources.
- Tourism is a functioning system composed of a demand (market) and supply side (attractions, transportation, services, information, promotion).

These principles gave rise to the tourism planning reality that not all geographical areas have equal potential. The geographer-planner Fagence (1991) has stated that: 'locations, regions, resources, amenities and infrastructure have an unequal potential and capacity for particular forms, types and scales of development'. For tourism, this means that a region will contain areas that vary greatly in potential. The concept of 'destination zone' attempts to define those areas that have greatest potential. The Upper Peninsula study resulted in delineating ten destination zones. In the ensuing years, most of the recommendations of this plan for zone development and resource protection have been implemented. Reflection suggests that a major reason for success was a process that combined local input with specialized study and concepts by professional designers and planners.

A destination zone can be conceived as having three major parts that need to be integrated: areas with *attraction potential*, a *community* that has adequate infrastructure and attraction potential, and can support new travel services, and *transportation* and access from market sources. Thus, a destination zone encompasses not only a community but its surrounding area as well. (Further discussion is provided in 'Destination scale' below).

It is conceivable, then, that the major thrust of a regional tourism plan should be the identification of key destination zone potential. With such new understanding in each potential zone, tourism development leaders can initiate their own local planning processes for expansion. Conversely, areas with little potential should not be given investment stimulation. A regional geographic assessment process, aided by computer geographic information systems (GIS), has been developed by Gunn (Gunn and Larsen, 1988) and applied to several regions in the United States in recent years: Texas (Gunn and McMillen, 1979), Oklahoma (Price Waterhouse and Gunn, 1987), Upcountry South Carolina (Gunn, 1990), Delaware (Gunn, 1991), and Illinois (Gunn, 1993b). The South Carolina example is used here to illustrate the process.

South Carolina Plan

The study area was a six-county portion of northwestern South Carolina, 3849 square miles in size and adjacent to the Blue Ridge Mountains of North Carolina. The major purpose of the project was to identify destination zones and potential development appropriate to the environment and suited to markets and to the production of tourism growth. The study included four major phases: (1) research of 'program' and 'physical' factors, (2) derivation of conclusions from research, (3) location of prime zones of potential, and (4) suggested development projects in zones and identification of other opportunities.

Program study included review of secondary data for information on (1) travel markets, (2) information systems, (3) promotional programs, (4) socio-environmental issues, and (5) planning and action agencies with ability to implement. Physical factor study was prepared for two groups of resources—natural and cultural. These physical factors were summarized in narratives and drawn on generalized maps. Because each factor has different relative importance these factor maps were weighted as shown in Table 2.1 for computer map overlays by GIS (geographic information system).

In order to show how the several physical factors aggregate, illustrating areas of greatest resource strength, these maps were digitized and then overlaid to produce composite maps as shown in Figure 2.1. For each series,

Table 2.1 *Weighting of resource factors*

For natural resource development		For cultural resource development	
Water	30	Prehistory	6
Vegetation/Wildlife	22	History	18
Topography	16	Economic development	20
Existing natural resource development	10	Existing cultural resource development	20
Transportation	18	Transportation	15
Cities	4	Cities	21
	100		100

Because the influence of factors varies, a differential weighting was assigned for aggregating computer maps.

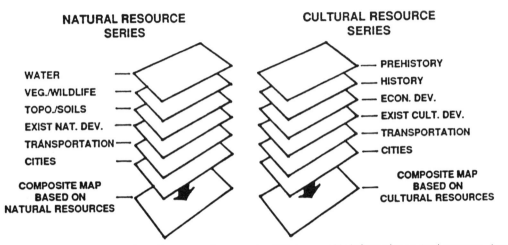

Figure 2.1 *Process for computer overlays. By means of a computer GIS (geographic information system) program, two series of map overlays were added, producing two composite maps*

maps of transportation and cities were included. By means of interpreting the narrative reports and GIS composite maps, zones were delineated based on natural and cultural resources as shown in Figures 2.2 and 2.3, respectively. By grouping these two maps, Figure 2.4 is produced, illustrating zones of greatest total potential.

Overall results from this regional study provided the following conclusions:

● Significant tourism development is already in place.
● Region has opportunity to compete well with others.
● Growth and popularity depend upon further planning and design.
● New cooperation of decision makers within and among zones is needed.
● Stronger linkage between rural attractions and cities is needed.
● Greater outside cooperation would help region.
● Small scale and slow growth is most adaptable to region.
● Needed are several important new steps: market research, training, education, public cooperation, regional and zone leadership and integration, and greater protection of resources.

Some observations on this process should be emphasized. Following this regional approach, it is the responsibility of all tourism forces at the regional level and within the delineated zones to take further steps. For example,

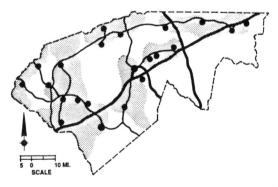

Figure 2.2 *Zones based on natural resources. From the composite map based on natural resources, several zones of greatest potential for tourism development were interpreted. Within these zones, leaders can stimulate attraction development to meet market demand for activities related to natural resources*

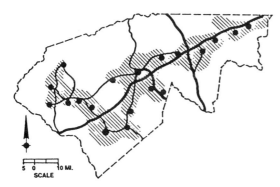

Figure 2.3 *Zones based on cultural resources. These zones represent interpretation of the cultural resource composite map. These zones have potential for new attraction development to meet market demand for activities related to cultural resources*

existing tourism capacities and limits to environmental stress must be determined. Existing political and tourism organizations may need to realign their boundaries or enter into new cooperative arrangements to follow through. Each zone contains one or more communities as focal points for expansion of services such as lodging and food. If several communities lie within a zone this suggests the need for cooperation in developing common themes. This process is proving its effectiveness in laying a foundation for regional tourism policy and development.

Other regional planning
Many other regions have become engaged in some form of regional planning for tourism development in the last few decades. A survey by WTO (World Tourism Organization) in 1980 revealed that 348 regional and 266 intraregional plans had been prepared at that time.

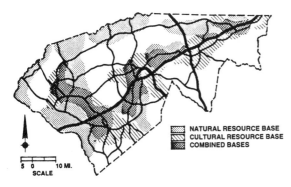

NATURAL RESOURCE BASE
CULTURAL RESOURCE BASE
COMBINED BASES

Figure 2.4 *Combined zones of potential. Overall tourism potential is revealed by adding together Figures 2.2 and 2.3. The darkest tone represents areas rich in both natural and cultural foundations for expanded tourism development to meet a wide range of travel market demand*

Japan (*Tourism in Japan*, 1992) reports that its planning division of the Department of Tourism is active in the following functions:

- Overall coordination and planning of tourist administration.
- Supervision of the Japan National Tourist Organization.
- Improvement of reception services for foreign visitors.
- Research and study on tourism.
- Subsidies to the tourist industry.
- Matters relating to the acquisition of stocks by foreign investors in the field of tourism.
- Collection and compilation of tourist-related documents.
- Handling of general affairs for the Council for Tourism Policy.

Special emphasis was placed on important natural and cultural resource areas. By 1989, 39 'Special Areas' (of cultural significance) had been designated and planned for tourism.

Australia has established a national plan (Commonwealth of Australia, 1992) that includes: marketing and coordination; research and statistics; economic and business issues; transport and facilitation; training, employment and standards; environment and social issues; and accommodation and market growth.

Another current GIS approach to the assessment of tourism potential is the 'Coastal Tourism Resource Inventory Project' (CTRIP) (ARA Consulting Group, 1991) for British Columbia, Canada. The purposes are: (1) to develop and implement a rigorous and credible tourism resource mapping methodology and (2) to ensure that the inventory provides a cost-effective tool to support tourism planning. It consists of two phases. The first phase is to develop, test and refine the inventory methodology. The second phase is to prepare a tourism resource inventory for the entire coastline of British Columbia.

Rather than generalizing for total tourism potential, this project focuses on eight categories of visitor activity, identified by consensus of consultants, operators, and recreationists:

sportfishing, overnight	kayaking
sportfishing, day charters	scuba diving
coastal overnight cruising	marinas
coastal cruising, day	cruise ships

For each category, specific site criteria were identified and used in resource evaluation. This step is followed by GIS overlays of factor maps specifically suited to the end-use category. Although this is in the experimental stage, it again shows the value of resource study and computer mapping tools for new tourism planning methodology.

Exemplary is regional tourism planning led by the Scottish Tourist Board (STB). In cooperation with 32 Area Tourist Boards, the STB provides planning and financial assistance for expanded development, including new golf courses, old town rejuvenation, fishing, the arts, cycling, access and transport (Scottish Tourist Board, 1993). A new Tourism Management Initiative includes plans for: newly designated tourist routes, priority destination area needs, town and village measures for improvement, scenic viewpoints, environmental awareness and protection, and facility design guidelines (Scottish Tourist Board, 1992).

Conclusions on regional tourism planning
Although not yet supported by a great groundswell of interest, tourism planning at the regional scale is the topic of more conferences, the concern of more policymakers, the subject of more technical study (such as use of GIS), and a beginning of serious implementation. Regional tourism planning is especially effective in creating national policy on transportation, marketing, interagency cooperation, and environmental and social issues related to tourism.

Destination scale

Even more popular has become planning and design at the destination scale—a community and surrounding area. Proper functioning of a destination includes three major parts: attractions, community, services and transportation. Tourism functions require integrated planning of the surrounding area and the city. Many recreational and cultural activities take place in rural areas as well as in cities, requiring cooperation among all political jurisdictions and private organizations.

Recently, several guides to planning and developing destinations have been prepared in the United States. The book, *The Community Tourism Industry Imperative: the Necessity, the Opportunities, its Potential* (Blank, 1989) contains twelve chapters of guidance information for individuals and organizations that wish to develop destination zones. The province of Alberta (Alberta Tourism, 1988) prepared its *Community Tourism Action Plan Manual* as a guide for organizations and a 24-step process for tourism planning and development. As of 1990, 250 of 429 eligible Alberta communities have developed their plans following this guide (Go et al., 1992). The US Travel and Tourism Administration, in recognition of dwindling rural economies, has developed

a tourism planning and development guide, *Rural Tourism Development Training Guide* (Koth et al., 1991). These and others are indicative of the new interest in making a more concerted planning effort at the destination scale than in the past.

Two important examples of planning at the destination scale are included in *New Challenges in Recreation and Tourism Planning* (Van Lier and Taylor, 1993). The Sils/Segl communities and surrounding areas in Switzerland have been planned to foster protection of mountain scenery of the Canton of Grisons by concentrating building areas (Jacsman et al., 1993). In France, Tarlet (1993) has reported on destination tourism progress in recent years. A major plan for the Aquitaine coast surrounding Bordeaux was prepared in 1967 and has met with reasonable success in years since. The tourism economy has improved at the same time that basic resource assets have been protected. Tarlet reports that planning of mountain tourist zones has met with mixed success. Many jobs have been created, new highways have improved access and the area has been revitalized. At the same time, some landscapes have been damaged, market studies were insufficient and sometimes development has not been adequately integrated with local communities.

Among destination plans, there appears to be no uniform approach. Some are prepared by governmental tourism agencies whereas others are the product of public–private cooperation. The Pacific Area Travel Association has sponsored several consultant task force projects at this scale. For example, a week of intensive study and evaluation of tourism in Moorea, French Polynesia, by a task force of four specialists resulted in specific recommendations for improvement (Kennedy et al., 1990). The study methodology included air and land reconnaissance, visits to tourism installations, interviews with proprietors, meetings with governmental officials and community representatives, and review of documents. Consensus was reached by the study team on 14 specific conclusions and recommendations including the establishment of a central sewage treatment plant to avoid beach and water pollution. The tourism sector was asked to provide better tourist access and interpretation for the significant natural and cultural resource areas, such as the beautiful central mountains and over 30 Polynesian archeological sites. Because hotel occupancy was already marginal (below 50%), the task force recommended denial of a proposed mega-resort that would do damage to the fragile environment. Since the report was issued, this proposal has been refused by official local action.

An excellent example of effective destination planning is the plan for Viborg County, Denmark (Munk, 1991).

The physical plan is described as a comprehensive land use and area plan that includes: directive on urban development patterns, infrastructure, and protection of wetlands and natural resources. The plan resulted from collaboration among the County Council, mayors of municipalities, and tourist association representatives. Essentials of the plan also include product development, marketing and information, education, public planning and administration, and organization and economy. The plan is integrated with plans of the Danish Tourist Board. Another worthy example of destination planning in Denmark is the plan for the region of Flyn (Thybo, 1991).

Conclusions on destination tourism planning

Comparatively recent is the proliferation of destination tourism planning. Now there is greater sensitivity to visitor capacity management, integration of tourism with the local society and economy, and protection of natural and cultural resources as foundations for more and better traveler experiences. New organizational mechanisms that foster collaboration on planning are appearing. More areas are seeing the value of planning that utilizes input from local citizens as well as planning specialists and consultants.

Site scale

Perhaps the greatest change emerging at the site scale is a new design paradigm that includes a combination of professional expertise and greater insight into social, behavioral, economic and environmental aspects of each tourism project (Motloch, 1991). This change implies less design elitism and more public participation in the design process. There is greater recognition that each site design and development is part of an environmental whole rather than an isolated entity. Certainly, the special talent and experience of professional designers is as essential as ever. But, the enduring test of a design is not merely a designer–client agreement but rather a satisfying and valuable experience by the visitor.

Critical to this new approach to design at the site scale is new awareness of place and placemaking. Each place has its own characteristics that provide a special foundation for development requiring protection of assets and unique design rather than thoughtless and uniform modification of land resources. From this design approach, new attractions and other tourism developments are being established that are endemic to place. This principle of local uniqueness creates development that is more competitive than a homogenized tourism landscape.

Another new design principle involves eco-design ethics. The burgeoning market interest in natural resource features is now requiring much greater design and management sensitivity to the environment. This new approach is not mere altruism—it is good tourism economics. For example, the collaboration between owner and architect for Maho Bay Camps, US Virgin Islands, has produced a popular, profitable and environmentally sound facility (Leccese, 1992). The owner-developer argues that it is more profitable to work with nature than against it and that when well-designed and managed, the environment can be a valuable marketing tool (Selengut, 1992).

An increasingly important design trend is greater involvement of those impacted by new development. In British Columbia, Canada, a 'Co-Design Approach' (Callaway and Kipp, 1990) has been applied to coastal planning. Several focus groups identified specific themes that led to design principles:

—use of natural landscaping with indigenous species;
—a marine architectural theme; and
—walkways to connect downtown with waterfront.

Artists then interpreted these into graphics, followed by specific plans for tourism that are likely to be implemented.

The Western Australian Tourism Commission (n.d.) has published *Public Involvement in Tourism Development: What Does it Mean for the Developer?* This guide states that all tourism developers have the obligation of letting the public know about plans by means of open houses, workshops, community liaison, and media releases.

Greater collaborative design and planning among professionals and many involved parties is taking place. An example is the Victoria & Alfred Waterfront, Cape Town, South Africa (Victoria & Alfred Waterfront, 1991, 1992). Hotel investors, civic officials, architects, planners and citizen groups have collaborated on major waterfront redevelopment for both local citizens and visitors. Of the first phase investment (R63 million) R35 million has been spent in infrastructure alone—roads, water supply, waste drainage, landscaping, and relocation of nonconforming structures. These plans have received many honors and awards for their innovative approach.

Greater public–private planning between tourism interests and national park administrators is taking place. An example is the site planning project for Orange Valley Resort, Antigua (*Orange Valley, Antigua*, 1991). The focus is on a resort complex but collaboration on plans for an adjacent national park is an important element of the project. Proposed for the national park are three zones: natural reserve, recreation zone, and a development zone (272 acres, 12% of total). The master plan objective is to create a world-class resort that is fully integrated into Antiguan way of life at the same time that it provides for visitors and adds to the economy. The plan concentrates buildings and facilities on 'hardened' sites and manages rare and fragile environmental assets for long-range resource protection.

Conclusions on site scale planning
The major change in site scale planning and development is greater integration with the physical, political and social setting. Local citizens and governmental agencies are now beginning to cooperate with owners and designers in the creation of plans. Better design is demonstrating that tourism development and environmentalism are compatible, even essential to each other. There is a growing trend toward more localized, small-scale and slow-paced development rather than externally imposed, large-scale and high-impact development. The special qualities of places are being protected as new site designs are prepared for tourist facilities, services and attractions.

Conclusions

The traditional tourism archetype of promotion as the sole key to development is now being modified by many forms of planning. Modern planning has broken away from the traditionally narrow image of elitist, dictatorial, and insensitive legal planning and has moved toward the concept of participatory goal-setting and strategic planning as a process. Nations, provinces and states are increasingly engaged in regional planning for greater overall good. Communities, as never before, are coordinating their tourism planning with design and planning for facilities and services is being modified with new concepts integrated with surrounding social and environmental factors.

These changes in planning, even though not universal, are a significant break from the past. For the first time in history they show that tourism developers must recognize several goals in addition to improved economy. Certainly, employment, wages, income and increased tax revenues will continue to motivate tourism development. But, the new interest in planning suggests that three other goals are equally important: increased visitor satisfactions, integration with existing local social and economic life, and protection and better utilization of basic natural and cultural resources.

Many challenges remain. Greater business success and economic impact are directly dependent upon stronger understanding of traveler's attitudes and preferences; greater sensitivity to all local social and economic impacts; increased realization and action to clean up and protect natural and cultural resources; new multidisciplinary educational programs; much more aggressive professional design and planning activity in the field of tourism; and a major shift from myopic to broad-scale understanding and practices by tourism investors and developers.

References

Alberta Tourism (1988) *Community Tourism Action Plan Manual*, Alberta Tourism, Edmonton.

ARA Consulting Group (1991) *Coastal Tourism Resource Inventory, Phase I: Mapping Methodology*. For Sustainable Development Branch, Ministry of Tourism, ARA, Victoria, British Columbia.

The 'Biodegradable Meeting' (1990) *Meetings & Conventions*, Nov., p. 63.

Blank, Uel (1989) *The Community Tourism Industry Imperative: the Necessity, the Opportunities, its Potential*, Venture, State College, PA.

Blank, Uel, Gunn, Clare A. and Johnson, Johnson & Roy, Inc. (1966) *Guidelines for Tourism–Recreation in Michigan's Upper Peninsula*, Cooperative Extension Service, Michigan State University, East Lansing, MI.

Bridges, J. G. (1959) 'A short history of tourism', *Travel & Tourism Encyclopedia*, H. P. Sales (Ed.), Travel World, London.

Callaway, Clive and Kipp, Sara (1990) 'The Salmon Arm Waterfront—a win–win project', Proceedings 'Planning for Special Places Conference', Banff, Alberta, 13–16 May, pp. 107–110.

Commonwealth of Australia (1992) *Australia's Passport to Growth: a National Tourism Strategy*, Ministry of Tourism, Canberra.

Fagence, Michael (1991) 'Geographic referencing of public policies in tourism', *The Tourist Review*, March: 8–19.

Frenon, Michel and Batisse, Michel (Eds) (1989) *Futures for the Mediterranean Basin—The Blue Plan*, Oxford University Press, New York.

Go, Frank, Milne, David and Whittles, Lorna J. R. (1992) 'Communities as destinations: a marketing taxonomy for the effective implementation of the tourism action plan', *Journal of Travel Research*, 30(4): 31–37.

Gunn, Clare A. (1965) *Concept for the Design of a Tourism–Recreation Region*. B. J. Press, Mason, MI.

Gunn, Clare A. (1990) *Upcountry South Carolina Guidelines for Tourism Development*, (self-published), College Station, TX.

Gunn, Clare A. (1991) *Delaware's Natural Resource Potential for Tourism*, (self-published for Price Waterhouse), College Station, TX.

Gunn, Clare A. (1993a) *Tourism Planning*, 3rd edn, Taylor & Francis, Washington, DC.

Gunn, Clare A. (1993b) *Illinois Zones of Tourism Potential*, A. T. Kearney, Inc., Chicago, IL.

Gunn, Clare A. and Larsen, Terry R. (1988) *Tourism Potential—Aided by Computer Cartography*, Centre des Hautes Etudes, Touristiques, Aix-en-Provence, France.

Gunn, Clare A. and McMillen, J. Ben (1979) 'Tourism Development: Assessment of Potential in Texas', MP-1416, Texas

Agricultural Experiment Station, College Station, Texas A&M University.

Hallowell, Roger (1992) 'Trust in travel and the "Boundaryless" travel agency', *The Annual Review of Travel*, American Express Travel Related Services, New York.

Hobbs, Pam (1992) 'Changing values of today's leisure travelers', *Annual Review of Travel*, American Express Travel Related Services, New York.

Jacsman, Janos, Schlichter, Rene and Semid, Wizzy (1993) 'New development and concepts in tourism and recreation planning in Switzerland', *New Challenges in Recreation and Tourism Planning*, Van Lier and Taylor (Eds), Elsevier, Amsterdam, pp. 141, 178.

Kennedy, Ian (Ed.) (1990) *Moorea and Tourism*, Pacific Asia Travel Association, Sydney.

Kiemstedt, H. (1967) 'Zur Bewertung der Landschaft für die Erholung', *Bertrage zur Landespfliege*, Sonderheft 1, Stuttgart.

Koth, Barbara, Craig, Glen and Semm, John (Eds) (1991) *Rural Tourism Development Training Guide*, Tourism Center, University of Minnesota, St Paul, MN.

Lawson, F. and Baud-Bovy, Manuel (1977) *Tourism and Recreation Development*, Architectural Press, London.

Leccese, Michael (1992) 'Can sightseeing save the planet?', *Landscape Architecture*, 82(8): 53–56.

Morrison, Steven A. and Winston, Clifford (1992) 'Cleared for takeoff: The evolution of the deregulated airline industry', *The Annual Review of Travel*, American Express Travel Related Services, New York, pp. 75–89.

Motloch, John I. (1991) *Introduction to Landscape Design*, Van Nostrand Reinhold, New York.

Munk, Inger (1991) 'Tourism and the regional plan for the county of Viborg', presentation, IULA Meeting, 17 September 1991, Paros.

Orange Valley, Antigua (1991) A proposal for a major resort within the Antiguan and Barbudian National Park, LDR International, Columbia, MD.

Price Waterhouse and Gunn, Clare A. (1987) *Proposed Master Plan for Travel Marketing and Development for the State of Oklahoma*, Vols 1 and 2, for the State of Oklahoma, Tourism and Recreation Department, Oklahoma City.

Rigterink, Richard (1992) Correspondence, May, Johnson, Johnson & Roy, Inc., Ann Arbor, MI.

Ritchie, J. R. Brent (1992) 'New realities, new horizons—leisure, tourism and society in the third millennium', *The Annual Review of Travel*, American Express Travel Related Services, New York, pp. 13–26.

Scottish Tourist Board (1992) *Tourism and the Scottish Environment*, STB, Edinburgh.

Scottish Tourist Board (1993) *Support Arrangements for the Tourism Industry in Scotland: The Views of the STB*, STB, Edinburgh.

Selengut, Stanley (1992) 'Building partnerships between protected areas and the tourism industry', Presentation, IVth World Congress on National Parks and Protected Areas, Caracas, Venezuela, 10–21 February 1992.

Slater, R. W. (1991) 'Understanding the relationship between tourism environment and sustainable development', *Tourism, Environment, Sustainable Development: an Agenda for Research* (Proceedings of Conference at Brock University, St Catherines, Ont. 27–29 October 1991), L. J. Reid (Ed.), Travel and Tourism Research Association, Canada.

Tarlet, Jean (1993) 'French planning for tourism and recreation—new perspectives', *New Challenges in Recreation and Tourism Planning*, Van Lier and Taylor (Eds), Elsevier, Amsterdam, pp. 35–68.

Thybo, Eva (1991) 'Guidelines for a regional tourism planning process for the Danish region, Flyn', dissertation, University of Surrey, Guildford, UK.

Tourism in Japan (1992) Japan National Tourism Organization, Tokyo.

Van Lier, H. N. and Taylor, P. D. (Eds) (1993) *New Challenges in Recreation and Tourism Planning*, Elsevier, Amsterdam.

Victoria & Alfred Waterfront (1991) *1991 Review*, The V&A Waterfront, Cape Town, SA.

Victoria & Alfred Waterfront (1992) *1992 Review*, The V&A Waterfront, Cape Town, SA.

Western Australian Tourism Commission (n.d.) *Public Involvement in Tourism Development: What Does it Mean for the Developer?* WATC, Perth.

World Tourism Organization (1980) *Report on Physical Planning and Area Development for Tourism in the Six WTO Regions*, WTO, Madrid.

3 Tourism development—a systems analysis

Z.-H. LIU

Introduction

Tourism development is a dynamic process and is conducted in an ever-changing environment, a blend of economic, political, cultural, technological and geographical realities and events. The central task of development is to keep a dynamic fit between the development opportunities and industrial capabilities, both of which are determined by its external and internal environment respectively. Nowhere has the tourism industry's lack of control (and, one might add, understanding) been more apparent than in the domain of trends and events in its external environment. A correct and accurate environmental study could contribute to an improved understanding and awareness of environmental changes and their implications for tourism development. It could also facilitate tourism practitioners and policy-makers in adopting a proactive approach in environmental monitoring and management.

However, the tourism environment remains an unduly neglected area in tourism studies as there has been no comprehensive research in this respect, though there are many publications discussing the various aspects of the tourism environment. A tentative attempt has been made here to establish a logical framework of environmental analysis for tourism development, to identify the major external factors influencing tourism development, and to discuss the interactions between the tourism system and its external environment.

As there are numerous factors affecting the development of the tourism industry and numerous complex interactions between them, it is important to approach the issue in a systematic way and with a holistic perspective. The systems approach is concerned with the resolution of any complex system into a number of simpler components and the identification of important linkages between them. It is holistic, general and dynamic (Jafari, 1987; Sessa, 1988). By adopting the systems approach, the researcher examines the development of tourism as a dynamic process of interaction between the internal and external environments of the industry.

The tourism system and its environment

Tourism is a dynamic open system consisting of many interrelated sectors and firms which serve the tourist market. It is generally held that the tourism system is composed of four elements—the tourists of the generating regions, the transit routes, the destination regions, and the industry—which are interwoven in functional and spatial relationships (Leiper, 1979; Mill and Morrison, 1985).

The system is like a spider's web—touch one part of it and reverberations will be felt throughout. Changes in demand, supply, access or marketing will inevitably affect the whole tourism system and successful tourism development requires all the components to function in harmony.

An understanding of the functioning of the tourism system is significant in the analysis of the tourism development environment. Demand for tourism in a society is determined by its population's ability and desire to travel. Tourism demand in terms of the total level and preference is largely determined by generating countries' factors while the spatial distribution of demand will be most influenced by those in destinations. The change in one destination's environmental factor will normally have little effect on the global level of tourism demand, but will certainly affect the demand to that particular destination.

The supply of tourism products is conditioned by the provision and marketing of tourism attractions, amenities and transport facilities. The various demand determinants push a tourist into a travel decision while the supply variables pull the tourist towards a particular holiday destination. Tourism development is partly supply-led.

The interaction between demand and supply is complicated by the forces of competition from other destinations and other industries. Although the travelling public may regard holidays as a near-essential part of consumer expenditure, tourist destinations have been facing increasing competition both from other destinations and from other leisure products, and consumer durables. Therefore, the task of each destination is to compete with the others for a larger share in the global tourist market.

Tourism development is a dynamic process of matching tourism resources to the demands and preferences of actual or potential tourists. Tourism development aims to maximise and optimise the overall performance of the tourism system which may be measured in terms of its direct, indirect and induced impacts on the economic, social and physical environment.

Obviously, the level and characteristics of tourism demand, supply, competition and impacts and the nature of tourism development process and patterns are conditioned by a host of factors many of which are external and out of the control of the tourism system itself. As Figure 3.1 shows, any changes in the environment will affect the inputs, the process, and the outputs of the tourism system.

According to general systems theory, a system's environment encompasses all factors both inside and outside the system that can influence progress toward the attainment of its objectives. The environment at any given time is a result of the interplay of many complex and continually changing forces. The tourism industry is an open system, environmental factors inevitably influence it, and it is up to the management to ensure that this influence is channelled in a positive direction and contributes to the industry's success.

The environment of the tourism industry may be partitioned into three distinct but interlocking levels: the internal environment, the operating environment, and the macro-environment. Figure 3.2 depicts the relations between the tourism system and its environments.

The internal environment of the tourism system (in this analysis, the tourism industry in a country) is the level of environment which exists inside the system and normally has immediate and specific implications for managing the tourism industry. The main components of the internal environment may include the following aspects: policy

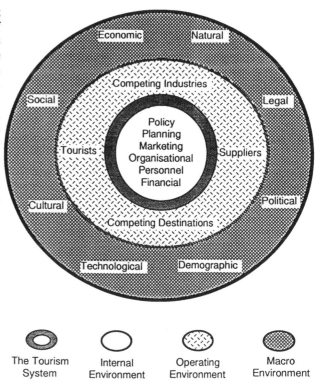

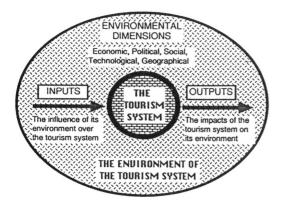

Figure 3.1 *The tourism system and its environment*

Figure 3.2 *The three environments of the tourism system*

(development objectives, policy-making procedures, coordination and implementation of policies); planning (development strategy and plan formulation, planning agencies, planning process, the role of national and regional plans in the industry); marketing (domestic and overseas tourist market segmentation, market positioning, product pricing, promotion and distribution strategies); organisational (industrial structure, communication network, public and private sector tourism relationships, competence of management); financial (profitability, capital formation, investment opportunities in tourism); and human (labour relations, recruitment practices, training programmes, incentive systems). The internal environmental variables determine the capability and capacity of the tourism system in adapting to its external environment and maximising the benefits and minimising the costs arising from external changes.

The operating environment is that level of the tourism system's external environment made up of components that normally have relatively specific and immediate implications for the operation and development of the system. The basic elements of the operating environment of a national tourism industry may include the domestic and foreign tourists; the suppliers of the input—capital, labour, land, technology, materials and power, etc.—required by the industry; the competition from other leisure sectors and consumer durables; and, internationally, the competition from other designations and transnational tourism corporations. These factors decide the immediate opportunities and threats to tourism development in a country. As external environmental variables, the national tourism sector has no control over them; however, to some extent it could influence them. For example, tourism development and promotion can stimulate the demand or alter the preference of tourists and a destination can reduce international competition by developing unique and differentiated tourist products.

The above two types of environments of tourism are extremely important to tourism development, the current researcher's effort is, nevertheless, concentrated on the discussion of the macro-environment. For the convenience of narration, the 'macro-environment' is here normally termed the 'environment', unless otherwise stated.

The macro-environment is that level of the tourism system's external environment made up of variables that are normally broad in scope and usually have less immediate effects on tourism and often influence tourism development through affecting its operating environment. The macro-environmental factors have here been categorised into economic, socio-cultural and demographic, political and legislative, geographical, and technological—five groups—and will be examined in the following sections respectively.

The economic environment

Tourism is first of all an economic activity and economic sector. The relevance of economic variables, such as economic development level, economic structure, economic cycle, trade balance, energy supply, etc., to tourism development is self-evident.

The economic development level

The economic level is the key environmental factor influencing tourism development since 'tourism cannot be considered outside the context of the different stages of development countries have reached' (Van Doorn, cited in Pearce (1989:12)). It affects virtually all aspects of tourism development, including the size and features of tourism demand, the availability and adequacy of tourism resources, the organisation and management of the industry, and the impacts of tourism development.

The positive relationship between the economic level and tourism demand is obvious in that the major origin regions of international tourists are the same regions where most of the developed countries are clustered—Western Europe and North America. The citizens in countries with a per capita GNP less than US $300 on average spent $0.96 on travel abroad while those in the nations with per capita GNP over $15 000 spent $265.42 on foreign travel in 1992. It appears that the threshold of international travel demand in GNP per capita terms was about $5000 in 1990. Any income level below that would normally not generate substantial outbound travel flows. Certainly, this threshold varies across time and countries.

There is also an important relationship between development level and the distribution of tourism demand between domestic and international tourism. It has been hypothesised that, along with the rise in economic development level, domestic tourism will stagnate and be overtaken in relative importance by a considerable expansion of foreign tourism; but with further increases in income and leisure time and the consequent growth of second and third holidays, there could be renewed growth in domestic tourism and the gap between foreign and domestic tourism may close (Williams and Shaw, 1991:6).

The level of economic development will largely determine the availability and adequacy of infrastructure, superstructure, capital and technology in a country, factors which have been considered as the 'dynamic' determinants of the attractiveness of a country (Meinung, 1989). Needless to say that in this respect developed countries are absolutely superior to developing countries. Poor access and inadequate infrastructure have been considered as the major obstacles of tourism development in developing regions (Heraty, 1989; Jemiolo and Conway, 1991).

However, a low level of economic development has certain advantages. First, underdevelopment itself is often a great source of attraction for tourism. 'Tourism, by its nature, tends to distribute development away from the industrial centres towards those regions . . . which have not been developed' (Peters, 1969:11) and the very consequences of lack of development can become positive resources of tourism such as the wilderness of the natural environment and undamaged traditional way of life. Secondly, lower living standards and low prices compared with those in the country of origin, or with those of competing tourist destinations, is a strong attraction, especially for undifferentiated or less unique tourist products such as beach holidays.

Economic development level also has implications for the degree of government involvement in tourism. Governments all over the world are involved in tourism and share many common responsibilities in tourism development, such as the coordinating, legislation, planning, and financing function (WTO, 1983). But governments in developing countries are more actively involved in tourism and have a wider range of functions. Besides supporting and regulating the industry, as their counterparts in most developed countries do, they 'have inevitably become both developers and managers to bridge the gap arising from a lack of innovations of the private sector' (Dieke, 1991:269–270).

The involvement of foreign capital and expertise in tourism development is also inversely related to economic level. In spite of the fact that in developed countries there are some forms of foreign involvement in tourism, it is not a desperate need and the investment across national boundaries is often a two-way flow. It is the developing world that depends heavily on foreign involvement 'to overcome two obstacles: their scarcity of domestic funds for investment in tourism, and their lack of tourism expertise' (Jenkins, 1982:91).

The economic development level of the destination is also closely related to the size and intensity of the tourism impacts, especially the social and cultural impacts. It has been suggested that developing countries are likely to experience more negative socio-cultural effects as a result of tourism development than developed countries (de Kadt, 1979).

Economic cycle

Although tourism has often been claimed as recession-resilient, the industry is inevitably affected by economic cycles and is especially highly responsive in general terms to changes in the level of disposable income in tourist-generating countries (Schulmeister, 1979). The global tourism statistics (see WTO, 1992, Table 1) indicate that the growth of international tourism throughout the postwar period has clear cyclical movements which average about 6 or 7 years and are fairly correlated to the world economic cycle.

Trade balance

International tourism has long been used as a means to promote exports and reduce trade deficit by many countries. The role tourism played in this respect is closely related to the balance of payments in general and the balance of the tourist trade itself. Generally speaking, the effort in promoting inbound tourism and restricting outbound tourism is closely linked to a country's balance of payments. A favourable trade balance is normally associated with no, or fewer, restrictions on outbound

travel, such as the case of West Germany since 1957 and Japan since 1964. The one hundred or so countries which have strict currency restrictions on foreign travel are usually less developed and often confronted with trade deficits.

Exchange rates

As inbound and outbound tourist demands, like the demands for all goods and services, are influenced by relative prices, they are bound to be affected by changes in exchange rates. A depreciation of a country's currency will normally make inbound travel more attractive and outbound travel more expensive. An appreciation has opposite effects: lower tourism receipts and higher tourism expenditure. It is worth emphasising that, in examining the effects of the volatility in exchange rates on tourists' destination choice, real exchange rates rather than nominal exchange rates should be used (Gibbons and Fish, 1985).

Energy supply

Tourism is an industry that is directly affected by changes in oil prices since the most popular forms of travel—air and automobile—are oil-dependent. Oil prices rose dramatically in the 1970s, then they fell somewhat less dramatically in the 1980s and they now appear to be fluctuating. The severe effects of oil price rises and the consequent gasoline shortages have excited intense discussion (see, for example, Maiden, 1986; Solomon and George, 1976). At the global level, the oil price shock in the mid-1970s could be one of the key factors which contribute to the levelling off in world tourism growth.

The political environment

Tourism development is strongly affected by political and legislative forces. Not only is tourism often manipulated for political purposes but 'political factors can create, alter or destroy the bases of comparative advantage' (Dicken, 1986:136) of tourism.

International tourism has long been used as a means of international influence, by both the generating and receiving countries. 'Tourism is not only a "continuation of politics" but an integral part of the world's political economy' (Edgell, 1990:37). Indeed, political consideration is often one of the key factors in a country's tourism development. 'Government leaders have perceived of tourism as a political bridge among nations' (Richter, 1989:7) and 'the flows of tourism between two nations can be used as a sign of the level of salience between the two nations and their people' (Stock, 1977:33).

The differences in attitudes about and control of tourism development throughout the world are mainly due to different political cultures, structures and situations. 'The ways in which tourism is organised, and its impacts, can be expected to differ considerably in countries with different political structure' (de Kadt, 1979:32). Political ideologies are often closely related to the perceptions of the impacts (especially the negative impacts) of tourism (Matthews, 1978; Nash, 1989). Liberals may be more likely to support tourism development, while conservatives seek to retain the existing economy (Snepenger and Johnson, 1991).

Tourism, especially mass tourism, is essentially a result of democratisation in the distribution of income, leisure time and human rights. It is no surprise, therefore, that tourism has often been promoted actively in democratic countries. In many authoritarian regimes, in contrast, both domestic and international tourism are often limited and strictly controlled, though authoritarianism is not always incompatible with tourism, as is exemplified by the Philippines under Marcos and Greece under the colonels after 1967.

In tourism development, political stability is a 'hygiene factor' in that it itself will not necessarily promote tourism development but its absence will certainly damage or destroy the industry. Numerous studies show that sharp downturns in the tourist traffic have often accompanied *coups d'état*, revolution, political upheaval, war and terrorist activity in different parts of the world. However, tourist memories have been shown to be relatively short, with a return to business as usual upon a resumption of normal conditions.

Tourism develops and functions within the legal framework which may be divided into two parts. The first is implicit tourism legislation, which involves legislation not normally thought of as having a tourism outcome but inevitably affecting tourism operation. The most common includes the regulations on investment, trade, competition, ownership, advertising, environment protection and land-use and various aspects of the labour market, such as minimum wages, work hours, working conditions, equal opportunity, and restrictions on overseas labour, all affect the supply and price of labour.

The second part is explicit tourism legislation—the laws and regulations 'targeted' at the tourism industry and dealing with the operation and management of tourist enterprises, such as the regulations on transport and travel service operations, special tourism taxes, financial and fiscal incentives, utilisation of land and other natural resources for tourism development, and generation of tourism demand (especially restrictions on outbound travel).

In recent decades, of special importance to tourism has been the transportation and tourist and environment protection legislation. Civil aviation regulation and deregulation, concerning both scheduled and charter operations, can play a major part in determining accessibility and the level and pattern of tourism demand. Tourist protection has attracted increasing attention from many governments and researchers (Anolik, 1991; WTO, 1981). At the international level, for example, the World Tourism Organisation (WTO) and the International Civil Aviation Organisation (ICAO) have been actively involved in assisting governments in developing legislation and policies to protect tourists (UN, 1993).

The socio-cultural environment

Tourism development is created and continuously modified within particular social and cultural settings. 'The social and cultural characteristics of a host society will influence its attractiveness to tourists, the process of development and the nature and extent of the impacts which occur' (Pearce, 1989:53).

As a social activity, travel and tourism is socially conditioned and socially differentiated. Social factors affect many aspects of tourism, ranging from travel patterns, lifestyles and demand preferences, to hospitality resources, social carrying capacity, and all the social impacts of tourism in a destination.

The increases in tourism demand closely corresponds to increasing social mobility, more free time, changing lifestyles and fashion. There has been an especially close link between the development of tourism and the increase in leisure time (Cross, 1990). Of particular importance to the travel trade is the growth in paid holidays, the longer weekend and the extension of retirement time.

Tourism development is also subject to the influences of social movements, such as the consumer and green movements. Tourist enterprises and other businesses have no alternative but to respond to the claims of consumerism and the rising expectations of tourists. Environmental conservation and protection is not only a social responsibility or legal obligation of the tourism business but also a sensible business principle, since most tourist attractions are based on the natural environment.

The effects of culture on tourism are multidimensional; it is not only a determinant of tourist attractions, but also a factor influencing the impacts of tourism.

'There is no tourism without culture' (WTO, 1985:6). The various aspects of culture, such as way of life, customs, traditions, language, religion, arts, etc., are valuable assets in attracting tourists to a country. This applies in particular to developing countries where traditional societies are different from the society where the tourist comes from. The great divergence of cultural characteristics between the tourist and the host population, however, also leads to more pronounced cultural impacts.

The attitude towards travel and perception of tourism impacts are also culturally differentiated and conditioned by national ideology and ethics. This is especially true in the introduction and tolerance of sex and gambling as tourist attractions, which have usually been regarded as immoral and having severe negative impacts (Eadington, 1976; Hall, 1992; Symansk, 1981).

Historical contacts with the outside world, especially with the major tourism generating and receiving countries, will generally strengthen the likelihood of tourist movements between them. For example, the historical ties between European countries and their former colonies have been influential in attracting tourists to the latter from their former suzerains; but they could also lead to more severe negative political and social impacts, as western tourists may easily stimulate the feeling of a new colonialism.

Tourism is fundamentally a business of people. Any demographic change in a society may have repercussions on tourism in one way or another. People are both providers and consumers of tourist services. The size of the population in a country, under given social and economic conditions, is a rough indicator of the size of human resources and the tourist-generating market. Changes in population structure, however, are more influential on tourism development.

Age structure

Age can play a significant part in the types of holidays and activities that appeal to an individual. Generally speaking, the influence of age on the propensity to holiday is most obvious among the elderly. The role of ever more numerous retired people in the developed countries has not yet been clearly defined, but it is clear that the senior travel market is one with great potential for growth.

The spatial structure of population

The pattern of the spatial distribution of population, and especially the level of urbanisation, has a strong influence on the size and structure of tourism demand. Residents in the major cities are more frequent holidaymakers than those people living in small or medium-size towns or rural areas (Tuppen, 1991). The level of urbanisation in a country may also affect its citizens' preferences for tourist attractions, especially the appreciation of the countryside landscape (Smith, 1984).

Educational and occupational structure

Education and occupation are important factors in influencing the perception of attractions, the motivation of and the demand for holidays (Pearce and Moscardo, 1985). Surveys in Western Europe show that the propensity for holidaymaking, and especially multiple departures, is much higher in the upper occupation and income categories while regular non-holidaymakers are much more numerous in the low-income groups and amongst farmers and fishermen (TPR, 1991).

The geographical environment

Travel is motivated by unknown and different places and tourism is about an experience of place. Geographical variables set broad limits within which tourism development takes place. It is possible to relate patterns of tourist activity to the opportunities and constraints presented by the country's nature. The degree of dependence on physical environment as attraction, however, varies with different forms of tourism.

It has been argued that natural environmental assets are the 'very foundation upon which all tourism rests' (Gunn, 1989:1) and scenic landscapes are usually the most successful in attracting tourists. Some special forms of landscape are of particular importance to tourism; they are pleasant beaches, snowy mountain slopes, health spas, wildness areas and attractive urban built environment.

Topography and physical features not only determine the distribution of tourist attractions but also have significant influences on the accessibility of a destination and the transport routes and networks within the destination. The resilience and suitability of the natural environment for development are also of importance as it affects not only the feasibility of but also the carrying capacity for tourism.

The relationship between tourism and climate has long been recognised (Mieczkowski, 1985; Yapp and McDonald, 1978). The roles of climate in tourism and other activities can be generally viewed as a hazard, a resource and a determinant (Kates et al., 1985). Climate is a given and stable backdrop to life on earth and a dominating influence in the moulding of human behaviour. Pleasant climate conditions are major tourist attractions. The growth of mass tourism in Europe is characterised by the mass movement of tourists from the cool and cloudy north to the warm and sunny south. Climate is also a key force shaping the seasonality of the industry as it determines the seasons of the tourism attractions and even influences the institutional factors such as school holidays. Extreme climatic events—drought, avalanche, cyclone, flood—may cause disastrous damage to the tourism industry, such as those reported in many island destinations.

Location is important in tourism development because monetary, physical, and temporal resources have to be invested to overcome the friction of distance, which is a major constraint in tourism destination selection decisions (Anastasopoulos, 1991). The location of a country, as far as tourism is concerned, has three dimensions:

Geographical situation

The geographical situation of a country largely determines its topography, climate and other natural features. The tropical and subtropical regions are often considered to be unfavourable for general industrial development (Courtenay, 1985) but have been very attractive to tourism development as the passion for sun and sea makes the tropical region the sun belt of mass tourist destinations. For landlocked states, an obvious disadvantage of their tourism industry is the lack of access to sea and beach. On the other hand, islands, especially small islands are comparatively better located for tourism than for most other industries. The limited resource endowment and development options also often lead island states to be specialised in a few industries, of which tourism is usually a viable one.

Distance to main tourist-generating regions

A country's relative location in terms of the distance to other countries usually has a significant effect on tourism. At the international level, proximity to developed nations is especially important. The tourism boom in countries like Austria, Switzerland and Spain is primarily attributable to their advantageous location as most of their neighbours are large tourist-generators. If the international tourist flow is understood as a movement from a few central places (namely, Western Europe and North America) that fans out over to other regions, the obvious distance decay effect can be observed: with intraregional traffic predominating in many parts of the globe and reciprocal flows developing between countries, particularly neighbouring ones.

Situation in the global transport network

Access and travel cost are not always proportional to physical distance; the availability and efficiency of transport routes are often more significant. The regional, national and global transport networks are not evenly distributed but are complex systems of hierarchically ordered centres which can be identified at a variety of scales. The higher a destination's position on the transport network hierarchy the more competitive its position in the tourism market. In international tourism, air routes are especially important. The availability, frequency, cost, closeness to key nodes and major routes, and provision of both charter and schedule flights all have significant impacts on the physical, temporal and economic accessibility of a destination.

The size of a country to certain extent determines the options, imposes thresholds, and influences the patterns of a nation's economic and tourism development. It has also a strong influence over the various aspects of tourism development, including the tourism resource base, the level of tourism demand, the significance of tourism in the economy, and the impacts of tourism development (Liu and Jenkins, 1993).

The technological environment

Tourism development is critically influenced by advances in science and technology, as 'almost all inventions and innovations in the world have in some way contributed to the increased ability of people to travel' (Hudman and Hawkins, 1989:3).

Technological advances have greatly improved the socio-economic life of modern societies. Indeed, the 'modernisation' of industrial society appears to have been in large measure synonymous with the march of technological 'progress' (Bairoch and Levy-Leboyer, 1981).

First of all, technological change is the volatile dynamic factor that permits a constant increasing productivity (Mowery and Rosenberg, 1989). 'Higher productivity, associated with technological advances, has made possible the development of leisure classes as well as an improved material apparatus for travel' (Nash, 1989:40). Technological advances have been successively reducing work hours, changing work patterns, altering housework and increasing leisure time for the mass population. A high level of social, occupational and spatial mobility is another feature of a society with modern technologies. Many western industrialised societies are being called 'nations on wheels' and the 'information revolution' has created a modern mentality characterised by broadened horizons and increased psychological mobility, and thus more prone to travel.

Technology developments have been creating new attractions and new forms of tourism and help to fully utilise existing attractions. Technology progress has contributed new and more efficient methods of opening up the potential of tourism resources. It has brought an increasing number of attractions into the circle of tourist activity by increasing accessibility, especially to remote areas. Technology has also created a variety of new tourist attractions: man-made wonders, theme parks, water sports, and so on.

Technology progress has improved tourist facilities and brought about changes to all areas of the hospitality industry (AHMA, 1983). Modern air-conditioning and central heating are among some of the technological developments that have reduced the influence of adverse climatic conditions and improved the comfort of hotels, so helping to boost tourism. Developments in food and catering technology have increased the variety and improved the quality and convenience of food and food services for the expanding tourist market (Glew, 1989; Storey and Smith, 1990).

The accessibility of a destination is critically important in its tourism development. Advances in technology have increased the speed and capacity and lowered the cost of transportation and communications and traditionally underpinned the worldwide development of tourism (Halshall, 1992; Hoare, 1991). Indeed, the three epochs in tourism development are identified with three transportation revolutions: railway, automobile, and aeroplane.

Technological innovations over the years have not only increased accessibility but also reduced journey times between two points, a process known as 'time–space convergence' (Janelle, 1968), and lowered travel cost, a process known as 'cost–space convergence' (Alber, 1971) though to a remarkably lesser degree. Obviously in terms of time and cost distance the world is 'shrinking'. The global tourism industry has benefited much from this time–space and cost–space convergence as travel time and cost are major deterrents in travel decisions.

Progress in technology, especially information technology has contributed tremendously to the management of tourism (Bennett and Radburn, 1991; Poon, 1988). The computer has obviously been the greater single technological change this century to affect businesses (Sheldon, 1987). It has been argued that the tourism industry in general is ideally suited for computer technology (Holloway, 1989). The administration of the world tourist industry has been radically altered by the development of world telecommunications services that provide travel agents with instant access to information about schedules, prices, flight availability and hotel and car rentals. Internal functions are increasingly performed by accountancy and administration systems, internal networks and extensive databases, while communication within the industry is now principally conducted through the medium of computerised reservation systems (CRSs)

and viewdata, which together have already replaced the use of telephones and the post.

A comparative analysis of environmental factors

Economic, social, political, geographical, technological—all of these factors, and others, affect tourism development; but the nature, extent and patterns of their influences on the industry are divergent. The various environmental factors tend to differ in the following respects.

(1) The relevance and significance to tourism development. Although it could be said that all macro-environmental factors are somewhat related to tourism, the closeness of their connection to and importance of their role in influencing the industry are widely varied. For example, in terms of the effects on tourism demand determination, income level, paid leave entitlements and social structure are far more important than most of the other environmental factors.

(2) The nature of the impacts on tourism development. The environmental variables could be classified into two groups: positive or motive factors which often stimulate demand and create development opportunities; and negative or hygienic factors which usually impose or reduce environmental threats. Some environmental factors do not positively motivate tourists and attract tourism development but where they are absent tourists will be put off.

(3) The scope of influence. Tourism is a multidimensional activity. All the environmental factors do not (at least not to the same extent) influence all the areas and aspects of tourism development. Changes in some environmental factors, such as national economic recession, may mainly affect the capability of a country of originating tourists, while others, such as higher relative price compared to competing destinations, may largely condition its capability of receiving tourists. The location of a destination determines its accessibility while cultural distance between tourists and hosts has influenced the cultural impacts of tourism.

(4) Patterns of change—the causes, frequency, pace and form of change. Changes in some factors may be caused by changes in others, such as changes in lifestyles and leisure patterns. Some others are more independent, such as technological advances and climate changes. Some factors, such as population size, change in a gradual and often smooth process, while the trends of other factors may be disrupted frequently, such as political instability.

With regard to the pace or cycle of change, there is also wide variation between different environmental factors. The natural environment is usually static in the short term, while exchange rates may change every day. As various factors change in different cycles, their effects on tourism development can only be examined in 'proper' time period because there is always a time lag between the causes and the effects.

(5) Scale of influence—world, regional, national or industrial. Some changes in the external environment will have global impacts, such as the greenhouse effect and ozone layer depletion; some have mainly regional effects, such as those in the EU policies on the European Union: others usually have only national implications such as those in a national economic and political situation; and some changes may have effects only on the tourism industry, such as a change in specific tourism legislation or policies.

(6) Controllability of change—the extent to which it may be influenced by the effort of the tourism system. Some factors such as the location and physical conditions of a country are impossible to change by human effort, whereas some others may be affected by tourism development such as lifestyle and leisure fashion; and changes in government policy toward tourism are often caused by the tourism system itself.

(7) The measurability and predictability of changes. Some environmental factors, such as income and price levels, are fairly measurable, while many others are difficult or impossible to quantify, such as changes in social value, cultural norms and political climate. Some variables, notably demographic ones, function in a fairly constant way throughout time and across the globe; while changes in most of the environmental elements are difficult to predict, though sometimes signs indicating the future trends may emerge in advance, such as those in economic, political and technological spheres.

Tourism system–environment interaction

All the environmental factors identified above are parts of a single whole. These environmental factors can only be adequately analysed in a holistic context as these factors do not intervene in tourism in a straightforward process of succession but occur through an aggregate or counterbalancing process. Therefore it is extremely difficult to isolate the contributions to tourism development of a single factor or separate the effects of one factor

from another. It must also be stressed, at this juncture, that it is not possible to present a comprehensive survey and an exhaustive list of all the factors contributing to tourism development. Emphasis has therefore been placed on a better understanding of the interactions between the tourism system and its environment rather than on a detailed picture or elaborated model of the tourism environment.

The interaction between the tourism system and its external environment may be seen from the tourism development mechanism. Tourism development is a continuous process of keeping a dynamic balance between tourism demand and supply and, in a broader context, between the development opportunities and the industrial capabilities. The effective and efficient development and operation of tourism in a destination will further improve its competitive position and open more development opportunities to the destination.

Obviously, the existence of development opportunities is vital to the success of an industry. But the mere existence of opportunities will not necessarily lead to successful development. This is because, first of all, a destination may fail to identify attractive opportunities; secondly, it may fail to mobilise sufficient resources for conducting the necessary development activities to exploit the opportunities; and thirdly, mismanagement and the consequent low efficiency may turn the development activities into an unsuccessful exercise.

It is therefore clear that while the opportunities and threats of tourism development are determined by the external environment, the exploitation of the opportunities are neither automatic nor inevitable, but are dependent upon a number of preconditions. The most critical ones are the scale, structure and capability of the tourism system itself. Moreover, external constraints or threats, which are normally thought of as something outside the system, if managed properly, may be converted into opportunities (Gharajedaghi and Ackoff, 1986). For example, the state of underdevelopment and remoteness could be well exploited as attractions for small-scale and high per visitor spending tourism.

Conclusions

The study has briefly explored the variety and complexity of environmental factors associated with tourism development. It has found that the tourism system is constantly influenced by various environmental variables, these including economic, political, social, cultural, demographic, natural and technological; each has unique features in terms of the nature, the intensity and scale of effects on tourism, and the patterns of change.

The author believes that a systematic approach to the analysis of the environment is necessary if we are to advance our understanding of the characteristics and change patterns of tourism. There is, of course, no sense in which a study such as this can be definitive; rather it is indicative. Much research and development work is necessary before the full potentials of the approach can be realised. There appear to be three issues of particular interest as they are at the heart of the more generic study of tourism environment.

First, the interaction between the three environments of the tourism systems, that is, the internal, operating and macro-environment, since without the effective interaction, the development opportunities created by the external environment will not be, at least not fully be, capitalised by the system. In order to achieve a better understanding of these interactions, multivariant techniques and factor analysis may be deployed to permit simultaneous analysis of sets of interacting variables.

Secondly, a more rigorous effort to codify and quantify the various environmental factors and their influences on tourism is needed as the development or adaptation of consistent and well-tested measurement techniques is an important part of the maturing process of any science (Ritchie, 1975). It goes without saying that many environmental variables are extremely difficult to conceptualise, let alone measure, in any clear and precise fashion. Yet, given the widespread belief that such variables are important, it is useful to attempt some quantification of such variables.

Thirdly, there is an urgent need to improve the reliability and accuracy of environmental trends prediction and forecasting. The increasingly turbulent environment requires tourism policy-makers and practitioners to adopt a proactive approach in scanning, monitoring and managing the tourism environment. Without the proper identification and prediction of environmental changes, any proactive approach could be fruitless. The ideal environmental trends scanning and forecasting should also indicate the specific implications to tourism development of the possible changes in various spheres of the tourism environment.

Of course, our knowledge of the tourism environmental factors and their changes is very limited. The potential behaviour of environmental variables and their implications for tourism development have not yet been properly identified, categorised, or analysed. Only after a large pool of systematically researched tourism environmental studies have been made available could researchers hope to seek for answers for the above three key issues.

References

AHMA (1983) *The State of Technology in the Lodging Industry 1983*, Educational Institute of the AHMA, East Lansing, MI.

Alber, R. F. (1971) 'Distance, intercommunications and geography', *Proceedings of the Association of American Geographers*, 3: 1–4.

Anastasopoulos, P. (1991) 'Demand for travel', *Annals of Tourism Research*, 18(4): 663–666.

Anolik, A. (1991) 'Preventive legal care within international legal systems', in *World Travel and Tourism Review*, Vol. 1, D. E. Hawkins and J. R. B. Ritchie (Eds), CAB International, Oxford.

Bairoch, P. and Levy-Leboyer, M. (1981) *Disparities in Economic Development since the Industrial Revolution*, Macmillan, London.

Bennett, M. and Radburn, M. (1991) 'Information technology in tourism: the impact on the industry and supply of holidays', in *The Tourism Industry*, M. T. Sinclair and M. J. Stabler (Eds), CAB International, Oxford.

Courtenay, P. P. (1985) 'Geography and development', in *Geographical Studies of Development*, P. P. Courtenay (Ed.), Longman, Harlow.

Cross, G. (1990) *A Social History of Leisure since 1600*, Venture, State College, PA.

Dicken, P. (1986) *Global Shift: Industrial Change in a Turbulent World*, Harper & Row, London.

Dieke, P. U. C. (1991) 'Policies for tourism development in Kenya', *Annals of Tourism Research*, 18(2): 269–294.

Eadington, W. R. (1976) *Gambling and Society*, Thomas, Springfield, IL.

Edgell, D. L. (1990) *International Tourism Policy: an Agenda for Managers and Executives*, Van Nostrand Reinhold, New York.

Gharajedaghi, J. and Ackoff, R. L. (1986) *A Prologue to National Development Planning*, Greenwood Press, Westport, CT.

Gibbons, J. D. and Fish, M. (1985) 'Devaluation and US tourism expenditure in Mexico', *Annals of Tourism Research*, 12(4): 547–561.

Glew, G. (1989) 'Developments in food technology', in *Progress in Tourism, Recreation and Hospitality Management*, Vol. 1, C. P. Cooper (Ed.), Belhaven, London.

Gunn, C. A. (1989) *Vacationscape: Designing Tourist Regions*, Van Nostrand Reinhold, New York.

Hall, C. M. (1992) 'Sex tourism in South-east Asia', in *Tourism and the Less Developed Countries*, D. Harrison (Ed.), Belhaven, London.

Halshall, D. (1992) 'Transport for tourism and recreation', in *Modern Transport Geography*, B. S. Hoyle and R. D. Knowles (Eds), Belhaven, London.

Heraty, M. J. (1989) 'Tourism transport: implications for developing countries', *Tourism Management*, 10(4): 288–292.

Hoare, A. G. (1991) 'Transport, trade and tourism', in *Economic Activity and Land Use*, M. J. Healey (Ed.), Longman, Harlow.

Holloway, J. C. (1989) *The Business of Tourism*, Pitman, London.

Hudman, L. E. and Hawkins, D. E. (1989) *Tourism in Contemporary Society*, Prentice Hall, Englewood Cliffs, NJ.

Jafari, J. (1987) 'The tourism system: sociocultural models for theoretical and practical application', *Problems of Tourism*, 10(3): 3–17.

Janelle, D. G. (1968) 'Central planned development in a time-space framework', *Professional Geographer*, 20: 5–10.

Jemiolo, J. J. and Conway, D. (1991) 'Tourism, air service provision and patterns of Caribbean airline offer', *Social and Economic Studies*, 40(2): 1–43.

Jenkins, C. L. (1982) 'The use of investment incentives for tourism projects in developing countries', *Tourism Management*, 3(2): 91–97.

de Kadt, E. (1979) *Tourism: Passport to Development?*, Oxford University Press, New York.

Kates, R. W., Ausubel, J. H. and Berberian, M. (Eds) (1985) *Climate Impact Assessment*, John Wiley, Chichester.

Leiper, N. (1979) 'The framework of tourism: towards a definition of tourism, tourist and the tourist industry', *Annals of Tourism Research*, 6(4): 390–407.

Liu, Z.-H. and Jenkins, C. L. (1993) 'Country size and tourism development: a cross-nation analysis', paper presented at the International Conference on Sustainable Tourism in Islands and Small States, Malta, November.

Maiden, S. (1986) 'Oil prices and air travel', *Travel and Tourism Analyst*, July: 5–17.

Matthews, H. G. (1978) *International Tourism: a Political and Social Analysis*, Schenkman, Cambridge, MA.

Meinung, A. (1989) 'Determinants of the attractiveness of a tourism region', in *Tourism, Marketing and Management Handbook*, S. F. Witt and L. Moutinho (Eds), Prentice Hall, London.

Mieczkowski, Z. T. (1985) 'The tourism climatic index: a method of evaluating world climates for tourism', *Canadian Geographer*, 29(3): 220–233.

Mill, R. C. and Morrison, A. M. (1985) *The Tourism System: An Introductory Text*, Prentice Hall, Englewood Cliffs, NJ.

Mowery, D. C. and Rosenberg, N. (1989) *Technology and the Pursuit of Economic Growth*, Cambridge University Press, New York.

Nash, D. (1989) 'Tourism as a form of imperialism', in *Hosts and Guests*, V. L. Smith (Ed.), University of Pennsylvania Press, Philadelphia, PA.

Pearce, D. (1989) *Tourist Development*, Longman, Harlow.

Pearce, D. L. and Moscardo, G. M. (1985) 'The relationship between travellers' career levels and the concept of authenticity', *Australian Journal of Psychology*, 37(2): 157–174.

Peters, M. (1969) *International Tourism*, Hutchinson, London.

Poon, A. (1988) 'Tourism and information technologies', *Annals of Tourism Research*, 15(4): 531–549.

Richter, L. K. (1989) *The Politics of Tourism in Asia*, University of Hawaii Press, Honolulu.

Ritchie, J. (1975) 'Some critical aspects of measurement theory and practice in travel research', *Journal of Travel Research*, 14(1): 1–10.

Schulmeister, S. (1979) *Tourism and the Business Cycle*, Austrian Institute for Economic Research, Vienna.

Sessa, A. (1988) 'The science of systems for tourism development', *Annals of Tourism Research*, 15(2): 219–235.

Sheldon, P. J. (1987) 'Computers: tourism applications', *Tourism Management*, 8(3): 258–262.

Smith, N. (1984) *Uneven Development*, Basil Blackwell, Oxford.

Snepenger, D. J. and Johnson, J. D. (1991) 'Political self-identification and perceptions on tourism', *Annals of Tourism Research*, 18(3): 511–515.

Solomon, P. J. and George, W. R. (1976) 'An empirical investigation of the effect of the energy crisis on tourism', *Journal of Travel Research*, 14(3): 9–13.

Stock, R. (1977) 'Political and social contributions of international tourism to the development of Israel', *Annals of Tourism Research*, 5 (Special No.): 30–42.

Storey, M. and Smith, C. G. (1990) 'Developments within the catering equipment industry', in *Progress in Tourism, Recreation and Hospitality Management*, Vol. 2, C. P. Cooper (Ed.), Belhaven, London.

Symansk, R. (1981) *The Immoral Landscape: Female Prostitution in Western Societies*, Butterworths, Toronto.

TPR (1991) *The European Tourist: A Market Profile*, Tourism Planning Research Associates, London.

Tuppen, J. (1991) 'France: the changing character of a key industry', in *Tourism and Economic Development: Western European Experiences*, A. M. Williams and G. Shaw (Eds), Belhaven, London.

UN (1993) 'Consumer protection: report of the Secretary-General of the United Nations', *Journal of Consumer Policy*, 16: 97–121.

Williams, A. M. and Shaw, G. (1991) 'Tourism and development: introduction', in *Tourism and Economic Development: Western European Experiences*, A. M. Williams and G. Shaw (Eds), Belhaven, London.

WTO (1981) *Consumer Protection and Information for Tourists*, WTO, Madrid.

WTO (1983) *The Framework of the State's Responsibility for the Management of Tourism*, WTO, Madrid.

WTO (1985) *The State's Role in Protecting and Promoting Culture as a Factor of Tourism Development and the Proper Use and Exploitation of the Natural Cultural Heritage of Sites and Monuments for Tourism*, WTO, Madrid.

WTO (1992) *Yearbook of Tourism Statistics*, WTO, Madrid.

Yapp, G. A. and McDonald, N. S. (1978) 'A recreational climate model', *Journal of Environmental Management*, 7: 235–252.

4 Financing for tourism projects in developing countries

O. BENNETT

Introduction

Financing tourism projects is a frequently discussed issue. There are many instances of tourism schemes considered to be worthwhile by their promoters which are languishing for lack of finance. In this paper it is argued that the simple availability of cash is far from being the only factor in constraining development; more often than not, sensibly planned and executed schemes can be readily financed, given an appropriate regulatory framework and political stability. In this discussion we are primarily concerned with capital-intensive forms of tourism development, particularly hotels and resorts and related transport and other infrastructure, but consideration is also given to other aspects of the tourism industry, including funding for travel agencies and for marketing and promotion.

The role of government

In developing countries the way governments act is fundamental to tourism financing. What they actually do is more important than what they say they do. Tourism is peculiar in that it is a fragmented industry, involving many small businesses, but one which competes internationally. This in itself means that the way in which a government approaches tourism is especially important as compared to other industries.

There are a number of roles governments can play. First, they can act as a facilitator to the tourism industry, providing a suitable climate against which private sector development can take place. This may extend to the provision of soft-loan financing. A second role is in the provision of supporting infrastructure such as roads, airports and utilities. A third role is in marketing support. A fourth is in the operation of tourism businesses themselves. The way in which government functions will largely determine the level of opportunity for the private sector, and the means whereby new developments can be financed.

Government as an owner/operator

In many countries it has been argued that for a tourism industry to develop government should not only fund new developments, but it should act as an owner and operator too. This has gone well beyond having a nationally owned airline, to state-owned resorts and hotels managed by a government-owned hotel company. Countries which still have state-owned and state-run hotels range from Kenya and Uganda to India and Indonesia. The rationale for such state intervention includes a view that it is necessary in the initial stages of tourism development, against a background of capital shortages and lack of entrepreneurial talent. It is also argued that government action is needed to open new areas for tourism where the risks are too high for the private sector.

Government-owned hotel companies have rarely been good performers. There have been numerous reasons for this, ranging from a lack of a requirement to act commercially, poor management, political interference and corruption, to decisions as to the siting of new developments being made on political rather than commercial grounds. The operation of hotels by international management companies where the property has been wholly or partially government-owned has been more successful: among examples are the Sheraton in Kampala, and the Hilton and the Intercontinental Hotels in Nairobi. The widespread privatisation of government-owned hotels indicates that there is now a realisation that the private sector is a better manager of tourism businesses. This leaves government to act as a facilitator rather than as an operator.

Government as a facilitator

The first question for government is, do they genuinely seek tourism development? There is often confusion as to whether this is really the case. Governments such as Singapore which have established clear goals in conjunction with the private sector have done well; those where there has been uncertainty as to the objectives have done badly. Even in Europe, a recent comparison of tourism in the twelve member states of the European Union identified a clear, coherent tourism policy as one of the key factors in the success of the three states (France,

Ireland and Portugal) which have experienced the most rapid growth in international tourism revenues in the past decade.

Among the objectives which governments typically have in tourism development are:

—obtaining foreign exchange earnings;
—distributing economic benefits more equitably between regions;
—providing employment;
—protecting the physical and social environment.

In order to achieve these objectives, control mechanisms have been evolved to:

—maintain environmental quality;
—monitor foreign exchange movements, the employment of expatriates, payment of taxation, and other dues;
—promote quality standards.

These control mechanisms tend to change slowly, whereas the character of the tourism industry in a country can change much more quickly. There are numerous instances of control mechanisms being outdated, or no longer achieving the originally desired objective. (At the same time measures to protect the environment are not necessarily strong enough.)

Planning for tourism

Some form of tourism development planning is practised in most developing countries. Among its advantages can be providing:

—a clear set of objectives of what government wishes to achieve;
—a context for operations by both the public sector (including prospective donors) and the private sector;
—a framework for tourist development which allows for environmental protection, and seeks to avert damage to the social and cultural environment for tourism;
—individual projects, or groups of projects, appropriate for donor funding in support of potential private sector development.

Among the drawbacks can be:

- the Plan is not sufficiently flexible to cope with changes in the tourism industry. The tourism industry is a fickle business, and there is a limit as to how much governments can plan for its development. Forecasts of future visitor numbers in particular are prone to error;

—the Plan is too ambitious, and concentrates on tourism potential, ignoring what can be realistically achieved.

The benefits of development planning are exemplified by the Master Plan for tourism in Fiji. Prepared almost twenty years ago, this Plan is still being used today. The forecasts of visitor numbers have proved to have been wildly optimistic, and the scale of development was over-ambitious. The value of the Plan has been in selecting areas for development, and in setting design guidelines. Resorts in Fiji are sympathetic with local styles, and high-rise development has been avoided, a direct result of the original Plan and a determination to implement it.

Other tourism development plans have done little more than to expand the bookshelves of Ministers of Tourism. One way in which tourism development plans have failed in the past is for the opportunities for tourism development to be investigated in detail, but without an appraisal of how new developments are to be implemented, or projects to be financed. If development planning is to be of practical value, it often needs to include the consideration of the likely commercial viability of projects, and how they are to be paid for.

Assessing financial reality may require an outline financial and economic analysis of prospective projects, incorporating an initial assessment of financial rates of return, and, for public sector projects, the economic rate of return. Likely capital costs, equity funding, and rates of interest need to be taken into account in evaluating the reaction of the private sector to development concepts. Using computer models, it is possible to test the effectiveness of different incentive structures on the viability of potential projects, and from this to evaluate whether incentives may need to be revised in order to achieve the set development objectives.

Government tourism departments tend to be weaker in implementation skills than those responsible for the provision of major infrastructure such as roads or water. Tourism very often tends to follow infrastructure provision rather than lead it; a key component of development planning is to ensure that agencies responsible for providing infrastructure are aware of the role and needs of the tourism sector.

Regulatory control

In controlling the tourism industry, and the private sector in particular, it is vital that governments understand what their objectives are if they wish to achieve successful tourism development. Equally, regulation can be used as a mechanism for dealing with apparently conflicting objectives such as a stated objective of promoting foreign investment to gain foreign exchange while catering for an underlying reluctance to see such investment. This may be because the repatriation of dividends to foreign investors is perceived as causing a net loss of foreign exchange and employment; it may simply be a feeling that national control is being lost.

Investors are not necessarily put off by sensible control mechanisms. Promoting investment requires legislation which is simple and easily comprehensible, and an approach by government which is designed to help the investor. There are several approaches. One is minimising the amount of legislation and control, concentrating on environmental protection while operating a relatively liberal foreign ownership and foreign exchange regime. Fiji is an example of this. Another is to adopt a 'one-window' approach to licensing, as in Indonesia, which reduces the risk of contradictory regulations being issued by different ministries. A third is for separate pieces of legislation to be relatively uncoordinated, and for licensing of the tourism sector to be the responsibility of different parts of government. This has been the case, for example, in Nepal.

Fiji has an essentially 'open door' approach where the majority of investment has been from overseas, and where there are no restrictions on foreign ownership, apart from limitations on outright land-ownership. Indeed the industry was first established on the basis of foreign investment by the private sector. The government has sought to promote investment, and to minimise control and regulation. Unlike in Indonesia, there is no hotel classification system nor any licensing of travel agents.

As a result of the way in which foreign investment has been encouraged, and regulation kept to a minimum, there is very substantial foreign ownership in both the hotel sector, and in ground-handling operations. In Fiji control concentrates on environmental protection; not only are there design guidelines derived from the original Master Plan, but an Environmental Impact Assessment is required for all new resort developments.

Indonesia has a more complex regulatory regime, including a requirement for all foreign investment to be in a joint venture with an Indonesian company. The Investment Co-ordinating Board (BKPM) has become the only government agency responsible for investment applications and approvals. Not only does it operate nationally, but in every province there is a regional investment coordinating board. BKPM is responsible for the issue of investment permits required to start a new development. In addition, in recent years government has sought to deregulate and simplify rules for both domestic and foreign investors. This 'one window' approach

combined with deregulation has led to significant inflows of foreign investment in recent years.

This contrasts with a country like Nepal, where control concentrates on hotel licensing, control over equity share holdings, the remittance of profit and capital, the employment of foreign labour and institutional arrangements. These controls are the responsibility of different ministries and departments, and there is no single body for the investor, domestic or foreign, to deal with. This has tended to discourage foreign investment; indeed, unlike in Indonesia or Fiji, there has been very little foreign investment in Nepal's tourism industry.

Foreign exchange controls can work against a country's best interests. In countries with strict foreign exchange regimes the local currency may be depreciating. If a travel business has to translate foreign currency earnings into the local currency at the time of receipt, when it requires to draw on those earnings for an item of foreign expenditure, the value of the foreign income will have fallen. This encourages travel businesses to hold illicit accounts in foreign countries to which earnings are remitted, to the detriment of the country concerned. This kind of regime, where remittance of profits may also be difficult, discourages foreign investment.

Investment regime

There are a number of ways in which government can directly promote investment. One is to provide soft loan facilities through a government-owned financial institution. Others, where no direct financial expenditure is required, are through the investment incentives and a favourable tax regime.

State-owned development banks are a common feature of developing countries, and for those countries where tourism plays an important part in the economy, they are generally active in the tourism sector. All of the countries discussed above have such an institution. The Fiji Development Bank and the Fiji National Provident Fund have both invested in tourism businesses. The state-owned Development Bank of Indonesia (BAPPINDO) and the Nepal Industrial Development Corporation (NIDC) both perform a similar role in providing longer-term financing than commercial banks and generally on more favourable terms. In Kenya there is a government-owned financial institution devoted solely to tourism, the Kenya Tourist Development Corporation. These bodies are discussed further below.

Incentives typically consist of such measures as investment allowances, duty exemptions or concessions, and tax holidays. Grant finance is relatively rare. A common complaint in several countries is that incentives focus on the hotel industry, and they are not extended to the travel sector as a whole. To attract foreign investment, incentives, and the tax regime, need to be internationally competitive. Countries which are unsuccessful at attracting foreign investment, even when they genuinely wish to do so, may find that their investment regime is not competitive internationally. It is very common that once an investment regime is in place it remains unchanged for a relatively long period, even though external circumstances may have changed significantly.

The private sector

One of the most important advantages of the private sector, as compared to government operation, is its flexibility and its ability to adapt to change at a speed which are beyond most civil services. Privately owned businesses are more adept at satisfying customer requirements. Domestically owned businesses have the advantage that a higher proportion of earnings may be retained in the country concerned, but in many developing countries the capital market is small, and mobilisation of capital is weak. Capital may be available, but there is no mechanism to group individuals' capital into a sufficiently large pool to provide an equity base for new tourist resorts and hotels. Foreign capital can bring expertise in international markets, and assist a country in being competitive, as well as providing financing for larger developments.

Sources of finance

Direct government financing for its own projects apart, financing comes from a variety of sources:

—multilateral and bilateral grant, loans and aid;
—commercial banks;
—development banks;
—foreign investors;

as well as from the mobilisation of domestic capital.

The allocation of funding to the tourism sector from government budgets has primarily been for infrastructure which is multisectoral in dimension as it benefits almost all other sectors. Direct investment in tourism infrastructure such as hotels has been limited to state-owned corporations, and in recent years this has tended to be directed more at financing operating losses rather than new developments. Otherwise, direct tourism expenditures by government tend to cover research and development and marketing. Typically the amounts involved are very small in relation to total government budgets, and are dwarfed by allocations to other sectors.

The Indonesian Government is one that has invested directly in hotels and resorts. They have done this through direct share holdings in state enterprises which own airlines, hotels, resorts, travel trade operations and land designated for resorts. Part of the reason is historical as tourism was in the very early days a pioneer industry and was assisted by government-to-government funds received for war reparations.

Multilateral and bilateral aid

Multilateral and bilateral loans are generally government-to-government, although development banks frequently obtain funds from international multilateral sources to lend on to the private sector. Aid direct to the tourism sector is most commonly in the form of technical assistance to governments. Examples are support given by the United Nations Development Programme (UNDP) and the World Tourism Organisation in support of tourism development planning, by the Commission of the European Communities in longer-term tourism development programmes (including marketing support), and by the UNDP and International Labour organisation in tourism training. Bilateral aid has also most commonly been in the form of technical assistance. Examples of grant aid provided to the tourism sector other than for technical assistance are Australian aid to build a new tourism school in Nadi in Fiji, and Chinese aid to build a Convention Centre in Kathmandu, Nepal, and Suva, Fiji.

A major agency providing funds and technical assistance direct to the private sector is the International Finance Corporation (IFC), an arm of the World Bank; an agency directing itself at smaller-scale projects is the African Project Development Facility which aims to assist indigenous African entrepreneurs. The Asian Development Bank has also recently established a soft-loan financing arm to lend to the private sector and the African Development Bank has a similar private sector arm. Other institutions which have lent to tourism enterprises include: the European Investment Bank in African, Caribbean and Pacific countries within the framework of the Lomé convention; the French Caisse Centrale de Coopération Economique in francophone Africa; and the British Commonwealth Development Corporation.

A combined approach of lending to government but in support of the private sector was taken by the World Bank in its funding of the Nusa Dua area of Bali in the 1970s. A Development Corporation was established, which used soft-loan finance to develop infrastructure for Nusa Dua, and to provide serviced sites on which resort development could take place. The success of Nusa Dua, after a slow start, has led to this formula being adopted for other areas of Indonesia, such as Lombok, albeit without World Bank support. A similar pattern has been adopted for the much more recent World Bank loan to Egypt for tourism development on the Red Sea coast. This major project is to support infrastructure development for resorts which are to be built by the private sector; a newly established public sector agency is responsible for the overall scheme, with commercial Egyptian companies undertaking specific development projects within that overall framework. International operating companies, such as Sheraton and Robinson's Club, are expected to operate the resorts.

Commercial banks

The role played by commercial banks in developing countries varies from country to country and even within a particular country from bank to bank. The role that each bank takes is influenced by its perception of the potential of the tourism industry in the country where a loan is requested and of its own experience in financing the industry, not only in the country concerned but also in other parts of the world where it operates. For example a large bank in Australia which faces major problems with non-performing loans in the hotels sector there is going to look very hard at any loan proposal received by a branch in, say Fiji, for a new hotel development.

All well-managed commercial banks manage their risk through having strict policies on country risk and sector limits. Most bank managers of branches of foreign-owned banks have limited authority to commit the bank. Hence loans to the tourism sector which are normally large need to be approved by a loans committee at the head office in the foreign country concerned.

It is common practice for private sector commercial banks to provide loans of less than five years. This is too short a period to finance many new tourism facilities as their gestation period is long and the payback period normally exceeds five years and, depending on the location, may even exceed ten years. In some countries, such as in Kenya, they will provide loans for soundly based projects to existing known and well-managed businesses for a five-year term, with a willingness to re-schedule a loan should this prove necessary. Commercial banks do play an important part in providing working capital financing in the form of overdraft facilities to hotels and travel companies or short-term loans to financially viable hotels for upgrading of their facilities.

In Fiji it is common to get a commitment for long-term financing for a new resort or hotel development from either the Fiji National Provident Fund (FNPF) or the Fiji Development Bank (FDB) of up to 15 years. However, it is the policy of these two institutions to lend on first mortgage on land and buildings only. In these cases it is common for commercial banks such as ANZ Bank or Westpac Bank to provide finance during the construction phase and upon completion the FNPF or FDB takes over after discharging the loan of the commercial bank.

State-owned banks in Nepal are very active in providing medium-term loans, normally of seven years' duration, to the private sector for development of new tourism facilities or the extension of existing facilities. They are also active in financing travel companies for the purchase of tourist coaches and providing overdraft facilities to travel and trekking companies. An interesting recent development is the emergence of syndicated loan financing in Nepal. Under this financing instrument, several banks, including state-owned and private sector commercial banks, jointly finance a development. The use of syndicated financing there is necessary, owing to the relatively large amount normally involved in financing the development of a new hotel or a major extension and the limited financing capacity of any one bank as a consequence of the low capital base of banks in Nepal.

Commercial banking has been dominated by state-owned banks in Indonesia. National private banks in Indonesia traditionally have a low capital base and hence they have not been too involved in financing of tourism facilities. Following deregulation in 1988, many new local banks and foreign-owned banks have entered the commercial banking scene and it is likely that in the longer term the private sector banks will assume a bigger role.

Development banks

While commercial banks tend to provide loans for short periods of less than five years and at commercial rates, development banks generally provide longer-term loans at competitive interest rates. They frequently take as collateral a first mortgage on land and building.

The Indonesian Development Bank, BAPPINDO, provides loans to the tourism sector with repayment terms of between 8 to 10 years. In Nepal, the NIDC provides long-term loans at lower than commercial rates of interest to the tourism sector. The loans have generally been for 10 to 15 years.

It has been a feature of development banks in a number of countries that they have incurred losses because of poor quality loans to the tourism industry and slack collection procedures. In Kenya, the Kenya Tourist Development Corporation (KTDC) had a successful initial period when it provided equity finance to new hotels largely in Nairobi.

Difficulties have subsequently arisen as a result of lending to much smaller tourism businesses undertaken as part of a desire on the part of government to develop rural areas. Had normal commercial banking practice been adopted, it is unlikely that these loans would have been made. The subsequent difficulty in obtaining loan repayments, combined with slow legal processes of placing businesses in insolvency, has led to the KTDC being unable to finance new loans. As a result its role has largely been taken by other institutions, including multisectoral development banks.

Further difficulties encountered by national development banks have related to a weak legal framework for business operation, including inadequate insolvency laws and a lack of recognised accounting standards in some developing countries. This has meant it can be difficult for the bank to repossess a hotel which is performing badly and unable to repay its loans. The lack of recognised accounting standards may make it possible for a business to produce accounts which show it is profitable in order to obtain funding, whereas it may in reality be trading at a loss or even insolvent. Alternatively it may show it is loss-making to justify defaulting on loan repayments, when the business is actually able to meet its obligations. This may be associated with political pressure from influential individuals. By not repaying capital and interest, some tourism businesses effectively obtain free financing, which distorts the whole industry. Such businesses are able to quote relatively low prices, making it difficult for new entrants to compete.

Foreign investment

Most countries in the world need foreign investment to maintain or improve economic growth. Such investment may be directly in tourism businesses, or it may come through local commercial or development banks. Difficulties are still encountered in attracting foreign investment, particularly in some countries. Why do investors prefer certain countries and not others? Work by the author and by David Tong on behalf of the Asian Development Bank and the World Tourism Organisation suggests that the major factors that will influence the level of foreign investment into a country are those that are well known, namely:

—political stability;
—a pro-business environment;
—the prospect of an adequate return on investment;
—the ability to remit earnings.

A potential investor looks at all the factors including other matters such as the tax regime, availability of trained manpower and management–labour relations, efficiency of the civil service in processing his application and the cost of investment and operation before he decides to invest. Normally he is courted by several countries competing for foreign investment at the same time. He will then make a decision based on all the facts before him and normally after having done a market and financial feasibility study. Those countries which are ambivalent about foreign investment, either on paper and/or in practice, may well not be considered at all.

Problems and constraints

The problems and constraints which apply to the private sector are often brought about by the public sector, which in turn faces its own financing problems. Tourism has to compete for funds with many other areas of government. It is relatively rare that major investment in infrastructure can be justified on tourism grounds alone, although more local investments may be. It is important that tourism interests are taken into account when relevant non-dedicated infrastructure is being considered. Too often tourism departments suffer from twin failings:

—they are not given a high priority in government, and their voice is not strong enough;
—they do not have a sufficiently clear sense of direction as to what infrastructure needs to be given priority, and what the benefits to tourism would be from a particular development. One problem for the public sector is that there are invariably political pressures to undertake investment that the private sector will not consider. A particular difficulty is drawing the line between catalytic investment in new destinations, which the private sector is not prepared to undertake, and making perverse investments for political reasons, for example because it is felt that the benefits of tourism should be dispersed more widely, when either the location or the nature of the investment is simply not viable in either the short or the longer term.

The key to private sector investment is a sound project, with good management, that is likely to make money. Generally investors and their bankers look for profit performance that is sustainable on a medium- to long-term basis and with an adequate return on capital and safety of that capital. If there is a project that can satisfy these criteria, then in general there should be no problem obtaining finance for the project.

Key objectives in financing are to achieve a good return and to minimise the project risk. Allied to this is the need for a recovery mechanism if things go wrong.

The following trends in financing for the private sector are evident in work carried out by the author and David Tong:

—financial institutions are likely to require higher levels of equity in order to reduce a tourism project's gearing or leverage and minimise their risk;
—shorter-term loans are becoming the norm, and loans over ten years will be more difficult to obtain;
—there will be a greater scrutiny of project proposals prior to approval of any finance;
—it will be difficult to obtain lending in developmental areas where the risk is high;
—in the case of foreign investment, the local partner will generally provide the land and will expect the foreign investor to arrange for the finance and to provide a guarantee;
—the private sector will become increasingly involved in infrastructural development as part of the resort development. However, government will need to provide appropriate incentives such as making land available to the investor at nominal cost.

Guidelines for the future

With few exceptions the poor performance of publicly owned tourism enterprises has demonstrated that it is most advantageous for tourism development if government is to act as a facilitator. This means government funding policy planning and research; tourism-related infrastructure; marketing; environmental conservation; and training. The private sector should fund travel companies and tourist attractions.

The inclusion of marketing as a public sector activity should not be regarded as ignoring the role of the private sector. However, the fragmentation of the tourism industry in most countries has led to market failure in tourism marketing. There are very few countries in the world, even those with the most free market capitalist inclinations, which do not provide a public sector framework for tourism marketing.

The same can be said of tourism training. There are a few countries, notably Singapore, where practical tourism training is provided by joint effort by the private sector. However, again because of the fragmentation of the industry, tourism is one area where training has to be carried out under the auspices of the public sector. If the private sector is made wholly responsible for training then the 'free loader' problem, of trained personnel moving on to employers who have not contributed towards the cost of training, is difficult to avoid. It is however possible to impose a levy on all employers to contribute towards the cost of training, as in Fiji and Kenya, for example.

Airlines in developing countries are normally government-owned enterprises. Given the limited scale of local capital markets, it is often difficult to privatise businesses with a substantial value and high capital requirements, although such privatisation may be desirable in making the airlines more responsive to customer needs and in becoming generally more efficient.

Hotels and resorts are an area of difficulty because commercial banks are often reluctant to lend on a sufficiently long-term basis for hotel construction. Government-owned development banks have tended to fill this gap. As the difficulties in funding hotel development are not expected to ease in the future, it is particularly important that development banks are well run and managed, and directed to operate in as commercial a manner as possible.

Guidelines for the public sector

The following guidelines are suggested for the public sector.

Clear leadership
Ministries and departments of tourism need to have a clear set of objectives for tourism development, and to know what their priorities are. It is unlikely this can be done without involving the private sector.

These objectives need to be conveyed to other branches of government, so that the role of new infrastructure in tourism development is properly understood, and so that priorities for tourist development are properly included alongside priorities for other sectors of the economy.

Legislation which is easy to understand
Government needs to legislate in such a manner that the private sector investor can clearly understand what is required of him. In some countries, laws are contradictory, and it is very difficult for prospective investors to know where they stand.

Legislation is likely to include some form of control of foreign investment. This needs to give businesses as much freedom to operate as possible. Promotion of the interests of the indigenous population may be necessary, but this needs to be balanced against the international nature of the tourism business.

Helping the investor
The private investor, whether domestic or foreign, needs to know where to go to get the necessary permissions, and what he (or she) has to do to get them. The

'one-window' system, where one agency carries out all the necessary work on behalf of the investor, should be pursued. There are few countries where given determination it cannot be put into effect.

Taxation and fiscal incentives

A clear and well-managed tax regime promotes investment. A reluctance on the part of tax authorities to accept audited accounts, and a perception by prospective investors that taxation is arbitrary, does not encourage investment.

Fiscal incentives need to be treated as one component of an overall investment package; they are not enough in themselves to promote tourism investment. They should not be fixed in stone, but rather be reviewed regularly against development objectives and against the offers of competing countries.

The efficiency of various forms of incentives can be tested by appraising the impact they would have on the profitability of sample tourism projects. This can be done as part of an outline feasibility study for a hotel, for example. The implications of one set of incentives against another for total tax collection can be examined at the same time.

Fiscal incentives very often apply only to hotels, and exclude other components of the tourist product, such as tourist coaches or secondary tourist facilities such as attractions or handicraft manufacture. They can also be less advantageous than those applying to export processing industries. There is often no logic to this, particularly as the leakage from foreign trade processing zones can be higher than that from tourist resorts. Indeed, there is an argument that hotels be treated as export processing zones, as they are often operating in foreign currency and exporting all their production (i.e. available room nights).

Exchange control

Exchange control can be a significant disincentive to invest. If applied over-zealously it is self-defeating, as management in the tourism industry—where most income is earned abroad—can find ways of avoiding it. They then simply waste management time finding ways of doing so. Exchange control rules need to be as simple as possible, and approvals under those rules need to be given quickly.

Controlling foreign investment

Most governments in developing countries feel the need to exercise some control of foreign investment, through requiring joint ownership, maintaining ultimate control over land-ownership, or other measures. Foreign investment is best encouraged where these controls are kept to a minimum.

Monitoring national development banks

National development banks are an important agent in tourism financing. Central government needs to ensure that they are properly managed, and if loans are not being repaid, that appropriate action is taken. Mismanagement will eventually lead to disillusion on the part of supporting donors.

Proper control of loans, both from development banks and from other banking institutions, requires a proper accounting system, and mechanisms for failing businesses to be repossessed. If businesses are not allowed to fail, it will prejudice future investment. If there is no appropriate mechanism for firms being placed into receivership, then this should be put in place.

Promoting domestic investment

Domestic investment is sometimes being constrained by a lack of appropriate vehicles through which to invest. The development of domestic capital markets is particularly valuable in encouraging tourism investment.

Development planning and finance

Tourist development plans can express the preferences of government for location, type and style of new hotels, resorts, and other facilities. At the same time they cannot dictate the pace of development. They need to be commercially realistic, and to take account of what is financially viable and where finance is to be obtained. The role of donor finance, and its relationship with private sector funding, should be considered. Tourism in a number of countries has suffered from over-rapid development, and the importance of environmental protection has now become more widely recognised. It is appropriate that Environmental Impact Assessments are required of hotel and resort developers. Such measures need to be implemented efficiently, so that government procedures are not excessively burdensome. Civil servants need to be trained so as to have an understanding of the implications which delays can have for the private sector.

Making the best use of donor funding

Donor finance in the tourism sector has most often been used for technical assistance. Such technical assistance has often been of less value than was anticipated. Technical assistance can play a valuable role in setting policies and programmes; marketing; training; and project implementation.

It can also assist in enhancing the overall awareness of the benefits and needs of the tourist industry. This has been done with Australian assistance in Fiji.

To succeed, there needs to be a clear understanding between all parties at the outset over what a particular item of technical assistance is to achieve, and how progress is to be monitored. Technical assistance in such fields as training and marketing needs to be carried out with a clear idea of how nationals are to take over. One foreign technical assistance project that simply leads to another is likely to be of limited lasting value. A set of recommendations is of little value if no one has any idea of how they are going to be achieved, and who is going to do it. Too many technical assistance projects fail because of this.

Guidelines for the private sector

The following guidelines are suggested for the private sector.

Providing support to government

The private sector needs to work with government, and to provide government with the guidance it needs to develop its policies. The private sector is always likely to be closer to market trends and developments than any government agency.

Acting with responsibility

If government acts responsibly towards the private sector, the private sector must reciprocate. If rules and regulations are well framed, and clearly understandable, the private sector needs to be prepared to abide by them.

Repayment

Repaying loans, to whatever institution, should be regarded as a prime responsibility of the private sector. It is as much a responsibility of the private sector to ensure that loans are repaid as it is of the organisations which make those loans. A lax repayment regime prejudices the future of tourism investment.

Roles of financing institutions

At its simplest, funding comes from government (including donor finance and development banks), from state and private banks, and through local equity capital and foreign investment. Commercial banks are unlikely to fund the full needs of the tourism sector in developing countries, because lending periods are often too short, and the funding requirement is too high as compared to the bank's capital base. Loan syndication is a means of partially overcoming this which should be encouraged.

Foreign investment is best suited to the larger and more substantial projects, where the funding requirement is greatest. This is likely to include airline finance as well as larger hotels and resorts. Development banks will need

to continue to support private sector ventures which require longer-term finance than commercial banks can provide.

Government has a prime responsibility for infrastructure provision. In developed tourist resorts, there is scope for the private sector to fund infrastructure provision either in whole or in part, as has taken place on Bali. Bilateral and multilateral aid is appropriate to the financing of tourism infrastructure, such as airports, roads, water and drainage and training facilities. Problems have arisen with donor finance in the tourism infrastructure where the scale of the investment has been large, but without an adequate commercial basis.

In some countries, pre-sale has been used as a means of finance. This can be through the pre-sale of timeshare units, or through the pre-sale of beds to tour wholesalers. This form of finance should be monitored carefully, as it limits flexibility and if problems arise they can be damaging to the country as a whole by undermining the confidence of investors.

Mechanisms for implementation

One of the best ways in securing successful tourism investment is to ensure that there is coordination between all the parties involved, and that all work is with a clear sense of direction towards a common goal. It is one of the reasons why, with such slender physical resources, Singapore has been so successful in tourism development.

Mechanisms for implementation include:

—an intergovernmental liaison structure, which is implementation oriented;
—a marketing body which is separate from government, and which has professional marketing staff, and which maintains close consultation with the private sector;
—a forum which brings together the public and private sectors on a regular basis;
—establishing links between trade associations, so that they work together, and are encouraged to do more than pursue the professional interests of a single sector.

Coordination which promotes sound market growth and soundly based construction projects is highly likely to generate financing. Countries such as Japan and Singapore have demonstrated the benefits of government and the private sector working together to an agreed goal.

Acknowledgements

The author would like to thank: the Asian Development Bank and the World Tourism Organisation for funding case studies in Fiji, Indonesia and Nepal on which this paper is partially based; David Tong who worked with the author on formulating many of the conclusions drawn from those case studies; and Michael Nevin in Touche Ross, previously with the European Investment Bank, for his comments. However, the views expressed are those of the author and do not necessarily reflect the views of the above organisations or individuals.

References

Akehurst, Gary, Bland, Nigel and Nevin, Michael (1993) 'Tourism policies in the European Community member states', *International Journal of Hospitality Management*, 12(1): 33–66.

Belt Collins Associates and others (1973) *Fiji Tourism Master Plan*, United Nations Development Programme/Government of Fiji, Suva.

Bennett, Oliver and Tong, David (1992) *Tourism Financing Study*, Asian Development Bank, Manila, and World Tourism Organisation, Madrid.

Nevin, Michael and Wason, Graham (1993) 'Success factors in European tourism policy', *Insights*, September 1993, English Tourist Board, London.

5 Tourism and small island states: problems of resource analysis, management and development

P. F. WILKINSON

There is plenty of evidence that almost anything we do on islands makes them worse.
Bill Newman, Professor of Oceanography,
Scripps Institute (Gosnell, 1976)

Introduction

It is clear that tourism is a resource-based industry. It is even clearer, however, that tourism is unlike other industries which are largely dependent on a particular natural resource(s), e.g. trees for forestry, alumina ore and hydroelectricity for the aluminum industry; petroleum deposits for the oil and gas industry; coal, limestone, iron ore, and water for steel fabrication; etc. Rather, tourism in its various forms and at its many destinations is dependent on complex combinations of intersecting resource characteristics: climatic (sun, snow), physiographic (mountains, lakes), floral (rainforests, prairies), faunal (big game animals, birds), aquatic (reefs, white-water rivers), terrestrial (deserts, glaciers)—and to extend beyond the biophysical environment, human (urban, rural), historical–cultural (fortifications, arts and crafts) and aesthetic (sunsets). As a result, tourism both shares many of the problems of other resource-based industries and yet is unique because of this complexity.

Over the years, several interesting analogies have been made between tourism and other resource-based industries in terms of their roles in the social and economic development of small island states. Usually, these analogies focus on a single natural resource and, as a result, both illuminate and mask the realities of tourism and its implications.

The 'stock' (or non-renewable) resource to which tourism is most often compared is oil. For example:

> Tourism earned poor countries about $55 billion in 1988, according to UN estimates. That makes it their second biggest earner of foreign exchange, after oil ($70 billion). But, unlike oil, tourism is still booming: the Economist Intelligence Unit reckons spending on international tourism, fares excluded, will grow by 4½–5% a year, in real terms, for the rest of the century. The third world's share of this should grow even faster. (Anonymous, 1989:19)

Despite this prediction of continued growth, there have been many warnings that economic dependence on tourism—or any other single resource—is not necessarily a safe route to take, for two reasons (e.g., Wilkinson, 1987b). First, like the fixed amount of oil in the world which is subject to depletion, the 'tourism resources' of small island states are susceptible to destruction because of the characteristics of small islands, particularly tropical ones: small physical area, fragility of ecosystems, strong interrelationships between terrestrial and marine environments, and—perhaps most important—limited institutional, legislative, and management capabilities. Second, small states of any kind, but particularly small islands, are at the mercy of what Trist calls the 'external environment' (Emery and Trist, 1965), that is, those global forces over which the small state has no control. For example, oil is again used, along with sugar cane, to trigger a useful analogy to tourism:

> For small countries too—just as for oil sheikhdoms—there is a risk of overdependence on one industry: tourism is not secure, any more than growing sugar-cane is. Exchange rate shifts and swings of fashion in the rich countries, a world energy crisis or a local political one—any of these can make nonsense of the sums. Ethnic conflict slashed tourist arrivals in Sri Lanka by nearly half between 1982 and 1986. The fear of AIDS cut business last year on the Kenyan coast, sometimes marketed as a sex resort. Thailand, notorious as such, also has been badly hit. (Anonymous, 1989:21)

These unexpected downturns in tourism are not limited to single countries or even regions, as witnessed by the global impact on tourism of the Gulf War in 1990–91, when the fear of air terrorism seriously cut travel to tourism destinations that were not involved in or even close to the conflict itself.

Sugar cane, as noted in the above quotation, is used as another frequent analogy to tourism. The comparison of tourism to 'a new kind of sugar' was first used by Rev. Abraham Akaka when blessing a new Hawaiian hotel (Finney and Watson, 1975:v). Undoubtedly, the original hope was that tourism represented a new form of prosperity for Hawaii, particularly in the wake of decreased global sugar prices after World War II as a result of competition from sugar beet production in other countries. In the Eastern Caribbean, the phrase could just as easily have been 'a new kind of bananas' because, after the sugar market collapsed in 1954 for the Windward Islands, there was a rapid switch to bananas. This continuing dependence on export monocrops led in the long term to precarious economic times for many of these islands with the only obvious economic alternative being tourism; even today, the European Economic Community's economic union in 1992 leaves the future of their banana markets to Great Britain in doubt. In any case, this analogy is both simple and dangerous: tourism, like bananas or sugar cane, is a 'monocrop' export industry, the base price for which is determined externally;[1] much of the profit leaks out of the economy; and no matter how capable an island is of attracting tourists or growing a crop, it is a small player in a global system rife with substitutes and intervening opportunities.

Because they focus on a single natural resource, these analogies, can be seen as a simplistic resource interpretation of tourism, its impacts, and its interrelationships with other sectors of national and global economies. A more accurate interpretation of tourism and resources requires a return to basic resource theory before a more comprehensive view of the resource problems related to tourism can be adequately and meaningfully discussed. This involves four stages:

- defining 'resource'
- going beyond the traditional concept of 'resource management' through the inclusion of the stages of resource analysis and resource development
- discussing the 'resource problems' related to tourism
- calling for an integrated approach to examining and potentially solving those problems.

The meaning of 'resource'

There are many definitions of 'resource', but the most commonly accepted one—and the one that is most clearly related to tourism—is that of Zimmermann (1951). He provides a functional interpretation of resources, arguing that neither the environment as such nor parts of the environment are resources until they are, or are considered

to be, capable of satisfying human needs. In this sense, resources are an expression of appraisal and represent an entirely subjective and anthropocentric concept;[2] in Zimmermann's (1951:15) words, then, 'resources are not, they become; they are not static but expand and contract in response to human wants and human actions'. Resources are attributes of the natural world that are no more than 'neutral stuff' until a combination of increased knowledge, expanding technology, and changing individual and societal objectives results in their presence being perceived, their capacity to satisfy human wants and needs being recognized, and the means to utilize them being devised:

> natural resources are defined by human perceptions and attitudes, wants, technological skills, legal, financial and institutional arrangements, as well as by political customs. What is a natural resource in one culture may be 'neutral stuff' in another culture. Resources, to use Zimmermann's words, are subjective, relative and functional. (Mitchell, 1989:2)

Clearly, tourism fits this concept of resources. Take the example of scuba-diving: coral reefs clearly have functions that are non-human (e.g., ecological) and non-recreational human (e.g., habitats for species that are food for humans), but their function as a tourism resource came about largely in the last 40 years because of human interests in the sea (including television films by Jacques Cousteau, the co-inventor of the scuba regulator), new technology (rubber and plastic fins, masks, and wet-suits; scuba gear; and jet airplanes which made reefs around the world accessible to potential tourists), training systems (PADI, NAUI), and institutional arrangements (marine parks, reef management plans).

But what is *the tourism resource*? With oil or sugar cane or hydraulic potential, the resource is obvious: it is the petroleum product or the plant and soil or the waterfall. With tourism, it is not so simple. As argued above, the tourism resource is not a single 'good' or 'service', but rather a *bundle* of goods and services, natural and human, social and cultural, economic and spiritual, fact and fiction, systemic and contextual. From a geographer's point of view, therefore, the tourism resource could be characterized as being 'the place'— the combination of factors which attract tourists to a destination and sustain their experience while they are there.

For example, the tourism resource of the Caribbean country of Dominica could be described as including: the flora and fauna of rainforests and coral reefs; Carib, African, Créole, and European culture and history; and small airports and small hotels. The result is a relatively small-scale and low-key tourism industry, with many regional visitors, and an emphasis on the natural environment and culture. That is Dominica. But it is not the other islands of the Caribbean. Each has its own combination of factors which makes it attractive to tourists of different kinds and numbers, e.g., the international airport, casinos, and condominiums of St. Maarten/St. Martin; the white and pink sand beaches of Anguilla; and the international airports and the mass-tourism multinational hotels of Jamaica. Even within a single country such as the Bahamas, there are great differences, e.g., the high-rise hotels, casinos, and nightclubs of Paradise Island, the exclusive Club Med and Windermere Club of Eleuthra, and the small scuba-oriented hotels of Andros.

The argument can be extended to suggest that the tourism resource also includes other factors which do not fit into the traditional conceptualization of 'natural' resources: legislation and fiscal incentives that permit and attract tourism development; the policy and planning system that guides the form and location of development; the transportation sector (airports, seaports, roads); the educational system (both general and tourism-related); the service sector (water, electricity, garbage, sewage); the not-for-profit sector that is involved in history, arts, and culture; the private sector which provides taxis, hotels, restaurants, stores, nightclubs, computers, construction material; and finally even the illegal or underground sector that fuels the tourist-oriented sex or drug trades in some locations.

Not all of these factors need to be in place for a particular location to be created as a tourism resource, but there must be some basic characteristics, including a physical environment that is conducive to a specific form of tourism. This was the case with greenfield sites such as Cancun, Mexico and Freeport, Bahamas, which were attractive sites for 'sun and sand' destinations, but had little or no history of tourism and no infra-structure.

Another characteristic of tourism resources is that they can be destroyed by over-use and mismanagement or be rendered obsolete as they are replaced by more attractive and interesting alternatives. There is also the possibility that, as Butler's (1980) tourist area cycle of evolution argues, they can be rejuvenated, as was the case in Atlantic City, New Jersey.

Resources such as oil or sugar cane are generally regarded as tangible and individual commodities, the supply and demand for which is determined in the marketplace. In contrast, tourism must be seen in the context of what O'Riordan (1971:16) terms a newer, more modern concept of resources which

places greater emphasis upon the intangible values, such as quality, variety, and ecological harmony, and visualises resources as 'bundles' of existing and potential uses (the multipurpose concept), where the importance and variety of the constituent functions vary over time in accord with changes in technological and organisational ability and social appraisal (the dynamic concept).

O'Riordan goes on to argue that, because such resources are neither tangible nor individual, nor entirely products of the natural environment, this newer concept introduces serious management problems because they cannot be owned or valued in the marketplace, nor expropriated, without creating external effects (either positive or negative) impinging upon other users or the natural environment, nor readily packaged and sold as individual units. Because there is not a competitive free market in which such resources can be priced, the given demand situation for such resources cannot be assessed at any given point in time, nor is the available supply (in terms of quantity and quality) known. In this sense, tourism resources have many elements of

public goods or 'common property resources' . . . [which] include such commodities as air, water, and the landscape, which exist in myriads of different combinations and are employed and evaluated in myriads of different ways. . . . [T]hese are resources that count, but they are so much more difficult to define, to evaluate, and to allocate than the old ones. As such proper management and clear social guidelines are urgently needed, and the creation and implementation of such guidelines represent the present challenge in resource management. (O'Riordan, 1971:17)

In conclusion, then, it can be seen that comparing tourism to resources such as oil or sugar cane has some utility, but such analogies are dangerously simplistic unless the analysis goes much deeper into the complex nature of tourism and its many connections into virtually all facets of a small island's environment.

Beyond the traditional concept of 'resource management'

Traditionally, resource management has been seen as an all-inclusive process which begins with locating a potential resource, planning its exploitation, financing the operation, and then carrying out the development. Best exemplified by the work of Mitchell (1989), more recent thinking divides the process into three stages, all of which are applicable to tourism: resource analysis, resource management, and resource development.

Resource analysis involves an understanding of 'the fundamental characteristics of natural resources and the processes through which they are, could be, and should be allocated and utilized' (Mitchell, 1989:3).

Analysis, as the 'examination of a thing's parts to find out their essential features' (*World Book Dictionary*, 1975), could involve four types of studies:

● surveying, mapping, and measurement of the supply of and demand for resources, as well as their characteristics and properties
● alternative (spatial, temporal, functional) allocations in terms of users, facilities, and activities
● biophysical, technological, economic, social, political, institutional, and legal variables which condition resource allocation or development
● the impacts of specific resource allocations (Mitchell, 1989:2–3).

Resource analysis, therefore, is clearly a 'research' activity, undertaken by academic, consulting or professional researchers.

Resource management 'represents the actual decisions concerning policy or practice regarding how resources are allocated and under what conditions or arrangements resources may be developed' (Mitchell, 1989:3). O'Riordan's (1971:19) definition, while it would probably be supplemented today by a phrase such as 'all within an ecological context' at the end of the first sentence, fits well with the situation related to tourism:

> a process of decision making whereby resources are allocated over space and time according to the needs, aspirations, and desires of man [*sic*] within the framework of his technological inventiveness, his political and social institutions, and his legal and administrative arrangements. Resource management should be visualized as a conscious process of decision involving judgement, preference and commitment, whereby certain desired resource outputs are sought from certain perceived resource combinations through the choice among various managerial, technical and administrative alternatives.

Resource management, then, is about power and politics (Fernie and Pitkethly, 1985:vii), in the sense that it may involve either the management of production from a specific resource, as in the case of a forest, or the overall planning of the development and use of resources in an area or region (Mitchell, 1989:3), as in the case of tourism in an island state. The process is usually undertaken by elected or appointed officials in the public or private sector.

In contrast, resource development is 'the actual exploitation or use of a resource during the transformation of "neutral stuff" into a commodity or service to serve human needs and aspirations' (Mitchell, 1989:5) through the building or providing of desired facilities and activities. This stage may be carried out singly or in combination by either the public or private

sector and occurs at the operational level, as opposed to the research or policy levels suggested by the earlier stages.

Each of these three stages of the resource process is briefly discussed below in the context of tourism in small islands. The purpose here is to highlight some of the more significant problems, rather than to provide an exhaustive examination, and to demonstrate that each of the stages is linked. While the Caribbean will be used as the focus of the discussion, many of the problems noted are equally applicable to other islands throughout the world.

Tourism and resource problems

> if the process of change is to be managed and sustainable island ecodevelopment is to become a reality, then the skills, expertise and accrued learning of islands, continental scholars and development specialists need to be applied in the search for island growth, resource management and survival strategies. (Towle, 1985b:596)

Resource analysis

There are vast gaps and many disagreements about the physical nature of small islands, as Towle (1985b:594) notes:

> island system literature and documentation, in the aggregate, is so diverse and inconsistent and lacks both a unified theoretical and empirical base. There has been little consensus.

This information and agreement problem, however, is occurring as islands around the world are experiencing strong development pressures

> based chiefly on tourism, on extractive enterprises, on their use as nodes for international air transportation and satellite tracking networks, and on the increased demands for and upon local resources generated by rising affluence and expectations among rapidly growing island populations. Additional driving forces include continentally based initiatives seeking waste disposal sites, deep-water petroleum transhipment sites, cruise ship ports, offshore banking centers, low-cost labor for materials processing and assembly, and expanded supplies of harvestable high-value marine species (like tuna, lobster, conch, and certain seaweeds). The availability of multinational and bilateral aid programs has also contributed to accelerated development activities.
> One by-product of this current development phenomenon has been a dramatic deterioration of island coastal environments, accompanied by a decline in the quality of life on islands, as measured by means other than such traditional economic indicators as gross national product (GNP) and average per capita income. On islands, as elsewhere, progress has its price. (Towle, 1985b:595)

There is a problem here more fundamental than just lack of information in that there is an absence of both methodological and theoretical understanding of island systems:

> [an] increasingly apparent cause of the decline [of environmental quality of island systems and their littoral zones] is a serious methodological failure in the omission of environmental resource values in planning and development strategies. The principal question now is how. (Towle, 1985b:597)

To a large extent, this absence is related to the focus of resource analysis research on continental systems and the assumption, both implicit and explicit that continental data can be applied to islands; Bacon (1985:46), for example, argues that

> Because of this interrelatedness Caribbean islands, particularly in the Lesser Antilles, can be thought of as large ecosystems (or as microcosms of all the characteristics and problems of continents or perhaps of the whole biosphere!). This has important implications for development and management of resources because the potential impacts must be sought through a whole range of interrelated and interdependent ecosystems.

In the Caribbean, there have been some outstanding examples of attempts to begin to fill this vacuum of knowledge, several of which will just be noted here as examples of work undertaken by academic, non-governmental, and governmental organizations at both national and regional levels. Summarizing a project designed to create a basic level of mapping conservation priorities in the Lesser Antilles in order to provide information to begin to devise a strategy for conservation action, Putney (1982) reviews the results of preliminary data atlases for the 24 islands or groups of islands, based on research conducted by the Eastern Caribbean Natural Resources Management Program (ECNAMP) for the Caribbean Conservation Association (CCA). The results include a common database for each island (e.g., such tourism-related data as tourism zones, reefs and dive sites, game species, beaches, archeological and historic sites, parks and protected areas, land ownership), identification of the largest remaining samples of the major habitats of the region, identification of priorities for action, and a listing of major resource persons and bibliographic sources.

Another example deals with baseline data on the institutional and legal structure of individual islands. The Natural Resources Management Project (NRMP) of the Organization of Eastern Caribbean States (OECS) undertook a second kind of information collection process

in its analysis of six country reports (Antigua and Barbuda, Dominica, Grenada, St. Kitts and Nevis, St. Lucia, St. Vincent and the Grenadines) designed to provide information on existing natural resource-related legislation in each country and to make preliminary recommendations on areas needing revision or strengthening. For example, the report on St. Lucia (OECS–NRMP, 1986) provides an identification and analysis of existing legislation (e.g., tourist industry development, beach protection, national parks) and government structure related to natural resources, and then preliminary observations on the overall picture, followed by recommended follow-up steps.

The most comprehensive resource analysis research in the eastern Caribbean was undertaken by the CCA and the Island Resources Foundation (IRF), with a separate 'environmental profile' (including information on tourism) being published for each of eight OECS countries (e.g., CCA, 1991); in each case, the research team and the island government was supported by a local organization (e.g., the National Research and Development Foundation in St. Lucia). The summary report for the series notes that the

> Profiles have highlighted gaps in the existing information base, suggested new guidelines for the design and funding of development programs, pinpointed weaknesses in regulatory or planning mechanisms, and illustrated the need for changes in policies. Most importantly, the process of carrying out a profile project has in many cases helped establish new working relationships and even consensus among governmental and non-governmental bodies concerned with environmental issues. It has also served to strengthen local institutions and improve their capacity for incorporating environmental information into development planning. (CCA and IRF, 1991:1)

This latter point is particularly important, as this project clearly demonstrates the feasibility of utilizing local and regional expertise, rather than depending solely on external consultants or international organizations. Another example of a similar country environmental profile has been done for Jamaica (Government of Jamaica, 1987).

There have also been a number of studies focusing on the supply and demand aspects of the tourism industry in the Caribbean, in terms of both the region (e.g., McElroy and de Albuquerque, 1991; Wilkinson, 1990) and individual islands (e.g., Dominica (Weaver, 1991) and Montserrat (McElroy and de Albuquerque, 1988)).

Resource management

Obviously, resource management decisions related to tourism are taken daily by officials in both the public and private sectors: policy is formulated, legislation is passed, development proposals are accepted, concessionary loans or tax incentives are granted, building permits are granted, bank loans are arranged, etc. There is not, however, a great deal of literature which discusses the power and politics issues related to tourism resource management decisions. This is true not just for the Caribbean, but for the tourism literature in general. A notable exception is Richter's (1989:2) *The Politics of Tourism in Asia*, which includes chapters on such large and small island states as Sri Lanka, the Maldives, and the Philippines; she argues that

> tourism is a highly political phenomenon, the implications of which have been only rarely perceived and almost nowhere fully understood. Furthermore, it matters a great deal whether the public and key policymakers are able to grasp the fact that, although tourism may have a frivolous carefree image, the industry is huge, intensely competitive, and has acute social consequences for nearly all societies.

While numerous studies have examined the policy aspects of tourism in particular islands in the Caribbean (e.g., Weaver, 1991), there has been very little in-depth comparative work focusing on the historical development of tourism resource management policies and planning in order to see whether there were common threads in tourism across islands or whether each case is unique. As a result, this author is in the final stage of comparative case studies in the Commonwealth Caribbean, focusing on Anguilla, Bahamas, Barbados, Cayman Islands, Dominica, Jamaica, and St. Lucia. These seven island microstates were selected based on their variety of patterns of tourism arrival statistics in terms of Butler's (1980) concept of a tourist area cycle of evolution (Wilkinson, 1989b). The individual island studies are in draft form and the results will be synthesized, pending verification of preliminary material distributed to participants in the study throughout the region.

Conclusions from this research are too preliminary to present at this time, but there are some analytical problems that can be highlighted here. First, in no case did there exist either a comprehensive overview of the situation, no matter how brief, or a collected set of all the relevant historical documentation. This demonstrates that such research is extremely time-consuming and can only be done in person and *in situ*. Second, and related to the first point, no matter how small the island, the number of individuals or organizations who had been and are currently involved in tourism policy and planning in some way was, quite simply, incredible; as a result, several research trips were required for each island and to regional

organizations in order to complete the picture as it emerged. Third, and not surprising given the complexity of the situation, contradictions and inconsistencies abound between stated policy and planning directives on the one hand, and actual implementation on the other.

Resource development

Tourism resource development is clearly a fact of life for many small islands around the world; indeed, for many such islands, tourism is the dominant economic, social, and biophysical reality that shapes their lives and landscapes. While there is a vast and excellent literature on impacts of tourism in general (e.g., Mathieson and Wall, 1982; Pearce 1989), there is no major text which focuses on small islands alone, although Britton and Clarke (1987) devote most of their book to islands. The impacts of tourism in the Caribbean have a long history of research (e.g., Hills and Lundgren, 1977) and there is a great deal of relevant literature on the Caribbean, but it is widely scattered and often in publications that have not received widespread circulation.

A few examples of the literature on tourist development are noted below. First, however, three caveats are noted by Dixon (1991) about the nature of tourist development: environmental concerns, externalities, and size.

> Given the important role of nature and natural resources to tourism in many Caribbean states, environmental concerns should be at the forefront when considering development projects. However . . . population growth, the imperatives of economic growth, and intensive exploitation of certain natural resources are all leading to increased stress on the resource base. These stresses, if they result in degradation of the resource, will result in economic losses due to both decreased productivity of the resource base, and decreased attractiveness of the locale to outsiders and resultant loss of tourism revenue. (Dixon, 1991:90)

Since tourism is an industry that sells a service that is heavily dependent on the environment, analyses of tourism projects are more likely than in many other cases to internalize what would normally be economic externalities. The industry is not completely self-policing, however. Overcrowding and congestion are one common externality, and the cumulative impact of many small investment decisions (the so-called tyranny of small decisions) may be a major concern. The 'next' project, for example, may create traffic congestion and impair views such that the economic value of existing projects is reduced. This is an example of negative economic externality.

In resort development one has the somewhat unusual situation where the biggest projects may be of relatively less concern (especially if they are remote from other developments): major megaproject resort developers are very aware of the fragility of what they sell and the necessity to take appropriate safeguards. Their physical size may also be such that they internalize what would normally be externalities. Developers of smaller hotels, however, may have less incentive to take appropriate environmental safeguards; these projects, therefore, deserve greater attention from planners and analysts. (Dixon, 1991:99)

The last point is particularly controversial, as is highlighted by examples given below which show that any development of any kind or size on a coast can have serious resource implications.

Among the greatest problems for Caribbean islands are direct impacts of tourism development on coastal resources, for the obvious reason that most island tourism occurs on or near the coast (Hunte, 1985). Cambers (1985), for example, documents the impact of the 308-room Heywoods hotel complex on Barbados's northwest coast in terms of beach erosion, reef damage, and water pollution. Similar problems on Grand Anse Beach in Grenada are described by Vincent et al. (1988), while Towle (1985a) and Devaux (1987a) discuss the impacts of the dredging of Rodney Bay (for a sailboat harbor and marina basin) and the construction of a causeway (originally designed as a site for a major hotel complex, but which remains vacant) linking Pigeon Island with the mainland on St. Lucia's northwest coast. The OECS (1988) describes the damage to shorelines and yacht marinas in the harbor at Castries, St. Lucia, due to the construction of the cruiseship dock at Pointe Seraphine. De Albuquerque (1991) discusses the results of the dredging and filling of two salt ponds in Antigua for the construction of major hotel/condominium projects, including increased turbidity and siltation, destruction of sea grass beds and mangroves, lower numbers of fish and birds, and coral die-back. It is important to note, however, that not all coastal problems are directly related to tourism; for example, Williams (1985) describes the long history of beach sand mining in St. Lucia for construction purposes, only a portion of which is related to tourist development. Whatever the causes, the end result is that many of St. Lucia's beaches show signs of increasing instability, with Grand Anse Beach, the largest on the island, experiencing severe structural instability (Devaux, 1987b).

Indirect or partial impacts of tourism development also have effects on coastal resources. For example, much of Barbados's prosperity that began in the mid-1960s was a result of its mixed economy, with a blend of agriculture (sugar cane), light industry, and tourism. One output of such prosperity was increased levels of sewage,

particularly in Carlisle Bay in Bridgetown, which caused massive coral destruction and loss of fish. As a result, a major sewerage project was implemented for the area of the capital city and has led to improved levels of water quality and marine habitats (Archer, 1988); however, given Barbados's recent economic difficulties, it is unlikely that this project will be extended in the near future along the west and southeast coasts where similar problems have been caused directly by extensive hotel development.

Aside from coast resources, there are other types of tourist development-related impacts on the resource base. One example of a direct impact is trail erosion and vegetation damage due to hikers. For instance, in the area around Dominica's Emerald Pool, a small but beautiful waterfall only a short walking distance from a main road, faces these problems as rapidly increasing numbers of cruiseship tourists (following the recent construction of the cruiseship facility at Cabrits National Park near Portsmouth) visit the site by tour bus. While there are other more spectacular natural sites in Dominica (e.g., the Boiling Lake, the world's second largest such lake), they require strenuous and long hikes and are, therefore, not well-suited to the short stays of cruiseship tourists. As a result, accessible sites, such as the Emerald Pool, are likely to deteriorate seriously.

Other indirect impacts result from developments that are related to, but not solely a result of tourism. For example, airport and road construction requires large amounts of sand and gravel, which in most cases has to be mined locally. Another example involves forest resources. In St. Lucia, rising standards of living (in large part, as a result of the tourism industry) have resulted in growing demands for energy, which in turn has caused higher prices for electricity, oil, and gas; however, this has led to serious concerns about deforestation as poorer people are forced out of the market for commercial fuels and increase their use of wood and charcoal (an act which, of course, is in itself a form of resource development). Wood and charcoal are often obtained illegally from government forests, including protected watersheds. The circle came about full a number of years ago when increased siltation resulting from deforestation-caused erosion knocked out a small hydroelectric facility in the southern part of the island (Wilkinson, 1984, 1987a).

Conclusion: the need for an integrated approach to tourism resource problems

Recently, there has been growing recognition that a new integrated approach is needed to deal with the kinds of problems noted above. For example, the Caribbean

Community's (CARICOM, 1989:3) Port of Spain Accord on the Management and Conservation of the Caribbean Environment states as follows:

> We strongly recommend to all governments of the Community that they establish arrangements that would permit an integrated approach to environmental management at the political, technical and administrative levels, and that such arrangements should include a designated focal point which would relate in a coherent manner to the regional and international levels.

While focusing on the conservation of wildlife resources, Butler's (1985) 'cornerstones' of conservation—legislation, environmental education, research, and establishment of reserves—appear also to be applicable to tourism resources and to form the basis for such an integrated approach.

Legislation

Calls for serious government involvement in tourism-related resource problems are not new. McElroy (1975:48), for example, noted that, without strong policy intervention, the contemporary island tourism economy system is non-sustainable because the nature of the macro-disequilibrium involves 'the following basic incompatibility: the imposition of an expanding, open, tourist-consumption-biased throughput economic system upon a closed, fragile, finite environment'.

Many Caribbean countries seem to recognize this need for policy, legislation, and administrative structures, but few have adequately addressed the issues. Chakalall (1985:56), in the context of the Lesser Antilles, makes a comment that is applicable to much of the rest of the Caribbean:

> All the governments of the Lesser Antilles have some sort of policy on the conservation of natural resources, even though most of them are not clearly and concisely expressed and up to date. No country appears to address the question of trade-offs between uses or multiple outputs of a particular natural resource.
> Government policies are directed at maximising the earning capacity of the major sectors of the economy that utilise natural resources: policies seem to be economically based rather than socially and environmentally based. However, recently, there has been an increased interest and some degree of commitment on the part of governments, particularly in relation to the natural environment. This has been reflected in the establishment of varying degrees of institutional support required to implement government policies.

Nevertheless, many countries have a long way to go in developing structures to deal adequately with resource problems; McElroy et al. (1987:93–94) present a dismaying picture:

> In addition to the routine lack of data, overburdened staff, skill deficiencies, and crisis management styles (Shaw, 1982), the planning function has frequently been fragmented unproductively, causing jurisdictional disputes and needless compromises to satisfy the competing claims of rival agencies. In some cases, long-term policy has been divorced from the land-use planners most knowledgeable about the environmental suitability for sustaining various activities. . . . [L]and-use and environmental planners often have little policy input and control over the legislative initiatives, incentives and subsidies that cause resource depletion and/or non-renewable uses.

Clearly, legislation alone—no matter how well crafted—is not sufficient to deal with the types of problems facing islands unless it is backed up by strong government support and institutions which are capable of managing the situation.

Environmental education

Jackson (1984:17) argues that the institutional support described by Chakalall will remain inadequate until Caribbean governments have greatly increased numbers of personnel trained to deal with the impacts of tourism and to monitor them over time:

> Although there is still much to learn about the intricacies of coastal environments, documentation points to relationships between certain tourism uses and the natural resources they affect. Understanding these relationships requires the training of personnel in appropriate fields. Training of such personnel should be viewed in most islands as a priority equal to the demand for engineers, nurses and doctors. Unfortunately, this is not the case presently.

While such professional training is clearly needed at the post-secondary level, basic environmental education—including the relationship between tourism and resources—is not an important focus of primary and secondary curricula in the Caribbean (CCA, 1990). Because of their inherent fragility, islands need both qualified professionals and a citizenry which is aware of and sensitive to their environment, more so than even do continental nations.

Research

The general lack of knowledge of natural processes in the literature on islands (OTA, 1987) is a serious problem both because resources ultimately determine the capacity of islands to support livelihoods (Beller, 1987) and because

> the failure to explicitly incorporate such knowledge in the decision-making process prevents planners from adequately addressing all the critical site-specific questions that circumscribe sustainability. These issues include:
>
> —selecting suitable locations for economic activities, residential settlements, and infrastructure;
> —defining renewal rates of resource use/extraction;
> —determining appropriate technologies to avoid damaging sustainable marine yields; and
> —devising compatible multiple resource uses that complement biological productivity and economic potential and so on.
>
> Unless these key resource decisions are carefully customized to fit the integrated natural processes of terrestrial and marine ecosystems, the risk of destructive spillovers and nonsustainability will continue. (McElroy et al., 1987:99)

The only way to overcome this problem is through systematic and long-range research on island resource issues (Thorsell, 1990). As noted above, there have been some excellent beginnings on some islands and for some topics, but more attention should be directed to strengthening both regional and national research capabilities, particularly through cooperative ventures.

Establishment of reserves

On the surface, the establishment of terrestrial and marine reserves in the form of national parks and other protected areas may appear to be the solution for protecting fragile, endangered resources. There are, however, at least three serious barriers to overcome. First is the institutional problem noted earlier: even if an area is designated a reserve, its protection and management in reality will depend on the degree to which there are problems of adequate legislation and management agencies, trained personnel, and available data. Second, McNeely and Thorsell (1988) note that the smallness of many islands means that suitably large areas without human habitation are not available to set aside as national parks; they suggest that other forms of management may be needed to conserve natural values while permitting certain human uses, giving the example of paying local landowners on Yadua Taba (Fiji) not to graze goats or slash and burn for agriculture in order to save a unique iguana species. Third, through their very creation, reserves attract resource users, albeit often ones who exert different kinds of pressures on the environment. For example, the creation of a marine park may keep out local fishermen,

but it may also attract foreign scuba-divers who, in sufficient numbers and without adequate controls, could seriously damage a reef.

Nevertheless, there are several interesting examples of reserve systems in the Eastern Caribbean. Dominica, which established the Morne Trois Pitons National Park over twenty years ago (Thorsell, 1984; Thorsell and Wood, 1976), recently established a second national park at Cabrits (James, 1985) and is considering extending the system into forest reserves. St. Lucia is currently developing a plan for a system of parks and protected areas that would include national parks, marine reserves, forest reserves, and protected forests (Romulus, 1990). Two examples of successful marine parks/reserves are to be found in the United States Virgin Islands (Towle, 1989) and Saba (Van't Hof, 1989).

The flip side of reserves is the creation of tourist development zones designed to concentrate the industry in particular parts of an island. Barbados, for example, has such zones on the west, south, and southeast coasts, in order to keep development away from the rugged east coast which has been declared a national park (Government of Barbados, 1988). Concentration through zoning also makes the servicing of hotels with water, sewers, and roads much easier; on the other hand, the concentration of tourists could exacerbate social conflict with local people.

Acknowledgement

Appreciation is extended to the Social Sciences and Humanities Research Council of Canada for their ongoing support.

Notes

1. In fact, in the case of sugar in the Caribbean, price reflects politics rather than demand. For many years, the export price of sugar has been a function of United States guarantees of sugar purchases under the Caribbean Basin Initiative. For example, the 1985 production price of sugar in St. Kitts-Nevis was 156% of the world market price (Corbett et al., 1985), yet profits were made by supplying sugar to the guaranteed American market.
2. It is recognized that this view of 'resource' as an anthropocentric concept is in contrast with other, ecophilosophic views of the world which would view this approach as being 'resourcist' and economic, rather than ecological. The argument is valid and deserves debate, but will not be discussed here, not only for reasons related to time and length, but also because the discussion here is framed in the context of tourism which is *ipso facto* an anthropocentric phenomenon. Moreover, given the nature of tourism, it seems appropriate to extend Zimmermann's focus on 'natural' resources to 'human-made' resources as a similar functional process takes place; for example, the potential for tourism can turn the 'neutral stuff' of a derelict military establishment into a resource.

References

de Albuquerque, K. (1991) 'Conflicting claims on the Antigua coastal resources: the case of the McKinnons and Jolly Hill Salt Ponds', in Girvan and Simmons (1991:195–205).

Anonymous (1989) 'Third World tourism: visitors are good for you', *The Economist*, March 11: 19–22.

Archer, A. B. (1988) 'The impact of land-based sources of pollution on the marine environment', in International Association for Impact Assessment (1988:264–279).

Bacon, Peter (1985) 'Interpretation of the physical and biological characteristics of the Caribbean from an environment-development perspective', in Geoghagan (1985:42–53).

Beller, W. S. (Ed.) (1987) Proceedings of the Interoceanic Workshop on Sustainable Development and Environmental Management of Small Islands, United States Man and the Biosphere (MAB) Commission, Washington, DC.

Britton, S. and Clarke, W. C. (Eds) (1987) 'Ambiguous alternative: tourism in small developing countries', University of South Pacific, Suva, Fiji.

Butler, P. (1985) 'Conservation of natural resources in St. Lucia', in A. E. Lugo and S. Brown (Eds), *Watershed Management in the Caribbean*, Proceedings of the 2nd Workshop of Caribbean Foresters, St. Vincent, March 19–23, Institute of Tropical Forestry, Rio Piedras, San Juan, Puerto Rico, pp. 111–117.

Butler, R. W. (1980) 'The concept of a tourist area cycle of evolution: implications for management of resources', *Canadian Geographer*, 24:5–12.

Cambers, G. (1985) 'A major tourist development on the west coast of Barbados at Heywoods', in Geoghagan (1985: 267–269).

CARICOM (Caribbean Economic Community) (1989) The Port of Spain Accord on the management and conservation of the Caribbean environment, issued by the First CARICOM Ministerial Conference on the Environment, Port of Spain, Trinidad and Tobago, May 31–June 2.

CCA (Caribbean Conservation Association) (1990) *Towards an Environmental Education and Communications Strategy for the Caribbean*, CCA, St. Michael, Barbados.

CCA (Caribbean Conservation Association) (1991) *Antigua and Barbuda: Country Environmental Profile*, CCA, St. Michael, Barbados.

CCA and IRF (Caribbean Conservation Association and Island Resources Foundation) (1991) *Environmental Agenda for the 1990's: a Synthesis of the Eastern Caribbean Country Environmental Profile Series*, CCA and IRF, St. Michael, Barbados, and Red Hook, St. Thomas, USVI.

Chakalall, B. (1985) 'Natural resource management problems and needs in the Lesser Antilles', in Geoghagan (1985: 54–59).

Corbett, V. F., Goodwin, G., Trevor Hamilton and Associates, Klaus Hardtke Associates, and Smith, P. G. M. (1985) Inter-island transportation study, prepared for Economic Affairs Secretariat of the Organization of Eastern Caribbean States and the Inter-Agency Resident Mission, Antigua, United Nations Development Program.

Devaux, R. (1987a) 'The impact of the Rodney Bay project on coastal processes', in C. Wereko-Brobby (Ed.), *Coastal Zone Management of the Caribbean Region*, CSC Technical Publication Series No. 227, Commonwealth Science Council, London, pp. 117–131.

Devaux, R. (1987b) 'Conservation of St. Lucia's national and cultural heritage', unpublished manuscript, St. Lucia National Trust, Castries, St. Lucia.

Dixon, J. A. (1991) 'Project appraisal: evolving applications of environmental economics', in Girvan and Simmons (1991: 83–106).

Emery, F. and Trist, E. (1965) 'Searching for new directions, in new ways . . . for new times', in J. Sutherland (Ed.), *Management Handbook for Public Administrators*, Van Nostrand Reinhold, New York, pp. 257–301.

Fernie, J. and Pitkethly, A. S. (1985) *Resources: Environment and Policy*, Harper & Row, London.

Finney, B. R. and Watson, K. Z. (Eds) (1975) 'A new kind of sugar: tourism in the Pacific', East–West Technology and Development Institute, East–West Culture Learning Institute, East–West Centre, University of Hawaii, Honolulu.

Geoghagan, T. (Ed.) (1985) Proceedings of the Caribbean Seminar on Environmental Impact Assessment, Caribbean Conservation Association and Institute for Resource and Environmental Studies, Dalhousie University, St. Michael, Barbados, and Halifax, Canada.

Girvan, N. P. and Simmons, D. (Eds) (1991) Caribbean ecology and economics, Caribbean Conservation Association, St. Michael, Barbados, pp. 143–164.

Gosnell, M. (1976) 'The island dilemma', *International Wildlife*, 6(5): 24–35.

Government of Barbados (1988) 'Barbados physical development plan' (amended 1986), Town and Country Planning Office, Ministry of Finance, Bridgetown, Barbados.

Government of Jamaica (1987) 'Jamaica: country environmental profile', Natural Resources Conservation Division, Ministry of Agriculture, and Ralph M. Field Associates, Inc. on behalf of the International Institute for Environment and Development, Kingston, Jamaica.

Hills, T. L. and Lundgren, J. (1977) 'The impact of tourism in the Caribbean: a methodological study', *Annals of Tourism Research*, 4(5): 248–267.

Hunte, W. (1985) 'Marine resources of the Caribbean', in Geoghagen (1985:38–41).

International Association for Impact Assessment (1988) Proceedings of the International Workshop on Impact Assessment for International Development, 31 May–4 June 1987, Barbados.

Jackson, I. (1984) 'The importance of tourism', in Organization of American States (OAS), *Enhancing the Positive Impact of Tourism on the Built and Natural Environment*, Vol. 5, OAS, Washington, DC, pp. 2–41.

James, A. (1985) 'Flora and fauna of the Cabrits Peninsula', Forestry and Wildlife Division, Ministry of Agriculture, Commonwealth of Dominica, Roseau, Dominica.

Mathieson, A. and Wall, G. (1982) *Tourism: Economic, Physical and Social Impacts*, Longman, London.

McElroy, J. (1975) 'Tourist economy and island environment: an overview of structural disequilibrium', *Caribbean Educational Bulletin*, 2(1): 40–58.

McElroy, J. and de Albuquerque, K. (1988) 'Planning and management of land resources in Montserrat', Island Resources Foundation, St. Thomas, USVI.

McElroy, J. and de Albuquerque, K. (1991) 'Tourism styles and policy responses in the open economy–closed environment context', in Girvan and Simmons (1991:143–164).

McElroy, J., de Albuquerque, K. and Towle, E. L. (1987) 'Old problems and new directions for planning sustainable development in small islands', *Ekistics*, 323/324: 93–100.

McNeely, J. A. and Thorsell, J. W. (1988) 'Jungles, mountain, and islands: how tourism can help conserve the natural heritage', in L. J. D'Amore and J. Jafari (Eds), *Tourism—A Vital Force for Peace*, First Global Conference, L. J. D'Amore and Associates Ltd, Montreal.

Mitchell, B. (1989) *Geography and Resource Analysis*, 2nd edn, Longman, Harlow.

OECS (Organization of Eastern Caribbean States) (1988) 'Coastal dynamics: Castries Harbour', Natural Resources Management Project, Castries, St. Lucia.

OECS–NRMP (Organization of Eastern Caribbean States–Natural Resources Management Project) (1986) 'Harmonization of environmental legislation: 1. St. Lucia', OECS–NRMP, Castries, St. Lucia.

O'Riordan, T. (1971) *Perspectives on Resource Management*, Pion, London.

OTA (Office of Technology Assessment, United States Congress) (1987) 'Integrated renewable resource management for U.S. Insular Areas', OTA-F-325, United States Government Printing Office, Washington, DC.

Pearce, D. (1989) *Tourist Development*, 2nd edn, Longman, London.

Putney, A. D. (1982) 'Survey of conservation priorities in the Lesser Antilles: final report', Caribbean Environment Technical No. 1, Caribbean Conservation Association, St. Michael, Barbados.

Richter, L. K. (1989) *The Politics of Tourism in Asia*, University of Hawaii Press, Honolulu.

Romulus, G. (1990) 'A system of parks and protected areas for St. Lucia', St. Lucia National Trust, Castries, St. Lucia.

Shaw, B. (1982) 'Smallness, islandness, remoteness, and resources: an analytical framework', Special Issue of Regional Development Dialogue, on Regional Development in Small Island Nations, pp. 95–109.

Thorsell, J. W. (1984) 'National parks from the group up: experience from Dominica, West Indies', in J. A. McNeely and K. R. Miller (Eds), *National Parks, Conservation, and Development: the Role of Protected Areas in Sustaining Society*, Smithsonian Institution Press, Washington, DC, pp. 616–620.

Thorsell, J. W. (1990) 'Research in tropical protected areas: some guidelines for managers', *Environmental Conservation*, 17(1): 14–18.

Thorsell, J. W. and Wood, G. (1976) 'Dominica's Morne Trois Pitons National Park', *Nature Canada*, 5: 4 (reprint).

Towle, E. L. (1985a) 'St. Lucia—Rodney Bay/Gros Islet', in Geoghagan (1985:228–243).

Towle, E. L. (1985b) 'The island microcosm, case study eight', in J. R. Clark (Ed.), *Coastal Resources Management: Development Case Studies*. Renewable Resources Information Series—Coastal Management Publication No. 3, Research Planning Institute, Inc., for National Park Service of the United States Department of the Interior and the United States Agency for International Development, Columbia, SC, pp. 589–749.

Towle, E. L. (1989) 'Case study on the Virgin Islands Biosphere Reserve', IRF Occasional Paper #50, Island Resources Foundation, St. Thomas, USVI.

Van't Hof, T. (1989) 'Making marine parks self-sufficient: the case of Saba', Conference on Economics and the Environment, Caribbean Conservation Association, Barbados, 6–8 November 1989.

Vincent, G., Huber, R. M. Jr and Meganck, R. (1988) 'The management challenge of Grand Anse Beach erosion, Grenada, West Indies', in International Association for Impact Assessment (1988:280–291).

Weaver, D. B. (1991) 'Alternative to mass tourism in Dominica', *Annals of Tourism Research*, 18(3): 414–432.

Wilkinson, P. F. (1984) 'Energy resources in a Third World microstate: St. Lucia Household Energy Survey', *Resources and Energy*, VI(3): 305–328.

Wilkinson, P. F. (1987a) 'The environmental impact of energy use on forest resources: St. Lucia', in J. G. Nelson and K. D. Knight (Eds), *Research, Resources and Environment in Third World Development*, Publications Series No. 27, Department of Geography, Faculty of Environmental Studies, University of Waterloo, Waterloo, pp. 187–192.

Wilkinson, P. F. (1987b) 'Tourism in small island nations: a fragile dependence', *Leisure Studies*, 6: 127–146.

Wilkinson, P. F. (1989a) 'Le tourisme dans les petites Antilles anglophones', in A. Huetz de Lemps (Ed.), *Iles et tourisme en milieux tropical et subtropical*, Collection 'Iles et Archipels' No. 10, Société l'Etude, la Protection et l'Aménagement de la Nature dans les Régions Inter-Tropicales, Le Centre d'Etudes de Géographie Tropicale du Centre Nationale de Recherches Scientifiques de France et le Centre de Recherches sur Les Espaces Tropicaux de l'Université de Bordeaux III, Talence, pp. 105–124.

Wilkinson, P. F. (1989b) 'Strategies for tourism in island microstates', *Annals of Tourism Research*, 16(2): 153–177.

Wilkinson, P. F. (1990) 'Tourism and integrated national development: the case of the Caribbean', in P. F. Wilkinson and W. C. Found (Eds), *Resource Analysis Research in Developing Countries: the Experience of Ontario Geographers*, Faculty of Environmental Studies, York University, Toronto, pp. 83–97.

Williams, M. (1985) 'Beach sand mining in St. Lucia', in Geoghagen (1985:143–164).

Zimmermann, E. W. (1951) *World Resources and Industries* (rev. edn), Harper and Brothers, New York.

6 Tourism in sub-Saharan Africa: development issues and possibilities

P. U. C. DIEKE

Introduction

Tourism in Africa exhibits many features of tourism in underdeveloped countries generally. African tourism economies, however, have their own particular problems. The present paper will explore these specific characteristics and also the more general development problems faced by these African countries as part of the developing world. Some of the constraints have a lengthy pedigree, being a legacy of the colonial past; others are fairly current. For instance, economic and political exploitation of this continent, real or imagined, has been a common subject of discussion (Hopkins, 1973; Rodney, 1981, 1989), and in recent times, African countries have been remarkably rocked by political instability (Teye, 1988).

Commentators on African economies (World Bank and UNDP, 1989) have suggested that the solution to the region's development slide lies in the introduction of a broad, comprehensive, and country-by-country-based set of reforms, usually under the auspices of the International Monetary Fund (IMF) and the World Bank. These measures, variously called Economic Reform Programmes (ERPs), Structural Adjustment Programmes (SAPs), or Programmes for Sustained Development (PSD), highlight the influence of market trends on development policy, with governments providing the broad economic and political support necessary for the forces to flourish. The changes have important implications for the tourism sector, and these will be discussed below.

The above problems and difficulties are rooted in factors that are both endogenous (e.g. mismanagement of funds) and exogenous (e.g. declining terms of trade). In a tourism context, the constraints are to be explained less by Africa's lack of development resources, particularly investment capital, among others, than by international market pressures and demands. The latter do exert a strong influence on the scale, type and nature of tourism to be encouraged. Seen in this light, one wonders whether African countries can, in Britton's words, meet the 'organisational and commercial requirements of incorporation into the international tourism industry' (1987:113).

This paper analyses some of the factors that inhibit and facilitate tourism development and the opportunities associated with the industry in Africa. These perspectives are considered within the context of international tourism demand characteristics with Kenya and The Gambia as case-study countries. These two sub-Saharan African countries, although variegated in the scale of their tourism, nevertheless share certain resource and policy orientations. A comparison of these countries will therefore show examples which are relevant to other countries where tourism is developing rapidly. First, the paper presents a perspective on global and African tourism trends and then sets out some background to the two countries of study. In the third place, it compares and contrasts the similarities and variations in the tourism sectors, and, lastly, discusses the relevance of the wider planning and policy principles resulting from the analysis.

World and African tourism: scope and significance

World and African tourism trends can be identified by reference to Tables 6.1–6.3. The tables show the growth rate of international tourist arrivals, receipts and regional groupings for selected years. As can be seen (Tables 6.1 and 6.2), global tourism arrivals and receipts in 1991 were 455 million and US$261 billion, respectively, making the sector the second constituent in international trade after oil. Also the dispersion of tourism is highly skewed in favour of the developed countries of Europe and North America, which received a total of 62% of the arrivals and 73% of receipts in 1991. By contrast, Africa had only 3.5% of arrivals and 1.8% of total receipts from tourism in 1991.

Within the African continent, the dispersion of tourist arrivals and receipts by subregional groupings in 1991 were respectively as follows (Table 6.3). Africa received a total of over 15 million international tourists in 1991, of which eastern part received 2.9 million, middle 0.4 million, northern 8.5 million, southern 2.5 million, and western 1.3 million. Again, in 1991, receipts in that order were: US$1.0 million, 0.06 million, 1.8 million, 1.2 million, and 0.6 million. Based on these figures, four general observations can be made.

Table 6.1 *International tourist arrivals, volume, average annual growth rates and world shares by country groupings: 1980, 1985, 1991*

	Volume (000 arrivals)			Growth rates (percentages)			World shares (percentages)		
	1980	1985	1991	80–85	85–91	80–91	1980	1985	1991
World	287 771	329 636	455 100	2.8	5.5	4.3	100.0	100.0	100.0
Developed countries	180 234	214 105	283 682	3.5	4.8	4.2	62.6	65.0	62.3
Developing countries	57 954	68 309	112 264	3.3	8.6	6.2	20.1	20.7	24.7
North America	35 376	38 588	57 712	1.8	6.9	4.6	12.3	11.7	12.7
West Europe	150 357	182 828	227 789	4.0	3.7	3.9	52.3	55.5	50.0
Eastern and Central Europe	39 473	31 436	50 115	−4.5	8.1	2.2	13.7	9.5	11.0
Latin America & Caribbean	26 011	27 907	39 791	1.4	6.1	3.9	9.0	8.5	8.7
Africa	7337	9706	15 845	5.8	8.5	7.3	2.6	2.9	3.5
Middle East	5992	6242	6712	0.8	1.2	1.0	2.1	1.9	1.5
Asia and Pacific	23 225	32 929	57 136	7.2	9.6	8.5	8.1	10.0	12.6
OECD	178 619	213 426	285 199	3.6	5.0	4.4	62.1	64.8	62.7
EC	115 063	138 199	181 534	3.7	4.7	4.2	40.0	41.9	39.9
EFTA	25 110	30 585	35 429	4.0	2.5	3.2	8.7	9.3	7.8
ASEAN	8300	10 011	19 643	3.8	11.9	8.2	2.9	3.0	4.3
Mediterranean countries	90 171	107 875	145 834	3.7	5.2	4.5	31.3	32.7	32.0

Source: World Tourism Organisation, *Compendium of Tourism Statistics*, 13th edn, 1993.

Table 6.2 *International tourist receipts, average annual growth rates and world shares by country groupings: 1980, 1985, 1991*

	Receipts (US$ million)			Growth rates (percentages)			World shares (percentages)		
	1980	1985	1991	80–85	85–91	80–91	1980	1985	1991
World	102 008	115 424	261 070	2.5	14.5	8.9	100.0	100.0	100.0
Developed countries	72 788	80 560	191 437	2.1	15.5	9.2	71.4	69.8	73.3
Developing countries	25 842	31 199	63 342	3.8	12.5	8.5	25.3	27.0	24.3
North America	12 342	21 040	51 088	11.3	15.9	13.8	12.1	18.2	19.6
West Europe	59 946	59 556	135 341	−0.1	14.7	7.7	58.8	51.6	51.8
Eastern & Central Europe	1708	1625	2893	−1.0	10.1	4.9	1.7	1.4	1.1
Latin America & Caribbean	11 813	11 550	20 933	−0.5	10.4	5.3	11.6	10.0	8.0
Africa	2711	2601	4593	−0.8	9.9	4.9	2.7	2.3	1.8
Middle East	3470	4803	3971	6.7	−3.1	1.2	3.4	4.2	1.5
Asia & Pacific	10 018	14 249	42 251	7.3	19.9	14.0	9.8	12.3	16.2
OECD	71 538	80 501	191 641	2.4	15.6	9.4	70.1	69.7	73.4
EC	45 043	44 610	102 633	−0.2	14.9	7.8	44.2	38.6	39.3
EFTA	12 004	10 758	26 627	−2.2	16.3	7.5	11.8	9.3	10.2
ASEAN	3140	5014	14 307	9.8	19.1	14.8	3.1	4.3	5.5
Mediterranean countries	30 136	33 024	72 750	1.9	14.1	8.3	29.5	28.6	27.9

Source: World Tourism Organisation, *Compendium of Tourism Statistics*, 13th edn, 1993.

Table 6.3 *Africa's tourist arrivals and receipts, 1987–91*

	Arrivals (thousands)					Receipts (US$ millions)				
	1987	1988	1989	1990	1991	1987	1988	1989	1990	1991
Subareas										
Eastern	2132	2335	2481	2875	2943	864	805	871	1056	1023
Middle	247	264	349	362	409	71	54	48	71	62
Northern	4953	7313	7920	8398	8595	1722	2458	2188	2297	1799
Southern	1348	1379	1795	2037	2583	669	745	801	1136	1155
Western	1169	1172	1206	1301	1315	471	506	441	515	554
Total	9849	12 463	13 751	14 973	15 845	3797	4568	4349	5075	4593

Source: World Tourism Organisation.

(1) The statistics highlight the competitive nature of international tourism in which countries, developed and developing, are fiercely wanting to increase their share of the market.

(2) It is obvious that visitor arrivals and receipts are heavily concentrated in the developed countries, particularly North American and European.

(3) The figures point to relatively small arrival and receipt share of African countries. In fact, between 1980 and 1991 Africa's share of tourist arrivals and receipts have not changed much. And even in Africa itself, North Africa has retained its dominance of both visitor arrivals and receipt figures.

(4) Unlike the countries of south Asia, east Asia and the Pacific, Africa depends highly on interregional tourism from the developed countries of the North (WTO, 1986).

In the following section, the paper will be reviewing some of the reasons behind Africa's poor performance in international tourism, and asking a question: What is the way out of this dilemma?

Macroeconomic context of tourism in sub-Saharan Africa

There are a number of structural deficiencies which characterise many, if not most, sub-Saharan African countries and developing countries elsewhere. These constraints include undiversified economic base, dependency on very few primary export products, deteriorating terms of trade, population pressures, and unrealisable political aspirations (UNCTAD, 1990). Other problems, briefly summarised, are a scarcity of foreign exchange for investment purposes, low gross national product (GNP) per capita, high rural–urban migration, a debt crisis, a lack of expertise, and a low human development index (HDI) (UNDP, 1993).

For the sub-Saharan African region as part of international economy, the 1980s were a period of major economic upheaval. The pressures described above intensified during these periods and, together with world recession, drought (e.g. in Ethiopia), civil conflict (e.g. in Somalia), poor economic policies (e.g. in Zambia), all combined to depress the economic conditions of the continent. The result—mounting debt, unsustainable deficit, crippling inflation, increasing unemployment and therefore shrinking incomes. The resultant scenario suggests two possibilities. First, the extent of the problem can be likened to the biblical 'Four Horsemen of the Apocalypse'—war, famine, disease, and pestilence—now let loose on the continent. Second, they are a reminder of the disasters which confronted African society and

economy at the dawn of colonialism, aptly described in Chinua Achebe's *Things Fall Apart* (1958). Indeed, the world has fallen apart again for most of the peoples of the region, with little or no hope for the immediate prospects (World Bank, 1989).

Against this difficult background, several African countries embraced the IMF/World Bank-inspired stabilisation and structural adjustment programmes in the 1980s (see Table 6.4). Basically, the reforms sought to ensure that these countries returned to a 'proper' economic development path and thus became viable members of a global system. To attain these objectives the reform measures placed strong emphasis on four areas: first, devaluation of national currencies; second, removal of government interference; third, elimination of subsidies; and fourth, liberalisation of trade. In essence such actions meant, in operational terms, allowing market mechanisms to prevail over state involvement. To some degree in some of these countries the record on the macroeconomic programmes has been successful (e.g. The Gambia) but discouraging in others (e.g. Nigeria). Although it is beyond the scope of this paper to probe these matters in any great length, the austerity changes introduced do have far-reaching consequences for the tourism sector, which are worth noting.

There is now an increase in private sector profile to initiate and develop the tourism industry along profitable lines. By implication this diminishes the operational influence of state capitalism in tourism. This imperative is justified on the ground that government should rationalise its use of scarce resources. Put differently, the withdrawal by government connotes that the public sector should not do what the private sector is able and willing to do. But the key to private sector investment in the tourism industry is confidence, emphasising the need for an assurance that, for instance, investment incentives, tax holidays, repatriation of profits, and so on are in place to stimulate their participation in tourism. Clearly, such functions are within the power of governments to perform. In this sense, therefore, the government's role is seen as 'enabling' rather than operational. It is common knowledge that for these 'enabling' functions to succeed in practice, it is required that governments should have a clear policy vision, setting out the sound parameters within which the private sector will operate.

Finally, one important dimension to the reforms is the increased emphasis which African governments have given to tourism as a viable development option, for a number of obvious reasons, which are widely recognised, although not wholly accepted. Goverment support for tourism is because of the economic benefits which the sector is expected to generate: foreign exchange,

Table 6.4 *IMF programmes in sub-Saharan Africa, 1980–1991*

Nation	80	81	82	83	84	85	86	87	88	89	90	91
Angola												
Benin										x		x
Botswana												
Burkina Faso												x
Burundi							x		x	x		x
Cameroon												
Central African Republic	x	x		x	x	x		x	x		x	
Chad		x				x		x		x	x	
Congo							x				x	
Côte d'Ivoire		x		x	x	x	x	x	x	x		x
Djibouti												
Equatorial Guinea	x	x				x			x			x
Ethiopia		x				x					x	
Gabon	x						x					x
Gambia, The		x	x		x		x	x	x	x	x	
Ghana			x	x			x	x	x	x		
Guinea			x					x		x		x
Guinea-Bissau		x						x		x		
Kenya	x		x	x		x		x	x	x		x
Lesotho									x	x	x	x
Liberia	x	x	x	x			I	x			N	
Madagascar	x	x	x		x	x	x	x	x	x	x	
Malawi	x		x	x	x			x	x	x	x	x
Mali	x		x	x		x				x		
Mauritania	x	C				x	x	x		x		
Mauritius	x	x		x		x		x				
Mozambique								x	x	x	x	x
Niger			x	x		x	x	x		x		
Nigeria								x		x		x
Rwanda												x
Sao Tomé and Principe										x		
Sénégal	x	x	x	x		x	x	x	x	x		x
Sierra Leone		x	C	x	x		x	S	I			
Somalia	x	x	x			x		x	I			
Sudan	x	x	x	x	x		I	x			N	
Swaziland						x						
Tanzania	x	x					x	x	x		x	x
Togo		x		x	x	x	x	x	x	x	x	
Uganda	x	x	x	x				x	x	x	x	x
Zaire		x	x	x	x	x	x	x		x		I
Zambia		x	x	x				I			x	
Zimbabwe		x		x								

Source: International Monetary Fund, *IMF Survey*, published 23 times annually, 1 Jan. 1980–31 Dec. 1991.
Key: x: at least one programme began that year—Compensatory Financing Facility (CFF), Compensatory and Financing Facility (CFF), Structural Adjustment Facility (SAF), or Extended SAF (ESAF). C: programme cancelled. I: declared ineligible by the IMF. S: declared suspended by the IMF. N: declaration of non-cooperation.

employment, income, government revenue and regional development. To some extent, these are debatable issues and need not concern us here. What is relevant in an African context, however, is that these benefits will, if realised, be used to overcome the resource problems as seen, increase the region's economic wellbeing, and thus facilitate the development process. Otherwise, the region will inevitably continue to depend on international aid to support development efforts.

In considering the above circumstances *vis-à-vis* tourism development in sub-Saharan Africa, several questions arise. How has tourism developed and what is the nature of the development? What are the problems of tourism development? How do the authorities concerned react to these problems in the planning policies they adopt for the tourism sector? Do their policies work? What lessons can be learned to guide future tourism development planning? These questions form the basis for the analysis presented below, are considered in relation to Kenya and The Gambia. In both countries tourism is of strategic importance in economic development. Second, both countries are regarded as pace-setters in the field of tourism in Africa. They would therefore be representative models for the wider group of countries in Africa wanting to develop their tourism potential.

Tourism development in Kenya

The country

Kenya is a country of 25 million people, situated on the east coast of Africa on the Indian Ocean. It shares boundaries with Uganda to the west, Tanzania to the south, and Ethiopia in the north. It is also bordered by Sudan in the northwest and Somalia in the east. Occupying an area of 582 646 km², two-thirds of which are either semi-deserts or deserts, the surface land for habitation is indeed limited. Administratively, the country is divided into seven provinces with Nairobi, the capital, as the only provincial district unit. The country is principally an agricultural nation; over 80% of the population depend on it. The two export commodities are coffee and tea, tourism another. Present estimates (Kenya, 1991; World Bank, 1991) indicate that agriculture's and tourism's share in GDP in 1990 was respectively 28% and 11.2%, while the manufacturing sector contributed 13.2%. The open nature of the country's economy has permitted Mosley (1983) to describe Kenya's economy as a classic example of 'the settler economies'. Once a British colony, Kenya achieved statehood in 1963. In politics Kenya used to be a one-party democracy; ironically, now the country has opened up to other political parties.

Evolution of tourism

Kenya is, perhaps by any international standard but certainly African comparison, one of the highly developed, most visited and probably successful tourism destinations. To promote itself, the country relies on two major tourist resources, beach and wildlife, which are concentrated in three prime areas: Nairobi, coast, and up-country game parks and reserves. Wildlife attractions are extensive and dispersed in 57 locations, which currently occupy about 10% of Kenya's surface land area. The four major beach areas on the 400-mile Indian Ocean coast are Diani Beach on the south coast, Mombasa in the north, Malindi/Watamu, and the Lamu archipelago. The coast resources also include palm-fringed sandy/white beaches, protected by coral reefs.

Over the years the tourism industry in this country has expanded considerably in many ways (Kenya, 1991). For instance, between 1970 and 1990, tourist arrivals showed an upward trend: in 1970 Kenya received over 0.3 million tourists, about 0.4 million in 1980 and by 1990 slightly above 0.7 million. The primary tourist markets have been from Germany, the UK, the USA, and Switzerland, in that order. While the purpose of visit varied, ranging from leisure (beach and safari), to business, to transit, overall it was the holiday tourists who contributed most to the increased traffic volume. For example, in 1990 holiday visitors increased by 13.5% over 1989; whereas business and transit visitors declined by 21.2% and 33%, respectively.

Tourist traffic was also spatially concentrated and, based on bed-night figures, tourists from the USA and the UK were significant in the Nairobi area, whilst in the coastal parts of the country, the Germans were predominant. For the lodges, the major shares of demand came from American, German and, to a lesser extent, UK tourists. Most tourists to Kenya arrived on an all-inclusive price basis, with relatively fixed itineraries usually determined in the developed generating countries; in 1990, average length of stay hovered around 14.3 days. This figure was only slightly higher than the 13.6 days in 1989 and lower than the 16 days recorded between 1986 and 1988, thus reflecting visitors' reaction to increased costs of travel and maintenance.

The supply of tourist facilities and services by area and category was both a reflection of this demand pattern as described and also an indication of a shift in the regions of tourist interest in Kenya. It again reinforced the profile of tourists themselves as well as what attracted people to vacation in this country. For instance, there was a considerable growth in the supply of accommodation establishments and bed-stocks (Kenya, 1990). Part of the reason was government purchase of hotels in the mid-1970s recession (Dieke, 1993a). It can be further observed that these facilities were spatially concentrated, first in the coastal areas, followed by Nairobi, for a number of reasons (Dieke, 1991): first the popularity of beach holidays which mostly appealed to the western European tourists; second, Nairobi has good conference facilities and is also a centre for many incoming tours. It attracted a large number of visitor bed-nights precisely because game-viewing tours originated and terminated in the city.

In the wider context of development, tourism is of fundamental importance to Kenya's economy in export earnings terms, among other benefits. From the point of view of gross domestic product (GDP), the sector contributed to it, from 1986 to 1990, an average of 14%

(at constant 1982 prices) (Kenya, 1991:19). Comparatively, coffee, tourism, and tea are, as stated above, the three main exports of Kenya. From 1985 to 1986, earnings from coffee surpassed those from tourism; but from 1987 onwards, tourism has become the most dominant sector, with coffee and tea taking second and third positions, respectively. Best available estimate of tourism employment (Kenya, 1991:40; see also Kenya, 1990:26–27) indicates that in 1990 tourism employed about 114 000 Kenyans, directly and indirectly. All considered, the above statistics do provide an indication of the place of tourism in the economy of this country.

Policy, organisation, and planning framework

In Kenya at present there is no comprehensive, nationwide tourism policy, and no clear policy guidelines for the tourism sector exist. However, government statements of national objectives are usually set out in national plans (Kenya, 1973, 1978, 1983, 1988) which also include tourism, or made in parliamentary sessions (Kenya, 1990), or further are contained in numerous policy documents (Kenya, 1965, 1980, 1981, 1982, 1986, 1988). From these official statements and sources, it is possible to discern several features of (tourism) policy as generally defined (see Jenkins, 1991; Rose, 1984) pertaining to Kenya. At best these are seen in the main as a by-product of larger government policies relating to other issues in the national interest, as Richards (1980:142) has acknowledged: 'Sector development planning in Kenya is much influenced by national economic and social development priorities, as laid down in the objectives of the country's development plans'.

In this connection, Kenya's development tourism policy objectives are to

> increase tourism contribution to the growth of GDP (Gross Domestic Product); raise the foreign exchange earning capacity; create more employment opportunities; increase Kenya ownership and management of the industry; reduce any undesirable social or environmental consequences; and conserve, protect and improve environment and wildlife. (Kenya, 1983)

One notable feature of the tourism targets is the economic *raison d'être* as the starting point for tourism development in Kenya. There are of course socio-cultural considerations as well. It is sufficient to say that since everything in tourism is not emergency-related, it follows therefore that Kenya's tourism policy measures need not be ad hoc and uncoordinated. Rather they should emerge out of careful examinations of several imperatives—an overriding need to maintain Kenya's market share of international tourism, the existence of destination substitution possibilities, intense competition among developing countries to attract more foreign tourists, etc.

To further those aims, Kenya has taken a number of steps, notably programmes to develop and expand hotel capacity along the coastal fronts, resulting from the work of two study groups established by government in 1971 and 1974 (see Kenya, 1971; Richards 1980) and other programmes associated with wildlife development. In brief, the government of Kenya passed a significant number of relevant laws which created institutions responsible for tourism development and growth. Three examples can be cited. The Ministry of Tourism and Wildlife (MTW) was created in 1966 as the main policy-making organ of the Kenyan government in tourism and wildlife matters. Part of its brief was to allocate tourism resources to cover activities carried out by other public bodies whose responsibilities impinged on tourism. Second, the Kenya Tourist Development Corporation (KTDC) was set up in 1965 to monitor the operation of hotels, lodges, and other forms of accommodation.

The KTDC and its subsidiary, African Tours and Hotels (AT&H), are in fact the investment arms of the government. Third, created in 1990 out of the defunct Wildlife Conservation and Management Department of 1976, Kenya Wildlife Service (KWS) was charged with responsibility for wildlife matters. To complement the efforts of the above government department and parastatals, there exist several quasi non-governmental organisations (QUANGOS, for short). Some are voluntary organisations, others trade associations whose contributions to Kenya's tourism sector are also important. Since the regulation of Kenya's tourism is the responsibility of a variety of organisations, public and private, operating within unclear policy guidelines, this does prompt a number of critical questions. First, do the policies work and if not, why not? Second, does the proliferation of tourism organisations hinder the coordinated development of tourism in Kenya? It is to these questions that the next section now turns.

Tourism development constraints

Several demand- and supply-related problems confronting Kenya's tourism industry can be identified, including:

(1) Spatial concentration in demand means severe strains on tourist facilities and services, especially at peak periods; and it may possibly also result in the resident–visitors irritants situation in Doxey's 'IRRIDEX' model (1975) generally associated with tourism development.

(2) Kenya depends more on holiday tourism than business tourism, even though business tourists are generally regarded as big spenders. Thus seasonal decreases in demand relate to business and holiday tourism and their impact on revenue generation, although business tourism in Kenya exhibits a much less seasonal pattern. A consequence of the lack of demand is almost total paralysis of the market. It means not only the prevalence of unemployment or labour under-employment but perhaps also under-utilisation of tourist facilities and, hence, inadequate returns on investment capital.

(3) Over-dependence on tourists from certain countries implies that Kenya runs the risk of reduced tourist receipts occasioned by a fall in demand from such countries.

(4) Spatial concentration and haphazard supply of accommodation outlets is a grim reminder of what Richards (1980:154) has described as the 'unplanned ribbon development'. This uncontrolled, unplanned development of specific areas will result in a deterioration of Kenya's tourism image and wildlife resources, or will further dilute the quality of Kenya's tourist attractions and may point to a lack of land-use planning and the non-existence of a zoning policy. Without this policy overview, sustainable tourism in Kenya will not be realised.

(5) Further difficulties for Kenya arise from the nature and extent of foreign involvement in its tourism industry. As would be expected, Kenya receives a relatively smaller share of tourist spend, especially relating to the inclusive tours. As a consequence of this, the onus on Kenya is perhaps to persuade people to stay longer in the country. By implication the achievement of this strategy does require the country to diversify the local attractions base available. Of course, tourists must be made aware of their existence and, if possible helped with relative access to them, within an affordable price range.

(6) As for the institutions managing the tourism sector, there is the worrying aspect, as ever, of budget and expenditure constraint, especially when compared with government expenditure on other sectors. Low budget means Kenya has a limited involvement in overseas trade fairs. It would be wishful thinking to pretend that, for example, with a promotional budget of K£3 million for the Tourism Department and also US$31 000 for the marketing of the Kenyatta International Conference Centre, all is well for tourism in Kenya in terms of publicity. The realities of international tourism are such that promotion is critical to survival in an intensely competitive market.

After all, tourism is the bedrock of Kenya's economic lifeline and so needs to be guarded jealously. If this country is to increase its economic gains from tourism, it needs to adopt more proactive measures to remain competitive.

(7) What is worse, the KTDC's investment programme to encourage Kenya participation in commercial ventures without alienating foreign partners—the much-rehearsed policy of 'indigenisation without confrontation' (Sinclair, 1992:557)—has fallen on hard times, in part due to budget problems as noted. Not surprisingly, the corporation now favours relatively large enterprises in investing in the hotel property development. Thus the KTDC is no longer seen as a catalyst to local investment but instead a reactionary force whose ad hoc response to opportunities does not augur well for Kenya's tourism.

Tourism development in The Gambia

The country

The Gambia, located on the West African coast, is a small country by any international comparison. Sandwiched on its three landward sides by Sénégal, it occupies a narrow, 350-km land strip on both sides of the Gambia River. The population in 1990 was estimated at 875 000 and, between 1980 and 1990, it grew at an annual rate of 3.3% (World Bank, 1991). With a land area of 11 295 km², much of which is saline marshes, the country has a population density of 73 people per km², reportedly one of the highest in mainland Africa. The climate is tropical with a rainy season from April to October and a dry season from November to March. A former British territory, The Gambia achieved political independence in 1965 and is currently a democracy; multiparty politics have always been permitted.

With very limited natural resources, the country's economy is based on agriculture, essentially groundnut production, the dominant sector. In 1989 groundnuts accounted for about 55% of the GDP and employed about 80% of the natural workforce. The industrial sector is small and is based largely on agro-processing, such as palm-oil and fish products, which for the period in review provided 9% of the GDP. The tourism sector now ranks second among the three foreign exchange earners for The Gambia, with the sector contributing 10% of the GDP in 1989. Since agriculture is the 'power-house' of the Gambian economy, the implications for the local economy are clear. Vagaries of the weather, such as drought, might decrease harvest and lead to low foreign currency accrual for investment. A low harvest means insufficient food production and so increased food imports are needed to feed the increasing population.

Evolution of tourism

The main tourist attractions of this country are a good combination of affordable beach assets, and a wide variety of birds for ornithologists, in addition to all-inclusive packages. Tourism began in 1965, when the Swedes first 'discovered' this country and 300 tourists visited there. Ten years later tourist arrivals increased to 21 000 and by 1990/91 season the total rose to 101 419 (The Gambia, 1992). The major source markets are from northern Europe, predominantly British and Swedish, whose arrivals in 1990/91 tourist season represented 57% and 13% respectively of total arrivals on organised holidays. For the 1990/91 period, average length of stay was estimated at slightly below 14 days. There is considerable seasonality, with November–April as peak months and the rest of the year as low period.

Tourism in The Gambia is regarded as a particularly important economic sector (The Gambia, 1990). In 1989 it contributed more than 10% of the country's GDP and net earnings of US$25 million (about one-half of the country's foreign exchange earnings). In this period also an estimated 7000 Gambians were employed directly and indirectly in the tourism sector. The direct jobs are in hotels and restaurants because of the need to supply and serve tourists. The jobs provided earnings for workers and investors in the form of wages and profits. Indirect employment was in a spectrum of activities like handicrafts, taxi transport, etc. In relation to tourist plants, at present, there is a capacity of about 5000 tourist beds in 17 hotels located mainly in the Greater Banjul Area, along the Atlantic coast, where much tourism has taken place.

Policy, organisational and planning framework

The first conscious effort to develop tourism in The Gambia was in 1972, with technical and financial assistance from the United Nations Development Programme (UNDP) and the International Development Agency, of the massive 'Tourism and Infrastructure Project' (TIP) of 1975–80, otherwise labelled the 'Bafuloto Project' (Coopers and Lybrand, 1974; World Bank, 1975). The aim of the project was to provide the basic infrastructure required for tourism, as a result of which land (750 metres wide and 15 km long) west of Banjul (formerly Bathurst), the capital, along the Atlantic

beach fronts, was designated as a Tourism Development Area (TDA) in 1974. Thus, the main dimensions of The Gambia's tourism policy objectives are in the spheres of economic growth, full employment, income generation, balance of payments, and narrowing the rural–urban structural imbalance (The Gambia, 1981). The belief is that tourism will contribute towards that achievement.

Since indigenous Gambians do not have access to the capital or training to enter into the tourism sector on a large scale, the policy of the government therefore has been to allow foreign overseas investors, perhaps single-handedly or in partnership with either the government or local Gambians, a role in tourism development. In support of the above policy objectives government has taken a number of useful steps: first, to encourage *supply* of tourism assets, it has provided basic infrastructure, facilities for manpower-training and granted generous incentives to investors, or even acted as guarantor for full loan to secure financing for hotel construction. Other measures are direct project aid, hotel investment and management, and perhaps protecting natural, historic and cultural attractions. To stimulate tourism *demand* for The Gambia, social and economic situations in the major developed tourism-generating countries have been critical, in addition to the development of inclusive tours and the relative loyalty of major European 'trigger' markets.

Furthermore, the Government has passed a series of laws, including, for instance, the 1988 Development Act (The Gambia, 1988) aimed to make it possible for investors to have all the approval they need to invest in the country within 90 days of application and also to provide them with the necessary information. To implement tourism policies the government has also introduced specific organisations: the Ministry of Information and Tourism (MIT) to determine overall tourism policy at home and abroad, and to deal with marketing, product development, product quality control, and overseas activities. Two boards, the Tourism Advisory Board (TAB) and the Tourism Area Development Board (TADB) (formerly Tourism Liaison Board), are both established under the aegis of the MIT.

The TAB, comprising representatives of public and private entities, acts in an advisory capacity to the MIT on all matters pertaining to the tourism sector. The TADB/TLB organises and coordinates development related to tourism, particularly in respect of land allocation in the TDA. The National Investment Board (NIB) handles government interests in hotel investment ventures. Planning of tourism in The Gambia is done within the overall framework of national objectives; it follows a five-yearly cycle, requiring 'an annual rolling revision to adjust targets and meet contingencies'

(Jenkins, 1991:110). Thus, there is, whenever possible, an integration of tourism policies with national development policies, thereby strengthening the links between national development planning and tourism planning (The Gambia, 1981, 1987, 1988).

Tourism development constraints

One factor which inhibits or constrains tourism, and possibly the implementation of policies, is the weak operating framework. As noted, responsibility for the sector involves many organisations whose cooperation is critical. There is the difficulty not only in coordinating their different activities but perhaps more importantly in implementing policies, partly attributable to differences in interests. For example, it is argued (World Bank, 1986) that major decisions regarding administration in the TDA do not follow a clear and well-defined administrative path. There are also instances where land areas in the TDA have been widened without previous permit from the TDAB/TLB, or where the Ministry of Local Government and Lands have sought to preserve lands against the wishes of other members of the TLB; such cases are an indication of disunity among tourism planners and executives.

In such instances, they point to confusion within the tourism sector, perhaps because the powers or decisions of the TLB are often ignored. It is also possible that many other bodies do not always comply with TLB's indications. It may well point to the impotence of the MIT as the custodian of public sector interest in tourism. Without enlisting the support and cooperation of these agencies, or having an appropriate structure to control operational standards in the tourism sector, it is doubtful whether the realisation of the planned objectives, as seen above, will occur. Probably as a consequence of these difficulties, an administrative decision has now been taken by the Government of The Gambia to replace the TLB with a new body, Tourism Area Development Board (TADB).

In the same way that the lack of an effective administrative with power structure impedes progress, so also does government under-funding of tourism. With current tourism budget of D650 000 (about US$76 000), it can be said that this sum is, relative to government expenditure on other sectors of the economy, inadequate (see The Gambia, 1992:33). Thus the MIT will be hard-pressed to provide the required promotion that is crucial to survival. The reasons are clear. In a highly competitive market in which destinations offer similar products, there is the danger that The Gambia might be sidelined or substituted by other similar destinations.

It is therefore imperative that, for the country to remain competitive, protect its market share, differentiate its product, and diversify its markets, it will require an increased budget provision. Unless the present figure is substantially improved, financial constraints will continue to hamper overall achievements and serve to make progress difficult.

Other problems of tourism in The Gambia include seasonality, low wages, and foreign domination which, taken together, may raise a further question of whether tourism has a 'development' impact on The Gambia. Because tourism to this country is highly seasonal, most tourist hotels are closed down, about fifty per cent of the staff are laid off, others are paid less or sometimes paid on a daily basis. These problems have implications for the local economy, the labour force and their families. Since the low period parallels the rainy season when intense farming activities take place in The Gambia, then one assumes that these hotel workers would return to farm work when tourist demand reduces. Quite the opposite, as Farver (1984:254) had found out: 'There is no evidence to suggest Gambia hotel workers return to the land to farm . . . the harvesting of annual crop coincides with the beginning of the tourist season. This makes farming and tourism an either/or situation. There is no trade-off possibility'. What is not clear though is how workers support themselves during the six-month off-season; this is an area that requires further research.

The concern about low-pay/skill and foreign domination, though not unusual, appears to be an inherent feature of the tourist industry in The Gambia. There is a correlation between low pay and unskilled jobs. Increase in pay in The Gambia does not necessarily reflect individual merit but rather is a function of national minimum wage regulations. Progression to management positions is often impeded through expatriate recruiting for such high posts. On foreign domination, it has been estimated (World Bank, 1986) that in the larger hotels which are run by the international hotel chains, most of the key positions are occupied by expatriates. This dilemma is understandable: expatriate employment policy is apparently governed by the hotel managers' belief that a larger number of expatriates can raise the standard of service. While this idea is probably true, it does raise doubts (Green, 1979) as to the realisation of government's Gambianisation policy to give the native population a major say in the affairs of the country, including tourism. And so, even if individual Gambians achieve the relevant qualifications to fill the management positions, such posts will, in the foreseeable future, be a 'closed shop' to expatriates as the need is to placate external partners.

Development issues

On the basis of the analysis described, a number of tourism development issues can be considered. The focus will be on areas of similarity and contrast, aimed to identify and assess their strategic implications for many African countries facing identical tourism situations and development potential.

1. In general the countries' respective tourism developments have, in the main, taken quite similar forms, determined largely by what they believed would serve the best interests of their respective communities. Thus, both countries developed their tourist industries with the object of overcoming the problems of development resources, particularly in the area of accumulating foreign exchange. Included in those tourist policies was the objective of establishing a degree of local control— be it labelled 'Kenyanisation', 'Gambianisation', or 'indigenisation without confrontation'. Consequently Kenya and The Gambia counted on exports to lead to their overall development strategy, and they also related local controls to state and private capitalists and enterprises in the context of closer—but less unequal— integration into the present capitalist international economy (de Kadt, 1979).

Hence, in the reform programmes discussed above, the private sector was given a predominant role to develop the tourism sector along profitable lines. This is not surprising, given that overseas private investors 'are not philanthropists or fools, and they themselves take as few risks as possible' (UNDP/ICAO, 1977). In this sense they need guarantees relating to repatriation of profits, capital, and even business confidence to invest in the tourism sector. The evidence is that this policy is working because in operational terms, there is now less state participation than before; government participation is limited to an 'enabling' role in setting out the sound parameters within which the private sector will operate. However, measured in volume and value terms, Kenya may be regarded as a model for a successful tourism development in sub-Saharan Africa, although at some cost: rapid development and over-development of tourism, succinctly characterised by Richards (1980:154) as 'unplanned ribbon development'. The Gambia is aware of this problem and wants to avoid it; hence a phased development approach to tourism.

2. Part of the success of Kenya and, to some degree The Gambia, is related to the extent of foreign commercial involvement in developing their tourism resources, and the policy of the countries has been to allow foreign investors in national economic development. This involvement, severally called 'ownership', 'partnership', or 'management contract', especially in the hotel subsector, is higher in Kenya than The Gambia (Dieke, 1991, 1993b). This variation between the countries is reflected in differences in their historical structural conditioning under British tutelage. One is therefore reminded of the suggestion (Britton, 1982:340) that 'where foreign enterprises were present in a country's tourist industry they would be the most successful', consequently 'pioneer' facilities for tourism development were in place because Kenya had a vigorous expatriate community which sought to advance foreign commercial interests, including tourism.

3. Similarly to Kenya, tourism in The Gambia was also externally stimulated, with conglomerates in countries with established connections with the country planning significant roles. Examples included the Scandinavian Vingressor group and the UK Copthorne Hotels (formerly British Caledonian Hotels), although at first this participation might have been limited. Important differences between the countries are the amount of capital invested and the extent of foreign participation in tourism. Compared with their Kenyan counterparts, the industry in The Gambia is so small in scale that it cannot sustain large-scale capital enterprise. In addition, the country has had no tradition of an expatriate community, because of climatic and epidemiological variations between east and west Africa, much to the disadvantage of The Gambia. East Africa has a cooler climate than the west and is also not as mosquito-infested. The result is that Europeans not only found Kenya conducive and so settled there in large numbers but that they were also central to the economic 'life line' of this country, again, as Mosley (1983) has recognised.

4. In terms of planning deficiencies in these countries, clearly tourism is an important economic sector. But its full potential is constrained by a number of exogenous factors, ranging from over-reliance on single markets to seasonal fluctuations in demand. There is also the problem associated with increasing emphasis on tourism development at the expense of other economic sectors, which would be putting one's proverbial eggs in one development basket. Bryden (1973) highlights the problem and argues that public sector resources can be diverted to tourism and implies that this can be to the detriment of other more socially advantageous forms of capital formation. Myers (1975) echoes this sentiment and states that tourism serves to increase the GDP no more than would similar investments in agriculture.

5. Just as the above are perceived as impediments to tourism, so also is the lack of an enforcing structure. The cases demonstrate that the tourism sector growth has been rapid and, particularly for Kenya, large-scale. The implication is that control of the industry, either in terms of scale or type of tourism development policy, lies outside these countries (see Dieke, 1993b:438–441). This problem is further exacerbated, especially when local manpower's ability to grasp the planning idea involved is deficient, as de Kadt (1979) has noted. In terms of tourism planning, the policy response has been belated, described as 'shutting the stable door after the horse has bolted'. These issues form the basis for a consideration of the lessons drawn from the paper, which may point to the way forward for these countries' tourism industries.

Conclusions—the way forward

To achieve the strategic objectives set for the tourism sector and thereby provide the springboard for a realisation of the 'basic needs' of the citizens of Kenya and The Gambia, there seem to be three possibilities. First, there is a need for forward planning, second, for flexibility in planning, and third, for considerable caution in monitoring and reviewing the effects of tourism to serve national development goals.

Need for forward planning

The issue of planning is largely one of how to ensure that best use is made of available resources. This is critical especially, as seen, where development resources in Kenya and The Gambia are scarce and there are many competing needs for what is available. Furthermore, part of the planning process requires that the benefits of tourism should be optimised and the disbenefits minimised. To ensure that these do happen, it is also essential that the institutional and organisation structures with relevant mandate are in place; there are several reasons for this. One relates to the need to ensure operational standards in the tourism sector, and the other to the need to coordinate the various activities which impinge on tourism. As a basis for the exercise of such functions, tourism objectives have to be developed and policies to implement those objectives formulated.

The development difficulties of these two countries dictate that, at the initial stages of tourism development, the above tasks are undertaken by the government sector (Jenkins and Henry, 1982) to provide the dynamic for tourism development and growth, within a national framework. Without a defined tourism policy, planning does become ad hoc and lacking in focus. As the

economic reform programmes noted above demonstrate, the comprehensive nature of policy planning does also involve a recognition by these governments of the axiom that they should not do what the private sector is able and willing to do. In the context of tourism planning, this implies an enhanced private sector profile to initiate and develop the tourism industry along financial profitability— the origin of the so-called 'withdrawal policy'. Of course, it needs to be stated again that the smooth functioning of the government 'enabling' role depends largely on its having a clear tourism policy vision. In brief, as Jenkins (1987:3) has succinctly put it, planning 'permits options to be considered . . . helps avoid the continuous situation of having to take emergency actions . . . provides some element of stability to future operations'.

Need for flexibility in planning

In the tourism policy process, planners must respond flexibly to external pressures over which they have no control, especially relating to the market distribution network—tour operators, airlines, and hotels. Essentially, these tourism transnationals, because of their extensive market connections, established reputations, and recognised expertise, can make or break tourism in most developing countries, including Africa. For instance, as surrogates for foreign tourists, overseas tour operators decide which destinations to 'sell', or even which holiday and tourist kinds to offer. Part of their business objectives is to ensure that host destinations provide the facilities and services of requisite international standards, acceptable to their clients. Such compliance is a *sine qua non* for future sales and possible repeat business, given the discretionary and exogenous nature of tourism demand. Discretionary because taking a holiday is voluntary, and exogenous because tourism is induced from outside of the host country.

It is also evident from the case studies that most tourists to The Gambia and, to a lesser extent Kenya, arrive as part of an inclusive tour, using foreign air carriers. The result is that much of the total holiday price paid by tourists does not accrue to these countries. Many researchers have suggested imprecise figures of what accrue to a host developing country, ranging between 15% and 46% (Britton 1982; Farver, 1984; Sinclair, 1992). Competition is another area of tourism policy concern. The international tourism sector is very competitive, partly because, as seen, taking a holiday is discretionary and partly because destinations offer undifferentiated products and even similar price ranges. This makes destination substitution a real possibility. Cognisant of these constraints, flexible tourism policies are likely to advance the cause of tourism and improve standards and quality of products. Flexible tourism policies need to be formulated and executed in a manner that does not alienate the proverbial goose that lays the golden egg, be it the market (tourist) or the market intermediaries (the travel trade), or even international organisations.

Need for caution

In advocating caution in tourism development, two issues closely related to the earlier discussions of planning and flexibility may be mentioned, because of their implications for tourism policy. The first is the question of scale, about which much has been written (see Jenkins, 1982; de Kadt, 1992; Richter, 1989). Expressions such as 'eco or green tourism', 'alternative tourism', 'sustainable tourism', 'enclave tourism', 'carrying capacity' encapsulate some of the current thoughts on tourism. What may be inferred from these catch-phrases is the notion that tourism development carries with it considerable economic and non-economic costs and benefits. Since resources are limited, careful resource use and management of them are critical, not least because of the need to ensure future availability and also to enhance the benefits of such an activity. Clearly, without careful, sensitive, and planned utilisation and management of the resources, destinations will, in environmental terms, become unattractive, with all the economic consequences that go with it.

Community involvement in tourism is a second area of relevance to this section, in order to make the tourism sector reasonably self-sustaining. De Kadt (1992), while supporting local participation in the tourism decision process, nevertheless questions the idea on three grounds. First, 'such calls for community participation gloss over the well-known tendency for local elites to "appropriate" the organs of participation for their own benefit'. Unless relevant safeguards prevail, it is possible that this pattern will hamper progress. Second, local experience of tourism is negligible; and third, even public servants, who hold their positions in trust on behalf of the government, similarly lack expertise and competence in tourism matters. The logical outcome of all this is that tourism policy planners 'are largely at the mercy of the opinions of those who are presented to them, or who present themselves as "experts"' (de Kadt, 1992). Hence the need for caution in regard to policies and institutional arrangements for the tourism sector.

References

Achebe, Chinua (1958) *Things Fall Apart*, Heinemann, London.

Britton, Stephen G. (1982) 'The political economy of tourism in the Third World', *Annals of Tourism Research*, 9: 331–358.

Britton, Stephen G. (1987) 'Tourism in Pacific-island states: constraints and opportunities', in Stephen Britton and William C. Clarke (Eds), *Ambiguous Alternative: Tourism in Small Developing Countries*, University of the South Pacific, Suva, pp. 113–139.

Bryden, John M. (1973) *Tourism and Development: a Case Study of the Commonwealth Caribbean*, Cambridge University Press, London.

Coopers and Lybrand (1974) *Tourism Infrastructure Studies*, Coopers and Lybrand, London.

Dieke, Peter U. C. (1991) 'Policies for tourism development in Kenya', *Annals of Tourism Research*, 18(2): 269–294.

Dieke, Peter U. C. (1993a) 'Cross-national comparison of tourism development: lessons from Kenya and The Gambia', *The Journal of Tourism Studies*, 4(1): 2–18.

Dieke, Peter U. C. (1993b) 'Tourism and development policy in The Gambia', *Annals of Tourism Research*, 20(3): 423–449.

Doxey, G. V. (1975) 'A causation theory of visitor–resident irritants: methodology and research inferences', in *Proceedings of the Travel Research Association, 6th Annual Conference*, Travel Research Association, San Diego, pp. 195–198.

Farver, Jo Ann M. (1984) 'Tourism and employment in The Gambia', *Annals of Tourism Research*, 11: 249–265.

The Gambia, Republic of (1981) *Five-Year Plan for Economic and Social Progress, 1981/82–1985/86*, Government Printer, Banjul.

The Gambia, Republic of (1987) *Tourism Statistics*, Central Statistics Office, Banjul.

The Gambia, Republic of (1988) *Development Act, No. 4 1988*, Government Printer, Banjul.

The Gambia, Republic of (1990) *Budget Speech*, Government Printer, Banjul.

The Gambia, Republic of (1992) *The Statistical Abstract of The Gambia 1991*, Central Statistics Department, Banjul.

Green, Reginald H. (1979) 'Toward planning tourism in African countries', in Emanuel de Kadt (Ed.), *Tourism: Passport to Development*, Oxford University Press, New York, pp. 79–100.

Hopkins, Antony (1973) *Economic History of West Africa*, Cambridge University Press, London.

Jenkins, C. L. (1982) 'The effects of scale in tourism projects in developing countries', *Annals of Tourism Research*, 9(2): 229–249.

Jenkins, C. L. (1987) 'Manpower planning in tourism', Lecture presented to UNDP/WTO Regional Seminar/Workshop on Tourism Training, in Colombo, Sri Lanka, September 1987.

Jenkins, C. L. (1991) 'Tourism development strategies', in *Developing Tourism Destinations: Policies and Perspectives*, Leonard J. Lickorish, Alan Jefferson, Jonathan Bodlender and Carson L. Jenkins (Eds), Longman, Harlow, pp. 61–77.

Jenkins, C. L. and Henry, B. N. (1982) 'Government involvement in tourism in developing countries', *Annals of Tourism Research*, 9(3): 499–521.

de Kadt, Emanuel (1979) *Tourism—Passport to Development? Perspectives on the Social and Cultural Effects of Tourism in Developing Countries*, Oxford University Press, Oxford.

de Kadt, Emanuel (1992) 'Making the alternative sustainable: lessons from development for tourism', in *Tourism Alternatives: Potentials and Problems in the Development of Tourism*. Valene L. Smith and William R. Eadington (Eds), University of Pennsylvania Press, Philadelphia, pp. 47–75.

Kenya, Republic of (1965) *African Socialism and its Application to Planning in Kenya*, Government Printer, Nairobi.

Kenya, Republic of (1971) *Proposed Tourist Resort on the Kenya Coast*, Government Printer, Nairobi.

Kenya, Republic of (1973, 1978, 1983, 1988) *Development Plan*, Government Printer, Nairobi.

Kenya, Republic of (1980) *Economic Prospects and Policies*, Sessional paper 4, Government Printer, Nairobi.

Kenya, Republic of (1981) *National Food Policy*, Sessional paper 4, Government Printer, Nairobi.

Kenya, Republic of (1982) *Development Prospects and Policies*, Sessional paper 4, Government Printer, Nairobi.

Kenya, Republic of (1986) *Economic Management for Renewed Growth*, Sessional paper 6, Government Printer, Nairobi.

Kenya, Republic of (1990) *Statistical Abstract*, Central Bureau of Statistics, Nairobi.

Kenya, Republic of (1991) *Economic Survey*, Central Bureau of Statistics, Nairobi.

Mosley, P. (1983) *The Settler Economies: Studies in the Economic History of Kenya and Southern Rhodesia 1990–1963*, University of Cambridge Press, Cambridge.

Myers, N. (1975) 'The tourist as an agent of development and wildlife conservation: the case of Kenya', *International Journal of Social Economics*, 2(1): 29–40.

Richter, Linda K. (1989) *The Politics of Tourism in Asia*, University of Hawaii Press, Honolulu.

Rodney, Walter (1981) 'Problems of third world development', *Ufahamu* 11(1): 115–142.

Rodney, Walter (1989) *How Europe Underdeveloped Africa*, Heinemann, Nairobi.

Rose, R. (1984) 'Comparative policy analysis: the programme approach', Studies in Public Policy No. 138, University of Strathclyde, Glasgow.

Sinclair, M. Thea (1992) 'Tour operators and policies in Kenya', *Annals of Tourism Research*, 19: 555–558.

Teye, Victor B. (1988) 'Coup d'état and African tourism: a study of Ghana', *Annals of Tourism Research*, 15(3): 329–356.

UNCTAD (United Nations Conference on Trade and Development) (1990) *Problems of Island Developing Countries and Proposals for Concrete Actions: Issues for Consideration*, UNCTAD, Geneva.

UNDP (United Nations Development Programme) (1993) *Human Development Report*, UNDP, New York.

UNDP/ICAO (United Nations Development Programme/ International Civil Aviation Organisation) (1977) 'Studies to determine the contribution that civil aviation can make to the development of national economies of African states', project RAF/74/021 final report, ICAO, Montreal.

World Bank (1975) *The Gambia Appraisal of an Infrastructure and Tourism Project*, The World Bank, Washington, DC.

World Bank (1986) *The Gambia: Tourism Impact Study*, The World Bank, Washington, DC.

World Bank (1989) *Sub-Saharan Africa; From Crisis to Sustainable Growth: A Long-Term Perspective Study*, The World Bank, Washington, DC.

World Bank (1990) *World Bank Annual Report*, The World Bank, Washington, DC.

World Bank (1991) *The World Bank Atlas*, The World Bank, Washington, DC.

World Bank and UNDP (1989) *Africa's Adjustment and Growth in the 1980s*, The World Bank, Washington, DC.

WTO (World Tourism Organisation) (1986) *Economic Review of World Tourism*, WTO, Madrid.

WTO (World Tourism Organisation) (1993) *Compendium of Tourism Statistics*, 13th edn, WTO, Madrid.

7 Tourism and sustainable regional development

P. KOMILIS

Introduction

Against a rich background of research work which has been undertaken in the various categories of developmental studies, research work to explore the development dimensions of tourism is descriptive and not very extensive. Of course, there is a considerable volume of research pertaining to specific tourism impact studies. However, the 'coverage' of tourism in regional science and regional economic development theories, or, deep and perceptive analytical research (of a theoretical, or empirical nature and at a micro- or macro-level) which relates the phenomenon of tourism growth to the development process, seems increasingly necessary in order to advance further. Existing 'limitations' of knowledge about the contribution and role of tourism in the development process implies that policy recommendations should be, as a general rule country-specific, or region-specific, relating types of tourism to the stage and characteristics of a country's or a region's development.

A systems approach views sustainability as an 'exercise in the conditional optimization and fine-tuning of all elements of the developmental system (including tourism) so that the system, as a whole, keeps its bearings without one of its elements surging forward to the detriment of the others' (Farrel and Runyan, 1991). However, research on sustainable development is patchy and has advanced little beyond the stage of formulating and discussing various principles and assumptions. In spite of the challenge to put the principles into operation and practice, what is perhaps a priority in this area is the development of more systematic, methodological, approaches to study specific situations from which to derive concrete concepts and theories.

The aim of this paper is to explore and interlink the dynamics of tourism's growth with those of sustainable regional development. In the first part, the synoptic and critical review of literature focuses on issues of tourism's spatial dimensions and regional development effects, as well as on concepts and main parameters which define conditions of tourism and sustainable development. The second part provides an overview of tourism's regional structure in Greece while the third part discusses a set of criteria related to modes and types of tourism which could support or be conducive to sustainable regional development. Finally, the fourth part deals with strategic issues of planning for tourism and sustainable development.

Conceptual, theoretical and methodological contexts

As has been noted elsewhere (Stegger, 1980) the place of tourism within the 'traditional' theories of regional economic development is very limited. Generally, drawing on the relevant literature (Miossec, 1976; Britton, 1980; UN 1982; Mansfeld, 1990), the theoretical and empirical research background for interpreting the spatial dimensions of tourism can be distinguished into three categories:

(a) locational theories, spatial interaction and demand models, seeking to explain tourism's spatial distribution or incidence and assess demand or flows at the international, national or regional scales;
(b) behavioural and descriptive–ideographic models, attempting to explore tourist spatial behaviour and the diachronic–physical evolution of tourist places;
(c) holistic (integration of historic, socio-economic and political elements), or political economy frameworks, aiming at discerning 'dependence–relation' issues in the development of tourism worldwide.

The regional developmental effect of tourism, the whole spectrum of socio-economic benefits or disbenefits of tourism's growth for host communities, regions and countries, is a significant and somehow complicated field of inquiry. The issues involved are many and diverse and the evidence from research and studies, in certain cases, inconclusive. For example, the effectiveness of tourism as a 'tool for regional development' in developing countries, but also in backward or peripheral regions, is an issue raising doubts and contradictory arguments (see, for example, Clarke (1981)). In this section a synoptic and selective review of literature is presented focusing on the themes of regional economic impacts and intersectoral linkages of tourism.

Specifically, from the review of certain tourist impact studies (see, for example, Archer (1974), TRRU (1975), Wheeler and Richards (1974), Loukissas (1982) and Tsartas (1992)), apart from the general positive effects of tourists' expenditure on the local and regional economy, one should also note the following:

—The uneven distribution of tourism's economic impact over a region; i.e. the high spatial concentration of the tourists' economic impact on the locality where they stay and spend money.
—The existing variations in the size of the impact that relate to the types of tourists and modes of travel used, as well as, to the type of accommodation.
—The incidence of a large part (often more than 50%) of the direct income and employment generation outside the accommodation sector or the tourist industry.
—The relative prominence of tourism on the creation of female employment opportunities.
—The difficulty in making cross-industry comparisons, as noted elsewhere (TRRU, 1975): 'the absence of a standard procedure for preparing multipliers poses considerable difficulties in any attempt to compare the multiplier effects of different industries'.
—The size and type of a tourist destination region (i.e. its socio-economic structure), as well as the types of tourists/visitors, are the major factors shaping the impact of tourism in the case of the Greek islands.

The debate on tourism's regional impact, concerning research and studies which apply the regional multiplier concept, centres on issues of data availability and quality, as well as on the relevance and applicability of region-specific findings to other regions or geographical contexts. Generally, it seems to have been ascertained that the extent of income and employment generation is positively affected by certain socio-economic characteristics of the local community (size, production structure or diversification, etc.).

The structural effects of tourism's growth is a less-studied issue, although of great importance for assessing tourism's role in regional development. Of the various methods and techniques employed to estimate regional economic benefits, or income and employment multipliers, it seems that input–output models provide the best results as to the interlinkages among the different sectors of the regional economy. Such models, analysed comprehensively by Fletcher (1989), have been employed in different case studies. For example, Stegger (1980) using such techniques to assess tourism's impact on Spain's regions, has evidenced tourism's limited ability to influence and enlarge, in a substantial degree, a region's productive structure. He argues that, apart from certain favourable impacts on the service sector, the existence of weak intersectoral links (backward linkages) show tourism's inability to play a leading, or a 'mobilizing' role for a region's development. In the case of Latin American countries it was found (Gormsen, 1988) that tourism's economic linkages with other sectors of the local/regional economy remain small.

With regard to one sector, viz. agriculture, and in places where tourism was expected to stimulate the agricultural sector by creating new markets or by expanding the already existing ones, the results, in general, seem to be negative; there was a further decline of the agricultural sector. Only in a few cases did tourism successfully assist agricultural employment, and this mainly in places where small tourist businesses were created with a large participation of local interest (Austria). Perhaps, strictly from the agricultural point of view, tourism and highly efficient agricultural development are mutually exclusive, since, as it is held (White, 1975), the additional income provided by tourism affects, with diminishing returns, the further development process of agriculture and rather assists in preserving traditional small agricultural units, etc.

Alternative or sustainable development (AD, SD), as well as alternative or sustainable tourism (AT, ST) are concepts and terms that have been used in many ways. In spite of diverse interpretations, there are certain themes or issues frequently appearing in the relevant literature (see, for example, Turner (1988) and Moffat (1993)) on sustainable development: ecologically sound or ecology-oriented development objectives; regionally conforming or territorially adjusted scale and forms of equity in terms of access to economic social and environmental goods and opportunities, or, distributive equality of development benefits; scientifically sound resource use and renewability-supporting uses or activities. However, the placing or the environment dimension (a dominant issue in the sustainable development arguments or paradigms) within the conceptual–theoretical frames of development studies does not yet assume a central position; most theorists in the discipline of Development Studies continue to treat environmental issues or management as marginal issues (Brookfield, 1988). Also, drawing on case studies of The Netherlands, England and Catalonia (Spain), the limited role played by regional spatial planning in environmental policy has been documented in a recent review (Marshall, 1993), along with suggestions and supportive arguments for a new spatial planning approach to guide environmental change.

With reference to tourism *per se*, sustainable is considered (Spiegler, 1990) the kind of tourism that fits to the given natural, cultural and social structures of a region or landscape. The concept of sustainability in tourism is frequently related to eco-tourism or eco-touristic activities—in the sense of being considered as a determining factor or criterion of an eco-touristic development. Among the numerous and diverse criteria defining eco-tourism and eco-touristic activities those gaining wider recognition (see, for example, Butler (1980) and (1991), Cater (1991), and Ruschmann (1992)) pertain to (a) sustainability of resource development in economic, socio-cultural and environmental terms, (b) the educational character of the recreational-tourism experience, and (c) the local participation in the tourism development process.

Empirical observations: international and national contexts

One could view modern international tourist flows as 'massive geographic displacements of seasonal or temporal nature' (Lundgren, 1975) affecting different spatial levels and appearing within a frame of interacting pull and push forces that pertain to: (a) a metropolitan-based travel system which initiates, controls and channels demand to chosen destinations and (b) the particular regional structure of the tourist product (TP), its competitiveness, attractiveness and ability to cope with and adjust to changing requirements of tourism-consumers.

Within the European context, tourism's growth and spatial structure reflects a process of leisure division (tourism demand and consumption differentiation) attributed to (i) marked inter-country differences, regarding socio-economic, supply-attraction and accessibility factors, and (ii) the international organization of the tourist industry: the influential role of tour operators and airlines in controlling market size, price of the TP, and transport links. The nature of the tourism trade (non-monopolistic), particularly within the south European–Mediterranean region, means that the existence of many alternative 'sunlust or beach-resort' destinations increases competition among Mediterranean regions and reinforces the probability of a substitution effect, under the influence of certain factors pertaining to price changes (exchange rates, domestic price levels, etc.) and to the tour operators' practices.

Taking Greece as a case study, we have argued elsewhere (Komilis, 1987) that tourism's regional structure is influenced by both endogenous and exogenous factors: (i) the country's socio-economic development process, territorial structure and regional accessibility, as well as the organizational mode of the tourist industry and

relevant government policies (e.g. investments), and (ii) the way the Greek regions are connected with the international travel system, and are affected by tour operations—the latter building on existing locational advantages, and reinforcing development in 'established' places.

Within the above context it is in order here to outline certain points pertaining to the main characteristics of tourism's regional structure.

At an earlier stage (the 1960s), tourism's spatial growth in Greece could be described in terms of a 'centre–periphery' dichotomy growth pattern—a dominant centre (Greater Athens region), and certain peripheral areas of two types: (a) small holiday-resort areas (usually small islands), depending upon the centre for their tourist transport links and logistics, and areas of a 'short-visiting-touring' character, and (b) a few areas or regions (Rhodes, Corfu, nothern coastal Crete) emerging as 'independent' in the sense that these peripheric destinations outside Athens were supported by strongly seasonal international tourism demand and were linked, on a seasonal basis, with the international air-based travel system. This distinction, however, appears to have changed, in the sense that certain peripheral areas are evidencing higher growth rates, while the centre is stagnating or exhibits slower growth rates. Such an apparent decentralization of activity, interregionally, is highly polarized spatially, that is, at the intraregional level it exhibits a high concentration of tourist activities in a few places and is absent in many other areas.

In spite of the significant changes observed in the regional patterns of tourism, it is difficult, owing to the unavailability of data (regional statistics on tourist expenditures and tourism's inclusion in the regional accounts), at the regional level to draw any conclusions as to whether or to what extent the growth of foreign tourism has corrected or reinforced interregional imbalances or development inequalities. Apart from 'crude' estimates, or hypotheses of tourism's favourable economic impact on particular areas (mostly island prefectures), on the basis of observed changes in population and internal migration (stabilization or relative increase) and employment (considerable increase), an accurate assessment of tourism's regional impact, or interregional effects is difficult.

The very few estimates of tourism's interlinkage with other production sectors at the national level seems to differ considerably. Certain estimates (Zacharatos, 1984) of the direct demand inputs from other sectors show such inputs to be higher than 30% of the gross value of the domestically produced tourism consumption—in contrast to earlier studies (KEPE, 1976) where the percentage was estimated to be in the region of 13%. Although regional estimates do not exist, one could generally infer that tourism's impact on the local-regional production system of the Greek regions, or the contribution of these regions' sectoral inputs to the gross value of the regionally produced tourism consumption, varies considerably from region to region. Of course, an assessment of such differences presupposes a detailed analysis of each region's particular consumption patterns and productive structure. However, following the discussion earlier on tourism's interlinkages we may advance the following argument in the form of an untested hypothesis for further discussion.

> The extent of tourism's demand for commodities and services being met by local-regional inputs, or, the spread range of economic effects are greater in regions with (a) a 'strong' and diversified economy (e.g. Crete versus other Aegean island regions) and (b) a particular articulation of the tourist clientele and the TP, i.e., a mix of different tourist market segments (instead of depending on a few nationalities) corresponding to a diverse development of the region's main components of its TP: accommodation, attractions, transport-networks.

Generally, the Greek TP, sold in the form of independent components, has not assumed to any significant degree its own regional identity—an identity that would result from a mobilization and utilization of all kinds of regional inputs and resources (economic, socio-cultural and physical), or that would result from consideration of the country's spatially diverse, natural, cultural and man-made tourist landscape, as fixed assets of the national and regional economy. Specifically, the Greek regions supply only certain components which constitute separate consumption inputs making up a final holiday package; the latter, which determines the particular mode of the regional product's consumption, is designed and marketed at extra-regional (national, or international) level.

The regional TP exhibits a certain diversity, mainly due to the natural and cultural particularity of regional landscapes, but in general it is undifferentiated and spatially uneven. Its lack of differentiation pertains to the almost exclusive development of conventional beach holidays and related accommodation forms, as opposed to a multifaceted development corresponding to and valorizing regional resources suited for such activities as nautical tourism, agrotourism, cultural–educational travel, health and congress tourism.

A second point worth noting is that the activities and policies of tourism development agents (tour operators, local tourist agents, the state), as well as the nature of relations developing among these agents, are such that they are conducive to the above-outlined forms of the TP articulation, through the external influence of the economic terms of its consumption, through the promotion of particular, stereotyped, consumption patterns (beach holidays–coastal resorts), or through the particular regional policies and practices (public investments, incentives) and the unplanned growth of tourist superstructure.

Tourism production and consumption patterns and sustainable development

Drawing on the main issues and points discussed earlier, the discussion in this section focuses on modes and types of tourism production and consumption processes which are believed to support or be conducive to sustainable regional development. However, it should be clarified here that the discussion does not offer 'operational' suggestions as to the concrete types or modes of tourism development that should be advanced. Instead, a set of sustainability 'specifications' is outlined to serve as a frame for integrating specific proposals. In other words, within the context of tourism's growth and the sustainability of regional development, we are assuming certain common 'denominators' or development criteria which underlie the selection of both the market- and product-related modes or types of tourism growth and the goals or policies of a regional development strategy.

The interregional differentiation and diversity of the regional tourist production is the *first criterion* in the selection and promotion of tourist products and sustainability—related regional development goals. Here, we are referring to a continuous process of enriching and innovating the tourist products in such a way as to enhance each region's 'tourist identity' and increase the range of its attractions and its competitiveness within the international tourism market. This is seen as a process which contributes to or presupposes valorization of the diverse regional/indigenous resources.

For example, it is worth noting within the above context the rich potential of cultural resources—related to particular types of tourism such as urban tourism and cultural travel—with which many regions of Greece are endowed, but have not valorized, for generating economic benefits to particular cities and localities.

The *second criterion* pertains to maximizing the economic benefits of tourism over an entire region, by providing the best interlinkages of tourism to the other sectors of the regional economy. In such a process the various categories and the scale of tourist production and consumption patterns are adjusted to, and integrated within, the regional production system.

Of the many growth sectors or areas which may support and promote sustainable regional development, or which may be included in the selected strategies or policies, tourism is of course not the only one of major importance. Depending on a region's specific geographic and socio-economic characteristics, as well as on its resource endowment, the entire resource potential should be identified and explored before making choices and designing appropriate sectoral interlinkages or integrated-activity complexes for sustainable development. For example, in the case of several peripheral Greek regions, certain areas of equal significance, such as land resources and agriculture, aquatic resources and coastal areas, renewable energy resources may be viewed and planned in conjunction with tourism.

Also, within the context of this criterion, one should critically explore the particular role of both the formal and informal tourism sectors regarding the extent of their integration within the regional economic structure, or their capability to produce higher or lower multiplier effects on the local economy. The significance or, better, 'performance' of the informal sector, which has been documented by Oppermann (1993) for certain third world countries, should be investigated to discover whether it applies to countries like Spain and Greece with a sizeable informal tourist sector.

A *third criterion* relates to equity and local involvement conditions that should prevail when tourism's growth is related to sustainable regional development. In the first case, one is referring to those conditions which should exist among the various social groups of the regional population—regarding available opportunities and the possibilities of access to economic, socio-cultural and environmental assets resulting from tourism development, or with regard to the spread range of socio-economic and environmental benefits accruing to the local community.

Regarding the creation of local involvement conditions, the aim should be to minimize social conflicts by avoiding any negative consequences of tourism's growth, in cases where ownership and management of the tourist product has been passed on, to a large extent, to non-locals from the initial phase of tourism's growth. Usually, this results in the creation of a parallel tourist economy, which develops independently of the local economy. In these cases the characteristic features are:

(a) The majority of the products or services necessary to satisfy tourist needs, are imported from other regions or even foreign countries.
(b) Investments in tourism are made predominantly by non-locals and enterprises increasingly use imported, better-trained labour, while locals are employed in low-quality, unspecialized jobs.
(c) The growth of tourist enterprises, shops, etc., as well as labour distribution, tend to evolve into two separate compartments: one servicing the tourists, the other servicing local residents.

The *fourth criterion* focuses on environmental considerations taken into account in policy-making and tourist product development. It involves the setting of constraints or limits, as well as adjustments or trade-offs, in the various relevant development or decision-making processes.

Such a criterion could be further 'elaborated' by distinguishing the different scales of intensity attached to the environmental problems. The various interpretations or value judgements given by policy analysts of the intensity scale of environmental problems seems quite important since it may influence the type of sustainability adopted or the priorities attached to social, economic or environmental goals (Marshall, 1993:71).

In connection with this criterion, there are two major and interrelated issues, of a methodological and operational nature, discussed extensively in tourism research and development studies: the issue of capacity (mainly of tourist resources or landscapes) and the issue of the various tourism impacts.

Tourism, or outdoor recreational capacity, seems to be a complex concept that borrows principles from both the social and the biological/physical sciences. Most definitions incorporate two basic elements of a desired condition: (a) maintaining the integrity of the resource base, or use resources at a sustainable yield level, and (b) providing or securing conditions for a recreation experience of high quality to the user or visitor. The subjectivity or value-judgements involved in defining these two elements, as well as the various capacity categories or procedures for its assessment, are discussed by Pigram (1980) and Sowman (1987).

In examining tourist capacity issues, it is important to view them within the context of the whole range of parameters which form the TP of a region—the TP being defined in this case as an economic, socio-cultural and physical entity with spatially discernible differentiations. With reference to capacity studies, and from the planning practice point of view, it is worth noting here certain 'technical requirements' described elsewhere, namely that

in the overall landscape analysis the physical presence of tourist-related matter (visitor volume and attributes) is weighted against local, or regional components crucial to place character. These local components are important in sociological–demographic terms, in the context of the cultural–historical environment, as well as, in relation to how the various pressures are felt in the more prominent parts of the ecological system. (Lundgren, 1979)

In spite of their great number and considerable progress in certain areas (e.g. methods and techniques of EIA) most impact studies in tourism are quite specific, i.e., they focus on analysing one dimension of tourism's impact without exploring existing interrelationships among them (e.g. socio-economic and ecologic parameters of tourism). In this context, the relevant issues could be approached on the basis of certain methods outlined elsewhere (Komilis, 1988) as well as by selectively drawing on specific methods or techniques, e.g. those exploring economic–ecologic relationships employed in particular studies (Isard et al., 1972). The use of input–output frameworks, or matrix techniques for analysing 'activity-resource' complexes are, generally, considered useful in estimating environmental changes (as a result of various processes) and assigning economic values to such changes.

Finally, a *fifth criterion* refers to continuity and adjustability of a region's tourist development within its wider environment. It refers to particular properties such as flexibility and responsiveness, concerning types or modes of a tourism development capable to meet and respond to the requirements or conditions of the international tourist market.

A tourist destination region develops its products according to the preferred, in the market, destination attributes and in such a way as to secure and maintain a continuous attractiveness within the destination choice patterns of tourists. However, regarding this criterion, it should be clarified, that sustainable development does not imply that a given process of economic growth, or in our case certain tourist activities, products or projects, should be able to continue indefinitely. Tastes and lifestyles change; so do vacation motives and holiday patterns, in a period perhaps smaller than a generation. Therefore, the essence and appeal of sustainability and of this criterion pertains to keeping certain choices open for the future (or, even trying in certain cases to match the exploitation of finite resources with developing substitutes or alternatives) while at the same time developing a region's socio-economic and environmental assets in response to changing demand conditions within a highly competitive environment. Two areas which could provide, as 'planning tools', useful insight in elaborating certain of the above criteria are the 'strategic marketing planning' (involving decision-making as to product positioning and market segmentation) and the 'life cycle' approach (drawing on the initial product life cycle method

used in the business sector). However, in the literature (Butler, 1980; Haywood, 1986; Calantone and Mazanec, 1991) we do not find any 'case studies' which employ such approaches to study, e.g., the 'effect of introducing strategic and environmental changes on the tourism life cycle of a region'.

Strategic issues of planning for tourism and sustainable regional development

As has been noted elsewhere (Breheny, 1991) strategic planning is in the foreground today, not only among academics and planning professionals but also on the political agenda, even in countries, such as the UK, with a conservative government. The reasons seem to be diverse: intensity of environmental problems and undesirable consequences of an unplanned development, but also the pressure of 'big business' which demands from the public sector support and creation of more stable and secure conditions within the operating environment.

The formulation of strategic choices and related policy guidelines and instruments is a complex process, which presupposes various interactions among diverse views and decisions, of different development agents and decisions makers, among which the politicians play a dominant role.

From the discussion so far, certain points emerge as instrumental parameters of a strategy framework for sustainable regional development. In this section we put forward and delineate a strategic spatial planning approach linking tourism's growth with sustainable regional development—an approach which could be interlinked with or incorporate sectoral (tourism) policies as well as other policy means of financial instruments (e.g. those taken at the EU level).

In connection to the above, a significant issue which appears frequently in relevant discussions pertains to selecting appropriate spatial levels and approaches of strategy of policy formulation and intervention. In our case, which is the best approach to bringing sustainable development objectives, or for incorporating the sustainability criteria, discussed in the previous section, into public policies?

Generally, an appropriate approach would depend on the particular character of each case and on the variable geographic, political economic and administrative-organizational contexts of each country.

Although the various approaches (e.g., sectoral, national/EU level, spatial or regional) are not mutually exclusive (often even co-exist to varying degrees) and, although certain issues and associated policies should be considered at several levels, the regional level appears to be more suitable in our case. This level seems more appropriate for addressing the complex issues involved in mixing and interrelating various dimensions (economic, environmental, social) of the policies pursued, for making certain intersectoral connections, or for considering and assessing ecosystemic and socio-economic impacts.

Among the strategic goals of tourism and sustainable regional development, the processes of innovation and restructuring of the entire tourism system (market, industry, product) assume dominant positions. The process of innovation involves new departures in markets, products and operating systems (management, marketing) of the tourist industry; while restructuring (market and product), pertains to structural changes in the composition, articulation and spatial distribution of tourist consumption patterns.

Specifically, the essence and scope of such processes lies in (i) the diversification and qualitative upgrading of tourist supply and demand (articulation or mix of different market segments, of international tourists), (ii) the interweaving of tourism and other tourism-related sectoral activities into regionally identifiable and differentiated tourist products, and (iii) increasing the competitive advantage of the Greek tourist industry.

A major policy implication emerging from the discussion of tourism's spatial structure is that Greek tourist destination regions should always consider, when developing international tourism, that they are entering a highly competitive international market which leaves them susceptible to outside economic forces. A successful national or regional tourist development strategy would require, in our opinion, a careful consideration of exogenous forces, in addition and in relation to more direct and endogenous concerns: scale of development, range of regional or community benefits, resources availability and investments allocation, etc. What seems to emerge as a major planning task and challenge relates to the regional structure of the tourist product: the way of developing and articulating its main components—accessibility, accommodation facilities, environmental attractions—according to the capacity and potentiality of regional resources and the developing new tourist markets in Europe. We believe that through a restructuring of the Greek tourist product, and through appropriate marketing policies, the main exogenous determinants of tourist flows could be influenced.

However, such a restructuring should take place along two major policy directions in such a way as to:

(a) liaise with the major process of economic restructuring and the heightened levels of territorial competition,

which develop among European countries and regions today and exhibit certain contrasting spatial characteristics: increasing globalization and centralization of the production system, but also flexibility regarding specialization or localization in particular industries and spatial contexts (Amin and Malmberg, 1992).

(b) contribute to the maximization of regional development benefits in a way that utilizes and mobilizes the regional resource base, realizes regional intersectoral linkages and is compatible with local-regional economic interests, societal values and environmental assets.

The frame of policy objectives

Current discussions on the need to reorientate planning action towards 'postmodern' practices are predominantly preoccupied, regarding their spatial dimension, with regional economic restructuring, taking place within the production system—a restructuring associated with Post-Fordism and characterized by flexibility of production, high capital mobility and the growth of tertiary activities (Cooke, 1986). Also, it is argued (Marshall, 1993), the increasing awareness and intensity of environmental problems and the need to guide environmental change, demands a more active role and reorganization of regional spatial planning in Western Europe. Within the Greek context, the regional planning's organizational and coordinating functions are in need of better instruments, mechanisms and management systems capable of (a) removing constraints or causes that give rise to policy divergencies and conflict situations among various actors, and (b) dealing with specific policy issues, e.g., EU's regional policies, allocating and monitoring funds, land use, or land and environment management policies.

It is far from this paper's scope to advance proposals for the organization restructuring of the regional planning system. Instead, we delineate below certain policy guidelines to serve as an orientation frame for the elaboration of the most appropriate mix of three types of policy instruments: financial instruments, i.e., the entire range of investments and incentives policies, sectoral or tourism-specific instruments, for the optimum management and regulation of tourist infrastructure, and spatial or physical planning instruments, predominantly land-use and environment regulatory measures.

Thus, on the basis of the strategic goals and the sustainability criteria outlined earlier, a reorientation of policy instruments, as to their scope and content, should involve certain adjustments or new departures along the following lines:

—place identity versus uniformity: work against homogenization forces to preserve and enhance diversity and unique regional elements (physical and socio-cultural), as opposed to superimposing a uniform standardized network and equipment of infrastructure.

—complexity or multiplicity of urban and rural functions, as well as intersectoral and interfunctional (between land uses) complementarities and coexistence, as opposed to distinctive sectoral or functional separation and monocultural development orientation.

—balance between (i) regional self-sufficiency (for indigenous resource valorization and socio-economic risks minimization (ii) dependency on external inputs (for the functioning of a region) and (iii) integration within the EU's competitive environment.

Concluding remarks

The literature and relevant studies do not provide, as yet, sufficient material and means—on the basis of theory and practice—for building, on a sound foundation, an efficient structure of policy instruments of wider applicability, to support a tourism-related sustainable regional development.

However, based on existing information and observations from country-specific paradigms, we are suggesting a strategic spatial planning approach for an appropriate linking of tourism with sustainable regional development. Such an approach envisages departures from existing, within the regional setting, modes or types of tourism's growth—introducing innovation and restructuring processes in the entire tourism system (markets–products–industries) on the basis of a set of sustainability principles.

References

Amin, A. and Malmberg, A. (1992) 'Competing structural and institutional influences on the geography of production in Europe', *Environment and Planning*, 25: 3.

Archer, B., Shea S. and Devane, R. (1974) 'Tourism in Gwynedd: an economic study', Wales Tourist Board, Bangor.

Breheny, M. J. (1991) 'The renaissance of strategic planning?' *Environment and Planning B: Planning and Design*, 18: 233–249.

Britton, S. G. (1980) 'A conceptual model of tourism in a peripheral economy', in Pearce, D. G. (Ed.), *Tourism in the South Pacific: the contribution of research to development and planning*, NZ MAB Report No. 6, NZ National Commission for Unesco/Dept. of Geography, University of Canterbury, Christchurch.

Brookfield, H. (1988) 'Sustainable development and the environment', *Journal of Development Studies*, 25: 1.

Butler, R. W. (1980) 'The concept of a tourism area cycle of evolution: implication for management of resources', *Canadian Geographer*, 24: 5–12.

Butler, R. W. (1991) 'Tourism environment and sustainable development', *Environmental Conservation*, 18: 3.

Calantone, R. and Mazanec, J. (1991) 'Marketing management and tourism', *Annals of Tourism Research*, 18(1): 101–119.

Cater, E. (1991) 'Sustainable tourism in the third world: problems and prospects', Discussion Paper No. 3, Dept. of Geography, University of Reading.

Clarke, A. (1981) 'Coastal development in France: Tourism as a tool for recreational development', *Annals of Tourism Research*, 8(3): 447–461.

Cooke, P. (1986) 'The changing urban and regional system in the United Kingdom', *Regional Studies*, 20(3): 243–251.

Farrel, B. and Runyan, D. (1991) 'Ecology and tourism', *Annals of Tourism Research*, 18(1): 26–40.

Fletcher, J. (1989) 'Input–output analysis and tourism impact studies', *Annals of Tourism Research*, 16(4): 514–529.

Gormsen, E. (1988) 'Tourism in Latin America—spatial distribution and impact on regional change', *Applied Geography and Development*, 32: 65–80.

Haywood, K. M. (1986) 'Can the tourist area life cycle be made operational?', *Tourism Management*, 7: 154–167.

Isard, W., et al. (1972) *Ecologic–Economic Analysis for Regional Development*, The Free Press, New York.

KEPE (Centre of Planning and Economic Research) (1976) Economic and Social Development Plan 1976–1980, Special Report on Tourism (in Greek), KEPE, Athens.

Komilis, P. (1987) 'The spatial structure and growth of tourism in relation to the physical planning process: The case of Greece', PhD. Dissertation, University of Strathclyde.

Komilis, P. (1988) 'The system of tourism's territorial profiles: a methodological approach, for the spatial analysis and organization of tourism', Papers, 2nd Symposium on Quantitative Methods, University of the Aegean, Chios, Greece.

Loukissas, P. J. (1982) 'Tourism's regional development impacts. A comparative analysis of the Greek islands', *Annals of Tourism Research*, 9: 523–543.

Lundgren, I. (1975) 'Tourist penetration/tourist product/ entrepreneurial response', in *Tourism as a Factor in National and Regional Development*, Occ. Paper 4, Dept. of Geography, Trent University, Peterborough, Canada, pp. 43–52.

Lundgren, I. (1979) 'The tourist product—how to measure its successful consumption', *The Tourist Review*, AIEST publ. I.

Mansfeld, Y. (1990) 'Spatial patterns of international tourist flows: towards a theoretical framework', *Progress in Human Geography*, 14: 372–390.

Marshall, T. (1993) 'Regional environmental planning: progress and possibilities in western Europe', *European Planning Studies*, 1(1): 69–90.

Miossec, J. M. (1977) 'Elements pour une théorie de l'espace touristique', *Les Cahiers du Tourisme*, C-36, CHET, Aix-en-Provence.

Moffat, I. (1993) 'Sustainable development: conceptual issues, an operational model and its implications for Australia', *Landscape and Urban Planning*, 23: 107–118.

Oppermann, M. (1993) 'Tourism space in developing countries', *Annals of Tourism Research*, 20(3): 522–556.

Pigram, J. J. (1980) 'Environmental implications of tourism development', *Annals of Tourism Research*, 7: 554–583.

Ruschmann, D. (1992) 'Ecological tourism in Brazil', *Tourism Management*, 13: 125–128.

Sadler, P., Archer, B. and Owen, S. (1971) 'The Anglesey Study: a preliminary report on the multiplier', Research Paper, Institute of Economic Research, University College of North Wales, Bangor.

Sowman, M. R. (1987) 'A procedure for assessing recreational carrying capacity of coastal resort areas', *Landscape and Urban Planning*, 14: 331–344.

Spiegler, A. (1990) 'Sustainable tourism', in *Environment, Tourism and Development: an Agenda for Action?* Workshop Papers, Centre for Environmental Management and Planning, University of Aberdeen.

Stegger, M. (1980) *Fremdenverkehr und Regionalentwicklung, dargestellt am Beispiel Spanien*, Verlag Weltarchiv, Hamburg.

TRRU (Tourism and Recreation Research Unit) (1975) 'The economic impact of tourism—a case study in Greater Tayside', University of Edinburgh/Scottish Tourist Board.

Tsartas, P. (1992) 'Socioeconomic impacts of tourism on two Greek islands', *Annals of Tourism Research*, 19(3): 516–533.

Turner, T. (Ed.) (1988) *Sustainable Environmental Management*, West View Press, Boulder, CO.

UN (United Nations–Centre on Transnational Corporations) (1982) *Transnational Corporations in International Tourism*, UN, New York.

Wheeler, B. and Richards, G. (1974) 'Tourism in Cardiganshire: an economic study', Wales Tourist Board.

White, P. E. (1975) 'Aspects and effects of tourism on the economic and social geography of small host communities', D.Phil. Dissertation Oxford University.

Zacharatos, G. (1984) *Tourismus und Wirtschaftsstruktur Dargestellt am Beispiel Griechenlands*, Peter Lang, Frankfurt-am-Main.

8 Tourism in Greece and Turkey: an economic view for planners

H. SEZER AND A. HARRISON

Contribution of tourism to a country's economy: a global view

Tourism: the product

Since Professors Hunzinger and Krapf attempted a first definition of 'tourism' in 1935 numerous scholars and institutions have endeavoured to refine and redefine tourism and the tourist in an endeavour to provide an internationally acceptable standard by which research, writing and data collection can be undertaken—and thereby bear comparison between and among countries and institutions. What has emerged, however, despite the WTO recommendation of March 1993, is a conviction that 'tourism' is as difficult to define as the 'tourist'— the human person who undertakes and consumes the tourism experience.

Because of the intangibility of the 'tourism product' and the inseparability of that 'product' from the consumer or co-provider—without whom there would be no tourism—then tourism is as varied and as variable as the tourist—who is the key player in the whole of tourism. The tourist brings to the consumption—or co-provision of tourism—the whole range of experiences, expectations, beliefs and prejudices of his life and social and cultural influences. In the terminology of services marketing, this makes each tourist heterogeneous and thus the tourist experience undertaken or consumed as heterogeneous as that tourist (or group of like-minded tourists).

The concept of the tourism 'product' is fundamental to the organisation and planning of the tourist industry. It has critical implications for the business plans— specifically in respect of marketing plans—of governments, commercial organisations and national, regional and local tourist organisations. Without an understanding of what constitutes the tourism product, and how that 'product' varies with the needs and wants of the consumer, the tourist, plans would have no focus and thus no direction or meaning. Product decisions in any industry are the focal point of any business activity, around which all other decisions must be made.

In tourism the tourist product can be conceptualised on two levels (Smith, 1989):

1. The total tourist product, a combination of all the elements of service which a tourist consumes from the time of leaving home to the time of return. This product then is a complex interaction of all the service elements, including the tourist's expectations and attitudes to the consumption process. At this level the product is an idea, a series of expectations or mental constructs in the mind and psyche of the tourist, inextricably interlinked with the provision and consumption of the tourist experience which is unique to that tourist at that time and place.
2. The specific, mainly commercial, products which are components of the total tourist product, such as the offers of accommodation (including food and drink), transport, attractions (natural and man-made), facilities, support network (including information and the destination's infrastructure).

To incorporate both concepts then, one could concur with Middleton (1990) that the total tourist product is a bundle or package of tangible and intangible elements of the tourist experience, based on activities undertaken whilst being a tourist. The package is perceived by the tourist as an experience, a bundle of elements available at a price.

Tourism: economic considerations

Trying to establish the contribution of tourism to a country's development is not an easy task. In addition to the definitional problems regarding tourist and tourism, there are also measurement problems in assessing tourist receipts and expenditures. Despite such difficulties observed data indicate that there has been a tremendous growth in international tourism during the last forty years. It is fairly easy to identify two factors which gave rise to such a trend. One is the considerable improvement in living standards in the West and the other is the recent technological advances in air transport. In 1950 there were 25 million recorded tourist arrivals; by 1991 this number increased sixteenfold to 450 million (Harrison, 1992:3). Tourism is currently the third largest item in world trade with its share of world exports exceeding 7%.

Tourism assumes special significance in the context of less-developed countries (LDCs) since international tourism is a means of promoting economic growth. However, international tourism for LDCs also means people from rich countries visiting relatively poor countries. This might accentuate the differences in lifestyles and wealth between the two groups of countries and possibly leave an impact—positive or negative—on the people of recipient countries. Thus, tourism is not just an economic but also a social, political and moral issue. Therefore, it is not surprising to observe that some of the theoretical approaches, particularly to the measurement of tourism's impact in LDCs, emphasises the latter aspects. In fact it is possible to divide these theories into two broad categories.

The first group would include those which are basically neoclassical in nature. This approach is also known as the modernisation theory (Harrison, 1992:8), or the functional approach (Lea, 1988:16). According to this approach tourism is an economic activity which occurs mainly in the context of a market economy. Therefore it is a question of using a given economic potential for maximum gain (=profit), as in the case of any other economic activity. However, in the context of LDCs, tourism is a vehicle for 'modernisation' which is equated with development. It is a means of acquiring not only capital, entrepreneurial skills and technical knowledge but also 'modern' values which are prerequisites for development. As the economic structure changes from that of a predominantly agricultural one to an industry- and/or service-dominated one, tourism acts as a catalyst in bringing about this change.

The alternative approach to tourism in LDCs looks at tourism from a historical perspective and is inspired by the dependency theories of development. It is radical in nature and emphasises the social, political and environmental as well as the economic aspects of tourism. This radical approach regards tourism as a special part of the international economic relations between the rich capitalist countries and the LDCs and is concerned about the increasing tendency of international tourism to serve the interests of the rich North at the expense of the LDCs, and its role in aggravating the inequalities between the two groups of countries. However, both approaches have, separately, much to contribute to the assessment of the impact of international tourism on the economies of the LDCs. The traditional approach has developed some highly sophisticated techniques which are used in measuring the impact of tourism, such as the multiplier analysis, input–output models and forecasting techniques. The radical approach, on its part, introduces a historical perspective to the analysis, focuses on the macroeconomic aspects of tourism development and emphasises the non-economic factors such as the social and cultural and environmental impact of international tourism. Thus, in a sense the two approaches complement, as well as compete with, each other.

The economic and social impact of tourism

Despite a considerable amount of controversy regarding the magnitude of the economic impact of tourism, it is generally agreed that international tourism affects several aspects of the economy concerned.

An obvious variable to be affected by international tourism is gross domestic product (GDP). According to one estimate, tourism was directly responsible for 4% of GDP in the nine countries of the EC in 1979. With the indirect effects this is thought to be as high as 10% (Williams and Shaw, 1991:30). The total effect—which can be estimated by multiplier analysis—of tourism on the GDP of a country is a combination of direct and indirect effects and depends upon its size and importance as a destination country and its economic structure, i.e. the linkages and leakages which exist in the economy.

Employment is another variable which is affected by tourism, although it is rather difficult to estimate this impact. According to the World Tourism Organisation (Williams and Shaw, 1993) 15.5% of total employment in Europe in the early 1980s was accounted for by tourism and tourism-related activities.

WTO figures also suggest that in 1985 direct and indirect employment in tourism constitute two-thirds of the labour force in Bermuda, 50% in Virgin Islands, 37% in Jamaica and 35% in the Bahamas (Williams and Shaw, 1991:34). However, these figures are viewed with scepticism by some. Particular criticism is made of the fact that direct tourism employment is largely related to semi-skilled and unskilled jobs and also dominated by the female labour force. Moreover, much of tourism employment is seasonal and thus not full-time. Finally, in certain circumstances tourism employment may actually take employees away from the other sectors of the economy.

Another obvious area of influence for international tourism is balance of payments, since international tourism is generally regarded as an important source of foreign exchange for many countries, including some large ones. For example, in Barbados, Jamaica, Morocco, Costa Rica, Thailand, Mexico, India, Kenya and Egypt, the ratio of tourist receipts to total export earnings exceeds the world average of 7% by a large margin (Harrison, 1992:11–12). If one considers that in these countries export earnings also constitute a relatively high proportion of GDP, the significance of international tourism becomes clear. However, the impact is not altogether a desirable one. To begin with the combination of a high tourism/export ratio and a high export/GDP ratio contributes to the problem of dependence and this makes the economy rather vulnerable. Moreover, a high tourist receipts/export earnings ratio could be counterbalanced by high outgoing tourist expenditure. Furthermore, tourist receipts could have high imported 'input' content such as imported food, tour operators' and travel agents' (foreign-owned) fees, remittances by foreign employees, etc. In fact some studies indicate that the net foreign currency earnings could be as low as 50–60% of the gross earnings in some countries of the Caribbean and the Pacific (Lea, 1988:46).

Environment is another issue on which tourism has a strong effect one way or another. For example, tourism might make a positive contribution to the conservation and rehabilitation of historic buildings and sites since usually these are tourist attractions. Tourism might also help the conservation of environment because it encourages the introduction of planning and control procedures without which it is difficult to preserve anything. Another positive contribution of tourism to creating better environment is that it encourages the development of infrastructure and social services such as roads, airports, water and sewage systems, electricity networks, medical services, etc. However, tourism is also likely to have a damaging impact on the environment. Mass tourism can put considerable strain on the existing resources which might result either in the pollution of water and air or in building new infrastructure such as a leisure complex, an airport or a motorway, which might not only spoil the landscape but also destroy a large area of natural habitat for many biological species.

For many countries tourism is a welcome economic diversification which reduces the external dependence of the country on a small number of, usually agricultural, commodities. However, for those countries where tourism is an important source of income and foreign exchange tourism itself becomes a factor just like an important agricultural commodity on which an economy depends. In such circumstances tourism is a potential source of instability. Not only is tourism a seasonal activity but it is also susceptible to changes in fashion or random external factors. For example, the internal political situation in the early 1980s and the Gulf War in the 1990s, badly affected tourism demand in Turkey and thus had adverse effects on the economy. Although these adverse effects were not terribly important for Turkey, because of its size, such a negative impact can be devastating for some of the small countries in the Pacific or the Caribbean.

Another adverse effect of international tourism is its potentially inflationary impact in an economy. Since incoming tourist expenditure is an addition to the injections into the circular flow of income, it can create inflationary pressures of a Keynesian type in the economy. To the extent that this extra demand gives rise to imported input, international tourism can also cause the cost-push type of inflation. It is a well-observed fact that some retail prices tend to rise during the tourist season. It is also well-known that land prices tend to rise in step with tourism demand and that accommodation becomes expensive.

A highly controversial issue regarding international tourism is its impact on the cultural and social life of the host country. It is generally accepted that tourism plays an important role in changing social structures, traditional values and socio-economic attitudes in the host country in favour of Western values and modes of behaviour. The wholesale term for such an impact is 'demonstration effect' which usually means a Western pattern of consumer, and even investment, behaviour. It might include anything from Hilton and Sheraton to Nescafé and Levis (jeans). The traditional view of international tourism would welcome 'the demonstration effect' as a contribution to the development effort of the country since it is an indication that it is changing its old values and ways. The radical view, however, regards it as cultural imperialism and commoditisation of traditional culture. For example, international tourism is associated with the disappearance of traditional art forms and their replacement by 'airport art' culture. Although tourism has encouraged the financial success of traditional art and artisans it is claimed that the commoditisation of indigenous arts and crafts under market pressures (Harrison, 1992:20) leads to a decline in the quality of craftsmanship and to the production of cheap imitations known as 'airport art' (Lea, 1988:71). However, it is also argued that tourism encourages new forms of creativity and artistic endeavour and new designs and materials, which are not necessarily any less artistic.

One of the socio-economic effects of tourism is its association with increased prostitution and crime. Particularly in countries such as Thailand, Taiwan, South Korea and the Philippines, marketing of tourism is explicitly or implicitly based on the sale of sex and therefore prostitution is claimed to be tourism-related by some people. Others argue (Harrison, 1992:32) that prostitution in the above countries may be encouraged by tourists but is not tourism-specific. For example, in Thailand it is attributed partly to the relaxed attitude towards sex in the traditional Thai culture and Buddhism and partly to the Vietnam War. Nevertheless, sex tourism is a reality and the traditional term 'three Ss' (sea, sun

Table 8.1 *The measurement of tourism impact: selected countries 1988 (%)*

	TIR	TPR	TDR	CR
Bahamas	604.50	6.60	1.20	95
Singapore	161.00	1.30	34.40	31
Jamaica	27.00	0.74	1.60	92
Mexico	6.80	0.19	0.08	94
Kenya	3.00	0.13	0.05	41
UK	27.60	0.75	1.80	41
Greece[a]	86.60	1.00	76.40	47
Turkey[b]	9.70	0.01	6.46	45

[a]1990.
[b]1991.
Sources: Harrison (1992:Table 1.8:12); *Bulletin of Tourism Statistics*, 1991, Turkey.
TIR = tourist intensity rate

$$\frac{\text{International tourist arrivals}}{\text{Population}} \times 100$$

TPR = tourist penetration rate

$$\frac{\text{Average length of stay} \times \text{No. of tourists}}{365 \times \text{Population}} \times 100$$

TDR = tourist density ratio

$$\frac{\text{Average length of stay} \times \text{No. of tourists}}{365 \times \text{Area in km}^2} \times 100$$

CR = concentration ratio—percentage of all tourist arrivals of top three sending countries.

and sand) to describe seaside holidays has been changed to 'four Ss' to include sex.

Measuring the impact of tourism

Economists have developed various techniques to measure the economic impact of tourism. These usually concentrate on how tourism affects the GDP, employment and the balance of payments of a country but the inflationary impact is also gaining importance.

Ratios

The most popular variables used in measuring the significance of tourism in a country are the number of tourist arrivals and/or the amount of tourist expenditure. However, using absolute numbers in international comparisons makes little sense. For example, 10 million visitors per annum to Greece and Turkey each would, *ceteris paribus*, have different environmental impact owing to the difference in the size of the two countries. It is therefore common to use ratios for comparisons rather than absolute numbers (Harrison, 1992:11). Table 8.1 provides alternative ratios for measuring the impact of tourism for selected countries. TIR measures the number of tourists visiting a country on a per capita basis.

TPR takes into account the length of time tourists spend in the country. It is not surprising to observe from Table 8.1 that the TIR for Greece is many times that for Turkey because, although only twice as many people visit Greece as the number visiting Turkey, the population of Greece is only a fraction of that of Turkey.

Direct, indirect and induced effects of tourism

Tourism affects almost all parts of an economy. Domestic tourism expenditure is part of household consumption while tourism investment by firms is part of total private investment. Inbound international tourist expenditure would be part of exports and outbound tourist spending part of imports. Any grants or loans given to the tourism sector or any taxes paid by this sector would also involve government (Bull, 1991:113).

The direct impact of international tourism will depend upon the ownership pattern of the tourism sector, the type of tourism provided, and the structure of the economy. For example, in some LDCs the effect of international tourism may be to increase employment but not wages, if the economy concerned happens to be a labour-intensive, low-wage economy, such as Tunisia's. On the other hand, in a high-wage economy international tourism might encourage sophisticated technology in transport and telecommunications, or an increase in demand for land and capital. The net direct impact will also depend upon the negative effects of international tourism such as those mentioned above, e.g. the demonstration effect, inflationary impact, environmental pollution, etc.

The secondary effects of tourism are usually analysed by tourism income multipliers (TIMs) and the input–output method. TIMs are nothing but the application of the usual Keynesian concept of multiplier to tourism expenditure. That is, an increase in inbound tourism expenditure will cause an increase in national income by an amount larger than the original increase in tourism expenditure.

$$\Delta Y = k\Delta E_{\text{tr}}$$

$$\therefore k = \Delta Y / E_{\text{tr}}$$

where ΔY is the increase in national income, ΔE_{tr} is the increase in tourism expenditure, and k is the multiplier.

The value of k, of course, depends on the leakages from the system, such as the amount of saving, taxes and import spending related to a given increase in national income (Bull, 1991:140). However, there are special leakages from the system in tourism. For example, some of what tourists spend may immediately go to foreign-owned transport firms, hotels, tour operators as profits and interest payments, and some to food and drink imports which might be required by tourists. Thus the TIM can be written as follows:

$$K = \frac{1 - MPM_{tr}}{t + s + [(1 - t - s)m]}$$

where t is the marginal tax rate, s is the marginal propensity to save, m is the marginal propensity to import, and MPM_{tr} = all the direct leakages from the tourism expenditure mentioned above.

It is clear that in general the lower the import content of consumption, and in particular the more an economy can supply the goods and services demanded by foreign tourists—small MPM_{tr}—the higher the final increase in incomes. Many LDCs which depend on tourism are small economies with heavy dependence on international trade, i.e. large m and MPM_{tr}, such as the Bahamas, Fiji, Bermuda, etc., have low TIMs. Turkey, on the other hand has one of the highest TIMs because it is a big country with a diverse economy and perhaps good linkages with the tourism sector.

Input–output method aims to show the secondary effects of tourism through the specific demand and supply requirements and linkages between different industries of an economy (Bull, 1991:142) in which tourism is regarded as a separate industry. The problem with this method is that it requires detailed sectoral data which is not easy to obtain. Moreover, the assumption of fixed inputs is particularly unrealistic for tourism in which production functions change rapidly. Furthermore, the input–output method ignores the possibility of excess capacity which is common in tourism.

Forecasting techniques are also used in estimating the impact of tourism, in particular in measuring demand for tourism. The latter is, of course, essential for policy and planning decisions by both the government and the private sector. The forecasting techniques in tourism can be quantitative or qualitative. Among the former, theory-based ones use econometric models and input–output analysis while pure statistical ones include time-series analysis, the gravity model and the probabilistic travel model. Among the latter, the Delphi technique is the most popular one.

Significance of tourism in Turkey and Greece

Turkey offers tremendous tourism potential as it has 778 000 km^2 of land surrounded by sea, larger than France and three times as big as Great Britain. Mountains in the north and south run parallel to the coast with very few passages. Thus the northern and southern coasts are characterised by long beaches, whereas, in the west, mountains are at right-angles to the coast, making it a very scenic coastline of a fjordic nature. Climatic conditions vary from typical Mediterranean in the west and the south to tropical in the eastern Black Sea region. Anatolia, also known as Asia Minor, has been the birthplace—and the death place—of dozens of civilisations, including Greek, Roman, Hittite, Phoenician, Seljuc and Ottoman. One archaeological excavation alone has been reported to have uncovered seven different civilisations on top of each other near Troy. Thus Turkey has considerable potential for all forms of tourism, including Mediterranean tourism, alpine tourism, rural tourism and cultural tourism.

Until recently tourism played only a minor role in the expansion of Turkey's economy. However, in the 1980s Turkey's receipts from international tourism grew more rapidly than those of any other major nation involved in tourism. Table 8.2 indicates that in 1963 the number of tourist arrivals was just under 200 000 with the associated income of $7.7 million. In 1992 these figures were 7.1 million and $3.7 billion respectively. In 1963 income from tourism constituted 0.1% of GNP and 2.1% of export earnings. In 1990 the former rose to 3.3% and the latter exceeded 26%.

Table 8.3 provides information for comparing tourism earnings with other forms of foreign currency earnings. As can be seen from the table, tourism is more or less as important to the balance of payments of Turkey as the Turkish workers working abroad (row 3). It can also be observed from Table 8.3 that tourism is a more important source of foreign currency earning than direct foreign investment. The table also points to the share of tourism in domestic investment hovering around 4% which the government is trying to increase.

Table 8.2 *The importance of Turkish tourism*

Year	Tourism arrivals (million)	Tourism receipts ($ million)	Share of receipts in GNP (%)	Share of receipts in export earnings (%)
1963	0.119	8	0.1	2.1
1970	0.725	52	0.5	8.8
1983	1.625	441	0.8	7.0
1986	2.391	1215	2.1	16.3
1988	4.173	2355	3.3	20.2
1990	5.389	3308	3.0	25.5
1992	7.100	3640	3.3	26.2

Sources: (1) *Bulletin of Tourism Statistics*, 1991, Ministry of Tourism, Turkey. (2) State Planning Organisation, 1985. (3) *Facts and Figures, 1993*, Ministry of Tourism, Turkey.

Table 8.3 *Tourism income and capital movements ($ million)*

	1988	1989	1990	1991	1992
(1) Tourism income	2355	2257	3308	2654	3640
(2) Workers remittances	1865	3138	3325	2901	3074
(3) (1)/(2)	1.27	0.81	0.99	0.91	1.18
(4) Foreign investment	824.5	1470.5	1784.0	1909.0	1295.3
(5) (1)/(4)	2.86	1.74	1.85	1.39	2.81
(6) Share of tourism in domestic investment	3.2%	4.0%	3.9%	3.9%	3.4%

Source: State Planning Organisation: Main Economic Indicators, April 1993.

Currently around 8 million tourists are expected to visit Turkey annually, generating around $4.5 billion of direct tourism income. The licensed bed capacity of 500 000 is offered by around 3180 licensed establishments. Turkey's share of (world) international tourism income is 1.4%.

In 1992 the main countries of origin of tourists arriving in Turkey were Germany, Bulgaria, Romania, Great Britain and the CIS. Still around 70% of arrivals occur between April and October, which creates the problem of excess capacity for the rest of the year. Although this concerns the authorities, they have not so far succeeded in finding a solution to the problem. Attempts to organise winter breaks have not met with success because Istanbul hotels are not prepared to reduce prices, since they obtain enough custom from business visitors. However, the present Minister of Tourism, Abdülkadir Ateş, stated (TRT Radio Interview, Ankara, 17 May 1993) that there are new attempts to develop rural and alpine tourism in Turkey, particularly around Erzurum and Van, which would help not only the problem of excess capacity but also in reducing the economic regional discrepancies.

Basic statistical figures for tourism in Greece are given in Table 8.4

Tourism development strategies in Turkey and Greece

Tourism as a conscious economic activity at both the governmental and entrepreneurial level is a relatively new phenomenon. Below is a brief discussion of what is meant by tourism policy and a brief history of government strategies regarding Turkish tourism.

The general principles and aims of tourism policy

Any tourism policy in Turkey must acknowledge the fact that the Turkish economy is a predominantly private enterprise economy; it is also a mixed economy; and any economic policy including those relating to tourism is formulated and implemented within the context of five-year development plans which are imperative for the public sector but only indicative for the private sector (Olali, 1990:58).

However, the general aims of a tourism policy in any country are bound to be a mixture of economic, social, and cultural considerations. Thus the aims of any tourism policy in general can be summarised as follows.

(1) To help achieve such economic objectives as full employment, price stability, and a more even distribution of income and wealth.
(2) To contribute positively to the balance of payments by increasing the diversification of exports and the foreign currency earnings.
(3) To enable maximum number of citizens to benefit from the cultural, recreational and leisure activities of the tourism sector.
(4) To protect and develop the natural and the historical resources of the country.

Tourism development strategies in Turkey

It is possible to identify four significant periods in considering the tourism strategies of Turkey, namely the pre-planned period; the planned period in the 1960s and the 1970s; the 1980s; and the 1990s.

Before 1963

Until the beginning of the planned period in 1963, there was no well-developed tourism strategy in Turkey. Various bodies tried to achieve modest aims with their own resources. For example, the most important

Table 8.4 *Basic statistical information for Greece 1992 figures*

Population	10.2 million
Employees in servicing and agriculture	2.8 million
GNP	$79.2 billion
Imports	$22.9 billion
Exports	$9.7 billion
Tourist arrivals	9.8 million
Tourist income	$5.8 billion
Ratio tourist income/GNP	7.3%
Ratio tourist income/exports	52%

Notes: (1) 70% of the Greek workforce is employed in services, often on a seasonal basis. (2) Tourist arrivals are expected to be between 13 and 15 million by the year 2000, or 2.3% of total world tourist numbers.

institution in Turkish tourism until 1930 was the Turkish Institute of Touring and Automobile which dominated the tourism policy in Turkey. After 1930 the Turkish Office took responsibility for any policy formulations. It should be noted that these two institutions were private sector bodies.

Government involvement in tourism began in 1949 with the meeting of the First Tourism Advice Committee whose report constituted the basis of the national tourism policy. The report was such an important document that it even influenced tourism policy in the planned period. Until 1963 Turkish tourism policy was developed by the subsequent Tourism Advice Committees.

Planned period

With the political change of 1960 came the economic and social changes set out in the new Constitution of 1961 and Turkey entered the planned mixed economy period with the First Five-year Plan of 1963–67.

The First Five-year Plan (1963–67) set out certain principles and objectives for the tourism sector. It proposed that the share of tourism investment in total investment was to increase, with the state sector shouldering the responsibility of building the infrastructure and the private sector that of the superstructure. The plan also decided, owing to limited resources, to intensify investment in high tourism potential areas, such as the Marmara and Ege districts and the city of Antalya. To help achieve these objectives the plan proposed market research into demand and supply conditions in tourism, establishing links with foreign firms and governments for promotion, and enacting the necessary legislation to facilitate investment and to create a ministry for tourism. The Second Five-year Plan (1968–72) endorsed the objectives of its predecessor and in addition introduced the notion of physical planning, the concept of internationally competitive pricing policy, and the principles of mass tourism for transport and accommodation policy. The Third (1973–77) and the Fourth (1979–83) Five-year Plans emphasised the leading role of the private sector in tourism investment and the importance of the banking system outside the Tourism Bank in providing finance for the sector. They also proposed the intensification of skill-based training programmes, extending physical planning in order to prevent haphazard development and increasing efforts to develop a superstructure suitable for mass tourism.

However, despite all the policy decisions and the encouragement and support given to tourism the expected improvements did not materialise and the plan targets were by and large not achieved during the 1960s and the 1970s. Moreover, the tourism initiatives in this period never managed to utilise Turkey's historic and natural wealth, neither did they respond to economic requirements.

The 1980s

Thus it was decided in the early 1980s that a radical change in the overall tourism strategy was needed. Consequently the government issued the Tourism Encouragement Framework Decree in 1980 and the Tourism Encouragement Law was passed in 1982. However, by 1985 it was realised that existing legislation was not going to provide the necessary impetus for the tourism sector. Consequently, tourism was included among the 'sectors of special importance for development' and some monetary incentives were introduced (TYD, 1992:VIII).

The strategy adopted by the government in the 1980s and hence incorporated into the Fifth and the Sixth Five-year Plans was in line with the general economic policy of Turgut Özal's government which was highly 'Thatcherite' in nature. It was based on the usual principles of the privatisation of the public sector, deregulation of industry and services, the liberation of import and export regimes, simplification of investment procedures, and the creation of a contemporary tourism culture based on the modern principles of tourism.

Within the context of this general economic philosophy, the Fifth (1985–89) and the Sixth (1990–94) Five-year Plans set out the following objectives for the tourism sector for the 1980s and the 1990s. Turkey will seek to establish closer links with the Balkans and the LDCs; the international capacity of Izmir and Antalya airports will be increased; charter transport will be developed; domestic tour operators and travel agents will be given encouragement and support; tourism training centres will be modernised and special hotel management schools with emphasis on foreign languages will be established. Necessary measures will be taken to improve the quality of statistical data, to reduce idle capacity, and to extend the tourism season.

The government also introduced the following incentives in order to achieve a significant increase in tourism investment.

1. Allocation of public land to investors on a long-term basis.
2. Soft loans provided by the Turkish Tourism Bank.
3. Exemptions from various taxes including customs and export taxes.
4. Preferential tariff rates for electricity, water and gas consumption.
5. Priority for communication needs, i.e. telex, telephone, fax, etc.

6. Allowance of foreign personnel employment up to 20% of the total workforce.
7. Casino operation licence for accommodation facilities.
8. Investment allowance.
9. Special incentive premium for foreign investors (Türkmen, 1988:12)

The 1992 coalition government

The coalition government of 1992 has criticised the developments of the past decade in the tourism sector and proposed changes in both objectives and strategy. It has been stated that the increase in the bed capacity has not been matched by improvements in the areas of marketing, air transport, training and technical infrastructure. The number of travel agencies is continuing to increase and yet they are dominated by foreign tour operators. Moreover, only 30% of air passengers use Turkish airlines. Consequently, more than half of the tourism income generated in Turkey goes abroad, shared between the foreign tour operators and airlines. There is acute shortage of skilled personnel, up to 70% of the demand from establishments. There is regional imbalance in tourism development in favour of the west and south-west at the expense of the north and the east. This has produced undesirable environmental results as well as aggravating economic discrepancies between regions. There is also bias in the incentives policy for big investment against small, medium and local investments.

The main objectives and the policies of the present government regarding tourism are briefly stated as follows.

(1) The share of Turkey in world tourism income will be increased from 1.4% to over 2% by 1994. This will be achieved by improving the competitive position of Turkish tourism. This will require better marketing methods and a concerted effort to improve the image of Turkey abroad.
(2) A comprehensive and coherent employment and training policy for tourism will be introduced. As part of this the number of training courses in educational establishments will be increased.
(3) The dependence of Turkish tourism on incentives schemes and subsidies as well as the existing excess capacity in tourism—up to 60% in some places—will be reduced. In this context alpine tourism, cultural tourism and rural tourism as well as domestic tourism will be encouraged. This diversification into different types of tourism will be complemented by geographical diversification.
(4) Prevention of environmental damage will be given priority in a multidimensional way. For example, in hotel building not only the location, height and the architecture of the building but also the activities of the hotel will be examined from an environmental perspective, e.g. the use of recycled paper, biodegradable detergents, and packaging, etc.
(5) The infrastructure of the tourism sector will be improved and the use of modern telecommunication systems will be maximised. This, it is hoped, will help the competitive position of domestic firms and thus the retention of tourism income within Turkey.
(6) Further diversification of the tourism product will be achieved by opening up new centres for winter tourism, in places such as the Kars–Erzurum–Bayburt triangle and in Cankiri and Kastamonu, by encouraging festival tourism, thermal tourism, and in particular the third-age senior citizen tourism.

To achieve the above objectives the following steps are being taken.

(a) TUSAP (Tourism Sector Development Plan). This is a project group made up of experts from different universities in order to determine a dynamic planning system in which the goals, strategies and policies can be revised and adopted according to future developments in the sector (*Silk Road*, Ministry of Tourism, Turkey, No. 2, Winter 1993, p. 38).
(b) The budget of the Ministry of Tourism will be increased and a new category of skilled personnel, called 'tourism specialists', will be created. These specialists will be graduates with special training in tourism and will be employed by the Ministry in Turkey and abroad as technical personnel.
(c) New legislation is being introduced to reorganise the structure of both the public and the private sectors of Turkish tourism. For instance, the International Relations Office of the Ministry of Tourism will gain the status of a separate Department; and various private sector institutions such as hotels for tourists, guides, travel agents, etc., will assume the status of 'Public Service Institutions'.
(d) Promotion activities will be intensified and several different promotion campaigns through TV advertising, press conferences, expositions, fairs, and bulletins and other publications will be launched in various European cities.
(e) Consultations have already started regarding the establishment of a private sector bank specifically designed to meet the financial needs of the tourism sector.

Tourism development in Greece

There are three main factors which have influenced recent policy-making decisions in Greece:

1. The Single European Market which provides new opportunities and challenges for Greece.
2. An acknowledgement of the changing needs and demands of tourists to Greece, along with a growing number of competitors who are responding to those changing demands.
3. A desire and a willingness to respond to external influencing factors by devising and implementing a unified tourism development strategy which will enable an informed decision making by all those involved in the tourism industry.

The key issues of the new approach to tourism development are:

1. Upgrading of standards, facilities and general infrastructure, along with a broadening of the spectrum and services available, e.g. from hotels.
2. Developing the tourist industry by investment in and building of new facilities, e.g. marinas, spas, golf courses, conference centres, etc.
3. Transferring the entrepreneurial activities to the private sector via leasing and incentive schemes, and thereby hoping to establish and develop a climate of confidence for investment and development.
4. Establishing and maintaining controls to ensure services are delivered according to promised standards.
5. Updating and adjusting legislation to respond to the needs of tourism—both providers and consumers.
6. An incorporation of the need for responsibility for safeguarding the environment into the masterplan for development of tourism, now with the Greek Centre for Programming and Research.
7. An acknowledgement of certain areas as being already saturated, and the transfer of development funds to underdeveloped areas, so as to spread visitor numbers throughout the country.
8. A refocusing on traditional types of accommodation and cultural activities, especially when original buildings, skills and customs are under threat of demise.
9. An acknowledgement of the importance of an integrated and coherent communications strategy, to reflect the key changes proposed for Greek tourism and controlled by the GNTO and presented according to international guidelines in the relevant country overseas.

All of these issues have been incorporated in a new legal framework which provides for the new mechanisms to enable these new initiatives to be enacted, primarily via the new spirit of cooperation between the state and the private sector. In addition, and in parallel, the new law for Investments in Industry in Greece has been passed.

Comment on the tourism strategies in Turkey and Greece

The historical position of the Turkish state with respect to tourism has been fairly inconsistent. Before the planned period the state failed even to acknowledge the phenomenon of tourism. In the 1960s and the 1970s, by contrast, the development plans adopted a highly *étatist* and centralised approach to tourism. Despite identifying the problems of inadequate infrastructure, illegitimate and environmentally damaging development, and the lack of physical planning, the state failed to take effective measures to solve these problems. In the 1980s the approach to tourism planning changed with the change in the economic and political philosophy of the government, and the state adopted a decentralised and liberal attitude to tourism. This means transferring some of the responsibility of planning to local authorities on the one hand, and providing incentives to encourage the private sector to have a leading role, not only in investment but also in the pricing policy, on the other. However, owing to the lack of sectoral planning, ineffective control, the lack of participation by local people, the abuse of political power, the get-rich-quick mentality coupled with dubious practices, inconsistencies in the planning criteria and procedures, and the general lack of appropriate tourism culture resulted in missed opportunities and inadequate and inappropriate tourism development.

The experience of the past three decades indicates that the approach to Turkish tourism failed to evaluate the domestic and the international sector in a consistent and integrated manner. Many organisations have been allowed to be set up and then to disintegrate. Even at the ministerial level, organisations have not been given the appropriate power and responsibility to achieve the desired objectives in tourism. The haphazard approach to tourism is reflected not only in the organisational structure but also in the legislation which is introduced in a piecemeal fashion (TEK, 1992:113). Perhaps the most tragic failure of the past three decades has been the environmental damage allowed to happen to the Marmara Sea and its coastline, including Istanbul and the Bosphorus, and to the Aegean coast, particularly around Izmir. Although this is subject-matter for another paper in its own right, it should be stated that the economic, social, and cultural repercussions of this negligence (criminal?) are likely to extend well into the next century and even further.

There are, however, reasons to be more optimistic in the 1990s. The planning approach, although still decentralist, appears to be more consistent. It seems to encourage the development of social consciousness regarding tourism, and a responsible attitude on the part of the citizens. It appears to adopt an integrated view of sectoral, regional and local planning, to take tourism education and training seriously, and thus to be prepared to commit resources to achieve the stated objectives.

However, it should be borne in mind that today tourism is a race for quality in a ruthlessly competitive world on a global level. The competitors of Turkey today include not only Greece, Portugal, North Africa and the Middle East but also some of the countries of Africa, of Asia and even of the Americas. It is not as easy to succeed as a tourist destination in this climate as it was twenty years ago. True, some developments present excellent opportunities, such as increased leisure, more efficient transport systems, increased popularity of nature and culture, new markets, such as some of the ex-Soviet republics, and the polluted coastline of the western Mediterranean. However, one should also be aware of possible threats, such as the possibility of increased costs, another oil crisis, the fortress EU, the dominance of the MNCs, and political instability in the region (TEK, 1992:114). All these factors necessitate a systematic, rational and even more diligent planned approach to tourism in Turkey today.

Greece has also acknowledged the importance of a planned approach to tourism development in order to best provide guidelines for all of the key providers (and consumers) in tourism and tourism-related industries. However, in a country which has acute economic problems and severe unrest among the working population —most of whom hope to obtain benefit from employment in tourism, the new framework for developing and controlling tourism in Greece is broad-ranging and ambitious. It is commendable for a government to decide on a policy which will improve the quality of the tourist experience, whilst at the same time providing a legal environment in which the tourist will be protected. However, to be committed to these policies whilst at the same time aiming to upgrade the product on offer to appeal to more affluent tourists, to aim to encourage new investment in previously neglected areas of the country and in new facilities and attractions, all the time conveying a unified message as to what Greece is and has to offer, is demanding a great deal from a country which is coming only now to the realisation that the tourist population is not infinite, and to ensure a continued success among

the targeted groups of tourists requires an adaptability and a responsiveness to tourists' needs not hitherto considered important. The government's first task then is to effect this change in philosophy, then to obtain a concerted and cooperative approach from providers at local, regional and national levels. Once these basic but critical issues have been addressed, then the government can embark upon the new tourism development strategy; but an outsider might recommend that they undertake only one or two of the development issues at a time, in order best to ensure total success of the new policies, and also to be able best to measure the success or otherwise of the changes.

Conclusion

What emerges from the previous pages is that tourism is not only a multidimensional phenomenon but also a highly elastic concept. Thus measuring its contribution to the development of the economy has all the pitfalls of any cost–benefit analysis regarding an economic project with social and environmental dimensions.

It is obvious that tourism is vitally important to the economics of both Greece and Turkey, and this importance has been recognised both at the local and at the national level, although the recognition is relatively recent in the case of Turkey.

What this initial examination of the respective tourism strategies and of the measurement of the economic benefits indicates is that there is a responsibility in every country for every decision maker to be aware of the issues surrounding the definition and measurement of tourism. With that responsibility there is also a need for decision makers to be informed of factors internal and external to the tourism industry which will influence the nature of tourism and demand for the various elements of tourism services.

The tourism planner then must be economist, marketer, strategist, accountant, environmentalist and communicator. There is a need for all these functions in the forming of tourism development plans if all the various facets of the complex tourism product are to be addressed and to be developed in line with the countries' natural and man-made resources and the propensity of its people to continue to offer tourism as an important and sustainable industry to ensure the future economic stability of the country.

There are reasons to be both optimistic and cautious regarding the future. One would like to think that past lessons have been learned well and that future challenges can be met with the rationality of long-term considerations rather than the economic and political expediency of the short term.

References

Archer, B. H. (1976) 'Demand forecasting in tourism', Bangor Occasional Papers in Economics, University of Wales Press.

Aricanli, T. and Rodrik, D. (1990) *The political economy of Turkey: Debt Adjustment and Sustainability*, Macmillan, London.

Britton, S. (1982) 'The political economy of tourism in the Third World', *Annals of Tourism Research*, 9(3):331–358.

Bull, A. (1991) *The Economics of Travel and Tourism*, Longman, Harlow.

Edgell, D. L. (1990) *International Tourism Policy*, Van Nostrand Reinhold, New York.

GNTO (Greek National Tourist Organisation) (1993) 'Strategy for the promotion of Greek tourism abroad'.

Harrison, D. (1992) *Tourism and the Less Developed Countries*, Belhaven Press, London.

Kaynak, E. and Macaulay, J. A. (1984) 'The Delphi technique in the measurement of tourism market potential', *Tourism Management*, 5(2): 87–101.

KEPE (Centre of Programming and Research for Greece) (1991) 'Master plan for tourist development'.

Lea, J. (1988) *Tourism Development in the Third World*, Routledge, London.

Liu, J., Var, T. and Timur, A. (1984) 'Tourist income multipliers for Turkey', *Tourism Management*, Dec.:280–287.

Mathieson, A. and Wall, B. (1982) *Tourism: Economic, Physical and Social Impacts*, Longman, Harlow.

Middleton, V. T. C. (1990) *Marketing in Travel and Tourism*, Heinemann, Oxford.

Olali (1990) *Turizm Politikasi ve Planlamasi* (Tourism Policy and Planning), Istanbul.

Özdemir (1992) *Tourizmin Turkiyenin Sosyo-Ekonomik Yapisina Etkileri* (The Effect of Tourism on the Socio-economic Structure of Turkey), Ankara.

Smith, S. L. J. (1989) *Tourism Analysis: A Handbook*, Longman, Harlow.

Türkman, M. (1988) 'The Turkish plan for tourism', A British Travel Trade Seminar on Turkey, 21 July 1984, London.

TEK (Economics Institute of Turkey) (1992) 'Turkish economy —sectoral developments', Ankara.

TYD (1992) *Tourism Yatirimlarinin Ekonomiye Katkilari* (Economic Contribution of Tourism Investment), TYD, Istanbul.

Uysal, M. and Crompton, J. L. (1984) 'Determinants of demand for international tourist flows to Turkey', *Tourism Management*, Dec.:188–277.

Var, T., Mohammad, G. and Icoz, O. (1990) 'Factors affecting international tourism demand for Turkey' (Research notes), *Annals of Tourism Research*, 17(4): 606–610.

Williams, A. M. and Shaw, G. (1991) *Tourism and Economic Development*, Belhaven Press, London.

Witt, S. F., Brooke, M. Z. and Buckley, P. J. (1991) *The Management of International Tourism*, Unwin Hyman, London.

Witt, S. F. and Moutinho, L. (Eds) (1989) *Tourism Marketing and Management Handbook*, Prentice Hall, Hemel Hempstead.

Witt, S. F. and Witt, C. A. (1992) *Modelling and Forecasting Demand in Tourism*, Academic Press, London.

World Tourism Organisation (1993) *Compendium of Tourism Statistics*, WTO, Madrid.

9 Turkish tourism development

M. KORZAY

Introduction

Is there a development in Turkish tourism?

When the available statistics are examined one can say that there has been a quantitative development of hospitality units, an increase in the number of tourists visiting Turkey and a considerable development in the infrastructure as well as an increase in tourist revenues.

The next question would be what the standing of Turkish tourism is among the tourism trends worldwide in Europe between the years 1980 and 1992. The main trends that will be compared are based on:

—arrivals/nights overstay
—international tourist flows
—international tourism revenues

Following this brief comparison, the importance of tourism for Turkey will be illustrated with figures indicating the evolution of tourism from 1955 until today, with reference to marketing, management, tourism education and employment, will be discussed.

The research findings on middle-sized hotels with up to 100 rooms and the managers' evaluation of the hospitality industry development, their concern with envouragement policies, the environment, personnel training, management styles, marketing approaches and their impact on tourism development will be considered.

This paper is based on a literature survey of secondary data supported by empirical studies on the progress of Turkish tourism and the impact of various features in the development process of the tourism phenomenon.

The importance of tourism for Turkey

Tourism has become a vital component of the Turkish economy. The following facts underline the tremendous economic importance of tourism to Turkey.

1. Between the years 1980 and 1992 the growth rate of Turkish tourism in Europe has increased by 17.95% (WTO, 1993).
2. Foreign exchange earnings from tourism account for 2.4% of GNP as of 1992, whereas it was 0.1% in 1963 (Turkish Ministry of Tourism, 1992b).

3. The share of Turkey in international tourism is 1.40% with 6 675 000 million guests. Turkey ranks seventeenth in the top thirty tourism destinations, whereas she was ranked twenty-ninth in 1980 (WTO, 1993).
4. The number of hospitality units were 511 in the year 1980 and by the year 1992 they had increased to 1498 which, is a twofold increase in 12 years. The number of beds were 56 000 in the year 1980 and by the year 1992 the number had increased to 219 900 which is a threefold increase (Turkish Ministry of Tourism, 1992a) (refer to Figures 9.5 and 9.6 for the types of accommodation).
5. According to the accommodation statistics (1992) the total number of nights spent by foreigners were 16 785 455 and nights spent by foreigners by their nationalities are respectively:

—Germany (FR) 7 573 318 (45.1%)
—France 1 447 251 (8.6%)
—Benelux countries 1 118 657 (6.7%)
—Scandinavian countries 985 526 (5.9%)
—Austria 921 678 (5.5%) (Figure 9.1)

The longest stay was realized by:

—Austrians, 8 nights
—Germans, 7.3 nights
—Switzerland, 7.2 nights
—Scandinavian countries, 6.1 nights
—United Kingdom, 5.1 nights

6. According to OECD statistics, employment in the field of hospitality in Turkey is 8% of the total active population and its share in the total service industry is 3.2%. Presently (1992) hospitality units in Turkey employ 63 000 people and the tourism secondary supporting industry employs about 95 000 people. However, unregistered hotels, camping sites, yachting facilities, travel agents and transportation companies employ people indirectly for the tourism industry. A rule of thumb estimation would be that 400 000 people are directly and indirectly employed within the service industry. This figure constitutes 10% of the people in the service sector and also is equivalent to 3% of the active population.

7. According to unpublished estimates the bed capacity has increased to 297 611 beds and 126 695 beds are under construction. 600 000 registered beds are forecast for the year 1999. So a 179 694-unit increase is expected for the coming five years. Therefore, by the year 2000, 302 389 bed units will create a job potential for 100 000 people (if we assume one employee per three bed units). Supposing these circumstances last till 1999, there will be an employment potential for 20 000 people for each year. One also needs to take into consideration the employment capacity that will be created by the unregistered hospitality units, travel agents and tourism supporting industries which will simultaneously be developing with the registered bed capacity.

These few figures and arguments may justify the importance of tourism for the Turkish economy.

The Turkish tourism development phenomenon

Two new marketing terms became popular in the second half of the twentieth century: 'Social marketing' and 'Organizational marketing'. Marketing was no longer by definition limited to the promotion and sales of goods and services but had a wider connotation. The marketing of policies, of parliamentarians, of colleges, universities and teachers, of education systems, of social and moral values and of lifestyles became its features. What actually has taken place in the last twenty-five years with the tourism phenomenon in Turkey is organizational marketing of tourism policies, management styles, education and employment.

The need for coordinating manpower and education outputs with the planned physical development of tourism, to avoid acute future shortages of skilled personnel and management staff and to ensure high standards of performance, was pointed out all through the awareness and advocacy stages of the tourism phenomenon. Unfortunately policy-makers were a little late in perceiving that tourism planning and the management of the established tourist infrastructure are two different topics which require different educational and skill development training programs. Furthermore, most of the hoteliers were not fully aware of such

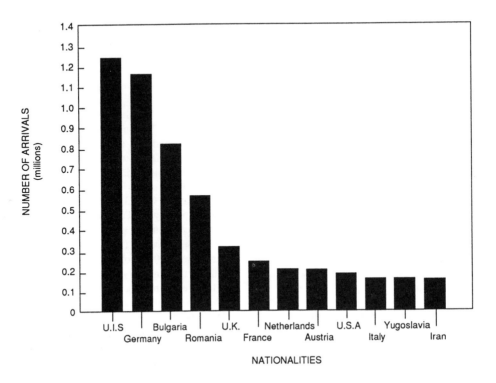

Figure 9.1 *Foreign visitor arrivals by nationalities*

far-sighted recruiting policies as: (1) consideration of manpower needs; (2) knowledge of the promotional ladder within the organization; (3) a prediction of future turnover rates on the basis of past experiences and future growth expectations; (4) understanding the type of person who seems to be best suited to specific positions in the organization (Armatas and Lundberg, 1983:89).

This approach is the outcome of dynamic market research and evaluation which did not exist in the Turkish tourism phenomenon at the awareness and advocacy stages (Table 9.1). Since most of the hotels, with the exception of the chain hotel units, in Turkey do not have organizational charts and job descriptions or work analysis, recruiting and personnel selection is based on rule-of-thumb manpower needs and on the personal evaluation of the managers.

The extreme shortage of personnel at all levels in the service industry has forced the policy-makers and the managers to adopt a dynamic market policy. Research on tourism manpower need and education at all levels were strongly felt to be necessary. Since 1955 the managers of the International chain of hotel units and the universities have tried to market the tourism phenomenon to policy-makers and to the public. Now we can turn our attention to the stages that the Turkish tourism phenomenon has gone through (Table 9.1).

Awareness stage (1955–1970)

All marketing strategies were put into effect at the awareness stage to raise positive interest for tourism assets, education, employment agencies, government bodies, universities, and in the eyes of the public (refer to Table 9.1).

As a result of the awareness stage, scholars, educators at the institutes, tourism sector members and families started to recommend strongly vocational subjects such as travel/hotel/tourism management for their youngsters.

Advocacy stage (1970–1982)

At this stage the following features were continuously marketed.

—Profitable utilization of tourism assets
—Sound inventory of tourism assets
—Tourism education, problems of:

(a) lack of specialized teachers at the universities
(b) too many courses being offered with limited sources
(c) lack of concentrated teaching of vocational subjects, which required enormous investment in laboratories and attracting specialists. The cost of the investment in education was never justified

—The necessity for tourism encouragement policies
—Integration of activities with tourism supporting services, goods and industries
—Area development plans
—Pricing policies
Price cuts for special business have been advocated for the purpose of eliminating drastic falls in market cycles. Also warnings have been given on:

(a) 'Prices being competitive and at the same time be able to produce adequate revenue to meet fixed obligations'.
(b) 'Wide scale price cuts being, by-and-large ill-advised' (Coffman and Recknagel, 1983:162).

—Area development plans, with the collaboration of public administrative bodies and international organizations, which took place at the advocacy stage had a positive/voluntary impact on the related bodies. Many of the above issues were put into action in the succeeding years.

Action stage (1982 to present)

—Very successful application of the investment encouragement policies caused a sudden increase in physical capacity.

(a) The allocation of public land on long-term leasing basis through the BOT (build operate and transfer) model.
(b) Grants reaching 40% of total investment cost.
(c) Low interest loans.
(d) Various tax exemptions and import facilitation.

—Dynamic market research gained popularity.
—Integration of tourism services and products encouraged the formation of incorporated corporations.
—Serious measures were taken on an area inventory of tourism assets.
—Development of resort complexes as well as development of malls.

Also by the year 1990 such other significant developments took place as:

—liberalization of air transportation
—ongoing market prices for room and package tour rates
—decentralization of planning authority to local bodies
—establishment of local investors' unions with the aim of realizing local infrastructure for public facilities at resort areas.

Table 9.1 *Turkish tourism development phases as to tourism education, marketing, management and employment*

Evolution process of Turkish tourist phenomenon	Marketing/ management	Tools	Education	Tools and sources	Employment	Tools	Sources
I. AWARENESS STAGE (1955–1970):							
A. Awareness of tourism phenomenon at: 1. Government 2. Public administrators 3. University 4. Private sector 5. Public level B. Awareness of tourism assets: 1. Sea, sun, sand 2. Cultural heritage 3. Anatolia is the cradle of civilization 4. Turkish hospitality C. Awareness of tourism education: 1. Secondary school level 2. Advanced vocational school 3. Undergraduate/graduate level 4. Public/Government level D. Authority of regional tourism planning was transferred to Ministry of Tourism in 1970	A. MCT[a] B. Travel agencies C. Chain hotels D. Tourism bank E. Static marketing policies in application F. Tourist profile unknown G. Tourist sources vague and unknown	A. Brochures B. Information offices abroad C. Local information offices D. Embassies and consulates E. Very limited international tour operators F. No market research G. Rule-of-thumb method in market estimation H. Land-use plans were prepared for western and southern coastline I. Various infrastructure investments both at national and regional levels were realized by the related government agencies	A. Very limited formal education 1. Undergraduate programs 2. Secondary level trade schools B. No-informal education C. Tourism Bank: on-the-job training programs	A. Under the auspices of business administration schools —On the job training at the establishments of Tourism Bank	A. Very limited need for executive jobs B. Limited need for managerial jobs C. High need for qualified personnel and skilled workers	A. No tools of training B. Informal training 1. Sending the management group abroad to other units of the chain hotels 2. On the management training at developed units C. Short courses 1. Türems 2. On-the-job training	A. Foreign chain hotel executive rotation program B. 1. Minority groups with good knowledge of foreign language and service 2. Foreign secondary school graduates with a good knowledge of English/French but no university degree. C. Local people with primary or secondary school diploma
II. ADVOCACY STAGE (1970–1982):							
A. Advocate the profitability of tourism assets to: 1. Public 2. Bureaucrats 3. Universities 4. MCT[a] 5. MEYS[b] B. Inventory of tourism assets C. Integrating activities with tourism supporting services goods and industries D. Research orientation for tourism marketing plans	A. MCT B. Travel agencies C. Hotels D. Educational institutes E. University senates F. Continuation of static marketing policies G. Generalizing tourist source and profile based on observation and previous tourist history	A. Awareness tours for people in tourism industry —Brochures —Information offices B. Integrate activities with foreign tour operations —advertise in foreign magazines C. Area advertisement and rotating of guests —New releases D. Exchange visits with tourism dept. instructors/administrators	A. Increase informal education 1. Advanced vocational schools 2. Undergraduate programs B. Management training programs C. Development of Türems D. Popularity of on-the-job training	A. Slide films local seminars B. Train the trainer programs and centers C. Tourism Bank and Türem training programs and centers	A. High demand for executive managers B. High demand for supervisory level jobs C. High demand for qualified personnel at big Hotels	A. Inventory and forecast of human resource needs (research in process) 1. Formal education outlets 2. Management trainee programs B. On-the-job training 1. Supervisory training at chain hotels C. Short seminars	A. Business schools with hotel management major options 1. Business administration hotel management majors from USA and England B. Advanced vocational schools (11) C. Türems D. Personnel management and department heads training sessions in big hotels on

1. Vocational
2. Behavioral
3. Security issues

E. Advocate:
1. Tourism education of formal/informal institutions abroad
   (a) Extension programs
   (b) International seminars
2. Tourism encouragement policies
   (a) Financial
   (b) Legal
   (c) Educational
   (d) Environmental
3. Pricing policies
   (a) Skimming the cream
   (b) Penetrating prices
   (c) Market prices
   (d) Price cuts
4. Area development plans with coordination and integration of:
   (a) World Bank
   (b) UNDP
   (c) ILO
   (d) Foreign and local universities
   (e) State Planning Board
   (f) MCT

H. The responsibility of Ministry of Tourism extended:
1. Planning, certification and controling of investment of tourist facilities
2. Training the personnel
3. Certification of the professional tourist guides
4. Determination of room rates and basic fares for package tours
5. Physical development
   1. Holiday villages
   2. Chains of marinas were developed by Tourism Bank as pioneering facilities

E. Curriculum development and exchange programs with foreign universities
F. MCT feeding market strategies to their representatives abroad
G. Observation and activity reports from MCT representatives abroad

III. ACTION STAGE (1982 to present):

A. Integration of tourism services and product
B. Area inventory of tourism assets
C. Development of market plans based on market research
D. Area development plans with special emphasis on resort development
E. Application of encouragement policies
1. Investment on infrastructure and physical capacity
2. Investment of education
3. Investment in human resource development program
F. Soft tourism approach with special emphasis on preservation of environment and the socio-economic values of the community
G. Sustainable development
H. Other significant developments

A. MCT
B. TURSAB
C. Hotels and TUROB
D. Universities
E. Development and implementation of dynamic marketing
F. Soft tourism approach with special emphasis on preservation of environment and the socio-economic values of the community
G. Sustainable development
1. In terms of geographical regions
2. Sub-sectors

A. Professional display organization at international tourism fairs and workshops
B. Emphasis on culture tours
C. Local/international workshops
D. Use of dynamic marketing policy with special emphasis on market research on tourist sources and profile
E. Incentives from the government are more selective
1. In terms of geographical regions
2. Sub-sectors

A. 44 advanced vocational schools
   —10 undergraduate programs
   —Some graduate projects
B. Private hotel schools
C. Türems
D. TUGEV

A. Limited demonstration area. Mostly theoretical instruction
   —Demonstration and on-the-job training at big hotels
B. Seminars/conferences and short-term crash courses
C. Hotel schools
D. Development of audio/visual educational material
E. Feasibility study on computer-assisted education and use of interactive video

A. Personnel need hierarchy as to different levels
1. Managerial level (7.8%)
2. Supervisory level (31%)
3. Qualified personnel (39%)
4. Skilled worker (22.2%)

A. Rotation of qualified managers or promotion of qualified supervisors
1. Management training programs at home and abroad
B. University curriculum development
C. Professional and systematic on-the-job personnel training program
D. Collaboration and coordination of government and public and private sector and foundations and universities

A. Formal education
1. 44 advanced vocational schools
2. 10 undergraduate hotel programs
3. 9 vocational secondary schools
4. 5 graduate programs
B. On-the-job training
C. TUGEV
D. Service oriented or specially trained migrant workers and their children from European countries
E. Unemployed central Europeans and people from new republics of former Soviet Union
F. Refugees from (former) Yugoslavia and Bulgaria

Continued overleaf

Table 9.1 *(Continued)*

Evolution process of Turkish tourist phenomenon	Marketing/ management	Tools	Education	Tools and sources	Employment	Tools	Sources
4. Investment in educational material development 5. Collaboration with local and foreign tour operators and investors 6. Build–operate–transfer policy 7. Grants reaching 40% of total investment cost 8. Low-interest loans 9. Various tax exemptions and import facilitation F. Hot issues of this stage (1990 on) 1. Participatory planning 2. Privatization 3. Decentralization 4. Increasing local initiatives 5. Competitiveness 6. Productivity 7. Sustainable development 8. Quality 9. Reducing the dependency of private sector on government subsidies	1. Liberalization of air transportation 2. Free determination of room and package tour rates 3. Decentralization of planning authority to local bodies 4. Establishment of local investors unions with the aim of realizing (a) Local infrastructure (b) Operating public facilities in resort areas	3. Investment types 4. Priority is given (a) To relatively less developed areas (b) The completion of existing investments (c) Maintenance and modernization of existing facilities (d) Diversification of supply 1. Emphasis on increasing 1. Quality of life 2. Quality of service 3. Diversification of services/products		F. Development of exchange and extension programs with foreign universities G. Quality of education 1. More hotel schools, with labs 2. Adaptation of simulation method		1. Establishment of continuing education programs 2. Extension programs 3. Short crash courses	

[a]MCT, Ministry of Culture and Tourism.
[b]Ministry of Education Youth and Sports.

The above three stages had positive as well as negative impact on the evolution of the Turkish tourism phenomenon.

The sudden increase in the physical capacity without proper area and infrastructure development plans brought about considerable socio-economic, as well as environmental, difficulties, together with a severe shortage of qualified manpower at all levels of the hotel/travel management grid.

Without sound market research, many businessmen from other sectors were attracted to invest in tourism. The most popular investment areas have been the resort complexes and five-star, big-city hotels.

The sudden development of resorts and big-city hotels with convention centers brings about two possible future market segments: congress and conference tourism and third-generation (senior citizens) health and culture tourism.

If the rich cultural heritage and the environment could be preserved and improved, the continuity of demand for Turkish tourism will have a positive multiplier effect on the creation of jobs and on the negative balance of payments of Turkey. On the other hand, the need for

education and training of the personnel for the diversified services, together with increased employment possibilities in sustainable tourism marketing and management, should not be overlooked (Korzay, 1988a:55–56).

Where does Turkish tourism stand in relation to worldwide tourism trends?

Foreign visitor arrivals in Turkey from 1981 to 1992 increased from 1 800 000 to 7 076 096, a threefold increase. In the case of world trends, guest arrivals of 572 418 000 in 1981 increased to 959 330 000 in 1992, which is only a 67% increase (Figures 9.1 and 9.2). In 1991/92 the annual growth rate in world tourist arrivals was 4.8% and the annual growth rate of tourist arrivals in Turkey over the same period was 28.24% (Figure 9.3). Tourist arrivals compared to world trends show a greater increase in the case of Turkey.[1]

As stated previously, during the 1980–92 period, the fastest growing tourism destinations in Europe were Turkey (+17.96%), Portugal (+10.32%), Hungary (+7.53%) and The Netherlands (+6.53%). Even though

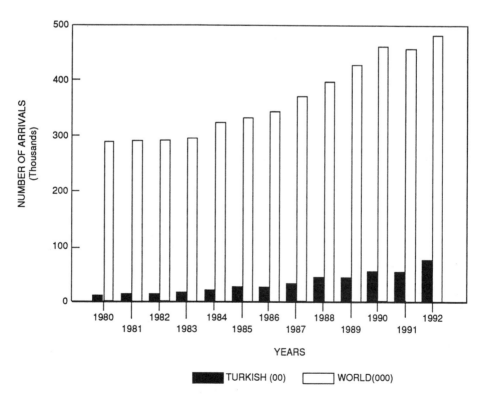

Figure 9.2 *Trends of tourist arrivals*

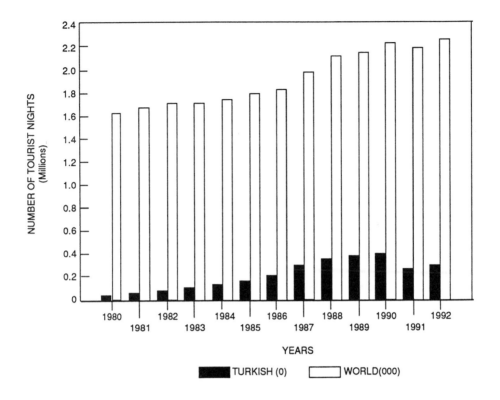

Figure 9.3 *Foreign visitor arrivals (1991–1992)*

Turkey does not have a leading share of arrivals worldwide, her growth rate is the fastest.

In 1981 Turkey had 0.6% of the worldwide tourist arrivals and in 1992 her share increased to 1.4%, which is a more than twofold increase (Figure 9.2). Worldwide tourism revenue has increased 173% from 102 to 279 million dollars whereas Turkish tourism revenues increased 1014% from 326 654 000 to 3 639 000 000 dollars, between 1980 and 1992.

Another comparison may be made on trends of arrivals and tourist nights. As international tourism generates over 2 billion nights worldwide, between 1980 and 1992 tourist nights have increased by 37% (1 630 285 000 to 2 226 629 000 nights) compared with a 65% increase for tourist arrivals. In the case of Turkey, tourist nights increased by 16-fold between 1980 and 1992 (1 000 000 to 17 000 000 nights) as against the twofold increase of tourist arrivals.

This may be a good indication that, as more people take trips worldwide they tend to take shorter trips, whereas in the case of Turkey a twofold increase in tourist

arrivals has been accompanied by a 16-fold increase in tourist nights, pulling the length of stay from 1.8 nights to an average of 2.5 nights. Even though it shows only a 0.7% increase, it is an indication that most tourists have short stays in Turkey; the exceptions are the package tours to the coasts of the west and the south where the registered average length of stay by the dominant package tour groups from Germany 7.3 nights, from Switzerland 7.2, from Scandinavian countries 6.1, from the United Kingdom 5.2, and from Austria 8 nights (Ministry of Tourism, 1992b). As a result we may generalize that the growth rate of tourist arrivals, nights of stay, and tourist revenues is more favorable in Turkey compared to worldwide trends (Figure 9.4).

The important issue is to introduce feasible and wise policies to provide for the continuation of sustainable and well-balanced tourism growth until the year 2000 in Turkey.

Therefore, attention should be concentrated on the development of the infrastructure and superstructure of touristic areas and of the role of middle-sized hotels, as

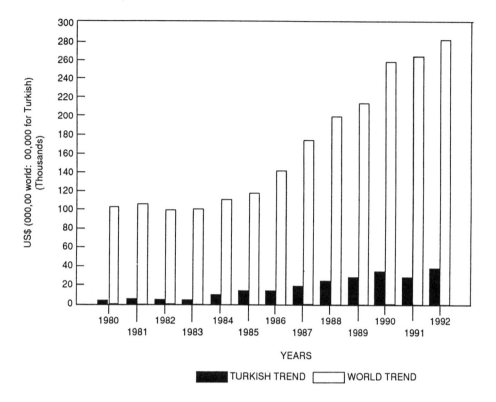

Figure 9.4 *Trends of tourism revenues*

well as second homes, as accommodation potential for the coming years, and the development of the attitude of the managers and the second home-owners towards the tourism phenomenon.

The middle-sized hotels and their impact on tourism development

Turkey has 1498 registered touristic establishments, with 219 940 beds as of 1992. The breakdown of the hotel categories are

—five-star hotels (326) 22%
—four-star hotels (63) 4%
—three-star hotels (425) 29%
—one- and two-star hotels (684) 45%

Their breakdown as to accommodation types and number of beds in each type is shown in Figures 9.5 and 9.6.

Also the map of Turkey shows the distribution of beds and nights spent by region (Figure 9.7). The findings of the research (Korzay, 1993, December, unpublished) on

middle-sized and small hotels up to 100 rooms in Turkey may raise some questions for consideration for the further development plans of tourism in the country.

The objective of the survey has been to:

(a) evaluate the role of the Ministry of Tourism and authorities in development of the hotel sector
(b) analyze the level of concern of the hoteliers for the environment
(c) evaluate the attitudes of the hoteliers to training
(d) evaluate the attitudes of the hoteliers to management styles
(e) evaluate the understanding of hoteliers to the tourism marketing phenomenon

The sample size was 9.3% of the whole population. Hoteliers believe that (39.4%) there has been a moderate tourism development in the last five years. Incentives were considered (39.4%) to be very important in this development process. Marketing support (53.2% 'very important'), public support (53.2% 'important'), risk-

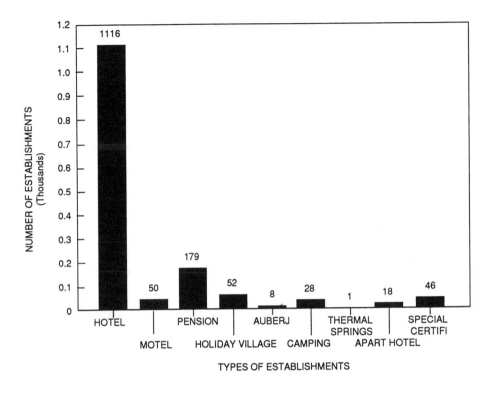

Figure 9.5 *Number of accommodation establishments by types*

sharing (44% 'important'), staff support (39.4% 'important') have been considered as important features of development.

The hoteliers' attitude and rating on various training features were: marketing training (62.4% 'very important'); staff training (45% 'very important'); catering training (44% 'important'); finance training (41.3% 'important'). On the other hand, hoteliers' evaluation of the marketing features were: market improvement (56.9% 'very important'); public relations (50.5% 'very important'); advertising (43.19% 'very important'); service differentiation (51.4% 'important'); segmentation (45% 'important'); new products (41.3% 'important'); positioning (36.7% 'important'); dynamic marketing approach had a higher rating (39.4% 'important') than static marketing approach (34.9% 'important').

The hoteliers' approach to management styles were: M.B.O. (42.2% 'important'); cooperational management (36.7% 'important'); functional management (35.8% 'important'). Risk management, non-risk management, static management, and ad hoc management were of moderate importance, varying from 37.6% to 30.3%.

The attitude of the hoteliers toward environmental issues were all rated as being very sensitive: preservation of environment (78.9%); over-building (67.0%); preservation of global environment (64.2%); preservation of architectural styles (61.5%); overcrowding (61.5%).

The results on environment sensitivity rates were very high. But the present level of environmental measures in respect to environmental codes contradicts the evaluation. Therefore, it can be said that hoteliers are aware of the importance of the sustainable environment for the success of their business but they have not been able to surpass the awareness stage and reach the action phase of sustaining the environment. Therefore this is one of the dominant threats to Turkish tourism development.

In short we may say hoteliers with hotel size of 51–100 rooms, 53% full-time employees, a moderate past profit, and an expectation of moderate profit in the future believe firmly that the development of tourism in Turkey rests on:

—encouragement policies
– subsidies from the public authorities and government

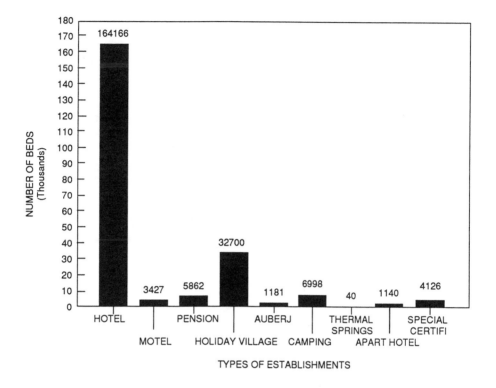

Figure 9.6 *Number of beds by types of establishments*

to the marketing process of the tourism product and services
—priority of training in marketing
—market improvement
—management by objectives

When we shift our attention to the present policies of the Ministry of Tourism we see that the government in Turkey is now aiming at reducing the dependency of the private sector on government subsidies. In this respect the incentives are made more selective in terms of geographical regions, subsectors and investment types (Ateş, 1993:138).

However, on the other hand, the government policy on giving priority to relatively less developed regions and to the finalization of the existing investments, the modernization of the existing facilities and the diversification of the tourism product, together with a high support for marketing and training of personnel and also environmental protection (Ateş, Abdülkadir, WTO 1993, p. 138), complements the expectations and the need hierarchy of the middle-sized hoteliers.

When the results of a similar survey in Spain and Great Britain/Ireland are compared to the Turkish survey on the perception of the hoteliers as to the key management contribution factors to the future developments of the hotel industry, one may notice a slight variation as to the general contributions the hotel development had with different rating in three different nations. Moral support from family members in GB/I has 70% rating of the very important scale 'polar' (along the seven-point attitude scales), whereas in Spain it is 52% and in Turkey it is only 18.3%. The moral support of the family in Turkey is not considered to be a significant contributor to hotel development, whereas encouragement policies are of vital importance. In all three countries, tax exemptions, staff subsidies provided by government agencies, and marketing support provided by tourist boards have high ratings of 50% to 60% as being very important.

While catering training has the highest priority, of 70%, in GB/I, Spain has personnel training as the highest, 83% priority, and Turkey has marketing training (62.49%) as the highest priority. In the case of environmental

96

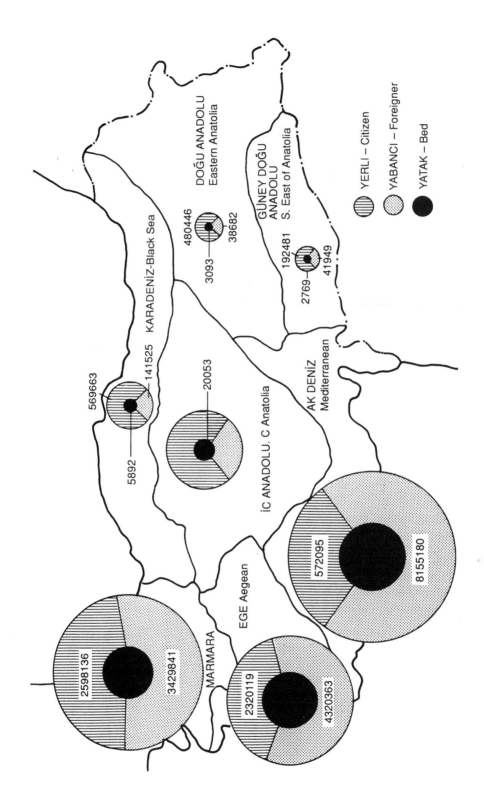

Figure 9.7 *Distribution of beds and nights spent by regions of Turkey*

concerns, GB/I's highest rating (67%) is for the conservation of architectural styles and in the case of Spain 'cultural heritage of the region must be preserved' has the highest rating (79%), whereas, in Turkey, preservation of the natural landscapes has the highest rating (78.9%) and the next very important rating is the avoidance of overcrowding (67%) whereas in the case of Spain its significance is shown with 36% and in GB/I with 41%. The Spanish hoteliers, as well as the Turkish, have a slightly pessimistic view about the development of the hotel industry. This rests on the evaluation of only modest profits in the last three years. But the expectation of the future sales evolution in the next three years is more optimistic.

The common denominator for all is tax exemptions and a system of financial encouragement policies, as well as support in marketing and training of personnel and staff with close collaboration of public authorities and tourist boards.

Impact of second homes as tourist accommodation on the development of Turkish tourism

Since the financial encouragement policies as to the development of physical capacity on the west and south coast of Turkey will be limited to the completion of the ongoing construction and the maintenance of the old ones, the great number of second homes along these coastlines may be utilized as accommodation capacity in the coming years. A few surveys have been undertaken on the issue (Korzay et al., 1989; Korzay, unpublished results, 1993).

As to the study undertaken in 1989, the results pointed out that there is a significant demand for using second homes at Marmara, at Ege and on the Mediterranean coast as accommodation units by tourists who prefer to interact more with local people and are more concerned with an economic vacation in a seaside resort house with its own privacy rather than being one of the mass in a resort village. It has also been perceived that senior citizens feel very comfortable with and prefer to rent a second home at a resort area. Most tourists rent the homes on their own without using the travel agencies as intermediaries.

According to the survey carried out at Çeşme (Aegean coast) most second-home-owners are willing to rent their homes to foreign tourists (Korzay et al., 1989). According to the latest survey at Kuşadası-İzmir (Doğan et al., unpublished, 1993) home-owners are using their homes mostly in July and August (50%) and most of them are not willing to rent (54.9%) their homes to tourists. The ones who are willing to rent their homes prefer to rent them on a daily or weekly basis rather than on a monthly

basis. Tourists prefer to spend their vacation in the months of August, October, June and November. According to the survey, second homes are highly requested by foreign tourists. It is only a very small (5%) group that seek very luxurious facilities and are not interested in the rental of the second homes. The second survey findings of Kuşadası (Doğan et al., unpublished), show that the second home availability dates correspond to home owners preference of renting dates.

Besides increasing the accommodation potential, second homes also provide an opportunity for the development of soft tourism through the sound interaction of the local people with tourists. Therefore, if necessary financial encouragement policies and insurance measures are developed and environment pollution and high-carrying capacity problems are solved, together with cooperative marketing efforts with travel agents, public authorities and local second-home-owners, there will be a high accommodation capacity along the west and south coastline without a high investment in physical capacity in these tourist destination points.

The role of travel agents in tourism development

Travel agents in Turkey are quite high in number (1432 by May 1992), and they provided 20% of the gross tourism revenues in the year 1992. There are no big tour operators, but one may find functionally specialized travel agencies on congresses and conferences, yachting, culture, senior citizens, package, educational and youth tours.

The marketing function of Turkish tourism is mainly undertaken by the travel agencies with the encouragement policies of the Ministry of Tourism and the European-based tour operators that have Turkey as their main destination for their groups.

The collaborative efforts of the travel agents with airline companies and public authorities had a positive impact on the development of the tourism marketing. On the other hand, the limited adaptation of high technology in communications, data development and dissemination of the information are the main hindrances to travel agents in tourism marketing of Turkey. Also too many small Turkish airline companies make it difficult to compete in the international air-travel market with regard to pricing policies, marketing and service quality.

When the global growth trends of professional, profitable, large travel corporations and their sustainability in the global market is considered, the unfavorable standing of Turkish travel agents becomes clear. For the sustainable growth of Turkish travel agencies there is a need to merge and form large tour operators and travel cooperations in order to compete profitably in a field structured by the professionalism and high technology communications systems that lie behind successful customer service.

The limitations and barriers that Turkish tourism needs to overcome for further development

A. The main tourism development limitations in Turkey are:

1. Limited adaptation of high-quality service and communications technology.
2. The negative image of Turkey created by economic migrant workers and the media in continental Europe and Great Britain and Ireland.
3. Insufficient launching and image building of Turkish tourism in North America and in the southwest Pacific, as well as Japan.
4. Poor segmentation of the global market in defining the need hierarchy of the segments and developing marketing strategies and tactics that would be compatible with each segment.
5. Limited diversification of services and the tourism product.
6. Terrorism and high inflation rates.
7. Limited high-quality service orientation for transportation modes and accommodation facilities.
8. Limited marketability of second homes as a tourist accommodation capacity.
9. Awareness of environment concerns has not been complemented by the necessary legislation and action-oriented projects.
10. The sudden increase in the number of tourism education institutions has not been complemented by global hospitality and travel education quality and high technology use in the development of the education systems.
11. As Turkey's share in the tourism market in Europe increases she should not overlook the fact that Europe's share in the global market will be declining as the southwest Pacific will be taking a greater share in the years to come.
12. Quality and time management in developing the tourism product is not satisfactory.
13. Education/training of the personnel and staff is limited.
14. Certification that is compatible with international standards is still at the debating stage.

B. Positive contributors to the development of Turkish tourism:

1. New touristic facilities along the coastline and big five-star hotels in the main cities equipped with latest technology and with necessary measures planned for sustainable environmental concerns.
2. Marketable cultural destinations in a sustainable environment.
3. The hospitality of the local people.
4. Trade barriers with most Western countries being abolished.
5. Turkey's becoming part of regional/business co-operations such as EMTA (Eastern Mediterranean Travel Association), EFTA, and the Black Sea Economic Cooperation.
6. Preliminary studies on the development of a tourism database and information dissemination centers have been undertaken.
7. Serious measures are being undertaken in developing a master plan for tourism.

The pros and cons of tourism development in Turkey to some extent counterbalance each other. One may have an optimistic view of Turkish tourism development, when the standing of tourism in Turkey is examined in terms of sustainable environment, preservation of cultural heritage, price advantages, the newness of the establishments, diversified tourist attraction products/destinations and the growth in tourist arrivals, revenues and overnight stays compared with the global trends and growth rates.

Conclusion

In this paper the main global trends in tourism development have been to some extent compared with tourism development features in Turkey. The compatibility of Turkish tourism development with global trends is satisfactory with respect to:

1. Development of information and communications technologies.
2. Greater interest in futurism and high technology concepts.
3. Significant development of congress and conference/convention tourism.
4. Aging population and increase in pre-health-care treatment programs.
5. Appreciation of and concern with the preservation of historic areas, traditional culture and the cultural environment.
6. The changes in political structure of the former Soviet Union and central European countries.
7. Unstable existence of peace.
8. Growth of second homes as a tourism accommodation potential have been discussed.

9. Perception of key management contribution factors to the future development of the hotel industry.
10. Globalization of trade and business community.

Based on a survey on secondary sources with some supportive empirical studies it can be concluded that the problem areas in Turkish tourism development are:

1. Image building.
2. Service/product launching as to different market segment needs further in-depth market research.
3. Horizontal and vertical collaboration of travel/hospitality and other service companies need to be researched as to their merging feasibility.
4. The ways and means of emphasizing the cultural heritage of Turkey in a marketable product mix have not been diligently manipulated yet.
5. No development of comprehensive brochures by the joint efforts of airlines, travel operators, travel agencies, hoteliers and national tourist boards.
6. Turkey's share in interregional tourism developments have not yet been clearly defined.
7. Measures to overcome or to localize terrorism are still not very well known publicly.
8. The reasons for limited conference business within the region needs to be analyzed and measures to overcome this need to be defined.

In short it may be said that the collaborative work and strenuous efforts of the Ministry of Tourism, investors, owner/managers, travel agents, airlines, public bodies, educational institutions and vocational trade associations and foundations contributed in gaining a momentum for Turkish tourism development in the last ten years.

The whole Turkish tourism development phenomenon needs to be more professionally planned, and put into action; and it needs to be very competitive with the ongoing global trends if the Turkish tourism trade is to survive in the interregional and global tourism markets.

Note

1. Estimated figures are based on WTO (1993) and Turkish Ministry of Tourism (1992b).

References

Armatas, James P. and Lundberg, Donald E. (1983) *The Management of People in Hotels, Restaurants and Clubs*, p. 89.

Ateş, Abdülkadir (1993) Address as the Minister of Tourism: 'Tourism development and the responsibility of the state', WTO, Budapest, pp. 136–139.

Coffman, David and Recknagel, Helen J. (1983) 'Marketing for a full house', Cornell University, School of Hotel Administration, Cayuga Press, Ithaca, NY.

Dalli, Özen (1992) 'Turizmin Türk ekonomisindeki yeri' Tourism Workshop IIIrd İzmir Economic Congress, pp. 237–249.

Dünya ve Türk Turizmine Genel Bakış (1988) TUGEV Durum Değerlendirmesi, Ocak.

Evans, McDonagh, and Moutinho, (1991–1992); McDonagh, Moutinho, Evans, and Titterington, (1992); Den, Ryan, and Moutinho, (1991a,b) 'Perception of key contributing factors to the future development of the hotel industry: a comparative analysis of British/Irish and Spanish samples', World Marketing Congress, Vol. VI, 1993—Proceedings of the sixth Bi-annual International Conference of the Academy of Marketing Science.

Korzay, Meral (1988a) Tourism Education Consultation Meeting, I: TUGEV-Humber College/Boğaziçi University 1988, pp. 56–58.

Korzay, Meral (1988b) 'Turizm'de İstihdam ve Eğitimi Politikası' TUGEV Danışma Toplantısı, 19 March 1988.

Korzay Meral (1988c) 'Üst Düzey Turizm Yönetici Eğitimi' *Ekonomik Bülten*, 20 Nisan 1988.

Korzay, M., Tanur, Gülçin, and Yamak, Sibel, (1989) 'Pansyonculuk ve ikinci Konutların Turizm Amaçlı Kullanımı' (Use of pensions and second homes as tourism accommodation units), Seminar Proceedings on the Share of Pensions and Second Homes in Turkish Tourism, pp. 84–91.

Tourism Workshop (1992) IIIrd İzmir Economic Congress.

Turkish Ministry of Tourism (1992a) *Bulletin of Accommodation Statistics*.

Turkish Ministry of Tourism (1992b) *Bulletin of Tourism Statistics*.

Turkish Ministry of Tourism (1992c) General Directorate on Investments: Department of Research and Evaluation, *Bulletin of Yacht Statistics*.

WTO (1993) *Tourism Trends Worldwide and in Europe 1980–1993* WTO Commission for Europe, pp. 6,7,9,10,11, 21,23.

10 Contemporary efforts to expand the tourist industry in Cuba: the perspective from Britain

S. BLEASDALE AND S. TAPSELL

Introduction

Cuba is the largest island in the Caribbean, stretching some 1200 kilometres from east to west. Physically the island has much to recommend it as a tourist destination. There are an estimated 289 beaches, including some that can claim to be among the best in the world. Cuba has numerous offshore islands, many of which conform to the tourist's ideal Caribbean image with palm-fringed white sand beaches lapped by warm and gentle turquoise seas. In addition Cuba has mountainous areas of great beauty, notably in Pinar del Rio. Rich tropical flora and fauna enhance Cuba's scenic attractions. Cuba also has a rich and diverse cultural and historical heritage developed in the context of piracy, slavery and colonialism, including some of the world's best examples of Spanish colonial cities and having the unique distinction of being the first of Columbus's New World discoveries. More recently (since 1959) Cuba's uniqueness has been reinforced by the imposition of a socialist experiment in development led by one of the world's most charismatic leaders—Fidel Castro.

In common with other Caribbean islands, Cuba's climate features the warm dry winters (average temperature from December to March = 26°C) which are so appealing to international travellers from Europe and North America. Not surprisingly, therefore, Cuba has long been an important destination for international tourists. This paper looks at the historical context of Cuban tourism and at recent attempts to place tourism in the forefront of Cuban development, and presents some thoughts on the difficulties facing this development strategy, with special reference to UK tourism to Cuba.

Cuba has attracted international tourists throughout the twentieth century. However the volume, origins and characteristics of this trade have varied and it is logical to divide tourism development in Cuba into three distinct phases.

Pre-revolutionary tourism (up to 1959)

In the late nineteenth century Varadero on the north coast of Cuba was developed as a tourist centre for middle-class families from the nearby town of Cardenas and quickly became very popular. This development consisted largely of family villas and bathing facilities. During the War of Independence with America (1895–98) many of these families lost their fortunes and after the war, when Cuba became a 'semi-colony' of the USA (1902), the way was open for Americans to purchase property very cheaply in Cuba (Jimenez, 1990). This marked the beginning of Cuba's international tourist trade.

From 1902 to 1959 Cuba was the main Caribbean destination for tourists from the USA. The nature of this tourism was quite different from today's tourism. There were two main centres of tourist activity—Varadero and Havana (Hinch, 1990). Varadero was largely developed during this period by American capital (notably the DuPont family). Early development consisted of boarding houses and family villas. Each family would swim in front of its own house and houses were isolated or built in small groups. The resort became well-known for yachting, bathing, carriage rides, music and theatre activities and was characterised by the distinctive, rather ornate clapperboard houses of which only a few remain today.

From 1926, after Du Pont bought a large block of land, the area became more developed and the 1930s and 1940s saw 'development fever' with land being bought cheaply and subdivided for development. During this period many exclusive neighbourhoods were developed (such as Kawama beach and the Surf club) incorporating family mansions and excluding the local population who were forced further south. 1950 saw the opening of the International Hotel as high-class tourist accommodation and in 1956 the Varadero Tourist Centre Authority was set up which was to oversee further development of the resort. By this time Varadero had developed into a sophisticated resort for rich Americans with facilities for gambling, several nightclubs, numerous restaurants and a reputation for Mafia connections.

The second main location for international tourism during this period was Havana, and Havana dominated the island's tourist hotel provision. The 1950s saw a dramatic increase in the building of tourist hotels, mostly financed and owned by foreigners, and a large proportion of these were concentrated in Havana. Like Varadero, Havana also attracted those seeking a sophisticated nightlife (such as was available at the renowned Tropicana cabaret) and was a major gambling centre. In addition Havana attracted a lively literary clientele, through its association with Hemingway. A third tourist centre at Santiago de Cuba was insignificant by comparison (Jimenez, 1990).

In 1957 Cuba recorded some 355 000 international tourists, over one-third of all tourists to the Caribbean at that time (Hall, 1992). These were largely the rich and famous, as the era of mass tourism had not yet arrived, and principally from the USA (Hall, 1992; Hinch, 1990).

Revolutionary tourism (1959–1987)

In February 1959 the People's Department of Beaches was established bringing to an end the era of private beach ownership and in March 1959 Law number 270 established the right of all Cuban nationals to enjoy all beaches (Jimenez, 1990). These changes set the scene for many of Cuba's tourist activities in the 1960s. In addition Cuba was outlawed as a travel destination for citizens of the USA thus eliminating over 80% of Cuba's foreign tourist market at a stroke. Socialist ideals heavily influenced tourist activity throughout the 1960s. The Cuban state recognised the right of everyone to enjoy leisure and so the main emphasis in the 1960s was on domestic tourism and a large number of camp-sites and other similar types of accommodation were developed.

The people of Cuba were encouraged to take part in tourism with educational and political aims so that social and group tourism was a feature of this period. Because of constraints on public and private transport this led to a much wider geographical dispersal of tourist facilities including some new resorts, e.g. Isla de la Juventud. Many of the more sophisticated facilities of the earlier period were abandoned or fell into disrepair, while some survived and became part of the domestic tourist industry. Foreign ownership and investment disappeared almost overnight.

International tourism fell away sharply (Hinch quotes 3–5000 foreign visitors in the early 1960s). Cuba looked to those nations who were politically sympathetic for visitors and a significant number of tourists came from the USSR (some for 'health' tourism) Czechoslovakia and East Germany, often in the context of cultural exchanges. Visitors from other countries were largely restricted to group tours organised by institutions such as trades unions, church groups, intellectual groups or political associations. Such 'political' tourism serves a number of purposes. For the host nation, political tours provide a

good opportunity to demonstrate the benefits of a particular political regime—a task made easier by the widespread practice in socialist countries (and adopted by Cuba) of strictly limiting the movements of such group tours and exercising strict control over sites visited, accommodation, transport and guides. Opportunities to mix freely with members of the public were reduced by putting tourist facilities off-limits to ordinary Cubans.

In many ways these tours resemble the 'Friendship' tours which used to characterise international tourism to the USSR and China. For the visitor tours will usually reinforce pre-existing sympathies, though clearly the impression of Cuba given by such visits is highly distorted (Hollander, 1986). Some small independent UK tour operators who were politically sympathetic to the Cuban regime began to organise tours to Cuba.

From the mid-1970s Cuba began, for economic reasons, to slowly rebuild a more broadly based international tourist industry, after setting up the National Institute of Tourism (Intur). Initial success was based on marketing winter package tours in Canada and then boosted by a relaxation of the ban on USA citizens travelling to Cuba during the Carter presidency.

Tourism since 1987

In 1987 tourism development was formally elevated to the top of the list of Cuba's economic priorities and dramatic increases in the targets set for the tourist sector were introduced (e.g. to reach 500 000 tourists by 1992, to increase bed spaces in Varadero to 35 000 by 1995, both objectives quoted by Intur). A major problem facing Cuba in trying to achieve these targets has been lack of capital. Many of the inputs required to expand Cuba's tourist facilities must be imported and this requires hard currency. In order to overcome this problem the Cuban government has introduced legislation and other mechanisms to generate external financing. The Cubanacan organisation was set up to facilitate joint ventures and other tourist-based ventures.

Changes in the constitution in 1982 made joint ventures with overseas corporations possible, allowing overseas companies to hold a 49% share in a Cuban venture and some repatriation of profits. Holdings of up to 100% are now allowed if the venture is considered sufficiently attractive. New incentives are being offered such as repatriation of profits and extensive tax holidays. Naturally this reduces the level of financial benefits to Cuba. Since 1987 many such ventures have been initiated through Cubanacan, principally to assist in the construction of additional hotel and resort capacity. Cuba has entered into agreements with a wide range of partners

Table 10.1 *Origin of international arrivals to Cuba*

Country of residence	1979	%	1984	%	1989	%
North America	33 794	44.73	39 959	19.34	79 623	24.40
Canada	25 355	33.56	23 772	11.51	66 724	20.44
USA	8 439	11.17	16 187	7.84	12 908	3.95
Latin America	8 243	10.91	47 929	23.20	73 483	22.58
Mexico	5 440	7.20	25 823	12.50	31 331	9.60
Venezuela	1 849	2.45	3 240	1.57	6 649	2.03
Europe	26 211	34.69	99 886	48.35	161 443	49.47
Czechoslovakia	4 972	6.58	4 675	2.26	4 647	1.42
GDR	1 521	2.01	6 013	2.91	11 655	3.57
FDR	800	1.06	17 570	8.51	45 564	13.96
Spain	1 919	2.54	22 278	10.78	36 037	11.04
USSR	11 012	14.58	21 928	10.62	16 269	4.98
Total	75 547	100.00	206 575	100.00	326 301	100.00

%, of market share.
Sources: World Tourism Organisation, *Yearbooks of Tourism Statistics*, 1981, 1985, 1992.
N.B. There is no direct comparison between 1979 and years after 1983 as changes were made in the collection of Cuban statistics.

but Spain and Mexico dominate. In addition the Government has also set up organisations such as Cubatur, Transtur and Havanauto to ensure the provision of improved services for tourists (Intur promotional material, 1992).

Problems remain with flights, especially with Europe, but these and other problems are gradually being overcome. Staffing problems are being overcome through the development of hotel training schools and tourism employment is now providing an increasing number of high-status jobs for Cuba's highly educated and multilingual graduate population (personal communication, Cuban tour guide, 1992). Considerable success has been achieved in a short time, particularly in increasing the hotel capacity of Varadero, Cayo Largo and other resorts and the government has also been investing in infrastructure to support tourism, as in the new international airport at Varadero. Tourist numbers have risen steadily and some diversification of the source areas has been achieved (World Tourist Organisation, 1981–1992).

Although Canada still dominates overseas arrivals, significant increases have been achieved in the number of travellers from Europe, especially Spain and West Germany, and from Central and Latin America, particularly Mexico (see Table 10.1). Clearly a major factor in the future will be Cuba's ability to compete in what is now a much more developed and sophisticated market for international tourism. Since 1959 tourism has entered the era of mass tourism and other islands in the Caribbean have established themselves in the marketplace. Entering the marketplace relatively late, Cuba will face considerable problems. However, Cuba is in a position to learn from the experiences of other major tourism destinations and should be able to avoid some of the problems and pitfalls (such as overdevelopment, cultural degradation, environmental damage) that other countries have suffered. However, the urgent need for hard currency now is forcing a more hurried short-term view.

Economic and political context of current tourism development

Before discussing the results of our research, it is important that the economic and political context within which current tourist development in Cuba is taking place is established. Until *perestroika*, and then the collapse of the Soviet Union, the Cuban economy was closely tied to that of Eastern Europe. Eastern bloc trading accounted for 80% of Cuba's imports and exports. Cuban sugar was purchased by the USSR at a higher price than that on the world market and in return the USSR supplied Cuba with essentials such as oil, which it was allowed to purchase more cheaply.

Cuba's pursuit of international tourism can be seen as a response to these changing world conditions over the last few years. The first main consequence of the economic reforms in the USSR to hit Cuba was the imposition of new rules for trade agreements; all exchange was to be in hard convertible currency. In addition, shortfalls in oil deliveries have added to the worsening economic situation, which further deteriorated in 1991 with tougher new trade terms that linked prices more closely to world market prices. Deliveries of many other Soviet goods have also been erratic since 1990, including grain and construction materials (Cross, 1992).

The chronic shortage of oil is probably the most serious problem facing the Cuban economy, causing the greatest slump in output. Public transport has been cut to a minimum and petrol for private use is virtually non-existent. Agriculture has been badly hit, without fuel for tractors or the transportation of produce. Less oil means less sugar and less sugar means less oil. Cuba has had to suspend much of its export shipments of sugar to international buyers, meaning that hundreds of millions of dollars' worth of hard currency earnings will be forfeit.

The lack of agricultural and other production has also led to domestic food shortages and to the existing rationing of basic foodstuffs and goods being extended to many other items. Economic problems were further complicated by a bad storm that struck the island in early 1993, causing more than one billion dollars' worth of damage, destroying homes and devastating crops, and also by unexpected rainfall that destroyed the last of the sugar harvest.

As a result of the economic hardships the Revolution is said to be in 'a special period'. Prospects for raising or maintaining food output have further been put in jeopardy by a lack of the means with which to pay for imports such as animal foodstuffs and wheat. In addition, the continued operation of many of Cuba's Soviet-designed industries depends on spare parts only the CIS countries can provide. Moreover, Soviet aid to Cuba has also been considerably reduced, further exacerbating the crisis (Cross, 1992).

The Cuban government has begun a new development strategy based on expanding as rapidly as possible three sectors seen to hold out the best prospects for foreign currency earnings (Cross, 1992). One of these sectors is the food programme, which seeks significantly higher agricultural productivity through the further application of science. However, it is hard to see how the food programme can succeed with the current chronic fuel shortages. The second sector is that of biotechnology and pharmaceuticals. Cuban expectations for this sector were based on exports worth 300 million roubles to the USSR in 1990. The final, and arguably the most important, sector to be developed is tourism. With the formerly tarnished image of the sector now apparently cleansed, exploitation of the sea, sand, sun and 'carnival' is expected to reap rich rewards (Cross, 1992). The role of tourism in contemporary Cuba is therefore central and

could be seen to be critical to the survival of the present Cuban state.

The Cuban model of tourism development

How does tourism development in Cuba compare with other areas? More specifically how does Cuban tourism compare with other third world countries and other islands, particularly other Caribbean islands? How does it compare with other socialist states? How has the Cuban approach to tourist development changed over time?

The answer to these questions can greatly assist in assessing the level of success that Cuban tourism can hope to achieve. It can also assist in predicting the sort of problems that might arise. A review of tourism research reveals a number of generalisations which might be expected to have relevance to a study of Cuba.

(1) Tourism in third world countries is often characterised by a high level of dependency on external factors, notably markets, capital and human resources. The role of multinational corporations in creating this dependency is emphasised (Pearce, 1987; Britton, 1982). Cuba is no exception—tourist growth is increasingly dependent upon external financing through joint ventures and upon Cuba's ability to develop an overseas market.

(2) Tourism in many third world countries is 'enclavic' in nature. In essence this means that tourists visiting third world countries are often confined to isolated enclaves separated from most of the local population. This tendency is especially noticeable in island resorts and areas where 'beach' tourism dominates. This results from a number of factors. Firstly, it is related to the external finance, markets and administration upon which much third world tourism depends, i.e. it is linked to the concept of dependency introduced under point (1). Secondly, it is linked to the increasing tendency of international tourism to be dominated by package tours. Enclavic tourism is perhaps best illustrated by the totally self-contained tourist villages that are now found in many locations. Enclavic tourism is also often characterised by the use of international currency (especially the US dollar) in resorts rather than local currency. Clearly enclavic tourism is closely related to the structure of the international tourist industry and the nature of the tourist market (Britton, 1982; Lea, 1988).

In Cuba recent government plans have focused upon developments in Varadero, thus potentially increasing both the geographical concentration of tourism and reinforcing the enclavic tendencies of the resort. Varadero shows many of the features of enclavic tourism. Tourists arrive at the new airport and no longer pass through Havana. Most only experience other parts of the island through group excursions. Tourists find it hard to spend local currency since all tourist shops, restaurants, car hire and taxis deal only in US dollars. New developments tend to be large self-contained hotels within the confines of which the tourist can spend the entire vacation (e.g. Superclub).

The decision to concentrate expansion in the resort of Varadero is based upon the fact that it offers the best opportunity for becoming a successful competitor in the international resort market, having a wonderful beach and an amenable climate. Concentrating upon one resort in this way makes it easier to separate tourists from the local population and thus reduce the unsettling effects that they might otherwise have on the local Cubans.

The Cubans are seeking to develop tourism in other areas, e.g. Cayo Largo, but these areas also tend to have many of the characteristics of resort enclaves. Elsewhere tourist development is focused on Havana where tourists are less isolated from the Cuban population but will still find many of the characteristics of 'enclavism' (such as the lack of places to spend local currency and dependence upon 'tourist' transport).

(3) Tourism in island locations (including Caribbean islands) shows a marked tendency towards a high degree of geographical concentration, usually coastal and often close to the main urban centre and international airport. These tendencies are particularly marked in small islands where packaged holidays dominate and especially if reinforced by high levels of external financing and management. The implications are that tourism benefits are unlikely to spread far beyond the tourism 'enclave' (Hills and Lundgren, 1977). Varadero illustrates these findings very neatly.

(4) Tourism in the Caribbean is dominated by the North American market, which reinforces the tendency to build enclavic resort areas catering largely for packaged holidays of the sun and sea variety. External financing from Europe, the UK and North America dominates the tourist industry in the Caribbean (Pearce, 1989; Hills and Lundgren, 1977). Cuba is somewhat exceptional in this respect because of its exclusion from tourists and capital from the USA. However, since the mid-1970s, Cuba's tourist industry has been heavily dependent upon the Canadian market. Recent years have shown some signs of increasing diversification towards Europe.

(5) Tourism in socialist states has been characterised by highly centralised planning and state ownership. Until the 1970s these countries concentrated more on domestic tourism and international tourism has been held back by low standards of service, poor infrastructure and excessive bureaucracy. Much tourist activity in these areas has been tightly controlled and packaged affording little

opportunity for the 'wanderlust' tourist. Based on the 'prescriptive' model and set in a Stalinist framework the objectives were to maximise hard currency earnings whilst minimising the possibilities for ideological contamination of the local population (Hall, 1984).

The political tours of Cuba from 1959 had many features of prescriptive tourism and Cuban tourism is still very centralised in terms of planning and direction. The tourist industry in Cuba is struggling with these issues and, whilst facilities have improved markedly, there remain some features of 'Socialist' tourism, e.g. Cuban bureaucrats' desire to control tourist movements and activities. In many ways the 'enclavic' tourist resorts of the free-market forms of tourism lend themselves to retaining some of this control.

We can see, therefore, that many of these research findings have some relevance to Cuba, and as Cuba becomes more closely involved with the mainstream of international tourism it seems likely that some of these features will become more evident. In effect both the free-market international tourism industry and socialist tourism display some of the same features—geographical concentration, enclavic resort development, separation of spending of local and tourist populations, dependency upon the global market which is dominated by North America and Western Europe. It is not therefore surprising to find such features developed or developing in Cuba.

Results of a survey of UK tour operators

Many problems face Cuba in trying to establish a place in international tourism, but we have chosen to start by looking at Cuba through the British travel industry. A preliminary analysis of Cuba–British travel links throws light on many of the problems which the Cuban tourist industry faces and suggests some alternative approaches to tourism. Our survey shows that British travel links with Cuba can be divided into two groups, each of which tends to cater for a different type of tourist:

(1) Tours organised by small, independent tour operators. These can be subdivided into two divisions. The first contains those organisations which have a relatively long history and which are motivated to a large extent by political sympathy with the Cuban revolutionary government. The second contains those companies that are looking to exploit the 'difference' factor that Cuba provides and for them the lack of a well-developed tourist industry is a plus factor.

(2) Large package tour operators offering tours to the developing resort areas. These have only entered the

arena in the last 2–3 years having been strenuously encouraged by Intur (the Cuban tourist authority).

Ten British tour operators were interviewed for the survey, all of which provide tours or travel arrangements for tourists to Cuba. The study involved several in-depth qualitative interviews, interviews by telephone and the completion of qualitative postal questionnaires. Three of the operators came under the first category of companies motivated by political sympathy with Cuba, four were small companies interested in promoting 'alternative' independent or small group travel and three were large well-known package-tour companies. In addition several other operators who do not operate tours to Cuba were approached to establish the motives behind their decisions.

Small independent tour operators

Politically motivated operators

Operators in this group had been sending tourists to Cuba since the early days of the Revolution. Often the tours started as cultural exchanges or as links between trade union groups. Both the companies and the tourists travelling with them tend to be sympathetic to the Cuban regime.

The number of tourists using these smaller operators tends to be small but constant: for one operator between 80 to 100 per year; for another more, at around one thousand. Many tourists take study or political tours where they can visit schools, clinics and factories and meet with members of the Communist Party, or even take part in Work Brigades. A few tourists travel to seek medical treatment while some have other special interests such as bird-watching, steam railways, music or dance. New bicycling tours of Cuba, which one operator has recently begun, have so far been extremely successful with clients, as well as being very practical with the current restrictions on fuel. Few tourists using these operators visit Cuba for the beaches, although the operators will arrange this type of holiday if requested. One study tour, which is run in conjunction with Cubatur and uses Cubana flights and nationally owned hotels, is able to transfer approximately 85% of all their payments directly into the Cuban economy. Another operator not approached for this study, is said to donate 10% of its profits to Cuba to help finance domestic holidays for Cuban people.

Tours for tourists using these operators often tend to be tailor-made for small groups, couples or individual travellers, although some packages are also available.

The cost of a package can therefore vary greatly; depending upon the request of the client, and the operators will arrange accommodation in any part of Cuba and in any category of hotel. Prices can start at around £600 or less for a two-week trip, which includes the air fare and bed and breakfast hotel accommodation. The operators use Cuban guides and transport companies when in Cuba, such as Cubatur for coaches and excursions and Havantur for car hire.

The operators interviewed felt that their holidays were a success from their point of view, with a steady flow of interest and positive feedback from the clients, many of whom often return to Cuba. From the Cuban viewpoint, although being positive as far as cultural exchange is concerned, it was felt that the small numbers of tourists visiting Cuba on this type of holiday only bring a limited amount of foreign exchange and will do little to improve the economic situation. However, it was suggested that small tour operators often open up a tourist destination, promoting the investment in infrastructure which is then able to accommodate the big tour operators. In this sense the small operators can offer the potential for the mass package at a later date.

All three operators felt that there was great potential for tourism development in Cuba, and one reported substantial increases in interest over the last year or two. However, it was acknowledged that red tape and bureaucracy were a problem at times, as were poorly maintained facilities. Another problem was the lack of cheap flights; however, this situation is improving all the time and there are currently several airlines who now operate regular flights to Cuba from the UK.

It was suggested that heritage and ecological tourism had great potential for development. Most of the tourists said that they were interested in the architecture in cities like Havana and Trinidad, others expressed interest in the Cuban landscape. Many also said that they enjoyed meeting the Cuban people, and for some this was the main focus of their trip. Poor food was given as the main aspect tourists disliked about their trips.

It was generally felt that the type of tourist travelling with their companies had different expectations from those on a beach package tour, and most were well aware of the political and economic situation in Cuba, and were aware that the infrastructure and facilities on offer to tourists were not of the same standard found in Europe or even other Caribbean islands. Therefore, the majority of the tourists were very positive about their experiences in Cuba.

From an operator's point of view, dealing with the Cuban authorities was at times difficult and communications can be poor and unreliable. One operator said that she found it difficult to get a response at all, despite speaking Spanish. For another, the fact that they had been operating in Cuba for many years and had built up a number of personal contacts there was very beneficial.

It was thought that Cubans need to do more market research. The issue of the 'image' of Cuba portrayed in the British media was also seen to be a problem and one operator felt that the British still prefer to holiday in former (safer?) British colonies. The image of Cuba as a threatening, military-run, repressive, communist society is still pervasive.

There appeared to be some resentment on the part of one operator over the changes in Cuban policy regarding tourism and a feeling that after years of supporting the regime they were now being ignored and passed over for the larger tour operators with their bigger markets.

Alternative/independent operators

The alternative/independent operators began running tours to Cuba from two to six years ago. Three of the operators specialise in travel to Latin America and for them Cuba was seen as a natural extension to what they already offered. In addition the island was seen as an unusual destination where none of the large tour operators had a footing. It was this last factor which had particularly interested one of the companies. Cubatur in London had also contacted at least one of the companies to promote Cuba and the charter flight they were beginning.

Tourist numbers visiting Cuba had been low—for two of the operators between 250 to 300 per year. These stated that their initial expectations had been exceeded and that they had seen a steady increase in interest, particularly due, they felt, to the events in Eastern Europe over the last few years. Another operator, however, said that they had only sent around 20 tourists to Cuba and that this had not matched up to their expectations of it as a travel destination.

The operators specialised in independent tailor-made tours, similar to those offered by the politically sympathetic companies, including special interest, health and cultural tourism. The prices of the tours again varied greatly, depending upon the itinerary and demands of the tourists. One operator felt that the interest in beach holidays would also increase in the future. For many of the tourists it was the 'unknown' and the 'difference' factor that attracted them to Cuba, and these tourists were said to be more adventurous than those on a normal package deal. A view frequently held by those wanting to visit Cuba was that they wanted to visit the island 'before everything changes'. One company did, however,

feel that some tourists were put off by the image of Cuba as a police state.

From the point of view of two of the operators the tours had been successful, particularly if the tourists were well informed of the limitations before they arrived in Cuba. There was still a degree of reluctance evident in committing themselves to sending too many people to the island because of the political and economic situation there, and concern for the safety of the tourists had to be considered as well as their own expenditure. One operator had mixed feelings about the success of their tours and still found dealing with the Cubans very unpredictable and difficult; there was still the idea in Cuba that tourists should 'fit into the system'.

From the tourists' point of view it was felt that 'different people get different things out of going to Cuba' depending upon their expectations. Most complaints received were concerned with the choice and availability of food, the hotel facilities and service, problems with getting petrol, and bad roads. The aspects of Cuba that tourists had enjoyed most were the architecture and cities, the culture and general ambience, the beaches and the people.

From the Cuban point of view these tours were very successful and helped to create a dollar income. All the operators felt that Cuba held great future potential as a travel destination, offering a cheap holiday in the Caribbean sun. Charter flights would need to be improved, as would the hotels and other facilities. One operator felt that their specialist type of tourism would wane as conditions improved and catered more for the mass market.

The recent political changes by the Cuban authorities were thought to encourage tourism development. One company reported that they had sold more tours in 1993 than in previous years, and that, with the introduction of a new charter from Gatwick in May 1994, they expected more interest in the next couple of years. There was still the feeling, however, that tourism in Cuba was very uncertain. When re-contacted in January 1994, one operator reported a tailing off of interest in the last couple of months of 1993 and another said that their early high expectations were no longer being fulfilled.

Large package tour operators

The Cuban experience offered to tourists by the large package tour operator is very different to that of the smaller operators. The large package tour operators generally appeal to the mass tourist, both at the lower and the higher ends of the market. Enclave tourism is their speciality. Increased consumer and travel trade press coverage, as well as conversations with trade colleagues, had led one operator to believe that Cuba was 'ripe' for tourism two years ago. This company set up an all-inclusive package at the Club Varadero hotel as part of a two-centre holiday with Jamaica. This holiday appeals to the more up-market tourist, as the price of the package starts at around £1600 and rises to over £2000 in the high season. All the ground handling in Cuba is done by Super Club and all meals, drinks, sporting and leisure activities are included in the price of the package.

Reaction from the consumer has been mixed. Tourists reported dissatisfaction with food, hassles from local people and difficulty in getting about the island unless on an organised tour; but they did enjoy the beaches and city sightseeing.

Two of the three operators, when approached in 1992, said that they hoped to expand their Cuba operations in the future if business potential appeared positive. They felt that there would be a future demand by tourists and one envisaged a boom within the next five years. It was felt that, as the infrastructure is developed, more hotels are built and supplies on the island improve, the potential for tourism will also increase. However, when re-contacted in 1993, one said that tourist demand has not matched up to expectations. Less space and information has now been provided on the holiday in the company's 1994 brochure, although there are no plans as yet to withdraw from Cuba.

The other operator, when re-contacted in December 1993, said that it had now pulled out of Cuba completely for 1994 to concentrate on promoting its packages to other Caribbean islands, such as the Dominican Republic. The reasons given for this decision were the feasibility and unreliability of charter flights and low demand from tourists. In 1991 around one thousand tourists travelled to Cuba with this company, which accounted for around 8% of the company's total passengers to the Caribbean.

The poor image of Cuba appears to have contributed to the lack of demand experienced by these operators. One commented that Cuba is still a new resort to many UK tourists and therefore it needs to be marketed rather better to the British public. Cuba was still felt to be an unknown and unreliable area for large-scale package tourism. The current political circumstances were felt to scare the public and prevent them from booking a holiday in Cuba. Positive changes in Cuban government policy towards international tourism could trigger a boom.

At the lower end of the market, another company has recently been heavily promoting its new packages in Cuba. These start at £299 for a two-week trip in the low season to over £600 in the high season. Prices include direct flights from the UK, local transfers and hotel accommodation in Varadero with breakfast only. The company is marketing Cuba as 'the pearl of the Caribbean, a unique island rich in colour and variety and a sun and sea worshipper's paradise.

As with the tours offered by the other large companies, these tours are basically beach packages where tourists are encouraged to 'explore, relax and enjoy' the local facilities. These holidays are therefore primarily based on recreation and leisure with the emphasis on relaxation and escape from the stress of everyday living. Additional cultural and historical day excursions to Havana, Trinidad, Santiago de Cuba and Pinar del Rio are also available. At the time of writing no details were available of the take-up and likely number of tourists this operator would be sending to Cuba in 1994, but follow-up research is planned in this area.

Operators not using Cuba as a destination

Several operators were interviewed who do not organise trips to Cuba. The operations director of one well-known British tour operator that specialises in small-group 'alternative' types of holidays said that there were several reasons why they did not consider Cuba to be suitable as a tourist destination. Firstly, the lack of reasonably priced reliable flights were seen as a problem. Secondly, it was felt that the Cuban government is not 'consumer oriented' and 'commercially minded'. Again it was suggested that the Cubans should be doing market research and encouraging more companies like themselves. He saw the Cubans as unreliable and unresponsive and personally did not have the time to keep visiting Cuba and using the 'personal touch' as some of the smaller operators are able to do. It was also felt that tourism in Cuba is too controlled and that there are too many restrictions placed upon both tour operators and tourists.

In conclusion, the operations director did feel that there will be a demand for travel to Cuba in the future and that he will be happy to send tourists there. Before this can take place, however, the Cubans will need 'to get their act together'.

Conclusions

Many changes are currently under way in Cuba. Cuban citizens can now vote for the first time directly for candidates to the provincial assemblies and the National Assembly. These reforms and other reforms are, according to Cross (1992), inextricably linked to the economic changes affecting Cuba.

Accelerating the drive to obtain desperately needed foreign currency, the Cuban government in July 1993 announced the lifting of tight restrictions on travel to the island for Cuban-American exiles. The exiles will be allowed to carry an unlimited amount of dollars with them, play host to their relatives in tourist hotels and shops, and return as often as they like. In the same month it was also announced that Cubans may legally possess and use hard currency for the first time in three decades (Lopez-Vigil, 1993).

Moreover, Cuba has taken another cautious step towards establishing a mixed economy by allowing limited private enterprise by individuals in a range of some 100 services, trades and crafts, provided that they do not employ other people. Foreign diplomats in Havana say that the 100 trades and services now opened up represent a large step towards allowing private initiative in an economy dominated by the state.

According to the Cuban leadership, economic growth must be maintained, even if social programmes have to be restricted. Priority in the future must be given to sectors of the economy that can generate hard currency income quickly, such as tourism; for example, scarce building materials must therefore be used for hotels rather than hospitals.

Results from our survey indicate a relatively steady supply of tourists via the small tour operators, although these are still uncertain, while the larger operators are finding it difficult to meet their targets because of problems with charter flights, shortages resulting from the economic situation, and resistance from the British public. What this suggests is that in the short term it might be more effective for the Cubans to target the small operators and build on the potential for niche marketing which they provide, whilst at the same time investing some effort in the UK to overcome the image problem which is holding back the growth of the British package tour market.

Of course this does not address the underlying problem of the lack of time available to the Cubans for the rational development of the tourist sector. What is being done in Cuba in the tourist industry is happening so fast that one suspects little thought has been given to a rational long-term plan, and decisions taken now may not be the best for the longer term. One could question the emphasis on substituting dependence from one cash crop, sugar, on to a new one in the form of tourism. However, under the present circumstances the Cubans have few alternatives.

The question remains as to whether Cuba can establish market enclaves rapidly enough to forestall further economic chaos, yet slowly enough to ensure the containment of the politically destabilising influence of the enclaves (Gunn, 1992). Research on tourism in Latin America shows that the Latin American market is divided. Latin American tourists go to Mexico for culture and heritage, and to the Caribbean for sun and sea. Spanish-speaking Cuba could provide both. This suggests a good potential market for tourists from Latin America.

Much depends upon the USA and its stance on the current trade embargo which was tightened with the Torricelli Bill (Cuban Democracy Act, 1992) which also sought to penalise third world countries that carry out trade with Cuba. The Bill, however, provoked strong international protest and, in November 1993, 88 countries voted to support Cuba's UN resolution calling for an end to the economic boycott by the USA.

Despite current economic problems, the future for tourism development in Cuba is full of possibilities and in many respects the island has many advantages over other tourist destinations that it has yet to fully explore. There is great potential for heritage tourism, cultural packages, eco-tourism and naturalist holidays, craft production, health tourism and tourism linked to sport.

Compared with other Caribbean islands, Cuba is larger, more diverse and cheaper. This should help to develop a broadly based tourist sector which would be sustained and less vulnerable to trends in the travel industry. Tourist information does, however, need to be greatly improved, with more up-to-date and accurate guidebooks, maps and leaflets. Information in museums is currently only in Spanish and there appears to be little available on Cuba's National Parks and ecological attractions.

One major advantage for Cuba is the non-seasonality of tourism demand on the island. While the domestic tourist season peaks in August, the international season does so in December. Therefore it should be possible to have a year-round tourist industry which benefits employment and optimises resource use. The hotel occupancy rates in WTO annual figures show very small seasonal variation in Cuba, which further supports this point.

Several areas for future research in Cuba can therefore be identified: the image problem of Cuba in the UK; the potential of alternative tourism strategies, including sustainable tourism, eco-tourism and responsible tourism; explorers versus the mass tourist; and, finally, the environmental social and cultural impacts of tourism.

The Cuban leadership, however, appears optimistic. According to Castro 'we still have an awful lot to learn about tourism . . . [it] will be the leading industry, and since we haven't found those big oil deposits, it is marvellous to have at our disposal these extraordinary deposits of natural resources for tourism' (*Granma Weekly Review*, 27.5.90). In spite of all its economic and political problems, Cuba continues to defy those who had predicted that Castro and the Cuban Communist Party would be out of power by 1993. The role that tourism may play in that change is debatable; will it help to ensure the survival of the current political regime by giving the Cuban economy the boost it so badly needs, or will it turn Cuba full-circle back to the gambling casinos, nightclubs and crime of the pre-revolutionary years?

References

Boniface, B. and Cooper, C. (1987) *The Geography of Travel and Tourism*, Heinemann, London.

Britton, Stephen (1982) 'Political economy of tourism in the third world', *Annals of Tourism Research*, 9:331–358.

Calder, Simon (1990) *Traveller's Survival Kit: Cuba*, Vacation Work, Oxford.

Cochran, Cate (1984) 'Escape from the whorehouse', *New Internationalist*, December, 18–19.

Cross, Peter (1992) 'Soviet perestroika: the Cuban effect', *Third World Quarterly*, 13(1): 143–158.

Dunleavey, M. P. and Penenberg, A. (1993) 'Castro's green gamble', *Green Magazine*, February, 12–17.

Ferrer, Eugenio (1989) *Guide to Cuba*, Gianni Constantino, Italy.

Ferrer, Eugenio (1989) *Guide to Havana*, Gianni, Constantino, Italy.

Granma Weekly Review, 27.5.1990.

Gunn, Gillian (1992) 'Cuba's search for alternatives', *Current History*, February, 59–64.

Hall, Derek R. (1992) 'Tourism development in Cuba', in Harrison, D. (Ed.) *Tourism and the Less Developed Countries*, Bellhaven, London.

Hall, Derek R. (1984) 'Foreign tourism under socialism: the Albanian "Stalinist" model', *Annals of Tourism Research*, 11: 539–555.

Hills, T. L. and Lundgren, J. (1977) 'The impact of tourism in the Caribbean: a methodological study', *Annals of Tourism Research*, 4: 248–267.

Hinch, Thomas (1990) 'Cuban tourism industry', *Tourism Management*, 11(3): 214–226.

Hollander, Paul (1986) 'Political tourism in Cuba and Nicaragua', *Society*, May/June: 28–37.

Jimenez, Antonio (1990) *Guide to Varadero*, Gianni Constantino, Italy.

Lea, John (1988) *Tourism and Development in the Third World*, Routledge, London.

Lopez-Vigil, Maria (1993) 'Is Cuba resisting or retreating?', *Journal of the Jesuit University of Central America, Managua*, September: 23–41.

Molinet, Joaquin (1992) 'Three cheers for a new 5 star', *Prisma*, no. 1, April–May: 13–14.

Pearce, Douglas (1987) *Tourism Today: a Geographical Analysis*, Longman, London.

Pearce, Douglas (1989) *Tourism Development*, Longman, London.

Population Reference Bureau Inc. (1993) *World Population Data Sheet*, Population Concern, London.

Prevost, Gary (1993) 'Communist Cuba's defiance', *The World Today*, August–September, 142–144.

Sol de Cuba (1992) 12(1): 12–13, 25–26.

World Tourist Organisation (1981–1992) *Yearbook of Tourism Statistics*, Vols 34–43.

11 Development theory applied to tourism in Jamaica

K. WOODCOCK AND L. FRANCE

Traditional development theories, it has been suggested (Harrison, 1992:18), could prove a useful framework whereby the processes and patterns of tourism development may be described and explained, especially in the less developed countries. Modernisation theory and underdevelopment theory are applied to the resort of Ocho Rios in Jamaica in order to test their validity within a tourism context. Some of the principles of sustainable development are also examined, an established approach in studies of development whose use in relation to tourism is more recent and more controversial, but increasingly fashionable. A number of socio-economic criteria are used to examine the extent to which tourism accords with the selected theoretical approaches to development. These include: ownership, management, employment characteristics and some of the physical consequences of tourism relating to accommodation and to a range of appropriate services.

It is appropriate that Jamaica should be used as an exemplar to test development theories. The country lies firmly within the less developed world, struggling with a huge debt burden and with an economy dependent upon export commodities largely controlled by multinational companies based in the developed world (Bayer, 1993; Ferguson, 1990). The majority of the population have little control over the pace or direction of the development of Jamaica's economy which has come to rely heavily upon tourism for much-needed income and employment (Bayer, 1993).

However, tourism in Jamaica is not a new phenomenon. Writing in the 1920s, Sir Algernon Aspinall described the increasing popularity of the island as a sunshine destination for the 'leisured classes' (Aspinall, 1930:207). Undoubtedly the Cuban revolution of 1959 that diverted North American holidaymakers to other areas led to the growth of Jamaica's resorts, included Ocho Rios (AA/Baedeker, 1992). By the mid-1960s, a group of hotels in the neighbourhood of Ocho Rios had firmly established the village as a resort, with the nearby Dunn's River Falls already a significant tourist attraction (Graves, 1965). Political unrest in Jamaica during the 1970s,

followed by the 1980 world recession led to a decline in tourism, which began to revive as the 1980s progressed (Bayer, 1993). It was at this time that mass package tourists came to supplement, and then replace, those more elite members of society whose presence on the island had created a fashionable image upon which its popularity with the new type of tourist was established.

It is therefore in the resort of Ocho Rios, by 1991 Jamaica's second-largest stopover visitor destination and the most important cruise venue (Planning Institute of Jamaica, 1991), that the selected development theories will be applied.

Development theories and tourism

According to Harrison (1992:18) development strategies are based on a variety of approaches towards 'modernisation' and 'development'. The issues can be examined across major perspectives of modernisation theory, underdevelopment theory and environmentalism.

Modernisation theory essentially focuses on the process of westernisation within which less developed countries seek to replicate Western development patterns with an evolving industrial sector, a growth of the role of money in the economy and a reduction in traditional family structures (Harrison, 1992:9). Elites and other 'change agents' play a pivotal role in the transfer of ideas, practices, technology and capital from the West and in the breaking down of those aspects of traditional culture believed to block economic growth.

Underdevelopment theory juxtaposes development and underdevelopment, propounding the contention that metropolitan centres exploit peripheries through the medium of unequal exchange (Harrison, 1992:9). The neocolonial role of multinational companies based in the developed world leaves the less developed countries in a dependent position from which there is no easy escape until they de-link from global capitalism.

Although superficially opposed, these theories (summarised in Table 11.1) have much in common, especially in relation to the concept of core and periphery

Table 11.1 *Summary of major theories*

Modernisation theory	Underdevelopment theory	Sustainable approaches
1.1 Tourism is a mode of modernisation enabling LDCs to develop along 'Western' lines.	1.2 Tourism is a new form of imperialism. It leads to the development of DCs at the expense of LDCs. Overdependence on tourism.	1.3 A useful economic activity that benefits hosts and guests. Tourism is not a panacea and should be part of a balanced economy.
2.1 Capital, expertise, technology and ideas originate outside LDCs where they are brought via MNCs. Tourism controlled by MNCs.	2.2 MNCs are main change agents of neocolonialism. MNC control of tourism is a concern.	2.3 Sensitive to needs and aspirations of host population. Local participation in decision-making. Local employment at all levels. Tourism controlled by host community.
3.1 Modernity and tradition seen as antithetical. Culture blocks development. If barriers are removed or minimised, growth can occur.	3.2 Disregard of culture and tradition is a loss to the host community.	3.3 Socially and environmentally considerate. It draws appeal from the total character of the host destination—scenery, history and culture.
4.1 Tourism is large-scale, mass package form for foreigners. Market-led.	4.2 Tourists distinct from host population. Mass tourism. Competition among LDCs.	4.3 Scale and pace of tourism development respect character of the destination. Asset-led tourism. Balance between foreign and domestic tourism sought.
5.1 Minorities within destination country seen as change agents —as modernising elite.	5.2 Existence of minority elites seen as a barrier to development for population as a whole.	5.3 Elitism is not favoured.
6.1 Tourism seen as a generator of employment, hence a benefit.	6.2 Tourism is seen as an exploiter of local labour.	6.3 Tourism seeks to bring varied, attractive and well-paid jobs.
		7.3 Recognition that the physical and cultural environment have an intrinsic value that outweighs their value as a tourism asset: enjoyment by future generations should not be prejudiced by short-term considerations.

and to the role of multinational companies and other elites in the developed process. They are enlarged by the more recent evolution of environmentalism whereby change is directed towards a more idealised and greener future.

Tourism has often been perceived by less developed countries as a viable route towards modernisation and development. Nevertheless, within the Caribbean there are mixed views about whether this sector can alleviate the region's economic problems and be developed and controlled as part of a comprehensive programme that will produce benefits which outweigh its negative socio-cultural effects (Gayle and Goodrich, 1993:168). Such attitudes tend to focus upon large-scale, capital-intensive, foreign-owned mass tourism as the principal option. Increasingly, however, a greater variety of approaches to tourism are becoming recognised, each of which has its own characteristics (Table 11.2) and offers a variety of possibilities appropriate to a range of economic and political priorities. There is considerable debate as to whether these are simply stages along a continuum from underdevelopment to development, or whether they are realistic sustainable options (Owen, 1991; Wheeller, 1991, 1992). Caribbean countries have themselves joined this debate through the annual series of ecotourism conferences organised by the Caribbean Tourism Organisation. These were initiated in 1991 in an endeavour to maximise benefits and minimise costs by seeking an alternative approach that would maintain the image of a thriving and desirable tourism destination. Nevertheless, the implications of the various approaches identified in Table 11.2 are clearly different. If the planning process can encourage those which are low-impact yet high-return then tourism may become more widely accepted as a positive development route by those groups and individuals who currently take an equivocal attitude towards this process within the context of the

Table 11.2 *Alternative types of tourism*

1. Large-scale enterprises owned and controlled by state agencies. Conventional approach. Often relevant on imported goods and capital. Provide international-standard facilities. *In theory* state control ensures profits are retained locally.
2. Large-scale enterprises owned and controlled by national private capital. Conventional approach. Profits further private wealth. Public gains indirectly from taxation and employment.
3. Medium-scale enterprises controlled by local companies and individuals. Small version of (2).
4. Small- and medium-scale enterprises organised as cooperatives at community level. Used as a way of increasing and diversifying community income and employment. Materials, labour and management supplied on a collective basis. Profits may be distributed to individuals or held as community funds. Facilities typically spartan.
5. Small-scale enterprises organised as individual or family concerns. Limited capital and expertise available so facilities tend to be of a low standard. On margins of marketing networks of conventional tourism.
6. Small-scale enterprises organised by individuals and families as a supplement to commodity production. Facilities provided by those in transition from a non-capitalist to a partially capitalist economy. Facilities rudimentary and reflect the resources available.

Source: after Britton (1987).

many less developed countries that have limited resources and few development options in a democratic state in which the local population quite naturally demands the higher material standards of wealthier nations within the world economic system.

The context for tourism in Jamaica

Many of Jamaica's economic problems are a result of the open, dependent and therefore vulnerable nature of that country's economy (Bayer, 1993).

The combination of structural inertia, imposed during the colonial period, and rising consumer expectations has made trade a crucial activity. Balance of payments constraints are one of the more important limitations to the achievement of development goals.

While the volume of exports grew in the early 1990s, their value fell slightly, due mainly to a decline in the international price for aluminium, a severe blow since bauxite is a major export earner for Jamaica. The lack of local processing of bauxite in an industry dominated by foreign-owned companies has clearly left Jamaica exposed to the politics and economic uncertainties of world commodity markets (Bayer, 1993).

By 1992 tourism had replaced bauxite as the largest foreign-exchange earner, making a crucial contribution to the economy (Bayer, 1993; Caribbean Tourism Organisation, 1993). While there is concern that the economy should not be overdependent on tourism, if careful planning restricts development the diversification of the national economic base is a valuable consideration (Table 11.1: 1.2, 1.3).

Indeed, tourism in Jamaica offers ways to meet economic development goals (Table 11.1: 1.1, 1.3) since it meets a number of primary needs: the generation of foreign exchange, diversification of the economic base and of exports, and the expansion of employment.

Further advantages may include attracting overseas investment and the provision of a mechanism whereby increased numbers of local people can participate in the monetary economy.

However, the role of tourism has been questioned. There are those who see the tourist as simply another 'cash crop' that has been substituted for sugar—the traditional staple commodity of colonial times (O'Grady, 1981). Structural problems common to these two 'cash crops' include: dependence on a developed world market; high levels of capital export; and a tendency to exploit local labour (Table 11.1: 1.2) (Ferguson, 1990).

Case study of Ocho Rios

Situated on the north coast of Jamaica, Ocho Rios was originally a small fishing village. Its development as a tourist resort began with the opening of the Tower Isle Hotel in 1948, although the nearby Dunn's River Falls was already a great attraction.

Spontaneous growth characterised the resort until 1964 when a development plan was ordered. In 1967 the St. Ann Development Company, a wholly-owned subsidiary of the government's Urban Development Corporation, was formed to undertake the redevelopment of Ocho Rios Bay and the surrounding areas ('Ocho Rios Development Plan', 1982).

As elite tourism was superseded by mass package forms, the original fishing village has been totally replaced by an artificial beach overlooked by hotel tower blocks. There are modern shopping plazas intended to serve the needs of both tourists and residents, as well as housing areas for those who work in the town. With a resident population of 110 000, Ocho Rios is the island's second largest stopover destination, accounting for 28.7% or 242 111 visitors, and the busiest port with 286 calls bringing 352 461 passengers (Planning Institute of Jamaica, 1991).

Table 11.3 *Affiliation between taxi services and accommodation establishments in Ocho Rios*

	No affiliation	Hotels' own transport	Private owners	Local tour companies	Total
Number of establishments	7	3	2	11	23
Percentage of establishments	30	13	9	48	100

Source: Survey, August 1992.

Tourism employment: significance and structure

The difficulties of distinguishing between direct, indirect and induced employment in an economic activity that transcends sectoral boundaries compounds the inaccuracy of estimates. Figures from the World Tourism Organisation in 1988 suggest that at that time direct and indirect tourism employment accounted for 37% of the total labour force in Jamaica (Planning Institute of Jamaica, 1990). By 1991 direct employment alone was gauged to be 38% of total employment (Planning Institute of Jamaica, 1991). This confirms an overall increase and clearly demonstrates the role of tourism as a generator of employment (Table 11.1: 6.1) and the dependence of the economy on this activity (Table 11.1: 1.2).

During 1991 22 788 were employed directly in tourism, an increase of 10.8% over the previous year (Planning Institute of Jamaica, 1991). In the tourism accommodation sector, Ocho Rios led the other Jamaican resorts in terms of direct employment. Survey work in 1992 suggested that of the 8130 people in this category, 95% were Jamaican with only a very small proportion coming from other Caribbean Islands (3%) or from the United States (2%). However, the pattern of origin of managers in relation to tourist rooms was rather different. While the majority were still Jamaican, they comprised a much smaller proportion of the total (60%), while those from Europe (35%) and North America (5%) assumed greater significance. In part this situation is a result of the dominance of the management contract by multinational companies, but there are also grounds for suggesting that barriers such as inculcated attitudes and education (*Daily Gleaner*, 17/8/92) have, so far, prevented a greater level of involvement by Jamaicans and especially by black Jamaicans. This accords with the underdevelopment theory (Table 11.1: 5.2) and highlights the need for a greater emphasis on management skills training to enable a larger number of Jamaicans to obtain more skilled and therefore higher-paid jobs. Typically critics of tourism, especially in the less developed countries, focus upon this problem and assert that while the industry may create employment (Table 11.1: 6.1), the jobs it produces are principally of an inferior nature

(Table 11.1: 6.2) (Mathieson and Wall, 1982; Lea, 1988; Pearce, 1989). Development, it is argued, does not stem from a nation of waiters, bellhops and chambermaids (Harrison, 1992).

The sale of relaxation and luxury through tourism in former colonies like Jamaica can replicate the old colonial problems of servitude, with a perpetuation of master/servant relationships. The unequal power inherent in such a situation is highlighted by the racial and colour differences between the two groups, with poor, local black workers inevitably resenting the luxurious lifestyles of wealthy, largely white, foreign visitors (Ferguson, 1990). So tourism can reproduce an oppressive history in microcosm. Mass tourism, exemplified by package tours, and often spatially concentrated into enclaves, reinforces this social separation and clearly circumscribes the possibility of realistic cultural interaction (Taylor, 1975) to the extent that voyeurism can lead to local conflicts (Table 11.1: 3.2) (Ferguson, 1990).

Other forms of tourism employment in Ocho Rios are typified by taxi services. The relationship between accommodation establishments and taxi provision is shown in Table 11.3. It is evident that a considerable proportion of establishments have links with local tour companies, especially JUTA Taxis. A small number of properties are affiliated to private taxi owners, while other establishments either have no particular links or largely use their own transport. Not unexpectedly it is the large, all-inclusive establishments (Sandals, Ciboney and Couples) that utilise their own transport facilities. Although overall employment is generated (Table 11.1: 6.1, 6.3), it does appear to benefit the larger, more exclusively tourism-oriented companies rather than private individuals plying for hire more generally. There also appears to be a danger of a reduction in such employment, especially for individuals, as the growing number of all-inclusive hotels provide their own transport (Table 11.1: 6.2).

Employment in the informal sector tends to be unofficial and often 'makeshift'. It varies in time and space and is extremely difficult to research and quantify. Such employment frequently occurs in handicraft production, food vending and beach trading. It has been

Table 11.4 *Accommodation types in Ocho Rios*

Accommodation type	Number of establishments	%	Number of rooms	%
Luxury hotels (100 rooms+)	10	48	2283	83
Luxury hotels (<100 rooms)	5	18	281	10
Budget hotels	4	17	107	4
Guest houses	3	13	60	2
Hostels and campsites	1	4	26	1
Total	23	100	2757	100

Source: Survey, August 1992.

suggested (MacKay, 1987) that many informal sector activities are 'non-jobs' in that they fail to provide a reasonable means of subsistence but are the survival strategies of the very poor (Table 11.1: 6.2). Surveys in 1992 have shown that the informal sector vendors and the market-women or higglers in Ocho Rios and the surrounding area are finding it increasingly difficult to operate as the facilities supporting mass tourism become more closely regulated and formalised. Many are unable to afford the rent and lighting for stalls in the specially constructed shopping malls. The removal of their traditional, randomly sited street stalls has been a severe blow. Similarly, the privatisation of beaches by accommodation establishments has provided further difficulties.

Accommodation: structure and ownership

Tourist accommodation is the largest source of tourism revenue in Ocho Rios where a mixture of types of provision is clearly evident. Accommodation guides (Tourist Information Office, 1992) and survey work suggest that a categorisation of accommodation types based on a combination of quality and size is the most practical. Hence a division into: luxury hotels with over 100 rooms; luxury hotels with less than 100 rooms; budget hotels; guest houses; hostels and campsites has been adopted (Table 11.4).

As Table 11.4 shows, it is the large luxury hotels with over 100 rooms that predominate, with nearly 50% of establishments and 85% of the total rooms available in the resort. It is within this sub-sector that, not surprisingly, foreign tourists are the most dominant— generally they comprise 90%, although overall within Ocho Rios approximately 82% of visitors were from overseas. This confirms the position of large-scale mass package tourism oriented towards an overseas market and providing international-standard facilities (Table 11.1: 4.1). Essentially this structure has remained unchanged since the nineteenth century when wealthy white visitors

from Europe and North America dictated the pattern of accommodation provision. The industry has adapted to the less affluent package tourists, but they remain racially, economically and spatially distinct from the majority of the Jamaican population (Table 11.1: 4.2).

Although there is comparatively little foreign ownership (Table 11.5) within the accommodation sector in Ocho Rios, there is considerable foreign influence on the extent and pattern of hotel development. The number of tourist rooms are linked in some way to multinational companies totalling 53%. The relationship between these rooms and the multinationalists is shown in Table 11.6. Superficially such a situation fails to accord with conventional beliefs that multinational firms bring capital and expertise to developing countries (Lea, 1988; Mathieson and Wall, 1982; Pearce, 1989). The experience in Ocho Rios is that they have undertaken relatively little direct capital investment or ownership. Instead, involvement has been confined to management contracts (61%) and franchises (17%), making use of expertise rather than capital in an increasingly competitive business environment within a country with a reputation for political instability and social unrest (Ferguson, 1990). However, through management contracts multinational companies are able to exert considerable control in countries such as Jamaica. They operate at a lower cost than indigenous firms, as a result of their size, diversity and breadth of experience, and have built up a set of intangible assets, logistical skills and managerial expertise (Poon, 1988). As change agents they have been instrumental in the growth of mass,

Table 11.5 *Ownership of tourist rooms in Ocho Rios*

Ownership	Number of tourist rooms	%
Jamaican	2298	84
North American	385	13
European	74	3
Total	2757	100

Source: Survey, August 1992.

Table 11.6 *Relationship between multinational companies and tourist rooms in Ocho Rios*

Type of MNC involvement	Number of tourist rooms	%
Ownership	184	12
Part ownership	139	10
Management contracts	886	61
Franchises	252	17
Total	1461	100

Source: Survey, August 1992.

standard tourism in Jamaica, but their presence may well have hindered the entry and subsequent likely survival of small indigenous enterprises and led to accusations of dependency and a lack of autonomy in the early development process.

The involvement of multinational companies in Ocho Rios demonstrates some of the basic principles of modernisation theory through the diffusion of ideas, practices and expertise (Table 11.1: 2.1) via management contracts and franchises, and the spread of mass standard international tourism (Table 11.1: 4.1).

Concern as a result of leakages due to foreign involvement (Table 11.1: 2.2) relates partly to multinational involvement in management, but also to the employment of foreigners in key positions, to government provision of infrastructure and of incentives for overseas investment, together with imported materials and food. This last is a result of tourist preferences for high quality and familiar accommodation, food and transport, aggravated by a poorly developed domestic productive structure that has failed to provide a reliable supply of goods of an acceptable quality. Foreign exchange leakages associated with hotel food purchases in Jamaica were estimated at 54.2% in 1988 (Wyer et al., 1988) and there is no reason to suspect that this figure has greatly changed since that time. The inability of Jamaican agriculture to supply hotels with the majority of their food requirements (Belisle, 1984) is simply part of a larger problem.

Although tourist accommodation in Jamaica is largely Jamaican-owned, surveys indicate that such ownership tends to be confined to white or Asian ethnic minorities rather than to the black majority. Typically, the highly successful all-inclusive organisation, Sandals Resorts, is owned and managed by a Syrian Jamaican (Barker, 1992, personal communication). This ownership pattern appears to be a direct outcome of the colonial past, when entrepreneurial activity was inhibited for those of African descent and was a deliberate policy measure intended to focus power in the hands of the minority ruling classes (Ferguson, 1990). Indeed, old attitudes that created the so-called 'slave psyche' have persisted (*Daily Gleaner*, 17/8/92), especially amongst the less-educated members of the black community, and have created mental barriers that are not easily overcome. Perhaps it is these barriers to black ownership and investment that underlie the relatively low levels of black involvement in the tourism accommodation sector, highlighting the underdevelopment of a specific racial group within a less developed economy and society (Table 11.1: 1.2). However, the perpetuation of old colonial systems is being broken down and improved education and a deeper understanding of the route to power on the part of the black majority has widened their influence and facilitated progress towards a more equitable distribution of wealth and power (Table 11.1: 5.3).

Other service sector ownership patterns

Similar patterns of ethnic ownership to those found in accommodation are apparent in the catering and retail sectors. This is clearly illustrated in terms of supermarkets, where two of the three establishments in Ocho Rios are owned by Chinese Jamaicans. Much of the retail trade is focused into purpose-built centres that combine shops offering high-quality, expensive souvenirs with craft stalls stocking a range of local handicrafts from wooden carvings and straw goods to paintings, alongside food vendors selling traditional jerk pork, rice and peas, and curried goat. While the high-class shops are owned and operated by ethnic minority groups, the majority of the stalls belong to black Jamaicans. In the past these stalls have been located at random along the streets. Now restrictive by-laws have made this more difficult. Instead vendors are concentrated into a purpose-built arcade constructed in 1991 on the site of the old food market on Main Street. This development was financed by USAID (US$600 000), the Local Development Programme (US$250 000), the Tourism Action Plan (US$25 000) and the vendors themselves (US$25 000). It is the vendors who are responsible for the maintenance of the arcade which they rent from St. Ann Parish Council, the site owners (*Jampress*, 26/5/91).

Infrastructure: costs versus benefits

It can be argued that tourism has been a major catalyst for infrastructural improvement in the former fishing village of Ocho Rios. This suggestion exemplifies some of the ideas of modernisation theory, whereby tourism can be seen as a process of modernisation along Western lines (Table 11.1: 1.1). At the same time, it is possible to assert that uncontrolled growth and a lack of planning in tourism development have led to the creation of an infrastructure that often benefits the tourists at the expense of the local population. Newspaper reports have stressed both the lack of an adequate water supply for local people when cruise ships are in port (*Sunday Gleaner*, 6/12/87) and the contrast that exists between the standard of construction of tourist properties and of those intended to house the resident population of the town (*Sunday Gleaner*, 14/5/89).

Such an inequality in terms of access to resources demonstrates the exploitation of the host community by tourism developers and supports notions of under-development theory (Table 11.1: 1.2) and a lack of the principles of sustainable development (Table 11.1: 1.3).

In recognition of some of these difficulties, a number of programmes have recently been financed by development loans for the longer-term improvement of Ocho Rios:

1. In September 1991 a contract was signed for the design of a sewage system. This project was funded by the European Community and involved a British firm of consultants who conducted an impact assessment of the options for waste disposal in the town (*Jampress*, 29/9/91).
2. A major development programme launched in August 1992 included the construction of a bypass for Ocho Rios, the expansion of the cruise-ship pier, the completion of the Greater Ocho Rios Water Supply Scheme and the development of an urban plan. Funding for these projects is via loans from, respectively, the inter-American Development Bank, Japan, the Economic Community through the Lomé Convention, and the United Nationals Development Programme (*Daily Gleaner*, 2/8/92). However, it seems likely that without tourism development, Ocho Rios would have been unlikely to receive the substantial loans necessary to fund this level of infrastructure provision. Both the finance and consultancy expertise originate outside Jamaica, supporting the principles of modernisation theory (Table 11.1: 2.1). But protagonists of underdevelopment theory might clearly identify such a situation as a demonstration of the power of the developed world over the less-developed countries (Table 11.1: 1.2).

Social effects of tourism development in Ocho Rios

Britton suggested that 'if all participants in tourism obtain some benefit, increased inequality is not necessarily problematic' (1982:346). Unfortunately, tourism develop-ment can increase social inequality and lead to other consequences commonly regarded as unacceptable. Such social consequences can arise from alterations in the physical environment made to accommodate and entertain tourists. This can be illustrated through land alienation in Ocho Rios.

Residents from Brook Green district in Ocho Rios filed an action suit in the Supreme Court to prevent the modification of the covenant on land next to their property which had been reserved for private residential development. The Urban Development Corporation and the Richfield Corporation had applied to remove the restriction to permit resort development. This would include the relocation here of a jerk pork centre which the residents believed would generate noise. Reflecting their views, the daily newspaper claimed that no consideration was given to Jamaican residents where tourism interests were involved (*Daily Gleaner*, 2/8/92). Also affected by this proposed development would be the schools and sports clubs formerly allowed to use part of the land as a playing field.

Further conflicts resulting from the loss of land to tourism include: the purchase of an area once a play-ground for the construction of the Sandcastles Hotel; the private ownership of stretches of beach (see Table 11.7) by hotels that either totally prevent access to local people or that charge an entrance fee for the use of the facility (*Daily Gleaner*, 9/11/91).

It would seem, therefore, that tourism development in Ocho Rios has led to a reduction in amenities previously available for the benefit of the local community. In this instance, tourism is acting as a 'metropole' by exploiting the 'satellite' or local community (Table 11.1: 1.2).

Principles of long-term sustainable tourism are not evident, with the tourist appearing to benefit at the expense of the host community (Table 11.1: 1.3, 2.3). This disregard for the needs of the host population may also lead to feelings of annoyance and antagonism postulated by Doxey (Murphy, 1985) and reinforced by evidence from Bayer (1993), the *Sunday Times* (19/12/93) and the *Daily Gleaner* (2/8/92), all of whom suggest that tourism can lead to crime.

Theory and reality

As is inevitable, the reality of the case study of tourism in Ocho Rios fails to accord precisely with specific

Table 11.7 *Beach ownership by accommodation establishments*

Number of establishments on a beach	Private beach		Public beach	
	Number	%	Number	%
16	9	56	7	44

Source: Survey, August 1992.

development paradigms. Nevertheless, a measure of agreement with each of the theoretical approaches to development can be identified.

Modernisation theory

Tourism appears to offer a mechanism whereby economic development goals can be achieved through the generation of foreign exchange, the diversification of exports and the expansion of employment opportunities. Existing tourism in Ocho Rios is predominantly large-scale, mass tourism for overseas visitors who demand facilities of an 'international' standard. The spread of this type of tourism could be perceived as a modernising force, facilitating the development of the town along Western lines with high-class hotels and an appropriate supporting infrastructure.

Although the capital for tourist accommodation provision does not, in general, originate outside Jamaica, as modernisation theory postulates, the ideas, practices and expertise frequently appear to be brought from overseas by multinational companies through management contracts and franchises. Aid, development loans and the expertise of consultants from developed world countries support much of the infrastructure established in Ocho Rios largely, at least initially, for tourism purposes. Whilst owners of major hotels are largely Jamaican, they are drawn disproportionately from white and Asian minorities. This accords closely with modernisation theory, whereby minorities are regarded as change agents and a modernising elite. The black majority are generally perceived as incapable of initiating the development process since they are assumed to be bound by tradition and culture, factors considered a barrier to development.

Underdevelopment theory

Foreign-owned, mass package tourism can be regarded as a mechanism whereby the developed world dominates the less-developed countries. It is a form of imperialism, with the tourists and the multinational companies as neocolonialists. Such an approach stresses the way in which tourism shares some of the structural problems of the old colonial system. This provides parallels with cash crops such as sugar which were equally dependent upon the whim of the world market, with similar high levels of capital export and a tendency to exploit local labour.

It has already been demonstrated that tourism in Ocho Rios follows this characteristic pattern, whose structure seems to have changed little since the nineteenth century. Tourists in general are racially, economically and spatially distinct from the majority of the population. This may recreate historical problems of servitude dating from the colonial past. Within such a 'master/servant' context the possibilities of meaningful cultural interaction between mass package guests and poor hosts are highly circumscribed and in such circumstances cultural voyeurism can lead to local conflicts and accusations of imperialism postulated by underdevelopment theory.

There is a relatively high degree of multinational involvement in the provision of tourist accommodation which leads to concern over leakages from the local and national economies. Leakages occur through: foreign-ownership and/or management; the employment of foreigners in key positions; government incentives to multinational companies; and imported food and materials. The reliance on imports is due to tourist preferences for international, standardised types of accommodation, food and transport. These factors are seen as the mechanisms by which surplus is transferred from the less-developed countries to the developed world.

Multinational involvement in Ocho Rios is predominantly in the form of management contracts and franchises. These less well understood types of dominance have led to concern over the extent of control of multinational operations in Ocho Rios, as well as in Jamaica overall.

Barriers to local black ownership of major accommodation establishments mentioned above may stem from either the structural inertia of the colonial past, or to educational barriers, or both. Whatever the underlying cause, the constraints on full participation in economic advance through tourism is evident on the part of the black majority of the population. This is further exacerbated in terms of employment where this section of the Jamaican community finds difficulty in securing the more skilled management posts. A consequent concern exists over the value of employment achieved by this group, especially in the informal sector where questions are raised about whether such jobs are a means of subsistence or merely a survival strategy of the very poor. The loss of land, resources and amenities from the local community of Ocho Rios for the benefit of tourists is seen as a demonstration of imperialism, with the global metropolitan countries gaining at the expense of the less developed world.

Concern also exists over the economic dependency of Jamaica on tourism both as a generator of foreign exchange and of employment, and fear of the neglect of other sectors of the economy. Like the other major national mainstay of the economy, bauxite, tourism is dependent upon a buyers' market. Aid and development loans from developed world countries often act to reinforce these entrenched patterns of dependence.

Sustainable approaches to tourism

Tourism in Jamaica, as well as in Ocho Rios, can offer a way of meeting economic development goals whilst bringing a measure of benefit to the host community through employment opportunities. Yet the marked national and local dependence upon tourism undermines the sustainable aim of using tourism as merely part of a more balanced economy.

Although the government has attempted to facilitate local involvement through loans and the leasing of hotels, and through a general improvement in development and in skills programmes, there is evidence of a lack of application of sustainable principles in the pattern of ownership and process of decision-making. Tourism in Ocho Rios has also fostered elitism amongst minority groups, being insensitive to the needs and aspirations of the majority of local people. At times, tourism takes disproportionately from the host community, as in the case of the loss of land, of resources and of limited infrastructural provision mentioned earlier. The scale and pace of tourism growth has been so great that the local infrastructure has been unable to support such development adequately. Greater planning and control are required so that long-term survival is not prejudiced by short-term considerations.

While proponents of modernisation theory may regard tourism in Ocho Rios as a modernising force and supporters of underdevelopment theory might perceive it as a form of neocolonialism, there may well be some common ground in sustainable approaches. Like modernisation theory, such approaches suggest that tourism has the potential to act as a catalyst for economic progress. In Ocho Rios this is demonstrated through the ability of tourism to bring employment and income to local people, as well as ensure a level of satisfaction for tourists. However, an examination of sustainable approaches suggest that they also share some of the concerns of underdevelopment theory in the nature of employment and ownership, and in the loss of amenities to the host population exemplified in the case study.

Conclusion

The death of dynastic politics and a decisive break in the colonial legacy of the island's ruling families occurred in March 1993 when a new Prime Minister secured the largest-ever electoral victory in Jamaica based on the slogan 'black man's time has come'. Increasing political independence and a removal of ingrained attitudes towards the black majority of the population are among the aims of this government, together with economic growth (*The Times*, 1/4/93). Such a policy could help to remove barriers to investment, involvement and employment in the tourism industry for a much wider section of the population.

There is also a need for asset-led tourism to replace market-led forms imposed and/or supported by the multinational companies, foreign governments and overseas tourists (Owen, 1991). A recognition of such a refocusing of new tourism developments has been made by the Jamaican government, both in its active participation in the annual Ecotourism Conferences run by the Caribbean Tourism Organisation since 1991, and in its amalgamation of the Ministry of Tourism with that of the Environment in 1992 (*Travel Weekly*, 4/3/92:59). These are the first steps in a doubtless hesitant and faltering progress towards the attainment of more physically, culturally and socially sensitive forms of tourism that benefit a greater number of local people and are more sustainable. Lessons learned from experience in resorts like Ocho Rios can be used to inform this progress and ensure that mistakes from the past are not repeated too frequently in the future.

References

AA/Baedeker (1992) *Caribbean*, Jarrold and Sons Ltd, Hampshire.

Aspinall, Sir A. (1930) *A Wayfarer in the West Indies*, Methuen, London.

Bayer, M. (1993) *Jamaica. A guide to the People, Politics and Culture*, Latin America Bureau, London.

Belisle, (1984) 'Food production and tourism in Jamaica: obstacles to increasing local food supplies to hotels', *The Journal of Developing Areas*, 19(1): 1–20.

Britton, S. G. (1982) 'The political economy of tourism in the Third World', *Annals of Tourism Research* 9(3): 332–358.

Britton, S. G. (1987) 'Tourism in Pacific Island States: constraints and opportunities', in Britton, S. and Clark, W. C. (Eds), *Ambiguous Alternatives: Tourism in Small Developing Countries*, University of the South Pacific, Suva, pp. 113–139.

Caribbean Tourism Organisation (1993) *Caribbean Tourism Statistical Report 1992*, Caribbean Tourism Organisation, Barbados.

Ferguson, J. (1990) *Far from Paradise*, Latin America Bureau, London.

Gayle, D. J. and Goodrich, J. N. (1993) *Tourism Marketing and Management in the Caribbean*, Routledge, London.

Graves, C. (1965) *Fourteen Islands in the Sun*, Leslie Frewin, London.

Harrison, D. (Ed.) (1992) *Tourism in the Less Developed Countries*, Belhaven, London.

Lea, J. (1988) *Tourism and Development in the Third World*, Routledge, London.

Mathieson, A. and Wall, G. (1982) *Tourism: Physical, Economic and Social Impacts*, Longman, Harlow.

Mackay, L. (1987) 'Tourism and changing attitudes to land in Negril, Jamaica', in Besson, J. and Momsen, J. (Eds), *Land and Development in the Caribbean*, Macmillan Caribbean, London.

Murphy, P. E. (1985) *Tourism: a Community Approach*, Methuen, London.

'Ocho Rios Development Plan' (1982) Ocho Rios Town Planning Department.

O'Grady, R. (1981) *Third World Stopover*, World Council of Churches, Geneva.

Owen, R. E. (1991) 'Strategy for sustainable tourism, the theory and the practice', paper to the International Conference on Tourism: Development Trends and Prospects in the 90s, Kuala Lumpur, 16–18 September 1991.

Pearce, D. (1989) *Tourist Development*, Longman, Harlow.

Planning Institute of Jamaica (1990) *Economic and Social Survey, Jamaica*, Planning Institute Publications Department, Kingston, Jamaica.

Planning Institute of Jamaica (1991) *Economic and Social Survey, Jamaica*, Planning Institute Publications Department, Kingston, Jamaica.

Poon, A. (1988) 'Innovation and the future Caribbean tourism', *Tourism Management*, 9(3): 213–220.

Taylor, F. (1975) *Jamaica, the Welcoming Society: Myths and Reality*, University of the West Indies, Mona.

Tourist Information Office (1992) *Tourist Accommodation Guides 1992*, Jamaican Tourist Information Office, Kingston, Jamaica.

Wheeller, B. (1991) 'Tourism's troubled times', *Tourism Management*, June: 91–96.

Wheeller, B. (1992) 'Is progressive tourism appropriate?', *Tourism Management*, March: 104–105.

Wyer, J. et al. (1988) *The UK and Third World Tourism*, Third World Tourism, European Ecumenical Network, Kent.

12 Appraising tourism projects

S. R. C. WANHILL

Introduction

The great variety in the components of the tourist product means that tourism projects may take many forms, each with its own particular features and trade norms in terms of operation. Traditionally, the private sector gives priority to the development of accommodation as this is a major source of revenue generation. As a rule of thumb, the hotel sector expects entry when room occupancies are in the range 70–80% and exit when they fall between 40–50%. For governments interested in expanding international tourism, airport developments are of critical importance. Airport facilities are designed around aircraft types, passenger flows and levels of congestion, termed standard busy hours. In addition, destination development includes a whole range of infrastructure and superstructure projects such as parks, sea-front promenades, improvements to historical attractions, the provision of restaurants, entertainment and speciality shopping. A variety of man-made recreation forms such as ski resorts, yacht marinas and golf courses may also be found at the destination.

The diversity of tourism projects may generate induced effects on competing and complementary businesses and projects. Thus, the development of a water resource for leisure purposes will almost certainly attract complementary enterprises such as a garage, boating operator, restaurants and cafes, and probably accommodation. Tourism development will create a stream of benefits and costs over a wide range of projects. The purpose of this paper is to review the different principles, as opposed to individual aspects, of appraising the benefits and costs flowing from tourist projects, commencing at the general level of sector analysis.

Sector analysis

For well over a decade, many governments around the world, faced with burgeoning public sector deficits, frustrated economic policies and the need to maintain international competitiveness, have sought to redefine their sphere of economic influence in terms of what should be left to market forces and what constitutes the 'market failure' case for intervention. This issue is considered by Choy (1991), who argues that government planning efforts might be better spent on resolving three kinds of market failure:

- The provision of public or collective goods: the principal feature of such provision is that it is non-excludable. If a good or service is to be provided at all, it may be consumed by everyone without exception and usually without charge at the point of use.
- Positive and negative externalities which impact on individuals not directly involved with the project or activities.
- Costs and benefits which are not reflected in market prices.

However, in tourism, care should be taken not to define the analytical framework of cost–benefit analysis too strictly by considering market failure only in terms of, say, the valuation of recreational space, social effects or the intrinsic benefits from the environment. Broadly defined, cost–benefit analyses takes a wider and longer look at the consequences of economic decisions. For example, one of the main planks of tourism policy, in many countries, is to develop a balanced growth of facilities at tourist destinations to meet the many and changing needs of visitors. The expected outcome, as in the case of growth poles, is to produce agglomeration benefits, by virtue of the synergy of one project with another and its linkages with the rest of the economy, which makes the sum of the whole much greater than the individual parts that would apply if the resources were devoted to an equivalent number of dispersed projects. The generation of agglomeration externalities underpins the Wales Tourist Board's (WTB, 1987) Local Enterprise and Development (LEAD) initiative, whereby a substantial portion of the Board's Section 4 funding, as prescribed by the 1969 Development of Tourism Act (House of Commons, 1969), was earmarked for integrated tourism development on a partnership basis with other agencies and the private sector in a number of resorts, tourism action areas, historic towns and small communities.

Governments have to make everyday decisions on the appropriate economic sectors to support and their respective projects. There are several direct measures

Table 12.1 *Direct and indirect value-added effects of principal export sectors in Mauritius*

Industry	Per Rs 1000 of export sales		
	Agriculture	Manufacturing	Tourism
Agriculture, hunting, forestry and fishing	761	283	44
Mining and quarrying	—	1	—
Manufacturing	9	325	29
Utilities	5	5	37
Construction	6	7	11
Wholesale and retail distribution	22	29	74
Local handicrafts	—	—	6
Hotels and restaurants	—	—	272
Transport and communications	59	42	39
Tourist transport	—	—	61
Financial and business services	16	19	85
Social, community and personal services	9	12	26
Recreation and cultural services	—	—	25
Total	887	723	709

Source: Archer and Wanhill (1981).

of economic worth, but a major criticism of direct ratios (Wanhill, 1982) is their failure to account for complementary effects of output expansion on the rest of the economy. The counter-argument is that indirect economic effects from development will be broadly similar from one project to another. This may be approximately true within an industrial sector, but it is hard to justify when considering projects located in different sectors of the economy. This aspect is illustrated in Table 12.1, which is drawn from a World Bank study (Archer and Wanhill, 1981). It may be seen from the table that linkages are an important aspect of tourism development because of the much wider spread that is achieved by income measures, such as value-added, when compared to agriculture or manufacturing, where the latter impacts are more narrowly focused. The significance of such linkages carries over into tourism project evaluation with the use of multiplier values to account for household income and employment creation. Multipliers are measures of the intensity of linkages within an economy and of the ability of the economy to retain the benefits of tourism.

At the sector level, it is possible to examine the overall effects of tourist expenditure within a generalised tourism model by defining the following system:

$$X = RAX + RT$$

$$P = \left[\frac{B_{m-1}}{i'(1-R)A + b_m} \right] X$$

$$= B^*X$$

$$L = EX$$

where

T = diagonal matrix of the categories of tourist expenditure;

X = matrix of gross output levels generated by tourist expenditure;

P = matrix of primary factor inputs;

L = matrix of employment created by tourist expenditure;

R = matrix of restrictions on local production capability;

A = matrix of intermediate consumption coefficients;

B^* = partitioned matrix in which the first $m-1$ rows are coefficients of primary factor usage and the last row, b_m, represents import requirements augmented by the deficits in domestic production capability, $i'(1-R)A$;

E = matrix of employment coefficients.

On its own, the input–output approach to analysing the impact of tourist expenditure embodies the assumption that resources are readily available to meet additional tourist demands. The value of multipliers is reduced if domestic supply constraints inhibit the ability of an economy to provide goods and services to tourists from local sources. This problem was first addressed by Bryden (1973) in his study of Antigua. He was particularly concerned with domestic agriculture and dealt with the matter by excluding this sector from the input–output table and transferring purchases from this sector into imports. This was picked up by O'Hagan and Mooney (1983), who imposed zero–one restrictions on the A matrix, representing traded and non-traded sectors. The model is, however, more general, than this (Wanhill, 1988). The **R** matrix imposes restriction coefficients that vary between zero and one according to whether there is no domestic supply capacity available or whether existing sectors can continue to supply the tourism industry as before. Provided domestic goods and services purchased by the tourist industry enter into international trade, the cumulative deficits in domestic production capability may be placed into the import row to simulate how tourist businesses would overcome local shortages. Restrictions on non-traded goods or services would act as an absolute constraint on tourism development. The system is solved in the following manner:

$$\mathbf{X} = (1 - \mathbf{RA})^{-1}\mathbf{RT}$$

$$\mathbf{P} = \mathbf{B}^*(1 - \mathbf{RA})^{-1}\mathbf{RT}$$

$$\mathbf{L} = \mathbf{E}(1 - \mathbf{RA})^{-1}\mathbf{RT}$$

In order to consider tourism in its totality, it is necessary to look not only at the performance of direct investment in tourism but also at the complementary bunches of investment required to support the tourist sector. The model discussed so far may be extended to cover this aspect. Define **v** as the vector of value-added coefficients and **K** as a diagonal matrix of capital–output ratios. Then the statistic

$$S = \frac{\mathbf{v}'(1 - \mathbf{RA})^{-1}\mathbf{RT}}{(\mathbf{Kv})'(1 - \mathbf{RA})^{-1}\mathbf{RT}} \qquad (1)$$

is a measure of the economic benefit–cost ratio arising from both the direct and complementary effects of tourist expenditure on the economy. Table 12.2 presents the S statistic for the three export sectors of Mauritius that were considered in Table 12.1. Per unit of capital, tourism generates a larger value-added than the other two sectors, thus making a greater unit contribution to economic growth in terms of the productivity of capital investment.

The value of S defined by Eqn (1) is made up of two parts: the numerator is the benefit stream (B) and the denominator is the capital investment requirements (K). Given estimates of the future progress of B, it is possible

Table 12.2 *Economic benefit–cost ratios for principal export sectors in Mauritius*

Industry	Ratio
Agriculture	0.305
Manufacturing	0.256
Tourism	0.397

Source: Wanhill (1982).

to liken Eqn (1) to an aggregate tourism project in which the net present value criterion (NPV) for acceptance is:

$$-K + B\left[\frac{1}{1+r} + \ldots\ldots + \frac{(1+g)^{n-1}}{(1+r)^n}\right] \geq 0 \qquad (2)$$

where

g = growth rate of the benefit stream, which could be positive, zero or negative;
n = length of the discount period;
r = economic discount rate.

Simplifying Eqn (2) gives:

$$-1 + \frac{S}{r-g}\left[1 - \left(\frac{1+g}{1+r}\right)^n\right] \geq 0$$

and solving for n,

$$n \geq \frac{\log\,[1 - (r-g)/S]}{\log\,[(1+g)/(1+r)]} \qquad (3)$$

By making n a variable in Eqn (3), the macro project is defined in terms of its pay-back. This implicitly introduces uncertainty as to the generation of future benefits into comparisons between one sector and another. Sector choice will depend on demand circumstances, and the values of g and S. It is to be expected that r will be uniform across sectors: in the United Kingdom, r is set by HM Treasury guidelines (1991) and is known as the 'Test Rate of Discount'. The latter is calculated to reflect the opportunity cost of capital in the economy at large.

With regard to the application of the results shown by Eqns (1) and (3), their estimation has become easier in recent years with the advent of modern computing power and the fact that more and more countries are collecting data suitable for the construction of tourism impact models by virtue of the need to improve their national accounts. Within the tourism sector, Eqns (1) and (3) set a macro standard for comparative performance of individual projects. Thus if S has a value of 0.397, g is 2% and r is 6%, then it will be two years and nine months before the value-added covers the capital outlay.

Nationally and regionally economic growth is measured by value-added. The latter includes within it the ability to generate investible funds, local income creation and hence employment. Governments normally employ a variety of criteria when assessing support for tourism projects, but, using the value-added concept, performance may be measured on three counts:

- The extent to which tourism projects have a higher value-added per unit of investment than other kinds of projects.
- How tourism projects match up to the macro standard depicted by Eqns (1) and (3).
- Tourism schemes receiving government assistance should do better than rejected projects, other things being equal. This comparison should exclude projects which are rejected because they are 'non-additional', that is, they are considered not to need state assistance as a condition of implementation.

Project analysis

Building on the work undertaken by the United Nations Industrial Development Organisation (UNIDO, 1972, 1978), Little and Mirrlees (1974), and Squire and van der Tak (1975), it is now generally accepted that the cost–benefit approach to project analysis has three distinct phases which may need to be covered in order to encompass both private and public sector interests:

- Financial analysis which examines the ability of the project to sustain itself in the market place.
- Economic efficiency analysis which measures the worth of the project to the economy as whole in terms of real resource flows, as opposed to transfer payments and receipts between one sector of the economy and another.
- Social analysis which looks at those aspects which the market mechanism is unlikely to account for, namely the distribution of the benefits and costs between different income groups, different economic agents and from one generation to another.

Financial analysis

Evaluation of the financial aspects is essential to any tourism project which is designed to attract substantial amounts of commercial funds. There are several ways of allocating economic resources other than the market mechanism. These include central planning, voting systems, dictatorship, gambling and even corruption. But the dominant theme in recent years has been for governments to leave economic decision to the market. To this extent, privatisation has been introduced as a way of reducing public sector deficits, increasing the efficiency of state industries and signalling to both domestic and foreign investors that the government is intent on setting the appropriate economic climate to attract private capital. Even with infrastructure projects lying within the public domain, for example, airports and harbours,

governments are concerned with cost recovery policies. Hartley and Hooper (1992) have taken this theme a step further by suggesting that the market failure argument in tourism policy may be no more than political lobbying. The implication here is that economic justification is, in practice, no more than the provision of persuasive ideas to rationalise political decisions and beliefs. There is no doubt that political opportunism is a source of project failure, but this line of argument works both ways: the belief that the market will optimise the provision of goods and services overlooks the point that the theoretical rules for the perfectly competitive model are not found in the commercial world. Thus, for example, joint venture public and private infrastructure projects may end up as being undersize and too costly because the private sector is unwilling to take long-term risks and the fact that commercial borrowing is, in almost every case, more expensive than government borrowing.

When considering the financial evaluation of tourism projects, it is important to distinguish between feasibility and viability. This distinction rests on the dominant cost structure of the industry which is one of a high operating leverage, that is, a high ratio of fixed to variable or running costs. In most instances, this feature is an outcome of the relatively high initial capital investment required. Where much of this investment is borrowed, the principal concern of the project's owners usually becomes one of servicing the debt. The concept of a high operating leverage is illustrated in Figure 12.1. R is the revenue line and C the total cost schedule attributable to running the project in a given year. The line $C-k$ represents the costs of operation after provision has been made for capital recovery. Mathematically, the latter is

$$k = \frac{Kd(1+d)^n}{(1+d)^n - 1}$$

where

K = initial capital investment
d = commercial cost of capital;
n = length of the discount period (life of the project).

In Figure 12.1, at a level of V_1 visitor days the scheme is feasible, since it generates a surplus BC over its running costs less capital servicing, but it is not viable, as there is a gap of AB in funds available to repay the initial capital investment. To the left of X, the project is neither viable nor feasible and conversely for point Y. But viability depends on d, which can fluctuate considerably by virtue of government economic policies, the financial structuring (funding package) of the capital investment and methods

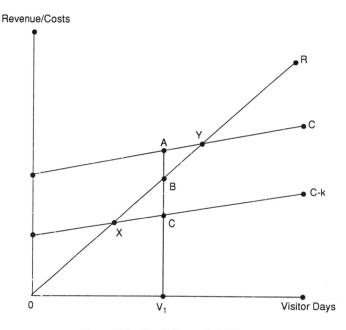

Figure 12.1 *Feasibility and viability*

of repayment. Thus, the owners of equity may be prepared to accept a lower return in order for the project to succeed, as is frequently the case in small businesses, or the project may generate particular economic benefits which could make it eligible for a 'soft' loan or grant-in-aid from tourism development agencies. Some projects may generate low revenue streams only in their early years and so will require a special form of finance such as a 'balloon' loan (see, for example, Ward and Dillon (1991)) whereby part or all of the principal is put aside to be repaid as a lump sum at the end of the loan period. As Ward (1989) observes, it is rare for specialist consultancy practices to return a negative project study. Unless the market assessment shows the concept to be totally inappropriate, in that it is, say, simply an 'ego trip' for the proposer, then, given the flexible and varied nature of tourism technology, it is often possible to revise the concept, costings and financial arrangements to assess what needs to be done to make the project viable.

There is a further aspect of viability which needs to be addressed and that is the possibility of capital appreciation. Tourism is, perhaps, more than any other industry involved with the development of real estate, particularly the accommodation sector which is normally the key area for private sector activity. Thus, there exists the possibility of substantial capital gains through property appreciation and there are a myriad of examples around the globe of hotel developments which were

primarily influenced by asset and site appreciation. In an early study, Andronicou (1979) shows that the development of the resort of Famagusta in Cyprus produced an increase in seaside land values of 3750% over 8 years, representing on average 57.3% per annum. Caution needs to be exercised here, for, although it is true that hotels have out-performed the rate of inflation in the longer term, to give hotels the same attributes as property investment is a mistake, as they are much more sensitive to downturns in consumer demand, are prone to seasonal cash-flow difficulties and usually have limited alternative use values. The essential steps in undertaking hotel feasibility and viability studies are shown in Table 12.3 and they are well covered in the sources that are listed.

In sum, the financial analysis of tourism projects is made up broadly of three components. First, the scheme

Table 12.3 *Procedures for the financial appraisal of an hotel*

- Overview of the local economy and social climate, including accessibility
- Evaluation of the site
- Market evaluation and demand analysis
- Competitive position
- Design concept and recommended facilities
- Financial analysis
- Risk assessment

Sources: Kendell (1982) and Ward (1989).

should be examined as a business proposition to see whether the concept is feasible and at a scale which is viable. This should normally be carried out at constant prices, which is the equivalent of assuming a uniform rate of inflation. Further, market prices are used throughout as real resource costs or 'shadow prices' are economy-wide concepts. Next, the impact of the funding arrangements (including available tax incentives and subsidies) on rates of return and the NPV are examined to assess how they may reduce any financial risk inherent in the project or increase its attractiveness to investors. At this stage, there may be 'hidden agendas' that should be taken into account, for example, in less-developed countries where restrictions on the convertibility of currencies are imposed, an international tourism project may give the owner access to a foreign exchange account, which is likely to be a considerable trading advantage. Finally, differential rates of inflation on costs and revenues are assessed in order to identify sources of gains and losses. A common gain occurs when debt repayments are not structured to keep up with inflation so their real burden declines as time goes on. Losses may accrue in situations where costs are rising faster than the ability of the operator to pass on increases in the form of higher prices to visitors—in short, cost-push inflation makes the project increasingly uncompetitive. In countries where there is high inflation it is not uncommon for businesses to quote prices in a 'hard' currency, in the knowledge that increases in domestic prices are countered by depreciation in the exchange rate.

Economic efficiency analysis

The process of economic efficiency analysis is implemented by taking an economy-wide view of the impact of the tourism project. Care is required in specifying the boundary of the project; thus, for example, a benefit stream at the regional level may be simply a transfer payment at the national level. It is customary in market economies to measure project benefits in terms of consumers' willingness to pay (WTP) plus any external gains. The former is considered to be some aggregation of individual preferences and is calculated from the area under the market demand curve. It is important to distinguish between 'demand' and 'need': demand is expressed in terms of WTP, whereas need is a concept applicable to the public provision of merit goods, such as recreational amenities, for the purpose of encouraging consumption because there are considerable social benefits that can be enjoyed by the population even though the WTP in the market-place may be somewhat limited.

Project costs are evaluated as real resource flows, including any costs external to the project, such as negative environmental impacts. The most common way in which market prices fail to indicate true costs is through taxes and subsidies. These are transfer payments and so input prices need to be adjusted to production costs by deducting taxes and adding transfers. For further consideration, there is the opportunity costs of a resource or the forgone alternative. If an area of land has no alternative use then its economic cost to the project is zero. Similarly, an unemployed person taken on by a tourism project has zero opportunity cost apart from the personal effort cost of work. Note that any savings in social security payments as a result of employment generation may be of benefit to the government treasury but, from the perspective of the economy as a whole, they are transfer payments.

On the other hand, the valuation of WTP is in market prices, since these are the basis upon which the demand schedule is drawn up. The main exception to this, whereby the WTP is not reflected in the demand curve, would be in circumstances of physical rationing, which artificially constrains demand.

In order to prevent the decision-maker from having to read through large amounts of data, it is the job of the project analyst to express all benefits and costs in a common 'yardstick'. Cost–benefit analyses requires that these effects are expressed in money terms and, while van Pelt et al. (1990) are theoretically correct in arguing that this approach is limited in dealing with environmentally sustainable tourism development, proposing instead multi-criterion analysis, in practice most cost–benefit appraisals recognise incommensurables, intangibles and project constraints. If it were possible to reduce all aspects of a scheme to monetary values then there would be little need for a decision-maker. All that would be required is a monetary accept/reject hurdle, set by the discount rate and the availability of capital funds. Incommensurables are those aspects of a project which can be quantified, but not in money terms. For example, the recreational benefits of a park may be measured in user hours. Intangibles are those benefits and costs which are either difficult to measure or purely qualitative in nature. As an example, Table 12.4 presents the kind of regional benefits that can arise as a result of airport improvement on one island within a group of Caribbean islands.

As regards constraints, these may often be stated by the decision-maker in the 'terms of reference' for the project or explained at the initial briefing. Examples include developments which might create irreversible environmental damage, impact unfavourably on the host community by, say, restricting beach access or compromise

Table 12.4 *Regional benefits from island airport development within a group of Caribbean states*

- Additional foreign exchange earnings within the Organisation for Eastern Caribbean States
- Improved operational efficiency and networking for Leeward Island Air Transport within the region
- Increased accessibility for domestic tourists (all purposes) as well as international tourists
- Raising the quality of the tourist product by making multi-destination tours easier and reducing the need to change transport modes from air to sea
- Multiplier effects on regional gateways through increased tourist spending and trade effects on other islands through expansion of intraregional purchases

safety standards, or be morally unacceptable, such as casino gambling.

In economic efficiency analysis, the economic net benefit (*ENB*) is defined as the difference between the *WTP* and the resource costs (*C*), plus or minus any net external effects. Ignoring the latter, for convenience of presentation, gives

$$ENB = WTP - C \qquad (4)$$

But the *WTP* is made up of an effective payment made by consumers at the market price, which is the revenue (*R*) and consumer surplus (*CS*), which is the difference between the market price and the price the consumer would be willing to pay. Thus Eqn (4) becomes

$$ENB = R + CS - C \qquad (5)$$

Producer surplus (*PS*) is the excess of the market price over the price at which the supplier is willing to sell, which in total is $R - C$. Hence, Eqn (5) may be simplified to

$$ENB = CS + (R - C)$$
$$= CS + PS \qquad (6)$$

Thus in economic efficiency analysis, because distributional effects are not considered, the economic net benefit is calculated as an increase in the total amount of consumer plus producer surpluses. A reduction in such surpluses would imply an economic net cost which would make it hard to justify the project unless the direct costs were outweighed by considerable external benefits.

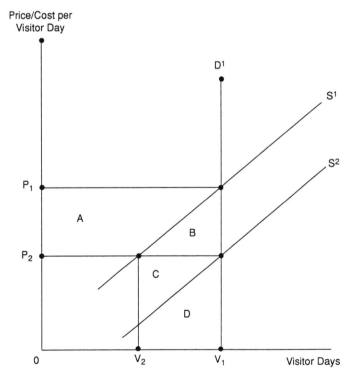

Figure 12.2 *Domestic visitors*

In measuring the *ENB* of a tourism project, there are a number of issues to consider. Figure 12.2 illustrates the purely competitive or displacement situation, where the output of the project does not enlarge market size at V_1 but rather displaces existing suppliers through efficiency gains that reduce the prevailing price from P_1 to P_2. The project takes $V_1 - V_2$ visitor days away from previous suppliers. It is assumed that the project benefits domestic tourism with the relevant impact divided into a number of areas. The significance of these areas is as follows:

A   = loss of old producer surplus;

A + B = gain in new consumer surplus;

C   = project producer surplus;

D   = project supply costs;

C + D = project revenue.

Thus, using Eqn (6)

$$ENB = (A + B + A) + (C + D - D)$$

$$= B + C$$

Alternatively, the *ENB* is the benefit from the resources saved from replacing $V_1 - V_2$ domestic production (B + C + D) less the general project cost (D), which is the reduction in supply costs (B + C).

The most common model used in tourism project appraisal is the market expansion case. This is shown in Figure 12.3. Demand is expected to grow from D^1 to D^2 in a situation where capacity is limited to V_1 visitor days as shown by the supply schedule S^1. Without the project,

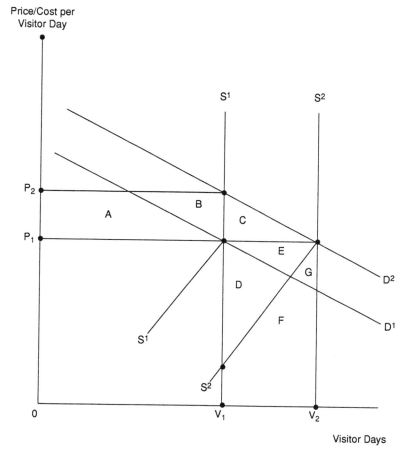

Figure 12.3 *Domestic visitors*

existing businesses face the possibility of increasing prices to P_2, thus those who see no benefit to themselves from expanding visitor numbers to V_2 are likely to oppose any development. This tends to bring tourism authorities, who wish to expand the market to capture the economic benefits of tourism growth, into conflict with private sector operators, who see demand growth as an opportunity for increasing the profitability of existing capacity. With the project prices remaining the same at P_1 and demand expanding to V_2, the meaning of the areas on Figure 12.3 from developing the project are:

A + B = loss of producer surplus from existing suppliers;

A + B + C = gain in consumer surplus to domestic visitors;

D + E = project producer surplus;

F + G = project production costs.

From Eqn (4), the *WTP* is C + D + E + F + G and so the *ENB* from developing the project is

$$ENB = (C + D + E + F + G) - (F + G)$$

$$= C + D + E$$

If the growth in demand is conditional to the project in the sense that design concept is aimed at attracting different market segments, then there is no displacement of potential profit increases to existing businesses. There will thus be no consumer surplus generated and so the *ENB* is simply the producer surplus from the project (D + E).

In appraising tourism projects there is, therefore, a requirement to exercise judgement as to the target market for the project and the nature of the market adjustment mechanism. The term 'fix-price' has been given to markets which are more likely to meet demand changes through adjustments in capacity. Such a description would apply to the growth in the mass tourism destinations, since suppliers have been largely price-takers in response to international market conditions. On the other hand, tourism capacity is long-lived and responses to downturns in demand are usually met in the first instances by rapid discounting as the variable costs of production are low, leaving a wide range of price discretion on the part of the supplier. 'Flex-price' markets are those where price is the principal means of adjustment to demand changes. Tourism is an experiential product

and there are resorts around the world that use price as a sign of exclusiveness so that capacity varies only marginally. Bermuda, for example, imposed a moratorium of large hotel buildings in the early 1970s.

In dealing with projects designed for international visitors (Powers, 1974), which is the case for most less-developed countries, the domestic model needs to be adjusted to discount benefits that are outside the national frame of reference. A similar situation would apply in terms of domestic tourism if the project boundary was only defined for a local area or region. The position of the market expansion model with respect to foreign visitors is presented with complete generality in Figure 12.4. Here the project displaces existing capacity by an amount of $V_2 - V_1$ visitor days, at the same time supplementing capacity by $V_3 - V_2$ visitor days. Without the project, existing suppliers would expand sales along the supply curve S^1, raising both output and price, and earning $P_2 V_2$ foreign exchange. The implementation of the project generates $P_1 V_3$ foreign exchange and savings in production costs of $V_2 - V_1$ visitor days' worth of domestic resources. The areas shown in Figure 12.4 are the following:

A + B   = loss of producer surplus for existing suppliers;

D + E + F   = project producer surplus;

C + D + G   = savings in domestic resource costs;

G + H + I   = project supply costs;

A + B + C + D + G = foreign exchange gain without the project;

D + E + F + G + H + I = foreign exchange gain with the project.

The *ENB* of the project may be presented as the net foreign exchange gain $(P_1 V_3 - P_2 V_2)$ plus the domestic resource savings [this is approximately $\frac{1}{2}(P_2 - P_1)(V_2 - V_1) + P_1(V_2 - V_1)$], less the project supply costs. Thus

$$ENB = [(D + E + F + G + H + I) - (A + B + C + D + G)]$$
$$+ (C + D + G) - (G + H + I)$$

$$= (D + E + F) - (A + B)$$

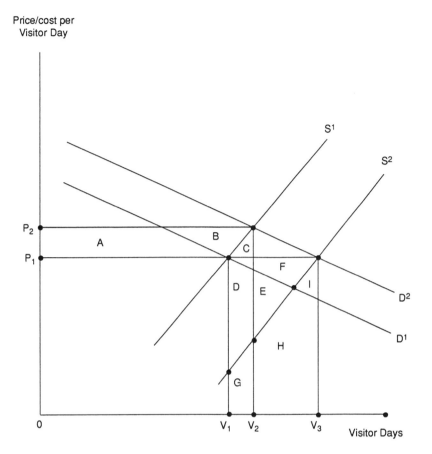

Figure 12.4 *Foreign visitors*

Consumer surplus is not included in this model as it accrues to foreign visitors. Hence, the economic net benefit of the project is ultimately made up of the project producer surplus less the producer surplus forgone by existing businesses. The latter is often neglected by private investors during the expansion phase of tourism development. The implied assumption is that market growth is conditional upon extra capacity so that only returns to the project are counted. The accommodation sector is particularly prone to this failing, which results in overbuilding, falling occupancy rates and falling profits. This has further consequences in that the hotels association will often put pressure on the government to give way on charter flights in order to boost occupancies, as well as discounting room rates. In turn, the expansion of charter flights is likely to reduce scheduled passenger traffic and so affect the profitability of the national carrier.

To complete the analysis, suppose the international tourism project also attracts domestic visitors. The economic benefits that accrue from the latter will differ from those generated by foreign visitors since the value of additional tourist services will depend on their *WTP* for them plus any savings in domestic resources that may arise through the project supplanting, in some part, existing capacity. The model is depicted in Figure 12.5 and may be interpreted in the following manner:

K	= domestic consumer surplus;
$K + M + N + P + Q$	= domestic willingness to pay;
$L + M + N$	= project producer surplus;
$J + L + O$	= domestic resource savings;
$O + P + Q$	= project supply costs.

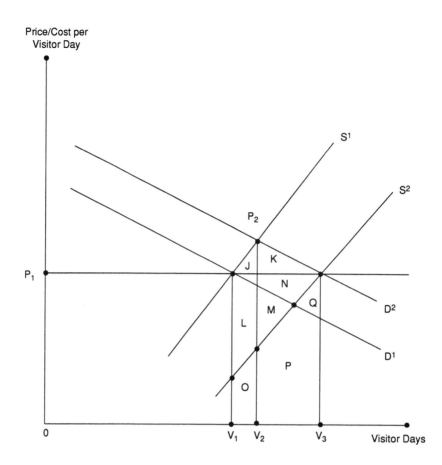

Figure 12.5 *Domestic visitors*

Using Eqn (4), the *ENB* is

$$ENB = (K+M+N+P+Q)+(J+L+O)-(O+P+Q)$$

$$= K+(M+N)+(J+L)$$

The *ENB* of the project to domestic users is therefore composed of consumer surplus [which is approximately $\frac{1}{2}(P_2-P_1)(V_3-V_2)$], the producer surplus created by the additional visitor days (V_3-V_2) and the efficiency savings resulting from the reduction in supply costs $(J+L)$. One further point to note is that the international project may not only be shared by domestic visitors, but may also induce domestic tourists to stay at home rather than take a trip abroad. In such instances, the benefits to the project are the foreign exchange costs that have been avoided, which treats this category of tourist in the same manner as foreign visitors.

In general, the further the product or service is from the market-place, the more difficult it is to evaluate the benefits, for the less likely is it that private-user benefits correspond to economy-wide benefits. If the project is an intermediate good or an infrastructure scheme, such as an airport, which reduces input costs and/or encourages market growth, then the relevant net benefit measure is made up of the impact on the project on the producer surplus for the whole industry, plus any monetary benefits and consumer surplus bestowed on domestic users. Early studies on appraising airports (Adler, 1971) concentrated on time-savings for passengers and reductions in transport costs in comparison with alternative travel modes. However, in many instances the most significant impacts of airport developments are indirect through facilitation of the tourism industry and the air-freight market. Bridger and Winpenny (1983) argue that it is difficult to ascribe all the surpluses arising from additional tourism activity to the airport development, and to ascribe only part makes the appraisal very arbitrary. They suggest that the cost of the airport should be included within a larger scheme for tourism development, which implies the insertion of a dummy resort complex to run alongside the airport appraisal. An alternative procedure is to use input–output analysis to disaggregate the components of tourist expenditure, then to allocate imputed payments to the owners of capital in the tourist industry to measure the economic costs of committing resources in the form of capital, and finally to attribute to the airport investment the residual of tourist expenditure over the economic input costs for the generated level of activity. The latter is defined in the usual manner as the difference between 'with' and 'without' the project.

The Brundtland Report (World Commission on Environment and Development, 1987) brought to the general attention of governments the issue of sustainable development which is about maintaining the balance between economics and the environment. One of the problems concerning the provision of outdoor areas for leisure purposes on a large scale is that they are rarely commercially viable in terms of the investment costs and operating expenditure necessary to establish and maintain them. The reasons for this lie in their periodic use (weekends and holidays) and the political and administrative difficulties of establishing private markets in what are perceived by the public as gifts of nature. This suggests that if it is left to market forces there is more likely to be under-provision of natural resources for leisure purposes than over-provision. Yet there are many social benefits to be gained from the availability of recreational amenities and from the control of land use to prevent unsightly development spoiling the beauty of the landscape.

If recreational and environmental resources are provided at no charge, the problem that is raised for project analysis is the measurement of the demand curve. Research in this area has centred upon three principal methods (Pearce et al., 1990):

- Travel-cost approaches.
- Hedonic pricing.
- Contingent valuation method (CVM).

The travel-cost method is based on constructing the demand curve from what is termed the 'generalised user cost' plus any consumer surplus. This is shown in Figure 12.6. At a level of V_1 visitor days the WTP is

$$WTP = C_1 V_1 + CS$$

which corresponds to the areas $A + B + D$ on the diagram. The generalised user cost represents the price of the facility and includes the value of time spent travelling to the resource, the value of time spent at the site and any monetary outlays. The benefits incurred by a reduction in the generalised user cost from C_1 to C_2 as a consequence of an improvement project are measured by the change in consumer surplus. This is in two parts: additional consumer surplus accruing to existing users (B) and that which accrues to induced and diverted demand (E). The former is calculated as $(C_1 - C_2)V_1$ and the latter as approximately $\frac{1}{2}(C_1 - C_2)(V_2 - V_1)$. If any diverted demand causes an increase in the generalised user cost to any other site, then this must be deducted. The change in consumer surplus is the benefit measure to be compared against the project costs.

Clawson and Knetsch (1966) extended the above analysis in an ingenious way by first estimating the trip generation equation in Figure 12.6 from data on visit rates and the generalised user cost according to distance zones from the recreation area, and then using the marginal response rate of visits from different zones, together with hypothetical increases in user costs, to simulate a 'final' demand curve for the recreation site. The area under the simulated curve is used as a measure of surplus. Needless to say, there are a number of theoretical criticisms aimed at the strong assumptions used in the Clawson model, particularly, the uniformity of trip behaviour from one zone to another. Empirical estimates have shown that the model is very sensitive to alterations in its parameters, which then imposes the requirement for more detailed data to be obtained with greater precision.

Hedonic pricing relies on there being a marketed surrogate for the free resource being evaluated. Pearce et al. (1990) tabulates the monetary effects of aircraft noise levels in terms of reductions in house prices. The problem here is to ensure consistency of comparisons, because there are many factors affecting the housing market, including institutional constraints.

Contingent valuation takes a direct approach by setting up hypothetical markets for the resource in question and asking individuals their WTP for improvement projects. CVM may be used to elicit valuations not only for actual use, but also option demand and existence values for, say, wildlife. An exploratory study for CVM in the context of the built environment has been undertaken by Thomas (1992).

Methods for discovering empirical demand curves for natural resources are open to the general question as to whether the environment is an economic issue or a constraint that is intangible as far as cost–benefit analysis is concerned. Giving the environment an economic value

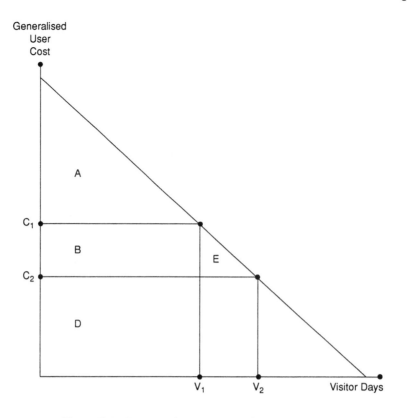

Figure 12.6 *Zero priced recreational and tourist facilities*

exposes it to possibilities of substitution by man-made capital with a higher market price. As many features of environmental damage appear to be irreversible, mistakes could ultimately prove to be extremely costly. It is for this reason that environmental impact assessments are now largely mandatory for projects funded by multi-national aid agencies.

Social analysis

Economic efficiency analysis looks at the project from the standpoint that market prices are not a reflection of true resource costs. The method does not examine the effects of the project on:

- Rate of economic growth, that is, the distribution of consumption between one generation and another.
- Distribution of the *ENB* between the private and public sectors.
- Distribution of income, namely, whether a unit of income accruing to a rich person should be valued equally to a unit accruing to a poor person.

There is a presumption in welfare economics for income equality, based on the notion that the marginal £1 is worth more to the poor than the rich and so, when transferred from the latter to the former, it serves to increase social welfare. The everyday expression of this concept is to be found in progressive income tax schedules. The World Bank method (Squire and van der Tak, 1975) is designed to take distributional issues into account by adjusting project inputs and output from market through economic accounting prices and then to social accounting prices. Numerical procedures and methods for calculating social accounting prices can be found in Weiss (1988) and Saerbeck (1988).

The World Bank method is designed for developing countries. Accounting prices provide for corrective action to two kinds of market price distortions:

- Protectionist trade policies working their way through to relative prices in all domestic markets, including those for factors of production.
- Factor market distortions relating to the opportunity cost of labour and public funds.

The approach adopted by Squire and van der Tak is to measure social surplus as uncommitted public income at world prices, the latter being regarded as the most efficient available price set. Uncommitted public income represents future investible funds in terms of foreign exchange. Private sector funds, to the extent that they are re-invested, can be regarded as equivalent. The philosophy behind the calculation of social accounting prices is that less-developed countries are normally faced with an adverse balance between investment and consumption, which they are unable to rectify because of inadequate institutional structures and a low savings base (as a result of low per capital GDP), and this in turn compromises future growth.

Project selection, usually funded by foreign borrowings and aid, may be used to correct for the consumption/investment imbalance by giving greater weight to the generation of investible funds than to consumption. Hence, social accounting prices for factors of production must reflect not only their opportunity or real resource costs, but also any additional consumption costs. For example, the shadow wage for a newly employed worker in the tourism sector would be made up of the employee's foregone marginal output (normally in agriculture), but which could be zero if the worker was previously unemployed, plus any additional consumption arising, less the social value of this consumption. The latter element is computed in terms of investment equivalents and is a measure of the benefit society deems that the individual receives from being able to consume more, appropriately weighted by an income distribution parameter. The implications of this line of analysis can be appreciated by supposing, for example, that there is an absolute priority on the generation of investment funds so that all consumption benefits are considered a cost. In which case, while the economic resource cost of employing an unemployed person is zero, the shadow wage rate in social terms will be close to the market wage if the worker is likely to consume most of his or her wage packet. In developed economies, where markets and institutional conditions work to bring the balance between investment and consumption into line with what is deemed appropriate in terms of government macro-economic policy, and there exist democratically agreed welfare and tax programmes concerning the distribution of income, then ideally there would be no difference between economic and social accounting prices. Thus, the shadow wage rate for an unemployed person is zero and the wage packet of this person would be counted as an economic benefit to be included within the definition of producer surplus.

Coming from the developed country perspective, and given the advocacy for tourism as a job generator in government economic policies, it becomes a matter of economic logic to link value-added, household income and employment, so as to evaluate the social benefits of publicly assisted tourism projects in terms of job creation. For example, within the European Union (Wanhill, 1993) the principles governing the bidding process for European Regional Development Fund (ERDF) grants for productive investment are:

- An indication of the market outlook in the sector concerned should be given.
- Effects on employment should be examined.
- An analysis of the expected profitability of the project should be undertaken.

In practice, local income and employment creation are the most significant factors affecting project acceptability, since the primary use of ERDF monies is to correct for regional imbalances. In terms of profitability, project feasibility is the main consideration, because the objective of ERDF is to make up for shortfalls in finance to ensure viability. A similar principle has always applied to grant-in-aid or loans offered by the Tourist Boards in the United Kingdom. Projects are expected to achieve viability after funding has been given. If the project was already viable, it would not receive public funds since it would not satisfy the 'additionality' criterion which lays down that eligibility can only apply to projects that would not proceed without investment support.

The starting point for evaluating tourism projects from an employment perspective is to measure the economic impact of tourist spending to derive employment multipliers. To illustrate the methodology, suppose there exists a tourist destination with an hotel and scenically attractive countryside. It is proposed that an attraction should be established, with the help of public funds, to develop the destination. Visitors are surveyed at the hotel and at key viewing points to ascertain what motivated them to come to the area and the potential drawing power of the attraction.

Total spending at the destination (T) will amount to expenditure at the attraction (A) plus expenditure at the hotel (H) plus all remaining expenditure (F). The pull factor (reason for visit) for the attraction is estimated to be x and for the hotel, y, leaving $1-x-y$ as the significance of the countryside. It follows therefore that attributable tourist expenditure by drawing power is:

$$\text{Attraction} \quad = xA + xH + xR$$

$$\text{Hotel} \quad = yA + yH + yR$$

$$\text{Countryside} = (1-x-y)\,(A+H+R)$$

$$T = A+H+R$$

The benefits (B) of developing the attraction are the difference between with and without the project. The without situation is:

$$\text{Attraction} = 0$$

$$\text{Hotel} = yH + yR$$

$$\text{Countryside} = (1 - x - y)\,(H + R)$$

$$T_w = (1 - x)\,(H + R)$$

Hence

$$B = T - T_w$$
$$= A + x(H + R) \tag{7}$$

If visitors to the attraction would have come to the area anyway then the benefits would simply be A.

The benefits shown in Eqn (7) are in two parts. The first term on the right-hand side is on-site expenditure and the second, off-site expenditure. The amount of off-site expenditure attributable to the attraction depends on its ability to generate additional visitors. Hence, this may be termed the visitor additionality factor. The application of employment multipliers per unit of tourist spending to Eqn (6), either on a full-time equivalent (FTE) or employment headcount basis, will give the gross employment (E) generated by the project. These multipliers are calculated so as to measure the direct employment effects of the project, the indirect effects arising out of intermediate purchases made by the project and the induced effects on the local economy as a result of the re-spending of local incomes derived from the project, and similarly for off-site expenditure. Thus:

$$E = Ae_a + xOe_o \tag{8}$$

Where e_a is the employment multiplier appropriate to the attraction, O is the sum of off-site expenditure ($H + R$) and e_o the required employment multiplier.

However, Eqn (8) ignores any business displacement from elsewhere in the area or from another publicly supported project located outside the area. This emphasises the importance of defining the boundary of the project, for what may be a net gain from the standpoint of a local authority may be merely a transfer if the reference area is taken as the national economy. If p is the proportion of local diverted demand in Eqn (7) then the net employment effects (N) are

$$N = E - pE$$
$$= (1 - p)\,(Ae_a + xOe_o) \tag{9}$$

Applications of Eqn (9) can be found in Johnson and Thomas (1992) in their study of Beamish Museum in the North of England and Lowyck and Wanhill (1992), which looks at the assessment of the New Theatre development in Cardiff, South Wales, for ERDF funding.

The obvious performance measures in terms of ranking projects relate to factors such as the number of FTEs created, job patterns in terms of educational attainment and skill levels, male/female ratios, the amount of part-time and seasonal work in relation to year-round, full-time employment, and so on. In addition, a number of financial indicators have been used in respect of the capital investment (K). The most common is the capital cost per job (K/N) but others include the grant cost per job (G/N), the private capital cost per job ($(K - G)/N$) and the grant leverage effect ($(K - G)/G$).

Conclusions

The appraisal of tourism projects has been considered at the sector level, with the measure of net benefit being the contribution to economic growth through value-added, and then at the project level. Three approaches were examined at the project level, namely, financial analysis, economic efficiency analysis and social analysis. Financial analysis looks at the project as a business proposition from the standpoint of the private sector. The project has to be viable in terms of achieving a hurdle rate of return on invested capital. Once the funding package is accounted for, then ability to service debt and meet the hurdle rate set by the owners of equity capital become the relevant criteria.

Economic efficiency analysis takes a wider and longer look at the net benefit stream from the position of the economy at large. The appropriate economic measures of the real resources flows to tourism projects were examined. Modern cost–benefit analysis, as exemplified by the World Bank, uses world prices as the yardstick for measuring real resource flows. This is based on the view that world markets are competitive and so international prices are the most efficient price set available. The net benefit stream measured in this manner corresponds to a surplus of foreign exchange.

Social analysis constitutes the last stage in appraising a tourism project. The surplus of foreign exchange, measured by the economic efficiency analysis, is adjusted to account for differential weights attached to the availability of the surplus for investment and consumption, the distribution of gains and losses between the private and public sector, and the distribution of personal income.

In practice, the 'terms of reference' of many tourism projects may only require the analyst to appraise the financial and economic aspects of the scheme, with consideration of the impact of tourism on government revenue, the balance of payment and employment. The distribution of income is normally a political issue and governments may have mechanisms other than project selection to achieve distributional objectives. Alternatively, governments may see economic growth as the maxim and rely on the market to deal with distributional issues through the 'trickle down effect'. However, the market has no inbuilt mechanism to deal with distribution and so there is no guarantee that economic growth will solve the problem. Finally, sustainable development requires the project to be assessed for its impact on the environment, which in tourism must also include impact on the host community.

References

Archer, B. H. and Wanhill, S. R. C. (1981) *The Economic Impact of Tourism in Mauritius*, World Bank, Washington, DC.

Adler, H. A. (1971) *Economic Appraisal of Transport Projects*, Indiana University Press, Bloomington, IN.

Andronicou, A. (1979) 'Tourism in Cyprus', in E. de Kadt (Ed.), *Tourism—Passport to Development*, Oxford University Press, Oxford, pp. 237–264.

Bridger, G. A. and Winpenny, J. T. (1983) *Planning Development Projects*, HMSO, London.

Bryden, J. M. (1973) *Tourism and Development: a Case Study in the Commonwealth Caribbean*, Cambridge University Press, London.

Choy, D. J. L. (1991) 'Tourism planning: the case for market failure', *Tourism Management*, 12(4):313–330.

Clawson, M. and Knetsch, J. L. (1966) *Economics of Outdoor Recreation*, Johns Hopkins University Press, Baltimore, MD.

HM Treasury (1991) *Economic Appraisal in Central Government: a Technical Guide for Government Departments*, HMSO, London.

Hartley, K. and Hooper, N. (1992) 'Tourism policy: market failure and public choice', in P. Johnson and B. Thomas (Eds), *Perspectives on Tourism Policy*, Mansell, London, pp. 15–28.

House of Commons (1969) Development of Tourism Act 1969, HMSO, London.

Johnson, P. and Thomas, B. (1992) *Tourism, Museums and the Local Economy*, Edward Elgar, Aldershot.

Kendell, P. J. (1982) 'Recent experiences in project appraisal', *Tourism Management*, 3(4):227–235.

Little, I. M. D. and Mirrlees, J. A. (1974) *Project Appraisal and Planning for Developing Countries*, Heinemann, London.

Lowyck, E. and Wanhill, S. R. C. (1992) 'Regional development and tourism within the European Community', *Progress in Tourism, Recreation and Hospitality Management*, 4:227–244.

O'Hagan, J. and Mooney, D. (1983) 'Input–output multipliers in a small open economy: an application to tourism', *The Economic and Social Review*, 14(4):273–280.

Pearce, D., Markandya, A. and Barbier, E. B. (1990) *Blueprint for a Green Economy*, Earthscan, London.

van Pelt, M. J. F., Kuyvenhoven, A. and Nijkamp, P. (1990) 'Project appraisal and sustainability: methodological challenges', *Project Appraisal*, 5(3):139–158.

Powers, T. A. (1974) *Appraising International Tourism Projects*, Inter-American Development Bank, Washington, DC.

Saerbeck, R. (1988) 'Estimating accounting price ratios with a semi-input–output table: Botswana', *Project Appraisal*, 3(4):190–198.

Squire, L. and van der Tak, H. G. (1975) *Economic Analysis of Projects*, Johns Hopkins University Press, Baltimore, MD.

Thomas, J. (1992) *Tourism and Environment: an Exploration of the Willingness to Pay of the Average Visitor*, Oxford Brookes University, Oxford.

UNIDO (1972) *Guidelines for Project Evaluation*, United Nations, New York.

UNIDO (1978) *Guide to Practical Project Appraisal: Social Cost-Benefit Analysis in Developing Countries*, United Nations, New York.

Wanhill, S. R. C. (1982) 'Evaluating the resource costs of tourism', *Tourism Management*, 3(4):208–211.

Wanhill, S. R. C. (1988) 'Tourism multipliers under capacity constraints', *The Service Industries Journal*, 8(3):136–142.

Wanhill, S. R. C. (1993) 'European regional development funds for the hospitality and tourism industries', *International Journal of Hospitality Management*, 12(1):67–76.

Ward, T. J. (1989) 'The hotel feasibility study: principles and practice', *Progress in Tourism, Recreation and Hospitality Management*, 1:195–205.

Ward, T. J. and Dillon, M. (1991) *Guidelines to Hotel and Leisure Project Financing*, World Tourism Organisation, Madrid.

Weiss, J. (1988) 'An introduction to shadow pricing in a semi-input–output approach', *Project Appraisal*, 3(4):182–189.

World Commission on Environment and Development (1987) *Our Common Future*, Oxford University Press, Oxford.

WTB (1987) *Tourism in Wales—Developing the Potential*, Wales Tourist Board, Cardiff.

13 Evaluating public resources used in tourism

E. SMERAL

Introduction

Tourism demand affects many goods and services as well as the environment; in most cases, the realization of tourism demand requires some attributes of the environment as an input.

The inflexibility of our socio-economic systems coupled with the fact that society is not ready yet to bear the full external costs of their different activities—especially regarding its consumption of the environment—are having a negative impact on the quality of many natural resources used in tourism. Given that visiting natural attractions is an important travel motive and that the desire to spend one's leisure time in an intact environment promises to become a mega-trend, the safeguarding and maintenance of an intact environment is vital for the tourism industry and consumer satisfaction.

Evaluating public resources used in tourism and the estimation of the total willingness to pay for them provides an important factual basis for developing new tourism policies, estimating their effects and determining the optimal steps of actions.

In this paper, three methods for evaluating public resources are covered: the travel cost approach, the hedonic-price method and the contingent value method.

The travel cost approach

The travel cost method is based on the assumption that the use of a natural resource will decrease as the travel (distance and time) costs increase. Utility gains from travelling *per se* or the costs of the equipment for various activities such as fishing, skiing or sailing are not considered.

The demand for a natural resource used in tourism can be estimated from models relating its use (mostly in the form of visits by the inhabitants of different zones of origin) to the travel costs in money terms—the shadow prices for the resource—to the socio-economic factors and, when necessary, to a set of dummy variables for special conditions as well. For the evaluation, the specific site must be defined. The exact definition of the origins of visitors (i.e. cities or countries) and the total population of each zone of origin are also necessary. If the capacity

of a resource does influence the total usage levels, the observed values might reflect the true value of the site; the effects of congestion are then measured instead.

Many authors have emphasized that travel costs should include the opportunity costs of travel time in addition to the pure money costs for a trip (i.e. petrol or ticket costs, meals, maintenance, overnight stops, etc.); the 'cost' of travel time is a significant determinant in an individual's decision to choose a certain destination. Some authors suggest further that a variable expressing the competition between different natural resources should be included in the use function, arguing that the willingness to pay is biased upwards in the case of single site evaluations.

Other studies show that the degree of substitutability between different natural resources is very low. Reasons for this are the inherent special qualities of the different destinations; special qualities might be the size of a natural resource in connection with a wide range of amenities, well-developed facilities or attractions.

Formally expressed, one assumes that a representative consumer maximizes a quasi-concave utility function, subject to income and time constraints (McConnell, 1985):

$$\text{Max } u(v,q)$$

subject to

$$y = cv + pq$$

and

$$T = 1 + v(t_1 + t_2)$$

where

v = number of visits to a given site,

q = Hicksian commodity bundle of other goods,

l = working time in hours

t_1 = travel time per visit in hours,

t_2 = time spent on the resource per visit in hours,

c = costs per visit,

p = price of q,

T = total time,

w = wage rate,

y_0 = exogenous determined income,

y = money income: $y = y_0 + wl$.

This basic theoretical model assumes that consumers can choose between work and leisure at a constant wage rate; if l is working time in hours, then t_1 and t_2 must be hours spent for the resource use and travelling.

Following the rules for constrained maximization problems, the Lagrangian expression is set up by combining the different constraints as follows:

$$L = u(v,q) + \lambda(y' - c'v - pq)$$

where

$$c' = w(t_1 + t_2) + c \text{ and } y' = y_0 + wT$$

Setting the partial derivatives of L to zero yields $n+1$ equations, representing the necessary conditions for an interior maximum. These $n+1$ equations can usually be solved for v, q and λ (assuming that the second-order conditions ensuring a maximum are fulfilled). The resulting relevant general resource use function is:

$$v = f(c',p,y')$$

Under the assumption that, in a cross-section analysis, p has the same value for all consumers, the general resource demand function becomes:

$$v = f(c',y')$$

This equation is used in many studies as an underlying approach for the travel cost method.

The basic empirical model for an isolated site with visits from j different zones of origin relates the use of a resource in terms of visitation to explanatory variables like population, income per capita and travel costs (time costs are included). Visits should be of constant length. When the lengths of stay vary, the length becomes a choice variable and needs an additional explanatory equation.

The basic empirical model can be expressed as follows:

$$V_j = f(POP_j, Y_j, C_j) \qquad (1)$$

where

V_j = number of visits of the resource from zone of origin j,

POP_j = population of the zone of origin j,

Y_j = income per capita in the zone of origin j,

C_j = travel costs in money terms from zone of origin j to the resource,

j = 1, . . . , n.

The hedonic-price method

The hedonic-price approach is based on the fact that different locations with different environmental attributes have different property values. With the hedonic approach it is possible to estimate the portion of a property value differential which arises from a particular environmental difference between properties, how much people are willing to pay for an improvement in the quality of the environment and what the social value of the improvement is (OECD, 1989).

In applied tourism research, the identification of (hedonic-)price effects occurring due to a difference in pollution or noise levels in vacation areas is usually done with the support of the OLS technique. With this technique data on either residential properties (e.g. house and land prices, renting fees for apartments) or tourism facilities (e.g. room rates, renting fees for vacation homes, restaurant prices) could be used.

The first stage of the hedonic-price approach is an estimation of an equation with the following form (Brookshire et al., 1982):

$$P_i = f(X_i, Y_i, Z_i, Q_i)$$

P_i could be the value of a property i, the room rate of a hotel i or the meal price in a restaurant i, X_i is a collection of site and/or quality variables (e.g. age of building, amount of rooms, lot size, quality of the hotel rooms or the service), Y_i is a collection of neighbourhood variables, Z_i summarizes accessibility and infrastructure variables and Q_i is a collection of indicators of environmental attributes in this vacation area under study (an increase in Q_i implies a higher noise or traffic level or a higher level of pollution).

The above equation is usually estimated on cross-section data and problems of multicollinearity and heteroscedasticity can be quite severe; further the researcher has to very careful in choosing the functional form as this has a great impact on the results.

Let us assume all necessary variables are statistically measurable and that the price equation has been satisfactorily estimated. The marginal willingness to pay (WTP_i) for a reduction in Q_i (or improvement of the environment quality) is given by the partial derivative.

$$\delta P_i / \delta Q_i = WTP_i$$

In the next stage, WTP_i is regressed on variables such as the socio-demographic (S_i) and economic characteristics (Y_i) of the individuals, the characteristics of the leisure behaviour (L_i), including activities, motives, spending patterns, etc., and an indicator of environment quality to obtain an inverse demand function

$$WTP_i = f(S_i, Y_i, L_i, Q_i)$$

As an example, let us suppose that the pollution and/or the noise level falls from Q_{i0} to Q_{i1}, then the gain in consumer surplus for each household or visitor at Q_{i0} is the welfare triangle under the WTP-function; by adding up all these increases in consumer surpluses we obtain the overall value of the environmental improvement.

The contingent value method

One of the central assumptions of the contingent valuation (CV) method is that individual responses to hypothetical markets are completely comparable with individual responses to actual markets. A goal of the CV method used in tourism research is to obtain the surveyed individuals' consumer surplus for a natural resource. The application of the CV method requires potential visitors to give an estimate of their willingness to pay for access to a particular natural resource used for tourism purposes; it is also important to make sure that the answers are given in relation to what the respondents would be willing to pay for the next best alternatives (if any exist).

The CV survey applied in tourism research should consist of three main parts (Mitchell and Carson, 1989):

— a scenario describing the hypothetical market in detail
— questions about the socio-economic characteristics of the consumers, their preferences, planned activities, motives, etc.
— questions for determining consumers' willingness to pay for the access to a site

The main question of the CV survey is concerned with how much the consumer is willing to spend for the use of the site or how much travel expense is the consumer willing to incur before he would prefer to go without visiting the site or the recreational area. The problem making it difficult for the respondents to pick realistic values has led to experimentation with different elicitation techniques.

In principle, there are two different CV elicitation techniques (Mitchell and Carson, 1989):

— whether the actual maximum amount or a discrete indicator of willingness to pay is obtained, and
— whether a single willingness to pay question or an iterated series is asked.

The bidding game, the payment card method and the open-ended question are common examples of the first technique.

The bidding game simulates an auction situation where individuals are asked to state the amount they are willing to pay. For example, the respondents are asked if they would be willing to pay an entrance fee of 100 ECU for a natural resource (per person, per day) in order to prevent a substantial quality loss from occurring. The next entrance fee categories proposed are 200 ECU, 300 ECU, 400 ECU, etc. until a negative response is obtained. Then the sum is decreased by 10 ECU until a positive response is obtained once more. Such a bidding process could measure the full consumer surplus, as the process will cover the maximum price a consumer is willing to pay. This method has a strong bias in that the starting bid influences the perceived value of the natural resource.

The payment card method gives the respondent a visual aid with a wide range of potential willingness to pay amounts. The question is then asked: 'What amount on this card expresses the maximum amount you are willing to pay?' This approach avoids the disadvantage of the starting point bias.

In the open-ended question method, the consumers are simply asked to state their maximum willingness to pay.

The 'take it or leave it' approach, with or without follow-up, and the checklist method represent the second measuring technique.

The 'take it or leave it' approach is based on predetermined prices chosen as approximate indicators for the maximum willingness to pay amounts of most respondents for the site. Each person is asked about their willingness to pay a specific predetermined price for the natural resource in question on a 'take it or leave it' basis, with no further iteration. But values obtained by the 'take it or leave it' method are only discrete indicators of the maximum willingness to pay rather than the actual maximum willingness to pay amount. The elaboration of the 'take it or leave it' method with a follow-up approach offers the possibility of making the estimation more exact. In this approach, when the respondent accepts a given price, another willingness to pay question is asked using a higher price randomly chosen from a list, and so on. If the respondent does not accept a price, a randomly chosen lower price is asked.

In the checklist method, the respondent simply checks off the amount reflecting his willingness to pay from a list.

Deriving the aggregate demand curve for a special natural resource could be done by applying the rules of a system of coordinates where the horizontal axis measures the number of respondents and the vertical axis measures the maximum prices (fees, costs) hypothetically paid per person. Using this aggregate demand curve, one could estimate the aggregate consumer surplus of the users (visitors) living in a certain zone. The aggregation over all living zones from which visitors come results in the total consumer surplus. When visitors are not homogeneous (varying amounts of trips per visitor, different levels of disposable incomes, different travel costs, etc.), one should be very careful that different segments for aggregation are defined in the derivation of the aggregate demand curve for all visitors as well as for the relevant population.

Many authors argue that the results of a CV survey may be biased by the strategic behaviour of the respondents. Minimizing the possibility of playing games is one of the most important challenges for the researcher. The various types of strategic behaviour in CV surveys are dependent on (Mitchell and Carson, 1989):

—the payment obligation, perceived by the individual: the respondent believes that the supply of the good is contingent upon the amount of willingness to pay he reveals, and
—the expectations of the respondent about the supply of the good when he assumes he has to pay the actual amount he offers, that the payable amount is uncertain or that he will have to pay a fixed amount.

According to these conditions, there are six different possibilities for strategic behaviour:

—The respondent will tell the true amount of his willingness to pay if he believes that the supply is contingent on his revealed preference and that he will have to pay the amount offered.
—The respondent makes no real effort to reveal his true preference if he is convinced that the supply is

inevitable and that there will be no connection between what he will actually pay and what he offers to pay.
—The more a respondent believes that the good in question will be provided regardless of his willingness to pay and the more the respondent believes that he will have to pay the amount he offers, the more the tendency for free riding behaviour (to underbid or pay nothing) increases.
—Another form of free riding can take place when the respondent believes in the availability of the good, but is not sure if he will have to pay what he offers.
—The tendency for overbidding increases the more a respondent believes that the amount offered will influence the supply of the good and that a lower amount offered will influence the final amount needed to pay.
—The last type of strategic behaviour is very sophisticated. Assuming that the amount of payment is uncertain and that the supply is contingent upon the revealed preference, the direction of the strategic behaviour would take depends on where the individual perceives the fact of uncertainty to lie; furthermore, a person's averseness to risk also influences the direction of the strategic behaviour.

References and bibliography

Brookshire, D. et al. (1982) 'Valuing public goods: a comparison of survey and hedonic approaches', *American Economic Review*, 72 (March):165–177.
Burt, O. et al. (1971) 'Estimation of net social benefits from outdoor recreation. *Econometrica*, 39:813–827.
Cesario, J. (1976) 'Value of time in recreation benefit studies', *Land Economics*, 52:32–41.
Cesario, J. and Knetsch, J. (1970) 'Time bias in recreation benefit estimates', *Water Resource Research*, 6:700–704.
Clawson, M. (1959) *Methods of Measuring the Demand for and Value of Outdoor Recreation*, Resource for the Future, Washington, DC.
Clawson, M. and Knetsch, J. (1966) *Economics of Outdoor Recreation*, Johns Hopkins University Press, Baltimore, MD.
Coase, R. (1960) 'The problem of social costs', *Journal of Law and Economics*, 3:1–44.
Dolan, E. (1971) *TANSTAAFL, The Economic Strategy for Environmental Crisis*, New York.
Eberle, W. and Hayden, F. (1991) 'Critique of contingent valuation and travel cost methods for valuing natural resources and ecosystems', *Journal of Economic Issues*, 25:3.
Johansson, P. (1987) *The Economic Theory and Measurement of Environmental Benefits*, Cambridge.
Kerr, G. N. et al. (1986) 'Economic benefits of Mt. Cook national park', Centre for Resource Management, University of Canterbury and Lincoln College.
Mitchell, R. and Carson, R. (1989) *Using Surveys to Value Public Goods: the Contingent Valuation Method*, Washington, DC.
McConnell, K. (1985) 'The economics of outdoor recreation', in Kneese, E. V. et al. (Eds) *Handbook of Natural Resource*

and Energy Economics, Vol. II, Elsevier Science Publishers, Amsterdam.

OECD (1989) *Environmental Policy Benefits: Monetary Valuation*, OECD, Paris.

Pigou, C. (1923) *The Economics of Welfare*, London.

Schreiner, D. F. (1985) 'Recreation benefits measured by travel cost method for the McClellan–Kerr Arkansas river system and application to other selected Corps lakes', Oklahoma State University.

Smeral, E. (1988) 'Tourism demand, economic theory and econometrics: an integrated approach', *Journal of Travel Research*, 4.

Smeral, E. (1992a) 'Why we discuss the environmental impact of tourism? Reasons and strategies for reducing', in Pillman, W. and Predl, S. (Eds), *Strategies for Reducing the Environmental Impact of Tourism*, Proceedings, Envirotour, Vienna, 1992.

Smeral, E. (1992b) 'Entrance fee for nature?', in AIEST (Ed.) *The Freedom of Travelling: Rights and Duties of the Tourists in the Year 2000*, St. Gallen.

Smeral, E. (1994) 'Measuring and managing tourism demand for public resources', in Witt, S. and Mountinho, L. (Eds), *Tourism Marketing and Management Handbook*, Prentice Hall, Englewood Cliffs, NJ.

Smith, S. (1989) *Tourism Analysis: a Handbook*, Longman, Harlow.

14 The economic impact of travel and tourism in a mountain area: the case of Vorarlberg, Austria

S. BAIER

Introduction

Vorarlberg is one of the nine federal states of Austria. In terms of size, it is the smallest state in the country. Approximately 80% of its area is mountainous with the greater part belonging to the 'Hochgebirge' (high-mountains). For the most part, tourism in the high-mountain areas is dominated by ski tourism, while the lower valleys have a twin season supply.

The impact of travel and tourism on the economy of an area or state is best described through the use of input–output analysis. However, in the case of Vorarlberg, a lack of input–output statistics available at the regional level caused some complications. The only solution was to use estimates based on the national input–output table, which were then adapted through the use of relevant regional values for the net quotas of involved industries, their different sales structures and labor productivities. The goal of the study was to find the value-added effects, the tax effects and the employment effects of tourism in Vorarlberg.

Basic assumptions

The basic concept behind the input–output model is that the demand for products of an industry determines more than just its own output: it also influences indirectly the production in the delivering industry. Such an induced output results again in input deliveries. Additionally, the delivering industries require products from the other industries for their own production, resulting in demand cycles. In other words, an autonomous increase in demand results in a multiplier process which creates direct and indirect income and employment.

The smaller the direct and indirect leakages outside of the area, the greater the domestic effectiveness of an increase in demand (the domestically induced net production, or value added). For a given region, in this case Vorarlberg, an autonomous increase in demand results is not just imports from foreign countries but also imports from other areas to which a part flows back.

In other words, the cumulative import quota of an area (i.e. Vorarlberg) is higher than for Austria as a whole.

The use of input–output analysis results in many useful results; however, the interpretation of the results must take into consideration the different restrictive assumptions of the input–output model. In principle, the assumptions are as follows (Skolka, 1974; Richter, 1981). The quantity relations of the inputs among themselves as well as with respect to the output are constant and independent of the production level. That means, the input–output analysis is based on linear-limitational conditions of production. Substitution possibilities of the inputs do not exist. The assumption of a linear-limitational production technique means that demand and supply elasticities are not considered. Economies of scale are also excluded from the analyses and the profit share is constant and independent of the production level. The output of each industry is homogeneous and produced with one technology.

Because of the restrictive assumptions, the results of the input–output analysis can only be cautiously applied with respect to practical problems, especially for marginal demand increases. This is also true for the employment effects resulting from a demand increase as the input–output technology does not take into consideration capacity utilization important for tourism. In practice, capacities often exist which allow employment and the capacities themselves to react to demand change when the capacity utilization has for a given time period a given level. An additional consideration is that labor force and physical capital is viewed as a whole unit and cannot be divided into smaller units.

The quantitative impact of tourism in Vorarlberg

Receipts and value-added

The receipts of Vorarlberg from tourism in 1993 totalled 18.4 billion Austrian schillings, approximately 8.5% of the Austrian total receipts. About 90% of the figure consists of foreign tourism, with a relatively smaller part belonging to domestic tourism. The impact of the tourist demand on the Vorarlberg economy can be seen best in an input–output table.

As shown in Table 14.1, the hotel and restaurant sector received around half of the tourist expenditures. Almost 40% of the whole tourism demand is spread among five other sectors. The most important are the food and beverage and wholesale/retail sectors, followed by transportation and communication, the oil industry, and the textile/clothing sector. The share of the other sectors on the tourism demand is just 10%. The most important differences in the demand structure regarding both domestic and foreign demand exist in the food and beverage sector and in the hotel and restaurant industry. The discrepancy in the hotel and restaurant industry is caused by the fact that the weight of business trips in domestic travel is significantly higher than in international travel and that this form of travel has a higher concentration of expenditures in hotels and restaurants than does recreational travel.

The tourist expenditure flows to domestic industries as well as to foreign industries (direct imports). All these sectors must spend a share of their receipts for inputs so that they can produce goods and services demanded by the tourists. These induced deliveries originate either from domestic producers or from producers abroad (indirect imports).

The results of the cumulative process generated by tourism demand can be calculated with the help of input–output analysis: For example, 1000 schillings of tourism demand generates in Austria a value added of 794 schillings (see Table 14.2). From this sum, the biggest amount ends up in the hotel and restaurant industry (around 30%). Following the hotel and restaurant industry, the wholesale/retail and food and beverage sectors received the next largest amounts of the induced value added. These sectors are followed by banking and insurance, agriculture and wood industries and transportation.

Around 20% of the tourism demand is imports. 14% is indirect and 7% direct.

The multiplier of 0.794 is the starting point for calculating the value-added effects of tourism in Vorarlberg. After weighing all factors and different models simulations, the resulting value-added multiplier for Vorarlberg was around 0.45. In other words, 1000 schillings of tourism expenditure results in 450 schillings of value added. The remaining 550 schillings are spent on imports from abroad or from other Austrian states.

The application of the value-added multiplier for tourism expenditures in Vorarlberg results in a value added which amounts to 8.3 billion schillings. In total the value added from tourism in Vorarlberg amounted

Table 14.1 *The structure of tourism demand in Austria (in percentage at 1990 prices, without value-added tax)*

	Foreign	Domestic	Total
(1) Agriculture	3.1	2.0	2.9
(2) Mining	—	—	—
(3) Food and beverage	11.7	7.6	11.0
(4) Textile and clothing	4.1	6.2	4.5
(5) Lumber	1.2	0.8	1.1
(6) Pulp and paper	2.0	1.4	1.9
(7) Chemical industry	1.2	1.9	1.4
(8) Oil	6.9	6.5	6.8
(9) Stone and glass	0.2	0.1	0.2
(10) Metal	0.4	0.5	0.4
(11) Machinery and equipment	3.2	2.5	3.1
(12) Energy	0.1	0.1	0.1
(13) Construction	—	—	—
(14) Retail	9.2	8.6	9.0
(15) Hotel and restaurant	48.2	53.1	49.0
(16) Traffic and communication	7.1	7.3	7.2
(17) Banking and insurance	0.2	0.1	0.1
(18) Other services	1.2	1.3	1.3
Total	100.0	100.0	100.0

Table 14.2 *Distribution of the induced value added of tourism demand per 1000 schillings in Austria (in percentage at 1990 prices, without value-added tax)*

	Foreign	Domestic	Total
(1) Agriculture	76.7	65.7	74.7
(2) Mining	1.1	1.1	1.1
(3) Food and beverage	84.1	74.0	82.2
(4) Textile and clothing	11.6	16.8	12.5
(5) Lumber	6.1	5.0	5.9
(6) Pulp and paper	8.8	8.0	8.6
(7) Chemical industry	10.2	11.4	10.4
(8) Oil	34.5	32.9	34.2
(9) Stone and glass	4.3	4.2	4.3
(10) Metal	3.6	3.8	3.7
(11) Machinery and equipment	26.6	24.2	26.1
(12) Energy	18.3	19.1	18.6
(13) Construction	11.3	11.6	11.3
(14) Retail	88.0	84.7	87.4
(15) Hotel and restaurant	233.2	256.3	236.9
(16) Traffic and communication	73.7	75.6	74.4
(17) Banking and insurance	79.7	78.0	79.3
(18) Other services	22.5	23.1	22.6
Value-added total	794.2	795.5	794.3
Direct imports	69.1	67.3	68.9
Indirect imports	136.7	137.2	136.8
Total	1000.0	1000.0	1000.0

to 8% of the regional GDP. Owing to the relatively high tourism intensity in Vorarlberg, the tourism share for all of Austria is 7% lower than in Vorarlberg.

The share of the value added of the Vorarlberg hotel and restaurant industry has a value of 5.5% lower than that of the whole tourism share (8%). These two figures are just comparable on a limited basis, as only a certain part of the hotel and restaurant industry belongs to the tourism sector; certain expenditures in this industry belong to private consumption (lunches, dinners and drinks) as well as business meals and receptions. In Austria as a whole, the part of tourism in the hotel and restaurant industry is around 75%.

Taxes

Accompanying tourism demand are the many taxes to be paid. In addition to direct and indirect federal taxes, many special state and local taxes must be paid as well.

Different calculations show us that 34.4% of the tourism expenditure in Vorarlberg consists of taxes (see Table 14.3). This calculated 'tourist tax rate' is 4.5 percentage points higher than the average for the Austrian economy as a whole. This higher tax rate in tourism is caused by a cumulation of both the indirect taxes and the relatively high value-added taxes. From 1000 schillings of tourism expenditures in Vorarlberg, 133 schillings must be paid for value-added taxes, 90 schillings for direct taxes, and also 90 schillings for employee social insurance. 85 schillings are left remaining in the category of indirect taxes. Of that, 44 schillings go to the federal state and 41 schillings to the states and their towns. In total, per 1000 schillings 398 schillings result in taxes; however, the relatively high subsidies in the tourism sector (above all for the hotel and restaurant industry and food and beverage production) must be considered here, amounting to 42 schillings, as well as the relatively low import taxes (192 schillings); this adds up to the 344 schillings.

Employment

The input–output employment multipliers of tourism demand are higher than those of private consumption and final domestic demand. The above-average employment multiplier of tourism results from the relative low import quota and the relatively low labor productivity in the hotel and restaurant industry. This is a result of the relatively low rationalization possibilities.

The employment multiplier of tourism demand (at current prices and value-added tax included) was in 1993 1.9 persons per 1 million schillings. The multiplier for the employed persons was 1.4 and for self-employed persons, 0.5 (per 1 million schillings).

The calculations for Vorarlberg result in an employment multiplier of 1.2. That means that, in the year 1993, 1 million schillings of tourism expenditures resulted in 1.2 persons employed in Vorarlberg. For employed people the multiplier was 0.9, and for the self-employed, 0.3.

These multiplier values must be interpreted very cautiously as the calculated multipliers answer just the question of how many persons in the past were employed through tourism expenditure. Forecasts should also take into consideration the fact that the capacity utilization is normally far less than 100% and that reactions to a demand increase do not occur immediately. Instead of an immediate response, it will take a certain time operating at a higher level of capacity utilization before one can see actual adaptations to the higher demand level.

However, disregarding all the abovementioned problems, the application of the calculated employment multipliers would have the following results: In the year 1993, tourism in Vorarlberg employed around 22 000 persons. From that figure, 16 500 persons are employed and 5500 are self-employed. The calculated employment figures are per definition full-time *working places*, not persons, which are partly dependent on tourism.

Table 14.3 *Taxes per 1000 schillings of tourism expenditure*

Direct taxes	90
Employee social insurance	90
Indirect taxes	85
Federal	44
State and local	41
Value-added and import taxes for intermediary deliveries	133
Taxes in total	398
Subsidies	− 42
Taxes and subsidies on the domestic production	356
Direct imports	192
Total	344

References

Richter, J. (1981) *Strukturen und Interdependenzen der österreichischen Wirtschaft*, Vienna.

Richter, J. and Zelle, K. (1981) Interregionale Lieferverflechtungen in Österreich.—Möglichkeiten der Schätzung einer multiregionalen Input–Output-Tabelle durch ein 'information minimizing model'.

Schulmeister, St. (1981) *Reiseverkehr und Wirtschaftsstruktur*, Vienna.

Skolka, J. (1974) *Anwendung der Input–Output-Analyse*, Vienna.

Skolka, J. (1981) *Entwicklung der Arbeitsproduktivität in Österreich 1964 bis 1977*, WIFO-Monatsberichte.

Skolka, J. (1987) *Der Steuergehalt der Endnachfrage*, WIFO-Monatsberichte.

Smeral, E. (1986) *Reiseverkehr und Gesamtwirtschaft*, Vienna.

15 The destination capacity index: a measure to determine the tourism carrying capacity

N. SALEEM

Introduction

The application of threshold concepts or the carrying capacity existed in the engineering field long before it was borrowed by other disciplines. For engineers, architects or builders, it usually meant the maximum capacity that a facility, infrastructure or a building could sustain in terms of the number of users. In this respect, the use of carrying capacity approaches were targeted primarily to facilitate the development of structures and it therefore remained a planning tool. Its application to assess the capacity of 'space', that is of the built and natural environment, possibly could have evolved from different perspectives: as an evaluative tool from urban planners and as a site/facility management tool from recreation organisations. It would become clear from later discussion how and when its application as a management tool expanded to include other areas and dimensions, i.e. from the area of physical carrying capacity to social, ecological and economic carrying capacities.

Our concern here is with the carrying capacity issues of tourism destinations. This immediately poses the question of what capacity we are concerned about—is it physical, social or economic? The aim of this paper primarily is to establish and explore a framework to examine the overall tourism capacity of a destination from a socio-economic perspective. But social issues and impacts of tourism cannot be studied independently and in isolation without also considering the other overlapping and intertwined issues and impacts. It is believed that the level of economic benefits/disbenefits of tourism and the degree of tourism activity determined by the volume of visitors and the amount of land used or exposed to tourism activity can have a bearing on the socio-psychological environment of the resident population and the ecological capacity of the destination.

In order to examine the concept of tourism carrying capacity from a socio-economic perspective for any specific destination, it is important to ask some key questions. How is tourism income shared between the local and the migrant employees and entrepreneurs? What sort of social relationship exists between the residents and the visitors due to differences in attitudes, status and cultural values? And how equitable is the distribution and allocation of resources such as land, facilities and infrastructure? Having these questions in mind, the author puts forward three postulates which link the determinants of the above issues and their impacts to the destination's tourism capacity (which is measured as an index) by a simple mathematical formula. The resulting index, however, does not tell us about the magnitude of the tourism capacity but it does help to compare capacity over a period of time and among similar destinations, and to assess how much has changed and in what direction the capacity has changed.

Tourism carrying capacity

Initial discussion on the application of the carrying capacity concept in the field of recreation management probably dates back to the 1960s. Butler and Kundson (as quoted by Williams and Gill (1991)) point out the use of carrying capacity approaches in establishing recreation management strategies to alleviate environmental and social impacts. Carrying capacity is mainly referred to as the threshold or limit of capacity of certain facilities such as a swimming pool or infrastructure or ecological environment like the national parks. Traditionally, it is said to determine the maximum number of users that can be accommodated at a given time by a certain facility or a specific site. In the 1960s, even in the recreation field, it was meant to indicate the physical carrying capacity rather than other derivatives such as the social carrying capacity or ecological carrying capacity. Further, in the recreation area, carrying capacity methods were used primarily as a management tool and its applications were essentially site-specific. It does not mean that the concept was not intended for use as a planning tool in pre-development stage. Piperoglou's suggestion (cited in Pearce 1989) that capacity assessment should be carried out before development takes place dates back to 1967.

In tourism too, the carrying capacity concept was applied in the early days to determine the physical capacity of tourism facilities. Later developments, as in the area of recreation management, expanded the concept to include environmental and ecological carrying capacity. In the 1980s, the idea of determining environmental carrying capacity became almost synonymous with the concept of environmental impact assessment. In the tourism arena at the same time, we saw new developments such as psychological and social carrying capacity emerging in academic circles. In fact, the social environment in tourism destinations has recently become the focus of many tourism academics involved in the research of carrying capacity.

Cooke and d'Amore, as cited by Pearce (1989), define social carrying capacity as 'that point in the growth of tourism where local residents perceive, on balance, an unacceptable level of social disbenefits from tourist development'. This may also be interpreted as the social-economic condition where the perceived psychological impacts of tourism are no longer considered as beneficial or worthwhile by the majority in the community. Certain variables such as the number of visitors, or type of visitors, that constitute the tourism environment, and the degree of development measured by volume of economic activity, and the level of tourist development can have a direct bearing on the social-economic conditions mentioned above.

In most recreation sites, the visitors are mainly the local residents. While in some cases, the use of facilities is limited only to the residents, much research in recreation management has been undertaken to examine facilities and sites where the users were both locals and outsiders. Considering these situations as similar to those of tourism activities, potential management issues and strategies can be examined from tourism management perspectives. One such issue would be to determine the acceptable level of tolerance between the visitors and residents when it comes to using public facilities and recreational or tourism facilities.

It is not intended here to review and analyse the environmental and ecological impacts nor the carrying capacity of a tourism destination at a micro-level. However, this is not intended to discount the importance of the ecological carrying capacity. Ecological capacity refers to the limits on the effects of tourism or recreational activity on flora and fauna, earth, water and air. As it will be noted later, this study is confined to examining and determining the tourism capacity on a broader scale rather than at micro-level where ecological impacts are assessed carefully.

One major objective of this article is to examine the tourism impact from a socio-economic perspective assuming that the degree of development and activity have a bearing on the tourism capacity of a destination in general. For this reason, it becomes necessary to include measures of economic impacts and to consider evaluating the system's economic carrying capacity. Surprisingly, the literature does not provide much evidence of using the word 'economic carrying capacity' within a socio-economic context. But Jansen-Verbeke (1991) discusses the economic carrying capacity of historic cities as having an impact on the use of buildings and land, leading to changes in use, loss of housing capacity, invasion of tourism-oriented shops, rise of property values etc., all of which can have a bearing on the social conditions.

Potential determinants of tourism carrying capacity

Socio-economic environment: income multipliers

Although carrying capacity is not often used in terms of economic dimensions, it is useful to introduce the concept to determine the limits of beneficial economic impacts. This immediately warrants discussion on adverse economic impacts. As in other areas, the laws of diminishing utility can be applied here. Should the marginal economic benefit of tourism diminish during the process of tourism development, it becomes necessary to determine the specific level of tourism activity when the net total economic benefit will be at an optimum. The reasons for diminishing economic benefit are more than one, but one key factor is benefit leakage from the system or the destination. If the destination attracts outside entrepreneurs and immigrant labour who would eventually repatriate the benefits from the system in the form of profits and wages, and if the system demands luxurious imports to satisfy the needs of incoming visitors, then the destination's economy can have a substantial amount of benefit leakage.

It is therefore necessary to determine the threshold level beyond which the local economy cannot be sustained without a substantial amount of benefit leakage. The economic carrying capacity can be said to refer to the threshold point which provides the highest level of benefit or earning retention to the system (regardless of whether it is an historic city in a larger state or an island in its entirety). When the economic disbenefits are higher than the net benefits, adverse socio-economic impacts can begin to develop. The following trends might provide some foresight as to what would constitute an adverse economic outcome:

—increase in imports from outside, particularly food items
—influx of migrant labour
—influx of outside entrepreneurs and vendors
—unplanned and spurious over-development

—increasing property values due to speculation
—inflationary tendencies

If these trends remain persistent and continue, the tourism destination could soon begin to see the shoots of adverse economic impacts. These impacts may be not merely economic disbenefits but also adverse social conditions. Visible symptoms of such adverse social-economic conditions can be characterised by the following:

—low-paid jobs and economic hardship for some, leading to social polarisation
—competing migrant labour associated with resident hostility and aggression
—social tensions between the have and have-nots
—antagonism towards the outside entrepreneurs and vendors by the locals
—perceived economic disbenefits by the locals
—high leakage of earnings from the system due to repatriation of profit/wage and imports of luxury goods
—inefficiency and effectiveness of the system in general

It is extremely difficult to establish a system for monitoring local social conditions that may emerge from changing social-economic consequences described above. However, changing social conditions in a locality leading to irritations and antagonism among locals towards the migrant workers, social polarisation between the have and have-nots, and demonstration effects etc. can be easily observed over a period of time. When an economy (either local or national) is booming, potential employees from the surrounding area could see this as a green pasture. In the tourism industry, it is essentially less difficult not to woo the relatively cheaper migrant labour when the employers are concerned about efficiency of operation rather than to whom they give the jobs.

It is often the local unemployed youth who resort to crime or other socially undesirable activities if opportunities are denied to them. Social irritation and aggression by the locals can be demonstrated against not only the migrant workers and entrepreneurs but also the tourists. Further, among the local entrepreneurs, there is always a feeling of tension in the air when outside entrepreneurs move in to exploit the economic benefits. Tourism opportunities always seem to attract outsiders to destinations in the form of investors, vendors, and employees.

What about the increase in the cost of living and inflated property values? Not all local residents are dependent on tourism to earn their living. Social polarisation, which can divide the residents into have and have-nots, can threaten the entire industry because of economic disparity where the have-nots cannot afford a reasonable standard of living. The crux of the argument is that economic factors can influence the social conditions. This means adverse economic outcomes of tourism activity and the linking resident behaviour and attitudes can cause the locals to feel uneasy about the visiting guests that they are supposed to host. One of the theses of this paper is that the 'income multiplier' can be used as a barometer to gauge the socio-economic condition of the destination. The 'income multiplier' derived from Keynesian principles can be said to represent the level of economic activity as well as the benefit level that the locality or host country as a whole can enjoy. According to the Keynesian concept of income multipliers,

$$M - 1/(1 - mpc)$$

where M is the multiplier and mpc stands for marginal propensity to consume. Since $(1-mpc)$ is the benefit leakage from the system, we can re-write the above as:

$$M = 1/L$$

where L is the leakage factor.

Socio-cultural environment: relative visitor density

Socio-cultural impacts of tourism can occur at different levels and dimensions. The extent to which the locals are affected socially or culturally depend on a number of factors. Here our inquiry ponders the significant impacts that may arise out of human interaction. In this respect, we are primarily concerned with the exchange of views, ideas, ideology, customs, traditions and lifestyle—not to mention the exchange of any tangible materials that symbolise the above-described attributes. The direction in which these attributes will flow depends on the intensity of exchange and the number of participants and it always tends to flow from the strong to the weak. Losing or gaining one's social or cultural traits or attributes may depend on the size of the visiting population as much as on the type of visitors.

The ratio of visitor number to the resident population, therefore, can be said to signify the degree of socio-cultural impact in the form of alien traits that the visiting population may deposit on the local people. This becomes an obvious fact if we look at most small states and islands where tourism dominates the national economy. The islands and small states in the tropics, particularly the micro-islands, have no viable economic resource-base or potential for economic diversity and heavily rely on the visiting tourists from the industrialised West. Some Mediterranean islands and coastal regions can also be categorised into this group of micro-states. In many of these micro-states, the local resident number becomes negligible when compared with the number of visiting tourists, particularly during the holiday season. In Malta, for example, currently there is a resident population of about 350 000 and the number of visitors per year is around 800 000. This gives a high visitor to resident ratio of 2.5 : 1. In some of the Caribbean islands, this ratio is even higher. In many macro-states where tourism is popular, this ratio may not be as high as in the micro-islands, but a similar situation can exist in the tourism destination areas such as the seaside resorts of the French Riviera and the Amalfitan coast of southwest Italy or the historic cities of York and Bruges.

However, tourism does not always bring about social-cultural impacts, particularly when it takes place within a country of a homogeneous social-cultural structure. Tourism within Europe or North America, for example, might not produce any changes in the social environment. Nevertheless, too many visitors who are in fact alien to the social structure of a specific locality, whether from the same country or not, can tilt the balance of the social-cultural fabric as well as the socio-economic structure and thereby cause a state of irritation, hostility and antagonism towards the visitors. It can also be speculated that increasing visitor numbers would attract social misfits and vice from elsewhere. Furthermore, individuality and privacy and the territorial integrity of individuals, which Western culture desires so much, can also be threatened by crowding, particularly by outside visitors. If there is one measure that can readily indicate the degree of crowding due to migrant population, it is the ratio of the visitor to the resident numbers. This ratio is theoretically arrived at from population density, i.e. number of people per square kilometre. By comparing the resident density with visitor density, it becomes possible to derive the relative density of visitors, i.e. visitor density to resident density which, when simplified, becomes the ratio of visitor numbers to resident numbers in one square kilometre. Thus: relative visitor density (RVD) becomes

$$RVD = \text{(Visitor density)}/\text{(Resident density)}$$

i.e.

$$RDV = \text{Visitor number}/\text{Resident number}$$

or

$$RDV = N_t/N_r$$

where, N_t is the number of tourists and N_r the number of residents.

Ecological and socio-psychological environment: relative land-use intensity

Socio-economic conditions as well as physical and ecological aspects of a geographical location can be affected also by the degree of development activity that tourism might bring in. The degree of development in the form of attractions, facilities, and infrastructure can be correlated to the amount of land used for tourism development and the amount of space that is allocated to visitor activities. Of course, the greater the amount of land used by tourism programmes, the less that becomes available for resident use. Constraints in resident use of land and public space could cause social tensions, anxiety and dismay among the locals, particularly when there is fear of dislocation. This would not only instigate perceived social-economic disbenefits but also lower the residents' psychological carrying capacity. If there is an indicator that would help determine the state of the above conditions realistically, it is the intensity of land-use by both the tourists and the residents. We may define land-use intensity as the percentage of the total land used by a specific sector or group, directly as well as indirectly. It is measured as the ratio of the amount of land area used by resident to the total land available or the area under tourist development and therefore exposed to tourists' use to the total available land. This means, the ratio of resident land-use to the total land area can be represented by (LU_r/LU_a) and that of tourist land-use to the total land area can be expressed by (LU_t/LU_a), where LU_r, LU_t and LU_a are resident land-use, tourist land-use and total land-use by all, respectively.

Therefore, the relative intensity of land use ($RILU$) becomes:

$$RILU = (LU_t/LU_a)/(LU_r/LU_a)$$

i.e.

$$RILU = (LU_t/LU_r)$$

Measuring the tourism carrying capacity

The more we get into subjective areas, the more we get away from developing methods to measure the carrying capacity objectively. Some researchers have attempted to use econometric models to determine the carrying capacity where the input variables ranged from visitor numbers to the tolerance level of both the resource system and the resident population. While most of these studies have been in the areas of recreational facilities or sites like national parks, recent attempts have been made to determine the tourism carrying capacity of historic cities as well as coastal areas.

In the case of environmental pollution or ecological effects, the application of scientific knowledge (physics, chemistry and biology) has proved successful in establishing some measures to determine the carrying capacity. For example, sea pollution level in coastal areas due to effluent discharges can be measured by counting a certain type of bacteria in the beach water, or air pollution due to traffic emissions by the amount of carbon monoxide in the air. Further, it is also possible to monitor and measure the impacts of this pollution on the ecosystem by scientific experiments.

Unfortunately, any measures to determine hostility or aggression levels of residents towards visitors in a tourist destination or social impacts of economic deprivation or social polarisation cannot be easily developed. Concepts and models from behavioural science and social science are, however, widely used in this area; but the subject matter under investigation becomes very subjective and the decision-making process is essentially judgemental.

Researchers from various disciplines have tried different approaches to describe and assess tourism carrying capacity. For some tourism carrying capacity is market driven (Plog, 1991) and it seems to reach the threshold when the visitor number approaches a point beyond which the destination fails to provide quality visitor experience. The 'critical range of elements of capacity' in Butler's (1980) cycle of evolution model describes such a threshold level of visitor numbers. Hawkins (as quoted by Williams and Gill (1991)) takes another step forward to include socio-psychological variables where the residents/tourists relationship plays a significant role. His model stresses the values the community perceives in the effects of tourism but it fails to consider the importance of economic benefits and disbenefits of tourism which could have had an impact on these perceived values.

In the end, what we are witnessing here is the subjectivity of the entire concept: when it comes to determining the carrying capacity we are moving from somewhat tangible indicators to rather subjective measures. Then, what about those simple indicators which some of us still may refer to to determine the tourism carrying capacity? Lozato-Grotart (1992) notes that the use of traditional indicators such as visitor density measured as ratio of tourist numbers per acre per year/month, tourist activity index measured as a ratio of the number of tourist beds per resident population in a given destination, or the ratio of number of tourist homes to the total number of properties etc. can determine the capacity of tourist destinations. The number of visitors, the bed-occupancy rate, the ratio of visitors to residents or visitors per acre, and developed land as a percentage of total land can also be used to assess whether or not a site or location has reached its capacity. If measured and monitored using these indicators within a destination context, it can obviously provide some idea whether or not the tourism threshold has been reached in a destination. These indicators, however, may not provide any useful measures to assess or compare the state of the social environment or the degree of social impacts of tourism. Nonetheless, some links that might indicate any relationships between these data and the prevailing social conditions, or even the physical capacity, can be established using certain postulates.

The destination capacity index of tourism

In this article, the author will attempt to establish a framework and a simple mathematical formula to determine the tourism carrying capacity of a destination using previously discussed indicators (leakage factor, RVD and $RILU$) as input variables. The proposed framework is derived from three postulates. These postulates are expected to establish a relationship between the destination's carrying capacity and its determinants.

The objective here is to establish a measure that would provide information about the 'global' tourism carrying capacity of the destination. The tourism carrying capacity in question is the level of tourism activity in a destination that we would like to maintain without exerting any adverse socio-economic impact on the community. Although it may be possible to establish some links between the environmental or ecological impact of human activity and interaction in a destination and the traditional indicators that are used to develop this framework, the primary aim of this paper is to establish an index that can be used to determine the tourism capacity of a destination within a 'global' context. Consequently, the proposed index would seem to dominate the socio-economic attributes. Further, this index is to be called simply the 'destination capacity index' (DCI) of tourism and is to be derived mathematically from the following postulates:

1. The DCI is directly proportional to the income multiplier of the destination.
2. The DCI is inversely proportional to the relative visitor density (RVD) of the destination.

3. The DCI is inversely proportional to the relative intensity of land-use ($RILU$) of the destination.

The first postulate states that the capacity of a destination (mainly in socio-economic terms) to accept and tolerate visitors increases proportionately with the level of net economic benefits which can be measured by means of the 'tourism multiplier'. Here, based on the Keynesian principles of income multipliers, the 'leakage of economic benefits' factor is used as the input variable. Therefore, using the previously defined symbols mathematically we may write the postulate as:

$$DCI \propto M \quad \text{i.e.} \quad DCI \propto 1/L$$

This means,

$$DCI = k_1/L$$

where k_1 is a constant, M is the multiplier and L the leakage factor.

The second postulate states that the capacity of a destination to absorb tourists decreases proportionately with increase in the relative visitor density (RVD) which is measured by the ratio of tourist numbers (N_t) to the resident number (N_r). This means mathematically:

$$DCI \propto 1/RVD \quad \text{i.e.} \quad DCI \propto 1/(N_t/N_r)$$

This means,

$$DCI = k_2 \times 1/(N_t/N_r) \quad \text{i.e.} \quad DCI = k_2 \times N_r/N_t$$

where k_2 is a constant.

Finally, the third postulate states that the capacity of a destination to receive outside visitors decreases proportionately with increase in the relative intensity of land-use ($RILU$) by the visitors measured by the ratio of tourist land-use (LU_t) to the resident land-use (LU_r) potential. Mathematically, as before, we can write this as:

$$DCI \propto 1/RILU \quad \text{i.e.} \quad DCI \propto 1/(LU_t/LU_r)$$

This means,

$$DCI = k_3 \times 1/(LU_t/LU_r) \quad \text{i.e.} \quad DCI = k_3 \times LU_r/LU_t$$

where k_3 is a constant.

By combining the above three postulates, we can conclude that the destination capacity index (DCI) of tourism is directly proportional to the economic income multiplier and inversely proportional to the relative visitor density (RVD) and the relative intensity of land-use ($RILU$). This means:

$$DCI \propto 1/L \times 1/RVD \times 1/RILU \qquad (1)$$

where, $1/L$ is the income multiplier and L is the leakage.

By substituting the variables in Eqn (1) with the above-described indicators, we now have the following equation for DCI:

$$DCI = k \times 1/L \times [(N_r \times LU_r)/(N_t \times LU_t)]$$

i.e.

$$DCI = k/L \times \frac{N_r \times LU_r}{N_t \times LU_t} \qquad (2)$$

where k is a constant.

The proposed capacity measure (DCI) is essentially an index and refers to the eventual social-economic conditions of the destination and the psychological status of the residents. Ideally, the destination capacity index of tourism should help us determine the overall tourism carrying capacity or tourism threshold of the destination at macro-level. However, this may be misleading because there is no way one could conclude that the current carrying capacity of the destination is ideal. Further, for a number to be computed for the DCI, it is necessary to determine a value for k, which should remain a constant under normal circumstances. Also, it is mathematically possible to have a DCI equal to zero but in reality, the carrying capacity of a destination may not reach a zero value. In this context, the index, DCI, provides a comparative measure. Even without a value obtained for k, it is therefore possible to compare the tourism capacity of a destination for different time periods using appropriate variables in the equation.

For example, the DCI of a destination for a specific year can be compared with a 'base year' simply by assuming the base year index (perhaps, this can be the year when the capacity was considered to be ideal or most appropriate) to be 100. An index of less than 100 for a specific year would indicate that the tourism capacity has declined compared to the base or ideal year capacity and such a measure can be expressed as a percentage. The following example should help illustrate the function and role of DCI: Suppose that we could re-write the Eqn (2) as

$$Y_a = k/L \times X_a \qquad (3)$$

where, Y_a is the DCI for year a and X_a is the variable component of $(N_r \times LU_r)/(N_t \times LU_t)$ for the same year, a.

Similarly, for year b we can re-write the equation as below:

$$Y_b = k/L \times X_b \qquad (4)$$

In Eqns (3) and (4), X represents the independent variable and Y the dependent variable. Further, k/L can be considered as a constant if the leakage factor remains unchanged for a specific time period. If the L factor changes constantly, then it is required to be considered as a variable and should be incorporated with the X component. Assuming that there was no drastic change in the leakage of benefits, we may now write these equations as follows:

$$Y_a = K \times X_a \qquad (5)$$

and

$$Y_b = K \times X_b \qquad (6)$$

Now by dividing Eqn (5) by (6), we should get:

$$Y_a/Y_b = (K \times X_a)/(K \times X_b) \quad \text{i.e.} \quad Y_a/Y_b = X_a/X_b$$

Since values for X_a and X_b can be obtained, a comparative value for Y_b can be established by giving a DCI measure of 100 for Y_a, considering that Y_a stands for the DCI of the 'base year'.

Let us take an example of a hypothetical small island in the Mediterranean as receiving an annual average visitor number of 500 000, currently spread almost evenly over the year, owing to beach tourism in the summer months and a booming conference trade during the winter months. According to the historical records, let us also assume that the island received only 350 000 visitors five years ago and had a resident population of 250 000. Further, the current census data shows that the population figure remained constant during the last five years. Now, if the residents' former land-use capacity (the total land-use capacity is 160 000 acres) of 140 000 acres has been reduced to 120 000 acres due to new tourist development (which is an increase of 20 000 acres in tourist land-use pattern) in five years, then by applying Eqns (5) and (6) we have the following:

$$DCI \text{ for base year is } Y_a = K \times X_a$$

$$\text{and for year five is } Y_b = K \times X_b$$

Now by inserting appropriate values for X_a and X_b from the above example, we have:

$$Y_a = K \times (N_r \times LU_r)_a/(N_t \times LU_t)_a$$

and

$$Y_b = K \times (N_r \times LU_r)_b/(N_t \times LU_t)_b$$

i.e.

$$Y_a = K \times (250\,000 \times 140\,000)/(350\,000 \times 20\,000)$$

and

$$Y_b = K \times (250\,000 \times 120\,000)/(500\,000 \times 40\,000)$$

This means:

$$Y_a/Y_b = [K \times (5)]/[K \times (3/2)] = 10/3$$

If Y_a takes a value of 100 as the base year, then we get:

$$Y_b = 100/(10/3) = 30$$

This means, the current tourism capacity of the island is only 30% of the previous capacity of 100 five years ago. This shows that the DCI of tourism has declined 70% from the base year.

Should any change in the leakage of benefit or earning retention in the system occur, the K factor ought to change ($K = k/L$, where L is the leakage factor measured as a percentage of total tourism earnings both direct and indirect). The earning leakage indicates the outflow of benefits in the form of repatriation of profit and wage, payment for imports, direct and indirect taxes, and savings. Significant change in any one of the above factors or in the sum total of the above will have a drastic impact on the percentage benefit leakage rate. Such an impact can be examined in the above hypothetical example of the Mediterranean island by modifying the DCI formula to include the L factor in the equation.

Suppose the leakage rate was 50% (or 0.50) five years ago, but owing to new tax relief provided to the local businesses, and because the island's tourism industry is currently dominated by local entrepreneurs instead of foreign companies, the current leakage rate is only 0.35. This change would make Eqns (5) and (6) look like:

$$Y_a = k/0.50 \times 5 \qquad \text{and} \qquad Y_b = k/0.35 \times 3/2$$

i.e.

$$Y_a/Y_b = 35/15$$

As before, if Y_a takes a value of 100, then we get:

$$Y_b = 100/(35/15) = (100 \times 15)/35 = 43\%$$

This clearly shows that improvement in the earning retention rate (or growth in income multipliers) can, in fact, increase the tourism capacity. In the above example, in fact, the decline in the tourism capacity is relatively less compared with what it would have been if no change (decrease) in leakage had occurred.

Here, if a value for *DCI* for a specific year is needed, it is necessary to carry out an extensive comparative study of similar destinations so that an appropriate standard can be obtained, based on the value of *K*. But such a standard always remains a relative index and the purpose can be either to compare with a similar destination which enjoys the most appropriate level (standard capacity) of tourism or with a base year when the same destination apparently enjoyed the right amount of tourism activity. But, in the absence of a base year or the most appropriate 'standard capacity' to be compared with, the *DCI* computation becomes just another measure to assess if the capacity has changed, regardless of direction.

Discussion and conclusion

As noted elsewhere, it can be said that the *DCI* is intended to measure the socio-economic carrying capacity of tourism. This means, the degree of development which correlates to the extent of tourism activity, and therefore to the degree of adverse impacts, was not incorporated directly into the formula. It is primarily the level of impacts (both beneficial and adverse), tolerance level (or how indifferent the resident can be to the visitors and associated consequences they bring about), and the residents' perceived benefits/disbenefits, together with the eventual outcomes such as hostility and aggression towards the visitors, or undesirable social conditions such as economic deprivation and social polarisation, that the proposed framework, and hence the *DCI*, is expected to represent.

Apart from the apparent 'limits' of the proposed model, there are other factors that we may want to explore. By examining Eqn (2) one could consider how the carrying capacity might be improved by increasing the number of residents (N_r) or residents' use of land (LU_r) when the total land space (LU_a) remains unchanged. Such a situation can occur when one-time tourists become residents, as happens in many south coast resorts in England, and local authorities adopt relevant policies and programmes to re-allocate the 'tourist space' and tourism resources to the local residents. It is therefore imperative that we consider these factors as relative measures (linked to each other where one influences the other), i.e. in terms of the ratio of visitor numbers to that of residents and the extent to which the tourists are allowed to use the space in terms of resident land-use pattern. While growth in the area of land-use by tourists should be accompanied by a decline in the net available

land for residents' use, the number of tourists can increase together with growth in local population. However, the degree of impact that the visitors can have on the host community can be said to be directly linked to the size of the resident population and, in fact, to the ratio of visitor to the resident numbers at any given time in any given location.

As for the intensity of impacts in a micro-island or small state, the total number of people at any given time consisting of residents and visitors can be a determining factor owing to the sheer size of the land and space available. In some destinations, tourists-turned-residents can help improve the social carrying capacity of the destination by being part of the community and thereby reducing the social tensions and hostility. On the other hand, in some destinations, 'migrant-residents' owning second homes are still looked upon as visitors and the residents can continue to show hostility towards these seasonal or occasional residents.

As for the potential use of the *DCI* model and its implications for destination management, it can be used as a planning tool as well as a management tool. If a 'standard capacity' can be established by *ex ante* comparative studies, the *DCI* model would be useful to determine a relative value for the carrying capacity which should provide useful information to formulate impact management strategies. On the other hand, as a planning tool, its application can be useful to project and evaluate potential impact levels in terms of the index's value for similar destinations or the same types of development. Further, it can also be used for formulating future development strategies or development control strategies for existing destinations, depending on the direction in which the *DCI* moves.

References

Butler, R. W. (1980) 'The concept of a tourist area cycle of evolution: implication for management of resources', *The Canadian Geographer*, 14(1):5–12.

Jansen-Verbeke, M. (1991) Based on a paper ('Managing and monitoring the tourism carrying capacity in a historical city: the planning issues') presented at the ACSP-ACSOP International Conference held in Oxford, 8–12 July, 1991.

Lozato-Grotart, J.-P. (1992) 'Geographical rating in tourism development', *Tourism Management*, 13(1):141–144.

Pearce, D. (1989) *Tourist Development*, Longman, Harlow, pp. 169–174.

Plog, S. C. (1991) *Leisure Travel: Making it a Growth Market . . . Again!*, John Wiley, New York.

Williams, P. W. and Gill, A. (1991) 'Carrying capacity management in tourism setting: a tourism growth management process (prepared for Alberta Tourism). Centre for Tourism Policy and Research, Simon Fraser University, Barnaby.

Part 2

THE TOURISM INDUSTRY

Travel and tourism is already the world's largest industry and the world's largest employer. The World Travel and Tourism Council has proved with compelling evidence that the direct and indirect impact of travel and tourism on the global economy produces a massive 10.2% of GDP. Its contribution is forecast to more than double by the year 2005 and in 1994 it is estimated to be employing 204 million people, equivalent to one in every nine workers.

The industry encompasses a panoply of businesses—airlines, tour operators, travel agents and hotels are representative of the major sectors. However, there are a multitude of other businesses such as construction, engineering and entertainment which, though not totally geared towards tourism, contribute and benefit from this massive industry. It is this factor which makes it extremely difficult to estimate the true value and size of the travel and tourism industry.

As a multi-sectoral industry, it is governed by a set of rules and regulations purporting to act in the consumer's interests, which are subject to change. In the airline sector, for example, tight restrictive bilateral agreements are finally being relaxed in favour of liberalisation. Although the United States has been the torch bearer with deregulation of its domestic market in 1978, the rest of the world has been slow to follow. Europe is now the leading light in this respect offering the hope of more competition and lower competitively priced fares. For the consumer, this has to be good news but the wait is not over yet. First, full cabotage rights will not be introduced into Europe until April 1997 and, second, the issue of state subsidies is one that is still to be resolved. Until such time fair competition will remain elusive. Furthermore, wrangling between airlines on an international scale over the exchange of rights further hinders the opening up of real competition. We still have a long way to go then before this goal is obtained.

Tour operators and travel agents have not escaped the hand of EC law. One such example is the 1992 EC Directive on package holiday travel. Though conceived as a measure to protect those booking international package holidays, it has been seen by some industry representatives as imposing unrealistic burdens on leisure product providers. As a result, some sectors of industry believe that it will frustrate rather than help their customers by imposing complex legal conditions on brochures and by complicating the everyday facility of taking telephone bookings.

A key characteristic of this industry then is its state of constant flux. It is an industry which is exposed to external pressures. This is exemplified by the Gulf War and the impact it had on travel. With fewer people flying, the ramifications were felt throughout the industry. The ongoing war in the former Yugoslavia is further evidence of the dramatic changes that can occur outside the tourism industry's control. In the context of tour operators' planning holidays up to two years in advance, it highlights some of the difficulties this industry faces.

Of the key trends facing the industry today, perhaps the biggest is the increasing polarisation between the very large firms at one end of the spectrum and the very small at the other. Termed 'globalisation' in the airline industry, it is a term applicable to all sectors and is resulting in the emergence of key global companies. In the hotel industry this is not a new phenomenon as the internationally recognised names of Forte and Hilton demonstrate. What is apparent is that the large are getting larger although there will always be a place within the industry for medium sized and small niche players. British Airways, for example, has made no secret of its quest for a global market presence and has formed a series of strategic alliances in pursuit of this goal. Indeed, in this sector, it is a widely held view that by the turn of the century there will be only a handful of mega-carriers. What is interesting is that the tourism industry is one that has been characterised by a preponderance of small businesses. How then will they survive as globalisation tightens its grasp on the industry at large? The evidence so far suggests that those professionally run small businesses will still have a role to play. The small independently run hotel, travel agent, tour operator and indeed airline fills a niche left vacant by the giants. It is altogether a different style of business offering a different style of service and attracting a different sort of consumer. In this sense the two complement rather than compete with each other.

The burgeoning growth of this most dynamic of industries is reflected in the broad spectrum of papers presented in this part. Roehl, for example, provides an interesting insight into the world of gambling as a tourist attraction; Phelps does the same for museums, while Frew turns her attention to the new opportunities presenting themselves to Australian tourism arising from international charter flights. Remaining in the airline sector, Seldon and Seldon tackle the complex issue of airline pricing while Forbes delves into transport policy in the European Union. From airlines we turn to the conference industry with a paper by Munro that looks at the effects of conference centres on the local economy as well as speculating on this particular industry's future. Yet another contrast is provided by Prentice and Light and Swarbrooke in their papers on heritage tourism and again by Haylock with a state-of-the-art view of timeshare. Stevens then provides an interesting perspective on the often neglected subject of stadia tourism.

Evidence of the importance of information technology (IT) throughout the industry is provided by way of the number of papers concentrating on this theme (Archdale; Buhalis; Desinano and Vigo; Williams and Hobson). While the focus obviously differs, the unifying thread is the increasing penetration of IT in all sectors of the industry. Extending beyond the status quo and concluding this section Williams and Hobson look to the future and speculate on the impact of 'virtual reality' (VR). One of many buzz phrases in the nineties, it will be interesting to watch VR's progress in tourism into the 21st century. Whatever the outcome, one thing is clear: IT will continue to play an increasingly significant part in the world of tourism but quite how it develops remains to be seen.

What is perhaps most interesting about this part is the freshness of its approach to the subject in question. It is, in essence, an applied approach. Original and expansive in subject matter, it sheds further light on this most fascinating of industries.

The Hon. Rocco Forte
Dr Marion M. Bennett

16 Gambling as a tourist attraction: trends and issues for the 21st century

W. S. ROEHL

Introduction

People often travel to have experiences normally unavailable to them. For example, people who live inland travel to visit the coast and people who live on the plains travel to recreate in the mountains. Another experience people often travel to enjoy is legalized gambling. This is especially true in nations with a federal structure, such as Australia, Canada, and the United States, where the individual states or provinces have considerable freedom in regulating business and entertainment activities. One consequence of this decentralization is variation among states and provinces in policy toward gambling. This variation means that some individuals must travel away from their place of residence to engage in legal gambling activities (Jackson and Hudman, 1987; Leiper, 1989).

Today gambling appears to be a growth industry. For example, Australia, which had two casinos in 1984, is expected to have 14 in operation by the mid-1990s (Beagle, 1993). Similarly, in the United States gambling legalization has boomed since the mid-1970s. The number of traditional casino hotels in Nevada and Atlantic City, New Jersey, have increased, limited stakes casinos have opened in South Dakota and Colorado, river boat casinos have begun operations in several states, and casinos on Indian reservations have appeared across the country.

Many see gambling, and especially casino gambling, as a way to help destinations compete more successfully for tourists. Others see the spread of gambling as a way to create jobs. Supporters also praise the legalization of gambling as a way to raise new tax revenues through a popular voluntary tax. However, some worry that the increased availability of legal gambling will result in numerous problems to the host community which would include compulsive gambling, crime and corruption, etc. Furthermore, they are concerned that these externalities will not only affect participants and the host community, but will also diffuse into the broader society.

There are also many operational and strategic questions facing gambling tourism. As the number of jurisdictions offering gambling tourism increases, both the response of potential tourists and the response of competing destinations will change.

There is a need for an integrated body of research about gambling tourism in general and casino tourism in particular[1] to both help guide public debate and inform the private sector.

Historical perspectives on gambling and tourism

Gambling has long been recognized as a tourist attraction. Gambling played an important role at the spa resorts of the 18th and 19th centuries. Members of the elite who frequented these resorts demanded amusements to occupy the time between treatments. Typical amusements included food, socialization, and gambling (Lowenthal, 1962; Turner and Ash, 1975).

Historically, the locations of gambling-based resorts have always been influenced by the geographical patterns of gambling acceptance. During the age of the elite resort, resorts tended to be located in geographically peripheral areas, allowing the elite to isolate themselves from the middle and lower classes. Peripheral location also served to isolate activities at these resorts (such as gambling) from public scrutiny. Even after society had turned against gambling in most English-speaking countries in the late 19th century, many older resort areas maintained a reputation for providing relatively open, though officially illegal, gambling. Examples in the United States include the traditional, geographically peripheral, resort areas of Hot Springs, Arkansas, Galveston, Texas, and Atlantic City, New Jersey.

Geography also plays a role in that many successful gambling resort areas have been located near areas of high population or large visitor volume where gambling was not permitted (Leiper, 1989). Examples of this locational strategy include Macau, Monte Carlo, Las Vegas, and Reno. In fact, Eadington (1976) argued that successful casino tourism areas should be located far enough from their major markets to ensure that casino gambling remained a speciality, rather than a convenience, good. Eadington felt that if access from large markets was too easy the novelty and excitement would soon wear off.

Today, gambling continues to play an important role in the United States' resort industry. Roehl and Van Doren (1990) proposed that casino-based resorts exemplify many of the trends affecting American resorts in general. Mega-hotels (3000 or more rooms) are built to achieve economies of scale. To obtain the year-round high occupancy rates necessary to recoup this investment, markets must diversify. This diversification expands the market for casino resorts from the traditional high-roller to a broader, middle-class market.

Trends in the spread of casino tourism

Australia provides a good example of the trends affecting the spread of casino tourism. In 1968 two casino options faced the government of Tasmania. One option was to open a British-style, members' only club. This would have catered to hard-core gamblers and combatted illegal gambling without stimulating the demand for gambling. The second option was to use casino tourism as a tool to stimulate the economy at a time when traditional economic activities were in decline. Tasmania chose the latter and initiated casino tourism in Hobart in 1973 (O'Hara, 1988).

Other states in Australia followed Tasmania's lead by opening casino facilities targeted at tourists. The first mainland casino opened in the Northern Territory in fiscal 1979. Until the mid-1980s Australian casinos remained geographically peripheral; Hobart and Launceston, Tasmania, and Alice Springs and Darwin, Northern Territory. This changed with the opening of casinos in Western Australia, South Australia, and Queensland. By the mid-1990s casinos will have opened amidst the center of the Australian population in Canberra, Melbourne, and Sydney (Beagle, 1993; Mossenson, 1991; Tasmanian Gaming Commission, 1989).

The spread of casino tourism in the United States followed the broad outline of the Australian experience. Casinos were seen as tourist facilities and were located in peripheral locations. In contrast, however, the spread of casinos in the United States has been characterized by more variation in the forms of casino tourism that have been implemented.

Three key trends have influenced the spread of casinos in the United States. First, public attitudes toward gambling have become more favorable. Roehl (1991) illustrated how public attitudes toward gambling had evolved between 1974 and 1989. For example, only 28% of adults in the South supported the legalization of casinos in 1974. By 1989, 52% of adults in the South supported legal casinos. During this period

gambling participation also increased. Second, reductions in federal funding for state and local governments during the 1980s motivated a search for new sources of revenue. Tax revenue from gambling was seen in many jurisdictions as a publicly acceptable means to produce new tax revenues (Winn and Whicker, 1989). Finally, in reaction to the Supreme Court's ruling recognizing the rights of Native Americans to operate gambling on their reservations, the Indian Gaming Regulatory Act of 1988 instituted procedures for states and Native American groups to negotiate agreements on the operation of gambling on tribal land.

Because of these trends, there has been a substantial increase in the availability of casinos. Traditional casino hotels are found in Nevada and Atlantic City, New Jersey (and will be joined in the mid-1990s by New Orleans). Limited-stakes casino gambling is available in Deadwood, South Dakota, and Black Hawk, Central City, and Cripple Creek, Colorado. Riverboat gambling is legal in six states: Iowa, Missouri, Illinois, Indiana, Louisiana, and Mississippi. Four other states currently have bills before their legislative bodies to legalize river boat casinos. Finally, 53 Indian tribes have signed contracts with their respective state governments to implement casino-style gambling on their reservations. As an example of the extent of reservation gambling, Minnesota has become the largest casino center between Nevada and New Jersey. Reservation casinos enjoyed revenue of $0.9 billion in 1991 (Connor, 1993; Doocey, 1993; McQueen, 1993; Minnesota Planning, 1992).

Geographically, the spread of casinos in the United States repeats the pattern seen in Australia. Casinos have spread from the periphery toward the core. The major difference between the two nations is that, while Australia will have casinos located in the heart of its population (Melbourne and Sydney), attempts to legalize casinos in major American cities such as New York and Chicago have failed.

European and American approaches to casino tourism

Traditionally, two approaches to casino legalization have been recognized (Commission on the Review of the National Policy Toward Gambling, 1976; Eadington, 1986; Skolnick, 1979a, 1979b). One is limited, or European-style, casinos. Casinos are viewed as a complement, not as a replacement, for other, traditional tourist attractions. Casinos are geographically, economically, and socially segregated. Regulations restrict casinos' ability to advertise and respond to the market. Steps are taken to discourage local residents from gambling. This approach is in contrast to the American (or perhaps more accurately Nevadan) model. The American model argues that market forces should determine location, number and operating hours for casinos. Promotion to stimulate demand is seen as a necessary action in a market economy and does not exclude local participation.

These two orientations mark endpoints on a continuum. Legislation legalizing casinos typically falls somewhere between these two extremes. For example, some of the first jurisdictions to legalize casinos after Atlantic City, Deadwood, South Dakota, and Black Hawk, Central City, and Cripple Creek, Colorado, attempted to alleviate public concerns about the social impacts of casinos by implementing low stakes (i.e., low maximum bet limits) gambling. As more jurisdictions legalize casino gambling in the United States it will be interesting to see how the semi-European approach of limited stakes competes with more market-driven approaches to casino gambling.

Casino tourists' motivations

Understanding casino tourism requires an understanding of why people gamble. One insightful approach is centered on the dichotomy of gambling as entertainment versus gambling to beat the system and make a profit (Eadington, 1987; Walker, 1992). This perspective recognizes that for many people gambling is a form of entertainment. A Gallup Survey conducted in 1989 illustrates this point (Hugick, 1989). When a sample of 1208 American adults were asked the main reason they gambled, 39% responded that they gambled to have a good time, because it is enjoyable, or for recreation. 12% cited excitement as the main reason they gambled, while 11% mentioned challenge or competition. In contrast, 27% of respondents cited making money or getting rich as the main reason they gambled.

For many, gambling is a form of entertainment. While winning bets increases the entertainment value of gambling, winning is neither strictly necessary nor expected. Research indicates that among people who gamble for entertainment, budgets are often established as they would be for other discretionary activities (Downes et al., 1974).

The behavior of those who gamble to make money is more complex. Gamblers who are committed to winning are faced with a situation where the bets available have a negative expected value. In the long run returns to the gambler from winning bets will be less than losses from unsuccessful bets, due to the house advantage. Gamblers who are committed to winning must therefore develop a set of beliefs to rationalize their frequent losses.

Walker (1992) suggests three core beliefs that are necessary in the face of continued losses among those who gamble for economic gain.

1. That through persistence, knowledge and skill it is possible for a person to make money through gambling.
2. While many will fail in the attempt, the gambler believes that he or she, unlike those others, has the resources needed to win.
3. That persistence in applying oneself to the task will ultimately be rewarded (Walker, 1992; see also Walker, 1985).

These core beliefs are reinforced, in the face of negative results, through various forms of irrational thinking. These include a belief in luck, an illusion of control over random events, and biased evaluation of outcomes (success is attributed to skill, failure is attributed to bad luck) (Walker, 1992).

In one of the few attempts to understand gambling's attraction for tourists, Leiper (1989) applied Gray's (1970) thesis concerning sunlust and wanderlust tourists to gambling. Leiper argues that gambling is more often associated with sunlust tourism than it is with wanderlust tourism. This is because wanderlust tourism is inherently riskier to the traveler. By placing himself or herself into a new situation, the wanderlust traveler is exposed to real-life gambles. Exposure to real-life gambles of new destinations and multiple destination trips minimizes the appeal of the contrived gambles available in the casino. In contrast, the sunlust traveler typically stays closer to home and engages in repeat visitation to a single destination. The sunlust traveler also tends to 'cocoon' himself or herself in the resort hotel, cruise ship, or camper park. Since real-life gambles have been minimized, the contrived gambles of the casino are attractive. Basically, Leiper is proposing that risk-taking is a homeostatic trait. If too little risk is available in the environment, artificial risks are sought. If the travel environment is inherently risky, artificial risks are not valued.

Social impacts of gambling tourism

While early research on the effects tourism has on the host community concentrated upon the (typically positive) economic impacts, research since the mid-1970s has noted that economic growth is often accompanied by changes to the host community's way of life (Pizam, 1978; Ap, 1990). The literature on casino tourism parallels the broader tourism literature. Early efforts stressed economic growth related to casino tourism. For example, in a review of five reports prepared for various constituencies in New York State between 1973 and 1979, Riper and Mango (1979) note that, while all reports devoted considerable efforts to quantifying the economic benefits associated with the legalization of casinos in New York, most failed to quantify the social costs that could reasonably be expected. By ignoring the cost side of the equation, casino supporters left the issue of casino development's social costs to casino opponents.

A good example of casino opponents' evaluation of the social costs of casino tourism is provided by Pollock (1987). Pollock quotes an academic critic of Atlantic City casino tourism who begins by citing the increased number of meals served by a local shelter for the homeless and increased arrests for prostitution. The critic continued by saying that:

> the inevitable outcome of casino gambling is the creation of a glamorous sink-hole of human degeneracy, pandering to the worst sides of an alienated culture unable to give rise to meaningful relations; where mobsters and others with unreported cash come to purchase ersatz pleasures and, in doing so, increasingly corrupt an area and its environs in ways never imagined by many who opted originally for casino gambling. (Pollock, 1987)

This reaction to casino tourism is not unusual; social policy relating to the regulation of vice often seems to rely on 'personal experience and solidly formed prejudice' (Kallick-Kaufmann and Reuter, 1979). Kallick-Kaufmann and Reuter (1979) continue, 'Most people believe that they know so much about it [gambling] that further research is simply unnecessary'.

However, the spread of casino tourism has begun to generate a body of research literature that attempts to measure the costs associated with casino development. The picture that is emerging from this literature is not as simple as the black and white arguments made by casino supporters and opponents.

Casinos and crime

One of the standard criticisms of casino tourism is that casinos increase crime. Yet this simple assertion is not as straightforward as it may first appear. An increase in crime can result from several distinct processes. The number of crimes reported can increase because of: (1) changes in the population at risk, (2) changes in criminal opportunities, (3) changes in law enforcement, of (4) changes in crime elsewhere (Albanese, 1985). More visitors to an area means that there are more opportunities for crime to

occur. An increase in resident population and/or income levels may also create more opportunity. Increasing the supply of hotel rooms has a similar effect by providing more opportunity for burglaries (Albanese, 1985). Furthermore, when dealing with a destination area that receives millions of visitors a year it is very difficult to determine an appropriate base rate for crime statistics (Friedman et al., 1989).

Studies of crime in post-casino Atlantic City exemplify these problems. Crime rates in Atlantic City and surrounding communities have increased since the first casino opened in 1978 (Friedman et al., 1989; Hakim and Buck, 1987). Economic modeling suggests, however, that this increase in crime is statistically related to the opening of casinos in Atlantic City, as well as increased wealth in some communities and increased unemployment in others. Not all types of crime have responded in the same way. In the Hakim and Buck (1987) study, larceny, auto theft, robbery, and violent crime were statistically related to the presence of casinos, while burglary and total crime were statistically unrelated to the presence of casinos in Atlantic City.

This line of research may best be summarized by Albanese (1985):

> any city which undergoes a significant revitalization (whether it be casino-hotels, theme parks, convention centers, or other successful development) that is accompanied by large increases in the number of visitors, hotels, and/or other commercial activity, may experience in [creased crime].

Equity of casino taxes on residents

One of the reasons gambling is legalized is to generate tax revenues. One of the concerns about casino tourism is the fairness of this tax on local residents. Studies of the tax burden of legalized gambling suggest that the taxes often fall more proportionately on lower income groups (i.e., the tax is regressive) (Clotfelter, 1979; Suits, 1977). Using data from a national sample, Suits's (1979) analysis indicated that casino gambling was a progressive form of taxation in contrast to most other forms of legalized gambling.

However, in a pair of studies, Mason, Shapiro, and Borg (Mason et al., 1989; Borg et al., 1990) question this interpretation. In the 1989 study the authors estimated that residents of Las Vegas pay a more regressive tax than do other Nevada residents who gamble in Las Vegas or out-of-state residents who gamble in Las Vegas. But since Las Vegas residents are the largest beneficiaries of these taxes the budgetary incidence and benefits are far less regressive than the tax incidence alone. Furthermore, the degree to which casino taxes are regressive is much less than other forms of legalized gambling such as state-sponsored lotteries.

In their 1990 study, Borg et al. estimated the equity of casino taxes in Las Vegas and Atlantic City. Results were not disaggregated by place of residence; they represent the tax burden on all gamblers in Las Vegas or Atlantic City. The overall tax structure in Las Vegas was regressive while casino taxes in Atlantic City approached proportionality.

Casinos and social impacts

A good example of the types of impacts associated with the introduction of casino tourism is provided by three studies of local government and agency officials in Black Hawk, Central City, and Cripple Creek, Colorado (Callaway et al., 1992; Caro et al., 1992; Elger et al., 1992). These three communities are small, historic mining towns in the mountains of central Colorado. Small stakes ($5.00 maximum bet) gambling on slot machines, blackjack, and poker was implemented in 1991. Interviews soon afterwards with local officials indicated that businesses had shifted their focus from serving residents to catering to tourists. This impacted residents' social life in that 'local' bars and restaurants became tourist-oriented casinos. The availability of basic goods and services to residents also declined as business people shifted to casino operations. Consequently, attitudes toward tourists also changed. Before gambling, tourists were seen as a necessary evil. After less than one year of gambling, residents were even more disenchanted with tourists.

Two of the key findings of these reports were that residents failed to accurately anticipate what casino tourism would be like and that the elite group surveyed had conflicting attitudes about the impacts of gambling tourism. Respondents believed that gambling had not improved the quality of residents' lives and that only a small percentage of local people benefitted from gambling. Despite these perceptions, respondents also felt that gambling held great promise for the community and it would be a bright spot in the community's future.

Other studies have directly questioned residents about the perceived benefits and costs associated with casino tourism. Pizam and Pokela (1985) surveyed residents in two areas of Massachusetts where casino tourism was proposed. Residents believed that casinos would bring economic benefits such as more jobs and a better standard of living. They also anticipated costs such as deterioration of neighborhood quality, more street crime and organized crime, and more traffic. Similarly, Caneday and Zeiger

(1991) surveyed residents of the casino town of Deadwood, South Dakota, and found that respondents recognized both benefits and costs after the legalization of small stakes casino gambling. Furthermore, residents and entrepreneurs noted different impacts. Overall attitudes toward casino tourism were influenced by how much benefit the respondent received from tourism. Residents employed in tourism were more supportive of casino tourism than were residents employed in non-tourism jobs.

In perhaps the most insightful approach to understanding how residents perceive the legalization of casino gambling, Mascarenhas (1990) attempted to assess the ethical dimensions of legalizing casinos in Detroit, Michigan. Teleological justification (actions justified by consequences) of casino gambling was relatively weak. Residents were suspicious of the consequences of legalizing casino gambling. More support was expressed on dimensions of distributional justice (equitable distribution of benefits and costs). A slim majority of respondents would support the legalization of casinos if profits from casinos would be used to fight urban problems or fund needed improvements. Attempts to evaluate the deontological ethics (some actions are never ethical regardless of their benefits to society) were less successful. However, it did appear that almost two-thirds of respondents saw no social–moral principle that could justify casino gambling.

Another social impact associated with casinos is gambling by under-age individuals. Frank (1990) evaluated the gambling behavior of college students attending an institution in the suburbs of Atlantic City, New Jersey. Results indicated that a substantial number of students under the legal age of 21 gambled on a regular basis. Furthermore, 6% scored 'at risk' on the South Oaks Gambling Screen, indicating that they had the potential to develop a gambling problem. Frank was concerned that the 6% figure was relatively high for a sample in this age group. He suggested that, despite the large number of under-age gamblers Atlantic City casinos annually turn away, under-age gambling was a serious problem.

Finally, the 'big picture' of how casino gambling impacts the host community has been addressed by a number of authors. One of the first studies to attempt an objective evaluation of the social costs of casino tourism was published in 1974 (Richardson, 1974). Richardson noted that the Las Vegas area had higher than average rates of crime, suicide, alcoholism, child neglect, etc. However, he concluded that:

> the evidence consistently affirms, however, that the high rates reflect, not the availability of legalized gambling, but specific social and demographic characteristics of the Las Vegas area. (Richardson, 1974)

Richardson suggested three factors to account for Las Vegas' poor record of social well-being. First, because of high growth rates and mobility, many residents had few family and peer group ties to the community. Among more established residents there was 'no evidence to suggest that the availability of legalized gambling is destructive of social stability' (Richardson, 1974). Second, many of the people who moved to Las Vegas had backgrounds of social marginality, marital failure, or poor social skills. When placed into the 24-hour open-city atmosphere of Las Vegas, these problems were magnified. Finally, Richardson attributed much of the social instability to the very large number of visitors and transients passing through Las Vegas.

At approximately the same time the Commission on the Review of the National Policy Toward Gambling commissioned a major survey of gambling attitudes and behavior in the United States (Kallick et al., 1976). Both a national study (with 1749 respondents) and a study of Nevada residents (with 296 respondents) were conducted. Compared to the national sample, Nevada residents had higher levels of participation in legal gambling and bet more in total. The study of Nevada residents also examined the perceived benefits of legalized gambling in Nevada. The major benefits perceived by both Nevada bettors and non-bettors were more jobs and more government revenues. However, there was also strong agreement that gambling had social costs. The primary cost identified was that people gambled more than they could afford. Interestingly, Nevada residents saw no change in respect for the law, police corruption, or political corruption as a result of legalized gambling.

The casino industry in Atlantic City has generated a large volume of literature (Abt and Smith, 1983; Mahon, 1980; Pollock, 1987; Samuels, 1986; Skolnick, 1978, 1979a, 1979b; Stansfield, 1978; Teske and Sur, 1991). Much of this accurately documents the poverty and social marginality experienced by many Atlantic City residents. However, much of this literature fails to acknowledge the high rates of poverty that existed in Atlantic City prior to the legalization of casinos (Pollock, 1987). Furthermore, many of the economic benefits of casino tourism have gone to surrounding communities, rather than to Atlantic City (Pollock, 1987; Teske and Sur, 1991). Atlantic City has also been handicapped by its history of corrupt politicians and political bossism. Local leaders in Atlantic City have not provided strong leadership, nor has the state of New Jersey succeeded in forming a regional authority to provide the missing leadership. This lack of good public policy has been accentuated by the failure of the casino industry to take a leadership role. Instead of stepping into this leadership vacuum, casinos have acted with relatively little enlightened self-interest (Pollock, 1987; Teske and Sur, 1991).

The success of individual casinos, coupled with the unemployment, under-employment, and poverty suffered by many of Atlantic City's residents, has resulted in cynical perceptions of casino tourism in New Jersey. Reeling (1986) surveyed New Jersey residents in 1980 and 1985 regarding their attitudes toward gambling and the Atlantic City casino industry. By 1985 New Jersey residents were more critical of Atlantic City and the casino industry. They were less likely to believe casinos will revitalize Atlantic City or lower its unemployment rate.

Taken as a whole, the literature on casino tourism suggests a number of conclusions about the social impact of casino tourism on the host community. One of the key findings is that residents are often unprepared for the dramatic changes instigated by casino tourism. Even if residents are familiar with hosting tourists in their community, they seem to be unprepared for the scale of casino tourism. The number of gamblers in new gambling jurisdictions is often higher than originally expected. This may be due to unmet demand for gambling in the United States. This large volume of visitors is also accompanied by a shift among local businesses from providing basic services to local residents to catering to visitors.

A second finding is that casino tourism often has extensive externalities. Benefits and costs accrue to both the destination area and surrounding communities. The spread of these benefits and costs is not necessarily equitable. Some communities may receive more benefits than costs while other communities suffer nothing but negative externalities.

Third, residents tend to recognize both the benefits and costs associated with casino tourism. Economic growth is the primary perceived benefits of casino tourism. Perceived costs often involved quality of life issues. Furthermore, these perceptions are often influenced by the individual's relationship to the tourism or casino industry. Those directly benefitting from casino tourism are most likely to perceive relatively more benefits and relatively fewer costs.

Finally, there seems to be considerable ambivalence about casino tourism. Problems are recognized but tolerated. This tolerance seems based upon the expectation of future benefits. How long individuals will tolerate present inconvenience in anticipation of future rewards may be one of the most critical issues facing the casino tourism industry.

A comparative study of the social impacts of casino tourism

In order to further contribute to understanding the social impacts of casino tourism, data was collected on Nevada residents' casino participation and attitudes toward casino tourism. This data was collected to accomplish two objectives. First, it partially replicates the Kallick et al. (1976) study. Longitudinal data may provide new insights into how residents' behavior toward and attitudes about casino tourism change over time. Second, it partially replicates Milman and Pizam's (1988) study of the social impacts of tourism in central Florida. Comparing resident attitudes toward mass tourism in Florida with resident attitudes toward mass casino tourism in Nevada may help identify characteristics unique to casino tourism. Alternatively, similarities in the perceived impact of tourism between the two groups would suggest that casino tourism is, in many ways, similar to mass tourism in the ways it affects the host community.

The data: Nevada 1974, Florida, Nevada 1992

The data used by Kallick et al. (1976) was collected through personal interviews with 296 residents of urban Nevada during 1975. Respondents described their gambling behavior in 1974. Individuals were excluded from the sample if they had moved to Nevada in the previous one and a half years or if they had moved to Nevada primarily for gambling. Once responses were weighted to correct for disproportionate selection the response rate was 70%.

Milman and Pizam (1988) surveyed residents of a three-county area in central Florida that is the home to the Disney World/Epcot Center complex, numerous other themed attractions, and, at the time of the study, 58 000 hotel rooms. Data was collected through telephone interviews. Three attempts were made to contact each selected telephone number. Interviews were completed with 203 residents for a response rate of 58%.

The original data used in this study was collected by mail questionnaire during June and July, 1992. A questionnaire was designed that replicated items from Kallick et al. (1976) and Milman and Pizam (1988). In this study respondents described their gambling behavior in 1991. Standard questionnaire design strategies were used (Dillman, 1978).

The sampling frame consisted of three sources. First, a random sample of postal carrier routes in urban Nevada (greater Las Vegas area, Reno, Carson City, and Sparks) was made. Residential addresses were then randomly sampled from the selected carrier routes. Second, a random sample of rural Nevada residences was drawn from telephone directories. Third, a random sample of Las Vegas area residences was drawn from the Las Vegas area telephone directory. This was done to increase the geographic variation of potential respondents in the Las Vegas area since the sample from the postal carrier routes was clustered in a fairly small number of areas.

Survey administration began in June, 1992. Each questionnaire was accompanied by a cover letter explaining the purpose of the study, identifying the study's sponsor, and stressing the importance of participation. A postage-paid return envelope was included. One week after mailing the questionnaire packet, a postcard was mailed to all potential respondents. This postcard thanked those who had already replied and urged non-respondents to do so. Three weeks later a second questionnaire, cover letter, and postage-paid return envelope was mailed to non-respondents. (The second questionnaire was not mailed to rural Nevada residences since rural Nevada was heavily over-sampled.)

The total sample size was 528. Non-deliverable addresses reduced the sample size to 441. One hundred fifty one complete questionnaires were returned for a 34% response rate.

Descriptive characteristics of the 1992 Nevada sample

Table 16.1 describes the study's respondents. Compared to all residents of the state of Nevada, survey respondents were: more likely to have at least some college education, less likely to have not finished high school, less likely to be in their twenties, more likely to be in their forties, more likely to have incomes in the $35 000 to $74 999 range, and less likely to have incomes of $24 999 or less. Women were over-represented. Geographically, the sample was very similar to the population distribution of Nevada.

Nevada residents' behavior and attitude, 1974 v. 1991

In order to compare gambling behavior and attitudes in 1974 and 1991, the data collected in 1992 had to be manipulated to match the sampling and screening procedures used by Kallick et al.. Individuals in rural Nevada were dropped from this part of the analysis. Screening questions were included in the questionnaire that were identical to those used by Kallick et al. (1976). The data were then weighted to correct for the unequal gender distribution.

The screened and weighted data for gambling participation is shown in Tables 16.2 through 16.5. Table 16.2 compares casino visitation for dinner or a show in 1974 and 1991. Nevada residents more frequently

Table 16.1 *Characteristics of the 1992 Nevada sample and characteristics of the 1990 Nevada population according to the 1990 Census of Population*

Characteristics	Percentage of Nevada respondents in 1992[a]	Percentage of Nevada population in 1990[a]
		population over 16
Sex		
Male	39	50
Female	61	50
		persons 25
Education		or older
Less than high school graduation	2	21
High school graduate	26	32
Some college	45	32
4-year college degree or higher	27	15
Household income	in 1991	in 1989
Less than $15 000	10	20
$15 000 to $24 999	11	19
$25 000 to $34 999	17	18
$35 000 to $49 999	28	20
$50 000 to $74 999	27	15
$75 000 to $149 999	6	7
$150 000 or higher	1	1
Age		
20 to 29 years	9	23
30 to 39 years	25	24
40 to 49 years	25	19
50 to 59 years	15	13
60 to 69 years	15	12
70 years or older	11	9
Place of residence		
Clark County	61	62
Washoe County and Carson City	23	25
Remainder of the state	16	13

[a]Totals may not sum to 100% because of rounding.

Table 16.2 *Number of times Nevada residents went to a casino primarily for dinner or a show in 1974 and 1991*

Number of times	Percentage of sample in 1974[a]	Percentage of sample in 1991[b]
None, no answer	69	20
1 or 2	7	14
3 or 4	5	16
5 to 9	7	26
10 to 19	7	12
20 to 29	3	5
30 or more	2	7

[a]Data from Kallick et al. (1976:406).
[b]Data collected by author.

Table 16.3 *Number of times Nevada residents went to a casino specifically to gamble in 1974 and 1991*

Number of times	Percentage of sample in 1974[a]	Percentage of sample in 1991[b]
None, no answer	78	48
1 or 2	5	14
3 or 4	2	9
5 to 9	4	4
10 to 19	4	5
20 to 29	3	6
30 or more	4	14

[a]Data from Kallick et al. (1976:406).
[b]Data collected by author.

Table 16.4 *Number of days Nevada residents played slot machines in 1974 and 1991*

Number of days	Percentage of sample in 1974[a]	Percentage of sample in 1991[b]
Zero	28	22
1 to 5 days	18	26
6 to 20 days	21	20
21 to 50 days	16	17
51 to 100 days	8	8
100 or more days	9	7

[a]Data from Kallick et al. (1976:408).
[b]Data collected by author.

Table 16.5 *Place Nevada residents played slot machines most often in 1974 and 1991*

Place	Percentage of sample in 1974[a]	Percentage of sample in 1991[b]
Casinos	49	54
Stores	16	8
Bars	5	15
Rail, air, bus station	1	1
Slot machine parlors	0	0
Didn't play, no answer	29	22

[a]Data from Kallick et al. (1976:408)
[b]Data collected by author.

patronized casinos for these activities in 1991 than in 1974. Going to a casino specifically to gamble also became more frequent by 1991 (Table 16.3). Most of the change occurred in the extreme categories. For example, 4% of the respondents in 1974 visited casinos specifically to gamble 30 or more times. By 1991, 14% of the sample visited casinos to gamble 30 or more times. The percentage of the sample who reported no casino visits specifically to gamble declined from 78% in 1974 to 48% in 1991. Interestingly, although this category of participation declined over time, it still represents the most frequent participation category in 1991.

In contrast to the changing behavior displayed in Tables 16.2 and 16.3, the amount of slot machine play is relatively constant between the two time periods (Table 16.4). Casinos were the most frequent location for slot play in both 1974 and 1991 (Table 16.5). It is also interesting to note that a sizeable proportion of respondents in each period did not play slot machines.

Overall, measures of gambling behavior show both consistency and change between 1974 and 1991. Nevadans appear to be visiting casinos more often than in 1974. This may be due to marketing efforts aimed at local residents. Also, the number of places to gamble increased over time; there were 179 licensed non-restricted gambling locations in 1974 compared to 376 in 1992 (State Gaming Control Board, 1975, 1993). As has been repeatedly shown, opportunity plays an important role in gambling behavior (Kallick et al., 1976). While Nevadans may be spending more time in casinos, they are not necessarily gambling more on all activities. Behavior on one specific type of gambling, slot machine play, remained constant between the two time periods.

Nevada residents' perception of the effects of legalized gambling in 1975 and 1992 was also investigated (Table 16.6). Here too there are both similarities and differences between the two time periods. Responses are similar in that in both years Nevadans agreed that legalized gambling creates more jobs, generates more money for the government, and results in people gambling more than they can afford. Also, few Nevadans in either year believed that legalized gambling means that people are working less or that it creates more of a chance for the common man to get rich.

Residents' perceptions also displayed change over time. The largest change occurred on the item 'more money to

run the government'. While a majority agreed with this statement in both time periods the percentage declined 26 points by 1992. In 1992 Nevada residents also reported ambivalent feelings about legalized gambling and organized crime. The 1992 sample, when compared to the 1975 sample, believed there were fewer racketeers connected to gambling but were less likely to believe that legalized gambling resulted in less money for organized crime. This could be a context effect; Nevadans in 1975 were living at a time when Nevada casinos were evolving from control by organized crime to corporate control.

Social impacts of mass tourism: central Florida and Nevada

The 1992 Nevada questionnaire included a set of questions that replicated Milman and Pizam's (1988) study. Those questions dealt with general perceptions of tourism and perceptions of the impact tourism had on specific socio-cultural issues such as quality of life and drug addiction. Results from the entire Nevada data set (151 observations) were compared to the results reported in Milman and Pizam (1988).

Three items that measured residents' overall attitudes toward tourism are reported in Tables 16.7, 16.8, and 16.9. Results indicate that both Central Florida and Nevada residents support tourism. Table 16.7 shows that over 70% of respondents in both groups favor or strongly favor the presence of tourists in their community. Furthermore, a majority of both groups believe that the number of tourists should increase (Table 16.8). Finally, over 75%

Table 16.6 *Nevada residents' attitudes towards the effects of the legalization of gambling in 1975 and 1992*

Effect of legalized gambling	Percentage agreeing in 1975[a]	Percentage agreeing in 1992[b]
More jobs	88	90
More money to run the government	87	61
People gamble more than they can afford	78	70
Less money for organized crime	46	28
More of a chance that children will be influenced to gamble	42	46
More racketeers connected to it	41	27
More of a chance for the common man to get rich	22	9
People working less because they are gambling	21	11

[a]Data from Kallick et al. (1976:398). Percentages represent respondents answering strongly agree or agree from a four-point scale that included strongly agree, agree, disagree, and strongly disagree.
[b]Data collected by author. Percentages represent respondents answering strongly agree or agree from a five-point scale that included strongly agree, agree, neutral, disagree, and strongly disagree.

Table 16.7 *Residents' feelings about the presence of tourists in central Florida and Nevada*

How do you feel about the presence of tourists in your community?	Percentage of central Florida residents[a]	Percentage of Nevada residents[b]
Strongly oppose the presence of tourists	2	3
Oppose the presence of tourists	4	4
Neither oppose nor favor the presence of tourists	16	22
Favor the presence of tourists	36	35
Strongly favor the presence of tourists	42	36
Mean[c]	4.2	4.0
Standard deviation	0.9	1.0

[a]Data from Milman and Pizam (1988:195)
[b]Data collected by author.
[c]Mean score on a scale where strongly oppose equaled 1, oppose equaled 2, neither oppose nor favor equaled 3, favor equaled 4, and strongly favor equaled 5.

Table 16.8 *Central Florida and Nevada residents' opinion on the volume of tourists visiting their communities*

How do you feel about the volume or number of tourists in your community?	Percentage of central Florida residents[a]	Percentage of Nevada residents[b]
Significantly decrease	3	4
Somewhat decrease	9	5
Not change	30	30
Somewhat increase	43	33
Significantly increase	15	28
Mean[c]	3.6	3.8
Standard deviation	0.9	1.0

[a]Data from Milman and Pizam (1988:199).
[b]Data collected by author.
[c]Mean score on a scale where significantly decrease equaled 1, somewhat decrease equaled 2, not change equaled 3, somewhat increase equaled 4, and significantly increase equaled 5.

of both sets of residents support the tourism industry (Table 16.9).

Table 16.10 displays mean scores for perceived tourism impacts on 14 selected socio-cultural issues. Residents of the two areas agree about the effects tourism has on nine of these issues. Members of both groups agree that employment opportunities, income and standard of living, overall tax revenues, and quality of life in general have improved because of tourism (i.e., mean scores for both groups were significantly higher than 3.0 at the 0.05 confidence level). The two groups also agree that tourism has contributed to a decline in people's honesty, increased sexual permissiveness, alcoholism, drug addiction, and traffic.

Table 16.9 *Overall opinion about/of the tourism industry held by residents of central Florida and Nevada*

How do you feel about the tourism industry in your community?	Percentage of central Florida residents[a]	Percentage of Nevada residents[b]
I strongly oppose the tourism industry	1	2
I oppose the tourism industry	5	1
I neither oppose nor favor the tourism industry	15	22
I favor the tourism industry	50	41
I strongly favor the tourism industry	29	34
Mean[a]	4.0	4.0
Standard deviation	0.8	0.9

[a]Data from Milman and Pizam (1988:195).
[b]Data collected by author.
[c]Mean score on a scale where strongly oppose equaled 1, oppose equaled 2, neither oppose nor favour equaled 3, favor equaled 4, and strongly favor equaled 5.

Table 16.10 *Perceived impact of the current level of tourism on selected socio-cultural issues in central Florida and Nevada*

Issue	Central Florida mean (std. dev.)[a]	Nevada mean (std. dev.)[b]
Employment opportunities	4.0[d] (0.9)[c]	3.9[d] (1.1)
Income and standard of living	3.8[d] (0.9)	3.4[d] (1.0)
Overall tax revenues	3.6[d] (1.1)	3.4[d] (1.1)
Quality of life in general	3.4[d] (0.9)	3.2[d] (0.9)
Courtesy and hospitality toward strangers	3.3[d] (0.9)	2.9[e] (0.9)
Attitude toward work	3.1[d] (0.6)	3.0[e] (0.8)
Mutual confidence among people	3.0[e] (0.6)	2.7[f] (0.8)
Morality	2.9[e] (0.8)	2.7[f] (0.8)
Politeness and good manners	2.9[e] (0.8)	2.7[f] (0.8)
People's honesty	2.9[f] (0.6)	2.5[f] (0.7)
Sexual permissiveness	2.7[f] (0.7)	2.4[f] (0.8)
Alcoholism	2.6[f] (0.6)	2.3[f] (0.8)
Drug addiction	2.7[f] (0.7)	2.3[f] (0.8)
Traffic	1.6[f] (0.8)	1.9[f] (0.9)

[a]Data from Milman and Pizam (1988:196).
[b]Data collected by author.
[c]Mean score on a scale where significantly worsen equaled 1, somewhat worsen equaled 2, not make any difference equaled 3, somewhat improve equaled 4, and significantly improve equaled 5.
[d]Mean score is greater than 3.0 at the $p = 0.05$ confidence level.
[e]Mean score is not different from 3.0 at the $p = 0.05$ confidence level.
[f]Mean score is less than 3.0 at the $p = 0.05$ confidence level.

The two groups have different perceptions about five issues. Residents of central Florida believe tourism has improved courtesy and hospitality toward strangers and attitudes toward work. In contrast, Nevada residents believe that tourism has not really affected these issues. Furthermore, residents of Nevada believe that mutual confidence among people, morality, and politeness and good manners have all declined because of tourism. Residents of central Florida feel that these issues have been unaffected by tourism.

Overall, residents of both areas view tourism as having positive economic impacts, negative implications on social–moral issues such as honesty and drug addiction, and very negative consequences on traffic. In evaluating all these costs and benefits residents in both areas seem to believe that the benefits exceed the costs since they report that tourism has a slightly positive effect on the quality of life in general.

Conclusion: the social impacts of casino tourism

Casino tourism affects residents. It brings economic opportunity together with changes that inevitably result from having a large transient population such as social instability, crime, and traffic. Residents recognize both the positive and negative impacts associated with casino tourism. Interestingly, residents of casino tourism destinations report perceptions similar to those reported by residents of areas that receive non-casino mass tourism. This suggests that in many ways casino tourism is similar to other forms of mass tourism.

While casino tourism shares many characteristics with other forms of mass tourism there is one key difference—gambling. Some percentage of residents and visitors will likely develop gambling problems. This differentiates casino tourism from other forms of mass tourism. It also suggests that decisions to implement casino tourism deserve a detailed and specific public debate. This debate should center on equity issues concerning the fairness of the distribution of benefits and costs (including the distribution of problem gamblers) associated with casino tourism.

Equity issues are critical to casino tourism for two reasons. First, casino tourism is associated with a number of characteristics that may spill over to nearby jurisdictions. These include the 'anything goes' atmosphere facilitating gambling, drinking, drug use, and prostitution as well as the more mundane impacts of traffic, property speculation, etc. Second, the very popularity of casino tourism suggests that residents, even in an area with a long history of tourism, may be unprepared for the volume of visitors that casinos will generate. The apparently large amount of unmet demand for casino tourism also means that business development may ignore local markets to concentrate on the more lucrative casino tourism market.

Directions for casino tourism research

It appears that tourism researchers have not considered casino tourism part of the field. In order to better understand casino tourism, its impact on the community, and its place as an economic tool, a number of issues should be addressed. Some of these issues are briefly discussed below.

Equity issues

The fairness of casino tourism needs to be addressed. More research should evaluate the nature of casino gambling as a tax strategy since existing research suggests that gambling taxes tend to be regressive. The externalities of casino tourism should also be investigated. This is especially important if casino tourism is to be used as a tool for urban development. Furthermore, the implications of the shift from peripheral casino locations to locations in the midst of large populations needs to be addressed.

Social impacts of casino tourism

Social impacts need to be studied in more detail. Impacts should be disaggregated to differentiate impacts on residents, residents employed in tourism, residents employed in casinos, and visitors. Costs of problem gambling and under-age gambling need to be quantified. True longitudinal studies are needed to track impacts over the product life cycle.

Economic impacts of casino tourism

Economic analysis of casino tourism needs to become more sophisticated. Analysis needs to distinguish between local economic effects of casino tourism and net regional or national economic effects. Impacts casino tourism has on other industries, investment, and on other forms of legalized gambling (which may be taxed at higher levels) needs to be investigated (Eadington, 1986).

Casino tourism and traveler decision making

Research needs to address the role legalized gambling plays in travelers' decision making. This would include identifying how attractive different forms of gambling are to various market segments. It would also entail understanding the role that competition (both gambling and non-gambling) and intervening opportunity plays in travel decision making.

Casino tourism and public policy

The public policy objectives of casino tourism need to be explicitly stated and objectively evaluated. Specifically, is the goal of casino tourism to maximize state or local tax revenue? To attract the maximum number of tourists to a destination? To maximize on-site visitor spending? To diversify a local or regional economy? Since the success of casino tourism cannot be evaluated without understanding the objectives it was designed to achieve, this is a critical area for research (Clotfelter and Cook, 1990; Mikesell and Zorn, 1987).

Casino tourism, competition, substitution, and the product life cycle

Research is needed to clarify the relationship among the various forms of gambling. Informed policy must be based upon identifying activities that are competitive and complementary. As the novelty of legalized casino gambling declines issues of market growth versus cannibalization become critical (DeBoer, 1986; Mikesell, 1987; Ovedovitz, 1992; Stover, 1990; Thalheimer, 1992; Vasche, 1990).

Note

1. Gambling tourism takes many forms. People become tourists to experience horse races, to visit casinos, or even to purchase lottery tickets (Sullivan, 1989). While recognizing this variety, this paper concentrates on casino tourism, and argues that casino tourism is a form of mass tourism.

References

Abt, Vicki and Smith, James F. (1983) 'On the social implications of commercial gambling: is gambling just another form of play?', *Arena Review*, 7(3):17–28.

Albanese, Jay S. (1985) 'The effect of casino gambling on crime', *Federal Probation*, 49(2):39–44.

Ap, John (1990) 'Residents' perceptions research on the social impacts of tourism', *Annals of Tourism Research*, 17(4): 610–616.

Beagle, John (1993) 'Casinos play monopoly', *Gaming & Wagering Business*, 14(3):15, 16, 18.

Borg, Mary O., Mason, Paul M. and Shapiro, Stephen L. (1990) 'An economic comparison of gambling behavior in Atlantic City and Las Vegas', *Public Finance Quarterly*, 18(3): 291–312.

Callaway, Andrew, Gish, Julie Ann, Parker, Robert, Szychowski, Gwen, Long, Patrick T. and Nuckolls, Jonelle (1992) 'Assessing the social impacts of gambling, as perceived by local government and agency officials, on permanent residents of Black Hawk, Colorado', Tourism Management Program, University of Colorado at Boulder, Boulder, Colorado.

Caneday, L. and Zeiger, J. (1991) 'The social, economic, and environmental costs of tourism to a gaming community as perceived by its residents', *Journal of Travel Research*, 30(2): 45–48.

Caro, Peter, Howard, Colin, Kilzer, Bill, Sherwood, Katie, Wagor, Kristin, Long, Patrick T. and Nuckolls, Jonelle (1992) 'Assessing the social impacts of gambling, as perceived by local government and agency officials, on permanent residents of Cripple Creek, Colorado', Tourism Management Program, University of Colorado at Boulder, Boulder, Colorado.

Clotfelter, Charles T. (1979) 'On the regressivity of state-operated "numbers" games', *National Tax Journal*, 32:543–548.

Clotfelter, Charles T. and Cook, Philip J. (1990) 'Redefining "success" in the state lottery business', *Journal of Policy Analysis and Management*, 9(1):99–104.

Commission on the Review of the National Policy Toward Gambling (1976) *Gambling in America*, US Government Printing Office, Washington, DC.

Connor, Matt (1993) 'Indian gaming: prosperity, controversy', *Gaming & Wagering Business*, 14(3):1, 8–10, 12, 45.

DeBoer, Larry (1986) 'When will state lottery sales growth slow?', *Growth and Change*, 17:28–36.

Dillman, Don A. (1978) *Mail and Telephone Surveys*, John Wiley, New York.

Doocey, Paul (1993) 'An overview of riverboat gaming: full steam ahead', *Gaming & Wagering Business*, 14(11):1, 38, 40.

Downes, D. M., Davies, B. P., David, M. E. and Stone P. (1974) *Gambling, Work and Leisure: A Study across Three Areas*, Routledge & Kegan Paul, London.

Eadington, William R. (1976) 'Some observations on legalized gambling', in W. R. Eadington (Ed.), *Gambling and Society: Interdisciplinary Studies on the Subject of Gambling*, Charles C. Thomas, Springfield, IL, pp. 47–56.

Eadington, William R. (1986) 'Impact of casino gambling on the community: comment on Pizam and Poleka', *Annals of Tourism Research*, 13(2):279–282.

Eadington, William R. (1987) 'Economic perceptions of gambling behavior', *Journal of Gambling Behavior*, 3(3):264–273.

Elger, Heidi, Mossman, Rob, Schuiling, Dave, Van Imhof, Rudi, Long, Patrick T. and Nuckolls, Jonelle (1992) 'Assessing the social impacts of gambling, as perceived by local government and agency officials, on permanent residents of Central City, Colorado', Tourism Management Program, University of Colorado at Boulder, Boulder, Colorado.

Frank, Michael L. (1990) 'Under age gambling in Atlantic City resorts', *Psychological Reports*, 67(3):907–912.

Friedman, Joseph, Hakim, Simon and Weinblatt, J. (1989) 'Casino gaming as a "growth pole" strategy and its effect on crime', *Journal of Regional Science*, 29(4):615–623.

Gray, H. P. (1970) *International Travel, International Trade*, Heath Lexington Books, Lexington, MA.

Hakim, Simon and Buck, Andrew J. (1987) 'Do casinos enhance crime?', *Journal of Criminal Justice*, 17(5):409–416.

Hugick, Larry (1989) 'Gambling on the rise; lotteries lead the way', *Gallup Report*, 285:32–39.

Jackson, Richard and Hudman, Lloyd (1987) 'Border towns, gambling, and the Mormon cultural region', *Journal of Cultural Geography*, 8(1):35–48.

Kallick, Maureen, Suits, Daniel, Dielman, Ted and Hybels, Judith (1976) *Survey of American Gambling Attitudes and Behavior*, US Government Printing Office, Washington, DC.

Kallick-Kaufmann, Maureen and Reuter, Peter (1979) 'Introduction', *Journal of Social Issues*, 35(3):1–6.

Lavery, Patrick (1974) 'Resorts and recreation', in P. Lavery (Ed.), *Recreational Geography*, John Wiley, New York.

Leiper, Neil (1989) 'Tourism and gambling', *Geo Journal*, 19(3): 269–275.

Lowenthal, David (1962) 'Tourists and thermalists', *Geographical Review*, 52:124–127.

Mahon, Gigi (1980) *The Company that Bought the Boardwalk*, Random House, New York.

Mascarenhas, Oswald A. J. (1990) 'An empirical methodology for the ethical assessment of marketing phenomena such as casino gambling', *Journal of the Academy of Marketing Science*, 18(3):209–220.

Mason, Paul M., Shapiro, Stephen L. and Borg, Mary O. (1989) 'Gaming tax incidence for three groups of Las Vegas gamblers', *Applied Economics*, 21:1267–1277.

McQueen, Patricia A. (1993) 'North American gaming at a glance', *Gaming & Wagering Business*, 14(9):52, 56, 59, 60, 62.

Mikesell, John L. (1987) 'The effect of maturity and competition on state lottery markets', *Journal of Policy Analysis and Management*, 6(2):251–253.

Mikesell, John L. and Zorn, C. Kurt (1987) 'State lottery sales: separating the influence of markets and game structure', *Growth and Change*, 18:10–19.

Milman, Ady and Pizam, Abraham (1988) 'Social impacts of tourism on Central Florida', *Annals of Tourism Research*, 15(2):191–204.

Minnesota Planning (1992) *High stakes: Gambling in Minnesota*, MN Planning, St. Paul, MN.

Mossenson, Dan (1991) 'The Australian casino model', in W. R. Eadington and J. A. Cornelius (Eds), *Gambling and Public Policy: International Perspectives*, Institute for the Study of Gambling and Commercial Gaming, University of Nevada, Reno, Nevada.

O'Hara, John (1988) *A Mug's Game: A History of Gaming and Betting in Australia*, New South Wales University Press, Kensington, NSW.

Ovedovitz, Albert C. (1992) 'Lotteries and casino gambling: complements or substitutes?', in W. R. Eadington and J. A. Cornelius (Eds), *Gambling and Commercial Gaming: Essays in Business, Economics, Philosophy and Science*, Institute for the Study of Gambling and Commercial Gaming, University of Nevada, Reno, Nevada.

Pizam, Abraham (1978) 'Tourist impacts: the social cost to the destination community as perceived by its residents', *Journal of Travel Research*, 16(4):8–12.

Pizam, Abraham, and Pokela, Julianna (1985) 'The perceived impact of casino gambling on a community', *Annals of Tourism Research*, 12(2):147–165.

Pollock, Michael (1987) *Hostage to Fortune: Atlantic City and Casino Gambling*, Center for Analysis of Public Issues, Princeton, NJ.

Reeling, Glenn E. (1986) 'A five year comparison (1980–85) of attitudes New Jersey residents have regarding gambling, especially in Atlantic City', Jersey City State College, Jersey City, NJ.

Richardson, Philip (1974) *Effects of Legalized Gambling on Community Stability in the Las Vegas Area*, Twentieth Century Fund, New York.

Riper, LeRoy Van and Mango, James P. (1979) *Casino Gambling in New York State?: A Summary of Published Reports*, LeRoy Van Riper, Albany, NY.

Roehl, Wesley S. (1991) 'Gaming tourism in the USA', in K. S. Chon (Ed.), *Proceedings of Research and Academic Papers*, Volume III, *The Society of Travel and Tourism Educators Annual Conference*, STTE, Las Vegas, Nevada.

Roehl, Wesley S. and Van Doren, Carlton S. (1990) 'Locational characteristics of American resort hotels', *Journal of Cultural Geography*, 11(1):71–83.

Samuels, Jack (1986) 'Gambling and tourism in the USA', *Travel & Tourism Analyst*, June:39–48.

Skolnick, Jerome H. (1978) *House of Cards: The Legalization and Control of Casino Gambling*, Little, Brown, New York.

Skolnick, Jerome H. (1979a) 'The dilemmas of regulating casino gambling', *Journal of Social Issues*, 35(3):129–143.

Skolnick, Jerome H. (1979b) 'The social risks of casino gambling', *Psychology Today*, 13:52, 54, 57, 58, 63, 64.

Stansfield, Charles (1978) 'Atlantic City and the resort cycle: background to the legalization of gambling', *Annals of Tourism Research*, 5(2):238–251.

State Gaming Control Board (1975) 'Quarterly report for the fourth quarter of 1974 (October 1 through December 31) and year to date comparisons (January 1 through December 31)', Nevada State Gaming Control Board, Carson City, Nevada.

State Gaming Control Board (1993) 'Gaming revenue report, year ended December 31, 1992', Nevada State Gaming Control Board, Carson City, Nevada.

Stover, Mark Edward (1990) 'Contiguous state lotteries: substitutes or complements?', *Journal of Policy Analysis and Management*, 9(4):565–568.

Suits, Daniel B. (1977) 'Gambling taxes: regressivity and revenue potential', *National Tax Journal*, 30(1):19–35.

Sullivan, Maureen (1989) 'Sunshine gamblers', *American Demographics*, 11(2):48.

Tasmanian Gaming Commission (1989) *Australian Gambling Statistics, 1972–73 to 1987–88*, Tasmanian Gaming Commission, Hobart, Tasmania.

Teske, Paul and Bela Sur (1991) 'Winners and losers: politics, casino gambling, and development in Atlantic City', *Policy Studies Review*, 10(2/3):130–137.

Thalheimer, Richard (1992) 'The impact of intrastate intertrack wagering, casinos, and a state lottery on the demand for parimutuel horse racing: New Jersey—a case study', in W. R. Eadington and J. A. Cornelius (Eds), *Gambling and Commercial Gaming: Essays in Business, Economics, Philosophy and Science*, Institute for the Study of Gambling and Commercial Gaming, University of Nevada, Reno, Nevada.

Turner, Louis and Ash, John (1975) *The Golden Hordes*, Constable, London.

Vasche, Jon David (1990) 'The net revenue effect of California's lottery', *Journal of Policy Analysis and Management*, 9(4):561–564.

Walker, Michael B. (1985) 'Explanations for gambling', in G. T. Caldwell, M. G. Dickerson, B. Haig, and L. Sylvan (Eds), *Gambling in Australia*, Croom Helm, Sydney.

Walker, Michael B. (1992) *The Psychology of Gambling*, Pergamon Press, Oxford.

Winn, B. M. and Whicker M. L. (1989) 'Indicators of state lottery adoptions', *Policy Studies Journal*, 18(2):293–304.

17 Museums as tourist attractions

A. PHELPS

The relationship between museums and leisure has always been ambiguous. The view that a museum should focus on the conservation and research of a collection to the exclusion of concern for the visitors is outdated, if indeed it was every truly the case. However, finding a balance between the traditional practices of museumship and the newer demands of earning a living from entertaining the public has aroused controversy. Some argue that the informed visitor should be distinguished from the 'leisure' visitor, who may have no prior interest in the collection, with the implication that the former is welcome while the latter is a burden. The distinction may be important when dealing with marketing or decisions concerning the language of interpretation, but in terms of contribution to the life of a museum the origin and motivation of a visitor should be seen as less important than the benefit to be derived from a visit.

What has become known as 'heritage' is an important part of the tourist attraction for many parts of Britain and is the major draw for international visitors. The attraction is based on survivals from the past: of royal pageantry and buildings, country houses and their parkland settings, historic monuments, cathedrals and parish churches, and the collections in our national museums and galleries, as well as traditional events and cultural performance. But heritage tourism is more than observation of architecture, history or nature, it has to do with appreciating what makes people and places different (Hall and Zeppel, 1990). At its best an interest in heritage can be an essential component of an environment and people-friendly tourism, encouraging meaningful and respectful interaction between visitors, the local community and their surroundings, to their mutual benefit. However, heritage can all too easily be packaged in presentations divorced from context and devoid of meaning. Museums have an important role in presenting and interpreting the heritage to the public through the medium of their artefacts.

Despite the absence of coherent policy, there is no lack of encouragement for museums to engage in active marketing to attract this pool of would-be visitors. This chapter will examine the potential for tourist development based on museums, the consequences for the museum staff and operation, and the stress it may place on the

traditional function of such organisations. The study will also question the potential benefits to the tourists as visitors and consider the role museums may play in enhancing understanding of past and place. The role of international and domestic tourism, both holidaymaking and day-tripping, will be considered through examples based on visitor surveys in a special interest museum in the capital, a county museum in a provincial city and a social history museum in a village setting.

Promoting museums as tourist attractions: advantages for the tourist industry

In recent years tourism has become one of Britain's more important industries. After a period of significant growth in employment, current evidence suggests that the domestic tourism market is, at best, static; despite muted optimism for medium-term growth, the trend shows growth in the number of visits, but decline in the length of holidays and the spend per night (BTA, 1993). The last decade has seen modest growth in overseas tourism to Britain with expenditure growing more slowly than the economy as a whole; overseas visitors also are making shorter trips and spending less per night. Thus, within cautious predictions for tourism overall, the short break sector is showing much more encouraging trends.

Surveys of visitors to Britain show heritage and cultural attractions to be amongst the most frequently mentioned reasons for their trip; their importance is reflected in the conclusion from several research projects that heritage should be presented as the main attraction in promotion (NEDC, 1992a). Heritage is also important for domestic trips: visiting heritage sites (outdoor) and art and heritage exhibits (indoor) feature as casual activities in nearly a quarter of UK holiday trips (NEDC, 1992b). Indeed 'heritage and hikes' has been identified as one of five market segments within the longer holiday market. The grouping makes a characteristic assumption that 'hiking' equates with an interest in natural heritage and does not attempt to distinguish between the attraction of viewing the heritage in all its forms and taking active exercise in outdoor locations.

The potential of heritage tourism is also indicated in surveys of day-trips from home, with the observation that people attracted by culture are likely to visit historic houses, gardens, cathedrals and castles as well as museums. Such attraction is less likely to be affected by short-term external variations (fashion, weather), and is more likely to grow in future with the ageing of the population, so providing a secure longer-term market.

The patterns suggested in both domestic and international tourism agree with the Economist Intelligence Unit's identification of the 'leisure pioneers' as the most rapidly growing lifestyle group (EIU, 1990), amongst whom the desire for meaningful experiences accords with the attraction of heritage in its widest definition. This analysis may anticipate growth in the proportion of people likely to specify heritage as a reason for their visit, but it should be recognised that the 'sun and fun' tourists remain more numerous and should not be discounted; although the latter group may have other reasons for selecting their holiday location, they may well engage in a day-trip to a heritage attraction within a longer holiday.

The heritage businesses in their widest definition are well positioned to provide for the increasing demand for short breaks with activity or interest, and day-trips offering educational as well as entertaining experiences. Nevertheless the enthusiasm of the tourist boards for promoting short breaks will not necessarily result in more visits at heritage attractions. Although heritage potential may feature in the *choice* of location for a short break, more heritage *visiting* seems to occur on longer holidays (Prentice, 1993). This is likely to reflect the time available as demonstrated by surveys at popular day-trip destinations; for example in the Ironbridge Gorge a substantial number of day visitors never pay to enter one of the museum sites. It was partly in response to this finding that the Ironbridge Gorge Museum Trust developed their operations off the museum sites, with a shop and, more recently, a themed restaurant in the village of Ironbridge.

The evidence would suggest a two-level approach would be beneficial within tourism promotion: promote the general image of a place with an interesting heritage to attract visitors *into* the region, and then target attractions information at visitors *within* the region to translate a stay in the area into visits to specific heritage attractions. Museums should be an important part of such heritage marketing, by cooperating with Tourist Board promotions outside their area and linking with other heritage organisations for specific promotion within the region.

Promoting heritage tourism: advantage for museums

Our major museums were established with a curatorial function, to conserve and research collections of local,

national and international importance; most also accept an educational purpose although philanthropic support for the 'improvement' of the working classes did not prevent a thoroughly off-putting classical staging in many cases. Although some museums still retain an emphasis on protection, in recent decades most have moved to provide presentation and interpretation in a more accessible format. Recently the relative importance of the different functions has been called into question as many museums define mission statements and reconsider their purpose in the face of declining funding and increased competition. A common response is a repositioning within the leisure market with a greater emphasis on the role of the organisation in relation to its visitors.

Museums are faced with a future of declining financial support from central sources and greater competition from the increased number of attractions and the introduction of new leisure activities (Middleton, 1990; Audit Commission, 1991). Although the total number of visits made to heritage attractions seems to be holding steady in the early 1990s, the increased number of attractions means that many have experienced a decline in the last few years due to competition (BTA, 1993; Phelps, 1991). In 1994 the easing of the Sunday trading laws may create further competition for the leisure visit. Garden centres have already broken down the barriers between retailing and leisure by adding cafes and playgrounds; observation of Bank Holiday shoppers in supermarkets shows little evidence of planned shopping, but great similarities with the fairly aimless 'leisure' wander around a garden or museum. In the face of such varied competition, museums need to work hard improving their service to maintain the visitor numbers as gate money becomes a more significant part of the budget.

Heritage tourism offers museums an opportunity to attract new visitors, widening their market from the traditional audience of interested local people and travelling professionals. Studies have shown that holidaymakers are likely to spend twice as much as day-visitors, and three times as much as local visitors (Myerscough, 1988). When combined with an effort to improve the quality of catering and retailing, this provides an opportunity to increase income whilst extending the educational role to a wider public. The challenge is exemplified by a study in the West Country which indicates the particular demand on museums 'to offer comparable facilities, displays and interpretation to other attractions and experiences, while retaining their essential uniqueness and maintaining their other functions of collecting, documenting and preserving the heritage' (WCTB/AMCSW, 1993). Tourism should be seen as a means of supplementing the income of a museum to enhance its prime function, not a drain on resources.

But tourists are not simply a source of revenue; a future in tourism requires providing both a good-quality experience and value for money. Museums that have managed to resist the pressure to charge still need to consider value provided in relation to the time a visitor commits. Targeting tourists would require most museums to address a different audience, with a need to consider the relevance of presentations not only to a wider age and educational range, but also to visitors with different ethnic and cultural backgrounds; such evaluation should lead to improved presentations to the benefit of all visitors. Tourists may further assist the museum activities simply by their presence, by adding to the 'critical mass' required to justify the presentation of a large-scale touring exhibition, particularly significant in regions with a relatively low resident population but large numbers of seasonal visitors (WCTB/AMCSW, 1993).

Heritage and tourism—problems and possibilities

Thus an opportunity may be identified within the tourism market in this country where museums could have a significant role to play. At the same time museum staff have identified a need to relate more directly to their visitors to improve communication and encourage more visitors. There is the possibility of bringing these two needs together in a positive way. This is not a new concept, but the greater urgency of current financial pressures may help to create the atmosphere for more cooperation between activities previously seen as unrelated.

The objective of promoting tourism is to achieve benefits to tourists, the local economy and the museums without exploiting either the material heritage or the visitor. However, tourism is not a universal solution; museum managers must examine their operation to assess the suitability of tourism within the particular local circumstances.

Case studies

Design Museum, London

The Design Museum opened on Butler's Wharf in central London in July 1989; in the first year of operation it attracted over 100 000 visitors. As the capital available for the launch of the museum is used, there is an increasing need to generate income from the visitors. The original mission statement for the new museum identified four main categories of visitor: the design professional, the education market, particularly students of design and

their teachers, manufacturers and the public 'visiting to become better informed, more critical and therefore more articulate as consumers' (Design Museum Survey Report, 1987). Thus although the mission statement allowed for the presence of the general public, there was a presumption throughout that the purpose of the organisation was to serve the design profession and a corpus of interested people. There was no allowance for a leisure visitor with no specific interest in the process of design.

Despite this approach, surveys have shown a persistent and substantial number of leisure visitors, with just over half of the visitors declaring their visit to be a 'general day out' (Design Museum Survey Report, 1990). When visitors were questioned about the features they most enjoyed in their visit many specific objects or exhibitions were identified, justifying the emphasis on interest in design. However, a significant number of features mentioned relate to the pleasure of a day out: the attraction of the building itself with the riverside location, the variety of displays and facilities such as the cafe. This reflects the mixed nature of the audience and reinforces the need to be concerned with the general visitor as well as the design professional.

Approximately a third of the visitors throughout the year were from overseas; although there were a proportion of design professionals, the great majority were tourists with no stated prior interest in design. With a central London location, it is perhaps not surprising that the Design Museum attracts a significant number of foreign visitors. What is more surprising is that the management declare 'no policy' towards overseas visitors; although this is in keeping with the original mission of the museum, in reality it means that the specific needs of a substantial number of visitors are not considered.

The operation of the museum is driven by the sequence of temporary exhibitions, reflected not only in the number of visitors but also in their origin. New exhibitions prompt repeat visits from the design professionals and generate editorial that helps to raise awareness of the museum. Current marketing is targeted within the M25 orbital motorway which is seen as the main zone of operation. Some forms of advertising will reach people commuting into the capital for work as well as visitors staying in the capital (e.g. posters on the Underground); this approach does not reach the potential day-visitors living outside London. There is opportunist use of BTA initiatives for overseas publicity, but with no overt strategy.

Surveys show that word of mouth is the most frequent source of information, so there is a renewed effort to meet the needs and exceed the expectations of the visitors. Developments since opening have improved the shop and cafe in line with visitor comments; there has been some success in responding to requests to give more direct access to the objects in the permanent galleries (for example you are invited to sit on some of the chairs exhibited).

An effort to meet the perceived desire of the design professional for a rapid turnover in temporary exhibitions has proved expensive and counter-productive. Although the professionals can be encouraged to make more frequent visits, they are a relatively small proportion of the total audience. Leisure and educational visits show a much longer repeat interval and are less likely to be prompted by a new exhibition. Longer-running temporary exhibitions would provide more opportunity to capitalise on word-of-mouth publicity, with greater potential to increase the total audience.

The museum management recognise that their location is a weakness as far as the domestic market is concerned; British people tend to associate the Museum with 'docklands', perceived as peripheral to London, or see the Museum as being the 'wrong' side of the river. Overseas visitors are more likely to perceive the Design Museum in 'tourist London' with its proximity to the major attraction of the Tower of London. The survey found nearly a fifth of visitors arriving 'by chance' having set out to visit the Tower of London or Tower Bridge; some visitors reported seeing the museum from their hotel window across the river.

The tourism market could be more thoroughly exploited; the Tower is such a huge attraction that if only a small proportion of their visitors could be encouraged to cross the river a significant difference could be made to the Design Museum. There is a desire to capitalise on this location advantage, but it will be difficult to break into the 'Tower and Bridge' day. A visit to the Tower of London is time-consuming and unlikely to be combined with other activities in the same day, particularly as a high proportion of the visitors arrive by coach. Nevertheless there is a great opportunity to inform visitors to the Tower about the Museum, in a way that may be taken up for a subsequent visit. This could be particularly advantageous with overseas visitors, who are more likely to operate within a small area of 'known' London.

The Design Museum has established a position in the design world as an exhibition venue and research base. It also has a function as a tourist attraction, although this is largely ignored in current presentation. The museum offers a location and presentation that could be promoted to enhance its role within tourism, which could both increase the total number of visitors and provide an opportunity to expand interest in design. This could be an important matter for an organisation with increasing reliance on earned income. A re-positioning

of the presentation to attract the interest of leisure visitors is unlikely to occur as it would be seen as compromising the main mission of the Museum. Nevertheless as tourists already form a significant segment of the visitors, it could be argued that making more deliberate provision for them is an essential part of the service to existing visitors as well as exploiting opportunities for expansion.

The Castle Museum, Nottingham

Nottingham Castle is the prime tourist attraction of the city attracting some 700 000 visitors a year; it is also the county museum and art gallery and a venue for temporary exhibitions. The recently reorganised Arts, Tourism and Heritage Division of Nottingham City Council has an expressed mission giving the museum service a clear role in fostering a sense of place and identity for the multi-cultural community of Nottingham, whilst also embracing visitors to the city. This presents the Castle management with the need to cater for three main groups of visitor: local residents (including many school parties), day-visitors from the wider region and holidaymakers. The Castle has a strong appeal to family groups, most of whom are 'general interest, casual' visitors (NCM&AG, 1993). The high proportion of 'holiday' visits in comparison with the other museums in the city emphasises the Castle's role as a day-visit attraction; despite a programme of temporary exhibitions geared to attract local people, less than 10% of the visitors interviewed in a recent survey came specifically to see a new exhibition.

The Castle offers a range of permanent exhibitions, most of which have some particular connection with the City. The image of place is particularly addressed in the 'Story of Nottingham' presentation, which is popular with visitors. However, a greater number of visitors stated interest in the 'Body Adornment' exhibit; this successful display is going to be expanded with the redevelopment of the museum currently in progress. Although not so immediately relevant to the local heritage as the 'Story of Nottingham', the new gallery gives an opportunity to interpret and encourage the involvement of the different communities in the city.

Despite not being the idealised Norman castle of Robin Hood films, the Castle is still the prime tourist attraction of the city; although the survey found only 14% overseas visitors, this is considerably more than at any of the other museums in the City. Those overseas visitors who do reach the Midlands are likely to be visiting friends, or travelling to business conferences. The number of independent foreign tourists is too small to justify direct marketing abroad, although the Castle does contribute to the promotion of the heritage image of the East

Midlands. Marketing directed at local residents and the business community is likely to be more cost-effective than promotion in the country of origin in reaching this segment of visitors. Nottingham does have the strength of the well-known Robin Hood story, but the Castle has opted with the city to focus on industrial and social history and not stress the Robin legend. This is not expected to result in loss of market share as attractions such as the Tales of Robin Hood are seen as complementary, offering a subsequent visit. Future plans include linked promotions involving a number of attractions and accommodation within the city, particularly targeted at the short-break market.

The museum service is under considerable pressure to generate more income, which is a controversial matter with both the councillors and the public. While the council wants to maintain a service to the community, they are required to cut the budget; the result is a compromise with a confusing pattern of some free museums, free days and free events within a general move towards charging. Local people are rather resistant and visitor numbers are falling on 'charge' days; visitors from outside the region seem to be more prepared to pay, perhaps regarding the museum more as a tourist attraction than a local service. About a third of summer visitors to the Castle grounds never enter the museum, but on weekends and public holidays when there is a charge this proportion falls to less than a quarter. Although the policy of increasing charges will raise income, it may also tip the balance towards tourist visitors making it harder for the service to deliver the mission by widening the audience amongst the local community. Introducing 'welcome' interpretation in different languages is an obvious development to favour tourists, but may further signify a shift from local service to tourist attraction.

The Framework Knitters' Museum, Ruddington

This is a social history and industrial museum housed in a small complex of listed buildings, comprising two original frame workshops, outbuildings and a row of cottages in a village three miles outside Nottingham. The museum holds a good collection of knitting frames, many of which are in working order and frequently demonstrated to visitors. The displays interpret the rise and fall of the framework knitting industry and the social conditions of the workers, using personal information concerning the families who occupied the cottages in the last century. Two cottages are restored to different dates to present living conditions.

Ruddington Framework Knitters' Museum offers a genuine insight into the life and work of a significant community within the village throughout the last century. It holds considerable local interest, but attracts relatively few visitors from the immediate surroundings. There has been a concerted effort to improve marketing and build an audience, reflected in the steady growth of visitors to the museum to about 5000. Most of the casual visitors are on a leisure day out within the region; there are very few holidaymakers and foreign visitors are mainly found in groups, for example, from local twinning associations. The museum caters for a large number of booked parties, most of whom are educational groups; the educational role of the museum has increased in recent years, but with a shift in emphasis from craft and design courses to schoolchildren, with a deliberate effort to tie in with Key Stage 2 of the National Curriculum.

The small size of the museum is both its major strength and a weakness: the sense of place instilled within the courtyard is tangible, but the site is quickly overcrowded and any idea of 'pastness' lost. The museum has recently acquired a redundant chapel adjoining the site. Acquisition of the building has placed a considerable burden on the finances of the museum so restoration is not likely to take place for some years. Although this building provides an opportunity to expand the presentation, an increase in visitor income is necessary to cover the running costs before any benefit can be derived.

Future developments within the village of Ruddington will provide the opportunity for cooperative marketing. The new Country Park is expected to attract a quarter of a million visitors when fully established, with the Nottingham Railway Heritage Centre offering an added attraction. If only a small proportion of these visitors can be persuaded to move into the village, the potential market for the Framework Knitters' Museum will be considerably increased. There are plans for a consortium leaflet; if this is taken up by the wider promotion of short breaks in the region, it may be possible to increase the number of tourists visiting the site. This would be beneficial to the museum through the increased income generated, especially as tourists are more likely to buy the museum products, which include expensive frame-knitted shawls. The museum could provide a valuable heritage experience based on the restoration and research of a past industry in its original location.

Ruddington is an example of a museum that has all the attributes that would create a distinctive and rewarding heritage attraction for tourists, but its location and small size mean that such marketing would not be cost-effective. There has been a clear shift in emphasis targeting the schools and the leisure day trip. Marketing must be carefully judged to balance the number of visitors with the space available. One strategy is the special events programme, accounting for about 20% of the visitors last year. Problems of crowding have been avoided by making use of the courtyard and road outside the museum. Although the events have been successful in attracting new visitors, the trustees do not see them as central to the mission of the museum so they may not continue. The distinctiveness of the museum means that it is not felt to be in competition with other heritage attractions, but is competing for the use of leisure time. Development of the education market may provide a more secure future.

Discussion

The recognition of 'heritage' as a tourist attraction has prompted the creation of pastiche attractions and with them a debate about appropriate use of material heritage and the dangers associated with interpretation diverted primarily for entertainment. Local museums have a great opportunity to counteract the 'consumerist' version of place that often follows a themed promotion (Daniels, 1992). Local collections such as Ruddington can contribute to the celebration of distinctiveness that is often lost in the eclectic collections of larger museums, or is deliberately submerged in the 'some time/any place' presentations of constructs such as the Black Country Museum.

Much of heritage development has been *product* led, with an emphasis on education. This is certainly the case in traditional museums with the presentation geared to their collection. However, a greater emphasis on attracting visitors requires a *visitor* orientation, with an effort to make the place more 'user-friendly' in the face of competition. Inevitably this leads to pressure to attract through the style of presentation rather than the physical resource. The result has been a shift of emphasis from traditional museum collection presentation to a heritage centre approach of telling a story. Such a change may result in conflict with the prime mission of a museum and blur the boundary between a museum and an entertainment centre, compromising the greatest strength of a museum in presenting a collection.

Marketing museums as tourist attractions

Strengths

Museums can feed directly into the appeal of the cultural heritage, which underpins both domestic and international tourism and is increasingly important as both markets mature. The existence of a collection provides the fascination of genuine artefacts which can be interpreted in different ways offering endless variation. Small museums can make a significant contribution to a 'sense of place' which is important in generating a distinct tourist image for an area and helps to encourage repeat visits. Local and national networks already exist that could assist small museums in specialist functions such as marketing.

Weaknesses

Despite considerable progress with imaginative developments, museums still have a negative image, as boring, forbidding places. There must be an effort to improve information *about* museums, as well as the presentation *within* them. Many museums operate with a small permanent staff who may lack the time and expertise to develop marketing initiatives, particularly those intended to improve relations with non-visitors.

Opportunities

The growth in demand for short breaks, especially special-interest breaks for middle-aged people, has created a market gap that can be exploited by museums. Much of interest to tourists already exists, the major task is to improve information and interpretation. Tourism can provide a renewable source of visitors without the need for frequent change in presentations necessary to encourage repeat visits.

Threats

The major threat to museums currently is the pressure on funding, combined with the competition from other attractions. Developing tourism provides an opportunity to address this problem, directly by increasing the number of visitors and thus the total spend, and indirectly by widening the audience to improve support for the future. However, some perceive a threat to the heritage itself, through indiscriminate promotion of 'pastness' in tourist hype which may undervalue the resource and perpetuate misunderstandings (Fowler, 1992). Regional distinctiveness may be distorted by the promotion of selective 'pasts' by councils keen to change their image, too often summarised in a catchy slogan.

The interaction of special-interest visitors and leisure visitors may lead to confusion on a site, as the formal presentation of the collection for the first group may be diluted by the increasingly familiar atmosphere of the 'heritage centre' popular with the second group. A desire to increase the number of visitors may result in developments some find unpalatable; English Heritage in particular has attracted criticism for encouraging special events, some of dubious historic justification (Eastaugh and Weiss, 1989).

Others see the positive side of an opportunity to widen the audience, but worry that the enthusiasm to 'tell a story' risks the authenticity of presentation (Uzzell, 1989). Museums are an essential backbone to the survival of material heritage, including the less obvious categories of craft, performance art and primary production where there has been a significant development in new museums recently. However, perhaps because of the pull of tourism promotion, the trend in presentation has shifted towards a created 'experience', to the point where some fear any presentation without visual effects and 'authentic' smells will disappoint (Cooper et al., 1993).

The competition for ever-more-memorable experiences has put pressure on the traditional museums to change the style of their presentation, but there is no direct evidence to support the contention that to be successful all attractions should respond in the same way. Cooper states that 'historic properties, museums and gardens need to change their displays and to feature special exhibitions and events in order to maintain interest and encourage repeat visitors' (Cooper et al., 1993:211). This statement makes a dangerous assumption, as there is little evidence to support the contention that *all* places can benefit from new interpretation. People value variety; if all heritage presentation follows the increasingly familiar 'heritage' pattern there may be a loss of market share to other types of leisure activity. Also there is a risk that altering the style of presentation of a traditional museum may alienate the existing visitors.

These issues come to a head in the discussion of authenticity. It is generally assumed that the 'leisure' visitor is not very demanding, they may be easily satisfied by a 'fun' experience and not too interested in detail (Cooper et al., 1993). However, a museum has an obligation to deal correctly with its material and an expertise that can be used to enthuse visitors about its subject area. It has been the practice for some time to stage exhibits to give viewers an idea of period settings or the context of objects; what is new is the staging of events for a shared experience within a museum setting. In the former the staging is obvious and the purpose clear; in the latter the purpose may be more confused and difficult for a visitor to interpret. The message about a different period may be lost in the fun of dressing up or conversing with a period character as our late-20th-century knowledge provides a filter through which re-creations are experienced. It may be possible to 'step back in time' into the setting of Viking Yorjik; it is not possible to detach our education and cultural relationships to experience the setting in the mind of the people who lived at that time (Boniface and Fowler, 1993).

Another contentious issue is 'theming', popular with heritage centres and regional tourist board promotion, and increasingly featured in retail developments. Theming may be a locational convenience but often has little geographic meaning; selecting a theme encourages a dangerous over-simplification of the complex heritage of a place to one single idea, often itself based on fiction through myth, literature or television (Shaw and Williams, 1994). This is clearly a problem when the history of a region is submerged in the promotion of a fictional representation such as in 'Catherine Cookson Country' (Pocock, 1992), but the concentration on the Vikings in York is equally single-minded and risks undervaluing the important heritage of other periods.

Conclusion

Success in any new initiative may be counted in terms of the benefit to an individual organisation, but coordinated action in tourism could help revitalise a whole region; such a strategy is advocated in a recent report issued jointly by the West Country Tourist Board and the Area Museum Council for the South West. This study recognises the importance of convincing all concerned of the benefits of joint action claiming that 'the barriers are mostly in people's minds; there are prejudices against museums . . . and there are those who consider tourists a scourge' (WCTB/AMCSW, 1993).

The case studies show that it is possible to increase the number of visitors by targeting tourists, but that this will have an effect on the style of the museum and the experience of other visitors. Careful preparation needs to be made to establish that tourism is the best strategy for the museum and its public.

Strategies

Market research—museums need to understand their current visitors and their needs, as well as identifying potential new markets. Quantitative data on the number of visitors and their profile is a start, but more effort needs to be given to qualitative research identifying the needs of visitors and what they really get out of their visit.

Marketing—existing marketing is probably aimed at a close professional group, existing museum visitors or residents. Marketing must be widened but without alienating existing visitors by presenting a redefined image. A large proportion of domestic tourism is based around visits to friends and relatives; local services and advertising should be angled to present the museums as suitable places to take a visitor.

Service—presentation within the museum must be extended to include the tourists; this means identifying the likely groups and their needs, for example, by improving exterior signs; foreign language leaflets, orientation and panels. Staff retraining should be considered, for example in dealing with non-English-speakers.

If the museums are to benefit from tourism without damaging their prime function, certain steps must be taken to devise an action plan.

1. *Identify the museums with the greatest potential benefit*

Museums most likely to benefit are those that have already identified a need to raise income derived from visitors and can accommodate more visitors. If the museum has a very restricted capacity, other forms of increasing income may be more suitable, e.g. local business sponsorship.

Indicators of income need: high dependence on visitor income with increasing competition from other attractions.

2. *Identify museums with a potential tourist attraction*

Tourism is not a panacea; many museums operate in locations that are unlikely to attract many tourists. Some museums have a very specialist presentation that is unlikely to appeal to general visitors, or have other strengths that could be compromised by a move to attract tourists. Other opportunities should be given full consideration, for example, the education market by linking with the National Curriculum.

Indicators of tourist potential: good base of domestic visitors or existing international draw in the near vicinity; general interest collections or specific collections with a strong regional identity or unusual local story.

3. *Convince the museum staff in appropriate museums of the benefits of targeting tourists*

There is a need to work with staff to negotiate means of making the presentation more appealing to tourists without compromising other important aims. If there is a conflict with other activities, the staff need to be convinced of the benefit to the museum as a whole of focusing on tourists.

Indicators of potential: strong management conviction and good staff relationships.

4. *Identify suitable strategies*

People on holiday use their time in different ways to those at home or work. There may be a need to modify opening hours to enhance opportunities or offer additional activities linked to outside events, e.g. festivals.

Indicators of potential: flexibility in management and staffing, with an openness to new ideas and interest in the wider market.

Identifying museums likely to benefit from tourism promotion is only part of the work; a museum presenting itself as a tourist attraction does not exist in isolation but is part of the leisure provision for the district. The role the museum can play needs to be worked out within a regional strategy, probably involving the district councils and regional tourist board. Few museums have the national pulling power to generate additional visitors to a region, although grouping new museums to create a cluster of attractions may have that result. Without more visitors in total, promotion will only result in more competition. This may not be a problem where the pool of tourists is large, as in the case of the Design Museum, but may be counter-productive in an area where tourism is not growing. There is greatest potential for individual museums where there is a regional strategy to lengthen the season, or encourage day-trippers to extend their stay into a short-break, as in Nottinghamshire. Museums need to identify and work to their strengths; it is not worthwhile to gear interpretation to international visitors if there is greater potential to increase the number of local visitors. Targeting tourists may cause local people to disregard the museum as just a tourist facility; such a strategy may be justifiable if the location offers a good potential for increasing visitor numbers through tourism, but should be accompanied by events targeted at the more traditional museum support and local community, perhaps in the low season.

Good heritage tourism is about recognising differences, it is about valuing the characteristics that make people and places distinctive and about understanding our relationship with community, culture and environment. Such developments are much in keeping with recent initiatives in 'greening' tourism, with the opportunities for developing local, smaller-scale tourism in sympathy with the local community and using existing resources. Museums have much to offer in this, and can benefit from welcoming a wider range of visitors. The visitors, whether local people reinforcing their own community membership, or tourists learning about a new place, have much to gain from contact with the artefacts. Current fashions may emphasise telling a story through audio-visual representation and interactive exhibits; it does museums no harm to share in the excitement of rediscovery through utilising new methods, although care needs to be taken about the balance of expense between media and collection. Tourist development should not be seen as a threat to the heritage, but should be managed to support its survival. Many museums have opened in the last decade; some will not last beyond the enthusiasm of their originators, but others will endure and become part of the heritage for future generations. Market forces have always had a part in this pattern, but may now be more important than in the past. Rather than ignore that reality, museum staff have the opportunity to use their collections to prove their worth in the market-place, stressing the enduring value of the authentic object over the passing interest of fabricated experience.

Acknowledgements

My sincere thanks to the following, who supplied material for the case studies and willingly gave up time to engage in conversations about their experience of tourism: John Hendry, The Design Museum, Butler's Wharf, Shad Thames, London; Richard Sandell, Museums Marketing Officer, The Castle Museum, Nottingham Castle, Nottingham; Jason Doherty, Curator, Ruddington Framework Knitters' Museum, Chapel Street, Ruddington, Nottinghamshire.

References

Audit Commission (1991) *The Road to Wigan Pier? Managing Local Authority Museums and Art Galleries*, HMSO, London.

Boniface, P. and Fowler, P. J. (1993) *Heritage and Tourism in the 'Global Village'*, Routledge, London.

BTA (1991) *Guidelines for Tourism to Britain 1991–1995*, British Travel Association, London.

BTA (1993) *Sightseeing in 1993*, British Travel Association, London.

Cooper, C. et al. (1993) *Tourism: Principles and Practice*, Pitman, London.

Daniels, S. (1992) 'Place and the geographical imagination', *Geography*, 77:310–322.

Eastaugh, A. and Weiss, N. (1989) 'Broadening the market', in Uzzell, D. (Ed.), *Heritage Interpretation*, Vol. 2, Belhaven, London.

EIU (1990) *The UK Leisure and Tourism Market*, Economist Intelligence Unit, London.

EMTB (1992) *Raising the Standard: a Tourism Strategy for the East Midlands 1992–1997*, East Midlands Tourist Board, Nottingham.

Fowler, P. J. (1992) *The Past in Contemporary Society*, Routledge, London.

Hall, C.M. and Zeppel, H. (1990) 'Cultural and heritage tourism', *Journal of Travel Research*, 24:1.

NEDC (1992a) *Marketing the UK Holiday in the UK*, National Economic Development Council, London.

NEDC (1992b) *Marketing the UK Overseas*, National Economic Development Council, London.

Lumley, R. (1988) *The Museum Time-Machine: Putting Culture on Display*, Routledge, London.

Middleton, V. (1990) *A New Vision for Independent Museums*, AIM.

Myerscough, J. (1988) *The Economic Importance of the Arts in Britain*, Policy Studies Institute.

NCM&AG (1993) 'Visiting museums: a report of a survey of visitors to Nottingham city museums and art gallery'.

Phelps, A. (1991) 'Heritage attractions in the East Midlands', *Trent Geographer*, 13.

Pocock, D. (1992) 'Catherine Cookson Country: tourist expectation and experience', *Geography*, 77:236–244.

Prentice, R. (1993) *Tourism and Heritage Attractions*, Routledge, London.

Ryan, C. (1984) *Visitors to Nottingham Castle*, TBS.

Shaw, G. and Williams, A. M. (1994) *Critical Issues in Tourism*, Blackwell, Oxford.

Uzzell, D. (Ed.) (1989) *Heritage Interpretation*, Vol. 2, Belhaven, London.

WCTB/AMCSW (1993) *Rain or Shine: A Tourism and Museums Strategy*, West Country Tourist Board and Area Museum Council for the South West.

18 International charter travel—a new opportunity for Australian tourism

E. FREW

Introduction

The introduction of Britannia Airways charter flights to Australia in 1988 and new package deals by scheduled airlines has made Australia a much more accessible and affordable destination to large numbers of tourists worldwide. In addition, airlines now offer very comfortable economy class service to Australia. This has made long-haul travel to Australia more tolerable and has established Australia as a desirable holiday destination.

This chapter aims to demonstrate that international charter travel is an important means of transport for the tourist and makes a significant contribution to tourism in the destination country. The paper uses the example of Australia to illustrate the importance of developing a liberal approach towards charter travel.

To define charter travel it is necessary to distinguish between *scheduled* and *non-scheduled* flights;

—*Scheduled flights* are those flights offered to the public according to a published timetable, or that are so frequent or regular that they constitute a systematic and identifiable series.
—*Non-scheduled flights* are chartered or special remunerated flights undertaken in an irregular fashion (Spanish Civil Aviation Department, 1981a).

Charter travel occurs when the entire capacity of an aircraft is engaged by one or a limited number of charterers (e.g. by a tour organiser or a travel agent) for non-scheduled flights to and from a destination. The charterer then resells the seats on the aircraft to prospective passengers (Statistics Canada, 1983). The charter flight may constitute a round or circle trip and be one of a regular series of flights (European Civil Aviation Conference, 1981).

On a worldwide scale charter travel accounts for only 10% of air transport activity, but in Europe, among the European Civil Aviation Conference member states, charter travel is used by nearly half of all international passengers (Harrington, 1991). However, international charter services to and from Australia account for only about 2% of total passengers carried (Australia World Airways, 1989).

In 1992 the countries which generated charter passengers to Australia were Brunei, Bulgaria, Commonwealth of Independent States, Germany, Japan, New Caledonia, Papua New Guinea, Singapore, South Africa, United Kingdom and Vietnam. Some international charter airlines carried Australians holidaying overseas, but only flights which generated overseas visitors to Australia have been included in Table 18.1.

Advantages of charter airlines

Charter airlines are able to offer lower fares than scheduled operators because of several factors.

Scheduled airlines operate through bilateral agreements between countries and it is often difficult to develop new routes quickly to meet a change in demand.

Charter airlines can respond to a change in demand for an established route by flying more or fewer flights. They can also respond quickly to demand for new routes. This flexibility provides charter airlines with an advantage not available to scheduled airlines.

In addition, the substantial cost of ticketing, marketing and promotion of the charter airline services is not borne by the airline (as is the case with scheduled airlines). Instead these costs are met by the tour operator who charters the aircraft (Australia World Airways, 1989).

Scheduled airlines have high frequency but they have a low load factor as they are obliged to provide a regular service even when every seat is not filled. Charter airlines only fly on demand and therefore have high load factors—often up to 90% or greater. They are therefore more fully utilised then scheduled flights.

To keep airfares to a minimum it is important to utilise the aircraft all year round. In Europe much of the charter travel is concentrated during the summer months of June to September. To utilise the aircraft out of the peak season many European charter airlines lease out their aircraft. The airlines which hire the aircraft offer winter sun holidays, or are based in the southern hemisphere where it is the peak season.

Table 18.1 *International charter flights to Australia in 1992*

Charterer	No. of charter flights in 1992	Approximate no. of charter passengers carried	Destination in Australia
Japan			
Japan Travel Bureau	14	5100	Brisbane; Cairns; Sydney
Kinki Tourist Company	14	3100	Brisbane; Cairns; Sydney
Qantas	13	3050	Adelaide; Brisbane; Sydney
World Air Charter	7	1600	Cairns
Japan Air Charter	2	540	Cairns
JTB Kumamoto	1	330	Brisbane
Vietnam			
Vietnam Airlines	32	7200	Darwin; Melbourne; Sydney
Mr Nguyen Anh Tuan	23	5100	Melbourne; Sydney
Singapore			
Region Air	21	4300	Darwin; Hamilton Island; Canberra
Indian Ocean Airlines	8	270	Christmas Island
Bulgaria			
JES Air	17	3800	Melbourne; Sydney
United Kingdom			
Britannia Airways	12 (in 92)	3200	Adelaide; Alice Springs; Brisbane; Cairns; Darwin; Melbourne; Coolangatta;
	13 (in 93)	3500	Perth; Sydney
New Caledonia			
Air Caledonia International	18	820	Norfolk Island
Brunei			
Royal Brunei Airlines	3	600	Darwin
Commonwealth of Independent States			
Baptist Union of Victoria	2	330	Melbourne
Aeroflot	2	310	Melbourne
South Africa			
United Cricket Board of South Africa	1	150	Adelaide; Brisbane; Canberra; Melbourne; Perth; Sydney
Germany			
Hapag-Lloyd	1	70	Various locations in Australia
Papua New Guinea			
Air Niugini	1	60	Townsville

Source: Adapted from Department of Transport and Communications (1992c) *List of Charter Flights to Australia in 1992*, AVSTATS Aviation Division, Canberra.

Another method of utilising aircraft throughout the year is for the airline to develop charter operations to the southern hemisphere. This policy has been followed by Britannia Airways who, since 1988, have been operating charter flights from the UK to Australia from November to March each year. This helps to utilise their aircraft in the off-peak season in the northern hemisphere and avoids the expense of having idle aircraft.

Is was demonstrated by the chairman of Britannia Airways that in Britain the existence of charter flights on certain routes has provided competition for the scheduled airlines which has resulted in fares being kept at a lower level than on routes where no charter airlines operate (Table 18.2). Beachey (1990) supports this argument by stating 'Charter operators offer not only cheaper fares than scheduled carriers, but the competition they introduce also constrains any increases in the price of scheduled flights'.

Costs are further reduced for charter airlines by their ability to operate between secondary airports. In Spain

Table 18.2 *Comparison of European airfares (cost per kilometre in UK pence)*

	Distance (km)	Excursion fares	Full economy fares
London to airports and return on routes with significant charter competition			
Athens	5088	3.3p	11.0p
Faro	3576	3.4p	11.9p
Palma	2872	3.7p	11.5p
Rome	2953	5.2p	14.4p
Tenerife	6072	2.8p	8.5p
London to airports and return on routes with little or no charter competition			
Ajaccio	2605	6.2p	16.6p
Nice	2204	5.9p	14.5p
Oslo	2495	6.3p	14.6p
Stockholm	3074	6.1p	14.4p
Vienna	2637	6.1p	15.8p

Source: Reed (1988).

in 1979 (the destination which has historically received most of Europe's charter travel) many secondary airports received no scheduled flights but handled many charter flights. Examples of such airports in Spain were Almeria, Reus and Lanzarote, all of which are popular holiday destinations (Spanish Civil Aviation Department, 1981b).

In Australia in 1992 the secondary airports which received international charter flights but received no international scheduled flights were Alice Springs, Canberra, Coolangatta and Hamilton Island (Department of Transport and Communications, 1992a). Utilisation of the secondary airports spreads the benefit of tourism to these smaller gateways and eases the burden on major airports.

Charter airlines often fly from secondary airports at the country of origin. Flying from these airports provides easier access to customers who do not live in the large cities. For example, Britannia Airways operates from Luton Airport, north of London. In an interview in 1990 the Commercial Manager of Britannia Airways said that there were several advantages to flying from Luton. He explained that there was less congestion than at other airports and so there were fewer delays. There was quick and efficient handling of passengers and luggage, and efficient preparation of aircraft as Britannia had their own ground handling crew based at Luton (C. Roberts, personal communication, 3 July 1990). As an illustration of this, in 1989 99% of Britannia's take-offs were within 5 minutes of the planned departure time (Britannia Airways, 1989). In addition, secondary airports have lower landing fees and handling costs.

The country which generated the most charter passengers to Australia in 1992 was Japan. All of the

charter flights from Japan to Australia in 1992 originated from secondary airports. The airports utilised were Sapparo, Sendai, Akita, Okayama, Niigata, Kumamoto and Matsuyama. In comparison all scheduled flights from Japan to Australia in 1992 originated from major airports, i.e. Fukuoka, Nagoya, Osaka and Tokyo (Department of Transport and Communications, 1992a).

Growth in the charter airline industry

Charter airlines increasingly fly to new long-haul destinations. In Europe people are tiring of the traditional overcrowded resorts and have began to look further afield for holidays in more exotic locations. The Association of European Airlines (1992) states 'As the market becomes more sophisticated, there is a slow but steady drift away from the short-haul packaged seaside holiday, towards more distant destinations worldwide and more unfamiliar destinations in Europe'.

The move away from the traditional destinations is reflected in the number of British charter flights to Spain. In 1987 Spain received 10.2 million charter flights but by 1992 this figure had dropped to 6.3 million (*Economist*, 1992).

It is predicted that the growth in intercontinental or long-haul travel which, from the UK, is defined as journeys of longer than 3500 km (O'Brien, 1990) will continue in the near future. It is estimated that the total number of long-haul trips worldwide is expected to nearly double by the end of the century from 36.7 million trips in 1986 to 64.2 million in 1999 (Beachey, 1990).

The European charter airlines have responded to the change in taste by developing new long-haul destinations such as Florida, Canada, Thailand, Puerto Rico, Mexico, Jamaica, Barbados and Australia and in so doing appeal to a new, more adventurous market.

It has been suggested (Beachey, 1990) that one of the reasons that demand for long-haul travel is increasing from economically prosperous nations is that people are looking for more quality and exclusivity 'not just in terms of accommodation, etc, but in terms of clean, unspoilt and uncrowded beaches, countryside that is not covered by apartments and towns that are not swarming with tourists'.

With long-haul travel becoming more viable and attractive, Australia has the opportunity to capture a larger segment of the worldwide tourism market as the country provides an attractive alternative to traditional destinations by providing all the elements which the discerning traveller is seeking.

In Europe many airlines have had to lower their prices to compete in the short-haul sector. However, in the long-haul sector there is less competition so it is possible to make a profit. Many airlines are therefore looking at long-haul operations as a means of recouping financial losses caused by the downturn in demand for short-haul flights. The commercial manager of Britannia Airways confirmed this view when he said in 1990,

> Britannia see the long haul market as their new area of development. I am not scared to admit that the European short haul market is falling and Britannia must look elsewhere for business. As a result we are developing long haul travel. These long haul trips are not only to Australia but to Florida and Canada. (C. Roberts, personal communication, 3 July 1990)

Another critical reason for the growth in long-haul flights is that, with economies of scale, long-haul flights use equipment more effectively. High-cost segments of a flight are while the aircraft is on the ground, during take-off and when landing. The shorter the distance flown the greater the proportion of the operation is taken up with these high-cost segments.

During long-haul flights the proportion of time spent on the ground is less and more time is spent at the most economical part of the flight—flying at cruising altitude. Similarly, on long-haul routes the aircraft is more intensively utilised, with an average working day of 11 hours in the air compared with 6½ hours for short-haul flights (Association of European Airlines, 1992).

The factors which affect an aircraft's productivity are the speed and daily utilisation. Table 18.3 illustrates that from 1980 to 1991 the speed and utilisation of aircraft within Europe has decreased over time. This reflects increased congestion in Europe and the problems of delay and indirect flight paths. Aircraft used on long-haul routes on the other hand have, during the same period, increased utilisation and capacity and improved fuel efficiency.

There is an opportunity for charter airlines to capitalise on the demand for 'visiting friends and relatives' (VFR) holidays to Australia. The VFR market has great potential because of the large number of migrants in Australia who have friends and relatives in their home countries. Since 1971, 2.2 million immigrants have settled in Australia of whom 25.5% came from the UK and Ireland, 24.9% came from Asia and the Middle East and 17.3% from continental Europe (Bureau of Immigration Research, 1991). A recent study (Forsyth et al., 1993) confirmed that the greater the number of permanent migrants resident in Australia, the larger the pool of friends and relatives in the home country who have an incentive to visit Australia. The charter airlines operating to Australia therefore have the opportunity to cater for these VFR travellers from Europe, Asia and the Middle East.

The interest in travel to Australia for VFR purposes is reflected in the Britannia Airways survey of its passengers. The survey revealed that the majority of visitors had several reasons for visiting Australia but 84% of the respondents came to visit friends or relatives (VFR), 54% came for a holiday, 2% for business and 4% for other reasons. The most popular combination was holiday and VFR travel with 40% visiting for both purposes (Department of Transport and Communications, 1992b).

Charter airlines also have the capacity to handle the increased demand from international incentive travellers. Australia is an ideal country to cater for the incentive traveller as the country satisfies all the required criteria for a suitable incentive trip destination as set out by Cleverdon (1988).

It is suggested that to provide a suitable incentive holiday the destination should (Cleverdon, 1988):

—have the right price range for the budget;
—be fashionable, desirable or glamorous;
—provide good (four or five star) hotels and a reasonable varied selection of restaurants, recreation, shopping and entertainment facilities;
—have good access;
—provide a good local ground agent; and,
—have the local currency working in the visitor's favour.

In 1991 the main use of charter flights in Japan was for incentive tours, followed by company and school travel (March, 1993). The Japanese charter airlines therefore have the opportunity to capitalise on the demand for

Table 18.3 *Aircraft productivity among Association of European Airlines member airlines*

		European routes			Long-haul routes		
		1980	1991	Difference	1980	1991	Difference
Speed	(km/h)	522	502	−4%	791	781	−1%
Utilisation	(hours/day)	7.0	6.4	−9%	9.6	11.0	+15%
Capacity	(tonnes)	14.4	14.8	+3%	39.2	45.4	+16%
Fuel efficiency	(ATK/gal)	6.8	8.9	+30%	10.5	11.8	+12%

Source: Association of European Airlines (1992).

incentive travel by increasing the number of incentive travellers they carry to Australia.

Customer service

Traditionally, charter airlines used old, second-hand aircraft and were notorious for providing very basic service. However, to provide flights to the new long-haul destinations such as Florida and Australia the charter airlines have had to invest in new long-range aircraft such as the Boeing 767. By operating newer aircraft the charter airlines have been able to provide greater passenger comfort and provide quality in-flight service which equals or even surpasses that offered by the scheduled airlines.

A Department of Transport and Communications survey of Britannia Airways found that, with regard to the standard of service offered by Britannia on charter flights to Australia, most passengers were more than satisfied. About 81% of passengers rated the standard of service as excellent or very good and 18% as average to good. Only 0.7% of passengers considered the standard of service as poor (Table 18.4).

Of the people surveyed, 41% had previously travelled economy class on a schedule airline from the UK so were able to make a comparison. These people were asked how the Britannia service compared with the scheduled service. 33.5% of the passengers said that it was better than the scheduled service, 52.4% said it was the same as the scheduled service and 14.1% said that it was worse than the scheduled service (Department of Transport and Communications, 1992b).

Economic input

Charter passengers visit for a short period but are high spenders. The Britannia Airways survey showed that the average length of stay for a Britannia passenger in Australia in 1991 was 31 days, which is much shorter than the average UK visitor, who stayed 59 days. However, in this time Britannia passengers spend an average of $A1633 in Australia (ignoring pre-paid components and assuming an exchange rate of 46 pence = $A1). This compares with the average UK visitor who, in 1991, spent $A2431. Therefore, a Britannia passenger spent on average about $52 per day, while a UK passenger spent on average $41 per day (Department of Transport and Communications, 1992b; Bureau of Tourism Research, 1991). This suggests that charter passengers, at least from the UK, have the potential to be a lucrative market for Australia (Table 18.5).

In 1992 the country which generated the most charter passengers to Australia was Japan. Japanese visitors have a high expenditure and in 1991 spent an average of $1329 or $166 per day during an average stay in Australia of only 8 days (Bureau of Tourism Research, 1991).

The Britannia Airways survey also revealed that the charter programme to Australia had generated a market different from that of the scheduled carriers. The survey found that 24.7% of travel groups would not have come to Australia if the Britannia holiday package had not been available (Table 18.6). Respondents were also asked what they would have done if their package had been 20% more expensive (a price equivalent to that offered by scheduled carriers). 32.4% of the passengers would not have come to Australia if the price of the package had been increased by 20%. If it is assumed that the same people who answered 'no' to Q3 also answered 'no' to Q4, then the maximum value of these two results provides an upper limit for the total generated traffic, i.e. about 32% (Department of Transport and Communications, 1992b).

These results support the development of charter travel to Australia as they illustrate that charter travel is able

Table 18.4 *Standard of service offered by Britannia Airways*

Question		No. of 'yes' answers	Percentage of 'yes' answers
Standard of Britannia	Excellent	1083	41.3
Service	Very good	1038	39.6
The level of service on	Good	359	13.7
Britannia flights	Average	123	4.7
	Poor	18	0.7
Scheduled experience Have previously travelled economy class on a scheduled airline from the UK		1071	41.0
Relative service	Better than schedule	367	33.5
How the Britannia	Same as schedule	573	52.4
service was rated	Worse than schedule	154	14.1

Source: Adapted from Department of Transport and Communications (1992b).

Table 18.5 *Average length of stay and expenditure of UK charter and scheduled passengers to Australia in 1991*

Type of passenger	Average length of stay	Average expenditure in Australia	Average spend per day
Britannia Airways passenger	31 days	$1633	$52
UK scheduled airline passenger	59 days	$2431	$41

Source: Adapted from Department of Transport and Communications (1992b) and Bureau of Tourism Research (1991).

to generate a new and different market to the scheduled carriers.

Australian charter regulations

In October 1987 the Australian government decided to permit international charter traffic into Australia under certain conditions.

Charter travel was permitted as it was seen to be 'in the interests of encouraging inbound tourism [and would] complement the services offered by existing scheduled carriers' (Minister for Transport and Communications, 1989). Under the regulations introduced in 1987, charter flights required case-by-case approval unless they met the following requirements (in which case they received automatic approval).

The charter flights must (Minister for Transport and Communications, 1989):

—carry only foreign passengers to and from Australia;
—operate on routes not currently served on a scheduled basis by the airlines designated under the bilateral agreement existing between Australia and the country concerned;
—comprise up to four return services per month and

operate for up to three consecutive months, although further programs would be considered after a review of the initial program; and
—carry passengers who have pre-purchased a significant ground package.

These conditions were designed to encourage inbound tourism and to ensure that new business was generated rather than a redistribution of the scheduled airlines' business.

If a proposal was not eligible for automatic approval, and where it could be shown that the charter flight may have had an impact on the scheduled services, the Department of Transport and Communications would seek Qantas's view before giving agreement to the charter programme.

The other restriction which was imposed on charter airlines concerned the airports they could serve. The government placed restrictions on which airports could be served, emphasising that Melbourne, Brisbane and Sydney were 'adequately served by scheduled carriers' (Britannia Airways, 1989).

In September 1990 the Australian government decided to take a more liberal attitude towards international charter flights and amended the regulations concerning international charter flights. The government accepted that charter flights were beneficial for Australia as they were able to:

—target new markets;
—foster the development of inbound tourism;
—encourage increased competition between carriers serving Australia; and
—provide a wider range of competitive choices for Australian consumers (Department of Transport and Communications, 1990).

Table 18.6 *Traffic generation and price sensitivity*

Question		Yes (%)
1. Other destinations	Did you consider a holiday elsewhere before deciding on Australia?	17.4
2. Price motivation	Was the price of the holiday a consideration?	66.4
3. Traffic generation	Would you still have gone to Australia if Britannia Airways holiday packages were unavailable?	75.3
4. Price sensitivity	Would you still have come to Australia if the package had cost 20% more?	67.6
5. Length sensitivity What length of time would you have spent in Australia if answer to Q4 was 'yes'?	less time	9.2
	same amount of time	72.8
	more time	18.0
6. Package value	Was the holiday package value for money?	96.2

Source: Adapted from Department of Transport and Communications (1992b).

In comparison with the regulations in 1987 the present regulations concerning charter flights are much more progressive. Today, if the conditions below are fulfilled (and if operational and safety requirements are complied with), then the charter receives automatic approval to operate into Australia.

The application:

(a) is for an affinity group, own use or one-off flight; or
(b) is for a single programme of up to 25 flights and the operator has not conducted a similar charter programme in recent months; and
(c) has as an integral part one or more of the following characteristics:
—a requirement for passengers to purchase an accommodation package, the duration of which is at least half of the period spent in Australia;
—targets smaller gateways;
—targets markets not served by scheduled services to or from Australia.

The guidelines also state that the Australian policy now allows charter operations 'to be as free as possible' to operate 'genuine non-scheduled operations' and these can be either inbound or outbound traffic or a combination of the two (Department of Transport and Communications, 1990).

It may be noted that Britannia Airways, in its 1992–93 season, offered the full quota of 25 flights which is approximately one flight a week for 5 months. However, this falls short of the three flights a week to Australia, deemed necessary by Britannia in 1989, to make the exercise financially viable. Therefore, Britannia may feel that further liberalisation is required to increase the number of flights they can operate in a season.

In Britannia Airway's submission to the Australian Government 1989 inquiry into tourism, Britannia stated, 'The future development of inbound tourism to Australia may, based on European experience, hinge on accessibility for charter airlines' (Britannia Airways, 1989).

Britannia Airways has had an important role to play in the liberalisation of the international charter regulations in Australia. The Commonwealth Department of Tourism has recognised that role in the National Tourism Strategy which states that 'the recent charter programs undertaken and planned by Britannia Airlines are indicative of the benefits to Australia from a liberal charter policy' (Commonwealth Department of Tourism, 1992).

Conclusion

International charter travel is an important means of tourism transport for both the passenger and the destination country.

For passengers, charter travel offers cheaper airfares, convenient originating and destination airports, flights to new, long-haul destinations and a good level of customer service. For the receiving country, charter travel is beneficial as it generates business for smaller gateways, and creates a new high spending market.

Charter airlines have traditionally flown where the market has dictated (i.e. to where the tour operators have sold seats) and they have offered fares at very low prices. Now, the charter airlines are using the same strategy to fly to new, long-haul destinations by providing low-cost travel with a good standard of customer service.

Charter airlines, however, face competition from the scheduled airlines which are offering low airfares to cater for the needs of leisure travellers. These low fares, coupled with the advantage of a comprehensive network of destinations and frequencies, provide travellers with an alternative to the traditional package deal offered by the charter operators.

With increased competition on routes, many charter airlines will look elsewhere for markets and may begin to expand their long-haul operations. There is therefore an opportunity for Australia to receive long-haul flights, especially long-haul charter flights.

In addition, with the liberalisation of the airline industry, the differences between scheduled and charter travel have become less defined. Larger charter airlines may continue to become involved in scheduled operations and the scheduled airlines have begun to offer holiday package deals on regular services by selling a proportion of their seats to tour operators which is part-charter of the aircraft.

For the customer the existence of both charter and scheduled flights on holiday routes is an advantage as it offers a greater choice and encourages competition between the carriers in price and efficiency of service.

The 1992 National Tourism Strategy on International Charters states that the strategy is to 'ensure that international charter guidelines give adequate recognition to the needs of the tourism industry and the benefits to Australia from efficient charter operations' (Commonwealth Department of Tourism, 1992). Australia was slow to accept the importance of charter travel but has now introduced much more liberalised regulations which will encourage further growth and frequency.

References

Association of European Airlines (1992) *Association of European Airlines Yearbook*, AEA, Brussels, Belgium.
Australia World Airways (1989) 'Australia World Airways Submission to the Industries Assistance Commission Inquiry

into Travel and Tourism', no. 288, Australia World Airways, Melbourne, Victoria.

Beachey, A. (1990) 'The UK long haul market', *EIU Travel and Tourism Analyst*, no. 1:42–53.

Britannia Airways (1989) 'Britannia Airways Submission to the Industries Assistance Commission Inquiry into Travel and Tourism', no. 236, Michael Kellaway International, Air Transport Consultants, Melbourne, Victoria.

Bureau of Immigration Research (1991) *Australia's Population Trends and Prospects, 1990*, Australian Government Publishing Service, Canberra.

Bureau of Tourism Research (1991) *International Visitor Survey*, BTR, Canberra.

Cleverdon, R. (1988) 'International business travel', Economic Intelligence Unit (Great Britain), Special Report, no. 1140, Economic Intelligence Unit, London.

Commonweath Department of Tourism (1992) *National Tourism Strategy*, Commonwealth of Australia, Canberra.

Department of Transport and Communications (1990) *Guidelines for International Passenger Charter Flights*, International Aviation Policy Division, Canberra.

Department of Transport and Communications (1992a) *Air Transport Statistics—International Scheduled Air Transport*, AVSTATS Aviation Division, Canberra.

Department of Transport and Communications (1992b) *Britannia Airways Survey, November 1990 to March 1991*, AVSTATS Aviation Division, Canberra.

Department of Transport and Communications (1992c) *List of Charter Flights to Australia in 1992*, AVSTATS Aviation Division, Canberra.

Economist 1992, 'Unpackaged: changing holiday habits', *Economist*, 324(7768):57.

European Civil Aviation Conference (1981) *Statistics on Non-Scheduled Traffic Reported in ECAC States*, European Civil Aviation Conference, Paris.

Forsyth, P., Dwyer, L., Murphy, P. and Burnley, I. (1993) 'The impact of migration on Australian inbound and outbound tourism', *Building a Research Base in Tourism*, Proceedings of the National Conference on Tourism Research, University of Sydney, March, 1993, BTR, Canberra, p. 53.

Harrington, M. (1991) 'Charters struggle with schedules', *Interavia Aerospace Review*, March: 25.

March, R. (1993) 'Change and opportunity in the Japanese outbound tourism industry', *Building a Research Base in Tourism*, Proceedings of the National Conference on Tourism Research, University of Sydney, March, 1993, BTR, Canberra, p. 111.

Minister for Transport and Communications (1987) 'Domestic aviation; a new direction for the 1990s', Media Statement, 7 October, Attachment D, AGPS, Canberra.

Minister for Transport and Communications (1989) 'International aviation; maximising the benefits, Media Statement, 15 June, AGPS, Canberra, p. 3.

O'Brien, K. (1990) 'The UK tourism and leisure market: travel trends and spending patterns', Economic Intelligence Unit (Great Britain), Special report, no. 2010, Economic Intelligence Unit, London.

Pearce, D. (1987) 'Spatial patterns of package tourism in Europe', *Annals of Tourism Research*, 14(2):183–199.

Reed, A. (1988) 'Britannia speaks out for British charter carriers', *Air Transport World*, no. 4:46.

Spanish Civil Aviation Department (1981a) *Civil Aviation Statistics in Spain from 1979*, Subsecretaria de Aviacion Civil, Madrid, as cited in Pearce (1987).

Spanish Civil Aviation Department (1981b) *Regional Distribution in Spain of Arrivals from Europe from 1979*, Subsecretaria de Aviacion Civil, Madrid, as cited in Pearce (1987).

Statistics Canada (1983) *Air Charter Statistics*, Statistics Canada, Ontario.

19 Allies or adversaries? Airline pricing of leisure and business travel

J. R. SELDON AND Z. A. SELDON

Introduction

Leisure and business travellers often are portrayed as antagonists, with one group suffering the iniquities of cost shifting at the hands of the other. D'Ambrosio (1993a) and a host of other popular and business writers document the widespread perception that airlines charge some customers more so that 'favoured fliers' can pay less. Nevertheless, just who loses to whom often seems to be in dispute, and there appears to have been relatively little work documenting the effects of pricing strategies actually followed by the air carriers. A recent study by Evans and Kessides (1993) showed that median United States air fares per mile fell over the decade following the Airline Deregulation Act of 1978 while the highest fare levels rose. However, the authors did not address the issue of whether effects on the latter were in a meaningful sense caused by the former, were the result of the same market forces at work, or were linked merely by chance. Nor did they distinguish specifically between impacts on business and non-business fares.

There has been even less effort devoted to constructing systematic behavioural models useful for predicting and assessing airline pricing behaviour. This chapter contributes to the latter task by modelling air carriers' optimal price and output responses to fluctuations in the strength of business and leisure travel markets. Particular attention is paid to the prospects for subsidization of one segment by the other and for cost shifting between the two.

Formal investigation of intermarket spillovers dates at least to Viner's (1923, 1937) classic studies on international trade and price discrimination, while antecedents can be found as far back as Cournot's (1927) mathematical modelling of monopoly pricing, a work first published over a century and a half ago. More recent contributions include Shaffer's (1984) empirical work on cross-subsidization in banking and Seldon's (1986) theoretical examination of cost-shifting incentives in hospitals.

In the next section, we build upon that literature by developing a model in which airlines set fares (and thus, effectively, choose outputs and sales) in submarkets that are readily identifiable but not always distinct at their margins. We use the model to identify conditions under which cross-subsidization and cost-shifting between markets could be expected to emerge, finding both phenomena likely to be rare.

We next consider an environment with the identical cost and demand conditions but with airlines constrained by regulatory, technological, or cost factors to produce submarket outputs in fixed proportions. Again, we examine that environment in search of pricing spillovers. Our conclusion is that constraints on airlines' behaviour easily can lead to an equilibrium in which one market subsidizes the other, and when market conditions vary, cost-shifting between the two will be likely.

The basic model

Consider the production and pricing decisions of a typical airline, i, whose institutional goal is to maximize profit (Π_i) earned by supplying services to two distinct customer categories: business and vacation travellers. Business clients (B) are charged price P for each unit of standard-quality business service purchased. Vacation travellers (V) pay price R per standardized unit of vacation travel.

We assume that travellers are well-informed about the quality of services they purchase. That is, they are knowledgeable about such features as accessibility and convenience and are able to evaluate the personal importance of those characteristics. For simplicity, we assume that they adjust willingness to pay in direct proportion to expected quality differences. This simplification permits us to model the case as one in which, in effect, all customers in a category receive the same service at the same unit price. However, qualitative conclusions will be unchanged as long as willingness to pay rises with quality. We do not address the question of whether available measures of real-world airline activity accurately proxy the model's output variable. On the assumption that seat miles and passenger miles are monotonically related, we need not distinguish between them in deriving qualitative predictions. Further, since the focus is on spillovers *between* submarkets, we ignore the obvious potential for price discrimination *within* them.

Conventionally, each market's demand curve is taken to be negatively sloped. That is, after accounting for all other influences—in particular, for differences in expectations of future fares—quantity demanded is higher at lower prices and lower at higher prices. Demand interaction is captured by including the price of vacation travel as an argument in the business demand function and the price of business travel as an influence on vacation travel demand. We as yet make no assumptions about whether business and tourist transport are substitutes or complements in the eyes of consumers, and no restrictions are imposed on the signs or sizes of the second derivatives at this stage of the investigation.

Total cost is monotonically increasing in outputs. Again, no *a priori* restrictions are placed on the signs or sizes of the second derivatives. Airlines are assumed to be risk-neutral, so that they pursue policies they anticipate will yield maximum expected profit. The analysis is carried on in a comparative statics context, identifying initial and final equilibrium solutions without attempting to trace the path from one to the other.

Expressing demand functions in inverse form and omitting subscripts denoting individual firms, the objective of each enterprise is to maximize the expected value of the expression:

$$\Pi = P(B,S,V) \cdot B + R(V,B) \cdot V - C(B,V) \qquad (1)$$

Term S is an autonomous shift parameter capturing changes in the demand for business travel. Without loss of generality, we may establish $P_S > 0$ by definition. That is, higher values of S indicate the ability of airlines to charge a higher price for any specific level of sales and hence reflect increased demand for business travel. By assumption, P_B, $R_V < 0$ and C_B, $C_R > 0$. The signs of P_V and R_B will depend on whether business and leisure travel are substitutes or complements and on the directions and strengths of the income effect on the demand for each. In general, however, we may expect that these cross-price influences will be small relative to the own-price effects, not least because price discrimination is viable only if markets can be kept distinct.

Representing partial derivatives via subscript notation, first-order conditions for maximum profitability are:

$$\Pi_B = P(B,S,V) + B \cdot P_B + V \cdot R_B - C_B = 0 \qquad (2)$$

$$\Pi_V = R(V,B) + V \cdot R_V + B \cdot P_V - C_V = 0 \qquad (3)$$

Eqns (2) and (3) conventionally require that marginal cost equal marginal revenue in each market segments, taking both revenue and cost spillovers into account. More intuitively, they set out the principle that profit-seeking airlines should increase sales (attracting more customers by cutting fares) whenever extra revenues from expansion would exceed added costs, and should forego the sale of output (deterring potential customers by raising fares) that would contribute less to revenues than to costs.

Eqns (2) and (3) rule out one form of subsidization of either consumer group by the other: since prices cover incremental costs, no customer (at the margin) is served at a loss. Still, fares and markups can differ in equilibrium and, depending on demand conditions, can do so even if costs should by chance be identical across sub-markets. Further, since the incremental revenue derived from each customer includes changes derived from the other market, there could be cases of profits in one appearing to support losses in the other.

As an example, if demand in two sub-markets were strongly complementary ($R_B \gg 0$ or $P_V \gg 0$) so that more service in one induces large demand increases in the other, it could be worth serving the first at (what in isolation would be) a loss in order to stimulate profitable demand in the second. A similar outcome can occur when cost functions are not strictly separable. For instance, if average costs for the enterprise as a whole are declining in the neighbourhood of equilibrium, it might be worth having average cost exceed one sub-market's price to gain the benefits of larger-scale production. (This situation mirrors that of a single-market producer who might find it profitable to operate a flight the firm's accountants cite as money-losing because demand is robust and average costs fall with increases in output.)

Even under the circumstances above, however, customers in the sub-market that seems to be subsidizing the other would pay higher prices for the product if the second group were not served. Thus, the apparent subsidy actually would benefit those paying it.

Second-order conditions (sufficient to ensure a profit maximum if first-order requirements have been met) are that:

$$\Pi_{BB}, \Pi_{VV} < 0 \qquad (4)$$

$$D = \begin{vmatrix} \Pi_{BB} & \Pi_{BV} \\ \Pi_{VB} & \Pi_{VV} \end{vmatrix} = \Pi_{BB}\Pi_{VV} - (\Pi_{BV})^2 > 0 \qquad (5)$$

Taken together, these conditions dictate that each market's marginal cost must be rising more rapidly (or falling more slowly, if marginal cost is declining in the neighbourhood of equilibrium) than marginal revenue.

Intuitively, this condition guarantees that profit would fall with either expansion or contraction of output in either market. Eqn (5) specifies that for a solution in which both markets are served, interaction between them cannot be too strong, either positively or negatively, relative to responses in each alone. Real-world corner solutions certainly may exist and warrant investigation, but they are outside the purview of this paper and its focus on cross-effects.

Comparative statics in the basic model

Given that the necessary (first-order) and sufficient (second-order) conditions for a profit maximum have been satisfied, consider the impact on the optimum fare charged tourist travellers when there occurs a decline in the demand for airlines' business services. The shift is modelled as a reduction in the size of S for all values of B in the relevant range of outputs.

The investigation follows a two-stage process. The first step is to determine the profit-maximizing adjustment in outputs when S changes. The second is to solve for the corresponding price changes. Focus is on the short run, identified as a setting in which the number of airlines does not change. (Long-run outcomes, under various oligopoly conditions, would be identical to the behaviour modelled here, while under pure or monopolistic competition, a normal profits equilibrium would ultimately dominate.)

In the analysis to follow, it is assumed that a typical air carrier is able to earn at least normal profits both before and after the shift and hence is not induced to leave the business by the lessening of demand for its services. It is apparent that no such guarantee of economic viability protects real-world airlines. However, airline deregulation was promoted partly on the grounds that enhanced competition would reduce excess profits (i.e. financial returns greater than the minimum level needed to make it worthwhile continuing in business) and partly that the threat of lower profits or losses would be met by elimination of X-inefficiency. Thus, the existence of profit potential is taken as a reasonable starting point. A more pragmatic reason for the assumption is that the present work is aimed at examining inter-market spillovers, not predicting which firms may be driven out of business by market shifts.

Optimal changes in B

Given a shift in the demand for business travel, the optimal response in that market segment is shown in Appendix Eqn (A.2) by the expression:

$$\frac{dB}{dS} = \frac{-\{P_S + B \cdot P_{BS}\}\Pi_{VV} + P_{VS} \cdot B \cdot \Pi_{BV}}{D} \quad (6)$$

From second-order conditions, the determinant D must be positive and Π_{VV} must be negative. The expression $\{\cdot\}$ cannot be signed unequivocally for all firms, since we have not ruled out the possibility that its second term will be negative and large enough to outweigh the first, which is positive by definition. However, observe that P_{BS} is the effect on the slope of the firm's demand curve when S changes. With the same number of firms sharing a smaller market, both the market share demand curve and the typical enterprise's *ceteris paribus* demand curve become steeper. Thus, when existing enterprises suffer a downward shift in market demand, P_{BS} must be positive for the representative enterprise. Then, since a lower S implies a smaller (larger negative) value of P_B, we argue that $\{\cdot\}$ is positive and conclude that the first term in the numerator will be positive for a typical carrier.

If P_{VS} has a value of zero, so that the demands for business and tourist travel are effectively independent of one another, the second term vanishes and the overall expression must be positive. It will also be positive whenever P_{VS} is small, or when P_{VS} and Π_{BV} both are negative (business and tourism travel are substitutes in the eyes of consumers, while expansion in one adds to the profitability of the other at the margin) and when both are positive (the two are complements, but added output in one lowers the profitability of the other). In each of these instances, the optimal response of a typical firm to decreased business demand is to serve fewer business customers.

This prescription that (holding other factors constant) airlines should accept lower sales in a market where demand falls may seem intuitively obvious. There is no evidence to suggest that passenger air transport provides an exception to what seems a commonsense rule. Further, it is apparent from much casual observation of airline behaviour, such as D'Ambrosio (1993b), that airlines are perceived to react that way. However, observe that if P_{VS} and Π_{BV} have opposite signs, it is conceivable—although still not assured, since the second term of (6) also must be large enough to outweigh the first—that the best response to loss of demand could be to *increase* sales volume in the market segment experiencing the loss.

Optimum change in P

The optimum business fare change is given by totally differentiating the business market demand function with respect to S to obtain:

$$\frac{dP}{dS} = P_B \cdot \frac{dB}{dS} + P_V \cdot \frac{dV}{dS} + P_S \qquad (7)$$

Eqn (7) cannot be signed in general, even if P_V is zero, since the initial term typically will be negative and the final component is always positive. The intuitive explanation for this indeterminacy is that even when (as will be typical) declining demand calls for lower sales in the market experiencing the decline, the optimum reduction need not be exactly that occurring with price held constant. If a greater reduction is appropriate, a price increase is called for; if a smaller decrease, a price reduction. In the first instance, firms undoubtedly will be accused of charging their remaining business customers higher prices to make up for lost demand; in the second, they will be seen as cutting fares to fill seats.

Optimal changes in V

The change in the optimum number of vacation travellers, V, resulting from a shift in the demand for business travel is given by:

$$\frac{dV}{dS} = \frac{-P_{VS} \cdot B \cdot \Pi_{BB} + \{\cdot\} \Pi_{VB}}{D} \qquad (8)$$

Again, D is positive and Π_{BB} negative from second-order conditions, while it was established above that $\{\cdot\}$ will be positive for a typical firm. B is positive by definition. The signs of P_{VS} and Π_{VB} have not been specified, so in general it is not possible to sign Eqn (8). However, if P_{VS} is zero (a shift in demand for business travel has no impact on the slope of the vacation travel demand curve) the sign of the expression will depend upon Π_{VB}. That term will be negative under likely conditions—for example, with demand spillovers negative or relatively small and incremental costs that rise with aggregate output.

In light of the above results, and although exceptions are not ruled out, we deem it probable that the appropriate response of real-world carriers to a downward shift in business demand will be to serve a greater number of vacation travellers; while in the face of increased demand for business travel, fewer units of vacation service should be sold.

Optimum change in R

The change in optimum vacation fare, R, is given by:

$$\frac{dR}{dS} = R_V \frac{dV}{dS} + R_B \frac{dB}{dS} \qquad (9)$$

In the previous section it was argued that dV/dS generally will be negative. Given conventional demand relationships, R_V is negative. Then, the first term in (9) will be positive. Similarly, dB/dS typically will be positive. Thus, unless R_B should happen to be negative and large— meaning that business and leisure travel are close substitutes, and casting doubt on separability of the markets—$dR/dS > 0$ is to be anticipated. That is, the prescription is for airlines responding to changes in business travel markets to raise vacation travel fares when business demand rises and to cut those prices when business demand falls.

This prescription may seem counter-intuitive in view of popular cost-shifting notions, but the explanation flows directly from the conditions for maximum profitability and is relatively straightforward. A fall in business demand shifts that sector's marginal revenue curve downward. In turn, the enterprise's aggregate marginal revenue schedule is lowered, and the effect of this shift is to reduce the equilibrium (profit-maximizing) value of marginal cost. As before, marginal revenue in the vacation sector must equal marginal cost for maximum profit; and that equality is regained by lowering tourist fares and serving more vacation customers.

An implication of this result is that many perceived cases of real-world cost-shifting may be suspect. One possibility is that observations of falling (rising) business fares occurring with rising (falling) tourist fare levels may reflect relative price adjustments that would take place in any event. That is, although prices in one sub-market rise as another market contracts, they may be falling compared to levels they *would* have attained if the contraction had not occurred. A second possibility is that the analysis of airlines' behaviour needs extension to capture the realities of cost-shifting.

An extended model with cross-subsidization

The analysis presented above, modelling the behaviour of airlines maximizing profit in an environment free of regulatory constraints on pricing or output levels, evidenced no incentives for deliberate subsidization of any market segment by another. The profit-maximizing price of an identical basket of services could differ between categories of customers (a case of third-degree price discrimination), depending on demand functions. The optimal price charged one group could be higher or lower than were other groups not served, depending upon the nature of joint costs. Absolute or relative mark-ups over cost might be higher for one market than another, depending upon demand and cost together. However, the conclusion was that profit-maximizing outcomes never would occur with any group of customers deliberately charged a higher price so that others could be served for less. Further, it was concluded that a decline in demand from one sector would typically spill over into others by inducing a decrease rather than a rise in their prices.

Now, consider a setting identical to that modelled above but with one important exception: the outputs of the two sub-markets are linked to one another according to the rule $\alpha V \geqslant B$, where $\alpha > 0$. Since our purpose is to investigate the effect of constraints imposed on airlines' choices, and since unconstrained behaviour was examined above, we concentrate on cases in which the equality holds. It may for convenience be assumed that α is constant, since no qualitative conclusions are altered by that restriction.

The assumption that the two markets must be served in fixed proportions has clear advantages for mathematical tractability, but also captures elements of substance in air transport. For instance, since aircraft are available only in discrete capacities and varying seat configuration is costly, carriers often will find it worthwhile maintaining a particular mix despite changes in the ideal (long run) proportions when demand levels vary. Thus, whether the fixed proportions scenario is cost-driven is an inherent feature of the technology or results from regulatory fiat, output inflexibilities represent a factor influencing the behaviour of profit-seeking carriers.

The goal of each airline now is to maximize:

$$\Pi = P(B, V, S) \cdot B + R(V, B) \cdot V -$$
$$C(B, V) + \lambda [B - \alpha V] \tag{10}$$

so that first-order conditions become:

$$\Pi_B = P(B, V, S) + B \cdot P_B + R_B \cdot V - C_B + \lambda = 0 \tag{11}$$

$$\Pi_V = R(V, B) + V \cdot R_V + P_V \cdot B -$$
$$C_V - \alpha \lambda = 0 \tag{12}$$

$$\Pi_\lambda = B - \alpha V = 0 \tag{13}$$

From (11) and (12), it can be seen that whenever the constraint is binding (so that the equilibrium value of λ is non-zero) marginal cost must exceed marginal revenue in one market while marginal revenue will exceed marginal cost in the other. In short, except in the singular case where the unconstrained profit maximum happens to involve selling outputs in the exact proportion dictated by Eqn (13), one market will at the margin subsidize the other.

In effect, this setting is one in which airlines find it worthwhile supplying more than the profit-maximizing output to one market in exchange for permission to service the other. Observe that λ may be either positive or negative, so that the direction of subsidy will vary according to the relative strengths of demand in the two markets.

Then, in the model as perhaps in the real world, business customers sometimes will discover that they are subsidizing leisure travel and leisure travellers sometimes will have cause to complain that they are supporting business counterparts, depending on current demand.

Changes in B

The adjustment in the optimum number of business customers for changes in S is given (Eqn (A.5)) by the expression:

$$\frac{dB}{dS} = \frac{\{\cdot\} \cdot \alpha^2 + P_{VS} \cdot B \cdot \alpha}{D} \tag{14}$$

In the unconstrained case, it was argued that a positive value of $\{\cdot\}$ would make $dB/dS > 0$ likely for a typical airline. Eqn (14) shows the same behaviour in the constrained case. Second-order conditions again require the denominator to be negative. Then, unless P_{VS} is both negative and large enough that $|P_{VB} \cdot B| > \alpha \{\cdot\}$, the optimal response to an increase in business travel demand will be to decrease business sales. Since whether it is positive or negative, P_V will tend to be small, P_{VS} will be smaller still. Thus, as before, the anticipated relationship will be $dB/dS < 0$.

Optimal changes in P

The optimal adjustment in the price charged business customers is given by taking the total derivative of the business travel demand function with respect to a change in S:

$$\frac{dP}{dS} = P_B \frac{dB}{dS} + P_V \frac{dV}{dS} + P_S \tag{15}$$

In the unconstrained case, it was shown that sales typically would be lower in the new profit maximum than before a downward demand shift, but that the decline might be more than, less than, or precisely equal to that which would follow from holding price constant as demand declined. Thus, the optimum price could be the same as, higher or lower than before the shift. Eqn (15), which is identical in form to (7), reveals that when airline behaviour is constrained, identical reasoning applies.

Optimal changes in V

Since we are considering cases in which the constraint that ties the two markets is binding, the change in the optimal number of vacation customers resulting from a change in the business demand shift parameter, S, is given from Eqn (13) by:

$$\frac{dV}{dS} = \frac{1}{\alpha} \cdot \frac{dB}{dS} \qquad (16)$$

It was established that in the unconstrained case dV/dS was likely to be negative, although exceptions were possible given certain demand and cost-interrelationships. In contrast, Eqn (16) shows a positive sign whenever dB/dS is positive. This difference in behaviour flows from the link between the vacation and business markets. When the optimal response to declining business demand is to accept fewer sales in that market, then since tourist sales are constrained to a level α times the new level of B, they also must be reduced. In parallel, whenever it is appropriate to increase business sales, so too must tourism offerings be expanded to satisfy the constraint.

Optimal changes in R

The optimum vacation travel price adjustment for a change in the business travel shift parameter, S, is given by:

$$\frac{dR}{dS} = R_V \frac{dV}{dS} + R_B \frac{dB}{dS}$$

$$= \left\{ \frac{1}{\alpha} \cdot R_V + R_B \right\} \frac{dB}{dS} \qquad (17)$$

Now, R_V is strictly negative, while R_B may be of either sign but is small relative to R_V. It was argued that dB/dS generally will be positive. Then, unless $\alpha > |R_V/R_B|$ and R_B is positive, the expression dR/dS will be negative. The implication is that, in contrast to the unconstrained case and in keeping with common views of the way in which air travel markets function, vacation travellers typically will face higher prices when business demand falls and lower fares when business demand rises.

At a more intuitive level, consider the (highly probable) case in which falling business demand dictates a decrease in the number of business travellers served. Then, because

of the constraint, tourist sales also must be cut back; and because profit maximization requires that sellers charge the highest price possible for each given sales level, airlines will ration vacation travel by raising fares. Since the prescription for minimizing the effects of a slump in business demand is to provide less service in both market segments, we would expect to find carriers reducing capacity by cutting flights and shifting to fewer and smaller aircraft rather than merely reallocating service between markets. In parallel, growing demand in one market segment should foster expansion in both.

Thus, although the reactions may not be exactly those popularly anticipated, in each instance a visible form of cost shifting takes place. The connections are to quantities rather than prices and there still is no real sense in which the shift is a means of making up for losses or of passing along profits earned in the other market. However, when there is a rise in the optimum number of business travellers served, vacation fliers will pay more; when there is a decline, they will be charged less. That relationship holds whether business counterparts are paying higher or lower prices than before, and whether the increase in business sales is a response to weaker or stronger demand in the market for business travel. In distinct contrast with the unconstrained case, only if falling (rising) business demand calls for a reduction (rise) in that market's output level and a decrease (increase) in business fares will vacation travellers find fares moving counter to those in the other sub-market.

Conclusion

This paper has modelled production and pricing in segmented markets for airline services in order to investigate responses to demand fluctuations, focusing on the possibilities of cross-subsidization and cost-shifting between tourist and business travel segments.

The analysis shows that, in the absence of extra-market constraints or technical rigidities, airlines will not find it profitable to subsidize one market at the expense of another, either in total or at the margin. Further, it reveals that successful profit-seeking airlines generally will not charge vacation travellers higher prices merely because commercial markets become less profitable. Indeed, under plausible demand and cost conditions, profit-seeking airlines should react to declining business demand by *lowering* fares to their other customers.

In contrast, it demonstrates that carriers pursuing the same goal but subject to constraints on outputs would engage in a strong form of cross-subsidization and also engage in a form of cost-shifting. Although exceptions could exist under certain cost and demand conditions, the expected case would see lost business demand causing profit-seeking airlines to raise fares to non-business customers and increased demand generating lower vacation travel fares.

The number of different constraints with the potential to generate an equilibrium displaying cross-subsidization is unlimited, and it would be hazardous to infer from the results derived here that cost-shifting necessarily must be common in air transport. However, the results do provide evidence that the effect can be induced by cross-market linkages and suggest that popular perceptions of both cross-subsidization and cost-shifting may warrant further study.

Appendix: comparative statics

The basic model

Comparative statics are described by the equation system:

$$\begin{bmatrix} \Pi_{BB} & \Pi_{BV} \\ \Pi_{VB} & \Pi_{VV} \end{bmatrix} \begin{bmatrix} dB \\ dV \end{bmatrix} = \begin{bmatrix} -(P_S + P_{BS} \cdot B)dS \\ -P_{VS} \cdot BdS \end{bmatrix} \quad (A.1)$$

where:

$$\Pi_{BB} = 2P_B + B \cdot P_{BB} + V \cdot R_{BB} - C_{BB} < 0 \quad (A.1a)$$

$$\Pi_{VV} = 2R_V + V \cdot R_{VV} + B \cdot P_{VV} - C_{VV} < 0 \quad (A.1b)$$

$$\Pi_{BV} = \Pi_{VB} = P_V + P_{BV} \cdot B + R_B + R_{BV} \cdot V - C_{BV} \quad (A.1c)$$

Representing the expression $(P_S + P_{BS}B)$ as $\{\cdot\}$, then:

$$\frac{dB}{dS} = \frac{\begin{vmatrix} -\{\cdot\} & \Pi_{BV} \\ -P_{VS} \cdot B & \Pi_{VV} \end{vmatrix}}{D} \quad (A.2)$$

$$= \frac{-\{\cdot\}\Pi_{VV} + P_{VS} \cdot B \cdot \Pi_{BV}}{D}$$

$$\frac{dV}{dS} = \frac{\begin{vmatrix} \Pi_{BB} & -\{\cdot\} \\ \Pi_{VB} & -P_{VS} \cdot B \end{vmatrix}}{D} \quad (A.3)$$

$$= \frac{-P_{VS} \cdot B \cdot \Pi_{BB} + \{\cdot\}\Pi_{VB}}{D}$$

The extended model

With α fixed and a binding market share constraint:

$$\begin{bmatrix} \Pi_{BB} & \Pi_{BV} & \Pi_{B\lambda} \\ \Pi_{VB} & \Pi_{VV} & \Pi_{V\lambda} \\ \Pi_{\lambda B} & \Pi_{\lambda V} & 0 \end{bmatrix} \begin{bmatrix} dB \\ dV \\ d\lambda \end{bmatrix} = \begin{bmatrix} -\{\cdot\}dS \\ -P_{VS} \cdot BdS \\ 0 \end{bmatrix} \quad (A.4)$$

$$\Pi_{BB} = 2P_B + B \cdot P_{BB} + V \cdot R_{BB} - C_{BB} \quad (A.4a)$$

$$\Pi_{VV} = 2R_V + V \cdot R_{VV} + B \cdot P_{VV} - C_{VV} \quad (A.4b)$$

$$\Pi_{BV} = \Pi_{VB} = P_V + P_{BV} \cdot B + R_B + R_{BV} \cdot V - C_{BV} \quad (A.4c)$$

$$\Pi_{\lambda B} = 1 \quad (A.4d)$$

$$\Pi_{\lambda V} = -\alpha \quad (A.4e)$$

$$\Pi_{\lambda\lambda} = 0 \quad (A4f)$$

Substituting and using Cramer's rule:

$$\frac{dB}{dS} = \frac{\begin{vmatrix} -\{\cdot\} & \Pi_{BV} & 1 \\ -P_S \cdot B & \Pi_{VV} & -\alpha \\ 0 & -\alpha & 0 \end{vmatrix}}{D} \quad (A.5)$$

$$= \frac{\{\cdot\} \cdot \alpha^2 + P_{VS} \cdot B \cdot \alpha}{D}$$

References

Brandts, Jordi and Holt, Charles A. (1992) 'An experimental test of equilibrium dominance in signalling games', *The American Economic Review*, 82(5):1350–1365.

Cournot, Augustin (1927) *Researches into the Mathematical Principles of the Theory of Wealth* [1838], transl. by Nathaniel T. Bacon, Macmillan, New York.

D'Ambrosio, Richard (1993a) 'Airlines hike biz fares by 5 percent on most routes', *Business Travel News*, 265:2.

D'Ambrosio, Richard (1993b) 'Delta, TWA slash many fares from Atlanta', *Business Travel News*, 268:5.

Evans, John J. (1986) 'Commercial banks and the consumer services revolution', *Journal of Bank Research*, 16(4):182–185.

Evans, William and Kessides, Ioannis (1993) 'Structure, conduct and performance in the deregulated airline industry', *Southern Economic Journal*, 59(3):450–467.

Meyer, David (1993) '1993 fare breaks are a big success, airlines decree', *Meetings Today Supplement: Business Travel News*, 272:A1.

Miyazaki, Hajime (1977) 'The rat race and internal labor markets', *Bell Journal of Economics*, 8(2):394–418.

Rose, John T. and Wolken, John D. (1988) 'Thrift competition and the commercial banking line of commerce', *Atlantic Economic Journal*, 16(4):24–36.

Seldon, James R. (1986) 'Hospital cost-shifting under fractional reimbursement', *Atlantic Economic Journal*, 14(1):50–58.

Shaffer, Sherrill (1984) 'Cross-subsidization in checking accounts: a note', *Journal of Money, Credit, and Banking*, 16(1):100–109.

Spence, A. Michael (1973) 'Job market signalling', *Quarterly Journal of Economics*, 87 (August):355–374.

United States (1989) *Financial Institutions Reform, Recovery and Enforcement Act of 1989*, Public Law 101-73-August 9, 103 State pp. 183–554.

Viner, Jacob (1923) *Dumping, a Problem in International Trade*, University of Chicago Press, Chicago.

Viner, Jacob (1937) *Studies in the theory of international trade*, Harper, New York.

Wilson, Charles A. (1977) 'A model of insurance markets with incomplete information', *Journal of Economic Theory*, 16 (December):167–207.

20 Tourism and transport policy in the European Union

A. H. FORBES

Passenger transport and tourism

In view of the easily demonstrable link between tourism and passenger transport, it is perhaps surprising that the two are so seldom considered together by governments and other policy-making bodies. Much of the demand for passenger transport services and facilities may be considered as tourism-related, particularly if one of the broader definitions of tourism is accepted; however, it is not always easy to distinguish between tourism and non-tourism use of passenger transport when preparing statistics, especially with surface-transport modes. Definitions of tourism are generally either conceptual or technical. The key concepts involved are travel, stay, destination activities (distinct from those of the local population) and the temporary nature of tourism (Burkart and Medlik, 1981); many authors and tourism organisations have adopted definitions based on this conceptual framework, for example Mathieson and Wall (1982), Boniface and Cooper (1987), Cooper et al. (1993) and The Tourism Society.

Conceptual definitions generally imply that tourism includes movement for all purposes, whereas in practice it is usual to exclude certain categories of traveller from tourism statistics. Technical definitions may specify the length of time which must be involved in order to allow a journey to be classified as tourism, and also the types of traveller who are not counted as tourists. The best-known technical definition is that of the World Tourism Organisation (WTO), whose classification of travellers is cited by Holloway (1989) amongst others. To be a tourist, according to the WTO, a person must travel for at least 24 hours and for no longer than one year; amongst categories of traveller which the organisation does not consider to be tourists are nomads, refugees, diplomats, members of the armed forces on duty, transit passengers and border workers. Burkart and Medlik state in addition that tourism visits must be 'for purposes other than taking up permanent residence or employment remunerated from within the places visited' (1981:42).

Whilst there may be no universally accepted definition of tourism, it is clear that travel is a necessary pre-requisite for tourism; the relationship between the two is effectively summarised by Burkart and Medlik who contend that 'all tourism includes some travel but not all travel is tourism' (1981:42). Travel implies passenger transport, which may be defined as the means by which people reach their destinations and move around once at these destinations; it is therefore reasonable to consider passenger transport to be an integral part of tourism (Robinson, 1976).

Several factors affect the use of different passenger transport modes for tourism purposes. Purpose of visit (business, holiday, common interest) is an important determinant of modal choice, and Table 20.1 shows the usage of the various modes according to this criterion.

Overall, the principal passenger transport mode for domestic and international tourism within the European Union is the private car. The same applies in the United Kingdom for domestic tourism but geographical constraints mean that international travel to and from the UK has hitherto only been possible by air and sea; at the time of writing the Channel Tunnel is expected to open shortly, adding rail to the modes which may be selected by travellers bound for the Continent. Several forecasts have been made concerning the effect of the opening of the Tunnel on cross-Channel passenger traffic (see Page and Sinclair, 1992), but of course only when the link is actually operating will it become clear whether the predictions of Eurotunnel (the tunnel's operators) are unduly optimistic.

The European Union (EU) and tourism

The European Economic Community was created on the signature of the Treaty of Rome on 25 March 1957 by the six nations which were already members of the European Coal and Steel Community: France, West Germany, Italy, Belgium, The Netherlands and Luxembourg. A third Community, the European Atomic Energy Community (Euratom) was also established by a separate treaty; for convenience the three Communities are collectively known as the European Community, abbreviated to EC (Robertson, 1973). The initial signatories were joined in 1973 by the United Kingdom,

Table 20.1

Tourist type	Transport mode						
	A	B	C	D	E	F	G
Holiday: inclusive tour (IT)	Y	Y	*	Y	Y	Y	#
Holiday: independent	Y	Y	Y	@	Y		+
Business and conference	Y		Y				Y
Visiting friends and relatives	Y	Y	Y	@	Y		Y
Other common interest	Y	Y	Y	Y	Y		Y
Day visitors (excursionists)	Y	Y	#	#	Y	$	Y

Key to transport modes: A, car (private or hired); B, coach (scheduled or chartered); C, scheduled flight; D, charter flight; E, ferry; F, cruise ship; G, train.
General key: Y, mode frequently selected by this tourist type; *, long-haul ITs; #, mode rarely selected by this tourist type; @, charter flight on seat-only basis; +, often in connection with railpass, e.g. Inter-Rail; $, local 1-day sea, lake or inland waterway cruise.
Source: Adapted from Cooper et al. (1993).

Denmark and Ireland, in 1981 by Greece, and in 1986 by Spain and Portugal. The basis of all EC legislation was and remains the Treaty of Rome, together with subsequent amendments to that treaty. The Maastricht Treaty on European Union is seen by some as a basis for strengthening the EU's tourism role, although it is not specifically concerned with tourism (Fitzpatrick Associates, 1993); since the ratification of the treaty in 1993, the EC has generally been referred to as the European Union.

Articles 48–73 of the Treaty of Rome are concerned with 'the free movement of persons, services and capital' and Articles 74–84 with transport (Robertson, 1973:179–181). Transport and agriculture were the only two industries to receive specific provisions under the Treaty of Rome; as we have shown, passenger transport is inextricably linked with tourism so any common transport policy would inevitably affect the EU tourism industry.

In the late 1950s, when the European Community was founded, the phenomenon of mass tourism was still unknown, and for more than twenty-five years the Community took no action directly related to tourism. However, Akehurst (1992) points out that EU tourism receipts in 1989 totalled 75.3 billion ECUs, which represented an increase of 9.1% in real terms over the previous year, while Cooper et al. (1993) report that in 1990 tourism was the third most important industry in the world in terms of export earnings. By the following year the tourism sector had grown to become the largest in the economy of the European Community, according to the Head of the Tourism Unit of Directorate-General XXIII at the European Commission (Tzoanos, 1991). Total receipts for international tourism in the EC in 1991 have been estimated at 81.7 billion ECUs, whilst

expenditure by member states was approximately 77.8 billion ECUs (Fitzpatrick Associates, 1993).

Of the world's top ten tourist destination countries, five are members of the EC—France, Spain, Italy, the UK and Germany, in that order—and the EU accounts for approximately 40% of all international tourism arrivals. World Tourism Organisation estimates also show that the EC contains five of the ten most important tourism-generating countries in terms of expenditure: in order (world ranking in parentheses) Germany (2), UK (4), Italy (5), France (6) and The Netherlands (8) (Fitzpatrick Associates, 1993).

Although EU interest in tourism might be thought to stem from the economic importance of the tourism business, there is an important political dimension to the involvement of the Community. Edgell (1990:37) asserts that 'tourism is, or can be, a tool used not only for economic but for political means', and in the case of the EU tourism is clearly one possible way to bring about the Community's aim (stated in the Treaty of Rome, Article 2) of promoting closer relations between member states.

Responsibility for tourism in the European Commission

The Commission of the European Communities (European Commission) is responsible for initiating EC policy, which must be submitted to the Council of Ministers (representing the EU's member states) for consideration and possible legislation. The Commission is charged with upholding the EC treaties, and also undertakes various administrative functions. The activities of the Commission are divided into separate policy areas, in much the same way as, at national level, governmental responsibilities are divided between ministries; the Commission's basic units of organisation are its 23 Directorates-General (Nugent, 1991). Table 20.2 shows the Directorates-General of the Commission, and some of its special units and services.

Although responsibility for tourism in the EC officially rests with Directorate-General XXIII of the European Commission, Lickorish (1991:180) aptly describes tourism in the EU context as 'a wide ranging activity, a trade in people potentially affecting almost every aspect of Community life'. Prior to February 1989, the tourism unit was located within DG VII (Transport), and several other Directorates-General produce measures and policy which may affect the tourism industry. For example, DG IV is concerned with competition policies affecting the transport and tourism industries, DG VI is interested in rural tourism and countryside recreation, DG XI is concerned with the negative environmental impact of

Table 20.2 *Directorates-General and special units of the Commission*

DG I:	External relations
DG II:	Economic and financial affairs
*DG III:	Internal market and industrial affairs
*DG IV:	Competition
*DG V:	Employment, industrial relationships and social affairs
*DG VI:	Agriculture
*DG VII:	Transport
DG VIII:	Development
DG IX:	Personnel and administration
*DG X:	Information, communication and culture
*DG XI:	Environment, nuclear safety and civil protection
*DG XII:	Science, research and development
*DG XIII:	Telecommunications, information, industry and innovation
DG XIV:	Fisheries
DG XV:	Financial institutions and company law
*DG XVI:	Regional policies
DG XVII:	Energy
DG XVIII:	Credit and investments
DG XIX:	Budgets
DG XX:	Financial control
*DG XXI:	Customs union and indirect taxation
DG XXII:	Coordination of structural policies
*DG XXIII:	Enterprises policy, distributive trades, **tourism** and social economy

Special units and services:

Secretariat-General of the Commission
Legal Service
Spokesmen Service
Translation Service
Joint Interpretation and Conference Service
Statistical Office
Consumer Policy Service
Joint Research Centre
Task Force: Human Resources, Education, Training and Youth
EURATOM supply agency
Security Office
Office for Official Publications of the European Communities

* = DG with tourism involvement.
Source: Adapted from Nugent (1991:67).

tourism and DG XVI is responsible for regional policies which may involve development or redistribution of tourism (Fitzpatrick Associates, 1993).

The Tourism Unit of DG XXIII is mainly concerned with the coordination of EU activities concerning tourism and the provision of information, but it has also become involved in funding tourism research and promotion of the EU as a tourist destination. However, EC member states tend to consider tourism as primarily a matter for national governments, National Tourist Organisations and local authorities, with such inter-governmental bodies as the World Tourism Organisation (WTO) and the Organisation for Economic Cooperation and Development (OECD) exercising a tourism function in the international sphere. Whilst this situation persists, any extension in the Commission's tourism role will be hard to achieve, despite pressure from the European Parliament (Fitzpatrick Associates, 1993).

Development of European Union tourism policy

The Commission published its first guidelines for an EC tourism policy in 1982, and submitted them to the Council of Ministers for consideration (EC, 1982). Areas were identified in which EC action could stimulate harmonious tourism development, ensure freedom of movement and protection for tourists and improve the conditions of tourism industry employees. Certain priorities for action were outlined, including combating the problem of seasonality in tourism, possibly by staggering school holidays, preservation of European heritage especially in disadvantaged areas, and promotion of social, cultural and rural tourism.

According to Davidson (1992:25) the validity of the European Commission's involvement in the field of tourism was confirmed by a judgment of the European Court in 1984 to the effect that EU nationals travelling abroad within the EU are 'recipients of services'. This means that tourism is covered by Articles 48–73 of the Treaty of Rome concerning 'the free movement of persons, services and capital' (Robertson, 1973: 179–181).

Lickorish (1991) and Akehurst (1992) describe the Community tourism programme proposed by the Commission in 1986, after a period of consultation with bodies such as the European Parliament. In addition to some of the ideas in the initial guidelines, the Commission made proposals for better use of EC development funding, better information as well as protection for tourists, and establishment of consultation and coordination between the Commission and member states. Partly as a result of this last proposal, the EU's ministers responsible for tourism have met the Commission on a regular basis since 1988, to discuss Community tourism policy and to exchange information on the tourism policies of EC members (Davidson, 1992). Other recommendations arising from these proposals and subsequently adopted include ones on standardised information and fire safety for hotels, and one on harmonisation of legislation on package travel (Akehurst, 1992). This last led to the EC Directive on Package Travel, Package Holidays and Package Tours in 1990.

European Year of Tourism (EYT) 1990

The European Year of Tourism 1990 was an initiative by the European Parliament, agreed by the ministers responsible for tourism in their meeting with the Commission at the end of 1988. Lickorish (1991:181) lists the Year's objectives as follows:

- To promote the Single Market and tourism's role in this
- To develop the integrating role of tourism in creating a people's Europe
- To promote a better distribution of tourism over time and location
- To promote EC tourism particularly by encouraging travel from third world

During the Year, which was funded by the EC and participating non-EU European nations and partly sponsored by American Express, special events, competitions and themed months were organised (for example, April was designated Angling Month), and various projects were co-financed, especially in the areas of youth tourism, cultural tourism, rural tourism and environmentally considerate tourism (Davidson, 1992). The Year was generally thought a success, and towards the end of it the Council of Ministers asked the Commission to draft a Community action plan to assist tourism.

The Community action plan to assist tourism

The action plan was drafted by the Commission in 1991, and was adopted following a decision of the Council of Ministers on 13 July 1992 (EC, 1992a). The Council allocated a budget of 18 million ECUs to implement the plan over three years from 1 January 1993. The main objectives of the action plan are summarised by Lickorish (1991:182) as follows: (1) to strengthen the horizontal approach to tourism, and (2) to provide support for specific measures to assist tourism in the EU, through medium-term action to facilitate the 'diversification of tourism activities, the development of transnational schemes and better promotion of European tourism in international markets'.

As regards the horizontal approach, the Council wanted to stress the importance of cooperation between member states and the Commission, so that 'coordination of Community policies must go hand in hand with coordination at Community level of national policies to assist tourism' (Lickorish, 1991:182). The policies referred to here are any which may affect tourism in some way, not just tourism policies. Better cooperation with the

tourism industry itself was suggested, as was the development of EC tourism statistics; action would also be designed to produce an improvement in the seasonal distribution of tourism (EC, 1992a).

Following on from successful initiatives in the European Year of Tourism, specific measures were envisaged in the following areas: information and protection for tourists, cultural tourism, environmental awareness in tourism, rural tourism, social tourism, youth tourism, training and increased professionalism in the EC tourism industry, and promotion of Europe as a tourist destination (EC, 1992a:29–31).

European Community transport policy

The efficient operation of freight transport is of critical importance to any free trade area, even if there is a lack of reliable empirical evidence to support the hypothesis that improved transport generates new economic development (Whitelegg, 1988). As Despicht (1964:191) observed, 'the inclusion of transport in this Second Part (of the Treaty of Rome) indicates clearly that the Signatory States regarded the integration of their transport systems as one of the fundamental aspects of Economic Union'. Bell et al. (1984:300) quote the Treaty of Rome's Article 3(e), which shows that 'the adoption of a common policy in the sphere of transport' was one of the EC's initial objectives, and Articles 74–84 provide more detail on the Community's transport role; the provisions of the Treaty applied specifically to transport by road, rail and navigable waterway, but the Council of Ministers was permitted to decide what action should be taken on air and sea transport (Robertson, 1973:181).

The Treaty of Rome dealt particularly with freight transport. However, in April 1961 the Commission submitted a memorandum to the Council outlining the principles of a Common Transport Policy (the Schaus Memorandum, named after Lambert Schaus, then the Commissioner responsible for transport), and this was followed in 1962 by an action programme, the main objectives of which are outlined by Gwilliam (1964:247):

(1) The removal of any obstacles which transport might represent on the establishment of the general common market.
(2) The creation of healthy competition of the widest possible scope.
(3) The development of a transport system which will prove a powerful stimulant for the growth of trade and widening of markets.

The suggestions for achieving the above objectives, like the objectives themselves, apply to passenger transport as well as to freight transport. However laudable the objectives and proposals which emanated from the EC in its early years may have been, in practice it proved extremely difficult to make progress. In 1973, the European Commission told the Council of Ministers: 'The efforts which have been made to . . . create a common transport market have not fully succeeded, and the Common Transport Policy is at an impasse' (Bell et al., 1984:301).

As long ago as 1964, Despicht identified three main reasons for this lack of progress: firstly, the member states all saw their transport systems as special cases requiring exceptional treatment, secondly the transport sector was characterised by a high level of public sector intervention (both regulatory and in ownership of transport operators and responsibility for infrastructure), and thirdly transport operators varied widely in their structure and regulatory environment, from state monopolies with no internal competition (the railways) to small road and inland waterway operators, but the services of all types of carrier were often interchangeable (Despicht, 1964:207–209).

By 1983, efforts to establish the Common Transport Policy had borne some fruit, with harmonisation of such matters as road signs and vehicle type approval, and the introduction of tachographs and EC drivers' hours regulations, for example (Bell et al., 1984:302). By this time the Commission had adopted what Erdmenger (1983) describes as a pragmatic approach to transport, no longer insisting on policy adhering dogmatically to the letter of the Treaty of Rome, but allowing a certain amount of flexibility. It was this which enabled some of the transport provisions of the Single European Act to be agreed, for example, as Erdmenger (1983) predicted the EU did not attempt to introduce full-scale USA-style air transport deregulation, which is what the Treaty of Rome implicitly required.

The Single European Act

The Single European Act of 1987, paving the way for the Single European Market which took effect from 31 December 1992, had a marked effect on EU passenger transport policy (and therefore on tourism). Measures affecting tourism transport included the abolition of frontier controls, abolition of intra-Community duty-free sales, harmonisation of VAT rates, and liberalisation of air and coach transport services.

As regards frontier controls, full abolition has not yet been achieved. However, routine baggage checks have been abolished on intra-Community air services, and a blue customs channel has been introduced in addition to the existing red (goods to declare) and green (nothing to declare) channels at EU airports, for the use of passengers travelling from within the Community (Fitzpatrick Associates, 1993). Passport checks for immigration purposes still take place on intra-EC passenger transport services, although the European Commission is convinced that the Single European Act obliges member states to remove such controls. The reluctance of member states (particularly the UK, Ireland and Denmark) to do so stems from their suspicion that mushrooming illegal immigration would be the result, because certain member states would be unable to control immigration effectively at the borders of the European Union.

The abolition of duty-free sales within the EU has proved difficult to achieve, and it has now been postponed until 1 July 1999. Such sales are particularly important to charter airlines, according to Fitzpatrick Associates (1993): of the duty-free sales of 587 million ECUs made by Europe's top 30 airlines in 1990, over half was accounted for by charter carriers, mostly from intra-EU traffic. Many airports also rely on duty-free sales to ensure profitability: Manchester is expected to lose 83% of its duty-free sales when these are abolished for intra-EC traffic (Fitzpatrick Associates, 1993). Some progress has been made on harmonisation of VAT within the EC—transitional arrangements came into force on 1 January 1993, with all member states being obliged to have a standard VAT rate of not less than 15%, and being permitted one or two lower rates of not less than 5% for goods and services on an agreed list. This list includes certain tourism-related products such as hotels and transport. Extra-high and extra-low VAT rates will not be allowed after the transitional period (Fitzpatrick Associates, 1993).

EU liberalisation of air transport has been phased in over three 'packages', the first taking effect on 1 January 1988 and the third with the Single European Market from 31 December 1992, although the right of EC airlines to operate 'cabotage' services (i.e. wholly within the territory of a member state other than their own) has been postponed until 1997 (French, 1992). In essence, airlines may now charge any fare they deem appropriate for travel between EC destinations (EC, 1992b). Airlines owned by EC nationals may now operate anywhere in the EC (EC, 1992c), whereas previously an airline had to be substantially owned by one EC nation to be allowed to fly from that nation (Davidson, 1992). In addition, the Commission is now empowered to enforce Community competition rules in order to block certain air transport restrictive practices (EC, 1992d). New regulations on coach transport allow properly licensed coach operators from anywhere in the Community to operate 'cabotage' services in EC countries other than their own, subject to certain restrictions which will remain until 1995 (EC, 1992e).

Conclusion: EU tourism and transport policies

The history of tourism and passenger transport policy in the European Union has been extremely turbulent; even now there is no Common Tourism Policy as such, and the Common Transport Policy is still incomplete despite the Single European Market. The problems with the Common Transport Policy have served to aggravate the difficulties of those in the Commission who make provision for tourism; it could be argued that a common transport policy is necessary before a tourism policy can be formulated, in view of the link between passenger transport and tourism, but tourism was not specifically mentioned in the Treaty of Rome whereas a Common Transport Policy was always seen as essential.

The failure of the Community to get to grips with tourism at all until the early 1980s is undoubtedly in part a reflection of the low status given to tourism by the public sector in some member states, especially the more economically developed ones, and in part a result of the difficulty in identifying tourism. The 'tourism industry' is an amalgam of several other industries, such as accommodation and passenger transport, and the tourism phenomenon itself affects a wide selection of the EU's areas of interest. In addition, member states have traditionally held the view that tourism should be the responsibility of governments and national tourist organisations rather than the European Community.

Recent EC action in the tourism and passenger transport fields (which cannot easily be separated) has been provoked by two factors more than anything else. The first was the initiative by the European Parliament which led to the European Year of Tourism, and subsequently to the Action Plan to assist tourism which is currently in force. Indeed, the European Parliament has consistently led the way in recent years in achieving a higher profile for tourism as a European Union concern. The second was the EU's need to remove travel restrictions and harmonise competition and consumer protection regulations in readiness for the completion of the Single European Market.

Concerning the future, Lickorish (1991) points to the positive outcomes of the European Year of Tourism, particularly to the partnership which has formed between the EU bodies and tourism's commercial sector, as an indicator that further positive progress towards a Common Tourism Policy will be made. With passenger transport, liberalisation of air transport is now well advanced although some future refinements will be needed, and the opening of the Channel Tunnel may precipitate some policy developments on rail transport in the Community, and will encourage further intermodal competition. There is still a long way to go, but it is now certain that the European Union is moving in the right direction with increasing enthusiasm.

References

Akehurst, G. (1992) 'European Community tourism policy', in Johnson, P. and Thomas, B. (Eds), *Perspectives on Tourism Policy*, Mansell, London, pp. 215–231.

Bell, G. et al. (1984) *The Business of Transport*, Macdonald & Evans, Plymouth.

Boniface, B. and Cooper, C. (1987) *The Geography of Travel and Tourism*. Butterworth-Heinemann, Oxford.

Burkart, A. and Medlik, S. (1981) *Tourism, Past, Present and Future*, 2nd edn, Heinemann, London.

Cooper, C. et al. (1993) *Tourism Principles and Practice*, Pitman, London.

Davidson, R. (1992) *Tourism in Europe*, Pitman, London.

Despicht, N. S. (1964) *Policies for Transport in the Common Market*, Lambarde Press, Sidcup.

EC (1982) 'Initial guidelines for a Community policy on tourism' (communication from Commission to Council), COM(82)385 FINL, EC, Brussels.

EC (1992a) 'Council decision of 13 July 1992 on a Community action plan to assist tourism (92/421/EEC)', *Official Journal of the European Communities*, no. L 231, 13 August:26–32.

EC (1992b) 'Council Regulation (EEC) no. 2409/92 of 23 July 1992 on fares and rates for air services', *Official Journal of the European Communities*, no. L 240, 24 August:15–17.

EC (1992c) 'Council Regulation (EEC) no. 2408/92 of 23 July 1992 on access for Community air carriers to intra-Community air routes', *Official Journal of the European Communities*, no. L 240, 24 August:8–13.

EC (1992d) 'Council Regulation (EEC) no. 2411/92 of 23 July 1992 amending Regulation (EEC) no. 3976/87 on the application of Article 85(3) of the Treaty to certain categories of agreements and concerted practices in the air transport sector', *Official Journal of the European Communities*, no. L 240, 24 August:19–20.

EC (1992e) 'Council Regulation (EEC) no. 2454/92 of 23 July 1992 laying down the conditions under which non-resident carriers may operate national road passenger transport services within a Member State', *Official Journal of the European Communities*, no. L 251, 29 August:1–12.

Edgell, D. L. (1990) *International Tourism Policy*, Van Nostrand Reinhold, New York.

Erdmenger, J. (1983) *The European Community Transport Policy*, Gower Publishing, Aldershot.

Fitzpatrick Associates (1993) *Tourism in the European Community: the Impact of the Single Market*, Economist Intelligence Unit, London.

French, T. (1992) 'The European Commission's third air transport liberalisation package', *EIU Travel & Tourism Analyst*, (5):5–22.

Gwilliam, K. M. (1964) *Transport and Public Policy*, George Allen & Unwin, London.

Holloway, J. C. (1989) *The Business of Tourism*, 3rd edn, Pitman, London.

Lickorish, L. J. (1991) 'Developing a single European tourism policy', *Tourism Management*, 12(3):178–184.

Mathieson, A. and Wall, G. (1982) *Tourism: Economic, Physical and Social Impacts*, Longman, Harlow.

Nugent, N. (1991) *The Government and Politics of the European Community*, 2nd edn, Macmillan, Basingstoke.

Page, S. and Sinclair, T. (1992) 'The Channel Tunnel and tourism markets in the 1990s', *EIU Travel & Tourism Analyst*, (1):5–32.

Robertson, A. H. (1973) *European Institutions: Cooperation, Integration, Unification*, 3rd edn, Stevens & Sons, London.

Robinson, H. (1976) *A Geography of Tourism*, Macdonald & Evans, Plymouth.

Tzoanos, G. (1991) Formal opening speech at 'Tourism and hospitality management: established disciplines or 10-year wonders?', Tourism Management/University of Surrey conference, Guildford, 25 September 1991.

Whitelegg, J. (1988) *Transport Policy in the EEC*, Routledge, London.

21 Conference centres in the 21st century

D. MUNRO

In recent years the worldwide growth of conference centres capable of holding over a thousand delegates has been considerable, and is continuing. As an example close to home, Edinburgh is spending £38 million on its 1200-delegate centre to open next year; this is a small amount compared to Singapore's £210 million investment in a centre which will contain one 12 000 delegate conference room. The appraisal used by the Edinburgh International Conference Centre to determine the viability of a centre of this size clearly demonstrates the demand. International conferences worldwide, as defined and reported by the Union of International Conferences, have increased from 4684 in 1984 at a steady rate to almost 9000 in 1990.

The total value of the conference market to the United Kingdom was estimated at £735 million in 1984, which was expected to increase to £1 billion in 1987—a trend that would bring £2 billion in 1994. *Conference & Incentive Travel Magazine* stated that developments with investment exceeding £600 million had been announced in the month of April this year (1993) to cater for this demand. Money is (or appears to be) freely available: £24 million is to be spent on upgrading London's Albert Hall; Belfast invests £29 million in a new centre. Further afield, Hong Kong will double the size of its facilities for £211 million and expects a return in economic benefit of £600 million *per year*. These are optimistic figures and it seems that almost every city in the world is planning developments in conference facilities.

Why are cities so eager to join the battle for delegates? The astonishing figure above tells all: Hong Kong expects a return of £600 million per year in economic benefit on its investment. To be more realistic, the city of Glasgow estimated that earnings from conference delegates in 1993 totalled £16 million. To quote Jim McIntyre, Executive Director of the Edinburgh International Conference Centre,

Each year the centre will generate more than 100 000 new business tourists with over £3.5 million spent on accommodation, a multi-million pound boost to the city's hotel trade. Annually £1.75 million will be spent in bars and restaurants, up to £450 000 in local shops with an additional £300 000 being spent on taxis and local travel. Most importantly, the city will enjoy an employment boost of nearly 1000 jobs generated directly from conference centre business.

This clearly illustrates the confidence of developers that a conference centre will benefit not only the owners of the centre itself (which may struggle to trade profitably) but more importantly the local businesses: shops, restaurants, bars, even football grounds can share the benefit in increased gates. This is why the business is attractive to city councils—it is an ideal way of generating goodwill and economic benefit to local trade.

How accurate are these figures on which so much investment and development is based? Certainly they show an enormous variation from one survey to another. In any case, statistics will only tell us the present trends and there is always a danger in accepting present trends to forecast future demands. A conference such as this, held in the last century, debated the growth in horse-drawn traffic and concluded that if such growth continued the streets would become unusable due to the depth of horse manure. The arrival of the horseless carriage was not at that stage foreseen and when it did arrive it was no doubt condemned as a nine-day wonder.

Do we have an equivalent of the horseless carriage in the conference industry? Has videoconferencing the power to put all our conference halls out of business? Well, I certainly cannot prove by statistics that this is likely. In the first few years of its existence video and teleconferencing have not made too much impact on the large meeting business. There is, and will be, strong resistance to conferring by satellite. The conference business is supplier led and the suppliers have immense strength. The marketing budget of just one conference centre is probably equal to the GNP of an Eastern European country. This may well be subsidised from public funds, almost unaccounted for. We have seen that cities are interested in the spin-off, and if the cost of marketing per conference is higher than the actual spend of the conference, will anyone ever know or care? The centre has been built and the centre must be kept full at whatever cost. It is hard to argue with this; we are talking about a very high level of investment and it is important to make maximum use of the facility. Airlines may go broke by filling all seats at whatever price they can get and ignoring yield; but civic budgets can be bottomless, or can appear so when it comes to marketing their pet project.

The second reason why it would appear that conference centres will keep their seats filled is that delegates enjoy them. The seasoned delegate will grouse about the amount of travelling he is obliged to do to keep up to date, but watch him fight his corner if his attendance budget is threatened. Of course the Rio Congress is important, and how could he miss the European seminar in Paris let alone the Australian symposium which happens to take place the week before the Olympics, or in our own case a few days before the British Open Golf Championship at nearby Turnberry? It is no coincidence that conference centres are inclined to be in cities of tourist interest; it is no secret that the choice of venue for an event is based on the popularity of the destination. The social programme is a very important part of the conference: the non-delegate programme (do you remember when it was called the 'ladies programme', then 'spouse', then 'accompanying persons' or even 'significant others'?); the pre- and post-conference tours; the banquet venues; all are important in the choice of destination. Every conference centre promotional video and brochure spends an amount of time and space describing the joys of the area. We need the spin-off. The conference calendar for international associations is carefully put together; it would be dreadful if the International Chapter of the XXXXX was held in Thailand the week before the American branch met in Phoenix, no time for rest and recreation in between. Delegates spend a lot of time putting together their itinerary to take in as many events as possible in a round-the-world trip, no back-tracking allowed (certainly no back-packing); side-trip mileage kept to a minimum. Nevertheless it is a tiring schedule and it could not be maintained if first-class air travel were not available, or if hotels did not offer executive rooms with every comfort and a chocolate on the pillow. Who would voluntarily surrender this for a solitary day in front of a videoconference machine?

These are strong reasons for supposing that the conference market will continue for many years to come. But there are equally strong reasons to surmise that it will not continue for ever. Firstly, the cost: I have emphasised the importance of first-class travel. Recently, as recession makes its demands, there has been a move towards savings in executive travel expenses. The cost of a first-class flight from Glasgow to New York is at present £3948 return. The economy fare (with restrictions) is £756 (and better fares are available) making quite a difference. Companies are tactfully suggesting that their executives might consider the lower option, and many business travellers have been forced into these economies. However, it only takes one overbooked flight home, or one change of flight denied, to encourage the executive

to insist on full-fare travel. As companies search for economies, the costs of sending delegates to overseas conferences must be considered as possible savings. How can a Health Board whose cost-cutting has affected patient care possibly justify its conference budget? To date, the strength of the pro-conference lobby (as detailed already) has been sufficient and the strength of the travel-loving medical consultant is a force to be reckoned with. Also, I do not underestimate the learning experience. But the balance must be found between time spent in learning new skills and time spent putting this knowledge into practice. The public is no doubt familiar with the difficulty experienced in trying to pin down a medical practitioner (and many other professionals too) who is constantly away on business, and this generally means attending another conference. The collective noun for academics (or these other professionals) is aptly an 'absence' of professors.

What alternative is there? It is hard to imagine an international conference on television screens with delegates sitting thousands of miles apart. But not so very long ago it was difficult to imagine an accounting system without the need for manually kept books: sales ledgers, purchase ledgers, invoicing, all laboriously completed by hand. Accountants were sceptical about computer accounts; they ran a manual set of books at the same time for security. The technology for the video conference is developing fast and the sales force which will persuade us of the acceptability of long-distance conferring will work with budgets as large as the new conference centres now possess. British Telecom is one of the leaders in the international field and bases its developments on international compatibility. It has reached agreements with many countries and believes that with compatibility the speed of progress towards international meetings will increase quickly.

Cost savings will be enormous, but equally, if not more, important will be the saving in time. A British Telecom survey found that 60% of senior executives from small to medium-sized companies spend at least one day a week out of the office travelling to meetings. This is (or should be) a worrying statistic. It is only because we have grown used to the idea over many years that we accept a situation which ties up business people so unproductively. If a delegate travels to a conference, the time spent travelling must be in proportion to the time spent conferring. No one will fly the Atlantic for less than a three-day event. Now, it may be, and in fact it almost always is, that the three-day event includes many hours of irrelevant talk (irrelevant, that is, to our delegate), padding to make up the time, or simply talks on subjects which are not in his field. He may sit in and listen, or he may use the time in other ways, shopping perhaps. But he will spend his three days at conference and two days travelling for the sake of a small number of hours usefully spent. This is not a good use of an executive's time.

This, however, is not a criticism of the need for conferences. It is important for professionals to keep up to date, to learn quickly about new developments. However, what must be questioned is the amount of time spent on actual learning. Take one fairly typical example of a conference programme, a one-day seminar organised by the City of Edinburgh District Council, the Department of Environmental Services and the Public Health Alliance. The day starts at 09.00 with registration and coffee; many conference days start at 09.30—too early to go to the office first but not so early that a special effort has to be made. However, this one starts at 09.00 with, of course, registration and coffee . . . till 09.30. Then we have a welcome by the Chair of Environmental Services Committee and an Introduction to the Seminar by the Director of Environmental Services Department. This takes us to 09.45 when we have the first of two 25-minute sessions by the speakers. Then coffee for 20 minutes. We manage two more 25-minute sessions before time for questions, a further 20 minutes. Then lunch, one hour and twenty minutes. The afternoon starts with an introduction to the afternoon session, only 10 minutes. Two 20-minute sessions followed by 20 minutes for tea. Two more 25-minute sessions, followed by 25 minutes of questions, followed by (open-ended) closing remarks at 16.00. It is unlikely that the busy executive would manage to get into his office after this; anyway he will not have any letters to sign unless someone else wrote them in his absence. So the day consisted of 25 minutes of introductions, 3 hours 15 minutes of business, at least 50 minutes of question time and two and a half hours of coffee, tea and lunch!

The subject of this productive day, by the way, was 'Smoking in the workplace—can you afford to ignore it?' An important subject without doubt, but does it really justify the man-hours (person-hours) spent in organising the seminar; the preparation time by the (10) speakers; the day away from the office by all the delegates? Could this not have been effectively organised by television? The answer may be, not yet, but in future definitely!

It is worth comparing the time spent in attending an overseas conference with an alternative—an International Conference held in Tokyo, a four-day event with perhaps 20 papers. The conference title is the 'International Association for Dental Research' (which did in fact attract 2500 delegates to Glasgow last year and would possibly have an equivalent number in Tokyo). Our typical delegate is a lecturer at the School of Dentistry here in Glasgow and his application for funds to attend the conference has been granted. He will be missing from his desk for at least one week and his department will be out of pocket to the tune of £5000 minimum. The benefits will be perhaps five papers of great interest and five of minimum interest and ten of no interest. Alternatively, he takes a few hours off at the times the papers are being presented (using videotape if this happens to be during the night) and views in the video room at his place of work. The cost will be the registration fee and the cost of transmission; the time missing from his department—a few hours.

The argument is that face-to-face contact is essential and in some meetings of course it is. However, debate *is* possible by television, and in any case how much debate does an international conference encourage in the meeting hall? The most worthwhile debates take place in the bars after sessions, during the coffee breaks, over lunch. It must be appreciated that the discussion of a paper informally is of great benefit, and it is difficult to imagine these discussions taking place by television; but it can and will happen. In France, home-based computer workers are installing videoconferencing just so that they can 'network' with colleagues. It works! After all, the Victorians did not readily accept that the telephone would take over from personal correspondence. Did we realise how quickly fax would take over all our business mail?

We know that this march of progress cannot be halted, and yet we refuse to take action on changes which will take place over perhaps 20 or 30 years. If the telephone and the fax machine have revolutionised communications, then perhaps television and video will revolutionise the conference market.

At present videoconferencing is confined to small meetings, and often these are meetings which would not have taken place without this facility, so there is little or no loss of income to hotels. But in this field, it is growing—Rank Xerox has been operating a videoconferencing unit in England for contact with its US locations since 1988. They say that, quite apart from the saving in executive time and money in attending meetings, the advantages lie in quicker decision making and also in team building—two plus points for the technology. Hotels, sensing the danger, are participating. Forte has put lines into many of its properties; Scandic Hotels have been involved and Hyatt plans to invest 3.5 million US dollars in equipping many of its properties. Of course the use of this facility is no threat to conference centres, although it is a threat to hotels which rely on small business meetings. But it is the start of a course which must be unstoppable: as we become familiar with the use of new means of communication we will be happy and willing to push forward the boundaries.

Some services which depend on business travel are already aware of the possible decline in their market. Boston Airport decided not to build a new runway after a feasibility study showed that up to 25% of traffic would be lost to videoconferencing over the next five years. Picturetel, which supplies videoconferencing units worldwide, anticipates a growth from 15 000 units to 700 000 in 1997. As well as tight cost control, events such as the Gulf War can concentrate the mind on finding alternatives to business travel. We hope not to repeat the situation of empty planes when many companies banned all executive travel because of the inherent dangers.

The advantages of videoconferencing are thus seen to be many, but can they overcome the attraction of the international conference? It is true to say that so far only small meetings can be catered for; can we imagine an international event on video? It requires some imagination, but who could deny the possibility?

The previously mentioned Conference of the International Association of Dental Research is announced to take place on television. Mr Tooth studies the programme; two papers interest him greatly. He sends off his registration form and payment and he receives in return the code which will allow him to tune in at the time of his interest. The speakers may be invited to a conference centre but they may also give their address from their home unit. As well as watching the screen, delegates are of course also on camera as the conference chairman can put any delegate on screen by pressing the right button when his attention is caught by a buzzer. Thus a question-and-answer session is easily handled. The documents and graphs which were once shown on slide or overhead, to be seen by those in the front rows and by those with exceptionally good eyesight, will now be shown on the television screen and copies can be run off for later study. At the first interval (no need for coffee to be served, refreshments are always available in the Video Room) Mr Tooth wants to discuss the paper with a colleague in New York. He punches in the colleague's registration number, finds that he is already talking to a delegate in Tokyo, and joins in a three-way conversation. When the conference restarts, Mr Tooth is deep in an important discussion so he switches on the video facility and will watch the next session later—at his convenience.

With a little imagination the whole conference interaction can be handled without leaving home. Yes, it may be some time in the future; but now is the time to plan for this change. One should not regret the building of so many conference centres as many businesses have profited from the development of this industry. However, thought must be given to the future inevitable demise of the activity, bearing in mind the size of the industry which may be wiped out in 50 years. The benefits that a conference centre will bring to a city has been proved many times; now consideration must be given to the damage that the loss of a conference centre will bring. A Coopers & Lybrand survey in 1990 claimed that conference delegate overnights was the fastest growing sector of hotel business—approximately 36% of all sales. Universities too see this market as a major source of income. These industries will be among the first to feel the pinch if videoconferencing takes over.

In Victorian times, one of the growth industries was church-going, if it can be called an industry. Certainly church-building was an industry. It was an industry in cities and in remote areas; take a tour round Scotland and see the churches in the highlands and on the islands; it is often difficult to see where the congregation came from as there seem to be more churches than houses. And when there were sufficient churches for the population, the church divided and new buildings were required for different denominations. As times change, these buildings lie empty or are put to a different use. The effect on morals may be great but the effect on the local economy is slight. However, the closure, or even under-usage, of a conference centre will be devastating—more in line with the closing of a coal mine or factory in a town which relied on it for employment. In the mining industry it could be considered no bad thing that men would no longer be required to spend their working lives underground with all the harm that this can cause. The tragedy was, and is, that mines were closed overnight with little or no thought for re-training, for introducing new industry. Could this not have been foreseen? Some mines have now been turned into Industrial Heritage Centres. Many imaginative uses have been found for redundant churches. Any ideas for a disused conference centre? Can you imagine tour guides taking groups of overseas visitors round the empty conference centre, explaining the former use of break-out rooms, interpretation booths, audiovisual aids? What other use can be found for these massive and in many cases architecturally splendid buildings? A use that will bring comparable benefit to the local community? This is the challenge which must be considered. There is time, as all this will not come to pass in the next ten years; but it may happen sooner than we think. And it would be good to think that we will be prepared for it. Sadly, the Bournemouths, Blackpools and Brightons of the world, which so successfully replaced the traditional family seaside holiday business with conferences, may now have to look again.

22 Current issues in interpretative provision at heritage sites

R. PRENTICE AND D. LIGHT

Heritage tourism and heritage interpretation

Historic buildings and monuments have long been popular as sightseeing attractions. However, it is only comparatively recently that heritage tourism has attained such a scale that it can be identified as a distinct sector of the wider tourism industry. What has been termed the 'heritage industry' (Hewison, 1987) emerged in the 1980s, and was largely the tourism industry's response to the marked increase in popular interest in the past during that decade. There is now little doubt that heritage tourism is a highly significant economic activity throughout this country, as figures from the *English Heritage Monitor* (BTA/ETB, 1992) indicate. In 1991 over 1900 historic buildings in England were open to the public, £166 million was spent by visitors to such sites, and over 18 700 people were employed at them. The sheer extent and scale of contemporary heritage tourism make it a legitimate focus for applied research. Recent years have seen the publication of a number of research monographs which focus on heritage tourism (Herbert et al., 1989; Merriman, 1991; Prentice, 1993a).

Closely paralleling the rise of the heritage tourism industry has been the growth of heritage interpretation. This activity has a long history, although it was not formalised until the 1950s (Tilden, 1957). In its original form heritage intepretation was primarily an 'educational activity' which aimed to use a variety of presentational media (for example, display boards, guided tours, exhibitions, and audio-visual displays) to explain the meaning and significance of a heritage site to those people visiting it. Interpretation was a largely altruistic activity, and a service for those people who wanted to better understand the place they were visiting.

From the 1960s onwards interpretation was widely adopted in Britain. Its initial use was in the countryside, particularly National Parks where it was employed as a means of visitor management (Prince, 1982). Interpretation became centred around communicating a conservation message to visitors to the countryside, with the intended purpose of generating appreciation and sympathy towards conservation strategies. The main media of interpretation were the visitor centre and nature trails. Interpretation of the built environment was slower to become established and did not really take off until European Architectural Heritage Year in 1975. It also tended to emphasise a conservation message and largely used the same media as countryside interpretation: in an urban context the visitor centre became the heritage centre, while the nature trail became the town trail.

With the emergence of the heritage industry in the 1980s the practice of interpretation underwent major changes. Unlike earlier provision of interpretation which had largely been by the public and voluntary sectors, interpretation was increasingly adopted by the private sector. Consequently it was adopted for a variety of new purposes. As employed within the contemporary heritage industry the following distinct roles can be identified (cf. Light, 1987):

Informal education

Interpretation within the heritage industry has largely abandoned a concern with transmitting a conservation message, although the objective of a conservation message remains foremost to some (STB, 1993). Instead, at many heritage attractions (with the exception of those in some National Parks) there has been a return to its original, altruistic educational role. For many people, learning and understanding are important requirements of their leisure time, and such people visit heritage attractions with the aim of informally learning about, appreciating and understanding them (see Light, 1994a). Indeed, Urry (1990) notes that increasingly people are demanding learning activities from their leisure time, whether this be visiting a heritage site or learning to ski. Similarly, Martin and Mason (1993) argue that tourist attractions which offer the opportunity for learning and participation will be a growth area in the future. Interpretation, then, has an important role in catering for visitors' desires for informal learning from their visit to a heritage attraction.

Entertainment

Originally entertainment was not an aim of interpretation, although there was widespread recognition that good interpretation should be entertaining (see Sharpe, 1982).

However, in recent years considerably more emphasis has been placed on the entertainment value of interpretative media. This stems from the highly competitive nature of the largely private sector heritage industry, with the need for heritage attractions to satisfy their visitors and retain their market share. Interpretation has been increasingly used as a means to this end. Considerable importance is placed on interpretative media being entertaining and enjoyable in order to ensure the satisfaction of visitors. This new emphasis on entertainment has stimulated dramatic developments in the media of interpretation employed at heritage sites. In particular, sophisticated technology is increasingly employed to create a supposedly authentic historical 'experience' (Light, 1991a). However, many critics argue that now entertainment has come to eclipse an educational role at many heritage sites (Lumley, 1988; Walsh, 1992). In response some public agencies (for example the Scottish Tourist Board) are seeking to counter this move to what has been termed 'trivialisation' (STB, 1993).

Product development

A corollary of the importance now attached to the entertainment value of interpretation is that interpretation is increasingly seen, not as a means of helping visitors to better understand a heritage attraction, but instead simply as something that can be added to such an attraction simply to give it additional appeal to visitors and potential visitors. In marketing terminology then, interpretation has become a means of product development. In this respect interpretation is simply a 'value-added product of the tourism industry' (Uzzell, 1989) for an audience who are increasingly familiar with interpretation and expectant of it when they visit heritage attractions.

Material for promotional purposes

At some heritage attractions the interpretative media can be used in the site's marketing and, particularly, promotional strategies. When a heritage attraction employs interpretative media that are novel or distinctive in some way then these can be used to give the site a clear product image for advertising purposes. In particular, the site's interpretation can be strongly promoted and advertised so as to emphasise in the minds of potential consumers the distinctiveness of a visit to that heritage attraction.

As a contribution to economic regeneration

During the 1980s considerable emphasis was placed on the potential contribution of heritage tourism to local and regional economic redevelopment. Many areas, particularly those traditionally dependent on primary industry (for example North-East England and South Wales) or those cities which experienced a decline of their dockland industries (for example Liverpool and Dundee) turned to heritage tourism as a means of regenerating their economies and infrastructure. Within such strategies interpretation has an important role. It can be used to tell tourists about a site's history and current opportunities, but equally importantly it can inform local residents of current and future plans for an area, and encourage a sense of involvement and pride in the area (Uzzell, 1988).

Propaganda and public relations

Interpretation can be employed to communicate a public relations message, or can be used more blatantly for propaganda purposes (cf. Uzzell, 1989). For example, the nuclear power industry frequently provides interpretative visitor centres at its power stations to explain to visitors how the industry works. A less political example is the potential of interpretation at churches and cathedrals to explain the Christian faith to their visitors (cf. English Tourist Board, 1984).

Evaluation of interpretation

Although interpretation has been increasingly employed in Britain since the 1960s, there has been much less concern with ascertaining, or evaluating, its effectiveness. Instead, interpretation has generally been regarded as an 'art' (Tilden, 1957; Aldridge, 1989), and a legacy of this approach is that systematic assessment of it has been limited. Good practice has tended to be assumed, often on the basis of little evidence, rather than demonstrated by formal assessment. Despite widespread recognition of the need for evaluation of the effectiveness or success of interpretation, and a developing literature on the subject, particularly during the 1980s, actual studies of the effectiveness of different interpretative media are few and far between. Instead, concern for evaluating the impact of interpretative presentations frequently goes little beyond mere lip-service, and formal studies of the effectiveness of interpretation remain rare. Although interpretation may not be regarded by all as a science, there is no reason why it should not be held up to rigorous scrutiny, and in the view of the current authors this should be the pre-eminent contemporary issue in the presentation of heritage attractions to tourists.

There are several compelling arguments for evaluation of the impact of interpretative media (Light, 1992a). Firstly, evaluation is the essential process of investigating whether or not interpretation is successful in its intended roles. Evaluation provides basic data about how interpretation functions in relation to its aims and target audiences; it can identify problem areas, and provide basic data on which remedial action can be taken (Prince, 1984; Prentice, 1993a). Evaluation can focus on whether visitors make use of interpretation, whether some media are better at engaging and retaining visitors' attention, and whether interpretation is successful in communicating with its users and helping them to understand the place they visit. The results of evaluative research can also be used to make changes to a heritage attraction's interpretative provision, for example by providing media or an interpretative story which is more appropriate to the people who use it. Thus evaluation allows the provision of interpretation at a heritage attraction to be a dynamic and ongoing process. Interpretation can also generate 'feedforward' information to benefit future research and design of interpretation (Griggs, 1984; Prince, 1984).

Secondly, evaluation is necessary to demonstrate the accountability and cost-effectiveness of interpretation (Roggenbuck and Propst, 1981; Griggs, 1984). As the above discussion noted, heritage sites are attaching increasing importance to interpretation which as a result attracts ever-greater capital investment. Considerable importance is placed on the contribution of interpretation to ensuring visitor enjoyment and satisfaction, and it is not uncommon to find some heritage attractions spending millions of pounds on interpretation. The sheer amount spent on interpretation demands that the cost-effectiveness of such investment should be demonstrated through evaluative research. This itself is not a new argument, but is made all the more pertinent by the extent of current investment in interpretative media.

A wide variety of techniques for evaluation are available, which involve differing degrees of impact upon the visitor. For example, Wager (1976) identified twelve methods of evaluation, while Roggenbuck and Propst (1981) added a further four techniques to this inventory. On the basis of these discussions, Light (1992a) has identified four broad categories of evaluative methods. First are unsophisticated appraisals which do not make any impact on visitors. These include informal assessments by other professional interpreters, auditing by an expert, and the reviewing of the interpretation by a panel of people with characteristics similar to the target audience. Second are techniques involving various forms of observations of visitors' behaviour without their being aware of it. These include the unobtrusive tracking of visitors and recording their behaviour (Russell, 1989); the recording and subsequent analysis of visitors' conversations at attractions (McManus, 1989), time-lapse photography

(Vander Stoep, 1989), and studies of non-verbal communication as a means of feedback from visitor to guides providing verbal information (Risk, 1989). Third are those techniques which involve direct informal feedback with visitors. These include visitors' books, suggestion boxes, self-testing devices and self-administered questionnaires. Fourth are those techniques which involve direct *formal* contact with visitors. Most frequently this involves using a questionnaire and interview schedule to ask visitors which interpretative media they saw and used, and what report they would give of them (Herbert, 1989; Prentice, 1993a, 1993b; Light, 1994b). This method can yield high-quality data and is the most rigorous method of evaluation; equally it is the most expensive.

Several authors concerned with the theory and practice of evaluation have emphasised the need for the activity to be undertaken with reference to clearly defined objectives and have argued that these objectives can be ordered hierarchically. Putney and Wager (1973) proposed a three-level hierarchy of objectives where the first level is policy objectives, the second level is for selection of opportunities (e.g. appropriate media and message), and the third level is for undertaking evaluation. Prince (1984) expanded and refined this notion and proposed a five-level hierarchy of objectives comprising museum policies, general exhibition policies, specific exhibition objectives, individual display objectives, and specific learning objectives. The benefits of such a hierarchy are that it provides a clear conceptual framework within which evaluative research can be undertaken and also that evaluative research may be undertaken at any level (or levels) of the hierarchy depending on the aims of the evaluation project.

Clearly then a conceptual hierarchy can be an important framework for evaluation of interpretation. In this paper we seek to demonstrate the applicability of a different form of hierarchy, the Manning–Haas hierarchy of recreational demand, to the evaluation of interpretation. This hierarchy is concerned not with objectives but instead with the various components of the visit to a heritage attraction. This hierarchy derives from the North American recreational science literature and is relatively unknown in European recreational analysis (although see Prentice (1993c) and Prentice et al. (1994)). As such it is novel; its application to interpretation and the evaluation of interpretation is even more so. In this chapter we seek to demonstrate how this hierarchy may be applied to the investigation of interpretation, and data from studies undertaken in the Isle of Man and Wales is used to illustrate key concepts. The hierarchy is offered as one means of advancing the evaluation of interpretation at heritage attractions, and as a new approach to evaluation, building on arguments about the need for evaluation made over the past 15 years.

The Manning–Haas hierarchy of demand

The theoretical stance of this paper is based on the perspective that the *benefits* gained from visiting an attraction are generated from the *experiences* had from the *settings* of the visit and the *activities* pursued while visiting. These four aspects or levels of the visit, namely benefits, experiences, settings and activities, may be conceptualised in hierarchical terms (see Table 22.1) in that the levels are causal, levels 1 and 2 being the conditions for level 3 which, in turn, is the condition for level 4. From the authors of this conceptualisation, we may term the model the Manning–Haas hierarchy (Manning, 1986).

As is clear from Table 22.1, the Manning–Haas hierarchy of recreational demands provides a conceptual framework for linking the various aspects of the visit experience, namely activities and their settings with the experiences derived and the benefits (or outcomes) produced by these experiences. Implicit in this hierarchy is the need to look simultaneously at these four levels if visitor motivation and satisfaction are to be fully understood. The hierarchy has great potential as a means of defining visitors' satisfaction in terms of demands made, namely demands for the provision of activities, appropriate settings to facilitate experiences, the experiences themselves, and the benefits sought and gained. Moreover, at each level of the hierarchy the importance of interpretation, and in particular its impact and effectiveness, may be isolated and examined. In the sections of this paper which follow we consider each level of the hierarchy in turn and review the

Table 22.1 *The Manning–Haas hierarchy of recreational demands applied to two tourist segments (after Prentice* et al. *(1993)).*

Level	Segment 1	Segment 2
1. Activities	Fell walking	Sunbathing on beach
2. Settings		
–environmental	Uplands	Coastal beach
–social	Few people	Family/friends
–managerial	Minimal restrictions	Beach facilities
3. Experiences	Physical exercise	Group bonding
4. Benefits		
–personal	Enhanced self-esteem	Family solidarity
–social	Endearment to landscape conservation	Endearment to family values

implications of each level of demand for interpretative evaluation.

Activities—level 1 of the hierarchy

This level of analysis is concerned with the activities undertaken by visitors to heritage attractions, and asks simply 'What do visitors actually do when they visit a heritage attraction?' A wide range of opportunities are open to visitors which include simply wandering around the site, admiring the view, visiting the souvenir shops and cafes, and picnicking. Of particular interest is the role of interpretation within these on-site activities. This level of analysis is concerned with whether visitors notice interpretative media, and how much attention they pay to them. Evaluation at this level of the Manning–Haas hierarchy seeks to establish whether, given the opportunity to appropriate interpretative media and messages, visitors actually choose to do so.

Table 22.2 presents data from a case study undertaken by Prentice (1993a) on the Isle of Man. The table shows visitors' awareness of the various interpretative media present at the three sites where the survey was undertaken. The tourist visitors surveyed self-reported on the interpretative media they had seen and the attention they had paid to them. It should be noted in reading this table that the presentation of Castle Rushen was quite different in 1991 than in 1990, the castle's interpretative presentation having been completely changed between the two surveys.

Table 22.2 indicates high levels of awareness of the interpretative media, findings which are supported by other research at heritage sites in Wales (Herbert, 1989; Light, 1994b). The main media of which the tourist visitors were aware at the attractions were furnished rooms, models including costumed figures, introductory exhibitions, information panels around the sites, directional signs, live animals, music and the 'voices' of costumed figures (life-sized models of persons of the historic period presented). This array of media of which tourists were most aware at the attractions would seem to emphasise the importance of a multimedia presentation at attractions, stimulating a range of senses. Moreover, it suggests that the traditional way of presenting historic monuments by means of a site guide book and wall plates or panels naming towers and rooms is insufficient for contemporary heritage attraction visitors, or more strictly, for the tourists among them.

Visitors who had encountered an interpretative medium were asked to report the extent of their attention to it on one of the scales below:

—examined it carefully/just glanced at it/ignored it;

Table 22.2 *Presentational media provided at attractions seen or heard by adult holiday tourists visiting different Manx heritage attractions*

	Peel Castle	Castle Rushen		Cregneash
	1990 (%)	1990 (%)	1991 (%)	1990 (%)
Guide book(s)	11	33	–	69
Guide leaflet	89	87	–	82
Guided-walk leaflet	1	–	–	19
Directional signs	–	100	100	–
Tape player for personal use	–	–	–	8
Introductory film/video	–	–	97	81
Exhibition panel introducing site	–	–	100	96
Information panels around site	98	100	98	99
Model(s)/costumed figure(s)	–	98	100	–
Print(s), photograph(s), painting(s)	–	61	–	80
Map(s), plan(s)	–	49	–	76
Other displayed item(s)	–	88	–	94
Furnished room(s)	–	63	100	99
Person(s) in period dress	–	–	–	74
Demonstration of crafts	–	–	–	50
Music	–	–	100	–
'Voices' of costumed figures	–	–	100	–
Live animals	–	–	–	99
Reconstructed wooden buildings	–	–	93	–
N =	184	185	192	177

Note. In 1991 at Castle Rushen the panels were of two different types and were separately asked about.
Source: Prentice (1993a).

—listened to it carefully/listened to it casually/ignored it; and
—watched it carefully/watched it casually/ignored it.

The results are shown in Table 22.3. Of particular interest to heritage managers is the interpretative media which visitors pay least attention to, since if these findings are replicated elsewhere, these media represent potentially wasted investment. The most widely ignored presentational medium was found to be the tape players at Cregneash, with a third of the minority of tourists who claimed in 1990 to have seen these saying that they had ignored them. In 1990 guide books were also ignored by a fifth of those tourists who had seen them, once again suggesting the weakness of this traditional means of interpretation. Herbert (1989) similarly reports that only a minority of visitors examine guide books carefully.

Other media were only ignored in 1990 by very few tourists, and some by none at all. At Castle Rushen in 1991 media were infrequently ignored, the most frequent case being that of the reconstructed wooden buildings which were set in a part of the castle informally visited by the mass of tourists and not fully integrated into the 'managed' visitor flow at the refurbished attraction. One in seven tourists claimed to have ignored these buildings. The information panels around the castle were also less

popular than the other media with about one in ten tourists claiming to have ignored either sort of panel during their visit. The same did not apply to the introductory exhibition of similar panels, and this may imply that a minority of tourists had seen sufficient written information by early in their visit and were enjoying the other media used. In other words, for a minority of tourists a substitution effect was apparent, of one medium by another, similar to that identified elsewhere (Prentice, 1991).

Although in general terms visitors were found not to have ignored the interpretative media they encountered, it would be wrong to assume that all media had equal impacts in holding the attention of holiday tourists. Further reference to Table 22.3 shows that some media were only casually examined, listened to or watched by many tourists, most notably guide books, music, reconstructed buildings and, at some attractions, information panels around the site, prints, maps, introductory exhibition panels and guide leaflets. For example, of all tourists claiming to have seen the guide book at Peel Castle in 1990, nearly seven out of ten said that they had glanced at it, rather than had examined it carefully, and of the information panels around the site at this castle, almost exactly half of those tourists who had seen them had just glanced at them.

Table 22.3 *Attention paid to presentational media provided at attractions by adult holiday tourists who had seen or heard these media during visits to different Manx heritage sites*

	Holiday tourists visiting the sites having seen or heard presentation media, examining, listening or watching media carefully or casually							
	Peel Castle		Castle Rushen				Cregneash	
	1990		1990		1991		1990	
	(a) %	(b) %	(a) %	(b) %	(a) %	(b) %	(a) %	(b) %
Guide book(s)	32	68	5	48	–	–	20	71
Guide leaflet	48	46	54	45	–	–	61	35
Guided-walk leaflet	*	*	–	–	–	–	59	34
Directional signs	–	–	85	15	88	12	–	–
Tape player for personal tour	–	–	–	–	–	–	40	27
Introductory film/video	–	–	–	–	97	3	89	10
Exhibition panel introducing site	–	–	–	–	62	39	87	13
Information panels around site	47	51	98	2	66	34	–	–
Model(s)/costumed figures	–	–	98	2	88	12	–	–
Print(s), photograph(s), painting(s)	–	–	94	6	–	–	49	50
Map(s), plan(s)	–	–	88	12	–	–	42	56
Other displayed item(s)	–	–	97	3	–	–	72	27
Furnished room(s)	–	–	75	26	92	8	85	15
Person(s) in period dress	–	–	–	–	–	–	74	25
Demonstration of crafts	–	–	–	–	–	–	82	17
Music	–	–	–	–	31	67	–	–
'Voice' of costumed figures	–	–	–	–	57	41	–	–
Live animals	–	–	–	–	–	–	88	12
Reconstructed wooden buildings	–	–	–	–	14	72	–	–

N = varies, derived from Table 22.1

Key: (a) careful attention; (b) casual attention.

Notes. (1) The number of tourists ignoring can be found by subtracting the figures for careful and casual attention from 100%.

(2) *indicates a sample size too small to safely permit analyis.

Source: Prentice (1993a).

Analysis at this level of the Manning–Haas hierarchy indicates that encountering and paying at least some attention to interpretation is an important activity undertaken during a visit to a heritage attraction. From this it may be inferred that some degree of informal learning and understanding is important to many people who visit heritage sites (see Light, 1994a). The discussion of Tables 22.2 and 22.3 indicates that attention to different interpretative media is not equal, and this supports Light's (1991b) typology of principal and secondary interpretative media. Principal media are those which are encountered by a majority of visitors and which are generally an important component of on-site activities (for example, models, furnished rooms and video displays). Secondary media are those which are of less importance and are generally only used by those visitors with a greater concern for learning and understanding during their visit (for example guide books, tape players). As such, segmentation of visitors in terms of their experiences and benefits sought is implied as one basis for evaluating interpretation.

Having identified the ways in which visitors make use in different ways of interpretative media, the researcher's next stage is to attempt an account for these findings. In a detailed study of the ways in which visitors used the interpretative media they encountered at heritage sites in Wales, Light (1994b) discusses attributes of both interpretative media and also of visitors which had an influence on the extent of visitors' attention. Properties of the interpretative media which could influence attention included subject matter, the amount and readability of text and novelty. However, the interest and motivation of the individual visitor was also important, and those visitors who went to heritage attractions from a declared interest in such sites were likely to pay more attention to interpretative media. Such findings reinforce the above point of the need to evaluate effectiveness in terms of the experiences and benefits sought by visitors. Such analysis is necessary if a fuller understanding of visitor–interpretation interactions is to be obtained. Hence, evaluation at the 'activities' level of the Manning–Haas hierarchy provides key information on how visitors make use of interpretation as part of their visit and also provides context data for more detailed investigations of the experiences and benefits obtained from encountering interpretative media.

Settings—level 2 of the hierarchy

The various contexts within which recreational activities take place can be considered as 'settings'. The Manning–Haas hierarchy identifies three levels of settings, namely physical, social and managerial settings. Each type of setting will have relevance for interpretation, and therefore also for the evaluation of interpretation.

Physical settings

The physical setting for tourism and recreational activity is usually a tourist attraction. Walsh-Heron and Stevens have commented, 'Attractions come in all shapes and sizes, catering to a wide variety of tastes and leisure requirements' (Walsh-Heron and Stevens, 1990). Much the same comment has been made about heritage attractions which have been described as 'a bewildering variety' (Light, 1989:130). Essentially, heritage attractions are a heterogeneous group. However the widespread use of the term 'heritage industry' (after Hewison, 1987) serves to mask this heterogeneity. The categorisation of a diverse group of attractions as one 'industry' groups together attractions of varying compatibility in terms of size, theme, management objectives and funding. It is our contention that the diversity of heritage attractions needs to be more formally acknowledged so that the different interpretative strategies for different types of site can be recognised. Such recognition is essential if evaluation of interpretation is to be appropriate and meaningful to the type of site where it is undertaken and not uncritically extrapolated to other (or all) types of attraction.

In any discussion of the evaluation of interpretation it is important to ensure that any comparisons are made between attractions of similar type. The need therefore is for a classification or typology of heritage attractions. One such schema, based on main subject types has been developed by Prentice (1993a) and is illustrated in Table 22.4. This typology is offered as a model which may be further refined as research effort continues. The typology has, of necessity, to reflect the range of 'attractions' which are visited by tourists and other visitors; as such, it has to include some 'attractions' for which this very term may seem inappropriate. Foremost among such sites are those commemorating genocide. In this typology, the term 'attraction' is meant in no other way than to describe a site, theme or area which attracts

visitors. It should not be taken to imply that these sites and the like are otherwise thought to be attractive.

These 23 types of heritage attraction, and their potential subdivisions, clearly illustrate the diversity of the heritage 'product', and frustrate the meaningful classification of attractions as a single 'industry'. Aspects of places found attractive by tourists but which are not site-specific, such as indigenous languages (Light, 1992b), add further to this heterogeneity. Only when heterogeneity of attraction type is recognised can a comparative assessment of interpretative effectiveness begin, and in turn can it be sought to establish the effects of different dimensions of this heterogeneity on the success or failure of interpretative provisions.

Clearly, different types of heritage attraction will be interpreted in different ways; it is therefore also misleading to describe interpretation as an undifferentiated activity. Interpretative messages will vary by site: for example, a natural history attraction will present a fundamentally different message from an industrial heritage attraction. Some messages may be relatively uncontroversial (for example those at a science park), while others will be emotionally charged (for example genocide monuments). Similarly interpretative media employed will also differ by site. At uncovered attractions (for example, many ancient monuments) the interpretative media have to be simple and robust and able to withstand the elements. At covered attractions (for example heritage centres) more elaborate and technically sophisticated media may be employed where they will not experience damage from wind and rain. Interpretative policies will also differ among different types of heritage sites. At theme parks, for example, interpretation is often used almost exclusively as a medium of entertainment. At religious sites it often has a more serious educational (and sometimes propagandist) role.

These varying messages, media and policies of interpretation will, to a large degree, influence evaluative strategies employed at different sites. Clearly no one evaluative programme can be employed at all sites. Instead, evaluative strategies need to be tailored to the unique circumstances (with regard to message, media and policies) of individual sites: evaluation policies must be site-sensitive. This is not to deny the value of evaluation 'packages', but such packages need to be confined to similar types of attraction if their use is to be appropriate.

Social settings

Social settings are the second type of setting important to interpretative evaluation in which visits take place. Various authors have emphasised that visits to heritage

Table 22.4 *A typology of heritage attractions (after Prentice, 1993a)*

Natural history attractions, including nature reserves, nature trails, aquatic life displays, rare breeds centres, wildlife parks, zoos, butterfly parks, waterfowl parks; geomorphological and geological sites, including caves, gorges, cliffs, waterfalls.

Science-based attractions, including science museums, technology centres, 'hands on' science centres, 'alternative' technology centres.

Attractions concerned with primary production, including agricultural attractions, farms, dairies, farming museums, vineyards; fishing, mining, quarrying, water impounding reservoirs.

Craft centres and craft workshops, attractions concerned with hand-made products and processes, including water and windmills, sculptors, potters, woodcarvers, hand-worked metals, glass makers, silk working, lace making, handloom weaving, craft 'villages'.

Attractions concerned with manufacturing industry, attractions concerned with the mass production of goods, including pottery and porcelain factories, breweries, cider factories, distilleries, economic history museums.

Transport attractions, including transport museums, tourist and preserved railways, canals, civil shipping, civil aviation, motor vehicles.

Socio-cultural attractions, prehistoric and historic sites and displays, including domestic houses, social history museums, costume museums, regalia exhibitions, furnishings museums, museums of childhood, toy museums.

Attractions associated with historic persons, including sites and areas associated with writers and painters.

Performing arts attractions, including theatres, street-based performing arts, performing arts workshops, circuses.

Pleasure gardens, including ornamental gardens, period gardens, arboreta, model villages.

Theme parks, including nostalgia parks, 'historic' adventure parks, fairytale parks for children (but excluding amusement parks, where the principal attractions are exciting rides and the like).

Galleries, principally art galleries.

Festivals and pageants, including historic fairs, festivals, 'recreating' past ages, countryside festivals of 'rural' activities.

Field sports, traditional field sports, including fishing, hunting, shooting, stalking.

Stately and ancestral homes, including palaces, country houses, manor houses.

Religious attractions, including cathedrals, churches, abbeys, priories, mosques, shrines, wells, springs.

Military attractions, including castles, battlefields, military airfields, naval dockyards, prisoner-of-war camps, military museums.

Genocide monuments, sites associated with the extermination of other races or other mass killings of populations.

Towns and townscape, principally historic townscape, groups and buildings in an urban setting.

Villages and hamlets, principally 'rural' settlements, usually of pre-twentieth century architecture.

Countryside and treasured landscapes, including national parks, other countryside amenity designations; 'rural' landscapes which may not be officially designated but are enjoyed by visitors.

Seaside resorts and 'seascapes', principally seaside towns of past eras and marine 'landscapes'.

Regions, including *pays*, counties, or other historic or geographical areas identified as distinctive by their residents or visitors.

Source: Prentice (1993a).

attractions are not solitary activities but are usually undertaken in groups (Uzzell, 1988; McManus, 1987). Survey evidence lends ample support to this claim. For example, Prentice (1989) noted that less than 5% of visitors to heritage attractions in Wales were alone. Clearly most visitors are in a group of some kind, although family groups are not always the most common (Light and Prentice, 1994). Furthermore, for some visitors to heritage attractions an element of social interaction is an important reason for their trip. Thomas (1989) noted that around a quarter of visitors to heritage attractions in Wales gave a child-orientated reason while 18% visited in order to show the site to relatives or friends. In such situations group members will clearly interact with one

another and, for some, being part of a group may be more important than the activity itself (Uzzell, 1988; Prentice et al., 1993).

The social context or setting of the visitor group will have important influences on how visitors behave with regard to interpretation. A study undertaken in a museum by McManus (1987) noted that single visitors were more likely to read exhibitions comprehensively, as were couples. Groups containing children were likely to spend a long time looking at an exhibition and to talk about it for a long time, but were less likely to read interpretation. Adult groups were less likely to read text closely. Similarly Light (1994b) noted that groups containing children were less likely to enter exhibitions and read less of the interpretation while couples had the opposite behavioural characteristics. McManus (1988) also noted that groups that showed strong cohesive behaviour (i.e. evidence of intimacy and bonding among group members) were more likely to read exhibition texts comprehensively.

Clearly then, the character and composition of groups of people cannot be excluded from any evaluative study, and this raises some important issues for evaluative research. When evaluating the effectiveness of interpretation it is also important to recognise that effectiveness will depend as much on the visitor and their social setting as the interpretative medium, and existing research has demonstrated that some visitors will be likely to pay more attention to interpretation, depending simply on the people they are with. In other words, some aspects of the 'effectiveness' of interpretation may be completely independent of the interpretative medium itself. Evaluation of interpretation should be sensitive to the ways in which different visitor groups make use of interpretation. When seeking to explain why visitors behave in a certain way with regard to interpretation, it is important to consider attributes of both the interpretative media and the visitors themselves (Light, 1994b; cf. Alt, 1977).

Management settings

Heritage attractions are managed environments, and tourists' activities at such attractions take place within management settings. These management settings will vary considerably among different attractions, reflecting the different philosophies of site presentation adopted by different managers, and this acts to further reinforce the heterogeneity of heritage attractions. For example, managerial values emphasised in such settings can range among preservationist, regulative, redistributive and marketing (Ashworth and Voogd, 1990).

Interpretation is often an important component of visitor attraction management and can be used to achieve various management objectives. Organisations such as English Heritage use interpretation to educate and inform the public, so fulfilling its statutory duty to promote wider public knowledge of England's heritage. At many private sector sites a high emphasis is placed on ensuring the satisfaction of visitors so that they are more likely to visit again and recommend the site to friends and relatives. Interpretative media can be used to achieve this objective through being entertaining and stimulating. Interpretation may be used as a medium of visitor management with the aim of telling visitors of the pressures facing the rural environment and generating thoughtful and sympathetic behaviour and sympathy for management objectives. As

noted above, some organisations use interpretation to accomplish public relations and propaganda objectives. Therefore the interpretative media which visitors encounter at a heritage attraction and the messages they contain will reflect implicit or explicit management policies.

There is also evidence that visitors to heritage attractions anticipate management settings of some kind. Some indication of the management settings expected by tourists from their visit may be seen in terms of the information required by them when asked on the Isle of Man. Asked in 1990 about the need for all historic attractions to have information available for visitors, almost all visitors were in favour of interpretative provision of this kind, with 70% strongly agreeing with the need for information (Prentice, 1993a). Clearly, one expectation is that of an informed visitor experience, and not simply enjoyment of the ambience of, or views obtainable from, castles and other similar attractions. Other research evidence supports this claim. Herbert (1989) reports that among visitors to ancient monuments in Wales, 45% stated that the main purpose of their visit was 'to be informed', 20% said 'to relax', 17% said 'to be educated', and 14% said 'to be entertained'. These findings are significant and indicate that almost two-thirds of the respondents (62%) required some element of (informal) education from their visit. Similarly, in a review of relevant research Light (1994b) suggests that the desire for informal education and understanding is an important motive for visiting heritage sites. For such people, intepretation is an important requirement and expectation of their visit and one aspect of the management setting that they will anticipate encountering.

A further dimension of customer expectation of settings concerns the importance given by visitors to the interpretative media provided at attractions. Table 22.5 presents data from surveys undertaken on the Isle of Man (Prentice, 1993a) regarding the proportion of tourists describing an interpretative medium as important or very important. Those media most frequently thought by tourists to have been very important to their understanding of an attraction can be seen from Table 22.5 to include an introductory film or video and models including costumed figures supplemented by furnished rooms and 'other' displayed items. Other media frequently thought to be important by those tourists having seen or heard them include prints, maps, directional signs, a guided walk leaflet, craft demonstrations and live animals. Conversely, other media were disproportionately rated as unimportant, or the tourists interviewed had no strong feelings either way concerning their importance or unimportance. Notable among these media were the reconstructed wooden buildings at Castle Rushen in 1991,

Table 22.5 *Adult holiday tourists' views on the importance of presentational media seen or heard to their understanding of the sites at different Manx heritage sites*

	Holiday tourists visiting the sites having seen or heard presentational media important or unimportant to their understanding of the sites							
	Peel Castle		Castle Rushen				Cregneash	
	1990		1990		1991		1990	
	(a) %	(b) %	(a) %	(b) %	(a) %	(b) %	(a) %	(b) %
Guide book(s)	6	94	10	28	–	–	42	34
Guide leaflet	14	73	18	34	–	–	59	38
Guided-walk leaflet	*	*	–	–	–	–	74	27
Directional signs	–	–	75	24	77	22	–	–
Tape player for personal use	–	–	–	–	–	–	42	37
Introductory film/video	–	–	–	–	88	11	80	19
Exhibition panel introducing site	–	–	–	–	46	50	77	22
Information panels around site	12	68	97	3	52	43	–	–
Model(s)/costumed figures	–	–	96	4	87	11	–	–
Print(s), photograph(s), painting(s)	–	–	78	22	–	–	50	48
Map(s), plan(s)	–	–	74	24	–	–	50	48
Other displayed item(s)	–	–	96	4	–	–	69	29
Furnished room(s)	–	–	58	41	90	7	78	21
Person(s) in period dress	–	–	–	–	–	–	67	33
Demonstration of crafts	–	–	–	–	–	–	74	22
Music	–	–	–	–	14	61	–	–
'Voice' of costumed figures	–	–	–	–	31	59	–	–
Live animals	–	–	–	–	–	–	72	27
Reconstructed wooden buildings	–	–	–	–	6	31	–	–

N = varies, derived from Table 22.1

Key: (a) very important; (b) important.
Note. *indicates a sample size too small to safely permit analysis.
Source: Prentice (1993a).

for whom more than six out of ten tourists who had seen them thought them either to be unimportant to their understanding of the castle or towards which they had no feelings as to their importance or otherwise. A third of tourists likewise did not think the site guide books important to their understanding of the sites. Other media were rated as unimportant by smaller minorities of tourist visitors. These included the guide leaflets, which were thought to be unimportant by a fifth of tourists who had seen them, and the tape players at Cregneash, which were similarly rated. Of the new media at Castle Rushen in 1991, not only were the wooden buildings disproportionately thought to be unimportant to an understanding of the castle, but a quarter of tourists interviewed did not think that the music which they had heard had been of importance, and a tenth thought the same about the 'voices' of the costumed figures. However, we should be careful not to over-emphasise a perspective of unimportance. Except for the wooden buildings, for example, at Castle Rushen in 1991 a majority of tourists, and in some cases *all* tourists who had seen or heard the presentational media thought them

to have been of some importance in their understanding of the castle.

At sites where interpretation is used to fulfil management objectives, evaluation of interpretation can be undertaken with reference to the management settings of the individual site and can be designed to investigate how effectively objectives are being met. For this to be possible, however, the site must have formulated clear objectives for its interpretation, since, as several authors have argued, without objectives evaluation is not possible (e.g. Putney and Wager, 1973; Prince, 1984; Uzzell, 1985). All too often this is not the case, and at best objectives have to be inferred from site media and their messages. The effectiveness of interpretation at achieving management objectives seems to have been assumed rather than having been the subject of formal assessment.

In addition to being concerned with management expectations of interpretation, evaluation of interpretation can also be undertaken with respect to visitors' expectations from it. To date this is one approach to evaluation that has had few proponents. Instead evaluation frequently proceeds on the basis of assumptions about what visitors require from interpretation, rather than definite knowledge of these requirements. A visitor-expectations approach to evaluation necessitates establishing what visitor requirements from interpretation actually are. Evaluation can then be undertaken with respect to these requirements. This would involve asking visitors whether the provision of interpretation at a heritage attraction (one aspect of the management setting) was what they had expected to find; whether it compared well with that encountered at other, similar attractions; whether it was adequate for their needs for understanding of the attraction; whether it told them what they wanted to know; and whether in fact it did help them to an increased understanding of the attraction. Only when interpretation is designed with a knowledge of the requirements, expectations and background knowledge of the people who will use it can it start to be fully effective.

Experiences—level 3 of the hierarchy

The experiences sought and gained by visiting heritage attractions vary among consumers (e.g. Prentice et al., 1993). For example, when visiting a social history museum, experiences can include feeling a sense of pride in past achievements, appreciating the quality of life today by comparison with past conditions, being impressed by dangers faced in the past, feeling nostalgic, and feeling sympathetic to past situations. These experiences differ from benefits which can include having learnt something of importance, having an enhanced sense of identity with the past, and having an enhanced desire to learn about the past. Clearly, since visitors are a heterogeneous group, they will experience a heritage attraction in different ways, although as yet comparatively little is known of visitors' experiences. We can, however, suggest that the experiences sought and gained will have some influence on how people respond to and learn from interpretative provisions.

We can get an initial indication of the kind of experiences visitors expect and anticipate from heritage attractions by examining the perceptions they hold of the functions of such sites. Table 22.6 presents data from surveys undertaken in the Isle of Man (Prentice, 1993a) where both visitors at heritage attractions, *and* on the Douglas sea front (i.e. not in the vicinity of the attractions surveyed) were asked for their opinions on the roles of heritage attractions on the island. In one respect, these findings stem from survey differences: in 1990 higher frequencies for functions ascribed at the attractions were recorded than two years earlier, as a consequence of prompting. More than a single function could be ascribed to the sites by the tourists interviewed. Among those fluctuations commonly ascribed to sites by the tourists

visiting them, conservation clearly ranked as important, being rated second to education as the most commonly perceived function in both 1988 and 1990. This was not the case, however, for tourists in general on the island, for whom education, information, the pleasure of viewing and a diversity of 'other' reasons are given as functions either of historic monuments or of museums. A substantial minority of the tourists interviewed on Douglas sea front in 1988 were found to have no perception of heritage attraction functions, and generally tourists interviewed in Douglas were less able to name multiple functions than were those tourists interviewed at the attractions. The information presented in Table 22.6 suggests then that a significant proportion of visitors consider heritage sites to have educational or informational functions; this suggests that some degree of information and informal education will be important components of their on-site experience and also a benefit from the visit. Interpretation is therefore an important aspect of the visit experience.

Table 22.7(a) presents data from a study undertaken at four heritage attractions in Wales in 1988 (Light, 1991b). At each attraction visitors were asked to respond to a number of statements concerning their experience of the site and its interpretation. The statements were designed to ascertain whether visitors were satisfied or dissatisfied with the visit experience. The figures presented in Table 22.7(a) show the proportion of visitors whose responses to the statements indicated that they were satisfied with the visit.

The table immediately indicates that a majority of visitors may be described as broadly 'satisfied' at all sites, but also that the extent of satisfaction differs among the sites. For example, satisfaction with the visit experience is highest at Tretower where the largest proportion of respondents considered that the site had lived up to expectations, that it was better than others visited, and that it was not spoilt by overcrowding. Conversely, at Caerphilly satisfaction was lower with fewer visitors (although still a majority) saying that the site had not lived up to expectations, and fewest saying that the site was better than others. Both Raglan and Tintern occupy intermediate positions. Similarly, Table 22.7(b) shows enjoyment of the visit. Although in some senses enjoyment may be considered a benefit of the visit, it can also be regarded as an indication of the quality of the visit experience and the satisfaction with that experience. The table shows that once again enjoyment was highest at Tretower and least at Caerphilly.

The reasons for differing experiences and levels of satisfaction are multifarious and, as discussed above, will be dependent on a number of site-specific and

Table 22.6 *Perceptions of the functions of heritage sites by adult holiday tourists to the Isle of Man*

	Holiday tourists visiting sites		Holiday tourists visiting IOM Douglas sea front 1988	
	Site survey 1988 %	Site survey 1990 %	Historic monuments %	Museums %
Pleasure of viewing	24	63	13	17
Education	48	74	15	27
Conservation	36	68	6	6
Information	34	44	11	20
Unspecific visits/days out	5	3	5	3
Tourism	–	22	8	2
Other	12	1	31	28
Don't know	1	–	24	19
N=	1942	547	342	342

Note. More than one function could be given.
Source: Prentice (1993a).

person-specific factors. However, there is reason to believe that interpretation is an important component of a visit to a heritage site and that satisfaction with interpretation can influence satisfaction with the overall visit (and vice versa). Table 22.7(c) presents visitors' responses to three statements concerning satisfaction with interpretation. Once again, large majorities of respondents were satisfied with interpretation. However, for all three statements this satisfaction is lowest at Caerphilly, while for two statements (2 and 3) it is highest at Tretower. Again Raglan and Tintern are in an intermediate position. The experiences of interpretation therefore appear to mirror those of the visit in general, with satisfaction being highest at Tretower and lowest at

Table 22.7 *Aspect of visitors' experiences of heritage sites*

(a) Proportion of respondents indicating satisfaction with aspects of the visit

	Caerphilly Castle %	Raglan Castle %	Tintern Abbey %	Tretower Castle %
Statement 1	77 (N=319)	90 (N=340)	90 (N=360)	91 (N=141)
Statement 2	37 (N=312)	52 (N=344)	43 (N=336)	61 (N=147)
Statement 3	93 (N=325)	96 (N=356)	92 (N=369)	99 (N=151)

Statement 1:	'This site has not lived up to your expectation' (disagreement is taken to indicate satisfaction)
Statement 2:	'This site is more interesting than others you have been to' (agreement taken to indicate satisfaction)
Statement 3:	'The presence of too many other people here has spoilt your visit' (disagreement is taken to indicate satisfaction)

(b) Proportion of respondents indicating that they had found their visit 'very enjoyable'

	Caerphilly Castle	Raglan Castle	Tintern Abbey	Tretower Castle
	46%	63%	58%	71%
N=	331	357	373	154

(c) Proportion of respondents indicating satisfaction with interpretative facilities

	Caerphilly Castle %	Raglan Castle %	Tintern Abbey %	Tretower Castle %
Statement 1	87 (N=324)	96 (N=355)	94 (N=369)	91 (N=149)
Statement 2	82 (N=319)	94 (N=353)	92 (N=365)	98 (N=110)
Statement 3	64 (N=317)	74 (N=347)	80 (N=359)	93 (N=111)

Statement 1:	'You have not learnt anything from our visit here' (disagreement is taken to indicate satisfaction)
Statement 2:	'The [interpretation] here has not enhanced your visit' (disagreement is taken to indicate satisfaction)
Statement 3:	'The information here is not presented in any clear theme' (disagreement is taken to indicate satisfaction)

Source: Light (1991b).

Caerphilly. Significantly, at the time of this study, the interpretative media employed at Tretower and Caerphilly were very different. Tretower featured a state-of-the-art stereo audio tour which was highly praised by the visitors. Conversely, Caerphilly was representative of a more traditional approach to interpretation and featured two exhibitions with a strong emphasis on the written word (although since the time of this study the interpretation at Caerphilly has been considerably extended and updated). Visitors appeared to respond to different interpretative strategies in different ways. Overall we can tentatively suggest from these research findings that experiences of interpretation are an important component of the overall visit experience and that satisfaction with interpretation is an important influence on satisfaction with the visit as a whole. The experience of quality and novel interpretation may serve to boost the experience of the visit as a whole, an important consideration for heritage managers at attractions that may not be intrinsically exciting. In the same way poor interpretation may depress overall satisfaction, even at sites which are of high interest to their visitors.

Once again these findings have implications for the evaluation of interpretation. Evaluation of how visitors make use of any interpretative medium cannot be divorced from the overall experience of, and satisfaction with, the visit as a whole. In particular, visitors expressing dissatisfaction with a particular piece of interpretation *may* in fact reflect a wider dissatisfaction with the visit experience. Moreover, some of the reasons for this stance may be entirely unconnected with interpretation, and may be wholly or partly beyond the control of site managers (for example, poor weather, overcrowding). Evaluation of interpretation needs therefore to be sensitive to the wider experiences of visitors and should attempt to take consideration of these experiences. In particular, the relationship between the various components of the visit experience (and satisfaction with these components), and responses to, and benefits obtained from interpretation is one which merits fuller investigation and should be an important part of future evaluative research.

Benefits (outcomes) of visits—level 4 of the hierarchy

Visiting a heritage attraction and the experiences received during the visit will produce a range of benefits (or outcomes) for the visitor. In particular, different components or aspects of the visit may produce different benefits. Of relevance to the present discussion are those benefits which result from encountering interpretative facilities. As Light (1994b) has noted, a study of the reasons given for visiting heritage attractions indicates

that, for many people, a desire to informally learn and understand about the past are important motivations for visiting heritage attractions. Many tourists wish to benefit from their visit by increasing their understanding of how people in the past lived and how those buildings which today have survived to be presented as sites to visit, originally functioned. Similarly, past industries attract visitors seeking the benefit of having understood the processes involved and the conditions of work (Prentice et al., 1993).

The benefits obtained from an encounter with interpretation may be examined in several ways. At one level the extent to which intepretation enhances the visit experience may be examined. As Table 22.7(c) indicated, over 80% of visitors at heritage attractions in Wales considered that interpretative facilities had indeed enhanced their visit. More specifically it is possible to investigate the extent of visitors' learning from an encounter with interpretation. This may be achieved simply by asking visitors whether they thought that they had learned anything. Again Table 22.7(c) indicates that over 87% of visitors at the four Welsh sites were of the opinion that they had learnt from their visit. A more rigorous and accurate assessment of visitors' learning may be obtained through the use of formal recognition and recall test questions. This form of benefit has been investigated in some detail by both the present authors.

The procedures for investigating visitors' learning from interpretation are both problematic and highly important. Light (1988) has reviewed the problems encountered when assessing the educational impact of presentational media and the key points are worthy of report here. Firstly, clear objectives of some kind are needed as to what a visitor can be realistically expected to have learnt following an experience of interpretative media. For example, in general terms visitors may be expected to give some indication of having acquired some new information from their visit. A more specific study might investigate how effectively interpretation has communicated key concepts, for example, a knowledge of the century in which a castle was built. Secondly, decisions have to be made about the selection of test questions. Are they to be taken from all of an attraction's interpretation, or just part of it? A problem arises when asking visitors' test questions, since there is no way of being certain that they had seen and read the part of the interpretation from which the questions were taken. One alternative approach is to ask visitors to specify the part of the interpretation they found most interesting and then ask questions based only on that display (e.g. Prince, 1982). This ensures that the visitors have seen the part of the interpretation from which test questions are taken. However, the strategy creates problems of comparability between respondents for it is impossible to know, in assessing recall, whether the questions pertaining to one part of an attraction are of equal difficulty to those for other parts. Also, such a strategy may not in effect be comparing those parts of an attraction's interpretation found most interesting but rather for some visitors, those found the least uninteresting (particularly for those visitors who were in a hurry). Further, to allow visitors to select that part of the interpretation found most interesting implicitly assumes galleries or other multiple displays are being studied, from which sufficient information can be extracted to form an evaluation for each component part: it is not a practical technique at the many monuments that lack large discrete displays of this kind. Another problem is taking some consideration of prior knowledge. Some visitors to a heritage attraction may arrive with extensive prior knowledge of it, while others may know almost nothing. When attempting to assess visitors' learning it is important to be able to differentiate between what was known before the visit and what was learnt during the visit. One approach is to interview two samples of visitors, one before the visit (to establish a baseline of prior knowledge) and one after the visit (to establish any increase on this baseline). However, this method fails to identify the extent to which each individual has learnt new information (Prince, 1982) and so is inadequate for assessing the benefits of an encounter with interpretation. An alternative approach is to ask visitors a series of test questions and if they answer correctly to ask them if they knew the answer before the visit. This allows each individual to establish their own levels of prior knowledge and subsequent learning (Prince, 1982).

The present authors have investigated learning by visitors to heritage attractions in the Isle of Man and Wales (Prentice, 1993a; Light, 1991b). Here we present some of the key findings from the Isle of Man studies. In order to investigate learning, recognition tests have been employed. These took the forms of multiple-choice questions (Miles et al., 1988; Prentice, 1991). Respondents were asked a series of questions and were asked to select the correct answer from a choice of five possible answers for the Manx surveys (four for the Welsh surveys). The location of the correct answer within the set choices was varied to avoid spotting by respondent tourists. Seven multiple-choice recognition tests were used at each attraction surveyed on the Isle of Man, namely at Peel Castle and Cregneash in 1990 and at Castle Rushen in 1990 and 1991. At each attraction, the questions were drawn from around the sites, each visitor interviewed being asked at any one attraction the same questions, thereby producing a summary picture of aspects of

visitors' knowledge when leaving each attraction. Visitors were asked to indicate any prior knowledge of the answers selected in the recognition tests.

The extent to which the tourists interviewed in the Manx surveys selected the correct answer is shown in Table 22.8(a)–(d). Some questions were much more frequently answered correctly than were others at the attractions. Strictly speaking, the frequencies are incomparable between attractions as they are derived from differing presentations and the questions may be more or less difficult to answer correctly at different sites. However, it would seem reasonable to conclude that the tourists interviewed were more informed when leaving Cregneash in 1990 and when leaving Castle Rushen in 1991 than when leaving the two castles in 1990. However, in interpreting these findings as indices of comparative interpretative success, we cannot assume that tourists visiting the attractions were equally uninformed about them prior to their visit. As noted earlier, it may be that at some attractions tourists arrive with substantial prior knowledge, but at others with little. In fact, for most of the recognition questions asked, the extent of prior knowledge admitted to by tourists who chose to answer a question was slight.

Clearly then, many visitors do learn something new when they visit a heritage attraction, and we are justified in identifying informal learning and understanding as benefits from the visit. The concern for heritage managers is how these benefits can be maximised, especially among those people who particularly require them. Are there certain properties of interpretative media which can assist and facilitate greater learning among visitors? If such can be identified then future interpretation can be designed with a greater concern for effective communication.

Similarly, are there characteristics of visitors themselves which make them more likely to learn during a visit to a heritage attraction? Indeed, in many ways the characteristics of visitors (for example, age, social class, motivation) may be as important as those of the interpretative media in promoting learning. If key learning characteristics of tourists can be identified and also can be found disproportionately among tourists visiting certain attractions, the presentation of these attractions could not be considered the sole factor in learning effectiveness. In short, in terms of the present discussion, are certain of the Manx attractions disproportionately visited by tourists who are more likely to learn from on-site presentation?

A problem in looking for determinants of this kind among the survey data is the strict incomparability of the recognition test scores between attractions. This may be overcome, however, by standardising between attractions

Table 22.8 *Recognition of interpretative information by adult holiday tourists when leaving Manx heritage sites*

(a) Peel Castle in 1990 ($N = 184$)

Question	Percentage of tourists giving the correct answer
With what country does the herringbone masonry found in St Patrick's Church suggest a link in the eleventh century?	1
To what use was this site put in the twelfth century?	34
To what use was this site put in the nineteenth century?	63
On what landscape feature is the castle sited?	64
What was the principal use of the round tower?	62
What evidence of links with Viking Ireland were found by archaeologists working on the site in the 1980s?	2
What unusual jewellery was found by archaeologists in the grave of the 'Pagan Lady of Peel'?	27

(b) Castle Rushen in 1990 ($N = 185$)

Question	Percentage of tourists giving the correct answer
Who rebuilt the castle in the fourteenth century?	38
From where is it thought the craftsmen came who built the castle?	10
Of what stone is the castle mainly constructed?	74
What is the function of the sloping grass bank on the outside of the curtain wall?	32
What was the function of the bends in the barbican (the entrance passageway to the castle)?	42
What is the main function of the outer courtyard of the castle?	5
For what purpose was the castle used in the nineteenth century?	84

(c) Castle Rushen in 1991 ($N = 192$)

Question	Percentage of tourists giving the correct answer
For whom was the present castle built?	66
Which period does the room with the peacock portray?	43
Bishop Wilson was imprisoned in this castle. What is he shown doing in the display?	88
What is the function of the sloping grass bank on the outside of the curtain wall?	75
What was a presence chamber?	83
What was the main function of the outer courtyard of the castle?	8
For what purpose was the castle used in the nineteenth century?	63

(d) Cregneash in 1990 ($N = 178$)

Question	Percentage of tourists giving the correct answer
On what did the community's livelihood at Cregneash mainly depend?	91
How was agriculture organised at Cregneash?	85
How was grain traditionally threshed at Cregneash?	88
What was the focal point of a Manx cottage?	77
What is thought to be the age of Harry Kelly's cottage?	46
What were the cottages at Cregneash traditionally roofed with?	71
What preservation activity at Cregneash preceded in the 1930s the preservation of buildings?	67

Source: Prentice (1993a).

in terms of the average (median) scores obtained by tourists at each site. In effect, the average score, although different between attractions, is the element of comparability. This enables a comparison of the characteristics of respondents attaining average or below-average (median) total scores across the seven tests at the Manx attractions with those of tourists obtaining above-average (median) scores. In this way site-specific differences are countered. Comparing the recognition test scores of tourists in this way confirms for the Isle of Man the success of the new presentation of

Castle Rushen, for at the attractions surveyed in 1990 both social class and age of completion of full-time education had direct effects on learning, but not at Castle Rushen in 1991. The presentation in 1991 clearly affected on-site learning irrespective of these background determinants, and succeeded in overcoming the effect of these otherwise important factors.

Once again, these research findings raise implications for evaluation of interpretation. The need is for a fuller understanding of the ways in which visitors learn from interpretative media at heritage attractions. Existing research, including that undertaken by the authors, has established that learning does occur, and has pointed to some of the attributes of interpretative media and visitors themselves which influence this learning. However, this research is in its early stages, and more research effort will be necessary to unravel the complex nature of interactions between visitors and interpretative media. For this reason we urge that considering the educational impact of interpretation is an issue which needs to be given priority on any future research agenda.

The Manning–Haas hierarchy implies that benefits are the outcome of experiences, settings and activities. Clearly the need is for a much enhanced understanding of the nature of benefits, such as learning, understanding and appreciation. However, the relationship between these benefits and the other elements of the hierarchy (activities, settings and levels) is also an issue for further research. For example, the relationship between benefits (learning) and experiences is one which warrants further investigation. How does the overall visit experience at a heritage attraction have an influence on learning? Does enjoyment of the attraction as a whole facilitate learning? The relationship between learning and enjoyment has been identified by other researchers (see, for example, Moscardo and Pearce (1986)) but the exact relationship between the two is ambiguous. Similarly, the relationship between learning as a benefit and social settings (group composition and behaviour) is also one that is little understood. Some recent work, however, has considered the impact of experiences on formal learning as part of higher education field visits to an attraction (Prentice, 1993b; Prentice, 1994), although this is specific to a single site (Kidwelly Castle) and may or may not be generalisable.

Summary and conclusions

The principal contemporary issue in interpretative provision at heritage attractions is the continuing insufficiency of attention to the effectiveness of investments in heritage presentations. This insufficiency manifests itself both in a deficiency in the *volume* of research effort

directed to evaluation and in the failure to date to develop a *conceptual* framework of evaluation. In this paper we have attempted to address both of these deficiencies. Firstly, research into the effectiveness of interpretation was reported. Secondly, we have demonstrated the application of the Manning–Haas hierarchy of recreational demand to the study of heritage interpretation. For the development of evaluative studies it is the usefulness of this framework which should take prominence in a future research agenda. The Manning–Haas hierarchy proposes that a visit to a heritage attraction can be broken down into a number of interlinked components. The activities undertaken at a heritage attraction will take place in various settings, including the physical setting of the attraction itself, the social setting and context of the visit, and the management setting which underpins the activities. The activities undertaken will generate a range of experiences, and these experiences will themselves produce various benefits to the visitor.

The roles and use of heritage interpretation can be considered at each level of the hierarchy. Making use of interpretation is an important activity undertaken at heritage attractions. Interpretation is also an important component of the physical and management settings of an attraction. Interpretation can contribute to the experiences of the visit as well as producing benefits for the visitor in the form of enhanced understanding and appreciation of the attraction.

Consequently, issues of the effectiveness of interpretation can be considered at the various levels of the Manning–Haas hierarchy. Indeed the hierarchy provides a powerful conceptual framework for the evaluation of interpretation. It allows a comprehensive evaluation of all the aspects and roles of interpretation at a heritage attraction in comparison to the conventional approach which has tended to focus individual aspects of interpretation in isolation. However, the Manning–Haas hierarchy is more than just an alternative framework for evaluation: instead it generates some new approaches and perspectives on evaluation.

At the activities level of the Manning–Haas hierarchy research seeks to identify the ways in which interpretation is a component of the activities undertaken when visiting a heritage attraction. This includes visitors' awareness of, and attention to, the interpretative media they encounter. Such an understanding is a prerequisite for an understanding of the way in which interpretation contributes to the experiences of the visitor, and the benefits they receive. At the settings level of the hierarchy, the physical setting of the attraction will influence the general scope and objectives of the evaluative programme. The social settings will influence the activities undertaken and is an important variable to consider in evaluative research which seeks to understand the nature of visitors' activities with regard to interpretation. The management settings of an attraction will influence visitors' expectations with regard to interpretation, and so evaluation can be undertaken with respect to these expectations. At the experiences level of the hierarchy, interpretation will be an important component of the visit experience for many people, and evaluation can seek to ascertain the impact of interpretation on these experiences. The activities and social settings of the visit will also be an important influence on experiences. Finally, many of the benefits obtained from visiting a site will result from interpretation, most notably an enhanced understanding of the site, and evaluation can seek to identify the nature of such learning and the attributes of both visitor and interpretative medium which influence it.

The Manning–Haas hierarchy then has many implications for evaluation of interpretation and raises several considerations for a future research agenda. First is the need for comprehensive and holistic investigations to be undertaken which consider all the various components and contributions of interpretation to the visit rather than considering each part in isolation. The Manning–Haas hierarchy also allows the linkages and relationships between the different contributions of interpretation to the visit to be identified. Secondly, there is a need for a fuller understanding of the importance of interpretation to experiences and benefits of the visit. Such an understanding is of direct relevance to heritage managers in allowing them to plan with a thorough knowledge of the attributes, expectations and behaviour of their visitors. As much of the resource base of United Kingdom (and particularly Scottish and Welsh) attraction-based tourism is accounted for by heritage attractions, the need to develop an alternative conceptual framework for investigating interpretative effectiveness extends to the whole UK tourism industry and, indeed, beyond to other tourist areas with similar attraction bases. It does not need the present authors to remind the tourism sector that an ineffectual attraction base can undermine a region's accommodation resources as tourists go elsewhere.

References

Aldridge, D. (1989) 'How the ship of interpretation was blown off course in the tempest: some philosophical thoughts', in Uzzell, D. (Ed.), *Heritage Interpretation*, Vol. 1, Belhaven, London, pp. 64–87.

Alt, M. B. (1977) 'Evaluating didactic exhibits: a critical look at Shettel's work', *Curator*, 20: 241–258.

Ashworth, G. and Voogd, H. (1990) 'Can places be sold for tourism?', in Ashworth, G. and Goodall, B. (Eds), *Marketing Tourism Places*, Routledge, London, pp. 1–16.

BTA/ETB (British Tourist Authority/English Tourist Board) (1992) *English Heritage Monitor 1992*, BTA/ETB Research Services, London.

English Tourist Board (1984) *English Churches and Visitors: A Survey of Anglican Incumbents*, English Tourist Board, London.

Griggs, S. A. (1984) 'Evaluating exhibitions', in Thompson, J. M. A., Bassett, D. A., Davies, D. G., Duggan, A. J., Lewis, G. D. and Prince, D. R. (Eds), *The Manual of Curatorship: A Guide to Museum Practice*, Butterworths, London, pp. 412–422.

Herbert, D. T. (1989) 'Does interpretation help?', in Herbert, D. T., Prentice, R. C. and Thomas, C. J. (Eds), *Heritage Sites: Strategies for Marketing and Development*, Avebury, Aldershot, pp. 191–230.

Herbert, D. T., Prentice, R. C. and Thomas, C. J. (Eds) (1989) *Heritage Sites: Strategies for Marketing and Development*, Avebury, Aldershot.

Hewison, R. (1987) *The Heritage Industry, Britain in a Climate of Decline*, Methuen, London.

Light, D. (1987) 'Interpretation at historic buildings', *Swansea Geographer*, 24: 34–43.

Light, D. (1988) 'Problems encountered with evaluating the educational effectiveness of interpretation', *Swansea Geographer*, 25: 79–87.

Light, D. (1989) 'The contribution of the geographer to the study of heritage', *Cambria*, 15: 127–136.

Light, D. (1991a) 'The development of heritage interpretation in Britain', *Swansea Geographer*, 28: 1–13.

Light, D. (1991b) 'Heritage places in Wales and their interpretation: a study in applied recreational geography', unpublished Ph.D. thesis, University of Wales.

Light, D. (1992a) 'Notes on evaluating the effectiveness of interpretation', *Swansea Geographer*, 29: 99–108.

Light, D. (1992b) 'Bilingual heritage interpretation in Wales', *Scottish Geographical Magazine*, 108: 179–183.

Light, D. (1994a) 'Heritage and informal education', in Herbert, D. T. (Ed.), *Heritage and Tourism*, Mansell, London (forthcoming).

Light, D. (1994b) 'Visitors' use of interpretative media at heritage sites', submitted to *Leisure Studies*.

Light, D. and Prentice, R. (1994) 'Who consumes the heritage product', in Ashworth, G. and Larkham, P. (Eds), *Building a New Heritage: Tourism, Culture and Identity in the New Europe*, Routledge, London (in press).

Lumley, R. (1988) 'Introduction', in Lumley, R. (Ed.), *The Museum Time Machine: Putting Cultures on Display*, Routledge, London, pp. 1–23.

Manning, R. E. (1986) *Studies in Outdoor Recreation*, Oregon State University Press, Corvallis.

Martin, B. and Mason, S. (1993) 'The future for attractions: meeting the needs of the new consumers', *Tourism Management*, 14: 34–40.

McManus, P. M. (1987) 'It's the company you keep: the social determination of learning-related behaviour in a science museum', *The International Journal of Museum Management and Curatorship*, 6: 263–270.

McManus, P. M. (1988) 'Good companions: more on the social determination of learning-related behaviour in a science museum', *The International Journal of Museum Management and Curatorship*, 7: 37–44.

McManus, P. (1989) 'What people say and how they think in a science museum', in Uzzell, D. (Ed.), *Heritage Interpretation*, Vol. 2, Belhaven, London, pp. 156–165.

Merriman, N. (1991) *Beyond the Glass Case: The Past, the Heritage and the Public in Britain*, Leicester University Press, Leicester.

Miles, R. S., Alt, M. B., Gosling, D. C., Lewis, B. N. and Tout, A. F. (1988) *The Design of Educational Exhibits*, 2nd edn, Unwin Hyman, London.

Moscardo, G. and Pearce, P. L. (1986) 'Visitor centres and environmental interpretation: an exploration of the relationships among visitor enjoyment, understanding and mindfulness', *Journal of Environmental Psychology*, 6: 89–108.

Prentice, R. C. (1989) 'Visitors to heritage sites: a market segmentation by visitor characteristics', in Herbert, D. T., Prentice, R. C. and Thomas, C. J. (Eds), *Heritage Sites: Strategies for Marketing and Development*, Avebury, Aldershot, pp. 15–61.

Prentice, R. C. (1991) 'Measuring the educational effectiveness of on-site interpretation designed for tourists', *Area*, 23: 297–308.

Prentice, R. C. (1993a) *Tourism and Heritage Attractions*, Routledge, London.

Prentice, R. (1993b) 'Evaluating interpretation by considering the consumer', *Interpretation Journal*, 53: 9–11.

Prentice, R. C. (1993c) 'Motivations of the heritage consumer in the leisure market: an application of the Manning–Haas hierarchy', *Leisure Sciences* (in press).

Prentice, R. C. (1994) 'Heritage as formal education', in Herbert, D. T. (Ed.), *Heritage and Tourism*, Mansell, London (forthcoming).

Prentice, R. C., Witt, S. F. and Hamer, C. (1993) 'The experience of industrial heritage: the case of *Black Gold*', *Built Environment*, 19.

Prentice, R. C., Witt, S. F. and Wydenbach, E. G. (1994) 'The endearment behaviour of tourists through their interaction with the host community', *Tourism Management* (in press).

Prince, D. R. (1982) 'Evaluating interpretation: a discussion', Centre for Environmental Interpretation Occasional Paper No. 1, Centre for Environmental Interpretation, Manchester.

Prince, D. R. (1984) 'Approaches to summative evaluation', in Thompson, J. M. A., Bassett, D. A., Davies, D. G., Duggan, A. J., Lewis, G. D. and Prince, D. R. (Eds), *The Manual of Curatorship: A Guide to Museum Practice*, Butterworths, London, pp. 423–434.

Putney, A. D. and Wager, J. A. (1973) 'Objectives and evaluation in interpretative planning', *Journal of Environmental Education*, 5: 43–44.

Risk, P. (1989) 'On-site real-time observational techniques and responses to visitor needs', in Uzzell, D. (Ed.), *Heritage Interpretation*, Vol. 2, Belhaven, London, pp. 120–128.

Roggenbuck, J. W. and Propst, D. B. (1981) 'Evaluation of interpretation', *Journal of Interpretation*, 6: 13–23.

Russell, T. (1989) 'The formative evaluation of interactive science and technology centres', in Uzzell, D. (Ed.), *Heritage Interpretation*, Vol. 2, Belhaven, London, pp. 191–202.

STB (Scottish Tourist Board) (1993) *Site Interpretation: A Practical Guide*, Scottish Tourist Board, Edinburgh.

Sharpe, G. (1982) *Interpreting the Environment*, 2nd edn, John Wiley, New York.

Thomas, C. J. (1989) 'The roles of heritage sites and the reasons for visiting', in Herbert, D. T., Prentice, R. C. and Thomas, C. J. (Eds), *Heritage Sites: Strategies for Marketing and Development*, Avebury, Aldershot, pp. 62–93.

Tilden, F. (1957) *Interpreting our Heritage* (3rd edn 1977), University of North Carolina Press, Chapel Hill, NC.

Urry, J. (1990) *The Tourist Gaze*, Sage, London.

Uzzell, D. (1985) 'Management issues in the provision of countryside interpretation', *Leisure Studies*, 4: 159–174.

Uzzell D. (1988) 'The interpretive experience', in Canter, D., Krampen, M. and Stea, D. (Eds), *Ethnoscapes*, Vol. 2, *Environmental Policy, Assessment and Communication*, Avebury, Aldershot, pp. 248–263.

Uzzell, D. (1989) 'Introduction: the visitor experience', in Uzzell, D. (Ed.), *Heritage Interpretation*, Vol. 2, Belhaven, London, pp. 1–15.

Vander Stoep, T. (1989) 'Time-lapse photography', in Uzzell, D. (Ed.), *Heritage Interpretation*, Vol. 2, Belhaven, London, pp. 179–190.

Wager, J. A. (1976) 'Evaluating the effectiveness of interpretation', *Journal of Interpretation*, 1: 1–18.

Walsh, K. (1992) *The Representation of the Past: Museums and Heritage in the Post-modern World*, Routledge, London.

Walsh-Heron, J. and Stevens, T. (1990) *The Management of Visitor Attractions and Events*, Prentice Hall, Englewood Cliffs, NJ.

23 The future of the past: heritage tourism into the 21st century

J. SWARBROOKE

Introduction

Heritage tourism is an activity with a long history that can be measured in centuries if not millennia. On the other hand, the term itself is a relatively recent invention, for the word 'heritage' only began to be used commonly in the 1970s, in Europe at least. Heritage Tourism as a recognised industry is a modern development.

The scope and nature of heritage tourism

Heritage tourism is a loose term that can be interpreted broadly or narrowly. For the purposes of this discussion it will be defined as tourism which is based on heritage where heritage is the core of the product that is offered and heritage is the main motivating factor for the consumer. It is based on the view that heritage is only heritage in tourism terms when it is of interest to, and accessible to, tourists.

In this context heritage is taken to mean history, culture, and the land on which people live. It includes both tangible and intangible elements and therefore includes the following, for example:

- historic buildings and monuments
- the sites of important past events like battles
- traditional landscapes and indigenous wildlife
- language, literature, music and art
- traditional events and folklore practices
- traditional lifestyles including food and drink and sport

It covers the aspects of heritage that are consciously owned and managed by the public, private, and voluntary sectors and those elements which are not owned, by anyone.

How old something has to be to be considered as heritage is an arguable point, but the period seems to be becoming shorter and shorter. There are museums now which have exhibits based on life in the 1960s and even later.

Heritage is not homogeneous. It exists at different levels, namely, global, national, regional, and local. Because it is a personal subjective and emotional concept as well as an objective and functional one, each individual views heritage in a different way. In the Deep South of the USA two old men living in the same town will have a different view of the heritage of their area if one is poor and black and the other rich and white. The tourism industry needs to be sensitive to such issues if it is to be managed in a way that is socially acceptable and does not reinforce prejudice, discrimination and resentment.

Heritage also means different things to the various sectors of the tourism industry. For many attractions it is their core product while many destinations have developed on the basis of their historical and cultural appeal. To tour operators it is a commodity that helps to sell holidays.

Interestingly, now that travel and tourism is a well developed activity, it is beginning to have its own heritage artefacts. Examples of this include the following:

- trains and rail services such as the Orient Express
- veteran airliners such as the DC-3
- the architecture of the luxurious hotels on the French Riviera, and 18th- and 19th-century health resorts
- long-established attractions such as, museums and galleries, in that now the buildings and institutions are regarded as being as much a part of the nation's heritage as the collections they contain

The historical development of heritage tourism

Tourism based on history and culture is not new, although it was often the preserve of small elite sections of society. In the time of the Romans there was a relatively well developed pattern of travel for culture and pleasure.

In the Middle Ages in Europe, religious heritage, in the form of pilgrimage sites, was perhaps the main motivation for travel. Such pilgrimage tourism was on a relatively large scale and was 'served by a growing industry of networks of charitable hospices and mass produced indulgence handbooks' (Feifer, 1985:29). The pilgrimages in the Christian world, such as those to Rome and to the Holy Land, were paralleled in the Islamic world by pilgrimages to Mecca and other holy sites.

By the start of the 18th century, the 'Grand Tour' had become a well-established activity for the sons of the aristocracy and the gentry. It was based on visiting sites of artistic importance around Europe and was seen as part of a young man's education. The 'Grand Tour' also resulted in a large number of eye-witness accounts by people who undertook the Grand Tour. By the 19th century the Grand Tour had developed and widened and become part of the Romantic movement and acted as a catalyst for the rise of what might be called, 'scenic tourism', based on landscapes.

The end of the 19th century saw the beginning of packaged heritage tourism with Thomas Cook's first holidays to see the ancient historical monuments of Egypt.

Heritage tourism continued to develop at a steady pace throughout the first half of the 20th century, in more and more locations. Its most spectacular period of growth has, however, undoubtedly been in the last fifty years, alongside the dramatic growth in international tourism and leisure activities. The car has made historic buildings and sites accessible to a mass domestic market, while the rise of the overseas package holiday allowed more and more people to visit heritage attractions in other countries. Some of the most popular package holidays have been to those places which have a reputation for heritage such as Paris, and the Renaissance cities of Italy.

In the last two or three decades, heritage tourism has changed in a number of ways particularly in terms of the product, as follows:

1. The growth of open-air museums, such as Skansen in Sweden, Ironbridge in the UK, and the Ecomusées of France. These have particularly been based upon traditional architecture, industrial heritage, and social history.
2. The development of heritage centres which tell the story of an area or a specific theme, often using novel methods of interpretation such as interactive video.
3. The rise of 'living history' where paid or voluntary 'interpreters' dress in costume and explain sites and events to visitors, perhaps in the language of the appropriate period, particularly in the USA.
4. Competition from heritage centres and pressure on funding have stimulated traditional museums to become more imaginative, 'user-friendly', and entrepreneurial.
5. Heritage tourism has become a tool of government regional and economic policy with historic docklands being developed as tourist attractions in the USA, and UK, and the use of rural traditions and gastronomy to attract tourists so that farms can be kept viable in rural France.
6. The exploitation of scientific and technological heritage to attract visitors, for example, La Villette in Paris.

7. The linking of the arts and heritage to create new tourist attractions such as live theatre performances at National Trust and English Heritage properties and opera performances amongst the Pyramids or in the Roman Theatre at Orange in France.
8. The increasing efforts which are being put into conserving and enhancing the environment of whole towns or city centres which makes them attractive heritage destinations.
9. An increasing fascination with the earth's natural environment and wildlife heritage which has led to wildlife 'watching' and conservation holidays.
10. The development of car and walking trails that link together heritage attractions.
11. A growth in interest in the history of 'the Common Man' as well as a continued interest in the heritage of the few, what might be termed, 'the history of Kings and Queens'.

The growth of heritage tourism has not been a homogeneous activity across the whole world. The bulk of the market tends to come from what might be called the 'developed countries' of North America, Europe, Japan, and Australasia. This is also where the majority of the most highly developed heritage products are found. Nevertheless, most national tourism organisations are now using heritage to attract tourists to their countries. Boniface and Fowler note:

> in the area of tourism, countries have courted a world market; with the chosen object of enticement, more often than not, heritage. How else to be a distinctive 'product', distinguished from others, on a world scene? So far so easy, but of a heritage, what features should be selected? What is attractive to a chosen market? And, just as important, what will be repulsive and to whom? (Boniface and Fowler, 1993:1)

The reasons for the growth of heritage tourism

Heritage tourism has grown rapidly in recent years because of many of the same reasons that have led to the growth of tourism generally including: increased leisure time, more disposable income, the development of the package holiday, and increased mobility due to the growth of car ownership.

There are also other more specific reasons for the growth of heritage tourism as follows:

● higher levels of education
● media representations, particularly on television, of heritage themes in their own and other countries, including buildings and monuments, people's lifestyles and special events.

- the development of new types of heritage tourism products
- The status which is attached to heritage tourism by individuals and society
- a growing desire amongst holidaymakers to learn something new whilst they are on holiday

The nature of the heritage tourism product

The heritage tourism product is heterogeneous. Sometimes it is tangible and takes the form of buildings and monuments, while at other times it is an intangible such as a folklore event or a particular language. The product can be natural or man-made and may be a single attraction, a destination area, or a whole country. Some heritage is consciously owned and managed so as to attract tourists while other heritage features are managed with the aim of reducing the problems caused by unwanted tourism. The heritage product is controlled by different types of organisations with differing objectives. Private-sector-owned attractions are often driven by the profit motive, while those in the public sector tend to be managed with wider social objectives in mind, including education and providing leisure facilities for the community. Those in the stewardship of the voluntary sector are often only made available to tourists as a means to another end, for example, to generate revenue to fund conservation work. Finally, some of the heritage products are totally authentic, while others are less than authentic.

Even if we focus just on single-site, individual, man-made heritage attractions rather than destinations, there is great diversity. Prentice has identified seventeen different types, ranging from nature trails to 'historic' adventure theme parks, and from historic gardens to breweries (Prentice, 1993:39–40). These attractions also vary in that some are themselves old while others are very recent developments. Some charge a market price while others make no charge.

One of the major ways in which the heritage product is almost infinitely varied is in terms of the benefits bestowed on users and those which users seek from it. These tend to vary depending on the type of attraction but include the following: status, inexpensive family day out, an opportunity to learn something new, relaxation, healthy exercise, nostalgia, aesthetic pleasure, exhilaration and excitement, being awe-inspired, entertainment, participating in activities, meeting like-minded people.

The amount of heritage tourism product available has increased dramatically in recent years in two ways, firstly through the opening of many new heritage attractions in the past decades or so—in the UK alone the number of museums has more than doubled in the last twenty years.

Secondly, the tourism industry has increasingly packaged heritage products to make them more accessible to more people. In particular, there are now organised short breaks in the UK and abroad based on visiting all kinds of heritage attractions and destinations as well as longer 'study type' holidays.

The market for heritage tourism

The heritage tourism market is also heterogeneous and again varies depending on the type of heritage. Some of the ways in which the market is heterogeneous include the following:

1. Some tourists are almost obsessed by heritage, for others it is a minor interest, while for some people it holds no interest whatsoever.
2. The market for some heritage attractions and destinations means mainly a day-trip market, while the market for others is made up, almost exclusively, of people on holiday.
3. Heritage may appeal to an international or to a mainly national, or even just a local audience.
4. The market for different types of heritage can often be segmented on the basis of factors such as age, sex, class, and race.
5. Certain sorts of heritage appeal to mass markets while others have narrow, small niche markets.
6. Differences in people's ability and willingness to pay to enjoy heritage products.

The marketing of heritage tourism

Heritage has only been marketed as a tourism asset on any real scale in recent years as the tourism industry has realised that the packaging of heritage can be lucrative and as public sector bodies have realised that heritage can be used to attract tourists, so that the economic benefits can be enjoyed by the community. Many commentators are concerned that the marketing of heritage as if it were any other commodity can cause serious problems, as well as being morally suspect. These commentators have two main worries. Firstly, that the artificial 'branding' of areas with heritage themes such as 'Herriot Country' and 'Brontë Country' can lead to visitors seeing areas in terms of one-dimensional stereotypes that never change, rather than as complex places that are constantly changing. Secondly, they are concerned that marketing to a mass market can lead to a trivialisation of heritage, and even the fabrication of heritage, designed to entertain the market.

Current debates and issues in heritage tourism

As we noted earlier, heritage tourism is at an important crossroads today, and faces a range of key issues, and debates, which we will now consider.

Heritage and nostalgia

Museum professionals and writers like Robert Hewison fear that many of the newer types of heritage attractions, which are more 'populist' than traditional museums and galleries, are sacrificing history to nostalgia. The accusation is that such attractions are not presenting 'true', professionally researched history which can sometimes be uncomfortable, but are rather offering a cosy, selective, nostalgic view of history. This accusation has particularly been levelled at the modern social history and industrial heritage attractions that have been developed in northern England. The main criticisms of nostalgia are twofold, namely that it gives people a false impression of history and that it encourages the population to look backwards rather than focusing on the challenges of the present and the future.

However, these criticisms assume there is something that can be called 'true' history. Perhaps this view is right in terms of traditional 'Kings and Queens and important dates' history, but it could be argued that in terms of social history, every person should be seen as an individual with a unique history or life story.

People's unique experiences mean they often have different opinions on a particular period, so that it could be argued that there is no one social history but rather a myriad of individual social histories. The critics of nostalgia also appear to hold the controversial view that the views of professionals born since the events they are interpreting took place, are more relevant than those of non-professionals who lived through the events. This can perhaps be seen as a rather élitist and patronising viewpoint.

Heritage and authenticity

It has been argued that as interest in heritage has grown the tourism industry has sacrificed authenticity in its desire to 'milk' this lucrative 'cash cow' by providing non-authentic heritage experiences to meet the desires and fantasies of the tourists. Authentic heritage is sometimes easy to identify such as traditional landscapes or traditional events that have carried on continuously for many years. However, in other cases the distinction between authentic and non-authentic, can be difficult to judge. What about traditional events that have been forgotten for some years but are then started up again by enthusiasts, or refurbished docklands, such as the Albert Dock in Liverpool, where the buildings have been heavily restored and are no longer used for their original purpose? There are also occasions when authenticity is either not possible (for example, fire regulations may not permit authentic reproductions of mining conditions in an industrial heritage museum) or undesirable (reconstructions of Nazi treatment of the Jews, to give but one illustration).

On the other hand, some attractions adopt a heritage theme, without any pretence of authenticity. This is particularly true of theme parks, for example, the Camelot and American Adventure theme parks in the UK.

A good example of the authenticity dilemma is whether ruined monuments should be left as ruins or should be reconstructed to look as near as possible to how they would have looked in their heyday.

The concept of authenticity is a particularly difficult one in the case of what Boniface and Fowler have called the 'moving object story' (Boniface and Fowler, 1993:121). This means when artefacts are moved from their original (authentic) geographical and cultural context to another one which is alien to that context. The object is now authentic but its context is not, therefore is it truly authentic heritage? There are numerous examples, particularly many paintings that have been bought and sold over the years, and countless artefacts in the stately homes and museums of Europe that were plundered from Africa, India, and the Far East during the colonial period. If these were all to be returned to their original homes, the heritage tourism map of the world would be changed overnight and many European cities that sell themselves as major museum cities might have to find new selling points!

Heritage—education or entertainment?

Traditionally, there has been a view that heritage was about education while entertainment was the province of theme parks and theatres. However, with the growth of what has been called the 'heritage industry' and the growing interest of entrepreneurs in heritage, the techniques of the theme parks and the theatre have been applied to some aspects of the heritage product. Some traditionalists believe that as entertainment arrives, serious history and education disappear while other people believe that you cannot educate unless you entertain. The blurring of the distinction between entertainment and education, as that between authenticity and fabricated heritage, has been seen by commentators such as John Urry, as a manifestation of post-modernism.

Heritage tourism, trivialisation, and commodification

The growth of international tourism has led to heritage being packaged as just another part of the tourism product. However, in order for it to meet the needs of tourists, heritage often has to be changed in ways that trivialise its content or value. For example, long traditional dances that have deep meaning are shortened to meet the schedules of tour groups and, in doing so, lose all their true meaning. Heritage tourism can also lead to heritage sites losing some of their original purpose, particularly in the eyes of visitors. Notre Dame is not seen as a place of worship for the local community but as a tourist attraction.

Heritage tourism as an agent of cultural change

Tourism which is motivated by a desire to view heritage can be an agent of cultural change. The number of visitors to the area that has been branded 'Dutch Country' in Pennsylvania, USA, has led some residents to start to offer services for visitors on a commercial basis which has changed, for ever, their own society and their relationship with the outside world. On perhaps a deeper level, people who buy second homes or eventually migrate to another country in the hope of becoming part of a community they see as traditional, ensure these communities will become a little less traditional, because of their own actions. This is being seen with the many British people who are buying second homes in, or migrating to, rural France at present (Swarbrooke, 1993b).

Heritage and sustainable tourism

There is a general belief that heritage tourism and sustainable tourism are complementary as heritage tourism is perceived to be 'intelligent' tourism carried out by educated people. However, heritage tourism currently has some aspects which are definitely not green or sustainable. Many sites are overcrowded and overused with resulting deterioration in their physical fabric. This is true of historic cities as well as individual sites; this has led to calls for the de-marketing of such honeypot sites as well as the use of visitor management techniques. The trivialisation and falsification that can come with tourism is also hardly compatible with the principles of sustainable tourism. So-called 'traditional' souvenirs are often bought in from other countries rather than being made locally, or local crafts have to be modified to make them acceptable for tourists, in other words, souvenirs have to be small enough to allow them to fit into a tourist's luggage.

However, if one takes the view that sustainability in tourism is about local control and the maximising of the economic, social and environmental benefits of tourism for the local community, while minimising the costs, France has some interesting examples to offer, in the field of heritage tourism, including:

● Lascaux II, a copy of the original Lascaux caves which were closed due to the damage being done to them by visitors' breath! This faithful reproduction gives visitors a good impression of the real thing and attracts 200 000 visitors a year.
● Cinéscénie, at Le Puy du Fou in Vendée, is an annual event where a local volunteer cast recreates scenes from the history of their community for tourists. All the profits from the event are used to fund local community projects.
● Ecomusées, where themes in local history are interpreted through the use of authentic sites and buildings, and visitors are encouraged to see the links between human history and the physical environment that have shaped human history.
● Local voluntary associations designed to protect the heritage of 'Pays' or areas that develop heritage-based activities and attractions for tourists, so that local history is interpreted by local people. A good example is the Hyelzas village in Lozere which is a recreated village based on a real community that became deserted. It is run by Le Mejean Association and the village also has *gîte* accommodation and local food products are sold. The proceeds are used to further the work of the Association (Boniface and Fowler, 1993:91–94).
● The development of rural tourism in France, based on traditional landscapes, lifestyles, and regional gastronomic traditions that is being used by the government as a way of sustaining the viability of rural economies and local agricultural economies.

Clearly there can be a symbiotic relationship between heritage tourism and the concept of sustainable tourism. Heritage needs the economic benefits that tourism can bring while tourism needs heritage as a tourist resource or raw material. However, achieving this relationship is an infinitely more difficult task, which involves a number of ethical questions.

Ethical issues and heritage tourism

Heritage tourism involves many ethical dilemmas, some of which we have already touched on such as authenticity and the branding of areas with historic theme labels. However, there are others. Firstly, who decides what, and whose, heritage should be portrayed for tourists? Also, who decides who should be allowed access to heritage sites? For example, do we have the moral right to stop Druids celebrating the solstice at Stonehenge when it could be argued that in many ways they are carrying on the traditional purpose of Stonehenge?

The role of the media and heritage tourism

It is clear that the mass media in all its forms is now a major determinant of tourist behaviour. Holiday programmes on television and features in newspapers and magazines make people aware of heritage, particularly in other countries and create a desire to visit the places concerned. In addition, the books written by people who have moved to other countries are also increasingly influencing tourism flows. The books about life in Provence, written by Peter Mayle, with their vivid and romanticised images of traditional village life have encouraged many people to visit the village mentioned in the book.

The funding of heritage

Traditionally most heritage has been conserved by the public sector. However, in the UK at least, government and local authorities are finding it increasingly difficult to pay for the conservation of the nation's heritage. English Heritage faces difficult choices in deciding what it can afford to conserve while the theatrical world which is a major tourist attraction in the UK, is struggling to survive on inadequate funding. At the same time, in the face of government-imposed financial restraints local authorities are struggling to maintain their subsidies for museums which in 1991 amounted to about £4.50 per museum visitor (Audit Commission for Local Authorities and the National Health Service in England and Wales, 1991:19). In this situation the public sector is having to become entrepreneurial, which is leading to some uncomfortable compromises between traditions of conservation and scholarship and the need to attract and entertain visitors. The pressures on public sector funding are also placing more emphasis on the role of the voluntary sector to conserve the nation's heritage, hence the growth of heritage trusts and Friends organisations. There is also a growth of public–private sector partnerships in the heritage field.

Talking about the funding of heritage leads us on to the debate about who should ultimately pay for heritage. Should it be the heritage tourist who uses the heritage resources, or the community as a whole, including those who never use such resources? This is at the heart of the debate about museum charges.

The quality of heritage management

Given the growing pressures on heritage managers (financial, competition, and changes in consumer behaviour) doubts are growing about the ability of many heritage managers to cope. Many are professionally trained scholars or conservationists who need financial and marketing skills to flourish in the new entrepreneurial world of heritage. In recognition of this, much work on training is being undertaken by the professional bodies in the heritage field.

The quality of heritage attractions

At a time when quality and public access are buzz words in the heritage field, many attractions are simply not of a good enough quality to justify charging people to visit them. There are weaknesses in customer care, interpretation and support services such as catering, particularly in the small private museums or those sites which have inadequate budgets. Such attractions may find it hard to survive in the increasingly competitive heritage tourism market.

The saturation of the heritage tourism market

There is a growing feeling that the boom in new heritage products coming on to the market in the 1980s and early 1990s may soon lead to the market becoming saturated. In Britain, it has been estimated that between 1979 and 1989 well over 1000 new attractions opened (there are now around 5000 in Britain). This has led to predictions that we may see closures and bankruptcies of heritage sites and organisations in the years to come, particularly if the problems of quality are not tackled.

What of the future?

In the years to come, the concept of what constitutes heritage may well change in response to political, social and cultural developments around the world. These changes may include the following:

- The growing influence of mass popular culture, as represented by popular music, cinemas and television, will become increasingly recognised as an element in the heritage of people and places. This trend has already begun with museums like the National Museum of Photography, Film and Television in Bradford.
- As consumerism becomes an ever more important part of people's lives, all over the world, the purchase and use of consumer goods will in time become a part of

the shared heritage of individuals and societies. This will include things as diverse as food products, household appliances, and even the package holiday itself. Both of these forms of heritage will be solidly based upon nostalgia rather than a serious interest in the history of popular culture or the consumer society.

- In the future, there is a danger that heritage will become globalised and more homogeneous. Mass communication, global marketing, and political changes such as the growing influence of the European Union and the 'Westernisation' of Eastern Europe will all reduce the differences in culture and lifestyle between local areas, regions, and even countries. Given that such diversity is the key to attracting heritage tourists to a particular destination such a development would be a real threat for the tourism industry. Over time, such homogenisation of heritage could perhaps reduce the motivation of many tourists to travel, to see different cultures. Such a development would kill for ever the concept of living heritage, where history shapes current cultures and guides an area's future, for homogenisation and globalisation of heritage would destroy this continuum.

- Modern phenomena which are currently seen as negative, may with time, become valued heritage artefacts. For example, much modern architecture may one day be viewed as a treasured part of the national heritage, either because of its form or its monumental scale. It is not hard to imagine the Antigone complex in Montpellier in France, which is based on classical styles and daring modern approaches to architecture, being seen in the future as an architectural treasure.

The future may also see changes in the definition of how old something has to be to be seen as heritage. As the pace of life and the speed at which it changes is perceived to become ever faster, we may decide that our concept of 'history' should begin nearer and nearer to the present day. The world has changed so much in recent years that already media coverage of events in the 1970s looks as if it is talking about a place that seems as far away as newsreels of the Edwardian era would have seemed for people in the 1970s. One day, heritage could literally mean events that happened just a few years ago, or even less. Having considered changes in the concept of what is heritage and when is heritage, we must now look at the question of whose heritage and who should control its interpretation. There is a view that much of the heritage tourism product is highly political and even discriminatory in that it is selective in what and whom it chooses to emphasise. This recognition together with concerns over issues such as racism and sexism will lead to

a redressing of the balance so that the heritage of minority groups and women for example, may be given more prominence. Heritage may thus become a less cosy, neutral subject than it has been seen as in the past and heritage tourism in the future may become the focus of political controversy. This trend may be intensified by the rise of nationalism in areas like Eastern Europe where heritage and heritage sites may become even more important as symbols of political and nationalistic ambitions. The growing role of voluntary bodies in heritage and the principles of community tourism may combine and result in the growth of heritage products where local people who are amateurs, rather than heritage professionals, decide what stories will be told and how they will be told.

However, the heritage-motivated tourists themselves will probably change too. More and more of them will not only be interested in passively learning more about an area's heritage, but will also want to be active heritage tourists participating in heritage. They will want to try local crafts or help restore heritage sites.

The protection of both the natural and built heritage will not be able to rely solely on local voluntary initiatives and the changing nature of behaviour amongst tourists. There will have to be some form of constraint over the use of some heritage sites and destinations. This could take the form of taxes on heritage tourists, constraints on visitor numbers, pre-booking for heritage sites, pricing policies designed to reduce numbers, and the de-marketing of heritage sites.

In the future, the distinctions between education and entertainment, and between authentic and non-authentic, and even the differences between light-hearted leisure and sensation-seeking and heritage will become ever more blurred. This will happen partly because of the use of new technologies such as 'virtual reality'. It will also be a reflection of other factors like the recognition by theme parks for example, that they need to offer more opportunities for visitors to learn something to meet the aspirations of both adult tourists and school parties alike.

This trend will also reflect pressures on public-owned heritage organisations to become more entrepreneurial and changes in the attitudes to heritage on the part of consumers. This development is, at the same time, both the greatest potential opportunity and perhaps the most serious threat ever to heritage tourism. It could either bring masses of new people into the market, or 'debase' the product so much that existing customers might leave the market.

Conclusions

If heritage tourism is to remain as a flourishing tourism market and a socially acceptable and healthy activity it seems to the author that two things must happen.

Firstly, partnerships need to be developed between all the stakeholders in heritage tourism, including 'heritage professionals', funding bodies, destination marketing agencies, governments, local communities, tour operators, and the tourists themselves. A common sense of purpose needs to be created if heritage tourism is to become truly sustainable.

Secondly, we need to see heritage as something that is not just about the past. Otherwise we might become obsessed with the past at the expense of the future, and simply use heritage tourism as an excuse for wallowing in nostalgia. Instead, we should seek to link the past with the present and the future. In the field of industrial heritage, for example, we should not only look at the past industrial life of a community. We should see how the past has shaped the present industrial life of the area and look at how local people hope their community will develop in the future. Heritage must be seen as a continuum that has a present and future dimension. Otherwise heritage will become just like a fossil, dusty and lifeless, and giving no indication of the rich and exciting story that led to its creation, and the dramatic events that grew out of its existence.

References and bibliography

Andreux, J.-Y. (1992) *Le Patrimoine Industriel. Que-sais Je?*, Series, number 2657, Presses Universitaires de France, Paris.

Ashworth, G. J. and Tunbridge, J. E. (1990) *The Tourist-Historic City*, Belhaven, London.

Audit Commission for Local Authorities and the National Health Service in England and Wales (1991) *The Road to Wigan Pier*, HMSO, London.

Boniface, P. and Fowler, P. J. (1993) *Heritage and Tourism in the Global Village*, Routledge, London.

Boylan, P. (Ed.) (1992) *Museums 2000—Politics, People, Professionals and Profit*, Routledge, London.

English Tourist Board (1992) *English Heritage Monitor*, English Tourist Board, London.

Feifer, M. (1985) *Going Places*, Macmillan, London.

Hewison, R. (1987) *The Heritage Industry: Britain in a Climate of Decline*, Methuen, London.

Johnson, P. and Thomas, B. (1992) *Tourism, Museums and the Local Economy*, Edward Elgar, Aldershot.

Lumley, R. (Ed.) (1988) *The Museum Time Machine: Putting Cultures on Display*, Routledge, London.

MacCannell, D. (1989) *The Tourist: a New Theory of the Leisure Class*, 3rd edn, Macmillan, London.

Prentice, R. (1993) *Tourism and Heritage Attractions*, Routledge, London.

Swarbrooke, J. S. (1993a) 'The future of heritage attractions', *Insights*, January: D15–D20.

Swarbrooke, J. S. (1993b) 'The socio-cultural impact of British visitors in rural France', conference paper presented to the Thirteenth International Congress of Anthropological and Ethnological Sciences, Mexico City, July 1993.

Turner, L. and Ash, J. (1975) *The Golden Hordes*, Constable, London.

Urry, J. (1990) *The Tourist Gaze: Leisure and Travel in Contemporary Society*, Sage, London.

Uzzell, D. (Ed.) (1989) *Heritage Interpretation*, Vols 1 and 2, Belhaven, London.

Vergo, P. (Ed.) (1989) *The New Museology*, Reaktion, London.

24 Timeshare—the new force in tourism

R. HAYLOCK

It is hard to imagine a tourism activity of greater contradictions than timeshare: a 'bad press' in many countries, with a correspondingly poor public image, yet delivering by far the highest consumer satisfaction rates when compared with most holiday products.

But despite both image problems and widespread recession in many markets, timeshare sales continue to be big business. Since the early 1970s, the timeshare industry has grown steadily. In Europe, the growth rate has been between 12% and 15% year on year over the past five years—totally outstripping the growth of the rest of the European travel and tourism sector.

Between 1980 and 1992, the number of timeshare resorts increased by almost 600% worldwide; annual sales of timeshare intervals increased by more than 300% worldwide; annual gross sales volume increased more than 650%; roughly 3.3 million timeshare weeks were purchased, representing a total sales volume of almost $4 billion. Based on this data, timeshare sales are predicted to reach £30 billion over the next 12 years (Ragatz Associates, 1992a).

Current size of the industry

More than 2.5 million households all over the world now own timeshare, in almost 4000 resort properties. Over 2600 of these resort properties are 'affiliated' to the RCI exchange system. Given that the average size of household is 3.5 people, a quick calculation reveals that more than 8 million people take timeshare holidays each year. That is a significant number in the tourism industry. Indeed, to take the UK as an example, people travelling on timeshare holidays abroad now equate to 9% of British package holidaymakers going abroad.

History and development

If you play golf, you do not need to buy a golf course to indulge in the sport: you join a club and play when you want to. The principle of timeshare is very similar.

The concept of holiday timeshare started in the late 1950s, with an idea conceived by a Swiss, Alexander Nette, and put into practice in a hotel which he ran in Ticino. The idea evolved into Hapimag, a Swiss-based company, which offered its shares for sale, the proceeds of which were used to buy holiday properties throughout Europe. The ownership of shares conveyed the right to use the holiday properties on a regular basis. Hapimag is now a successful business with more than 90 000 shareholders and 45 holiday resort properties throughout Europe.

In 1967, an enterprising hotelier at Superdevoluy in the French Alps started what has become the more common form of timeshare—the sale of right-to-use 'fixed' weeks in the hotel for holiday purposes—sold with the slogan 'stop hiring a room, buy the hotel, it's cheaper!'

At that time, however, the idea did not spread any further in Europe. As so often happens with Europe's creative ideas, it took America's entrepreneurs fully to exploit the potential of timeshare.

Property developers in Florida in the early 1970s were enjoying a sales boom in holiday condominiums and proceeded to plan and build a vast inventory of condominiums for subsequent sale. The second major oil crisis of the mid-1970s hit the American economy hard and condominium sales collapsed almost overnight. Developers looked desperately for new and creative ways of selling their empty properties. They discovered holiday timeshare and thus began the evolution of special marketing and sales techniques which require the sale of one apartment 50 times over—for each week of the year.

Salesmen soon came up against a particular problem: while the potential client liked the timeshare accommodation and the resort on offer, he did not like the prospect of having to return to the same place at the same time for his holiday year after year.

At the same time, in Indianapolis, Jon and Christel DeHaan had begun a private 'swap' system with their friends, trading weeks in each others' holiday homes. When this swap system was applied to the timeshare idea, the timeshare sales problem was solved. Thus, a company called RCI was founded in 1974 as a timeshare exchange organisation to enable purchasers of timeshare to exchange the weeks they owned each year for weeks in different resorts. A second exchange organisation, Interval International, came along two years later. Between them, these two companies acted as the catalyst which started a boom in timeshare sales in the USA during the following 10 years.

Meanwhile, in 1974, the UK's first timeshare development was begun quite independently by a British entrepreneur, Frank Chapman. This was the Loch Rannoch development in Scotland, completed in 1976. Without any clear sequence of events, timeshare developments began to emerge in France, Italy and Scandinavia. The European timeshare industry was born.

By the early 1980s, the timeshare boom in Florida and other US holiday destinations was reaching its peak. As a result, a number of experienced and successful marketers came to Europe and persuaded owners of holiday resort properties in the Algarve and the Canary Islands to try the concept of timeshare, and began selling mainly to British holidaymakers.

For 20 years now, timeshare sales have shown a quite amazingly consistent upward trend as the business has spread to all four corners of the world.

USA

In the USA, the entrepreneurial beginnings are being followed by the entry into the business of operators with a more established profile. As the largest and most mature market in the world, the USA is now seeing less spectacular growth, but the image of the industry has become better established, strict regulation has been introduced and the industry has learned to live with the consequences. Some of the very well known names in the international hospitality industry have moved into timeshare—bringing with them a welcome air of respectability and stability, with established brands and substantial credibility. So it is that major hotel chains such as Marriott, Hilton, Sheraton and Radisson have moved into timeshare, as indeed has the Walt Disney Organisation with its Disney Vacation Club at Walt Disney World in Orlando.

Marriott is now one of the largest sellers of timeshare in the world, estimated to have sold $160 million in 1993. Hilton Hotels is now developing a series of hotel-related timeshare resorts in the USA, under the banner of the Hilton Grand Vacations Club. The first of these is a purpose-built timeshare resort next to its existing hotel and casino properties in Las Vegas.

Europe

Europe is the second-largest market area in the world for timeshare sales. The European timeshare business had its roots in Britain, since the English-speaking entrepreneurs who started the boom sold mostly to British holidaymakers in the Canary Islands. The Canaries certainly still contain the highest concentration of timeshare development in Europe.

The largest number of European timeshare owners is British, but other markets in Europe are now growing rapidly.

Germany is Europe's second-largest market after Britain. The size of the population and its propensity for travel and holidays make this a fertile marketplace—though growth has been somewhat slowed in recent years owing to economic and political circumstances.

A welcome resurgence in the long-established French and Italian markets over the past three years has seen a significant increase in timeshare resorts in both countries—though the French are showing a greater inclination than before to buy in traditional holiday areas such as Spain.

Spain itself saw phenomenal growth in domestic timeshare ownership from 1990 to 1992, with the number of owners escalating from 3000 families in 1990 to 23 000 by the end of 1992. The trend has been similar, though less dramatic, in Portugal and a domestic market is emerging in Greece. The Scandinavian markets have been hit by severe recession and have not realised their potential, but smaller markets like Switzerland and Austria are showing promise.

As in the USA, well-known names are giving credibility to the business in Europe: Barratt in the UK; the giant Metro group in Germany, known for its chain of cash-and-carry stores as well as its wide-ranging investments in European tourism; France's Club Méditerranée; the Banco Bilbao Vizcaya in Spain (a recent entrant into the business); the Berlusconi group in Italy; and the giant Sol hotel group in Spain, which has announced that it is to begin its entry into the timeshare market through two of its Melia resort hotels.

New opportunities for further growth of the timeshare business are appearing with the liberalisation of the various countries forming Eastern Europe. A number of marketing companies are already selling Spanish and Canary Islands timeshare weeks to East Germans, Hungarians and Poles—and even to residents of the former Soviet Union. What is more, timeshare resorts are being developed in these countries: a new resort is being planned in Moscow; several are coming on-stream in Hungary. Turkey is another country with huge potential, given its population of 60 million, including a well-off middle class, and its increasingly important role in European tourism.

South Africa

Timeshare has been popular in South Africa for many years and this is therefore one of the maturer markets. The penetration of eligible households rate is high.

Despite that fact, and despite political and economic uncertainty, sales are still being achieved at a reasonable rate, with a turnover of $60 million in 1993.

The image of the industry has improved markedly since the introduction by the self-regulatory Timeshare Institute of South Africa (TISA) of a five-day cooling-off period which came into force on 7 October 1992. This has had the effect of reducing the level of presure by sales people on consumers without affecting sales dramatically.

New resort development is now slow. RCI affiliated five new timeshare resorts in 1993 and expects a similar trend to continue during the first half of 1994 when a number of new developments are expected to come on-stream, particularly in the area of the Western Cape, where demand exceeds supply some two and a half times over.

Latin America

Having spread to Mexico in the mid-1970s, as American holidaymakers in Mexican resorts proved willing buyers, timeshare in Central and South America is at last taking off in a number of countries. Mexicans themselves have discovered the concept, to the extent that some 125 000 Mexican families are owners (Ragatz Associates, 1992a). About 50% of the available tourist beds in Cancun are now timeshared and the Mexican Ministry of Tourism has recognised timeshare as an important contributor to the national economy.

As buying power recovers in the rest of South America, its sheer size means huge openings for timeshare. By the end of 1992, Latin America had nearly 500 timeshare projects, with significant developments in Argentina, Venezuela, Brazil and Chile. The development curve is currently much steeper than in the early years: Venezuela has developed 60 timeshare projects in five years while it took Mexico 13 years to reach the same total. Mexico now sells more than 100 000 weeks a year and Venezuela almost quadrupled its annual rate of sales between 1990 and 1992 from 13 000 to 50 000 weeks. There are now timeshare projects in Peru, Costa Rica, Uruguay and Chile and projects are under consideration in Ecuador and Columbia.

Asia Pacific

The last link in timeshare's global chain of active leisure markets is the Asia Pacific region. This developing region has, since the late 1980s, seen a tremendous growth in leisure spending and tourism, and timeshare ownership and resort development is expected to follow the wave of tourism growth as it has in other markets.

The market for timeshare in Asia is still very new, but many feel it is ready to grow rapidly as one of the 'hot' new timeshare markets for the future. Timeshare resort growth (outside of Japan and Australia) will have doubled annually during the last two years as demand for resorts in or close to key urban destinations, such as Singapore, Bangkok and Hong Kong, or well-established holiday locations, such as Bali, is being driven by both existing timeshare owners in Europe, the Americas, Japan and Australia and the growing affluence of indigenous travellers.

Unlike the other markets of the world, Asia Pacific is already seeing more sophisticated companies and hotels participating during the early growth stages. On the other hand, the condominium developer is still able to sell all he can build in a very active and speculative real-estate market. The growing middle class in east and south Asia will continue to fuel this region for many years to come.

Australia, which led timeshare growth through the 1980s is currently showing little progress on account of the recession there and high administrative costs related to strict regulation. Australian developers and industry specialists are looking towards Indonesia as a new frontier and catalyst for timeshare growth in Bali and Jakarta.

India

India is potentially one of the world's biggest timeshare markets, since some 20 million households have been identified as eligible buyers. In addition, it is expected that a number of non-resident Indians, such as those living in the Gulf area, Europe and the USA, will be interested in buying timeshare in their home country.

India's first timeshare resort was opened at Kodaikanal in 1988, by Sterling Holiday Resorts Ltd of Madras. The same company now has nine resorts with eight more planned by 1995. In the past year, around 10–12 new companies have emerged in various parts of the country. Those wishing to enter the holiday timeshare market include some well-known names in the Indian business world, such as Oberoi hotels and Mahindra Holdings.

Views of tourism organisations

A fundamental justification of the planned growth of the tourism industry is its ability to stimulate local economies. This objective is especially true of the timeshare industry.

The World Tourism Organisation and many national tourism organisations around the world recognise the contribution which timeshare is making to the tourism economy of many countries. The benefits of timeshare have been acknowledged by the National tourist bodies of

Spain, Portugal, Greece and France. In addition, the head of tourism at the European Commission has publicly demonstrated his support for the industry, recognising how timeshare helps to meet the objectives of his unit in terms of quality of tourism, extension of the traditional season and the higher economic stimulus compared to traditional holiday products.

Economic benefits

A considerable amount of research has been carried out, all of which demonstrates that timeshare has a positive economic effect in the areas where resorts are developed, creating jobs in both the construction and operational phases of resort building and attracting to the area relatively affluent and high-spending visitors throughout the extended season.

The financial contribution made by timeshare developments to their local economies includes sales of timeshare, maintenance fees, local taxes, the purchase of travel facilities and the payroll on-site. The developments create permanent full- and part-time jobs on-site, and temporary jobs are created in the community.

A review of timeshare in Europe, commissioned towards the end of 1993 by the European Timeshare Federation (Lifestyle, 1993), concluded that 700 000 European owners of timeshare generate some £387 million a year in visitor revenue, and that the timeshare industry sustains at least 20 000 full-time equivalent jobs in Europe.

A report carried out for the then Canary Islands Timeshare Resorts Association (Ernst & Young, 1990) demonstrated clearly the economic benefits of timeshare to the islands, both in terms of expenditure in development of the timeshare units and of expenditure in the islands by timeshare owners. The report showed a total investment in construction of 67 273 million pesetas (£373m); in promotion and advertising of 79 850 million pesetas (£443m) and a visitor spend of 25 152 million pesetas (£139m).

The report showed that 239 550 households purchased timeshare properties in the Canary Islands; the average number of families owning timeshare intervals in each unit was 30 (some would own more than one week). Given that the size of the party using the timeshare interval on each occasion was at least 2.5, that means some 598 875 timeshare visitors travelled to the Canary Islands in 1990.

Owners in northern England resorts spend some £714 per annum on their timeshare holiday (Ernst & Young, 1991). From this beginning, Ernst & Young went on to say,

around 42 000 timeshare holidays are taken in British resorts annually, generating almost £30 million of visitor expenditure. Applying conventional multipliers, under which one full-time equivalent job is created for every £20 000 of expenditure, this implies that timeshare sustains 1500 full-time equivalent jobs in this country. However, this takes no account of the jobs created as a result of the initial injection of spending arising from the purchase price paid for the timeshare unit, which amounted to £6380 on average in the north of England. We estimate that over the past ten years this has added a further 13 400 full-time equivalent jobs which can be associated with British timeshare resorts, and that on current growth trends this figure will increase by a further 3000 jobs a year as a result of new owners buying in new and existing British resorts during the remainder of the decade. On this basis, timeshare would be responsible for supporting up to 50 000 full-time equivalent jobs in Britain by the year 2000.

In California, the timeshare industry generated about 1.2 million room nights of occupancy in 1991, involving about 515 000 occupants; was responsible for 6735 full- and part-time jobs and $91 500 of expenditures per unit (Ragatz Associates, 1992b).

The Canadian economy benefits from timeshare to the tune of $124 000 of expenditures per unit and 4872 full- and part-time jobs (Ragatz Associates, 1993a). In Puerto Vallarta, Mexico, a contribution of $241 000 of expenditures per unit plus 3950 jobs are attributable to timeshare (Ragatz Associates, 1993b).

Extending the season

Most timeshare resorts (except in Italy which generally has relatively short summer and winter seasons) sell 50 weeks of timeshare throughout the year, therefore ensuring visitor levels year-round.

Even if the owner is unable to take up the option of using his week's ownership, or wishes to travel elsewhere, the exchange system, like that operated by RCI, ensures that a timeshare owner from elsewhere will probably come and use the accommodation.

Ragatz Associates' studies of Mexico, California, Hawaii and Canada show that the number of repeat visits made to a destination by timeshare owners is significantly greater than for other forms of holiday.

Within the UK, the even distribution of timeshare occupancy levels exceeds 70%. This compares favourably with serviced accommodation (hotels have barely exceeded 60% in the 1990s) and is much greater than self-catering accommodation (where second-home occupancy rates are around 10–15% per annum).

In the maturer US market, timeshare occupancy rates exceed 85% (Miner, 1987). These higher occupancy rates are especially beneficial in traditional resort and holiday areas, as opposed to urban locations, because of the reduction in the seasonality of local employment.

The peak season is also extended. Timeshare developments in capital cities can have 100% year-round occupancy levels. In England, 68% of resorts have a peak season running in the five summer months of May to September inclusive; and in Scotland the pattern is the same, with over half of resorts having an additional two and a half months between February and mid-April for skiing.

A study of timeshare-related tourism in Malta (Dean, 1993) shows the effect of timeshare development on the island's tourism statistics, both in terms of increasing visitor numbers and of extending the usual summer high season into a five-month shoulder season, together with an active winter season. Tourist arrivals to the island rose from 746 000 in 1987 to over 1 million in 1992, an increase of 34%, and occupancy levels rose to 70% following the conversion of several of the island's hotels to timeshare.

The same author identifies similar benefits in Mexico where the stay of Mexican hotel visitors in most coastal destinations averages about 3.5 nights and that of a foreign visitor four to five nights. Timeshare, with a typical minimum guest's stay of seven nights, produces an extension to the average tourist's stay and the prospect of repeat visits.

A further study of Mexico, specifically of Puerto Vallarta (Ragatz Associates, 1993b) concluded that average occupancy of timeshare accommodation was 75% compared with 46% for the local hotel industry. Similar studies showed occupancy rates in Canada of 80% and in California of 82%.

Improving the quality of accommodation

Timeshare developments are usually built to a higher specification than most other types of tourist accommodation. They are often built in secluded areas and are designed to blend in with the local countryside. Environmentally, one timeshare unit used for 25–50 weeks during the year is less damaging than the 10–20 holiday homes that would be required to meet the same demand on a whole-ownership basis.

Research shows that consistent quality of accommodation is an important reason for buying and is a factor which is becoming increasingly important to the sophisticated consumer.

It has been acknowledged that a timeshare is probably the most expensive item that many families would buy after a house and a car. They therefore expect to receive value for money, often manifested in the quality of the accommodation, the location and setting and the overall facilities.

Timeshare developers, owners' committees and the exchange organisations all have a long-term interest in maintaining the quality of resorts, not only to protect the values of the initial investment but also to ensure ongoing access to the flexibility of the exchange system.

At RCI, requests are matched for holiday exchange accommodation on the basis of the quality of the holiday weeks deposited by the timeshare owner. It is clear that an owner at a top-quality resort will tend to get top-quality exchanges, while owners at more modest resorts would receive exchanges of an equivalent quality.

RCI operates a sophisticated system of customer feedback to monitor the quality of its affiliated resorts and to encourage the pursuit of the highest possible standards.

On returning home from an exchange holiday, RCI's customers (they are 'members' of RCI's holiday club) are asked to complete questionnaires, rating the resort they have just stayed in across a number of key factors: check in/out; hospitality; quality of unit; quality of resort; and housekeeping. All the data is analysed and a set of monthly ratings derived for each resort affiliated to RCI. These ratings are sent to the resorts for their use in quality control.

The company's 'resort recognition programme' results in the conferring of awards—'Gold Crown Resort' or 'Resort of International Distinction'—on those resorts which consistently receive the most positive feedback from RCI members who have stayed there on exchange visits.

Legislation

Recognising the growth and impact of timeshare, a number of jurisdictions have enacted, or are about to enact, legislation to embrace the timeshare concept.

The entrepreneurial spirit which has done so much to advance the rapid growth of timeshare has also led in certain instances to unacceptable practices, particularly regarding sales and marketing. It is this, rather than any unsatisfactory aspect of the product itself, which has tarnished the name of timeshare in many parts of the world. It is therefore these practices which legislation has sought to tackle in the interest of consumer protection.

The seminal consumer protection legislation was the Florida law, introduced by the State of Florida in 1983 shortly after the timeshare industry became established and used as a model by almost every other US state. This landmark legislation, regarded as draconian, included provision for a mandatory 'cooling-off period' of 14 days, during which the prospective purchaser can cancel the purchase agreement.

In Europe, the picture is mixed according to jurisdiction, with the European Union awaiting, at the time of writing, a directive which will govern the sale of timeshare in all EU countries. The draft directive includes the basic principles of a cooling-off period after purchase and a restriction or ban on the acceptance of cash deposits during the cooling-off period. In the short term, the directive when implemented is likely to dampen sales volumes for a while. However, timeshare has proved itself to be an infinitely adaptable business and there can be no doubt that companies will come to terms with the new legislative parameters in the marketplace, provided that the final legislation is reasonable and well-balanced. The current 13 national timeshare trade associations throughout Europe have formed the European Timeshare Federation (ETF) which has been putting the industry's case to the authorities in Brussels.

A further measure which will affect many jurisdictions is planned legislation in the Isle of Man. Many timeshare resorts in Europe selling under the 'club trustee' legal structure, of which there are about 200, are governed by Isle of Man law because the trusts used for this effective consumer protection vehicle are based in the Isle of Man. A new bill expected in autumn 1994 will also incorporate a cooling-off period and a limit on deposits as well as measures relating to the provision of consumer finance. It is likely that the Isle of Man government will keep the provisions of their law in line with those of the EU directive.

Most European countries currently do not have specific laws covering the sale and operation of timeshare. In these jurisdictions, developers, and all of those connected with the industry, find their own ways to reconcile the legal aspects of their projects with any existing laws on the sale of property.

In France, ineffective legislation has tended to stunt the growth of the business to some extent. In Austria, Switzerland and Denmark the law prevents land or property ownership—and therefore timeshare ownership— by non-nationals. The timeshare industry in Denmark is lobbying the government to halt this restriction, which would open up new opportunities for the otherwise stagnant timeshare market. In Austria, a review of this particular piece of legislation also looks likely.

In Spain—a major market for European timeshare resorts sold to a range of nationalities—a draft law to regulate timeshare sales has been in the hands of the Ministry of Tourism for some time, but is unlikely to be passed in advance of the EU directive.

A stringent new Portuguese timeshare law was passed in August 1993. Long and complex, it is aimed both at curbing hard-sell techniques and at dealing with the financial problems of some major Portuguese resorts. Unfortunately, it had the instant effect of severely curtailing timeshare sales. The likely future consequence of this legislation could be to halve the number of new resorts able to undertake timeshare development.

In the UK, a Timeshare Act came into force in October 1992, introducing a mandatory cooling-off period of 14 days—and virtually nothing else. While the industry as a whole acknowledges the need for a cooling-off period to curb the worst excesses of the hard sell, 14 days is thought to be unnecessarily long. The UK Act singularly failed to protect the consumer in any other way, such as by insisting on full disclosure to the purchaser of the exact nature of the timeshare week being purchased.

It is inevitable that the introduction of legislation will put a brake on growth for a period. In some cases, those sales people active in markets which become regulated move out and go elsewhere; Eastern Europe, for example, currently provides rich pastures. In other cases, the growth of the timeshare business will slow down considerably. A report for the European Timeshare Federation found that the sales volume in the UK timeshare industry was halved in the first 12 months after the introduction of the Timeshare Act, with cancellation rates increasing two- to three-fold and only a handful of the previous 60 off-site sales offices still doing business.

Further potential for growth

Despite certain misgivings concerning the effect of legislation in Europe in the short term, there is no significant factor in sight which would seriously dampen the growth of timeshare sales on a global basis within the foreseeable future. The significance of the timeshare industry is increasing rapidly and the trend is set to continue around the world. In the next few years, analysts believe that timeshare may grow up to 10 times faster than the tourism industry as a whole.

A report carried out in the UK for RCI (Henley Centre, 1993) identified a number of socio-economic trends, including trends in the pattern of holiday-taking, which bode well for the future of timeshare. The report forecasts a modest recovery of consumer spending in the 1990s, with spending on leisure likely to grow slightly faster than consumer spending as a whole. A more numerous, active and affluent group of people aged 45-plus will also have the advantage of being the first generation to benefit in any general sense from inheritances resulting from the fact that their parents were property owners.

Furthermore, the report points out that holidaymakers will be taking more initiative in organising their holidays, seeking more excitement as well as benefiting from longer holiday entitlement.

In 1990, Projection 2000 forecast continuing growth for timeshare in the late 1990s, stimulated by more frequent holiday-taking, the maturity of the exchange mechanism, relatively lower air travel costs and the inheritance factor. The same report recognised vast untapped potential across Europe.

RCI has a longer list than ever before of timeshare developers wanting to affiliate new resorts to its exchange programme. A number of untapped markets are emerging within which timeshare is burgeoning: Israel and the Middle East, Eastern European countries, India, South America, the Far East and South-East Asia.

Even within established markets there is astonishing potential for future business. Joachimsthaler's study (1992b) earmarked Germany as one of Europe's most important markets. Predicting a penetration rate of 5% of all German households likely to be interested in owning timeshare, Joachimsthaler estimates that 573 000 households will have bought timeshare in the next 20 years, equivalent to a market value of more than 11 billion DM. In the short term, recession and the economic problems associated with German reunification have meant that the rate of growth has slowed over the past year. Nevertheless, the long-term outlook for Germany remains strong. Economic difficulties aside, reunification has significantly increased the total potential.

Growth in France will be slower (Joachimsthaler, 1992a) but still significant, with an estimated 260 000 new French owners likely to buy timeshare over a 20-year period.

The UK market is expected to be worth some £385 million per annum in new sales by 1997 (Mintel Leisure Intelligence, 1993).

The growth of various European markets means that the dominance of the UK is gradually declining as the business matures and growth becomes slower while other markets in Europe catch up.

The advent of new products, bringing greater flexibility to the industry, will further increase future business levels. 'Classic' timeshare has to date been handled in one-week fractions. However, with the trend in the holiday market moving more towards short breaks—long weekends and mid-week breaks—there is some demand for a system of 'holiday points'. By buying groups of points instead of units of time, timeshare owners are able to decide how many days' holiday to take at any one time, and are able to trade up or down in both size of unit and season, by 'spending' more or fewer of the points they have purchased. Points systems have been in place in South Africa since 1987, operating a variety of flexi-swap, re-packaged weeks, multi-ownership and resort ownership systems.

Such systems will lend themselves particularly well to hotel groups, several of which have already been mentioned. There is no doubt that the entry of these well-established companies into the timeshare business is important both for the image of timeshare and for future timeshare development.

It is very likely that several other major hospitality companies will enter the timeshare business in the next five years. Nor is there any doubt that these international companies will extend their timeshare product to other parts of the world in due course.

Further prospects are being created as an ever-wider range of companies enter timeshare: banks, financial services companies, industrial conglomerates, media companies and a pension fund are just a few of the sectors which have taken on timeshare interests in the recent past.

The business of timeshare has already proved itself not just resilient to recession but particularly able to adapt to crisis. The flexibility of the business means it can be a source of solutions to problems in other areas. Consequently, many new timeshare developers now entering the business are doing so because they cannot sell their holiday developments for whole ownership or because their hotels are in a distressed state.

Despite worldwide recession, timeshare has proved that there is always a market for the right sort of holiday product, especially since there is a growing tendency in the mind of the customer to regard holidays not as a luxury but as a necessity.

The one fact which is likely to restrict growth in Europe in the short term is the advent of new legislation in the European Union (Henley Centre, 1993). But there is little doubt that the industry will adapt to the new climate and will forge ahead after a period of readjustment.

In other parts of the world, the possibilities are virtually endless. Timeshare is clearly a force which is changing the way many people plan their holidays. It is improving the quality of holidays and therefore increasing consumers' expectations. As it continues to grow, so the influence of this extraordinary business on the rest of tourism will increasingly be felt.

References

Dean, Paul (1993) 'Timesharing opportunities for the hotel sector', *Travel & Tourism Analyst*, Economist Intelligence Unit, London.

Ernst & Young (1990) 'Economic study of the activity of timesharing in the Canary Islands', Santa Cruz de Tenerife.

Ernst & Young (1991) 'The financial and economic impact of timeshare', London.

Henley Centre, The (1993) 'Attitudes to timeshare and future prospects for the timeshare industry', London.

Joachimsthaler, Erich (1992a) 'Timeshare a pre-competitive analysis of the French market', Alza Ltd, Barcelona.

Joachimsthaler, Erich (1992b) 'Tourism and timeshare: a pre-competitive analysis of the German market', Alza Ltd, Barcelona.

Lifestyle Marketing Associates (1993) 'A report on the likely effect of certain regulations resulting from the proposed EC legislation regarding timeshare', Surrey.

Miner (1987) 'Timesharing in the USA', *Travel & Tourism Analyst*, Economist Intelligence Unit, London.

Mintel Leisure Intelligence (1993) 'Report on timeshare', London.

Ragatz Associates (1992a) 'An annual report of the worldwide timesharing industry', Eugene, Oregon.

Ragatz Associates (1992b) 'The resort timeshare industry in California', Eugene, Oregon.

Ragatz Associates (1993a) 'The resort timeshare industry in Canada', Eugene, Oregon.

Ragatz Associates (1993b) 'The resort timeshare industry in Puerto Vallarta', Eugene, Oregon.

25 Sports stadia and arenas: the sleeping giants of tourism

T. STEVENS

Introduction

Sports stadia and arenas are increasingly being recognised as a fundamental feature of urban or regional regeneration with significant touristic potential and importance. The realisation of the stadium as a tourism asset is primarily founded upon the economic impact generated by regular sporting occasions and, more recently by the hosting of mega-events, such as the Olympic Games or Superbowl (Weiller and Hall, 1992; Hall, 1992). In addition, Stevens (1992) used the Annual CHRIE Conference in Orlando to launch the concept of the Stadium as 'The Sleeping Giant of Tourism'—a giant capable of realising its inherent potential through the development of an integrated sporting visitor attraction, a more sophisticated version of the traditional Sports Hall of Fame (Redmond, 1991; Balliet et al., 1993).

The importance of the stadium's contribution to enhancing a city's image to attract tourists and corporate business investment, or relocation, has been examined in detail by Petersen (1990) and Lipsitz (1984). More recently, Kitchen (1994) analysed the potential contribution that the new Olympic Stadium would make in reshaping Manchester's tourism prospects, advancing the traditional economic perspective discussed by Hall (1992) and Bale (1989).

The stadium is becoming more readily integrated and accepted as a fundamental component of the leisure industry in general. Although we have been building stadia for over 2000 years the historical and primary focus of attention has been upon the design and function of the building rather than upon its management. Ancient Greece is credited with the construction of the first significant arena with a grandstand for a sporting event at Olympia between 400 and 300 BC. Indeed, Fletcher in *A History of Architecture on the Comparative Method* describes the structure and reminds us that the word 'stadium' is derived from an ancient Greek name for a footrace observed by spectators.

Inglis, an advocate of a creative approach to the design of the sports stadia, in his paper 'New directions in stadium design' (1993), which was published to accompany the 'Making a Stand' exhibition held in London (1993) and Swansea (1994), writes of stadia, 'great buildings demand even greater vision'. This refers to the opportunity for stadia to be fully embraced as part of the leisure industry.

'Making a Stand' exhibition reflects upon the societal influences shaping the design and place of stadia in our communities. The classically inspired, often multipurpose venue of continental countries producing inspiring landmarks and civic centrepieces is compared with the single-use, pre-defined model that typifies British stadia.

Inglis (1993) speculates that this lack of tradition, or appreciation of the stadium, may stem from the fact that sport in Britain evolved facilities based upon existing sports grounds. There is no history of stadium development. He says, 'The Romans did not bequeath to these islands a significant amphitheatre, circus or hippodrome. Britain had no stadium as at Olympia or Delphi, no Colosseum as in Rome, no arena as in Arles, Nimes or Verona'. He goes on to point out that under Napoleon's instructions a 30 000 capacity arena was designed for Milan by Luigi Canonica. Significantly, and ironically, these historic stadia are vital components of the tourist industry in their regions (see, for example, Luciani (1990)).

If contemporary and new stadia are to realise their inherent tourism potential, management becomes as critical as the original design. There is a growing recognition, however, that the management of the stadium or arena is an essential prerequisite if the enormous capital and real-estate asset of the facility is to be realised (Lipsitz, 1984). Stadia must be regarded as a microcosm of the hospitality industry in general, reflecting most of the trends in the socio-cultural leisure environment. They are rapidly becoming multi-faceted complexes hosting a diversity of events that involve a wide range of hospitality services and management skills. Arguably only theme parks involve such a broad range of management inputs (Stevens, 1993).

The importance of integrating management considerations within the design process was recognised in 1956 by Homer T. Borton, the president of the Osborn Engineering Company and one of the world's foremost designers of ballparks. He wrote in the *Consulting Engineer Magazine* of the need for ingenious stadium design to recognise that in the years to come 'the people [who visit ballparks] will be the same but with new and different wants which must be satisfied' (Borton, 1956). Lowry (1992), in his compendium of ballparks, *Green Cathedrals*, described as 'the ultimate celebration of 273 ball parks in North America', discusses the inadequacies of stadium management in the mid-1950s. He says, 'Amenities were certainly sparse by today's standards. Limited concession menus, long waits in toilet lines, stiff hard chairs or bleacher seats, and sudden downpours were expected'. Ironically what Lowry describes for the 1950s in North America would provide a suitable picture for stadia in Europe 30 years later.

For Lowry the radical liberalisation of the 1960s brought the social–cultural changes which heralded in the new 'needs and wants' predicted by Borton. These factors of change spawned a new generation of stadium. This was a trend repeated with the onset of the 1990s and the realisation that appropriately located, designed and managed stadia were capable of achieving dramatic positive impacts for a community.

Borton's recognition of the need for market orientation accepted that stadia were special places that had to capture the spirit of the event and provide the stage upon which *heroes* could create the *legends*. The technocrats (architects and engineers) as well as those charged with achieving commercial viability (managers and marketers) had to accept that the hardware solutions to most public demands for safety and comfort were founded upon less tangible, or mechanistic, aspects of 'going to the ball park' . . . atmosphere, sense of occasion, evocation, emotion. Indeed, the essential fabric recaptured in Director Phil Alden Robinson's 1989 film, *A Field of Dreams* and Costner's portrayal of *Bull Durham* in the film of the same name. This testimony to the 'sense of place' that transcends these cathedrals of sport has been reflected in a new genre of sports literature in Britain. Tom Watt's (1993) story of the heritage of the North Bank at Arsenal's Highbury Stadium in London, and the best-selling chronicle of the life of a soccer spectator by Hornby (1992) detail the essence of the stadia.

The magnitude of the challenge facing stadia managers is becoming apparent. In essence, the need to adopt a strategic overview of the potential of the facility to contribute to broad economic and physical planning whilst at the same time meeting aesthetic, comfort, and amenity objectives at an operational level. Furthermore, the bottom line is primarily that of sustaining an environment within which the anchor sport(s) can perform successfully.

In 1993, for example, the Cardiff Arms Park, hosted three International World Cup Soccer matches, three 50 000 capacity pop concerts (including U2, the Rolling Stones and Phil Collins), and the Bruno–Lewis heavyweight world title fight. It is estimated that this range of activity contributed in excess of £52 million to the local economy. The host governing body, the Welsh Rugby Union, remains unequivocal, however, that the maintenance of the 'hallowed' turf for rugby football remains the pre-eminent objective when programming multiple use, and despite the commercial imperatives.

The revival of the Olympic Movement in 1896, the growth of spectator sports generally, and the development of media interest in sporting events gave impetus to stadia development in Europe and the USA in the 1890s. This heralded the start of a century of stadium development and evolution. It is possible to identify, at least, five clearly defined eras of stadia development over the past 100 years. Whilst the actual chronology of the eras varies on each side of the Atlantic, the sequence remains constant. The stages of evolution reflecting Borton's changing wants and needs and the evolution of major league sports as populist spectator events.

The tracking of the five eras in the evolution of the modern sports stadium and arena is possible via a number of key sources, particularly the documentation produced by *Panstadia* (quarterly), Lowry (1992), Twydell (1993), Inglis (1987, 1990), and Neilsen (1986). For the purposes of this paper, examples of each era are drawn from North America:

(1) *The classic ballpark*
    Neighbourhood focus, dedicated single sporting activity, basic and limited range of amenities for spectators, groundsmanship key management task, e.g. Forbes Field (1909), Griffith Stadium (1911), Tiger Stadium (1912) and Wrigley Field (1914).

(2) *The modernist super stadium*
    Greenfield or out-of-town locations, dramatic visual presentation of design, accommodating a range of events and sports, commercial/funding demands reflected in sponsors' boxes, increased attention to spectator safety and comfort, tendency to be soulless places for the spectator and the sportsman, e.g. Candlestick Park (1960), RKF (1962), The Astrodome (1965), Busch Stadium (1966) and the Riverfront Stadium (1970).

(3) *The neo-classical ballpark*
    Post-modernist recognition of the strengths of the classic stadium, an attempt to combine the quality

and amenity requirements of the late 1980s with the features of the early parks, e.g. Comiskey Field, Camden Yards, and the Arlington Stadium.

(4) *The regenerated stadium*

Generally category (2) parks which are receiving a secondary phase of investment to upgrade, thereby accommodating new sports (such as soccer for World Cup USA '94) or multiple events to enhance viability (such as exhibitions, fairs or concerts), e.g. Citrus Bowl in Orlando, Rosebowl in Los Angeles, Meadowlands in New York.

(5) *The millennium stadia*

Multipurpose venues based upon innovative design and sophisticated management in which every traditional assumption about stadia is challenged (see later), embraces the qualities and strengths inherent in the three previous eras and produces an environment that is managed for high-quality leisure experiences, e.g. Skydome in Toronto, the Olympic Stadium and Georgia Dome in Atlanta, and the American West Area in Phoenix.

The innovative characteristics of each era were provoked by a complex interaction of market, technical and socio-economic variables, many of which transcend the entire spectrum of leisure provision. These include: personal mobility; disposable income; sports participation, trends and fashions; quality of experience and, implicitly, of safety and comfort. They also reflect (i) the geography of franchise sale and purchase arrangements, (ii) the politics of stadium ownership, (iii) city aspirations to be recognised as a vibrant, significant place, (iv) the felicitations of broadcast media, and (v) the exceptional demands of the growing number of global mega-events (such as Superbowl, the Olympic Games, and World Cup Soccer).

An essential feature of a city's ability to host one of the 105 major league teams (see Table 25.1), or, indeed, a primary sporting event or festival, is the provision of modern, high-capacity stadia and arenas. The economic rewards inherent in major sporting activities in a city (Bale, 1989; Getz, 1992) have stimulated considerable development in facilities throughout the USA over the past 20 years. The public sector has recognised the added value of investment in stadia and accept that they can rarely be expected to make a profit (Herbert, 1992) but accept that the political risk involved is outweighed by wider economic gains to the community.

There is increasing recognition amongst municipal and state governments that new facility development, or re-financing to upgrade an existing facility, is essential in attracting or retaining a major league sport. Interest in

stadia product development is, therefore, considerable. Stadia development allied to inter-regional franchise redistribution is spawning new facilities and encouraging the relocation. Stadia and arenas are being used as a catalyst for urban regeneration or sub-regional economic development (via mixed facility complexes in suburban locations). The 'new' stadia are also potent visual images and landscape features contributing to positive destination imagery, considered so essential in tourism destination planning and marketing (Gunn, 1988). The Olympic Cities of Barcelona (1992), Atlanta (1996) and Sydney (2000) are fully exploiting these linkages. Indianapolis is, on a more modest scale, also trading on this potential (Indianapolis Chamber of Commerce, 1992).

As Lipsitz (1984) has identified: 'The mass popularity of sports and the close relationship between civic identity and local teams makes the construction of sports facilities an important tool for promoting public and private spending aimed at solving the problems of civic development'. These sentiments are particularly well expressed in the Indianapolis example (see above).

The growth in the popularity of sports has led to increased attendances over the past decade in the USA. In the period 1980 to 1990 attendances at baseball, football, basketball and hockey have increased by 25.7%, 25.4%, 62.8% and 32.3% respectively (NSGA, 1993) as can be seen from Table 25.2. It should be recognised, however, that the US population has a narrower range of sporting interest with a wide cross-section following and participating in fewer sports (NSGA, 1993). In the UK attendances at sporting events has similarly increased over the past 5 years despite a significant decline in the mid-1980s (see later).

Professional sports leagues have long-term strategic reasons for expansion, particularly in terms of adding to their fan base and building national TV ratings, both of which create revenues. The growth in the number of teams, major sporting events and attendance levels has spurred interest in renovating or developing modern facilities—facilities which have to address the comfort, amenity and safety requirements of the spectators as well as the physical demands of multiple use.

As a result of this research, it is estimated that there exist in the USA between 86 and 90 stadiums for professional sports teams (excluding arenas used for professional motor racing and horseracing and amateur track and field or swimming). This represents 4% of the total of 2223 multi-use facilities used by not only professional teams but also college sides, and minor league teams. Herbert (1993) estimates there to be 25 to 35 cities actively involved in building or refinancing a major facility, representing a financing market of $15 billion (see Table 25.3).

Table 25.1 *Distribution of major league sport franchises in the USA, 1988*

1984 population rank	Metropolitan area	1984 population (in thousands)	Franchises 1988				
			Baseball	Hockey	Basketball	Football	Total
1	New York	17807	2	3	2	2	9
2	Los Angeles	12373	2	1	2	2	7
3	Chicago	8035	2	1	1	1	5
4	Philadelphia	5755	1	1	1	1	4
5	San Francisco	5688	2	—	1	1	4
6	Detroit	4577	1	1	1	1	4
7	Boston	4027	1	1	1	—	3
8	Houston	3566	1	—	1	1	3
9	Washington	3427	—	1	1	1	3
10	Dallas–Ft. Worth	3348	1	—	1	1	3
11	Miami	2799	—	—	—	1	1
12	Cleveland	2788	1	—	1	1	3
13	St Louis	2398	1	1	—	1[a]	3
14	Atlanta	2380	1	—	1	1	3
15	Pittsburgh	2372	1	1	—	1	3
16	Baltimore	2245	1	—	—	1	2
17	Minneapolis	2231	1	1	—	1	3
18	Seattle	2208	1	—	1	1	3
19	San Diego	2064	1	—	1	1	3
20	Tampa	1811	—	—	—	1	1
21	Denver	1791	—	—	1	1	2
22	Phoenix	1715	—	—	1	—[a]	1
23	Cincinnati	1674	1	—	—	1	2
24	Milwaukee	1568	1	—	1	—	2
25	Kansas City	1477	1	—	—	1	2
26	Portland	1341	—	—	1	—	1
27	New Orleans	1319	—	—	—	1	1
28	Columbus	1279	—	—	—	—	—
29	Norfolk	1261	—	—	—	—	—
30	Sacramento	1220	—	—	1	—	1
31	Buffalo	1205	—	1	—	1	2
32	Indianapolis	1195	—	—	1	1	2
33	San Antonio	1187	—	—	1	—	1
34	Providence	1095	—	—	—	—	—
35	Charlotte	1,031	—	—	—	—	—
36	Hartford	1030	—	1	—	—	1
37	Salt Lake City	1025	—	—	1	—	1
	Totals		24	14	23	27[b]	

[a]In 1988 the Cardinals moved from St Louis to Phoenix.
[b]The football total does not include Green Bay (Packers).

The Urban Land Institute of America suggests that the majority of this new interest in large facility development is public-sector-focused. Public-sector projects representing 56 (65%) of the 86 identified earlier (see Table 25.4).

Table 25.2 *Attendance at major league sports in the USA, 1980–1990 (millions)*

	Baseball 162 games	Football 16 games	Basketball 82 games	Hockey 80 games
1980	43.7	14.1	10.7	10.5
1985	47.7	14.1	11.5	11.6
1990	54.9	17.7	17.4	13.9

Table 25.3 *Total finance market, USA, 1992*

(a) Size of US multipurpose area market
Number of professional facilities ($ billions)

Existing and projected	New	Existing re-finance	Total
59	$1.5	$4.4	$5.7

(b) Size of US domestic stadium market
Number of professional facilities ($ billions)

	Existing or projected	New	Existing	Total
	57	$2.5	$7.7	$10.2
Total	116	$4.0	$12.1	$15.9

Table 25.4 *The ownership of stadia and arenas (compiled from various sources)*

USA (35 cities)	Stadia		Arenas		Total
	Baseball	Football	Basketball	Hockey	
Public	20	25	7	4	56
Private	5	3	12	10	30
Total	25	28	19	15	86

This impetus has created a range of funding models to produce capital monies. Significantly, in the context of this research, a key feature of sporting finance is the ability to produce (a) contractual sources of finance, and (b) a growing realisation that there are other sources of income to create a revenue stream independent of the actual use of the facility. The concept of a visitor attraction as an inherent feature of a stadium clearly holds potential to contribute to this independent revenue stream as well as adding a facility adding appeal to other 'sales' and market opportunities using the facilities.

The two critical aspects of this new stadium activity is (i) its design and (ii) its management. The economic survival imperative requires stadia designers and operators to understand user demands and to optimise and create new revenue opportunities. Stadium owners cannot tolerate new facilities that are loss-leaders or added cosmetics to an already complex funding equation (Herbert, 1993).

Linked to this aspect is the shift towards the privatisation of the management of facilities. A recent report on privatisation concluded that 85% of state agencies were expecting to introduce privatisation in the next 2–3 years and 95% of the top 24 cities were contracting-out leisure services within excess of 20% of all publicly owned stadia and arena already out to private contractors. Clearly, therefore, arrangements for managing any new attraction within the stadium complex must be a key consideration in the marketing approach. Stadium owners are unlikely to wish to manage the attraction and are likely to prefer to include its operation in the overall contract for the management of the facility.

The past 15 years has, therefore, witnessed a shift in emphasis towards the provision of facilities that are designed *and* managed in a holistic fashion (as implied above). Management interests are now involved in the conceptual and design process. In addition, and most significantly, private sector management organisations have emerged as a major growth sector of the hospitality industry. These include a number of US-based market leaders who are now active in a global context and include: Ogden Entertainment Services, ARA and SMG.

Similarly, a new generation of stadia designers has emerged which is sympathetic to and actively embrace a managerial inputs. Leading the field are a clutch of American companies, notably Ellerbe Becket (Missouri), the Olympus Group (N. Carolina), and the Hellmuth Obata and Kassabaum Sports Facilities Group. Not surprisingly, the need for professional representation and recognition of the stadia management business has stimulated a number of professional bodies (see Table 25.5). It is worth noting, however, that two or three of the main US representative bodies were founded in the first quarter of the century. Significantly, those funding and financing current stadia investment welcome the recognition of management expertise and involvement (Herbert, 1993).

The importance of appropriate management for the new generation of facilities features in the National Football League's schedule of requirements to host Superbowl and in the International Olympic Committee's questions asked of ACOG the Atlanta Organising Committee (Catherwood and Kirk, 1992). It is perhaps surprising to note, however, that key texts on sports facility, or recreation management refer to stadia management (see, for example, Epperson (1986), Horine (1991), and Torkildsen (1993)). Recently, however, leisure industry magazines have begun to include stadia management features (notably *Panstadia International Leisure Management* and *European Sport*).

In Europe there has been a recent (past 10 years) and urgent, need to re-examine the role and place of the stadium

Table 25.5 *The main professional bodies (see* Panstadia, *Vol 1, No. 2, 1993)*

Acronym	Title	Founded	Primary geographic sphere
IAAM	International Association of Auditorium Managers	1924	N. America
IASLF	International Association for Sports and Leisure Facilities	1965	Global
ICMA	International City/County Management Association	1914	N. America
AFDM	Association Facility and Development Management	1992	Europe

Table 25.6 *The post-modernist challenge to traditional assumptions about stadia*

- that they have to be outdoor facilities
- that staging of sport alone is the prime function
- that stadia should be removed from urban centres
- that the target audience is predominantly young/male/cash-paying/interested in the event itself
- that spectators with disabilities cannot be fully or safely accommodated
- that only basic levels of amenities or services are sufficient
- that the stadium is only operational for events or special occasions

in both a spatial and societal context. Although a number of the casual factors requiring this re-evaluation are similar to those occurring in the USA over the past 100 years, several have been provoked by dramatic, often tragic events.

The changing scenario has been created, firstly, by the inheritance of technological advancements from North America—innovations which have been backed by a post-modernist Europe's willingness to accept creative solutions in which every traditional assumption about 'the stadium' is being re-evaluated (see Table 25.6, based upon 'Making a Stand' exhibition in London and Swansea 1993/94).

Second (this as with the first causation, is a global trend) is the momentum discussed earlier created by the desire of cities and countries to host mega-events. Atlanta's preparation of new stadia for the 1996 Olympiad (Delfon, 1993) precipitated similar grand schemes in all prospective host cities for the 2000 Games (Panstadia, 1993) including Manchester's abortive bid (Jorgensen, 1993). Italia '90, the 1990 World Cup Soccer finals, provided Italy with the opportunity to reassess, regenerate and replenish its stock of stadia. The result was the dramatic new chapter in European stadia with the new Stadio Giuseppe Meazza in San Siro, Milan, the Stadio Nuovo Comunale in Turin, and the Stadio Luigi Ferraris in Genoa.

The dramatic development of these, often beautiful, structures provided the backcloth against which a series of tragedies were being enacted in other stadia across Europe—tragedies which highlighted the aged (see Figure 25.1) and decrepit state of repair of many stadia, especially in Britain. The tragedies (see Table 25.7) fatally demonstrated failures to appropriately manage, to provide even basic amenities, and to have more than scant regard for spectator comfort and safety (Lischer, 1992).

The publication of the Taylor Report (see Table 25.7) in 1990 was undoubtedly the single most influential advocacy for a serious review of stadium design and management in Britain. The demand for all-seater stadia

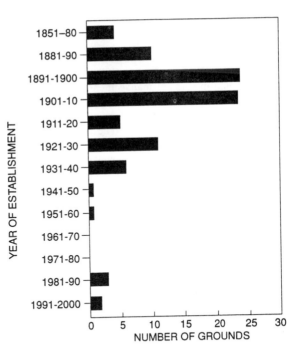

Figure 25.1 *Soccer grounds of Britain—origins as at 5 January 1993*

for crowds in excess of 10 000 by 1994/95 has prompted unprecedented activity in Britain. The report's recommendations have, however, reverberated around the world, calling attention to the issues of customer amenity, safety and comfort.

The requirements to significantly improve spectator comfort, safety and other amenities, especially the need

Table 25.7 *The tragedies at European stadia*

Year	Stadium	Deaths
1972	Ibrox Stadium, Glasgow (crowd crush, panic and stampede)	66
1975	Safety at Sports Grounds Act	
1985	Kenilworth Road, Luton (televised riots)	—
	Valley Parade, Bradford (fire in wooden grandstand)	50
	Elland Road, Leeds (hooliganism)	1
	Heysel, Brussels (crowd riots leading to panic and crush)	39
	European Convention of Soccer Violence	
1986	Poppelwell Report in UK on Safety at Sports Grounds	
1989	Hillsborough, Sheffield (many causal factors)	95
1990	Lord Justice Taylor's Report on Safety at Sports Grounds	

for all-seater stadia by the 1994/95 season, has provoked unprecedented investment in upgrading facilities. The commercial, as well as the legislative imperative, has brought stadia firmly into the diverse world of the leisure industry, requiring management skills hitherto severely unrepresented in stadium management.

The government's insistence that clubs invest in their facilities has prompted the 130 soccer league clubs in Britain to evaluate their stadia. The current situation indicates that the majority of clubs are investing to improve their existing grounds; however, 26 are actively considering relocation. The Football Trust has, since its inception in 1990, made available £89.7 million of grant aid as a contribution to over £300 million investment in soccer stadia over the past three years. Similar upgrading involving major investment is taking place elsewhere. For example, the Scottish Rugby Union has a £40 million programme for Murrayfield and the English RFU an £80 million investment in Twickenham, whilst Bradford's Odsall Stadium has a £100 million scheme proposed. Stadia represent the largest single area of investment in leisure in the UK. This investment embraces facility upgrading of sporting venues throughout the country.

The policy and investment to date, despite the comments by Taylor on the need for improved management, has been for improving the structural hardware of stadia. The need to upgrade the strategic and operational skills of those responsible for stadia management has to be met if the full benefits of the investments are to be realised. This is particularly important because of the volumes of customers/spectators involved. For example, on Saturday 15 January 1994 when a full football league and international rugby programme was to be played it was estimated that over 750 000 people would visit stadia in the UK.

Within the equation postulated by Taylor (HMSO, 1990) is the clear belief that, 'the importance of good management cannot be emphasised too strongly'. The three quotations are from sources represented on the Stadium Management Project's Steering Committee (see later). All reflect upon the role of improved management skill requirements in stadia and arenas.

> if the Taylor Report has been the primary motivation to press ahead with the development and advancement of stadia for football, it has also had a major effect upon the management responsible for stadia, prompting a reconsideration of their role.

> In the aftermath of the Taylor Report managers of such venues are finding themselves responsible for increasingly diverse facilities which will require the acceptance of new commercial opportunities and the continuing evolution of attitudes.

> Commercial pressures have served to bring these stadia and their management within the diverse world of the leisure industry, competing for business in new areas and having to adopt attitudes that have previously been alien.

Preliminary research by the Football Stadia Advisory Design Council (established in Britain by the government to pursue the recommendations of the Taylor Report) indicated that the provision of management education and training programmes for the growing numbers involved in managing, planning and licensing stadia were non-existent in Europe. In North America programmes existed but were composite of recreation degree schemes or were of short duration organised by the professional bodies (see Table 25.5). There is little consistency or pedagogic structure to this uncoordinated provision.

It was against this complex backcloth that The Stadium Management Project (SMP) was conceived in 1993 by staff in the Faculty of Leisure, Tourism and Health Care at the Swansea Institute of Higher Education, Wales, in the UK. The Faculty is a recognised 'centre of excellence' in the field of leisure training and education and carries out a wide range of research and consultancy for the leisure industry, including pioneering research into safety through its 'Safety in Leisure Research Unite' (SAIL). The opportunity to undertake the project has been facilitated by the 'Pick-Up Select Initiative', a scheme administered by the Higher Education Funding Council (Wales) to stimulate higher education collaboration with industry. SMP has been endorsed by the main professional bodies on both sides of the Atlantic and its work is guided by an industry-led Steering Committee, chaired by the Group MD of Wembley plc. The project is designed to focus upon the strategic management of stadia as leisure, tourist and community resources and is primarily focused upon the UK, although it is acknowledged that there is potential for international transferability of the outcomes. Consequently, relationships have been established with the USA and with Europe. The project is also asked to reflect upon the need to embrace a wide variety of sporting venues and to consider the diversity of provision.

The study is producing a 'template' for the development of management, management structures and management practices at the strategic and corporate level for the future management of stadia. The 'template' will then be used to identify training needs. The 'template' will be produced by evaluating the management, management organisation, management practices and management issues affecting stadia. An analysis will be carried out using a procedure involving the gathering and analysis of information by panels of 'experts' and has proven application in the evaluation of educational, social, environmental and managerial options. The expert panel concept is an adaptation of the Delphi technique which has emerged as a particularly acceptable methodology in the hospitality industry (Thompson, 1993). This particular project adapts the Delphi process and introduces a triangulation approach based upon 'testing the template' against selected perspectives considered vital to the training needs analysis.

The remarkable transformation achieved by the Indiana Sports Movement, translating 'Indiana-no-place' to 'the star of the snowbelt', is testimony to the power of an integrated tourism and leisure strategy featuring world-class sports facilities. The emergence of successful tourism programmes centred upon stadia and arena development is also evidenced in St Louis, Chicago, and Calgary. Sheffield (World Student Games), Barcelona (Olympic Games) and Vancouver (Commonwealth Games) have restructured, or intend to restructure, their tourism product based upon their stadia infrastructure. New domed facilities for example in Atlanta (Georgia Dome), in Toronto (Skydome) and in Japan (Fukuoka Dome) extend this concept by providing real multiple-use options, especially for convention and conference markets.

Stadia and arenas provide cities and regions with opportunities to host major events of both a sporting and cultural nature. They are the venues for national and international sports teams. Stadia are architectural landmarks with significant social–cultural connotations. As places where heroes perform and legends are created they contribute to the area's heritage. The result is a powerful relationship between tourism and stadia—a relationship still to be fully developed. Stadia are the sleeping giants of the tourism and hospitality industry.

References

Bale, J. (1989) *Sports Geography*, E. & F. N. Spon, London.
Balliet, W. et al. (1993) *Gousha Sports Atlas*, USA Today.
Borton, H. T. (1956) 'Ballpark design', *Consulting Engineer Magazine*, August.
Catherwood, D. W. and Kirk, R. L. (1992) *The Complete Guide to Special Event Management*, John Wiley, Chichester.
Delfon, R. (1993) 'The master plan', *Panstadia*, 1(3).
Epperson, A. F. (1986) *Private and Commercial Recreation*, Venture Publishing.
Getz, D. (1992) *Special Event Tourism and Festivals*, Van Nostrand Reinhold.
Gunn, C. (1988) *Tourism Planning*, Taylor & Francis, New York.

Hall, C. M. (1992) *Hallmark Tourism Events*, Belhaven, London.
Herbert, W. (1992) 'Creative financing of sports facilities', *Panstadia*, 1(1).
Herbert, W. (1993) 'Finding the funds', *Panstadia* 1(3).
HMSO (1990) *The Taylor Report: The Hillsborough Stadium Disaster*, Cmnd 962, HMSO, London.
Horine, L. (1991) *Administration of Physical Education and Sport Programs*, W. C. Brown.
Hornby, N. (1992) *Fever Pitch*, Gollancz, London.
Indianapolis Chamber of Commerce (1992) *Beyond the Games*, Indianapolis.
Inglis, S. (1987) *The Football Grounds of Great Britain*, Willow Books.
Inglis, S. (1990) *The Football Grounds of Europe*, Willow Books.
Inglis, S. (1993) *New Directions in Stadium Design*, Building Centre, London.
Jorgensen, P. (1993) 'After the event', *Panstadia*, 1(3).
Kitchen, T. (1994) Manchester's Olympic Bid Review and Proceedings Town and Country Planning Summer School.
Lipsitz, G. (1984) *Sports Stadia and Arenas*, Urban Land Institute.
Lischer, M. (1992) 'Herding them in', in *European Sport*, Vol. 1, Sports Council, London.
Lowry, P. (1992) *Green Cathedrals*, Addison-Wesley, Wokingham.
Luciani, R. (1990) *The Colosseum*, De Agostini.
NSGA (1993) *Sports Participation in the USA 1992*, NSGA, Chicago.
Neilsen, B. (1986) *Dialogue with the City: The Evolution of the Baseball Park*, Landscape 29.
Panstadia (1993) 'The flame still burns', *Panstadia*, 1(3).
Petersen, D. D. (1990) *Convention Centres, Stadium and Arenas*, Urban Land Institute, New York.
Redmond T. (1991) 'The changing styles of sports tourism', in Stabler M. (Ed.), *The Tourism Industry*, CAB International.
Stevens, T. (1992) 'Stadia—the sleeping giants of tourism', CHRIE 1992 Conference Proceedings.
Stevens, T. (1993) 'Theme parks' in Buswell, J. (Ed.), *Case Studies in Leisure Management*, Longmans, Harlow.
Thompson, L. (1993) 'A Delphi study to identify skills in the commercial foodservice industry in the year 2000', CHRIE Conference Proceedings 1993 Annual Awards.
Torkildsen, G. (1993) *Leisure and Recreation Management*, E. & F. N. Spon, London.
Twydell, D. (1993) *Football Grounds*, Aerofilm Guides.
Watt, T. (1993) *The End*, Mainstream Publishing, London.
Weiller, B. and Hall, C. (1992) *Special Interest Tourism*, Belhaven, London.

Further reading

FSADC (1991) *Football Stadia Bibliography 1980–1990*, Football Stadia Advisory Design Council, London.

26 Destination databases: issues and priorities

G. ARCHDALE

The Pacific Asia Travel Association (PATA) is a non-profit entity organized to encourage and assist in the development of the travel industry throughout the Pacific area. Its 1992 conference had the theme 'Synergy: service and technology' and addressed a number of issues relating to electronics in tourism marketing. Subsequently PATA commissioned an in-depth study entitled 'Destination databases, issues and priorities'. This chapter is a shortened and updated version.

Background

The travel industry's business processes have been greatly altered by developments in computing and telecommunications during the last twenty years. The role of the public sector, which does not process reservations as a prime activity, has been mainly limited to the development of product databases, containing destination data. A limited amount of marketing activity using customer databases has also been undertaken.

Recently, increasing attention has been paid to the potential for combining these product and customer databases in an integrated fashion with a reservations function. Such developments go under the generic term of 'destination databases'.

The astonishing developments in the twin technologies of computing and telecommunications over the past twenty or so years have had a major impact on all kinds of business practices worldwide. The travel and tourism industry, as a major user of both data and communications, is fundamentally affected by these developments.

The airline Computer Reservation Systems (CRSs) are the most notable example of change. Their core business remains the sale of airline tickets, though both the CRSs themselves and major-non-air vendors such as hotel groups and car rental companies are making increasing efforts to exploit the distribution opportunities the CRSs provide.

Tourism industry systems

Unlike airlines, tourism vendors do not necessarily have 'systems'. Whether a company operates a reservation system is a function of the type of business it is.

Significant tourism systems (those requiring substantial investment, specialist development and/or operational staff) can be divided into three main types: tour operator systems, major vendor systems (e.g. hotel groups' systems) and intermediaries' systems (e.g. those used by hotel representation companies).

Tour operators need systems for the same reasons as airlines. Consequently their systems share important characteristics. Inventories are normally fully computerised. Inventory control is centralised with all bookings normally having to be made from this inventory.

However, unlike airline seats, the majority of tour operators' products are normally only sold in one country. Consequently tour operator systems have been developed on a much less international basis than airline systems.

Many major vendors have invested heavily in computerised central reservations systems, particularly multinational companies. The driving force behind these investments has been the importance of central control and efficient management. A good reservation system also enables these companies to develop marketing uses of their database, a process long-exploited by airlines and others such as retailers of consumer goods.

An issue which has occupied much attention in recent years has been the need for these systems to be linked into the airline CRSs. However, the lack of an agreed format for inter-vendor communication similar to the teletype messages used by airlines, the many proprietary systems operated by these vendors and the differing technical requirements of each CRS has meant that achieving effective links is a complex and expensive process.

The use of intermediaries is a common business practice in the travel industry. Many of these have developed their own system-related services. Some have automated their systems to provide a better service to their existing clients. Others have entered the market by offering a 'new' service, often based on a technology application.

An example of the former is Utell, the world's largest hotel representation company. Utell acts as the intermediary between a travel agent in one country and a hotel in another. It also offers a range of marketing services on behalf of its hotel clients. For Utell, maintaining a central database with up-to-date information on the properties it represents, their prices, location, facilities and availability, is crucial to its successful operation.

An example of the second type of intermediary is Avis. Avis initially developed its own central database and communications links with the major CRSs. It later sought to recoup some of its investment by establishing a subsidiary, WizCom, to offer similar facilities to other companies, primarily large hotel groups.

Another example is THISCo, The Hotel Industry Switch Company, a joint venture between a number of the larger US hotel chains and the Reed Publishing Group. THISCo was set up in order to provide a simple connection between the various central reservations systems (CROs) that belonged to member hotel groups and the CRS systems. A key objective was to reduce the cost of developing and maintaining such links. The majority of these developments have been gradual evolutions of existing commercial activity. They have been carried out by the private sector, in the main with multinational business patterns. In all cases processing reservations has been a core part of the business.

The role of the public sector

In contrast, the activities of government tourist offices (NTOs), responsible for destination marketing, have been limited by the fact that these bodies neither operate on a commercial basis nor have reservations activity as a core business. Any reservations activity that is carried out has normally developed as an 'after-sales' service. Where there are systems these have usually been implemented as a processing aid to an existing activity such as publishing rather than as an integral part of the destination-marketing effort.

There are a few exceptions to this, such as the Queensland Travel and Tourism Commission's (QTTC) ATLAS subsidiary and the now-defunct HI-LINE, the specialised reservations service set up in 1984 by the Highlands and Islands Development Board.

The main focus of NTO computerisation (apart from the inevitable finance and accounting systems) has been on 'product' databases. The most common tasks that have been computerised are the data management ones associated with publishing, or administrative functions such as the registration of hotels. These databases have normally been regarded as an internal management activity and are rarely integrated into the marketing function.

The last few years have seen a trend to make this computer-held data more widely available, using a range of IT techniques including stand-alone kiosks, viewdata or other networks and, in a few cases, interactive media.

In most cases, though, this kind of development has not been seen as a primary marketing activity. It is only really in the area of customer databases that NTO marketing departments have been active. Several NTOs make their customer databases available for use directly by the private sector, often on a commercial basis.

Some NTOs have experimented with the use of CRS systems and other networks, such as Prodigy in the USA, to deliver information electronically to travel agents or the general public. Some claim some success. However, in general, this has been additional to their existing publishing activities. The result is that they have incurred extra costs.

Destination database developments

The majority of destination database developments have been at a local level. The total number of systems in existence is now well in excess of two hundred. However, the vast majority are limited in their scope and ambition either by their ownership or by their technology.

The overall impression is of a diverse, geographically disparate and generally reactive pattern of systems development, confused business objectives, a marked absence of technical, commercial or data definition standards, a plethora of often-conflicting developments within individual countries and little evidence of inter-NTO cooperation or even informal discussion of the issues.

Despite a long history of studies, proposals and projects addressing what have variously been described as National Computerized Reservation Systems, National Bed Banks, etc., no truly 'national' systems based on advanced technology and delivering applications and services commonplace in the commercial sector have yet been established as businesses with a secure long-term future.

The earliest study this author has found was carried out in 1968 in Britain. It proposed using surplus capacity on the National Coal Board's mainframe computer with terminals located in hotels, tourist centres and travel agencies and connections to the main air and sea carriers. No costs were quoted in the summary of the study and it was not pursued further. However, the general operating principles, of accumulating product and vendor inventory data and making it widely available to users through individual terminals and travel industry networks, are virtually identical to many 'new' proposals now being made over twenty-five years later!

Two ambitious national start-up operations that have been attempted, BRAVO in the UK and Swissline, have, for different reasons, failed to start operating. The Irish Gulliver project was launched in 1992 and is developing slowly rather than spectacularly. In France the Découverte de la France initiative has found considerable difficulties in attracting product vendors to use its (relatively expensive) services.

Analysis of specific systems (listed in Table 26.1) in the original report resulted in the development of a basic four-stage classification.

1. Destination-based visitor servicing systems:
   systems in this generic category include MINNESOTA VAES and ULYSSES.
2. Tourism and travel information systems for professional use:
   systems in this generic category include DANDATA, NZ HOST, TIS and BOSS-Tourism.
3. Mature product reservation systems for professional use:
   systems in this generic category include ATLAS, NEWTRACS, CHARMS, HI-LINE and TIBS.
4. Fully structured destination databases:
   systems in this generic category include GULLIVER and Découverte de la France.

These categories are not an attempt to identify a 'best' approach, but are simply a way of classifying the variety of systems currently operational and showing the gradual evolution of destination databases.

Several issues emerged from the survey. These included the need for airline CRS connections, for systems redevelopment as well as the role of the public sector, particularly in regard to funding.

Many of the systems reviewed were planning or have implemented CRS connections. There are significant difficulties associated with such connections. In the redevelopment context many commented on the need to update their systems. This partly reflects the more flexible and effective software now available. The extent of this

Table 26.1 *List of systems surveyed*

ATLAS (Australia)
BOSS (Canada)
CHARMS (Caribbean)
DANDATA (Denmark)
ETNA (England)
GULLIVER (Ireland)
HI-LINE (Scotland)
MINNESOTA VAES (USA)
NEWTRACS (Australia)
NZ HOST (New Zealand)
SWISSLINE (Switzerland)
TIBS (Germany)
TIS (Austria)
ULYSSES (France)

work will vary between systems and will depend on the original software and operating system platforms chosen. A recurrent problem is securing the necessary resources for such work.

A similar set of challenges faces the developers of the newer systems as they seek to extend destination database functionality. The pace of technology change is increasing. Successful systems establishment requires that the correct system approach is chosen; new approaches must be consistent with currently accepted as well as with emerging communications and information technology standards.

The public sector role in the development of destination databases is complex. A consistent element of the responses reflected increasing reluctance by governments to provide funding beyond an initial start-up period and pressure to expand the financial involvement of commercial partners. This trend can be expected to continue. If it does, ensuring the early involvement of appropriate commercial interests should help future initiatives.

Four fundamental facts about the current status of the development and application of destination databases emerged from the survey:

(a) there is an extraordinarily wide variety of systems, objectives, ownerships, funding levels/methods and applications;
(b) the relative success or failure of superficially similar initiatives has been influenced as much by 'political' as by commercial factors;
(c) the majority of destination databases at present play at best a subsidiary role in the actual marketing of destinations, representing only a tiny percentage of total destination product sales value;
(d) the development of destination databases, or central elements of them, is nevertheless proceeding apace worldwide. Commercial actors are beginning to play a greater role in an arena traditionally the preserve of the public sector.

The historical perspective

In considering the potential for any new technology application it is instructive to take a historical perspective. In the context of destination databases, which combine a radically improved and rapidly evolving methodology (computing) with new or better communications (tele-communications networks) in order to satisfy a growing market (tourism), the parallels with the early days of similar advances in technology and application such as the railways, the motor industry and in a more modern context, the French videotex initiatives, are significant.

In the last century the early development of the railways in Europe and America was characterised by extreme entrepreneurship, the rapid development and duplication of services, eventual success for only a few large operators, the early emergence of substantial barriers to entry and a national approach to control and organisation which persists to this day.

A later transport revolution, the emergence of the motor car, was characterised by similar entrepreneurship. This time, however, it was the provision of vehicles and the necessary services for their use which fostered intense competition.

The users of these vehicles had a relatively unrestricted and low-cost communications network, namely the road system (one which was and still is the subject of heavy public sector investment). This could be exploited for a range of purposes. Although individual national standards, such as which side of the road to drive on, still apply, in general the provision and use of motor vehicles is now an international business.

Similarly the development in France of an open and standardised network, the Transpac service, and the easy availability of vehicles to use on it, the Minitel terminal (over seven million now in use) and the 'kiosk' chargeable database, stimulated the provision of a vast range of services by entrepreneurs of all kinds.

Essential points that can be concluded are that:

1. entrepreneurs will always attempt to develop and deliver new services;
2. competition is a normal feature development;
3. the provision of an open highway (e.g. roads or telecommunications) facilitates this competitive process of service development, market evaluation and eventual commercial success.

The future for destination databases

Regarding the relatively limited impact to date of destination databases, probably reflects the fact that these entrepreneurial and competitive phases have only just begun.

Secondly, the only realistic open highway or communications network available to destination databases until now has been the airline CRSs. But the CRSs do not yet provide a fully effective service to non-airline vendors (see below).

These limitations are compounded by the commercial environment in which destination databases operate. Major vendors such as large hotels normally anticipate an average achieved room rate of only 60–70% of their quoted full tariff. Part of the reason for this is heavy distribution costs and commission payments to inter-mediaries. Although this is naturally a concern to them, and may well be a price-inflator, it is an expected and budgeted-for cost.

However, the smaller vendors, who make up the majority of product suppliers with which a destination database is dealing are not only reluctant to pay large commissions and booking fees but also cannot afford them. Thus the revenue available to destination databases is limited.

The factors affecting the development of the destination databases examined in the study were many. It would be both invidious and unsound to extrapolate conclusions from their different performances as to whether particular destinations or systems were intrinsically more suited to such developments.

However, it is worth making some general observations about different destination profiles. Where a destination has a significant supply of large hotels and a substantial international visitor flow, e.g. London, Hong Kong, New York, a highly developed and diverse distribution chain has to be already in place. It is probable, although not necessary, that individual properties or hotel groups will be on the CRS systems. It will certainly involve many different intermediaries, both at the destination, in the visitor originating countries and in the different market segments (leisure, business, inclusive tour, etc.) that both the destination and its individual businesses attract.

Secondly, a destination with a preponderance of inclusive tour visitors will have a highly structured, and possibly very vulnerable, distribution chain. While this type of arrangement can produce high visitor volumes, the destination's ability to price its accommodation at the most advantageous prices will be limited by the purchasing power of large tour operators.

Thirdly, a destination particularly attractive to the independent traveller is often one with an underdeveloped tourism business infrastructure, including a substantial number of small and independently owned businesses. Such a destination is theoretically well placed to benefit from a fully functional destination database. But it is unlikely that there is an adequate commercial basis from either the supply or the demand side to support it.

In considering the prospects for destination databases we can look at current trends in the various 'markets' for tourism products. Traditionally these have been assessed as geographical (e.g. the American market) with some segmentation (e.g. the senior citizen market).

Several factors are making these rather crude definitions obsolete. Both tourism demand and supply have expanded geographically through the provision of new transport services as well as physical developments within many destinations.

Secondly, there is an expanding propensity to travel, not least within the PATA region itself. This is primarily the result of greater prosperity. In the older travel-generating countries such as Europe and the USA there is an increasing fragmentation of the marketplace. New leisure and work patterns mean that the types of holiday taken and the timeframes within which they are taken are losing their previously rigid constraints.

This is matched by increasing market volatility. Destinations are clearly affected by customer reaction to economic and political factors, such as tourism-associated violence. Leisure tourists are able and willing to decide on destination and product nearer and nearer to their departure date. There is also an increase in 'environmentally aware' tourism, reflecting growing concern at destructive development.

All these factors affect the information requirements of the travel industry and the tourist. They lead to an increase in the amount of information required before travel decisions are made. Also the timescale in which this information is required is shortening.

Large elements on the demand side of the equation for destination database developments can therefore be termed positive. The provision of improved destination information is clearly essential.

The requirement to deliver availability and price data on a shorter timescale and to implement transactions is increasing. Finally the emergence of new market sectors, such as the environmentally conscious, offers excellent opportunities for implementing the type of targeted marketing techniques that suit effective destination databases.

The role of the airline CRS systems

The 1980s were characterised by rapid growth in the size and influence of the CRS companies. In their 'home market', the USA, virtual 100% penetration of travel agencies had been achieved by the CRSs by 1991. In Europe the Galileo and Amadeus systems became operational around the end of 1991 and today there is scarcely a corner of the world where one or more CRS systems do not have a presence.

The CRSs have a pressing need to increase their leisure sales. They cannot realistically expand their subscriber numbers in their mature markets. In their new markets they are locked in a competitive battle with other networks and with other sales channels for leisure products. But the process of handling leisure is different from processing airline seats. The CRSs need to have the right information in their systems, provide the user with a means of finding it and provide a secure transaction and payments path.

The unmanaged world of vendor data, the absence of accepted data presentation and communications standards, the lack of established reservations and payments channels other than those that are in competition with them and the cost and control issues facing vendors when they use the CRSs are all major inhibitors of the expansion of leisure sales.

The CRSs themselves have a relatively poor record in this field. The CRS companies would doubtless argue the opposite, as they have developed specialist 'products' to handle hotel, car rental and other travel-related booking requirements. But the operation of these 'products' is severely constrained by the particular systems architecture used by the CRSs. The consequences of this are:

- a high level of proficiency is required to process a reservation;
- a high level of database maintenance is required from businesses selling their products through CRSs;
- severe constraints are imposed on the way in which properties or products can be described or special offers promoted;
- connection to the CRS systems is costly and complex for even the largest vendors and prohibitive for the majority.

Until recently there has been relatively little effort by the major CRS companies to develop specialised leisure databases. This is partly because of the structure of the US leisure travel market. The USA has a relatively fragmented inclusive tour operator industry. By contrast the accommodation sector is dominated by large groups with strongly branded products. These brands are intensively marketed and promoted. They are sold by agents in combination with the discounted scheduled airline fares (95% of all domestic airline tickets in the USA are now sold at a discount to the full fare) obtainable via the CRSs. Even the commission for an air ticket sold in combination with a ground element is higher (11%) than for an air ticket sold on its own.

As the US systems expand globally they have recognised different market requirements. Notwithstanding this and the need to develop their leisure sales, the CRSs have many competing demands on their technical and human resources. They have to make continuing enhancements to their core systems as well as justifying the diversion of their development resources for new 'products' which will serve an unproven marketplace.

For practical purposes, therefore, the CRSs lack effective leisure databases and are reluctant to develop them. This has led to the development and provision of external databases, either on-line or at the point-of-sale.

The United States is now seeing a veritable explosion of new travel-related databases and point-of-sale (POS) applications. Examples of these include: Worldview TripPlan, a PC-diskette based information service on more than 160 destinations, primarily cities, worldwide. A recent development is Worldview's Automated TripPlan Software (WATS). WATS links the destination data Worldview to agency-held customer database details. This is activated by the passenger name record (PNR) created by a seat booking. Thus opera enthusiasts travelling to Vienna can be given bespoke information on opera while theatre buffs travelling to London can be automatically provided with details of the latest West End show—as well as the agency being given a prompt to offer tickets. Customised reports are produced at the modest cost of between US$9 to US$6 depending on monthly volume.

City Travel Guides is a similar operation but with the added twist that there is a specific software programme ('Travel Data') which can analyse the 'best buys' from the data contained within the basic database.

Weissmann Travel Reports added electronic access, initially via System One in 1992, to its destination reports which are designed for agency FIT clients.

The common feature of most of these POS applications is that they are being developed by entrepreneurial companies rather than the CRSs themselves.

CD-Rom-based services are flourishing. Since October 1993 one service in New York, World Travel Online, has even allowed its users to download video-clips and other destination data from a dial-up database service to their own PCs.

When considering the overall level of leisure-related information provision on the CRSs, note should be made of the continuing success of the various printed media and the intensive use of toll-free numbers by agents. This supports the conclusion that the CRS systems do not provide either an adequate information or reservations service for the leisure sector at present.

There is, however, a much-voiced argument which is a chicken and egg question. If data (or a relevant system) is not readily available, then it cannot be used. It is also true that publishers such as Reed are making major efforts to develop effective electronic media; the hotel industry, especially the US chains, are developing electronic links to CRSs and there is a groundswell of activity to develop networked databases.

From other quarters too there is a number of other initiatives in relation to CRS distribution of leisure products. In 1991 in the USA several major hotel groups formed HEDNA to improve their expertise re the CRSs. A related initiative, the Hotel Industry Standards Association (HISA) was announced in December 1993.

Major car-rental companies have also cooperated to develop screen and tariff display standards through the ACRISS initiative.

Also certain developments undertaken for the airlines themselves, such as the new Automated Ticket and Boarding Pass (ATB2), lend themselves to adaptation by other industry sectors.

The following conclusions were drawn from this complex environment:

1. The CRSs are the major existing travel-related networks. There are considerable barriers to entry for 'new' CRSs.
2. The travel industry is increasingly dependent on CRSs.
3. Vendors of all kinds, whether destination or product-oriented, private or public sector, are making increasing efforts to take advantage of the distribution and sales opportunities that the CRS/travel agency network provides. This activity is paralleled by many initiatives in the fields of commercial and data standards by international bodies such as IATA, the IHA and the ISO.
4. Thus leisure sales via the CRSs, though relatively modest to date, can be expected to increase sharply as a result of vendor, CRS and point-of-sale developments.

Issues for PATA and its NTO members

The key issue for PATA and its NTO members is the nature and level of their activity. Essentially there are three basic choices—inaction, reaction or proaction.

Few NTOs have no responsibilities in the fields of product information, direct customer (tourist) contact, relationships with air and sea carriers or vendors of all kinds. Some have legal duties in these areas and their reputation and funding may depend on how they carry out their functions and demonstrate their relevance in a rapidly changing world. Inaction, therefore, was not regarded as a possible option.

It is less easy to distinguish between reaction and proaction. A reactive requirement to consider new issues can quickly become a proactive plan to take advantage of new opportunities.

The best approach for an NTO is likely therefore to be a blend of proactive and reactive work. Its scope will be dependent on a range of internal and external factors. These will include the priorities and pressures it faces, the level of human and financial resources available, its constitution, expertise, previous experience, indigenous industry, main tourism markets and, not least, the personalities and interests of those with influence within it.

The type and level of any NTO's involvement in these issues therefore will be only partially determined by itself. The environment in which it is operating will also play a large role. A body such as PATA is in an excellent position to influence this environment. As a well-established, authoritative, international organisation with a broad cross-section of membership, PATA can build on these strengths to take a leading role in assisting its members in addressing destination database issues.

What initiatives should PATA undertake in order to bring the maximum benefit to its members? Specific recommendations were made in the study, based on the following issues.

Knowledge base

There is a widespread lack of knowledge and understanding of the 'science' of destination databases. This is an entirely normal feature of the development and implementation of any new technology. It affects all the many parties involved, system operators, their commercial clients, the owners and developeres of such systems as well as users.

However it can be highly dangerous. Ignorance of some of the main issues, such as the need to avoid an obsolete technology approach, can be fatal. Duplication of the learning curve imposes a heavy overhead.

At present there is a very inadequate knowledge base and few mechanisms whereby appropriate intelligence can be gathered, exchanged and exploited.

Standards

The absence of standards is evident at all levels, including CRS connectivity, presentation and data exchange, the commercial and legal frameworks in which destination databases operate and not least the commercial relationship between destination databases and their clients.

At the same time there is a range of bodies, including WTO, IATA, PTC, IHA and ISO, as well as regional and national associations of all kinds, who are addressing some elements of these problems. Are they adequately taking into account the needs and requirements of destination database operators?

Commercial and strategic issues

A fundamental issue is that of control. This includes an individual destination's freedom to control its own marketing and distribution strategy, control over its own data as well as over the costs of developing, maintaining and operating a destination database.

A related issue is the involvement of the *public sector*. The survey carried out for PATA demonstrated that there are increasing pressures on public sector bodies to find new sources of revenue. A destination database may appear an attractive opportunity to do just that but should it compete with or supplant the private sector?

The position of small and medium-sized enterprises (SMEs)

This is of particular relevance in tourism because of the extensive role that SMEs play, both in providing visitor services and facilities and spreading the economic benefits of tourism within the host community.

The relationship between the average SME and a destination database operator can be problematical. The normal business patterns of an SME sit uneasily with the commercial and operational requirements of a destination database, not to speak of other elements of the tourism distribution chain.

These issues are simplified and are not an exhaustive list. However they do cover some human resource aspects, the technical and commercial environment and elements of the industry structure within which destination databases operate.

Conclusions and recommendations

Experience in Europe, the scene of the largest number of individual destination database developments to date, has shown that these are likely to be disparate, often conflicting, inefficient in operation and expensive. In many cases they have failed to achieve their expressed objectives.

This reflects the confused commercial environment, the multiplicity of different technical platforms available, the relative maturity and intensity of European tourism developments and barriers to cooperation such as language, currency, cross-border restrictions, telecommunications regulation, etc., that still exist.

Indeed despite some efforts to develop coordinated national or international public sector systems the opposite trend appears to be gathering speed—that of an ever-increasing range of local applications. In France, for example, it has been estimated that there are over 350 different local systems in operation. Not all of these are full destination databases but this does demonstrate an intensifying competition to develop applications in product distribution, sales and customer marketing.

As noted above, however, this grass roots diversity, competitive activity and explosion of development is a normal phase in the implementation of new technological applications. As such it is generally regarded as having a beneficial effect, for example by attracting entrepreneurs and new service providers, thereby increasing overall sector investment and activity. In turn this speeds up the necessary process of product development, market evaluation and commercial acceptance.

In considering possible proactive roles for PATA, therefore, it was essential to distinguish between activities and initiatives which would assist this dynamic process, to PATA's own and its members' benefit, and those which, despite superficial attractiveness, were in fact doomed to failure.

A single study cannot realistically be expected to make a series of recommendations which are both uncontestable and exclusive of all others. What the author did therefore was to identify areas of priority focus for PATA activity consistent with the findings of the study and to provide a framework against which these could be assessed. These recommended areas of priority focus were as follows:

1. *Education and intelligence programme*

   While an improved knowledge base will inevitably develop in time there is a clear opportunity here for PATA to play a proactive role in developing a properly constructed education and intelligence programme. The lack of any similar activity at present, coupled with the need for it, suggested that such a programme could be a revenue-generator for PATA.

2. *Cooperative action plan for all PATA region destination databases*

   A feature of the European destination database scene is the marked lack of contact between the different actors involved. However, interdependence is synonymous with the travel industry and the relatively small market share that the majority of destination databases have in relation to the total business of their 'destination' implies that their real competitors are other methods of providing reservations and customer service rather than each other.

   Cooperation between existing and nascent systems' operators would bring significant benefits in dealing with the CRS systems as well as in other technology related issues. In particular, without cooperation and

correct identification of solutions (and who better to do this than those most experienced in the matter), the necessary knowledge base grows far too slowly and there is little that can effectively be contributed to the work of other bodies.

3. *Destination database forum with other international bodies*

   This recommendation primarily relates to the lack of standards of all kinds as noted earlier in the paper. The lack of these not only creates unnecessary overheads at all levels but also means that there is no 'level playing field' or the kind of open highway so necessary for the effective emergence of new technologies.

   Note that this in no way implies that the creation of 'regulations' is required. This would almost certainly be counter to the acknowledged dynamics of development. However, individual countries or companies normally do not have either the knowledge or the resources necessary to initiate and support the lengthy process of standards setting that is required. Similarly PATA clearly cannot carry out such activity in isolation from other bodies involved in these issues.

   PATA has the advantage of existing relationships with many of these bodies already. The successful implementation of the first two recommendations would enable PATA to bring a properly researched, authoritative and relevant focus to the work of these other bodies.

The suggested framework under which these recommendations should be evaluated is as follows:

1. The need for PATA's involvement; i.e. would it happen anyway without PATA?
2. The value of PATA's involvement; i.e. can valid benefits to PATA's members be identified?
3. The risk/reward ratio to PATA; i.e. what is the probable cost and likelihood of failure compared to the rewards of success?

The author believes that the above recommendations, while not exclusive of all others, pass this evaluation on all three counts.

27 Information and telecommunications technologies as a strategic tool for small and medium tourism enterprises in the contemporary business environment

D. BUHALIS

Abbreviations

CRS	computer reservation systems
DMS	destination management systems
EU	European Union
GDS	global distribution systems
ITA	incoming travel agencies (local handling)
ITT	information telecommunications technologies
OTA	outgoing travel agencies
RICIRMS	regional integrated computer information reservation management systems
SME	small and medium enterprises
SMTE	small and medium tourism enterprises
THI	tourism and hospitality industries
TO	tour operators

Introduction—situation analysis and methodology

Developments in information and telecommunication technologies (ITT) and computer reservation systems (CRS) undoubtedly change rapidly both business practices and strategies. Unexceptionally, the tourism industry has received several influences from these developments. This chapter concentrates on the implication of ITT for the tourism and hospitality industries (THI) and more specifically for the small and medium tourism enterprises (SMTE) section of the market. Further, the chapter concentrates on the contribution of SMTE to the prosperity of destinations. Examining SMTE's advantages and disadvantages, the chapter explores the major threats for the SMTE which jeopardise their future welfare, namely changes in consumer preferences, ITT and CRS domination, emergence of multinational corporations, and rising conflicts within the distribution channels of tourism products. ITT is proposed as a potential strategic tool for strengthening SMTE's competitive position in the international tourism arena. Computer reservation systems (CRS) in particular have a leading role in contemporary issues, effecting the best practices in the industry. An overview and a classification of the existing CRS is offered.

Hitherto, most ITT applications have concentrated on improving efficiency within the organisation context, though SMTE can achieve great benefits by building electronic networks for destination coordination. Thus, the idea of the regional integrated computer information reservation management systems (RICIRMS) is analysed. The chapter is based on on-going research aiming to provide strategic solutions and strengthen SMTE. It benefits from a pilot field research survey which incorporated 'in-depth semi-structured' personal interviews with 18 hospitality SMTE and eight incoming travel agencies (ITA) in two Aegean islands (Kos and Hios). In addition, four British tour operators (TO) (both small and large) and four outgoing travel agencies (OTA) (both chains and independents) have been interviewed in early 1993. The first results of a proper survey in more than 300 Aegean SMTE are also incorporated. Furthermore, lengthy discussions with academics, consultants, entrepreneurs, information technology experts and computer reservation system representatives of the last three years contribute also. Useful inferences from the pilot application of a RICIRMS on the Greek Aegean islands (AEGEO) are also drawn. The emphasis is to explore the information and reservation needs by the entire distribution channel and to identify specific requirements for every member. In addition, practices and conflicts in the existing channels are investigated. The paper does not aim to provide a quantitative analysis or statistically accurate results, owing to the small sample, but provides insights into the perspectives and needs of the various actors. Quantitative analysis based on a larger sample is due at a later stage in this research.

Information and telecommunication technologies in the tourism and hospitality industries

ITT and business strategy

Since the early 1970s ITT has played a radical role in the competitiveness of enterprises worldwide and it became one of the most important strategic weapons of organisations. Empirical data have demonstrated that ITT is used as a strategic resource in the following areas: cost competitiveness (66.67%), customer service (64.29%), product/service differentiation (45.24%), market segmentation (41.67%), new product planning (32.14%), supplier relations (28.57%), other (26.19%) (King et al., 1988:82).

Thomas (1988:4) defines technology as 'consisting of society's pool of knowledge concerning the industrial, mechanical and practical areas'. In addition, 'tele-communications networks provide the information highways over which new products and services can be offered, thereby redefining concepts of customer service, opening up new arenas of innovation, and altering the economies of distribution' (Runge and Earl, 1988). Porter (1989) recognises that ITT is reshaping the nature of industrial competitiveness by changing the nature or conduct of business. Consequently, 'the primary use of strategic information systems is to support or shape the competitive strategy of the organisation and its plans for gaining (or maintaining) competitive advantage' (Wiseman, 1985), especially if ITT can deliver cost advantage or differentiation against competitors (Porter, 1985).

However, ITT is not a panacea for organisational problems. Strassmann (1990) proves that there is little correlation between spending on information systems and profitability. Moreover, there is criticism that ITT often fails to add value to the organisation's operations, while the associated cost (capital, training staff) exceeds the benefit (Gamble, 1988a). High technology by no means guarantees profitability and it may even worsen a firm's competitive position in industry attractiveness (Porter, 1985). A variety of organisational redesigns and alterations on management control systems may be required in order to benefit from ITT (Freedman 1991). Moreover, managers' attitude and degree of capitalisation on ITT's potential play a critical role in the successful contribution to the organisation (Gamble, 1992; Pine, 1993a; Bruce, 1989).

Information and telecommunication technologies in tourism

The ITT revolution had severe implications to the tourism and hospitality industries (THI) as it changed the 'best operation practices' and provided opportunities for business expansion in the geographical marketing and operational sense. THI has become more flexible, quicker in response to consumer requests, more efficient. ITT has also reduced the costs of operations while it has delivered tools for flexible and competitive pricing. The rapid increase of the reliability, capabilities and capacity of telematics, combined with the decrease of their cost, has encouraged THI to adapt and use these new strategic tools heavily. 'A whole system of ITT is being rapidly diffused throughout the tourism industry and no player will escape its impacts' (Poon, 1993; Chervenak, 1993; World Tourism Organisation, 1988).

Further, adoption of ITT is forced by the enormous growth of the THI. Millions of schedules and prices are applied in the deregulated transportation industries daily, while numerous tourist destinations and unlimited tourist products have been developed lately. All these international business activities could never be handled without using ITT. Moreover, the proliferation of computers in society and the fierce competition force enterprises to increase efficiencies and consequently drive ITT in the THI (Go and Welch, 1991; Truitt et al., 1991). Poon (1993) probably describes it best: 'Tourism is a very information intensive activity. In few other areas of activity are the generation, gathering, processing, application and communication of information as important for day-to-day operations as they are for the travel and tourism industry'. Unlike durable and industrial goods, the intangible tourism service cannot be physically displayed or inspected at the point of sale before purchasing. Tourism services are normally bought well before the time of their use and away from the place of consumption. In the marketplace, tourism products are almost completely dependent upon representations and descriptions (information) in printed and audio-visual forms. Thus, communications and information transmission tools are indispensable to the tourism trade.

On the tourism demand side, a new/experienced/ sophisticated/demanding traveller is seeking more destinations and experiences. Consequently, tourists request a wide variety of specific information on the areas, accessibility, facilities, attractions, and activities at destinations. Timely and accurate information relevant to the consumer's needs is often the key to successful satisfaction of tourism demand (Williams, 1993). Therefore, it can be concluded that radical development of ITT usage in the THI is driven by both the development of the size and complication of the tourism demand as well as by the rapid expansion and sophistication of tourism and hospitality supply.

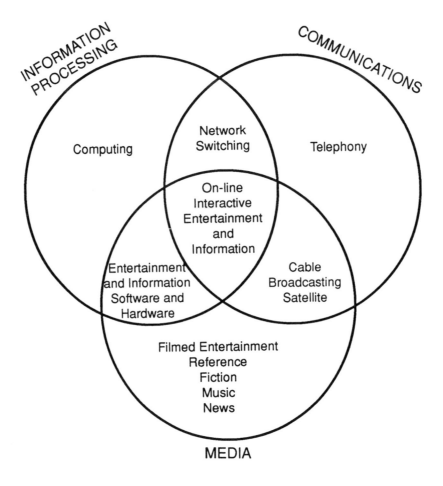

Figure 27.1 *Multimedia environment (from Cassidy (1993))*

The rapid growth of multimedia technology (Figure 27.1) which combines time-based media such as voice animation and video—along with space-based media such as text, graphics and image—provides the opportunity for interaction between the system and the user (Rochester and Douglas, 1991; Manchester, 1993) and thus will have radical effects on the tourism industry. Integrated services digital networks (ISDN) will formulate high-speed networks which will be able to handle large data volumes offering a revolutionary medium for distribution of tourism products (Haines, 1993).

ITT and home holiday shopping: a new trend
Although until recently consumers were reluctant to utilise home holiday purchasing (Gilbert, 1990) the increasing computer literacy of the younger generations, the wider availability of information technology in more households and the rapid growth of ITT's capabilities are expected to increase the direct involvement of consumers with ITT, in order to get a wider range of information on destinations and their attractions/facilities before making their ideal choice. Holiday shopping at home is gradually becoming a serious alternative or complement to

traditional travel agent visits. It is estimated that 2.9 million viewers in the UK use the travel section of the teletext. In addition, the wide spread of videotex technology, such as Minitel in France, has also provided a convenient communication media for home holiday shopping. Minitel claims 42% of travel reservations in France, with agents just one point ahead with 43% of bookings. The development of shopping channels through satellite and cable TV is another potential method of home shopping (Hyde, 1993).

Several authors believe that ultimately direct booking by the customer via home computer and interactive systems will become a reality (Haines, 1993; Go and Welch, 1991; Andereck, 1992; Pelletier, 1993). Holiday home shopping through ITT incorporates several advantages which can support its growth. Firstly, it enables the consumers to access a wider range of information, enabling them to acquire specific replies to their personal needs. The provision of some tangible elements, such as video sights and music from destinations, hotels, attractions and local environment, instead of relying on small, inadequate and often ill-informed or misleading brochures produced by tour operators (*Holiday Which*, 1988), can reduce some of the 'intangibility' of the tourism product, especially for destination-naive tourists. Moreover, ITT offers a greater flexibility, as travelling partners do not need to visit a travel agency together, at what are often inconvenient shopping hours or location, to discuss and book their holidays. Consumers have often suffered from travel agencies' inadequacies in providing quality service for various reasons, such as: inexperienced staff; holiday sold out of the brochure without any effort to customise the product; bias towards operators who provide higher commissions or special incentives; and lack of back-up information resources (*Holiday Which*, 1989). Holiday home shopping will never replace traditional high street travel agencies though, but it complements them and forces them into travel consulting. Thus, ITT is more likely to offer an additional distribution channel, targeted at ITT-literate consumers, those who have used the travel services before and therefore feel somewhat secure with the destination environment and those with specific requirements which cannot be accommodated by mass products. Destination-naive travellers, elderly people and ITT-illiterate customers would probably keep to the traditional paper brochure and travel agency combination.

Multi-integration of ITT and tourism and hospitality industries

Leisure destinations often consist of SMTE networks producing a blend of independently provided services,

which are combined in order to create an integrated product—the tourism experience (Buhalis, 1991). THI are regarded as highly value added chains where the performance of one activity affects the cost and effectiveness of the other (Go, 1992). ITT plays a dominant role in interconnecting SMTE and provides the communication network which enables the THI to perform their services delivery. In this sense, ITT is the lifeblood or the cement that holds together the producers and the distribution channels (Poon, 1993; Sheldon, 1993). Thus it enables the creation of a multi-integrated business and technology network (Figure 27.2) in which integrated ITT provides the platform for efficient communication in an integrated tourism industry, which in its turn is integrated with the local business and economic community.

Porter (1989) suggests that 'the world of the next decade is going to be a world where people struggle with how to connect systems, how to make them compatible, how to deal with the complexity of systems that span many activities within the firm and cross functional boundaries'. This could not be more applicable than in the THI. ITT is effectively playing an executive role in managing and unravelling the complexity generated by the inter-relationships within the tourism industry (Williams, 1993). The systemic adoption of ITT by all segments of the industry provides the necessary ground for a total system of wealth creation for the supply side (Poon, 1988b) and a total system of consumer satisfaction for the demand side.

Small and medium tourism enterprises

Importance and definitions

Small and medium enterprises (SME) dominate the global economy. It is estimated that 70% of turnover generated within the European Union (EU) is produced by the small business sector, 22% by micro enterprises (< 10 employees), 48% by small and medium enterprises (< 500 employees) and only 30% by large companies (> 500 employees); while 70% of Europe's workforce is employed by small business (29% by micro enterprises, 41% by SMEs and 30% by large companies). Almost 92% of all EU enterprises are micro enterprises (13.6 million), 6 million of which had no salaried employees; 7.9% of all enterprises are SMEs (911 000 small and 70 000 medium firms), while large enterprises account for only 1 in 1000 companies (13 000 in total). The average size of an EU enterprise is seven persons (Page, 1993; EIM, 1993; EC, 1993).

Classifying enterprises into small, medium and large is not an easy task. Two major approaches can be employed: a quantitative/objective and a qualitative/ subjective approach. In the first case, three criteria are

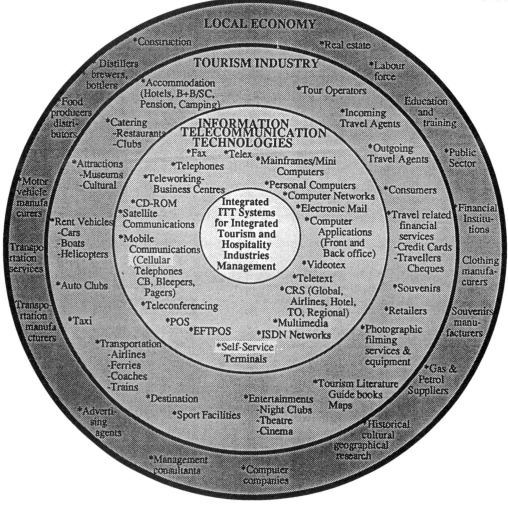

Figure 27.2 *Multi-integrated ITT systems for integrated tourism and hospitality industries in an integrated local economy*

normally used: number of employees, annual turnover and number of beds, especially for hotels. The European Union characterises as SMTE all enterprises which have less than 500 employees, less than 75 million ECUs net fixed asset, less than 38 million ECUs net turnover and less than one-third of the company being held by a larger firm (EC, 1991). When the employment criteria are applied then companies with 0–9 employees are characterised as micro, or very small, and the ones with 10–99 employees small, while 100–499 employees signifies a medium company and more than 500 employees a large enterprise (EC, 1993; Nijkamp et al., 1988; Page, 1993; Giaoutzi et al., 1988). When hotels are classified, the number of beds criterion can be applied.

Most authors seem to agree that accommodation establishments with less than 50 beds are small (Go and Welch, 1991; World Tourism Organisation, 1988; Moutinho, 1990). Further Moutinho (1990) characterises as small all hotels and travel agencies employing fewer than 10 people. When qualitative methods are employed, a wide range of criteria can be used, such as the organisational structure, participation in hotel consortia or chains, turnover, responsibility distribution in decision making, financial strength, operational procedures, recruitment and training practices, decision-making process, entrepreneurial involvement and control, integration level, family domination in running the property, internationalisation of operation; marketing functions and managerial experience (Buhalis, 1993; Poon, 1988a).

Contribution of SMTE in tourism and hospitality industries

Traditionally, SMTE have played a dominant role in the THI. They are particularly important in destination development, not only by providing tourists with direct contact with the character of the destination, but also by facilitating rapid infusion of tourist spending into the local economy (Cooper and Buhalis, 1992). It is estimated that more than 90% of hotels are SMTE and family-managed (Shaw and Williams, 1990; Go and Welch, 1991; Sheldon, 1993). Most of the hotel establishments throughout Europe are small, independent, flexible and seasonal (Go and Welch, 1991). More than 90% of Swiss hotels have 50 rooms or fewer and only 2% have more than 100 rooms. In France, 80% of the tourism firms employ fewer than 10 people (Williams and Shaw, 1988). The average hotel in the UK has 25 rooms (Lockwood, 1989) while 70% in the Scottish Western Isles have fewer than five letting bedrooms (Cooper and Buhalis, 1992). The average hotel and restaurant establishment in Greece employs 2.5 persons (Leontidou, 1991) while on the Greek Aegean islands the average number of beds per hotel is 63 (Buhalis, 1991). Finally, almost 90% of US hotels have fewer than 149 rooms (Go and Welch, 1991).

SMTE have, in most cases, informal organisational structures with great involvement by the proprietor's family. Often it is found that household traditional roles are adopted in the everyday running of the business. Research in small Greek hotels demonstrated that in many cases women have cooking, serving, cleaning and room setting responsibilities, while men look after the reception, the bar, construction, technology, negotiating prices and signing up contracts, purchasing, marketing and financial functions (Williams and Shaw, 1988). As a result, businesses are run on family principles rather than proper business practices while people in the SMTE rarely have formal education or training. This often causes both managerial and emotional problems.

Competitive position for SMTE: strengths and weaknesses

A wide range of strengths and weaknesses of the SME are due to their size (EIM, 1993; EC, 1993). More specifically, in the THI a range of strengths are often attributed, such as flexibility, direct control of service delivery, personalised and tailor-made service, entrepreneurial activity, strong local character, catering for special interest groups, employment of family members, flexible timetable and multi-skilled personnel

(Buhalis, 1991, 1992; Cooper and Buhalis, 1992; Go and Welch, 1991; Morrison, 1990; World Tourism Organisation, 1988; Lowe, 1988; Williams and Shaw, 1988).

However, SMTE have significant weaknesses as well. Management often suffers because of inadequate education or vocational training, ignorance of modern management and marketing techniques and lack of strategic planning. Family domination in SMTE can be a weakness because rational decisions have to be avoided in order to preserve family cohesion. The small size of operation provides little opportunity for the division of tasks, professional employees and proper training. Since no quality standards are introduced, service delivery varies according to the occupancy, service provider and timing. Moreover, SMTE face financial weaknesses, lack of economies of scale in purchasing raw material, low bargaining power, and lack of advanced facilities (World Tourism Organisation, 1991a, 1988; Shaw and Williams, 1990; Buhalis, 1991; Morrison, 1990; Williams and Shaw, 1988). As the THI becomes more professional, embraces quality management and responds to an increasingly discerning customer, the SMTE's typical lack of business expertise and minimal standardisation may become a liability (Cooper and Buhalis, 1992).

Current trends and potential threats

Distribution handicaps and tour operators' dominance

Marketing, and specifically the distribution channels, is the greatest weakness and threat for the SMTE. Unable to understand the consumer behaviour process, they rely on a canonical and seasonal demand, until of course it dries up. Consequently, they offer a 'product-oriented' service rather than one which is market-oriented. Moreover, SMTE cannot afford to launch their own marketing campaign and they lack the know-how. Inability to follow current trends and developments in the distribution channel field is evident. In a recent research study of more than 250 hospitality establishments only a handful had ever heard of computer reservation systems and one of them had such a misunderstanding that it had installed a travel agencies' version of a major CRS. Recent field research by this author on the SMTE of the Aegean islands provides plenty of evidence that this marketing weakness is capitalised on by members of the distribution channel in tourism, namely tour operators (TO) and major travel agencies. Being aware of SMTE's handicap, TO promote themselves and in fact are regarded by SMTE as the only way to fill empty rooms (Williams and Shaw, 1988). However, TO rarely pay deposits to guarantee their bookings and no formal obligation is normally given to fulfil their allotment. In addition, there is a 'release period' of only one to two weeks, which is insufficient for hoteliers to sell their rooms elsewhere in the event of their not being used. In most cases no compensation or cancellation fees are offered if rooms are not used. These practices are followed almost globally, regardless of the destination (Aegean islands: Buhalis, 1991; Kenya: Sinclair et al., 1992). As a consequence, TO minimise SMTEs' profit margins by negotiating discounts of up to 70% on the official rates of hospitality enterprises. Special offers, contributions to advertising and brochure production, representatives' expenses at destination and complimentary hospitality for 'educational trips' are also requested. In several Aegean hotels, TO offered a 0% increase for the 1994 rates. As there had been an inflation rate of almost 15%, an increase in labour cost of 22% and a capital cost of up to 35%, there was little room for optimism. In addition a constant devaluation of the drachma increases the profit margins for TO and allows them to offer reduced prices to their customers in order to compete in their market. In other tourist enterprises, such as restaurants, bars, night clubs, jewellery, souvenir and fur-leather shops, heavy commissions and/or a fee per tourist are requested by locally based representatives in order for the particular enterprise to be included in the 'suggested list' or to be made one of the stopovers in the city bar crawl organised at the destination. This 'blackmailing' situation is evident, specifically in destinations where supply exceeds demand and the area is reaching its maturity stage. Several TO practices, utilised in order to preserve their power in the distribution channel, were reported consistently by Aegean SMTE. The most common ones are: quoting that a particular hotel is full in order to promote committed hotels; downgrading customers' ratings for a hotel and consequently reducing its appeal; offering a disadvantageous space in brochures; offering a very short release period and thus minimising the opportunities for a hotel to sell its unused rooms; timing contract signing in low periods in order to achieve minimum rates; and leading tourists to different resorts every year, in a periodical way, in order to suppress demand and prices in all regions. Reducing the profit margins of the SMTE affects other enterprises in the area through multiplier effects. Consequently the entire local economy is endangered should SMTE fail to achieve a successful performance owing to inabilities to distribute their products adequately.

Globalisation and international competition

Moreover, the rapid development of the THI and global competition has increased the professionalism required

in the market. Transportation technology has removed the geographical barriers in travel behaviour, while media have reduced the distances and increased the understanding between different countries and cultures. Consequently, tourists have a much wider spectrum of destinations to choose from, most at very competitive prices. Furthermore, globalisation of the industry suggests that SMTE compete in a multinational environment where only organisations which can provide exceptional value or cost advantage, would be able to survive. The rapid development of ITT is often regarded as a facilitator for the globalisation of the THI (Ritchie, 1991; Olsen, 1991; Mowlana and Smith, 1992).

The opportunity of gaining economies of scale in all non-operational functions of the hospitality industry, such as distribution channels, reservations, marketing, advertising, administration, personnel management, technology adaptation, new product development, training and bulk purchasing of raw material and equipment, has forced the creation of major hotel chains, international consortia, management contracts and multinational franchising companies, and placed the independent operator at a disadvantage. The overall trend in the hotel industry is towards a gradual but steady switch from independently owned and operated hotels to hotel chain affiliation (Go and Welch, 1991). Unfortunately for the SMTE, globalisation goes hand in hand with increased concentration in the THI as large corporations consistently gain market share and market influence (Cooper and Buhalis, 1993). SMTE seem to be the weakest and most vulnerable members of the industry, and therefore need to seek competitive advantages to be able to compete in the international arena and maintain their market share.

Transformation of tourism demand

The development of the 'new' tourist who is becoming knowledgeable and is seeking exceptional value for money and time, and participation in special interest activities is another major challenge for SMTE. Thus, the relative importance of package tours which are based on low-quality, low-prices, is expected to decline in favour of independently organised tourism (Moutinho, 1990, 1992; Poon, 1989; Buhalis, 1991; Cooper and Buhalis, 1993). Poon (1988a, 1989 and 1993) has led the debate on tourism metamorphosis by suggesting that the 'old tourism' is gradually replaced by the 'new tourism'. The *old tourism* is characterised by 'mass, standardised and rigidly packed' tourism with little attention to tourists' personal needs, capitalising on the Ford model of mass production. It has been appealing to the mass markets, based on economies of scale and has primarily served the sunlust and inexperienced consumer. Using charter flights and undifferentiated, inexpensive accommodation, TO gather all elements of a trip in a 'package' which they sell as a commodity in its own capacity. However, since the 1990s the *new tourism* has emerged, offering new best practices. It is characterised as 'flexible, segmented, customised and diagonally integrated'. Utilising new technology, the tourism industry is able to offer a much more tailor-made product to a new/experienced/ sophisticated/demanding tourist who is looking for authentic experiences and has a wanderlust as well as an independent attitude. A relatively new movement towards environmental preservation and appreciation for the local society is also evident. Tourists tend to participate in the experience by being active and spend their time on their special interests. Flexibility in both consumer choice and the service delivery process is a key element. Brackenbury (1991) President of the IFTO, recently admitted that

the traditional annual family holiday, mostly in a Mediterranean beach resort, will not play a dominant role in the future. We have to accept that multi-interest travel is replacing part of our present bread and butter products. At least it has to be a combination of beach holidays plus pleasure of some kind or culture.

Every tourist is different, bringing a unique blend of experiences, motivations and desires. Jones (1993) suggests that 'leisure lifestyles are inconsistent, contradictory and individual'. In the 1990s tourism is following the trend towards customisation. Cooper and Buhalis (1993) suggest that 'to an extent the new sophisticated traveller has emerged as a result of experience. Tourists from the major generating regions of the world have become frequent travellers, are linguistically and technologically skilled and can function in multicultural and demanding environments overseas'.

In a similar sense Buhalis (1991) proposed that the traditional '4Ss' of the tourism industry (Sun–Sea–Sand–Sex) are transformed into Sophistication–Specialisation–Segmentation–Satisfaction. Hitherto, holidaymakers from northern countries escape to the sunny south to 'recharge their batteries' for a heavy winter back home. However, *Sea* pollution, health dangers resulting from *Sun* exposure, *Sand* degradation and modern *Sexually* transmitted diseases gradually limit the appeal of these elements. An increasing demand for more individualised, authentic and enriched tourist experiences signify the transformation of the traditional '4Ss' to four modern ones which framework the trends of the emerging tourism demand. Educated, experienced and demanding tourists require *Sophisticated* tourism products which can satisfy

their cultural, intellectual and sporting interests. As a result a demand for tailor-made, authentic and enriched experiences is leading the tourism industry to a sophisticated market place. Since every prospective tourist has almost unique needs and wants a certain amount of *Specialisation*, it is expected to dominate the future tourist product. Thus, the focus is turned to individuals and mini-mass markets which can share common activities and desire to experience similar activities. The identification of these mini-markets can only be achieved through detailed market *Segmentation*, based on lifestyle rather than on demographics. This process could demonstrate the similarities of the consumers and result in the formulation of feasible specialised activities. The ultimate aim for every tourism enterprise and destination should be the total customer *Satisfaction* throughout the tourist consumption chain, i.e. before, during and after the holiday. An integrated approach within the tourism industry is, therefore, required in order to ensure the coordination of the various enterprises and individuals involved in the tourist product delivery. SMTE and destinations which fail to serve and facilitate the transformation of tourism demand will be marginalised and suffer significant losses in their market share.

ITT and CRS implications for the SMTE

Finally, ITT and CRS pose a potential threat to the SMTE. Go and Welch (1991) fear that SMTE can be 'left out in the cold by the rapid advantages in modern hotel technology, especially in the area of reservation systems'. Recent research on the Aegean islands demonstrated clearly that SMTE are unable to follow the ITT developments and capitalise on potentials, owing to lack of know-how and capital. As most entrepreneurs or experienced managers have little education or training they tend to ignore the opportunities just because they cannot control it. They often feel that computer programmers will be 'external controllers' in their property. Consequently, they marginalise themselves, believing that ITT can be utilised only by larger organisations which have more divisions, funds and know-how. In this way, both their market shares and profit margins are jeopardised.

Perhaps, complicated *CRS developments* are the most influential of all ITT applications on tourism, changing the best business practices worldwide. CRS facilitate the distribution of tourism products and assist transportation/ hospitality/entertainment enterprises to handle their inventory efficiently and profitably. CRS offer the opportunity for instant update as well as the ability to provide information and support for the request/

reservation/confirmation/purchase processes for a combination of tourist products worldwide. It is estimated that 95% of US travel agencies are linked to at least one CRS and 88% of all airline tickets are issued through a CRS (Taylor, 1993). There are several types of CRS serving different enterprises, namely: airlines, hotels, rent-a-car organisations, tour operator and regional CRS.

Airlines were pioneers in CRS development and have benefited vastly since the 1970s. The growth of schedules and tariffs as well as the frequent alterations, forced by deregulation in the USA, made airlines' planning and operation unbearable without CRS. Most airlines developed their own systems, while the need for networking forced them to upgrade their systems to global distribution systems (GDS). All airline services, several hotels, major car hire companies and ancillary services such as entertainment worldwide are coming under the same 'umbrella' system which facilitates the distribution of a wide range of these products (Truitt et al., 1991; Feldman, 1987; Wardell, 1987; Boberg and Collison, 1985). Furthermore, *hotels* installed hotel information systems or property management systems in order to facilitate management of their inventory. Maximising profits requires a maximisation of both occupancy rates and tariffs. Hotel CRS can contribute to this task, in both property and corporate levels, by improving capacity and operational efficiency, controlling inventory centrally, providing last room availability, producing extensive marketing and operational reports, supporting pricing decisions, promoting to certain segments and organising distribution channels effectively (Chervenak, 1991). Several types of hotel CRS can be identified: *in-house CRS* operating for a single property, *hotel chain CRS*, integrating the rooms of an entire chain, *independent hotel reservation agents CRS* facilitating bookings in a wide range of interconnected hotels, and finally *hotel representation and consortium CRS*, promoting subscribed hotels (Braham, 1988; Chervenak, 1991; Beaver, 1992; Gamble, 1990; Lattin, 1990; McGuffre, 1990a, 1990b; Hickey, 1988; Go, 1988). Similar CRS have been developed by rent-a-car firms, ferry and railway companies and every tourism product which needs to be booked in advance. Moreover, tour operators have introduced CRS, where tourism products are held in a form of bundles, distributed to the travel retailers through videotex networks, and monitor the availability of 'holiday packages' (Bennett, 1993; Bennett and Radburn, 1991; Bruce, 1987; Hitchins, 1991; Deng and Ryan, 1992).

Finally, *global distribution systems* (GDS) have emerged through the integration of most of the above-mentioned systems with the most powerful airline CRS. Consequently, GDS can offer access to major hospitality

and tourism firms worldwide, while they can provide one-stop travel shopping opportunity. In this sense they can be characterised as 'travel distribution supermarkets' (Collier, 1993; Pelletier, 1993; Sloane, 1990; Truitt et al., 1991; Wheatcroft and Lipman, 1990; Archdale, 1991b). The competition of GDS has forced them to consolidate and experts believe that 'we are now seeing the development of a global framework or maybe three global distribution networks based upon SABRE, AMADEUS/WORLDSPAN and GALILEO' (Collier, 1993). Pelletier (1993) suggests that 'the signs are that it will prove very hard to prevent the large and powerful players in the business most of whom will have their own or shared systems from gaining advantages over the non-vendors'.

The brief analysis of the existing CRS illustrates that there is a great complexity in the market (Figure 27.3). Interconnections between CRS, loosely finalised procedures, and little understanding of CRS operation led SMTE to misunderstandings and little utilisation of the potential provided by CRS. Hitherto, CRS and GDS have targeted the business traveller market and consequently incorporate exclusively scheduled airlines, hotels which belong to chains or consortia and multinational rent-a-car firms (Peroni, 1991; Sheldon, 1993). The product standardisation and the existence of their own CRS, has established these firms' existence within the GDS (Archdale, 1991b, 1992a). Consequently, the budget-oriented and flexible leisure market is only being served by the tour operators' systems and has attracted little attention from other CRS or GDS. Thus, both the growing independent leisure market and the SMTE are inadequately served and suffer from isolation (Buhalis, 1993).

Page (1993) proposes that 'to function in the knowledge economy, small businesses need straightforward access to information-market intelligence as well as databases of market opportunities prospective customers and clients, supplies, possible distributors, agents and partners'. SMTE are often lost in a competitive and tricky CRS jungle where every system is marketed as the solution to their distributional problems. Lack of computer literacy, in most SMTE, in combination with little understanding of potential use of these networks 'place SMTE at a severe disadvantage, effectively barring them from the main stream of business' (Cooper and Buhalis, 1992). Go and Welch (1991) suggest that SMTE are 'the weakest and most vulnerable part of the hotel industry', while the Economist Intelligence Unit (1992) warns that

> while the independent property paradoxically may continue to offer the levels of personal services, they may at the same time find it much more difficult to remain in contact with their markets. If it becomes increasingly

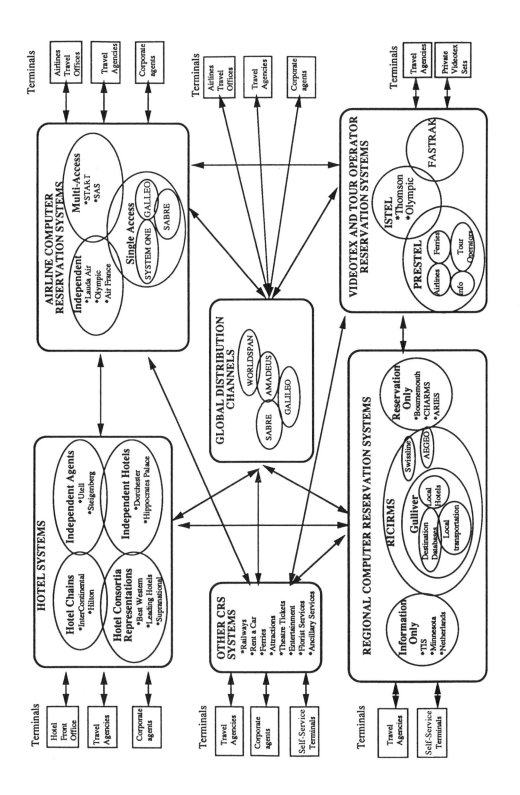

Figure 27.3 *The complexity of the computer reservation systems (Note: only a few names of CRS are provided to demonstrate the interrelations)*

normal to use computerised systems to reserve and even pay for hotel space, there is the possibility that the small properties will be left out in the cold.

Small and independent hotels need to enhance their distribution channels without losing their distinct character and their ability to provide uniquely delivered services. Perhaps Go and Welch (1991) express this threat clearly, 'Romantic, distinctive and charming as the private country hotel may be in almost any country in Europe, all that will count for little if there are no customers. All hotels must ensure that they are put before their market in the most effective way'. As, on the one hand, the vast network of family-run properties in Europe need to ensure their presence in the GDS systems (Go and Welch, 1991) and, on the other, they cannot afford to have individual membership, CRS stand as an opportunity for SMTE to initiate the desperately needed cooperation.

From computer reservation systems (CRS) to destination management systems (DMS) to regional integrated computer information reservation systems (RICIRMS)

> The airline-owned CRS of the North are generally biased in favour of origins, airlines and trans-national travel companies and against destinations, non-airline land service companies, and small and medium sized national companies which cannot afford the price of entry and transaction costs of the international airline CRS network. (Hansen-Sturm, 1991)

As CRS and GDS have a business traveller orientation and offer chain-multinational corporations, homogeneous, expensive, standardised products, they effectively marginalise SMTE. Hurst (1992) proposes that

> we must focus on creating a system which meets the needs of a whole accommodations industry both for the lesser known locations, the small to medium sized properties, catering to the leisure market, as well as city centre hotels catering to the business traveller. It is these properties, more so in some ways than the large business city centre hotels already well served by the CRS, which require the support of a destination database system.

In this sense, several destinations initiated a slow process of developing destination-oriented information and reservation systems for the local tourism enterprises and their attractions.

RICIRMS definitions and classifications

Destination management systems (DMS) primarily offer leisure and sensibly priced products, with heterogeneous and customised attributes, primarily served by independent SMTE (Peroni, 1991; Sheldon, 1993; Buhalis, 1993; Archdale, 1993). Several names have been attributed to these systems namely: *destination information systems* (Sheldon, 1993; Andereck, 1992); *destination management systems* (Vlitos-Rowe, 1992; Sussmann, 1992; Haines, 1991); *destination databases* (Archdale, 1993; Sussmann, 1992; Peroni, 1991, Yee, 1992; Jones, 1992).

There is hardly any adequate definition describing the concept or the existing DMS but 'a destination database is, in its simplest form, a collection of information, probably computerised and interactively accessible, about a destination' (Sussmann, 1992). Vlitos-Rowe (1992) quotes Haines's definition:

> A new breed of information technology that attempts to combine information and reservation by using artificial intelligence to link the two and, at the same time, derive a powerful marketing database with detailed customer preferences. These systems combine destinations information and produce databases with enquiries or client databases and offer a combined information retrieval and reservation capability. (see Haines, 1991, 1992, 1993; Jones, 1993)

Furthermore, Vlitos-Rowe (1992) suggests that 'DMS is intended to provide complete and up-to-date information on a particular destination. These complete data ensure that smaller establishments, as opposed to international hotel chains and other land services associated with travel are included'. Several DMS case studies are described in various documents (Buhalis, 1993; Vlitos-Rowe, 1992; Sheldon, 1993; Archdale, 1991a; Hansen-Sturm, 1991; Beaver, 1992; Vogel, 1991; Batle and Serra, 1992; Sussmann, 1992; Yee, 1992). Most of these systems can be divided into several categories according to:

(1) *Services they provide*: *information only*, where only information for certain products can be retrieved; *reservation only*, where only availability can be checked and reservations can be made; *information and reservations*, where both the above functions are available; and, finally, *multiple services systems*, which undertake an integrated role of information technology requirements for both tourism supply and demand (see RICIRMS description below).

(2) *Sectors they serve*: *hospitality systems*, which undertake hotel reservations only; *transportation only systems*, which provide timetables, availability, fares and ticketing for either aeroplanes, ferries, trains or coaches; *attraction systems*, offering information and ticketing facilities for specific attractions in a certain area; and, finally, *integrated systems*, which offer

the opportunity to retrieve information and make reservations in all services which can possibly be used by tourists at the destination.

(3) *Vendor of system*: systems developed by or under the support of the *public sector* dominated the existing systems; however, *private enterprises* have been set up as well; while *cooperation* between public, private sectors and local professional associations is another form of development.

(4) *Automation and technology utilised*: *semi-manual* systems utilise traditional ITT such as telephones, telex, fax, while *computerised networks* provide the opportunity for online response to any requests. These networks can utilise simple text or multimedia interfaces, enabling the user to retrieve a range of texts, music, video, computer animation, photographs, maps, etc.

RICIRMS features and benefits for SMTE and consumers

The DMS concept can be taken a step forward to RICIRMS, by proposing a very wide range of services for both tourism enterprises and consumers (Buhalis, 1993). Acting at a *regional* level the system should incorporate and coordinate the entire population of tourist services providers. Both individual products, such as hotels, restaurants, transportation and 'packages' created by principals, travel agencies, tour operators and other companies should be displayed. Failure to do so would remove the completeness of the system and would jeopardise the confidence that the system can provide the 'best available deal' (Buhalis, 1993; Haines, 1991; Peroni, 1991). Moreover, the system should be *multi-integrated*, i.e. utilise all available ITT to coordinate SMTE and integrate with the local economy. Although several DMS are not computerised, it is suggested that full benefits can only be gained when the system is utilising latest ITT. *Computerisation*, and networking of the entire population of enterprises at the destination would be essential for establishing an online network. The consistent reduction in ITT prices will make basic equipment affordable even to tiny organisations (Chervenak, 1993), and, consequently, it is unlikely that they will be disadvantaged unless they choose to be so by ignoring these developments. Several authors have emphasised that RICIRMS should provide *information*, about everything in relation to the destination (Buhalis, 1990, 1993; Peroni, 1991; Haines, 1991). Information can be classified in a '5A' framework: Accommodation–Accessibility–Attractions–Activities–Ancillary services. *Reservations* and purchasing of tourism products through an RICIRMS should also be

encouraged. It is vital that all required tourist products display their updated availability and price and can be purchased via the system. Tourists could either use self-service terminals and home computers to make reservations or they could ask booking agents or travel agencies to make the reservations for them. When no agencies are involved a fraction of their normal commission should be passed to individual customers as special discount. Bookings should be guaranteed against adequate deposit and a cancellation policy should clarify the obligations of both tourists and suppliers.

The system should also have a *Management* function for both the SMTE and the entire destination. Destination-wise, the maximisation of tourists' facilities usage and the maximisation of tourists' expenditure per capita is important for the local economy as it generates public and private income, employment, multiplier effects and foreign currency. Thus, RICIRMS can be utilised in order to promote the destination, announce specific events, make tourists aware of attractions, activities and local festivities and stimulate their spending in order to maximise the economic benefits of the tourism activity. Equally important, destinations should inspire tourists' sensible behaviour and exchange of socio-cultural experiences. RICIRMS can diffuse information on the host society, local culture, history, customs, codes of behaviour or dressing, and everything that would bring the host community and tourists towards a closer relationship and mutual understanding. Furthermore, destination management techniques can be introduced through an RICIRMS. Visitor management techniques could be incorporated and proper distribution of tourists within the destination should be attempted. Warnings of overbookings, over-crowded areas, sold-out facilities, events or attractions, as well as traffic jams, should be displayed on the system. Alternative routes or services should be then proposed, by the system, in order to save customers' dissatisfaction and destination deterioration. The major impact of RICIRMS on SMTE is the efficient *management of the SMTE* inventory and the opportunity they provide for SMTE marketing (Crombie, 1992). As the most important objective of every tourist enterprise is to maximise occupancy and average expenditure, RICIRMS can help by providing a comprehensive and up-to-date availability plan as well as by rationalising the pricing process. Yield management can be utilised, while marketing techniques such as direct mail, guest histories and frequent customer databases can increase the income of both the SMTE and the destination (Jones, 1993). The development of an alternative distribution channel will effectively reduce the tour operators' monopolistic buying power and will offer SMTE fair profit margins. The latter point is made consistently by researchers in the Mediterranean destinations (Aegean islands: Buhalis, 1990, 1991; Balearic islands: Batle and Serra, 1992). The diffusion of off-season attractions, combined with sensible pricing would stimulate demand for the 'low season' and thus would increase SMTE profitability (Buhalis, 1993). In addition, the system should provide managerial assistance for the SMTEs' functions. RICIRMS have the capacity to incorporate various databases or networks which could assist entrepreneurs such as purchasing networks, where not only can data for raw material suppliers be kept but also an online purchasing system could be in place, providing the opportunity to access directly and effectively the best producer. In addition, the system can provide the essential network for telebanking and thus reduce waiting time in banks as well as provide flexible banking hours. Moreover, RICIRMS can facilitate the centralisation of several SMTE functions such as accounting, marketing and recruitment to external contractors who would develop an expertise in the needs of these enterprises and split the cost between subscribed members. Teleconsulting might also be facilitated, where SMTE could place an enquiry and a specialist consultant would provide an appropriate answer within hours. The benefit of having experts managing several functions of geographically spread SMTE, especially for island destinations such as the Aegean archipelagos, at an affordable cost is tremendous. Finally, a wide range of information such as tourist statistics, new legislations, incentive policies, grant opportunities and special requests for cooperation would be enormously helpful. These business services can enhance the management expertise of SMTE, as well as reduce telecommunications costs, the need for entrepreneurs to travel and the unproductive time radically. Most of these services can attract public or European Union funding.

In recent field research on the Aegean islands' SMTE the vast majority suggested that a RICIRMS should be developed. They concentrated its benefits in provision of information to prospective tourists and the travel trade worldwide, reduction of dependency on tour operators, promotion of tourist products abroad, attraction of better 'quality' and wealthier tourists, coordination of destinations SMTE, and reduction of islands' isolation. Most of them were interested in getting reservations through a similar system. Furthermore, a considerable portion was willing to co-finance the development of a RICIRMS, depending on the cost and size of the SMTE, while a commission was readily offered for every reservation coming through the system. Unfortunately, they were unable to predict the benefits of networking and value added chains formulated by RICIRMS.

From the *consumer point of view*, destination information is a vital element of the consumer decision-making process, while it is a critical component of the destination's marketing mix (Sheldon, 1993; Andereck, 1992; Manfredo, 1989; Chon, 1991; Perdue, 1985). Murray (1991) suggests that 'the greater the degree of perceived risk in a pre-purchased context, the greater the consumer propensity to seek information about the product'. This is particularly the case for 'destination naive tourists' and especially for the infamous or new resorts where little public knowledge exists (Snepenger et al., 1990). Moreover, individuals seek travel information in order to make judgements regarding the possible payoff of a product purchase, given perceived risks as well as to remove some of the intangibility in the tourism product by getting more information on aesthetic, affective and imaginative aspects of the product. In addition, tourists use information in order to facilitate their travel planning and maximise their experience 'efficiency' while at destination (Fesenmair et al., 1992). Stanton (1992) suggests that 'current market trends such as increasing volatility, fragmentation and customer sophistication, imply an ever-increasing need for destination database developments to take place in order to properly meet customer demands and preferences'.

RICIRMS is the most suitable tool to provide tourist information to the new/sophisticated/experienced/demanding tourist who is travelling independently and requires more information to be available. In the current hectic business environment consumers tend to be equally time- and cost-conscious. Consumers want better returns on the time they spend as well as better value for money. As the market for shorter but more frequent holidays is growing rapidly, consumers will consistently need more flexibility and last-minute arrangements. This trend would require a vast amount of information to be instantly accessible as well as an opportunity to check availability and make reservations from one point of sale. Convenient payment methods, through global financial institutions such as credit card corporations, would be basic prerequisites for purchasing any product. Of course, a 'user-adoring' interface (rather than just 'friendly') would need to be in place. Vogel (1991) concludes that there is a great demand for 'easy access to transparent and easy to compare information on a wide variety of choices of destinations, holiday packages, travel, lodging and leisure services, the actual prices and availability of such services. Customers also want immediate confirmation and speedy documentation of their reservations'. RICIRMS can serve tourists in the pre-trip decision period as well as during their trip. A wide range of information should be on display such as transportation schedules, facilities, accommodation–catering–entertainment establishments, last seat/bed availability, description of resorts and enterprises, weather reports, travel regulations, exchange rates (Sheldon, 1993; Buhalis, 1990; Jones, 1992). The data should be displayed in a flexible way, where users can set their priorities and preferences for their specific needs. Moreover, users with different expertise should be able to customise the system to their pace. In order to acquire consumers' confidence this data should be up-to-date, unbiased, precise, complete and accurate, and they need to offer the 'best available deal' for the consumer. Furthermore, expert systems technology can be incorporated in order to propose specialised tourist product bundles, based on key parameters or preferences set by the user, or his/her past consumer behaviour (Buhalis, 1990, 1993; Crouch, 1991). Users should be able to acquire a printed copy of all relevant information and material they need for their trip. Furthermore, a consumer database can be incorporated in order to work as a marketing tool for both destinations and SMTE. Advanced segmentation, direct mail and customised marketing techniques can be utilised (Jones, 1992, 1993). Once at the destination, consumers can utilise RICIRMS's massive computing facilities for other purposes, such as communications and file transfer with their working environments, forwarded electronic mail address, teleworking, electronic bulletin boards discussing issues and experiences about the destination.

Distribution of RICIRMS

An extensive network should be developed in order to distribute RICIRMS within the destination and the prospective tourists' countries of origin, as demonstrated in Figure 27.4. *Locally*, intelligent tourist kiosks with self-service multimedia and interactive capabilities can be conveniently located in hotel lobbies, and at key tourist locations, providing 24-hour information and reservation services for tourists searching for suitable accommodation, transportation or activities. Moreover, the system can be within local SMTE and regional tourist information offices computer systems (Buhalis, 1990; Hwa, 1992). The ultimate aim should be that every single SMTE should have a computerised system which would be able to access the RICIRMS and acquire a wide variety of services for both tourists and entrepreneurs. SMTE who cannot afford to install a computer system or who lack capable personnel should be able to communicate via conventional media, such as telephone, fax or telex through a dedicated operator, or should be given incentives to acquire a terminal. Access to banking systems is of equal importance in order to facilitate payments by credit card

(Buhalis, 1991, 1993). Perhaps the most important function of RICIRMS would be to distribute information and enable reservations at prospective *tourists' place of origin*. In this function it will stimulate and administrate demand for the destination and the SMTE. The system can be distributed through a national node in the most important countries of origin. This node can be hosted by a specific enterprise distributing the RICIRMS, the flag airline's offices of the destination country or the national tourist organisation office in this market. RICIRMS should encourage access by both individual and institutional customers, namely travel agencies and tour operators. The system should ensure that both computer and videotex interfaces can be connected. In addition, a dedicated operator should be available to deal with requests emerging through conventional telecommunication media.

Undoubtedly, airlines lead the technology diffusion in the tourism industry (Poon, 1993). CRS and GDS can host RICIRMS in order to provide the opportunity for consumers and travel agencies to have access to destination-related comprehensive information. GDS would benefit by selling airline tickets and perhaps getting a fair commission on other reservations through RICIRMS. Jones (1992) suggests that 'the emphasis is not on the question of the storage of the destination's full product in the airline CRS but on enabling that CRS to draw on the product the destination has to offer, when the situation arises'. GDS can also gain a significant competitive advantage by becoming a one-stop point of sale, promoting any type of tourist products worldwide. Since technology, expertise and networking are in place, GDS need comparably minor investments to enhance their potentials. An expansion into the 'low margins–high volumes' leisure market would be inevitable. GDS would eventually become a platform for travel information and reservation for both business and leisure markets. It is evident that GDS are getting more involved in various RICIRMS pilot projects while GDS speculate the most appropriate direction (Peroni, 1991; Buhalis, 1991; Archdale, 1993, Oliver, 1991; Haines, 1991).

The most significant problem RICIRMS distribution has to overcome is compatibility. Several CRS, GDS and DMS operate already, utilising different software and working processes, creating unnecessary overheads at all levels. Some of these systems are incompatible deliberately in order to discourage users to swap between systems. Thus, 'information technology islands' are formulated, trapping the 'best deal' within the borders of the 'island'. This will be intolerable to both customers and industry in the near future. The days of capitalising on consumer lack of information and knowledge are definitely limited.

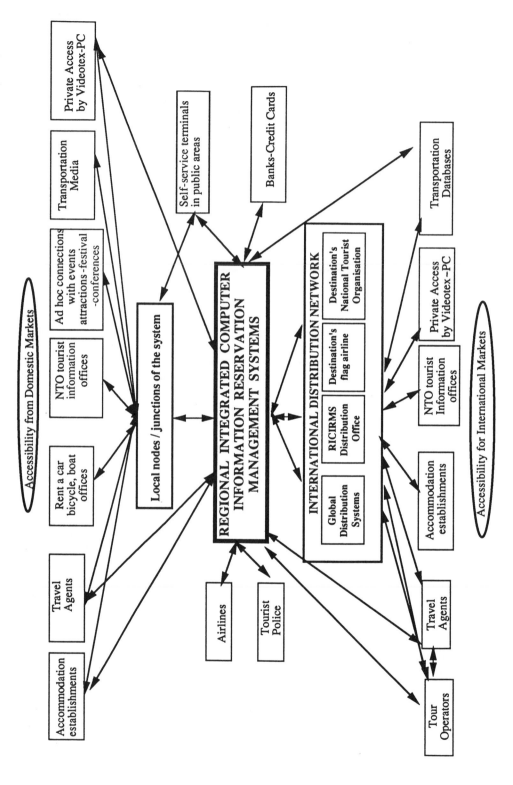

Figure 27.4 *Distribution of RICIRMS (adapted from Buhalis (1990, 1993))*

CRS and RICIRMS interface standards should be established and thus, a global compatibility between systems should eventually be reached (Quee, 1992). Industry should be able to use the very same equipment to access various systems. User-friendly interfaces would reduce the need for specific training and make it easier for everybody to benefit from the system. Experienced and educated users will be able to operate various systems and therefore benefit from its potentials. In conclusion, systems and vendors should open their accessibility and consistently compete on the value they can offer, rather than restricting users to limited options.

RICIRMS organisation

The organisational framework of an RICIRMS is very significant for its success. Since public sector and national tourist organisations are normally responsible for the marketing and the strategy of a destination they are often regarded as most appropriate to undertake the development and maintenance of RICIRMS (Peroni, 1991, Archdale, 1991a, 1993). Sheldon (1993) suggests that similar systems can be nationally centralised, regionally centralised or regionally networked. Hitherto, the public sector has dominated the development and operations of DMS, mainly because SMTE cannot afford to develop an RICIRMS for themselves. Massive investments in equipment, data collection, engineering, art-work and maintenance are required. Moreover, SMTE lack the expertise and the experienced personnel to oversee such a project. Research in the Aegean islands suggested that RICIRMS should be driven by non-profit cooperation schemes, such as the local hoteliers and travel agencies associations and should be backed by public sources such as national tourist organisations. Other local tourist enterprises can contribute while universities and research institutes might be able to assist in both ITT and tourism marketing sides.

Several interviews with SMTE suggested that an individual vendor could develop an RICIRMS. Apart from the fact that development costs are prohibitive, it is strongly believed that an RICIRMS should be a non-profit organisation, which, however, should be able to break even. The existence of an individual vendor who would be interested in maximising his return on investment or perhaps influencing prospective tourists towards certain more commissionable or profitable products would be disastrous for an RICIRMS. In this sense no advertising should be permitted in an RICIRMS. An index form representation, equal for all participants, should be adapted. In order to avoid discrimination, tourism products should not be listed alphabetically.

Instead, a random generator should be utilised to rank the entire population of enterprises meeting customers' criteria. A consumer watchdog should ensure neutrality and fair representation for all participants. Lessons should be learnt by CRS role in the airlines competition and the regulation framework in the USA and the EU. More importantly RICIRMS should be driven by multi-skilled managers who can understand both demand and supply needs, technology and tourists and tourism consumer behaviour. SMTE should build up trust in RICIRMS and support it by allocating it a fraction of their capacity and honouring reservations arising from the system. They might also need to be prepared to sacrifice some of their independence and accept the operation conditions imposed by the system.

RICIRMS economics

The question of who pays for the RICIRMS development and operation is not an easy one. The feasibility of RICIRMS is under scrutiny, especially since the few promising projects collapsed due to lack of funding. Sheldon (1993) divides the RICIRMS economics into developing and operating economics. Hitherto, the public sector has played a dominant role in RICIRMS development. A wide range of private sponsors has financed research and RICIRMS pilot research projects. Perhaps a blend of private and public resources should provide the most adequate financial form. However, since RICIRMS should not be profit-making organisations, the private sector cannot have high returns on investments. The involvement of telecommunication companies in RICIRMS (such as Cable and Wireless in CHARMS and BRAVO), demonstrates that there may be fruitful benefits arising from RICIRMS, mainly for supporting services.

On the operation side there is a trade-off between charges made to principals and competence of the system. It is quite apparent that 'a fully comprehensive system can only occur if no listing fees are demanded' (Sheldon, 1993). However, a minimal joint fee combined with reasonable commission on bookings is perhaps the most appropriate way. Research at hospitality SMTE on the Aegean islands demonstrated that only a very small fraction refused categorically to pay some money to join an RICIRMS. Several SMTE were willing to co-finance the development and operation of such a system. A few conditions were normally demanded such as a contribution according to hotel size, unbiased representation, the entire population of SMTE at destination be included, and public sector involvement, *inter alia*. Other considerations, such as the increase of booking volumes, the reservations generated for the low period, the rates achieved through RICIRMS, and the coverage of the international market, would affect entrepreneurs' willingness to pay for RICIRMS services. Interviewees who refused any payment to a RICIRMS often had committed most of their rooms to tour operators or had financial problems and mortgages. Most SMTE viewed RICIRMS as another advertising medium while the major synergies of distribution and operation functions were missing from the picture. Almost the entire population of SMTE interviewed could happily pay commission for bookings made through the system. The level of commission could be greater during low periods but it was stiff in the peak period. Commission levels could reach up to 25% but the 10% norm was usually followed. McGuffre (1990a) and Go and Welch (1991) warn that bookings through CRS can cost, either customer or principal, up to 30% of the product prices, when all commission payments to travel agencies, CRS and credit card companies involved are paid. However, in bookings where no CRS is used the situation is similar, when two or more travel agencies are involved. Moreover, hoteliers normally have no choice but to offer more than 50% discount/commission to tour operators. Consequently, hoteliers who use RICIRMS should be able to increase their profit margins without increasing the final consumer price. In addition, incoming or handling travel agents, at the destination, were also prepared to pay a joining fee and a commission in order to promote their services, namely local transfers, excursions, and packages at the destination. Tour operators on the other hand who organised trips to destinations could see little benefit from an RICIRMS, apart from providing a more realistic and appealing destination image for consumers and train travel consultants. Thus, they were reluctant to pay for RICIRMS services. Outgoing travel agencies (OTA) regarded RICIRMS as an information tool for destinations, while the reservation facility was perceived differently by independent and chain OTA. Thus, their willingness to pay was different as well. However, an annual fee, equivalent to the cost of information manuals currently used, was offered unreservedly. In addition, payment according to usage could be in place for information retrieval and bookings.

Finally, consumers could pay a small amount whenever they use the system for information retrieval or bookings. The charge may be incorporated in the product price or may be separated. Litinas and Vourgaridis's (1992) research on usage of the AEGEO's pilot projects suggests that only 7% of the individual users were reluctant to pay at all, 55% could pay the equivalent of 30–50 pence, 6% around one pound, 22% up to £1.50 and 10% between three and six pounds. That proves that consumers

appreciate the services provided by RICIRMS and are willing to pay for their usage. A RICIRMS-literate user could benefit from identifying better product prices and therefore justify the cost of system's usage. Lessons can be learned by examining videotex payment systems in countries like France.

In general, pricing of RICIRMS should be based on the examination of different participants' cost and benefits between currently used resources/practices. The more savings on information resources, communication costs, labour costs and training expenses occur, or the more value is added in a product and the greater profit margins that emerge, the more the willingness to pay would increase among the parties involved.

RICIRMS limited development and failures

Despite RICIRMS' promising future there is little successful development to date. Several reasons can be posited. RICIRMS represent a very modern approach to destination management, which redefined the best practices in the industry. The immaturity of the industry to capitalise on this change, combined with the opposition of some distribution channel members who benefit more from the existing situation, is also evident. Technology is another factor, as RICIRMS require massive computing, storage and networking capabilities at an affordable cost which have become available only recently. GDS demonstrated effectively that the best practices in the tourism business lie with the multi-integration of ITT and the tourism industry. Consequently, RICIRMS became the next reasonable step.

On the tourism demand side, the sophistication of the customers and their desire for specialised products, which could offer exceptional value, became evident only in the early 1990s. As holidays are becoming a more inelastic product, the price of the package will be less important in the decision making while value added products will dominate. The growth of tourism demand, due to the consistent desire of Westerners to travel and the democratisation or development of other parts of the world such as the Communist bloc, suggests that computerised systems will be required to handle the vast volumes of emerging tourists.

On the supply side, the dominance of the package and the existing distribution channels has made both principals and NTO idle and reluctant to initiate any aggressive marketing strategy. However, changes in consumer preferences combined with the fact that multinational companies aim to please their shareholders, rather than develop sustainable destinations and look after SMTE, initiated a process of identifying strategic tools for destination prosperity. In addition, deregulation in air transportation essentially means that fares in scheduled airlines can be reduced to levels competitive with charter prices. This will enable individual travellers to make their personalised leisure arrangements without paying inflated prices. The ITT training and understanding of THI managers is improving gradually and it provides them with new methods for performing their tasks. THI growth globally means that more information is required by tourists and trade, while new efficient methods to match tourism demand and supply are desperately needed in order to identify the best product for each customer. Finally, concern for SMTE's survival in the contemporary business environment has forced both private and public sectors towards cooperation and utilisation of all potential resources for achieving competitive advantages (Buhalis, 1993).

Nevertheless, only a few systems can survive the fierce competition in both THI and CRS industries. Several reasons have been identified for RICIRMS' failures including: lack of adequate finance for development and operation; incomplete representation of enterprises at the destination; incomprehensive presentation of facilities offered; inaccurate pricing and inventory of tourist products; delays in confirmation; lack of easy access and use of system; inconvenient methods of payment; ignorance of international CRS industry standards; unsuccessful cooperation with CRS; lack of involvement, support and coordination with tourist boards; small SMTE interest; limited training; inappropriate technology; limited knowledge of the tourism industry by developers; and conflict with dominant interests (Buhalis, 1993; Haines, 1991; Hansen-Sturm, 1991).

Conclusion

Although SMTE play a dominant role in the international THI they are very vulnerable in the contemporary, demanding business environment. The distribution handicaps they face, as well as the fierce competition stimulated by the globalisation of the THI and the transformation of the tourism demand, place SMTE in a disadvantaged position. In addition, radical developments in ITT and CRS fields, which SMTE cannot follow, effectively exclude them from the 'opportunity set' of prospective tourists.

However, information and telecommunications technologies can be utilised as a strategic tool for the development of both the SMTE and the destination, while RICIRMS seems to be the answer to the threats faced by SMTE. It can provide a strategic tool for SMTE by developing a coordinated regional integrated system which can facilitate both destination and SMTE strategic management and marketing. The system should support information and reservation functions while a wide range of value added services can be incorporated. The aim of RICIRMS should be: maximisation of the long-term business revenues for the SMTE of the area; satisfaction of the new/experienced/sophisticated/demanding tourists' needs; and enhancement of benefits for the local area and the host society. A wide range of organisational and attitude changes should be in place in order to allow SMTE to gain maximum benefits from this potential. It is perhaps the only chance for SMTE to promote their services competitively and recover from their disadvantaged position, in comparison with the large multinational enterprise. Therefore RICIRMS is a strategic tool for both SMTE and destinations which they cannot afford to ignore. Failure to understand and adopt these systems might cause competitive disadvantages and neo-colonialism where large multinational corporations will squeeze profit margins and challenge SMTE's existence in the next century.

Acknowledgements

The author would like to acknowledge Dr C. Cooper, Dr J. Fletcher, and Mrs S. Sussmann, MSTHI, University of Surrey, Professor N. Litinas, DBA, University of the Aegean, and Mr M. Friel, Oxford Brookes University, for their valuable contribution to this paper. Financial support for this research project has been provided by the Surrey Research Group, ConTours Consultants and it is gratefully appreciated.

References and bibliography

Andereck, K. (1992) 'Researching consumer information: comments on researching consumer information', *Proceedings of Travel and Tourism Research Association: Tourism Partnership and Strategies: Merging Vision with New Realities*, 23rd Annual Conference, 14–17 June, Minneapolis, pp. 50–52.

Archdale, G. (1991a) 'The promotion of the destination and the tourist products through information and the role of the public offices for the support of the necessary infrastructure', *Proceedings of the International Conference on Computer Networking and the Public Tourist Organisation*. Assisi-Perugia, Italy, 18–20 November.

Archdale, G. (1991b) 'Computer reservation systems: the international scene', Part 1, *Insights*, D15–D19.

Archdale, G. (1992a) 'Computer reservation systems', Part 2, *Insights*, D21–D25.

Archdale, G. (1992b) 'A new direction for effective destination marketing and quality customer service' keynote address, in Yee (1992), pp. 13–18.

Archdale, G. (1993) 'Computer reservation systems and public tourist offices', *Tourism Management*, 14(1): 3–14.

Batle, F. and Serra, A. (1992) 'Computer reservation systems: their impact on the Mallorcan tourism industry', *Proceedings of IV World Congress of Regional Science International*, University of Balearic Islands, Palma de Mallorca, 26–29 May.

Beaver, A. (1992) 'Hotel CRS—an overview', paper given in the conference: *Tourism and Hospitality Management: Established Disciplines or 10-year Wonders*, 25–28 September 1991, University of Surrey: *Tourism Management*, 13(1): 15–21.

Bennett, M. (1993) 'Information technology and travel agency: a customer service perspective', *Tourism Management*, 14(4): 259–266.

Bennett, M. and Radburn, M. (1991) 'Information technology in tourism: the impact on the industry and supply of holidays', in Sinclair and Stabler, M. (Eds), *The Tourism Industry: an International Analysis*, CAB International, Oxford, pp. 45–67.

Boberg, K. and Collison, F. (1985) 'Computer reservation systems and airline competition', *Tourism Management*, 6(3): 174–183.

Borsenik, F. (1993) 'Hospitality technology in the 21st century'. *Hospitality Research Journal*, 17(1):258–259.

Brackenbury, M. (1991) 'The preferences of tourists in the European market', presentation in conference: *Strategic Development of European Tourism towards 2000*, Crete, 18–20 May.

Braham, B. (1988) *Computer Systems in the Hotel and Catering Industry*, Cassell, London.

Bruce, M. (1987) 'New technology and the future of tourism', *Tourism Management*, 8(2):115–120.

Bruce, M. (1989) 'Technological change and competitive marketing strategies', in Witt, S. and Moutinho, L. (Eds), *Tourism Marketing and Management Handbook*, Prentice Hall, London, pp. 455–458.

Buhalis, D. (1990) 'The new telecommunication technologies in the tourism industry of the Aegean islands', University of the Aegean, Research programme STAR, Chios, August (in Greek).

Buhalis, D. (1991) 'Strategic marketing and management for the small and medium tourism enterprises in the periphery of the European Union. A case study for the Aegean islands in Greece', M.Sc. dissertation, University of Surrey, UK.

Buhalis, D. (1992) 'SWOT analysis for the small and medium tourism enterprises: the case study of the Aegean islands, Greece', *Hospitality Management Education: Hospitality and Tourism Industry Research Conference*, Birmingham Polytechnic, April, 1992.

Buhalis, D. (1993) 'RICIRMS as a strategic tool for small and medium tourism enterprises', *Tourism Management*, 14(5): 366–378.

Cassidy, J. (1993) 'Bell rings multimedia revolution', *Sunday Times*, 17 October, section 4:2–3.

Chervenak, L. (1991) 'CRS: the past–the present–the future', *Lodging*, June:25–43.

Chervenak, L. (1993) 'Hotel technology at the start of the new millennium', *Hospitality Research Journal*, 17(1):113–120.

Chon, K. (1991) 'Tourist information seeking behaviour and its marketing implications', *Hospitality Research Journal*, 14(2):485–490.

Collier, D. (1993) Presentation to WTO Americas seminar on Trends and Challenges of International Tourism, Montreal, 27–28 May, *Viamericas*, 2(June):5.

Cooper, C. and Buhalis, D. (1992) 'Strategic management and marketing of small and medium sized tourism enterprises in the Greek Aegean islands', in Teare, R. Adams, D. and Messenger, S. (Eds), *Managing Projects in Hospitality Organisations*, Cassell, London, pp. 101–125.

Cooper, C. and Buhalis, D. (1993) 'The future of tourism', in Cooper, C., Fletcher, J., Gilbert, D. and Wanhill, S. (Eds), *Tourism: Principle and Practice*, Pitman, London, pp. 265–276.

Crombie, P. (1992) 'Industry perspective–NTO and SME perspective: national tourist offices (NTO) and small and medium establishments (SME)—an interdependency', in Yee (1992), pp. 49–53.

Crouch, G. (1991) 'Expert computer systems in tourism: emerging possibilities', *Journal of Travel Research*, 29(Winter): 3–10.

Deng, S. and Ryan, C. (1992) 'CRS: tool or determinant of management practice in Canadian travel agents?', *Journal of Travel and Tourism Marketing*, 1(1):19–38.

EC (1991) 'Impact of completion of the internal market on the tourism sector', Tecnecon Consultants, European Community, DG XXIII, November, Brussels.

EC (1993) 'Communication from the Commission: the European Observatory for SMEs—Comments by the Commission on the First Annual Report (1993)', European Community (COM993) 527 final, 5 November, Brussels.

Economist Intelligence Unit (1992) 'International hotel prices and cost structures', *Travel and Tourism Analyst*, No. 5:66–83.

EIM, 1993, 'The European Observatory for SMEs, first annual report', Report submitted to the European Community, DGXXIII, Small Business Research and Consultancy, Netherlands.

Feldman, J. (1987) 'CRS in the USA: determining future levels of airline competition', *Travel and Tourism Analyst*, No. 3:3–14.

Fesenmair, D., Vogt, C. and Mackay, K. (1992) 'Researching consumer information: exploring the role of pre-trip information search in travel decisions', *Proceedings of Travel and Tourism Research Association: Tourism Partnership and Strategies: Merging vision with New Realities*, 23rd Annual Conference, 14–17 June, Minneapolis, pp. 32–36.

Freedman, D. (1991) 'The myth of strategic IS', *CIO*, 4(10):42–48.

Gamble, P. (1988a) 'Tourism technology: developing effective computer systems', *Tourism Management*, 9(4):317–325.

Gamble, P. (1988b) 'Culture shock, computers and the art of making decisions', *International Journal of Contemporary Hospitality Management*, 2(1):4–9.

Gamble, P. (1990) 'New developments in computer technology and their application to the hospitality industry', in Cooper, C. (Ed.), *Progress in Tourism Recreation and Hospitality Management*, Vol. 2, Belhaven, London, pp. 222–231.

Gamble, P. (1992) 'The strategic role of information technology systems', in Teare, R. and Olsen, M. (Eds), *International Hospitality Management: Corporation Strategy in Practice*, Pitman, London.

Giaoutzi, M., Nijkamp, P. and Storey, D. (1988) 'Small is beautiful—the regional importance of small scale activities', in Giaoutzi, M., Nijkamp, P. and Storey, D. (Eds), *Small and Medium Size Enterprises and Regional Development*, Routledge, London, pp. 1–18.

Gilbert, D. (1990) 'European tourism product purchase methods and systems', *The Service Industries Journal*, 10(4):664–679.

Go, F. (1988) 'Key problems and prospects in the international hotel industry', *Travel and Tourism Analyst*, No. 1: pp. 27–51.

Go, F. (1992) 'The role of computerised reservation systems in the hospitality industry', *Tourism Management*, 13(1):22–26.

Go, F. and Welch, P. (1991) 'Competitive strategies for the international hotel industry', Special Report No. 1180, The Economist Intelligence Unit, London.

Haines, P. (1991) 'Qualities needed by destination management systems', *Proceedings of the International Conference on Computer Networking and the Public Tourist Organisation*, Assisi–Perugia, Italy, 18–20 November.

Haines, P. (1992) 'Case studies and status reports—international experience—introduction', in Yee (1992), pp. 66–69.

Haines, P. (1993) 'Destination databases: the Pacific Asia Travel Association perspective', Paper No. 6, PATA Occasional Papers Series, Pacific Asia Travel Association, San Francisco.

Hansen-Sturm, C. (1991) 'Control of computerised information and reservation network as instruments of strategic development and transparence in the market, public strategy for tourism electronic markets', *Proceedings of the International Conference on Computer Networking and the Public Tourist Organisation*, Assisi–Perugia, Italy, 18–20 November.

Hickey, J. (1988) 'Hotel reservation systems and source of business', *Travel and Tourism Analyst*, No. 2:23–36.

Hitchins, F. (1991) 'The influence of technology on UK travel agents', *EIU Travel and Tourism Analyst*, No. 3:88–105.

Holiday Which (1988) 'Brochures, tricks of the trade', March:108–113.

Holiday Which (1989) 'Travel agents, Consumers Association', May:138–141.

Hurst, S. (1992) 'Industry presentation—Accommodation and attractions perspective', in Yee (1992), pp. 42–48.

Hwa, K. (1992) 'National Computer Board's welcome speech', in Yee (1992), pp. 9–12.

Hyde, J. (1993) 'Shopping around for a product that is a home from home', *Travel and Trade Gazette, UK*, No. 2080, 13th October:6.

Jones, C. (1992) 'Destination databases as keys to effective marketing', in Yee (1992), pp. 19–30.

Jones, C. (1993) 'Applications of database marketing in the tourism industry', Paper No. 1, PATA Occasional Papers Series, Pacific Asia Travel Association, San Francisco.

King, W., Hufnagel, E. and Grover, V. (1988) 'Using information technology for competitive advantages', in Earl, M. (Ed.), *Information Management: The Strategic Dimension*, Clarendon Press, Oxford, pp. 75–86.

Lattin, T. (1990) 'Hotel technology: key to survival', in Quest, M. (Ed.), *Horwarth Book of Tourism*, Macmillan, London, pp. 219–223.

Leontidou, L. (1991) 'Greece: prospects and contradictions of tourism in the 1980's', in Williams, A. M. and Shaw, G. J. (Eds), *Tourism and Economic Development: Western European Experiences*, 2nd edn, Belhaven, London, pp. 94–106.

Litinas, N. and Vourgaridis, A. (1992) 'Integrated tourist development of the Aegean islands: the role of telematics', *Proceedings of the Conference Tourism and the Environment*, University of the Aegean, Dept. of Environment, Mytilini, 23–24 October.

Lockwood, A. (1989) 'Quality management in hotels', in Witt, S. and Moutinho, L. (Eds), *Tourism Marketing and Management Handbook*, Prentice Hall, London.

Lowe, A. (1988) 'Small hotel survival—an inductive approach', *International Journal of Hospitality Management*, 7(3):197–223.

Manchester, P. (1993) 'Bell rings multimedia revolution', *Sunday Times*, 17 October, section 4:2–3.

Manfredo, M. (1989) 'An investigation of the basis for external information search in recreation and tourism', *Leisure Sciences*, 11(1):29–45.

McGuffre, J. (1990a) 'CRS development and the hotel sector', Part I, *Travel and Tourism Analyst*, No. 1:29–41.

McGuffre, J. (1990b) 'CRS development and the hotel sector', Part II, *Travel and Tourism Analyst*, No. 2:18–36.

Morrison, A. (1990) 'The utility of consortia to the entrepreneur operating within the hotel industry', M.Sc. thesis, University of Stirling, UK.

Morrison, A. (1992) 'The small firm sector within the UK hotel industry—an endangered species?', *Conference of Hospitality Management Education: Hospitality and Tourism Industry Research Conference*, Birmingham Polytechnic, April 1992.

Moutinho, L. (1990) 'Strategies for destination development—the role of small businesses', in Goodall, B. and Ashworth, G. (Eds), *Marketing Tourism Places*, Routledge, London, pp. 104–122.

Moutinho, L. (1992) 'Tourism: the near and future future from 1990s to 2030s or from sensasision TV to skycycles', *Conference proceedings: Tourism in Europe*, Newcastle Polytechnic, 8–10 July.

Mowlana, H. and Smith, G. (1992) 'Trends in telecommunications and the tourism industry: coalitions, regionalism, and international welfare systems', in Ritchie, B., Hawkins, D., Go, F. and Flechtling, D. (Eds), *World Travel and Tourism Review: Indicators Trends and Issues*, Vol. 2, CAB International, Oxford, pp. 163–167.

Murray, K. (1991) 'A test of services marketing theory: consumer information acquisition activities', *Journal of Marketing*, 55(1):10–25.

Nijkamp, P., Alsters, T. and van der Mark, R. (1988) 'The regional development potential of small and medium sized enterprises: a European perspective', in Giaoutzi, M., Nijkamp, P. and Storey, D. (Eds), *Small and Medium Size Enterprises and Regional Development*, Routledge, London, pp. 122–139.

Oliver, J. (1991) 'Leisure SABRE: a global means of distribution of tourism products', *Proceedings of the International Conference on Computer Networking and the Public Tourist Organisation*, Assisi–Perugia, Italy, 18–20 November.

Olsen, M. (1991) 'Environmental scan: global hospitality industry trends', in Hawkins, D., Ritchie, B., Go, F. and Flechtling, D. (eds), *World Travel and Tourism Review: Indicators Trends and Issues*, Vol. 1, CAB International, Oxford, pp. 120–124.

Page, A. (1993) 'Global small business—a focus for economic recovery', paper presented in Conference: *Overcoming Isolation-Telematics and Regional Development*, 30 April–2 May, University of the Aegean, Business Administration Dept., Chios Island, Greece.

Pelletier, J. (1993) 'GDS within our reach?', *Viamericas*, No. 2, June.

Perdue, R. (1985) 'Segmenting state travel information: inquirers by timing of the destination decision and previous experience', *Journal of Travel Research*, 23(3):6–11.

Peroni, G. (1991) 'Problems and prospects for the renewal of public tourism marketing in the computer network era', *Proceedings of the International Conference on Computer Networking and the Public Tourist Organisation*, Assisi-Perugia, Italy, 18–20 November.

Pine, R. (1993a) 'Technology transfer in tourism', in Ritchie, B., Hawkins, D., Go, F. and Flechtling, D. (Eds), *World Travel and Tourism Review: Indicators Trends and Issues*, Vol. 3, CAB International, Oxford, pp. 206–210.

Pine, R. (1993b) 'Technology transfer in the hotel industry', in Jones, P. and Pizam, A. (Eds), *The International Hospitality Industry: Organisational and Operational Issues*, Pitman, London, pp. 226–240.

Poon, A. (1988a) 'Flexible specialisation and small size—the case of Caribbean tourism', SPRU, DRC Discussion Paper, No. 57.

Poon, A. (1988b) 'Tourism and information technologies', *Annals of Tourism Research*, 15(4):531–549.

Poon, A. (1989) 'Competitive strategies for new tourism', in Cooper, C. (Ed.), *Progress in Tourism, Recreation and Hospitality Management*, Vol. 1, Belhaven, London, pp. 91–102.

Poon, A. (1993) *Tourism, Technology and Competitive Strategies*, CAB International, Oxford.

Porter, M. (1985) 'Technology and competitive advantage', *The Journal of Business Strategy*, Winter:60–70.

Porter, M. (1989) 'Building competitive advantage by extending information systems', *Computerworld*, 23(41):19.

Quee, T. (1992) 'Industry presentation—transportation perspective: destination databases', in Yee (1992), pp. 38–41.

Ritchie, B. (1991) 'Global tourism policy issues: an agenda for the 1990's', in Hawkins, D., Ritchie, B., Go, F. and Flechtling, D. (Eds), *World Travel and Tourism Review: Indicators Trends and Issues*, Vol. 1, CAB International, Oxford, pp. 149–158.

Rochester, J. and Douglas, D. (1991) 'The emerging world of multimedia', *I/S Analyser*, 29(3):1–12.

Runge, D. and Earl, M. (1988) 'Getting competitive advantages from telecommunications', in Earl, M. (Ed.), *Information Management: The Strategic Dimension*, Clarendon Press, Oxford, pp. 125–145.

Shaw, G. and Williams, A. M. (1990) 'Tourism, economic development and the role of entrepreneurial activity', in Cooper, C. (Ed.), *Progress in Tourism, Recreation and Hospitality Management*, Vol. 2, Belhaven, London, pp. 67–81.

Sheldon, P. (1993) 'Destination information systems', *Annals of Tourism Research*, 20(4):633–649.

Sinclair, T., Alizadeh, P. and Onunga, E. (1992) 'The structure of international tourism and tourism development in Kenya', in Harrison, (Ed.), *Tourism and the less developed countries*, Belhaven, London, pp. 47–63.

Sloane, J. (1990) 'Latest developments in aviation CRSs', *EIU Travel and Tourism Analyst*, No. 4:5–15.

Snepenger, D., Meged, K., Snelling, M. and Worrall, K. (1990) 'Information search strategies by destination-naive tourists', *Journal of Travel Research*, 29(1):185–208.

Stanton, R. (1992) 'The PATA survey report "Destination databases: issues and priorities"', in Yee (1992), pp. 31–37.

Strassmann, P. (1990) *The Business Value of Computers: an Executive Guide*, The Information Economics Press, Connecticut.

Sussmann, S. (1992) 'Destination management systems: the challenge of the 1990s', in Cooper, C. and Lockwood, A. (Eds),

Progress in Tourism, Recreation and Hospitality Management, Vol. 4, Belhaven, London, pp. 209–215.

Taylor, P. (1993) 'Operators locked in battle', *Financial Times*, 9 November, Business Travel section:5.

Thomas, M. (1988) 'Innovation and technology strategy: competitive new technology firms and industries', in Giaoutzi, M., Nijkamp, P. and Storey, D. (Eds), *Small and Medium Size Enterprises and Regional Development*, Routledge, London, pp. 44–70.

Truitt, L., Teye, V. and Farris, M. (1991) 'The role of computer reservation systems: international implications for the tourism industry', *Tourism Management*, 12(1):21–36.

Vlitos-Rowe, L. (1992) 'Destination databases and management systems', *Travel and Tourism Analyst*, No. 5:84–108.

Vogel, H. (1991) 'Computer networking and new ways of tourism promotion and marketing for the public system in Holland, Austria and Germany', *Proceedings of the International Conference on Computer Networking and the Public Tourist Organisation*, Assisi–Perugia, Italy, 18–20 November.

Wardell, D. (1987) 'Airline reservation Systems in the USA: CRS agency dealerships and the gold handcuff', *Travel and Tourism Analyst*, January:45–56.

Wheatcroft, S. and Lipman, G. (1990) 'European liberalisation and world air transport: towards a translational industry', Special Report, No. 2015, Economist Intelligence Unit, London.

Williams, A. M. and Shaw, G. J. (1988) 'Western European Tourism in perspective', in Williams, A. M. and Shaw, G. J. (Eds), *Tourism and Economic Development: Western European Experiences*, Belhaven, London, pp. 12–38.

Williams, P. (1993) 'Information technology and tourism: a dependent factor for future survival', in Ritchie, B., Hawkins, D., Go, F. and Flechtling, D. (Eds), *World Travel and Tourism Review: Indicators Trends and Issues*, Vol. 3, CAB International, Oxford, pp. 200–205.

Wiseman, C. (1985) *Strategy and Computers: Information Systems as Competitive Weapons*, Dow Jones-Irwin, New York.

World Tourism Organisation (1988) *Guidelines for the Transfer of New Technologies in the Field of Tourism*, WTO, Madrid.

World Tourism Organisation (1991a) Seminar on Small and Medium Sized Enterprises, Report on WTO in Milan, 16–17 December 1991.

World Tourism Organisation (1991b) 'Tourism to the 2000. Qualitative aspects affecting global growth: a discussion paper', Executive Summary, Madrid, WTO.

Yee, J. (1992) *Proceedings from PATA Destination Database Conference*, Singapore, 9–10 December, PATA Intelligence Centre, San Francisco.

28 Developing information technology options in the hotel industry: the value chain approach

P. DESINANO AND C. VIGO

Introduction

Information technology (IT) applications greatly affect businesses, including the hospitality industry, and a critical issue concerns the relationship between technology and business. The way of conceiving the business environment (e.g. the firm, the corporation, the competition and so on) becomes the driver of IT applications. The aim of this chapter is to briefly discuss the drivers of IT in the hospitality industry, to pinpoint current problems and sketch the more meaningful trends in the near future. Recent important criticism would suggest broadening our perspective and inserting the hotel business within the context of the service business.

The evolution of IT applications in the hospitality industry

The works of Gamble (1984, 1991), Kasavana and Cahill (1987) and Moore (1989) represent a valuable basis for an outline of the evolution of IT applications in the hospitality industry. Each of these works describes hotel computerisation as a step-by-step process. At the first stage, in the 1960s, IT was interpreted as a powerful tool for the automation of basic hotel functions. Influenced by the experience drawn from other business sectors, particularly industry, the first functions to be automated were concerned with highly structured and repetitive tasks. In the hotel industry these functions included accounting, payroll, reservation and inventory control. The declared aim at this stage of IT application was operational efficiency, primarily time-saving and personnel reduction. At that time the hardware available was not user-friendly and the rare attempts to automate the typical front office operations ended unsuccessfully. The failure of attempts at hotel front office automation at the New York Hilton in Manhattan in 1963 is a symbolic event. On the other hand, computerised hotel reservation systems provided good results.

Later, during the 1970s, the advent of the minicomputer made the use of IT in the hotel industry cheaper and more accessible. IT applications were extended to marketing and control functions. Management, through the detailed and precise recording of front office transactions, were able to draw accurate guest profiles thus making marketing segmentation more effective. Furthermore the quantity of data produced by back office procedures provided timely and analytic control information. In this stage of its evolution the management found IT to be a useful tool for monitoring hotel operations.

At the end of the 1970s and during the 1980s the PMS (property management systems) evolved. Integration became the main requirement: integration within the individual firm and integration between the firm and the outside world (e.g. other corporate firms, CRS, external data sources, etc.). Managers were very sensitive to integration between front office and back office systems. This goal was achieved by integrating front office and back office procedures within a single database. Sometimes a more advanced level of integration was achieved with the concept of CIB (computer intelligent building). This chapter tackles the management of technological equipment such as energy-saving systems, alarm systems, access authorisation and other typical devices. Furthermore the early 1980s saw the definitive achievement of turn-key PMS, off-the-shelf systems produced and marketed by specialised software houses.

The brief history of hotel computerisation we have sketched shows how some guidelines have directed IT applications for the hotel business. First, structured and repetitive operational activities were automated. At a later stage, computer applications were extended to a larger range of operating activities, including front office, but the focus was placed on control, which is the typical function of middle management. Further developments, as Gamble (1991) argued, are related to the extension of IT to the firm's strategic level, the level of strategic planning executed by top management. Hence the computerisation process has evolved from the lower to the upper hierarchical level of the firm's organisational chart.

Wiseman (1988) observes that this perspective of the computerisation process, characterised by various hierarchical levels as we explained, is based on a specific way to view a firm proposed by Anthony in 1965. This approach has not only strongly affected management studies in the late 1960s and most of the 1970s but, Wiseman adds, has also inspired the information system design of the last twenty years. Anthony's view suggested isolating the firm from its environment for a better understanding of planning and control mechanisms. In addition, he considered IT a valuable tool for operational support to management activities. This paradigm became an unspoken assumption accepted by the majority of information system managers—and information systems for the lodging industry have not been an exception. Wiseman called this approach the 'conventional perspective'.

Conventional versus strategic perspective

The strategic management studies achieved in the 1980s highlighted many cases where IT played an essential role in the strategic behaviour of the firm and not simply an operational one. A large number of these classic cases are documented (Wiseman, 1988). In the early 1980s these experiences, joined to new tools for economic analysis, determined a turning-point in the ways of considering IT within a business. In the light of those changes Wiseman (1988) strongly criticised the 'conventional perspective' and proposed an alternative perspective he defined as 'strategic'. The key to understanding the fundamental distinction between the conventional and the strategic perspective is related to the conceptual difference between the function and use of IT. The strategic value of an IT application is not related to the technical functions involved in the application itself but to the manager's use of this technology to tackle a specific competitive issue. For example the hotel financial statement may be considered a boring legal constraint or a powerful tool to carefully analyse the cost trends of a business to support the low-cost strategy chosen by hotel management. In the strategic approach IT is not merely evaluated as a tool, but as a fundamental building-block of the strategic structure. In this sense the strategic value of an IT application lies in its positioning inside the strategy of the firm.

Wiseman criticised Anthony's paradigm-based IT applications because the paradigm represents a kind of 'prison' for strategic thought, reducing the range of possible uses to the limits of technical functions. Instead new business can also be generated by a paradoxical use of IT. To synthesise one can say that the user's applicative horizon is broader than the IT system's designers.

To use IT in a strategic perspective, one must recognise the opportunities available in a specific competitive context. The famous IT consultant, James Martin, within his information systems construction methodology known as 'information engineering', dedicated a specific chapter to the so-called 'strategic systems vision' (Martin, 1990). In order to accomplish this task Porter and Millar (1985) suggested two conceptual tools: the information intensity matrix and the value chain. The first tool assesses the high or low information content of the product/service under analysis. The value chain, on the other hand, is a tool to systematically analyse those activities of the firm that are able to give a competitive advantage within the selected basic strategy. In this paper attention is focused on the value chain because recently heavy criticism has been directed towards this.

The value chain

The value chain configuration enables the firm to improve, in efficiency and effectiveness, the final value to the buyer. Value is measured by the number of clients willing to buy the firm's offerings. In such a way, a firm competes in the competitive arena to reduce costs or to increase value by setting a higher price. The firm's competitive advantage can occur within the chain of value activities in producing goods or performing and delivering services. Value created by the firm increases the competitive margin in the chain. Comparing its value chain with that of its competitors, the firm highlights differences. Differences in the competitive arena are sources of differentiation.

Porter (1985) divides value activities into primary activities and support activities (see Figure 28.1). The former, primary activities, are those involved in the physical production of a firm's output. The latter support the primary activities. As Porter (1985) states, the firm's value chain is a linkage of interdependent activities. This interdependency can improve the performance of each activity in reducing related costs or enhancing differentiation.

The firm's value chain, within a particular industry, is part of a broader value system (see Figure 28.2). Suppliers create upstream value for the firm and this can eventually create downstream value, through the (distribution) channel value, to the buyer's value chain. Differentiation is the liaison between the firm's value chain and the buyer's value chain. Value, for the buyer

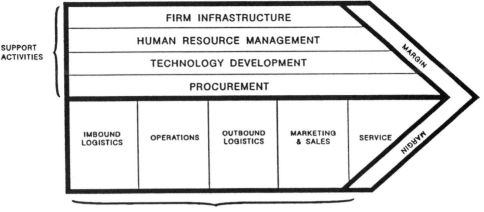

Figure 28.1 *The generic value chain (from Porter (1985))*

is to buy the same perceived 'product' or 'service' at lower price, or to obtain 'uniqueness' at whatever price. In this sense Porter argues: '"Quality" is too narrow a view of what makes a firm unique, because it focuses the attention on the product rather the broader array of value activities that impact the buyer' (Porter, 1985).

Developing the strategic use of IT

The value chain is the basis on which Porter and Millar (1985) have designed a specific approach to the strategic use of IT. Of course the strength of this perspective of IT employment is related to the strength of the value chain theory.

Porter and Millar (1985) observe that in every product or service an information component and a physical component are distinguishable. The same observation is possible for each strategic relevant business activity. When IT can support such information contents then it becomes a strategic weapon for the firm. The main strategic effects of IT are:

- cost reduction;
- differentiation increase:
- change in the relationship within the competitive arena.

The IT issues are strategic if they support or shape the firm's selected basic strategy for achieving the various targets defined. For example, the first hotel chains equipped with a CRS introduced a strong item of differentiation about the way to make reservations compared to the traditional way based on telex or phone technology. Furthermore, IT can also change the structure of the competitive arena. For instance, a CRS that provides direct booking from the customer by personal computer technology modifies the relationship between service provider and customer, reducing the role played by delivering channels such as travel agencies.

The value chain is a powerful tool for pinpointing all the strategic activities able to create value for the customer or differentiating or decreasing the cost of the product/service.

Normann versus Porter

Porter and Millar (1985) assert that the value chain model is applicable to every kind of business and this position is confirmed and *specified* in Porter (1985). Recently Porter's approach to business strategy has met with strong criticism on the part of Richard Normann (1991) who discussed the argument more extensively in Normann and Ramirez (1993). *Harvard Business Review* organised a mini-forum on this issue (Perspectives, 1993).

Figure 28.2 *The value system (from Porter (1985))*

The focal point of Normann's criticism is the difficulty in designing clear interfaces among the various value activities within the value chain. Normann (1991) declares that it is not possible to conceive of service distribution as a linear sequence of separate activities because service distribution is characterised by strong interaction between clients and personnel. This interaction is like a dialogue that is difficult to break down without losing the specific nature of service businesses.

This criticism is more clearly defined and explained in three case histories given by Normann and Ramirez (1993). In this paper the authors argue that the focal point is reinventing value not producing it. More precisely the core business is the promotion of social innovation through the dynamic reconfiguration of the relationships, the roles and the number of business 'players'. No longer then is it a *value chain* but a *value constellation*. On this issue Normann and Ramirez consider the value chain obsolete for every type of business and classify Porter's approach as belonging to the old industrial era as opposed to the value constellation approach belonging to the new post-industrial era.

Normann's thesis undermines the basis of a successful management paradigm and, at the same time, poses an important problem related to IT management. To which reference scheme must we refer in developing effective IT applications in business? If Normann is right, the value chain approach should be refuted as a paradigm to direct IT applications and research towards other directions.

Redefining the value chain in business services: the case of the hotel industry

Normann's criticism is well-founded but does not address the basis of the value chain concept. Porter's approach does not simply focus on added value but enlarges the concept to define a firm's activities as the key to get an advantage over competitors. The diagnosis should be made considering all the value activities in the firm's performance as part of a single-industry value system. Reinventing value, as Normann and Ramirez (1993) recommend, does not necessarily mean abandoning a strategic tool for the assessment of the firm's current position in the competitive arena. The reinvention of a business could be the result of an analysis of the firm's value chain or of the competitive arena, reconsidering for example new entrants or substitute products/services. There is no 'new logic of value', but only a new starting point, a new positioning of a business. Instead Normann's considerations are very important in adapting the value chain when it must be applied to service businesses such as the hotel industry.

Porter (1985) configures all value activities from a 'manufacturing industry' viewpoint. Even a manufacturing firm which does custom rather than mass production would be difficult to fit into the generic value chain scheme. His suggestions for redefining the value chain, and Normann and Ramirez's criticism have stimulated us to reinterpret Porter's strategic approach in the hotel industry.

Combining the definition of service performance, production and delivery with the nature of service itself, we have attempted to fit Porter's general theory into a specific service industry. In this approach all references are made, in an unambiguous way, to the hotel business.

It is essential to define the value chain or identify value activities in each individual case, since these may differ considerably from industry to industry, and even between two different business units within the same industry.

Take, for example, two hotels in the same urban area delivering similar services to business travellers. Hotel service is a bundle of activities, consisting of a core product—a quiet and clean bedroom—plus a set of services. Lovelock (1992a) proposed a figure (Figure 28.3) that encompasses the core and supplementary services offered to business travellers by a good hotel. If the two hotels do not belong to the same chain, one is not likely to find the same check-in procedures, the same restaurant services, the same personnel policy, the same distribution channels or the same suppliers. These differences in packaging and delivering hotel services could contain the key to gaining competitive advantage over one other.

As Lovelock (1992a) points out, in managing services, differences between the manufacturing industry and the service industry lie in the 'front office' operations where the customer interfaces with the service operations, and this is particularly true for hotel guests. 'Back office' operations are sealed off from the hotel guests; they are managed in not very dissimilar ways from those of manufacturing firms. Other important features in managing services business, and hotel services in particular, such as the nature of product–service, people (staff and customer) as part of the product, the customer involvement in service production and delivery, the importance of the time factor, quality control problems, different distribution channels, simultaneous production and consumption and absence of inventories for services are evidenced by Lovelock (1992a) and Reid (1989). Though, for the last item, in the hotel industry, Reid (1989) emphasises that some elements of the service-product mix are tangible and inventories must be maintained.

From this viewpoint, hotel services are the result of the mix at the set-up and delivery phase of physical,

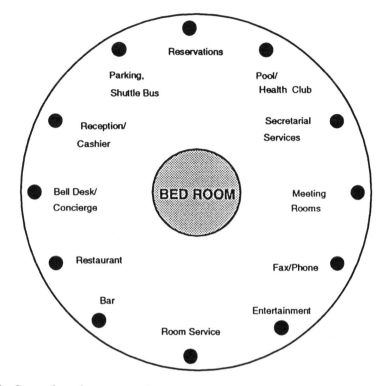

Figure 28.3 *Core and supplementary services at a hotel for business travellers (from Lovelock 1992a))*

organisational and labour activities, interfacing necessarily with hotel guests for the global performance.

In other words, Porter's theory is different from Normann and Ramirez's because each one is a specific answer to a specific problem. Porter poses the problem of understanding how the firm creates value for the buyer. The answer to this question is the identification of those activities that create value permitting the firm to perform its chosen basic strategy. Instead Normann and Ramirez (1993) suggest identifying the right offering, e.g. combination of products and services, reinventing new ways to create value for the customer, ways reflecting the complexity of the actual business environment. In a sense Normann and Ramirez focus on the offering while Porter focuses on the process to perform it.

The value chain configuration in hotel businesses

Defining the value chain for the hotel business means identifying value activities that can be potential sources for lowering costs or to enhance differentiations. In our case we have disaggregated a generic hotel firm identifying those activities which can bring a hotel business to gain

a certain amount of margin and value in the competitive arena. This arbitrary interpretation is particularly suited to the hotel industry and is related to the characteristics of hotel firms, as capacity constrained firms where guests come for the services. A good outline to identify the strategic activities of hotel business is the hotel guest cycle as described in Kasavana and Cahill (1987). Five primary activities were identified (see Figure 28.4).

Distribution and sales

Unlike a manufacturing firm, where distribution and sales concern the marketers when the product actually leaves the production line, a hotel firm, which delivers its services to the guest on the premises, is involved in this activity from the moment the marketing plan, to attract people to the property, is formulated. This activity starts a relatively long time earlier, before physical service production and consumption begin. Occasionally, this period becomes shorter when a walk-in customer comes in asking for a bed overnight.

Accessibility, sales systems and procedures, as well as distribution channels, sales personnel and reward systems, form the distribution and sales activity.

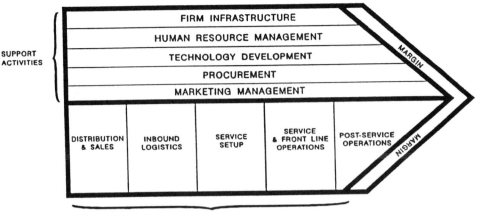

Figure 28.4 *The hotel value chain*

Inbound logistics

Since some elements of the product–service mix are tangible, and inventories of food and beverage items as well as sheets, towels, soap, sanitation products, and general furniture must be maintained, inbound logistics become a fundamental activity in hotel operations. Receiving, checking and stocking goods and raw materials as well as their distribution to department stores are some of the initial steps in preparing the tangible mix of hotel service.

Service set-up

This activity concerns the pre-arrangement of service and front line operations. This activity is carried out mainly by back-of-the-house personnel who do not come into contact with the guest. It includes food preparation, housekeeping operations, maintenance, cleaning and sanitation of common areas, and so forth. What happens backstage is of little interest to the guests, but it is a strategic activity for the hotel as a whole.

Service and front line operations

This activity is 'the moment of truth' for the overall hotel services and operations because it directly involves the physical person of the guest. Service operations can be divided into those relating to the service personnel and those relating to the physical facilities and equipment. This activity allows the firm, through the service personnel, facilities and equipment, to deliver the value service to the guest. Every deed, every action or performance is a potential source to enhance quality. Each point of contact could also be a source of differentiation for the method of delivering services.

Post-service operations

Post-service operations are those activities performed when the guest has checked out, or better yet when he has already left the premises. They are performed by the firm to upgrade the value service and to remind the guest of the hotel 'experience'. This activity is centred in the marketing-oriented hotel organisation and has a tremendous impact on the guest: consider follow-up activities, special programmes for repeaters, birthday or special-event mailings, the rapid restitution of lost or forgotten property, and so forth. These acts complete the marketing cycle, stimulating the guest to repeat reservations or toward positive word-of-mouth promotion.

Primary activities cannot be performed without support activities. These pervade the whole firm and its service performance. We have identified the following support activities (see also Figure 28.4).

Marketing management

With increasing competition in the service industry, many authors (Lovelock, 1992b; Reid, 1989; Wind et al., 1992; Eiglier and Langeard, 1987) recommend that firms be marketing-oriented in managing services. In this respect Lovelock (1992b) states: 'many service firms have developed an effective marketing function to act as a bridge between the organisation and the environment within which it operates'.

Nowadays hotel businesses tend more and more to be marketing-oriented firms, and the marketing function is involved not only with identifying needs and trends within the market-place but also with the product concept, distribution and pricing strategies, sales activities, the development of communications programmes and monitoring the activities of competitors, as well as control of internal and external operations. On the whole, the marketing function takes part in all hotel operations and acts to support them.

Procurement

This activity concerns the acquisition of all elements, physical and non-physical, that make hotel services feasible. Procurement is a part of many sub-activities such as linkages with suppliers, raw material control, product and service positioning and image, as well as the monitoring of all personnel and equipment performance in the hotel business, either in backstage activities or in front stage activities. In this view, procurement is spread over many activities performed by the firm and is not limited to the purchasing function.

Technology development

In every business, sector, or industry, each activity is performed with a heavy dependence on technology. Technology is embedded into the firm's know-how, into production and service procedures, into support facilities and equipment. The technological support is now part of each hotel department and activity: reservation procedures, guest and supplier database maintenance, conservation, cooking and cleaning technology, and so on. Not only is technology itself an integral part of this activity, but every process to improve service and the product line becomes a part of technology development. We also consider research and development part of this activity, because considering R&D strictly as an engineering department is a very narrow view. In the hotel business, technology development includes the search for new food products or new menus at a restaurant, packages or special programmes, new communications systems or new service delivery procedures.

Human resource management

Human resource management concerns staff recruiting and training policies as well as the personnel management function. This activity can no longer be considered a mere handling of wages! High-quality recruiting and training, with related costs, are essential activities in the hotel business because of the high personnel turnover and the related waste. Personnel is a key and irreplaceable element

in delivering hotel services, and personnel could be a strategic source of competitive advantage for the hotel business. Therefore the role of HRM in identifying and exploiting personnel skills becomes a winning resource to implement the firm's strategy.

Firm infrastructure

This concerns a number of basic activities necessary to run a firm: from general management to budgeting, from general accounting to financial planning and legal aspects, from contacts with regulatory bodies to the monitoring of the firm's overall affairs. It does not deal with any specific activity, but it supports the whole chain. Generally the firm's infrastructure is seen to be above hotel operations, but it can achieve a strategic role in creating a very strong advantage in the competitive arena. Consider the strategic role of general management in creating liaisons with regulatory bodies, state agencies or local boards or in influencing the administrative 'environment'.

Reconfiguring IT strategic impact in hotel industry

In the light of the above statements, it is possible to reconfigure a new scheme to guide the strategic use of IT.

Normann and Ramirez's (1993) observations are very useful in analysing the competitive arena and in designing the offering by integrating Porter's concept of the assessment of economic sector attractiveness. The IT impact on the offering can be evaluated by joining Porter and Millar's (1985) considerations with Normann and Ramirez's. In this sense it becomes a 'value creation designing'.

The value chain model, reconfigured on the basis of each specific business, remains a fundamental tool for designing the business process to achieve the offering. The value chain can be interpreted as 'value creation engineering'. Thus Porter and Millar's (1985) considerations about IT support within the value chain continue to be valid.

Conclusions

After over eight years from its first publication, the value chain continues to be an effective paradigm to guide IT business applications, Normann's (1991) criticism notwithstanding. Of course, the generic model proposed by Porter (1985) had to be rethought and adapted for each particular competitive arena. This chapter has attempted to propose a possible generic value chain for hotels that meets the particular characteristics of service businesses, so different in many points from manufacturing businesses. Normann and Ramirez's (1993) observations are very valuable when management must define and analyse the competitive arena to design a new product or service or to reconfigure roles and the relative relationships among competitors. Both approaches are important for the design of IT applications from a strategic perspective.

References

Anthony, R. N. (1965) *Planning and Control Systems: a Framework for Analysis*, Harvard University Press, Boston, MA.

Eiglier, P. and Langeard, E. (1987) *Servuction—Le marketing des services*, McGraw-Hill, Paris.

Gamble, P. R. (1984) *Small Computers and Hospitality Management*, Hutchinson, London.

Gamble, P. R. (1991) 'Innovation and innkeeping', *International Journal of Hospitality Management*, 10(1):3–23.

Kasavana, M. L. and Cahill, J. J. (1987) *Managing Computers in Hospitality Industry*, The Educational Institute of the AHMA, East Lansing, MI.

Lovelock, C. H. (1992a) 'Basic toolkit for service managers', in *Managing Services*, Lovelock, C. H. (Ed.), Prentice Hall, London, pp. 17–30.

Lovelock, C. H. (1992b) 'The search for synergy: what marketers need to know about service operations', in *Managing Services*, Lovelock, C. H. (Ed.), Prentice Hall, London, pp. 392–405.

Martin, J. (1990) *Information Engineering*, Vol. II: *Planning and Analysis*, Prentice Hall, Englewood Cliffs, NJ.

Moore, R. (1989) 'Information systems in the hospitality industry: an Ever-changing Phenomenon', in *Proceedings of the International Meeting 'Informatica e informazione'*, Perugia, Italy, 18–20 May 1989; published in *Quaderni di Politica del Turismo*, 1(1):105–107 (Maggioli, Rimini, Italy).

Normann, R. (1991) *Strategic Management Services*, John Wiley, Chichester.

Normann, R. and Ramirez, R. (1993) 'From value chain to value constellation', *Harvard Business Review*, July–August: 65–77.

Perspectives (1993) 'Strategy and the art of reinventing value', *Harvard Business Review*, September–October:39–51.

Porter, M. E. (1985) *Competitive Advantage*, Free Press, New York.

Porter, M. E. and Millar, V. E. (1985) 'How IT gives you a competitive advantage', *Harvard Business Review*, July–August:149–160.

Reid, R. D. (1989) *Hospitality Marketing Management*, Van Nostrand Reinhold, New York.

Wind, J., Green, P., Shifflet, D. and Scarbrough, M. (1992) 'Courtyard by Marriott: designing a hotel facility with consumer-based marketing models', in *Managing Services*, Lovelock, C. H. (Ed.), Prentice Hall, London, pp. 118–137.

Wiseman, C. (1988) *Strategic Information Systems*, Irwin, Homewood, IL.

29 Tourism—the next generation: virtual reality and surrogate travel, is it the future of the tourism industry?

A. P. WILLIAMS AND J. S. P. HOBSON

Introduction

The term 'virtual reality' (VR) was first coined by Myron Krueger in the mid-1970s to describe a theoretical approach to understanding the human/computer interface. Today, the VR concept has emerged and stands as the vanguard of a new technological revolution. Describing VR, Kuffel (1993) observed, 'Virtual reality grabs your imagination by the throat. This is the final frontier for silicone junkies, a place which never existed and yet there it is right in front of you—and behind, below and above. This is the looking glass through which Alice fell'. Whether creating new worlds, or re-creating 'real world' environments, VR technology is likely to have a major impact on the future tourism industry. It may potentially redefine the nature of tourism as we understand it today.

Technology and Tourism—redefining the relationship

The wind of change is blowing.

Harold Macmillan

Technology has already had a dynamic effect on the tourism industry. For example, computer systems were installed in many tourism operations, with their main function being to support the front-line staff in carrying out their jobs. These systems were designed to make improvements in clerical and administrative efficiency, and as Gamble (1984) noted, 'the only difference being that they [computers] work at electronic speeds'. These early systems focused on the main data-processing functions, such as input, storage, and retrieval of large amounts of information. Consequently, these systems became prominent in reservation departments and accounting offices, where there was a large amount of data to be processed. Despite the technology playing an essentially passive role, operators gained substantial improvements in efficiency and in many cases this resulted in competitive advantage over other tourism suppliers.

As the price of technology has fallen, and the processing power of computers has improved, the relative competitive advantages have been slowly diminished. Consequently, suppliers have looked to new technological developments to maintain their position in the market. A new generation of systems have evolved, which are now playing a more significant role in operations and management of the whole tourism industry than their predecessors. The position of computer systems has changed from playing a largely passive and supporting role, to a more strategic and proactive role.

The central focus of present and future technology developments lies within communication systems. Computerised reservation systems (CRS) which were instigated by the airlines, now provide many tourism suppliers with an increasingly global distribution of their products and services. In fact, it is argued that the dramatic impact of CRS is actually redefining the marketing and distribution channels of tourism products and services (Bitner and Booms, 1982; Go and Williams, 1993). In many cases the early investment in CRS created substantial competitive advantages for the owners of the CRS. In the case of American Airlines, through its CRS system (SABRE), it has created such a large competitive advantage, that the CRS division now generates more profit for the company than the airline division (Hopper, 1990).

Poon (1988) also highlights that the tourism industry is impacted by a complex system of information technologies (SIT). She points out that the SIT affects four components of the tourism system; these are the delivery of tourism services, the management of tourism, the marketing of tourism, and producer/consumer relationships. It can thus be deduced, that the whole tourism industry is, in some way, affected by, or entirely dependent on, developments in information technology. Williams (1993) goes further by suggesting that information technology is the dependent factor for business survival in the tourism industry of the future.

As communication technologies continue to evolve, there will be growing impacts from technology on different sectors of the tourism industry. Developments such as artificial intelligence, electronic data interchange (EDI), and ISDN technologies are likely to play key roles in shaping the future tourism industry. For example, ISDN technology is creating some exciting opportunities with the ability to transmit graphics and digitised images (video images) over long distances. The major CRS companies are already investing in and researching into the potential of ISDN. American Airlines' SABREVISION, has started an initiative in this direction, by combining the pictures and video images of destinations, with the availability and price information of the CRS. Other CRS companies are sure to follow this latest development.

Obviously, the continued pace of rapid technological change creates a dilemma for operators and suppliers. While, on the one hand, it creates new opportunities, on the other hand, it makes existing technologies obsolete, which creates investment and cost difficulties. The potential competitive advantages gained may be short-lived, or even non-existent, which then questions the need to invest at all. However, Shafer (1987) makes some relevant observations, 'To many tourism professionals the past seems immaterial and the present obsolete. Technology—in the form of new innovations, information, techniques, procedures, and/or equipment—has accelerated the pace of change within the tourism industry to the point where the future seems to arrive faster every day'. Thus, it is clear that advanced technologies have become an integral part of the tourism industry, and will play an increasingly prominent role in the future.

Tourism—the road ahead

> *For my part, I travel not to go anywhere, but to go. I travel for travel's sake. The great affair is to move.*
> Robert Louis Stevenson

Despite the recession in the Western industrialised countries and Japan, international tourism is still growing at a faster rate than international economic growth (WTO, 1993). Between 1970 and 1990 tourism grew by nearly 300% and it is expected to grow by half as much again by the end of the century. In 1991, 450 million tourists travelled internationally; but this only represents 8% of the world's population (UNEP, 1992).

Looking at the world in population terms, in 1992 the world's population stood at 5.4 billion people. It is expected to grow to 7.1 billion by 2010, and 8.5 billion by the year 2025. Most of this population growth will be in Asia, and it is estimated that Asia will represent 60% of the world population by the end of the century. Asia is also the fastest-growing economic region of the world. As Andrews (1993) pointed out, 'By almost every yardstick Asia has become home to the most impressive economic growth in history'. With such economic growth predicted, tourism is set to enjoy further increases. In east Asia and the Pacific, tourism growth is already surging, with tourism arrivals there growing by 8.2% in 1992, well above the world average (WTO, 1992). It has been noted by some observers that it is not beyond the realm of possibility that by 2010, China's travel market could be larger than the USA (Cleverdon, 1993). Meanwhile, with the recession failing to dampen the demand for travel in the developed industrialised countries, the tourism industry seems well placed to take advantage of the economic upswing. The future long-term growth of the tourism industry, from a demand point of view, looks promising.

The developments of new transport technologies have allowed us to travel further, faster. Each new technological breakthrough, has allowed us to make another leap forward in our travel patterns (Hobson and Usyal, 1993). However, it is already clear that the world's tourism infrastructure is being increasingly stretched and overloaded. As Cleverdon (1992) observed, 'the scale of growth in tourism will place great pressure on the facilities and amenities required by tourists'. Currently, many countries are facing large budget deficits ('Fear of finance', 1992), and the sheer scale of the required infrastructure projects is becoming too financially daunting. Furthermore, local and environmental groups are becoming increasingly successful in their objections to such projects, slowing developments further. As Hobson (1993), pointed out, 'it is clear that future infrastructure projects will be developed at a slower rate than in the past. It will also not be at a pace that will keep up with the projected growth of tourism'. Therefore, looking into the future, the growth of the tourism industry is likely to face more constraints from the supply side than the demand side.

Whether it is in industrialised countries, or in developing third world countries, traffic congestion appears to be a worsening problem. Furthermore, with the majority of European and American airports already reporting congestion problems, and forecasting even more difficulties in the coming decades, long-distance travel may already be losing its allure. As the main generating tourism markets are becoming increasingly sophisticated and demanding, potential tourists are already looking at alternatives to long-distance travel. During the 1980s, the most noticeable trend was the increase in short-break tourism, and this is expected to continue into the next century (Frechtling, 1987). It is also becoming clear that tourists are becoming less willing to put up with the problems of travelling long distances. As Boorstin (1975) pointed out, the English word 'travel' was originally the same word as 'travail' (meaning 'work' or 'torment'). And travail, in turn was derived from the Romans and the Latin word 'tripalium', which was a three-staked instrument of torture. Perhaps, they knew something about travel at the end of the 20th century.

It may not be surprising to see, that alternatives to the 'actual' travel experience already exist—for example, substitute and surrogate tourism. Substitute tourism has existed for some time and can be defined as where 'one destination takes the place of another destination'. For example, The English Riviera concept was created and marketed by the Great Western Railway (GWR), to offer a British substitute to its continental rivals in France and Italy. Similarly, Montreal in Quebec, Canada, has marketed itself as a French-speaking substitute destination to Americans, who are unwilling or unable to travel all the way to France.

Surrogate tourism on the other hand, can be defined as, 'a whole travel experience, where tourists make trips to imitations of actual destinations or to fictitiously created places or events'. For example, Disney's EPCOT offers an imitation of the Eiffel Tower in Paris, and it also offers created experiences such as its 'Star Tours' to outer space. Looking at the current developments of theme parks, Stevens (1993) observed that, 'So many theme parks are offering themed areas which are based on faraway places, offering a surrogate travel experience. . . . Who needs to travel the world when you can achieve "virtual reality" in the more comfortable, palatable environment of a theme park?'

Predicting the future, Anthony Smith (1993), President of Magdalen College, Oxford, sees two parallel trends of opposite kinds that are converging to impact leisure and entertainment, and consequently the tourism industry. On the other hand, the development of large-scale public events with impressive venues and media aided by technology that can deliver convincing representations of historical, contemporary or fantasy events. On the other hand, he saw people demanding more choice, and becoming more comfortable with interactions with technology. He observed that,

> If you attempt to link these two tendencies—the public spectacle and the capacity for individual choice—you arrive at a medium of dial-up virtual techniques to gain access to an intangible but wholly enthralling experience, giving the solitary individual the feeling of being present at

a spectacle in the illusory company of a large number of others. Somewhere in Japan you may be sure that someone is thinking hard about VOD (video on demand) and VR (virtual reality).

Virtual reality—the emerging technology

> *I see no reason to suppose that these machines will ever force themselves into general use.*
> The Duke of Wellington (referring to steam engines)

VR or cyberspace as some prefer to call it, has become a recent 'buzzword' amongst computer technology academics and industry practitioners alike. It has been identified as one of the most exciting technological developments of the future, where different experiences can be created through the use of computer-mediated imaging and graphical environments. Potentially, there are an infinite number of 'experiences' which VR technology can create. Recent literature on VR (Rheingold, 1991; Helsel and Roth, 1991; Krueger, 1990; Laurel, 1990) has discussed the many implications of the VR experiences for the psychological and sociological impacts on human behaviour. This chapter will focus primarily on the current technological aspects of VR and how they may impact tourism in the future.

VR: the link with entertainment

Early developments in VR were closely linked to the film and entertainment industries, especially the computer and video games market. Film distributors and producers have experimented with various imaging technologies in the quest to offer the 'complete' or 'whole' experience for consumers of entertainment. Advances such as 3-D glasses, sound and high-quality imaging technology within cinemas have emerged and production teams have recently created some amazing computer-generated graphics and special effects in movies such as *Star Wars* and *Jurassic Park*.

However, the implications of VR are far more wide-reaching than the entertainment industry, since, it is argued, 'we are on the brink of having the power of creating any experience we desire' (Rheingold, 1991). Despite the fact that it has been the entertainment giants of Sega Enterprises and Nintendo who have 'kickstarted' the VR revolution into action, many other industries and companies are now investigating the potential of VR. Banks, retailers, tour operators, and government agencies are all looking at VR developments. As consumers we may all be using VR in the future; from shopping to banking, from relaxing to exercising, from travelling to staying at home. VR can potentially create images and experiences which are so realistic, it may redefine the whole philosophy of the way we live our lives.

VR: a realistic experience

VR will provide an experience which is beyond the normal capabilities of an individual. It will enable participants to enter computer-generated environments that offer three-dimensional perspectives through the use of sound, sight and touch technology. VR uses a selection of different hardware and software technologies to create the simulated experiences which the participant actually believes are in fact real. For example, participants will soon be able to enjoy the VR experiences such as flying an F-16 jet fighter, or playing a round of golf at St Andrews, all within a realistic, but simulated environment.

Although there are many questions which remain to be answered about VR, there are several features which can be clarified. Firstly, a VR experience is a simulation, it is not 'real', but for authenticity and immersion it should look or feel 'real'. Caneday (1992) notes that VR is oxymoronic, that something must be virtual or real but not both. This raises some interesting philosophical questions, such as what is and what is not a 'real' experience in this world? However, these are questions beyond the scope of this chapter.

Heim (1991) argues that human imagination is the key difference between reality and virtual reality, suggesting that, 'virtual reality needs to be not quite real or it will lessen the pull of imagination . . . which allows us to take what we read or hear and reconstitute the symbolic components into a mental vision'. He also states that 'virtual realities may be all the richer for preserving some relationship to a real world without however becoming boring or mundane' (Heim, 1991). It is this difference between a real experience and a VR experience which is in fact the attraction of VR. Similarly, Walser (1991) argues that 'the whole purpose of cyberspace technology is to trick the human senses and sensibilities, to help people believe and sustain an illusion'.

Secondly, VR acts as an interface between human beings and technology. As Kuffel (1993) notes, 'much as the Macintosh operating system and now Windows for PCs made computing easier for computer semi-literates, virtual reality has the potential to expand the relationship between humans and computers into three-dimensions'. Spring (1991) agrees claiming that 'virtual realities represent a natural evolution of interface design with increasing control of the interface being placed with the computer system'. VR is thus helping to overcome some of the barriers between human uses and applications of technology in the world.

The final important component of VR technology is that it serves as a massive information processor, which creates pictures and visual images of information for users to understand the data being presented. It has been found that 'the human mind can assimilate about 100 bits of information per second from text, but takes in about one billion bits per second merely observing the world. Virtual Reality seeks to open the text bottleneck by describing complex information visually' (Kuffel, 1993). The use of pictures, images, graphics, sound and interactive environments can create much more meaningful information and better understanding for participants.

Virtual reality—the technology involved

Any sufficiently advanced technology is indistinguishable from magic.
                                                    Arthur C. Clarke

The technologies involved in producing VR experiences include a combination of visual, audio and kinetic effects. The core of every VR simulation is a large database which stores the relevant data. A powerful computer with a sophisticated graphics capability is then used to create the virtual world, in three dimensions, and presents the data precisely as required. As technology costs decrease and computer power increases, the development of VR experiences is coming much closer. The quality of computer-generated visual images has improved enormously over the last few years, with graphics, animation and digitised video images having clearer resolutions than ever before. This imaging technology is continuously improving and will play a key role in future VR developments.

The use of high-definition television (HDTV) offers an insight into the quality of computer-generated images of the future. The technical capability of HDTV is 1920 pixels per line for 1000-line resolution. This creates superb quality pictures which, 'have more depth, definition and texture. The colours are richer . . . it presents imagery so clear it's startling' (Brill, 1993). HD imagery will have a strong emphasis in the creation of future VR experiences. Similarly, the quality of digitised sound has improved dramatically with compact disc (CD) quality now possible in many computer simulations. As the quality of visual images and sound improves, the degree of immersion and realism in the VR experience will be enhanced.

VR technologies differ considerably from the technologies used in simple computer games and advanced motion pictures, through their interactive capabilities and kinetic effects on the human body. A series of different sensory effects can be created to allow the VR participant to interact with the technology in different ways. Props, such as joysticks and steering columns, have been developed to create realistic kinetic effects. Currently, most VR developments have focused on a variety of head-mounted displays (HMD), which allow a person to look around in a virtual room by simply turning the head. A sensor detects head movement and the direction of the eyes, and the software re-configures the vision being seen by the participant. As these head-mounted displays evolve, they are becoming increasingly portable and user-friendly. Recent technologies are even more advanced, such as the 'dataglove' and 'datasuit' which are still under development. but will be able to detect movement of the arm and, eventually, whole body movement.

Other VR technology designs have centred on the 'pod'-based enclosed shell. Here, the participant enters into a semi-closed environment, such as a flight simulator, in addition to wearing an HMD. In the future, advances of VR technology may include developments such as sensory floors, which can detect the location and body position of the participant. Another important upcoming development is where multiple participants can share the same VR experience. Maloney (1992) notes that consumers want more out of the 'experiences'—group participation, control and intellectual stimulation will be more important than sensory overload. These technologies will create even more realism for the VR experience, which is likely to speed up VR's commercial availability.

Towards a paradigm for the complete virtual reality experience

> *Experience is never limited, and it is never complete.*
>
> Henry James

As technologies have improved, the degree of realism in VR is even closer to becoming the next best thing to the real experience. However, it is important to isolate the VR experience from the simple simulations and video games, which have so far been developed for the home computer market and amusement arcades. The complete or true VR experience includes several features.

Visualisation features

There are several components of the VR visual experience which must be incorporated into the complete VR experience. Spring (1991) notes, 'fundamental to much of the virtual reality work is research on visualisation—the animated display of symbolic information in the form of concrete objects and physical relations'. The quality

of a virtual reality interface depends on the following visualisation factors identified by Cruz-Neira et al. (1992):

- *stereoscopic vision*—three dimensions
- *visual acuity*—a measure of the resolution and field of view
- *linearity*—the ability to bend light and expand the field of view
- *look-around capability*—to view objects from different angles (unlike a CRT screen)
- *communication*—the ability to be able to visualise other participants in the experience

Immersion features

Cruz-Neira et al. (1992) suggest that immersion is 'the degree of suspension of disbelief', in the experience. They argue that the degree of immersion of a VR participant within the experience is based on:

- *a field of view*—the visual angle a viewer can see without head rotation. It is a critical component in the VR experience for creating realism
- *panorama*—the ability to surround the viewer. This has been an important aspect of most VR developments so far, and is an advancement from the early developments such as the OMNIMAX theatres and the Disney Star Tours
- *A viewer centred perspective*—where the technology and images can react quickly and accurately to the participant's actions
- *body and physical representation*—of the participant is important. In many VR experiences it is possible to see the hands of the participant
- *intrusion*—the isolation of the viewer within a closed environment

Interactivity features

Rheingold (1991) has suggested that interaction in VR is vital to give the feeling of presence. Interactivity, which is based on the degree of control the participant holds in the experience, is probably the key differentiating factor of VR from early gaming simulations. Spring (1991) notes that interactivity arises from the naturalness of user involvement and whether it is artificial or natural. The development of kinetic sensors and graphical manipulators have helped to create realism and naturalness in the interactive experience. Heim (1991) notes 'the degree of realism is in principle unlimited. This very realism may turn to irrealism where virtual worlds are indistinguishable from real worlds, where virtual reality gets bland and mundane'. Coates (1992) argues that at present 'we are able to create and enjoy images, but we are beginning to go beyond images used passively'.

Despite being in the early stages in the development of VR technologies, it is possible to see heavy investment in its future from major companies such as Sega and VP Industries. At this stage, there are seen to be some weaknesses with VR technology, especially with some of the visualisation features, such as graphics quality. However, there is a general optimistic consensus amongst industry practitioners and academics, that the technology is rapidly improving and the true VR experience is likely to be available not too far into the future.

How will virtual reality affect the future of the tourism industry?

I never think of the future. It comes soon enough.
Albert Einstein

For readers of science fiction novels, or avid viewers of the TV show *Star Trek—The Next Generation*, the concepts of VR and the hologram images of the 'Holideck' may seem all-too-familar. It is also clear that VR offers many possibilities to a range of businesses and society in general. The ability to view, explore, and alter the design of a house while it is still on the architectural drawing board is just one example of an industry which is about to be revolutionised by VR. When considering its future application within the tourism industry, VR will offer the ability not only to view a destination (as in a video), but also to become immersed in the activities that are going on. The tourist will move from being an observer to being an active participant.

VR technology will eventually allow the participant to visit existing environments or, as in the case of 'Alice in Wonderland' stories, create totally new realities and worlds. Looking to the future possibilities of VR, Welter (1990) pointed out that VR participants, 'can touch, pick up, and manipulate virtual objects in the computer with their hands. They can fly or ride bicycles in the sky. They can hear cars whizzing by them. . . . These aren't pie in the sky. The adventures of Alice may no longer be fiction'.

Already applications of VR technology are being touted in the tourism industry. For example, Sega plans to develop 50 theme parks in Japan over the next few years with the aim of 'making its attractions interactive, letting people shoot and steer to give them the incentive to try again' ('Sega amusement', 1993). Similarly, Disney are promising to use VR technology in their proposed historical America Park outside Washington, DC. As Robert Weiss ('US history', 1993) senior vice-president

of Walt Disney Imagineering pointed out, 'We can make you a civil war soldier. . . . We can make you feel what slavery was like during that period, and what it was like to escape on the underground railroad'.

Looking at the future role of theme parks, Jones and Robinett (1993) acknowledged that 'When one looks ahead at the large number of tourists who are expected to travel to new destinations (particularly within the Asia-Pacific region), there will be increasing pressure on sensitive environmental and social resources at the destination'. The tourist system is going to have a more difficult time in meeting these demands. Furthermore, as tourists become more sophisticated and mature, it is arguable that they are becoming more dissatisfied with the full 'actual tourist experience' and are instead opting for the 'surrogate travel' experiences that the 'let's pretend worlds' can offer (Caproni, 1993). As Stipanuk (1993) points out, 'the tourism experience is potentially fragile and vulnerable to events which might fracture this experience . . . tourists wish to have safe and secure experiences'.

As further pressures are placed on the tourism system, it is perhaps likely that tourists will become increasingly disenchanted with the tourism experience because of the gap that often exists between their expectations and reality. Surrogate travel, within the security of some form of location-based entertainment (LBE) centre is one way of ensuring the best tourism experience is 'guaranteed'. Bruce (1987) supports this, claiming that 'with the developments in communication technologies it may be that the amount of movement of people will start to decrease. Instead business people may well hold teleconferences, and other potential travellers will take instant trips with audio visual images'.

Once the cost of VR further decreases, it will be possible to enjoy the experience from the comfort and familiarity of the home environment, much as Anthony Smith predicted. As Caneday (1992) goes on to point out, it will allow travellers to participate in their fantasies through VR with 'the dream of making worlds, of visiting environments and living inside stories, without leaving the living room'.

Conclusion

We stand together on the edge of a new frontier.
J. F. Kennedy

Currently, many of the VR experiences on offer can be viewed as no more than advanced military games. This is no accident. Leaps in technology have often come from the perception that the technology would give some form of military advantage. Boeing's civilian aircraft came as a spin-off from its technological development of military aircraft. The jet engine was developed for fighter aircraft during World War II, just as the US and Russian space programmes grew out of the German V2 rocket initiatives. The US military, through its Advanced Research Projects Agency has invested large sums with such companies as Hughes Aircraft Company, in the development of VR to train pilots and tank crews in a cost-effective way (Brill, 1993). With the end of the cold war, US defence contractors are not alone in trying to find alternative uses for their advanced technologies. As Tamiya (1993) observed, 'Mitsubishi Precision Co. isn't the only Japanese defense contractor being forced to use its technology—not to mention its imagination—to stay afloat. And many are focusing on the entertainment market'. So, while many of today's VR experiences are military-based, they will quickly evolve into more commercial leisure and tourism applications.

The full impacts of VR on society are only just beginning to emerge, and the tourism industry will be only one small part of the global impact of this technology. While VR potentially offers a vast array of benefits, undoubtedly there will also be drawbacks. But these have yet to fully emerge, be appreciated and understood. As Stipanuk (1993) has already pointed out, 'whilst the travel/tourism purist would probably disclaim the Disney-like experience as artificial and shallow, it may be one form of appropriate tourism'. In the future, technology inspired surrogate travel is a strong possibility, and this will have major implications for the tourism industry. On the other hand, the standard definitions of a tourist has always involved some form of travel as being implicit. VR has the potential to offer the tourism experience without having to travel. Is this even tourism? Can it be described as 'artificial tourism'?

In conclusion, the VR technological revolution has been compared to an aircraft leaving an airport, 'speeding down the runway seconds before ascending into the sky', (Brill, 1993). It should be clear by now, that the tourism industry should not only book its seat, but should also have a good idea of where the flight is going to take us.

References

Andrews, J. (1993) *Pocket Asia, The Economist*, London.

Bitner, M. J. and Booms, B. H. (1982) 'Trends in travel and tourism marketing: the changing structure of distribution channels', *Journal of Travel Research*, 20(4): 39–44.

Boorstin, D. J. (1975) *The image: a guide to pseudo-events in America*, Atheneum, New York.

Brill, L. M. (1993) 'Virtual reality: get real', *Funworld*, July: 22–29.

Bruce, M. (1987) 'New technology and the future of tourism', *Tourism Management*, 8(2): 115–120.

Caneday, L. (1992) 'Outdoor recreation: a virtual reality', *Parks and Recreation*, 27(8): 48–52.

Caproni, J. (1993) 'Travel as theater: a challenge to the credibility of tourism', *Journal of Travel Research*, Winter: 54–55.

Cleverdon, R. (1992) 'Global tourism trends: influences and determinants', in *World Travel and Tourism Review*, 2nd edn, Ritchie, R. and Hawkins, D. (Eds), CAB International, Wallingford, Oxford, p. 90.

Cleverdon, R. (1993) 'Global tourism trends: influences, determinants and directional flows', in *World Travel and Tourism Review*, Vol. 3, Ritchie, R. and Hawkins, D. (Eds), CAB International, Wallingford, Oxford, p. 85.

Coates, J. F. (1992) 'The future of tourism: the effect of science and technology', *Vital Speeches (VSP)*, 58(24): 759–763.

Cruz-Neira, C., Sandin, D. J., Defanti, T. A., Kenyon, R. V. and Hart, J. C. (1992) 'The cave: audio visual experience automatic virtual environment', *Communications of the ACM*, 35(6): 65–72.

'Fear of finance' (1992) *The Economist* (Survey of the World Economy), 19 September: 1.

Frechtling, D. C. (1987) 'Key issues in tourism futures: the US travel industry', *Tourism Management*, 8(2): 106–111.

Gamble, P. R. (1984) *Small Computers and Hospitality Management*, Hutchinson, London.

Go, F. M. and Williams, A. P. (1993) 'Competing and cooperating in the changing tourism system', *Journal of Travel and Tourism Marketing*, Summer.

Heim, M. (1991) 'The metaphysics of virtual reality', in Helsel, S. K. and Roth, J. (Eds), *Virtual Reality: Theory, Practice, and Promise*, Meckler, Westport, CT, pp. 27–34.

Helsel, S. K. and Roth, J. (Eds) (1991) *Virtual Reality: Theory, Practice, and Promise*, Meckler, Westport, CT.

Hobson, J. (1993) 'Transport, infrastructure and tourism—are there private solutions to public problems?', in *World Travel and Tourism Review*, Vol. 3, Ritchie, R. and Hawkins, D. (Eds), CAB International, Wallingford, Oxford, p. 175.

Hobson, J. and Usyal, M. (1993) 'Infrastructure: the silent crisis facing the future of the tourism industry', *Hospitality Research Journal*, 17(1): 209–218.

Hopper, M. (1990) 'Rattling SABRE—new ways to compete on information', *Harvard Business Review*, May–June: 118–125.

Jones, C. and Robinett, J. (1993) 'The future role of theme parks in international tourism', *World Travel and Tourism Review*, Vol. 3, Ritchie, R. and Hawkins, D. (Eds), CAB International, Wallingford, Oxford, pp. 144–150.

Krueger, M. W. (1990) *Artificial Reality*, Addison-Wesley, Wokingham.

Kuffel, C. (1993) 'Games without frontiers', *Expression*, August/September: 42–45.

Laurel, B. (1990) *The Art of Human–Computer Interface Design*, Addison-Wesley, Wokingham.

Maloney, J. (1992) 'Are we having fun yet?', *Digital Media: a Seybold Report*, 2(2): 30–32.

Poon, A. (1988) 'Tourism and information technologies', *Annals of Tourism Research*, 15: 531–549.

Rheingold, H. (1991) *Virtual Reality*, Summit Books, New York.

'Sega amusement idea now virtually reality' (1993) *South China Morning Post*, 6 July: 6.

Shafer, E. L. (1987) 'Technology, tourism and the 21st century', *Tourism Management*, 8(2): 179–182.

Smith, A. (1993) 'The electronic circus', *The Economist*, 11–17 September: 72–76.

Spring, M. B. (1991) 'Informating with virtual reality', in Helsel, S. K. and Roth, J. (Eds), *Virtual Reality: Theory, Practice, and Promise*, Meckler, Westport, CT, pp. 3–18.

Stevens, T. (1993) 'Theme Parks: playgrounds or agents of social and cultural development', *The American Express Annual Review of Travel*, American Express, New York, pp. 64–71.

Stipanuk, D. M. (1993) 'Tourism and technology: interactions and implications', *Tourism Management*, August: 267–278.

Tamiya, A. (1993) 'Japanese defense contractor enters amusement market', *Funworld*, July: 32.

UNEP (1992) 'Industry and environment', *United Nations Environment Programme*, 15(3).

'US history gets Disney treatment' (1993) *South China Morning Post*, Business section, 15 November: 7.

Walser, R. (1991) 'The emerging technology of cyberspace', in Helsel, S. K. and Roth, J. (Eds), *Virtual reality: Theory, Practice, and Promise*, Meckler, Westport, CT, pp. 35–40.

Welter, T. (1990) 'The artificial tourist', *Industry Week*, 1 October: 66.

Williams, A. P. (1993) 'Information technology and tourism: a dependent factor for future survival', in *World Travel and Tourism Review*, Vol. 3, Ritchie, R. and Hawkins, D. (Eds), CAB International, Wallingford, Oxford, pp. 200–205.

WTO (1992) *Yearbook of Tourism Statistics of the World*, World Tourism Organization, Madrid.

WTO (1993) 'Background note', *Seminar on Tourism Trends and Marketing Strategies: East Asia and the Pacific*, Manila, WTO, Madrid, CAP/24/sem., p. 10.

Part 3

TOURISM MARKETING AND RESEARCH

Marketing is the process that brings together the buyer and seller of the tourism product in a satisfactory relationship based on correct decisions about product offering and presentation, effective distribution, appropriate pricing and adequate communication and promotional choices. It is associated with a number of specific techniques and methods including: market segmentation and consumer behaviour research, customer service provision, product positioning and branding, market analysis, market forecasting, competitive monitoring and environmental scanning (adapted from Go and Haywood, 1990).

At the practitioner level a great deal of marketing and research know-how has been acquired by NTOs, large travel companies (major airlines, rail and ferry firms) and the top end of the accommodation and hospitality sectors (e.g. hotel and restaurant chains). For many smaller organisations—the most numerous category of tourism enterprises—marketing is less widely applied and, where it is, it is often conceived mainly as promotion and publicity, rather than a more comprehensive kind of strategic, customer-orientation to the planning of markets and products, requiring integrated, organisational support.

The relatively slow adoption of market orientation in tourism is surprising since tourism marketing has always had one advantage that many other kinds do not—the comparative ease with which personalised databases on customers can be assembled. The booking of tourism commonly involves the submission and recording of detailed customer information (names, geographic location, gender, seasonal choice etc.) that can act as a valuable source of customer profiles and a predictor of future behaviour. Tour operators who have maintained and analysed past customer patterns have found that they are a reliable base for a significant amount of future business. Even a small bed and breakfast establishment can arrive at reasonable customer profiles by analysing the visitor book.

The academic literature of tourism marketing has had an even shorter life than general tourism managerial texts, most books being published in the 1980s and after (e.g. Middleton, 1988; Reid, 1989; Morrison, 1990; Burke and Resnick, 1991; Holloway and Plant, 1992), though marketing has featured strongly in tourism journals (Van Doren, Koh and McCahill, Chapter 31 in this book). The dominant approach has been an adaptation of service marketing theory to tourism, focusing on product features such as heterogeneity, perishability, inseparability and intangibility, which differentiate service goods from packaged goods and durables. There has been less emphasis on the ways in which tourism differs from other service products (e.g. the fact that it frequently involves the participation of several suppliers, is harder to evaluate, involves high risk, and can be partially designed by the consumer). There has been even less formulation of concepts and practices distinctive to tourism marketing, though Ashworth, Goodall and Voogd have edited interesting collections which have made a start at theorising destination marketing as a discrete field (Ashworth and Goodall, 1990; Ashworth and Voogd, 1990) and Lumsdon has produced a useful tourism marketing case study text (Lumsdon, 1992). Another recent area of marketing borrowing, rather than conceptual innovation, has been the application of strategic planning theory to destination marketing (Heath and Wall, 1992).

Of the four main elements of the marketing mix—product, place, price and promotion—promotional planning has probably received most attention. Promotion is central for a product that cannot be physically distributed and thus requires the customer to come to it. For the first-time visitor a destination or attraction is an abstraction, which is why the components and measurement of destination image have been key analytical foci (e.g. Echtner and Brent Ritchie, 1991). One of the major developments in promotional opportunities over the last ten years has been the increase of media time and space in Europe and North America devoted to travel (Seaton, 1994).

This part of the book includes papers addressing a wide variety of these marketing issues: an overview of tourism choice models (Ryan); a wide-ranging review of tourism research based on citations in tourism journals (Van Doren, Koh and McCahill); two papers on specific market segments, the youth market and VFR travellers (Seaton; Josiam, Clements and Hobson); a new look at seasonality (Butler); an update on the destination lifecycle—one of the few tourism-specific concepts to emerge in the discipline (Cooper); research on destination image (King); an appraisal of the environmental forces affecting the market for South American tourism (Lumsdon and Swift); five useful market-specific studies on the cultural tourism market (Richards); the business travel market in Europe (Davidson); two studies of the commercial short break market (Faché; Edgar, Litteljohn, Allardyce and Wanhill) and hotel competition in Southeast Asia (Schlentrich and Ng); a market forecasting model of Australian tourism demand (Bakalis, Morris and Wilson); two contrasting papers on the topical question of repositioning sun, sea and sand destinations in Spain (Hart; Amor, Calabuig, Abellán and Monfort); an endorsement of strategic management approaches to Spanish tourism planning (Bigné, Camisón and Monfort); and a welcome article on an underwritten area of media representation, the cinema and its influence on travel (Riley).

It is still too early to see tourism marketing as a field that is as developed as that of packaged goods, but the contributions here suggest how quickly knowledge and approaches are multiplying.

A. V. Seaton

References

Ashworth, Gregory and Goodall, Brian (1980) *Marketing Tourism Places*, Routledge, London.

Ashworth, Gregory and Voogd, H. (1990) *Selling the City*, Routledge, London.

Burke, James E. and Resnick, Barry P. (1991) *Marketing and Selling the Travel Product*, South-Western, Cincinnati, OH.

Echtner, Christine and Brent Ritchie, J. R. (1991) 'The meaning and measurement of destination image', *Journal of Tourism Studies*, 2(2): 2–12.

Go, F. and Haywood, K. M. (1990) 'Marketing of the service process: state of the art in tourism, recreation and hospitality industries', in C. P. Cooper (Ed.), *Progress in Tourism, Recreation and Hospitality Management*, Belhaven, London.

Heath, Ernie and Wall, Geoffrey (1992) *Marketing Tourism Destinations: a Strategic Planning Approach*, John Wiley, New York.

Holloway, J. C. and Plant, R. V. (1992) *Marketing for Tourism*, 2nd edn, Pitman, London.

Lumsdon, Les (1992) *Marketing for Tourism: Case Study Assignments*, Macmillan, London.

Middleton, Victor (1988) *Marketing in Travel and Tourism*, Heinemann, London.

Morrison, Alastair M. (1990) *Hospitality and Travel Marketing*, Delmar, USA.

Reid, Robert D. (1989) *Hospitality Marketing Management*, Van Nostrand Reinhold, New York.

Seaton, A. V. (1994) 'Tourism and the media', in Witts, S. J. and Moutinho, Luiz (Eds), *Tourism Marketing and Management Handbook*, Prentice Hall, London (in press).

30 Leisure and tourism—the application of leisure concepts to tourist behaviour— a proposed model

C. RYAN

Introduction

This paper is developed from a specific view of the holiday experience. The underlying *leitmotif* is that tourism is concerned with the quality of the holidaymaker's experience of travel and place. This experience includes travel to the place, the nature of the holiday destination, the return journey, and the interactions between tourist, host, fellow tourists and representatives of the tourist industry that occur in this process.

This perception of tourism is not the only perspective. Tourism can be construed as an economic activity, and might be defined as 'a study of the demand for and supply of accommodation and supportive service for those staying away from home, and the resultant patterns of expenditure, income creation and employment' (Ryan, 1991:5). But, from the experiential view it can be argued that the attitudes, expectations and perceptions of the holidaymaker are significant variables in setting goals, influencing behaviour and determining final satisfaction. It is also noted that tourists retain, while on holiday, the social skills used to establish acceptable parameters of action. Just as in daily life people adopt procedures for establishing compromises, disbelief, and readjustments to perceived, as distinct from desired, realities, so too these processes occur at the holiday destination. Martin (1992) has referred to the situation whereby 'in most marketplaces today, both consumer and seller play the characteristic post-modern game of collusive irony' (1992:24).

Accordingly, this paper reviews literature relating to motivations for recreational activities, and levels of satisfaction derived from such activities. Ryan (1991, 1994) notes that the relationship between motivation, performance and resultant satisfaction invites consideration of a number of variables, including:

(a) the expectation and perception of the place and its attributes;
(b) the importance of the activity to the individual in meeting personal needs;
(c) the expected outcomes of the activity;
(d) the role of intervening variables which are twofold in nature:
 (i) internal, personal factors such as perceived ability to bring about a desired outcome; and
 (ii) external factors which affect the probability of a desired outcome such as the availability of human and other resources;
(e) the presence of significant others, and the importance attached to them; and
(f) the degree to which an individual is able to adopt adaptive behaviour, such as goal adjustment and search behaviour, given the frustration of initial objectives.

The paper is also based on the assumption that variables thought to be appropriate to recreational activities by researchers in leisure studies can be of use in understanding the nature of holiday-taking and the satisfaction derived from it. Holidays include a series of behaviours (some of which are sporting in nature) in which needs for relaxation, skill acquisition, self-development etc. form a complex set of relationships; and it is argued that parallels with other leisure activities can be drawn.

Equally, any brief consideration of this area should take into account some theories of consumer behaviour. If satisfaction is seen as the congruence of need and performance, then dissatisfaction can be perceived as a negative gap between expectation and experience. Therefore, some form of gap analysis might be helpful in analysing tourist satisfaction. Equally, if cognitive dissonance is thought to play a role, then it is arguably 'triggered' by some event, some 'critical incident' in the holiday-taker's experience of place or activity. Research would apparently indicate that such events can serve as powerful 'confirmers' of positive experience (Bitner et al., 1990).

The concepts of fun and leisure

The question as to what are the roles and functions of leisure; its contents, the distinctions between leisure and fun, the motivations for, and determinants of, satisfactory leisure experiences are well recorded in the literature relating to leisure studies. For example, Podilchak (1991) examines the meaning of leisure and fun, and argues that there is indeed a distinction. Fun is perceived as being:

(a) doing things on the surface, being silly, laughing;
(b) as growing out of an activity, being purposeless; and
(c) exciting, exhilarating—unique, not everyday.

Fun is qualitative. Leisure, on the other hand, is seen as being more serious and more institutionalised and, since it involves choice, by implication is more premeditated. Podilchak argues that in the definitions of leisure as a means of 're-creation', the fun and instantaneous enjoyment associated with it has been deleted from the analysis of leisure and its role in contemporary society. Gunn (1988:13) makes a similar point when he writes:

> As it was formalized and institutionalized, recreation became whatever the proponents and agencies created as policy. Some recreational professionals draw a strong distinction between that which is an end in itself and that which is purposeful, claiming that the former is negative whereas the latter is positive. Leisure, engaged in for its own sake, provides no focus; those recreational activities accepted by society as wholesome, creative and uplifting are worthy of public support.

Yet, in the case of tourism, reference is made to tourism as a 'sanctioned escape route', a 'regression into childhood' (Cohen, 1979; Crompton, 1979), and in that sense the role of fun within the tourist experience has been recognised, albeit not always analysed in terms of its relationship with other components of the tourist experience.

Leisure and tourism—conceptual overlaps

As evidenced by a perceived need to devote a special issue of the *Annals of Tourism Research* (Vol. 18, no. 1, 1991) to the relationship between leisure and tourism studies, there have been few structured attempts to apply variables thought to contribute towards a satisfactory leisure experience to the phenomenon of holiday-taking. Tourism literature has tended to concentrate more on the determinants of tourism choice and holiday behaviour.

One reason may lie in the definitions of tourism used in both commercial and academic research. Tourism activity has been defined in terms of travel away from home requiring overnight accommodation. Such a definition attracts attention to questions of where people go, and seeks to explain travel in the language of economic variables and social processes as well as of motivational

drives. Equally, the objective or perceived attractiveness of destinations is viewed as being important, particularly from the geographical viewpoint of finding measures of attractiveness for spatial modelling. Arguably, the psychological perspective of tourism as an experience of place, and events at that place, has tended not to feature as strongly in the literature. A review of standard texts, such as those of Mathieson and Wall (1982), Murphy (1985), and Burkart and Medlik (1990), would seem to support this contention. This is not to say that psychological modelling is absent from the literature. Far from it, and the work of Pearce (1982, 1988) is a notable contribution here; but it might in part explain why the gap between recreational and tourism literature has occurred at a conceptual level. (In saying this, it is recognised that structural components of academic departmental organisation might well, in the final analysis, be at least as important a contributing factor.)

Also it can be argued that there is a distinct difference between leisure activities undertaken as part of one's daily life, and those undertaken whilst on holiday. Put simply, by definition, the holiday trip requires a stay away from home, and thus holiday activities occur within a geographical space with which the tourist may not be familiar. Thus, holiday experiences involve degrees of exploration which might not be present in the normal pattern of leisure activity. Yet even this argument must be modified. For example, Lyon (1988), in analysing the attraction of timeshare, argues that geographical familiarity and destination loyalty might be motivators for the use of such types of holiday accommodation. Gunn (1988), in common with many other authors, points out that the tourism experience has a time dimension. He argues that there are three stages: the creation of pre-image, participation and evaluation. Ryan (1991) refers to the fact that the holiday experience commences with the collecting of information about destinations prior to actual booking, and that the brochure is used as a source of reference and confirmation of the travel decision prior to departure. Pre-departure behaviour is characterised by special purchases, and post-participation is experienced through souvenirs, the development of photographs and other forms of behaviour designed to recall the holiday. Hence, holiday experiences have both spatial and time dimensions.

The overlap between leisure and tourism is, on the other hand, more apparent when the phenomenon of VFR (visiting friends and relatives) tourism is considered. It can be hypothesised that the trip activities so undertaken are akin to family day-trips; there are high degrees of familiarity with the holiday destination, and the nature of the activities may be more home-based than would otherwise be the case. Certainly in MacCannell's term the 'backroom' is certainly more open. Yet, from the viewpoint of an attraction operator counting visitor numbers, there may be little distinction between those on day-trips or those who come further afield, or in the nature of their activities once they arrive.

Yet even where familiarity with a destination is present, the experience of the visit is never the same. Interactions with different people can make it seem a different place, while the nature of the search for information about a place may be conducted less strenuously.

Having indicated some differences between tourism and recreation, Smith and Godbey (1991) emphasise their commonality. They write:

> Many authors link both recreation and leisure, as well as tourism to a spiritual search. The desire for authenticity as a driving force in tourism is a familiar hypothesis to tourism scholars, but the same theme exists in leisure studies. The two fields of study share the same dialectic between a theoretical, descriptive, cross-sectional and applied research to a new form of scholarship that emphasises theory, conceptual development, analytical rigour and eschews the concept of immediate application. It thus is attacked by academics as not having legitimacy, and from industry as not being practical. (1991:86)

Concepts drawn from leisure studies

There are many concepts drawn from leisure studies that can be of use to the tourism researcher seeking to understand the nature of the tourist experience, and some reviews of these can be found in the literature (Pearce, 1988; Smith and Godbey, 1991; Ryan, 1994). From the perspective of tourist activity classification, the concept of the Recreational Opportunities was expanded by Butler and Waldbrook (1991) into a Tourism Opportunity Spectrum.

These authors and others have identified a number of principles that might help to understand tourist behaviour and satisfaction. Dimanche et al. (1991) have noted the importance of involvement in the recreational activity, and this might be thought to be important in holiday-taking, given the levels of planning that might precede it and the anticipation which accompanies the period prior to departure. Laing (1987) found when analysing reasons given for independent holidaymaking, 'freedom' and 'independence' were the most quoted reasons (by 50% of the sample), while the primary reason for selecting a package holiday was that little planning was needed, and, in 16% of cases the primary reason was that 'no risk was involved' (Laing, 1987:173). Laing also found that for package holiday-takers, the lack of risk was the most frequently quoted secondary reason for taking package holidays, and concludes 'perceived risk . . . seems to play

an unique role as an enforcer rather than a prime motivator to stay at home' (Laing, 1987:146).

However, close analysis of Laing's data shows that, while risk aversion is a factor, other factors may be more important—notably the force of habit. He notes:

> for many people package holiday taking is an habitual action—they rarely consider the reasons behind the preference . . . (the) preference for packaged travel may be more an outcome of personal and highly individual factors which demand particular detailed analysis. (Laing, 1987:179)

Specific risk-aversion strategies and indeed the reliance upon habit are means of avoiding the stress associated with the unfamiliar. Yiannakis and Gibson (1992) identify as two of three dimensions in their model the strange–familiar axis and the high structure–low structure dimension. Their results show that organised mass tourists score high in their needs for familiar, highly organised structures—findings which support the work of Laing. The inexperienced tourist might also show similar preferences, and from this perspective the comment by Norton (1987) that the decline of transatlantic traffic in 1985 and 1986 in the face of aircraft hijackings and other terrorist action was in part due to the inexperience of American tourists is consistent with this contention.

Gray (1987) proposes a categorisation of four components of stress that is applicable to recreation and tourism. The 'stressors' are:

(a) *intensity*—the demands of the task and self-assessment of ability to cope with those demands;
(b) *social interaction*—the relationships incurred in being part of a group;
(c) *novelty*—the creation of concern by being in a new and unfamiliar environment; and
(d) *specific situations*—the development of perceived threat within a specific set of circumstances.

Each of these factors may be viewed as possessing the characteristics of a continuum ranging from high to low intensity, high or low social interaction etc. It may therefore be possible to plot the nature of the tourist experience upon each of the dimensions Gray identifies.

The overlapping nature of the debate relating to leisure motivation is further evidenced by the concepts of boredom and frustration which are reported in the leisure literature. Patrick (1982), Hill and Perkins (1985), Iso-Ahola and Weissenger (1990) and Voelkle and Ellis (1990), are amongst those who describe boredom as being a sense of dissatisfaction, disinclination to action, longing with an inability to designate what is longed for, a passive expectant attitude, a sense that time hangs heavy or stands still, and a sense of emotional bankruptcy and being found in situations characterised by high degrees of familiarity, lacking novelty, and having too much time for a task posing little challenge. Given such conditions it can be hypothesised that within a holiday experience low levels of *satisfaction* may be recorded. However, perversely, holidaymakers may also respond with low levels of *dissatisfaction*. Pearce (1988), builds upon the work of Langer and Piper (1987) in suggesting that large parts of a holiday may be accompanied by a degree of 'mindlessness'. This might be described as being akin to the state sometimes experienced by drivers when they arrive at their destination with little ability to recall the events of the journey. A process of automatic reaction has taken place.

Within the holiday, Pearce suggests, there are a large number of potential occasions for such mindless behaviour which induces little recall. Many are highly scripted occasions where a series of familiar steps are followed in a programmed sequence. The checking in of the baggage, the ordering of a hamburger at a fast food outlet, the driving of long distances through uniform scenery would be examples of little challenge, little novelty, and hence little cause for either high or low levels of satisfaction. Would it be true to argue that the experienced holidaymaker is likely to descend into such a state of mindlessness where diminishing returns to scale have been experienced? The first Gothic cathedral visited may be fresh in the mind, but what of the fifth, sixth or twenty-sixth?

In 1988 Pearce proposed the concept of the tourist career as a progression along Maslow's hierarchy of motivation, and from this perspective the 'self-actualised' tourist would indeed find something fresh and new in the fifth, sixth or indeed the twenty-sixth Gothic cathedral that is visited. However, the tension between familiarity on the one hand, and the degree of involvement on the other is more likely to be a predictor of the degree of satisfaction to be derived from such a visit. Hence, familiarity would induce boredom, unless there is a very strong interest in Gothic architecture. However, the evidence for Pearce's concept is weak—indeed the evidence from Pearce's study of visitors to Timbertown in Australia and the study he quotes by Mills are not conclusive. Mills in his study of skiers notes, 'The context validity in terms of numbers of items and diversity within some of the operational measures in this study is admittedly weak' (1985:197).

A significant concept that might incorporate the concepts of boredom, excitement, familiarity and involvement that is widely reported and used in the leisure studies literature

and which can be of help in understanding tourist behaviour is the concept of flow. The concept has, for example, been used by Mannell et al. (1988) in a study of retirees undertaking exercises in Ontario, while Chick and Roberts (1990) used the dimensions of challenge and skill and resultant 'flow' in a study of Americans playing in pool leagues in bars on a Monday night. Csikszentimihalyi (1975:36) defines the 'flow' experience as 'one of complete involvement of the actor with his activity' and identifies seven indicators of its frequency and occurrence (Csikszentimihalyi 1975:38–48):

(a) the perception that personal skills and challenges posed by an activity are in balance;
(b) the centring of attention;
(c) the loss of self-consciousness;
(d) an unambiguous feedback to a person's actions;
(e) feelings of control over actions and environment;
(f) a momentary loss of anxiety and constraint; and
(g) feelings of enjoyment or pleasure.

Additionally, for the flow experience to be felt there are four prerequisites:

(a) participation is voluntary;
(b) the benefits of participation in an activity are perceived to derive from factors intrinsic to participation in the activity;
(c) a facilitative level of arousal is experienced during participation in the activity; and
(d) there is a psychological commitment to the activity in which they are participating.

It is not difficult to assume that these prerequisites are present in many holiday environments. The perception of flow thus occurs where there is a balance between the skills of the participant and the challenge inherent in the situation. If the skills possessed are inadequate for the task, frustration results. Such frustration can be evidenced by a process of annoyance, anger and possibly a collapse into sullen lethargy. Does this describe the attitude of the package holidaymaker at a foreign airport faced with a delay of an unknown number of hours of his or her charter flight with no couriers or other representatives of the company at hand? On the other hand, a situation of insufficient challenge, or lacking in an ability to involve the tourist, results in boredom. The concept has its antecedents in the Yerkes–Dodson 'Law' (1908) of arousal, and so has a long pedigree of psychological support.

It is obvious that the concept of 'flow' is applicable to work settings, but Baldwin and Tinsley (1988:266) conclude it is 'more readily perceived in leisure than in work'.

If, however, it is to be argued that the concept of 'flow' is applicable to holidaymaking situations and not simply to sports-orientated leisure, and if the concept of involvement is thought to be important, a necessary addition to any model of tourist behaviour and resultant satisfaction is a recognition of the role of motivation. Csikszentimihalyi (1975:38–48) notes that a prerequisite is that the activity is voluntary, thereby implying that a decision to participate has been made. Mannell et al. (1988) also argue that the concept has to incorporate a role for expectation and purpose (motivation). Arguably, within a context of holidaying activities, it is a balance between challenge, skill, motivation, and expectation that determines the experience of flow. Mannell et al. found that 'there was strong evidence for the prediction that higher levels of flow accompany freely chosen activities . . . freely chosen activities are not only more likely to be labelled leisure, but to be accompanied by higher levels of flow' (1988:299).

The motivation for holiday-taking and holidaymaking

There are many studies of tourist behaviour that identify potential sources of holiday-taking and holidaymaking motivation. Incidentally, although the terms holidaymaker and holiday-taker are often used as interchangeable descriptions of the same thing, the distinction between the two could well be important—the 'holidaymaker' being proactive, the 'holiday-taker' more passive. Thus the abovementioned works of Yiannakis and Gibson (1992) and those of Pearce (1982) are amongst those who have proposed tourist typologies based on responses to motivational questionnaires subjected to cluster analysis or similar responses. As with all such questionnaires, the validity of the results depends not simply upon correlations of items, but upon the validity of underlying theory. The problem of reporting results simply based on the emergence of factors that are strongly correlated has been described by Bagozzi thus:

> One drawback with this procedure is its atheoretical character. Rather than proposing a structure of perceptions based on conceptual arguments and prior research, the researcher relies on the pattern of responses found in the particular data under scrutiny to arrive at perceptual dimensions. This can lead to fortuitous, but erroneous, solutions and tends to promote a multitude of variables and interpretations, since little consistency results across studies. A second drawback is that principal components and common factor analysis can sometimes generate many dimensions within any particular study and thus yield cumbersome models. (1988:166)

Again, there are motivational studies within leisure theory that may be applicable to tourism. One such concept that

has been tested by other than the original authors is the Leisure Motivation Scale of Ragheb and Beard (1982). This scale possesses four dimensions and is derived from Maslow's theories of motivation. The dimensions are:

(a) The *intellectual* component, which 'assesses the extent to which individuals are motivated to engage in leisure activities which involve . . . mental activities such as learning, exploring, discovering, thought or imagining';

(b) the *social* component 'assesses the extent to which individuals engage in leisure activities for social reasons. This component includes two basic needs . . . the need for friendship and interpersonal relationships, while the second is the need for the esteem of others';

(c) the *competence-mastery* component assesses the extent to which 'individuals engage in leisure activities in order to achieve, master, challenge, and compete. The activities are usually physical in nature'; and

(d) the *stimulus-avoidance* component of leisure motivation 'assesses the drive to escape and get away from over-stimulating life situations. It is the need for some individuals to avoid social contacts, to seek solitude and calm conditions; and for others it is to seek to rest and to unwind themselves'.

The content of these dimensions are similar to those identified by commentators on tourism motivation (e.g. Iso-Ahola, 1982), but the Leisure Motivation Scale has been replicated in other studies (Sefton and Burton, 1987; Loundsbury and Franz, 1990), and found to possess significant degrees of stability (Loundsbury and Hoopes, 1988). Ragheb and Beard also devised two other scales of Leisure Satisfaction and Leisure Attitudes, but these have not proved so consistent (e.g. Sefton, 1989). Within a UK context, Ryan (1993a) reported being able to replicate the factors of the Leisure Motivation Scale.

Given the dimensions identified by Ragheb and Beard, it becomes possible to incorporate them into a more conventional attitudinal model as identified by a series of writers including Vroom (1964), Fishbein (1967), Bagozzi and Warshaw (1988), and as have been developed within the tourism literature by various authors including Moutinho (1987) and Witt and Wright (1990), amongst others. These models seek to measure the strength of the attitude held by assessing the importance of product attributes to the respondent, and the respondents' perception of the degree to which a product actually possesses the attributes. Thus, for example, a holiday-maker's attitude towards say, Benidorm, may be gauged if they value peace and quiet highly, and perceive Benidorm as lacking these attributes. Given the attitude held, then the attitude may be a precursor to action—in this case to avoid having a holiday in Benidorm! The same distinction can also be held to be the basis of a gap analysis similar to that incorporated in part by the SERVQUAL model of Parasuraman, Berry and Zeaithaml (1985, 1988, 1993). Here satisfaction is measured as a gap between client expectation and client perception of a service—a congruence between the two being a measure of satisfaction. Given that the dimensions of the SERVQUAL model incorporate tangibles, reliability, responsiveness, assurance and empathy, the application of a gap approach using the two-dimensional modelling technique inherent in both the SERVQUAL and multi-attribute models begins to provide a methodology to implement a questionnaire that utilises the attitudinal concepts of these models with a content derived from flow theories, the Ragheb and Beard Leisure Motivation Scale with additional questions designed to measure familiarity and involvement.

In short, a number of potential approaches exist in the explanation of holidaymaker behaviour, but such paradigms must recognise the:

(a) constructs of risk aversion and risk taking inherent in travel;
(b) relationship between holidaymaker and significant others—e.g. family, other tourists;
(c) relationship between tourist and tourist;
(d) use of the tourist destination zone by the holidaymaker;
(e) relationships between tourist and agencies of the tourist industry;
(f) relationships between tourist and members of the host community not employed in the tourist industry;
(g) constructs of familiarity, mindlessness and novelty;
(h) constructs of involvement and flow;
(i) constructs of motivation;

even while adhering to an accepted mode of attitude measurement.

Towards a general model

To attempt a general model of such a nature is perhaps inconsistent with today's thinking, especially if one takes into account concepts of tourism as a postmodern activity devoid of consistency on the part of its participants as they indulge in role play. Indeed Foxall (1990:174) refers to the erosion of paradigms as psychologists have sought to refute, incorporate or improve understanding of human behaviour. He also comments that:

A comprehensive plurality of paradigms is inescapable if authentic understanding of consumer behaviour is preferable to the doctrinaire parochialism that would follow the domination of consumer research by one ontology and associated methodology.

Hence a general model can only serve a limited function in the sense of providing a context of behaviour and choice. Additionally, it must not only take into account the personal factors of individual choice as listed above, but also:

(a) marketing variables—product design, pricing, advertising/promotion channels;
(b) tourist variables—previous destination experience: life cycle, income, age, lifestyle, value system;
(c) destination awareness—unavailable or considered sets (inert, inept, evoked);
(d) affective associations of destinations—positive, negative;
(e) tourist destination preferences;
(f) formation of intention to visit;
(g) specific situational variables.

As a first stage towards model building, a conventional marketing model would indicate a process illustrated in Figure 30.1 where the tourist becomes aware of an effective set of choices that appeal by reference to the marketing environment, applies a series of emotive considerations to that set, formulates an intention to visit or not as the case may be, and makes a decision in the light of immediate situational variables.

However, the choice marks only the completion of the first stage of the model. The second part relates to the actual experiences as a result of that choice. As initially noted, the holiday consists of further components, namely:

(a) travel to the destination;
(b) the nature of the destination;
(c) the nature of the interaction with significant others; and
(d) activities undertaken.

The second stage of the model might be as illustrated in Figure 30.2.

Implications of the model

Once the outward journey begins, so too does a process of evaluation. The nature of the trip, its comfort, ease of journey, delays, and the ease of accessibility to the destination become part of the total experience. It is

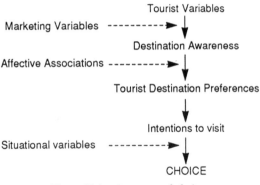

Figure 30.1 *A process of choice*

tempting to describe these experiences, in Herzberg's terms, as hygiene factors. That is, the availability of ease and comfort etc. are not in themselves predictors of high degrees of satisfaction, but their absence can generate dissatisfaction. They create dissatisfaction in two senses. Initially expectations are high, and an early disappointing experience might cause initial dissatisfaction. Second, on completion of the holiday, tourists become concerned about the need to return home in time for work, the need to make connections, or for the need to be picked up at airports by friends and relatives. Delays etc. at this stage of the holiday can cause a revaluation of the past, otherwise satisfactory, experience. If, however, the journey goes according to plan, then an expected service is delivered, but no addition to total satisfaction may occur.

This scenario may be true of mass package holidays, but not necessarily true of all types of holidays. For the 'explorer' type of tourist, the actual journey may be the purpose and rationale of the holiday. Indeed, acceptable levels of discomfort might actually enhance satisfaction with the holiday. Furthermore, the journey, like the rest of the holiday, consists of a series of events, and to refer to satisfaction with the trip as a whole implies a process of compensating between 'highs' and 'lows'. In short, inherent characteristics of the journey do not retain constant values, but can only be evaluated by reference to the tourists' needs and expectations.

The same is true of the destination tourist zone. Conventionally the tourist literature refers to destination attributes as having different appeals to different types of tourists (Cohen, 1972, 1974; Plog, 1977). Although a number of writers (e.g. Gyte, 1988; Ryan, 1991) have sought to modify this by reference to changing tourist behaviour within a tourist zone, or from evidence of search behaviour by tourists in terms of physical exploration of sites (Cooper, 1981), it is none the less recognised that the nature of the tourist destination is an important variable in determining satisfaction. It is the milieu of the goal-seeking behaviour, and must permit the sought goals to be achieved. If it does not possess this potential, the tourist will be dissatisfied. Thus, the inherent characteristics of the destination are evaluated against this matrix of needs, and expectations.

A destination may possess the right type of attributes, but still not generate a satisfactory holiday experience. This can arise for at least two reasons. The first is that the holidaymaker perceives the destination as lacking in quality. A mass tourist might view a zone as possessing hotels, bars, clubs, beaches etc., but also perceives them as being 'tacky', or over-priced, or otherwise not delivering 'value for money'.

A second reason for dissatisfaction might lie in the nature of the interactions between tourist and significant others. For example, the 'explorer' might find a destination to be 'authentically ethnic', but is unable, in McCannell's (1976) terms, to penetrate the 'back room'. The failure to establish contact with local people at what is thought to be a 'meaningful' level will leave the tourist frustrated, and hence dissatisfied. Equally, the mass-organised tourist returning to a destination which is known to meet the terms of both product mix and quality of provision, might have a less than satisfactory experience because of a failure to get on well with fellow tourists. Also, although both staff and destination characteristics remain the same, the staff cannot sustain the same quality of service as fatigue occurs on the part of service providers. Thus, the quality of the product towards the end of the high season might not be as high as at the beginning of the season (or at the end of season when pressures abate). (It is for this reason that some tour operators switch personnel at mid-season in an attempt to retain 'fresh staff' on site.)

However, the model does not predict that satisfaction will be generated by a congruence of expectation and

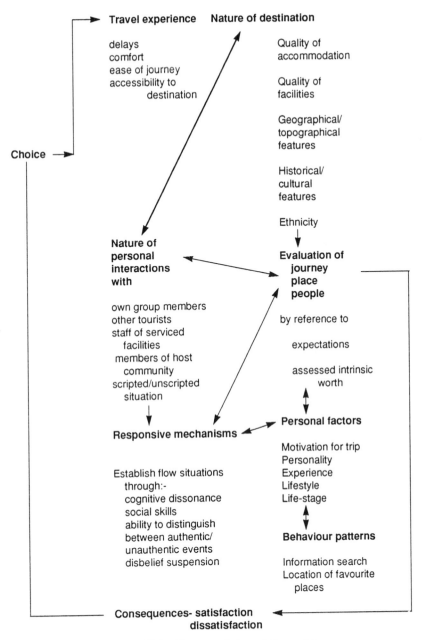

Figure 30.2 *The second stage of the model*

perceived reality at the time of the initial meeting of tourist and destination. It argues that there will be a process of information acquisition, evaluation of that information, and a process of either changing evaluations of place and/or behaviour. For example, if the 'explorer' finds that the destination is more built-up than expected, a choice of reaction exists—first, accept the destination on its own terms, and so have a 'relaxing' holiday by the swimming pool, and hence return both physically relaxed and satisfied; second, decide to use the destination as a base from which to explore surrounding areas; or third, leave the area altogether. Alternatively, they may complain bitterly to the tour operator. The model postulates a process of site evaluation, and a process incorporating an ability to suspend disbelief and a search for alternative and more satisfactory sources of potential goal solution. It does postulate a model of the tourist as a goal-seeking, active participant making either internal motivational or external behaviour changes where initial expectations are not met.

What is being discussed is some form of operant performance within complex and open social settings. In short a process of contingency management is involved. Contingency management may be defined as programmes of behaviour modification based on the negotiation and implementation of a contract that specifies rewards and punishments contingent upon the performance of particular behaviours (Lowe et al., 1987). The situation of the holiday is one where there is high motivation to achieve goals, within an at least moderately high informational context. Foxall (1990) proposes a behavioural perspective model which 'stresses the situational factors that are systematically related to such behaviours' (see Table 30.1). It is interesting to note that Foxall includes within the reinforcement component the level of informational content. It can be noted that almost by definition the holiday experience would form a 'pleasurable' context requiring hedonic responses. From the viewpoint of the above model the informational context provided by the tourist destination is important. Wearden (1988), reviews some of the literature relating to experimental reinforcement schedules with human respondents, and concludes that 'reinforcers' are informational rather than hedonic or response-strengthening; they inform subjects of the accuracy of their performance or that it has been otherwise satisfactory. Whether adopting Foxall's or Wearden's perspective, the conditions of the destination zone and consumer experience are such that they lead to extended problem solving (EPS).

Two apparent caveats to this approach might be mentioned. The first queries the degree to which the holiday experience is entirely one where EPS occurs, and the second is whether behavioural approaches are entirely valid bearing in mind Pearce's (1988) concept of the travel career based in Maslow's work. It was previously argued that at least parts of the holiday are characterised by 'mindlessness' and by scripted occasions. For example, it can be contended that frequently repeated actions become routinised, and hence are characterised by a lack of distinguishing features. It becomes difficult for respondents to differentiate between the same action carried out on different occasions. Here the concept of the 'critical incident' as developed by Bitner et al. (1990) may be significant. It can be contended that the scripted occasion is one which meets a set of not particularly high expectations—arousal levels are low, and the tourist goes with the 'flow' involved in a low arousal–low challenge–low skill situation. On the other hand, if the occasion becomes marked by a critical incident where performance either exceeds or is significantly below expectation, the situation ceases to be a scripted occasion.

If the characteristic of the scripted occasion is one of repeated action, then by definition it is unlikely to occur in the early stages of a holiday when a tourist is learning about the destination zone. Again, caveats need to be mentioned. The scripted occasion may occur early in a holiday if it is a situation where the tourist has repeatedly returned to the destination (e.g. a 'holiday home'). Assuming that in most cases tourists are exploring new situations, it can be hypothesised that scripted occasions tend to occur only in the latter part of the holiday period, or where the tourist has significant levels of past experience of that type of situation. In short, the scripted occasion occurs through familiarity, and, from the

Table 30.1 *Contingency categories, response patterns and reinforcement schedules*

Contingency category			Typical response pattern	Apparent reinforcement schedule
Setting component relatively	Reinforcement component			
Open Closed	} High	{ High hedonic Informational	EPS/new task gambling	High VI/VR High VR
Open Closed	} Low	{ High hedonic Informational	popular entertainment primary escape	Low VR Low VI
Open Closed	} High	{ Low hedonic Informational	LPS/modified rebuy Mandatory consumption	Low VI FI
Open Closed	} Low	{ Low hedonic Informational	RRB/straight rebuy secondary escape	Low FI/VI Low FI

Note: EPS = extended problem solving; LPS = limited problem solving; RRB = routine response behaviour; VI = variable interval; VR = variable ratio; FI = fixed interval.
Source: Foxall (1990:140).

context of information theory, not at points of discontinuity. Such an analysis is from the perspective of the tourist. From the viewpoint of the provider of the service, what is to the tourist a new situation, may in fact be a very familiar one, and the skill of the service provider is shown by their ability to 'persuade' the customer of the 'novelty' of the tourist experience. Essentially a situation perceived by the tourist as a 'scripted, mindless' experience is one that is not generating high levels either of satisfaction, or of dissatisfaction. It might be said to be satisfaction-neutral. On the other hand, a series of scripted encounters might generate satisfaction if the motivation for the holiday is primarily one of relaxation and escape from daily pressures of family and work life. The 'mindless' occasion requires little decision taking or mental exertion and poses little challenge and thus might be entirely appropriate as a holiday experience.

However, the question also remains as to the degree to which the above model can fully explain holiday satisfaction. It is a deductive model based on observation, and like many behaviourist models it can only make inferences about cognitive mediation. The question is important because the motivational models which are reviewed above, and which give rise to the items used in the Ragheb and Beard questionnaire, were based on concepts of autonomy and cognition associated with authors such as Maslow. But can such incidents be incorporated into the model of determinants of tourist satisfaction, and is it legitimate to incorporate concepts derived from humanistic psychology into a seemingly deterministic model? Skinnerian thought can be described as the proposition that observable behaviour can be explained in terms of contingent environmental stimuli; and the process whereby the rate of response is brought under the control of consequent stimuli (reinforcers and punishments). The model has not indicated the nature of reinforcement schedules, and is relativistic in its approach. It incorporates a plurality of paradigms. For example, while primarily arguing that the holiday experience by its nature uniquely meets a series of needs (for example, escape and fulfilment needs) and primarily consists of extended learning behaviours, as discussed above, it recognises routinised procedures where, arguably, Skinnerian approaches are apt descriptors. The model accords to cognitive, internalised processes important functions as motivators for holidays. The cognitive processes are also called into play as means of adjustment to initially less than satisfactory scenarios where the holidaymaker can subsequently derive satisfaction from the holiday. These internalised processes are important, because a basic premise in the argument is that similar motivations and similar holiday settings are not sufficient to predict either behaviour or the final level of satisfaction experienced.

Finally, it must be noted that the model is, at best, only a partial model. The outcome with which it is concerned is a measure of satisfaction, not behaviour. The link between satisfaction and behaviour is viewed as a reiterative process. That is, where performance meets or exceeds expectation, satisfaction is deemed to be an outcome. Where performance is inferior to expectation, then it is expected that adaptive behaviour results in achieving satisfaction because the motivation for satisfaction of wants is high within the holiday context. Where it is not possible to achieve those initial wants, alternative wants are substituted, behaviour changes, and again the goal is the satisfaction of those alternative wants. The consequence of achieving satisfaction from the holiday as to future holiday behaviour is not explored. Rather there is an implicit assumption that the link between satisfaction with a given type of holiday and repeat purchase of that holiday is, in fact, weak. The assumption is that holidaymakers use different types of holidays to meet different types of needs. The realisation of a satisfactory holiday is no guarantee of a repeat purchase. Repeat purchases may be a function of a changing prioritisation of the needs that motivate holidays, or the ability of a holiday type to meet different needs. Those needs are primarily determined not by the nature of past holiday experiences, but by other socioeconomic factors such as lifestyle, life-stage and the interpretation of the resultant experiences through the psychological network formulated by personality and learning abilities.

The model also lends credence to the theories of Plog (1977) in that specific destinations will be selected by tourists because those destinations possess the attributes that permit the fulfilment of primary leisure motivations.

The formulation of propositions

Having generally discussed some of the implications of the model, the question arises, does it help to formulate specific hypotheses that can be tested? Briefly the model utilises a gap analysis approach drawn from the SERVQUAL model that satisfaction is a consequence of expectation being met. The components of expectation, and the criteria against which performance will be judged is composed of two types of attributes. Extrinsic attributes refer to specific tangibles of the holiday destination—namely accommodation, scenic and other valued physical and cultural components of the destination, the types of people that reside in the resort (both indigenous people and other visitors). Intrinsic attributes refer to the motivations, which can be categorised on the basis of the four clusters described by Ragheb and Beard.

It is now possible to formulate a series of specific propositions. These are:

(a) satisfaction arises from the perceived attributes of the destination matching expectation;

(b) expectation is formulated by reference to four primary leisure motivations, as described by the Ragheb and Beard Leisure Motivation Scale, namely:

- the intellectual component;
- the social component;
- the competence-mastery component; and
- the stimulus-avoidance;

(c) the destination selected by a holidaymaker will possess attributes that match the primary source of motivation for that holidaymaker;

(d) the more experienced the holidaymaker, the better is the match between primary motivation source and destination attributes;

(e) the more experienced the holidaymaker, the better the match between perception and expectation, and the higher the level of satisfaction;

(f) less experienced holidaymakers will tend to have lower satisfaction scores, but a higher standard deviation of scores. Their inability to more correctly match destination with motivation will lead to a greater chance of disappointment or expectation being surpassed, hence the greater variation in the distribution of satisfaction scores;

(g) from the concept of the 'travel career' it is expected that more experienced holidaymakers will score more highly on intellectual motivations;

(h) more experienced holidaymakers will tend to show less evidence of adjustment behaviours at the holiday destination. Their ability to better select destinations that match needs requires less exploration as a sign of search behaviour designed to overcome initial disappointment;

(i) a congruence between expectation and perception of a place may not in itself lead to high levels of satisfaction being recorded. Intervening variables such as the need to select a holiday destination that meets the needs of significant others, or constraints imposed by availability of time or income, may mean the selection of a destination that does not meet the primary motivation of the holiday-taker. Therefore, where dissatisfaction occurs in spite of the congruence between expectation and perceived attributes of location, intervening variables can be identified as being important in the choice of location;

(j) where there is initial disappointment, higher levels of satisfaction are associated with higher levels of search behaviour;

(k) the more experienced the traveller, the smaller is the number of holiday destinations considered prior to choice; and

(l) the more experienced the tourist, the more homogeneous is the selection of holiday destinations considered before a choice is made.

Some findings

In a study of 1127 holidaymakers derived from the MOSAIC geo-demographic database in order to be representative of British holidaymakers, it was found that the concepts of the Ragheb and Beard Leisure Motivation Scale were applicable. Using a shortened version of the scale after a pilot study, as shown in Table 30.2, the four dimensions of the scale could be replicated. As Table 30.3 also indicates, the factors did not correlate with each other. Additionally the scale also possessed reliability as measured by Cronbach alpha coefficients, in that using a stepwise procedure which measured the total scale, and the contribution of each item to the scale, the score was consistently above 0.75. Ryan (1993a) also reports that it was possible to derive clusters of holidaymakers and that significant differences existed between them both in terms of their scores on the scale, and in their requirements of holiday destinations.

The gap concept as a measure of satisfaction was also used, as indicated in Table 30.4, when seeking to correlate the gap with other measures of satisfaction derived from

Table 30.2 *Mean scores on holiday motivation scale*

While on holiday I like to:	Mean	Standard deviation
relax mentally	5.9645	1.4656
discover new places and things	5.9290	1.3275
avoid the hustle and bustle	5.6335	1.6575
relax physically	5.5049	1.6905
be in a calm atmosphere	5.3895	1.7057
increase my knowledge	4.3913	1.6985
have a good time with friends	3.8385	2.0900
be with others of daily life	3.7054	1.7786
build friendships with others	3.4694	1.6855
use my imagination	3.4499	1.9033
gain a feeling of belonging	2.8066	2.6000
challenge my abilities	2.6939	1.8446
use my physical abilities/skills in sport	2.5617	1.9330
develop close friendships	2.4667	1.7424

Total number of respondents: 1127

Note. Scale runs from 1 to 7, with seven being the highest score.

Table 30.3 *Rotated factor matrix*

	1	2	3	4
be with others	**0.84050**	− 0.07896	0.02898	− 0.00210
have a good time with friends	**0.79335**	− 0.00803	− 0.10442	− 0.05877
build friendships	**0.72943**	0.03444	0.14009	0.10689
develop close friendships	**0.68307**	0.09004	0.14681	0.30176
gain a feeling of belonging	0.46475	0.27576	0.36594	0.13401
relax mentally	0.02713	**0.81445**	0.03478	− 0.02035
be in a calm atmosphere	0.04078	**0.75693**	− 0.01628	0.13337
relax physically	0.08999	**0.75024**	0.04655	− 0.28261
avoid the hustle and bustle	− 0.05031	**0.72714**	− 0.04895	0.04420
to increase my knowledge	− 0.05374	− 0.01105	**0.80329**	0.13756
discover new places and things	0.10357	− 0.04862	**0.72367**	− 0.24460
use my imagination	0.17943	0.04138	**0.67382**	0.35811
use my physical abilities	0.11174	− 0.01072	− 0.07794	**0.83814**
challenge my abilities	0.14200	− 0.05340	0.44655	**0.74025**

the conventional measures used on tour operator monitoring forms such as 'how strongly would you recommend this holiday to a friend?' and 'To what extent would you say you were satisfied with the holiday?', strong correlations emerge. In Table 30.5 the score of total satisfaction is the sum of responses to questions about:

(a) the extent to which they enjoyed the holiday
(b) the recommendation of the holiday to a friend
(c) satisfaction with accommodation
(d) satisfaction with the holiday area
(e) assessment of value for money
(f) perception of enjoyment of travelling companions

What is not supported by the results is the thesis that, given initial disappointment with the holiday destination, higher search activity occurs. There was no evidence that the less satisfied conducted higher levels of exploration activity, indeed the reverse was true—namely those who explored more had higher scores of satisfaction.

It has also been shown that the situational framework of the holiday is important. For example, using the same sample Ryan (1993b) reported that life-stage was an important consideration in holiday-taking decisions, and this confirmed the recent work of Lawson (1991) and Bojanic (1992).

Table 30.4 *Oblimin rotation*

Factor correlation matrix:

	Factor 1	Factor 2	Factor 3	Factor 4
Factor 1	1.00000			
Factor 2	0.10535	1.00000		
Factor 3	0.16798	0.06847	1.00000	
Factor 4	0.16963	− 0.01094	0.17381	1.00000

The research is continuing and currently the relationship between familiarity and tourist satisfaction and behaviour is being examined. Early results would seem to indicate that familiarity with the *type* of holiday being undertaken is not significant, but familiarity with the *destination*, as

Table 30.5 *F-ratios and probability scores—one-way analysis of variance for gaps between desired and perceived holiday experience against scores of total satisfaction*

Score of total satisfaction against:	F-ratio	Probability
Motivational factors		
relax mentally	12.97	0.0000
be in a calm atmosphere	8.02	0.0000
discover new places and things	6.94	0.0000
gain a sense of belonging	6.10	0.0000
increase knowledge	5.66	0.0000
relax physically	5.13	0.0000
use my imagination	5.00	0.0000
develop close friendships	4.67	0.0001
build friendships	4.33	0.0003
challenge my abilities	3.98	0.0006
use physical abilities	3.07	0.0055
Holiday destination factors		
comfort	33.08	0.0000
accommodation	32.34	0.0000
good weather	20.84	0.0000
beautiful scenery	19.07	0.0000
location	17.32	0.0000
interesting culture	14.77	0.0000
chance to get away from it all	10.23	0.0000
interesting history	7.35	0.0000
children's facilities	6.70	0.0000
good couriers	5.53	0.0000
having a good time with friends	5.33	0.0000
opportunity to mix with others	4.03	0.0005
being with others	3.02	0.0063
an active nightlife	2.64	0.0153
good bars	1.60	0.1420

measured by the number of previous visits to the same destination, is important.

Conclusion

Drawing upon concepts primarily found in leisure analysis, and utilising them within broad marketing theory and attitude measurement has produced a means of analysing tourist behaviour and satisfaction. The broad model of tourist behaviour suggested above has proved useful in that the contentions provided have led to measurable propositions. The results would seem to confirm that the practice of market segmentation is important, not only along the conventional lines of life-stage and psychographic profile, but also in terms of defining brochure messages that emphasise novelty or familiarity as is appropriate to the market segment. The research is continuing with particular reference to the nature of the perceived gap between expectation and perception of the holiday destination as this gap seems to correlate highly with conventional measures of satisfaction. Evidence from the SERVQUAL model studies implies that close study of these gaps can indicate areas where management might need to amend policies. Using a gap analysis of the factors inherent in the Leisure Motivation Scale and combining this with destination descriptions given by respondents it is hoped to obtain a better understanding of what constitutes an acceptable holiday environment.

What is also of interest is that the motivational scores shown in Table 30.2 reaffirm the primary need for relaxation. Given the attention being paid in the literature to emergent more active lifestyles and the supposed implications for new styles of holidays, the survey results and the cluster analysis previously reported provide little evidence of any real shift in holiday motivations. In this sense, it can be contended that reports of the demise of the outbound package holiday industry as it is known in the UK are premature.

References

Bagozzi, R. P. (1988) 'The rebirth of attitude research in marketing', *Journal of the Market Research Society*, 30(2): 163–196.

Bagozzi, R. P. and Warshaw, P. R. (1988) 'Broadening the theory of reasoned action to encompass goals and outcomes: an empirical comparison of two models and extensions', unpublished working paper, The University of Michigan.

Baldwin, K. S. and Tinsley, H. E. A. (1988) 'An investigation of the theory of Tinsley and Tinsley's (1986) theory of leisure experience', *Journal of Counselling Psychology*, 35(3): 263–267.

Beard, J. G. and Ragheb, M. G. (1980) 'Measuring leisure satisfaction', *Journal of Leisure Research*, 12(1): 20–33.

Beard, J. G. and Ragheb, M. G. (1983) 'Measuring leisure motivation', *Journal of Leisure Research*, 15(3): 219–228.

Bitner, M. J., Booms, B. H. and Tetreault, M. S. (1990) 'The service encounter: diagnosing favorable and unfavorable incidents', *Journal of Marketing*, 54: 71–84.

Bojanic, D. (1992) 'A look at a modernised family life cycle and overseas travel', *Journal of Travel and Tourism Marketing*, 1(1): 61–80.

Burkart, A. and Medlik, R. (1990) *Tourism, Past and Present*, Heinemann, Oxford.

Butler, R. W. and Waldbrook, L. A. (1991) 'A new planning tool—the tourism opportunity spectrum', *The Journal of Tourism Studies*, 2(1): 2–14.

Chick, G. and Roberts, J. M. (1990) 'Harmful and benign conflict in the Monday night pool', Proceedings of the 6th Canadian Congress of Leisure Research, University of Waterloo.

Cohen, E. (1972) 'Towards a sociology of international tourism', *Social Research*, 39(1): 164–182.

Cohen, E. (1974) 'Who is a tourist? A conceptual clarification', *The Sociological Review*, 22: 527–555.

Cohen, E. (1979) 'Rethinking the sociology of tourism', *Annals of Tourism Research*, 6: 18–35.

Cooper, C. P. (1981) 'Spatial and temporal patterns of tourist behaviour', *Regional Studies*, 15(5): 359–371.

Crompton, J. L. (1979) 'Motivations for pleasure vacations', *Annals of Tourism Research*, 6(1): 408–424.

Csikszentimihalyi, M. (1975) *Beyond Boredom and Anxiety*, Jossey-Bass, San Francisco.

Dimanche, F., Havitz, M. E. and Howard, D. R. (1991) 'Testing the involvement profile (IP) scale in the context of selected recreational and touristic activities', *Journal of Leisure Research*, 23(1): 51–66.

Fishbein, M. (1967) *Readings in Attitude Theory and Measurement*, John Wiley, New York.

Foxall, G. (1990) *Consumer Psychology in Behavioural Perspective*, Routledge, London.

Gray, J. A. (1987) *The Psychology of Fear*, Cambridge University Press, New York.

Gunn, C. (1988) *Tourism Planning*, Taylor & Francis, New York.

Gyte, D. (1988) 'Repertory grid analysis of images of destination: British tourists in Mallorca, Trent Working Papers in Geography, Nottingham Polytechnic.

Hill, A. B. and Perkins, R. E. (1985) 'Towards a model of boredom', *British Journal of Psychology*, 76: 235–240.

Iso-Ahola, S. (1982) 'Towards a social psychology of tourist motivation—a rejoinder', *Annals of Tourism Research*, 9: 256–261.

Iso-Ahola, S. and Weissenger, E. (1990) 'Perceptions of boredom in leisure: conceptualisation, reliability and validity in the Leisure Boredom Scale', *Journal of Leisure Research*, 22(1): 1–17.

Laing, A. (1987) 'The package holiday participant, choice and behaviour', unpublished Ph.D. thesis, Hull University.

Langer, E. J. and Newman, H. (1979) 'The role of mindlessness in a typical social psychology experiment', *Personality and Social Psychology Bulletin*, 5: 295–299.

Langer, E. J. and Piper, A. T. (1987) 'The prevention of mindlessness', *Journal of Personality and Social Psychology*, 52: 269–278.

Lawson, R. (1991) 'Patterns of tourist expenditure and types of vacation across the family life cycle', *Journal of Travel Research*, Spring: 12–18.

Loundsbury, J. W. and Franz, C. P. (1990) 'Vacation discrepancy—a leisure motivation approach', *Psychological Reports*, 66(2): 699–702.

Loundsbury, J. W. and Hoopes, L. (1988) 'Five year stability of leisure activity and motivation factors', *Journal of Leisure Research*, 20(2): 118–134.

Lowe, C. F., Horne, P. J. and Higson, P. J. (1987) 'Operant conditioning: the hiatus between theory and practice in clinical psychology', in Eysenck, H. and Martin, I. (Eds), *Theoretical Foundations of Behaviour Therapy*, Plenum, London.

Lyon, A. (1982) 'Timeshare—the decline', unpublished thesis, Nottingham Business School, England.

McCannell, D. (1976) *The Tourist—a New Theory of the Leisure Class*, Schocken Books, New York.

Mannell, R., Zuzanek, J. and Larson, R. (1988) 'Leisure states and "flow" experiences: testing perceived freedom and intrinsic motivation hypotheses', *Journal of Leisure Studies*, 20(4): 289–304.

Martin, B. (1992) 'Briskly up Plog's Scale', in *The Times Higher Educational Supplement*, 7 February: 24.

Maslow, A. H. (1970) *Personality and Motivation*, Harper & Row, New York.

Mathieson, A. and Wall, G. (1982) *Tourism, its Economic, Social, and Environmental Impacts*, Longmans, Harlow.

Mayo, E. J. and Jarvis, L. P. (1981) *The Psychology of Leisure Travel*, CBI Publishing, Boston, MA.

Mills, A. S. (1985) 'Participation motivations for outdoor recreation: a test of Maslow's theory', *Journal of Leisure Research*, 17: 184–199.

Moutinho, L. (1987) 'Consumer behaviour in tourism', *European Journal of Marketing*, 21(10): 1–44.

Murphy, P. (1982) *Tourism—a Community Approach*, Methuen, London.

Norton, G. (1987) 'Tourism and international terrorism', *The World Today*, February: 29–33.

Parasuraman, A., Zeaithaml, V. A. and Berry, L. (1985) 'A conceptual model of service quality and its implications for future research', *Journal of Marketing*, 49(4): 41–50.

Parasuraman, A., Zeaithaml, V. A. and Berry, L. (1988) 'SERVQUAL: a multiple-item scale for measuring consumer perceptions of service quality', *Journal of Retailing*, 64(1): 12–37.

Parasuraman, A., Berry, L. and Zeaithaml, V. A. (1991) 'Refinement and reassessment of the SERVQUAL scale', *Journal of Retailing*, 67(4): 420–450.

Parasuraman, A., Berry, L. and Zeaithaml, V. A. (1993) 'More on improving service quality measurement', *Journal of Retailing*, 69(1): 140–147.

Patrick, A. (1982) 'Clinical treatment of boredom', *Therapeutic Recreation Journal*, 16: 7–12.

Pearce, P. L. (1982) *The Social Psychology of Tourist Behaviour*, Pergamon Press, Oxford.

Pearce, P. L. (1988) *The Ulysses Factor: Evaluating Visitors in Tourist Settings*, Springer Verlag, New York.

Plog, S. C. (1977) 'Why destinations rise and fall in popularity', in *Domestic and International Tourism*, E. M. Kelly (Ed.), Institute of Certified Travel Agents, Wellesley, MA, pp. 26–28.

Podilchak, W. (1991) 'Distinctions of fun, enjoyment and leisure', *Leisure Studies*, 10(2): 133–148.

Ragheb, M. G. and Beard, J. G. (1982) 'Measuring leisure attitudes', *Journal of Leisure Research*, 14: 155–162.

Ryan, C. (1991) *Recreational Tourism, a Social Science Perspective*, Routledge, London.

Ryan, C. (1993a) 'Correlations between clusters based on the Ragheb and Beard Leisure Motivation Scale and the attributes of desired holiday locations', Proceedings of Third International Conference of the Leisure Studies Association, Loughborough University, 14–18 July 1993.

Ryan, C. (1993b) 'Life stage and family activities at holiday destinations', Proceedings of the Second Island Tourism International Forum, Bermuda College, 16–19 May 1993.

Ryan, C. (1994) *Researching Tourist Satisfaction—Issues, Concepts, Problems*, Routledge, Chapman & Hall, London (in press).

Sefton, J. M. (1989) 'Examining the factor invariance of Ragheb and Beard's Leisure Satisfaction and Leisure Attitude Scales', unpublished paper, Office of Research Services, University of Saskatchewan, June.

Sefton, J. M. and Burton, T. L. (1987) 'The measurement of leisure motivations and satisfactions: a replication and extension', Leisure Studies Division—The 5th Canadian Congress on Leisure Research, p. 29, Dalhousie University, Halifax.

Smith, L. J. and Godbey, G. C. (1991) 'Leisure, recreation and tourism', *Annals of Tourism Research*, 18(1): 85–100.

Voelkle, J. and Ellis, G. D. (1990) 'Use of criterion scaling in the analysis of experience sampling data, Proceedings 6th Canadian Congress on Leisure Research, Leisure Challenges, Bringing People, Resources and Policy into Play, Ontario Research Council on Leisure.

Vroom, V. H. (1964) *Work and Motivation*, John Wiley, New York.

Wearden, J. H. (1988) 'Some neglected problems in the analysis of human operant behaviour', in Davey, G. C. L. and Cullen, C. (Eds), *Human Operant Conditioning and Behaviour Modification*, John Wiley, Chichester.

Witt, C. and Wright, P. (1990) 'Tourist motivation: life after Maslow', *Proceedings of Tourism Research into the 1990s*, Durham University, pp. 1–16.

Yerkes, R. N. and Dodson, J. D. (1908) 'The relation of strength of stimulus to rapidity of habit formation', *Journal of Comparative Neurological Psychology*, 56: 98–121.

Yiannakis, A. and Gibson, H. (1992) 'Roles tourists play', *Annals of Tourism Research*, 19(2): 287–303.

31 Tourism research: a state-of-the-art citation analysis (1971–1990)

C. S. VAN DOREN, Y. K. KOH AND A. McCAHILL

Introduction

'It seems reasonable to assume that by the end of the century tourism will be one of the largest industries in the world, if not the largest' Kahn (1976:40). This prediction by Herman Kahn appears to be in the process of vindication as, indeed, both international tourism receipts and arrivals in 1992 reached the highest levels ever. In 1992, over 476 million tourists traveled internationally and spent over $279 billion. Expenditure on tourism services worldwide (including both domestic and international travel) reached over $2 trillion in 1992, representing approximately 12.5% of the world's consumer spending.

Statistics such as these clearly indicate the global volume and extent of tourism. However, to what extent is tourism research state-of-the-art in comparison to this global expansion? In keeping with the focus of the conference, this article analyzes reported research to help determine possible answers to the above question. In assessing tourism research as state-of-the-art it is necessary, like the god Janus, to look back as well as forward. The citation analysis reported in this research provides a backward view as well as possible indications for the future of tourism research.

History of tourism research

Despite the global volume and economic aspects of tourism, the research literature relating to this field of study presents a relatively brief and disjointed history. Before the 1970s, there was little cohesive presentation of tourism research. Tourism studies were reported in a wide variety of sources, from government documents to books. The only tourism journal in existence was *The Tourist Review* (first published in 1946). Consequently, scholarly articles on tourism appeared in a multitude of journals (e.g., from anthropology to transportation journals) and by authors from a multitude of academic and institutional backgrounds. Many governmental bodies, consulting companies and academic disciplines contributed to the 'hodge-podge' of reported tourism research.

In recent years there has been discussion regarding the possible maturity of tourism as an academic discipline. A focal point of such discussion concerns the extent and development of tourism research literature. Sheldon (1990:473) refers to tourism as a 'maturing field of study' and cites research as important for 'extending knowledge of the tourism phenomenon, and by contributing to the field's academic stature—an important consideration for a maturing field'.

In assessing the possible maturity of tourism, as with any growing discipline, it is crucial to periodically 'take stock' and analyze the extent and direction of its evolving research literature. This can lead to a better understanding of likely continued development (or possible lack thereof). Sheldon (1991) quotes Van Over and Nelson who summarize this viewpoint: 'In a relatively new field . . . it is periodically necessary to identify and evaluate major research contributions. Such an exercise serves not only to document the historical evolution of a discipline, but to give it a sense of its future as well'.

There are many routes to evaluating major research contributions to a growing area of study. These include analysis of conference presentations, proceedings, books, dissertations and academic journals. However, with tourism, as with most academic areas of study, the research journals are considered to be the major showcase of research in the field. Alternatively, as succinctly stated by Van Doren and Heit (1973), 'academic journals mirror the direction of a discipline's research'. The literature in the journals reflects, among other items, the authorship, institutional productivity and topical areas of study. Usually included is discussion of the methodology and statistical techniques employed in the research. Also, the use of citations provides valuable information as to who and what is being quoted. Journals typically represent state-of-the-art research, as the time lag for article publication is generally much shorter than is necessary for book publication or conference planning. Thus, in this citation analysis, journals were chosen for analysis as the best indicators depicting the evolution of tourism research.

Review of literature

The rationale of conducting a content analysis of journal articles to assess the growth of a discipline's research is not new (Sheldon, 1991). This methodology has been used in other fields of study, for example: by Vellenga et al. (1981) and Allen and Vellenga (1987) in transportation; and by Stahl, Leap and Wei (1988) in management (Sheldon, 1991). Other authors have analyzed academic journals by focusing on specific sections of reported research, for example: an analysis of the statistical techniques commonly used in the marketing journals (Grazer and Stiff, 1987); an evaluation of business journals (Ferguson, 1983); and an identification of the subject areas and research techniques used in hospitality-related journals (Crawford-Welch and McCleary, 1992). Several studies have been conducted in the recreation/leisure arena. A content analysis and appraisal of the *Journal of Leisure Research* was conducted to assess the match between stated goals of the journal and reported research (Van Doren and Heit, 1973). A citation analysis of the primary leisure journals was undertaken to provide insight into the structure and boundaries of leisure research (Van Doren et al., 1984).

Within the tourism literature itself, several authors have broached the question of identifying the state-of-the-art extent of tourism research and hence, hopefully of the field itself. Dann et al. (1988) consider the question from the interplay between theoretical awareness and methodological sophistication within tourism research. A meta-analysis was conducted for two journals (*Journal of Travel Research* and *Annals of Tourism Research*) over a 10-year period. Findings indicated a gradual increase in the reporting of scientific research (as opposed to descriptive feature articles) as well as a steady growth in the use of more sophisticated analytical and statistical tools. While showing promising growth, 'maturity' of field is not indicated as the authors claim that tourism researchers must continue to develop the balance between theory and method.

Some researchers have examined the titles of published doctoral dissertations in tourism (Jafari and Aaser, 1988) while others have concentrated in analyzing the choice of statistical methods (Reid and Andereck, 1989). The authors conclude that prior to 1984 journals tended to lack diversity and show an overwhelming dependence on the use of descriptive statistical techniques. Since 1984 there has been a definite trend to the usage of more sophisticated methods and analysis, Reid and Andereck (1989).

More recently, the work of Pauline Sheldon has contributed much to using journal analysis to provide vital statistics regarding the growth of the development of tourism literature. Her first study considered the perceptions of publishing faculty in both tourism and hospitality journals. The first portion of the study involved a ranking of the tourism and hospitality journals according to quality, frequency of referencing and frequency of publication. The second segment concerned the respondent's use of journals in allied fields which publish tourism research articles (Sheldon, 1990).

Sheldon's second study examined selected issues of three journals over a 10-year period (*Annals of Tourism Research*, *Journal of Travel Research* and *Tourism Management*). She presented the results in four segments: 'percentage of authors affiliated with academic and non-academic institutions, the geographic contributions of authors, the research contributions of different universities and the degree to which repeat authorship exists' (Sheldon, 1991:475). She concludes by stating that 'substantial progress' has been made towards developing tourism research and that this trend can be expected to continue: 'the 1990s can be expected to produce even greater gains' Sheldon (1991:483). The citation analysis conducted in this article may provide more insight regarding the progress that has been made in the evolution and development of tourism research.

Methodology

The citation analysis reported in this study is a portion of a larger unpublished research undertaking which involves a content analysis of tourism journals. It is a systematic, empirical analysis of six refereed journals (published in English) from 1971 to 1990. The journals have been selected to represent the four continents publishing tourism journal research (i.e., N. America, Europe, Asia and Australasia). The refereed journals analyzed in the study are: *Annals of Tourism Research* (ATR) and *Journal of Travel Research* (JTR) both published in N. America, the *Journal of Tourism Management* (JTM) and *The Tourist Review* (TTR) from Europe, *Tourism Recreation Research* (TRR) from Asia and the *Journal of Tourism Studies* (JTS) representing Australasia. All journal issues within the 20-year period were examined, including research notes which reported scientific research. When the first publication of the journal was later than 1971, the citation analysis was conducted from the first issue onwards. The journals in this category are as follows: the ATR (1973), the TTR (1976), the JTM (1980) and the JTS (1990). Due to unavailability of earlier issues of the TRR, only issues from 1984 onwards have been incorporated into this citation analysis.

For each journal article a complete content analysis was conducted. First the subject and authorship of the article was identified. All articles were then classified as either research (based on the principles of scientific enquiry) or feature (a narrative approach). For research articles the methodology and statistical techniques employed were also identified. A comprehensive citation analysis was conducted for all articles (both research and feature) reported in the above six journals over the 20-year period (1971–1990).

The citation analysis resulted in a total of 19 576 citations over the twenty years. The actual unit of analysis utilized, the 'citation' was considered to be any source listed by an author. Each reference was coded as a single entry, irrespective of the number of times it was cited in the article. This approach was adopted because the objective was to identify the diversity of sources which contributed to the literature over time, rather than to identify which citations were most heavily relied upon by any single author (Van Doren et al., 1984). This method of citation analysis has an extensive pedigree within the social sciences, e.g. Garfield et al. (1964), Blume (1977), and Goldman (1979).

Six indicators were utilized to assess the citations reported in the six tourism journals. The first indicator involved an overall comparison of tourism and non-tourism citations. The second considered the extent to which citations originated from tourism journals, including two non-refereed journals: *The International Tourism Quarterly* (ITQ) and the *Travel and Tourism Analyst* (TTA). The third indicator analyzed contributions from non-tourism academic journals in related social science disciplines or professional studies. The contribution from non-tourism journals is then further analyzed by reviewing each of the six refereed tourism journals to determine the academic subfields utilized. The fifth indicator relates to the use of non-refereed publications in tourism research. Finally, a comparison across time is provided, in increments of five years. This examines the evolution of tourism research by assessing the developmental growth patterns of the following: tourism journals, general tourism publications, non-tourism journals, non-English citations and other citations. All of the results of this study are presented in descriptive form.

Results and discussion

Citation analysis overview (1971–1990)

Frequently a new field of study, discipline or profession is measured by the degree to which it draws upon its own literature in scholarly writing. Table 31.1 provides an

overview of the citation analysis for the 20-year period. The six refereed travel and tourism journals draw approximately 15% of their citations from eight tourism journals. In addition to the six refereed journals, two non-refereed journals are also included—the *International Tourism Quarterly* (ITQ) and the *Travel and Tourism Analyst* (TTA). If the number of citations from tourism books is added to that of tourism journals, then almost one-quarter (23.5%) of all citations originate directly from tourism books and journals. When the remaining four tourism categories shown in Table 31.1 are included, the total contribution from the tourism literature rises to 39.95%. This indicates a substantial degree of quoting from within the field and is one of the indicators of maturity of a field (Van Doren et al., 1984). The interdisciplinary/professional base of travel and tourism is demonstrated by the 38% of citations that are from non-tourism journals (30.55%) and non-tourism books (7.73%). The category of 'Tourism government documents/reports' includes national and state/provincial government reports as well as items such as technical reports published by planning agencies. Trade publications refer to the variety of magazines and newspapers printed for the tourism industry. Tourism conferences are those sponsored by recognized tourism institutions (academic and industry). The remaining category, WTO/IOUTO reports, was included to determine the extent to which international reports and statistics are commonly cited in

Table 31.1 *Citation analysis overview (1971–1990)*

	Number	%Total
Tourism literature		
Tourism journals	2909	14.86
Tourism books	1714	8.76
Tourism govt. documents/special reports	1444	7.38
Trade publications	1024	5.23
Tourism conferences	519	2.65
WTO/IOUTO reports	210	1.07
Subtotal:	7820	39.95
Non-tourism literature		
Non-tourism journals	5982	30.56
Non-tourism books	1514	7.73
Non-tourism govt. documents/special reports	1286	6.57
Non-English citations	1107	5.65
Popular magazines	548	2.80
Newspapers	525	2.68
Non-tourism conferences	416	2.13
Other	378	1.93
Subtotal:	11756	60.05
Total:	19576	100.00

Journal citations (tourism and non-tourism) = 8891 or 45.42

tourism journals. This category provided the smallest contribution from the tourism literature and may be an indication of the time lag necessary to collect and assimilate international statistics regarding tourism.

The 'Non-tourism literature' section of Table 31.1 includes general sources of citations, e.g. magazines and newspapers. The section entitled 'Other' includes unpublished theses/dissertations, citations resulting from personal interviews and any other citations that could not be classified under the other stated categories.

A good indicator of the development of tourism research is the fact that a substantial portion of tourism citations originate from refereed journals (both tourism and non-tourism). The total number of journal citations in Table 31.1 is 8891, representing 45.42% of all citations. When this number is added to the citation of books (tourism and non-tourism) the total of citations emanating from these two categories is 12 119 citations or 62%. Thus journals and books are the predominant sources of citations in the tourism journals.

Citation analysis of the six refereed tourism journals

A comparison of tourism journal citations in the six refereed journals reveals that the four journals with the largest number of citations all have the highest number of citations from their own pages (shown by the underlining in Table 31.2). The remaining two journals, TRR and JTS both cite the ATR most frequently. However, due to the tender age of the JTS (first published in 1990), it was not possible for the JTS or any other journal to cite the JTS in the journal issues incorporated in this study. Clearly, the *Annals of Tourism Research* (ATR) is the premier journal referenced by scholars. It is both the most cited journal (1171 citations) and uses the most citations (1233 citations). Also, it is one of the top two cited journals for all journals except the JTM where the ATR is a close third (127 citations) behind the JTR (133 citations). The JTR, like the ATR, is widely

cited (941 citations) while the newer JTM is cited less (381 citations). However, on its own pages, the authors in the JTM use almost as many references from other journals (502 citations) as do the authors in the JTR (667 citations). These three journals (the ATR, JTR and JTM) together constitute 2493 citations, or an overwhelming 89.04% of all refereed journal citations. According to Goldman (1979) domination of an academic discipline by a small number of journals can be construed as evidence of a maturing academic field. Thus the increasing compactness of tourism research may indicate a burgeoning state of maturity. Another positive indicator of the evolution of tourism research is the fact that 96.25% of tourism journal citations were reported from refereed tourism journals. The two non-refereed tourism journals (ITQ and TTA) only accounted for 109 citations, or 3.75% of citations.

Non-tourism journal citations

Authors of tourism research often declare that the study of tourism is supported by a multidisciplinary contribution from a variety of other fields of academic study. This is substantiated in this research. Non-tourism journals account for 5982 citations or 30.55% of all citations (Table 31.1). A closer analysis of the contribution from other fields is shown in Table 31.3 which provides a more detailed overview of the sources of non-tourism journal citations and solidifies our knowledge that the subject draws its strength from other disciplines and professions. To assess the contribution of other subjects, nineteen academic categories and one miscellaneous/other category are identified in the population of non-tourism journals. All of the categories are from under the social science or professional umbrella and are ranked in Table 31.3 to reflect the appropriate contribution to tourism research. The miscellaneous/other category contained journals that could not be classified under the other 19 categories.

Table 31.2 *Citation analysis of the six refereed tourism journals*

Journal	Date of publication	ATR	JTR	JTM	TTR	TRR	JTS	Row total
1. ATR	1973	716	306	120	76	15	0	1233
2. JTR	1970	148	449	39	27	4	0	667
3. JTM	1980	127	133	161	61	20	0	502
4. TTR	1946	56	24	42	78	10	0	210
5. TRR	1976	75	23	10	3	11	0	122
6. JTS	1990	49	6	9	2	0	0	66
Column total		1171	941	381	247	60	0	2800[a]

[a]The total does not = 2909 as reported in Table 31.1 as the 109 citations from the two non-refereed journals (TTA and ITQ) are excluded.

Table 31.3 *Non-tourism journal citations*

Discipline	Number	%
1. Marketing	744	12.44
2. Sociology	694	11.60
3. Recreation/leisure	621	10.38
4. Economics	610	10.20
5. Geography	481	8.04
6. Management	454	7.59
7. Planning/development	356	5.95
8. Psychology	350	5.85
9. Anthropology	343	5.73
10. Hospitality	289	4.83
11. Environment/natural res.	221	3.69
12. Miscellaneous/other	176	2.94
13. History	122	2.04
14. Political science	115	1.92
15. Statistics	111	1.86
16. Parks/forestry	81	1.35
17. Transportation	72	1.20
18. General business	57	0.95
19. Education	52	0.87
20. Philosophy	33	0.55
Total:	5982	100.00

In the attempt to more closely identify links with other disciplines, the closest relative (that of business) was further subdivided into four categories: economics, marketing, management and general business. The total number of citations from these four categories is 1865 citations representing a substantial contribution of 31.18% to all citations in the refereed tourism journals.

Marketing was the clear leader in terms of contribution to tourism research (744 citations, 12.44%). Much of this contribution resulted from the reliance of business citations in the JTR and the JTM. Marketing is closely followed by three other disciplines, sociology (694 citations, 11.60%), recreation/leisure (621 citations, 10.38%) and economics (610 citations, 10.20%). When geography, the fifth-ranking discipline is added (481 citations, 8.04%), the top five contributors to tourism research account for over half of all non-tourism journal citations (3150 citations, 52.66%). Thus these five academic disciplines represent the most dominant subfields supporting tourism research. This clear identification of subfields may prove useful information to tourism authors in terms of possible joint partnerships for research and funding. Within the top five disciplines, the social sciences contributed the most—sociology, recreation/leisure and geography resulted in 1796 citations (57.02%) while marketing and economics resulted in 1354 citations (42.98%). Thus, it is clearly indicated that the tourism journals are based in the social sciences with a prominent secondary base in business management. The top ten

ranked disciplines shown in Table 31.3 represent 4942 citations, or 82.61% of all non-tourism journal citations.

Tourism journal citations from non-tourism journals

Table 31.4 provides insight into the nature and structure of each of the six tourism journals by analyzing the

Table 31.4 *Tourism journal citations from non-tourism journals*

	Number	%
ATR		
1. Sociology	459	16.29
2. Anthropology	281	9.97
3. Economics	275	9.76
4. Recreation/leisure	273	9.69
5. Geography	271	9.62
	1559	55.33
JTR		
1. Marketing	419	29.71
2. Recreation/leisure	167	11.84
3. Management	135	9.57
4. Psychology	121	8.58
5. Economics	115	8.15
	957	67.85
JTM		
1. Management	127	13.56
2. Economics	124	13.20
3. Hospitality	116	12.39
4. Marketing	104	11.10
5. Planning/development	93	9.90
	564	60.15
TTR		
1. Economics	66	14.40
2. Recreation/leisure	57	12.47
3. Sociology	45	9.84
4. Geography	43	9.40
5. Hospitality	40	8.75
	251	54.85
TRR		
1. Geography	37	13.75
2. Anthropology	32	11.89
3. Environment/natural res.	32	11.89
4. Sociology	27	10.00
5. Miscellaneous	23	8.55
	151	56.08
JTS		
1. Recreation/leisure	19	19.38
2. Environment/natural res.	13	13.30
3. Sociology	10	10.20
4. Economics	9	9.20
5. Miscellaneous	9	9.20
	60	70.50

proportions to which other fields of study are represented in each journal. The five prominent citation sources from non-tourism journals are listed and in every case the top five categories account for the majority of non-tourism citations. The range is from 54.85% with the TTR to 70.05% with the JTS. The academic structural strength of each of the journals is clearly reflected in the top five categories of citations represented in each journal. In all cases the structural underpinning of the journal is congruent with its stated objectives. For example, the Statement of Purpose contained in the ATR declares the journal to be a 'social sciences journal focusing upon the academic perspectives of tourism [and] . . . is structured by the research efforts of a multidisciplinary community of scholars'. This mission is reflected in the fact that the two highest sources of non-tourism journal citations are sociology and anthropology, followed by economics, recreation/leisure and geography. Similarly, the JTR, published by the Travel and Tourism Research Association, clearly demonstrates its marketing/promotional flavor with 30% of its citations directly from marketing. In addition, a further 10% of citations originate from management journals and another 8% from psychology. The JTM likewise is based in the management sciences with 37% of its citations originating from management, hospitality and marketing, subjects that reflect its purpose and contribution to this field of study.

The remaining three journals would seem to mirror strong social science orientations although *The Tourist Review* (TTR) does include hospitality and marketing citations that are not as evident in TRR and JTS. The Asian journal, TRR, appears to have a strong base in the social sciences rather than management sciences. This journal, and the JTS are the two tourism journals to feature environment/natural resources in the top five categories. It would appear that North America and Europe each have a social science and management science-based journal—the ATR and JTR for North America and TTR and the JTM for Europe, respectively. While all these four journals have an international purview, the researchers and journal editors in the two traditionally wealthy regions of the world have proceeded along two distinct paths of inquiry—academic and practical. Both paths are necessary and essential to tourism and travel knowledge. The appearance of two new refereed tourism journals in the 1990s (the *Journal of Travel and Tourism Marketing*, 1992, and the *Journal of Sustainable Tourism*, 1993), indicates that further frontiers and opportunities to fill needed research niches are essential.

Non-refereed publications

While approximately 45% of all citations are from refereed journals, a larger proportion is from other types of literature sources. Non-journal citations for the six journals are listed in Table 31.5. The highest proportion for each journal is indicated by underlining. The newest journal, *Journal of Tourism Studies* (JTS), has 28% of all non-journal citations from tourism books with three additional journals, ATR, JTM and TTR also having the most citations from tourism books. All the journals have more than 25% of all citations from a combination of tourism/non-tourism books. The highest is 36% by the JTS, followed by 34% in the JTR. The JTR has the highest percentage of citations from non-tourism books at 22% (many of these are basic marketing and statistical textbooks) and government documents. The JTR also has the highest proportion of all six journals regarding special report citations. In three journals, the authors using non-English citations ranged from a high of 26.19% for the TRR to 15% for TTR to 0.06% for the new JTS. The European journal TTR contained 14.90% of non-English citations followed by the ATR at 13.37%. Both the JTR and JTM had low rates of non-English citations. These two journals also have relatively high citations from trade publications, particularly the JTM at 15%. It could be inferred that these comparisons provide further evidence that the JTR and JTM have a more practical, applied orientation.

Citation analysis by half-decade

The study of tourism is a very new academic subject as evidenced by the age of the six premier tourism journals analyzed in this study (Table 31.2). Van Doren et al. (1984) emphasized that if a field of study has one or two journals predominant, this may indicate that the field of study has a developing identity with scholars that build on the work of others. This identity means that there is structure and compactness to the field. Goldman (1979) believes that a field is compact if scientific publications are limited to a few journals and if there are few subfields. Such compactness is not presently evident in tourism journals yet may be emerging. While Table 31.3 indicates there are at least ten subfields commonly utilized in non-tourism journal citations (representing 82.61% of such citations), the five dominant subfields did represent over half of all non-tourism journal citations (52.66%). Thus by Goldsman's criteria there is evidence that tourism as a field of study is maturing and becoming more compact in nature. Also, an analysis of how the types of citations, particularly those drawn from the tourism literature, have

Table 31.5 *Non-refereed publications*

| | ATR | | JTR | | JTM | | TTR | | TRR | | JTS | |
	No.	%	No.	%	No.	%	No.	%	No.	%	No.	%
Tourism books	766	17.16	264	11.89	327	16.94	196	18.06	113	13.83	48	28.07
Tourism conferences	157	3.51	115	5.18	151	7.82	65	5.99	21	2.57	10	5.84
Other	188	4.21	77	3.46	56	0.03	22	2.02	26	3.18	9	5.26
Special reports	485	10.86	302	13.60	258	13.36	133	12.25	88	10.77	20	11.69
Trade publications	362	8.11	189	8.51	281	14.55	118	10.87	46	5.63	28	16.37
Magazines	246	5.51	102	4.59	95	4.92	57	5.25	42	5.14	6	3.50
Newspapers	271	6.07	74	3.33	115	5.95	21	1.93	38	4.65	6	3.50
Government documents	533	11.94	481	21.66	248	12.84	82	7.55	83	10.15	17	9.94
WTO/IOUTO	65	1.45	9	0.04	54	0.02	47	4.33	25	3.05	5	2.92
Non-tourism books	555	12.43	480	21.62	220	11.39	147	13.54	98	11.99	14	8.18
Non-English citations	597	13.37	64	2.88	69	3.57	162	14.90	214	26.19	1	0.06
Non-tourism conferences	237	5.31	58	2.61	56	0.03	35	3.22	23	2.81	7	40.9
Totals	4462	100.00	2220	100.00	1930	100.00	1085	100.00	817	100.00	171	100.00

increased over time indicates that tourism as a subject may be gradually moving towards a more compact structure.

Figure 31.1 provides an overview of the growth of tourism literature over the 20-year period. To provide a more specific analysis of the development of tourism research, the five categories of citations are represented in increments of half decades.

The largest growth pattern is that of tourism general literature (see Table 31.1 for a classification of tourism literature). This attests to the growing availability of

tourism and travel publications. The increasing storehouse of tourism sources (from books to trade magazines) is being amply utilized by tourism researchers. Thirty-one per cent of the citations in the three journals of the first half decade are from the tourism literature. By the 1986–1990 period, this had increased to 40% from tourism within the TTR and the newest journal (JTS) which contained more than 50% from tourism citations. The overall use of tourism citations over the 20 years has grown to 39.93% of all citations. Included in this figure

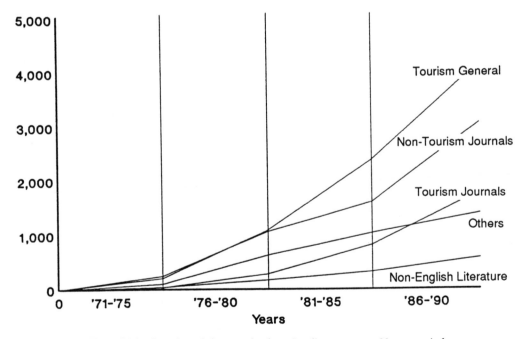

Figure 31.1 *Overview of the growth of tourism literature over 20-year period*

is the use of tourism journals which increased steadily in each five-year block to a total of 14.86% of all citations.

One measure of the maturity of a discipline is the proportion of citations from its own journals relative to journals outside the discipline. Previous studies have stated that physics draws almost all of its citations from its own literature, economics 70% and marketing and sociology 45% and 40% respectively (Van Doren et al., 1984). The data of Figure 31.1 indicate that, as the number of tourism journals have increased over two decades, the citations from tourism journals has increased correspondingly. This augurs well for the journal authors and indicates that tourism research as scholarly writing is being more widely disseminated.

The remaining two categories shown in Figure 31.1, 'Non-English literature' and 'Others', demonstrate a stable pattern but do not demonstrate the fastest growth patterns evidenced by 'Tourism general' and both 'Tourism journals' and 'Non-tourism journals'.

Summary

The citation analysis conducted in this study does reveal an emerging state-of-the-art level of development regarding tourism research. Tourism research is developing a tighter structure and more compact boundaries while still incorporating the diversity of disciplines and professions listed in Table 31.3. Indeed, the fact that many researchers in tourism have a training foundation outside this relatively new field of study may hasten the process towards research maturity. Whether these specialty 'building blocks' will continue to be influential in our research may be essential to the internal morphology of studies on tourism.

Acknowledgements

The authors wish to acknowledge the assistance of Professor Sheila Backman, Department of Parks, Recreation and Tourism at Clemson, for providing copies of *Tourism Recreation Research* and Professor Nick DiGrino, Department of Recreation, Park and Tourism Administration, University of Western Illinois, for providing copies of *The Tourist Review*. We are indebted to Sheila and Nick for their cooperation in completing this citation analysis.

References

Allen, B. J. and Vellenga, D. B. (1987) 'Affiliation of authors in transportation and logistics academic journals—an update', *Transportation Journal*, 26(2): 39–47.

Blume, S. S. (1977) *Perspectives in the Sociology of Science*, John Wiley, New York.

Crawford-Welch, S. and McCleary, K. W. (1992) 'An identification of the subject areas and research techniques used in five hospitality-related journals', *International Journal of Hospitality Management*, 11(12): 155–167.

Dann, G. M. S., Nash, D. and Pearce, P. L. (1988) 'Methodology in tourism research', *Annals of Tourism Research*, 15(1): 1–28.

Ferguson, W. (1983) 'An evaluation of journals that publish business logistics articles', *Transportation Journal*, 22(4): 69–72.

Garfield, E., Shor, I. H. and Torpie, R. J. (1964) 'The use of citation data in writing the history of science', Institute for Scientific Information, Philadelphia, p. 76.

Goldman, A. (1979) 'Publishing activity in marketing as an indicator of its structure and disciplinary boundaries', *Journal of Marketing Research*, 16: 485–494.

Grazer, W. F. and Stiff, M. R. (1987) 'Statistical analysis and design in marketing journal articles', *Journal of the Academy of Marketing Science*, 15(1): 70–73.

Jafari, J. and Aaser, D. (1988) 'Tourism as the subject of doctoral dissertations', *Annals of Tourism Research*, 15(3): 407–429.

Kahn, H. (1976) *The Next 200 Years: A Scenario for America and the World*, Morrow, New York, p. 40.

Reid and Andereck (1989) 'Statistical analyses use in tourism research', *Journal of Travel Research*, 28(2): 21–24.

Riddick, C. C., De Schriver, M. and Weissinger, E. (1984) 'A methodological review of research in journal of leisure research from 1978–1982', *Journal of Leisure Research*, 16(4): 311–321.

Sheldon, P. J. (1990) 'Journal usage in tourism: perceptions of publishing faculty', *Journal of Tourism Studies*, 1(1): 42–48.

Sheldon, P. J. (1991) 'An authorship analysis of tourism research', *Annals of Tourism Research*, 18(4): 473–484.

Stahl, M. J., Leap, T. L. and Wei, Z. Z. (1988) 'Publication in leading management journals as a measure of institutional research productivity', *Academy of Management Journal*, 31(3): 707–720.

Van Doren, C. S. and Heit, M. (1973) 'Where it's at: a content analysis and appraisal of the journal of leisure research', *Journal of Leisure Research*, 5: 67–73.

Van Doren, C. S., Holland, S. M. and Crompton, J. L. (1984) 'Publishing in the primary leisure journals: insight into the structure and boundaries of our research', *Leisure Sciences*, 6(2): 239–256.

Vellenga, D. B., Allen, B. J. and Riley, C. D. (1981) 'An analysis of author affiliation for publications in transportation and logistics academic journals, 1967–1979', *Transportation Journal*, 21(1): 44–53.

32 Are relatives friends? Reassessing the VFR category in segmenting tourism markets

A. V. SEATON

Novitiates into the arcane lore of tourism analysis learn an early catechism about the nature of travellers. Travellers, saith the catechism, fall into four main types: holidaymakers; those visiting friends and relatives; those travelling on business; and a heterogeneous body of people travelling for 'other' purposes. This quartet of Holiday, VFR, Business and Other is enshrined in the rubric of countless international, national and regional visitor studies and standard to their analysis.

The purpose of this paper is to explore the utility of one of these central categories, 'visiting friends and relatives', as an aggregate category for understanding tourist behaviour.

The evolution of the VFR concept

The VFR category has been around since the ark. Though it is difficult to date its origins precisely, VFR travel was a main feature of early Grand Tour tourism when many aristocratic and genteel travellers 'doing' the continent stayed with status peers and foreign relatives in places like Paris and Florence. The concept seems to have existed explicitly in tourism data since the war in visitor studies by both public and private sector tourism organisations. Today it is still a key segmental category used to classify an important proportion of tourist volume worldwide. In 1986 VFRs accounted for 21% of all vacation trips in the 12 European Community countries with some countries showing scores that were much higher, notably Portugal, 42%, France, 33%, and Spain, 32% (EC Omnibus Survey, 1986). In 1992 31% of all UK trips to Scotland and 19% of those from overseas were VFR (STB, 1993). In Northern Ireland in 1991, 47% of all tourist nights, 39% of all trips and 34% of tourist spending were classified as 'visiting friends and relatives' (NITB, 1991). The latest UK Tourism Survey shows that 22% of all tourist trips by purpose within the UK in 1992 were VFRs, with 45% claiming to have stayed with friends and relatives, even when doing so was not the main purpose of the trip (UKTS, 1992). It is not necessary to push this statistical trawl any further, only to note that similar figures on the importance of VFR travellers can be produced from data for most other destinations internationally.

So if the VFR category captures such an important volume of tourist behaviour why should it be questioned?

Before an answer can be given, it is worth looking at the rationale for having a VFR category in the first place.

The logic implicit in deploying the VFR category goes something like this: 'visiting friends and relatives' is a valuable segment for tourism organisations to disaggregate from total visitor data because it identifies a group of travellers who, by making their own accommodation arrangements, spend nothing on board and lodging, and less on tourism activity overall. Since tourism planners are interested in revenue-generation, it is important to differentiate those tourists who are likely to spend more ('holiday visitors', sometimes tagged even more forcibly as PHVs—'pure holiday visitors') from those who, paying nothing for their keep, will spend less.

The logic behind this argument has been tested many times, by comparing the visitor expenditures of PHVs v. VFRs. The results of such comparisons invariably suggest that PHVs do outspend VFRs, in the UK by almost 3 to 1 (in 1991 average spending per trip for VFRs was £39.42 v. £132.94 for overall trips (UKTS, 1992)).

The VFR category is thus based on grouping substantial numbers of people through an absence—not paying for accommodation—thus relegating them to diminished importance in tourism planning. Although quite extensive data on VFR activities and expenditures are gathered by NTOs, and the importance of the category in out-of-season tourism is widely recognised, in general VFR tourism does not attract the attention of some other categories. As Denman has noted: 'The VFR market is often a forgotten market . . . frequently treated as an irrelevance within any tourism policy or action programme' (Denman, 1988:7).

Problems with the VFR category

What are the weaknesses of current approaches to the VFR category?

One answer might be that market segmentation should be a positive force, the identification of opportunities rather than lack of them. The VFR category is, to some extent, a negative grouping rather than a segment defined by precise, positive characteristics.

Secondly, the VFR category can be seen as a classic example of what marketers call 'production-orientation', an administrator's convenience, developed from the perspectives of the supplier, rather than one that sheds very much light on subjective tourist behaviour, particularly the motivational aspects. People don't think of themselves as VFRs. They think of themselves as one or the other—visiting families *or* visiting friends—and the motivations, even within these two apparently similar groups, may be highly diverse. The VFR category can be seen as a conceptual aggregate, rather than a natural grouping that would be recognised by the actors who constitute it.

More than that, the category is ambiguous: visiting friends and relatives can be a primary motivation, the reason for a trip, or merely a trip descriptor, meaning simply that friends and relatives provided accommodation, irrespective of whether they were the main reason for the trip. In practice, these two are often hard to separate, though several NTOs make efforts to do so.

Overall then the VFR category is non-consumer-oriented and imprecise. Coming back to the original question, 'What is wrong with the VFR concept?', we can now venture a tentative answer which is that 'It may draw attention to a significant number of people, but tells us comparatively little about them except what they don't do, or worse, suggests common motivational characteristics which may not exist'.

At this point someone might object that all marketers, whatever their product, attempt to distinguish users from non-users and that this is, in effect, what the VFR category was designed to do in a tourism context. But this argument does not bear scrutiny. In other consumer-goods fields, non-purchasers are all equal— they have a value of precisely nothing at all. This is certainly not the case with VFRs who may spend nothing on accommodation (and even that is not completely true—in 1991 9% of UK VFRs stayed in some kind of commercial accommodation), but they may still eat out, buy presents, visit attractions, use transport facilities etc. etc. In short, they may still be highly desirable prospects for many kinds of tourism product, who would repay further study. In fairness a number of tourism planners have recognised this and have uneasily suspected that, despite their under-consumption in terms of accommodation, VFRs might constitute a major market opportunity, if only because they are so numerous. But to date nobody has successfully broken open the category for more precise scrutiny (although the European tourism statistics group, Eurostat has considered it).

The evidence

What would happen if one did so?

The quick answer is, that no one knows for sure but there are clues, tucked away in the nooks and crannies of studies into other things, that suggest interesting outcomes.

Firstly, there are good reasons for thinking that simply splitting the VFR category into three—(i) visiting friends, (ii) visiting relatives and (iii) visiting friends and relatives—would immediately improve our understanding of tourism behaviour. Try this simple test: first describe the last time you went to stay with a friend out of your area; then describe the last trip you made to see your mother, father or aged aunt. At Strathclyde University we have begun to ask people to do this and the results shown suggest some differences in behaviour patterns within a nominally homogeneous category. Here are two sets of verbatim responses from a middle-aged businessman, describing two trips, the first a visit he and his wife made to an old work colleague in Scotland:

> We stayed with John and Mary for a weekend at their house in the Scottish Borders. We arrived on the Friday night and had a meal with them at home. On the Saturday we all went to Edinburgh for the day where we visited Valvona and Crolla, an Italian delicatessen, and spent £35 on wine and food, paid for by credit card. Then we visited an exhibition at the Scottish Royal Academy (programme cost £2) and had lunch there (cost about £2 a head). In the afternoon we did some shopping and bought a blouse costing £17 for my wife, paid for by credit card, and then went back to the house. In the evening we went out for an expensive meal at one of the Good Food Guide restaurants near Biggar (£37 a head), paid for by credit card.

Compare this high-rolling account with the following week when Mr Brown went to the Midlands to see his father two weeks before Christmas:

> It was a duty visit I have to make two or three times a year. I drove down buying petrol on the way and two chocolate bars. When I arrived my father had prepared a meal which we had with my brother and his family. For two days we watched TV and stayed in, apart from a short walk round the park. The major expenditure was petrol, except for a bottle of wine I bought for the meal.

These accounts do not of course prove anything, but they highlight the differences—motivational and behavioural— that may lurk beneath the deceptively even surface of VFR classifications.

More substantial evidence comes from a four-nation Family Tourism Survey, also being carried out at Strathclyde. One of the findings from this is the distinctive vacation patterns of Asian, ethnic minorities in Britain. It suggests that virtually all long-haul main vacation trips designated VFRs are actually VRs—family trips back to

Pakistan or India and other ex-commonwealth countries where members of the extended family are living. Similarly, a paper by Jackson (Jackson, 1990) highlighted the fact that much VFR tourism to Australia may also comprise large numbers of family members visiting recent Australian immigrants from countries of origin (and also family visitor flows the other way from Australia to original country of origin). A comparable phenomenon is observable in the Shetland Isles where a significant number of VFR trips are actually 'hamefarins', people returning to their roots and staying with long-lost relatives—not friends (Mullay, personal communication). In 1992, Ireland actually set out to activate this latent relative market when the Northern Irish Tourist Board and Borde Fialte collaborated in staging a 'homecoming' festival encouraging people to return to their roots, and achieved 12 000 visitors.

In contrast to these instances where VFR trips were mainly to relatives, data on short breaks suggests the reverse—that it is friends rather than relatives who may predominate. Forty-six per cent of all UK short breaks were VFRs in 1991 (UKTS, 1992) but they were less likely to include young people and older people than main vacations, suggesting that family/relative factors played a smaller part; only 39% of trips included children v. 43% for long holiday trips; and only 7% included adults over 65, v. 17% for long holiday trips (UKTS, 1992). A similar pattern is suggested from German data: 34% of German short breaks were VFR (Lohmann, 1991), but teenagers were only half as likely to take short trips as young adults.

One of the biggest reasons for subdividing the VFR is the sheer diversity of tourism behaviour it conceals. VFR data gathered at Strathclyde and by Denman for the English Tourist Board (Denman, 1988) suggests some of the variety of activities and motivations that go under the VFR umbrella. Some of these activities/motivations are presented in Figure 32.1. One immediate impression that comes from looking at the list is that many of them fall naturally into an either/or category—visiting friends or visiting relatives. I have indicated the likely split between the two by designating friend-based trips with an F; relative-based ones with an R. This heterogeneous inventory must make any market analyst think hard about lumping them all together simply on the basis of one absence. There can be few forms of market segmentation where a single category covers such a multitude of motivations and behaviour.

Some provisional hypotheses

From this appraisal of VFR data it is possible to hypothesise some tentative differences between relative- and friend-oriented tourism.

Pen pals visiting and being visited F
City twinning group visits between different countries F
Nostalgia trips for ex-service personnel F
Alumni/school reunions F
Company and workmate reunions F
Fanclub conventions F
Interest groups (hobbies, collectors etc.) meeting together
    away from home F
Surprise birthday/anniversary parties away from home F/R
Couples meeting at weekends F
Short-stayers dropping in on friends overnight F
Academic visits to colleagues F
Children having friends to stay F
Ex-neighbours meeting up at either's home F
Homecoming trips R
Students coming home from college or school R
Long-haul migrant visitations R
Military personnel home on leave R
Furloughs from diplomatic duty R
Genealogy trips to look up ancestors R/F
GI brides homecomings R
Custodial visits for divorced parents and their children R
Weddings R/F
Funerals R/F
Weekend breaks R/F

F = friend event; R = relative event; F/R = either relative or friend event

Figure 32.1 *VFR activities and motivations*

Hypothesis 1: Relative-oriented, domestic trips are often motivated by obligation.

Hypothesis 2: As a result of 1, domestic relative-oriented trips may be less destination-influenced. They have to be taken wherever the relative happens to live.

Hypothesis 3: As a result of 1 and 2 relative-oriented trips may be difficult to influence in destination terms, but perhaps possible to affect in frequency terms.

Hypothesis 4: Long-haul relative-oriented trips may be more affected by destination factors (the glamour of a flight to Australia to see an uncle, for instance) than domestic ones.

Hypothesis 5: Domestic relative-oriented trips may occupy 'special time'—recurrent family rites of passage such as birthdays, weddings, funerals, as well as cyclic high days and holidays, and seasonal festivals, particularly Christmas.

Hypothesis 6: All relative-oriented trips may include greater amounts of in-home hospitality than out-of-the-house activity.

Hypothesis 7: Domestic, friend-oriented VFR trips, on the other hand, are less structured by obligation and have a greater voluntaristic element.

Hypothesis 8: Friend-oriented trips are less dependent on seasonal rituals.

Hypothesis 9: Friend-oriented trips may include more out-of-the-house activity (eating out, attraction visiting, socialising).

Hypothesis 10: Friend-oriented trips may consist of more short breaks and be more likely to take place at weekends.

Hypothesis 11: Friend-related trips may, as a result of axioms 7–10, be more susceptible to influence than relative-oriented trips.

Hypothesis 12: Friend-related trips may be more affected by destination and events factors than VRs.

We can contrast some of these hypothesised differences in the features of VF and VR travel as follows:

VF trips	VR trips
Freely chosen	Obligated
Associated with more hospitality outside home	Associated with more hospitality in home
Often weekend short breaks	Often seasonal short breaks
Ordinary, secular occasions	Sacred, ritual occasions
Destination-, event- and person-centred	Mainly person-centred
Associated with lower levels of long-haul travel	Associated with higher levels of long-haul travel

These are hypotheses all of which could be tested. If the differences between the two kinds of VFR trip were substantiated it might then be possible to put values to them that could result in different marketing priorities and programmes for each.

Moreover, once tourism planners began thinking in terms of VFs and VRs as two distinct categories with a third that included both, it would naturally lead to new questions about them and the possibility of further category refinements.

One difference that might well emerge is socio-economic. Sociologists have long suggested, in Britain at least, that entertaining non-family friends at home is more common among middle-class, middle/upper income groups, while lower-income groups tend to confine home entertaining to the family. A small-scale study at Strathclyde, which took 100 high and 100 low socio-economic respondents and compared their responses to questions about tourism behaviour, found some evidence of this. One of the findings was a marked propensity for C2DEs to stay with relatives, never friends, for main holidays; but for ABC1 respondents to visit friends, not family, for short breaks.

These socio-economic differences, arising from the VF/VR separation, may be particularly marked in analyses of the short break market. In Britain the short break market is upmarket, ABC1 rather than C2DE, and VFRs constitute about 57% of trips. It would be useful to know whether these VFRs are, in fact, mainly VFs, VRs or combinations of the two.

The hypothetical propensity pattern emerging from these socio-economic speculations might look something like those set out in Figure 32.2. Again these hypothesised relationships could be tested.

Another way of delving deeper into VF and VR behaviour, once the categories were split, would be motivationally. Why, for example, are some friends visited not others? It may be that VFR trips are a function of three variables: the destination, the event (e.g. a hallmark event, sporting trip) and the person. It should be possible to weight all three factors in assessing VF motivations. Research might indicate the need to subdivide the VF market into three segments: (i) person-centred VFs, (ii) destination-centred VFs and (iii) event-centred VFs. It is not hard to imagine a number of other behavioural subdivisions once VFs and VRs were constituted as independent categories. Are most ethnic and long-haul VFRs actually VFs as the Strathclyde data suggests? Do life cycle variations operate? Do young singles visit more friends or relatives? Do married couples visit more families? Do empty nesters—couples whose children have left home—engage in more VF or VR behaviour?

Another interesting possibility is that of adapting Pierce and Scott's trip index to differentiate patterns of family-based and friend-based trips. The trip index was developed as a way of quantifying what proportion of a total trip was spent in a particular place, and thus assessing the importance of particular destinations. Developed a decade ago (Pierce and Scott, 1983), it was arrived at by a simple formula:

$$\text{Trip index} = \frac{\text{Length of individual trip}}{\text{Length of total trip}} \times 100$$

	ABC1 VFs	C2DE VFs	ABC1 VRs	C2DE VRs
Vacation type				
Main holiday	Low	Low	Low	High
Short breaks	High	Low	Medium	Low

Figure 32.2 *Propensity for VF/VR trips by socio-economic status and vacation type (ABC1 = upper socio-economic groups; C2DE = lower socio-economic groups)*

This formula could be adapted, as follows, to determine what proportion of a trip was spent with a relative or friend.

$$\text{VF/VR index} = \frac{\text{Length of VF or VR trip}}{\text{Length of total trip}} \times 100$$

The formula would reveal to what extent VFs and VRs were discrete trips or merely components of longer trips and what, if any, were the differences between the two.

Finally, there is a category which currently eludes tourism data completely—'visiting *with* friends and relatives'. Though party size has been a feature of many visitor studies, the composition of the party has seldom been analysed. The Family Study at Strathclyde suggests that between 30% and 40% of families with children over 11 take friends on main summer vacations, in addition to family members. Clearly, family parties which include friends hold more volume potential for tourism planners than those which do not.

How important is the VFR category to the industry?

The industry has a vital interest in getting a better understanding of the VFR category. Though VFRs spend less per day they stay longer. In 1990 international visitors to the UK stayed on average 14.7 days v. 9.9 days for holiday travellers. Though they spend much less per day, their average expenditure per visit, £318.6, was only about 25% less than that of holiday visitors who averaged £410.2 (IPS, 1990).

There is hardly a tourism business which is not involved in VFR travel. Coach and train operators know that budget travel comprises high volumes of VFR passengers. Short break providers know that over half their market is made up of VFRs. Excursionist admissions to many tourist attractions peak at times when local people have friends or relatives staying. Credit card usage may be high when people are together for VFR activities. For people taking weekend breaks with friends a whole range of accessories ranging from wine, flowers, and presents may be bought before arrival and a lot more spent on 'living it up' later.

So what can be done?

The issues raised in this inquiry could be investigated through an ordered sequence of research. The research would involve three steps:

(a) Qualitative analysis, carried out with samples of VFR travellers through group discussions and/or depth interviews, exploring the range of motivational/behavioural factors that lay behind their trips to friends and relatives. This qualitative research would be designed to generate leads on such issues as: whether the VF or VR was long haul or domestic; a short break or a main vacation; whether the place, the person or the event was the main reason for the trip; when the trips took place and how long they lasted; what proportion of a total trip was a VF or VR stay; how expenditures varied for VF and VR trips; what motivated the trips; as well as standard demographic data including life cycle, socio-demographics etc.

(b) Small-scale quantitative experimentation with modified visitor studies which (i) for the first time, divided VFR respondents into three categories: visiting friends, visiting relatives and visiting both friends and relatives and (ii) added new motivational/behavioural categories which had emerged from (a).

(c) Provided (a) and (b) indicated the potential of refinements to the VFR category, adopting the improvements in full-scale visitor studies.

Conclusion

One final question remains—the extent to which the VFR market can be influenced by tourism planners. The received wisdom is that much VFR travel would take place anyway and that marketing activity may not substantially increase it. Two comments are in order:

1. First, it would be useful to know how susceptibility to influence would differ for friend- and relative-related travel, the hypotheses here being that friend-related trips may be more destination/event-influenced than relative-related ones.
2. Secondly, even if VF/VR/VFR trips all turn out to be difficult to influence motivationally *at source*, it might still be possible to influence their ultimate pattern (attractions visited, excursions taken, meals out etc.), by promotion and information delivered to hosts and travellers. This could only be done once both high propensity travellers *and their hosts* had been accurately identified.

Commentators are already recognising that tourism worldwide will not expand at the rate it has done since World War II. As more tourism providers compete for slices of the same cake, niche marketing will be necessary to achieve competitive advantage. There is *a priori* evidence to suggest that the VFR category may hide more variations than similarities and may well conceal a number of niches that could be activated if defined more clearly. A more tourist-centred approach might reveal opportunities—not just the one main accommodation absence that characterises the category at the moment. It is at least worth interrogating this long-established, portmanteau category.

Postscript

Since a draft of this paper was presented to the Scottish Tourist Board in March 1993 its major recommendation, that a test of splitting the VFR category should be undertaken, has been adopted. In late 1994 the UK Travel Survey is to include a special analysis of 2000 VFR travellers, split between Friends and Relatives. The Scottish Tourist Board expects to publish the results in 1995.

Acknowledgement

I would like to thank Dr Brian Hay, Research Manager of the Scottish Tourist Board, for his helpful comments on an earlier draft of this paper, while holding him in no way responsible for the final version.

References

BTA/ETB Services (1988) 'The shortbreak market'.

Denman, Richard (1988) 'A response to the VFR market', BTA/ETB consultancy report.

EC Omnibus Survey (1986).

IPS (International Passenger Study) (1990).

Jackson, Richard T. (1990) 'VFR tourism: is it underestimated?', *Journal of Tourism Studies*, 1(2).

Lohmann, Martin (1991) 'The evolution of shortbreaks in Europe', in Fache, W. (Ed.), *Shortbreak Holidays*, Conference symposium for Centre Parcs, Rotterdam.

Mullay, Maurice, Director of Shetland Tourism Board (1990) Personal communication.

NITB (Northern Ireland Tourist Board) (1991) 'Annual Report'.

Pierce, Douglas G. and Scott, Jeanette, M. C. (1983) 'The trip index', *Journal of Travel Research*, Summer: 6–9.

STB (Scottish Tourist Board) (1993) 'Tourism in Scotland', fact sheet.

UKTS (1992, 1993) 'United Kingdom Travel Surveys, 1991, 1992'.

33 Youth travel in the USA: understanding the spring break market

B. M. JOSIAM, C. J. CLEMENTS AND J. S. P. HOBSON

Youth travels—are they a clone of older travelers or are they different? Research in the areas of travel motivations, destination selection, and barriers to travel are typically conducted utilizing older travelers. Little information exists on youth travel trends (Aramberri, 1991). Does this mean that all travel is identical and that youth travel is unworthy of study? Economic impact projections indicate that one type of youth travel phenomenon, 'spring break', alone generates close to one billion dollars (Brosseau, 1984; Hayes, 1988).

As travel markets grow and as the youth of today are recognized as the adult travelers of tomorrow, the need for research on youth travel grows. As marketers attempt to reach the young and capture the millions of dollars they spend, they need to understand the motivations and barriers to youth travel. Knowledge of youth destination selection and travel trends are also important.

This research project sought to gain a better understanding of youth travel by studying the spring break phenomenon in the United States. While this phenomenon is only one portion of youth travel, it provides a convenient snapshot view. It is also an event that has been popular in the United States since the late 1930s and has significant economic impact.

The research, utilizing a national survey, analyzed youth spring break travel patterns during the 1993 spring break. The study surveyed travel motivations, travel barriers, expenditures, modes of transportation, and destination selections of student spring breakers. The results were intended to provide insights into this youth travel phenomenon that would be helpful to marketers and promoters. Progressive tour operators, destination cities, and local chambers of commerce may utilize the results to develop strategies that will capitalize upon opportunities presented by the market, while overcoming potential barriers. Airlines, accommodations and vendors of products and services targeted at youth may find the knowledge helpful to tailor their services to the needs of the youth market. The research was also designed to serve as a base for future longitudinal research on youth travel

trends. It will form the foundation of a detailed database upon which travel and marketing researchers can build.

Literature review

Youth tourism has been historically perceived as being similar to travel of older adults. The most evident difference is simply the chronological age of the tourist. This is supported by the definition frequently used for youth tourism: the traveling behavior of those independent travelers in the age group 15 to 25, whether they go individually or in groups (Aramberri, 1991). Research, while limited, now shows that youth travel may vary in more ways than just chronological age. Clarke (1992) delineates differences by referring to 'youth' as a person's social position which may be partially determined by age, but not completely by it.

Travel motivations, while varying between individuals, may also be somewhat different. Typical travel motivations for adult travelers can be categorized as: (1) escape from a perceived mundane environment; (2) exploration and evaluation of self; (3) relaxation; (4) prestige; (5) return to childhood; (6) enhancement of kinship relationships; (7) facilitation of social interaction (Crompton, 1979). However, Clarke (1992) indicates that youth need satisfaction centers around: (1) need for a 'fun time'; (2) need for companionship of people their own age; (3) availability of nightlife; (4) value for money. Youth are typically looking for a novel experience, low cost, easy access to culture, entertainment, places of historic interest, and youth-oriented tourist information (Ravon, 1991). Youth is a stage in the life cycle which allows the individual a greater amount of disposable time, a relative absence of responsibility and, typically, a lack of mental and physical constraints. While money may be limited for many youth, they typically have little commitment to housing or children and appear to be willing to pay for travel that holds the promise of adventure. Traveling away from a familiar environment enables youth to be exposed to new and different cultures and ideas. In many cases it forces the youth to evaluate their own culture and customs. It gives them a fresh look at themselves and their surroundings. Travel also allows the individual the opportunity to express their drive for independence from all sources of authority (Jafari, 1991; Clarke, 1992).

Just as travel motivations may be different for youth, so too may the barriers to travel. According to Vogt (1976) common barriers to adult travel are: (1) expense; (2) lack of time; (3) poor health; (4) old age; (5) children; (6) lack of interest and motivation. While expense may still be a barrier to youth travel, the remaining factors are perceived to be less constraining to youth.

The challenge for marketers is to understand the motivations and barriers involved in youth travel. The marketers strive to understand the youth market and the components of it. One component of youth travel in the USA is a popular phenomenon commonly known as 'spring break'. This paper analyzes this phenomenon to gain a better understanding of youth travel.

Spring break is a North American phenomenon, occurring on an annual basis. Each college campus has a spring vacation period of approximately one week in duration. During this break thousands of students migrate from their college campuses to relax, explore, and enjoy a different part of the country. However, since not all colleges close at the same time, destinations typically host visitors from March to late April. Spring break may therefore provide researchers with a snapshot picture of one segment of youth travel.

The American college ritual of spring break can trace its roots to the first college 'swim forum' of 1938. It was held in Fort Lauderdale, Florida, and approximately 300 students competed. Since that event swim forum, spring break has developed into a uniquely North American tourism phenomenon. The several-weeks-long student spring break period has become a major tourism market, with numerous destinations such as Fort Lauderdale, South Padre Island, Palm Springs, Daytona Beach, and Pensacola depending on this market for much of their tourism receipts. Both the demand and supply components of this travel phenomenon have grown quickly. As early as 1953, Fort Lauderdale attracted 15 000 spring breakers. By 1985, the number had grown to over 350 000 (McLeod, 1991).

Two Hollywood films, *Where the Boys Are* in early 1960s, and *Spring Break* in 1983, are credited with fueling this phenomenon. Each year the media has been filled with stories related to the antics of students on spring break in popular destinations. In many cases the articles identified the negative impacts of this annual migration of students (Roshan, 1990). However, the sole 'party' motivation of spring breakers seems to be changing. Having realized the economic impact of large numbers of spring breakers, many destinations are developing strategies to attract these youth travelers.

Research questions

This study, while attempting to build the body of knowledge in the area of youth travel, addressed one major research issue: what are the current spring break travel patterns of USA college students? Specifically, it was the objective of the study to study the demographic characteristics of travelers and non-travelers, identify motivations and barriers to spring break travel, identify modes of transportation and accommodations used, analyze travel expenditures and length of stay, and identify popular spring break destinations.

Methodology

A customized optically scannable survey was administered to college students throughout the United States. In order to obtain a national representation two universities were selected from each of the nine statistical regions of the USA (Figure 33.1). Colleagues and professional associates were requested to survey 200 students at each university.

The survey instrument was a revised version of one which was used in a pilot project by Hobson and Josiam (1992). The instrument consisted of a series of forced-choice items. The items related to demographic characteristics of travelers and non-travelers, student travel expenditure patterns, travel motivations, barriers to travel and destination selections. The survey was administered by an instructor in a classroom setting, one to two weeks after the students returned from spring break. All the students present, including those who travelled and those who did not, were requested to complete the survey.

Survey results were first analyzed by region, and then combined. The results presented are of the combined sample, unless otherwise noted. Where meaningful variations from the entire group were found for individual regions, they were reported as exceptions. This was done for two reasons. First, a large sample was needed to give meaningful interpretation for cross-tabulations and other procedures. Second, recognizing the limitation of the non-random sampling, researchers attempted to compensate for it by obtaining a large sample from a broad geographical base.

Results and implications

Sample description

While each campus was requested to complete 200 surveys, a total of 2960 surveys were returned. A balanced sample was obtained in terms of gender and age. However, the distribution was uneven across the 'year in

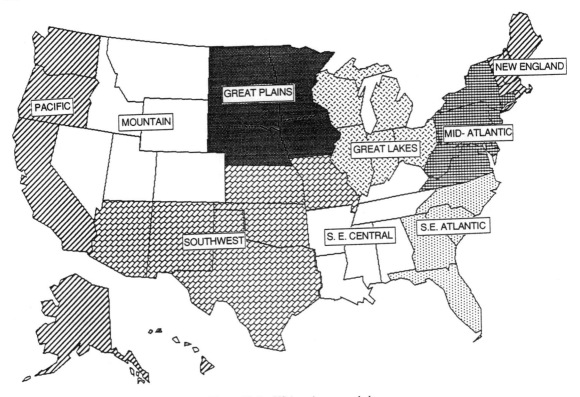

Figure 33.1 *USA regions sampled*

college' variable. More seniors and juniors completed the survey than sophomores and freshmen. This can be attributed to using convenience samples in the various campuses.

The demographic profile of the travelers, closely paralleled that of the non-traveling respondents. This suggests that demographic factors such as gender, age, and year in college do not discriminate between travelers and non-travelers.

Forty-six per cent of the respondents indicated that they had travelled for pleasure during the spring break of 1993 (Figure 33.2). The only exception to this pattern was found in the regions of Mountain, S. E. Atlantic, and Southwest, where the percentage of travelers was higher, at 67.8%, 54.4%, and 55.7% respectively. This variation can be accounted for by the proximity of popular destinations to

the campuses surveyed in the region. Proximity tends to reduce the cost, time, and problems associated with travel, thus increasing the propensity to travel. Many of the popular spring break destinations such as Daytona Beach, Fort Lauderdale, and Panama City are located in the S. E. Atlantic region. Other popular destinations, such as South Padre Island and Las Vegas, are located in the Southwest and the Mountain regions, respectively.

Barriers to travel

Non-travelers were asked to identify the main barrier to their spring break travel. The single most important reason for not traveling was work-related commitments (Figure 33.3). The second major reason selected was the

Figure 33.2 *Travel status (N = 2956)*

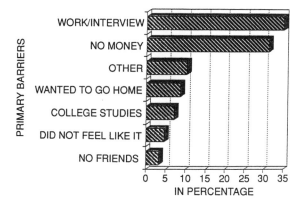

Figure 33.3 *Barriers to travel (*N = 1596*)*

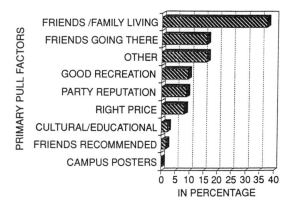

Figure 33.5 *Destination pull factors (*N = 1316*)*

lack of money. Results may also reflect a change in the way college education is financed in the USA. A growing number of students are required to work to support themselves through college. This finding appears to be contrary to the common assumption that youth are not constrained by work commitments.

Marketers can focus on this segment by using strategies enabling this segment to travel. A variety of payment strategies such as allowing payments in installments and/or allowing payments using credit cards may help overcome this barrier. At present, most trips are promoted for the entire break period. Promoting shorter trips to nearby destinations may also reduce costs. Further, shorter trips would enable some of those with work commitments to take a few days off.

Travel motivations

Travel motivators were addressed with two questions. Travelers were asked to indicate the factor that motivated

them to travel. The response items modeled Crompton's (1979) 'push' and 'pull' factors. The responses to these two questions were analyzed individually and collectively (Figures 33.4 and 33.5). A variety of conclusions were drawn.

The most common 'push' factor (Figure 33.4) was to 'get away' with just over 45% of the respondents giving it as the main reason. Related factors, such as a 'need to relax' and 'wanted a dose of sun, surf, sand' were also identified as motivating factors. When these three categories were added together, they accounted for almost 70% of the responses. Marketers can capitalize on these factors by pursuing relaxation and sun-seeking themes in their advertising campaigns.

'Visiting friends and relatives' was a push factor for only 10% of the respondents. However, 35% of the respondents selected 'friends and relatives living there' as the most important destination specific 'pull factor'. On closer examination it appears that the sequence of travel decisions is as follows. First, the choice is made

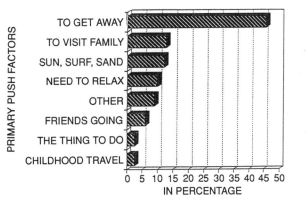

Figure 33.4 *Push factors (*N = 1316*)*

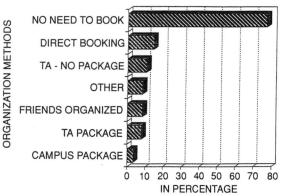

Figure 33.6 *Trip organization methods (*N = 1317*)*

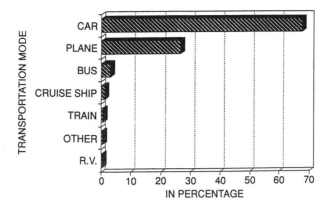

Figure 33.7 *Modes of transport (N = 1313)*

whether to travel or not. Second, having decided to travel, the individual selects a destination. Given a choice of equally appealing destinations, the scales are easily tipped in favor of one where friends or relatives live. Food and lodging expenses can be reduced by taking advantage of the hospitality of friends and relatives. Perhaps many students decide to make Florida their vacation destination because Uncle Harry or Grandma Millie live there.

It seems that peers have a great role to play in influencing the choice of destination (Figures 33.4 and 33.5). It is interesting to note that the posters on campus, which seem to be ubiquitous before the break, have little or no recognizable impact on destination choice. However, it is possible that these posters stimulate discussion and increase awareness. Word of mouth seems to play a much stronger role. This would suggest that the experience of one group of spring breakers influences those in the years to come. Destinations that want to attract this market would be well advised to focus their energies on ensuring a good experience for visitors.

Travel arrangements

Approximately 46% of the student travelers had no need to make prior bookings (Figure 33.6). This is consistent with the fact that most travelled by car and then stayed with friends or relatives at the destination. Advance travel arrangements, using direct bookings or packages, were made by approximately 25% of the travelers.

An additional 20% used the services of a travel agent. This shows a high awareness of the role of travel agents among this segment. Travel agents can capitalize upon this awareness.

Mode of transportation

The most common mode of transportation used by students to reach the destinations was the automobile (Figure 33.7). It is not surprising to see that cars have the greatest share. However, a quarter of the students traveled by air. This high figure bodes well for the future of the

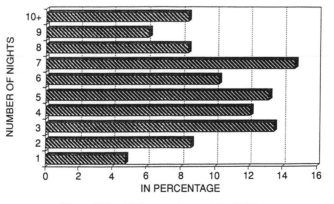

Figure 33.8 *Nights spent away (N = 1315)*

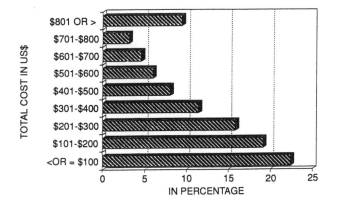

Figure 33.9 *Cost of trip in US$ (N = 1372)*

airline industry, with the younger generation showing such a high usage. Given the low cost of bus travel, it would appear that there is a lot of potential for bus companies in this market. Even the cruise ships, stereotypically associated with the older adult travelers, seem to have obtained entry in this market. There is potential for cruise lines to capitalize on this phenomenon. The two notable exceptions to this general pattern were the students surveyed in Hawaii and the S.E. Atlantic. Those in Hawaii traveled by plane rather than by car. This is to be expected, considering that one has to take a plane to get off the island, even to travel to another one. Students in the S.E. Atlantic region tended to use cruise ships more. Again, given that a large number of cruise ships are based on the Florida coast, this usage seems to be a function of proximity.

Length of trip

The average length of the trip was approximately five nights. The distribution follows a bell curve pattern with a peak of seven nights (Figure 33.8). It should be pointed out that most colleges are closed for nine days. As the expenses of the trip rise in proportion to the length of the trip, it is not surprising to find that very few students went away for all nine days. It was found that those who stayed longer had friends or relatives at the destination. Presumably, this is what enabled them to take a longer vacation. Marketers would be well advised to promote shorter trips to keep costs down. Travelers from the Mid-Atlantic region took a longer vacation, an average of about seven days. This can be attributed to the greater traveling time from this region to the popular destinations.

Average expenditures

The expenditure pattern showed that the largest percentage of students spent less than $100 (Figure 33.9). The mean expenditure was about $375. Once more, this shows the role of affordability. However, a quarter of the students spent over $500 per person. There was also a high number

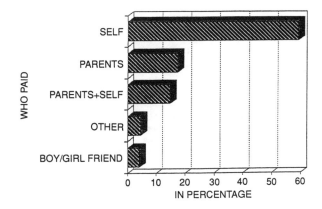

Figure 33.10 *Who paid for trip (N = 1303)*

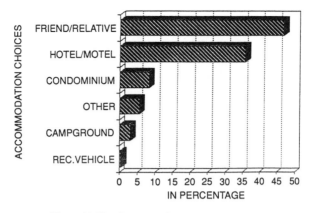

Figure 33.11 *Accommodations used (N = 1268)*

of student travelers who reported spending over $800. If these expenditures are multiplied by the massive number of students who traveled, the economic impact of this phenomenon was staggering.

There are approximately 5 million students at four-year colleges in the USA (Waldrop, 1992). If, as this study indicates, about 46% (Figure 33.2) traveled on spring break, spending an average of $375, the estimated direct expenditure is over 850 million dollars! This estimate seems to be realistic. In 1991, just one destination, South Padre Island, estimated that 250 000 students vacationing there would spend $75 million (Shinkle, 1991). Hobson and Josiam (1992) estimated that travelers from one campus of about 5000 students spent $1.11 million during the spring break of 1991.

Trip financing

Most students financed their trip with their own resources (Figure 33.10). However, parents also provided assistance

to many. Parents funded over a quarter of the trips, either completely or partially. One can only speculate as to the reasons. Certainly these respondents are the first generation of college students whose parents either went on, or wanted to go on, 'spring break'. Perhaps, by now travel is perceived as a 'rite of passage' which parents want their children to experience (Aramberri, 1991; Jafari, 1991). Parents may feel that their hardworking children deserve this trip. Perhaps, nostalgic parents are re-living their own spring break experiences through the travels of their children. This seems to be an opportunity for spring break promoters. Parents can be targeted directly with sales pitches. Spring break travel can be promoted as a Christmas gift or as an incentive for getting good grades.

Accommodations

Respondents were queried as to the accommodations they used, while on vacation (Figure 33.11). Most of them stayed with friends or relatives. However, over a third

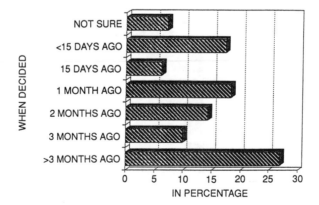

Figure 33.12 *When decided to travel (N = 1318)*

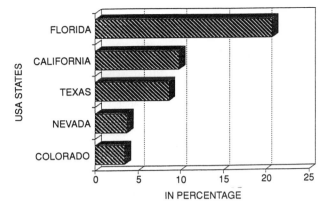

Figure 33.13 *Top five states in the USA (*N = 1228)

stayed in hotels or motels. Condominiums were the residence of choice for about 8%. With the proliferation of condominiums in most popular vacation spots, one expects this to increase in the years to come. It seems the campgrounds, capturing only 3% of these travelers, are a low-cost alternative that are missing out on this cost-conscious market. This suggests an opportunity for operators of campgrounds.

Time of decision making

Respondents were asked when they decided to travel. They were also asked when they decided upon a specific destination. It appears that the decision to travel was almost simultaneous with a choice of a specific destination. Approximately a quarter of the students decided to travel more than 3 months before the break (Figure 33.12). A further analysis revealed that those who decided to travel much later took shorter trips to nearby destinations, thus reducing the need for advance planning. This demolishes the stereotype of the happy-go-lucky student. Marketers may be well advised to start advertising before Christmas to reach the early planner.

Destinations

The five most popular destination states in the USA were Florida, California, Texas, Nevada, and Colorado

(Figure 33.13). Florida stands out with just over 20% of the market. This is not surprising, considering that it has a long history of hosting spring breakers. Florida also has many beaches within easy driving distance of each other. California and Texas were in close competition for the second place. Texas with one major destination, South Padre Island, seems to have a disproportionately high market share. This augurs well for other places which would like to promote themselves as destinations. The surprise showing here was that of Nevada, with a high number of students visiting Las Vegas.

A categorization of destinations revealed the type of destinations students visited (Figure 33.14). The results shatter the stereotype of spring break, by revealing that the majority of travelers actually went to metropolitan cities, rather than to beach destinations. Las Vegas and Los Angeles were the two most popular metro areas. Each captured over 5% of the students who identified a specific destination (Figure 33.15). Chicago, New York City, and Minneapolis/St Paul also were popular destinations. This finding reveals opportunities for marketers. They can selectively target campuses and promote short trips to nearby metropolitan destinations. But companies can get into this market by using the bus both for travel and for local sightseeing.

Traditionally, when spring break is mentioned, images of hordes of students tanning themselves on popular

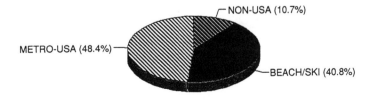

Figure 33.14 *Destination categories (*N = 595)

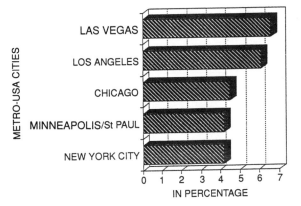

Figure 33.15 *Top five metro-USA destinations (N = 595)*

beaches come to mind. Figure 33.16 shows the popularity of these beach destinations. Daytona Beach topped the list, closely followed by Panama City, and the Florida Keys. South Padre Island in Texas was not far behind. Fort Lauderdale, where the phenomenon first began in the early 1930s, was a distant fourth in 1993.

Panama City, the Florida Keys, and South Padre Island are emerging spring break destinations that were virtually unknown just 10 years ago. A combination of aggressive marketing and bad word of mouth about treatment of students at Fort Lauderdale has served to create this market (Higgins, 1991). This is evidence that new destinations can tap into this massive market and displace complacent rulers who take their market share for granted.

Mexico was the most popular of the non-USA destinations, with a commanding lead over the Bahamas (Figure 33.17). Leading destinations in Mexico were Mazatlan, Cancun, and Puerto Vallarta respectively. Even though Mexico drew only 5.3% of the market, it attracted more students than did 47 of the 50 USA states.

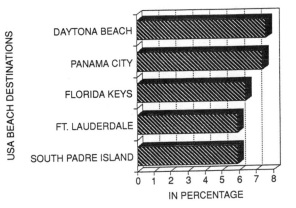

Figure 33.16 *Top five USA beaches (N = 595)*

Mexico could gain even greater share with properly targeted promotions featuring their warm climate, low cost, and close proximity to the USA.

It is surprising that Jamaica and the Bahamas, with their well-established tourism infrastructure and multi-million dollar tourism promotion budgets, are not more popular with the students. Is it by choice, or chance, that this well-defined market segment has been ignored by these countries?

Conclusions

This research study identified similarities and differences between adult travel and youth spring break travel. The main barriers to the youth travel were work commitments and lack of money. This is similar to the barriers adults encounter (Vogt, 1976). This shows that in the USA, college students are independent and possibly not totally financially dependent upon family financial support.

The main motive to travel during spring break was to 'get away'. This is similar to a need to 'escape from the mundane' which was identified as a predominant older traveler motive by Crompton (1979). A 'need to relax' and get a 'dose of sun, surf, and sand' were also strong motivators for the students. A need to travel as a result of traveling as a child, however, was not a strong motivator, as is frequently found in adults.

Youth choice of travel destinations was varied, ranging from metropolitan cities to beaches and to foreign locations. Metropolitan cities were found to have attracted the largest segment of this market. The traditional Florida destinations, however, continued to attract large numbers. The top states visited by the students are, however, similar to the top states in overall tourism receipts.

Many students were well-organized, and planned their trips well in advance. Trips were funded predominantly by the students themselves; however, many were aided by their parents. While 46% of students overcame the barriers to travel, lack of money was the most important barrier reported by non-travelers.

Families and friends played an important role in destination selection. In many cases it appeared that a destination was selected predominantly because friends/relatives lived there. While peers may have less influence on adult destination selections, 67% of activities planned for older travelers' vacation trips include friends and family (USTDC, 1993).

The most popular mode of transportation utilized by the students was the automobile. This appears similar to travel by older adults, as 75% of all travel is by car

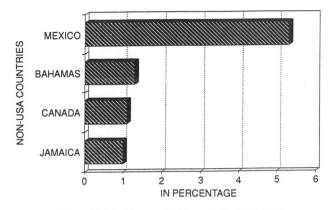

Figure 33.17 *Top non-USA countries (N = 1228)*

(USTDC, 1993). The emergence of students selecting cruises is also reflective of a market that has tripled in overall popularity since 1980 (USTDC, 1993).

The overall expenditures of the spring break phenomenon are staggering. However, average expenditures of about $375 are somewhat less than average adult travel expenditures. Average expenditures during the fall of 1993 were $906 per trip and the median expenditure was $635 per trip (USTDC, 1993). This does not mean that the youth expenditures are trivial and should not be pursued, rather marketers and promoters must be cognizant of the price-sensitive needs of this market.

Findings have significant implications for marketers and promoters. Those wanting to capture this multi-million dollar market can develop shorter-term packages, promote non-traditional destinations, market directly to parents, and develop inexpensive vacations.

This study lays the groundwork for further studies on the spring break phenomenon. Understanding this phenomenon will enable researchers and others to get a comprehensive view of youth travel. This study also provides the base for longitudinal comparisons, enabling researchers and marketers to identify trends in destination selection, changing motivations and barriers, and expenditure patterns. Further, the study can be extended to include: a comparison of youth travel patterns in the USA with other countries; a focus on special target demographic and psychographic groups; or comparative analyses of the travel patterns and motivations of subcultural and ethnic groups.

This study can also be followed up with qualitative studies. Qualitative studies will enable researchers to get a deeper understanding of the motivations and barriers to travel. Further, they will provide an in-depth look at the actual youth travel 'experience'.

Acknowledgements

Acknowledgement is made to all of the researchers' colleagues who distributed the surveys to students across the USA. The survey would not have been possible without their assistance. Acknowledgement is also made to the University of Wisconsin Faculty Research Initiative through which funding was provided.

References

Aramberri, J. R. (1991) 'The nature of youth tourism: concepts, definitions and evolution', keynote paper presented at The International Conference on Youth Tourism, New Delhi, India, January.

Brosseau, J. (1984) 'The students' rite of spring break', *USA Today*, 1 March: 1D.

Clarke, J. (1992) 'A marketing spotlight on the youth "Four S's" customer', *Tourism Management*, September: 321–327.

Crompton, J. L. (1979) 'Motivations for pleasure vacation', *Annals of Tourism Research*, October/December: 409–423.

Hayes, J. (1988) 'Daytona beach aims to expand', *Restaurant News*, 25 March: 3.

Higgins, S. (1991) 'Students take break from recession', *The News Herald*, Miami, 7 April.

Hobson, P. and Josiam, B. (1992) 'Spring break student travel—an exploratory study', *Journal of Travel & Tourism Marketing*, 3(1): 87–97.

Jafari, J. (1991) 'The significance of youth tourism: socio-cultural dimensions', keynote paper presented at The International Conference on Youth Tourism, New Delhi, India.

McLeod, L. (1991) 'Where the boys aren't', *Chicago Tribune*, March 29, pp. 1–2.

Ravon, Z. H. (1991) 'Incentives for youth tourism', keynote paper presented at The International Conference on Youth Tourism, New Delhi, India, January.

Roshan, M. (1990) 'Students inundate Key West', *Key West Citizen*, 11 March.

Shinkle, K. (1991) 'Spring break gets organized', *Tampa Tribune-Times*, Clearwater, Florida, 24 March.

USTDC (United States Travel Data Center) (1993) 'National and central states travel trends', presented by Suzanne D. Cook at the 14th annual Censtates TTRA Conference, Omaha, Nebraska.

Vogt, J. W. (1976) 'Wandering: youth and travel behavior', *Annals of Tourism Research*, 4(1): 25–39.

Waldrop, J. (1992) 'Spring break grows up', *American Demographics*.

34 Seasonality in tourism: issues and problems

R. W. BUTLER

Introduction

Seasonality has long been recognised as one of the most distinctive features of tourism, and indeed, after the movement of people on a temporary basis, may be the most typical characteristic of tourism on a global basis. Seasonality, in the context of this paper refers to a temporal imbalance in the phenomenon of tourism, and may be expressed in terms of dimensions of such elements as numbers of visitors, expenditure of visitors, traffic on highways and other forms of transportation, employment, and admissions to attractions. Seasonality has frequently been viewed as a major problem in the tourist industry, and has been held responsible for difficulty in gaining access to capital, for problems in obtaining and holding full-time staff, for low returns on investment and subsequent high risk, for problems relating to peaking and overuse of facilities and conversely to under-utilisation of the same resources and facilities, and difficulties in getting tourism recognised as a viable economic activity in many areas. Accordingly much attention has been paid and much effort made by both public and private sectors to reduce seasonality in destination areas through a variety of approaches.

In spite of this concern over seasonality and its perceived generally negative effects upon tourism and destination areas, there has been relatively little research devoted to this topic which appears in the published literature. It is clear that, while there is often general agreement about the seasonality 'problem', comparatively little study has been made of its detailed nature or all of its effects. Problems exist in identifying the basic causes of the phenomenon and reasons for its persistence, and in definition and measurement. Despite years of effort by the public sector through policy and aid, and the private sector through marketing and pricing in particular, seasonality continues to persist in many areas, suggesting that the causes are not being adequately addressed, if indeed it is appropriate to 'solve' this 'problem'. Very little research has been done on the positive aspects of seasonality, such as they are, to explore, for instance, if this phenomenon really is a problem for all parties involved in tourism. Equally little research has addressed the problem of whether seasonality varies in nature and intensity on a spatial basis, either within or between destination areas, although there has been speculation that such is the case.

The discussion which follows has four basic objectives, all related to resolving or clarifying the issues and problems raised above. The first is to discuss the causes of seasonality to provide a foundation on which the rest of the discussion can stand. The second is to discuss the nature and characteristics of seasonality, and to comment on it as a problem or benefit. The third is to examine briefly approaches which have been taken to reduce the level of seasonality and their general effectiveness. The fourth, and final objective is to assess whether there is a spatial aspect to seasonality, and if so, what its nature might be. A brief commentary on data gathered over a 20-year period on seasonal fluctuations in tourism in northern and western Scotland completes the discussion, and is followed by concluding remarks.

Causes of seasonality

It has been generally accepted that seasonality in tourism has two basic origins, one which may be called 'natural' seasonality, and one called 'institutionalised' seasonality (BarOn, 1975:2; Hartmann, 1986). The first relates to regular temporal variations in natural phenomena, particularly those associated with climate and the true seasons of the year. Typical variables included are cycles or patterns of differences in temperature, rainfall and snowfall, sunlight, and daylight (see, for example, Barry and Perry (1973) and Boucher (1975)). Seasonal variations are different from the daily fluctuations of the weather at a particular destination, and are regular and recurring. In general, seasonal differences increase with distance from the equator, and thus are more marked in high latitudes than in equatorial locations, and consequently have varying impacts upon human activity (Budyko, 1974; Mauss and Beuchat, 1979).

The second type of seasonality is that brought about by human decisions, and normally refers to traditional and often legislated temporal variations in activities and inactivity. Institutional seasonality varies much more widely and with much less regularity of pattern than does its natural counterpart. It is the result of religious, cultural, ethnic and social factors, in some cases representing links to natural phenomena, and in others nothing more than age-old whims or preferences. One of the most common forms of institutionalised seasonality which affects tourism is the public holiday, often based on one of, or a combination of, religious holy days, days of pagan significance, and the occurrence of natural features, e.g. solstices. Although public holidays used to be single days, and thus could be expected to have only minimal influence on tourism, over the years, particularly since the early nineteenth century, days have been expanded into weekends and breaks of longer duration, and assumed increasing relevance for tourism and long-distance travel.

The most significant elements of this form of seasonality are school holidays and industrial holidays, especially where the latter are associated with trade fairs. The origin of a lengthy mid-year school holiday stems from the necessity of students being available to assist with agricultural production, in particular the summer harvest, and periods of from six to ten weeks have been allocated for this. Despite the fact that such needs no longer exist in any western country, the summer school holiday continues to exist and to dominate the tourist industry in much of the world (Netherlands, 1991). This is for two main reasons. The tradition of a family holiday meant that for any family with children of school age, the only time when holidays could be taken without the children missing school, was during the summer recess. Coupled with this was the fact that in most countries that had such legislation, the summer months had the best weather for the traditional holiday, whether this was by the beach, the lake or in the mountains. Thus people not only had to go then, it was the time of the year when most desired to go. The second reason for the importance of this factor is that the bulk of world tourism is generated by the western industrial countries and these were the first to enshrine summer school holidays in legislation, thus as Hartmann (1986) suggests, tourist seasonality may be thought of as a western concept.

In a similar vein, as the Industrial Revolution progressed, and with it social reform and legislation, the idea of holidays with pay took root, and in most cases such holidays became tied to the main summer season to allow families to holiday together. In some urban centres whole industries would close for a one- or two-week period, a pattern seen very clearly in the industrial centres of Scotland, with the 'Fair Fortnights', during which time virtually all industrial activity would cease within a particular community, a pattern reflected in the visitation patterns to the Clydeside resorts (Pattison, 1969).

It can be argued, however, that there are other causes of seasonality beyond the basic two identified in the literature and discussed above. Another significant cause of seasonality is that of social pressure or fashion. In many societies the privileged elite often divided their year into specific 'seasons' during each of which it was considered socially necessary to participate in certain activities and be in certain locations. Examples include the season for taking waters at spas, a season for socialising in appropriate capitals, a season for hunting and fishing on country estates, and in Europe, a winter season on the Côte d'Azur (Nash, 1979). While such seasons may be regarded as institutionalised in one form or another, they do not normally feature in what is generally thought of as institutionalised seasonality. Rather, it can be argued, they form a third category, perhaps most appropriately called 'social' seasonality. While the process of the democratisation of leisure, or mass following class has done much to remove the significance of such seasons, other, perhaps smaller, but still significant seasons exist. The affluent and privileged still flock to specific recurring events, although inevitably the length of stay is much shorter than in previous decades. The shooting season on grouse moors, while still approximately the same length, is rarely observed in full by families, and while the 'Glorious Twelfth' may still be celebrated fervently, a week or two on the moors is probably all that most can afford, in either time or money.

In the late twentieth century it may be appropriate to recognise a fourth cause of seasonality in tourism, related to climatic factors, but also reflecting the changing patterns of recreational and tourist activity, and this is the sporting season. While the example of grouse shooting noted above may also be viewed as a sporting season, it has always been associated with social activities and privilege. In the last decade of the twentieth century the sporting aspects of activities have tended to replace social aspects in terms of importance to most tourists. Thus we see now the appearance of distinct seasons associated with at least one major sporting activity, namely snow skiing, and to a lesser degree ones associated with other popular activities such as surfing and golf. The combination of climatic and physical requirements, e.g. snow and hills, along with the necessary infrastructure for such activities has seen the appearance of distinct seasonal variations in tourism visitation in a significant number of destination areas across the globe.

To the above four causes of seasonality we may add a fifth, that of inertia or tradition. There can be little doubt that many people take holidays at what are peak seasons because they have always done so, and old habits tend to die hard. In some cases there may be good reasons for continuing a pattern even when one no longer has to do so, when, for example, children are no longer in school. The traditional holiday months may still be the best for weather, or for specific activities or events, or transportation and other services may not be available out of the conventional season. (These points will be commented on further below when discussing attempts to reduce seasonality.) In some cases, perhaps a large number in some societies, there is no specific reason for people continuing to take their holidays when they do, other than inertia or tradition. Failure to recognise this as a cause of seasonality may affect the ability to change or reduce seasonality.

Nature and characteristics of seasonality

The rather limited literature on seasonality in tourism that has appeared in print has several foci. These include: the relationship of seasonality to demand and visitation; particular regional and destination characteristics of seasonality; the effects of seasonality on employment and the financial well-being of tourism; its impacts upon destination areas; and policy implications and attempts to reduce the level of seasonality. Relatively little of the literature deals with concepts or theory (Hartmann, 1986), or with definitions and causes of seasonality, and only a few specific works examine problems of measurement (BarOn, 1975; Sutcliffe and Sinclair, 1980) or of seasonal variations in types of visitors (Bonn et al., 1992).

Most of the literature which examines the demand aspects of seasonality does so from the point of view of management of tourism and identifies seasonality as a problem of considerable magnitude (McEniff, 1992; Witt et al., 1991). It is seen as a major problem with respect to investment in tourism because of the frequent shortness of the business season in tourism destination areas, with potential investors being deterred because of the compression of the operating period into a few months. This poses problems in securing return on capital, and in inefficiency in plant operation, which must either run at low levels of use for much of the year or run at overcapacity during the peak season (Cooper et al., 1993).

Yacoumis (1980:84) is typical when he describes seasonality in tourism as 'an almost universal problem, varying only in the degree of its acuteness from one country to another', and his review of seasonality in tourism in Sri Lanka represents one of the few detailed discussions of this phenomenon in a specific location. By far the most exhaustive review of the problem is that by BarOn (1975) who examined the issue for 16 different countries using data covering a period of 17 years. Such

a study is unique in the literature, and most references to seasonality occur either as brief discussions in books on tourism (e.g. Cooper et al., 1993; Mathieson and Wall, 1982; Murphy, 1985; Pearce, 1989; Shaw and Williams, 1994; Witt et al., 1991), or in articles which have other main concerns (e.g. Bonn et al., 1992; Dieke, 1991; Hannigan, 1980; Kemper et al., 1983; Ronkainen, 1983).

The overwhelming consensus of opinion in such writings is that seasonality is a problem, that it has a number of facets and implications as noted above, and that it is something to be overcome, or at least modified and reduced in effect. Ronkainen (1983:421) notes that 'The encouragement of tourism outside the high season is one of the few recommendations [of a European conference] not having direct political connotation . . . [and that] seasonality of tourism is plaguing most of the signatory countries'.

The discussion of seasonality in specific destinations is often linked to the impacts and effects of seasonality in those locations (Belisle and Hoy, 1980; Dieke, 1991; Drakatos, 1987; Donatos and Zairis, 1991; Netherlands, 1991). In many cases the impacts discussed are primarily those dealing with either employment (Clarke, 1981) or with under-utilisation of physical plant (Van der Werff, 1980). Only in a very few cases (Mathieson and Wall, 1982; Mitchell and Murphy, 1991; Murphy, 1985; Pearce, 1989) is there discussion of the environmental effects of seasonality. In such cases the discussion is mostly generalised and notes the intensity of pressure on often fragile environments because of crowding and overuse during the peak season.

It is only in the discussions on employment and to a lesser degree of environmental and social effects, that any mention is made of the fact that seasonality may not be totally negative for tourism destinations. Murphy (1985:81) notes that 'seasonality is not necessarily bad for everyone', and goes on to add that, to some communities, the end of the tourist season is regarded as 'the light at the end of the tunnel'. In this vein he discusses the fact that individuals need release from stress and that some populations would not be capable or at least content to experience the stress of catering for tourists throughout the year. This is an argument echoed by Mathieson and Wall (1982) when they quote Jordan (1980) to the effect that 'locals view the approaching [tourist] season with mixed feelings and value the off season when only permanent residents are present'. Similar findings were made by Brougham and Butler (1981) in their study of the perceptions of residents of the Isle of Skye towards tourism.

The discussion on the effects of seasonality upon employment in the tourism industry in destination areas indicates two viewpoints. The majority opinion appears to be that the seasonal nature of tourism presents problems for employers, making it difficult to recruit full-time staff and to retain them (Pearce, 1989; Yacoumis, 1980), and that tourism related employment may create competition for labour with other seasonal employers such as agriculture (Mathieson and Wall, 1982). Other viewpoints exist, however. Mourdoukoutas (1988) argues that unemployment is not caused by seasonal employment, and that in the Greek islands a considerable number of employees choose seasonal employment because it pays better than alternatives, and also because in some cases it allows them to pursue other activities during the off-season. Ball (1989) notes that rural seasonal employment in tourism may offer a relief, albeit temporary, to urban unemployment, although such a relief has declined considerably over the past 50 years.

Perhaps the most strongly argued case for seasonal tourism employment being a positive rather than a negative factor is made by Flognfeldt (1988). He suggests that the essential employment needs of the tourism industry, particularly in remote and small communities, may complement traditional patterns of employment and unemployment, rather than compete with them. Shaw and Williams (1994:238–239) cite evidence from the Scilly Isles which supports this argument. Similar trends can also be seen in peripheral regions of many countries, where, for a variety of reasons, it has been necessary to import labour to meet seasonal demand from tourism and other economic activities. In Shetland, and elsewhere in insular Scotland, for example, employment plurality, combining jobs in a variety of fields, including tourism, oil-related activities and more traditional activities such as agriculture and fishing is not uncommon (Nelson and Butler, 1993).

Undoubtedly, however, the overwhelming impression from the literature is that seasonality in tourism is a problem. It is equally true to say that this viewpoint is primarily one taken from an economic position, and reflects concerns with the difficulty of attaining an efficient utilisation of resources (Sutcliffe and Sinclair, 1980). To managers and owners of tourism enterprises, seasonality compounds the problems of trying to make a living in a dynamic industry vulnerable to changes in fashion and external forces (Snepenger et al., 1990). From an environmental viewpoint there are advantages and disadvantages to seasonal fluctuations in demand and visitation. While areas may experience very heavy use during peak seasons, in the long run they may well be better off than having that use spread more evenly throughout the year. It has been shown that environmental impacts of recreation and tourism have heavy initial loadings, and that additional use has proportionally less effect for each additional unit

of use (Mathieson and Wall, 1982). A lengthy rest period, particularly where much of that period is still within climatic limits for growth, may allow almost complete recovery, or at least stability, to be achieved.

It is in human, and hence cultural and social, terms that the greatest benefits of a seasonal pattern of tourism, such as they are, may be identified. There is no doubt that tourism can disrupt traditional social patterns in a community, and have effects upon cultural activities (Mathieson and Wall, 1982; Murphy, 1985; Pearce, 1989). The off-season often represents the only time that the local population can operate in what to it is a 'normal' manner, and engage in traditional social and cultural activities. While this may be a relatively inefficient way of operating in economic terms, it may well be preferable to some communities, particularly those which have alternative sources of income, and do not rely entirely upon tourism for their economic survival.

Policy implications of seasonality

As noted earlier, there have been very considerable efforts made by both the public and the private sectors to overcome or reduce the seasonality aspects of tourism. A significant proportion of BarOn's comprehensive study of seasonality is devoted to discussing methods for improving the seasonal pattern of tourism (1975). The literature suggests that there have been a limited number of approaches to overcoming seasonality, including trying to lengthen the main season, establishing additional seasons, diversifying markets, using differential pricing and tax incentives on a temporal basis, encouraging the staggering of holidays, encouraging domestic tourism in off-seasons, and providing off-season activities such as festivals and conferences (BarOn, 1975; Smale and Butler, 1992; Sutcliffe and Sinclair, 1980; Witt et al., 1991).

Seasonality remains a difficult phenomenon to overcome. BarOn (1975:52) noted that 'the changes which have occurred in the range of seasonality indicate that despite the importance of reducing the seasonal peaks and the efforts that have been applied, the seasonal range has in fact increased for many countries with the growth of tourism'. His comments would appear to reflect what has been implied in other studies (Netherlands, 1991), namely that when a country is experiencing rapid growth in tourism, that growth is often of such magnitude that it swamps any efforts to redirect visitation into quiet periods of the year. It is likely that when countries are entering a period of rapid growth in tourism, often characterised by aggressive marketing, that little thought is given to trying to attract tourists at particular times of the year. Rather the emphasis is upon attracting tourists.

This viewpoint is supported by BarOn's comment (1975:53) that in the countries which he examined in the mid-1970s, 'The expansion of tourism has been largely an expansion of the main season'. A statement in another report (Netherlands, 1991:7) that northern European countries appeared to be the most successful at spreading tourism, probably because they had older-established industries which had already experienced peaking problems in the 1950s and 1960s is in a similar vein. In such countries tourism is no longer growing at the rapid rate which characterised Mediterranean countries from the 1960s onwards. When tourism plant and facilities are not being rapidly expanded, and when tourism numbers are relatively stable or only increasing slowly, then attention is more likely to be focused on the off-season and methods to spread tourism throughout the year.

The stubbornness of tourism in remaining seasonal, despite intensive efforts of the industry and governments, suggests that the problem is more complex than generally thought. It may also be that the reasons are somewhat simpler than may be expected. It was noted above that inertia and tradition may be causes of seasonality in some situations. Most efforts to overcome the temporal imbalance in demand have not been aimed at these factors, but rather have concentrated upon the destination areas rather than the consumer. Many efforts have been made to diversify the appeal and attractions of the destinations, presumably on the assumption that if they are made more attractive in relatively unattractive seasons, then tourists will come. This assumption would appear not to be entirely accurate.

It would appear that the shift to off-season holidays that has occurred has taken place because of an increase in the taking of additional holidays, rather than because of a shift of the primary holiday. The Netherlands report notes that the main restriction on the timing of trips is the school holiday (1991:6) and that 'Long holidays are more likely than other types of trip to be concentrated in the peak summer months' (1991:5). The author concludes that 'Unless the number of long holidays decreases significantly, which . . . seems unlikely, tourism congestion will continue to be a problem in the EEC' (1991:6).

It has to be borne in mind also that the provision of additional holidays will not necessarily reduce seasonality in any area, indeed, such a process may simply create seasonality in another location. There is no evidence to suggest that a person receiving an additional holiday is likely to spend it in the same location as he or she spent their primary holiday, but at a different season. Rather, they are likely to spend it at another location, perhaps at another season. Perhaps the best example of this is the increasing frequency of second holidays taken by North Americans, where the most common pattern is to take a primary (usually summer) holiday in temperate climes, and a secondary (usually winter) holiday in tropical climes, or perhaps at a winter sports resort. As a result of this pattern there is a marked seasonality in tourism in the Caribbean (CTRC, 1980). The relative level of affluence of residents of industrialised countries, coupled with legislated free time and ease of transportation has meant that many tourists can overcome real seasonal (climatic) problems and pursue the sun or snow at whatever time of the year they prefer, often creating inverse seasonal peaking in destinations with different climates to that of their home region.

The long-term nature of the seasonality characteristic of tourism tends to suggest that it is caused by more than climatic factors or institutional ones, although there is no doubt that these are major influences. Clearly the long school holiday in the summer remains one of the impediments, if not the largest single impediment, to reducing seasonal concentrations of tourists. However, even if this were removed or significantly changed, it is unlikely that there would be no seasonal fluctuations in tourism. Some people would not wish to go at alternative times, some would find the off-season weather at some destinations to be unattractive, and a full range of services and attractions may not be available in destination areas. Finally, there may well be reaction in host communities against a lengthening of the season or the attraction of more visitors at non-traditional times; thus policies designed to reduce seasonality need the support of destination area communities if they are to be successful in all aspects.

Spatial aspects of seasonality

It is clear that although seasonality may be an almost universal characteristic of tourism, it varies considerably from location to location. Climatic seasonality is much less marked the closer one gets to the equator, but even in equatorial destinations tourism may be seasonal because of seasonal factors (both climatic and institutionalised) in tourist origin areas. It is also clear that the degree of seasonality varies within destination countries and perhaps regions. Murphy notes that large cities such as London have a less seasonal pattern of tourism than do tourist resorts (Murphy, 1985:79), a view supported by the World Tourism Organisation which indicated that 'Tourist destinations supported by large urban centres, while having high points of activity, have more continuous operation throughout the year because they depend upon a more diversified demand' (WTO, 1984:43).

There are also indications that seasonality varies with the relative location of destinations within a country or major region. Snepenger et al. (1990) found that seasonality of demand in Alaskan tourism was almost 10% higher in the more remote interior than in coastal areas. In his study of Sri Lanka, Yacoumis (1980) suggested that it was necessary to analyse seasonality at three levels, national, regional, and sectoral, and went on to show considerable variations in a seasonality ratio on a spatial basis. Butler, in an early study of tourism in the Scottish Highlands and Islands also recorded significant variations in seasonality between central and more remote locations (1973).

This aspect of seasonality has not been explored to any degree in the literature. The World Tourism Organisation commented (1984:43) that 'the most specialised destinations . . . are usually the most seasonal' but did not pursue this theme further, nor discuss any spatial implications of the statement. Shaw and Williams (1994:184) make the point that *temporal polarization has the effect of reinforcing spatial polarization* (their emphasis) which can have serious implications for the environment. It is argued here that it is important to understand if seasonality has a spatial dimension as well as the required temporal one, if successful attempts are to be made to disperse tourism in time as well as space.

In this vein, it is suggested that remote or peripheral destinations are likely to experience seasonality in tourism to a greater degree than are more centrally located destinations for several reasons. In the first place, remoteness implies relative difficulty of access, which could involve longer time involved in travel. Given that most tourists have only limited vacation time available, and as travel consumes time, trips to such destinations can only be made when considerable time is available. As noted above, long trips tend to be made in the peak season much more than short trips. Remote locations generally receive relatively few visitors, and thus transportation and other services also tend to be limited, and may only operate at certain times of the year, when demand justifies their availability. Such a situation also encourages, if not mandates, visitation within limited periods. Finally, in some destinations, remote areas are climatically marginal, and visitation may be attractive, or even practical, only at specific and limited times of the year. The final section of this paper attempts to ascertain if there is a spatial pattern to seasonality by examining levels of tourism in a number of locations in northern and western Scotland.

Seasonality in tourism in Scotland

Scotland, as many parts of northern Europe, has a long history as a tourist destination, and a tourist industry which is characterised by a distinct and limited primary season. While skiing developments from the 1960s onwards have provided a winter season to a limited degree in a few specific areas, the tourism industry in Scotland is dominated by a summer peaking of visitation. This has been seen as a problem for many years by both of the public agencies most concerned with the development of tourism in Scotland, the Scottish Tourist Board, and Highlands and Islands Enterprise (the recent successor to the Highlands and Islands Development Board). Both of these agencies, over the last quarter of a century, have adopted policies aimed at reducing seasonality (Scottish Tourist Board, 1992; Highlands and Islands Enterprise, 1992) and have devoted considerable effort to attempting to reduce the level of seasonality, frequently by marketing and by inducements to potential visitors to come to the area out of the normal season. There does not seem, however, to have been any assessment of whether their efforts have been successful, in terms of whether the level of seasonality has in fact been reduced over this period, nor any real examination of whether seasonality is a feature common and uniform throughout Scotland, or whether it is more significant in certain locations than in others. This final section of the paper, therefore, examines briefly the pattern of seasonality in tourism for parts of Scotland from the 1960s to the present.

In undertaking such research two problems emerge, one of obtaining data which demonstrates seasonality, and the second, related to this, of obtaining data for a period going back a quarter of a century. While very considerable assistance and cooperation was obtained from a wide variety of bodies and individuals in trying to obtain such information, it was inevitable that the material collected would be incomplete and somewhat inconsistent. Few agencies collect data in the same format and manner over a period of decades; routes and highways change, railways close, hotels and other accommodation units change in size, class and opening times; some information is confidential and thus unavailable, and some has simply not been retained. Nevertheless, it is felt that sufficient data have been collected to indicate some trends and issues about seasonality of tourism in northern and western Scotland. The focus of the analysis is on the more remote areas of Scotland because of previous work done by this author on that region in the 1960s and 1970s, and the availability in that work (Butler, 1973) of some data on seasonality for that period.

It was decided to attempt to collect data which would show the dimensions of seasonality for 1970, 1980 and 1990, or as close to these dates for the same facilities and areas as possible. A simple index of seasonality was prepared (comparing peak month to quietest month), which would demonstrate the relative levels of visitation to locations on a monthly (or four-weekly) time period on a common base. The use of an index was necessary as it is not reasonable to compare actual numbers of tourists from year to year because of annual fluctuations in numbers, and because it is not appropriate to compare numbers of passengers on a ferry with numbers of entrants to an attraction or bed-night occupancy in an accommodation unit.

It is not possible in a paper of this length to present the sets of data which were used to examine seasonality over time and space. In all, some 67 sets of data were analysed, involving figures for air, sea, rail and road transport, entry figures for nine National Trust properties in Scotland, bridge and ferry crossings, employment and unemployment figures, and accommodation occupancy rates. While individual cases, as may be expected, go against the general trends, several broad patterns can be identified. In the first case, the pattern of seasonality, however measured, has not changed appreciably throughout the north and west of Scotland from the early 1970s to the present day. It is certainly true to say that visitation in the off-peak season, i.e. April, May, September and October has increased significantly in absolute terms during this period. On the other hand, so too has visitation during the peak summer months of June, July and August, and as BarOn (1975) noted in his earlier study, increases in the peak season have more than kept pace with increases in the shoulder- or off-seasons.

With respect to the spatial pattern of seasonality, some reduction in the seasonality index has been recorded in the last decade or so for locations closer to the core of Scotland (the central Lowlands), for example, the National Trust for Scotland sites at Bannockburn and Killiecrankie, compared to those in more remote locations such as Culloden and Inverewe. This is in line with the discussion above, where it was expected that the more developed tourist areas would be the first to be able to reduce seasonality by spreading visitation over the year. It likely represents an increase in short second holidays and mid-week breaks, during which periods visitors would not be as likely to travel considerable distances to northern and western locations as they would be to places in the central Highlands.

The overall spatial pattern of seasonality is less consistent, although it is possible to confirm the proposition that the more remote areas experience a stronger pattern of seasonality than more central locations in general terms. Many peripheral locations display appreciably higher seasonality indices than do central locations; however, considerable variation exists. A problem which needs to be resolved is a firm classification of relative remoteness, as distance from a central point is not a reliable measure of true remoteness. Travel time would be a better measure, and a ranking of locations based on such a criteria would probably yield more consistent results.

There are some difficulties in comparing the levels of seasonality from one location to another, unless the two locations are otherwise similar, particularly when traffic figures are used. Small absolute changes in seasonal tourist visitation can cause major changes in seasonality indices for communities in remote areas where total traffic volume and tourist numbers are very low. Areas which receive large numbers of tourists in a highly seasonal pattern could still receive low seasonality indices if the volume of seasonal tourist traffic is masked by high levels of non-tourist traffic throughout the year. It is best to compare different locations only in terms of similar measures of tourist seasonality, where possible controlling for differences in local populations and non-tourist factors.

Conclusions

This discussion has focused on the topic of seasonality in tourism, and in particular on aspects of this phenomenon which have not been examined in detail. Seasonality is a subject which is often discussed in the literature of tourism, but rarely analysed. One result of this is that there has been little development of theory or concepts pertaining to the topic, and much of the discussion has not been based upon empirical research but more on assumption and supposition. There can be little doubt that seasonality represents a problem of maximising the efficient operation of tourism facilities and infrastructure, and results in unnecessary excess capacity for most of the year in most destinations. On the other hand, very little research has been done to examine the advantages to destination areas of one or more off-seasons which provide periods of recuperation and restoration, and allow residents to prepare for the next tourist season.

Very little has been documented or reported in the literature on the causes of seasonality, beyond the very general assumptions discussed earlier. The relationship between seasonality and motivation of visitors has not been explored, and it is not known, for example, whether dissatisfaction with conditions in the origin region or the attractions of the destination play a greater role in shaping the seasonal patterns of tourism. It is not known with any certainty whether tourists travel in peak season because they want to, because they have to, or because they have been conditioned to. Considering the efforts and investments which have been made in attempting to reduce the level of seasonality in destinations across the world, it would seem appropriate for more attention to be given to research which might explain the phenomenon before continuing to attempt to modify what is essentially a poorly understood, if widely known, facet of tourism.

Acknowledgements

The author would like to acknowledge considerable assistance from a number of individuals who provided information, only some of which has been utilised in this study, Ms C. Fraser (Highlands and Islands Enterprise), Mr I. Young (Caledonian-Macbrayne), Mr J. Miller (Highland Region Transport Department), Mr B. Hay (Scottish Tourist Board), Mr I. Robertson (Loganair) and Ms S. Anderson (National Trust for Scotland), and staff of the Highlands Airports Authority, Orkney Shipping Company, and Shetland Island Council. Part of the field work for this study was funded by a grant from the Social Science and Humanities Research Council of Canada.

References

Ball, R. M. (1989) 'Some aspects of tourism, seasonality and local labour markets', *Area*, 21(1): 33–45.

BarOn, R. V. (1975) 'Seasonality in tourism', Economist Intelligence Unit, London.

Barry, R. G. and Perry, A. H. (1973) *Synoptic Climatology—Methods and Applications*, Methuen, London.

Belisle, F. and Hoy, D. (1980) 'The perceived impact of tourism by residents: a case study in Santa Marta, Colombia', *Annals of Tourism Research*, 7(1): 83–101.

Bonn, M. A., Furr, H. L. and Uysal, M. (1992) 'Seasonal variation of coastal resort visitors: Hilton Head Island', *Journal of Travel Research* 31(1): 50–56.

Boucher, K. (1975) *Global Climate*, English Universities Press, London.

Brougham, J. E. and Butler, R. W. (1981) 'A segmentation analysis of resident attitudes to the social impact of tourism', *Annals of Tourism Research*, 13(4): 569–590.

Budyko, M. I. (1974) *Climate and Life*, Academic Press, New York.

Butler, R. W. (1973) 'Tourism in the Highlands and Islands', Ph.D. thesis, University of Glasgow.

Clarke, A. (1981) 'Coastal development in France: tourism as a tool for regional development', *Annals of Tourism Research*, 8(3): 447–461.

Cooper, C., Fletcher, J., Gilbert, D. and Wanhill, S. (1993) *Tourism: Principles and Practice*, Pitman, London.

CTRC (Caribbean Tourism Research Centre) (1980) 'Caribbean tourism markets: structures and strategies', CTRC, Christ Church, Barbados.

Dieke, P. (1991) 'Policies for tourism development in Kenya', *Annals of Tourism Research*, 18(2): 269–294.

Donatos, G. and Zairis, P. (1991) 'Seasonality of foreign tourism in the Greek island of Crete', *Annals of Tourism Research*, 18(3): 515–519.

Drakatos, C. G. (1987) 'Seasonal concentration of tourism in Greece', *Annals of Tourism Research*, 14(4): 582–586.

Flognfeldt, T. (1988) 'The employment paradox of seasonal tourism', paper presented at Pre-Congress Meeting of International Geographical Union, Christchurch, New Zealand, 13–20 August.

Hall, C. M. (1991) *Introduction to Tourism in Australia*, Longman Cheshire, Melbourne.

Hannigan, J. A. (1980) 'Reservations cancelled: consumer complaints in the tourist industry', *Annals of Tourism Research*, 7(3): 364–384.

Hartmann, R. (1986) 'Tourism, seasonality and social change', *Leisure Studies*, 5(1): 25–33.

Highlands and Islands Enterprise (1992) 'Tourism—the way forward', Highlands and Islands Enterprise, Inverness.

Jordan, J. W. (1980) 'The summer people and the natives: some effects of tourism in a Vermont vacation village', *Annals of Tourism Research*, 7(1): 34–45.

Kemper, R., Roberts, J. and Goodwin, D. (1983) 'Tourism as a cultural domain: the case of Taos, New Mexico', *Annals of Tourism Research*, 10(1): 149–172.

McEniff, J. (1992) 'Seasonality of tourism demand in the European community', Economic Intelligence Unit, London.

Mathieson, A. and Wall, G. (1982) *Tourism: Economic, Physical and Social Impacts*, Longman, Harlow.

Mauss, M. and Beuchat, H. (1979) *Seasonal Variations of the Eskimo*, Routledge & Kegan Paul, London.

Mitchell, L. S. and Murphy, P. (1991) 'Geography and tourism', *Annals of Tourism Research*, 18(1): 57–60.

Mourdoukoutas, P. (1988) 'Seasonal employment, seasonal unemployment and unemployment compensation: the case for the tourist industry of the Greek Islands', *American Journal of Economics and Sociology*, 47(3): 314–329.

Murphy, P. E. (1985) *Tourism: A Community Approach*, Methuen, New York.

Nash, D. (1979) 'The rise and fall of an aristocratic culture, Nice: 1763–1936', *Annals of Tourism Research*, 7(1): 61–75.

Nelson, J. G. and Butler, R. W. (1993) 'Assessing, planning, and management of North Sea Oil development effects in the Shetland Islands', *Environmental Impact Assessment Review*, 13: 201–227.

Netherlands (1991) 'Improving seasonal spread of tourism', Netherlands Ministerie van Economische Zak, Rotterdam.

O'Driscoll, T. J. (1985) 'Seasonality in the trans-Atlantic vacation market', *Annals of Tourism Research*, 12(1): 109–110.

Pattison, D. A. (1969) 'Tourism in the Firth of Clyde', Ph.D. thesis, University of Glasgow.

Pearce, D. G. (1989) *Tourist Development*, Longman Scientific and Technical, Harlow.

Ronkainen, I. (1983) 'The Conference on Security and Cooperation in Europe: its impact on tourism', *Annals of Tourism Research*, 10(3): 415–426.

Scottish Tourist Board (1992) 'Development, objectives and functions', Scottish Tourist Board, Edinburgh.

Shaw, G. and Williams, A. M. (1994) *Critical Issues in Tourism*, Blackwell, Oxford.

Smale, B. J. A. and Butler, R. W. (1992) 'Geographic perspectives on festivals in Ontario', *Journal of Applied Recreational Research*, 16(1): 3–24.

Snepenger, D., Houser, B. and Snepenger, M. (1990) 'Seasonality of demand', *Annals of Tourism Research*, 17(4): 628–630.

Sutcliffe, C. M. S. and Sinclair, M. T. (1980) 'The measurement of seasonality within the tourist industry: an application to tourist arrivals in Spain', *Applied Economics*, 12(4): 429–441.

Van der Werff, P. (1980) 'Polarizing implications of the Pescaia tourism industry', *Annals of Tourism Research*, 7(2): 197–223.

Witt, S., Brooke, M. Z. and Buckley, P. J. (1991) *The Management of International Tourism*, Unwin Hyman, London.

WTO (World Tourism Organisation) (1984) *World Tourism Statistics*, WTO, Madrid.

Yacoumis, J. (1980) 'Tackling seasonality: the case of Sri Lanka', *Tourism Management*, 1(2): 84–98.

35 The destination life cycle: an update

C. COOPER

Introduction

In such a rapidly changing industry as tourism, commentators have struggled to derive generalisations of change and to seek patterns to explain the evolution of tourism in all its forms. Tourism is not alone in this attempt to generalise, indeed subject areas such as marketing, management and retailing are also attempting to build generalised theories. In marketing, for example, the product life cycle (PLC) describes the evolution of a product as it passes through 'introduction' and inevitably continues to 'maturity' and perhaps 'decline' (Day, 1981; Rink and Swan, 1979). In retailing, a variety of models have been derived to explain change including life cycle approaches and the wheel of retailing (Brown, 1987). Yet central to many of these approaches is the anthropomorphic cyclic theory.

In tourism, Butler's (1980) pioneering paper first applied the life cycle to tourist area evolution and the bare bones of his approach have sparked off much research work and elaboration of the concept. There is no doubt that the tourist area life cycle (TALC) is a scion of the PLC (Brown, 1987). In marketing, the PLC debate has largely been concluded with, on the one hand, proponents arguing the inevitable, inexorable and unavoidable progression of sales, whilst opponents stress the lack of operational validity, and the tautological nature of the PLC which, they say, renders it devoid of explanatory power (Brown, 1987; Hunt, 1976). This debate is much more recent in tourism, fuelled by attempts to apply the concept to resorts and tourist areas. It is the aim of this paper to provide an update and review of the status of academic writing on the life cycle as it applies to tourist destinations.

The tourist area life cycle

The modification of the PLC for tourism areas suggests that destinations also experience a 'birth to death' cycle. Here, numbers of visitors replace sales of a product (Figure 35.1). The first stage becomes 'exploration' where small numbers of adventurous visitors are attracted by the unspoilt natural beauty or culture at the destination. At this stage numbers are restricted by lack of access and facilities and the attraction of the destination is that it is as yet unchanged by tourism and contact with local people will be high. Also the visitors who arrive in the exploration stage will avoid the trappings of mass tourism by booking independently. Parts of Antarctica, Latin America and the Canadian Arctic are examples here; indeed physical conditions may dictate that some of these regions never pass beyond the exploration stage (Goodall, 1992).

In the 'involvement' stage, tourism acts as a catalyst for local initiatives to provide for visitors and later advertise the destination. This results in increased and regular numbers of visitors as a tourist season and market area emerges and pressure may be placed on the public sector to provide infrastructure. Minimal social and economic overhead capital initiates conversion of rural

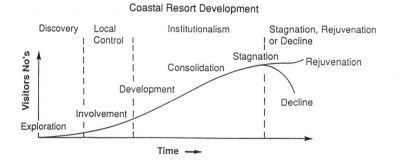

Figure 35.1 *Hypothetical tourist area life cycle (from Butler (1980))*

land to tourism uses (Goodall, 1992), and it is at this stage that community tourism initiatives and controls are at their most important. The smaller, less-developed Pacific and Caribbean islands are examples of this stage.

By the 'development' stage the area is experiencing an exciting and dynamic period of growth and evolution. Here, large numbers of new visitors continue to arrive, fuelling growth and, at peak periods perhaps equalling or exceeding the numbers of local inhabitants. If community initiatives have not been implemented the organisation of tourism will begin to change as control is passed out of local hands and external companies emerge to provide up-to-date facilities, which may alter the appearance of the destination. For a resort to be successful at this stage careful planning is necessary if the destination is to avoid problems of overuse and deterioration of facilities. Regional and national planning and control will have become necessary in part to ameliorate problems but also to market to the international tourist-generating areas. Distribution channels will also change as visitors become more dependent upon booking through the travel trade. Parts of Mexico and the north and west African coasts exemplify this stage.

In the 'consolidation' stage the rate of increase of visitors begins to fall although the destination is now a fully fledged part of the tourism industry with an identifiable recreational business district containing the major franchises and chains. Debbage (1990) provides an insightful analysis of the power relationships and the impact of international economic forces which occur at this and further stages in the life cycle, as resorts become straws in the wind of mergers and acquisitions in say, the hotel trade. Many Caribbean and northern Mediterranean destinations are examples here.

If the tourist destination has not developed in a sustainable manner then stagnation and decline will ensue. At 'stagnation' peak numbers have been reached and the destination is no longer fashionable. It relies on repeat visits and business use of its extensive facilities and major efforts are needed to maintain the number of visits. The destination may by now have environmental, social and economic problems (the Costa Brava typifies this stage). The stagnation stage has attracted research, particularly in an attempt to ameliorate problems and avoid decline (Cooper, 1990; Lane, 1992; Reime and Hawkins, 1979). Agarwall (1994) has suggested a post-stagnation phase where a range of possibilities exist. These include: continued decline; a complete change of function (to say a dormitory town, such as Clevedon for Bristol); or various forms of rejuvenation.

In Agarwall's 'continued decline' phase visitors are lost to newer resorts and the destination becomes dependent on a smaller geographical catchment for day-trips and weekend visits. Property turnover is high and tourist facilities such as accommodation are converted into other uses. Rejuvenation involves remaining as a tourist resort but deciding on new uses, new customers, new distribution channels and thus repositioning the destination. Changing the attractions such as introducing a casino (as at Scheveningen (The Netherlands) (Weg, 1982) and Atlantic City (USA) (Stansfield, 1978)), is a common response. Similarly some destinations capitalise on previously unused natural resources, such as winter sports, to extend the season and attract a new market. These facility developments often reflect joint public/private sector ventures to seek new markets and invest in the destination in order to reach a cycle/recycle pattern. Increasingly these responses are embedded within a strategic approach to turning the resort around, responses which require a major civic commitment (Cooper, 1990). Many UK and northern European resorts are examples here.

Of course, the resort cycle occurs with different timings and variations but is dependent upon the destination's rate of development, access, government policy and competing destinations—each of which can delay or accelerate progress through the various stages. Indeed development can be arrested at any stage in the cycle. For example the political events of 1974 completely halted the evolution of resorts in northern Cyprus. Only tourist developments promising considerable financial returns will mature to experience all stages of the cycle. In turn the length of each stage, and of the cycle itself, is variable. At one extreme instant resorts such as Cancun (Mexico) or timeshare developments move almost immediately to development and consolidation, thereby omitting earlier stages; whilst at the other extreme well-established resorts such as Scarborough (England) have taken centuries to move from exploration to rejuvenation.

Applications

Applications of the TALC and attempts to apply it to destinations fall into three main areas:

- as an applied model of destination evolution;
- as a guide for marketing and planning; and
- as a forecasting tool.

Explanatory model

The life cycle should be seen as one of a suite of explanatory models explaining tourist development (see, for example, Pearce (1989) and Goodall (1992) for evaluations). Whilst others have provided alternative explanations of resort evolution (Young, 1983; Smith, 1991), the life cycle provides an attractive intuitive explanation of the evolution of resorts and has generated the most research. An increasing number of writers have sought to examine destination evolution using the TALC approach (for recent attempts see, for example, Cooper and Jackson (1989), Choy (1992) and Weaver (1990)). Nor should these attempts be seen as a simplistic geometric analogy of visitor numbers. The life cycle is providing a useful framework for analysis of the growth of destinations, the interplay between markets and physical development and allows historical examination of the factors that lead to turning points in a destination's development and the characteristics and leadership styles at each particular stage of the destination's evolution.

One problem with the TALC is the tendency to focus on a single sector or product rather than the multisector approach taken by economic development models (Goodall, 1992). Less attention has been paid to utilising the life cycle within the broader framework of tourism development, although there are exceptions here. These include work by Lundgren (1982) who has linked the popular core/periphery model of tourist development with life cycles of destinations in a generalised framework but with no empirical validation. Butler and Waldbrook (1991) have applied the 'recreational opportunity spectrum' (Clarke and Stankey, 1979) to the life cycle to provide a broader interpretation of tourist development and possible planning responses. With this approach, the evolution of an area is calibrated along a number of variables such as access, management inputs, visitor types and visitor impacts and the necessary planning, management and marketing responses are mapped at each stage.

None the less, the tourist area life cycle is at its most useful as a framework for understanding how destinations and their markets evolve. The shape of the curve is dependent upon supply-side factors such as investment and capacity constraints, and the cycle can be used to conceptualise tourist impacts and planning responses at various stages. As has already been stated, the cycle also allows for an understanding of the appropriate timing and development of community-based and sustainable tourism strategies. Clearly, the involvement stage is important here but an appreciation of control and power within the resort at later stages may also assist in devising sustainable tourism strategies which are rooted in the realities of the complex politics of large resorts, or the local politics of say, rural areas. The cycle simply recognises that tourist destinations are dynamic and provides a framework for the analysis of changing provision of facilities and access matched by an evolving market in both quantitative and qualitative terms.

In terms of marketing, commentators have criticised the cycle on the grounds that it does not take into account market segmentation, in other words that different segments of the market will each experience a different resort cycle (Ward, 1984). On the contrary, the work of writers such as Plog (1991) clearly addresses this issue and amplifies the cycle's explanatory power. Plog (1991) suggests that tourists can be characterised as allocentric (adventurous, ever seeking new destinations), or psychocentric (seeking familiar destinations and the security of the travel trade). Midcentrics have some of both of these characteristics and represent the bulk of the market. Plog envisages a destination appealing to allocentrics in the early stages of evolution, to midcentrics in the later stages of 'development' and 'consolidation' and to psychocentrics in 'stagnation' and 'decline'.

This approach allows the linking of theories of the diffusion of innovations to the cycle with interesting results (Cooper, 1992). The resort can be thought of as an 'innovation' which is progressively adopted initially by the more 'adventurous' tourists in the early stages to be replaced by 'laggards' or more conservative tourists as the resort moves into the later stages of the cycle. Of course, the development of an increasingly standardised resort product over time will progressively appeal to low risk-taking, psychocentric-type visitors who prefer the security this provides. In other words successive waves of different numbers and types of tourists with distinctive preferences, motivations and desires populate the resort at each stage of the life cycle. The implications of these ideas are explored later in this paper.

Marketing and planning

Some argue that the true test of any explanatory theory in the applied social sciences is whether it can be operationalised. In the case of the TALC this would involve using the cycle as a tool for planning and managing tourist areas (Doyle, 1976; Reed, 1987). The TALC is useful in providing resort managers with a long-term perspective and illustrating the different driving forces of change at each stage, and also recognising for what it is the hiatus which often occurs as areas move from one stage to the next. In other words the explanatory nature of the TALC can be utilised as a versatile organising framework for product planning and strategy. The main determinant of strategy is expected market growth, and other factors include distribution of market shares, degree of competition and profitability (Cooper, 1989). It can therefore be argued that each of these vary at different stages and a different marketing mix is appropriate. In hospitality management for example the

Table 35.1 *Implications of the tourist area life cycle (Sources: Doyle, 1976; Ward 1984)*

	Involvement	Development	Consolidation	Decline
Characteristics				
Visitor numbers	Low	Fast growth	Slow growth	Negative growth
Private sector profit	Negligible	Peak levels	Levelling	Declining
Cashflow	Negative	Moderate	High	Declining
Visitors	Innovative/allocentric	Mass market (innovators)	Mass market (followers)	Laggards/psychocentric
Competitors	Few	Growing	Many rivals	Fewer rivals
Responses				
Strategic focus	Expand market	Market penetration	Defend share	Reposition
Marketing expenditures	Growing	High (declining %)	Falling	Consolidate
Marketing emphasis	Build awareness/ educate	Build preference/inform	Brand loyalty	Protect loyalty/seek new markets
Distribution	Independent	Travel trade	Travel trade	Travel trade
Price	High	Lower	Low	Lowest
Product	Basic/unstandardised	Improved/standardised	Differentiated	Changing
Promotion	None	Personal selling/ advertising/PR	Personal selling/ advertising/PR/sales promotion	Personal selling/ advertising/PR/sales promotion

PLC is beginning to be used in this way as a framework for strategic planning.

Table 35.1 summarises the relationship between life cycle stage, a destination's characteristics and possible marketing responses. In the early stages, growth of visitation is slow; gaining awareness takes time and some resorts may not progress beyond this stage. At involvement, promotion and accessing distribution channels will be important. Here, concern is with building up a strong market position before competitors enter. By development the emphasis changes to market expansion by building market share through increased visitor numbers, pre-empting competitors' customers but also relying on word of mouth promotion as early 'adopters' spread the word. Also, diversification of distribution channels is important, as is maintaining quality of the resort's products, continuing promotion to keep awareness high and adding new facilities. As consolidation approaches, defence of market share against competitors becomes important as does maintaining margins and cash flow by cost control and avoiding price wars. Competition for visits is intensive from a number of well-entrenched, mature resorts. In consolidation the strategy is to seek new users and encourage increased use amongst current visitors. This involves modifying the product through improvements in quality, features and style, and modifying elements of the marketing mix accordingly (Kotler, 1980). However, once visitor numbers stabilise, management should not await decline as inevitable but should seek to review options to revitalise the destination. By decline the task switches to preventing a cash drain in activities with no future, and the area may decide to disinvest in tourism and pursue other economic sectors.

The decline/rejuvenation stage points up the differences between dealing with a marketing 'product' and in tourism, dealing with the built fabric of a 'destination area'. Tourism is closely woven into the very way of life of the town and supports jobs, services and carriers (Cooper, 1990). The reduction of tourism thus places the architectural, economic and social future of these destinations in jeopardy and it is therefore difficult to argue that such resorts have reached the end of their useful life. Here, strategic thinking on the scale of the life cycle can provide managers with an historical perspective and prompt a new scale of strategic thinking (Diamond, 1988; Smith, 1991).

Forecasting

Cycles can also be used as forecasting tools, although here they are less successful because of the differing lengths of the stages and the difficulty of obtaining standardised sales histories or long runs of visitor arrivals data.

Use of the life cycle approach as a forecasting tool in tourism is less developed and somewhat discredited. The problem is that forecasting depends upon the ability to isolate and predict the forces driving the cycle. Most forecasts have highly limiting assumptions (such as constraints on long-run growth, an S-shaped diffusion curve, homogeneity of customers) and give no explicit consideration of marketing decisions or the competition. Also, the forecasts need long runs of visitor data which (with a few exceptions) are not normally available. Yet, frustratingly for forecasters, retrospective studies have shown that many resorts fit the TALC pattern. This empirical evidence can be summarised as: visitation of many destinations broadly follows the TALC pattern; profits peak during rapid growth and problems of competition increase as the cycle progresses; there is no regularity in the length of the stages of the TALC and the shape can be temporarily bent by heavy promotional expenditure. Work is continuing to evaluate the tourist area life cycle using empirical data but the scarcity of long runs of historic information on visitor numbers is a problem here.

Assessment

The life cycle approach has many critics, in part drawn by its very simplicity and apparent deterministic approach (Brownlie, 1985). Yet, as Brown (1987) has argued, the more the approach is refuted, the stronger it becomes, as each objection is absorbed. Some argue for example that far from being an independent guide for decisions the curve is determined by the strategic decisions of management and heavily dependent on external forces such as the competition, development of substitute products, swings in consumer taste and government legislation. Of course the counterargument to this is the explanatory framework approach, that by seeing the curve as a dependent rather than an independent variable, then it provides useful explanations of the processes which drive it.

Other more detailed criticisms (see Haywood, 1986; Cooper, 1989) include:

- The danger of reacting to warning signs which may have been misinterpreted, because there is poor empirical validation for shape or length and stages can only be identified accurately with hindsight. The TALC is destination-specific, with each stage varying in length and with differing shapes and patterns. The life cycle, it is argued, does not therefore provide sufficient insight into the development of policy or planning for tourist areas or products. It may also be imprecise as a guide for strategy because it ignores competitive settings and profit considerations.
- As noted above, its main uses for decision taking and forecasting are in doubt. In particular the wisdom of pursuing a standardised marketing strategy at each stage has been questioned and it is also imprecise as a forecasting tool and difficult to calibrate because of the lack of long runs of data on visitor numbers and sales.
- The identification of stages and turning points is difficult without hindsight, yet given the increased cost

of reacting as the need for change becomes more obvious this is an important point for practitioners. To some extent the use of leading indicators (such as growth rate of visitors, percentage of first-time visitors, number of competitors, levels of prices and profits, advertising, promotional expenditure) can assist here. However, the variety of possible shapes of the curve and acceleration or delay due to external factors make it difficult to identify the stage reached by a destination. What is needed here is the development of guidelines and ratios of variables which will assist destination managers.

- The level of aggregation is problematic and must be clearly addressed. Geographical scale is important for the tourist area life cycle as each country is a mosaic of resorts and tourist areas (which in turn contain hotels, theme parks etc.) and, depending on the scale taken, each may be at a different stage in the cycle. The unit of analysis is therefore crucial.
- As noted earlier, some argue that the life cycle assumes a homogeneous market but the market can be divided into many segments and a perfectly logical stance would be for, say, a destination to introduce segments sequentially. Equally, geographical segmentation would produce different curves for, say, domestic or international visitors.
- The concepts are vague and not developed for some points in the TALC. For example, the decline stage suggests that visitor numbers have exceeded the carrying capacity of the area. Yet capacity is a notoriously difficult concept to operationalise as it is dependent upon management inputs and no single capacity threshold exists for a destination—physical, environmental and psychological capacities may each be different. Of course, neither does this take account of spatial or temporal variations, such as seasonality with the attraction of crowd-tolerant visitors in the peak season and others in the quieter off-peak.

The use of the TALC as an operational guide for destination managers or forecasting is clearly problematic. Partly this is a result of the ill-defined concepts used in the TALC (such as carrying capacity and the tourist product—both are difficult to operationalise) and the illusory vagueness of the patterns which only emerge clearly with hindsight.

Extensions

It is evident that recent applications and extensions of the TALC are moving away from geometric forms towards managerial applications which embody a realistic assessment of the concept.

For example, it is possible to make the link of market evolution and the life cycle more explicit by analogy to the S-shaped diffusion curve—the life cycle approach is rooted in population ecology and the diffusion process (Lambkin and Day, 1989; Haywood, 1990). As mentioned above, it would be expected that, as it develops, a destination area would be progressively adopted by increasingly conservative visitors. Adoption of the resort would be expected to be related to learning, risk avoidance, market structures, the competition, existing markets, and the nature of the resort itself. Individuals can therefore be classified as early adopters—venturesome consumption pioneers—through to laggards bound by tradition. A visitor's position on the adoption curve will therefore be determined by both demographic and psychological characteristics along with the nature of the resort (Cooper, 1992). Of course these ideas have been championed by Plog with his ideas of allocentric, or early adopting tourist and psychocentric laggards (Plog, 1991). This approach to market segmentation based upon an individual's likelihood to visit a resort at a particular stage in its development is mirrored in Cooper's (1981) work where the risk-taking and learning behaviour of tourists to a small island was classified. In this study tourists minimised risk and maximised utility in resort choice. Clearly knowledge is not a free good and levels of information may be an independent variable in the process (Vernon, 1966). Equally, it would be expected that resorts will become increasingly standardised as they progress through the life cycle and will therefore appeal to low risk takers in the later stages of the cycle. A fruitful area for research is to examine systems of competing resorts, the characteristics of their markets and the influence of such factors as access, promotion and distribution systems.

A second area of research relates to the relationship between organisational structures and stage of the life cycle. In tourism, there is virtually no research linking these two areas (Cooper, 1992). The closest is Tse and Elwood's (1990) examination of strategy and life cycle stage in the hospitality industry. Here they suggest that, in the early stages of the cycle when organisations are small, the personality of the entrepreneur or leader is important whilst in the later stages when the organisation is larger, then more complex bureaucratic systems develop. Haywood (1990) agrees that young organisations manage by crisis and are action-oriented and opportunity-driven with few systems, rules, procedures or delegation. With progression through the life cycle there is a danger that the original aims and commitment are lost as others take over. Clearly the key is to achieve a successful transition from entrepreneur to manager by delegating to

a formal layer of middle managers with well-defined procedures (Tse and Elwood, 1990). For destination development the parallels are obvious, with increased complexity, larger organisations, and more stakeholders as the area moves through the cycle. Again the critical point is to move from the involvement stage to development and consolidation without loss of local control and sustainable development options. In this respect, Gormsen (1981) has examined the contrasting roles of local and external participation in coastal resort development.

A final approach is to utilise the life cycle as a way of thinking about resort development but to loosen the shackle of deterministic birth to death thought (Ioannides, 1992). Instead, an emergent school of thought suggests that products evolve through 'directed change' (Trellis and Crawford, 1981). The product is dependent upon certain forces but sales do not follow a fixed sequence of stages, rather it is possible to envisage a matrix of growth patterns where the unit of analysis is type of growth (slow positive growth, negative growth, no growth, average positive growth etc.) rather than the shape of the growth curve (Cooper, 1992; Jones and Lockwood, 1990).

Jones and Lockwood (1990) suggest a variety of forces which affect the type of growth: changes in consumer taste, economic influences, competitive forces and demographic change. Trellis and Crawford (1981) suggest that management/entrepreneurial influences generate growth or change, the marketplace provides a 'natural selection' in terms of consumers and competitors, and that government and other agencies then mediate and regulate the process of product growth and evolution. As a result the product displays an evolution of directed change with increased sophistication, efficiency and diversity over time. Both sets of authors thus suggest a dynamic process of growth which is not deterministic and still provides a conceptual framework for the understanding of the relationship between products and markets.

Conclusion

The tourist area life cycle has generated considerable debate and research since its inception in 1980. Despite many critics, acceptance of the concept appears to be strengthening, particularly as an organising framework for destination development. The concept is much less successful in providing detailed prescriptions for marketing or planning actions, simply because the life cycle is destination-specific and there is little empirical validation of its shape or length to allow generalisations to be made. It is in the explanatory power of the curve that the main utility of the life cycle approach lies. It provides a convenient and acceptable aid to understanding the evolution of tourist destinations and it should therefore provide guidance for strategic decision taking, at least in terms of driving tourism businesses and destinations towards the adoption of a long-term planning horizon. In respect of its explanatory framework the life cycle elegantly combines both supply and demand-side variables and may therefore provide the seeds of a generalised theory of tourism.

References

Agarwall, S. (1994) 'The life cycle approach and south coast resorts', in Cooper, C. and Lockwood, A. (Eds), *Progress in Tourism Recreation and Hospitality Management*, Vol. 5, John Wiley, Chichester, pp. 194–208.

Brown, S. (1987) 'Institutional change in retailing: a review and synthesis', *European Journal of Marketing*, 21(6): 5–36.

Brownlie, D. (1985) 'Strategic marketing concepts and models', *Journal of Marketing Management*, 1: 157–194.

Butler, R. W. (1980) 'The concept of the tourist area cycle of evolution: implications for management of resources', *Canadian Geographer*, 24: 5–12.

Butler, R. W. and Waldbrook, L. A. (1991) 'A new planning tool: the tourism opportunity spectrum', *Journal of Tourism Studies*, 2(1): 2–14.

Choy, D. J. L. (1992) 'Life cycle models for Pacific island destinations', *Journal of Travel Research*, 30(3): 26–31.

Clarke, R. and Stankey, G. (1979) 'The recreation opportunity, spectrum: a framework for planning, management and research', US Department of Agriculture and Forest Service Pacific North West Forest and Ranger Experiment Station, General Technical Report PNW-98.

Cooper, C. P. (1981) 'The spatial and temporal behaviour of tourists', *Regional Studies*, 15(2): 359–371.

Cooper, C. P. (1989) 'Tourist product life cycle', in Witt, S. F. and Moutinho, L. (Eds), *Tourism Marketing and Management Handbook*, Prentice Hall, Hemel Hempstead, pp. 577–581.

Cooper, C. P. (1990) 'Resorts in decline: the management response', *Tourism Management*, 11(1): 63–67.

Cooper, C. P. (1992) 'The life cycle concept and strategic planning for coastal resorts', *Built Environment*, 18(1): 57–66.

Cooper, C. P. and Jackson, S. (1989) 'Destination life cycle: the Isle of Man case study', *Annals of Tourism Research*, 16(3): 377.

Day, G. S. (1981) 'The product life cycle: analysis and applications issues', *Journal of Marketing*, 45: 60–67.

Debbage, K. G. (1990) 'Oligopoly and the resort cycle in the Bahamas', *Annals of Tourism Research*, 17(2): 513–527.

Diamond, N. P. (1988) 'A strategy for cold water resorts into the year 2000', unpublished MSc. thesis, University of Surrey.

Doyle, P. (1976) 'The realities of the product life cycle', *Quarterly Review of Marketing*, 1: 1–6.

Goodall, B. (1992) 'Coastal resorts: development and redevelopment', *Built Environment*, 18(1): 5–11.

Gormsen, E. (1981) 'The spatio-temporal development of international tourism: attempt at a centre–periphery model', *La Consummation d'Espace par la Tourisme et sa Preservation*, CHET, Aix en Provence, pp. 150–170.

Haywood, K. M. (1990) 'Resort cycles: a commentary', Paper presented to the American Association of Geographers Conference, Toronto, 1990.

Haywood, K. M. (1986) 'Can the tourist area life cycle be made operational?' *Tourism Management*, 7(2): 154–167.

Hunt, S. D. (1976) *Marketing Theory: Conceptual Foundations of Research in Marketing*, Grid, Columbus, OH.

Ioannides, D. (1992) 'Tourist development agents. The Cypriot resort cycle', *Annals of Tourism Research*, 19(4): 711–731.

Jones, P. and Lockwood, A. (1990) 'Productivity and the product life cycle in hospitality firms', Paper presented to the Contemporary Hospitality Management Conference, Bournemouth, 1990.

Kotler, P. (1980) *Principles of Marketing*, Prentice Hall, Hemel Hempstead.

Lambkin, M. and Day, G. S. (1989) 'Evolutionary processes in competitive markets: beyond the product life cycle', *Journal of Marketing*, 53: 4–20.

Lane, P. (1992) 'The regeneration of small to medium sized resorts', Paper presented to Tourism in Europe Conference, Durham, 1992.

Lundgren, J. J. (1982) 'The development of tourist accommodation in the Montreal Laurentians', in Wall, G. and Marsh, J. (Eds), *Recreational Landuse: Perspectives on its Evolution in Canada*, Carleton University Press, Ottawa, pp. 175–189.

Pearce, D. (1989) *Tourist Development*, Longman, Harlow.

Plog, S. C. (1991) *Leisure Travel. Making it a Growth Market Again!* John Wiley, New York.

Reed, R. (1987) 'Fashion life cycles and extension theory', *European Journal of Marketing*, 2: 52–62.

Reime, M. and Hawkins, C. (1979) 'Tourism development: a model for growth', *Cornell Hotel and Restaurant Administration Quarterly*, 20(1): 67–74.

Rink, D. R. and Swan, J. E. (1979) 'Product life cycle research: literature review', *Journal of Business Research*, 78: 219–242.

Smith, R. A. (1991) 'Beach resorts: a model of development evolution', *Landscape and Urban Planning*, 21: 189–210.

Stansfield, C. A. (1978) 'Atlantic City and the resort cycle', *Annals of Tourism Research*, 5(2): 238–251.

Trellis, G. J. and Crawford, C. M. (1981) 'An evolutionary approach to product growth theory', *Journal of Marketing*, 45: 125–132.

Tse, E. C. and Elwood, C. M. (1990) 'Synthesis of the life cycle concept with strategy and management style: a case study in the hospitality industry', *International Journal of Hospitality Management*, 9(3): 223–236.

Vernon, R. (1966) 'International investment and international trade in the product cycle', *Quarterly Journal of Economics*, 80: 190–207.

Ward, J. (1984) *Profitable Product Management*, Heinemann, London.

Weg, H. van de (1982) 'Revitalisation of traditional resorts', *Tourism Management*, 3(4): 303–307.

Young, B. (1983) 'Touristisation of traditional Maltese fishing villages', *Tourism Management*, 4(1): 35–41.

36 Australian attitudes to domestic and international resort holidays. A comparison of Fiji and Queensland

B. KING

Introduction

This paper examines the attitudes of Australian consumers to domestic and international island resort destinations. Two comparable island resort destinations were selected for study, the Mamanuca islands in Fiji and the Whitsunday islands in Queensland, Australia. Issues explored included travel experiences, the influences on holiday decision-making and the images held of the two destinations. Concepts to be investigated included the view that domestic destinations enjoy a higher level of awareness amongst consumers than their international equivalents, are perceived as more suitable for short break holidays, as more easily accessible, as cheaper and as less exotic. The view that short-haul sun, sea and sand resort destinations are highly substitutable from a consumer point of view was also evaluated. The two groups have common characteristics which make them suitable for comparative purposes, notably the rough equidistance from the key Australian source markets of Melbourne and Sydney, a subtropical location, close proximity between the various islands in the groups, and easy accessibility from a major airport (Nadi in the case of the Mamanucas and Hamilton Island—to a lesser extent Proserpine—in the case of the Whitsundays). Both are established resort holiday destinations for Australian travellers. The rest of this paper outlines the selection of methodology, its execution and then presents some preliminary results.

Literature review

There is a substantial body of literature written on the characteristics of tourism in developing countries, including Fiji. Much of this work evaluates relations between the major tourism-generating countries (predominantly in the developed countries and including Australia) and the world's tropical and subtropical destinations (predominantly in the developing countries and including Fiji). Such studies have included examinations of so-called 'centre–periphery relations' (Hoivik and Heiberg, 1980),

the role of transnational corporations (Dunning and McQueen, 1982), imagery (Britton, 1979), marketing authenticity (Silver, 1993) and the role of the tour operator. Within this literature, there are a number of works evaluating tourism in small island destinations (Cazes, 1987). Fiji, in particular, has been the subject of a number of such studies, notably by Britton (Britton, 1982; Britton and Clarke, 1987), whose work emphasised the links between tourism, dependency and underdevelopment.

As a developed country, Australia has been less frequently evaluated from the point of view of tourism's negative impacts, though Craik (1991), has examined the negative dimensions of tourism development in Queensland, notably in the Queensland islands. Barr (1990) has also examined the historical development of tourism in the Whitsunday islands, including its increasing dependence on externally generated capital. Whilst many of the studies previously referred to contain general comparisons and one or two some specific comparisons (Dieke (1993) compared Kenya and The Gambia), few studies have undertaken direct comparisons between tourism regions in developed and in developing countries (an exception is Pizam et al. (1994)). The present study attempts to fill that gap.

Another relevant literature is the body of work dedicated to the study of resorts. Because most resorts are self-contained and tend to view themselves as tourism destinations in their own right, the literature has studied the phenomenon from a variety of angles. Such approaches have included the study of the resort development process (Dean and Judd, 1985; Stiles and See-Tho, 1991), planning (Smith, 1992), assessment of local attitudes (Witter, 1985), marketing (King and Whitelaw, 1992), the resort life cycle (Butler, 1980), resorts as communities (Stettner, 1993), architecture (England, 1980) and landscaping (Ayala, 1991), to name but a few. A significant dimension of this literature is the role of resorts as 'enclave' developments, separated from the reality of daily life in adjacent areas.

The marketing of the Whitsundays and of the Mamanucas has not been the subject of any dedicated studies that could be ascertained by the author. However more general studies on Queensland (Sweeney, 1991) and on Fiji (Stollznow, 1990, 1992) have provided insights into the perceptions of the two areas by consumers. In both cases the research was commissioned by the relevant tourism authorities (the Queensland Tourist and Travel Corporation and Fiji Visitors Bureau respectively) and undertaken by a market research company.

Objectives

This research constitutes one phase of a larger research project. The purpose of this phase was to compare the marketing of two comparable groups of islands (the Whitsundays in Queensland and the Mamanucas in Fiji), and consumer responses to prevailing images within the Australian market. Subsequent stages involve an examination of travel agent attitudes, a detailed comparison of the promotional activities undertaken by the two destinations and interviews with tour wholesalers and resort managers. The travel agent survey has been completed and the two subsequent stages are currently underway. The results of these stages will be reported in subsequent papers and are not included in this study. Issues covered here are the images that Australians associate with subtropical island resorts generally and with the island resorts particular to the two relevant regions. The desirability of the destinations, the travel experiences of participants and the nature of their decision-making processes were also examined. A broader issue relating to this research, though not one which could be answered definitively was that of whether the availability of domestic subtropical island destinations makes overseas tropical island destinations less attractive to Australian consumers. Australia is one of the few major tourism-generating countries to have domestic subtropical islands which have been developed for tourism. In contrast consumers in countries such as Canada, New Zealand, Germany, Scandinavia, the United Kingdom and (to a lesser extent) the USA must travel overseas for their island resort experiences. Are such 'sun, sea and sand' destinations competitors with similar overseas destinations? Issues are raised about how Australians view their own country as opposed to their neighbours in the Asia-Pacific region and whether their stereotype of domestic destinations is more or less accurate than the views that they hold of overseas destinations.

Study methodology

The primary investigation involved the staging of eight consumer focus groups with equal numbers of participants in Melbourne and Sydney. A total of 60 consumers

participated. The main purpose of these groups was the generation of key ideas to take forward to the travel agent survey. This later stage was to involve a telephone survey of 200 travel agents, again with half each in Melbourne and Sydney. The travel agent survey would produce quantifiable results, unlike the focus discussion groups which have purely qualitative objectives and outcomes.

The focus discussion group method was selected for four major reasons. Firstly it is acknowledged as the best research approach for the generation of ideas and for the identification of key issues (Peterson, 1987; Gordon and Langmaid, 1988), particularly when quantification of responses is not required. Secondly the method is more cost-effective than personal interview. Thirdly it allows the researcher to segment respondents into key demographic and experiential characteristics. Finally, a reputed market research company with extensive experience in running consumer focus groups on travel to Queensland, Brian Sweeney and Associates, offered the researcher financial and logistical assistance with the groups. The groups' discussions were held in the offices of Brian Sweeney and Associates. The Melbourne groups were video-taped and the Sydney groups were audio taped. Recruitment criteria were drawn up by the author, though actual recruitment was undertaken by the company.

Certain limitations of the method must be acknowledged. Groups can be subject to the influence of an emerging collective mentality which may cause individuals to suppress their own views. It is also difficult to ensure that groups are genuinely representative of the demographic profiles that they are intended to represent. The quantification of responses is a questionable practice and often results in unrepresentative findings. In this research project, the groups were selected according to four key variables. Firstly equal numbers of groups (four each) were staged in Melbourne and in Sydney. It was intended that this geographical breakdown would help the researcher to identify any differences in consumers evident in the two areas. Also it was hoped that by selecting consumers in Australia's two major cities, that a reasonably representative segment of the Australian population could be examined. Groups were also segmented into those travelling with families, and those travelling as singles or as couples without children. Age specifications were placed on both types of respondent, with older (over 45) and younger (under 25) excluded from the study. Groups were also segmented according to their level of travel experience to the two relevant destinations. Three types of experience were examined, namely those who had visited both Queensland and Fiji, those who had visited one but not the other and finally those who had visited neither.

The method used in focus discussion groups to introduce particular subjects into the discussion is described as a 'line of inquiry'. In this research, the eight groups were guided into the topic gradually and were aware only that the discussion would centre upon resorts in their broadest sense. The line of inquiry used involved six stages. These sought to elicit participant views as follows:

1. Mental associations prompted by the terms resort and island resort.
2. The information-gathering and decision-making processes used in preparing for resort holidays were elicited.
3. The previous resort experiences of experienced travellers and the experiences anticipated by intending but inexperienced travellers.
4. Responses to various name prompts, both resort-specific and regional.
5. Perceived differences between the two destination areas and the circumstances in which a visit to one would be preferred over a visit to the other.
6. Word association. Participants were presented with a number of descriptions and asked to attach the most appropriate ones to the relevant destination area.

The choice of study regions

The nature of the investigation required the selection of comparable areas offering tropical or subtropical island resorts to the Australian market. It was advisable to select areas which were comparable in terms of accessibility (e.g. flight times), were already established destinations in the marketplace and which offered relatively substitutable experiences for consumers. Both Queensland and Fiji can be regarded as sun, sea and sand destinations and the Whitsunday and Mamanuca groups offer equivalent island resorts, nine in the case of the Whitsundays, twelve in the case of the Mamanucas. Fiji was chosen because of the author's familiarity with the destination. Also highlighting the relevance of Fiji for comparative purposes was the current move by the Fiji Ministry of Tourism and the Fiji Visitors Bureau to shift the focus of tourism marketing in Australia from the depiction of resort-based experiences, to a more diverse tourism product focusing on environmental and cultural experiences. It seemed an appropriate time to evaluate whether the dissatisfaction with the resorts in Fiji was as serious as indicated by previous research (Stollznow, 1990, 1992).

In the case of Queensland, substantial work had been undertaken for the Queensland Tourist and Travel Corporation (QTTC) on consumer attitudes to the island resorts. The present research offered the opportunity to re-evaluate some of the concerns raised in the QTTC research through direct comparison with an equivalent overseas destination.

Tourism in the Whitsundays and in the Mamanucas

The Whitsundays

The Whitsunday Islands are located off the northeastern coast of Queensland in northern Australia. In 1991–92 the State of Queensland accounted for the largest percentage (29%) of all nights spent by interstate travellers in Australia, followed by New South Wales (the most populous state) with 28%. Queensland is the major beach resort destination in Australia, particularly for Japanese tourists who spent 50% of their total Australian nights for 1992 in the state.

There are 74 islands in the Whitsunday group. The Whitsunday Shire (or local government division) incorporates sections of the mainland including the towns of Airlie Beach and Shute Harbour as well as the islands. The Whitsunday group includes small islands which are occupied substantially by a single resort (e.g. Daydream Island), larger islands housing a single resort (South Molle and Lindeman islands, for example), one larger island featuring multiple resorts (Long Island which incorporates Palm Bay Hideaway and the Radisson resort) and many with no resort development (such as Whitsunday Island). Most of the islands are designated National Park, with overall management being the responsibility of the Great Barrier Reef Marine Park Authority. Resorts cater for a variety of markets, including the exclusive (e.g. Hayman Island) the 'middle' market (e.g. Daydream Island) and the 'budget' market (Hook Island). The Whitsundays have been described as constituting one of the four main island groupings off Queensland (King and Hyde, 1989) or one of five according to Sunlover Holidays (Queensland Tourist and Travel Corporation, 1993) and are probably the best-known of the four or five groups.

The islands collectively attracted 146 700 visitors in 1992–93 (Queensland Visitor Survey, 1993), of whom 33% originated in NSW and 14.9% in Victoria. The average length of stay was recorded as 5.1 nights, though the average length of stay for NSW and Victoria residents is much higher. The average expenditure per visitor night was $186.78, higher than for any other Queensland region. 74.8% of all visitors arrived by air into the region, with a further 21.4% arriving by private vehicle. The total accommodation capacity of the eight resorts (Brampton is excluded from the data) is 1675 rooms, almost five times the capacity of the Mamanucas. Figures for the June quarter of 1993 (Australian Bureau of Statistics, 1993) indicate that the Whitsunday Shire (which includes some of the mainland properties) offers a total of 2417 rooms in the category 'licensed hotels, motels etc. with facilities', indicative that the bulk of the regional accommodation capacity is situated on the islands.

Most travellers to the islands arrive by air, either at Hamilton Island Airport, flying with Ansett Australia, or through Proserpine with Qantas Airways. Most of the islands have a close association with one or other of the airlines (a contrast with the Mamanucas where there is no direct equity or operational involvement). Hayman, Hook and South Molle islands are operated by Ansett, whilst Brampton is operated by Qantas subsidiary, Australian Resorts. Hamilton Island is independent of the airlines, but has a closer association with Ansett, since the island airport is a joint venture between the airline and the island.

Only three significant Australian wholesalers are involved with the Whitsunday island resorts. These are the two major domestic airlines, namely Ansett (through Ansett Holidays) and Qantas (through Australian Holidays) and Sunlover Holidays, a subsidiary of the Queensland Tourist and Travel Corporation. Until recently all three brands have been purely domestic operations. This has changed with Ansett Holidays introducing packages to Bali and the intention by Qantas to replace the Australian Holidays brand with Qantas Jetabout brand (previously a purely international operation). Table 36.1 indicates which of the resorts are featured in the various holiday brochures offered by the operators. Club Med Lindeman Island is the only Whitsunday island not packaged by either of the airlines or by Sunlover Holidays. Its operator, Club Med, features its own brand which is brochured and made available through travel agents. The narrow range of wholesalers stands out clearly in the table.

The Mamanucas

The Mamanucas are a group of islands located off the west coast of Fiji's main island, Viti Levu, close to the country's main international airport at Nadi. Fiji itself consists of 322 islands, of which one-third are inhabited. Of the total land mass of 18 272 square kilometres, the two largest islands Viti Levu (10 429 square kilometres) and Vanua Levu (5556 square kilometres) make up the bulk. The country was formerly a British colony and has been independent since 1970. Tourism is the principal foreign exchange earner, followed by sugar. Fiji is the major tourism destination in the South Pacific, accounting for twice as many arrivals as its nearest rival, French Polynesia and twelve times the number in Tonga. Its dominance is relative, however, with northern Pacific destinations attracting larger numbers—Hawaii attracts twelve times as many and Guam twice as many as Fiji. Australia accounts for over 30% of all visitor nights in Fiji, making it the dominant market source (Tourism Council of the South Pacific, 1993).

The Mamanuca islands range from seven to 40 kilometres off the Viti Levu coast and most of the inner islands can be accessed by boat departing from Denarau Beach (near Nadi). The more northerly islands can be reached by boat from Fiji's second city, Lautoka. An airstrip is located on Malolo Lailai Island, home of two of the Mamanuca resorts—Musket Cove Resort and Plantation Island Resort. The flight from Nadi International Airport takes 10 minutes and is operated on demand. Castaway Island, one of the more exclusive in the group can also be accessed by seaplane and Tokoriki and Matamanoa by helicopter. The Mamanuca resorts are smaller in scale than their Whitsunday counterparts with the largest (Mana Island) having a capacity of 132 units. Most are pitched at the middle rather than the upper end of the market, though the recent opening of the tiny Sheraton Vomo Resort (with a total capacity of 30 suites) has added an up-market alternative to the range. Accommodation is typically 'bure' style, often with thatched roofs.

The total number of rooms offered by the twelve resorts is 535 (this figure includes a recent expansion in capacity

Table 36.1 *Whitsunday islands featured in air-inclusive holiday brochures*

Resort	Qantas Australian Holidays	Ansett Holidays	Club Med	Sunlover
Hayman		X		X
Hamilton		X		X
Daydream	X	X		X
Palm Bay, Long Island	X			X
Radisson, Long Island	X	X		X
Brampton	X			X
Hook		X		
Lindeman			X	
South Molle		X		X

Sources: Sunlover Holidays 'Queensland's Islands' brochure; Ansett Australia's 'Queensland Islands' brochure; Australian Airlines Holidays 'Queensland Islands' brochure; Club Med 'Club Med Lindeman Island, Whitsundays Queensland' brochure.

at the Musket Cove Resort). This total of the twelve resorts is less than the capacity of the two major Nadi-based resorts (the Regent and Sheraton hotels), indicative that the bulk of accommodation capacity is located onshore, unlike the situation in the Whitsundays where the islands hold a dominant position. The Australian market is the dominant source of business for the islands within the group. Some have, however, succeeded in attracting substantial numbers from other markets. Mana Island, for example, attracts substantial numbers of Japanese. At this stage, figures are not available for the Mamanucas specifically, but their much smaller scale than the Whitsundays is put into perspective by the realisation that the Whitsunday island resorts alone attract a number of visitors annually (146 700) equivalent to over half of the total Fiji number (274 534 in 1992).

Unlike the Whitsundays, the Mamanucas are packaged by a number of international wholesalers specialising in outbound travel from Australia. These are listed in Table 36.2. Air Pacific, which is the national carrier of Fiji and the major airline servicing Australia and Fiji, does not package the island, apart from releasing 'specials' on a periodic basis with the individual resorts. Qantas packages Fiji and the Mamanucas under the Jetabout brand. A number of independent wholesalers also feature Fiji and the Mamanucas, including Viva!, Travelscene, Jetset, Orient Pacific Holidays and Venture Holidays, to name but a few. The historical division between Australian domestic packaging (dominated by the two domestic carriers) and international packaging (far more fragmented) is currently changing, though the existing pattern of many small operators featuring international destinations is likely to continue.

The key differences and similarities between the Whitsundays and the Mamanucas are highlighted in Table 36.3.

Focus discussion group findings

'Islands' and 'tropical' are the terms most closely identified with the term resort, with warm weather and water seen as essential elements. Ski resorts were mentioned in three groups, but almost as an afterthought. Most of the images expressed were positive ones. Cultural issues rated little mention and the environment was mentioned primarily as a backdrop to other active or passive activities.

Table 36.2 *Mamanuca island resorts featured in key air-inclusive holiday brochures (ex-Australia)*

Island resort	Wholesalers featuring the resorts
Treasure Island Resort	Connection Holidays Sportswell Holidays Jetset Jetabout
Castaway Island	Rosie the Travel Service Jetset Jetabout
Mana Island	Pacific Island Holidays Connection Holidays Jetset Jetabout
Plantation Island	Dive Adventures Orient Pacific Pacific Island Holidays Connection Holidays Jetset Jetabout
Tokoriki	Connection Holidays Jetabout
Matamanoa	Jetabout
Musket Cove	Jetabout
Club Naitasi	Connection Holidays Jetabout
Beachcomber	Rosie the Travel Service Jetabout

Source: Fiji Visitors Bureau, Sydney, and selected tour operator brochures. Some operators may have been omitted from the list.

Images most commonly associated with resorts

The following words were mentioned most frequently as encapsulating the resort experience:

Tropical	Being lazy or relaxed	Luxury/up-market
Lying in the sun	Sandy beaches	Warm weather
A relaxing drink	No clocks or schedule	A tropical island
Seclusion	Palm trees	Water

The dominant negative images were a fear of being trapped—whether it be physically (an inability to get off the island), economically (an inability to afford or unwillingness to pay the perceived high prices charged on the islands), socially (being surrounded by people with whom one feels little in common) or psychologically (a general sense of being 'hemmed in'). Participants repeatedly expressed their desire not to feel trapped. They wanted to be able to visit other islands and not to feel constrained financially, physically or psychologically. A feeling of freedom was important even for those who doubted whether they would actually take advantage of day-trips and tours. It should, however, be acknowledged

Table 36.3 *Contrasts and similarities between the two groups*

Contrasts Mamanucas	Whitsundays
International destination for Australians	Domestic destination for Australians
Weak concept of the region in Australia	Strong concept of the region in Australia
Small to medium sized resorts only	Small, medium and large sized resorts
Many tour operators featuring the islands	Few tour operators—airlines dominant
Part of a developing country	Part of a developed country
Marketing emphasis on local culture	Emphasis on natural beauty and relaxation
Travel agents officially paid 10% commission for air tickets	Travel agents officially paid 5% commission for air tickets
Insignificant presence of branded hotel chains	A number of brands present (SPHC/Australian resorts)

Similarities
Both regions are characterised by a tropical setting, pristine beaches and coral
Heavy dependence on a small number of airlines serving the Australian market
Easy accessibility of a major airport
Short-haul destinations
Direct access available via both water craft and aircraft
Both are constituted as established tourism regions
Cooperative marketing undertaken by the various resorts in the groups
Both have fabricated tourism island names (e.g. Castaway, Beachcomber, Daydream) plus traditional names (South Molle, Matamanoa)
Recent bankruptcies have occurred in both regions (Naitasi, Castaway and Hamilton islands)

that resorts were viewed predominantly in terms of positive associations. The negatives were generally beneath the surface and appeared predominantly a reflexion of underlying anxieties.

Top of mind awareness of island resorts

Respondents were asked which names first come to mind when the word resort is mentioned. The main differences between awareness of the two groups was that whilst the Queensland resorts were identified by their names (e.g. Daydream or Hamilton), most overseas island resorts were referred to in terms of countries (e.g. Fiji, Tahiti, the Cook Islands). Mention of the names of specific overseas resorts was very limited. Australian resorts have a higher brand awareness than overseas counterparts, even those overseas destinations which involve a flight of similar duration (such as Vanuatu and New Caledonia). The most frequently mentioned island resorts were Hamilton, Hayman, Great Keppel and (to a lesser extent) Daydream and Dunk. Three of the five are located in the Whitsundays, whilst Dunk and Great Keppel islands are not. When asked which resorts first come to mind, some groups suggested only Australian resorts. In these cases overseas resort areas were only mentioned following prompting.

In contrast, awareness of the Fiji resorts was extremely low. Almost no-one had heard of the Mamanucas, even those who had stayed there. Awareness of individual resort names was very patchy. Those who had visited parts of Fiji other than the Mamanucas also had a very low awareness of the names of individual resorts.

Perceived accessibility

The Whitsundays are perceived as far more easily accessible than the Mamanucas. Commenting on Fiji, one Melbourne respondent expressed his belief that 'you have to go via New Zealand don't you?' In fact there are almost daily four-hour flights direct from Melbourne to Nadi. Equivalent nonstop flights from Melbourne to the Whitsundays are only operated in peak holiday periods (and intermittently). The perception of the Whitsundays as more easily accessible is possibly based on the familiarity consumers appear to have of domestic destinations. Generally, consumers who have not previously visited Fiji, have little idea of how long it takes to get there. Some family respondents expressed their unwillingness to take children on flights in excess of four hours. This eliminates some competing destinations such as Hawaii and Bali which involve much longer flights than either the Whitsundays or Fiji.

The Whitsundays were viewed as better suited to short break holidays of three to five nights' duration, because of their easier accessibility, though a perception was evident that this was too short a period for a resort holiday, given the cost of the transport component. In the view of the author, there is no fundamental reason why the Mamanucas could not compete with the Whitsundays for the short break market, though some changes would be needed. Evidence of this is that one couple who had travelled to the Mamanucas for their honeymoon commented that their journey time was excessive and attributed this to not being made aware of the availability of shuttle flights from Nadi to the islands. Raising awareness of the easy accessibility of the Mamanucas would seem to be a logical promotional priority for the island group.

The holiday decision-making process

The key influences on decision-making were word of mouth and travel agents. It was perceived that travel agents provide good advice and do not particularly try to 'push their own products', but a strong preference was expressed for travel consultants who have visited resorts personally. This was seen as enabling them to provide worthwhile advice. Perhaps this issue relates to the concern about possible 'entrapment' on an island resort that is not suitable. Most consumers indicated that they would 'shop around' various travel agents.

Respondents viewed the choice of airline and tour operator as relatively unimportant. Most were unaware of which company had packaged the holidays that they had previously purchased. Brand loyalty was not much in evidence, and was connected with travel agency names, particularly chains, and not with tour operators or airlines. Almost all respondents indicated that the choice of holiday company/tour operator should be and is left to the travel agent.

Social interactions at resort destinations

Fiji is perceived as a 'friendly' destination for the interactions it offers amongst tourists themselves, and between tourism and resort staff and/or local residents. The 'Bula' (welcome) greeting and friendly smiles of the Fijian staff are emblems of such perceived friendliness. The Whitsundays are perceived as offering a more perfunctory style of service—certainly more professional and more efficient, but less friendly. The Whitsunday experience was perceived as a less social one. One telling comment was that 'Australians are more friendly to one another when they are travelling overseas' and it was stated that in the Whitsundays tourists tend to 'keep themselves to themselves'. It was perceived that those who would enjoy a rewarding social experience were watersports enthusiasts and 18–35s. Ironically, perhaps, the Australian resorts offering the best social experience were those which attracted a large international clientele. Dunk Island, which is in Queensland but not in the Whitsundays was mentioned as an example of this.

Another dimension of the social interactions was the view expressed by three female participants in one group (and not contested by the rest) that women needed to 'fit the image' to go to the very public environment of a resort. The need to be young, tanned, glamorous and scantily clad was seen as a barrier to enjoyment and relaxation for those who did not think of themselves in these terms. The view of resorts as an 'unattainable paradise' may appeal to the image makers, but clearly has some unfortunate by-products for certain women travellers. Other groups did not take this view and were more pragmatic, claiming that you choose the island suited to your own market segment.

Phrases most closely associated with the Whitsundays and the Mamanucas

Table 36.4 summarises the words most closely associated with the two areas. Judgements were arrived at via consensus with 'maybe' indicated where dissenting views were expressed. A number of cards were presented

Table 36.4 *Phrases associated with the two island groups*

Description	Whitsundays	Mamanucas
Interesting history	No	Yes
Interesting culture	No	Yes
Good food	Yes	Yes
Quality service	Perhaps	Yes
Lots to see and do	Yes	Yes
Interesting local customs	No	Yes
Diversity of accommodation	Yes	Divided
Glamorous	Yes/perhaps	Yes/perhaps
Expensive to get to	Yes	No
Exotic	No	Yes
Meet compatible people	Yes	Yes
Shopping opportunities	No	Perhaps
High on-island costs	Yes	No
Good-value packages	Perhaps	Yes
Prestige destination	Yes	Perhaps
Safe destination	Yes	Yes
No pressures	Yes	Yes
Overdeveloped	In some places	No
New sport and recreation opportunities to try	Yes	Yes
Plenty for kids to do	Yes	Yes
Too many kids	Sometimes	No
Casual	Yes	Yes
Too much high rise	In some places	No
Spectacular reef scenery	Yes	Yes
Chance to learn new things	Yes	Yes
Try new foods	No	Yes
Paradise	Yes	Yes/maybe
Environmentally friendly	No/perhaps	No
Romantic	Yes	Yes
Good to tell your friends about	Yes	Yes

containing words that participants were asked to match up with the two island groups. The positive phrases most closely associated with the Whitsundays are concerned with *relaxation* ('no pressures', 'casual' and 'safe'), to do with *sporting opportunities* ('lots to see and do', 'the opportunity to try new sporting and recreational activities'), *hedonism* ('good food' and 'romantic'), to do with *glamour/prestige* ('glamorous', 'prestige destination', and 'good to tell your friends about'), and a *beautiful environment* ('spectacular reef scenery' and 'paradise').

The negative images or images which failed to elicit a strong positive response were the issue of *expense* ('expensive to get to', 'high on-island costs'). The dominant image of high cost affected perceptions of other issues. The Whitsundays were seen as offering good-quality food 'but you certainly have to pay for it'. Despite the recent blitz of discounted short duration packages to the Whitsundays by the airlines, groups were reluctant to concede that good value packages were available.

Despite the fact that much of the Whitsunday region is designated national park, the area is thought of as being somewhat *overdeveloped*—it is 'overdeveloped' and has 'too much high-rise development' and is not 'environmentally friendly'. Hamilton Island was the only island consistently described as 'overdeveloped', though a number of participants associated the concept with the group as a whole.

The response to the issue of *quality service* for example might be typified by the comment in one group 'it's a bit iffy that one'. A clear perception emerged that service in Australian regions in a general sense is unreliable. The Whitsundays are seen as typical of this. One negative for the Whitsundays is that though consumers expect service in Australia to be more professional because of more stringent training, it is regarded as being less friendly and more perfunctory than in Fiji and other overseas destinations. Professionalism has the potential to be a selling point, though not immediately in view of the prevailing consumer attitudes. The Whitsundays are affected by the views that Australians have of their own country as a whole.

The Whitsundays are regarded as offering *less novelty* than Fiji, apart from the Great Barrier Reef and sporting facilities. A visit to the Whitsundays is not an 'interesting historical' or 'interesting cultural' experience. It is not 'exotic', or an 'opportunity to try new foods'. It cannot offer 'interesting local customs' or 'shopping opportunities'. One participant commented that to get 'real' culture, you would have to go up to the Torres Strait islands (home of the Torres Strait islanders, a group of indigenous Australians). The fact that Broome in Western Australia markets its multicultural background and influences is an indication that at least one Australian beach resort destination has sought to capitalise on its culture.

Whilst some respondents who had previously visited the Whitsundays commented that 'once you get to know a bit about the history of the area, it starts to get interesting', for most the Whitsundays are a place to go for total relaxation. This may be indicative of the fact that because Australia is a recently settled country by Europeans, its residents do not yet perceive its sights as offering historic interest.

A visit to the Mamanuca islands is seen as offering *greater diversity*. It offers 'interesting history' and 'interesting culture', 'lots to see and do' and 'interesting customs'. It also offers *plenty of other activities* having ample 'new sporting and recreational activities to try' and being a 'chance to try new things'. It is definitely different, being strongly 'exotic'. Nor is it seen as any less relaxing. It is seen as 'safe', 'casual' and as offering 'no pressures'. There is 'plenty for kids to do' which was favourably commented upon by families who also expressed the view that the availability of child-minding facilities and 'children-oriented' staff allowed the adults to relax. The perceived friendliness of the Fijian staff and their 'caring nature' was seen as a key attribute for dealing with children. One group commented that generally speaking, Australia (and hence Australian resorts) is/are 'safer' than overseas equivalents, but that security seemed more of an issue in Bali (security needed) than in Fiji. The Fiji military coups were only commented upon twice and then in passing. Fiji is not thought of as unsafe.

The Fiji island resorts were not associated with high-rise buildings nor with overdevelopment. On the other hand they were not seen as 'environmentally friendly' (possibly because of concerns about standards in a developing country). Participants appeared cynical about any close association between resorts and 'environmental friendliness'. The Mamanucas were regarded as offering spectacular reef scenery, but this issue did raise nationalistic impulses amongst respondents. A number commented that the Fiji reef scenery could 'not compare with what Australia has to offer' with the Great Barrier Reef. Most groups regarded Australia as having the 'biggest and the best' reef. The reality is that, though Fiji's barrier reef is certainly much shorter than Queensland's, there is greater variety of reef in close proximity to the actual resorts. The Great Barrier Reef typically involves a two-hour boat trip from the Whitsunday island resorts.

The Mamanucas were described as a 'wonderful' place for kids, 'you can let them roam entirely free with complete peace of mind'. Fiji is also regarded as lower cost than the Whitsundays. It is not 'expensive to get to', 'on-island costs' are not high, 'good value packages' are available. Groups were in agreement that the Whitsundays are a 'prestige destination' and that this is less the case of Fiji. Their hesitation (not outright objection) to this phrase is in line with the view that Fiji offers good value. One or two participants who had visited Fiji commented that it was not actually very cheap, but the Whitsundays have a greater problem than Fiji with this issue. Though the Mamanucas were not seen as being a prestige destination, they were 'good to tell your friends about', were 'romantic' and possibly (opinion divided) 'glamorous' and even 'paradise'.

The word sort revealed very few negative impressions of Fiji. Those negative impressions that did arise came up in general discussion.

Overall impressions

'It costs more to travel within Australia than to travel overseas': this oft-repeated view was clearly in evidence. The advent of airline deregulation has not yet eliminated the perception of high costs for travel within Australia. The high-profile advertising of short break packages to the Queensland islands using price leaders has had little apparent impact on *perceptions*, though some groups did mention that the deals looked cheaper than before. In contrast Fiji was depicted as a good-value destination, even though participants who had stayed in the Mamanucas commented that on-island costs were 'on a par' with those charged for meals in major Australian cities.

The perception of high costs in the Whitsundays is reinforced by the high profile of destinations such as Hayman Island. A number of participants likened their image of the Whitsundays to sitting by a large and luxurious yacht. The positive side of this is that the Whitsundays are regarded as a desirable destination, with an element of glamour and romance. The negative is that travellers are perceived as unfriendly and self-contained and that one cannot escape from 'monopolistic high on-island costs'. The perception of small, exclusive resorts offering highly personalised service such as Bedarra and Lizard islands, has translated itself across the board, though consumers do not actually believe that this is what they will receive themselves. They fear being trapped, either with people with whom they have little in common, or else in school holidays with thousands of kids. The image is a positive one, but it is the stuff of dreams and consumers seem to have difficulty relating the image to their personal experience.

Fiji still has a highly favourable image with consumers. There is no doubt in the minds of consumers that Fiji is 'exotic'. A couple of consumers had a negative perception of Fiji as somewhere that was suspiciously

cheap. The use of price leaders excluding airfares seems to have confused consumers, some of whom think the total package price can be less than say $300. Whilst prices must remain competitive, apparent excessive discounting can have a negative effect. The view that Fiji resorts are greatly overpriced (Stollznow, 1992) was not confirmed by the focus discussion groups.

Brand recognition awareness

The groups were presented with the names of the various Whitsunday island resorts to test their recognition and to explore the impressions evoked by the resort names, whether known or unknown. All groups recognised the name Whitsundays without difficulty and identified them as a group of islands in North Queensland. Most participants were aware of the general but not the specific location of the group. A number thought (incorrectly) that they are located off the north Queensland cities of Townsville and/or Cairns. The overall image is dominated by 'sailing through a myriad of green islands' with the 'Great Barrier Reef close by'. The resorts were regarded as vehicles for the experience of total relaxation in this highly coveted environment. In contrast, the name Mamanucas did not elicit recognition from any group. This was the case, even for individuals who had previously visited islands within the group. The only other regional name in Fiji which was mentioned was the Coral Coast which appears to have a stronger identity.

Despite strong awareness of the Whitsunday group and generally high recognition of certain resort names, group members had difficulty summarising the individual resort characteristics. Some resort descriptions were noticeably inaccurate. The only Whitsunday resort 'brands' with a high awareness were Hayman ('luxurious', 'exclusive', 'I would love to go there but could never afford it' and 'I picture big luxurious boats') and Hamilton ('Surfers on an island', 'up-market', 'expensive', 'didn't it burn down?'). Hamilton is the most built-up of the Whitsunday islands with two tower blocks and almost 700 rooms. Focus group participants were divided in their views on Hamilton between those who were strong supporters and those who strongly opposed what the island was seen as representing (the 'white shoe brigade' and false glamour). The focus groups confirmed the findings of previous research (Sweeney, 1991) that the Queensland (and Whitsunday) island resorts are perceived to a substantial degree as unattainably luxurious. In the case of the Whitsundays, this image is undoubtedly the result of image marketing by the two resorts Hamilton and Hayman plus the influence of yachting. The fact that the two dominant resort images are of extreme expense (in the case of Hayman) and overdevelopment plus dubious taste (in the case of Hamilton) is a problem, since it creates an overall image which is atypical of the true range of resorts on offer.

The medium-sized resorts lack brand awareness. Brampton (20 nautical miles south of the southerly boundary of the Whitsundays and not officially part of the group) is thought of as desirable but consumers are unclear about its target market. South Molle has some recognition as an 'all-inclusive' resort and as being targeted at families. For those with no awareness, it was commented that the name sounds 'boring'. The same cannot be said of Daydream which people said 'sounds good'. It did elicit some negative comment, however. A couple of individuals in different groups put Daydream in the same category as Hamilton ('overdeveloped'). Others said that the island is too small for a large resort and that as a tourist on the island one would feel 'cooped up'. It did receive praise for good quality and modern facilities, indicating awareness of its recent and total refurbishment. No single group was aware of the Club Med resort on Lindeman Island (opened in November 1992). All eight groups made comments such as 'sounds like wine' or 'alcohol'. This was despite the fact that some respondents had visited Club Med resorts overseas resulting in an apparent impression of Club Med as almost synonymous with overseas resorts. The Club Med philosophy of creating an ambience suitable for different types of consumer (for example families, couples and singles) was praised by most (it was criticised by a small number), but strictly in the context of overseas resorts. A challenge exists for Club Med to reinforce the consumer association between the concept and the island (Lindeman).

There was little apparent awareness of Hook Island Wilderness Lodge, though participants who had taken trips around the Whitsundays commented favourably on it. Finally comments were divided on Long Island, the only Whitsunday island with two separately owned and managed resorts located on it. The two are the tiny Palm Bay Hideaway (14 units) and the larger (106 units) Radisson Whitsunday resort. For two couples, Palm Bay was 'the perfect place for total relaxation', for another it was not luxurious enough ('we asked to be transferred to Hamilton'). There was generally low awareness of the Radisson property which had been taken over by the company only a year earlier and had four other recent owners. No-one had stayed at the Radisson, but each group expressed opinions to the effect 'Radisson, shouldn't they be in Florida?', 'money', 'American', 'an American hotel chain—what on earth are they doing there?' The fact that the Radisson offers arguably the lowest accommodation tariffs in the Whitsundays is

clearly out of step with consumer perceptions. The location on Long Island reinforced the North American connection for a number of respondents (another and better known Long Island is located in northeast USA). Such comments are an interesting insight into consumer expectations of a domestic destination, namely that names should sound authentic. Though both Palm Bay Hideaway and Hook Island Wilderness Lodge are promoted as being 'the way the Whitsundays used to be', there is little evidence of consumer awareness that these low key and basic alternatives are available in the Whitsundays. The Hayman and Hamilton-induced image seems to have crowded out the earlier concept of the Whitsunday resorts as places with small huts or cabins on the beach.

As previously mentioned, awareness of the individual Mamanuca resorts was low. Those who had visited various islands spoke highly of all of them. The only exception was one female respondent who had visited Castaway Island and said there were too many children. She said that if she returned it would be with a family. This comment aside, Castaway, Treasure, Mana, Matamanoa, and Plantation islands all received strong recommendations from all those who had been there. The group were divided on the names of the islands. A number expressed a preference for the 'Fijian-sounding names' (Matamanoa, Tokoriki, Tavarua, Mana) as opposed to the more anglicised (Musket Cove, Plantation, Treasure, Castaway, Beachcomber). Others said that without more information, the English names at least conveyed a sense of what they offer. The myths of the South Seas came out strongly when the names were proposed—all groups associated Musket Cove with pirates, or with an 'attractive bay infested with smugglers'. Most liked the name. Plantation Island conveyed an impression of 'the colonies' and of palm trees. Again the response was favourable. Two islands were thought to sound Japanese (Naitasi and Tokoriki), though the former also had Tasmanian connotations for one group!—Matamanoa sounded 'Polynesian or Hawaiian', Castaway 'sounds lovely and enticing' and Beachcomber and Treasure 'interesting', with the former also sounding 'relaxing'. The name Tavarua Island elicited no response with any group. The names clearly evoked the exotic, in comparison with the Whitsundays, in the sense that tourists have the prospect of experiencing 'otherness'.

When asked to compare the two lists of resorts, respondents commented that most of the Fiji destinations were called 'resorts', whilst the Whitsunday destinations were called simply 'islands'. This was not intentional on the author's part—the labels were taken directly from brochure titles—but resulted in some interesting comments. The name 'resort' may be likened to an international brand name—it is a source of reassurance in that it implies the necessary facilities will be in place. However, it is the word 'island' that conveys the romance, and perhaps the essence of the experience. Most respondents would probably prefer the use of the term 'island', provided the more descriptive promotional material provided reassurance about resort facilities. Consumers liked the 'exotic' dimension conveyed by the word 'island', whilst others felt reassured by the implication of developed facilities implicit in the word resort.

Conclusions

The conclusions of this stage of the research are of necessity tentative since the original objective and methodology was focused on idea generation and not on hypothesis testing or quantification. Nevertheless a number of potentially valuable findings can be observed.

The Whitsunday and Mamanucas examples suggest that Australians have a better knowledge of areas within their own country than of equivalent areas overseas. The familiarity of domestic destinations is simultaneously a strength and a weakness for resort and destination marketing. Familiarity provides consumers with reassurance about issues such as infrastructure, health and other services, language and currency to name but a few. The unfamiliarity of overseas destinations, however, is associated with the exotic, with 'otherness', with cultural diversity and with historical interest. Whilst the myth of the idyllic tropical island applies to some extent to both areas, it has greater power over the consumer imagination when applied to overseas South Pacific settings such as Fiji. This gives these destinations a marketing advantage.

Familiarity also seems to lead to an impression of proximity—the Whitsundays are perceived as much more easily accessible than the Mamanucas, though there is in reality little difference. This view of accessibility gives a natural advantage to the domestic destination in the short break (3–5-night stay) market. Heavy marketing of such packages has benefited Queensland relative to international destinations such as Fiji in this growing market area. The larger marketing budgets available to domestic promoters has assisted this trend.

One disadvantage faced by the domestic destination and one based on what is largely a misconception, is the view that domestic holidays cost more than equivalent international holidays. The perception is based on the previously high cost and highly regulated domestic airline environment and does not seem to have been greatly influenced, as yet, by the advent of domestic airline deregulation in 1991. There was evidence that attitudes are changing. Participants were aware of an 'increasing

number of special packages' to the Whitsundays. Whilst domestic means less exotic in the minds of consumers, the idea of the Whitsundays as a highly desirable tourist destination is growing. This is possibly symptomatic of an increasing interest in domestic holidays by Australian travellers.

The study has highlighted the minimal importance that Australians place on tour operators and/or tour wholesalers for both domestic and international holidays. This contrasts with the state of affairs in most European generating countries where tour operators play a pivotal role. The study reveals some insights into social attitudes ('Australians are more friendly when they are travelling overseas'). The preference by a number of participants for Australian resorts which attract an international clientele is an indication of the greater integration of Australia into world tourism, with the previously tiny number of overseas tourists growing rapidly and providing many Australian destinations with a more cosmopolitan atmosphere.

The study also highlights the danger of overdevelopment, even where it is geographically confined, in areas of great natural beauty. The influence of one highly developed resort (Hamilton Island) has coloured overall consumer impressions of an area which is otherwise notable for its world heritage qualities. Consumers perceive the smaller Fijian 'bure'-style resorts as more compatible with the environment, despite the lesser stringency of environmental regulations in Fiji. The whole issue of perceived and actual environmental standards is likely to play an increasing role in consumer choices between domestic and international destinations. Inaccurate imagery was also evident in the case of the Whitsundays to the extent that it was perceived to be dominated by high cost and luxurious resorts. The reality that most resorts cater to the middle of the market, has clearly been distorted by the large marketing budgets of specific exclusive resorts (Hayman and Hamilton). The resulting misconception is indicative of the dangers of individual resorts advertising heavily independent of the regions in which they are located. The need for greater collective marketing to bring about a more consistent image is evident. Despite this, caution should be observed over the choice of image to represent the destination. Queensland's current tourism logo is a palm tree, consistent with the stereotypical tropical island image. A number of respondents commented on the paucity of palm trees in the Whitsundays. In reality those that do exist were introduced, the typical vegetation is dominated by eucalypts! Images should not be based on stereotypes if consumer disappointment ensues.

The key findings of this consumer investigation will be carried forward to the subsequent survey of travel agent attitudes. This subsequent stage will enable measurement of the consistency of attitudes across the two target groups, including actual quantification of travel agent views.

References

Access Research (1992) 'Delivering the package', Australian Federation of Travel Agents, Sydney.

Australian Bureau of Statistics (1993) 'Accommodation statistics, June Quarter 1993', Australian Government Publishing Service, Canberra.

Ayala, H. (1991) 'Resort hotel landscape as an international megatrend', *Annals of Tourism Research*, 18(4): 568–587.

Barr, T. (1990) The development of the Whitsundays as a tourist destination to the early 1970's', *Studies in North Queensland History*, No. 15, James Cook University, Townsville.

Britton, R. A. (1979) 'The image of the third world in tourism marketing', *Annals of Tourism Research*, 6: 318–329.

Britton, S. (1982) 'Tourism and underdevelopment in Fiji', Development Studies Centre Monograph, Canberra.

Britton, S. and Clarke, W. (Eds) (1987) *Ambiguous Alternative. Tourism in Small Developing Countries*, University of the South Pacific, Suva, Fiji.

Butler, R. (1980) 'The concept of a resort life cycle of evolution: implications for management of resources', *Canadian Geographer*, 34(1), 5–12.

Cazes, G. (1987) 'L'Isle tropicale, figure emblematique du tourisme international', *Les Cahiers de Tourisme*, Series C, No. 112.

Craik, J. (1991) *Resorting to Tourism. Cultural Policies for Tourist Development in Australia*, Allen & Unwin, Sydney.

Dean, J. and Judd, B. (Eds) (1985) 'Tourism developments in Australia', Royal Australian Institute of Architects Education Division, Red Hill.

Dieke, P. U. C. (1993) 'Cross-national comparison of tourism development', *Journal of Tourism Studies*, 4(1): 2–18.

Dunning, J. H. and McQueen, M. (1982) 'Multinational corporations in the international hotel industry', *Annals of Tourism Research*, 9(1): 69–90.

England, R. (1980) 'Architecture for tourists', *International Social Science Journal*, 32(1): 44–45.

Gordon, W. and Langmaid, R. (1988) *Qualitative Market Research. A Practitioner's and Buyer's Guide*, Gower, Aldershot.

Hoivik, T. and Heiberg, T. (1980) 'Centre–periphery tourism and self-reliance', *International Social Science Journal*, 32(1): 69–98.

Hundloe, T., Neumann, R. and Halliburton, M. (1989) 'Great Barrier Reef tourism', Institute of Applied Environmental Research, Griffith University, Brisbane.

King, B. E. M. and Hyde, G. (1989) *Tourism Marketing in Australia*, Hospitality Press, Melbourne.

King, B. E. M. and Whitelaw, P. (1992) 'Resorts in Australia: a recipe for confusion?, *Journal of Tourism Studies* 4(1): 41–48.

Peterson, K. I. (1987) 'Qualitative research methods for the travel and tourism industry', in Ritchie, J. B. and Goeldner, C. R. (Eds), *Travel, Tourism and Hospitality Research. A Handbook for Managers and Researchers*, John Wiley, New York, pp. 433–438.

Pizam, A., Milman, A. and King, B. E. M. (1994) 'The perceptions of tourism employees and their families towards tourism. A cross-cultural comparison', *Tourism Management*, 15(1): (in press).

Queensland Tourist and Travel Corporation (1993) 'Sunlover holidays—Queensland's islands 1993-1994', Brochure, QTTC, Brisbane.

Queensland Visitor Survey (1993) National Centre for Studies in Travel and Tourism, Brisbane.

Silver, I. (1993) 'Marketing authenticity in third world countries', *Annals of Tourism Research*, 20(2): 302–318.

Smith, R. A. (1992) 'Beach resort evolution. Implications for planning', *Annals of Tourism Research*, 19: 304–322.

Stettner, A. C. (1993) 'Community or community? Sustainable development in mountain resorts', *Tourism Recreation Research*, 18(1): 3–10.

Stiles, R. B. and See-Tho, W. (1991) 'Integrated resort development in the Asia-Pacific region', *Travel and Tourism Analyst*, No. 3: 22–37.

Stollznow (Research Pty Ltd) (1990) 'Evaluation of consumer perceptions of Fiji as a travel destination', Fiji Visitors Bureau, Suva.

Stollznow (Research Pty Ltd) (1992) 'Qualitative investigation into the perception of Fiji in Sydney and Melbourne', Fiji Visitors Bureau, Suva, Fiji.

Sweeney (Brian, and Associates) (1991) 'Domestic tourism segmentation study report on the islands', Queensland Tourist and Travel Corporation, Brisbane.

Tourism Council of the South Pacific (1993) 'South Pacific tourism statistics 1992', Tourism Council of the South Pacific, Suva, Fiji.

Witter, B. S. (1985) 'Attitudes about a resort area: a comparison of tourists and local retailers', *Journal of Travel Research*.

37 Latin American tourism: the dilemmas of the 21st century

L. M. LUMSDON AND J. S. SWIFT

Tourism is not a new phenomenon in Latin America: the continent has been receiving visitors for well over two hundred years. It is unusual, therefore, that it is only during the past two decades that the region has come to be regarded as somewhere other than the domain of the wealthy or eccentric. It is only relatively recently that tourism has begun to be of significant economic importance throughout most Latin American countries.

Interest this century began at the end of World War II, but this was of a restricted nature, given the great distances between originating countries and Latin America. The basic problem of the 1950s centred around bringing together the market and the tourist offering. Intra-Latin American tourism was of a small scale, primarily due to low levels of disposable income available. Postwar economic stagnation and distance meant that Europe would be slow to develop. In contrast, the USA with its faster economic recovery and proximity to Cuba and Mexico was a far more promising prospect. The nearness of the USA to Mexico in particular (the two countries share a common land frontier) has since helped the latter to build a tourism base which continues to attract visitors in numbers far in excess of other Latin American destinations.

The next major step in international tourism development came in the early 1960s and was significant mostly in terms of the European markets. Social changes such as the popularity and status of holidays abroad, economic prosperity and the increasing acceptance of cheaper air travel meant a boom in tourism on a scale not known hitherto. Whilst Mediterranean destinations benefited greatly there was still relatively little interest in Latin America, distance and cost remaining as the two main barriers.

The 1970s, however, saw the real growth in long haul with destinations in the Far East, Australasia and the USA, the latter attracting the main focus of attention. Why did Latin America not gain from these rising trends? Instead of rapid growth there was a slow and erratic increase in visitor arrivals. The main reasons were instability and violence: they remain as fundamental question marks today.

From the 1950s through to the 1980s observers could have been forgiven for suggesting that the continent was on the brink of total collapse. Countries such as Colombia, Guatemala, Uruguay and Venezuala struggled with protracted guerrilla warfare throughout this period (Gott, 1973). Campaigns were long and fought with increasing intensity. Against this backdrop striking events such as the overthrow of governments by guerrilla groups (Cuba in 1959, Nicaragua in 1979) and military coups (Brazil in 1964, Peru in 1968, Chile in 1973, Argentina in 1975) were devastating to the economies and image of these countries. Add to this abuses in human rights, terrorist atrocities and natural disasters and it is surprising that the infant tourism sectors survived the turmoil.

Another major barrier to tourism development in the 1980s was the rampant hyper-inflation, experienced particularly in Argentina and Brazil. Argentinian inflation peaked at 4924% in 1989 (ABECOR, 1991) and Brazilian inflation reached 1038% in 1988 (ABECOR, 1989). This factor, in addition to those mentioned above, led to failing confidence that Latin America could ever be a major player in world tourism.

Ten years on there are grounds for greater optimism. Within the last five years, elected civilian democracies have replaced military dictatorships throughout most of the continent. Furthermore, these democracies have embraced economic reforms including extensive privatisation programmes. There would appear to be a genuine willingness to halt corruption. This process should be of benefit to tourism in the long term as it signals closer cooperation between government and private enterprise.

Current trends

An analysis of visitor arrivals (Table 37.1) shows the relative importance of the market as a whole, and the gradual rise in numbers towards the end of the 1980s, while exhibiting the erratic pattern of arrivals at some destinations. Supporting evidence suggests that tourist flows emanate mainly from neighbouring countries. For example, continued efforts by Argentina to attract overseas

Table 37.1 *Arrivals of tourists from abroad, 1981–1992 (selected countries (thousands))*

Country	1981	1985	1986	1987	1988	1989	1990	1991	1992
Argentina	1145	1503	1774	1472	2119	2492	2666	2870	2900
Bolivia	155	127	133	147	167	194	208	221	222
Brazil	1358	1734	1934	1929	1743	1272	1361	1352	1474
Chile	405	418	581	575	624	797	952	1349	1400
Colombia	477	784	732	541	829	733	784	857	800
Ecuador	245	238	267	274	347	306	327	365	363
Paraguay	267	263	371	303	284	279	291	361	350
Peru	335	300	304	330	359	334	298	232	200
Uruguay	928	1031	1149	1047	1035	1240	1267	1510	1550
Venezuela	200	269	311	338	373	412	446	598	550
Mexico					14 142	14 964	17 176	16 560	17 587

Source: World Tourism Organisation (1993).

visitors from Europe and North America have only had a moderate degree of success. The main market for Argentina is still Latin America (Table 37.2), and, within this, Uruguay is the most significant (Table 37.3). In turn Uruguay and Chile receive visitors mainly from neighbouring Argentina (Schluter, 1991).

The problem with intraregional development is that while significant in numbers the spend per capita is far less than with long-haul visitors. Furthermore, Lumsdon and Swift (1993) highlight the increasing problems faced by destinations, especially 'gateway cities', that deal with growing numbers of visitors: 'Tourism authorities are torn between volume and lesser spend in the local economy, or fewer long-haul visitors and a higher spend per capita'.

Table 37.2 *The world market for tourism to Argentina, 1991*

Region/area	Number of visitors to Argentina	As a percentage of total
Latin America	2 323 019	81
Europe	290 447	10
USA & Canada	139 857	4.9
Rest of World	117 023	4.1

Source: Dirección Nacional de Migraciones (1992).

Table 37.3 *Tourist arrivals—Argentina: periphery countries, 1991*

Country	Number of visitors	As a percentage of total
Uruguay	979 141	34.1
Chile	571 254	19.9
Brazil	303 414	10.6
Paraguay	257 245	9.0
Bolivia	70 760	2.5
Total	2 181 814	76.1

Source: Secretaria de Turismo de la Nación (1991).

Table 37.1 also emphasises the decrease in visitors to a number of Latin American countries at different times during the past ten years. There has been a sustained decline in Peru, for example, during recent years. The main factors underlying this instability are those mentioned above, but particularly the volatility of exchange rates and the potential threat of violence, which thwart potential investment for tourism and taint visitor perspectives. This is the heritage of tourism development in Latin America and regardless of the ongoing process of democratisation these factors will combine to retard plans to stimulate rapid growth in the short term.

Most commentators suggest that international tourist arrivals worldwide will continue to grow at 3–4% per annum despite natural disasters, regional wars and greater environmental awareness. In this context, it is necessary to examine the factors underlying the erratic growth rate in Latin America.

Geographical location

Despite widening horizons, Latin America is still considered to be distant from its current long-haul markets of Europe and the USA (10–16-hour flight times), and more so from some of the potential markets of the future such as Japan and Australasia. Despite technological advances in air transport, it is doubtful whether flying time could be reduced significantly during the next decade. This will be a limiting factor when targeting, for example, growth markets such as Japan.

Economic realities

The problems of Latin American economies are complex and cannot be addressed in depth in this paper. In general terms, the condition of most Latin American economies could well be described as poor, with the possible exception of Argentina and Chile. A recent survey undertaken by *The Economist* suggested that Brazil was still in the grip of hyper-inflation (1000% in 1993) while Peru was considered more stable at just over 50% (*Economist*, 1993a). A recent *Financial Times* assessment of the economic performance of Brazil commented that the country was 'struggling to stabilise its economy' (Barham and Foster, 1994) and even Chile, described as the model economy of Latin America in the late 1980s, is suffering: 'there are signs that the world economic downturn is starting to catch up with Chile. . . . There remains the nagging worry that Chile, the self-styled "Dragon" of Latin America, may be running out of puff' (Pilling, 1993).

Despite the continuous problems of the region, many observers suggest that the current removal of bureaucracy and the trend towards privatisation will regenerate local economies: 'Privatisation is the key ingredient in Latin America's plan to promote economic growth; only under the discipline of free-market capitalism will corruption and inefficiency that now runs rampant in many of its basic industries be eliminated' (Chu, 1993).

Political realities

The past five years has seen a period of relative calm in Latin America during the ongoing process of democratisation. There is peace but in some instances it is fragile. Until January, 1994, Mexico had been regarded as a stable democracy, governed by the institutionalised revolutionary party, and interested more in oil and tourism revenues than old revolutionary slogans. A minor insurrection occurred in Chiapas (*The Economist*, 1994) and was reported widely by the media prior to the main booking season with the predictable consequence of a downturn in visitors in 1994. Several pundits suggest that this regional revolt could be symptomatic of an underlying rift in the country. Political stability is delicate in several other Latin American countries, including Argentina where President Carlos Menem is attempting to change the constitution to ensure a second consecutive term of office, and this has generated an undercurrent of unrest. The events are more isolated than in earlier decades but point to an uneasy state of democracy which could well deteriorate in the short term.

Lack of tourism infrastructure

The level of tourism infrastructure varies from country to country, but is of particular concern in destinations which are specifically courting long-haul visitors, such as Brazil and Argentina. For example, attitudes of visitors to the capital city and major gateway of Argentina,

Buenos Aires, are gathered on a regular basis by the Buenos Aires Tourist Authority and most comments relate to the inadequacy of the infrastructure:

—Lack of hygiene in toilets and lack of public toilets
—Expensive taxi charges, especially from Buenos Aires airport
—A lack of long-distance public telephones, and overall lack of telephonic communications
—Poor state of repair of city streets and pavements
—Traffic congestion and noise
—Uncomfortable public transport[1]

Argentina is not unique in this respect. An overview of Latin American infrastructure in *The Economist* notes that: 'In Montevideo and Mexico City, businessmen fed up with inefficient public telephones have embraced cellular technology. In Buenos Aires and Caracas, private courier services compete vigorously with the state-run postal system' (*The Economist*, 1993b).

Empirical research conducted amongst tour operators[2] revealed a number of interesting insights regarding the level of infrastructure at several destinations. Operators rated the level of public transport in Cuba as very poor, and in Bolivia and Argentina as poor. Levels of infrastructure were cited as one of the worst aspects of Honduras and Guatemala. The same respondents were critical of hotel accommodation in several countries, specifically El Salvador, Guatemala, and Honduras. However, it should be pointed out that the problem has been identified and is being tackled in some countries, specifically Argentina (McDermott and McDermott, 1993) and in the mega-resorts of Mexico (Jesitus, 1993).

Market structure

The long-haul market is dominated by the airlines in three ways. Firstly, they determine the frequency and hence capacity on the long-haul routes. They are also directly or indirectly involved in tour operation. Aerolineas Argentinas, Iberia, Varig and Viasa, for example, work closely with tour operators and in some cases have their own packages. They also join forces to offer country and cross-continent airpasses. Thirdly, the airlines spend more heavily than others to promote travel to Latin America.

Most of the tour operators, however, are based in the generating countries and those dominating the marketplace offer a short- and long-haul portfolio from which their customers choose. There is a limit to the number of destinations which can be offered commercially and Latin America is not represented well in their brochures in comparison to the more established Caribbean islands or

Florida. The exception is Mexico where both the capital and resorts such as Acapulco or Cancun feature strongly.

If tour operators are the gatekeepers of long-haul travel then Latin American tourism providers have failed to gain their confidence completely. As mentioned above, initial research suggests that tour operators expect a much improved infrastructure and a less negative image. Many respondents commented that the greatest assistance received was from their own agents rather than government organisations, and many were particularly disparaging about Latin American tourism departments, as evidenced in the following three quotations:

—'Government organisations are useless'.
—'Government Tourist Boards are not helpful in terms of supporting literature'.
—'The Governments are very slow in offering help and assistance. Any encouragement that does help comes from the private sector'.

There was mixed opinion, however, regarding Peru. One explanation might be that smaller, specialist operators tend to spend more time in Latin America and therefore have greater opportunities to gain information and contacts at first hand. In this respect they are more positive in their appraisal although they still have doubts about the infrastructure available at major gateway cities such as Buenos Aires, Caracas, Lima and Rio de Janiero, the pivotal points on their multi-destinational tours.

Poor image

A poor image is of especial concern to tour operators, for continuous negative media attention can destroy years of investment in a market. The media reports mixed images of Latin America, but most are negative—the drug barons in Colombia, recent accounts of hundreds of youths rampaging across Copacabana Beach at Rio, the devastation of shanty towns in Caracas and the quelling of an uprising in Mexico are four recent listings from years of negative reports. Peru has suffered the most and has lost much of its USA market following the coverage of guerrilla warfare of the 'Sendero Luminoso' there. Peruvian tourism officials estimate that Britain is one of its most important markets, but in recent times the Peruvian Tourist Office in London has only been opening on a limited basis, so poor has been the interest in holidays to this beautiful country. Even the visual impact of Machu Pichu, colonial Cuzco and Cochabamaba in the High Andes fails to overcome the perceived dangers of travel.

Increasing competition

The major external threat to Latin America is the opening up of existing and new markets elsewhere in the world. Two examples are Australasia and Eastern Europe. The development in the old Soviet bloc will be slow, but from the Baltic states to Moscow tourism development is being planned. Thus, despite sustained growth worldwide, long-haul destinations will find it increasingly difficult to compete by the turn of the century. Not only will the range of destinations worldwide be far wider and accessible but also there is evidence that short-haul locations are repositioning themselves (such as Spain in Europe) to counter the loss of trade.

It is easy to generalise about Latin America as a region, for many of the problems do occur throughout the continent. But the pattern of development has been different from country to country, and it is important to recognise this. Uruguay, for example, has little natural potential for tourism in comparison to Colombia, which has great potential but is bedevilled by terrorism and drug-related violence.

Mexico is by far the market leader in Latin America. It retains one undeniable advantage: it borders the USA so has an achievable market within a relatively close proximity. From the 1970s onwards the government of Mexico has involved itself heavily in the generation of tourism, not only in the USA market but also in Europe. This has been achieved primarily through the direction of the Mexican Ministry of Tourism with its public face of 'Secretaria de Turismo' (SECTUR). Despite the criticisms levelled against the Ministry, i.e. inflexibility and ineffective use of resources, this state-dominated sector has delivered several major new products, such as the integrated resorts of Cancun, Ixtpa, Los Cabos, Huatulco and Loreto, which have been coordinated by the National Trust Fund For Tourism Development (FONATUR). The appeal of these resorts are to the USA mass market, but they are also prompted by way of European tour operators. Integrated resorts are not universally accepted as a positive development, the main criticism being that they are wealthy tourism enclaves separated from poor host communities. The sentiment is expressed in the following travel column:

> Say Hello to Cancun and bid adios to Mexico. You can play golf or tennis, enjoy watersports, pay 2 dollars for a cup of coffee, try on a pair of Gucci shoes, and let the doorman at the Hard Rock pour tequila down your throat to help pass the time in the queue. (Wickers, 1989)

The Mexican government has enjoyed greater recognition for the development of new cultural packages such as the Mayan Trail, and its new policy of 'Apertura' aims to bring private capital and skills to the marketplace, thus building on the successes to date.

Such priming activity has not been so prevalent elsewhere. Argentina like so many Latin governments has been willing to establish a bureaucracy to plan and promote tourism, but the emphasis has been primarily on private sector development. In Argentina the 'Secretaria de Turismo de la Nacion' is responsible for establishing an ongoing framework for tourism development. Its 'Plan de Marketing Estrategico, 1989' sets out the long-term objectives of tourism development in Argentina (Secretaria de Turismo de la Nacion, 1988):

A. To increase the numbers of foreign visitors to Argentina
B. To increase the per capita expenditure of such tourists within Argentina
C. To encourage repeat visits from these tourists
D. To break down the seasonality of tourism
E. To improve the national transportation and communication structure
F. To foster greater links between government and private enterprise in the development of tourism.

This is inevitably a broad-brush plan and regional and city tourism authorities are expected to develop more detailed strategies within an overall framework. This is where the main problem lies. Resources are limited and action is slow to follow.

Planning for the future

The following issues need to be resolved if tourism is to flourish in Latin American Countries.

Economic development

Tourism cannot generate economic gain in isolation. In fact, several commentators suggest that tourism follows economic success in other sectors. Much of Latin America is undergoing an extensive programme of privatisation, especially Argentina, Brazil, Chile, Colombia, Mexico and Uruguay. Tourism relies heavily on sectors which are going through the process of privatisation such as financial services, transport and public utilities including communications. It is a process fraught with the dilemmas of the management of change and this has undoubtedly affected tourism. Telephonic communication, for example, is very limited in many cities. In trite terms, it is not easy to 'phone home.

Privatisation has almost meant that tourism has slipped down the order of priorities for many governments. Government officials give credence to tourism as being important in terms of international status, image projection and foreign exchange, but in comparison to other emerging sectors of the economy tourism it is regarded as more ephemeral. It is only the Mexican government that has laid out plans which have been executed with a degree of persistence. It is not typical of Latin America, and its success in lifting tourism from such a low base to a recognisable international dimension is a considerable achievement. Elsewhere, there are plans but few resources to implement them. It is hard to penetrate beyond the rhetoric.

If Latin America is to succeed, then more concerted government backing will be required to invest in tourism infrastructure and to develop partnerships with the private sector. It is also important that they need to be accountable and offer a real return for the destinations as well as the investors of capital. There will also be a need to act in a more collective way as a region, rather like the ASEAN group of countries in the Far East.

Nature and type of tourism

The main question is what type of tourism should be developed? The issues of carrying capacities, host community involvement and cultural diffusion are important, but to date the agenda has focused more on spend per visitor and encouragement of tourism which requires little infrastructure but is highly priced to the customer. The adventure holiday or eco-holiday fits into this category. Several critics have pointed to the dangers of developing such holidays in an unplanned manner and across several countries. The scale is undeniably small at present but the environment which is being visited is extremely sensitive to tourist flows. Manaus is a classic example. While eco-holiday companies readily support the concept of conservation in the forest the impact is being noted. When does such tourism become large-scale? As Jesitus (1992) notes: 'unchecked ecotourism can devastate animal habitats and primitive cultures and perhaps upset entire nations'.

The problems exist elsewhere too. The attraction of tourism in Ecuador has been the rich wildlife adventure of the Galapagos islands but the dangers of numbers in recent years has redirected attention to the jungle or 'selva' regions of Ecuador which are in many respects equally fragile. National Parks are planned, but it looks as if they will follow tourism development. Such dilemmas will require resolution before the pace of tourism demand outstrips conservation measures.

Mass resort tourism

The argument has led some to suggest that the best way to develop tourism is by way of the development of integrated resorts built to Western standards and mass market expectations. Such resorts would also isolate tourists from host communities and sensitive areas, but would perhaps also deprive them of their reason for visiting the country in the first instance. It is also argued that existing destinations (rather than purpose-built new ones) should be developed to cope with increased numbers of overseas visitors but also to stimulate intraregional tourism. There is a very real danger that such destinations would lose their identity through the rapid influx of visitors. A case in point here is Uruguay which is periodically overwhelmed by tourists: 'With nearly two million tourists expected this year, Uruguay is only a million short of its goal of one visitor per inhabitant' (Honore, 1993). The local identity that Uruguay resorts once had is rapidly being sacrificed to satisfy beach-based tourists from Argentina: 'Nothing about Punta del Este is Uruguayan. At least not during the southern hemisphere's summer, when the sleepy resort on Uruguay's Atlantic Coast turns into a sprawling playground for Argentines' (*The Economist*, 1993c). Such development in recent years has prompted the Uruguayan tourist authorities to seek other markets, particularly from the USA and Europe. As the Deputy Tourism Minister observed: 'The problem is that we have few direct flights to Europe or the US, so travellers tend to pass us by' (Crawford, 1990). Tour operators are less favourable towards Uruguay's potential, commenting that the country generally has little to offer the long-haul traveller. There will be a tendency for countries to polarise their efforts either towards regional resort development or to encourage long-haul tours. This will require a greater coordination between tourism authorities than at present if it is to succeed.

Image projection

In the short term the major issue to overcome is image deterioration. The brokers of the marketplace need to be assured that the stories of violence and disorder are becoming less frequent. They need to be assured that petty crime and pollution in Latin America is no worse than elsewhere, no more than a consequence of urban dwelling.

Government officials often project an official image of such destinations but these are markedly different to the perceptions of tour operators. Countries such as Panama and Colombia suffer from drug-related images whilst Mexico, Dominican Republic and Costa Rica are generally associated with mass tourism from the USA. Bolivia, Brazil, Colombia and Peru have a poor image with regard to urban crime and associated violence. The authorities are desperately attempting to counter such images by projecting more positive aspects of their resorts and gateways through promotion. In some instances, firmer action has been taken to present a safer environment. For example, the city of Rio de Janeiro recently launched a 'Tourist Police Force' of some 475 officers, whose main task is to patrol the beaches and sea front (Vanvolsem, 1993).

If Latin American destinations are to break out of the declining spiral of negative media coverage, they need to address the issues first-hand in their own cities and then they need to manage a reversal of image through advertorial and editorial in overseas media. They also need to maintain a direct and genuine contact with tour operators. Such dialogue needs to commence as soon as possible and with firm support packages if tour operators are not to retrench to a position of minimal commitment to Latin America.

Conclusions

Tour operators are confident that demand will increase in Latin America but with one proviso—that the infrastructure improves considerably. This seems unlikely in the short term, for resources are being directed to other parts of the economy, particularly public utilities such as gas (Argentina and Chile); the management of such dramatic changes in the economic structure is likely therefore to take longer to implement than initially anticipated. In many respects, the problem of image with both tour operators and their customers presents the greatest barrier to development in the coming years. The first stage in improving this image has begun with the process of democratisation, but there is still a considerable amount of work to be undertaken to bring about a change in hardened attitudes formed over the last quarter of a century.

Latin America will slip into the 21st century without having created an impression in the long-haul market. It will, nevertheless, witness a modest growth in the intraregional and domestic markets as pockets of industrialised, urban areas gain greater wealth from the privatisation and stimulation of local economies. The irony is that many of the *nouveau riche* will continue to fly to destinations such as Europe or Australia (Tarul, 1993) for their main sojourn, leaving others to partake in beach holidays at home.

Notes

1. This, and other information relating to tourism surveys in Buenos Aires, is based on unpublished data held by the Subsecretaria de Turismo, within the Municipalidad Central de Buenos Aires. One of the authors was given access to this material at the Ministry Building and gratefully acknowledges the help provided by the Buenos Aires Tourist Authority.
2. The data relating to European and North American tour operators comes from empirical research undertaken by the authors during 1994.

References

ABECOR (1989) 'Brazil', ABECOR Country Report (December).

ABECOR (1991) 'Argentina', ABECOR Country Report (August).

Barham, J. and Foster, A. (1994) 'Teething troubles continue to nag at Mercosur market', *Financial Times*, 17 January.

Bergsman, S. (1992) 'Direct flights to tap Mexican market', *Hotel and Motel Management*, 207(21).

Chu, F. J. (1993) 'The rising tide of privatization', *The Bankers Magazine*, 176(1): 58.

Crawford, L. (1990) 'Waiting for the Europeans', Survey on Uruguay, *Financial Times*, 15 October.

Doulton, R. (1989) 'Nurturing the "Mexico Set"', Survey on Mexico, *Financial Times*, 13 October.

The Economist (1993a) 'A survey of Latin America', *The Economist*, 13 November.

The Economist (1993b) 'Infrastructure in Latin America: public services, private pesos', *The Economist*, 17 July.

The Economist (1993c) 'Snob value', *The Economist*, 13 February.

The Economist (1994) 'The clash in Mexico', *The Economist*, 22 January.

Gillette, B. (1993) 'Best Western set to take advantage of upswing', *Hotel and Motel Management*, 208(8).

Gott, R. (1973) *Rural Guerrillas in Latin America*, Penguin, Harmondsworth.

Honore, C. (1993) 'A Mickey Mouse site for URU Disney', *The Observer*, 20 June.

Jesitus, J. (1992) 'Unchecked tourism can be devastating', *Hotel and Motel Management*, 207(7).

Jesitus, J. (1993) 'Mega resort expected to boost Mexico's tourism', *Hotel and Motel Management*, 208(2).

Lumsdon, L. M. and Swift, J. S. (1993) 'The development of tourism in Latin American gateway cities', Paper presented to the VII General Conference of EADI, Berlin, 15–18 September 1993.

McDermott, J. and McDermott, B. (1993) 'Buenos Aires builds hotel supply', *Hotel and Motel Management*, 208(5).

Pilling, D. (1993) 'Latin America's dragon running out of puff', *Financial Times*, 19 August.

Schluter, R. G. (1991) 'Latin American tourism supply: facing the extra-regional market', *Tourism Management*, September: 222.

Secretaria de Turismo de la Nacion (1988) 'Argentina naturalmente: plan de marketing estrategico, 1989', Secretaria de Turismo de la Nacion, Buenos Aires.

Tarul, R. (1993) 'Os brasileiros se dao bem na Australia', *Jornal do Brasil*, 14 April.

Vanvolsem, W. (1993) 'Dance with danger in Rio', *Daily Telegraph*, 20 February.

Wickers, D. (1989) 'Gems among the high rises', *Sunday Times*, 8 October.

38 Developments in European cultural tourism

G. RICHARDS

Introduction

Cultural tourism is currently in vogue in Europe, and is frequently invoked in both urban regeneration strategies and rural development plans. The advantages of cultural tourism as a development tool are its reputation as a growth market, its place-specific nature, its role in image building, and the 'upmarket' nature of most cultural tourists (Richards, 1993). The resulting convergence of cultural tourism policy throughout Europe is evident at all policy levels, from the European Community (1992) down to local government (Myerscough, 1991). Forecasts of growing interest in cultural heritage, more urban tourism and more short-break tourism (Gratton, 1992; Van der Borg and Costa, 1993) seem likely to ensure the future of cultural tourism as a major sector of the European market.

Academic interest in cultural tourism, however, has developed somewhat more slowly. A recent review of the cultural tourism literature (Richards, 1993) indicated that there are relatively few studies which concentrate specifically on cultural tourism, and even fewer which can provide data on the development or significance of cultural tourism. This dearth of literature can partly be traced to the understandable definitional problems surrounding the subject (Bonink, 1992), and the resulting difficulties in identifying and measuring cultural tourism consumption and supply (Richards and Bonink, 1992a). One unfortunate consequence of this lack of analysis is that the causes of the apparent rapid growth of cultural tourism have been largely ignored. Cultural tourism is usually treated as a 'new market' or 'new product' (Myerscough, 1988; Frangialli, 1990) devoid of any social, economic, historical or political context. In the absence of such contexts, cultural tourism can easily be viewed as an overnight fashion or fad, in spite of its long history (Thorburn, 1986). Indeed, one researcher has suggested that the term 'Kultur Tourismus' was only used in Germany after re-unification in 1990 (Narhstedt, personal communication, 1993).

The argument presented here is that cultural tourism is more than a simple market trend. In order to identify the reasons why cultural tourism is currently the centre of so much attention, the phenomenon must be set in a wider social and political context. More specifically, the growth of cultural tourism can be traced to the processes of economic restructuring which have stimulated cultural development strategies in cities across Europe (Bianchini, 1990).

In their recent analysis of the role of cultural development in urban regeneration in Europe, Bianchini and Parkinson (1993) identify a number of trends in cultural policies, which can also shed some light on the motives for cultural tourism development. Firstly, increased leisure time and leisure spending by consumers in the 1960s and 1970s led to greater expenditure by city governments on leisure provision and cultural services. This has increased the range of cultural facilities available, and created a professional infrastructure with a vested interest in the expansion of cultural provision. Secondly, national policies of decentralisation created a climate in which 'city decision-makers saw the development of cultural policies as a valuable tool in diversifying the local economic base and achieving greater social cohesion'. The need for economic restructuring also marked a change in policy emphasis from the social and political concerns of the 1970s to economic and urban regeneration priorities in the 1980s. The promotion of urban culture therefore became driven by employment creation, as part of an attempt to 'cushion the negative effects of the painful transition from an industrial to a post-industrial economy' (Booth and Boyle, 1993). Finally, the realisation that culture could be used as a tool to achieve political objectives led to a move away from the narrow 1950s identification of culture with the high arts, towards a wider view in the 1970s, embracing both high and popular culture forms.

While Bianchini and Parkinson limit their analysis to cities, it is clear that economic restructuring is also having an influence on cultural development in rural areas. Cultural tourism has been identified as a major potential source of economic development and employment generation for rural areas in the EC (ECTARC, 1989), and this role is confirmed by the recent LEADER rural development initiative, which contains a substantial cultural tourism element (LEADER, 1993).

The growing economic emphasis in cultural policy means that cultural tourism forms an attractive area of development for urban and rural areas alike. Local economies need to attract inward investment and expenditure from outside the region in order to expand and diversify the economic base. Cultural tourism not only injects new money into the local economy through direct spending by tourists, but can also stimulate investment through improving the image of a city or region (Myerscough, 1988). Cultural tourism is also an important means of offsetting the high cost of providing cultural facilities, and cuts in public spending during the 1980s have made this rationale still more attractive. If the core funding for museums and other cultural facilities is declining, then other sources of income must be sought to fill the gap. Tourism is an obvious source of revenue, even though the degree of market orientation required to maximise tourist revenue is often resisted by the museums themselves (Cossons, 1989).

The developments described above have a number of implications for the analysis of cultural tourism in Europe. The first implication is that cultural tourism may not simply be a market trend related to greater consumer interest in heritage or culture, but can also be partly explained as an example of 'supply-led' demand, stimulated by the growth in cultural opportunities across Europe. Second, expansion of cultural facilities requires a concomitant expansion of market demand if visitor levels at existing attractions are to be maintained. Market expansion can be achieved either through attracting new participants by increasing the democratisation of culture, or by increased frequency of participation by existing cultural visitors. Thirdly, if cultural tourism is to effectively fulfil the new economic aims set for it, then the pressure to commercialise cultural facilities will increase.

Thus there are a number of key questions which need to be answered in respect of cultural tourism in Europe. Is the market for cultural tourism actually increasing, as many previous studies have claimed? Is any growth in cultural tourism being produced by an extension of participation to new groups of cultural tourists, or by more frequent consumption by existing participants? Is the cultural tourism product becoming more commercialised? This article attempts to answer these questions utilising new research on the scale and composition of cultural tourism in Europe.

The cultural tourism literature

The cultural tourism literature is very fragmented, because of the wide-ranging nature of the subject matter. The term 'cultural tourism' has been applied to every kind of cultural event, from opera (Hughes, 1986) to pop concerts

(Milestone, 1992). A review of definitions (Richards, 1993) suggests that cultural tourism can indeed encompass almost any form of cultural consumption, although in practice the term has been applied almost exclusively to elements of 'high culture'. The development and marketing of cultural tourism in Europe has been linked mainly to established cultural forms, such as museums, art galleries, historic houses, theatres and concert halls. Forms of 'popular' or 'mass' culture, such as pop music or football, rarely find a place in cultural tourism development (Boyle and Hughes, 1991). Until recently, therefore, the concept of cultural tourism seems to have been relatively limited in application, but there are now signs of the term being more widely applied. In the UK, for example, cultural tourism came to be closely associated with 'heritage' during the 1980s, thanks largely to the efforts of the British Tourist Authority. In the last few years, however, arts organisations have been showing more interest in tourism (Bonink, 1992), particularly as a means of augmenting declining public sector funding.

While the definition of cultural tourism may gradually be widening, the nature of the cultural audience has tended to remain narrow and elitist. Because of the basic high culture identification of cultural tourism, the participants tend to be drawn largely from the highly educated, high-income sectors of the service class (Hughes, 1987). This view is confirmed by research on cultural audiences for UK museums (Merriman, 1991) and arts events (Arts Council of Great Britain, 1991). Research in The Netherlands indicates that the major barrier to cultural participation is lack of cultural capital (Bourdieu, 1984), and to a lesser extent income (SCPO, 1991). Tourists coming from outside Europe, for example from the USA, also tend to conform to the highly educated, high-income profile (Berroll, 1981). Comparison with previous studies of cultural participation in Europe (e.g. Bourdieu and Darbel, 1991; Ganzeboom, 1989) indicates that the profile of cultural visitors has changed little in 30 years with respect to educational and income-related variables.

The term 'cultural tourism' therefore effectively identifies a group of high-income, highly educated consumers. Myerscough (1988) characterised the cultural tourism market as 'new, upmarket, expanding and fed by high levels of satisfaction and willingness to repeat the trip'.

If the profile of the cultural tourism market is clear, the picture of cultural tourism supply in Europe is far more fragmented. Because the organisations of cultural facilities is usually divided between 'heritage' and 'arts' sectors (Bonink, 1992), integrated information on cultural tourism supply is limited. An attempt was made by the Irish Tourist Board (1988) to review the supply of cultural tourism attractions on a European scale, but lack of comparative data meant that their database was compiled using information from guide books. There is also a lack of longitudinal data on the supply of cultural attractions in Europe. Individual national studies indicate that the supply of museums has increased rapidly in recent years (ETB, 1992), but again there is little comparative information available.

The ATLAS research project

The literature on cultural tourism reveals three major weaknesses of previous research. Firstly, studies of cultural tourism have often lacked a clear or operational definition of cultural tourism, which makes comparative research in the area difficult. Secondly, the research has been highly fragmented, dealing either with specific sectors in the cultural tourism market, or with particular facilities or regions. Thirdly, very little longitudinal research is available to allow trends in cultural tourism consumption or supply to be undertaken.

The Cultural Tourism Project undertaken by the European Association for Education in Tourism, Leisure and the Arts (ATLAS) attempted to address these deficiencies by collecting data on a European basis using a standardised definition of cultural tourism and a standardised questionnaire survey of 6400 cultural visitors across the European Community. The research was funded by DG XXIII of the European Commission as part of their initiative to develop rural and cultural tourism. The basic aim of the project was to provide a consistent measure of the scope and importance of cultural tourism in the EC, and to identify the nature of cultural tourist. The research is intended to establish a baseline against which future changes in cultural tourism consumption can be measured. More details of the research methods and data collected are given in Bonink and Richards (1992), and an analysis of the methodological problems involved in such transnational research is provided in Richards and Bonink (1992b).

The ATLAS project defined a cultural tourist as 'the temporary movement of persons to a cultural attraction outside their normal area of residence, with the intention to satisfy their cultural needs' (Bonink and Richards, 1992). For the purposes of measuring the volume and significance of cultural tourism, however, the analysis was based on visits to specific cultural attractions, which enable visitor numbers to be analysed. Although

the definition could be applied to a wide range of cultural institutions, the research reported here has tended to concentrate on the traditional 'high culture' heritage and arts attractions, since these tend to be most prominently featured in cultural tourism development. Extensive developments are also taking place in the area of 'popular culture' and tourism (Cohen, 1991), but there is currently relatively little evidence available on these developments.

The following sections utilise data from the ATLAS project to analyse the current nature of cultural tourism in Europe, and its relationship to wider issues of cultural and economic development.

The cultural tourism market

One of the key tasks for the ATLAS research project was to analyse the scale and composition of the European cultural tourism market. This was attempted through a combination of questionnaire surveys and collection of secondary data on cultural attendances. The attendance data provided a picture of the total cultural visit market, and surveys of cultural visitors allowed a crude assessment of the proportion of cultural tourists to be made. The questionnaire survey also enabled a profile of the cultural tourists to be assembled.

The questionnaire survey revealed that a high proportion of cultural visitors could be characterised as cultural tourists. About 20% of the cultural visitors interviewed could be characterised as 'specific cultural tourists', with a cultural motive for visiting the attraction. The average cultural tourist visited three cultural attractions during their stay. The ATLAS study thus estimated that there were about 25 million specific international cultural tourism trips in the EC in 1992 (Richards and Bonink, 1992a). The proportion of cultural tourists in the ATLAS survey is broadly consistent with previous estimates of the proportion of tourists visiting cultural attractions. In the UK, for example, the proportion of overseas visitors to museums in 1990 was 22%, and the proportion of overseas visitors attending historic buildings was 35% (Bonink, 1992).

An assessment of changes in the number of cultural tourists over time can only be made with reference to historical data on cutural visits. The ATLAS database has enabled a picture of cultural attendances in the EC to be compiled from different national sources. Although these sources vary in terms of their coverage and form (e.g. in some cases museums only, in others monuments and art galleries as well), the combination of these sources does allow an assessment of the general trends in cultural

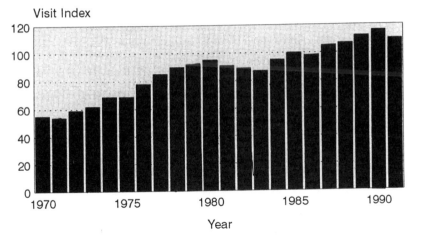

Figure 38.1 *Cultural visits in Europe (Visit index: 1985 = 100)*

visits over the last 20 years (Figure 38.1). The data indicate that cultural visits in Europe increased sharply in both the 1970s and the mid- to late-1980s. Cultural visits declined during the recession of the early 1980s, and the indications are of a further decline during the economic downturn of the early 1990s. The picture that emerges is of generally strong growth, which has weakened only in periods of economic adversity.

This general pattern is also evident to varying degrees at national level. In the UK, for example, heritage attraction visits grew by 9.5% between 1985 and 1992. Attendance growth was particularly strong in the late 1980s, but weakened between 1990 and 1992 because of the UK recession. In The Netherlands, visits to museums increased by almost 50% between 1980 and 1991 (Bonink, 1992), and performing arts attendances grew by 22% over the same period (CBS, 1993). In Italy, visits to cultural attractions increased by 18% between 1974 and 1991. Attendance growth was strong in the late 1970s (+34% 1974–1979), but attendances actually fell by 4% during the 1980s. Similarly, visits to cultural attractions in France rose strongly in the mid-1970s, but museum visits fell by a third in the late 1970s and early 1980s. The peak museum attendance in 1989 was therefore only 18% higher than 1978, the peak year during the 1970s. Almost all the countries studied show a fall in cultural visits in the early 1990s, concurrent with the economic downturn. The UK and The Netherlands also exhibited weaker growth in the 'arts' component of cultural tourism than for 'heritage' attractions such as museums. In his examination of the supposed growing interest in opera in the UK for example, Hodgson (1992) finds that while sales of

opera recordings have grown, attendance of opera performances has not. Cultural tourism growth is therefore evident in most countries, but does not seem to be as strong or as uniform as some authors have suggested.

This analysis raises some interesting questions about the nature of cultural tourism demand in Europe. For example, is cultural tourism actually a growth sector of the tourism market as a whole? What is the source of the market growth in attraction visits? Is growth produced by a widening of participation across all social groups? Is the growth in cultural visits stimulated more by tourists than local residents? Are international tourists responsible for a greater proportion of the growth in demand than domestic tourists? Not all of these questions can be answered at present, because the data required to answer them is not yet available. However, the following analysis provides some pointers as to where the answers might lie.

Although cultural tourism has clearly grown rapidly across Europe, there is less evidence to suggest that it has grown any faster than tourism demand in general. A comparison of the index of cultural visits with an index of international tourism demand in Europe, for example, shows a very similar pattern of growth (Figure 38.2). In The Netherlands, although 'historic buildings, churches and old cities' became increasingly important as a motivation for holiday trips during the 1980s, a growth of 38% in museum visits between 1985 and 1991 was closely matched by a 37% rise in domestic tourism over the same period (Bonink, 1992). In England visits to historic properties (+24%) and museums (+23%) grew more slowly than visits to tourist attractions as a whole (+35%) between 1976 and 1991 (ETB, 1992). The proportion of overseas tourists among UK cultural visitors

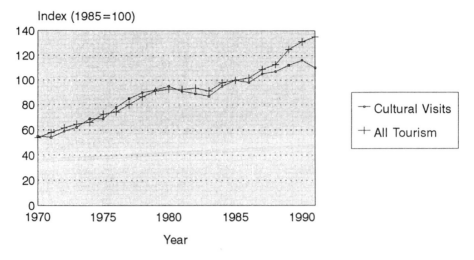

Index (1985=100)

Figure 38.2 *Culture and tourism in Europe (European indices: 1985 = 100)*

seems to have remained broadly steady, with the percentage of overseas visitors to UK museums being 19% in 1985, 19% in 1989 and 22% in 1990 and 1992 (Bonink, 1992; Hanna, 1993). Some studies have also demonstrated that growth in cultural attendances may be linked closely to special events. For example, the European City of Culture event led to a growth in cultural visits in the Glasgow region in 1990 and in Dublin in 1991 (Myerscough, 1991; MacNulty and O'Carroll, 1992). In the case of Glasgow, there was a 15% drop in cultural visits to the region in 1991, immediately following the Year of Culture event. This suggests that cultural tourism may produce significant tourism growth related to specific attractions or events, but there is currently no conclusive evidence that cultural tourism is becoming a more important segment of the European market in relative terms.

The absolute growth in the cultural tourism market might, however, be expected to produce changes in the composition of cultural participation. Cultural tourism is usually developed to bring new visitors into a specific region, and often attempts to broaden access to cultural infrastructure for both residents and visitors. If these aims were being achieved, one might expect changes in both the social and geographic distribution of cultural visits in Europe.

The ATLAS cultural visitor research, however, found little evidence of a broadening market for cultural tourism. The cultural visitors interviewed in all countries tended to be well-educated and from higher socio-economic groups. Over 80% had some form of tertiary education and almost a quarter had been educated to postgraduate level. Only 3.2% of the total visitors

interviewed were unemployed. Almost a third of inter-viewees came from the 20–29 age group, which is related to the high proportion of students in the sample. In addition, there was a strong tie to cultural occupations among visitors. Almost 12% of the total sample worked in occupations linked to heritage and museums, 10% worked in the performing arts and almost 18% were connected with the visual arts. For respondents classified as 'specific cultural tourists' the proportion having an occupational link with the cultural industries rose to 50%.

Not surprisingly, therefore, cultural visitors also tended to exhibit a high degree of continuity in their cultural consumption patterns at home and during tourism trips. The majority of cultural visitors visit museums and monuments both in their home area and on holiday, and they are slightly more likely to visit performing arts attractions at home than on holiday (Figure 38.3). The level of regular cultural consumption is much higher for cultural tourists than among the population as a whole. For example, almost 80% of English cultural tourists interviewed abroad indicated that they regularly visited museums in the UK, compared with 22% of the UK population as a whole (Mintel, 1991). Cultural visitors also tend to take more holidays than the population as a whole. Over 70% of respondents had taken at least one long holiday in the previous 12 months, significantly higher than the level of holiday participation for the EC as a whole (SCPO, 1991).

A comparison with the work of Bourdieu on the arts museum audience (Bourdieu and Darbel, 1991) indicates comparatively little change in audience composition over the past 30 years. Bourdieu's survey of European museums

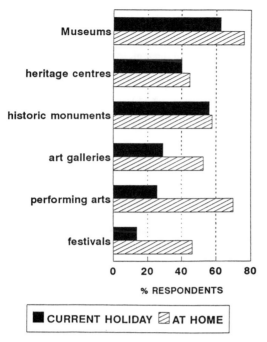

Figure 38.3 *Cultural attraction visits, on holiday and at home*

Table 38.1 *Attendance at UK cultural attractions by socio-economic group, 1991*

	Socio-economic group (%)	
	ABC1	C2DE
Performing arts	59	29
Museums and galleries	63	36
Frequency of museum visits		
4 or more times/year	27	16
2–3 times/year	41	37
1 visit or less	31	45

Source: Arts Council of Great Britain (1991).

indicated that frequent museum visitors tended to be well-educated and from professional occupations, and about 40% of visitors were students. He also found that 'arts specialists' were particularly likely to visit art museums in France. The broad similarities between the results of the two surveys indicates that little has changed in the composition of the cultural audience. In addition, the ATLAS surveys indicate that Bourdieu's original findings may be applicable to a wide range of cultural attractions, and not just museums of art. Evidence from museum and gallery surveys in the UK over the past 10 years show that visitors to all types of cultural institutions are still predominantly catering to the service class (Bonink, 1992; Merriman, 1991; de Mul; 1992, Mintel, 1991).

Some studies have indicated a widening base for the cultural audience over the past 30 years. In The Netherlands, the proportion of the population visiting museums has risen from 30% of the population in 1974 to 47% in 1991 (CBS, 1993), and in the UK Merriman found that over 80% of the population have visited a museum at some time in their lives. The proportion of performing arts attenders has also shown some increase, from 34.2% of the UK population in 1987 to 35.7% in 1990 (TGI, 1992). Frequent, cultural consumers, however, come predominantly from the higher socio-economic groups. In the UK, for example, museum visitors from the AB group visit museums much more frequently than

other museum visitors (Table 38.1). In The Netherlands the broadening of the cultural audience which was evident until the early 1980s has now ceased, and the performing arts audience in particular has become more 'elite' in recent years (Knulst, 1989). Merriman (1991) concludes that 'museums split the population into those who possess the culture to perceive them as a leisure opportunity and make sense of a visit, and those who do not'. In terms of cultural tourism, of course, the ability to take advantage of cultural tourism opportunities is further constrained by access to the resources needed to travel. Thus although cultural tourism may have helped to boost the number of cultural visitors, it may have done little to broaden the base of the cultural visitor market.

The picture that emerges of European cultural tourists is of frequent culture consumers, with a high level of education, often employed in cultural occupations, and with a high propensity to travel. It seems that the apparent growth of cultural tourism over the past 20 years has not broadened the basic market beyond the service class (Hughes, 1987), but rather has been fed by more frequent cultural tourism consumption on the part of already frequent culture consumers. Cultural tourism, therefore, does not seem to be based on the democratisation of culture, but rather on the continued monopolisation of high cultural forms by specific groups in society.

The supply of cultural tourism attractions

The problems of defining cultural tourism also make it difficult to identify cultural tourism attractions. An initial attempt to assess the scale of cultural tourism supply in the EC relied on Baedeker guide books to provide the classification of cultural attractions. This initial assessment identified large disparities in the supply of cultural attractions. For example, France, Germany, Italy and the UK accounted for 66% of the attractions listed in the inventory.

Over the past 20 years, the supply of cultural tourism attractions has grown strongly in Europe as a whole. If the supply of museums and other cultural attractions in The Netherlands, Italy, Germany, Portugal and the UK is compared for example, all show a significant increase in supply, with growth rates ranging from 10% to 97% over the last ten years or so. Data from periodic surveys by Unesco (1974–1992) also indicate an overall growth in museum supply across Europe as a whole in the last 20 years.

If the supply of cultural attractions in these countries is used to construct a combined index of supply growth, then a broad comparison can be made with changes in cultural visits over the same period (Figure 38.4). The indications are that the supply of cultural attractions has outstripped growth in cultural tourism demand in the last decade. In The Netherlands, the supply of theatres grew by 42% between 1970 and 1986, even though audiences for subsidised theatre fell by 50% over the same period (Knulst, 1989). Supply growth was particularly strong during the late 1980s. In The Netherlands, for example, the number of museums grew by 11% between 1980 and 1985, and then by 30% from 1985 to 1990 (CBS, 1993). A similar pattern is evident in Germany, where the number of museums grew by 21% from 1982 to 1986, and by a further 33% between 1986 and 1990. In England, investment in heritage and museum development grew significantly during the 1980s to reach 10% of total tourism investment by 1989 (ETB, 1991).

Much of the growth in supply has also been located away from the traditional tourist centres, as local governments have sought to harness cultural development for economic and image-building aims. In England, 60% of museum and heritage investment between 1987 and 1991 was located in the regions (ETB, 1991). In France, for example, the number of communes with at least one museum grew from 1437 in 1980 to 2009 in 1990 (Ministère de la Culture, 1991). Such localised cultural development can be traced to the fragmentation and regionalisation of cultural consumption noted by Robins (1991).

It seems, therefore that much of the growth in the supply of cultural attractions has been prompted by public-sector-led spending on cultural development. Over the past 10 years, cultural budgets in many European cities have grown substantially, and many of these developments have been specifically aimed at cultural tourists (Bianchini and Parkinson, 1993). In France, for example, cultural spending per inhabitant in the 'Grandes Villes' increased from 500FF in 1978 to 1225FF in 1990. Within this total, capital costs grew twice as fast as running costs (Ministère de la Culture, 1991). The impact of increased regional emphasis in cultural policy on participation has been mixed, however. In The Netherlands, extensive cultural tourism development in the province of Friesland produced a 16% increase in cultural attendances between 1990 and 1992, compared with a 15% increase for the area around Amsterdam. In Sweden, a specific policy aimed at broadening access to culture saw the market share of regional museums fall from 62% of visits in 1974 to 57% in 1985.

Public sector investment in cultural development during the 1980s has been largely linked to economic goals, such

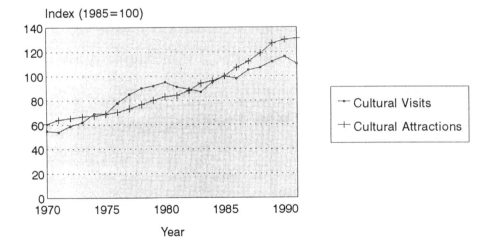

Figure 38.4 *Cultural supply and demand (European indices: 1985 = 100)*

as generating income and employment. Public sector investment has also begun to have strings attached. Cultural institutions must now adapt themselves to the needs of the market, and reduce their overall reliance on public sector funding.

The commodification of cultural attractions

Signs of the transformation of cultural institutions 'into a commodity called "heritage"' (Hewison, 1987) abound. In the UK, for example, the government has shifted responsibility for the Royal Palaces from the Department of the Environment to a non-government agency which has specific financial targets to meet. In The Netherlands, national museums are in the process of being transferred to the private sector. The Dutch Minister responsible for museums recently stated: 'Museums are going to operate in a more business-like way. That is particularly important for increasing the quality of the museum product. It is also necessary to help them survive in the market for culture and leisure, where the competition is becoming even fiercer' (Tweede Kamer, 1991:5).

In Italy, the Ronchey Act of 1993 has laid the foundations for making museums more 'entrepreneurially efficient' by introducing performance indicators, organisational reforms and private sector involvement. Such moves towards privatisation and market orientation in cultural attractions have produced complaints that culture is becoming increasingly commodified as part of a growing 'heritage industry' (Hewison, 1987), and is being moulded to the needs of the 'enterprise culture' (Corner and Harvey, 1991). In order for cultural attractions to become 'commodified', of course, a growing army of willing consumers is required. Although the basic market trends suggest that consumption of cultural attraction products is growing, we also need to examine the extent to which this consumption is actually more commodified as a result.

If the use of cultural attractions across Europe is indeed becoming more commodified, then one would expect to find evidence of increased revenue generation through entry charges and visitor expenditure, and there should also be a greater number of attractions attempting to replace subsidies with visitor-generated income.

There is evidence from diverse sources to suggest that such trends are occurring across Europe. Admission charges at historic properties grew by 71% from 1987 to 1992, double the increase in the retail price index. Even larger increases were recorded at popular public sector attractions, such as those owned by English Heritage and the Royal Palaces (Hanna, 1993). One effect of rising admission prices has been to boost the proportion of self-generated income at state-owned attractions. In the national museums, for example, self-generated income rose from 12% to 21% of revenue between 1986/87 and 1990/91 (de Mul, 1992). In The Netherlands, the average admission price for museums increased by almost 78% between 1980 and 1990. At the same time, the number of museums offering free admission fell from 27% to 22%. As in England, admission revenue has risen, from 8% of revenue in 1980 to 13% in 1989. In Italy, admissions to museums offering free entry fell by 24% between 1987 and 1991, while admissions to paid entry museums rose by 17% over the same period.

Entry prices, are only one measure of increasing revenue generation by cultural attractions. Some studies also indicate that income from merchandising, catering and other secondary spend sources is also growing. For example, public historic attractions increased admission revenues by between 1% and 5% between 1990 and 1991, but revenue from catering and merchandising grew by up to 15% (ETB, 1992). As Hewison (1991:165) notes: 'Thus museums are being forced into the market-place. If they remain free at the point of entry they must do more to justify their existence by the volume of visitors passing through their doors, and once inside, these must be exploited through the sale of souvenirs, refreshments, and so forth'.

As Kelly (1991) has suggested, however, a simple introduction or strengthening of the pricing mechanism does not automatically mean that consumers will blindly go along with the process of commodification. There has been some evidence of consumer resistance to commodification, and examples can also be found in the area of cultural attractions. Although a recent UK survey suggested that the majority of visitors do not object to increased charging in principle (Mintel, 1991), consumer behaviour indicates an avoidance of charging on the part of many cultural tourists. For example, the 6% increase in museum visits in the UK between 1990 and 1992 can be almost wholly attributed to a substantial rise in admissions at the British Museum, which has no entry charge (ATLAS Database, 1993). Attendances at national museums which introduced admission charges in the 1980s fell by up to 40%. In 1992, paid admissions at National Trust properties fell by 10% in 1992, while free admissions for members remained constant (Hanna, 1993).

It should be noted, however, that even in the face of advancing commodification, public funding is still by far the largest source of income for cultural attractions. Over the EC as a whole 66% of museum income is provided from state funds, and in Italy the proportion rises to almost 90% (Di Battista, 1993). Even though 'independent' museums have provided the biggest source of museum supply growth in the UK in recent years, over 50% of the funding for these institutions comes from the public sector (Hewison, 1991).

Discussion

The review of cultural tourism in Europe has identified a number of trends which appear to relate to the wider context of economic and social restructuring in Europe, rather than a simple tourism market demand trend.

There is no doubt that the overall demand for cultural tourism, as measured by visits to cultural attractions, has increased significantly across the EC. In spite of temporary reversals caused by adverse economic conditions or a drop in general tourism demand, cultural tourism in the EC appears to have at least doubled over the past 20 years. Although this growth is substantial, it is no greater than the growth in general tourism demand in the EC. Claims that cultural tourism is a new market or a particularly fast-growing sector of the tourism market cannot therefore be substantiated by the evidence currently available.

In fact, there are signs that the cultural tourism market may be less fruitful than many authors have suggested. As the supply of cultural attractions has been growing faster than demand over the past 5 years, there is now far more competition for the cultural visitor than was the case a decade ago. In addition, research on the profile of cultural visitors does not suggest much widening of the cultural market, but more frequent cultural participation by a relatively small group of consumers. The engine for growth in cultural tourism over the past 20 years has therefore been rising incomes, education levels and leisure-time availability among the service class. In this regard, cultural tourism is no different from other expanding areas of out-of-home leisure consumption over the past 30 years (Knulst, 1989).

Evidence from The Netherlands in fact suggests that although cultural visits have been increasing as an element of tourism consumption, cultural motivations for such trips are less important. Jansen-Verbeke (1988) demonstrates that while 10% of city trips involve a museum visit, visits to museums are a primary motive for only 1% of all city trips. This suggests that growth in museum visits can at least partly be explained by the growing supply of museums, which presents more opportunities for 'casual' museum visiting.

The growth in cultural consumption opportunities can be traced to the development of cultural policies in Europe over the past 30 years. In the 1960s and early 1970s cultural development was stimulated by a desire to achieve 'vertical equalisation', or a more even distribution of cultural consumption through all social groups (Ganzeboom, 1989). Vertical equalisation was attempted largely through subsidies to lower entry prices and support more 'democratic' forms of cultural reproduction. In the late 1970s and 1980s the growth of regionalism within Europe has placed increasing emphasis on 'horizontal equalisation' (Ganzeboom, 1989), or the attempt to distribute cultural consumption more evenly across all areas of a country.

Cultural policies oriented towards horizontal equalisation coincided in the 1980s with the growing use of culture as a tool for economic development, particularly in regional economies in Europe (Bianchini and Parkinson, 1993). The result has been a dramatic growth in the supply of cultural attractions in all areas of Europe. The growth in supply has been particularly strong in the late-1980s as cultural tourism became identified as an attractive source of income to finance economic restructuring. The result is that the supply of cultural attractions is now outstripping growth in demand, sharpening competition for cultural tourists.

This aggregate analysis of cultural consumption hides the fact that the demand for museums and other 'heritage' attractions often behaves very differently from the performing arts. In France heritage attractions increased their audiences by 60% between 1983 and 1989, while performing arts attendances fell by 8%. Italy is one of the few countries where growth in performing arts attendances has outstripped heritage demand, but this can be explained by the lamentable state of Italy's museum service (Di Battista, 1993).

Knulst (1989) explains the stronger growth of heritage attendance in The Netherlands in terms of the greater 'cultural competence' required from arts visitors compared to museum visitors. Museums and other heritage attractions allow visitors to structure their own experience, whereas arts performances are indivisible products requiring simultaneous production and consumption, and offering fewer concessions to individual taste. The ATLAS research has also demonstrated that the consumption of arts performances by tourists in Europe is additionally limited by information barriers. Not only do foreign visitors often face linguistic barriers to arts participation, but they also often lack the information required to access specific events. Museums and other heritage sites are usually open year-round, and can overcome language barriers through multilingual signs and guides. Arts performances are usually of limited duration, often need to be booked in advance, and can present substantial linguistic barriers to participation or enjoyment. The only significant exception seems to be the UK, where arts performances can cater for a substantial overseas English-speaking market.

There are signs, however, that the gap between 'heritage' and 'arts' tourism is beginning to narrow. As economic motives augment or replace cultural motives for the development and maintenance of cultural facilities, there are growing signs that arts organisations are joining the heritage industry in its search for tourist-generated income (Bonink, 1992). The work of Myerscough (1988, 1991) on the economic impact of the arts in the UK, for example, has prompted several new developments in 'arts tourism' in recent years (ETB, 1993).

Conclusion

This review has indicated that cultural tourism is neither a 'new' nor a particularly fast-growing sector of the European tourism market. What is new about cultural tourism is the way in which economic motives for cultural development have replaced cultural motives over the past 30 years. The new emphasis on economic development can be linked to the economic restructuring of the European economy and the growing competition for inward investment amongst the regions of Europe.

Cultural policies developed in the 1960s and 1970s aimed at the horizontal or vertical equalisation of cultural consumption have been replaced by cultural policies framed as an adjunct to economic policy. The target group for these new cultural tourism policies is usually the frequent culture-consumer among the service class, the group that earlier cultural development tried to avoid. The heritage market in particular has therefore benefited from rising incomes and leisure-time availability among the service class in Europe which has fed other areas of tourism demand. Cultural tourism appears to have been identified by tourism policy makers as an effective way of targeting high-spending, frequent tourism consumers (Richards, 1993). In order to attract these tourists, the development of cultural infrastructure, or the adaptation of cultural facilities for tourism promotion has increased in the 1980s, particularly in the regions.

The resulting expansion of the supply of cultural attractions and events has produced an element of supply-induced demand growth, particularly in the 'heritage industry' (Hewison, 1987). The fact that different sectors of the wider cultural tourism market have behaved markedly differently over the past 20 years makes it dangerous to generalise a wider 'cultural tourism industry'. Although pressures to cut public spending are enforcing a similar market orientation and commodification rationale on all cultural institutions, it is still clear that the reactions to these pressures still differ widely. Museums which require smaller amounts of 'cultural capital' (Bourdieu, 1984) or 'cultural competence' (Knulst, 1989) for their consumption appear to have been more successful at adapting to changing leisure and tourism demand in Europe. Arts tourism, by contrast, remains a more exclusive product, and the supply of arts attractions is still weakly articulated with market demand.

References

Arts Council of Great Britain (1991) 'Omnibus arts survey', London.

ATLAS Database (1993) Department of Leisure Studies, Tilburg University, The Netherlands.

Berroll, E. (1981) 'Culture and the arts as motives for American travel', Proceedings 12th Annual Travel and Tourism Research and Marketing Conference, Salt Lake City, pp. 199–200.

Bianchini, F. (1990) 'Cultural policy and urban social movements: the response of the "New Left" in Rome (1976–85) and London (1981–86)', in Bramham, P., Henry, I., Mommaas, H. and van der Poel, H. (Eds), Leisure and Urban Processes, Routledge, London, pp. 18–46.

Bianchini, F. and Parkinson, M. (Eds) (1993) Cultural Policy and Urban Regeneration: the West European Experience, Manchester University Press, Manchester.

Bonink, C. (1992) 'Cultural tourism development and government policy', MA thesis, Rijksuniversiteit Utrecht.

Bonink, C. and Richards, G. (1992) 'Cultural tourism in Europe', ATLAS Research Report, University of North London.

Booth, P. and Boyle, R. (1993) 'See Glasgow, see Culture', in Bianchini and Parkinson (1993), pp. 21–47.

Bourdieu, P. (1984) Distinction: a Social Critique of the Judgment of Taste, Routledge & Kegan Paul, London.

Bourdieu, P. and Darbel, A. (1991) The Love of Art: European Art Museums and their Public, transl. [from the French] by Caroline Beattie and Nick Merriman, Polity Press, Cambridge.

Boyle, M. and Hughes, G. (1991) 'The politics of "the real": discourses from the Left on Glasgow's role as European City of Culture, 1990', Area 23(3):217–228.

CBS (Centraal Bureau voor de Statistiek) (1993) Cultureel Jaarboek, CBS, The Hague.

Cohen, S. (1991) 'Popular music and urban regeneration: the music industries of Merseyside', Cultural Studies, 5(3):332–346.

Corner, J. and Harvey, S. (Eds) (1991) Enterprise and Heritage, Routledge, London.

Cossons, N. (1989) 'Heritage tourism—trends and tribulations', Tourism Management 10(3):192–194.

Di Battista, M. (1993) 'Arts museums as enterprises? The case of Italian museums', Paper presented at 2nd International Conference on Arts Management, Paris, France.

Dietvorst, A. G. J. (1992) 'Cultural tourism and time–space behaviour', Paper presented at VII ELRA Congress, Bilbao, Spain.

ECTARC (1989) Contribution to the Drafting of a Charter for Cultural Tourism, European Centre for Traditional and Regional Cultures, Llangollen, Wales.

ETB (English Tourist Board) (1991) 'Tourism investment report', ETB, London.

ETB (English Tourist Board) (1992) 'Sightseeing in 1991', ETB, London.

ETB (English Tourist Board) (1993) *Arts Tourism Marketing Handbook*, ETB, London.

European Community (1992) 'Community action plan to assist tourism', *Official Journal of the European Community*, L 231:26–32.

Frangialli, F. (1990) Closing Statement at the WTO Seminar on the Integration of Tourism in Europe, Istanbul, Turkey.

Ganzeboom, H. (1989) *Cultuurdeelname in Nederland: een empirisch-theoretisch onderzoek naar determinanten van deelname aan culturele activiteiten*. Van Gorcum.

Gratton, C. (1992) 'A perspective on European leisure markets', Paper presented at LSA/VVS Internationalisation and Leisure Research Conference, Tilburg, The Netherlands.

Hanna, M. (1993) 'Monitoring heritage', *Leisure Management*, October 21–22.

Hewison, R. (1987) *The Heritage Industry: Britain in a Climate of Decline*, Methuen, London.

Hewison, R. (1991) 'Commerce and culture', in Corner and Harvey (1991), pp. 162–177.

Hodgson, P. (1992) 'Is the growing popularity of opera in Britain just another nineties media myth? Market research provides the answer', *Journal of the Market Research Society*, 34(4):405–418.

Hughes, H. (1986) 'Tourism and the live performance of opera and classical music', *Journal of Arts Policy and Management*, 2(3):12–16.

Hughes, H. (1987) 'Tourism and the arts: a potentially destructive relationship?', *Tourism Management*, 10(2):97–99.

Irish Tourist Board (1988) *Inventory of Cultural Tourism Resources in the Member States and Assessment of Methods Used to Promote Them*, European Commission DG VII, Brussels.

Jansen-Verbeke, M. (1988) *Leisure, Recreation and Tourism in Inner Cities*, Katholieke Universiteit, Nijmegen.

Kelly, J. R. (1991) 'Commodification and consciousness: an initial study', *Leisure Studies*, 10(1):7–18.

Knulst, W. (1989) *Van Vaudeville tot video*, Sociale en Cultureel Planbureau, Rijswijk, The Netherlands.

LEADER (1993) 'Tourism at the service of rural development', LEADER, Brussels.

MacNulty, P. and O'Carroll, C. (1992) 'Visitors to tourist attractions in Ireland in 1991', Tourism Development International, Dublin.

Merriman, N. (1991) *Beyond the Glass Case: the Past, the Heritage and the Public in Britain*, Leicester University Press, Leicester.

Milestone, K. (1992) 'Popular music, place and travel', Proc. Internationalisation and Leisure Research Conference, Tilburg, The Netherlands.

Ministère de la Culture (1991, 1992) *Development Culturel*, Nos 90, 92.

Mintel (1991) 'Cultural visits', *Leisure Intelligence*, 3:1–25.

de Mul, S. (1992) 'Museums on the move', Dissertation, Tilburg University, The Netherlands.

Myerscough, J. (1988) 'The economic importance of the arts', Policy Studies Institute, London.

Myerscough, J. (1991) 'Monitoring Glasgow', Glasgow City Council.

Richards, G. (1993) 'Cultural tourism in Europe' in Cooper, C. P. and Lockwood, A. (Eds), *Progress in Tourism, Recreation and Hospitality Research*, 5, Wiley, Chichester, pp. 99–115.

Richards, G. and Bonink, C. (1992a) 'Cultural tourism development in Europe', Proc. 5th Council of Europe Routes de la Soie Conference, Macclesfield, UK.

Richards, G. and Bonink, C. (1992b) 'Problems of transnational research', Proc. Internationalisation and Leisure Research Conference, Tilburg, The Netherlands.

Robins, K. (1991) 'Tradition and translation: national culture in its global context', in Corner and Harvey, pp. 21–44.

SCPO (Social and Cultural Planning Office) (1991, 1993) *Social and Cultural Report*, SCPO, Rijswijk, The Netherlands.

TGI (1992) 'Target Group Index', London.

Thorburn, A. (1986) 'Marketing cultural heritage: does it work within Europe?', *Travel and Tourism Analyst*, December: 39–48.

Tweede Kamer (1991) 'Toegankelijkheid en behoud van het museale erfgoed', *Tweede Kamer vergaderjaar 1990–91*, 21,973, no. 1.

Unesco (1974–1992) *UNESCO Yearbook*.

Van der Borg, J. and Costa, P. (1993) 'The management of tourism in cities of art', *Tourist Review*, 2:2–10.

39 European business travel and tourism

R. DAVIDSON

During the 1980s, business travel emerged worldwide as one of the fastest-growing and most profitable sectors of the travel and tourism industry. Travel for business-related purposes—in the widest sense, including meetings and conferences, trade fairs and exhibitions, as well as incentive travel—was recognised as being one of the most effective ways of doing business, seeking out new markets, exchanging ideas, and communicating with customers and colleagues alike.

However, it is a characteristic of the business travel industry that it tends to follow very closely the fortunes of the economy as a whole—much more so than leisure tourism does. And of all the various forms of business travel, general business travel—getting employees from A to B, from sales presentation to contract signing, and so on—is the type which represents the most accurate indicator of general economic wellbeing.

Therefore, the recession which has characterised the European economy of the 1990s has had far-reaching implications for the structure and texture of the general business travel market of this continent.

This paper examines the profile of the European business travel market during these recessionary times, and investigates companies' attempts to control their spending on business travel, in response to the crisis. Conversely, the business travel industry's own response, in the form of its efforts to maintain or expand its share of the market, is also examined.

Introduction

The importance of business travel to the European tourism industry cannot be overestimated. Europe still ranks as the foremost private sector business travel market in the world, outspending the USA and all other regions. However, the period of rapid increase in spending on business travel during the late 1980s was brought to an end by the recession, which has stubbornly set in to cloud over the economy of every European country.

But even before the Gulf War and the onset of the current economic climate, there were signs that companies were starting to turn the spotlight on travel costs, which had long been a poorly tracked item in their annual balance sheets. One of the earliest signs of this increased scrutiny of travel spending was witnessed by the airlines who, even at the end of the 1980s, were already seeing evidence of downtrading from 'first class' and 'business class' travel. The last profitable year for European airlines was 1989. Between 1989 and 1992, European scheduled airlines lost about $4 billion, despite the fact that actual passenger numbers continued to rise: between 1980 and 1992, according to the Association of European Airlines, traffic as measured in passenger kilometres more than doubled (Branegan, 1993).

Oversupply was partly to blame for these losses, as airlines had been adding seats just as fast as, or even faster than, traffic had been growing. For example, among the major European carriers, traffic in 1992 actually grew by 11.5%; but capacity increased at the same pace, leading to the situation where only 56.8% of seats were filled. The only solution proposed by the airlines was a series of price wars, as they began lowering their fares in the effort to maintain market share. Consequently, revenues on a passenger-kilometre basis were badly hit, resulting in a marked reduction in yield. Europe's yields on international routes were 30% lower in 1993 than they were in 1985 (Branegan, 1993).

The airlines' problems were compounded by a severe drop in the European business community's demand for the high-profit first class and business class tickets which traditionally have subsidised cheaper 'economy' seats. Despite the European Community's airline deregulation measures, intra-European airfares remain among the world's most expensive, on a cents per kilometre basis. Downtrading in terms of class of travel was, therefore, a logical step for business travellers whose budgets were coming under pressure. If the airlines looked upon this new trend with dismay at the end of the 1980s, they would have been even gloomier if they had known that this was to be no short-term economy measure on the part of their best customers, but rather a foretaste of a radical restructuring of the entire business travel market.

In a sector dogged by a dearth of reliable intelligence and a lack of hard statistical information on overall supply and demand, it is extremely difficult to quantify trends with any degree of accuracy. Statistics from the Association of European Airlines portray the situation in one sector. However, another respected source of information in this field is the annual American Express European Business Travel and Expense Management Report, which gives a comprehensive insight into developments within the business travel market as a whole.

The 1993 European Business Travel and Expense Management Report published by American Express Europe Ltd was the result of by far the largest such research project ever carried out in Europe. Individual market surveys were carried out in ten European countries: Belgium, France, Germany, Hungary, Italy, The Netherlands, Spain, Sweden, Switzerland and the UK.

Business travel expenditure in Europe

In the countries surveyed for this report, private sector companies were found to be spending a total of $141 billion between them on business travel—almost exactly the same figure as for 1992. On average, 31% of this is spent abroad, on international business travel. The largest market is Germany, which spent over $38 billion, or 28% of the total; but the UK and France show significant expenditure levels, with $30.3 billion and $25.3 billion respectively.

What is this money spent on? Figure 39.1 gives the breakdown of spending by category, showing that airfares represent by far the largest item of expenditure, at 26% of the total, followed by hotel bills and fuel/kilometrage.

Business travel, after buildings and salaries, now ranks as the third largest cost facing most companies, accounting for 4.8% of the total costs of the average European company. But, apart from Hungary, which was expanding from a small base, only UK companies showed any significant increase in expenditure in 1993—and this was a recovery from the heavily depressed levels of 1991 and 1992. Sweden, Germany and Switzerland recorded sharp falls, while French spending on business travel remained static for the second year running.

European countries spend on average 2.5% of their gross domestic product on business travel, although there are wide variations in these percentages. The Swedes and the British spend proportionately more of their GDPs on this than anyone else (3.8% and 3.5% respectively), because of their geographical locations, which require air travel to get to their main markets, and the highly international character of their economies.

Who travels on business?

On average, 27% of employees of European companies travel on business at some time of the year. 9% of all employees travel on business abroad, with small countries such as Switzerland, The Netherlands and Belgium having the highest proportion of international business travellers among their workforces.

The ratio of travelling employees to total staff numbers also varies from industry to industry. In general, there

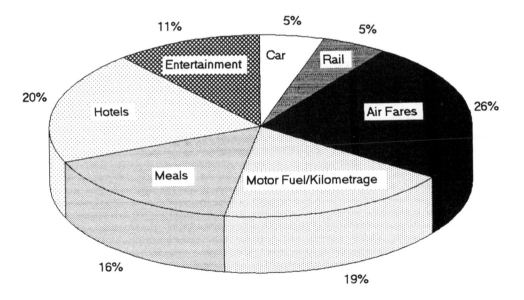

Figure 39.1 *Business travel by type of expenditure (American Express, 1993)*

is a high percentage of business travellers in the workforces of transport and communications, wholesale and retail trade and the energy and chemicals sectors.

Field and sales staff represent the largest single group in terms of their numbers, accounting for 27% of all business travellers. Although senior managers may be more frequent travellers, they account for a relatively small group among the population of all of those travelling for work-related purposes. However, the situation is different with regard to *international* travel, where senior management do represent a significant proportion (27%) of all business travellers. Middle and junior management account for a further 26% of all international business travellers.

An increasing proportion of those travelling on business are women. Over Europe as a whole, the average proportion of women among business travellers is 13%. Most countries are close to this figure, but the UK has the highest proportion of businesswomen on the move, at 23%. This percentage has doubled in four years, but there is still a long way to go in order to match the situation in the USA, where 40% of business travellers are women. Nevertheless, as European economies continue to shift away from manufacturing towards the service sector, where most women travellers are concentrated, the situation seems set to change.

Company measures to control travel costs

The recessionary business climate over most of the continent has led management of European companies both to tighten up their control of business travel expenses and to pursue greater value for money in this area. There is a general mood of austerity and belt-tightening, with an inclination to look for economies in all aspects of business travel.

The 'Business travel and expense management report 1993' published by American Express Europe Ltd (American Express, 1993) states that, in that year, 64% of companies had taken initiatives to control costs and manage their travel budgets more skilfully. The most commonly used techniques are the following.

Travel policies

A clearly written, comprehensive travel policy is seen by a growing number of employers as the cornerstone in controlling and reducing their travel-related expenses. Such policy documents provide staff with a vital point of reference to determine their employers' philosophy on business travel and enable them to organise their travel within clearly defined guidelines. 60% of European companies with ten or more staff regularly travelling on business now have a written travel policy. (On the other hand, 35% have only informal guidelines for staff and 5% have no travel policy at all.) In general, as might be expected, the larger a company is, the more likely it is to have a formal travel policy.

Travel policies most commonly contain specific rules governing the following aspects of business travel.

Air travel

56% of the companies surveyed by American Express were found to exercise some control of their employees' use of air travel. For long-haul flights outside Europe, only 12% of directors and senior managers now fly first class. The most usual class is business (or club) class for this level of management. Middle and junior managers are more likely to travel in economy. But there are some interesting variations in air travel policies between countries. Sweden, France, The Netherlands and Hungary allow very few senior managers to fly first class, but at the other extreme, one in five Spanish and Belgian managers still flies first class on long-haul flights.

The survey also showed that a remarkably high proportion of senior managers were now flying economy class on long-haul flights. 40% of Spanish senior executives were expected to travel in this way. Other economy-minded countries were The Netherlands (36% of senior managers), Italy (31%), Sweden (30%) and France (26%).

Hotels

48% of European companies have specific rules relating to the hotel accommodation which their employees are entitled to use while travelling on business. These normally deal with the highest grade of hotel allowed for the various levels of management.

Car hire

50% of companies regulate their employees' use of hire cars in some way. Of these, 56% require employees to use a designated car hire company, 37% insist on prior authorisation, and 19% permit car hire in an emergency only.

Special discounts and corporate rates

Just over half of all European companies have some sort of discount arrangement or special rates from travel suppliers—most usually hotels, airlines and car hire companies. But, countries tend to fall into two groups: those where it is very usual to have special rates (Sweden,

Italy, Spain, France and the UK) and those where only a minority of companies do so (Belgium, Germany, The Netherlands and Switzerland).

Those companies which spend the most on travel are also the most likely to have negotiated special rates. Only 42% of companies with under 20 staff travelling on business have these, while the proportion rises to 70% for companies with 50 or more roving employees.

A good example of a company finding itself well-placed to reap benefits from airlines and hotels in the form of discounts is Shell International, which has chosen to use this particular cost-saving strategy in preference to downtrading. The company's outlay on air tickets is £12.5 million a year, and on overseas hotels alone £5–6 million. Clearly, such levels of spending speak volumes around any negotiating table, and Shell International has been able to strike some very advantageous deals with travel suppliers (Skapinger, 1993).

In the UK, at the height of the recession, there were concerns in the business tourism industry that a 'discount culture' was evolving in the market, as customers increasingly tried to use their negotiating muscle to get reduced rates, primarily from hotels. At that time, even individual business travellers were often able to successfully negotiate reductions in hotel rates, sometimes on arrival at the reception desk.

Now, discounts tend to be limited to corporate buyers, who use the argument based on the volume of business they can provide, to get special rates from hotels. It is now common practice for companies to limit the number of hotels they use for their travelling staff. This increases the volume of employees they send to any given hotel, and this can be used as a negotiating strength.

As a result, very few business travellers pay hotels' published or rack rates. The extreme case of this is seen in the USA, where only 20% of guests pay the full rate (Skapinger, 1993). But the phenomenon is present throughout Europe. According to the 1993 'Euro cities survey' published by Pannell Kerr Forster, guests in Edinburgh hotels were receiving average discounts of 44.8% off the official rates. In Oslo, overall discounts of 44.7% were available, while business travellers could get 42.8% off their hotel bills in Manchester and 41.1% in Athens. Even the European cities with the firmest room rates were found to be offering substantial reductions to business clients: 12.5% off in Zurich, 14.5% in Prague and 15.5% in Berlin.

This looks like a trend which is set to continue. Compared with five years ago, business travellers are in a stronger position to negotiate reductions in hotel rates, because there are fewer of them now as a proportion of all hotel guests. Geoff Parkinson, a director of the

Horwarth hotel and leisure consultancy, has demonstrated how the worldwide proportion of hotel guests who are business travellers and conference delegates fell from 56% in 1988 to 49% in 1992. The other 51% are lower-spending leisure tourists. 'Although (leisure) tourists are clearly welcome, the tourist market is very competitive and many hotels will not be able to return to full profitability without an increase in business traffic' (Skapinger, 1993).

Trading down

Trading down is the path which has been followed by many companies in their crusades against high travel bills. Standards of comfort for business travellers have fallen, with restrictions on the use of first class and business class air travel and luxury hotels. According to travel agents Thomas Cook, in 1993, only 14.9% of UK companies allowed all staff to fly business class throughout the world, compared to 25.4% the previous year. Furthermore, it was predicted that the figure would shrink further, to 13.4% of UK companies in 1994.

In many cases, this trading down is not imposed from above—by the travel policy for example—but is voluntary. Many of the senior managers currently slumming it in four-star or even three-star hotels are doing so because they want to be seen as setting an example to staff. They do not want to risk the credibility of their company's cost-cutting policy by staying in exclusive establishments—even if, as is often the case, these offer special deals to business guests.

Centralised travel buying

In the effort to control spending on travel and at the same time improve their negotiating power with suppliers, many companies are moving towards streamlining their travel purchasing arrangements. Within the majority of companies, the responsibility for making travel arrangements is still largely left to the individual travellers themselves or their secretaries, resulting in a diffused and inefficient system. But centralised travel purchasing arrangements are gaining in popularity. 38% of European companies with ten or more staff travelling regularly on business now have their own internal 'travel manager'—a person responsible for negotiating and managing the travel arrangements for all employees.

74% of companies have an 'appointed travel agent' which employees are expected to use, and 1 in 10 has an 'implant' desk of the travel agent on their own premises. Those companies with the largest numbers of travelling staff are also the most likely to have appointed travel agents. These latter can provide their client companies with a range of valuable services, of which the most important are: lower-priced airfares through guaranteed booking at the cheapest fares or rates, bookings at very short notice, and lower hotel rates through volume rebates. As well as savings on air fares and accommodation, specialist business travel agents can deliver a range of other benefits, including corporate car hire, foreign currency and traveller's cheque provision, and passport and visa advice. Channelling all of its travel purchasing through a single travel agent also helps a company ensure that its travel policy is complied with by that agent.

Despite the range of cost-saving strategies open to them, only 54% of European companies as a whole claim to be 'extremely' or 'moderately' successful in controlling their travel costs. This figure dwindles to 26% in the case of France, where business travellers have yet to feel the full force of austerity measures to which their fellow Europeans have had to become accustomed. The business travellers least likely to endure additional pain in the future are the British, the Belgians and the Spanish, in whose countries the highest success rates were reported.

Travel industry moves to attract business

As the market becomes more demanding and more cost-conscious, the business travel industry has had to find new ways to win and keep customers. Following the principle that it is cheaper to keep existing customers than attract new ones (particularly when new customers are so thin on the ground), airlines and hotels are increasingly offering incentives to their most loyal clients.

One of the most important weapons in the airlines' armoury is the 'frequent flyer programme' (FFP). These reward systems were born and raised in the USA during the 1980s as a means of creating and maintaining loyalty to a single airline or group of airlines. The principle is that the buyer of a ticket earns points which can be accumulated and eventually exchanged for free flights and a range of other benefits—upgrade privileges, additional excess baggage allowances, expedited check-in, admission to airport lounges, etc.

During the 1990s, European carriers were forced into the FFP game, in response to the competition created by US airlines aggressively promoting their schemes. Even Asian and Far Eastern airlines which for years were able to command loyalty from passengers simply on the strength of their outstanding passenger service, have now been obliged to introduce their own FFPs.

The effectiveness of these incentive schemes was shown in a 1993 survey of European business travellers by Official Airline Guides, which reported 70% of business travellers as saying that, given a choice of airlines on a route, they would always choose the one to which their FFP belonged.

Other incentives designed to woo business travellers and keep them in first class and business class compartments fall into two categories: on the ground and in the air. Chauffeur-driven limousine transfers to the airport are increasingly used to pamper high-spending passengers. Once at the airport, the same business travellers are more than likely to spend some time in an exclusive lounge, away from the crowds, queues and noise. British Airways leads the airlines in its provision of lounge facilities. To its range at Heathrow—Clubworld, Speedbird for CIPs (Commercially Important People) and the Oasis lounge with showers—was added in 1992 what BA claims to be the largest business class lounge in Europe, complete with 40 telephones, fax machines and photocopiers.

In the air, airlines are coming up with ever more ingenious ways of justifying their business class and first class fares. In addition to having better food and wines and more comfortable seats than those in economy class, these passengers increasingly have access to a wide range of services made possible through sophisticated in-flight technology. This can provide on-board telephones, fax and computer links, and even air-to-ground teleconferencing facilities (Davidson, 1994).

Here, the airlines' strategy is clear. In an era of corporate cost-cutting, they find themselves under growing pressure to justify the considerable price differential between business class and economy class travel. Turning their aircraft into 'offices in the sky' provides the airlines with a way of linking this extra cost with greater productivity on the part of the individual business traveller.

Hotels have adopted the same strategy. Being more responsive to business guests' need to be seen to be industrious while travelling on company business, hotels no longer aim to be home-from-home, but rather offices away from the office. Office-like efficiency for guests can be assured through the provision of laptop computers, modems, and fax machines in rooms, with translation services and the more and more widespread 'business centres' which offer guests the full range of secretarial services during their stay.

Hotels have also seen the benefits that incentive schemes have brought the airlines and are beginning to offer their own 'loyalty clubs' for the frequent traveller. The benefits of belonging to such clubs can translate into substantial savings of both time and money. For example, the late check-out or early check-in facility offered to certain hotel cardholders can avoid the expense of paying for an extra night's accommodation, while express check-in/check-out facilities make for valuable time savings. Free room upgrades, discounts on laundry and telephone surcharges and free nights' accommodation at weekends are among the other perks now dangled by hotel chains in their effort to attract the business client.

Outlook

Most of the European companies participating in the American Express 1993 'Travel and expense management' survey were confident in their predictions that their spending on business travel would recover as the worst of the recession passes. Around 30% of them believed that their expenditure on this item was set to increase faster than total company revenue. This sentiment was particularly strong in the UK, perhaps reflecting the fact that the economic cycle is further advanced there than in continental Europe. In any case, companies were unanimous in regarding business travel activity as an essential condition of growth.

But will companies ever return to the heady, free-spending days of the 1980s? Juergen Bartels, chief executive of the Carlson Hospitality Group, which owns Radisson Hotels, is one of many in the industry who believe not. His prediction is that European and US businesses' painful restructuring in the face of growing competition from Asia will keep travel costs under pressure: 'There is no point in building any new four- or five-star hotels in the US or Western Europe. The demand will not be there' (*Financial Times*, 1993).

Kevin O'Brien, author of 'The West European business travel market 1993–1997' also believes that the new-found cost-consciousness will not diminish after the recession ends:

> The Gulf War educated the corporate sector as to the amount of non-essential travel expenditure incurred in previous years. The 1990s will witness the advent of the responsible, cost-conscious business traveller. Travel preferences will become less important to the corporate client as the benefits of cost reductions will increasingly outweigh them. (O'Brien, 1993)

References

American Express (1993) 'European business travel and expense management report 1993', American Express Europe Ltd.
Branegan, J. (1993) 'What ails Europe's airlines?', *Time Magazine*, 23 August:37.
Davidson, R. (1994) *Business Travel*, Pitman, London.
Skapinger, M. (1993) 'Don't pay what they charge', *Financial Times*, 9 November.
O'Brien, K. (1993) 'The West European business travel market 1993–1997', *Financial Times*.
Pannell Kerr Forster (1993) 'Euro cities survey', Pannell Kerr Forster.

40 Commercial short holiday breaks— the relationship between market structure, competitive advantage and performance

D. A. EDGAR, D. L. LITTELJOHN, M. L. ALLARDYCE AND S. WANHILL

Introduction

Short breaks in hotels have grown rapidly in size, value and sophistication since the 1960s (Bailey, 1990). They are now a valuable market to Scottish tourism in terms of contribution to hotel fixed costs, reduced seasonality, and high supplementary spend (Davies, 1990), accounting for £87.5 million in 1990, 70% of all short holiday spend (BTA, 1991).

This paper explores the nature and development of commercial short holiday breaks (CSHBs) within Scottish tourism, highlighting the range of marketing strategies employed by major operating companies, and through an understanding of the highly segmented market conditions forms a base for allowing further analysis of corporate performance relative to market and industry dynamics.

Methods

This section provides a definition of commercial short holiday breaks (CSHBs), and determines the methods used in the research to date.

Definition

The research concentrates on commercially-centred activities. CSHBs are therefore defined as 'hotel packages of one to three nights which for a single price together with accommodation include one or more of the following: meals; transport; entertainment; or a programme of activities'. This definition allows use of secondary sources for Scottish market background, and primary sources for more detail of supplier provision and performance. As hotels account for 78% of all spend in the CSHB market compared to other forms of accommodation (MSI, 1991), the definition is suitable for the purposes of this paper.

Methods

A review of CSHB literature was undertaken and revealed little systematic study on the subject. Most coverage was in the form of newspaper and trade press articles, conference papers, government publications, and industrial research documents. A computerised database containing the 30 largest hotel groups in Scotland (by room capacity) was therefore constructed from primary data drawn from company literature, group brochures, and company accounts. To compensate for differing demand patterns and operating environments, and to allow comparative analysis of performance, CSHB provision, regions, and market segments, the database was split into seven regions of Scotland, with boundaries determined by area tourist board boundaries.

To determine the relationship between market structure, competitive advantage and performance, a strategic framework was developed, based upon Scherer's structure–conduct–performance approach to industrial economics (Scherer, 1980). This framework was applied to the CSHB market using data of a competitive and strategic nature, obtained via structured telephone interviews with key personnel of 23 CSHB providers. These interviews were later supplemented by further interviews directed towards financial and non-financial performance. The samples accounted for 74% of the database room stock and 76% of the estimated CSHB revenue generated by the corporate sample.

The paper examines the key areas of Scherer's approach relative to the CSHB market supply, establishing the evolution of CSHBs, market structure, market conduct and market performance, and concluding with a suggested model of market performance.

Evolution of short breaks

To determine the relationship between market structure, competitive advantage, and performance, it is necessary to establish how CSHBs have evolved and the effect this has had upon the nature of the CSHB market. Full appreciation of CSHB evolution requires examination of developments from both supply and demand perspectives.

Supply perspective

The CSHB concept devolved from off-peak marketing efforts of hotel groups and associated intermediaries during periods of low demand where premium rates for accommodation and service could not be achieved (BTA, 1988), with the philosophy that any room sold during off-peak periods was contributing to fixed costs, emphasising the importance of marginal pricing as a strategy to boost occupancy and increase profitability (Hanks et al., 1992).

As the market matured, the off-peak concept developed into a market in its own right, companies actively attempting to compensate for low-season trade by offering short breaks to effectively extend their operating season.

Such developments continued throughout the 1970s and into the later 1980s, when it became evident that a combination of economic boom, international crisis, and the tendency to holiday two or three times a year, had resulted in major growth in the UK short holiday market, which by the end of 1989 accounted for up to 90% of the UK holiday demand of UK Hotel Groups Plc (Kleinwort Benson Securities, 1991). Suppliers were putting more effort into differentiating their product, seeking new markets and deliberately altering the off-peak image associated with short holiday breaks. As the market further matured so too did the means of marketing and distributing the concept. Thus suppliers have not only extended the variety and season of short breaks but have also increased the spread of market level and location, and used a greater variety of distribution channels to raise awareness of their efforts.

Demand perspective

The increased availability of CSHBs in number, variety, and perceived quality, combined with the increased levels of consumption and the experience of package holidays abroad, makes it reasonable to assume that customer knowledge would increase through experience, fuelling maturation of the market as consumers become more aware of alternatives, holiday more frequently, and demand new, value-for-money experiences.

Conclusions

The resulting effect of demand and supply developments has been the gradual evolution of a CSHB concept, away from the traditional off-peak image and representing a growth market in its own right, shown in Figure 40.1. In more recent years, a greater degree of market segmentation has arisen incorporating more sophisticated

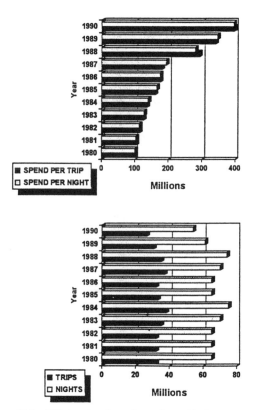

Figure 40.1 *UK short break market and spend index 1980–1990 (Source: BTS)*

marketing strategies and selective use of distribution channels, resulting in a highly varied and competitive market.

Short break market structure— a supply approach

This section examines the nature of CSHB supply by establishing the dominance of hotel groups followed by a market structure analysis based on Porter's 'industry structure' model (Porter, 1980). It concludes with a summary of the key elements of CSHB market structure.

While demand is important in terms of understanding market conditions, this paper focuses on strategic and competitive dimensions of supply and therefore deems the evolution of demand and related conclusions as an adequate demand perspective to the study.

Nature of supply

The following supply sources have been highlighted by the research as the main areas of CSHB provision.

- Corporate hotel group/chain: large, often publicly quoted hotel companies, who issue specialist brochures for CSHBs.
- Short break operator: specialist intermediaries, not owning hotels but obtaining revenue by brochure inclusion fees and commission; often used by hotel groups to supplement distribution.
- Hotel consortia: organisations often used by small privately owned hotels to gain marketing and purchasing economies. Gains revenue via membership fees and commission.
- Destination marketing: organisation designed to market a particular location area, thus providing valuable spin-off benefits for all local trade, and direct marketing for members.

From the identified supply base, corporate hotel suppliers in Scotland account for approximately 77% of CSHB revenue share from only 6% of unit share (Figures 40.2 and 40.3).

Hotel groups dominate revenue market share, pressurising smaller operators and causing many CSHB market features to reflect their own characteristics, including: market level of three/four star; density of location in major cities; tariffs based on accommodation with add-ons at cost; all-year availability, seven days a week; usually offering breaks via a corporate brochure, with 21 companies offering 24 brochures, 86 different packages and eight core segment themes 1991/2. Such results have been an evolutionary result of competitive and strategic activities and warrant investigation via a market/industry structure analysis.

CSHB industry structure

The purpose of this section is to determine the nature of competitive rivalry and form a grounding for determining competitive advantage. Figure 40.4 below shows a diagrammatic representation of the CSHB market/industry structure based on applying work by Porter. Each of the four forces acting on competitive rivalry are analysed in turn, establishing barriers to entry and level of threat or bargaining power.

Potential entrants

There are two forms of potential entrant, the entrant challenging physical provision and the entrant challenging distribution, the former being capital-intensive and marginal-contribution-based, the latter, more market-driven and commission-based. Physical provision, in this case the 'hotel', can be challenged from a number of

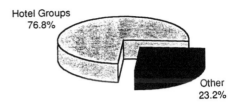

Figure 40.2 *Market share of CSHB revenue 1991 (Scotland) (Source: Database 1991/2)*

sources, the main of which are other hotel groups, independent unaffiliated hotels, and consortia.

Distribution is an area where, in the past, a number of operators have attempted to enter the market, some successfully, e.g. Goldenrail, Superbreaks, P&O, others not successfully—Stardust, and Camelot. These agents work for commission and include short break operators, travel and transport companies, and handling agents. While the basic concept of a CSHB is easily replicated by any hotel-based organisation the viability and levels of awareness generated by such organisations is highly dependent upon the size, or critical mass, the organisation can achieve, as such corporate hotel groups are in the ideal position to enter the market, while unaffiliated independents are less able to enter the market in a feasible or recognisable manner, and as such turn to consortia to gain the mass required. These characteristics have helped fuel the distribution entrants who, once established, are able to operate in a more cost-effective, less labour-intensive manner, spending a majority of expenditure on promoting and distributing brand concepts, and attempting to raise barriers to entry and hinder new entrants attempting to overcome start-up cost.

Barriers to entry. In the previous section, 'Evolution of short breaks', CSHB was established as potentially very lucrative, providing not only an additional market in a maturing holiday industry but also compensating for markets lost or lagging. To gain additional, and protect existing market share, operators create and raise barriers

Figure 40.3 *Market share of hotel units 1991 (Scotland) (Source: Database 1991/2)*

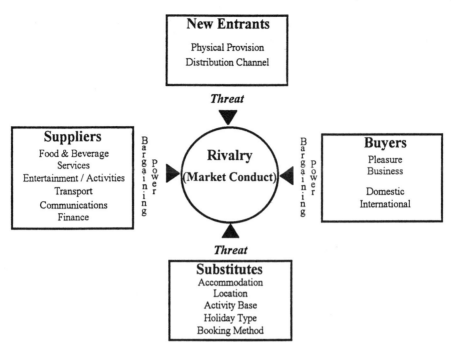

Figure 40.4 *Structural analysis of the CSHB market 1991/92 (Source: Application from Porter (1980))*

to entry. In the CSHB market these barriers are clearly evident, often forming the basis of suppliers' competitive strategy. The most evident barriers to emerge since the 1980s are location, market level, facilities/differentiation, and size, acting as barriers for both physical providers and distributors. These barriers are essentially the key competitive strategies of the 1960s to 1980s, suggesting that perhaps the strategies of the 1980s and 1990s may become the barriers to entry of the future.

Substitutes
Substitutes are evident in the 'prime functions' of CSHB provision: accommodation, location, activity, and reservations.

- Accommodation: in substituting accommodation, a number of alternatives to hotels exist, including caravans, VFR, and campsites. In addition, the level of accommodation can be changed, i.e. trading down. These threats of substitution are very high, however, as CSHB demand shifts more to cities and fully serviced accommodation packages are promoted, barriers to entry are raised.
- Location: as hotels are fixed in location they are under considerable threat if consumers substitute location, e.g. city/resort, national/international.

- Activity base: activities can be substituted, i.e. local attractions offering what may have been part of a commissionable hotel package at a cheaper price, or customers taking advantage of the basic hotel B&B package and making their own entertainment.
- Holiday type: trends and disposable income are the key instigators in substituting holiday type, with consumers deciding to try different types of holiday or fewer longer holidays.
- Booking method: booking methods are closely linked to distribution and commission. Methods include via travel agents, direct with hotels, through consortia, and through short break operators. With commission ranging from 0% to 30% this can be a costly area of substitution.

Substitutes can therefore be related to the physical properties of the hotel or are representative of the consumer/producer interface (distribution).

Barriers to entry. Barriers to entry vary considerably from company to company and segment to segment; main barriers are similar to new entrants, with the addition of specific strategies directed towards market share, expected standards, and group size, including brand loyalty, relocating breaks from resorts to cities, packaging, and introducing 'flexible breaks'. The type of barrier and the effectiveness of such barriers is dependent upon how well the organisation is able to monitor and adapt to the environment, resulting in groups using environmental complexity created via segmentation to deter entrants and substitutes (see the following section, 'Short break market conduct').

Suppliers

Suppliers take a number of forms, essentially constituting the component parts of any hotel or CSHB product. As hotels are reliant in varying degrees upon the provision of food and beverages, accommodation and support services, suppliers to hotels in these areas will have varying market powers. As CSHB markets are targeted emphasis is placed on different forms of supply, exposing areas of reliance on each type.

In addition to hotel suppliers, CSHB markets require additional categories of supply such as finance, entertainment/activities, and communications, e.g. booking methods. The former combine to constitute the supply of a CSHB segment(s), displaying differing market characteristics and determining the suppliers' bargaining power in the market.

Buyers

CSHB consumers are 'buyers' which, while predominantly domestic/pleasure based, do have elements of international inbound demand, differences in price sensitivity/elasticity, and basic requirements—by segment.

Competitive rivalry

The four forces identified (Figure 40.4) act upon the market, creating competitive rivalry; such rivalry is clearly identified in the type of strategies used by hotel companies to gain competitive advantage and forms the basis of the market conduct analysed later.

Key elements of CSHB market structure

The market structure analysis reveals key elements relative to CSHB market structure and competitive rivalry.

- The market is increasingly mature, with suppliers adopting sophisticated marketing strategies to gain market share.
- CSHB growth is in terms of market share of total hotel markets (Figure 40.5).
- Hotel groups dominate CSHB supply.
- As competitive rivalry intensifies, market complexity increases, resulting in a greater need for groups to inform and segment customers, often through branded packages.

The next section focuses on competitive rivalry and the means of gaining competitive advantage, through an analysis of market conduct.

Short break market conduct

An analysis of the main CSHB competitors and strategies adopted, indicates where and how competitive advantage is gained and sustained in the market. This section firstly establishes the main market CSHB competitors, before focusing on competitive advantage.

Competition

In the previous section it was established that competition takes a number of forms: hotel groups, independent

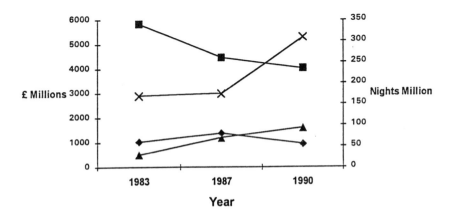

Figure 40.5 *UK holiday market 1983–1990 (Source: UKTS and BTS)*

hotels; other forms of accommodation; intermediaries; and locations. Figure 40.6 provides a breakdown of competition, emphasising the main CSHB suppliers. Hotel groups are the main form of competition, probably owing to their width of market coverage and predominantly high-profile supply base.

The four main intermediaties, Goldenrail, Superbreaks, Rainbow, and Highlife, are seen as major competitors, implying that smaller independent operators will find it difficult to compete, as the market further matures and begins to show tendencies of monopolistic competition, emphasised by the minimal representation of consortia.

Competitive advantage

This subsection is in three parts: competitive advantage explained; strategic activity; and value chain linkages—which when combined comprise the means by which groups gain and sustain competitive advantage.

Competitive advantage
'Porter argues that firm profitability is a function of industry attractiveness and the firm's relative position within it. Strong relative positions imply that the firm has a competitive advantage that can be sustained against attacks by competitors and evolution of the industry. Competitive advantage comes from creating value for buyers that exceeds the costs of generating it' (Hergert and Morris, 1989). Competitive advantage is therefore the edge created by an organisation to outperform competitors. To build competitive advantage is not enough; it must be sustained.

Strategic activity
As hotel groups dominate market share this section focuses on hotel group methods of competing, determining and categorising CSHB market strategies. Hotel groups compete against intermediaries and unaffiliated hotels

for market share via distinct competitive routes: broadly categorised into strategies that 'defend' market share, acting as barriers to market entry, and 'predator' strategies that expand market share by attracting or shifting market segments.

Defensive strategies

Defensive strategies are adopted by companies to help sustain market share. There are two key types: pricing and differentiation strategies.

Pricing
Pricing appears relatively unstructured (Figure 40.7) based primarily on location and market level, often at package cost plus margin. Essentially smaller operators are unable to compete on price, owing to the lack of flexibility for marginal contribution; thus groups are not forced to offer very low prices, as long as the customer is receiving perceived value for money.

Differentiation
Differentiation occurs in three forms, all raising perceived value, increasing market complexity (comprehension of the operating environment) (Duncan, 1972), and preventing new entrants/substitutes by setting basic standards and raising start-up costs.

Differentiation is by market level (setting standards, raising values/expectations), by location (i.e. city centre or resort), or by facilities (e.g. offering leisure facilities). These forms maintain basic price command and create barriers to entry causing non-price-based competition and therefore raising profitability.

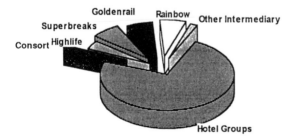

Figure 40.6 *Identified competition (1991/92) (Source: Questionnaires Phase I 1992)*

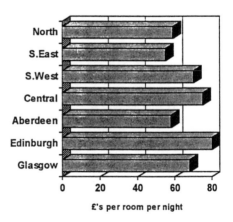

Figure 40.7 *Cost of CSHB by location 1991 (Source: Database 1991/92)*

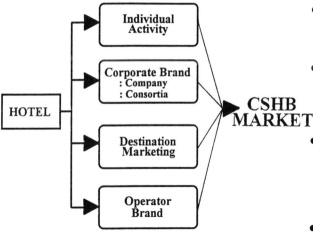

Figure 40.8 *Distribution channels for CSHBs 1991/92*

Predatorial strategies

Predatorial strategies are categorised under three headings: distribution, segmentation, and promotion. Their prime function is to gain market share.

Distribution
Distribution strategies are used to reach target segments as effectively or efficiently as possible; each form of distribution can be used in isolation, or more commonly in combination. Figure 40.8 shows distribution channels used

● Individual hotel activity. Independent actions of individual hotel units, including special offers, leaflet distribution, and press advertising. Cost is variable and therefore widely utilised by smaller units.

● Corporate activity: hotel group. Used by hotel groups to present a corporate image or brand, essentially in the form of CSHB brochures distributed by mail via the CRS and head office.

● Corporate activity: consortia. Small operators are limited to the consortia brochures, often racked in travel agents. Utilised in much the same way as hotel groups, to gain additional exposure, scale economies, and to present a group identity.

● Destination marketing. This distribution benefits both independent operators and hotel groups. There are a number of forms, ranging from area tourist boards to local authorities. The aim of the organisation is to market an area, through the use of local facilities, including hotels, resulting in many direct and indirect benefits.

● Operator brand. This refers to short break operator brochures used almost entirely by hotel groups, because of the commission, and associated charges. They have good travel agent racking, and brand by operator name, e.g. Superbreaks.

The importance and usage of distribution methods by hotel groups is shown in Figure 40.9. It can be seen that rankings one (hotel group brochure) and two (individual hotel activity) are very close, while ranking three (SBO) is almost half their importance, perhaps because of high associated costs, e.g. commission. Destination marketing is of less importance (four), with consortia used least, probably as they are essentially designed for and used by small operators. It therefore appears that hotel groups use the top three distribution methods most, while the lower ranking channels are used by independent, smaller hotels.

Segmentation
Predatorial strategies include segmentation, not only acting to segment the market, reducing or increasing

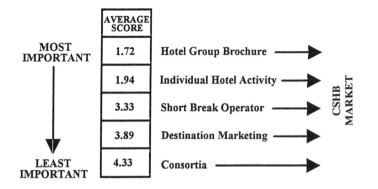

Figure 40.9 *Identified importance of distribution channels by hotel groups 1991*

Hotel group	CSHB brands	No. themes
Copthorne	1	1
Forte	1	4
Friendly	2	3
Gleneagles	1	6
Hilton	3	5
Holiday Inns	1	3
Jarvis	1	5
Marriott	1	3
Milton	2	4
Mount Charlotte Thistle	1	9
Principal	3	3
Queens Moat House	1	4
Scottish Highland	1	5
Sheraton	1	1
Stakis	1	5
Swallow	1	2

Figure 40.10 *Summary of number of CSHB segments and brands 1991*

complexity, but also raising the customers' perceived value of CSHBs by (a) raising the ease of purchase, (b) disguising contributions to fixed costs and enhancing product synergy (Ansoff, 1968) through packaging, and (c) creating identifiable and interchangeable target markets, with a variety of price and activity brackets while maintaining a degree of flexibility. Figure 40.10 shows the range of market segments targeted by various groups and their associated brand names.

A key method of achieving segmentation is via packaging, ranging in style, number, and components, an essential strategy adopted by many groups. Packages take two forms, (a) pure and (b) mixed. Pure packaging relates to a bundle of components offered as a single product, not added to or broken down, e.g. a coach touring break. In mixed packages a basic theme is offered, and the consumer is allowed to pick and mix various 'extras' to add to the theme, e.g. DBB with the option of golf. Mixed packages are most evident in the CSHB market with 16 groups producing 63 packages

under 22 brands. Key themes are special interest and DBB breaks; the most important package components, identified as being essential, are evening meals and child discounts.

In addition to pure and mixed packages, groups can utilise add-ons, additions to the perceived value of the break, not directly related to the principal theme. They increase the perceived value/price ratio at no apparent cost to the customer, e.g. toiletries, chocolates.

Promotion

Promotional strategies are based on brochure production, advertising, and branding and are closely interlinked.

Brochure production as the main media for distribution plays a differing role for groups. Figure 40.11 shows the relative percentage of groups' total promotion spend used on brochure production, providing some indication of priority to CSHB provision. (N.B. further analysis of actual spend is required.)

Advertising is becoming more widespread among hotel groups in attempts at non-price competition, establishing brand loyalty and therefore gaining market share. Branding is product-based, reflecting segments and brochures, and is used to reduce consumer decision complexity while maintaining supplier complexity.

Gaining and sustaining competitive advantage

Combining the former strategies the model illustrated in Figure 40.12 is created. It can be seen that lower-order defensive strategies are used to sustain and protect market share, essentially raising market complexity and reducing initial attractiveness, while the higher-order predatory strategies are used to gain market share by managing complexity and maximising achievable marginal contributions. Table 40.1 summarises key strategies adopted by various groups operating in the CSHB market.

The next subsection focuses on the value chain of organisations, and establishes areas of specific competitive advantage.

Value chain linkages

Examining the 'functional' aspects of gaining and sustaining competitive advantage via a value chain analysis (Porter, 1985) exposes areas of linkage occurring within or between organisation functions, allowing strategically important activities to be identified. Figure 40.13 shows the key value chain linkages within groups. Central reservation systems (CRS) are the most common linkage, followed by travel agents, and sport/activity, where the centre circle represents the CSHB market and the outer

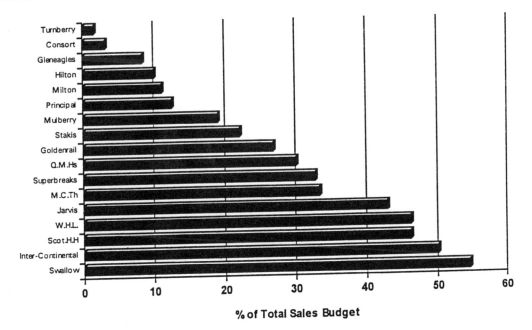

Figure 40.11 *Brochure production budget as a percentage of total sales budget 1991/92 (Source: Questionnaires Phase I 1992)*

circle the hotel company linkages, represented by blocks to the market. CRS has become the most common linkage through companies raising the environmental complexity by segmentation (to reduce new entrants), then attempting to raise, reduce, or manage the complexity within their organisation to gain market share (Figure 40.14).

Table 40.2 summarises main areas and number of sources of competitive advantage identified by hotel groups.

Conclusions

Strategies adopted by major companies vary between market segments, they appear relatively primitive, the packaging component being the most developed. While pricing, and differentiation exist, these seem to act more as barriers to entry, with value chain linkages creating cost economies essentially in the area of CRS for widening/targeting markets and reducing commission payable; packaging is used to gain additional market share.

CSHB strategies are adopted by a wide range of companies, all with differing levels of ownership, cost structure, location, market level, and tariff; yet some companies perform significantly better in the market than others. The next section seeks first to establish performance categories of 16 companies, and then relate such performance to the strategic dimensions established.

Short break market performance

This section examines the performance of hotel companies operating in the CSHB market in terms of (i) financial and (ii) non-financial performance, examining an industry and competitor/concentration approach before relating strategy to identified performance.

Financial performance

Industry financial performance of hotel companies operating in the CSHB market, is examined before focusing on CSHB performance in concentration terms. After completing the financial appraisal, non-financial performance is assessed in a similar manner before determining links between performance and competitive advantage.

Industry performance

The 16 groups established in the previous section with identified strategies are examined in terms of general industry performance. Performance is assessed using prime indicators of: revenue; profits; return on capital; gearing; and liquidity. Based on these indicators, Table 40.3 is created for financial year April 1991/92.

Having established basic performance indicators, the groups can be divided into performance categories. The criteria for these divisions is fully explained in the

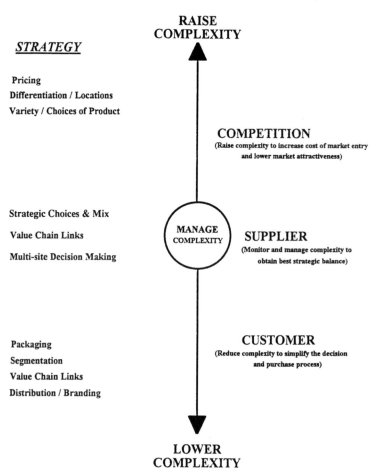

Figure 40.12 *Model of complexity and strategy in the CSHB market*

conference presentation, where each individual group is categorised into a single performance category, ranging from A (top performers) to D (lesser performers). While these measures are subject to environmental and scale issues, they form a basis for comparison at industrial level. Table 40.4 indicates which category (in ranked order) of industrial financial performance groups belong.

The next subsection establishes the performance categories of the groups, in the same way, when based on market concentration ratios in the CSHB market, after which non-financial performance categories are established and a summary of all performance categories provided.

CSHB market: concentration performance
This section determines group performance in the CSHB market, in terms of CSHB revenue concentration ratios. (Note that actual figures are not displayed at the request of some hotel groups surveyed.) Table 40.5 indicates the

concentration ratio for each group in terms of total CSHB revenue and CSHB revenue per room and per unit, before determining the performance category for each. From the former concentration ratios, CSHB market financial performance categories are established (Table 40.6).

With groups having been classified into financial performance categories, the next subsection establishes non-financial performance categories based upon two measures: portfolio concentration (rooms and units), and level of competitive identity.

Non-financial performance

Portfolio
It was established in the earlier section, 'Short break market structure—a supply approach', that greater market and strategic power is gained by larger hotel groups. Table 40.7 indicates the concentration ratios

Table 40.1 *Summary of key strategies and general strategic category for hotel groups 1991*

Hotel group	Key CSHB strategy	General category
Copthorne	Distribution	Predator
Forte	Promotion	Predator
Friendly	Promotion	Predator
Gleneagles	Segmentation	Predator
Hilton	Promotion	Predator
Holiday Inns	Promotion	Predator
Jarvis	Segmentation	Predator
Marriott	Distribution	Predator
Milton	Pricing	**Defender**
Mount Charlotte Thistle	Segmentation	Predator
Principal	Pricing	**Defender**
Queens Moat House	Promotion	Predator
Scottish Highland	Segmentation	Predator
Sheraton	Distribution	Predator
Stakis	Segmentation	Predator
Swallow	Distribution	Predator

for hotel company rooms and units (UK) 1991/92, indicating in terms of supply which groups are the main performers. Based on these concentration ratios, Table 40.8 indicates performance categories and ranking of the groups. In a similar manner, the performance measured in terms of competitive identity can be established.

Competitive identity

An indicator of non-financial performance can be seen to be the perceived level of threat that the company imposes on other companies within the market. This is identified in terms of whom companies see as their main

Organisation's Operating Environment

Figure 40.13 *Value chain linkages within the CSHB market*

form of competition. Figure 40.15 shows the competitors most identified by other groups. The larger hotel groups, as may be expected, are identified as most competition, with Forte (59%), Stakis (55%), and Mount Charlotte Thistle (50%). When these results are tabulated with most competition (higher performance) at category A, a ranking of competition performance of the sample companies is achieved. Note that 'other' has been removed and groups not mentioned are categorised D (Table 40.9).

Performance summary

Having determined the various categories of performance using financial and non-financial measures, the performance summary given in Table 40.10 is formed. From the table it can be seen that performance varies considerably between companies and between measures. The next section relates the strategies adopted in the section, 'Short break market conduct', to the identified performance in an attempt to explain these performance variances and allow the development of a performance model.

Strategy, competitive advantage and performance

This section identifies areas of linkage between established general strategy categories, more specific competitive advantage and level of performance achieved, first in financial, then non-financial terms, before concluding with a model of strategy and performance.

Financial performance related

Using measures of financial performance and relating them to strategy establishes the potential industry effect of offering CSHBs on corporate performance, before focusing on CSHB market concentration performance and specific competitive advantage/strategies.

Corporate performance links

There are three areas in this subsection, linkages between volume of CSHB business as a percentage of total revenue and identified performance, type of strategy adopted, and specific category of CSHB strategy adopted linked to performance.

● Percentage short break revenue
  When CSHB percentage of total revenue is compared to performance (Figure 40.16), the higher the percentage of revenue attributable to CSHBs the better the corporate financial performance. While this may be due

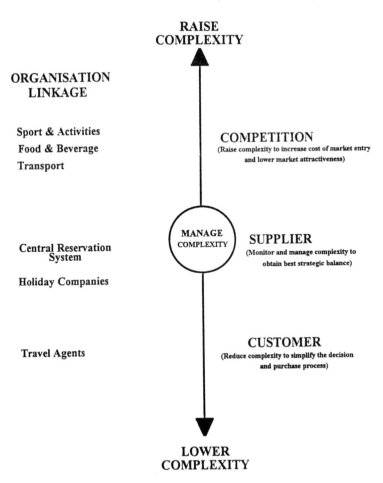

Figure 40.14 *Organisation linkages and the model of complexity*

Table 40.2 *Main areas and number of sources of competitive advantage*

Group	No. sources	Main competitive advantage
Forte	6	Image
Friendly	2	Image
Gleneagles	5	Image
Hilton	1	Image
Holiday Inns	2	Image
Jarvis	2	Skilled staff
Marriott	3	Location
Milton	1	Value
Mount Charlotte Thistle	6	Marketing
Principal	1	Low overheads
Scottish Highland	5	Image
Stakis	5	Image
Swallow	3	Location
Copthorne	2	Location
Sheraton	2	Location
Queens Moat House	2	Image

Source: Questionnaires Phase II 1993.

Table 40.3 *Corporate financial performance indicators (April 1991/92)*

Group	Revenue £000s	Profit AIT £000s	Profit % PAIT	OP.P	ROCE	G.RNG	Current ratio	Liquid ratio	RTA
Forte	835 000	35 600	4.3	9	4.1	50.34	0.62	0.54	2.3
Friendly	20 837	1889	6.6	15.5	6	34.3	0.45	0.43	3.5
Gleneagles	15 856	1272	8	10.8	2.96	123.2	0.26	0.19	2.6
Hilton	750 000	75 600	10.1	18.7	8.7	11.9	2.69	2.63	17.8
Holiday Inns	510 000	65 600	12.8	22.7	5.71	19.12	5.44	5.43	5.2
Jarvis	59 907	3374	5.6	28.2	1.38	325.5	0.9	0.87	1.29
Marriott	345.5	18 973	5.5	9.6	8.86	2.58	1.55	1.55	6.29
Milton	4891.5	149.4	3.1	13.2	5.28	325.5	0.20	0.18	3.04
Mount Charlotte Thistle	163 113	− 6222	− 3.8	30	− 1.28	161.0	0.26	0.25	− 0.49
Principal	22 102	1107	5	18	1.58	152.4	1.05	1.03	1.24
Scottish Highland	15 016	− 847	− 5.6	6.1	− 5.05	274.4	0.25	0.21	− 3.48
Stakis	83 198	234	0.3	16.6	6	48	0.21	0.2	4.6
Swallow	77 933	9800	12.6	16	7.9	36.4	0.89	0.76	5.2
Copthorne	46 469	497	1.1	11.6	0.34	92.63	0.43	0.41	0.27
Sheraton	4941	1753	35.5	52.5	81.9	58.7	1.32	1.32	43.7
Queens Moat House	492 900	73 600	14.9	30	7	100	0.13	0.13	4.44

Source: FAME (CD ROM).
Key: PAIT, Profit after investment and tax; OP.P, Operating profit; ROCE, Return on capital employed; G.RNG, Gearing; RTA, Return on total assets.

Table 40.4 *Category of industrial (financial) performance*

Category	Hotel company
A	Hilton; Holiday Inns; Sheraton
B	Swallow; Queens Moat House; Marriott; Forte; Friendly; Stakis
C	Jarvis; Copthorne; Principal; Gleneagles; Milton; Mount Charlotte Thistle
D	Scottish Highland

Table 40.6 *Category of CSHB market (financial) performance 1991/92*

Category	Hotel company
A	Queens Moat House; Gleneagles; Hilton; Holiday Inns; Scottish Highland
B	Forte; Principal; Stakis; Swallow
C	Mount Charlotte Thistle; Jarvis; Friendly
D	Copthorne; Sheraton; Marriott; Milton

Table 40.5 *CSHB market financial performance (concentration) 1991/92*

Group	CSHB[a] revenue Concentration Ratio	Revenue per room Concentration Ratio	Revenue per unit Concentration Ratio
Forte	17.9	2.6	2.2
Friendly	1.3	2.6	2.1
Gleneagles	0.8	15.1	25.0
Hilton	16.4	8.3	13.0
Holiday Inns	9.6	12.0	16.1
Jarvis	3.1	4.5	2.9
Marriott	0.02	0.2	0.3
Milton	0.3	2.3	1.5
Mount Charlotte Thistle	10.6	2.9	2.9
Principal	2.6	11.6	4.1
Scottish Highland	2.6	16.5	9.5
Stakis	6.7	7.0	6.7
Swallow	4.5	4.2	4.0
Copthorne	0.5	0.9	1.5
Sheraton	0.3	0.6	1.4
Queens Moat House	22.8	8.6	6.7

Source: FAME and Questionnaires Phase I/II.
[a]Commercial Short Holiday Break.

Table 40.7 *Hotel group room and unit concentration ratios 1991*

Group	Con. rooms	Con. units	Group	Con. rooms	Con. units
Forte	32.5	36.4	Mount Charlotte Thistle	17.4	15.9
Friendly	2.5	2.8	Principal	1.1	2.8
Gleneagles	0.3	0.2	Scottish Highland	0.7	1.2
Hilton	9.6	5.6	Stakis	4.6	4.4
Holiday Inns	3.9	2.6	Swallow	5.3	5
Jarvis	3.4	4.8	Copthorne	3	1.6
Marriott	0.5	0.3	Sheraton	1.8	0.7
Milton	0.6	0.7	Queens Moat House	12.8	15

Source: Company literature.

Table 40.8 *Categories of non-financial portfolio performance 1991*

Category	Hotel company
A	Forte (P); Queens Moat House; Mount Charlotte Thistle; Hilton
B	Swallow; Stakis; Jarvis; Holiday Inns
C	Sheraton; Copthorne; Scottish Highland; Principal; Friendly
D	Gleneagles; Milton; Marriott

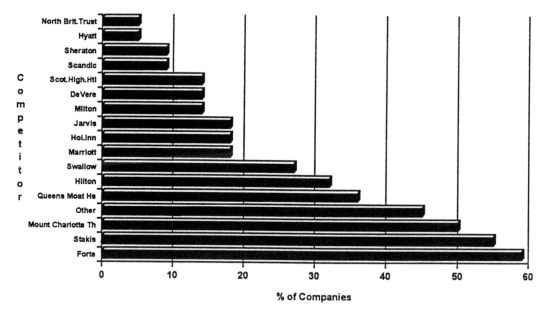

Figure 40.15 *Identified hotel group competition 1991 (Source: Questionnaires Phase I 1991/92)*

Table 40.9 *Categories of non-financial competitive identity performance 1991*

Category	Hotel company
A	Forte; Stakis; Mount Charlotte Thistle
B	Queens Moat House; Hilton; Swallow
C	Marriott; Holiday Inns; Jarvis; Milton; Scottish Highland
D	Sheraton; Copthorne; Friendly; Principal; Gleneagles

to a number of reasons, e.g. higher supplementary spend, more consistent markets, etc., the fact remains that groups with higher CSHB revenue percentage are better corporate financial performers. (Note that Scottish Highland Hotels and Principal Hotels are active in the market but, owing to high interest payments, have lower performance.)

- General strategies

  In terms of general strategies of predator and defender, Figure 40.17 shows that all the groups in higher corporate performance brackets A/B adopt predator strategies while those adopting defender strategies are in the C performance bracket.

- Specific strategic categories

  More focused, Figure 40.18 shows specific strategic categories adopted. The vast majority of high performers use distribution and promotion strategies while lower performers appear to rely upon segmentation and pricing

strategies. (Note that companies will adopt a number of strategies; the key strategy is their main focus.)

- Corporate (financial) performance summary

  While it is recognised that most of the corporate high performers (A) are groups with low total ownership, there also appears to be strong indications of linkages

Table 40.10 *Summary of performance categories 1991/92*

	Performance category			
	Financial		Non-financial	
Group	Corporate	Market	Portfolio	Identity
Forte	B	B	A(p)	A
Friendly	B	C	C	D
Gleneagles	C	A	D	D
Hilton	A	A	A	B
Holiday Inns	A	A	B	C
Jarvis	C	C	B	C
Marriott	B	D	D	C
Milton	C	D	D	C
Mount Charlotte Thistle	C	C	A	A
Principal	C	B	C	D
Scottish Highland	D	A	C	C
Stakis	B	B	B	A
Swallow	B	B	B	B
Copthorne	C	D	C	D
Sheraton	A	D	C	D
Queens Moat House	B	A	A	B

(p) = premier/outstanding performance. These measures are general, excluding seasonal, location, and operational variables.

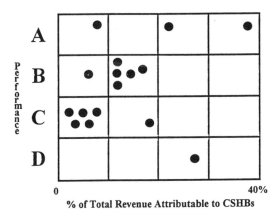

Figure 40.16 *Percentage of total revenue attributable to CSHBs linked to corporate (financial) performance*

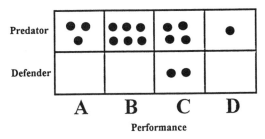

Figure 40.17 *General category of strategy linked to corporate financial performance*

between CSHB provision and performance, with groups that utilise promotional and segmentation strategies generally performing better.

The next section focuses on the CSHB market performance linked to specific strategies, number and type of competitive advantage areas, and organisation linkages.

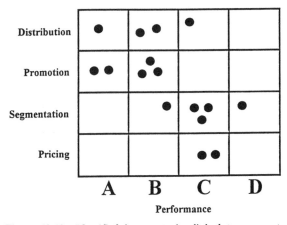

Figure 40.18 *Identified key strategies linked to corporate (financial) performance*

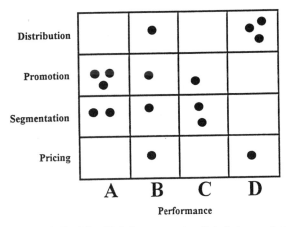

Figure 40.19 *Identified key strategies linked to market (financial) performance*

Market (financial) performance links
- Strategy category

  This section determines linkages between the strategic categories (promotion, segmentation, distribution, pricing) and market performance. From Figure 40.19, market performers (A) use mainly promotional strategies, followed by segmentation strategies, while the poorest performers (D) use distribution strategies. This may indicate the effects of commission, however; in an attempt to establish why such strategies are adopted, it is useful to relate performance to the number of sources of advantage and then link strategies adopted to the number of sources of advantage.
- Number of sources of advantage

  The relationship between performance and the number of areas of competitive advantage is shown in Figure 40.20. Category A performers are of two types, those with many areas (sources) of competitive advantage

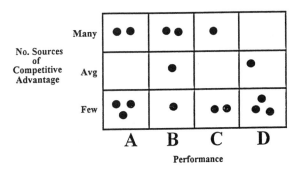

Figure 40.20 *Number of competitive advantage sources linked to market (financial) performance*

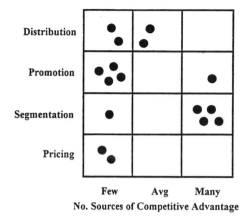

Figure 40.21 *Identified key strategy linked to the number of sources of competitive advantage*

and those with few. Closer analysis reveals that the A performers with many areas of competitive advantage use segmentation strategies, while those with few use promotion strategies. The D performers can be seen to have few areas of competitive advantage but adopt a distribution strategy, perhaps attempting to gain scale economies and critical mass; these groups should perhaps focus on developing promotional-based strategies to aid market performance. Combining the areas of competitive advantage and the strategic categories, a number of distinct characteristics are evident (Figure 40.21).

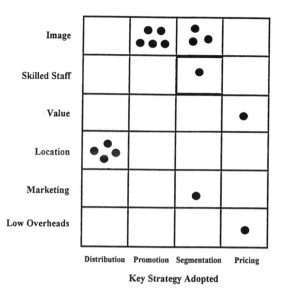

Figure 40.23 *Main form of competitive advantage linked to key strategy identified*

Groups adopting promotional strategies and pricing strategies have few sources of competitive advantage, while distribution strategies have medium to few sources, and segmentation many sources—resulting in the former strategies being more focused and the latter more broad and innovative, essentially driving and steering market development.

● Main type of advantage

Figure 40.22 shows that companies with enhanced performance (A) tend to identify image as their main competitive advantage. While A performers have main advantage of image, D performers main advantage is location.

Further analysis of advantage type relative to strategy reveals that companies adopting distribution strategies

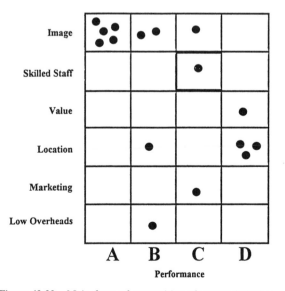

Figure 40.22 *Main form of competitive advantage linked to market (financial) performance*

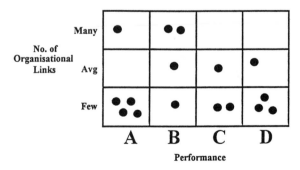

Figure 40.24 *Organisational linkages linked to market (financial) performance*

identified location as their main advantage, while those adopting promotion and segmentation strategies have the advantage of image (Figure 40.23).

● Organisational linkages

Organisational linkages appear to be secondary to strategies adopted. What appears to be the case, from Figure 40.24, is that performance in the market at corporate level is not greatly affected by linkages. In some cases, however, where strategies are similar but performance is different, linkages appear to enhance (financial) market performance, e.g. Milton and Principal Hotels; both adopt pricing strategies with few areas of competitive advantage yet Principal has considerably better market performance. This may be due to the fact that Principal identified many areas of organisation linkages while Milton identified few areas of organisation linkages.

● Market (financial) performance summary

It appears that the number of areas of competitive advantage determines strategies adopted, which in turn can be linked to financial market performance and the key form of competitive advantage. For example: a group with few areas of competitive advantage would essentially adopt promotional or pricing strategies; adopting promotional strategies (given the ability) would lead to enhanced performance and a concentration of efforts on image as the key competitive advantage.

In addition, as indicated by the Milton/Principal scenario, organisational linkages can enhance performance of certain strategies adopted; this is most likely to occur at the unit level and will form the basis of further study into unit/market-based performance.

These conclusions require further testing, with consideration of environmental variances; however, they

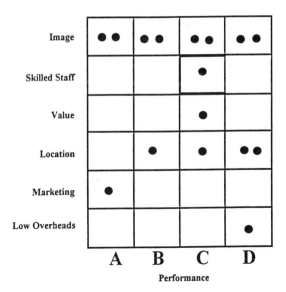

Figure 40.26 *Non-financial performance linked to main area of competitive advantage*

form the basis of the performance model and further research to be undertaken.

The next subsection establishes non-financial performance linked to strategy in terms of strategies adopted, main type of advantage, and organisation linkages.

Non-financial performance

While financial measures are often used to determine performance, alternative measures, i.e. non-financial, allow a more qualitative assessment of performance (Miles and Huberman, 1984). This section examines portfolio performance (market presence of groups) and competitive identity (perceived threat in the market) relative to identified CSHB strategies in non-financial terms.

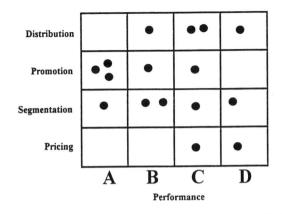

Figure 40.25 *Non-financial performance linked to identified key strategy*

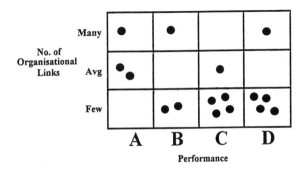

Figure 40.27 *Organisational linkages related to non-financial performance*

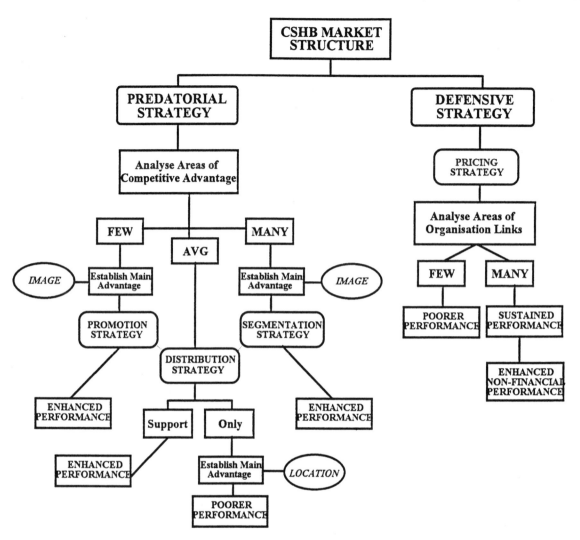

Figure 40.28 *Developing model of the relationship between strategy and performance*

Portfolio performance

From Figure 40.25, 'A' performers in terms of portfolio size concentrate on promotion and segmentation strategies, essentially establishing brands and using market size to increase coverage; poorer performers (D) tend not to use promotional strategies, perhaps owing to their limited portfolio, using only distribution strategies.

Competitive identity

High performers are characterised by identifying image and marketing as the main competitive advantage (Figure 40.26). These are also characteristics of A to D performers.

However, where performance appears to be enhanced, i.e. the difference between Forte, Stakis (A) and Holiday Inn, Scottish Highland (C), it is in the number of organisational linkages. This relationship is shown in Figure 40.27.

From Figure 40.27, it can be seen that higher performing companies with similar identified competitive advantages are better performers owing to their higher number of organisational linkages; so while the previous subsection established linkages as playing a minor role in terms of market (financial) performance, they would appear to adopt a more important role when achieving non-financial performance.

Performance summary

Performance has been examined on two levels relative to the strategic dimensions of the market. It was found that financial performance appears to be based upon the type and number of areas of competitive strategy, leading to the strategy adopted and resulting financial performance, while non-financial performance appears to be closely linked to organisation linkages.

The next section suggests a model for how companies can enhance their financial and non-financial performance in the market. This model is a working model, and still requires development and testing.

Conclusions

This section concludes the paper by presenting a model of strategy and performance in segmented markets (in this case the CSHB market) indicating where and how groups may develop and enhance their performance (financial or non-financial).

The strategy-performance model

Hotel groups will adopt either predatorial or defender strategies (Figure 40.28). Adopting predatorial strategies requires an analysis of areas of advantage and then selection of strategy, while defensive strategies are based upon achieving non-financial performance created via organisational linkages.

Enhancing performance in the CSHB market

While it is appreciated that the model requires testing, it is a step towards establishing links between segmented markets, strategic activity, and enhancing performance. In enhancing performance, consider a group at present adopting a segmentation strategy, based on main advantage of location and few areas of competitive advantage. Using the model it would be advisable for the company to either seek more areas of competitive advantage, and focus on image as the main competitive advantage, or adopt a promotional strategy based on image, or, alternatively, if there are a number of organisational linkages, fall back to a defensive pricing strategy and sustain financial performance while perhaps seeking new forms of advantage and enhancing non-financial performance.

This model will form the basis of future Ph.D. research, which will: (i) test and modify the model to determine performance in segmented markets based on the nature of the market and resulting performance; (ii) adopt a multi-site approach to analysing performance, thus establishing linkages and 'gaps' between the corporate perception and the unit/market perception—essentially focusing on the value chain and concepts of yield management; and (iii) expand the non-financial measures to include a more comprehensive list of variables, such as staffing, growth, promotional spend, etc.

The combined effect of the research developments will allow the performance model to be modified and the relationships between market structure, competitive advantage, and performance to be established more fully.

References

Ansoff, I. (1968) *Corporate Strategy*, Penguin, London.

Bailey, J. (1990) 'Short holidays', *Insights*, No. 1: B1.1–B1.7, London.

BTA (British Tourist Authority) (1988) 'The short break market', BTA/ETB, London.

BTA (British Tourist Authority) (1991) 'UK tourism statistics 1991/1', BTA/ETB/STB/WTB/NITB, London.

BTS (British Tourism Surveys) 1983–1989, NOP Research, London.

Davies, B. (1990) 'The economics of short breaks', *International Journal of Hospitality Management*, 9(2):103–109.

Duncan, R. (1972) 'Characteristics of organisational environments and perceived environmental uncertainty', *Admin. Science Quarterly*, 313–327.

FAME (Financial Analysis Made Easy), CD ROM Database, December 1993.

Hanks, R. D., Cross, R. G. and Noland, R. P. (1992) 'Discounting in the hotel industry: a new approach', *Cornell HRAQ*, February:15–23.

Hergert, M. and Morris, D. (1989) 'Accounting data for value chain analysis', *Strategic Management Journal*, 10:175–188.

Kleinwort Benson Securities (1991) 'Quoted hotel companies: European markets', KBS Ltd (6), London.

Miles, M. and Huberman, M. (1984) *Qualitative Data Analysis: a Sourcebook of New Methods*, Sage, London.

MSI (1991) 'Short break holidays', Marketing Strategies for Industry (UK) Ltd, London.

Porter, M. E. (1980) *Competitive Strategy*, Free Press, New York, p. 4.

Porter, M. E. (1985) *Competitive Advantage: Creating and Sustaining Superior Performance*, Free Press, New York.

Scherer, F. M. (1980) *Industrial Market Structure and Economic Performance*, 2nd edn, Rand McNally, Boston, MA.

41 Hotel development strategies in Southeast Asia: the battle for market dominance

U. A. SCHLENTRICH AND D. NG

Introduction

Hotel and tourism development in Southeast Asia has experienced rapid growth since the mid-1980s. Originally, foreign-based hotel chains provided development, marketing and operating expertise to Asian investors. The predominant market entry mode for these companies was the management contract without equity participation.

Most Asian countries imposed restrictions on foreign ownership of real estate forcing overseas developers and operators to find local partners for expansion in this region. Foreign hotel chains are now facing severe competition from evolving Asian operators who are willing to either develop properties on their own or enter into joint venture agreements with local developers, thus achieving income not only from management fees but also as a percentage of profits obtained from operations and through the appreciation of real estate.

Of the world's 200 largest hotel companies, 17 are based in central Asia and 11 are headquartered in Japan. Three of these companies rank among the top six in the world for quality standards and guest satisfaction.

The first part of this paper evaluates the evolution of the region's overall hotel development and analyses the present status of the industry in the different countries of Southeast Asia. The second part contains the results of a study analyzing the market entry and development strategies of international hotel groups.

Regional overview

Only three decades ago. Asia accounted for only 4% of the global economy but now provides 25% and by the year 2000 is projected to contribute one-third of all economic activity on earth. The rising powers in the region are developing countries—from Thailand and Malaysia to China—whose combined economies will expand an average of 8.7% this year versus projected world growth of 2.2% according to the International Monetary Fund. Southeast Asia is becoming an economic power in its own right. The GDP growth rate for the past

Table 41.1 *GDP growth rate for selected Southeast Asian countries*

	Average growth 1985–89	1989	1990	1991	(forecast) 1992
China	11.6	4.0	5.0	5.7	6.0
Hong Kong	8.9	2.3	2.3	3.5	4.5
Singapore	6.0	9.2	8.3	5.9	6.5
Indonesia	5.1	7.4	7.0	7.0	6.6
Laos	—	10.7	9.1	6.7	6.3
Malaysia	7.0	8.8	9.4	8.5	8.7
Philippines	2.8	5.6	2.5	2.1	4.1
Thailand	9.9	12.0	10.0	7.4	8.0
Vietnam	5.1	5.5	2.4	3.8	4.9

Sources: Asian Development Bank (1992) and Far Eastern Economic Review (1991).

seven years illustrates the dynamic growth for this region (Table 41.1).

The growth of world tourism tends to parallel the growth of the world's economy. While Europe, Japan and the USA have entered a relatively stagnant period of growth, central Asia's tourism receipts continue to achieve spectacular gains.

Three Southeast Asian countries (Hong Kong, Singapore and Thailand) are ranked among the top fifteen world tourism earners, followed closely by Malaysia and Indonesia (Table 41.2).

As a result of relaxed restrictions on overseas travel capacities and strong expansion of economic growth, outbound travel from Pacific Asian countries achieved a 10% annual growth rate in air passenger traffic from 1990 to 1993, while the world annual growth rate was 6–7% during that period, according to the International Air Transport Association (IATA).

Hotel operating results

Although the economic recession resulted in little growth in hotel occupancy globally, the average occupancy in the Asian region increased from 67.3% to 71.0% during 1991–93. The percentage of foreign visitors to the region also increased from 26.5% to 27.4%. North Asia (China,

Table 41.2 *World's top tourism earners, 1991. International tourism receipts (excluding international transport)*

1991 rank	Country	Millions of current US dollars		1986 rank	Average annual growth rate 1986–91(%)
		1991	1986		
1	USA	45 551	20 454	1	17.37
2	France	21 300	9724	4	16.98
3	Italy	19 668	9855	3	14.82
4	Spain	19 004	12 058	2	9.53
5	Austria	13 956	6954	6	14.95
6	UK	12 588	8163	5	9.05
7	Germany	10 947	6294	7	11.71
8	Switzerland	7030	4227	8	10.71
9	Mexico	5934	2984	10	14.74
10	Canada	5537	3860	9	7.48
11	Hong Kong	5078	2287	11	17.30
12	Singapore	4386	1767	13	19.94
13	The Netherlands	4300	2219	12	14.15
14	Thailand	4295	1421	14	24.76
15	Australia	4164	1300	15	26.22
	World total	260 763	140 023		13.24

Source: World Tourism Organization.

Korea, Taiwan and Hong Kong) achieved an average increase in occupancy of 10% from 73.4% to 83.4% in 1991–92 (Table 41.3).

The strong performance of the Asian hotel market makes this region a prime target for strategic hotel development for both Asian and foreign hotel companies.

The environment for hotel development

International hotel companies planning to enter the Asian market must understand that it is not a homogeneous market but one of great political, religious, legal and socio-economic diversity. In evaluating the environment for investment in Southeast Asia, the first point to note is the government's attitude toward foreign investment

Table 41.3 *Overall performance measurements*

	Asia	North Asia	Continental Europe	United States
Annual room occupancy (%)	71.0	83.4	62.4	60.1
No. of guests per room	1.45	1.59	1.33	1.11
Amounts per available room				
Total sales	$36 985	$35 459	$44 570	$17 794
Income before fixed charges	$14 130	$10 889	$10 243	$3551
Net income	$7944	$4743	$2792	$362

Source: Horworth International (1993a).

in tourism. All the Southeast Asian countries have officially welcomed such investments, although their effort in stimulating tourism demand varies in intensity.

With this in mind, it becomes necessary for hotel developers and operators to examine the following specific issues:

- Country risk, including past political behavior
- Strength of present government and rival political groups
- Restrictions on foreign investment
- Taxation and repatriation of profits
- Level of crime and corruption
- Level of government support of tourism
- Standard of infrastructure
- Availability of building materials and equipment, operating supplies and food and beverage goods
- Restrictions on work permits for expatriates
- Laws pertaining to the employment and training of staff
- Level of government bureaucracy
- Existing and potential ecological problems

Based on these factors, international investors must weigh political risks and the costs of regulatory compliance against the gains that can be achieved. Restrictions on investment may be partially offset by financial incentives for development and by other programs governments have implemented to encourage tourism, such as tax abatements and development subsidies. The activities of hotel companies in Southeast Asia so far, reveal a consensus that, in Hong Kong, Singapore, Indonesia, Malaysia and Thailand, political considerations are not a major obstacle to development. With regard to China, the Philippines and Indochina, however, no such consensus exists.

The laws governing foreign ownership of business and real estate vary from country to country in Southeast Asia. Hong Kong and Singapore have the fewest and most straightforward restrictions on foreign investment. Financial deregulation, the free exchange of currency and the presence of a large number of local and foreign banks and other financial services give these two countries an advantage over their neighbors in attracting foreign investment. Restrictions are more severe in Malaysia, Indonesia and Thailand. The effect on foreign investment, however, has generally been offset by substantial incentives for projects which governments deem worthwhile and by the high returns that are possible in spite of these limitations. Thailand's system is restrictive (maximum 49% ownership of land) but relatively unencumbered. Similar restrictions in the Philippines, however, in combination

Table 41.4 *Laws governing foreign ownership of real estate in Southeast Asia*

	Foreign ownership	Freehold	Leasehold
Hong Kong	No restrictions	No	Yes: to 1997 plus 50 years
Indonesia	80% initially, reduced to 49% over 15 years	No	Yes: 20 to 60 depending on rights
Malaysia	No restrictions on land	No	Yes: usually 66 or 99 years
Philippines	Maximum 40% on land	No	Yes: 100% on lease up to 25 + 25 years
Singapore	Restrictions on residential property only	Yes	Yes: usually 99 or 999 years
Thailand	Maximum 49% on land	No	Yes: 100% on lease up to 30 years

Source: Jones Lang Wootton (1990).
According to the Basic Law of Hong Kong after its reversion to China, the lease duration of all current and future leasehold properties can be extended for 50 years after 1997.

with this country's political instability, have made offshore debt-financing very difficult (Table 41.4).

In Indonesia, foreign investors may initially hold a majority interest in a new enterprise, but this must be gradually faded out to a minority position, usually within fifteen to twenty years. Indonesia's system of land-ownership is the most complex in the region. There is no concept of fee simple. The right to 'build', 'exploit' and 'use' can be registered, but disputes over such rights are common.

Under Malaysia's New Economic Policy (NEP), all businesses have been required to meet certain levels of participation (in terms of ownership and management) by bumiputras. The NEP was adopted as a means of correcting real and perceived inequalities in the distribution of the country's wealth. The NEP expired at the end of 1990, and the government has now announced a New Development Policy (NDP) to take its place. It appears that racial quotas will continue but will be de-emphasized in the future.

Regional overview

China

Although the 4 June 1989 Tiananmen Square massacre has been widely cited as an example of political instability in China, the absence of powerful rival groups gives the Communist Party the absolute mandate to extend their rule. The presence of corruption and cumbersome bureaucracy in China, however, has made hotel investment costly and time-consuming. Moreover, the Chinese government has become less generous in the terms it extends to foreign investors, especially in those cities where foreign investments are plentiful. Official Chinese figures show that some $44 billion of foreign money was invested in China between 1979 and the middle of 1993, almost $20 billion of it after the beginning of 1992. Funds from Hong Kong account for well over half the investment and the overseas Chinese are responsible for some 80% of total investment (*The Economist*, 27 November 1993). In October 1993, the government abandoned a three-month effort to achieve a slow-down in the economy. Industrial output alone was growing at a rate of 29.9% a year. The State Statistical Bureau projects that economic growth during the first half of 1994 will increase by a staggering 15%. China is aiming to slow the economy to a 9% rate of growth in 1994 and to cut inflation from about 17% to about 12%. This policy might result in a curtailment in the development of tourism infrastructure projects.

China's comparative advantage in labour-intensive industries and the easy access to capital have made it a threat to Western economies which struggle at present with high unemployment. It is essential that China rejoins the GATT negotiations which were suspended in 1988 as a result of the Tiananmen Square massacre. China has three inhabitants for every two in North America, Europe and Japan combined; economic and political instability could have extremely negative effects on the world economy as a whole. It is therefore, imperative that China's gradual economic transition is maintained through sustained market-oriented reforms. China seems to be making progress in its political and economic relationship with America. In January 1994 a three-year textile agreement between the two countries was finally signed, averting a potentially serious trade dispute. Such a dispute would have disrupted Chinese exports to the USA and American investment and travel to China, thus seriously affecting foreign hotel investment in China.

Hotel occupancies have been steadily rising in China's major urban centers since 1991, while secondary cities remained relatively static. Future growth in China's hotel sector will depend on factors such as improvements in its transportation infrastructure and further airline deregulation.

Hong Kong

In Hong Kong, the problem of the 1997 reversion to Chinese government is more a question of uncertainty than of quantifiable risk. The intent of the Beijing government is centered on one issue—internal political stability. In the interim, Hong Kong's role as a point of entry to China makes it sensitive to any events that affect travel to the mainland. As some critics put it, 'Hong Kong's hotel industry catches a cold when China sneezes'.

The prolonged argument about the financial arrangements for Hong Kong's new airport and related projects reflects the mistrust between the British and Chinese governments. Although they appear to be about finance, Hong Kong and British officials believe that China (which is concerned about political power in the colony), is using the issue to exercise leverage over Mr Chris Patten, Hong Kong's governor (*Financial Times*, 22 July 1992:4). It can be seen that further accusations between British and Chinese governments will continue if the Beijing government perceives that its sovereignty is being threatened by the complications of democracy in Hong Kong.

South China's explosive economic growth, particularly in the Guangdong Province, contributed significantly to Hong Kong's continued economic growth. Hong Kong is in its third year of an economic boom which has raised the Hong Kong stock market index by 239% since the end of 1990. In 1992, over 950 000 Chinese nationals visited Hong Kong while over 21.5 million visits were made by Hong Kong residents to mainland China, an average of more than three visits for each of the territory's 6 million inhabitants. Total visitor arrivals to Hong Kong reached a record high of 6.9 million in 1992 while total tourism receipts grew by 22%.

The addition of new hotel stock between 1989 and 1991 and the political upheaval of the Tiananmen Square massacre in China resulted in a decline in hotel occupancy to 68% in Hong Kong. In 1992, however, Hong Kong's leading luxury hotels recorded an increase in occupancy to 78–80% (Jones Lang Wootton, 1993).

Singapore

A stable business climate and a robust economy have been created in Singapore through pragmatic, fully orchestrated efforts to attract investment, combined with an authoritarian approach to internal politics. Largely as a result of the worldwide recession, the economic growth rate of Singapore was 5.8% in 1992, the lowest rate since 1986. Supported by a strong marketing campaign, 'Visit ASEAN Year', and a significant influx of intraregional travel, Singapore reported 6 million visitor arrivals in 1992. The Singapore hotel market is seen as one of the most stable in Asia, largely as a result of a stable political and economic structure and a consistent tourism policy.

The construction of the new international Suntec City conference and exhibition center, due to open in 1994,

and the development of a mega-resort which will include a marina, golf courses and more than forty hotels on the nearby Indonesian island of Bintan will further enhance Singapore's position as a key tourist destination. Additional room supply presently under construction or in the planning stage will result in an increase of more than 32 000 rooms, a 32% increase over a six-year period.

Malaysia

The history of independent Malaysia has pivoted on the necessity of accommodating the interests of several ethnic groups: the Malays, the Chinese and the Indians. The challenge for Malaysia's Prime Minister, Dr Mahathir Mohamad, is to maintain a harmonious balance between these ethnic groups. The current rise of Islamic fundamentalism could result in the reversal of the modern socio-economic policies which have so far achieved spectacular economic growth and stability.

Over the past five years, Malaysian share prices have risen by over 300%, making it one of the fastest growing economies in the world. A strong manufacturing and tourism market and a favorable economic investment policy have contributed to Malaysia's economic success. The highly successful 1990 'Visit Malaysia Year' promotion, which increased visitors by over 50% from the previous year to 7.4 million, will be repeated in 1994, demonstrating the government's support of tourism.

Major international hotel consortiums have targeted Malaysia, and especially Kuala Lumpur, as a sector for expansion. Marriott, Hyatt, Westin, Sheraton, New World, Nikko and Mandarin Oriental are among those who intend to open properties in Malaysia during the next two years, virtually doubling the supply of four- and five-star room inventory. The average occupancy of 72% achieved in 1992 is expected to decline drastically as a result of this oversupply. In view of the continued strong economic growth rate which is estimated to be 8% in 1994, hotel occupancies are expected to stabilize within a three-year period.

Thailand

Although Thailand is considered to be politically conservative, the military coup of 1991 shocked the local business community and foreign investors. This event serves as a reminder of the strong military ties which exist at all levels of government and throughout the economic system.

Thailand's primary challenge is to invest in and upgrade its infrastructure. Bangkok is hopelessly enmeshed in a continuous traffic jam while air and water pollution are threatening the environment. Within the next three years, the Thai government is projected to spend $25 billion on improvements to the airport, road and mass-transit systems. The island of Phuket, a popular resort destination for international tourists, will be further developed. In the north, the city of Chiang Mai has seen considerable hotel investment and its growth could be greatly enhanced by the opening of Vietnam and Cambodia.

Hotel companies who plan new projects in Bangkok include Ritz-Carlton, Peninsula, Sheraton, Westin and Melia-Sol. It is expected that another 2800 rooms will be added by the end of 1995, resulting in an oversupply. Thai tourism has suffered lately as a result of the weakening of the economies in Europe, America and Japan.

Philippines

The Philippines have a long history of political instability. Communist movements and military coup attempts have been common for the past thirty years. However, under the presidency of Corazon Aquino, the advent of democracy has led to the present resolution of problems with the communist and Muslim insurgents who agreed to a peace formula.

The Philippines continue to suffer from serious corruption both in the political and commercial sectors and from a high rate of inflation. These factors have had a negative influence on international hotel development. The government is presently supporting efforts to develop resort facilities in its southern islands.

Indonesia

Suharto was inaugurated as president in 1968, two years after he led the military in seizing power from Sukarno. The strength of Suharto along with the lack of an obvious successor has created some uncertainty. There is a sense that the regime is, in effect, masking problems in the society and the economy that may rise to the surface with the eventual change of government. The perception among many Indonesians that the benefits of economic reforms are not being equitably distributed became a major source of political tension in 1990. Not surprisingly, foreign investors have found the best Indonesian partners to be those with close connections to Suharto. This makes the succession question all the more critical for the international business community. Against this uncertainty must be weighed the high returns that are possible in Indonesia.

Indonesia has achieved substantial economic growth which was, however, largely financed through the assumption of foreign debt. The resulting liquidity shortage within the domestic banking sector caused interest rates to increase drastically to 30% in 1991. Indonesia's financial markets and investment opportunities are being opened more widely to foreigners as declining oil prices forced the Suharto government to make the economy more efficient and competitive.

Two million visitors, mainly from ASEAN countries, came to Indonesia in 1992. As a result of new hotel openings, occupancies in Bali declined significantly whereas Jakarta maintained strong occupancies and average rates. According to Horwath International (1993b), visitors to Bali declined from a high in 1980 of 890 900 to a low of 119 000 in 1990 (1991–92 figures were not available).

Indonesia, with its 13 700 islands of scenic beauty represents a promising market for future resort development. However, further improvements in its infrastructure and the deregulation of the airline industry are required. The opening of the improved Jakarta convention center and the addition of the new Hyatt and Le Meridien hotels in 1992 will further strengthen Jakarta as a primary convention destination.

Vietnam

The election of Vo Van Kiet as Prime Minister is certain to accelerate Vietnam's development and its transition to a more open market economy. Vo Van Kiet has stated that 'The greatest threat to Vietnam is slow, not fast development'. The uncertainty in Vietnam stems in part from the differences between the northern and southern parts of the country. It is true that the Vietnamese government wants foreign investment. Yet, while the south has a strong entrepreneurial tradition and, indeed, has a relatively recent history of international tourism, it is in Hanoi that decisions governing foreign investment are made. Despite the announced program of economic reform and plans to establish international development funds, there are doubts as to whether the north will relinquish central control over foreign investment or embrace the commercial culture and the south.

The Clinton administration and America's G7 partners have resumed their political and economic dialogue with Vietnam. Once full diplomatic relations are re-established, Vietnam is certain to experience substantial foreign investment and economic growth. Japanese, Hong Kong, Taiwanese and Korean investment groups are already actively developing projects in Ho Chi Minh City (formerly Saigon), Hanoi and Da Nang, Vietnam's existing hotel inventory is totally inadequate and hotel developments are presently in the planning and development stages by SAS, New World and Peninsula.

Mayanmar, Cambodia and Laos

In view of the political and economic uncertainty which still exists in these countries, investors and hotel management companies are taking a 'wait and see' attitude. Mayanmar seems to be moving slowly towards the liberalization of its economic policies towards foreign investors and appears to be encouraging hotel development.

Hotel development trends in Southeast Asia

The current supply of hotels and resorts in Southeast Asia reflects historical patterns of demand, both from business and leisure travelers. The international hotel industry within the region has been dominated for many years by luxury hotels in primary cities, owned locally and run by the large American international chains. Recently, however, the hotel market has become much more competitive and complex. The product segments and major players are now more numerous and diverse.

The economic growth in the region has fostered the development of new market segments and new destinations, thus creating a larger pool of opportunities. Overall, however, the development of new products particularly outside the luxury range, has tended to somewhat lag behind the emergence of new segments of the travel market. One reason is the time required to plan and complete a project. The international hotel industry in Southeast Asia continues to be dominated by four- and five-star city hotels. This is a reflection of the preference by property owners and investors for prestigious brand names, opulent surroundings and the highest levels of service. The deluxe hotels are the most differentiated, catering to the very highest yield business and leisure travelers and to the upper end of the local restaurant and banquet market. Aided by relatively low labor costs, the luxury market has traditionally enjoyed the greatest demand and the highest profit margins.

Although mid-scale demand is growing, rising land and construction costs have pushed developers toward the top end in regional gateway cities such as Hong Kong, Singapore, Bangkok and Kuala Lumpur. Development continues in these destinations, in part because a property in at least one of the cities is viewed by most hotel companies as a critical first step in establishing a presence in the region. Yet, the cost of development in these destinations cannot be recovered without a premium room rate. Moreover, it may be necessary to enter into some

type of multi-use development, combining hotel, shopping arcade, office and other facilities under the same roof in order to attract more people to use these facilities through cross-demand stimulation. An example of such a development is the New World Center in Hong Kong which comprises hotels, shopping, restaurants, entertainment, offices and residential space. The presence of the luxurious Regent Hotel gives the entire development an aura of quality and international appeal.

Despite a recognized need for accommodation in the three-star range, development of this type of property is out of the question in most central business districts due to the high cost of land. It is, instead, expansion into secondary cities and suburban locations that is resulting in a better balance between upscale and mid-price hotels. Secondary cities in the region are growing into important business and tourist destinations. These include Chiang Mai and Chiang Rai in Thailand, Surabaya and Jogjakarta in Indonesia and Kota Kinabalu, Kuching and Penang in Malaysia.

In new destinations where demand is still limited, the same property must be able to accommodate various market segments. Many hotel groups see opportunities in such locations to develop secondary brand names and mid-market products. Sheraton's plan for a chain of Sheraton Inns throughout Indonesia is an example of this approach. Others, like Accor and Holiday Inn and regional groups like Dusit Thani, are also expanding aggressively in this market sector.

With the increase in disposable income and available vacation time, the intraregional leisure market has also experienced expansion. The growth in income will be most striking in developing countries within the region. According to The ASEAN Tourism Industry Report (1992), 'The gross domestic products of East and Southeast Asia are expected to expand as much as 6.9% on average in both 1991 and 1992'. Another factor influencing the growth in demand is the likely increase in paid leave entitlement. According to a report on the world hotel industry in the 21st century by the International Hotels Association (1992), 'While Western Europe's paid leave entitlement is unlikely to grow much, there should be growth in North America and Asia where at present paid leave is no more than 30–40% of European levels'. Furthermore, the continued decrease in international airfares and ease of accessibility to the Asian region will stimulate new demand.

The supply cycle

Most management groups seeking to develop in Southeast Asia appear unworried by impending oversupply when choosing locations for new hotels. Their overriding strategy is focused on market penetration into every major gateway city thus allowing for cross-marketing and promotion throughout their network of properties. Management groups cite the cyclical nature of the hotel business in their defense. Room supply and demand are rarely in perfect balance and hotels in newly emerging economies tend to develop late in the economic cycle. It takes approximately three years to plan and build a hotel and it is therefore difficult to time an entry into the market at the optimum moment in the economic cycle.

Singapore, which in the mid-1980s suffered dramatic oversupply, has now moved back towards a better balance between supply and demand. Similarly Hong Kong, seriously oversupplied in 1983 and again in 1990–91, swung back to equilibrium in 1993. Mainland China could be an exception, however. Many hoteliers and analysts are pessimistic about oversupply in China both for primary and secondary cities which have been overdeveloped in the 1980s.

In general, hotel executives regard oversupply problems in Southeast Asia, as everywhere else, as temporary and cyclical. Nevertheless, even if this view is correct, those contemplating new development must be aware of market conditions and infrastructural constraints that can lengthen the down cycles, making the adverse effects of overbuilding more permanent (Table 41.5).

Table 41.5 *Existing (1991) and proposed hotel room supply in selected Southeast Asia locations (mid-1990s)*

City/country	Existing hotels		Proposed new hotels or expansion	
	No.	Rooms	No.	Rooms
Peking, China	28	15 925	35	16 142
Hong Kong	69	27 231	27	36 572
Malaysia[a]	977	45 453	9	1654
of which:				
Kuala Lumpur	22	12 902	3	1449
Singapore	65	22 937	12	6916
Thailand (4 + 5-star)	54	19 523	49	21 985
of which:				
Bangkok	21	10 802	26	10 695
Chiang Mai	10	2090	7	2750
Phuket	11	2701	4	1740
Indonesia (1–5-star)	410	34 971	24[b]	4905
of which:				
Jakarta	56	8759	7	2583
Bali[c]	187	9316	10	4359

[a]Proposed new rooms figures based on these facilities already under construction and scheduled to open in 1990.
[b]Foreign investment projects only.
[c]Hotel properties with 100 rooms or greater are included in this category.
Source: Pannell Kerr Foster Services Ltd, Hong Kong, and Directorate General of Tourism, Indonesia.

The international hotel giants

American hotel companies were the first major chains to establish operations in Asia, arriving in the 1960s and 1970s. Others followed more or less the same initial strategy, aimed at covering the relatively safe gateway cities of the Pacific rim with generally no more than one or two properties in each country.

Cited commonly as leaders in this region are Hilton International, Sheraton, Hyatt and Holiday Inns, companies which operate the largest number of properties. Conspicuously absent from the list of market leaders are Inter-Continental and Westin, early entrants whose presence has been eroded as management contracts have expired and been taken over by competitors or by the owners themselves. Companies who entered the Asian market very late include Marriott and the Four Seasons groups. Through a timely merger with Regent in 1992, the Four Seasons hotel group gained instant access to Regent's ten Pacific rim properties.

European chains have been slow to enter the Southeast Asian market. Accor has recently established a footing and intends to bring a range of hotel and resort products to the region. Meridien now has nine hotels in operation or under construction in Asia. SARA Hotels sold out its stake in Southeast Asia entirely, as did the British group, Grand Metropolitan, in 1987. Other European chains, including Moevenpick, SAS Hotels, Swissotel and Kempinski are regarded as newcomers to the area. All these groups, however, have undergone substantial restructuring, largely as a result of the weakness in their owning companies which, with the exception of Moevenpick, are airlines. The future of international hotel expansion for the Moevenpick group is still unclear due to its recent sale by the owner, Mr Prager. The demerger activities of the British-owned Forte chain will lead to a renewed focus of this group's hotel expansion plans into Asia. Club Mediterranée and the Spanish Sol group are continuing their development into the Asian region.

International hotel chains with a strong Asian presence and favorable market recognition have been able to achieve a proportionally high level of bookings originating from within the local Asian markets for their overseas hotels. Hilton International's company-wide occupancy by Asian guests was 26% in 1993 (20% Japanese and 6% other Asians). In response, Hilton has established distinctly branded guest rooms and service concepts in 50 of their non-Asian properties around the world to cater specifically for their Asian clientele.

The 'Wa No Kutsurogi' (comfort and service, the Japanese way) service concept features the following guest amenities in over fifty Hilton International Hotels:

- Japanese-speaking staff
- Japanese hotel information, from menus to fire safety instructions
- An oriental food selection
- Bottled, still mineral water in the guest rooms
- Green tea service
- Slippers, bathrobe and yukata (a lightweight gown) available
- Dedicated Japanese assistance telephone line
- Two-hour pressing service

Regional chains

The greatest challenge to the established market leaders and to new entrants from overseas is 'a barrage of new Asian based groups which can match them in service standards and outbid them with equity from their cash-rich owners' (Hunt, 1990:24). The Asian hotel companies have evolved from single properties to regional chains, some of which have set themselves global ambitions. Prime examples of companies which have expanded rapidly beyond their local borders are Shangri-La and Dusit Thani. The Mandarin Oriental, Peninsula and Regent/Four Seasons are already well-established regionally and are now focused on expanding globally. The Hong Kong-based New World Development Company has not only embarked on aggressively expanding its own branded hotel product but also acquired Ramada Hotels and, in 1993, Stouffer Hotels and Resorts. After acquiring the Omni group, the Hong Kong-based Wharf Holdings Ltd continues to seek Asian expansion (Table 41.6).

Japanese groups have shown the greatest interest in regional and international expansion. In fact, the first Asian hotel company to develop extensively was Japan's Tokyu Group which operates the Pan Pacific Hotels (Bailey, 1987:46). Other than Nikko, a division of Japan Airlines, most Japanese groups have expanded quite slowly in Southeast Asia. This may be due to a lack of interest by Japanese hotel companies in projects in which they do not own a substantial share. The general restrictions on majority ownership of real estate in most Southeast Asian countries may limit their speed of development (Table 41.7).

Hotel chains with strong financial backing

In competing for projects, the corporate affiliations of Asian hotel management companies give them considerable financial and local planning advantages. Many have been taken over or been created as subsidiaries of larger companies with substantial real-estate interests. An equity orientation combined with their understanding of the local and regional business environment gives such companies a competitive advantage in finding partners and establishing relationships with them. New World, for example, is backed by a real-estate development company based in Southeast Asia. Hotel groups such as Dusit Thani and Shangri-La have been created through technology transfer by owners who formerly employed foreign operators. Saunders (1991) described this evolution as fitting in quite naturally with the personal, entrepreneurial nature of Asian business owners and with the related reluctance to lose control to outsiders. Evergreen Hotels, a subsidiary of Taiwan's Evergreen Corporation, is another example. They are presently developing hotels throughout the region, tying into the flight route of Eva Airlines.

On the other hand, several well-known Western brand names whose fortunes in Asia seemed to be fading, may be poised for re-entry into the market under Asian

Table 41.6 *Southeast Asian hotel groups*

	Corporate base	No. of hotels
New World Stouffer Ramada	HK	174
Omni International	HK	45
Shangri-La Int.	Malaysia	21
Shanghai-Jin Jiang Group	PR China	15
Regal Hotels	HK	9
Mandarin Oriental Hotels	HK	9
Park Lane Hotels Int.	HK	8
Dusit Thani	Thai	14
Peninsula	HK	6
Amari Hotels & Resort	Thai	8
Equatorial Hotels Int.	Sing	5
Imperial Family Hotels	Thai	10
Century Interbat	HK	5
Singapore Mandarin Int.	Sing	5
Regent/Four Seasons	HK	13

Source: International Hotels Association (1993).
Groups listed in order of total number of rooms.

Table 41.7 *Japanese hotel groups operating in Southeast Asia*

Hotel group	No. of hotels
Tokyu Hotel Group	102
Prince Hotel Inc.	70
Fujita Kanko Inc.	65
Nikko Hotels Int.	33
Ana Enterprises Ltd	33
Sunroute Hotel Systems	72
Dai-Ichi Hotels Ltd	42
New Ontani Co. Ltd	22
Niyaji Hotels	16
Rihga Royal Hotels	15

Source: International Hotels Association (1993).
Groups listed in order of total number of rooms.

ownership. These include Ramada (now owned by new World Development), Inter-Continental (owned by Seibu-Saison) and Westin (owned by Aoki).

Competitive position and strategies

Apart from the few Asian based groups like Mandarin Oriental, Peninsula, Regent International and Shangri-La which are aiming for the top end of the market, most other Southeast Asian hotel companies are now focusing on the three- to four-start market. These companies are very effective in competing for contracts in the growing intraregional market. Their success is based on a combination of financial strength and market knowledge. Asian-based hotel companies generally understand Asian owners better than their foreign competitors do. Also, their willingness to be major equity partners allows them to accept lower management fees as they share in the appreciation of the real estate and the profit generated from operations. As intraregional travel continues to grow, these chains will be less dependent on Western marketing and reservation systems.

Elements of successful entry by foreign operators

No matter what forms of market entry and development strategy are chosen, the hotel-operating companies have to carefully evaluate the entire implementation process in order to achieve successful entry into this region. They must also realize that the investment required to establish a presence is considerable and that the returns may be slow to materialize as many locations have currently reached saturation.

Since gaining recognition and building personal relationships are essential to doing business in Asia, the international hotel company should establish a permanent base in the region, particularly an office with a developmental role and not just a hotel. A significant investment in establishing a local presence is viewed by the local business community as evidence of the company's sincerity and long-term commitment to the region. Very often, local partners and owners will want to get to know their foreign associates personally and meet with them on a regular basis. Hong Kong and Singapore are the most favorable sites for regional offices as they have an advanced infrastructure, good educational systems, public security and widespread use of English as the language of business.

In establishing a regional office, an international company must find a representative who will live in Southeast Asia on a permanent basis. Saunders (1991) commented that the common practice in North America

of rotating executives through two- or three-year assignments is anathema to the highly personalized way of doing business in Southeast Asia. Contacts and relationships that are developed by one person cannot easily be transferred to their successor. In-depth cultural knowledge in terms of customs, corporate culture and Asian negotiating skills are necessary elements for success in hotel development.

In this environment, executives deal with one another not as representatives of an organization but primarily as individuals. Business decisions may be made on the basis of intuition, pragmatism, personal loyalties, ego or any combination of the above. Thus, qualities such as open-mindedness and patience are all-important. In keeping with the highly personal and entrepreneurial culture of commerce in Southeast Asia, local owners will expect that the person who earns their trust has the authority to make business decisions that arise out of that relationship. In Southeast Asia, decisions are made at the top. Therefore, the head of a large company will expect the person they deal with to be of at least a similar level. It must be emphasized that strong, high-level personal relationships may easily outweigh the marginal difference in value between one hotel brand and another.

International hotel companies should prepare executives and their families for what they can expect in an Asian cultural environment. Personnel at headquarters must also recognize that the process of settling in and developing business relationships is costly and time-consuming. This understanding and support can eliminate the unnecessary pressure on the executives to complete deals with second-rate partners or on sub-optimal contract terms.

Hilton International and Hyatt International developed a strong foothold in the Asian market primarily by adhering to these principles. Their senior executives who were based in Asia over an extended period of time established credibility and long-term relationships with Asian investors which resulted in their company's successful rapid expansion into the region.

Market entry modes

In order to evaluate present market entry modes and forms of financial investment participation by international and Asian hotel groups, an unpublished empirical study was conducted (Ng and Schlentrich, 1993). Questionnaires were sent to twenty international hotel companies, that is, either hotel management companies or holding companies with hotel subsidiaries which have hotel operations in more than three countries apart from their home country and have hotel(s) in at least one country in the Southeast Asian region.

Nine completed questionnaires were returned for a 45% response rate. The responding companies were:

- Club Méditerranée
- Dusit Thani Hotels and Resorts
- Holiday Inn Worldwide
- Inter-Continental
- Mandarin Oriental
- Marriott Corporation
- Ramada International Inc.
- Regent International
- Ritz-Carlton Hotel Co.

Of this sample, three are Asian hotel groups, including Dusit Thani, Mandarin Oriental and Regent International, while the other six are non-Asian hotel groups. Ramada, which was acquired in 1989 by New World Development, a Hong Kong-based real estate/property development company, is regarded as a foreign hotel company, while Regent, after its merger with the Four Seasons Group, is still considered to be an Asian group.

Forms of involvement for existing properties

This study indicates that the current entry modes used by international hotel chains are management contracts, equity joint ventures, franchising and wholly owned ventures. The most common form of involvement is the management contract without equity participation. Companies plan to use this vehicle increasingly for future developments (Table 41.8). Management contracts were used when these companies entered into the Asian region in the early 1970s. According to a survey of hotel management agreements in Asia-Pacific by TransAct (June 1991, PATA (1991)), the average term of the initial period for the contracts was usually 20 years with renewal terms averaging 12 years. A substantial number of these contracts are still valid.

The value of a management contract with a substantial number of years remaining was clearly demonstrated when Hilton International's contract was bought out by

Table 41.9 *Level of equity participation*

Level of investment[a]	Current properties (20% of total)	Planned properties (10% of total)
Less than 10%	19%	17%
10 to 30%	41%	33%
Greater than 30%	45%	50%

$N = 9$ hotel companies (145 properties).
[a]Percentage of total development cost.
Source: Ng and Schlentrich (1993, unpublished).

Hutchinson Whampoa, the Hong Kong holding company, for $125 million in January 1994 in order for the existing site to be redeveloped. The contract was due to run for another 20 years, contributing approximately $6 million a year in management fees.

Level of equity participation

The results of both current and future projects show that international hotel investors prefer a higher level of equity investment for their joint venture projects. This may reflect the operators' desire to satisfy the requirement of the Asian owners/partners to share their risks. The operators may also want to gain a higher return on their investment apart from the basic management or franchising fees. Moreover, they may want to have increased control in operating the hotels. Another distinct feature found was that Asian groups tend to have a far higher equity component than their non-Asian counterparts (Table 41.9). This is also the result found by Hunt (1990).

Forms of equity participation

Operators stated that they have used all forms of equity participation and that they would be flexible in using different forms if needed. One operator described their position 'as a policy, we are open to whatever structure seems to be the best for each situation . . . every form of investment is possible and most have been utilized in some area of our region'.

Table 41.8 *Forms of hotel ownership and management*

	Before 1985	Current properties	Planned properties
Wholly owned	9%	8%	1%
Management contract with equity participation	19%	20%	10%
Management contract	44%	45%	67%
Franchise	28%	27%	22%

$N = 9$ hotel companies (145 properties).
Source: Ng and Schlentrich (1993, unpublished).

Table 41.10 *Forms of equity participation for hotel properties with equity investment*

Forms of equity participation	Frequency[a]
(a) Pre-opening technical assistance fee	2
(b) Pre-opening inventories and working capital	2
(c) Furniture, fixtures and equipment	2
(d) Internal or external funds	7
(e) Others	0

[a]More than one choice was allowed.
Source: Ng and Schlentrich (1993, unpublished).

Table 41.11 *Reasons for equity investment*

Reasons	Frequency[a]
(a) Requests by owners/partners to share the risks	3
(b) To have more flexible forms of development strategy in view of fierce competition for management contract	3
(c) To secure a longer-term management contract	4
(d) To have increased control in operating the hotel and reduce the interference by owners	3
(e) To seek a higher return/profit especially in those properties with the potential of long-term capital appreciation	4
(f) Availability of capital	1
(g) Risk of investment in this region has been reduced	0
(h) Others	0

[a]Companies could give more than one response.
Source: Ng and Schlentrich (1993, unpublished).

With regard to the forms of equity participation, the use of internal funds (i.e. reserves, retaining earnings) and external funds (i.e. bank loans, rights issues and bonds) was the norm (Table 41.10).

The two most commonly cited reasons for the use of equity joint venture were:

- To secure a longer-term management contract, and
- To seek a higher return/profit, especially in those properties with the potential for long-term capital appreciation (Table 41.11).

Constraints for future hotel development in Southeast Asia

The greatest concern for operators is oversupply of hotels in the region followed by worldwide and regional economic recession. It should be noted that the results of this question only reflect the concerns by hotel chains which focus on the four- to five-star market. Their perception of the constraints for future hotel development in this region may be different from other hotel chains which focus on three-star or budget hotel developments (Table 41.12).

Limitations

The sample size of this study is relatively small. Hopefully, more international hotel companies will be willing to participate in any future studies in order to reflect a more accurate picture of current and emerging market entry strategies. Furthermore, a separate study focusing on three-star or budget hotels should be undertaken.

As some of the questions could be viewed as too sensitive by most of the hotel companies, the respondents might not be willing to disclose their actual strategic plans in writing. Therefore, it is recommended that part of the study should be conducted through field interviews.

Summary and conclusions

Economic growth has resulted in a greater range of financing options in Southeast Asia. However, integration

Table 41.12 *Constraints for future hotel development*

	Strongly disagree 1	Slightly disagree 2	Slightly agree 3	Strongly agree 4	Score
(a) Lack of good sites		*			2.13
(b) Stringent financing requirement by financial institutions			*		2.44
(c) Lack of good joint-venture partners		*			2.33
(d) Oversupply of hotels				*	3.44
(e) Slow-down of demand		*			2.33
(f) Political instability (worldwide and regional)		*			2.22
(g) Economic recession (worldwide and regional)			*		2.78

Source: Ng and Schlentrich (1993, unpublished).

into the global economy has also exposed the region to worldwide conditions such as the current credit crunch. As indicated in Saunders's study (1991) there will probably be a shortage of both debt and equity for hotel projects during the 1990s. In the wake of hotel investment disasters, particularly in China, investors are scrutinizing new projects more closely. Japanese banks, the leading source of financing in the late 1980s, have virtually disappeared from the scene, owing to tremendous recent losses from bad debts incurred in both stock market and real estate portfolios.

Until very recently, most lending for hotel development in Southeast Asia was not conducted on a true project finance basis. Instead, foreign and regional banks lent money to the individuals undertaking development on the strength of their standing in the local business community. This reflects both the culture of commerce in Southeast Asia and the strength of demand generated by a booming industry. In today's more conservative climate, banks are scrutinizing hotel project financing closely, generally requiring:

- Detailed project proposals, including line cost development projections, financial projections, business plans and, recently, environmental impact studies
- Early selection of an operator/management company with a guarantee for achieving projected returns
- Incentive fees which previously were based on a percentage of gross operating profit (before debt service) but which are now increasingly based on a percentage of cash flow after debt service
- Increased levels of equity participation (from 30% to 50% of total project cost)
- Shorter-term mortgages (7–10 years) usually with a floating interest rate
- Restricted lending to high-risk regions (i.e. the People's Republic of China).

The emergence of strong Asian-based hotel companies will make market entry for European and American hotel operators seeking traditional management contracts (without equity participation) exceedingly difficult.

Environmental and cultural concerns

The negative impact of large-scale resort developments in the region have led to the destruction of environmentally sensitive coastal areas. The challenge for local governments and the tourist industry as a whole will be to ensure that fast expansion will not take place at the expense of the indigenous population and their cultural and natural heritage.

Bali, for example, a once unspoiled island of scenic beauty and diverse culture, is under siege from rampant commercialism due to its relentless pursuit of tourism revenue. Similar strategies have led to the downfall of resorts such as Acapulco, the Costa del Sol and entire stretches of the Adriatic coast.

Governments, in cooperation with developers, operators, environmental scientists and community representatives, should develop a master plan for regional development. Such a plan should include strict zoning regulations and developmental guidelines with regard to land use, infrastructure, amenity and support facilities (not only for tourists but also for the local community).

Responsible individual developers, notably the Thai Wah Group (which was awarded the 1992 International Hotel Association Environmental Award for their outstanding work at the Laguna Beach Resort) and the developers of the Puerto Azul Resort located on the outskirts of Manila lead the way in giving a positive example of what can be accomplished with commitment and sound environmental planning.

Segmentation and niche marketing

The popularity of Asia as an international destination will further increase as a result of demographic trends. According to the US Bureau of Census, the aging 'baby boomers' (45–55 years old) with a desire to travel, the availability of disposable income and increased time for travel will increase 63% in the coming ten years, a market of over 37 million Americans. The pattern is similar in the other wealthy G7 nations.

This market and the intraregional market are projected to give rise to the following niche market products:

- Asian-based cruise operations—the fast growth of the Florida-based cruise operators indicates that the use of market segmentation promotions could be successfully applied in the Asian region.
- Destination resorts with a timeshare or real-estate component—reputable hospitality companies (i.e. Hilton USA, Marriott, and Disney) are now entering this market.
- Golf, spas and leisure club resorts—the largest operator of private business clubs, Club Corporation of Asia, which is based in Hong Kong, is presently involved in over 18 projects in the Asian region.
- Gaming and entertainment resorts—given the concentration of increased wealth in the Asian region, a market seems to exist for a large offshore gaming and entertainment resort which could compete effectively with Macau and the Australian Gold Coast casinos.

● The convention market—Singapore and Hong Kong are already listed among the top ten cities in the world for conventions by the International Association of Professional Congress Organizers. The projected continuous economic growth and the network of global scientific ties will lead to a sharp rise in international conventions and exhibitions held in Asia. The development and expansion of centers in Hong Kong, Singapore and Jakarta will provide facilities of an international standard.

● Economy hotels—this sector of the hotel market has experienced the fastest growth in the United States, largely as a result of the economic recession. At present, this market is underdeveloped in Asia.

Tourism and hospitality development in Asia is projected to experience strong growth well into the next decade. Political stability, improvements in infrastructure and strict adherence to the maintenance of cultural and environmental factors will provide a solid foundation for the industry.

References and bibliography

ASEAN (1992) *ASEAN Tourism Industry Report*, ASEAN Tourist Information Centre.

Asian Development Bank (1992) 'Annual outlook report 1992'.

Bailey, Murray (1986) 'International hotel chain expansion in Asia: who will get their fingers burnt?', *EIU Travel & Tourism Analyst*.

Bailey, Murray (1987) 'Hotel chains in Asia', *EIU Travel & Tourism Analyst*, March.

Edwards, Anthony (1990) 'Far East and Pacific travel in the 1990's: Forecasts and analysis of potential constraints', Special Report No. 2030, The Economist Intelligence Unit, London.

Economist Intelligence Unit (1991) 'International tourism reports database', *EIU Travel & Tourism Analyst*, No. 4.

Economist Intelligence Unit, *EIU International Tourism Reports: Hong Kong, Thailand, Singapore, Malaysia, Indonesia, 1990–92*.

EIU International Tourism Reports (1990), China, No. 3.

EIU International Tourism Reports (1990), Malaysia, No. 3.

EIU International Tourism Reports (1990), Singapore, No. 2.

EIU International Tourism Reports (1991), Indonesia, No. 3.

EIU International Tourism Reports (1992), Hong Kong, No. 1.

EIU International Tourism Reports (1992), Thailand, No. 1.

Eyster, James J. (1988) *The Negotiation and Administration of Hotel and Restaurant Management contracts*, 3rd edn, School of Hotel Administration, Cornell University, Ithaca, NY.

Eyster, James J. (1993) 'The revolution in domestic hotel management contracts', *Cornell H.R.A. Quarterly*, 16–26 February.

Far Eastern Economic Review (1991) *Asian Yearbook 1991*.

Financial Times Survey (1992) *Indonesia*, 24 June.

Financial Times Survey (1992) *Asia*, 8 June.

Go, Frank and Welch, Peter (1991) 'Competitive strategies for the international hotel industry', Special Report No. 1180, The Economist Intelligence Unit, London.

Horwath International (1993a) *Worldwide Hotel Industry 1993*, New York.

Horwath International (1993b) *Worldwide Beach Resort Survey 1993*, New York.

Hunt, Jill (1990) 'Hotels in Asia', *EIU Travel & Tourism Analyst*, No. 4.

IHA (International Hotels Association) (1992) *International Hotel Trends*.

International Hotels Association (1993) 'Hotels 325: the world's largest 200 chains', *Hotels*, June:39–60.

Jones Lang Wootton (1990, 1992, 1993) *JLW Asia Property Review*, London.

PATA (1991) 'Management contrasts: marriage made in Heaven or Hell', *Travel News Asia Pacific*.

Saunders, Heather A. (1991) 'International hotel development in Southeast Asia: the emergence of a new model', Graduate School of Cornell University, Ithaca, NY.

Schlentrich, U.A. (1993) 'Trends in world hospitality', *Hospitality Management*, No. 135:14–16.

The World Bank (1992) 'Annual report 1992', Washington, DC.

WTO (World Tourism Organisation) (1992) *Yearbook of Tourism Statistics*, vol. 1, 44th edn.

42 Tourism trends to 2000 from the Antipodes to the Old Continent

S. BAKALIS, A. MORRIS AND K. WILSON

Introduction

The total Australian resident short-term departures (ARSTDS) experienced a 5.45% average annual growth (AAG) rate between 1980 and 1992. The growth rate of ARSTDS picked up substantially in 1992 after a very disappointing 1991. More specifically, according to Table 42.1 (see the Appendix for the tables), the number of such departures in 1992 totalled 2 276 300 persons, an 8.43% growth over 1991. This follows a decline of 3.26% in 1991, which was largely due to the Gulf War. It is also apparent that over the course of the last 13 years both America and Asia have surpassed the Old Continent in terms of AAG rates. Asia by achieving an AAG rate of 7.86% has moved from its position as the third most popular destination region in 1980 (behind Europe and Oceania) to the most popular in 1992. On the other hand, America's AAG rate of 7.26% in relation to Europe's modest 2.87% may result in America becoming the second most popular destination for Australians in the next few years if these trends were to persist.

However, looking at the very latest figures in 1992, it is worth noting that ARSTDS to Europe experienced a 12.31% growth over 1991, which compares quite favourably to Asia's 7.41% and America's 8.54% achieved over the same period of time. This may be an auspicious sign for the European destinations which have been suffering badly from the Australian tourists' turnaround towards Asian, American and Oceanian destinations during the 1980s.

It is also evident that travel to the Old Continent hit a snag in 1991 when there was a substantial 13.46% decline over 1990. This decline followed rather large increases of 10.29% in 1989 and 9.85% in 1990 and was due to the Gulf War and, of course, the continuing recession in Australia.

At an individual country level the United Kingdom (combined with Ireland) ranks as the third largest single destination for Australians and is by far the top European destination—accounting for almost half of the Australian visitation to Europe—despite a moderate 2.5% AAG rate

over the last 12 years. Other significant European destinations for Australians are The Netherlands, France, Germany, Italy and Greece.

Table 42.2 (in the Appendix) reveals that from these destinations France has been experiencing a high AAG rate of almost 10% while ARSTDS to Italy and Greece have simply flattened out with a very low AAG rate of 1.2% for Italy and zero AAG rate for Greece. Of course, it is also worth noting that both Italy and Greece (especially Italy) experienced substantial increases in 1992 in relation to 1991 following the end of the Gulf War. The AAG rates to the German Democratic Republic and The Netherlands have been 3.77% and 2% respectively, although as a proportion of the total ARSTDS to Europe the ARSTDS to these nations as well as Italy and Greece have remained rather stable.

In this paper, we generate a model which seeks to explain what determines ARSTDS to the Old Continent as a whole as well as to some of the major European destinations. The main aim is to discover and quantify relationships between ARSTDS and the determinant factors such as time, movements in the real value of the Australian dollar, disposable income and Australian tourists' attitudes towards European destinations in relation to other destinations that compete for the Australian tourist dollar.

Work of this kind can set the scene for undertaking accurate forecasting in an industry where uncertainty about the level of anticipated demand for tourist services represents one of the main obstacles in the process of developing planning procedures. Forecasting can provide at least some indications of the expected level of demand which consequently enables businesses to plan and control their resources accordingly.

The rest of this paper is organised as follows. The next section discusses the rationale for the choice of the adopted model in the context of the current literature. The functional form of the model and the estimation technique are then presented and some interesting empirical results (that are presented in the Appendix) are discussed, for Europe as well as for some individual European countries. Finally some concluding remarks are offered.

The model in the context of the literature[1]

The dependent variable

In the tourism literature the most frequently used dependent variables are the total number of visits (Kliman, 1981), visits per capita (Papadopoulos and Witt, 1985; Witt and Martin, 1985, 1987a, 1987b, 1987c), and total or per capita tourist expenditure (Artus, 1972; Loeb, 1982; Uysal and Crompton, 1984).

Data on an annual basis have been the most common data that appear in the literature (Loeb, 1982; Quayson and Var, 1982; Uysal and Crompton, 1984; Papadopoulos and Witt, 1985; Witt and Martin, 1985, 1987a, 1987b, 1987c, 1988a, 1988b, 1989a, 1989b). This is because explicit international tourism data are published mainly on an annual basis in most international publications. In addition, the use of yearly data provides the convenience of avoiding the effect of seasonality. In this paper, however, quarterly data (as in Smith and Toms (1978) and Chadee and Mieczkowski (1987)) of ARSTDS to Europe were used, in order to quantify not only demand determinants but also the seasonal effect on air travel to Europe.

Explanatory variables

Real per capita gross domestic product (GDP)

International travel is expensive and has been generally classified among luxury goods and services (Smith and Toms, 1978). Undoubtedly, the level of income determines the likelihood that an individual will undertake an overseas trip.

Theoretically, the larger the real per capita GDP of a country is, the more likely the citizens are to spend on pleasure and entertainment and consequently, the more likely is the undertaking of an overseas trip (Smith and Toms, 1978; Loeb, 1982; Uysal and Crompton, 1984; Var et al., 1990). Indeed, the majority of tourism studies have shown that the demand for tourism is invariably highly income-elastic (Boye and Gunadhi, 1986). However, there were cases in which an inverse relationship between real per capita income and arrivals at a destination had emerged. For example, Chadee and Mieczkowski (1987) found an inverse relationship between US income and US tourist arrivals from the USA to Canada. They justified their findings by making the assumption that Canada had been a quasi-domestic destination for Americans and they further concluded that in the face of a rise in US real per capita income US travellers were likely to visit other international destinations. The same situation emerged in the Var et

al. (1990) study when they examined the relationship between Canadian per capita income and arrivals of Canadians to Turkey.

Nevertheless, the findings of the abovementioned studies cannot constitute a rule as far as the relationship between per capita income and arrivals is concerned. Indeed, other empirical studies have shown that whenever the real per capita income is being used as proxy for the disposable income, the respective regression coefficient is positive and usually more than unity (Stronge and Redman, 1982; Loeb, 1982; Uysal and Crompton, 1984; Lin and Sung, 1983 (cited in Boye and Gunadhi (1986)); Anastasopoulos, 1990).

The price of tourism

The appropriate form of the price variable is by no means clear according to Witt and Martin (1987a). The cost that tourists bear for undertaking an overseas trip can be classified into two categories: firstly, the associated cost prior to the departure from the origin country and secondly the cost that emerges while at the tourist destination. The determination of the cost that comes into the second category is a complex one. This is because there is a need to estimate many influential factors that determine this cost component (i.e., time spent at the destination, quality of services, amenities used) and this can become a very troublesome task (Witt and Martin, 1987a).

Most studies in this area use retail price indexes (i.e., consumer price indexes (CPIs)) of the origin and the destination countries (Kliman, 1981; Papadopoulos and Witt, 1985; Loeb, 1982; Uysal and Crompton, 1984; Anastasopoulos, 1990) and/or exchange rates (Loeb, 1982; Uysal and Crompton, 1984; Chadee and Mieczkowski, 1987; Var et al., 1990) as proxies for the cost that tourists bear or the prices that tourists are likely to pay while at the destination.

The dilemma that one faces in including the exchange rate and/or relative prices[2] has been addressed by many researchers, who have expressed their views from different perspectives. Gray (1966) (cited in Witt and Martin (1987a:234)) in agreement with Loeb (1982) argues:

> Prices are seldom completely known in advance by travellers so that the price level foreseen by the potential traveller will depend predominantly upon the rate of exchange of his domestic currency and hearsay evidence. Thus, while the influence of the price variable is undoubtedly complex, the rate of the exchange rate can be expected to be a prime indicator of expected prices.

In addition, Artus (1970) (cited in Witt and Martin (1987a:233)) states: 'The consequences of a change in the exchange rate are immediately perceived by potential foreign travellers. On the other hand these persons are not well informed about recent price developments in foreign countries'. However, the inclusion of relative prices (as a variable) in determining tourism demand for a particular destination was adopted by other researchers and bolstered by Loeb (1982) who attempted to express international tourism demand (in the form of travel exports) as a function of the exchange rate, real per capita income and relative prices. His findings provided evidence that: 'relative prices, and not just exchange rates and real per capita income are an important contributing factor to real travel exports' (Loeb, 1982:18).

The use of relative prices (in the form of CPIs of the origin and destination countries) was also adopted and critically analysed by Witt and Martin (1987a). In their attempt to investigate the choice of an appropriate variable that would represent the tourists' cost of living, their results were found to be in agreement with those of Loeb's (1982). They stated that the empirical results that stemmed from their study did not 'provide evidence of clear superiority (between CPIs and exchange rates), but rather indicate that the consumer price index either alone or together with the exchange rate, is a reasonable proxy for the cost of tourism' (Witt and Martin, 1987a:245). In their conclusion, they stressed that the exchange rate on its own is not an acceptable proxy.

Overall, it can be said that both variables have been found to be significant determinants of tourism demand at a destination. There is no clear evidence to exclude one or the other. Consequently, in the context of our model it will be assumed that both relative prices and nominal exchange rates are expected to exert an influence on ARSTDS to Europe.

Trend and seasonal variables
As the data series that will be examined is a time series one (quarterly), the inclusion of variables that account for the seasonal and time effects, in the estimated model, is essential. The trend component, represents the long-run (upward or downward) movement that ARSTDS usually follow along with the economy's long-run growth. This component can also be affected by changes in travellers' preferences and in their real disposable incomes as well as by population shifts. Of course, seasonality is the cyclical behaviour that takes place on a regular, short-term basis. Baron (1972, 1973, 1974) has addressed the importance of studying the underlying patterns in trend and seasonality in the tourism industry which is heavily affected by them.

Total ARSTDS to America and Asia/Oceania
These variables are included in order to capture the association of the total ARSTDS to Europe in relation to other competing destinations such as America and Asia.

Overall, we will consider the Australian real per capita GDP as proxy for the Australian tourist's disposable income, the real exchange rate (i.e., changes in relative prices including the impact of exchange rates) between the origin and the destination country, time, seasonality and competing destinations as the main determinants of ARSTDS to Europe. Indeed, it is widely accepted that, as far as the destination area is concerned, these factors influence the tourist's opinion quite significantly (Loeb, 1982).[3]

Functional form and estimation techniques

Having taken into consideration what the literature review suggests, an international travel model would take the following general form:

$$ARSTDS = f(RPCGDP, RER, ARSTDSOA, \quad (1)$$
$$ARSTDSAM, TIME, S_1, S_2, S_3)$$

where Australian resident short-term departures (ARSTDS) is the dependent variable of the regression model and is measured by the total number of travellers that intend to stay overseas less than a year and Europe or a specific European country is the main destination that they will visit.[4] Real per capita gross domestic product (RPCGDP) is the total gross domestic product (GDP) of Australia divided by the product of the respective quarter's Australian consumer price index (ACPI) multiplied by the population of Australia in that particular quarter. The estimation of the RPGDP data points has been undertaken by using the following formula:

$$RPCGDP = (GDP/POP)/ACPI \quad (2)$$

Real exchange rate (RER) is the real cost of tourism in Europe in terms of Australian dollars. It is estimated by making use of the following formula:

$$REF = (NER_{AUD,FC} * ACPI)/FCPI \quad (3)$$

where $NER_{AUD,FC}$ is the nominal exchange rate between the Australian dollar and the foreign currency (which is expressed in units of the foreign currency per Australian dollar), and FCPI is the foreign consumer price index.

Indeed, assuming that the FCPI represents adequately the cost of tourism in a foreign country, the product of the ACPI multiplied by the NER when divided by the FCPI will give the real purchasing power of the Australian dollar at the European destination under consideration. Therefore when the RER decreases the Australian traveller would probably revise downwards his/her plans for a visit and therefore the number of ARSTDS would decline. The reverse would happen if there was a rise in the RER. As we have already mentioned, the inclusion of the variables ARSTDSAM and ARSTDSOA is aimed at capturing the association of the total ARSTDS to Europe in relation to other competing destinations such as America (ARSTDSAM) and Asia/ Oceania (ARSTDSOA). TIME is the time trend variable. Seasonal dummy variables (S_1, S_2, S_3) are included in order to account for the effect of seasonality on ARSTDS to Europe. An inspection of the graph of ARSTDS to Europe suggests that the seasonal pattern was fairly stable during the sample period (see Figure 42.1).

In econometric modelling the most widely used technique for estimating tourism demand is the ordinary least squares (OLS) method. However, there are variations in the functional forms of models that have been derived in the area of tourism. The log-linear models have been widely used by researchers of international tourism whenever an attempt was made to use an econometric model (Gray, 1966; Artus, 1970; Smith and Toms, 1978; Little, 1980; Loeb, 1982; Uysal and Crompton, 1984; Boye and Gunadhi, 1986; Chadee and Mieczkowski, 1987; Var et al., 1990).

We argue that ARSTDS are unlikely to adjust instantaneously to changes in RPCGDP and RER, and found that a one quarter lag of both variables performed best. On the other hand, ARSTDSOA and ARSTDSAM, being substitutes, ought to have their impact contemporaneously.

In this paper, we reject the use of a simpler linear model because, in the all-Europe model, autocorrelation was encountered; after re-estimation using the Cochrane–Orcutt technique,[5] the model exhibited heteroscedasticity.[6]

In the period under review, the economic regressors are strongly trended, and three of the four are highly correlated.[7] We therefore enter these variables as first differences in the model. The basic model we test is

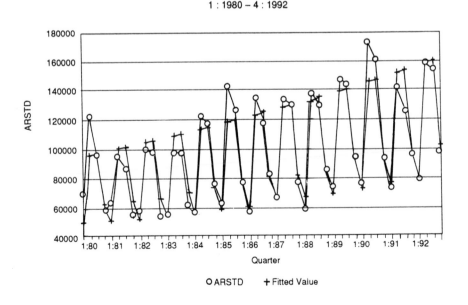

Figure 42.1 *Actual and fitted quarterly data of ARSTDS to Europe*

$$LARSTDS = \beta_0 + \beta_1 S_1 + \beta_2 S_2 + \beta_3 S_3 + + \beta_4 \, TIME$$

$$+ \beta_5 \Delta LRPCGDP_{-1} + \beta_6 \Delta LRER_{-1}$$

$$+ \beta_7 \Delta LARSTDSOA + \beta_8 \Delta LARSTDSAM + \epsilon$$

where

LARSTDS	= logarithm of ARSTDS
S_i	= seasonal dummy (S_i = in quarter i, 0 otherwise)
TIME	= time trend (TIME = 1, 2, . . .)
$\Delta LRPCGDP_{-1}$	= change in the logarithm of Australian real GDP per capital lagged by one quarter
$\Delta LRER_{-1}$	= change in the logarithm of the real exchange rate lagged by one quarter
$\Delta LARSTDSOA$	= change in the logarithm of ARSTDS to Oceania and Asia
$\Delta LARSTDSAM$	= change in the logarithm of ARSTDS to America
ϵ	= random error term

On the assumptions that tourism from Australia to Europe is a superior good and obeys the law of demand, and that travel to Oceania, Asia and America are substitute goods, the hypothesised signs of the coefficients are β_5, $\beta_6 > 0$ and β_7, $\beta_8 < 0$.

For example, the number of the ARSTDS to Europe is expected to increase (decrease) if there is a rise (fall) in the real exchange rate (i.e., in RER), *ceteris paribus*. The same is true with respect to changes in the real per capita gross domestic product (i.e., RPCGDP). On the other hand, one would expect a decline (rise) in the total ARSTDS to Europe in the presence of a rise (decline) in the total ARSTDS to competing destinations such as America, Asia and Oceania.

Finally, and before proceeding to the next section which presents the empirical results, it should be noted that the Australian Bureau of Statistics (ABS) publications on tourist arrivals and departures was the main source for gathering data for departures to Europe. The quarterly publication of the International Monetary Fund provided data on exchange rates and consumer price indexes of European countries and Australia, while ABS publications provided data on the Australian gross domestic product and consumer price index and the population of Australia. The period covered by the database is from January 1980 to April 1992.

Empirical results

We describe here the results obtained from the all-Europe model. The results for particular countries, which are broadly similar, may be viewed in the Appendix. All models were estimated using the Microfit3 program.

In models where autocorrelation presented problems, they were re-estimated using the Cochrane–Orcutt technique. Where this has been necessary, the diagnostic statistics are based on OLS tests of the models using Cochrane–Orcutt transformations of the variables. In all cases the diagnostics are satisfactory; however, we have chosen not to delete variables whose t values were not significant at the 0.05 level.

Interpretation of the coefficients of the economic variables is, at first sight, fairly difficult, since we are dealing with differences of logarithms. It is easy to show, however, that the first differences of the logarithmic regressors are the logarithms of ratios between successive periods.[8] Although we are not able to interpret the coefficients as simple elasticities with respect to, say RER, we can nevertheless draw some meaningful conclusions. If the ratio of RER to its previous level increases by 1%, the corresponding coefficient indicates the average change in ARSTDS, *ceteris paribus*.

The coefficient of real per capita income term, $\Delta LRPCGDP_{-1}$, has the expected sign, and a value of 2.2227. This implies that ARSTDS to Europe would be approximately 2.2% higher, on average and other things being equal, were the ratio 1.01 instead of 1.00 in the preceding quarter, in other words if the growth rate in real per capita income was 1% per quarter. This result is in agreement with the majority of the studies which have attempted to construct a suitable model for forecasting tourism demand (Gray, 1966; Smith and Toms, 1978; Loeb, 1982; Uysal and Crompton, 1984; Papadopoulos and Witt, 1985; Boye and Gunadhi, 1986).

We had no readily available basis for constructing a real exchange rate for the whole of Europe, and experimentation with the use of the Trade Weighted Index proved unsatisfactory. We used the pound sterling as a proxy and found that the coefficient of $\Delta LRER_{-1}$ had the expected sign, and a value of 0.29835. This implies that ARSTDS to Europe would be approximately 0.3% higher, on average and other things being equal, were the ratio 1.01 instead of 1.00 in the preceding quarter, in other words if the growth rate in the real exchange rate was 1% per quarter. During the sample period this term had a downward trend, hence the real exchange rate effect was largely negative.

The coefficient of the ARSTDS to Oceania and Asia term, ΔLARSTDSOA, has the expected sign, and a value of -0.31096. This implies that ARSTDS to Europe would be approximately 0.3% lower, on average and other things being equal, were the ratio 1.01 instead of 1.00 in the same quarter, in other words if the growth rate in ARSTDS to Oceania and Asia income was 1% per quarter. Since during the sample period this growth has generally been positive, we conclude that Australian tourism to Oceania and Asia has had a negative impact on tourism to Europe.

The coefficient of the ARSTDS to America term, ΔLARSTDSOA, did not have the expected sign, and had a value of 0.26020. This is puzzling because this variable is significant at the 0.01 level. It also has the wrong sign in the models for individual countries. Since Australian tourists are unable to nominate more than one main destination, it is not conceivable that ARSTDS to Europe and America are complementary goods, which might have explained the result. We offer the following speculation regarding this anomalous finding. People travelling through Europe and America as part of a single trip, may nominate their main destination arbitrarily; hence essentially the same factors have caused them to visit both places.

The trend coefficient was 0.010442 which indicates a trend rate of growth of approximately 1.05% per quarter or 4.27% per annum.[9]

The coefficient of the March quarter dummy was -0.22225. This corresponds to a seasonal index of 0.8007,[10] where the December quarter index is defined to be 1.0000. Seasonal factors appear to cause an approximate reduction of 20% in the March quarter, compared with the December quarter.

The coefficients for the June and September quarters were almost equal, and hence were replaced by a single dummy, S_{23}, which was defined to be 1 in the June and September quarters, and 0 otherwise. The coefficient of S_{23} was 0.46276 which corresponds to a seasonal index of 1.5885,[11] thus seasonal factors appear to have caused almost a 60% increase in ARSTDS to Europe in the June and September quarters, compared with the December quarter.

Next we used the all-Europe model to make some forecasts for the five years following the sample period. Since accurate forecasts of the values of the economic regressors is not possible, we construct several scenarios, all of which involve constant growth rates. The most likely scenario is that growth rates will continue at roughly the same average rates as those observed in the sample period (see Case D in Table 42.4). Figure 42.2 shows quarterly forecasts under the most likely scenario, and Table 42.5 shows annualised forecasts for the different scenarios.

What is clear from Table 42.5 is that the forecasts are not particularly sensitive to the scenarios used, or in other words the forecasts are determined largely by the trend and seasonal factors. Very large changes in the economic regressors would be required to bring about substantial differences in the forecasts, assuming of course that there are no structural breaks in the model during the forecast period.

Conclusions

Uncertainty about the level of anticipated demand for tourist services nationally or regionally represents one of the main obstacles in the process of developing planning procedures in the tourism industry. As a result forecasting, and more specifically accurate forecasting, has become an important element in tourism planning and management (Calantone et al., 1987).

In this paper, we have tried to stress (in the context of the literature in the area of tourism) the need for demand forecasting. The modelling approach that we have adopted (i.e., multiple regression analysis) has gone some way towards (i) identifying and quantifying relationships between ARSTDS to Europe and its major demand determinants and (ii) forecasting ARSTDS to Europe. These issues are not simply essential but of vital importance in the process of securing and enhancing a profitable future for a tourism business.

Generally speaking we have revealed that on the economic side Australia's real per capita GDP and fluctuations in the real exchange rates stand out as relatively important factors that affect outbound travel from the Antipodes to the Old Continent. Disposable incomes are in turn dependent upon factors such as wages, tax policy, interest rates and inflation levels. Within this context, outbound travel from Australia to Europe can be expected to remain subdued so long as the current recession in Australia continues. However, if the recent relief in interest rates is sustained, mortgage repayments will not impinge so markedly upon disposable incomes, and the probability of expenditure on travel may increase. Such an increase in travel may be further enhanced as Australia emerges from the recession, as some economic indicators seem to reflect recently. These findings are consistent with other work in this area (see, for example, BTR (1991)). However, if economic recovery in Australia

ARSTD EUROPE
1 : 1980 – 4 : 1997

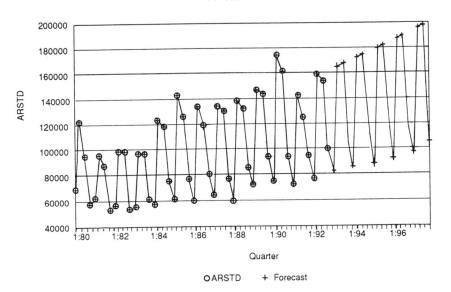

Figure 42.2 *Quarterly projections to 1996 coupled with the actual quarterly observations from 1980 to 1992 (Case A)*

is accompanied by a general depreciation of the Australian dollar against most European currencies and as long as inflation rates in European countries continue to outstrip Australia's very low inflation rate then a decline in the real purchasing power of the Australian dollar in Europe will continue. This may then result in any increased travel demand being expressed in domestic, rather than outbound, travel. In that case Europe could continue to have a decreasing share of the Australian overseas travel dollar.

We have also pointed out that apart from economic conditions, there are also trend time factors that influence the level of outbound travel. We have shown that these factors are quite strong. Seasonality as it was expected does influence considerably departures to Europe (especially) during the Mediterranean spring and summer. The relationship between ARSTDS to Europe and ARSTDS to other destinations such as (Asia/Oceania and America) are significant determinants of the ARSTDS to Europe.

Of course, it goes without saying that our projections for outbound travel from Australia to Europe may be totally immaterial in the presence of unforeseen exogenous factors as recent experiences (such as the Gulf War) have shown. None would deny that with Saddam Hussein still

at the helm in Iraq the situation in the Middle East is very sensitive and that the consequence of any hostilities in that part of the globe will adversely affect outbound travel from Australia to Europe. The same can be said with respect to the civil war in the former Yugoslavia, which up to this point of time is confined to that country only and has not spread to bordering countries. If this was to happen the prospects of outbound travel from Australia to Europe would be very bleak, especially for those European countries, such as Greece, that may be directly involved in such a conflict. And this is without mentioning any adverse developments in the former Soviet Union or within the European Economic Community.

Notes

1. In this section we draw extensively on material from Bakalis and Theodossiou (1994).
2. A relative prices variable is usually defined by the ratio of CPIs between the origin and destination economies (Loeb, 1982).
3. It is widely acknowledged (by many researchers) that international travel also depends upon major transportation costs. However, this variable is often excluded because the acquisition of data is not feasible and because of the possibility of potential multicollinearity problems (Uysal and Crompton, 1994).

4. This definition has been set by the Australian Bureau of Statistics.
5. $\rho = 0.34204$.
6. A heteroscedasticity test, which regressed squared residuals on squared fitted values, produced a Lagrange multiplier statistic $CHI\text{-}SQ_1 = 8.4146[0.004]$, and on an F test, $F_{1,50} = 9.6529[0.003]$.
7. The Pearson correlation coefficients are 0.88908 between LRPCGDP and LARSTDSOA, 0.84568 between

LARSTDSOA and LARSTDSAM, and 0.78896 between LRPCGDP and LARSTDSAM.
8. For example, $\Delta LRER_t = \log(RER_t) - \log(RER_{t-1}) = \log(RER_t/RER_{t-1})$.
9. Defining g = quarterly growth rate we have $1 + g = \exp(0.010442) = 1.0105$, hence $g = 0.0105$ or 1.05%.
10. $\exp(-0.22225) = 0.8007$.
11. $\exp(0.46276) = 1.5885$.

Appendix

Table 42.1 *Total departures and growth rates by region*

Year	Total	Europe	Asia	America	Oceania	Other
1980	1 203 602	349 496	315 468	165 353	354 422	18 863
1981	1 217 299	301 705	362 343	165 545	361 170	26 536
1982	1 286 908	311 966	386 424	181 884	386 144	20 490
1983	1 252 974	314 305	378 398	163 857	377 387	19 027
1984	1 418 600	375 200	425 400	174 000	422 600	21 400
1985	1 512 000	410 300	466 600	171 600	439 300	24 200
1986	1 539 600	396 700	520 100	185 600	415 300	21 900
1987	1 622 300	408 300	547 300	215 100	417 300	34 300
1988	1 697 600	417 000	599 900	243 900	407 200	29 600
1989	1 989 900	459 900	714 700	293 000	492 300	30 000
1990	2 170 000	505 200	759 200	348 200	529 900	27 500
1991	2 099 300	437 200	728 400	353 500	522 300	57 900
1992	2 276 300	491 300	782 400	383 700	546 300	72 900
Annual growth rates						
1980	—	—	—	—	—	—
1981	1.14	−13.67	14.86	0.12	1.90	40.68
1982	5.72	3.40	6.65	9.87	6.91	−22.78
1983	−2.64	0.75	−2.08	−9.91	−2.27	−7.14
1984	13.22	19.37	12.42	6.19	11.98	12.47
1985	6.58	9.36	9.69	−1.38	3.95	13.08
1986	1.83	−3.31	11.47	8.16	−5.46	−9.50
1987	5.37	2.92	5.23	15.89	0.48	56.62
1988	4.64	2.13	9.61	13.39	−2.42	−13.70
1989	17.22	10.29	19.14	20.13	20.90	1.35
1990	9.05	9.85	6.23	18.84	7.64	−8.33
1991	−3.26	−13.46	−4.06	1.52	−1.43	110.55
1992	8.43	12.31	7.41	8.54	4.60	25.91
AAG						
80–92	5.45	2.87	7.86	7.26	3.67	11.92

AAG = average annual growth.
Source: Australian Bureau of Statistics (1980–1992).

Table 42.2 *Total departures and growth rates for some selected European countries*

Year	UK	Netherlands	Italy	France	Germany	Greece
1980	188 317	13 010	38 695	8409	20 509	31 459
1981	155 698	11 221	33 544	9172	18 130	27 127
1982	155 167	11 977	35 373	10 857	20 716	27 185
1983	165 422	11 174	35 557	9660	18 654	24 963
1984	200 500	12 200	39 500	13 000	23 200	28 500
1985	218 600	13 400	43 800	14 000	24 900	32 400
1986	210 400	13 300	39 400	14 300	26 900	31 700
1987	214 100	14 100	40 200	15 800	26 200	33 900
1988	221 500	12 800	39 300	16 300	27 000	33 600
1989	247 500	13 200	41 500	20 500	30 700	31 600
1990	264 600	16 000	45 000	24 100	34 600	33 100
1991	231 300	13 800	37 500	22 400	31 500	27 400
1992	253 500	16 500	44 900	25 500	32 000	30 100
Annual Growth Rates						
1980	—	—	—	—	—	—
1981	− 17.32	− 13.75	− 13.91	9.07	− 11.60	− 13.77
1982	− 0.34	6.74	5.45	18.37	14.26	0.95
1983	6.61	− 6.70	0.52	− 11.03	− 9.95	− 8.85
1984	21.21	9.18	11.09	34.58	24.37	14.17
1985	9.03	9.84	10.89	7.69	7.33	13.68
1986	− 3.75	− 0.75	− 10.05	2.14	8.03	− 2.16
1987	1.76	6.02	2.03	10.49	− 2.60	6.94
1988	3.46	− 9.22	− 2.24	3.16	3.05	− 0.88
1989	11.74	3.13	5.60	25.77	13.70	− 5.95
1990	6.91	21.21	8.43	17.56	12.70	4.75
1991	− 12.59	− 13.75	− 16.67	− 7.05	− 8.96	− 17.22
1992	9.60	19.57	19.73	13.84	1.59	9.85
AAG						
80–92	2.50	2.00	1.20	9.68	3.77	0.00

AAG = average annual growth.
Source: Australian Bureau of Statistics (1980–1992).

Table 42.3a *Empirical results: Europe*

Estimation: Cochrane–Orcutt method AR(1)

Dependent variable LARSTDSEU

Regressor	Coefficient	Standard error
INTERCEPT	10.984 5	0.048 408
S_1	− 0.222 25	0.053 069 **
S_{23}	0.462 76	0.024 219 **
TIME	0.010 442	0.001 3268**
ΔLRPCGDP$_{-1}$	2.222 7	0.866 87 *
ΔLRERUK$_{-1}$	0.298 35	0.120 58 *
ΔLARSTDSOA	− 0.310 96	0.140 85 *
ΔLARSTDSAM	0.260 20	0.072 658 **

R-Sq	0.964 89	$F_{8,40}$	137.414 7 [0.000]
Adj R-Sq	0.957 87	SE	0.071 908
Resid SS	0.206 83	Mean Dep Var	11.451 6
SD Dep Var	0.346 77	Max Log-likelihood	64.429 9
DW	1.940 0		

Diagnostic tests

Test statistics		LM version		F version
Serial Cor	CHI-SQ$_1$	0.042 393 [0.837]	$F_{1,40}$	0.034 637 [0.853]
Funct Form	CHI-SQ$_1$	0.419 51 [0.517]	$F_{1,40}$	0.345 41 [0.560]
Normality	CHI-SQ$_2$	1.00 19 [0.606]	Not applicable	
Hetero	CHI-SQ$_1$	0.025 793 [0.872]	$F_{1,47}$	0.024 753 [0.876]

*Significant at 5%. **Significant at 1%.

Table 42.3b *Empirical results: United Kingdom and Ireland*

Estimation: Cochrane–Orcutt Method AR(1)

Dependent variable LARSTDSUK

Regressor	Coefficient	Standard error
INTERCEPT	10.322 7	0.057 785
S_1	−0.177 07	0.069 396 *
S_{23}	0.449 08	0.031 695 **
TIME	0.011 073	0.001 5476**
$\Delta LRPCGDP_{-1}$	2.884 5	1.124 6 *
$\Delta LRERUK_{-1}$	0.298 52	0.156 29
$\Delta LARSTDSOA$	−0.258 96	0.184 09
$\Delta LARSTDSAM$	0.208 30	0.094 605 *

R-Sq	0.938 01	$F_{8,40}$		75.653 2 [0.000]
Adj R-Sq	0.925 61	SE		0.091 630
Resid SS	0.335 84	Mean Dep Var		10.813 5
SD Dep Var	0.332 50	Max Log-likelihood		52.553 8
DW	1.942 2			

Diagnostic tests

Test statistics		LM version		F version
Serial Cor	CHI-SQ$_1$	0.108 88 [0.741]	$F_{1,40}$	0.089 079 [0.767]
Funct Form	CHI-SQ$_1$	0.857 1E-4 [0.993]	$F_{1,40}$	0.699 6E-4 [0.993]
Normality	CHI-SQ$_2$	1.290 6 [0.524]	Not applicable	
Hetero	CHI-SQ$_1$	0.810 01 [0.368]	$F_{1,47}$	0.790 00 [0.379]

*Significant at 5%. **Significant at 1%.

Table 42.3c *Empirical results: Germany*

Estimation: Ordinary least squares

Dependent variable LARSTDSGDR

Regressor	Coefficient	Standard error
INTERCEPT	8.232 1	0.048 337
S_1	−0.243 22	0.084 446 **
S_{23}	0.346 61	0.041 355 **
TIME	0.013 595	0.001 0341**
$\Delta LRPCGDP_{-1}$	1.733 0	1.315 8
$\Delta LRERGDR_{-1}$	−0.261 83	0.204 83
$\Delta LARSTDSOA$	−0.265 43	0.228 29
$\Delta LARSTDSAM$	0.140 67	0.115 84

R-Sq	0.917 59	$F_{7,42}$		66.805 4 [0.000]
Adj R-Sq	0.903 85	SE		0.102 17
Resid SS	0.438 44	Mean Dep Var		8.725 5
SD Dep Var	0.329 51	Max Log-likelihood		47.466 7
DW	1.641 0			

Diagnostic tests

Test statistics		LM version		F version
Serial Cor	CHI-SQ$_1$	1.484 4 [0.223]	$F_{1,41}$	1.254 4 [0.269]
Funct Form	CHI-SQ$_1$	0.049 837 [0.823]	$F_{1,41}$	0.040 907 [0.841]
Normality	CHI-SQ$_2$	1.546 2 [0.462]	Not applicable	
Hetero	CHI-SQ$_1$	0.092 748 [0.761]	$F_{1,48}$	0.089 204 [0.766]

*Significant at 5%. **Significant at 1%.

Table 42.3d *Empirical results: Italy*

Estimation: Ordinary least squares

Dependent variable LARSTDSITA

Regressor	Coefficient	Standard error
INTERCEPT	8.776 0	0.041 549
S_1	−0.209 30	0.072 810 **
S_{23}	0.567 40	0.036 289 **
TIME	0.003 4889	0.905 5E-3**
$\Delta LRPCGDP_{-1}$	3.962 2	1.132 7 **
$\Delta LRERITA_{-1}$	0.372 78	0.191 137
$\Delta LARSTDSOA$	0.025 593	0.195 79
$\Delta LARSTDSAM$	0.314 75	0.100 41 **

R-Sq	0.956 70	$F_{7,41}$	129.420 2 [0.000]
Adj R-Sq	0.949 31	SE	0.087 688
Resid SS	0.315 25	Mean Dep Var	9.130 1
SD Dep Var	0.389 48	Max Log-likelihood	54.103 8
DW	1.899 7		

Diagnostic tests

Test statistics		LM version		F version
Serial Cor	$CHI\text{-}SQ_1$	0.092 934 [0.760]	$F_{1,40}$	0.076 008 [0.784]
Funct Form	$CHI\text{-}SQ_1$	2.142 0 [0.143]	$F_{1,40}$	1.828 5 [0.184]
Normality	$CHI\text{-}SQ_2$	0.711 71 [0.701]	Not applicable	
Hetero	$CHI\text{-}SQ_1$	0.148 35 [0.700]	$F_{1,47}$	0.142 73 [0.707]

*Significant at 5%. **Significant at 1%.

Table 42.3e *Empirical results: France*

Estimation: Cochrane–Orcutt method AR(1)

Dependent variable LARSTDSFRA

Regressor	Coefficient	Standard error
INTERCEPT	7.456 7	0.059 881
S_1	−0.055 714	0.069 988
S_{23}	0.243 90	0.034 635 **
TIME	0.023 031	0.001 6469**
$\Delta LRPCGDP_{-1}$	−0.422 19	1.257 5
$\Delta LRERFRA_{-1}$	0.029 362	0.218 51
$\Delta LARSTDSOA$	0.366 78	0.188 73
$\Delta LARSTDSAM$	0.242 82	0.101 10 *

R-Sq	0.949 97	$F_{8,40}$	94.938 8 [0.000]
Adj R-Sq	0.939 96	SE	0.099 521
Resid SS	0.396 18	Mean Dep Var	8.213 3
SD Dep Var	0.405 29	Max Log-likelihood	48.506 1
DW	1.718 1		

Diagnostic tests

Test statistics		LM version		F version
Serial Cor	$CHI\text{-}SQ_1$	0.452 78 [0.501]	$F_{1,40}$	0.373 07 [0.545]
Funct Form	$CHI\text{-}SQ_1$	0.810 97 [0.368]	$F_{1,40}$	0.673 15 [0.417]
Normality	$CHI\text{-}SQ_2$	1.246 3 [0.536]	Not applicable	
Hetero	$CHI\text{-}SQ_1$	2.828 7 [0.093]	$F_{1,47}$	2.879 5 [0.096]

*Significant at 5%. **Significant at 1%.

Table 42.3f   *Empirical results: Greece*

Estimation: Ordinary least squares

Dependent variable LARSTDSGRE

Regressor	Coefficient	Standard error
INTERCEPT	8.492 4	0.054 177
S_1	−0.112 59	0.092 733
S_{23}	0.620 00	0.045 804 **
TIME	0.001 2445	0.001 1596
ΔLRPCGDP$_{-1}$	2.280 4	1.464 5
ΔLRERGRE$_{-1}$	−0.448 82	0.265 09
ΔLARSTDSOA	−0.248 63	0.250 43
ΔLARSTDSAM	0.775 95	0.132 00 **

R-Sq	0.943 00	$F_{7,42}$	99.259 3 [0.000]
Adj R-Sq	0.933 50	SE	0.113 31
Resid SS	0.539 27	Mean Dep Var	8.827 9
SD Dep Var	0.439 40	Max Log-likelihood	42.292 1
DW	1.565 9		

Diagnostic tests

Test statistics		LM version		F version
Serial Cor	CHI-SQ$_1$	1.407 9 [0.235]	$F_{1,41}$	1.187 9 [0.282]
Funct Form	CHI-SQ$_1$	3.608 4 [0.057]	$F_{1,41}$	3.189 0 [0.082]
Normality	CHI-SQ$_2$	1.919 7 [0.383]	Not applicable	
Hetero	CHI-SQ$_1$	0.326 86 [0.568]	$F_{1,48}$	0.315 85 [0.577]

*Significant at 5%. **Significant at 1%.

Table 42.3g   *Empirical results: Netherlands*

Estimation: Ordinary least squares

Dependent variable LARSTDSNET

Regressor	Coefficient	Standard error
INTERCEPT	7.706 3	0.068 874
S_1	−0.081 357	0.119 81
S_{23}	0.367 89	0.059 118 **
TIME	0.005 9913	0.001 4730**
ΔLRPCGDP$_{-1}$	0.778 62	1.878 4
ΔLRERNET$_{-1}$	0.093 076	0.293 42
ΔLARSTDSOA	0.022 626	0.323 27
ΔLARSTDSAM	0.577 12	0.165 50 **

R-Sq	0.836 52	$F_{7,42}$	30.701 5 [0.000]
Adj R-Sq	0.809 27	SE	0.145 61
Resid SS	0.890 50	Mean Dep Var	8.048 8
SD Dep Var	0.333 42	Max Log-likelihood	29.752 9
DW	2.039 7		

Diagnostic tests

Test statistics		LM version		F version
Serial Cor	CHI-SQ$_1$	0.026 861 [0.870]	$F_{1,41}$	0.022 038 [0.883]
Funct Form	CHI-SQ$_1$	0.514 53 [0.473]	$F_{1,41}$	0.426 30 [0.517]
Normality	CHI-SQ$_2$	4.906 2 [0.086]	Not applicable	
Hetero	CHI-SQ$_1$	5.422 6 [0.020]	$F_{1,48}$	5.838 9 [0.020]

*Significant at 5%. **Significant at 1%.

Table 42.4 *Alternative scenarios for the calculation of long-term forecasts (to the year 1997) of tourism trends**

	Case A	Case B	Case C	Case D	Case E
Trend/seasonal	Yes	Yes	Yes	Yes	Yes
RPCGDP	0	2%	4%	2%	2%
RER	0	0	0	−6%	0
ARSTDSAM	0	0	0	8%	8%
ARSTDSOA	0	0	0	6%	6%

*All changes are on an annual basis.

Table 42.5 *Projected departures and AAGs to Europe to 1997 in the presence of alternative economic scenarios*

Year	Case A	Case B	Case C	Case D	Case E
1992	491000	491000	491000	491000	491000
1993	518773	524556	530374	522469	524830
1994	540900	546929	552995	544753	547215
1995	563971	570257	576583	567988	570555
1996	588025	594580	601175	592214	594891
1997	613105	619851	626816	617474	620256
AAG					
92–97	4.5%	4.8%	5.0%	4.7%	4.8%

References

Anastasopoulos, P. (1990) 'Demand for travel', *Annals of Tourism Research*, 17:663–665.

Artus, J. R. (1970) 'The effect of revolution on the foreign travel balance of Germany', IMF Staff Papers, No. 17, pp. 602–617.

Artus, J. R. (1972) 'An econometric analysis of international travel', IMF Staff Papers, No. 19, pp. 579–614.

Australian Bureau of Statistics (1980–1992) 'Overseas arrivals and departures', ABS, Canberra, Australia.

Australian Bureau of Statistics (1980–1993) *Overseas Arrivals and Departures Australia Quarterly*, ABS, Canberra, Australia.

Australian Bureau of Statistics (1980–1991) *Australian Demographics Statistics Quarterly*, ABS, Canberra, Australia.

Australian Bureau of Statistics (1991) 'Australian economic indicators', ABS, Canberra, Australia.

Bakalis, S. and Theodossiou, K. (1994) 'Southern Europe as a tourist destination to the folks from downunder: the case of Greece', *Journal of Hospitality and Leisure Marketing* (in press).

Boye, C. K. and Gunadhi, H. (1986) 'Demand elasticities of tourism in Singapore', *Tourism Management*, 7:239–253.

BTR (Bureau of Tourism Research) (1990) 'Australian tourism trends', BTR, Canberra, Australia.

BTR (Bureau of Tourism Research) (1991) 'Australian tourism trends', BTR, Canberra, Australia.

Calantone, R. J., Di, Benedetto, C. A. and Bojanic, D. (1987) 'A comprehensive review of the tourism forecasting literature', *Journal of Travel Research*, 26(2):28–39.

Chadee, D. and Mieczkowski, Z. (1987) 'An empirical analysis of the effects of the exchange rate on Canadian tourism', *Journal of Travel Research*, XXVI (1).

Gray, H. P. (1966) 'The demand for international travel by the United States and Canada', *International Economic Review*, 7:83–92.

International Monetary Fund, *International Financial Statistics*, IMF, New York.

Kliman, M. L. (1981) 'A quantitative analysis of Canadian overseas tourism', *Transportation Research*, 15A:487–497.

Kucukkurt, M. (1981) 'Factors affecting travel destination choice: an expectancy theory framework for studying travel behaviour', U.M.I., Rensselaer Polytechnic Institute.

Little, J. S. (1980) 'International travel in the U.S. balance of payments', *New England Economic Review*, May–June:42–55.

Loeb, P. D. (1982) 'International travel to the United States: an econometric evaluation', *Annals of Tourism Research*, 9:7–20.

Papadopoulos, S. I. and Witt, S. F. (1985) 'A marketing analysis of foreign tourism in Greece', in *Proceedings of 2nd World Marketing Congress*, Shaw, S., Sparks, L. and Kaynak, E. (Eds), University of Stirling, pp. 682–693.

Quayson, J. and Var, T. (1982) 'A tourism demand function for the Okanagan, BC', *Tourism Management*, 3:108–115.

Smeral, E., Witt, F. S. and Witt, C. A. (1992) 'Econometric forecasts: tourism trends to 2000', *Annals of Tourism Research*, 19:450–465.

Smith, A. B. and Toms, J. N. (1978) 'Factors affecting demand for international travel to and from Australia', Occasional paper No. 11, Canberra, Australia.

Stronge, W. B. and Redman, M. (1982) 'U.S. tourism in Mexico: an empirical analysis', *Annals of Tourism Research*, 9:21–35.

Theodossiou, K. (1992) 'Forecasting outbound tourism from Australia to Greece' unpublished Masters Thesis, Victoria University, Melbourne.

Uysal, M. and Crompton, J. L. (1984) 'Determinants of demand for international tourist flows to Turkey', *Tourism Management*, 5:288–297.

Uysal, M. and Crompton, J. L. (1985) 'An overview of approaches used to forecast tourism demand', *Journal of Travel Research*, XXII:7–15.

Var, T., Mohammad, G. and Icoz, O. (1990) 'Factors affecting international tourism demand for Turkey', *Annals of Tourism Research*, 17:606–609.

Witt, F. S. and Martin, C. A. (1985) 'Forecasting future trends in European tourist demand', *Tourist Review*, No. 4:163–180.

Witt, F. S. and Martin, C. A. (1987a) 'Tourism demand forecasting models: choice of appropriate variable to represent tourists' cost of living', *Tourism Management*, 8:233–246.

Witt, F. S. and Martin, C. A. (1987b) 'International tourism demand models—inclusion of marketing variables', *Tourism Management*, 8:33–40.

Witt, F. S. and Martin, C. A. (1987c) 'Econometric models in forecasting international tourism demand', *Journal of Travel Research*, XXV:23–30.

Witt, F. S. and Martin, C. A. (1988a) 'Substitute prices in models of tourism demand', *Annals of Tourism Research*, 15:255–268.

Witt, F. S. and Martin, C. A. (1988b) 'Forecasting performance', *Tourism Management*, 9:326–329.

Witt, F. S. and Martin, C. A. (1989a) 'Accuracy of econometric forecasts of tourism', *Annals of Tourism Research*, 16:407–427.

Witt, F. S. and Martin, C. A. (1989b) 'Measures of forecasting accuracy—turning point error v size of error', *Tourism Management*, 10:20–28.

Witt, S. F. and Martin, C. A. (1989c) 'Demand forecasting in tourism and recreation, in *Progress in Tourism, Recreation and Hospitality Management*, Cooper, C. P. (Ed.), Belhaven, London, pp. 4–32.

43 Barriers found in repositioning a Mediterranean 'sun and beach' product: the Valencian case

F. AMOR, C. CALABUIG, J. ABELLÁN AND V. M. MONFORT

Barriers found in repositioning a tourist product

The understanding of consumers' wants and needs is the first step to gain insight about the nature of the actions to be taken in order to modify consumers' attitudes towards a product or service. The identification of the actual barriers found in the process of change of consumers' perceptions is an important tool for the task of repositioning a product or service. When repositioning a tourist product in the mind of consumers it is essential to take into account the different stages in the consumers' decision-making process.

Among others, Middleton's (1988) stimulus–response model of buyer behavior is an operative approach for the analysis of the different factors influencing the selection of a tourist destination since it implies a useful partition of the process. The analysis of these different determinants is the basis of identifying the barriers in repositioning a tourist product. These obstacles in changing consumer's perceptions can be ascribed to the diverse components resulting from this partition or, in other words, can be attributed to the different stages of the process (Figure 43.1).

Basically, the components of the model are the product itself, the competitors, the communication channels, the influential groups and post-consumption feelings. Using this model it is possible to identify the barriers in repositioning a tourist product.

The barriers inherent to the product itself are those characteristics which impede the achievement of the desired image owing to a lack of adequacy of the product to the desired repositioning, to an unrealistic desired repositioning, and/or to intrinsic inconsistencies of the product.

The barriers derived from the competition are mainly the result of the existence of already established products with a set of attributes with a similar positioning to the one desired for our product.

The barriers arising from the communication are twofold: firstly those derived from the communication of one's product; and, secondly, those resulting from the communication efforts made by competitors.

The inadequacy or inconsistency of the elements of the communication mix (advertising, promotion, public relations) are barriers derived from the communication of one's product. By the same token, the barriers arising from the communication of competitors' products are the adequacy or consistency of the communication mix and the support received by the competitors' messages, including the use of public relations.

The lack of distribution, or deficiencies in it, as well as inconsistencies in the distribution in regard to the desired repositioning, entail barriers for changing consumers' perceptions about a tourist product. In the same manner, an adequate and consistent distribution of competitors' product can constitute an obstacle in repositioning one's own product.

Influential groups, such as the family, peer groups, etc., can also generate obstacles by means of negative advice regarding the characteristics of one's product—based either on perceptions which oppose consumers' expectations, or experience, or both. In the same way, these groups can produce barriers in repositioning a tourist product by means of supportive influence in respect of the attributes of competitors' product.

Finally, the nature of post-consumption feelings—either negative or positive—concerning one's own or the competitors' product constitute a set of potential barriers in repositioning a tourist product in the mind of the consumers.

The Valencian case

Background on the Valencian case

Valencia is a Spanish region located on the Mediterranean coast which constitutes the southern extremity of the Mediterranean industrial arch. It is especially suited to tourism as it is situated at a strategic meeting point of the western Mediterranean key communications network. The Valencia region with its different resorts, attracts visitors not only from Spain but also from other European countries (Germany, United Kingdom, Benelux, France, Italy, etc.). The Valencian tourist product was developed during the 1960s, 1970s and 1980s on the basis of a set of natural conditions, e.g. its mild climate and its lengthy

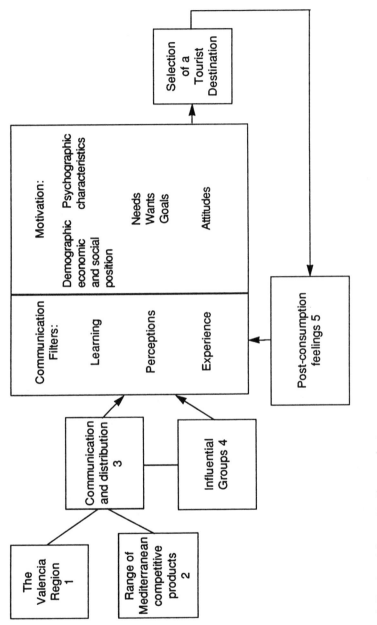

1. Barriers inherent to the product
2. Barriers derived from the competition
3. Barriers arising from: the communication of one's product/the communication of the competitors' product
   Barriers derived from: the distribution of one's product/the distribution of the competitors' product
4. Barriers arising from influential groups
5. Barriers arising from post-consumption feelings

Figure 43.1 *Adaptation of the stimulus–response model of buyer behavior developed by Middleton (1988)*

coastline, which has shaped its image as a 'sun and beach' tourist destination. The development of tourism as an industry in the region came with the discovery, by international tour operators, of the opportunities offered by some coastal resorts, such as Benidorm. What these resorts offered was an exotic product as well as low prices, which considerably appealed to the middle and lower segments of the market.

From the start the development of tourism in Valencia was not accompanied by any appropriate instruments to measure carrying capacity. Therefore, tourism development had the seeds of its own subsequent problems, by its failure to take into account factors that might affect its viability in the future.

When Valencia began to develop its tourism activity, Spain had a totalitarian government with limited political freedom. Tourism was used as a propaganda tool to create a good image of the regime. General Franco's regime used tourism to overcome the autarchy, to increase his popularity and to provide foreign exchange to finance an underdeveloped economy which was outside of the evolution taking place in the European context. There was also a lack of full powers to design a regional tourism policy for Valencia. For this reason, and because of the later Spanish political change, the decision to adopt an appropriate policy line in tourism was delayed. Nowadays, Valencia has a regional government with full powers to design its own tourism policy according to its interests. The organization in charge of the development and implementation of this policy is the Valencian Tourist Board (ITVA) where the authors of this paper currently pursue their professional careers.

It can be concluded that tourism in the Land of Valencia has been primarily driven for three decades by the market requirements generated by tour operators' needs. This has configured a basic model that relies fundamentally on the region's natural conditions and is showing signs of exhaustion. It must be pointed out that, as a Mediterranean tourist model based on 'sun and beach', the Valencia region suffers from an important degree of seasonality, shaped by the vacation habits of its main markets. This seasonality is particularly acute in Spain itself; other nations have reduced this problem by staggering their holidays.

The Valencian Tourist Board's current tourism policy attempts to reduce the seasonal nature of its product by carrying out promotional efforts during the low season, favoring conditions to make the offer more attractive for 'third age' and 'business and convention' tourism, in order to increase the profitability of the hotel premises in the low season. These initiatives are an attempt to solve the traditional and established model's shortcomings.

Valencia's tourism policy is designed to increase competitiveness by improving the quality of products and services, incorporating quality guidelines previously used by the industrial sector.

It is necessary to find elements to uplift this 'sun and beach' offer, to improve quality, and to diversify the tourist activity through new and alternative products for which it has resources and a potential demand in the market. In other words, the desired repositioning is based on the diversification of the product towards new segments of the market, such as the business, cultural, health, sports and adventure segments, and on increasing the quality of the service. In so doing, the Valencian government aims to develop a 'sun and beach' product addressed to segments of demand with a higher capacity to generate receipts.

Research objectives and methodology

The fundamental objective of this paper is to identify the barriers to repositioning a Mediterranean 'sun and beach' product, in particular the Land of Valencia.

In order to identify the obstacles to repositioning the Valencian tourist product in the mind of current and potential consumers, and given the lack of research in this field related to the Valencian case, qualitative research was carried out in those origin markets of particular importance for the Valencian tourist industry such as the United Kingdom and Germany.

Three instrumental objectives were defined: firstly that of determining the current image of Valencia as a tourist destination; secondly, that of identifying the group of Mediterranean tourist destinations with which it competes in the eyes of the consumer; and, lastly, that of detecting the factors which create a distance between the current positioning in the mind of the consumer and the desired positioning.

Two population groups were included in the study: end-users (holidaymakers) and professional advisers (tour operators/travel agents). Two group discussions in each country were held with end-users who had spent holidays in the Valencian region within the last five years. Recent visitors (within the last two–three years) were given priority. Each discussion lasted for about one and a half hours. Six depth interviews, in each country, with the most important tour operators (3) and travel agents (3) were carried out.

Current image of the Valencian tourist product

The current image of the Valencian tourist product can be summed up as follows: 'A compromise solution to the holiday problem—somewhere to go when the budget is limited'. This is undoubtedly an essential issue, given the increasingly demanding character of consumers who, on the basis of their greater experience, do make comparisons related to the cost of their holidays taking into account different destinations. Valencia is considered by consumers as a relatively cheap holiday venue, which offers sunshine and beaches—a place where one can find a mild climate and enjoy the beaches, as with most tourist destinations in the Mediterranean, and which, as Jenner and Smith (1993) put it, is suitable for families and a fun place to go to with a group of friends. For these authors, the most significant differences within the Mediterranean derive from distances from origin countries, with this factor having implications for the mode of transport used. On this subject tour operators' opinions differ. Valencia is on the one hand considered to be more for flight tourists, and on the other hand more for car-driving tourists.

There is also a lack of clear perception concerning the distinction between the summer or winter character of Valencia as a tourist destination. Tour operators do not have a concrete idea of how to categorize the Valencian tourist product.

A more detailed characterization, according to consumers and tour operators' perceptions, includes the following attributes:

- down-market, attracting visitors with a low socio-economic profile
- not high quality, although the service and the quality of accommodation services are seen to have improved lately, generating a better price–service relation; and the offer of sport activities is considered as very attractive, as a consequence of the high quality of the golf courses
- overcommercialized
- built-up, and consequently environmentally deteriorated
- mass tourism
- appealing to young people whose priority is nightlife (drinking and having a good time)
- safe, the security issue is not considered a problem in Valencia.

It is interesting and important to note that Valencia is not seen as a region. Consumers are more inclined to think of the region as Benidorm and its surrounding areas—if they think of the region at all. On the whole, they tend to think in terms of specific towns/cities they have visited and they sometimes use the nearest airport as a point of reference.

Consumers do see differences within the Valencian tourist product. The best-known resorts are classified into two different categories. On one hand, Benidorm is labeled as 'mass tourism' linked to the hotel industry. On the other hand, Denia, Altea and Jávea and other small coastal towns are perceived as tourist destinations characterized by self-catering apartment-style accommodation.

Benidorm is a clear example of a tourist destination focused on consumers of package products with a low level of involvement—people are put in the plane, disembarked and accommodated in the hotel. Benidorm has a bad image, even though consumers and tour operators have heard of the attempts to change this perception. Its reputation has mainly suffered because the city is completely blocked with skyscrapers (some consumers see it as a Little Manhattan) which make it unattractive; it had water problems in the past (there was no water available for hours during the day); its beaches are considered overcrowded; and it does not have the atmosphere of a Spanish town. It is also perceived as a cheap alternative to consider when looking for 'sun and beach' holidays, particularly for young tourists seeking a vacation with an important component of nightlife. Although Benidorm has a good image with respect to its tourist infrastructure, it is included in the programs of few tour operators. When the region as a whole is evaluated, it is clear that negative perceptions of the main resorts dominate the opinions of those whose exposure to the region has tended to be concentrated in such places.

However, consumers acknowledge the existence of pleasant, quieter spots away from the main tourist centers, and some mention the variety of things to do/places to visit if one knows where to look for them, particularly inland villages with natural and cultural attributes as well as big cities such as Valencia and Alicante. (It is important to realize that not all respondents wanted variety; in particular, some emphasized that their main priority at the present time was to find a location where there was plenty of sun and beaches, where their children could safely amuse themselves, and where they themselves could relax.)

Denia, Altea, Jávea—and in part also Calpe—are considered to be the exact opposite to Benidorm. These locations are regarded as quieter, because the vacation homes there mainly belong to private owners. These vacation homes are offered through certain travel organizers, who, as agents, manage the houses for private owners. These places are seen as more individual, equipped with Spanish charm, but also with a poorer tourist infrastructure. These smaller places, in which the richer home-owners enjoy their holidays, are also regarded as having a higher price level. Not surprisingly, in these resorts older and more solvent visitors who use the place as their mean of transport, are the norm.

Barriers found in repositioning the Valencian tourist product

Barriers inherent to the product

As perceived by visitors to Valencia, there appear to be some weaknesses in the configuration of the product, especially in the main tourist destinations. These are related to commercialism/lack of authenticity, visual pollution, acoustic pollution, beaches, activities, accommodation, service and the communications network.

- *Commercialism/lack of authenticity*

An aspect of particular importance for consumers is the authenticity of the components of the product—in the sense that they should reflect the character of the region—which is becoming an increasing requirement of the more demanding tourist we know nowadays. These educated tourists reject those destinations where commercialism has become pervasive, although some areas, especially away from the region around Benidorm, still show the soul of Spain.

Some signs of this phenomenon which are perceived by visitors to Valencia are the presence of crowds of English tourists, museums put there for the tourists rather than to house articles of genuine historical interest, and folklore adapted for the tourist rather than genuine/inherent to the region, to mention but a few of them.

- *Visual pollution*

Owing to the increasing awareness of the importance of the environmental aspects of a tourist destination, this is an obstacle to have in mind when facing future tourism developments. Unattractive buildings and high-rise blocks too close to the coast line, thereby obstructing the view, as well as waste spoiling the landscape, are evident obstacles to provide an image of a quality product.

- *Acoustic pollution*

The 'nightlife, discotheques, pubs' aspect is important for certain young consumers. They even make their holiday destination choice according to it. Nevertheless, a large entertainment offer can be a deterrent for visitors who search for peace and relaxation.

- *Beaches*

A general problem affecting all 'sun and beach' products is the deterioration of the ozone layer and its effect in reducing the desirability of the sun.

With regard to Valencia, overcrowding of some of its beaches—generally those in the main tourist centers—constitutes the only barrier related to them since beaches are considered clean by consumers and as having adequate facilities for the practice of water sports.

- *Accommodation*

In reference to the accommodation on offer, two issues could be considered as handicaps to the repositioning of the Valencia region in the mind of the consumers: firstly, accommodation provided in the region is perceived as fairly basic, probably due to the image of the hotels of Benidorm (low quality and prices), secondly, the existence of anonymous hotels which could be located in the coastline of any country. Consumers expect to find establishments which reflect the character of the region. This type of accommodation can be found in small villages which have the authentic Spanish spirit but are less prepared for tourism.

- *Service*

Basically, consumers perceive that there is a substantial credibility gap in respect of repositioning Valencia as a quality product where good service is provided. The main reason behind this perception is the association of Valencia with the consumption of package products which tour operators buy at low prices. This is a problem with many implications and it will be considered below.

- *Communications network*

Nowadays, the consumer of tourist products has high expectations related to the ease of access to the vacation site. Some consumers are discontented with the lack of direct flights linking their countries of origin with the Valencia region. While for the city of Alicante some charter services are provided, the problem is particularly critical in the case of the city of Valencia.

Barriers derived from the competition

Since the choice of holiday destination depends on several factors such as the circumstances in which the holiday is being taken, the budget available, the motivation to travel, whether the vacation is the main one of the year or an extra/top-up, and who one's companions are, etc., the profile of different destinations in the Mediterranean will have a strong influence on the decision-making process.

There is general acknowledgement that, in comparison with a few decades ago, when Valencia was one of the obvious choices of the consumer of 'sun and beach' products, there is much more choice these days; this is largely as a result of greater affluence and a reduction in the cost of travel in general.

Other resorts in Spain—Costa del Sol, Gulf of Almería, Costa Brava, Mallorca, etc.—Turkey, Greece and Portugal are considered by consumers as alternative holiday destinations in the Mediterranean area. The particular advantages and disadvantages of certain popular destinations in the Mediterranean that offer strong competition to Valencia are considered here.

- *Mallorca*
  Mallorca is better-known and easier to reach than Valencia because of the existence of direct communications with the origin markets. On the other hand, owing to its insularity, the visitor to Mallorca is more restricted and is not able to visit other big cities. Aspects shared by both destinations are the price and the contrast between small villages and big tourist centers.
- *Costa Brava*
  In comparison with Valencia, Costa Brava, on one hand, is perceived as offering better infrastructures for the visitor, in particular for family groups. Costa Brava is also better known and closer to the origin markets, and therefore easier to reach by coach. On the other hand, this region has a similar hotel and entertainment offer and the consumers' perception of cost is the same as that of Valencia.
- *Gulf of Almería*
  The Gulf of Almería is better known in some origin markets, such as Germany, than Valencia. Aspects these two regions have in common are the perceived cost, the contrast in the landscape and the wide provision of golf courses.
- *Costa del Sol*
  This area is better known than Valencia. Consumers' perception of other aspects of the product is quite similar to that of Valencia.
- *Greece and Turkey*
  The advantages of Greece and Turkey, according to the viewpoint of consumers, are the friendliness of the local people, the service and the authenticity of their products. Also, destinations corresponding to these countries are seen as less down-market, less overcrowded and less spoiled/commercialized. The opportunities for visiting places of historical interest are greater than in Valencia. Those destinations are also better known. Disadvantages of holidays in Greece and Turkey are the cost, the insecurity, the distance, which makes them less accessible, the quality of the accommodation and the primitive sanitation standards, in other words, the poor conditions of hygiene, which are found in some places.
- *The French Riviera*
  The south of France is better-known and is perceived to be more elegant and exclusive. It is also considered up-market and, therefore, full of affluent people. Consequently, it is seen as a more expensive destination than Valencia.
- *Portugal*
  Some destinations in Portugal such as the Algarve are better-known and have an image of being less commercialized and offering more authenticity than the Valencian region. A particular disadvantage is the distance from the origin markets.

Barriers arising from communication

An essential task to carry out in order to reposition Valencia as a quality-oriented and diversified tourist product is to make current and potential consumers aware of what it offers and the changes it is trying out.

Consumers' perceptions and the opinion of tour operators shed light on the degree of attainment of the communication efforts made by Valencia. The widespread impression is that, in spite of its potential as a Mediterranean tourist destination, this region is adequately communicating neither its natural advantages, such as its beaches, nor the competitive advantages it has developed during the last three decades (such as its know-how related to hotel management), to increase its market share. Some shortcomings have been detected in its marketing efforts (advertising, promotion, publicity and distribution), particularly the content and style of the message transmitted and the amount of information received by current and potential consumers about the Valencian tourist product.

Before discussion of the shortcomings mentioned above, it is worth taking some facts into consideration. Research carried out by the Valencian Tourist Board in the field of the patterns of consumption of packaged products (ITVA, 1993) reveals that this type of consumer operates under low-involvement conditions; in other words, they engage in virtually no active information search, either about the characteristics of the selected product or on alternative products. Furthermore, some of them prefer to discover the attributes of their destination choice while they are enjoying their visit.

The Valencian region has not engaged in huge advertising campaigns, but has concentrated its resources in text and paper-based information, due, among other reasons, to budget limitations. Nor has it developed effective promotional activities among prescriptors of trips to the Mediterranean—travel agencies—providing them with detailed information of the Valencian tourist product in order to facilitate their task of advising consumers.

Publicity, an inexpensive and enormously effective tool of communication has also been under-used. The absence of information about Valencia in the mass media is notorious. Only in a few cases, in which a tongue-in-cheek account of places like Benidorm is given, are consumers exposed to the product.

Considering the higher degree of notoriety reached by other Mediterranean competitive destinations, according to consumer and tour operator responses, it seems that competitive destinations are either making more effective communication efforts or laying out larger sums of money.

One of the main obstacles that can be imputed to communication shortcomings, seems to be that the Valencian region as a whole has no clear image, although particular spots are well-known. To some extent, this is probably a consequence of the low-involvement situation which characterized some consumers of the package product, as already mentioned above. Brochures do not identify Valencia as a region but as the area surrounding Benidorm. In any event, visitors are more likely to refer to specific resorts—Alicante, Benidorm, Calpe, Jávea and Denia.

Consumers and travel trade perceptions are that the communication efforts carried out by Valencia tend to reinforce existing images and stereotypes (chiefly because they are centered in the main tourist centers); thus the 'sun and beaches', cheap and cheerful image of the region prevails, with the result that other places more exotic and interesting are overlooked.

The communication efforts of other Mediterranean destinations which show particular regions of a country feature a wider variety of elements, that is to say, they present other aspects of the product besides 'sun and beaches', such as inland attractions, small villages, etc. Consumers and the travel trade consider this approach as the right one, even if, personally, visitors are not interested in variety at the current time.

The focus of communication efforts on the main resorts—featuring hotels and packed beaches—to the exclusion of other locations in the area is seen as an important obstacle in the repositioning of Valencia. The travel trade highlights the invisibility of the region other than Benidorm for consumers, since this resort is, in the mind of consumers, the 'tip of the iceberg' of the Valencian tourist product. Inland areas of Valencia should be featured more and there should be mentions of the different opportunities for tourists to know the real flavor of Valencia and, therefore, to enjoy their holidays.

Some shortcomings detected in the content of the communication efforts made by Valencia are related to the following issues: beaches, accommodation, cultural aspects, scenery, and activities.

There is a lack of detailed information about the beaches. Consumers are not aware of their quality and characteristics. There is ignorance of the existence of well-equipped and clean beaches along the whole coastline of Valencia, rather than just in the main tourist centers.

Owing to insufficient communication of the accommodation offer, consumers' knowledge is usually based either on previous experience or on word-of-mouth. Valencia is not perceived as having a quality hotel infrastructure. Basically, consumers only know the accommodation offer of the main tourist centers, which is perceived as low-quality and addressed to visitors with a low socioeconomic profile. Other components of the offer targeted to up-market consumers, such as charming small hotels and accommodation linked to golf courses, as well as stylish villas and apartments, are not present in the communication efforts.

Insufficient communication efforts are dedicated to the promotion of the cultural aspects of the Land of Valencia, given the perception of its richness and variety according to those consumers who have visited other places besides the main tourist centers.

Of relative importance, since a tourist destination is not usually selected for its gastronomy, is the difficulty of finding good Valencian cuisine. There is also a lack of information about natural scenery, specially, of the inland areas of the region and the possibility of practicing sports such as golf. Communication efforts could help to overcome these problems.

Barriers arising from distribution

One of the main obstacles to achieving the desired repositioning seems to be the exploitation of the Valencian tourist product by a few tour operators for their own benefit, hence, configuring an oligopoly of demand. These tour operators basically commercialize those destinations capable of carrying package products, because of the characteristics of their accommodation capacity, such as the existence of a considerable amount of bed-places in the down-market and/or mid-market segments. In this context, it is not surprising the image consumers have of Valencia, given the values attached to Benidorm which consumers link to the lower end of the market.

This process of exploitation has resulted in some cases in the creation of a 'concrete jungle' that is increasingly out of step with the demands of today's marketplace. Consequently, for this reason among others, demand for these resorts has decreased during the last four years to the point that tour operators have been excluding these destinations from their programs. Furthermore, this is not the only consequence related to the prevalence of tour operators in the commercialization process of the Valencian tourist product. Consumers' perception of a credibility gap in respect of repositioning Valencia as a quality product finds its roots in this phenomenon. For instance, tour operators have squeezed the hotel industry on price to the point where consumer complaints about food and service are growing. As a travel agent points out '10 pounds a day per head is canteen catering'.

Barriers arising from influential groups
When people are choosing a holiday, it seems that friends are a major influence, partly because they give honest opinions, but also because, to some extent, one expects one's friends to have values similar to one's own. Generally speaking, the main obstacles arising from this source are the negative perceptions these influential groups have regarding Valencia as a tourist destination. Related to this issue, research sheds light on two facts. Firstly, friends are unlikely to recommend Valencia unless the intended visitors are youngsters. And, secondly, in regard to the knowledge of different destinations in Valencia it is only through talking to friends and/or relatives that visitors learn about the less well-known areas.

Barriers arising from post-consumption feelings
People have predominantly negative perceptions based largely on previous visits to the main resorts. For the most part, exposure to the main tourist resorts is responsible for clouding the view. The key factor behind this perception is the circumstances in which they visited the region in the past. A cheap and cheerful holiday was appropriate at that moment but, not surprisingly, given the predominant image of Valencia most consumers would not choose to go there for a main holiday nowadays. On the contrary, consumers, unwaware of the variety that the region has to offer, seem to favor other holiday destinations that they had been to such as Turkey, the Greek islands, Cyprus or the south of France.

References and additional bibliography

Aguiló, Eugeni (1992) 'La posición competitiva de las regiones turísticas mediterráneas españolas: posibilidades de la política turística', in *Papers de Turisme*, No. 8/9, 1992, pp. 75–92, Valencia.

Ahmed, Zafar U. (1991a) 'Marketing your community. Correcting a negative image', in *The Cornell H.R.A. Quarterly*, 31(4):24–27.

Ahmed, Zafar U. (1991b) 'The influence of the components of a state's tourist image on product positioning strategy', in *Tourism Management*, 12(4):331–340.

Benidorm Town Council (1986), 'Ecología, economía y turismo en el Mediterráneo', Benidorm Town Council and Alicante University, Alicante.

Chon, Kye-Sung (1991) 'Tourism destination images modification process. Marketing implications', in *Tourism Management*, 12(1):68–72.

Fitzpatrick Associates (1993) 'Tourism in the European Community. The impact of the single market', The Economist Intelligence Unit, London.

Heath, Ernie and Wall, Geoffrey (1992), *Marketing Tourism Destinations. A Strategic Planning Approach*, John Wiley, New York.

ITVA (1990) *Libro Blanco del Turismo de la Comunidad Valenciana*, Institut Turístic Valencià (ITVA), Valencia.

ITVA (1991) 'El mercado turístico español. Aproximación a la demanda turística de la Comunidad Valenciana', in *Papers de Turisme*, No. 7, 1991, pp. 71–85, Valencia.

ITVA (1993) 'Test de marcas turísticas de la Comunidad Valenciana', Institut Turístic Valencià (ITVA) and Metra Seis, Valencia.

Jenner, Paul and Smith, Christine (1993) 'Tourism in the Mediterranean', The Economist Intelligence Unit, London.

Kotler, Philip, Ferrel, O. C. and Lamb, Charles (1987) *Strategic Marketing for Nonprofit Organizations. Cases and Readings*, Prentice Hall, Englewood Cliffs, NJ.

Lozato-Giotart, Jean-P. (1991) *Mediterráneo y Turismo*, Masson SA, Barcelona.

Middleton, Victor T. C. (1988) *Marketing in Travel and Tourism*, Heinemann, Oxford.

Monfort, V. and Morant, A. (1991) 'La actividad turística', in *Atlas Temático de la Comunidad Valenciana*, No. 32, pp. 621–640, Editorial Prensa Alicantina SA, Alicante.

Morant, A. and Monfort, V. (1992) 'La actividad turística y su promoción desde la Comunidad Valenciana', in *Papers de Turisme*, No. 8/9, 1992, pp. 47–74, Valencia.

Morgan, Michael (1991) 'Dressing up to survive. Marketing Majorca anew', in *Tourism Management*, 12(1):15–20.

Pearce, Philip L. and Stringer, Peter F. (1991) 'Psychology and tourism', in *Annals of Tourism Research*, 18(1):136–154.

Pedreño Muñoz, A. (Ed.) (1986) 'Perspectivas de la evolución del sector turístico en el contexto de la economía Alicantina', Banco de Alicante, Alicante.

Pedreño Muñoz, A. (dir.) (1990), 'Libro blanco del turismo en la Costa Blanca', Cámara Oficial de Comercio, Industria y Navegación de Alicante, Alicante.

Pollard, John and Dominguez, Rafael (1993) 'Tourism and Torremolinos. Recession or reaction to environment?', in *Tourism Management*, 14(4):247–258.

Vall, Josep F. (1992) *La Imagen de Marca de los Países*, McGraw-Hill/Interamericana de España, SA, Madrid.

Vera Rebollo, F. (1990) 'Turismo y territorio en el litoral mediterráneo Español', Estudios Territoriales no. 32, MOPU, Madrid.

Vera Rebollo, F. (1992) 'El turismo', in *Estructura Económica de la Comunidad Valenciana*, Espasa Calpe, Madrid.

Yin, Robert K. (1989) *Case Study Research: Design and Methods*, Sage Publications, Newbury Park.

44 How to use a mature tourism mix towards the healthy redevelopment of the traditional sun and sand resorts

M. HART

To talk of tourism in the year 2000, in the recessionary United States of Europe, is to talk of a completely different reality from the post-war economic climate which first gave rise to the phenomenon. For a start, tourism can hardly be looked upon as the well-deserved reward for work well done in a world where unemployment is the general tonic or affliction. For much the same reasons, neither can tourism be considered any longer an inevitable province of the young; in earlier days youth was equated with active employment and this, unfortunately, is very rarely the case nowadays. With the 21st century just round the corner, the world belongs more significantly to the 'babyboomers', to the generation born in the post-war baby boom, who grew up with tourism as a normal component of their existence and who have effectively changed every aspect of everyday life on which they have impacted up until now (hippies, flower power, the Pill, women's liberation, yuppies, test-tube babies, genetic engineering etc.). We have only to look at Europe (and for the purposes of this paper we will consider Europe as being composed of the present European Union plus the countries of EFTA) to see how different the demographic profile is nowadays from when the first international tourists of 'mass tourism' embarked on voyages abroad in the 1960s. At the time of writing this paper (the mid-1990s), the population over 55 years old is already far more numerous to the population with ages ranging between 13 and 19. By the year 2000, it is estimated that the imbalance will be even greater with an adult population in Europe of over 300 million, 100 million of whom will be over 55 years old. With a present proportion of four people in active employment for every retired person in Europe (1993 data presented at the celebration of the European 'Year of the Elderly and Solidarity between Generations'), whole parcels of everyday life need to be re-evaluated and re-thought, one of which, very evidently, is tourism.

It is not only the economic recession but also growing concern for the ecological 'climate' and environmental matters in general—everything 'green' in the widest sense of the adjective—which has forced upon us a need to reformulate theories and reappraise ideas. The mass tourism of the 1960s and 1970s was largely composed of sunseekers: the classic shopfloor worker in search of the three, or usually four, 'S's booked up a package holiday which afforded him just that with the minimum of problems and surprises. The major mass resorts of the 1960s such as Torremolinos and Benidorm in Spain and, now to a lesser extent thanks to a whole policy of rethinking and restructuring in time, Majorca, stand as testimony to the havoc wreaked by the mass tourists in the pursuit of their pleasures. The tour operators, in an attempt to eliminate perceived problems for the ordinary British or German 'man-in-the-street' unwittingly triggered off a process of standardisation of the product on offer with one common denominator, i.e. guaranteed sunshine. The result of packing them in to these resorts, apart from profits for the tour operators and the land speculators, was to wipe out differentiating features which may have attracted the discriminating tourist to the resort in the first place, with the result that a holiday to Torremolinos, Benidorm or Majorca in the 1970s was considered almost tantamount, from the point of view of exotic experiences and 'difference', to Bognor Regis with sunshine. Global warming, the depletion of the ozone layer, the greenhouse effect and the increased danger of skin cancer are all realities of our times which, logically, impact on the decision-making process of any potential tourist. The standard, and now largely standardized, resorts of the past are now faced with the grim reality that what represented their main pull in days gone by, i.e. their guaranteed sunshine, no longer is guaranteed, nor is it attractive for many potential tourists.

To some extent, it could be argued that the reformulation of past values and definitions has already begun in tourism, as can be witnessed in the upsurge in the last few years of literature relating to 'sustainable tourism' formulas or 'alternative tourism' recipes. The panacea for all our evils, if we are to believe everything we read, lies in 'quality not quantity'. In other words, 'mass tourism' is evil, no matter what form it takes, whether mass 'green' tourism or mass rural tourism. Whatever form it takes, it would seem, if it is 'mass', it is not resort-friendly.

The question which begs to be asked is what happens to the resorts of the past which grew up around mass tourism and which, although very clearly on the downward slope of their life cycles and reflecting varying levels of unsustainability due to the effects of mass tourism, depend almost exclusively on the income and employment afforded by this sector? On the one hand, they can hardly restrict quantity without losing revenue. On the other, they can hardly offer quality in their present state: neither from the point of view of exclusive accommodation and services, nor from the perspective of 'quality' seen as a different and exotic cultural experience. Nor can it be 'quality' from the perspective of 'quality of life' for the host population who can scarcely benefit in its present precarious situation of employment from a major fall-off in tourism numbers.

It is, perhaps, this last component of tourism, the host community, which has often been ignored in the past by those involved in the tourism planning process. 'Environmental impact assessment', which is a new tool in tourism planning, is still based on evaluation of damage to the physical (i.e. geographical) environment. The long-term damage wrought by mass tourism, in socio-cultural terms, is something which has less frequently been weighted in the evaluation of impact, but which far outbalances the short-term economic benefits which, in any case, rarely redound to the host population as such. Resorts such as those in the south of the islands of Tenerife (Los Cristianos, Los Gigantes) and Gran Canaria (Maspalomas, Playa del Inglés or Puerto Rico) obviously need reworking and rethinking for tourism if there is to be some way of benefiting and enriching the host population whilst offering a 'quality' product for the tourist. However, the 'club' formula (Oreja and McNutt, 1993) whereby you restrict your market to the 'quality' tourist, apart from being elitist, equates (wrongly in our opinion) socio-cultural and ecological responsibility with greater consumer power, besides scarcely representing a solution which can be applied overnight. As with any long-term solution to shortsighted or haphazard planning, an improvement in quality demands sacrifices and therefore full information for, and the active collaboration of, the host population which is precisely the component of the tourism product which has most consistently been ignored over the years in Spain. Far less is the 'club' formula a solution on islands whose fragile economies may be shattered by a massive pull-out of any of the major tour operators, no matter how tyrannical their conditions for remaining may be.

The other great issue which has been addressed recurrently in the tourism literature of the last decade has been the need to break the deadlock of seasonality. This problem does not affect the Canary Islands, which is perhaps the only region within Europe, particularly in the sun and sand sector, that is not influenced economically by the changing of the seasons. The grossly misnamed 'third age' tourism has been considered to be the solution to the problem, in this case. Which sector of society has free time all the time? Obviously, those who are retired from active full-time employment and can take their holidays whenever they please, i.e. mature tourists. No-one has ever bothered to consider whether, in fact, these resorts which are unattractive to every other sector of the population outside their peak seasons, basically because they lack the organised entertainment, full service and climatic conditions which usually complement the physical draw of the resort, should be found appealing by our older generations. This lack of consideration for the needs of the mature tourist is intimately linked to the idea of 'economic usefulness' of the person in our consumer society. Once a person fails to produce, he is no longer useful and therefore must make do with what society sees fit to bestow upon him. The changing demographic profile of Europe, Japan, Canada and the United States of America, however, render this conception of society debatable. The mainstream tourism of the future will be mature. To look upon mature tourism as a stopgap remedy for breaking the deadlock of seasonality is grossly shortsighted. What is more, as surveys have shown, when left to their own devices even mature tourists who participate in so-called social tourism ventures (highly subsidised tours, perhaps more widespread now in Spain than in any other European country) would still prefer to travel in the peak season.

The changing demographic picture in the world, demands that we redefine tourism and the tourist. The young have time to travel but no money. The adult population in active employment has the money but not the time. The mature population has both. It is time to tap this market which even back in 1985, Scott Supernaw, then the President of Olson Travelworld, described as: 'The gray market, it's been such a mystery to us for so many years . . . I don't know of a bigger, more lucrative, more misunderstood, more confused market that everybody in the US covets at this time.'[1]

The Malta Conference of 1991, co-financed by the European Commission together with American Express and Tourism Canada (both of whom, plus the Hilton chain of hotels, have carried out important research programmes into the needs and wants of mature tourists)[2] revealed that mature tourism accounted for over 20% of the total tourism in Europe in 1990—142 million domestic trips and 41 million international. In the USA, the population over 55 years of age in 1990 accounted for some 21% of the total population. This 21% accounted for 28% of all the international trips taken by Americans in 1992. Even more revealing is the fact that, should the age be brought down to fifty, then mature tourism represented 49% of all international trips taken by Americans. Some seven million American tourists visited Europe in 1990, two million of whom were mature, i.e. over 55 years old. It is estimated that this figure will go up 78% by the year 2000, thereby representing some 3.5 million mature American tourists. In the same period, 1990, some 400 000 mature Canadian tourists chose Europe as their holiday destination with clear preferences being shown for the UK, France, Germany and Italy. It is calculated that this figure will double by the year 2000, a fact of greater importance when we consider that the Canadians spend approximately double the amount the Americans do per capita. The 'silver market', which is how the Japanese refer to their 12 million citizens over 65 years of age, accounted for approximately 18% of the international trips contracted in 1990, i.e. 200 000 of the 1.3 million, a figure which will probably double by the year 2000.

This gradual ageing of the populations in the developed countries has several repercussions, all of which will necessarily be reflected in future trends in tourism. First and foremost, the growing social costs of an inactive population in times of recession and rampant unemployment will prove to be an excessive burden for any of the developed countries' governments to bear. Instead of early retirement programmes, the age of retirement will probably rise, as it already has in Japan. The accrued experience of a lifetime's work will no longer be blown out with the candles on the 65th birthday cake but will be used by companies who will place their senior members in consultancy and executive posts. A prolonged working life, though not necessarily full-time or office-bound, will provide extra income over a longer time for a generation which, in any case in most of the developed countries, had subscribed to equity and pension schemes to see them through their old age in comfort. The mature citizen has less family commitments, usually owns his residence and is not, therefore, burdened by a mortgage and, in this day and age, is a market-conscious and aware person. The scarce economic resources and fragile states of health, accountable between them in surveys for over 62% of the mature tourists who did not travel[3] in 1990 are part and parcel of the profile of old age and senior citizens which has predominated up until now but is hardly applicable to the 'babyboomers'.

The 'babyboomers' are people like Jane Fonda, Richard Gere and the Billary duo (Bill and Hillary Clinton) who have enjoyed a greater awareness of the need to work and play hard. These are the people who first investigated yoga, aerobics, alternative medicine and macrobiotic food. It is the generation of women who expect to work outside the home owing to improved educational circumstances, and who have had greater economic independence than their forefathers (or foremothers). It is the generation with a greater cultural baggage than any before it, thanks to the massive introduction of computers in all walks of life and a much expanded media system. The generation which radically changed lifestyles in the 'swinging sixties' will hardly do less when they swing into their sixties. Wayne Haeffer, the Director of the American Association of Retired People said in the Mogán conference on Mature Tourism in 1993, 'Shattering stereotypes about ageing will mean better trips for mature travellers and better business results for all of you'.[4]

Mature tourists of the future will be much more likely to be participating in polar bear safaris and white water rafting in the Grand Canyon (to mention only two of the possibilities on offer in the Association's magazine *Modern Maturity*) than to be rocking themselves to sleep in a rocking-chair on the porch of the spa where they have gone to 'take the waters'. The report carried out by the Centre for Policy on Ageing in the UK called 'Living Dangerously' (1991) revealed that this enhanced state of wellbeing and health is accompanied by an improved psychological profile. In the words of the American financier, Bernard Baruch: 'To me, old age is always 15 years older than I am' (pronounced when he had already attained the ripe old age of 85). Just as the post-war definition of tourism is no longer valid for us in this day and age, so our definitions of older people, coined in the post-war years, in a culture which idolised youth above all things, must now be reappraised. The mature person may come to be considered again as the 'elder' in society, i.e. elder from the point of view of wisdom and accumulated experience. Mature tourists are experienced and discerning consumers who look upon international travel, not as an escape from the drudgery of everyday routine, but as a 'gateway to experience'. As such, they are more prepared to become involved in local culture, to participate in the holiday experience and even to contribute to its success. The older people are, the less materialistic they become and the greater the value they attach to quality experiences: quality of service, for example, the personal touch and local hospitality. The resort that caters for mature tourists, not as a profitable sideline to fill in the gaps when other tourists are not forthcoming, but rather as a mainstream activity, will be rewarded by a tourism which is genuinely respectful of the physical and socio-cultural environment. Apart from the obvious rewards for the host community, there is also the fact that a spin-off of improving conditions to meet the requirements of quality service demanded by the mature tourist is an overall betterment for all tourism.

Current trends in tourism have indicated an ever-greater segmentation of the market in general (Marchena, 1993). This is also the case in the demands of mature tourists. Whereas in the past the industry tended to segment tourists by age, the demographic, socio-political and economic pointers would seem to indicate that from now on it will have to segment the sector of mature tourism (and tourism in general) by lifestyles and attitudes. By the year 2025 in Western Europe alone, the people between 40 and 59 years of age will account for 26% of the total population and the people over 60 for another 26%. Therefore any attempt which is made to cater for this sector's needs, apart from meaning good healthy tourism practice, will also make good economic sense. Here we are dealing with the occasional mature traveller as opposed to that sector of the market known as 'retirement tourism' and second home owners, already dealt with more than capably by other authors (De Albuquerque and McElroy, 1993). According to the data of ETIC (European Travel Intelligence Centre), most mature tourists travel for purely recreational and leisure motives: 80% in the cases of the UK, Germany, The Netherlands and Finland but slightly less than 60% in the cases of Spain, Greece and Portugal (all of which are countries with high indices of domestic tourism). The average percentage of business travel is 8% though there is a tendency for this figure to vary widely with age, from over 13% for people between 55 and 59 years of age falling to 3% for the over 75s. For leisure travel abroad, the three/four 'S's variant is the most popular, accounting for 31%, followed by touring holidays (29%) and city breaks (11%), with sporting and other holidays lagging a long way behind (1% and 5%). Therefore, if the present trends persist, this would represent a new lease of life for the traditional resorts, a fact borne out by recent market surveys and research carried out in the island of Gran Canaria, Spain.[5]

The mature tourist represents a boon for the travel industry in that the large majority of this sector opt for all-inclusive package tours, with transport either by plane or by coach contracted through their local travel agency. Even when travelling by private car, the mature tourist will still have recourse to the agency to reserve hotel accommodation. Because they have more time at their disposal to do so, and also owing to the fact that they are highly value-conscious, the mature tourists will use the travel agency's brochures and staff to much greater effect than other sectors of the population. They also tend to stay longer in any one place than other tourists: the average stay for long overseas trips is 12.2 nights and for short trips, 2.1 nights. Eighty per cent of mature international tourists make trips of over four days' duration whilst a substantial 14% stay for longer than two weeks in any one destination. The mature tourists prefer hotel accommodation on their trips abroad (64%) and 83% of the tourists who opt for hotels, stay in four- or five-star establishments. Four- and five-star hotels are much more labour-intensive, which bodes well for employment figures in resorts which specialise in this kind of tourism. Since many mature tourists travel alone, the four- and five-star hotels that specialise in conference tourism (perhaps the most lucrative form of tourism and most certainly of shortest duration) can more than cover costs on single-room accommodation without economic penalty to the mature tourist who opts for the same.

All told then, the prospects for the traditional resorts could hardly be brighter—if, indeed, the host population has been made aware of the long-term advantages of accommodating mature tourism and can revitalise its characteristic hospitality patterns. To achieve a healthy socio-cultural balance in the resort, the tourism authorities should strive to accommodate all sectors of the tourist demand to a greater or lesser extent. The tourists who are known to seek merely sun, sand, cheap booze and holiday romances, i.e. the real consumer tourists, can be accommodated in areas which cater for their needs, always allowing, nevertheless, for variation, above all in spending power of this sector. Enough surveys have been carried out for us to know that the package tourist will spend directly proportionally to the amount s/he originally laid out on the holiday abroad, with the Germans spending most, in the case of the Canary Islands (they also pay most for their package), and the Irish and the Finns spending least. Incentive tourism should also be encouraged since, although a low consumer power area, this type of tourism is positive in that the tourists participate actively in making the long-sought trip a success and are anxious to investigate the resort to the full without being disrespectful of local customs and countryside. Conference tourism, as we have already mentioned, which can be highly controlled, has little environmental impact on the resort and economically contributes greatly (this sector represents the greatest source of souvenir, as in craft, buying). However, as has been proved in resorts such as Majorca, the change from the traditional formulas of 'S' tourism and unsustainability as the result of too much of the same is not untraumatic and demands firm commitment on the part of both public and private sectors of the industry. Also, care must be taken not to throw the baby out with the bathwater; in other words, the standard 'S' tourism and all the progress made up until now in the development of 'alternative tourism' variants are totally valid for the mature tourists of the future as long as the common denominator of *quality* and *value service for money* are borne in mind. If the public authorities make road traffic signals easier to read and comprehend, they must see that they are contributing towards a better quality tourism for all age groups, not only the mature. By making minibus travel more available for groups of six to eight people in car-hire firms—in order to avoid the problems of car insurance for mature tourists and yet ensure safety levels whilst allowing for a certain margin of independence— exclusively tailored to their needs and wants, not only are we contributing towards improving employment figures plus reducing road congestion and pollution, but also we are providing a more personalised attention to the guest.

For although, as the Senior Vice-President of American Express Travel Related Services for Europe Middle East and Africa, John E. Stuart, pointed out: 'The good news is, we're pushing at an open door. In survey after survey, older Americans list travel as their top priority for their retirement years . . . they *spend more money* on travel and recreation than any other age group. . . . And they now see travel as a *regular repeat purchase*'. This sector values more highly than any other the hospitality side of travel. Tourism is, after all, a service industry and, just as SAS airlines realised, summed up in the words of their President and CEO, Jan Carlson: 'We stopped flying airplanes and started flying people', so the leisure sector has to shake up, rethink and begin again to welcome guests (Smith, 1977) instead of merely catering for temporary clients. A better quality product can only be offered by a host population which is firmly convinced of the beneficial and positive effects of tourism. This perhaps is easier to achieve in a pristine unexploited resort than in a region, such as the Canary Islands, which has 'suffered' the onslaught of the golden hordes for long and, more seriously, the constant straining in different directions of the public and private sectors to the detriment of local interests for even longer.[6] However, the fact borne out by the results of various Delphi projections carried out by the ULPGC, that the host population still continue to look upon tourism as something positive (though perhaps solely from the economic and employment perspective and then again only if the local people can regain control of their heritage) and that there is an awareness of the positive

need to recover traditional community values, does not bode ill for this destination either.

The 'global village' and a United Europe demand of us that we view all of our activities in a much wider geographical context than the merely local or national level upon which we worked before. The consumer society and the system of mass production which underpinned all the definitions and concepts of the 1960s are far removed from the highly automated, workforce reductive 1990s. As such, it is no longer valid to consider all activities and component factors of our everyday existence in terms merely of their economic relevance. Just as the European Economic Community of the 1970s evolved in time from a principally economic necessity to the European Community, where socio-cultural and ethnic values took the forefront to the European Union, so tourism (the 'play' component of the balance of work and play, vital for a healthy existence) must now be viewed not as just an economic tool, but rather as a service sector which brings a community together in pursuit of an improved wellbeing in the future and a greater defence of its characteristic past.

Notes

1. Taken from his speech at the XVI Annual Conference of the Travel and Tourism Research Association.
2. The Hilton Hotels Corporation has even developed a 'Senior Honors Program' for people over 60, possibly in response to the excellently comprehensive study presented by the US Travel Data Center (1990) 'The mature market: a report on the impact of the changing mature market in the US travel industry', Travel Industry Association of America.
3. Delphi study carried out for the Spanish Government's Department of Tourism and another by the Saga Tours Company in the UK.
4. Haefer, W. (1993) 'Changing perspectives on older Americans', Paper given at the III International Conference on Mature Travel and Tourism in Mogán, Gran Canaria, Spain.
5. COECAM (1993) 'El Análisis de la demanda turística en Gran Canaria: temporada invierno 1992–93'. Also the recent study on tourist trends carried out by the research team at the Master Internacional de Turismo at the University of Las Palmas de Gran Canaria.
6. Perhaps best exemplified in a recent statement by the President of the Autonomous Government of the Canary Islands pronounced in a press conference held (22 October 1993) to celebrate the inauguration of the Hotel-School (and I quote):

no podemos privar a nuestra tierra de contar con unas instal- aciones como las de estos centros de formación, que permitan atraer un turismo de calidad y culto, que nada tiene que ver con el de sol y playa. (Underlining is the author's own)

we must actively strive to equip our islands with training centres which will allow us to attract a refined, quality tourism far removed from the sun and sand tourism of the past.

References

De Albuquerque, K. and McElroy, J. (1993) 'Sustainable alternatives to insular mass tourism: recent theory and practice', Paper presented at the Malta Conference on Sustainable Tourism.

ETTC (European Tourism Travel Commission) (1993) 'Europe's Senior Travel Market', Brussels.

Marchena, M. (1993) *New Tourism Trends and the Future of Mediterranean Europe*. TESG Tijdschrift, Amsterdam.

Oreja Rodríguez, J. and McNutt, P. (1993) 'Economic strategies for sustainable tourism in islands: the case of the Canary Islands', Paper presented at the Malta Conference on Sustainable Tourism.

Smith, Valene (1977) *Hosts and Guests: the Anthropology of Tourism*, University of Pennsylvania Press, Philadelphia, PA.

45 The Spanish tourism industry: analysis of its strategies and the efficacy and achievements gained from them

C. CAMISÓN, E. BIGNÉ AND V. M. MONFORT

Introduction

Spain is one of the top tourist regions of the world. Proof of this is the known facts of places in accommodation (7.1 million in 1991), number of foreign tourists per year (53.5 million in 1991) and 19 000 million dollars generated by tourism in 1991, as well as its leading position in the European market for Mediterranean holidays. Also, following the new trends, there has been a process of diversification of supply, other modes such as golf tourism, sports tourism, green tourism or cultural tourism, which have contributed towards a process of geographical diversification of supply, attenuating the problems of localization derived from the priority given to the development of mass sun-and-sand tourism.

Despite the privileged competitive position it has occupied for the last two decades, Spanish tourism is at this time going through a transitional phase, which in the opinion of some analysts indicates some worrying future trends. There are several causes. The evolution of demand towards a more diversified touristic product offering better value for money, the growing concern for the environment which contradicts the degradation of the surroundings, a fragmented sector structure with low levels of professionalism, and a substantial growth of competition (especially new destinations which compete in its traditional market segments and enjoy comparative advantages in costs/prices), have changed the setting of Spanish tourism by constituting a serious threat to its competitiveness.

However, these future trends, though worrying, can be considered as opportunities to remodel the strategy of supply of Spanish tourism. The change in the competitive framework may serve as a vehicle for the correction of its weaknesses and a greater concentration on its strengths.

The objective of this paper is to analyze the strategic approach as an instrument of research into tourism. In it we will examine the strategic changes adopted by Spanish tourism, analyzing their contributions and defects.

Tourism research and the strategic approach[1]

An essential starting point for this purpose is a broad identification of the determinants of Spanish tourism's competitiveness, as well as a more systematic analysis, useful for the designing of suitably focused public policies. The diagnosis of the causes of those trends in supply and demand cannot be made on the basis of national statistics, which measure very partially and with limited efficacy the real situation of tourist activity. However, tourism research has in the past inclined clearly towards a macro-economic viewpoint, analyzing the problems and the facts from an aggregate perspective, using national statistics as the main source of information. This traditional approach to tourism analysis has led to general conclusions such as reduction in the average spend per tourist or decrease in the share of the world market. These conclusions have been the basis of generic diagnoses of the causes of the competitiveness problems of Spanish tourism: the generally low quality of the supply, over-valuation of the real effective exchange rate, etc.

The consideration of the 'industry', 'branch' or 'sector' as the most appropriate framework for analysis (Mason, 1939; Bain, 1972) is a key point of industrial economics. Its theoretical basis was the hypothesis that the structural characteristics of the industry such as conditions of supply, production technology, import and/or export barriers, or the needs of the capital factor and the labour factor, limited sufficiently the range of strategic options available, ensuring homogeneity among business internal to the industry. This approach has resulted in different industrial classifications, whose framework of analysis differ according to variables in production processes, inputs, finished products or services, and even physical appearance (Day et al., 1979).

Both this traditional methodology and other lines of research into the phenomenon of tourism from sociological, geographical, town-planning or land-use standpoints, though useful for the identification of the problems of tourist activities, have two fundamental weaknesses:

(1) They ignore aspects currently vital to any analysis of competitiveness.
(2) Their non-validity as rules, given their inability to move from identification of problems to recommendations or strategies, in order to generate policies for practical and specific action (for a particular difficulty in a certain area).

On the other hand, there is very little tradition, especially among Spanish researchers into tourism, of the use of the strategic approach, based on the methods provided jointly by management and marketing.[2] This paper rests on this methodological substratum, which allows an innovative vision of the history, challenges and perspectives of the tourism business.

Curiously enough, the public administrations of tourism have been innovative in the use of the strategic approach for the diagnosis of the activity, the knowledge of its competitive position and the determining of feasible strategies for the improvement of the competitive capacity of tourist firms. The studies by the Spanish General Secretariat of Tourism (Secretaria General de Turismo, 1989, 1992) for the drawing-up of the 'Tourism marketing plan 1990' (Gilbert, 1989) and of the 'Framework plan for competitiveness in Spanish tourism (FUTURES)' at the national level, or at the regional level by the Valencian Tourism Institute (ITVA, 1990), in its 'Strategic plan for tourism in the Land of Valencia', and by the Monitor Company—founded by that high-priest of 'strategic management', Michael Porter—for the Regional Government of Catalonia (Monitor Company, 1992), are experiences to be recommended.

Thus, the FUTURES plan indicates: 'Competitiveness is not a quality which can be attributed generically to a country or sector; these will be competitive to the same extent as the majority of businesses based in them. Consequently, the basic unit of analysis for studying competitiveness is the firm' (Secretaria General de Turismo, 1992:15).

These analyses agree that a useful knowledge of the strategic behavior of the various businesses involved in Spanish tourism requires rigorous technical studies which go beyond the usual focus on the destination point. In particular, three directions show great promise:

1. Research into the *strategic segments* of world tourism, in order to later analyze those found in Spain. One line of work of growing importance is the application of formal methods of analysis of the portfolio of business units or strategy centers, with creative (never deterministic) aims, for strategic diagnosis. Also, it is very important to know and understand the trends (prospects) and the factors of success in each strategic segment (at a worldwide level), for the purpose of defining the relative competitive positioning of Spanish firms in these factors, and from there to evaluate their real competitiveness and their capacity to assume the strategies needed to triumph in each segment.

2. Particularly since Porter's study (1990) on *The Competitive Advantage of Nations*, growing importance has been given to the geographical area (locality, district, region) or 'home base', from which the strategic decisions of the firm are made, and the social and economic conditions of this setting. From this standpoint, the conditions determining the competitiveness of a tourist service (whether accommodation, catering, a theme park, a wholesale travel agency, etc.) and the holiday experience of a tourist, find meaning in a certain geographical area, defined by a multidimensional relationship among firms and industries involved, transport and communications infrastructure, complementary activities (commercial infrastructure, tradition of fairs, etc.), support services (training, information, etc.), natural resources and institutional policies. Porter calls the complex grouping of these elements a 'cluster', its analysis being fundamental for determining the sources of competitive advantage for the firms involved, as well as for formulating specific strategic recommendations.

The main tool for analysis of the 'clusters' is Porter's famous 'diamond' *for the analysis of factors determining competitiveness*. Thus, once the objective strategies and the vehicles required in each segment have been identified, a detailed analysis must be undertaken of the determinants of competitiveness (strategy, structure and rivalry of firms, demand conditions, conditions of the factors, and connected and supporting sectors) which for each 'cluster' make up the competitiveness profile. From the conclusions will arise detailed strategic proposals for each level (locality, district, region, and national) and the type of responsibility (public and private).

The competitiveness of a sector is thus not measured on the basis of global information, nor is it understood to be a generic whole, but as referring to specific strategic systems (business units) organized in homogeneously defined geographical areas.

Spanish tourism has before it an interesting challenge: to detect and describe the existence of these 'clusters' or specific tourism strategy systems, organized in homogeneously defined geographical areas.

3. Research from the standpoint of the tourist-consumer, with the aim of finding the commercial reasons for evaluation and presentation of the tourism product

consumed in each space or territory, as well as the decision processes of the customer who is in a position to choose between similar alternatives at his/her level of tastes/income.

The strategic approach: strategic segmentation and conceptualization of business in tourism

Although the study of change in management systems, in concordance with the transformation of the setting and of the nature of the firm itself, has been the object of attention in business literature,[3] the attempt to adapt the strategic management approach to tourism has far fewer precedents. Outstanding studies in this line are those of Blomstrom (1983), Reichel (1983), Schaffer (1985, 1986), Tse (1988), Tse and Olsen (1988, 1989), Woodside (1988), and Nanus and Lundberg (1988).

The process of adoption of good administrative practices has generally been slow in tourism firms. A plausible explanation is the reluctance of management in the sector to accept the universality of the administrative function. Gamble (1992) explained this reluctance by problems of perception or of loss of contact with the setting, problems of organizational structure and problems of inertia. Slattery and Olsen (1984) also point out the unmoving and defensive attitude to changes in the setting which is typical of tourism management. However, the prevailing opinion has been the acceptance of the value of strategic management, emphasizing especially:

(1) Its values of flexibility and global analysis. This seems to be an important advantage in businesses like hotels, where the success of the units rests in large part on the roles of 'strategist' and 'entrepreneur' of the management (Schaffer, 1985).
(2) The greater need for tools to assist administration owing to the complex nature of the products–markets amalgam typical of tourist systems and organizations (Webster and Hudson, 1992:14–15). The growth of tourist chains has increased their complexity, which Sasser and Morgan (1977) illustrate by the 'Bermuda Triangle' typical of service businesses, whose vertices are services, markets and locations.

The central idea of the concept of strategy lies in conceiving it as a method for integrating the system or the firm in its setting. The establishing of connections between the firm or system and the setting form the essence of strategy, and takes the following form:

(a) The selection of the area of action or activity of the firm or system, i.e. the extent and nature of the productive relationships between the firm/system and its setting. This first phase, which we could call the *conceptualization of the service* or the *definition of the business*, attempts to define the *business* in which the firm or system wishes to participate, or to answer the question, 'What business are we in?'
(b) The determining of the way to compete in each business, its *competitive strategy*, consists precisely of the structured set of actions which the firm or the system intends to carry out, in order to gain and maintain a strong and sustainable competitive position against the rest of the industry. The determining of how to compete is equivalent to deciding how the firm or system will try to obtain and preserve *competitive advantages*.

The concept of strategy thus conceived highlights the importance of a suitable definition of the *scope* or field of activity of the system or firm, since it is here that they will seek to create competitive advantages.

A business is characterized by its identifiable, congruent and homogeneous strategic behavior towards the competition, and in general towards the market (Thiétart, 1990). To enable more accuracy in identifying divergences in customer motivation, buying or information processes, models of use of the service, keys to success and organizational settings, allowing differential treatment for each tourist business, it seems to us expedient to rely on the conceptualization of a business offered by Abell (1980) and Ansoff (1976), in conjunction with the *servuction* methodology developed by Eiglier and Langeard (1989:175–216). From this viewpoint, the businesses of a system or firm are construed in terms of products and markets.

The *conceptualization of the service* or *definition of the business or activity* in which the firm or system is present consists of establishing what in strategic terms is called the product–market binomial. A *product* is the result of the definition of a business concept, certainly the most complex decision to be taken in an organization since it demands great creative capacity and is the key to competitive success. A business concept is the definition of the primary function to be fulfilled by the product and bought by the customer. It constitutes the nucleus of the firm's supply of services (basic, peripheral, derived and complementary), as well as the central element in the proposed positioning to be taken up against the competitors in the market. Given that any tourist enterprise (and in general any firm in the service sector) is always a *multiservice enterprise*, the demarcation of what to do and what not to do is a fundamental decision (Chías, 1991:15–16). Likewise, at the level of tourist systems, we can understand that there are substantial differences between the products of sun-and-sand tourism, cultural tourism, and sports or ecological tourism, since the basic need to be satisfied by the consumer-tourist differs appreciably, and with it the business concept.

We can further enrich the definition of product by considering that a tourism product is described, as well as in terms of the functions or services which it offers to consumers to satisfy certain of their needs, by the technology used. The technology thus becomes the nexus linking products and markets, as each specific way of satisfying a basic need frequently gives rise to a different market. For example, in the case of the 'sports tourism' product, the same basic need can be satisfied in quite different ways: golfing, horse-riding, sailing, 'rafting' etc. Each of these distinct ways of satisfying the same basic need (technology) constitutes a product (in a more complete definition), it being possible then to talk of the products golf tourism, horse-riding tourism, water tourism, mountaineering tourism, etc.

A *market* is distinguished by the groups of customers served and the services or functions provided. Therefore, the second major decision in the strategic process is the selection of the *target clientèle*. We understand by this term the grouping of potential customers, with a high level of homogeneity in their behavior, which the firm has defined and selected (based on the comprehension of the potential market and of its segmentation) and towards whom will be directed all the action of the firm. Tourist markets are differentiated by distinguishing behavior models of the consumers, the competitive forces and the keys of the success of a business.

This three-dimensional focus (Figure 45.1) demonstrates that the process of definition of a business is begun by the tourism firm or system establishing a list of possible groups of customers, services to be supplied (primary needs to be satisfied) and available technologies.

Next, the tourism firm or system must decide the *strategic range of its activities*, that is, the extent to which a business seeks to satisfy one or more needs for one or more market segments, and it uses for this purpose one or several technologies (Abell and Hammond, 1979: 392–393). The defining by a tourism firm or system of the businesses in which it wishes to be present will thus be the result of the combined replies to three questions:

(1) Whom is it desired to satisfy? target clientèle.
(2) In what is it desired to satisfy them? services to be rendered or needs to be met.
(3) How they are to be satisfied? technologies to be used.

Once the functions to be supplied, the technologies that are going to be used for this purpose, and the groups of customers to be served, have been chosen, the tourism firm must decide if it offers the same supply of services to each segment of the market included in its target clientèle, or opts on the other hand for a *differentiation*

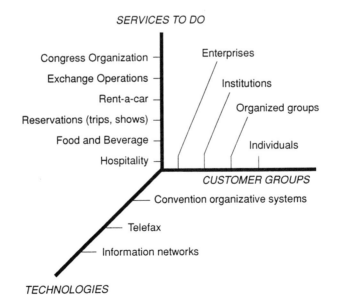

Figure 45.1 *An approach to the hospitality business*

of the product by adjusting the offer to the profile of each homogeneous group of customers. Thus a firm which has opted for golf tourism can differentiate its offer depending on the segmentation of its target clientèle, being able to adapt to the specific playing habits and behavior of children, the elderly, or professionals.

Although the definition of the business in which the tourism firm positions itself is very important for the strategic diagnosis, in the real economy tourism firms do not compete for business, nor even for markets, but for market segments with dissimilar consumption and information habits. This strategic view therefore underlines the importance of a *specialization* of the tourism firm with the aim of positioning itself to compete in specific segments (Figure 45.2). From this viewpoint, gaining competitive advantages in the development of new products will require firms capable of identifying and reacting to the changes which occur in their setting (Go, 1992).

The concern to break down the *scope* of a tourism firm or system into simpler parts, in order to improve its strategic analysis and the quality of decision-making, has increased as awareness has grown of two facts:

(1) The *multiservice firm* nature of any tourism organization, and consequently its greater complexity.
(2) Spanish tourism, as a result of the very diversity of its people/villages, its natural and cultural wealth, and the drive to diversify the supply side of tourism, as

mentioned earlier, currently has a pronounced *'multi-activity'* or *'multi-business'* nature. In this sense we must reject totally the existence of a tourist business. Here there lies a serious conceptual error, the germ of later competitive failures. Tourism is too broad and heterogeneous to be analyzed globally. There exist different tourist businesses aimed at satisfying different basic needs, with completely dissimilar behavior patterns and settings. In this first approach, we can understand the substantial differences between the sun-and-sand tourism business through tour operators, the cultural tourism business of central Europe, or the business of residential tourism for the elderly.

(3) Certain strategic problems are typical of large-scale tourist chains or multi-site operations. Jones and Lockwood (1992) detected two approaches in strategic management in these organizations. The first approach, predominant in the past, consists of a centralized control, which has led to rigid hierarchical control systems, a large head office which supposedly achieves economies of scale, a product with a strong brand and a high degree of standardization. The second approach consists of returning control to the post of manager of each unit, in an attempt to reduce one of the dimensions of the complexity. The strategies for achieving this aim have consisted of reducing effectively the impact of having many locations, by delegating decisions and responsibility

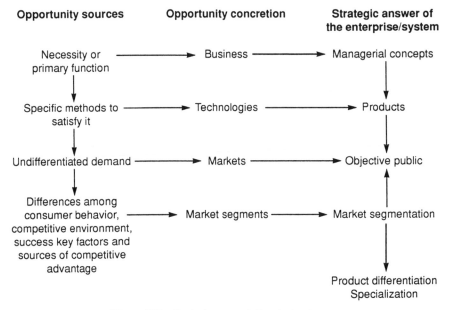

Figure 45.2 *Strategic segmentation in tourism*

to the level of the establishment, or reducing the number of market segments, splitting the organization into divisions with responsibility for specific segments, after the fashion of Trust House Forte's Inns, Post House or Family.

For these reasons, the essential starting point for the analysis of the Spanish tourism system, in order to formulate a competitive strategy aimed at finding and exploiting opportunities in each tourist business, is *strategic segmentation*: its division into *strategic segments* (Boston Consulting Group, 1976), 'strategy centers' (Wright, 1974), 'strategic business units' (Hax and Majluf, 1984a, 1984b; Wind and Mahajan, 1981; Ohmae, 1983), 'strategic domains or fields of activity' (Thiétart, 1990), or 'strategic business areas' (Ansoff et al., 1982).[4]

The tourism system must be split into strategically differentiated segments, understood as tourist product/market segments which compete for the same consumers, distribution channels or sources of competitive advantage, since it is here that the true competition is found. There are three fundamental reasons for the need to identify strategic units of businesses, with specific weight in the Spanish tourist system (Menguzzato and Renau, 1991:90):

(1) There is no overall competitive position of the country, but different competitive positions for each strategic segment.
(2) Each strategic segment exists in a specific competitive setting and requires particular distinctive competences (abilities and assets). The decision-making and action situation is thus dissimilar in each case.
(3) The identification of strategic units of businesses does not mean that several activities should not be regrouped when factors critical for their success coincide, in order to exploit synergistical possibilities and not to multiply the number of different work points in national tourism planning.

The Spanish tourist system: strategic segments and portfolio models

Since strategic segmentation is one of the most difficult and delicate tasks of a strategy (of a firm or of the national tourism system) (Thiétart, 1990; Sicard, 1987), it requires the aid of techniques with a sensible balance of capacity for dissection and globality.

The demarcation of strategic segments for a tourism system requires attention to detail, avoiding two opposing errors. The first one is excessive segmentation, which would cause confusion between strategic segmentation and market segmentation, leading to overestimation of the national competitive position in the strategic tourism units thus defined. The second is an excessively global segmentation, which would lead to confusion between the statistical notion of 'sector' or 'industry' and that of strategic segment, masking the differences which exist (Porter, 1976; Coate, 1983).

One procedure for tackling strategic segmentation full-scale is to use 'activity matrices' or *portfolio models*. These models aim to provide a formalized support for the basic decision regarding the make-up of the business portfolio of the tourism firm or system, and for the analysis of its positioning in each strategic segment as against its competitors. The conclusions to be drawn refer to the evaluation of the competitive interest of each segment for the firm or system, their specific weight when designing the optimum portfolio, the distribution of resources and, consequently, to the specific strategies to be designed and implemented, seeking always the maximum equilibrium in the portfolio of activities and to optimize global performance.

There is nowadays an abundance of models for strategic analysis of the portfolio, dating from the late 1960s and early 1970s, inspired by major consulting firms and large companies.[5]

One of the most popular models for portfolio analysis is the *General Electric–McKinsey approach*. This contribution was a decisive milestone for considering each system as a network of interrelated strategic business units. It took the specific form of a matrix, which received the name of 'Business Assessment Array', which was useful for classifying the centers of strategy by their competitive position and the strength of the market.

The 1990 Marketing Plan for Spanish Tourism used this tool to design the business strategy for the Spanish tourism system (Figure 45.3). Specifically, its construction of the matrix is based on the definition of strategic areas proposed by Ohmae (1982), with the strategic objective of identifying the forces acting in the setting of the firm and exploiting them in order to reach an optimum differentiation from competitors.[6]

The 'White Book on Tourism in the Land of Valencia' has taken the same path. In a first phase, it classified the level of attraction of the possible segments as indicated in Figure 45.4; it can be appreciated that the most attractive market is business tourism, which is, however, the only one not controllable from the point of view of the planning of tourism, as it is closely linked to social, economic and cultural activity. Subsequently, it expressed the strategic diagnosis on the matrix 'attraction/competitive position of the Land of Valencia' shown in Figure 45.5.

We have found three major defects in these applications. First, quite different assessments of the levels of attraction

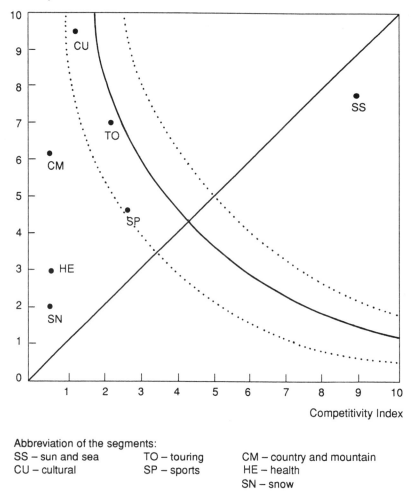

Attractivity index

Competitivity Index

Abbreviation of the segments:
SS – sun and sea   TO – touring   CM – country and mountain
CU – cultural   SP – sports   HE – health
                                            SN – snow

Figure 45.3 *Attractivity—competitivity array of the Spanish tourist system (Source: Secretaria General de Turismo (1989))*

of segments such as cultural tourism, health tourism, or sun-and-sand tourism, although in this last case the differences can be explained by the division into 'mass sun-and-sand tourism' and 'individual sun-and-sand tourism'. These contradictions are caused by the process of quantification of the index of attraction or strength of each strategic segment, which suffers from oversimplification. In the identification of relevant factors, the list established (Figure 45.6) is too short, compared with the already small list of 15 factors in Wind and Mahajan (1981). Thus there are no indices of quality, cost, profitability, competence, segment structure, technology or social and political context. The list of

factors in competitiveness is more complete. Finally, there is an excessively generic definition of competitive strategies for each strategic segment, with no attempt to make use of the information supplied by the positioning map to offer more specific strategies for each strategic area, in line with the studies by Channon and Jalland (1978) or Hofer and Davoust (1977).

All in all, we believe that, properly used, the portfolio analysis models are a suitable instrument for achieving a balanced tourism system and a base for designing selective investment policies, to consolidate the competitive position in the traditional markets at the same time as improving it in new markets.

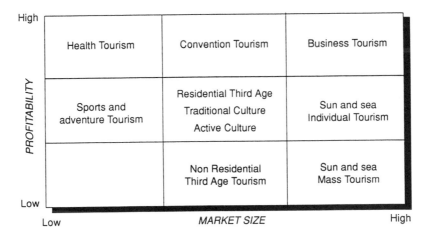

Figure 45.4 *Attractivity level of the strategic segments in tourism (Source: ITVA (1990))*

The strategic advertising of the brand-name 'Spain'

The quantitative importance which advertising receives in budgetary terms, as well as its character as expression and form of the global strategy of the brand-name 'Spain', led us to pause over the analysis of the most recent advertising strategies.

The 'White Book on Spanish Tourism' of 1990 reflects the principal motives for visiting Spain. Among these the two most relevant are the sun and the climate (quoted by 82% of respondents). On the basis of this clear motivation and considering the strategic option of diversification suggested by the 'Marketing Plan for Spanish Tourism', the core of the communication was defined: diversity and sun, which finally became transformed into 'Spain. Everything under the sun'.

The visual elements chosen were Miró's sun with the red and yellow colours of the flag of Spain. The logo of the brand-name of Spanish tourism communicated the value of the brand and its competitive positioning. Spain's

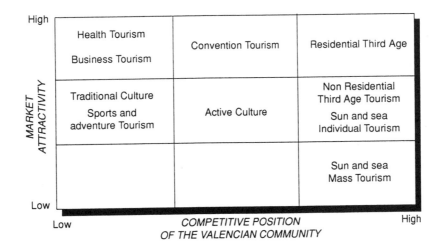

Figure 45.5 *Attraction–competitive position array of the Valencian tourist system (Source: ITVA (1990))*

	Attractivity factors	**Competitivity Factors**
Spanish Tourist System	1. Market size. 2. Market growth. 3. Level of spending. 4. Seasonality.	1. Market share 2. Relative index of offer. 3. Relative index of communication.
Valencian Tourist System	1. Market size. 2. Market profitability. 3. Degree of development.	1. Renown and image. 2. Climate and beaches. 3. Substructure. 4. Environment. 5. Public services (tourist orientation). 6. Offer (capacity). 7. Quality / price. 8. Service quality. 9. Welcome, orientation and information services. 10. Nearness to source markets. 11. Promotion in source markets.

Figure 45.6 *Key factors for the assessment of attractivity and competitivity indicators in each segment (Source: Secretaria General de Turismo (1989) and ITVA (1990))*

competitive advantage was diversity and the sun—the sun for reasons well known to tourists, and diversity including sports such as skiing, sailing, golf, diverse cultures and traditions, and a number of traditional dishes and regional cuisines.

The 'everything under the sun' campaign was carried out at an international level in the principal markets for seven years, with media investment levels close to 1600 million pesetas in 1988. The diffusion was done basically in magazines and newspapers because of the lower effective cost to reach the various markets (Parkinson and Martin, 1993).

In 1992 a new approach was adopted to reposition the brand. The slogan chosen for the advertising campaign was 'Spain—Passion for life'. The fundamental values of the brand were diversity, dynamism, and creativity, which although not in contradiction with the previous campaign, did require a repositioning in consumer perception.

The campaign aimed to emphasize the creativity and dynamism of the country, and the variety it offered, which differentiated it from its competitors. The objectives of the campaign were to show a country with growing and intense development, capable of providing for the various needs of tourists, to communicate a country with great traditions, culture, history and natural resources, and to manifest a country with personality and enthusiasm for life (Parkinson and Martin, 1993).

Based on the concept of 'Passion for life', various tourist activities related to sports, art, climate, nature,

food, etc., are shown in all their intensity. In this campaign once again, magazines and newspapers were the principal media used, with 80% of the budget, but the remaining 20% was also devoted to television in the European market.

Conclusions

In this study we have carried out an analysis of the different approaches to research into tourism and of the strategies adopted by the Spanish tourism industry, and their positive and negative influences on the market. From this we can draw the following conclusions:

—The diverse lines of research into the phenomenon of tourism carried out from macroeconomic, sociological, geographical and town-planning viewpoints, among others, are useful to the extent that they contribute to the analysis of the situation of tourism. These approaches, the most usual among Spanish researchers, become inadequate for competitive development of the products and firms of Spanish tourism.

—The strategic approach is, in our opinion, a more innovative approach which allows the analysis of the weaknesses and strengths, opportunities and threats, and competitive development of the firms and their products.

—Spanish public administrations have been innovative in the use of the strategic approach for the diagnosis of the activity, the knowledge of its competitive positioning and the determining of strategies.

—The 1990 'Marketing Plan for Spanish Tourism' used portfolio models, and in particular the Business Assessment Array matrix to define the business strategy of the Spanish tourism system. Likewise the 'White Book on Tourism in the Land of Valencia' classified the level of attraction of the segments, to subsequently express the strategic diagnosis on the matrix 'Attraction/ competitive position of the Land of Valencia'. Although some defects can be observed in their application, they constitute an adequate instrument for defining a balanced system of tourism.

Notes

1. This paper forms part of a research project entitled 'Spanish tourist industry: application of DELPHI method to the analysis of its strategic behavior, efficacy and results', carried out by the Department of Business Management of the University of Valencia. We wish to thank the Directorate-General of Scientific and Technical Research of the Spanish Ministry of Education and Science.
2. Among the very few papers taking this line, we may mention: Bordás (1993), Bordás and Araya (1992), Camisón and Monfort (1993), Bigné and Miquel (1992), Moutinho et al. (1994), and Oreja (1992).
3. A review of the diversity of strategic approaches can be found in Choffee (1985).
4. These concepts are not completely equivalent, the differences lying in their definition as conceptual bases of diverse models of strategic analysis (see Gouillart, 1989; Marten, 1987). But all agree on the idea of creating units of analysis for strategic segmentation.
5. Various attempts at classification have been made by Wind and Mahajan (1981), Choffray and Wagner (1983), Sallenave (1983) and Marten (1987).
6. Other structurings of strategic areas, different from the original proposal by General Electric–McKinsey, are those of Hax and Majluf (1984b), Wind and Mahajan (1981), Rothschild (1979), Pessemier (1977), and Hofer and Schendel (1978).

References

Abell, D. F. (1980) *Defining the Business: The Starting Point of Strategic Planning*, Prentice Hall, Englewood Cliffs, NJ.

Abell, D. F. and Hammond, J. S. (1979) *Strategic Market Planning. Problems and Analytical Approaches*, Prentice Hall, Englewood Cliffs, NJ.

Ansoff, H. I. (1976) *La Estrategia en la Empresa*, EUNSA, Navarra.

Ansoff, H. I., Kirsch, W. and Roventa, P. (1982) 'Dispersed positioning in portfolio analysis', *Industrial Marketing Management*, 11:237–252.

Bain, J. (1972) *Essays on Price Theory and Industrial Organization*, Little, Brown, Boston, MA.

Bigné, E. and Miquel, S. (1992) 'La empresa hotelera española: factores de desarrolla', *Papers de Turisme*, 10:63–77.

Blomstrom, R. L. (1983) *Strategic Marketing Planning in the Hospitality Industry: a Book of Readings*, The Educational Institute, American Hotel and Motel Association, East Lansing, MI.

Bordás, E. (1993) 'Nous negocis turistics per a l'any 2000: les claus de l'èxit', Actes del II Simposi Internacional de Turisme 'La competitivitat de l'empresa turistica davant els nous escenaris inmediats', ESADE, Barcelona, 21–22 January, pp. 25–35.

Bordás, E. and Araya, M. (1992) 'Los planes de márketing turísticos. La nueva herramienta clave para el desarrollo', *Revista Valenciana d'Estudis Autonomics*, 13(March):39–73.

Boston Consulting Group (1976) 'Pay off on the corporate portfolio', *Perspectives*, 135.

Camisón, C. and Monfort, V. (1993) 'La empresa turistica valenciana: diagnóstico estratégico y posicionamiento competitivo', *Papers de Turisme*, 12 (in press).

Channon, D. and Jalland, M. (1978) *Multinational Strategic Planning*, Macmillan, London.

Chías, J. (1991) *El Mercado son Personas. El Marketing en las Empresas de Servicios*, McGraw-Hill, Madrid.

Choffee, E. E. (1985) 'Three models of strategy', *Academy of Management Review*, 10(1):89–97.

Choffray, J. J. and Wagner, P. (1983) 'Definition et révision d'une stratégie de developpement industriel', *Révue Française de Marketing*, 92:5–17.

Coate, M. B. (1983) 'Pitfalls in portfolio planning', *Long Range Planning*, 16(3):4–56.

Day, G. S., Shocker, A. D. and Srivastava, R. K. (1979) 'Customer oriented approaches to identifying product-markets', *Journal of Marketing*, 43 (fall):8–19.

Eiglier, P. and Langeard, E. (1989) *Servuction, Le Marketing des Services*, McGraw-Hill, Paris.

Gamble, P. (1992) 'Estrategias comerciales en mercados neuvos y tradicionales', *Revista Valenciana d'Estudis Autonòmics*, 13:217–246.

Gilbert, D. (1989) 'Plan de estrategia de marketing para el turismo en España', *Estudios Turísticos*, 104:83–100.

Go, F. (1992) 'El paradigma de los nuevos productos turísticos y las ventajas competitivas', *Revista Valenciana de'Estudis Autonòmics*, 13:75–102.

Gouillart, F. (1989) *Stratégie pour une Entreprise Competitive*, Económica, Paris.

Hax, A. C. and Majluf, N. S. (1984a) 'Le planning stratégique après le Boston Consulting Group', *Harvard-L'Expansion*, 33:53–66.

Hax, A. C. and Majluf, N. S. (1984b) 'Planification stratégique et matrice économique', *Harvard-L'Expansion*, 33:92–105.

Hofer, C. W. and Davoust, M. J. (1977) *Gestion Stratégique Couronée de Succès*, A. T. Kearney Inc., Chicago, IL.

Hofer, C. W. and Schendel, D. (1978) *Strategy Formulation: Analytical Concepts*, West Publishing, St Paul, MN.

ITVA (1990) 'Libro blanco del turismo de la comunidad valenciana', Generalitat Valenciana, Conselleria d'Industria, Comerç i Turisme, Valencia.

Jones, P. and Lockwood, A. (1992) *The Management of Hotel Operations. An Innovative Approach to the Study of Hotel Management*, Cassell, London.

Marten, I. (1987) *Planificación Estratégica en Empresas Diversificades: Análisis de la Cartera*, Ediciones de la Universidad Autónoma de Madrid, Madrid.

Mason, E. (1939) 'Price and production policies of the large scale enterprise', *American Economic Review*, 29(March):61–74.

Menguzzato, M. and Renau, J. J. (1991) *La Dirección Estratégica de la Empresa. Un Enfoque Innovador del Management*, Ediciones Ariel, Barcelona.

Monitor Company (1992) 'Reforçament de l'avantatge competitiu del sector turístic a Catalunya', Generalitat de Catalunya, Departament de Comerç, Consumi i Turisme, Barcelona.

Moutinho, L., Miquel S., Bigné, E. and McDonagh, P. (1994) 'Key factors contributing to the future development of the hotel industry: a comparative analysis of the views of British/Irish and Spanish hotel managers', *Journal of Hospitality and Leisure Management*, in press.

Nanus, B. and Lundberg, C. (1988) 'In QUEST of strategic planning', *Cornell Hotel and Restaurant Administration Quarterly*, August.

Ohmae, K. (1982) 'Foresight in strategic planning', *The McKinsey Quarterly*, Autumn: 14–31.

Ohmae, K. (1983) 'The strategic triangle and business unit strategy', *The McKinsey Quarterly*, Winter: 9–24.

Oreja, J. R. (1992) 'Tenerife hospitality firms: current situation and competitive strategies', Instituto Universitario de la Empresa (IUDE), University of La Laguna, La Laguna, Tenerife.

Parkinson, S. and Martin, M. A. (1993) 'The development of Spain as an international tourist brand', *Proceedings of the 22nd Annual Conference of the European Marketing Academy*, Barcelona, 25–28 May, pp. 1229–1243.

Pessemier, E. A. (1977) *Product Management: Strategy and Organization*, John Wiley, New York.

Porter, M. (1976) *Interbrand Choice, Strategy and Bilateral Market Power*, Harvard University Press, Cambridge, MA.

Porter, M. (1990) *The Competitive Advantage of Nations*, The Free Press, New York.

Reichel, A. (1983) 'Strategic management: how to apply it to firms in the hospitality industry', *Service Industries Journal*, 3.

Rothschild, W. E. (1979) *Strategic Alternatives*, AMACOM, New York.

Sallenave, J. P. (1983) *Gerencia General y Estrategia Empresarial*, McGraw-Hill, Mexico City.

Sasser, W. E. and Morgan, I. P. (1977) 'The Bermuda Triangle of food service chains', *Cornell Hotel and Restaurant Administration Quarterly*, February: 56–61.

Secretaría General de Turismo (1989) 'Plan de marketing del turismo 1990', Ministerio de Transportes, Turismo y Comunicaciones, Madrid.

Secretaría General de Turismo (1992) 'FUTURES: plan marco de competitividad del turismo español', Ministerio de Industria, Comercio y Turismo, Madrid.

Schaffer, J. D. (1985) 'Strategy, organisation structure and success in the lodging industry', *International Journal of Hospitality Management*, 3(4):159–165

Schaffer, J. D. (1986) 'Structure and strategy: two sides of success', *Cornell Hotel and Restaurant Administration Quarterly*, February:76–81.

Sicard, C. (1987) *Practique de la Stratégie d'Entreprise*, Hommes et Techniques, Paris.

Slattery, P. and Olsen, M. (1984) 'Hospitality organisations and their environment', *International Journal of Hospitality Management*, 32:55–61.

Thiétart, R. A. (1990) *La Stratégie d'Entreprise*, rev. edn, McGraw-Hill, Paris.

Tse, E. (1988) 'Defining corporate strengths and weaknesses: is it essential for successful strategy implementation?', *Hospitality Education and Research Journal*, 12(2):57–72.

Tse, E. and Olsen, M. D. (1988) 'The impact of strategy and structure on the organisational performance of restaurant firms', *Hospitality Education and Research Journal*, 12(2):265–276.

Tse, E. and Olsen, M. D. (1989) 'Relating Porter's business strategy to organisation structure: a case of US restaurant firms', *Proceedings of the Launch Conference of the Journal of Contemporary Hospitality Management*, Dorset Institute, pp. 87–105.

Webster, M. and Hudson, T. (1992) 'Strategic management: a theoretical overview and its application to the hospitality industry', in Teare, Richard and Boer, Andrew (Eds) (1992) *Strategic Hospitality Management. Theory and Practice for the 1990s*, Cassell, London, pp. 9–30.

Wind, Y. and Mahajan, V. (1981) 'Designing product and business portfolio', *Harvard Business Review*, January–February: 155–165.

Witt, S. F. and Moutinho, L. (1989) *Tourism Marketing and Management Handbook*, Prentice Hall, Hemel Hempstead.

Woodside, A. G. (1988) 'Consumer decision making and competitive marketing strategies: applications for tourism planning', *Journal of Travel Research*, 26(3):2–7.

Wright, R. V. L. (1974) 'Un systeme pour Gérer la diversité, Arthur D. Little Inc.

46 Movie-induced tourism*

R. W. RILEY

For a destination—a small hotel or an entire continent—there's no finer publicity than that generated by a major motion picture. Not only do most tourism entities lack the big bucks to finance a far reaching advertising campaign, but no pocket brochure can match the wide screen miracle of Technicolor, Dolby, and high profile spokesmen

(Williamson, 1991)

The golden years of the silver screen are said to have passed but movies have recently been recognized as powerful forces when publicizing and promoting consumable items. Large volume sales of *Batman* and *Jurassic Park* memorabilia provide some evidence of the influence that movies can have on consumptive behaviors. Airlines, motor vehicle manufacturers and beverage companies have long recognized this influence and often compete for the right to have their products used during movies. There also appears to be a suggestion that movies can influence the travel preferences and destination choices of some people who attend movies (Riley, 1992). Despite these suggestions, there has been no empirical investigation of the phenomenon. Using anecdotal observations, popular media articles and the attendance figures gathered at movie locations, this paper advances a prima facie case that some movies are valuable tourism publicity and promotion tools. In consideration of this suggested phenomenon, an attempt is also made to explain why movies are effective as publicity and promotional mediums for attracting visitors.

One inference from increased visitorship to movie locations is the positive economic impact on the movie location and surrounding areas. To local tourism administrators and marketers, this suggestion would seem to be intuitively correct; however, no evidence has been collected to confirm this intuition. The organizations most likely to gain from the collection of this data are film commissions, tourism promotion bureaus and economic development units. These organizations are often charged with attracting movie production companies because of the money injected into the film location's economy. Unfortunately, these organizations appear to have been remiss when justifying the economic importance of location movies. To date, the film commissions' primary justification for existence has been the money spent by production companies when filming on location. No studies have been conducted to assess the secondary economic effect of tourist spending generated from visitation to movie locations. Using evidence similar to that already stated, this paper will explore the economic justifications that film commissions have used in the past.

A lack of research about the relationship between feature-length location films, increased post-film visitation and economic impact poses the question of how evidence should be collected. A brief outline of data-gathering problems is offered to assist film commissions who wish to better justify their existence.

The ensuing discussion is initiated by advancing the case of motion pictures as pseudo-tourism attractions. Advertisements and movies are then compared to understand why movies can be effective publicity and promotional tools. Evidence of increased visitorship and film commissions' economic justifications are offered in brief case studies using North American and Australian examples. Finally, some brief remarks are made about particular methodological problems and possible solutions when attempting to assess visitation effects and economic impacts.

Movies as tourism-inducing events

Natural and man-made attractions have traditionally been recognized as the two main types of tourism pulling agents. Ritchie has identified 'hallmark events' as another type of attraction that enhances a destination's image and therefore acts as a luring device for tourists. He defines 'hallmark events' as: 'Major one-time or recurring events of limited duration developed to primarily enhance the awareness, appeal and profitability of a destination in the short and/or long term. These events rely for their success on uniqueness, status, or timely significance to create interest and attract attention' (Ritchie, 1984). For inclusion in this attraction category, Ritchie identifies the typical 'hallmark events' of international trade fairs (Expos), festivals (Carnival in Rio), culturally unique events (Oktoberfest), historical commemorations (centennial celebrations), major socio-political happenings

---

*Some of the data presented in this article was first published in *Tourism Management*, 13(3):267–274 and is reproduced here with the kind permission of Butterworth-Heinemann, Oxford, UK.

(papal visits), and sporting events (soccer's World Cup). It could be argued that some of these events are undertaken primarily to commemorate the historical, social or cultural importances of the host population. However, it is equally arguable that the original purposes of many such events have now been usurped by the purpose of the short and long-term economic impacts they generate.

Not included in Ritchie's 'hallmark' examples are a type of event that meets all but one of his criteria. Motion picture films make up this event category by showcasing the attributes and attractions of destinations within two-hour scripted stories. The showcasing of destination attractions, within the frame of a story, allows potential travelers to develop a more complete destination image through vicarious consumption.

Motion picture films possess one departure from Ritchie's definitional criteria. Films are a passive involvement entertainment medium, rarely used to 'primarily enhance the awareness, appeal, and profitability of a destination'. Full-length feature films are not commissioned to showcase the attributes of locations or countries, they showcase a story line and oftentimes the principal actors in the hope of profitability. One advantage of motion picture films is their ability to fulfill Ritchie's reoccurrence criterion. Audiences can choose to view the movie repeatedly, in the theater, on video cassette or when released for television viewing. With each audience encounter there is potential to attract a new flock of visitors to the film location.

Advertising versus publicity engendered by movies

Promoting tourist destinations, to potential vacationers, is a difficult proposition. Developing favorable images of destinations through short segments of radio advertising, newspaper articles, television and brochures is a very expensive proposition. Most products and services use advertising to entice buyers and they all compete for the limited time and attention of the media-harried consumer. Indeed, consumers are said to be exposed to a range of '250 to 2000' print and broadcast advertisements each day (Assael, 1987). This deluge of sales-speak makes differentiation confusing amongst the blur of consumptive options.

Through advertising, tourism marketers hope that consumers will be favorably impressed with destinations although exposure to thirty-second television spots and print advertising is unlikely to be the necessary amount of information needed to induce visitation.

Current tourism advertising lacks the resources needed to prolong destination exposure in order to capture awareness and sustain the interest of potential consumers. On the other hand, motion picture films can fulfill the deficiencies of prolonged exposure and sustained interest. In successful box-office films, the increased awareness of destinations can be substantial and the received value of increased tourism can also be substantial when compared to the budgets needed for advertising the same destinations.

Butler (1990) suggests that audio-visual information such as television shows, and video cassettes are becoming increasingly significant as knowledge sources. Fewer people are relying on written information to gather knowledge. In this sense, the instant gratification of effortless movie viewing and the involvement nurtured through a cinematic storyline can be far greater than any promotional brochure can manage. Through feature length movies, destinations such as Fiji (*Blue Lagoon*), the stately homes of Atlanta (*Driving Miss Daisy*), and the Amish country of Pennsylvania (*Witness*) have been brought to the attention of many viewers who were not previously aware of their existence.

Movies, as a type of publicity and promotion, are effective to wide market segments of the population for the reasons explained previously but also as passive, non-sales-oriented forms of communication. Consumers need not vacate the most comfortable chair in the house or go further than the local cinema to enjoy an extended spectacle. Essentially, movies are attractions even though they are displayed in tourism-generating areas. Through movies, the attractions of a destination are transferred in a story-like, 'living' form to the locations of potential consumers. The destination has enhanced appeal through the viewers involvement in the storyline. Within the medium of movies, it is relatively easy to be captivated by the beauty of the South Dakota plains where native Americans once roamed (*Dances with Wolves*), or by the incredible natural spectacles of rock formations at Devils Tower National Monument in eastern Wyoming (basalt rock outcrops from *Close Encounters of the Third Kind*). When viewing movies, consumers become vicariously attracted without leaving the security of home and without the 'hard sell' impressions inherent in paid advertising. By using motion picture films, the barriers of information and time lack are reduced while destination images are enhanced. For the viewing public, successful movies can be 'hallmark events' and attractive devices for tourist destinations.

Film commissions' current justification

Most film commissions, reporting the impact of location films, have focused on the money spent in communities by film production companies and their respective entourages. Some film commission news releases have expounded the $10 000 000 dollars per year spent on location while filming *Dallas* (Hodges, 1991), the $30 000 rental for the house in *Driving Miss Daisy* (Patureau, 1991), and the $15 000 spent each week in local grocery bills for *Steel Magnolias* (Jones, 1991). Total location spending for *Steel Magnolias* resulted in a $4 000 000 investment for the city of Natchitoches. Unfortunately, the secondary economic effects of tourist visitation have never been calculated by film commissions. Recently, twelve weeks of shooting for *Weekend at Bernies II*, benefited the economy of the US Virgin Islands by an estimated total of $12 000 000. The value of the subsequent publicity was estimated at $25 000 000 (*Travel Weekly*, 1993). The Virgin islands did not, however, report any plans to track the potential effect of increased tourism visitation. Inevitable, it would seem, is a need for tourism bureaus, film commissions and economic development units to jointly track the effects of a film as they apply to increased visitor arrivals, motel rentals, attraction admissions fees, restaurant meals and souvenir shop receipts. It is logistically difficult to gather data about a motion picture film's contribution to tourist visitation, but particular cases of visitation data and anecdotal information lends some support to these attempts. This type of research would also present a justification for film commissions when seeking the monetary resources needed to encourage further movie production at tourist locations.

North American movies—case studies of film locations

Ray, people will come Ray. They'll come to Iowa.
They'll turn up in your driveway and they won't be
sure why they're doing it. They'll be right at your door.
(Actor James Earl Jones in the movie *Field of Dreams*.)

In 1989, movie-makers focused their lenses on a baseball diamond among the expansive cornrows of Iowa—4 miles along a graveled farm road and one half hour drive from the nearest city. The baseball diamond location for *Field of Dreams* was situated in the heartland of a largely ignored agricultural hinterland—one that has rarely been considered as a tourist attraction. The only recognition for this geographical area was the book, *Little House on the Prairie*. At the time of lensing, the Iowa economic development department trumpeted the windfall based on an estimated $5 000 000 spent by the production company in the surrounding communities (Jones, 1991). Although the baseball diamond has become a destination for nearly 140 000 visitors to date (1989, 7500 visitors; 1990, 15 000;

1991, 35 000; 1992, 50 000; 1993, 40 000), little has been done to assess the economic impact due to tourist visitation (Boekensted, 1994). It is said that the diamond in Iowa has become a shrine to baseball. 'Fathers bring their sons. They go out and swing a bat, run the bases, take pictures. . . . I've heard it described as a shrine, but I don't know why' (Lansing, 1989).

Rayburn County, Georgia, was the site of *Deliverance*, a story which followed the ill-fated trip of three men canoeing a river. Their personal disasters were in stark contrast to the surrounding environmental beauty and the novelty of white-water river riding. *Deliverance* became the catalyst for a thriving river rafting operation and Rayburn County has experienced significant visitor increases since the film was released in 1972. Local people involved in accommodation services say that the movie has realized an estimated 20 000 tourists per annum, with gross annual revenues exceeding two million dollars (Dillard, 1991). Despite this movie-generated phenomenon, no formal studies were ever conducted to verify the visitor increases and secondary economic impact.

Visitation statistics from Historic Fort Hays, Kansas, a site briefly used at the start of *Dances with Wolves*, recorded a 25% increase in 1991 and a further 18.9% increase in 1992. These figures compared favorably with an annual average increase of 6.6% for the previous four years. The drop in visitations for 1993 was attributed to problems with snow accumulation which limited visitation for three months (Wilhelm, 1994). According to the superintendent of Historic Fort Hays, the site still attracts a primary audience of interstate passers-by, but these people now have prior knowledge and interest in the site and are therefore more likely to interrupt their travel. Their willingness to turn off the interstate is greater than it had been in the past. For South Dakota, the filming of the movie had an estimated impact of $12 000 000 from money spent by the cast, crew and production company (Brost, 1992). Since the release of *Dances with Wolves*, there has been a recorded 341% increase in British lead package tours. Some foreign tour packages are now advertising South Dakota as 'Indian country' (South Dakota Economic Development and Tourism Department, 1994). Unfortunately, there has been no attempt to track the economic impact from the increased visitation attributed to the movie. Production spending for *Roxanne* had a similar economic impact on the town of Nelson in Canada. Ten million dollars was the reported investment in the community and tourism was observed to increase rapidly after the movie's release (Haupt, 1992). No studies were commissioned to track the increased visitorship or the economic impact.

The most comprehensive evidence of a movie's attractive ability relates to *Close Encounters of the Third Kind*. The spectacular basalt rock outcrops of Devils Tower National Monument were central to the storyline and provided an imposing backdrop to many scenes. Recorded increases in visitation hold more weight when the relative isolation of the site is considered. Located in Wyoming, Devils Tower National Monument is approximately 300 miles from Denver, the closest metropolitan area. Visitation statistics reflected a dramatic increase due to the movie's release in 1977. The release resulted in a 75% visitor increase in 1978. After *Close Encounters* was released to television in 1980, the National Monument recorded a 34% visitation increase over the previous year. Over the ten-year period before the film was released, average visitation increased at 6.35% annually. After the movie's release to television, visitation dropped for three years before rebounding to an annual average growth rate of approximately 3% (Devils Tower National Monument, 1994). The extreme influx of visitors on each of the releases is difficult to explain for any other reason than film-induced attractivity. Once again, no study was conducted to capture the economic impact and the visitation figures only exist because the site is managed by the US National Park Service.

The enduring effect of the movie was illuminated in a study conducted at Devils Tower, eleven years after the film premiere. Researchers asked a question which focused on visitor's initial source of knowledge about Devils Tower. Their conclusion was:

> The most frequently identified means of initial awareness was 'word of mouth at home'. Over one fourth of all respondents indicated that they had first learned about Devils Tower through verbal contact in their home area. Considering that another one-fifth of the respondents indicated the movie *Close Encounters* was their point of initial knowledge pertaining to Devils Tower, discussion concerning that movie may have influenced the vast majority of people to visit the national monument. (Workman et al., 1990)

Eleven years after the movie was released, 20% of visitors to Devils Tower National Monument credited the viewing *Close Encounters of the Third Kind* as their primary source of destination knowledge.

Steel Magnolias, filmed in Natchitoches, Louisiana, premiered in November of 1989. Based on three data sources collected by the Natchitoches Parish Tourism Commission, there was a recorded 39.7% increase in visitors for 1990. Since this time, tourism has increased at a yearly average of 20% and the curiosity to explore the movie sites has prompted the development of special city tours and brochures. The local tourism commission reported that $4 000 000 was spent by the production company while in Natchitoches; they have never attempted to assess the secondary economic impact of movie induced visitation (Natchitoches Parish Tourist Commission, 1994). A movie in the same genre was *Fried Green Tomatoes*, a story that chronicled the relationships of women and their struggle for self-sufficient legitimacy. According to the owner of the Whistle Stop Cafe, one of the primary locations, the tourism attracting quotient of the movie was not spectacular scenery but 'a search for something they [visitors] have lost, like strong friendships and family traditions' (Goodman, 1993). Although no spending totals have been released for location filming or for tourist visitation, there is now an estimated influx of 600 visitors per day. Juliet, Georgia, population 500, has been transformed from a ghost town into a tourist destination (Mayfield, 1993).

Visits to Southfork Ranch, the family home portrayed in the *Dallas* television series, are a high priority for many Americans and Western Europeans visiting the city of Dallas. Foreigners insist on visitation despite the limited spectacle and a one-and-one-half-year closure to on-site inspection. Apparently foreigners relate Southfork to a validation of the 'American dream' that anyone can be wealthy. The program epitomized open spaces, rich people, western lifestyles, cowboys, and opportunity (Elam, 1991). Southfork has an estimated 400 000–500 000 visitors each year (Golden, 1992) despite the cancellation of the show. The television show has been called 'an hour-long commercial for Dallas and Texas, all over the world' by one city official (Hodges, 1991).

For the final North American case, it has recently been noted that visitation to Dinosaur National Monument has benefited from the release of *Jurassic Park*. Even though no scenes were shot at the Monument, visitors set record attendance figures. Visitation increases of approximately 10% were recorded for 1992 and 1993, after relatively stable yearly increases of approximately 2% over the preceding three years. The interest in dinosaurs is thought to have increased visitation and the effect has been so marked that the title of the park newsletter is now underscored with 'A Real Jurassic Park' (Excell, 1994).

Australian movies

Between 1981 and 1988, Australia experienced an annual visitor increase of 20.5%, from the United States (Lassiter, 1990). At the same time, United States movie viewers experienced and made box-office successes of several Australian films. Despite the 1989 decline in visitation to Australia, an American Express study identified Australia as the 'most desired single destination for travel out of the U.S.' (Anon, 1990). This statement was confirmed through research conducted by the Market Project Group of New York who described Australia and New Zealand combined, as the most desirable destinations for American citizens (Schoolmaster, 1989). A recent survey of travel agents revealed that 30% of US agents mentioned *Crocodile Dundee*, unprompted, when asked about factors influencing the growth of tourism from the United States in the 1980s (Curtis, 1993).

Following the premise of this paper, it would seem that in the 1980s, Australian film productions were significant 'pull' factors. Promotional literature and other popular media were rife with references to, *Mad Max* (1980, release date in the United States), *The Road Warrior* (1982), *The Man from Snowy River* (1982), *Mad Max: Beyond the Thunderdome* (1985), and most recently *Crocodile Dundee I* (1986) and *Crocodile Dundee II* (1988). The influence of these movies was so pervasive that the Economist Intelligence Unit of England lamented the end of the 'Crocodile Dundee era' in overseas publicity and promotion (The Economist Intelligence Unit, 1990). The high profile enjoyed by Australia in the United States was estimated at 'fifty dollars worth of publicity for every dollar spent on advertising' (Coster, 1990). In the Australian situation, movie-induced tourism data was too difficult to gather. Many other factors could have impacted visitation.

The Australian films which attracted attention in the United States have common elements which may be stimulating factors in motivating Americans to travel. These include the use of natural environments as a spectacular backdrop to action, a portrayal of uncomplicated indigenous lifestyles, and lastly, the interaction and struggle of man with the environment.

For film commissioners

The anecdotal evidence is difficult to ignore. Data for United States and Australian cases suggest that motion picture films act as 'hallmark events' and produce a surge in visitation from tourist-generating areas. However, further evidence needs to be accumulated to verify these assertions. In order to justify and solidify their existence, film commissions need to reach beyond their reliance on the amount of money spent in movie production. They need to research the ripple effect that tourists cause when quelling their film-engendered curiosity. Film commissions, tourism promotion agencies and economic development units need to cooperate in developing documentation of visitation. The concurrent collection of visitor spending may show that the economic impact exceeds the original movie production expenditures.

Several problems need to be addressed when conducting a study of the movie-induced visitation phenomenon. Some of these problems and possible solutions are outlined below:

(1) Problem: How do film commissions isolate the magnitude of increases attributed to movie-induced visitation?

Solution: Conduct studies at sites that have a history of collecting year-round visitation data. The average increases from previous years can be compared to those recorded during movie production and after the movie's release.

Solution: Gather baseline data for at least one year before filming begins?

(2) Problem: If the site already attracts a significant number of visitors, how do commissions identify the movie-induced visitors?

Solution: Survey visitors to find their initial source of information and their primary reason for visitation.

(3) Problem: Are visitors primarily attracted to the movie site or is it one of many stops in a more extensive visit?

Solution: Survey at movie locations that are remote destinations or those sites that have never been considered as tourist attractions.

Solution: Compare visitor data with other sites in close geographical proximity for increases of similar magnitude.

(4) Problem: Are other events contributing to the increased attendance figures?

Solution: Inventory the surrounding area for other tourist-attracting events and attempt to assess their attractive pull by gathering visitation figures. If these events occur regularly, gather visitation statistics from prior years.

(5) Problem: When is the attractive pull initiated?

Solution: Gather baseline data before, during, and after location filming. The curious movie-induced visitor, may be lured by pre-shooting publicity or the chance to see movie stars and movie production.

References

Anon (1990) 'Tourism promotion offices plot marketing strategies for 1990s', Supplement to *Travel Weekly*, 49(8):20,28.

Assael, Henry (1987) *Consumer Behavior and Marketing Action*, P. W. S. Kent, Boston, MA.

Boekensted, Betty (1994) Personal communication—visitor book manager, Dyersville, Iowa.

Brost, Kristin (1992) Personal communication—public relations coordinator, South Dakota Economic Development and Tourism, Pierre, South Dakota.

Butler, Richard (1990) 'The influence of the media in shaping international tourism patterns', *Tourism Recreation Research*, 15(2):46–55.

Coster, Heather (1990) 'The inbound market under the microscope', *Australia Tourism Outlook Forum Report*, Australia Tourism Commission, Canberra.

Curtis, Rosemary (1993) Personal communication—research manager, Australian Film Commission, Sydney.

Dillard, Tom (1991) Personal communication—hotel owner, Rayburn County, Georgia.

The Economist Intelligence Unit (1990) 'Australia International tourism reports', Economist Intelligence Unit, London.

Elam, Greg (1991) Personal communication—public relations officer, Dallas Visitor and Convention Bureau, Dallas.

Excell, Anne (1994) Personal communication—concession and visitor statistic specialist, Dinosaur National Monument, US National Park Service, Colorado/Utah.

Golden, Fran (1992) 'TV, movie fans turn locations into popular tourism sites', *Travel Weekly*, 51(8):1, 12–13.

Goodman, Mark (1993) 'Fried green tomatoes, hon?', *People Magazine*, 8 February.

Haupt, Jennifer (1992) 'Reaping the benefits of celluloid magic', *Profiles, A Magazine of Continental Airlines*, September: 20, 51.

Hodges, Anne (1991) 'Dallas, TV's ultimate soap', *Houston Chronicle*, 12 April:1F.

Jones, Betty (1991) Public relations release, Natchitoches Parish Tourism Commission, Natchitoches, Louisiana, 27 March.

Jones, Tom (1991) 'Dubuque hosts première for field of dreams'—public relations release, Department of Economic Development, Des Moines, Iowa, 28 March.

Lansing, Don (1989) in 'People do come to the field of dreams', Greg Smith, *Brunswick News*, Georgia, 9 September 1989.

Lassiter, E. (1990) 'After strike, Australia tries to pull itself back on top', *Travel Weekly*, 49(65):1, 24, 26–27.

Mayfield, Mark (1993) 'Movie magic revives GA town', *USA Today* 25 May: 6A.

Natchitoches Parish Tourist Commission (1994) 'Tourism statistics—yearly totals', Natchitoches, Louisiana.

Patureau, Alan (1991) Personal communication—staff writer, Atlanta Constitution, Atlanta, Georgia.

Riley, R. (1992) 'Movies as tourism promotion: a "pull" factor in a "push" location', *Tourism Management*, 13(3): 267–274.

Ritchie, Brent (1984) 'Assessing the impact of hallmark events: conceptual and research issues', *Journal of Travel Research*, 23(1):2–11.

Schoolmaster, R. (1989) 'Short, cheap trips still reign', *USA Today*, 13 November: 1A.

South Dakota Economic Development and Tourism Department (1994) 'Statistical report for 1993', Pierre, South Dakota.

Travel Weekly (1993) 'More than scenery', 30 August: 6.

Wilhelm, Robert (1994) 'Annual report—visitation statistics', Historic Fort Hays, Hays, Kansas.

Williamson, Judy (1991) 'Where the scenery steals the show', *Houston Chronicle*, 24 March: 1H, 5H.

Workman, Colleen, Zeiger, Jeffrey, and Caneday, Lowell (1990) 'Analysis of visitation: report of Devils Tower Tourism Association', Black Hills State College, Spearfish, North Dakota.

47 Short break holidays

W. FACHÉ

Introduction

The short break market is almost certainly the fastest growing sector of the travel industry in Europe. Although there are increasing numbers of people who take—besides a long holiday—another short holiday, the tourism industry stays nevertheless to a large extent focused on the main holiday during the summer. This has been the strategy since the 1960s when the summer holiday was still the only holiday in the year. So far as short holidays did get attention they were mainly seen as weekend trips with only a marginal importance for the travel industry. But the growth of the short holiday leads to the fact that fairly recently the travel industry has woken up to the future potential of this new market.

In this chapter we will describe the volume of the market and the characteristics of the short holiday, and analyse who it is that mainly takes a short holiday, with what motivation and in what accommodation. Also we will point out, when it is of interest, the consequences of this trend for the travel industry.

No consensus on the definition of a short break

Despite the lack of a clear, international definition, short holidays are frequently defined as trips of one to three nights away from home, primarily for holiday purposes.

In some surveys short holidays are defined as holidays up to three nights, taking place in a commercially provided accommodation, i.e. hotels, guest houses or self-catering; or a stay at the homes of friends or relatives; or a stay in a caravan or other accommodation used by its owners. Other surveys use the term short break in relation to short holidays exclusively in commercial accommodation. Short breaks are then a sector of the more comprehensive category short holidays. In the UK in 1991 44% of short holidays were short breaks in commercial accommodations (ETB, 1992). For the purposes of this chapter we also use the term short break for a holiday taken in commercial accommodation.

The definition is one problem in comparing surveys of different countries. Also the methodological approaches are different in surveys. As short trips tend to be forgotten fairly soon (or not reported) by interviewees, it is not feasible to record them accurately within a yearly survey.

Therefore some research institutions are working on representative surveys carried out several times a year and register the trips made in the respective period, for example, in the UK the BTSM (which has been replaced by the UKTS) worked with monthly surveys; in West Germany (KONTI RA) and The Netherlands (CVO), surveys are carried out every three months. All of this makes the comparison of statistical findings rather problematic.

Growth of the short break market

According to some tourism experts (e.g. Schweizerische Verkehrszentrale, 1989; OPT, 1989; Eichwalder, 1988; Middleton and O'Brien, 1987; Cockerell, 1989), in many European countries the growth rates of short holidays are much higher than in other segments of the travel market. Commercially accommodated short breaks are said to be growing much faster. This is a rather common point of view, but it is difficult to provide detailed statistical evidence for each European country. In many countries the holiday surveys do not cover short holidays which last for less than four nights away from home.

In the UK short holidays have shown until 1988 more growth than holidays as a whole, and most of this growth has been concentrated in short breaks, taken in commercial accommodation. Table 47.1 shows this relative growth of different segments of the market over the past decade. Owing to a change in the statistical basis in 1989, it is only possible to examine long-term trends up to 1988, and 1989 figures are not comparable with the ones from 1988 (Beiosly, 1991).

Table 47.1 *Relative tourism trends*

	Percentage change 1979/80–87/88	
	Trips	Real spend
All tourism	+6	+4
All holidays	0	−4
Short holidays in home of friends or relatives, or in commercial accommodation	+20	+58
Short breaks in commercial accommodation only	+45	+76
Short breaks in licensed hotels	+52	+92

Source: BTS (quoted by Beiosly, 1991).

While it is difficult to quantify, there is, according to Beiosly (1991), some evidence to suggest that commercial short break packages (i.e. commercially marketed packages comprising accommodation, meals and other services at an inclusive price) have been growing at even faster rates than the above table would suggest. Some sources estimate growth rates of between 15% and 20% per annum have been realised during the 1980s.

The same trends can be ascertained in West Germany. According to Lohmann (1990), more than one-third of the West German population aged 14 and above took short holidays in 1985 (38.9%). This is equivalent to about 18 million persons. However, the actual number of trips is much higher, as several trips per person have been made. This equals 43.7 million trips in 1985 and a calculated 50 million trips in 1987 (for 1988 some 57 million short trips). In the past 15 years the number of short trips in Germany has been growing faster than the number of longer holiday trips (5 days and more).

A similar development can be seen for The Netherlands. In 1985 16.9% of the population took a short break in commercial accommodation. After six years this figure is nearly double (1985: 16.9%; 1986: 17%; 1987: 22.9%; 1988: 25.6%; 1989: 27%; 1990: 28.2%; 1991: 29.3% (CVO, 1992)).

Also in Belgium, we notice during the period 1982–1991 a continuous growth. In 1991 more than twice as many Belgians took a short break than in 1982 (1982: 10.9%; 1985: 13.0%; 1988: 18.5%; 1991: 24.1%). This growth appears mainly from 1985 onwards, and concerns short breaks during both the winter and the summer (WES, 1992).

In the future, short break holidays will become more and more important. Leisure time has undergone many changes. The amount of leisure time that people have now has increased slowly but steadily and it looks as if this trend will continue throughout the 1990s.

One important factor for the tourism industry is the change taking place in the time that people have free from work to take holidays. The key word here is flexibility. Working patterns are more and more flexible, resulting in greater variety in the timing of tourist patterns. Changes to the work pattern include more flexible hours for those in full-time employment and a distinct growth in part-time working and shared jobs.

However, a more important consequence for short break holidays is the psychological attitude of people towards weekend or midweek holidays. Research shows that besides income and time considerations, the psychological threshold of a first-time short break holiday is an important one to cross.

All statistics indicate that we are going through a process of recruitment, because before the decision to go on a short break holiday is taken, the time factor and income situation must be considered. However, once people have actually experienced a short break holiday, they are much more open to continue taking short breaks, even though income and time still play an important role.

Once the first steps have been taken, people will continue to participate in short break holidays because the threshold, in fact, was lower than expected.

Does the future really look that bright for each country? For some countries (e.g. Germany, Austria, The Netherlands), at the moment, Lohmann (1990) does not see an end of the quantitative development of short break holidays, which does not mean that there are no limits. In other European countries a certain plateau has been reached (e.g. Great Britain, Ireland) and a further quantitative development seems to be unlikely there. On the other hand, growth rates of short break holidays may be high in countries of southern Europe (e.g. Italy, Spain) but because of a considerable lack of reliable data nobody seems to be able to calculate or to predict them at the moment.

The relative volume of short breaks

This information is of great importance for the commercial sector. For the UK, Victor Middleton made an estimate of the size of the commercial short break holiday in 1986.

> Adopting a minimum level of spending as a logical basis for defining a commercial holiday, he stressed that most of the estimated 33 mn short holidays taken in 1985 were not commercial in nature and that the 'true size' of what realistically can be considered the commercial U.K. short-break market is probably between 5 mn and 8 mn holidays, split between hotels, holiday parks and centres, and self-catering. (Middleton and O'Brien, 1987)

Research suggests that short holidays are mostly additional holidays rather than substitutes for a main holiday. Beiosly (1991) mentioned, as a support for this hypothesis, a study carried out for the Wales Tourist Board in 1986. In this study it was found that frequent short break takers were more likely to have had a long holiday in the same year and more likely to have been abroad. Research-findings from The Netherlands also support this hypothesis (Lohmann, 1990).

Characteristics of short holidays

Short trips do not replace longer holidays. Destinations of short holidays are mainly within the home country. For example, in West Germany some 80% of the short trips registered are within the Federal Republic; trips abroad are made mainly by people living near the borders (Lohmann, 1990). Also in very small countries, the vast majority of the people take a short holiday in their own country: for The Netherlands, 83% (NRIT, 1990), and Belgium, 63% (WES, 1989). Because of the short duration of the short break, people mainly look to take them near to the place where they live.

Bearing in mind these destinations, it is not surprising that private cars are the main means of transportation. Aircraft and trains are more important for destinations abroad, especially for city trips.

Short breaks are taken throughout the year and do not show the intense peaking of longer holidays. Short holidays in Germany have their peak in May and December and a significant low in July, so they generally tend to be more off-season (see Figure 47.1). They have significant potential to contribute to off-season business.

It has to be kept in mind, however, that the number of overnight stays during these short trips with a maximum of three nights is comparatively small. Also, gains within this market segment lead to significant traffic growth, mainly in private cars, evoking both traffic flow and environmental problems with all their economic impacts (Lohmann, 1990).

In the UK there are two periods with above average short break taking: April and May, and August to October (Figure 47.2).

Short break takers are relatively high spenders. Average spending on short breaks in Britain, for example was £73 per trip in 1987, or £35 per night.

Gratton (1990) argues that shortbreak holidays are likely to generate greater economic benefits and fewer economic costs than conventional tourism. For Northern European countries, international tourism has an adverse balance of payments effect (i.e. there is net outflow of

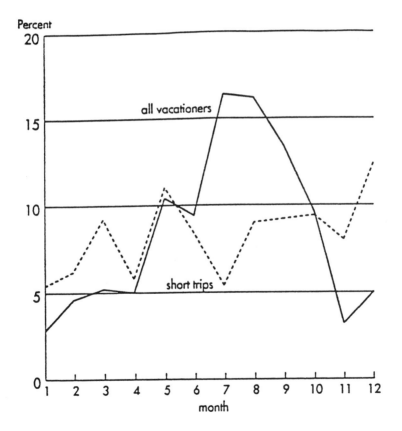

Figure 47.1 *Month of holiday trips (main and additional trips, 1988 and short holidays, 1989) of West German Tourists (Source: Reiseanalyse 1988 and Kontinuierliche Reiseanalyse 1989 des Studienkreises für Tourismus, quoted in Lohmann, 1990)*

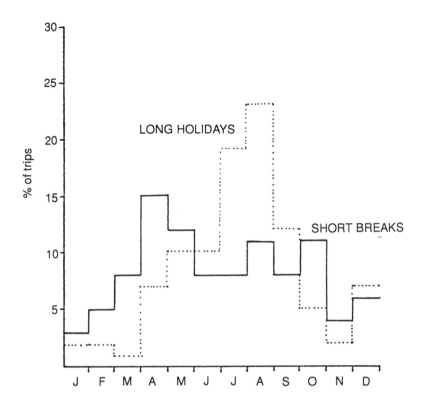

Figure 47.2 *Month of holiday in Britain (Source: British Tourism Survey quoted in Gratton, 1990)*

tourist expenditure). Since the major share of short break holidays is domestic tourism, the increasing tendency to take short break holidays at home is likely to improve the adverse balance of payments implications of tourism. The major economic benefit of short break holidays, however, is in the income and employment generated in local economies. Statistics show that short break holidays are associated with the highest expenditures per person per night of any other sector of the domestic tourism market. Hence the potential for employment generation through this form of tourism is greater than for conventional domestic tourism.

Concerning the planning and booking of a holiday there is a general trend towards more spontaneous decisions. The growing number of people who travel spontaneously, who book late or travel standby or at the last minute is, according to Opaschowski (1990), indicative of a radical change in the attitude to holiday travel: to get away from scheduled obligations and set holiday times. More spontaneous, more frequent, shorter—this is the best way of describing the new attitude to tourism, the holiday formula for a new self-confidence.

Travel is no longer a long-planned enterprise, but a relatively spontaneous decision. Depending on travellers' whims, finances or the weather, decisions and bookings are put off to an increasing extent. The 'new tourist' does not want to be pinned down to set times.

A third of all holiday travellers in West Germany (32%) represent the view: 'I prefer a spontaneous trip, without any planning or pressure of set times'. The groups which most display this spontaneous attitude to travel are young adults (50%) and singles (52%). The shorter the trip, the more spontaneous the concomitant decision. Someone who is going away for a few days does not want to plan far ahead. Half of the UK short holiday takers booked their trip less than one month in advance, or did not book at all (Table 47.2) (ETB, 1988).

Profile of short break takers

So far as data are available for different countries, the characteristics of short break takers are pretty much the same. We present here statistical evidence for two countries: the UK and West Germany.

Table 47.2 *Booking moment of short holidays*

	All short holiday takers (%)
When short holiday booked	
Less than one month	47
Within one month	14
Within two months	12
Within three months	5
More than three months	15
Did not book	4

Source: The short holiday market (quoted in ETB (1988)).

The profile of British short break takers is set out in Table 47.3, drawing on UKTS data. Compared to the population as a whole, short break takers in commercial accommodation are

—more up-market: managerial and professional (AB) and clerical and supervisory (C1) groups.
—young and middle-aged travellers: The over-65s are under-represented. But the coming generation of senior citizens may show a different travel behaviour as part of a different lifestyle.

Short break takers are less likely than holidaymakers generally to have children with them and are more concentrated in the 35–54 age group.

Table 47.3 *Profile of short break holiday takers in the UK—1989*

	Long holidays (%)	Short holidays (%)	Short breaks (%)	UK population (%)
AB: professional, managerial	26	29	28	17
C1: clerical and supervisory	26	24	25	22
C2: skilled manual	26	28	30	29
DE: unskilled manual and state pensioners	22	18	18	32
15–24	14	26	24	20
25–34	22	21	19	17
35–44	21	22	25	17
45–54	12	14	16	13
55–64	14	11	11	13
65 +	17	7	5	19
Children present in household	43	39	40	32
15–34, S, NC	11	22	19	16
15–34, M, NC	3	5	5	4
15–34, C	22	20	19	18
35–54, NC	13	17	20	17
35–54, C	20	18	21	13

S single, M married, C children under 15, NC no children.
Source: UKTS, 1989 (quoted in Beiosly, 1991).

Traditionally, the target market for commercial short break packages has been characterised as empty-nesters— middle-aged ABs with no dependent children and high disposable incomes. Whilst this group will undoubtedly remain important, Beiosly (1991) believes there will be a broadening out of the market for commercial short breaks in the future as the market sees:

- The increasing involvement of self-catering and holiday centre operators in this area.
- The development of more products aimed at families and younger age groups.
- A growing number of over-65s who have both the income for and habit of taking short breaks.

In Germany we notice that the short holidaymakers have about the same profile as in the UK (see Table 47.4).

Table 47.4 *Profile of short holiday makers in West Germany—1989*

n = 4000	Population (%)	Short holiday makers (%)
Sex		
female	53.3	50.6
male	46.7	49.9
Age		
14–19	10.5	10.1
20–29	17.9	22.2
30–39	14.2	15.7
40–49	17.0	19.9
50–59	14.9	14.9
60–69	13.7	11.1
70 and older	11.9	6.0
Marital status		
single	27.0	30.9
married	57.4	57.6
widowed/divorced separated	15.7	11.4
Occupation		
independent/self-employed	4.8	5.6
clerical/supervising	25.7	33.6
skilled manual	12.8	12.5
unskilled	5.2	3.3
farmer	0.5	0.2
housewife	20.2	16.2
in education	13.7	15.7
pensioners	17.2	12.6
Monthly net income		
less than 1500 DM	10.7	9.0
1500–2500 DM	26.1	20.0
2500–3000 DM	15.2	15.7
3000–4000 DM	20.3	20.6
4000–5000 DM	11.9	14.7
5000 DM and more	9.4	13.9

Source: Kontinuierliche Reiseanalyse 1989, StfT, 2nd Quarter, quoted in Lohmann, 1990.

Short break motivations

According to research quoted in a publication of the British Tourist Authority (ETB, 1988), there seem to be two main reasons for taking a short holiday. First, short holidays often have some kind of purpose or 'trigger' that may be a special offer seen in a newspaper or magazine or on television or the occurrence of a special event, sporting fixture or exhibition around which a holiday is built. The second main reason for taking a short holiday is to 'get away for a break' or a 'change of scene' (see Table 47.5).

Whilst 'getting away from it all' was identified as a major motivation for taking a short holiday, the research also suggested that getting about and seeing things was important on a short holiday. That means that the holiday location must have things to do and see, whether it is a city, countryside or seaside.

Asked to rate a number of factors in order of importance for a short holiday, off-peak, 'to get away from it all' emerged as the single most important factor. Other factors varied in importance for short holiday takers who had chosen different types of destination for their short holidays. This suggests that short break takers are not all of a kind, but can be subdivided according to a variety of important needs (see Table 47.6).

Accommodation for short breaks

For accommodation on short holidays, the homes of friends and relatives play an important role, as Table 47.7 shows for the UK. However, this is changing, as was the case for the longer holiday some years ago. In 1989, 42% of short holiday trips were in commercial accommodation. In 1991, 44% of the short holidays are commercially accommodated (ETB, 1992). For previous years there are no comparable figures.

Table 47.6 *Factors sought in a short holiday, off-peak*

| | Location of short holiday | | | | |
	Total (%)	London (%)	Abroad (%)	Seaside resorts (%)	Country areas (%)
To get away from it	55	46	50	59	62
Beautiful countryside	39	12	34	40	52
Lots of things to see	32	44	47	26	30
Hot weather	28	20	31	31	27
Good restaurants	22	29	22	21	20
Lots of entertainment	20	32	19	19	15
Foreign/different	12	10	36	9	9
Nightlife	12	12	12	12	9
City sights	11	24	14	9	7

Source: ETB (1988).

There are relatively few products tailor-made for the short break taker (Cockerell, 1989). A first attempt started in the 1970s when urban hotels introduced special weekend rates. Business-oriented hotels find demand concentrated on Monday to Thursday nights during the week, a problem referred to as periodicity. This situation encourages them to offer special weekend deals to short break holidaymakers (Goodall, 1989). Large hotel chains especially offer incentives to tourists; for example, in 1991, Pullman, Altea and Arena hotels reduced prices for weekends from 3 November 1990 till 24 March 1991 at all their hotels throughout Europe. On top of that, in each country they deployed one collective reservation-phone. The Inter-Continental Hotels launched the 'Heart of the city weekends', in its 36 hotels at very reduced prices on 1 April 1991.

In the UK 14 big towns (Portsmouth, Plymouth, Cardiff, etc.) agreed to offer a 'Great British City Break': reduced hotel-prices, a collective hotel-booking phone number, information on special events and travel arrangements by rail, coach or air.

Table 47.5 *Main reasons for taking a short break*

	Base: 813 100%
Special event to attend	27
Get a break after winter	16
Had a few days off work	13
Get break between summer holidays and Christmas	9
Just for a break	6
To visit or holiday with friends or relatives	6
Had holiday left over	4
Get a break from the children	4
Celebrations (wedding, anniversaries, etc.)	2
Other reasons	13

Source: Mas: North West Short Break Holidays Research, 1988 (quoted in ETB (1988)).

Table 47.7 *Accommodation used on short holidays in 1991 in the UK by British residents*

	Short holiday trips (1–3 nights) 26.1 million (%)
Serviced	
Licensed hotel	12
Other hotel	5
Self-service	
Rented flat, cottage, etc.	4
Camping, caravan	11
Non-commercial (homes of friends or relatives, second homes, and others)	68

Source: *The UK Tourist: Statistics 1991*, London 1992.

Nowadays, however, the short break market would seem to demand much more than a price reduction for a weekend stay in a business hotel. People want something different, which comes more up to their leisure needs. Price is often not the overriding factor in determining choice of short break options. The periodicity effect encourages some hotels therefore rather to innovate by offering diversified leisure facilities and cultural entertainment in their hotel.

These innovations are not only for the benefit of short break holidaymakers; the facilities also attract business travellers and conference participants.

But the most successful innovations are related to new forms of accommodation. During the 1960s a totally new breed of holiday villages emerged in northern Europe: *the four-season holiday village*. These holiday villages of the second generation originated, when, apart from the open-air recreational facilities, indoor leisure facilities, such as heated indoor swimming pools, indoor tennis courts, etc., were introduced in the villages as well. Apart from this fundamental difference with the holiday villages of the first generation, another major innovation of the second generation must be cited. In holiday villages of the second generation the self-catering bungalows are now also suitable for winter occupation, thanks to their construction and central heating.

Thanks to these developments, holiday villages became centres offering possibilities for holidays whatever the weather. Thus the holiday operators came to terms with the unpredictability of the weather in countries with a temperate climate; and thus this new generation of holiday villages became a significant provision for short break holidays during all seasons of the year.

The introduction of all-weather leisure facilities has given rise to all-year-round holiday villages of two different types. The first, most spectacular type is the large-scale holiday villages with extensive indoor leisure facilities (e.g. the super water-leisure centre) and ranging in size from 400 to 700 bungalows. The second type concerns villages with fewer and smaller indoor facilities, and of a smaller scale (100 to 250 bungalows). We would like to discuss the former category (large-scale projects) in more detail here, since these have been subject to the most fundamental innovations.

The most spectacular aspect of the large-scale projects has been the introduction of a whole new breed of super indoor water-leisure facility. The Dutch company Center Parcs first introduced the innovative 'Subtropical Water Paradise' in 1980 at the new holiday village of Eemhof in The Netherlands. The success of so many large-scale second-generation holiday villages as short-break holiday provisions can be primarily attributed to the presence of these indoor water-leisure centres, which constitute the centrepiece of most of the second-generation holiday villages and are their unique selling proposition.

In 1987 Center Parcs integrated the 'Subtropical Water Paradise' in a new concept of village centre under a transparent dome. Under this dome three different areas can be found: a large subtropical water-leisure 'paradise', as mentioned above, a leisure sports centre and a 'Parc Plaza'.

In addition to the extensive indoor leisure centre, the large-scale innovation holiday villages also have within the village itself a broad range of outdoor recreational facilities for tennis, miniature golf, golf, skiing, surfing, sailing, canoeing, bowling, children's games. . . . This extensive range of indoor and outdoor leisure facilities is the key element of such holiday villages.

The development of holiday villages is not only characterised by the creation of an extensive indoor and outdoor leisure infrastructure within the holiday village. Some have also created a natural forest environment within the holiday village itself.

This spacious forest setting, the relatively low building density and the extensive range of indoor and outdoor recreation facilities on site within the village itself, means that a leisure world is created within the holiday village. This is a holiday village of the self-contained concept. This does not mean that holidaymakers never leave the premises during the course of their stay: they do, to a limited extent.

In addition, a great variety of accommodation options is offered. There are bungalows, for 2, 3, or up to 10 persons. Alongside bungalows, some holiday villages have also integrated onsite three-storey hotels. With this innovation the concept of holiday villages has come full circle. In the 1950s the first generation villages attempted to provide an alternative to hotel holiday accommodation. Today they are completing the circle themselves, by building hotels as part of their village complexes.

Center Parcs International let villas in 13 holiday villages in four countries (The Netherlands, Belgium, France and the UK) with a unit occupancy rate of 90–95%. The percentage of loyal quests (those who have stayed at one of the villages five times or more) was 28.3%. This means that this group is as large as the group of first-timers (29.6%). Of the visitors who had stayed at Center Parcs before, 56% had returned within a year (Center Parcs, 1990). According to a survey in The Netherlands, the following visitor groups are the most strongly represented: the 25–39 age group (62%), families with young children (41.9%), ABC1 socio-economic income groups (75%).

The Parc Plaza is an important component of the village centre. In a subtropical setting one can find restaurants, a café, a discothèque, bowling-alleys, terraces, gardens with living tropical trees and plants, a pond with real tropical vegetation and birds (for example, flamingoes), and shops. The temperature in the Parc Plaza is 22 to 23°C.

A third significant component of the village centre is the indoor leisure sports area, with courts for tennis, squash, badminton, volleyball and table tennis, a fitness centre and a beauty salon.

Water-leisure, leisure sports, casual social activities, eating, drinking, walking and leisure shopping are no longer compartmentalised in different locations. All these activities are possible in an indoor 'Mediterranean' resort.

Another innovative accommodation is the new generation of country hotels with extensive leisure facilities. Country Club Hotels of the UK brewery company Whitbread, for instance, are hotels with 100 to 120 3-star hotel bedrooms, an 18-hole golf-course and an indoor swimming pool. In Germany Aldiana who operates holiday clubs in Mediterranean countries, Senegal and Thailand, will open in 1994 country clubs in Germany for short breaks.

Another innovation for the short break taker relates to the introduction of the midweek period for the renting of a bungalow in a holiday village. Short breaks are still considered too often as synonyms of (extended) weekend breaks. This is, for instance, especially the case in France. But different factors, including the increasing flexibility of working hours in various countries, the increasing number of one-person households, the earlier retirement and the changing lifestyle, lead to the fact that more and more people take a short break outside the weekend. But a short break in midweek is only possible when changes take place at the supply side. Until recently it was common that the renting-periods for a bungalow in a holiday village were arranged for a full week, from Saturday to Saturday, or from Friday to the Friday of the next week. It was almost impossible to book midweek (Ward and Hardy, 1986). Nowadays there is in the holiday village and holiday centre sector an increasing trend to give accommodation for a weekend or midweek. In The Netherlands the increase in stays in holiday villages is mainly caused by the increase in midweek holidays.

The findings above put the definition of short breaks and short holidays in a different light. The adoption of three nights as the dividing-line between long and short holidays is somewhat arbitrary, as Table 47.8 shows. In many ways four nights would reflect better the increasing tendency of accommodation operators to split the week into weekend breaks of three nights and midweek breaks of four nights.

Table 47.8 *Length of UK holiday trip*

Nights	Percentage of holiday trips
1 night	12
2 nights	23
3 nights	12
4 nights	9
5 nights	6
6 nights	6
7 nights	17
8 + nights	15

Source: UKTS (1989), quoted by Beiosly (1991).

An innovation which closely relates to the 'impulsive' booking behaviour of short break takers is the introduction of the 'short-term line' by Center Parcs. This is a central phone number, which is being equipped on working days from 8.45 till 22.00 and on Saturday, and Sundays and holidays from 10.00 till 15.00. Via this telephone line one can rent a bungalow which was being reserved for short-term bookers until 6 weeks before the date of their stay. One has to pay a late-booking additional payment for this service.

In addition to the mainstream short break products, such as city trips and seaside and countryside resort breaks, there is a need for innovation in programmes which appeal to specific market groups. Middleton and O'Brien (1987) refer, for example, to 'educational' breaks, offering the chance to learn or improve a skill, such as painting or foreign languages, or health and fitness breaks.

Conclusions

The concept of short break holidays represents a major marketing breakthrough for the tourism industry. The short holiday trend is important from both micro and macro economical points of view, because short holidays show a stagger over the whole year, mostly in the off-season and because they are mainly domestic holidays.

The short break takers' needs are not uniform, however; a segmented approach may be the most appropriate marketing strategy.

The specialist short break market is particularly interesting as it is possible to package a short break programme around any specialist activity for which a demand can be identified.

References and bibliography

Association Française d'Experts Scientifiques du Tourisme (1988) Première Forum sur le tourisme de proximité et de cours

séjours, 23–24 Septembre 1988, Sainte-Maxime, AFEST and Chambre de Commerce et d'Industrie du Var.
(Report on the first conference on the short break in France.)

Beiosly, S. (1991) 'Short holidays', in *Insights* (published by the English Tourist Board), September.

Center Parcs (1990) 'Naambekendheid en markt penetratie, 1990', Center Parcs, Rotterdam.

Cockerell, N. (1989) 'Outbound markets/market segment study, the short break market in Europe', in *EIU Travel & Tourism Analyst*, no. 5.
(This study looks at the market, country by country, in Europe.)

CVO (Continue Vakantie Ondergoet) (1992) Quoted in NRIT op. cit.

Eichwalder R. (1988) 'Reisgewohnheiten der Österreicher im Jahr 1987', in *Statistische Nachrichten*, 7:512–524, and 8:623–631.

ETB (English Tourist Board) (1988) 'The short break market', ETB/BTA Services, London, December.

ETB (1992) *The UK Tourist, Statistics 1991, ETB, NITB, STB, WTB*, London.

Faché, W. (Ed.) (1990) 'Shortbreak holidays', Center Parcs, Rotterdam.
(In this book five scientists analyse: the different aspects of short breaks; the market in different European countries, the economic aspect; the importance of the short break for the family with children; innovations in holiday accommodation for short breaks.)

Goodall, B. (1989) 'Tourist accommodation', *Built Environment*, 15(2): 78–91.

Gratton, C. (1990) 'The economics of short break holidays' in Faché, W. (Ed.), *op. cit.*, pp. 29–42.

Lohmann, M. (1990) 'Evaluation of short break holidays in Western Europe' in Faché, W. (Ed.), 'Shortbreak holidays', Center Parcs, Rotterdam, pp. 7–27.

Middleton, V. and O'Brien, K. (1987) 'Short break holidays in the U.K., packaging the fastest growing sector of the U.K. holiday market', in *Travel & Tourism Analyst*, The Economist Publications Limited, London.
(Analyses the market size, the marketing and development in the packaging of short breaks.)

Nederlands Bureau Voor Toerisme (1992) 'Toerisme in cijfers 1992', NBT, Leidschendam.

NRIT (Nederlands Research Instituut voor Recreatie en Toerisme) (1990) *Trendrapport Toerisme*, Breda.

Opaschowski, H. W. (1990) 'Urlaub 89/90, Trendwende im Urlaubsverhalten? Die Grenzen grenzenlosen Reisens', BAT Freizeit-Forschungsinstitut, Hamburg.

OPT (1989) 'Plan de promotion', OPT, Brussels.

Schweizerische Verkehrszentrale (1989) 'Touristischer Lagebericht der Schweizerischen Verkehrszentrale für das Jahr 1989', SVZ, Zurich.
(Detailed statistics on the short break market.)

Ward, C. and Hardy, P. (1986) *Goodnight Campers, the History of the British Holiday Camp*, Mansell Publishing Ltd., London.

WES (Westvlaams Economisch Studiebureau) (1992) 'De evolutie van het korte vakantiegedrag in de periode 1982–91, deel 5: reisgedrag en opinies van de Belgen', WES, Brugge.

Part 4

TOURISM, THE PUBLIC SECTOR AND SCOTLAND

The tourism industry lies mainly in the private sector. Yet the policies and functioning of the public sector exert powerful influences on what happens in tourism. This is true for both developing and advanced countries. Much more is involved than simply the economic policies of governments, although these obviously affect the state of both demand and supply. Governments seek to optimise benefits and reduce the costs of tourism in all sorts of ways, some of which are overtly formulated as tourism policies, others not.

The basic reasons for the complexity of the interaction between public and private sectors have to do with the varied nature of tourism, both in the sense of the wide range of visitor-oriented businesses which make up the industry, and in terms of the variable impact of visitors on the physical and cultural environment. Among the more obvious considerations prompting public sector intervention are concerns about foreign exchange earnings, employment creation, the regional and seasonal spread of costs and benefits, consumer protection issues, the safeguarding and development of tourism resources and elements of infrastructure. Also relevant are concerns relating to the health and welfare of the population as a whole, although few governments have progressed beyond basic legislation to ensure a minimum annual holiday entitlement for the employed.

The effective functioning of a national tourism industry is generally held to demand a degree of government-led coordination of marketing effort, research, development and training. Although there are a number of supranational organisations working internationally to achieve related objectives, national government involvement in tourism is mostly focused on national structures, often supplemented by dependent regional organisations. Most nation states have seen fit to establish a national tourist organisation to promote the image of the country both at home and abroad and carry out a range of functions intended to meet some of the policy aims set out above. National organisations can range from a full-scale 'Ministry of Tourism', through a variety of types of national tourist organisation, to a minimalist 'Marketing and Convention Bureau'. The variants of dedicated tourist organisations and of the increasing number of partnership arrangements are a matter of growing academic interest.

Less closely examined but of continuing significance is the role of local government. Many local authorities are deeply involved in destination marketing, infrastructural provision, facilities development and training. Through the exercise of land-use control policies within the remit laid down by central government, local government is also able to influence the shape of tourism development. It

has been a striking feature of the recent evolution of tourism supply in the United Kingdom that city councils of hitherto unregarded destinations have taken a proactive role and worked imaginatively with other agencies and the private sector to develop and sell new tourism products. The primary motivation has been to promote a broad economic development in order to compensate for the decline of traditional industries. That this can be combined with environmental improvements and increased support for selected cultural activities is seen as a bonus for both residents and potential visitors. An outstanding example of this approach has been that of the host city for the Tourism—the State of the Art Conference, Glasgow.

The United Kingdom is also notable in that rather against the general non-interventionist trend of its government policy, government-sponsored economic development agencies have often committed substantial resources to high-profile development projects, particularly in difficult inner-city areas. Again tourism has been embraced both for its regenerative economic value and for its quality of life-enhancing potential.

There remain many governmental, official and voluntary organisations exerting important influences on the conservation of tourism resources. In many cases the work of such bodies relates to aspects of what has come to be called the natural and built heritage. The United Kingdom can show several leading examples of the voluntary type of organisation. The mass-membership National Trust and the National Trust for Scotland have as their primary aim the preservation of lands and buildings of historic or national interest or natural beauty. In doing so they exercise responsibility for many areas of great attraction to tourists and function as the nation's leading visitor attraction operators.

The distribution of key tourism functions between government agencies varies from country to country. It can also vary over time. In Scotland the lead agency, the Scottish Tourist Board, is celebrating its twenty-fifth anniversary with, among other activities, its sponsorship of the Tourism—the State of the Art Conference. Scotland ceased to be an independent nation state through the 'voluntary' union with England in 1707. Yet the semi-devolved nature of government for Scotland ensured that when the United Kingdom parliament enacted the 1969 Development of Tourism Act, a Scottish Tourist Board was created with, among other responsibilities, the remit of marketing Scotland as a tourist destination within the UK. The functions of the STB have been progressively added to and extended. For many years the Highlands and Islands Development Board and its successor organisation played a crucial role in the marketing and development of tourism in the Highland area of the country. This included the pioneering of a system of locally supported area tourist organisations. They were used as a model for a Scotland-wide network of ATBs developed in the early 1980s. In 1993 an adjustment of responsibilities between STB and the National and Local Development Agencies has produced a more clear-cut division where the marketing and coordinating roles are held by the Scottish Tourist Board, including oversight of the entire Area Tourist Board system, while local development and training responsibilities reside substantially with Highlands and Islands Enterprise, Scottish Enterprise and their network of Local Enterprise Companies. At the same time, as part of a reorganisation of local government, it has been made necessary for councils wishing to promote their areas as tourist destinations to do so only through a revised Area Tourist Board structure consisting of a smaller number of Boards than the previous 32 separate units.

The interplay of public sector agencies in Scottish tourism, although simplified, could still be perceived as complex. Subsidiarity notwithstanding, in the years ahead the European Union is likely to have a greater effect on public tourism policy in all member states. It may be that for Scotland the main impact will be felt less in the areas addressed by the single market legislation, consumer protection requirements and the Commission's Action Plan initiatives, than in the potential to be realised through increased payouts to various areas of Scotland under the European Union's regional development programmes.

As long as Scotland remains in full incorporating union with the rest of the United Kingdom, the parameters of tourism policy will continue to be set by Westminster. Since the mid-1980s tourism has moved some way up the UK political agenda, although there is little evidence of a qualitative change in how tourism is seen by legislators. The emphasis has been on removing barriers obstructing the growth of tourism businesses and obtaining greater leverage of private funding through careful targeting of public funds. The fragmented nature of the industry, the variation in quality of provision and service delivery by both public and private bodies, the restrictions in funding for the marketing of the United Kingdom overseas by the relevant public agencies, the difficulties in securing adequate investment in transport infrastructure—all of these factors have been identified as problems for the UK industry. Within the United Kingdom domestic leisure tourism seems likely to continue to move away from main holidays towards additional holidays and short breaks, implying a further evolution in the approach and provision of public and private sector alike. Meanwhile public policy for tourism in the other sense, that of

seeking to devise measures to raise the level of social benefits through access to participation in tourism by excluded groups, remains largely confined to pressure on the industry to provide for the physically disabled and privately inspired charitable endeavour.

This section contains a variety of papers relating to the role of the public sector as well as some aspects of the operation of the tourism industry in Scotland. Drawing largely, but not exclusively on UK experience, Hughes provides a comprehensive review of the literature on the relationship between tourism and government, with additional reference to the wider field of government policy related to leisure. Adams and Hay supply an organisational history of the lead public sector tourism body in Scotland (forthcoming, 1995), the Scottish Tourist Board. Long sets out some perspectives on organisations which straddle the public/private divide—local area tourism partnerships. Travis also explores the partnership concept, this time in the context of Scotland's contribution to tourism development in Eastern Europe and the countries of the former Soviet Union. Durie's paper examines the development of Scotland as a tourist destination in the nineteenth century, a time of minimal public sector intervention. Pringle's investigation of the failure of the ambitious and pioneering Hi-Line destination marketing system demonstrates how difficult it is for such a venture to achieve long-term viability without public sector support. An exposition of some of the factors affecting visitor attraction development in Scotland is undertaken by Smith, highlighting the importance of public sector support. McBoyle detains us on the private sector side to illustrate how the Scotch whisky industry has come to operate an important component of Scotland's tourism infrastructure—visitor centres at malt whisky distilleries. By contrast, at a time when the United Kingdom railway system is undergoing privatisation, Stewart-David provides a highly readable insight into the problems facing any organisation undertaking to operate a very important section of the transport infrastructure in Scotland, the scenic West Highland Line. Finally, Tagg and Seaton have extracted findings from the ambitious Family Holiday Survey in order to illustrate the differences between Scottish and English family holidays.

Ronnie Smith, Scottish Hotel School
Brian Hay, Scottish Tourist Board

Reference

Adams, G. and Hay, B. (1995) 'History and development of the Scottish Tourist Board', Scottish Tourist Board, Edinburgh, forthcoming.

48 Tourism and government: a subset of leisure policy?

H. L. HUGHES

This paper is a review of published literature covering the relationship between tourism and government. The aim is to determine and evaluate the approaches adopted in analysing that relationship. The analysis will be undertaken within the context of the separate literature on the relationship between leisure and government. The perspectives utilised in both the tourism and leisure studies will be identified and the degree to which they are congruous will be examined; this may indicate whether the approach to tourism should be modified.

The relationship between government and tourism is relatively recent in any formal specific sense. Much of the academic literature in the UK on the government–tourism relationship focuses on the work of the organisations that have been specifically established for a tourism purpose: the national and regional tourist boards. These owe their existence to the Development of Tourism Act 1969 which remains in force. Analysts commonly itemise the Act's sections, describe the structure and functions of the boards and discuss subsequent changes.

Development of tourism act 1969

The Act established four statutory boards—British Tourist Authority (BTA), English Tourist Board (ETB), Wales Tourist Board (WTB) and Scottish Tourist Board (STB)—which were to undertake the work previously done by voluntary trade associations. (The Northern Ireland Tourist Board had been in existence as a statutory body since 1948.) The bodies were created by statute and were to be financed largely by government. (Regional tourist boards in England and the equivalent elsewhere in the UK were not established by statute but followed the formation of the '1969' boards.)

The main function of the boards was, and remains, that of marketing/promotion. The BTA was to encourage foreign tourists to the UK whereas each of the national tourist boards was to direct its marketing effort at the domestic market. The Act also brought into operation a scheme for financially assisting the construction of new, and redevelopment of existing, hotels. This was relatively short-lived, though extremely effective. A more limited scheme of grants for tourism projects (under section 4

of the Act) continued, though only until 1989 in England. It was implemented via the national tourist boards which thus had development functions as well as marketing functions.

The structure of the boards has changed little since 1969, though the BTA and ETB have been reorganised and have, since 1984/85, shared common services. The STB has been permitted since 1984 to promote in overseas markets (in consultation with the BTA). Since 1989 the role of the ETB has diminished and more emphasis (and financial support) has been placed on the role of the regional network. The most recent organisational change of significance has been the creation, in 1992, of the Department of National Heritage (DNH). The DNH embraces responsibility for sport, heritage, broadcasting, the film industry and tourism; responsibility for these was previously scattered across several government departments whose main concern was usually something other than 'leisure'. The BTA and ETB, for instance, were responsible to the Department of Employment. The BTA and ETB are now responsible to the Secretary of State of the DNH though the other national tourist boards remain responsible to their respective national Secretaries of State (i.e. of Wales and of Scotland).

Commentary on the government–tourism relationship has focused on three main areas: changes in organisation and structure, the policy itself and the rationale for government involvement.

Structure, organisation and policy

There has been a particular concern with the unsatisfactory nature of the Act itself which, it is felt, led to confusion of role and duplication of effort by the boards (Cooper, 1987; Middleton, 1986; Wanhill, 1988). There has been no single minister responsible for tourism in the UK and coordination has been complicated. The BTA and ETB were originally responsible to the Department of Trade and Industry and, during 1985 to 1992, to the Department of Employment, whereas the other national boards have always been responsible to their respective national Secretaries of State. The division of responsibilities has led to a disproportionate funding of the national boards

(Wanhill, 1988). The differences in funding owe more to political pressure than to any overall strategic decision.

Added to this is the inevitable dispersal of interest in tourism among many other government departments. Medlik (n.d.), however, believed that since tourism is not a discrete activity it did not need a separate ministry but a 'sponsor' ministry.

The separation of responsibilities between the national tourist boards is an inevitable consequence of nationalist feeling and the structure of government in the UK. As a corollary it is clear that any unified structure might cause resentment in Wales and Scotland. The structure and division of responsibility remains unaltered despite the recent shift of tourism into a 'Ministry of Leisure', the DNH. At the least there is now a unified government department with a Secretary of State of Cabinet rank. This development had not, however, been widely canvassed by tourism observers. It still leaves the issues of inter-board rivalry and confusion and of inter-government-departmental interests in tourism unresolved. The policies and actions of many government departments have a bearing on tourism, despite some interests and responsibilities having been transferred to the DNH.

The lack of coordination, purpose and direction has been aggravated in Scotland by the existence of other powerful bodies with an interest in tourism (Heeley, 1985). The Highlands and Islands Development Board (HIDB) was established pre-STB and because of its powers to give financial assistance to tourism projects and to market the Highlands and Islands, the STB's remit in the region was considerably limited. Coordination of activities has been difficult.

In addition to structural and organisational issues a further recurring theme has been the absence of policy. The 1969 Act created bodies which were, in effect, left to create policy; no policy guidelines were included in the Act (Shaw et al., 1991; Heeley, 1986b). This lack of central direction has added to the confusion at the level of the tourist boards, which have been able to devise their own separate responses to tourism (Middleton, 1974).

Shaw et al. (1987, 1991) consider that governments have reacted to opportunities and problems as they have arisen rather than developing a long-term coherent strategy for tourism in the UK. Government policy is seen as no more than generally supportive. There have been a number of reviews of tourism but they have dwelt largely on organisational and efficiency issues rather than on matters of policy and strategy.

The weaknesses implicit in the 1969 Act remain (Wanhill, 1988; Medlik, 1990). There is no single body capable of developing a tourism policy for the whole of the UK; policy guidelines have not been set by governments;

there is inequitable treatment of the boards in terms of funding; there are limited links with or guidance on how to link with other government bodies and local government concerned with tourism.

United States of America and Europe

Commentary on experience in other countries such as the USA has also focused on the lack of concern of government and the uncoordinated and underfunded activity. In the USA the National Tourism Policy Act (NTPA) 1981 was considered to be a landmark inasmuch as it was an attempt to provide a coordinated administrative structure for tourism (Airey, 1984). The US Travel and Tourism Administration (USTTA) established by the Act was not the first such federal body but the NTPA did see tourism as an activity with wide-ranging effects. In reality the USTTA has concentrated on international and commercial aspects. The USTTA is part of a government department (unlike the UK experience) and is headed by an Under-Secretary of Commerce. This in itself was seen as an elevation of the importance of tourism in government circles (Edgell, 1984). The USTTA is, though, only a very small part of the Department of Commerce and resources devoted to its work have been meagre (Airey, 1984; Ronkainen and Farano, 1987) in part perhaps because of the unsympathetic approach of the (Reagan) government (Richter, 1985).

In addition to national government the policies of the European Union (EU) (ex European Community) may also have a bearing on tourism in the UK. There is a consensus that the EU needs to develop its tourism policy further (Robinson, 1993). Each of the member states adopts a different approach to tourism and they have been slow to develop a European approach. The actions of the EU in general, and in the area of tourism in particular, have been such as to facilitate the free movement of people and thus tourism on a large scale rather than to encourage the development of alternative forms of tourism or to develop appropriate responses to the excesses of tourism.

Akehurst et al. (1993) conclude that, within the EU, those countries that have been the most successful in promoting their tourism (France, Portugal and Ireland) have been those which shared several features. These included clear government strategy and organisational structure and strong government financial support for promotion and investment. Tourism policies were coordinated with policies in other associated areas such as transport. Swarbrooke (1993a) concurs with the view that the success of France as a tourist destination is attributable in large part to the role played by the public sector.

Local government and regional tourist boards

Comparatively little has been written about the local government dimension of tourism or about the regional tourist boards (England). Local government in the UK has had an interest in tourism for much longer than has national government, though it remains a discretionary function of local government. It dates, in many cases, to the development of (seaside) resorts in the 19th century. Local authorities have been suppliers of part of the tourist product in the form of recreational facilities as well as having responsibility, as planning authorities, for the overall development of their areas. Many local authorities have, in addition, been responsible for the marketing of the resort as a tourist destination.

Commentary on local government has usually stressed the past concentration on 'product and place' which is changing only slowly to an emphasis on 'promotion and price' (Heeley, 1986a). It may not, however, be appropriate for local government to have sole responsibility for marketing since the ethos of local government is often unhelpful in developing a commercial approach to marketing (Hughes, 1989). Swarbrooke (1993b) has been particularly scathing about the standard of local government marketing, describing it as 'ineffective and lacking in professionalism'. He suggests that if local government is not prepared to do the job properly, or cannot afford to do it, then they should seriously consider whether they should undertake it all.

Local authorities have been criticised for not adopting a 'strategic' approach to tourism development (McVey, 1986) at least as evidenced in their structure plans when first developed. Local government has often been seen by commercial tourism firms as unduly restrictive through the exercise of their planning duties (Shaw et al., 1987). Local government reorganisation underway currently (1993/94) provides little evidence that many local governments have thought any more clearly about tourism as a strategic issue (Bacon and Le Pelley, 1993).

Hudson and Townsend (1992) have observed a growing interest by local government, especially outside the traditional resort areas, in tourism as a basis for local economic development. This interest, they believed, was not based on a sound information base but was pursued more on an unsubstantiated belief that tourism was a 'good thing'. Heeley (1988) had earlier commented on the necessity for local governments to critically and objectively evaluate their pursuit of tourism development. They should be prepared to cooperate with and leave responsibility to the private sector where appropriate. An increasing interest in tourism in local government is confirmed by Richards and Wilkes's survey (1990) of local government in England.

In the same way as at the national level, tourism has been observed to impinge upon several aspects of local government policy and operation, including recreation and the arts, planning, transport, etc. Despite the increased interest in tourism, local governments frequently leave responsibility for tourism split between several departments without coordination or clear strategic guidance (Bacon and Le Pelley, 1993).

The role of local government in tourism has been questioned, in particular, since the development of the Regional Tourist Boards (RTB). Those in England have occasionally met with indifference or resistance from local government (Bowes, 1988). Most observers welcomed the RTBs as reflecting the shift in tourism participation away from one-destination stays towards a wider geographical area, touring-type tourism. It was also acknowledged that the efforts of regional boards might be more effective and economic than those of a larger number of smaller local government bodies.

RTBs in England are not statutory bodies, though they receive some of their funding from the ETB. The remainder of their financial support is from local government and the commercial sector. The Scottish Regional Tourist Associations encouraged by the STB disappeared with local government reorganisation in 1975 to be followed by statutory area tourist boards, but only in 1981–82. The shift of funding from the ETB to the RTBs (post-1989) may be of some concern (Medlik, 1990). In particular it might be that there would be a loss of expertise at the centre and reduced opportunities for an effective, coordinated national strategy. The devolution may have the effect of an unnecessary duplication of activity across the country.

National tourist offices

Little of the discussion and debate about government and tourism touches on the rationale for government involvement. There is an implicit assumption in much of the work that government should be involved (Bull, 1991; Holloway, 1985). Few commentators question that government should have a role in tourism and most are content to observe the role without comment on its form or extent. Discussion is often limited to an identification of factors that might have influenced the structure and form of government intervention (Choy, 1993), such as the political system and the stage of economic development.

Government intervention in tourism often takes the form of a national tourist office (NTO) such as the BTA. Such an NTO may have several roles but common to most countries is a marketing function and, occasionally, a development function, if only in the form of infrastructure (Pearce, 1992). Choy (1993) considers that the role of the NTO should alter with the product life cycle.

Jeffries (1989), in debating the role of the NTO, concluded that the BTA, for instance, may be more a 'facilitator' than a 'dynamic creator' of demand. Additionally the product it is selling is very much beyond its influence and it is suggested that the emphasis of activity should shift from destination marketing to rather more 'behind-the-scenes' activity including market research.

Dwyer and Forsyth (1992) sought to subject tourism promotion by government to 'rigorous economic analysis'. The costs and benefits of promotion were examined and, although in the Australian case there were net benefits, it was recognised that any gains to private sector operators might be offset by wider resource costs.

Whilst there seems to be a consensus on the marketing function of NTOs (as agents of government) there is less agreement on the developmental and other roles. Central government need not be directly involved in tourism at all, of course. At the least it may seek only to set guidelines for the development of tourism, leaving tourism as a private sector activity. It may see its role as a facilitator of the development of tourism and creating a positive climate within which it may operate, i.e. to remove unnecessary obstacles and correct market failure.

Whatever form of activity an NTO might engage in, it faces the problem that most of the tourist industry is currently owned by the private sector and the component organisations are numerous. It is likely, therefore, that any policy can only be 'indicative' (Shaw et al., 1987).

Rationale

It is sometimes argued that government is involved anyway, however indirectly, in tourism as policies on transport, the arts, heritage, etc. have implications for tourism and, at the least, government should be aware of these implications.

Government's general concern for environmental matters and consumer protection will invariably have an impact on tourism. Many environmental issues may be precipitated by tourism and may be interpreted as the property rights issue discussed earlier. The requirements and interests of the tourist need to be articulated by some 'collective' voice.

Frequently, the intervention of government is justified by reference to the merits of tourism itself—its contribution to economic growth, the balance of payments, employment, regional development, inner city regeneration, etc. (Middleton, 1974). Governments are, therefore, bound to have an interest in tourism because of its potential in contributing to the achievement of government objectives. It may, however, be difficult to justify government involvement on these grounds since there are many other forms of activity which may have the same merits (Graham, 1988). Tourism either has to demonstrate a superior performance or seek justification in some other way.

Choy (1991) argues that governments should leave the private sector to be responsible for tourism and should seek only to resolve issues of 'market failure'. Market failure may arise because of externalities. These are the effects (both positive and negative) upon those other than the consumers of a product. In tourism they may include noise, congestion (Hartley and Hooper, 1992), preservation of facilities for potential future users, and degradation of the environment (Johnson and Thomas, 1992a).

'Public goods' are a particular form of externality; here the benefits of provision are available to the entire community regardless of who finances the purchase, e.g. parks, historic sites, landscape, scenery, beaches, etc. It may be appropriate for government to intervene to ensure provision since, left to the market, some citizens could be excluded.

The service provided by a national tourist office (NTO) is widely considered as a public good in that if left to the private sector it may be underfunded and underprovided. They usually have a marketing function and the marketing of a destination will benefit all regardless of any individual organisation's contribution to that function.

Negative externalities may give rise to issues of 'property rights' (Johnson and Thomas, 1992a), issues which may only be resolvable by government. Tourism may be related to the presence of scenery, beaches, mountains, etc. but the tourists usually have no financial influence over these resources to ensure that they are preserved. Those (if anyone) who own the natural resources may not be directly concerned with the tourism aspect since the resources have other functions (e.g. agriculture). In such cases government intervention may be considered appropriate as a form of collective action on behalf of the tourists who are unable either individually or collectively to exercise any property rights, e.g. National Parks in the UK (Hartley and Hooper, 1992; O'Fallon, 1993).

Government intervention may also be considered desirable in the case of 'merit goods', i.e. 'they are so important to the wellbeing of the individual that consumers should not because of low income or ignorance be prevented from consuming them' (Hughes, 1984). Social tourism policies common in many European countries reflected such a view—that holidays, in some way, were beneficial to the individual (and society) and should be available to all (Hughes, 1991).

Even where market failure is acknowledged to occur it is not self-evident that government should intervene. The intervention requires resources and may even, itself, generate further distortions (Johnson and Thomas, 1992a). O'Fallon (1993) applies a 'public choice theoretical framework' to considering the role of government in tourism and observes that in seeking to serve the interests of politicians, bureaucrats and interest groups, government intervention may not improve on the market failure situation. The concept of market failure is vague and imprecise, may prove very little guidance to policy-making and may be used to justify many forms of intervention by vested interests (Hartley and Hooper, 1992).

Other rationale presented for government intervention has included reference to the structural characteristics of the tourist industry. There is a large number of organisations involved in the provision of the tourist product, spread across a wide variety of activities (Pearce, 1992), not all of whom have a primary interest in tourism. In the case of destinations there may be a very practical need for some 'catalytic agent' to take the initiative and coordinate the actions of the numerous individual agents if coherent, uniform product development and image promotion is to occur (Hughes, 1989).

There may well be a reluctance of the private sector to finance tourism investment (Dwyer and Forsyth, 1992). The magnitude of the sums required and the risk involved for some forms of investment may be such as can only be borne by government (Williams and Shaw, 1991a; Graham, 1988). If standards of existing facilities are to be raised and/or new facilities provided, then some government intervention may be necessary.

Politics

The political reality of why governments become involved or how the structures and policies are derived are infrequently discussed and analysed. Tourism policy as the outcome of political pressure has been touched on by a number of US writers (Edgell, 1984, 1990; Richter, 1985, 1989, 1993) and only more recently in the UK (Greenwood, 1993).

Both Edgell and Richter recognise the political implications of tourism itself whereby governments may seek to intervene in order to maximise political advantage, for example, governments discourage tourism to political enemies and encourage tourism to foster international understanding. Richter (1989) recognises that 'little empirical work has been done to demonstrate the validity of the myth' of the goodwill and understanding that are often claimed for international tourism. She also points out that frequently policies have a pro-business bias, reflecting the more powerful voices in the political process. As a consequence, tourist policies may not be serving the public interest in anything other than a very narrow sense (Richter, 1993).

Greenwood (1993) recognises the existence of a large number of interest groups in tourism in the UK and believes that they have made, individually and collectively, a significant contribution to government's approaches to tourism. Despite this, their influence may have been limited compared with that in other industries, because of their number and variety of interests.

This concern for the political dimension is more usual in leisure studies than in tourism studies. Studies of leisure and of tourism have focused on similar issues but they have generally been conducted independently and have adopted different approaches to their respective areas of study.

Leisure and government

A focus of attention common to both the leisure and tourism literature has been the analysis of organisation, structure and policy. Some concern has been expressed, for instance, about the lack of central government policy on leisure (Travis, 1979). No government has had a coherent comprehensive leisure policy; governments have had policies directed in an uncoordinated way at various aspects of leisure, most notably sport and the arts, but also gambling, drinking and entertainment. Central government policy and organisation for leisure remain fragmented despite the creation of the DNH (Henry and Bramham, 1993). The role of central government in leisure has always been minor in respect of provision of facilities and it has been more a regulator and subsidiser. Local government has, since the 19th century, been the main provider of public sector leisure facilities, though the bulk of leisure provision has been by the private commercial sector and voluntary bodies.

There has also been a diffusion of leisure interests and powers across local government departments (Travis, 1979; Travis et al., 1981). Local government did move towards a more integrated view of their leisure services during the 1970s, in the form of establishing 'leisure' committees. Departments, however, often continued to be unintegrated.

A further aspect of work on leisure policy has been the growth of the 'leisure professional and manager' especially associated with the growth of local government services. It may be that they have become bureaucratised and absorbed into 'the establishment'. They had, perhaps, become too preoccupied with the management of the facilities and not concerned enough with identifying needs and responding to the communities they served (Travis et al., 1981; Benington and White, 1986). The leisure professionals, whether in local government or in central government bodies, may of course have a vested interest in preserving the status quo and advancing middle-class interests and pursuits (Wilson, 1988).

There has been, in the literature on leisure policy, a particular interest in the rationale for intervention. The interpretation of the rationale has, though, been different from that adopted in studies on tourism in that commentators have focused on the historical and political dimensions of policy and the role and significance of leisure.

Government intervention in leisure has, however, been rationalised in the same way as involvement in tourism by reference to market failure and externalities (Bramham et al., 1993; Henry and Bramham, 1993). Social benefits such as health, community unity, civic pride, national prestige, social cohesion, etc., and public goods in the form of public spaces, National Parks, etc. may be deemed desirable and, if left to the market, consumption might be suboptimal.

Current government interest in leisure can be traced to the period of industrialisation in the late 18th and 19th centuries. Government restricted certain forms of leisure and encouraged others (Henry and Bramham, 1993; Coalter, 1984). There was a concern for public order and moral welfare and this showed itself in the form of intensified control over the sale of alcohol, the designation of streets as thoroughfares rather than as public social spaces, and the provision of museums and art galleries, swimming pools and baths. 'Public' sports were restricted and regulated. Non-leisure objectives were being pursued through leisure-related policies; they had moral overtones and recreation was to be purposeful, to build character, discipline and responsibility (Clarke, 1992). With the upheavals of industrialisation and urbanisation there was clearly a concern on the part of the government for social stability and that the population should be both 'responsible' employees and law-abiding citizens.

Policies have been interpreted by some as legitimising and bolstering the capitalist system (Wilson, 1988; Coalter, 1986; Clarke and Critcher, 1985) with government operating in the interests of the dominant capitalist class. The pursuits encouraged by the government were those which epitomised the forces of capitalism (e.g. competitive sports) and the arts and heritage supported and preserved

were those of the middle and upper classes (Bramham and Henry, 1985). Governments have seen the promotion of particular forms of leisure as binding society together in a common culture; sport and arts policies have continued to promote the tastes of the middle classes with the aim of encouraging others to experience and to identify with (or acquire) those tastes too. By regulating the pursuits of the working class, by exposing them to the 'high arts' and channelling activities into regulated forms, the state was ensuring that the workforce was instilled with a respect for authority and discipline and was discouraged from engaging in activities that might interfere with the pattern of the working day and week.

The legacy of 19th-century policy remains in the second half of the 20th century. Buildings remain and similar rationale is expressed for government intervention in leisure (Bramham and Henry, 1985). More recent pronouncements have seen leisure provision as part of a programme to alleviate social problems, to curb vandalism, delinquency and urban riots. (It has, though, never played a major role in social policy (Roberts, 1992).)

During the latter part of the 20th century leisure provision by the state has been regarded by many as a 'right'. The development of the universal provision of many services by the welfare state has shifted the emphasis away from government 'control' of leisure towards a more positive view of ensuring access for all (Coalter, 1984, 1986; Henry and Bramham, 1993; Wilson 1988). Leisure came to be regarded as something worth pursuing in its own right, as compared with the view that it should be controlled or encouraged in order to achieve other (extrinsic) goals. Since the mid-1970s, however, there has been a replacement by the 'market imperative' (Henry and Bramham, 1993; Ravenscroft, 1993). Local government is now required to offer its leisure services out to tender so that a rather more commercial approach to the provision has developed. This may be interpreted as part of a wider drive towards an enterprise culture. Those who do not succeed generally in the free enterprise capitalist system will not be able to afford the leisure services; there is thus an incentive to become a successful participant in that system (Ravenscroft, 1993).

Conclusions

The literature on leisure has not dealt specifically with tourism and has adopted perspectives different from those in the tourism literature. Much of the commentary on the relationship between tourism and government has been restricted and narrowly focused compared with that on leisure and government. Leisure analysts have tended to adopt a rather wider approach though this difference in approach may, in part, reflect a relative lack of government attention to tourism. Tourism in the UK has experienced comparatively little government intervention either in the form of direct provision, subsidy of private enterprise or regulation.

Structure and policies have been one focus of the tourism literature. Discussion has been in the form of which organisational structure is 'best' or desirable for tourism, without questioning whether government should be involved at all, and without identifying the criteria by which structures are being assessed. Most of the discussion has taken place without identifying the interests of the parties concerned—consumers, producers, government, citizens, etc.—and assumes that the 'tourist interest' would be best served if the existing structure were better coordinated and clear policy established. It is widely assumed that tourism is worthy of support and requires some intervention.

The second focus, rationale for support, has been couched mostly in economic and pragmatic terms. There is no doubt that government's main concern with tourism has been economic. Given a failure of the market to generate an effective marketing organisation and to ensure an appropriate stock of quality hotels then the 1969 intervention may appear justifiable.

The reasons commonly expressed for intervening in leisure generally may not be so justifiable in the case of tourism. It is possible, but by no means certain, that there has been a relatively widespread provision by the private sector (compare sport) and widespread opportunity for cheap holidays (compare the arts). 'Regulation' was not deemed necessary as 'threatening' activities did not arise specifically in the holiday situation; holidays would be regulated by employers along with other aspects of the discipline of the working week and year. It is equally possible that the lack of government attention can be accounted for by a lack of interest and a belief that tourism was of little significance. The perspectives of the leisure-policy analysts may be illuminating in the case of tourism, if only to explain fully the lack of government involvement.

Such government intervention as has occurred has been positive, e.g. the 1871 Bank Holiday Act and the 1938 Holidays with Pay Act, and could be interpreted as ensuring that the workforce is refreshed and re-created for the productive process. However, governments have not gone so far as to 'underwrite the costs of capitalism' by encouraging subsidised holidays. In view of the concern for the welfare of the working class some more positive form of policy towards holidays might have been expected to emerge; holidays may have a positive effect on the physical and mental wellbeing of the participants.

Leisure analysts have recognised that governments have intervened because of the role that leisure plays in lives—giving meaning, fulfilment, social cohesion, sense of community, belonging, etc. There seems to have been a failure on the part of government and commentators to recognise that tourism may perform similar roles and, therefore, should be encouraged.

The very lack of government intervention in tourism may reflect implicit support for the capitalist system insofar as the holiday industry is a private enterprise activity and the holiday parameters have been set by collective bargaining within industry. The generally favourable attitude towards holidays could also be interpreted as part of a wider and continuing class domination, in that holidays and other consumer goods and services distract the working class from their lack of political power.

Whatever the rationale for (or interpretation of) government policy, existing institutions and organisations are open to analysis from the 'political' perspective. The formation or implementation of policy in the UK is delegated to non-government organisations—tourist boards. They operate at arm's length from government and members are appointed by the appropriate government minister. It may be claimed, as a consequence, that they are undemocratic and unaccountable to those they might claim to represent. It is possible to argue, too, that the membership of the boards is narrow and is representative only of the interests of industry.

The political reality of the government–tourism relationship has not been considered at any great length, though such an analysis may provide considerable insight into that relationship. There are, undoubtedly, dimensions and perspectives to the study of government–tourism relationships that remain to be explored. Approaches and interpretations utilised in the leisure policy field could well be profitably transferred and applied to tourism policy. Analysts need to approach the study of the government–tourism relationship as one wherein social, economic and ideological influences are recognised more explicitly.

References

Airey, D. (1984) 'Tourism administration in the USA', *Tourism Management*, 5(4): 269–279.

Akehurst, G., Bland, N. and Nevin, M. (1993) 'Tourism policies in the European Community member states', *International Journal of Hospitality Management*, 12(1): 33–66.

Bacon, M. and Le Pelley, B. (1993) 'Local government reorganisation—tourism's chance or peril?', *Insights*, July: A5–A13.

Benington, J. and White, J. (1986) 'Leisure. Functional paper 4: the future role and organisation of local government', University of Birmingham, Institute of Local Government Studies, Birmingham.

Bowes, S. (1988) 'The role of the Tourist Board', in Goodall, B. and Ashworth, G. (Eds), *Marketing in the Tourism Industry: the Promotion of Destination Regions*, Croom Helm, London.

Bramham, P. and Henry, I. (1985) 'Political ideology and leisure policy in the UK', *Leisure Studies*, 4(1): 1–19.

Bramham, P., Henry, I., Mommas, H. and van der Poel, H. (1993) 'Leisure policies in Europe', in Bramham, P., Henry, I., Mommas, H. and van der Poel, H. (Eds), *Leisure Policies in Europe*, CAB International, Wallingford.

Bull, A. (1991) *The Economics of Travel and Tourism*, Pitman, Melbourne.

Choy, D. (1991) 'Tourism planning: the case for market failure', *Tourism Management*, 12(4): 313–330.

Choy, D. (1993) 'Alternative roles for national tourism organisations', *Tourism Management*, 14(5): 357–365.

Clarke, A. (1992) 'Citizens, markets and customers: a post Welfare State view of leisure', in Sugden and Knox (1992).

Clarke, J. and Critcher, C. (1985) 'The devil makes work: leisure in capitalist Britain', Macmillan, Basingstoke.

Coalter, F. (1984) 'Public policy and leisure', in Tomlinson, A. (Ed.), *Leisure: Politics, Planning and People*, Vol. 1., *Plenary Papers*, Leisure Studies Association, London.

Coalter, F. (1986) *The Politics of Leisure*, Vol. 3 of The Proceedings of LSA Conference, Brighton, 1984, Leisure Studies Association.

Cooper, C. (1987) 'The changing administration of tourism in Britain', *Area*, 19(3): 249–253.

Dwyer, L. and Forsyth, P. (1992) 'The case for tourism promotion: an economic analysis', Discussion paper no. 265, Centre for Economic Policy Research, Australian National University, Canberra.

Edgell, D. (1984) 'US government policy on international tourism', *Tourism Management*, 5(1): 67–70.

Edgell, D. (1990) *International Tourism Policy*. Van Nostrand, Reinhold, New York.

Graham, C. (1988) 'Tourism and leisure projects: criteria for government support', in McDowall and Leslie (1988).

Greenwood, J. (1993) 'Business interest groups in tourism governance', *Tourism Management*, 14(5): 335–348.

Hartley, K. and Hooper, N. (1992) 'Tourism policy: market failure and public choice', in Johnson and Thomas (1992b).

Heeley, J. (1985) 'Tourism: a Highland stramash', *Quarterly Economic Commentary*, 10(4): 57–59.

Heeley, J. (1986a) 'Tourism in England: a strategic planning response?', in Houston (1986).

Heeley, J. (1986b) 'An overview of the structure of tourism administration in Scotland', in Houston (1986).

Heeley, J. (1988) 'Planning for tourism: what should be the role of the local authorities?', in McDowell and Leslie (1988).

Henry, I. and Bramham, P. (1993) 'Leisure policy in Britain', in Bramham, P., Henry, I., Mommas, H. and van der Poel, H. (Eds), *Leisure Policies in Europe*, CAB International, Wallingford.

Holloway, J. C. (1985) *The Business of Tourism*, Macdonald & Evans, Plymouth.

Houston, L. (Ed.) (1986) 'Strategy and opportunities for tourism development', Occasional paper no. 22, Planning Exchange, Glasgow.

Hudson, R. and Townsend, A. (1992) 'Tourism employment and policy choices for local government', in Johnson and Thomas (1992b).

Hughes, H. L. (1984) 'Government support for tourism in the UK: a different perspective', *Tourism Management*, 5(1): 13–19.

Hughes, H. L. (1989) 'Resorts: a fragmented product in need of coalescence', *International Journal of Hospitality Management*, 8(1): 15–17.

Hughes, H. L. (1991) 'Holidays and the economically disadvantaged', *Tourism Management*, 12(3): 193–196.

Jeffries, D. (1989) 'Selling Britain—a case for privatisation?', *Travel and Tourism Analyst*, 1: 69–81.

Johnson, P. and Thomas, B. (1992a) 'Tourism research and policy: an overview', in Johnson and Thomas (1992b).

Johnson, P. and Thomas, B. (Eds) (1992b) *Perspectives on Tourism Policy*, Mansell, London.

McDowell, D. and Leslie, D. (Eds) (1988) *Planning for Tourism and Leisure*, Proceedings of first international conference, University of Ulster at Jordanstown.

McVey, M. (1986) 'The strategic role of local authorities in tourism: the Welsh experience', in Houston (1986).

Medlik, S. (n.d.) 'Organisation for tourism in Britain'.

Medlik, S. (1990) 'Government and tourism', in *The Tourism Industry 1990–91*, The Tourism Society, London.

Middleton, V. (1974) 'Tourism policy in Britain: the case for radical reappraisal', ITQ Special No. 1, Economist Intelligence Unit, London.

Middleton, V. (1986) 'England and Wales', *International Tourism Reports*, (2): 5–26.

O'Fallon, C. (1993) 'Government involvement in New Zealand tourism: a public choice perspective', *Geojournal*, 29(3): 271–280.

Pearce, D. (1992) *Tourist Organisations*, Longman, Harlow.

Ravenscroft, N. (1993) 'Public leisure provision and the good citizen', *Leisure Studies*, 12: 33–44.

Richards, G. and Wilkes, J. (1990) 'The role of local authorities in tourism development and promotion in England', Centre for Leisure and Tourism Studies, Polytechnic of North London, London.

Richter, L. (1985) 'Fragmented politics of US tourism', *Tourism Management*, 6(4): 162–173.

Richter, L. (1989) 'The politics of tourism in Asia', University of Hawaii Press, Honolulu.

Richter, L. (1993) 'Tourism policy-making in South-East Asia', in Hitchcock, M., King, V. and Parnwell, M. (Eds), *Tourism in South-East Asia*, Routledge, London.

Roberts, K. (1992) 'Leisure responses to urban ills in Great Britain and Northern Ireland', in Sugden and Knox (1992).

Robinson, G. (1993) 'Tourism and tourism policy in the European Community: an overview', *International Journal of Hospitality Management*, 12(1): 7–20.

Ronkainen, I. and Farano, R. (1987) 'United States' travel and tourism policy', *Journal of Travel Research*, XXV(4): 2–8.

Shaw, G., Williams, A., Greenwood, J. and Hennessy, S. (1987) 'Public policy and tourism in England', Tourism in Cornwall project discussion paper no. 3, Department of Geography, University of Exeter, Exeter.

Shaw, G., Greenwood, J. and Williams, A. (1991) 'The United Kingdom: market responses and public policy', in Williams and Shaw (1991b).

Sugden, J. and Knox, C. (Eds) (1992) 'Leisure in the 1990s: rolling back the Welfare State', LSA publication no. 46, Chelsea School Research Centre, Brighton Polytechnic, Brighton.

Swarbrooke, J. (1993a) 'Public sector policy in tourism—a comparative study of France and Britain', *Insights*, March: C33–C46.

Swarbrooke, J. (1993b) 'Local authorities and destination marketing', *Insights*, July: A15–A20.

Travis, A. (1979) 'The state and leisure provision', Sports Council and Social Science Research Council, London.

Travis, A., Veal, A., Duesberry, K. and White, J. (1981) 'The role of central government in relation to the provision of leisure services in England and Wales', CURS, University of Birmingham, Birmingham.

Wanhill, S. (1988) 'Politics and tourism', in *The Tourism Industry 1988–89*, The Tourism Society, London.

Williams, A. and Shaw, G. (1991a) 'Tourism policies in a changing environment', in Williams and Shaw (1991b).

Williams, A. and Shaw, G. (Eds) (1991b) *Tourism and Economic Development: Western European Experiences*, 2nd edn., Belhaven, London.

Wilson, J. (1988) *Politics and Leisure*, Unwin Hyman, London.

49 Perspectives on partnership organisations as an approach to local tourism development

P. LONG

Background

References to partnerships between public and private sectors in the development, marketing and management of tourism in local areas are now commonplace in reports and strategies produced by local authorities, tourist boards and other organisations with interests in tourism. Local tourism partnerships have recently been promoted by government (Employment Department et al., 1992) and national tourist boards (English Tourist Board, 1991; Northern Ireland Tourist Board, 1992; Scottish Tourist Board, 1992; Wales Tourist Board, 1993) and have been established in a variety of locations and organisational formats across the United Kingdom.

As Turner (1992) notes, the concept of public/private sector partnership in tourism development is not new, with many resort towns developing in the Victorian era with a blend of municipal and individual entrepreneurialism. However, the ubiquity of 'partnership' policy statements in local tourism plans and strategies in the 1980s and 1990s and the introduction of organisational arrangements for local initiatives bears examination and has to date received limited attention in the academic tourism literature.

This paper examines local area tourism partnerships in England and specifically those sponsored by the English Tourist Board (ETB), the former Tourism Development Action Programmes (TDAPs) and the successor Local Area Tourism Initiatives (LATIs). These have resulted in formal organisational arrangements and share certain defining characteristics (Bramwell and Broom, 1989):

- They seek collaboration and cooperation between a wide range of public and private sector organisations located in, or having an interest in, their areas' tourism, drawing on local knowledge and expertise.
- They are action-orientated with the programme emphasis on implementing initiatives rather than on prolonged and detailed research and strategy formulation.
- They are comprehensive and integrated in approach encompassing the range of interrelated aspects which affect tourism in the programme area. Consequently, they normally include development, marketing, information and environmental advisory and training remits.

- They are corporate in approach and involve objectives and work programmes which are shared both among and within organisations. This is particularly important when tourism-related activities are the functions of several different local authority departments and where the programme area transcends administrative boundaries.
- They are short-term programmes with a limited duration, usually 3 years, with the aim of establishing sufficient momentum for progress to be sustained in the longer term, based on local resources. Between 1984 and 1990, 20 different areas within England were designated as TDAPs by the ETB in consultation with local interests. The locations of these programmes varied considerably in scale, physical characteristics and settlement patterns, but may be categorised as:

- Traditional coastal resorts such as Torbay and Bridlington.
- 'Heritage' towns—Carlisle, Norwich and Lancaster.
- Larger industrial urban areas—Bristol, Bradford, Tyne and Wear, Portsmouth, Cleveland and Leicester.
- Remote rural areas—North Pennines and Kielder.
- Mixed economy rural areas—Forest of Dean, Shropshire, Wiltshire.
- Traditional rural and resort destinations—Isle of Wight, Cornwall, East Kent (adapted from Bramwell and Broom (1989)).

Since 1990, a number of additional programmes have been designated under the new title of Local Area Tourism Initiatives (LATIs). An interesting locational feature of four of these programmes is their narrowly focused area definition within an urban context. These are Greenwich and Islington (districts within London), Leeds Waterfront and the Castlefield district within Manchester.

In April 1993, a further programme entitled Tourism Challenge was announced by the ETB. This programme is also designed to support the formation of partnership organisations in locations which can demonstrate potential for tourism and economic development. The partners in all LATIs include:

- The local authority, or several local authorities within the LATI area.
- Local private sector operators and associations such as chambers of commerce and travel associations.
- The relevant regional tourist boards.
- English Tourist Board.

Other organisations directly involved vary between each LATI, but have included:

- National Park authorities.
- Urban development corporations, and economic development and enterprise agencies (themselves partnership organisations).
- Local community groups and associations, e.g. Weymouth Civic Society, parish councils, North Pennines Heritage Trust.

The strategies pursued by these local initiatives vary according to the environmental, economic, social and political characteristics of the area and the priorities identified by the partners. However, programmes commonly involve marketing development, training provision for operators, and improvements to the quality and supply of accommodation as well as to accessibility, environment, attractions and infrastructure (Bramwell and Broom, 1989).

The interest in participating in partnership arrangements for local authorities is portrayed by Turner (1992) as resulting from central government policy directing them to act as 'enablers' and not 'providers' of services and from restrictions on local government spending, with tourism regarded as 'discretionary' (i.e. non-statutory) expenditure.

On the private sector side, anticipated difficulties in achieving the desired rate of return from tourism developments, particularly from innovative schemes, has led private enterprises to look to local authorities either to contribute to capital costs or to offer favourable rental terms (where they are the landowners) in recognition of the wider economic benefits of new developments. There has, additionally, been a realisation that there needs to be a pooling of resources in what is a very fragmented industry in order to compete with spending on the promotion of overseas holidays. There is also a recognition, within both public and private sectors, that for many of the complex infrastructure problems which confront tourist areas a simple solution is insufficient, or such a solution requires a partnership between the institutions which make up the local community (Turner 1992: A85/86). As Inskeep (1991: 412) puts it, 'Because tourism is a complicated, multisectoral activity, achieving coordination among the government agencies involved in the various aspects of tourism and between the government and private sector enterprises is a major consideration'.

A rationale appears to exist for the establishment of partnership arrangements and for programmes to assist in their formation. However, detailed discussion is lacking in the academic literature of issues such as agreeing the definition of objectives, organisational design and processes, sustaining programmes in the long term, factors which may influence success or failure, the identification of areas (and actors) which might benefit from a partnership approach (and those who might lose) and the outcomes of local area tourism initiatives.

Such research that has taken place has usually either been commissioned or conducted internally by partner organisations, is place-specific, policy-driven and action-orientated, and is focused on the characteristics of the area, marketing and development opportunities, the design of the programme of action and monitoring and evaluation arrangements. This pragmatic approach to research in part reflects the need to achieve results in what is commonly a limited time scale.

This paper seeks to broaden the study of local area tourism partnership organisations from specific policy considerations in particular locations by examining the potential contributions from several disciplinary perspectives. These include:

- Political analyses of local partnership approaches to policy formulation and implementation, particularly in relation to local economic development using area-based initiatives.
- Political geography approaches, notably in terms of the identification of tourist regions, the definition of boundaries and territorial characteristics.
- Aspects of organisation theory, particularly in terms of organisation–environment relationships, inter-organisation and network analysis, and organisational approaches to local planning.

Only a brief examination of these perspectives is possible here. The paper therefore outlines major themes rather than detailing methodological approaches, and proposes a research agenda that may help to guide future studies of this emergent and important subject.

Policy studies and local tourism partnerships

Political theories and ideologies provide rationales and competing perspectives on policy formulation, processes and implementation. The subject will be addressed here only insofar as it appears relevant to the study of local area tourism partnerships. Parallel initiatives in, for example, local economic development which have adopted partnership approaches, provide interesting comparative material, as well as placing tourism programmes within a wider context.

The changing role of local goverment and the growing importance of partnership approaches in local economic development and urban regeneration have received considerable attention in the policy studies field in recent years (see, for example, Campbell (1990), Chisholm (1990), Cochrane (1991), Edwards and Deakin (1992), Meyer (1991) and Smallbone (1991)). Common themes in these studies include the emergence of local initiatives as a consequence of legislative changes affecting local government passed during the 1980s and the associated development of institutions, instruments and financial regimes aimed at 'levering' private sector contributions into public programmes.

The range of organisations involved in these partnerships with origins in the 1980s include City Action Teams, Task Forces, Urban Development Corporations, Training and Enterprise Councils, local enterprise agencies and trusts and Business in the Community. Studies of policy approaches adopted by these organisations might usefully be extended to LATIs. Sellgren (1990), for example, examines local economic development initiatives in terms of their origins, activities, legal structures, participants, sources of finance and budgeting. Others have drawn on case studies to illustrate policy processes and outcomes and the roles of partnership organisations in local areas (Gaunt, 1991; Harloe et al., 1990; Smallbone, 1990; Valler, 1991).

Other perspectives from policy studies which might be applied to the examination of local tourism partnerships include:

- State-centred in contrast to class-centred analyses of local politics (Fasenfest, 1991). The former examines the roles of professionals and bureaucrats in overcoming local economic development policy constraints. The latter is concerned with the capacities of local interest groups to influence policy implementation. The role of local elites, 'growth coalitions' in local economic development (Meyer, 1991) is a similar research area, as is the study of local corporatism.

> A corporatist framework would stress: the increasing use of non-elected agencies, the downgrading of the lead role of local authorities and the rise of business interests and the particular role of property interests in developing growth strategies and additionally, the closed nature of local politics, the networks of power involving business, political and labour interests and the concern with economic development. (Shaw, 1992)

- Concern with the factors which influence local partnership-building. These factors may include: levels of autonomous decision-making capacity, ability to gain access to non-local resources, the influence on national and regional organisations, the range of participants and their respective motivations, the process of bargaining, goal-setting and institutional development, the policy tools used and performance evaluation methodologies (Harding, in Campbell (1990)) (see also Coulson, in Campbell (1990), on 'social audit', 'social cost–benefit analysis', 'impact analysis' and 'action research methodologies').
- Explaining policy variation between localities (Urry, in Harloe et al. (1990)) and the examination of the particular historical and political circumstances within local areas which may represent constraints and opportunities for the development of partnership approaches (Harloe et al., 1990; Fasenfest, 1991).
- The political balance within local authorities, changes to that balance and the extent to which this may be a factor in influencing council roles within partnership structures (Smallbone, 1991).

Political geography and local tourism partnerships

In contrast to a policy studies approach which places primary emphasis on political processes underlying local initiatives, political geographers generally stress specific territorial features which distinguish regions and local areas (Paddison, 1983; Taylor and House, 1984).

As previously noted, the boundaries of local area tourism initiatives may not necessarily coincide with administrative borders and may be devised in terms of their actual or potential recognition as tourist areas (for example, North Pennines, Settle–Carlisle). Others are defined as sub-areas within larger districts (Castlefield in Manchester, the Waterfront in Leeds, Islington and Greenwich within London). The identification of viable subregions which have the conditions to achieve recognition or to operate as coherent tourist areas in marketing and management terms is clearly important in securing tourists, industry and community support for local tourism initiatives. The contribution of political geographers might usefully be examined in this context.

Paddison (1983) outlines a framework which examines political systems in territorial, in contrast to policy or organisational, terms. In this approach, 'territory (space) is a politically organising factor, providing identity, a sense of place, security and stimulation' (1983:15). The development and promotion of a 'sense of place' or local identity is a key component of much tourist literature and many tourism strategies. Paddison's framework for the

Table 49.1

Problems/issues	Defining features	Examples
Identity	Mutual sentiments by territorial communities towards local initiatives	Subregional identities
Legitimacy	Acceptance of local initiative programmes	Authority questioned by some
Participation	Those who contribute to decision-making	Subregions/localities/population groups relatively advantaged/disadvantaged
Penetration	Effectiveness of local initiative programmes	Spatial impacts of programmes
Distribution	Extent of resource distribution	Transfers between 'rich' and 'poor' areas

Adapted from Paddison (1983):9.

analysis of territorial political development includes this and other issues which are relevant to the study of local area tourism initiatives and is adapted in Table 49.1.

A feature of this framework for the study of local area tourism initiatives is the emphasis upon local community perspectives. The framework might therefore be employed to consider issues of equity in local political systems, including partnership arrangements, in addition to economic development considerations.

Variations in public sector spending programmes between local areas may also be examined from a political geography perspective. Variables which might explain differences in spending between areas include:

- The identification of local needs in terms of, 'the objective conditions that demand ameliorative action by governments. These should include conditions generated by the physical and socio-economic character of the jurisdiction that arise either within the community at large or *from a specific area* or demographic sub-group within it' (Paddison, 1983:157; emphasis added).
- The 'territorial extent' of resources available to meet 'needs'.
- Local politicians, professionals, business and community dispositions towards the identification of needs and the deployment of resources.

This analysis might include: (a) perceptions of needs and associated service requirements, (b) attitudes towards service recipients and, (c) attitudes towards the desirability and legitimacy of local initiatives to deal with these needs.

Political geography may therefore provide an organising framework for the definition of local area tourism initiative boundaries to take account of the issues highlighted in Table 49.1 and for the analysis of variations between different areas in resourcing partnership initiatives. The issues of local equity, accountability and participation may be overlooked in initiatives which emphasise marketing and economic development objectives. The approaches outlined here may therefore be of value in taking these considerations into account.

Organisation theories and local tourism partnerships

The TDAPs and LATIs which have emerged during the 1980s and 1990s have resulted in formal organisational arrangements for programme administration and management. This has generally involved a steering group comprising representatives from partner organisations and a working group (or groups) responsible for programme implementation (Bramwell and Broom, 1989). LATIs have few direct employees, involving staff on secondments from partnership organisations or with personnel allocated to partnership responsibilities as part of their jobs with partner organisations. Nevertheless, LATIs can be considered as organisations in their own right with their own identity, management and objectives, albeit with a high degree of dependency on the sponsoring partners and with a possibly limited life span. The study of local tourism partnerships might therefore be developed with specific reference to organisation theories. In particular, research which has focused on organisation–environment relationships and inter-organisational analysis is considered below, these being aspects of organisation theories having particular relevance to the specific nature of partnership organisations.

As Pearce (1992) observes, 'there has been comparatively little research on tourist organisations, whether in the tourism or the organisation literature' (1992:1). Moreover, 'in general tourist organisations at regional or the smaller, local scale have attracted even less attention than the national organisations' (1992:2). Pearce has made a valuable and timely contribution to the study of tourism organisations. However, his treatment of organisation theory is limited largely to a functionalist/open systems approach which has recently been challenged by organisation theorists. Thus, for Pearce, 'the concern is with what tourist organisations actually do, a concern expressed by focusing on their goals and functions' (1992:19). While this is a perfectly reasonable objective and is under-researched in tourism studies, the recent undermining of the functionalist orthodoxy in organisation theory is not addressed. The nature of this challenge and its implications for the study of tourism partnership organisations is briefly presented here before turning to organisation–environment relationships which Pearce correctly identifies as having significant relevance for the study of tourist organisations.

The origins of the functionalist paradigm of organisational research can be traced to the 'scientific management' movement associated with Taylor and Ford in the 1920s/30s. This asserted, in brief, that corporate officers, starting with given goals or desired outcomes, *design* the organisation, including its structure, control systems (technical and social) and work processes to achieve measurable ends (Warriner, 1984:4). The basic assumptions of the approach were: managerial control, agreement of purpose, and organisational autonomy. The task of social scientific research was to suggest ways of improving organisational rationality.

The basic functionalist model was challenged from the 1950s/60s from three directions:

● A 'human relations' approach emphasising non-rational interpersonal factors within organisations and recognising that managerial decisions are only one element of an organisation's operations.
● Analyses of purpose which examined the legitimacy of managerial goal definitions. The focus here was on interest groups and 'political processes within organisations by which divergent interests are resolved, accommodated, or co-opted in order to achieve a consistent pattern of action' (Warriner, 1984:12).
● The recognition of the significance of external environment influences upon organisations. This developed into an 'open systems' approach derived from ecological, evolutionary and natural selection theories. However, the functionalist model was largely maintained by a weakening of environmental considerations. This involved conceiving the environment as a passive 'sink' for outputs and 'reservoir' of inputs, using managers' perceptions as surrogates for the environment, and conceiving the environment only insofar as it provides management information (Warriner, 1984:15).

There is a tendency, therefore, for functionalist organisational research to focus on practical solutions to practical problems as defined by management. Studies are based upon actors' accounts and documents without reference to possible biases resulting in 'bureaucratic abstracted empiricism'—the use of data without adequate regard to the socio-economic and institutional context (Martins, 1986:144).

New research agendas in organisation studies emphasise plurality, diversity and ambiguity in organisation structures. Burrell and Morgan (1979), for example, argue that organisational courses of action are a consequence of the relative power of competing interests. Furthermore,

> although each of these interest groups may be rational with respect of its own interests . . . the organisation as a whole is not rational, since by definition, the dominant coalition is not the entire organisation and the satisfaction of its interests is not the same as the satisfaction of the interests of other groups nor . . . for the maintenance of the organisations as a whole. (Burrell and Morgan, 1979:215)

Other research themes currently attracting attention are concerned with processes of organisational change which reject the linear, rational models dominating systems-based research (Barrett and Srivastva, 1991; Hassard and Pym, 1990; Leifer, 1989) and concentrate on uneven, irregular paces of transition in different aspects of organisations. 'This form of analysis draws on theoretical resources sensitive to the multiple and contested organisational rationalities which underpin structural transition and their embeddedness within wider frameworks of political power and cultural control' (Reed, 1991:124).

According to Reed, systems theory has an acknowledged predisposition to view systems as ordered structures resulting in a failure to recognise paradoxes, contradictions and ambiguities—the 'dis-organisation in organisations'. The emergence of novel and innovative organisational forms, breaking with bureaucratic rationalisation and centralisation, exemplified by partnerships, support the case for pluralist research approaches. At the extreme, 'a powerful intellectual undercurrent . . . is the belief that the time may be ripe to abandon the concept of organisation altogether as the central problematic in the study of organisations' (Reed, 1991:129).

Whether one accepts this position or not, attention to the environment in which local tourism partnerships operate must represent a major consideration in future studies.

In this context, the central problem is the specification of environmental considerations that are relevant to the focal organisation. Warriner (1984) presents a 'transactional field' or 'niche analysis' approach which is, 'based on the assumption that organisations are affected by (and affect) their environments only through transactions between the organisation and other social actors' (1984:157). In this approach the 'contents' of the environment are specified by the two-way flows of physical, social and symbolic materials, other social actors represent the 'elements' of the environment and organisational interconnections its structure.

The analysis of organisation–environment relationships is therefore defined by transactional networks in this framework. Local tourism partnerships are likely to be involved in several kinds of organisational relationships and a variety of networks, giving a complex structure to the environment. These networks and relationships might be considered in terms of local communities, governmental networks, institutional fields (other tourism and related organisations) and private sector interests. This observation leads to an assessment of a further aspect of organisation studies—inter-organisational analysis.

Local tourism partnerships represent a formalisation of inter-organisational relationships between partners. Additionally, partnerships are engaged operationally with external organisations. Analysis of relationships and networks between organisations may therefore provide insight into the dynamics of local tourism partnerships. As Pearce comments, 'given the multi-faceted nature of tourism and the many different activities that tourist organisations . . . engage in, questions of coordination and inter-organisational interaction are likely to be critical in any analysis of tourist organisations' (1992:16).

An additional consideration here is the novel and innovative form of LATIs, transcending administrative and organisational domains, thus partnerships may not necessarily reflect the established political and administrative frameworks, boundaries and divisions of power which Pearce assumes (1992:20).

According to Karpik (1978:6), 'the notion of a network . . . designates a set of organisations which exercise their effects upon a focal organisation, or the system or interaction itself, whose composition, configuration, equilibrium and change are to be examined'.

This 'system of interaction' may be applied to the examination of LATIs, as follows (adapted from Benson in Karpik (1978:76–88)):

- In terms of the bases of differential power within a partnership. This involves assessment of the centrality and peripherality of partnership members, patterns of cooperation, coordination and conflict between members and the extent to which a partnership has achieved inter-organisational equilibrium. Benson identifies the dimensions of equilibrium as being: agreement about the roles and scope of partnership members, 'domain consensus'; agreement on the nature of the tasks facing the partnership and appropriate objectives, 'ideological consensus'; positive evaluation of other partnership members; and effective coordination of operational programmes.
- By definition of the partnership environment with reference to the concentration and/or dispersal of resources and powers, levels of partnership autonomy and/or dependence, dominance patterns within a partnership and externally imposed control mechanisms.

- Identification of factors which may result in changes to partnership arrangements (for example from recession, local government reorganisation and altered tourist board funding) and the nature of change (cooperative, disruptive, manipulative, authoritative).

Inter-organisational relationships may also be examined from a structuralist perspective, for example in terms of relational aspects of political structures. 'The basic objective of a structural analysis of politics is to explain the distribution of power among actors in a social system as a function of the positions that they occupy in one or more networks' (Knoke, 1990:9). An alternative conception of structuralism is to consider partnerships as 'continuous flows of conduct in time and space' (i.e. actions and meanings) (Knoke, 1990:16). This approach is associated with Giddens's 'structuration' theory; however, Knoke observes that its 'usefulness is severely limited by Giddens's failure to specify a research methodology for testing its arcane theoretical formulations' (1990:16).

A critique of inter-organisational research approaches is provided by Martins (1986) who argues that a concern with procedural aspects of inter-organisational conflicts and coordination, decision-making processes, etc. runs the risk of reification (taking the organisation as the central problematic as opposed to wider processes of institutional and social change). 'Organisations are mere empirical realities and their study cannot define a self-contained theoretical problematic. Rather it must be used as a springboard for analysing the historical processes of institutional and social production and reproduction of which organisational phenomena are, perhaps, the most expressive manifestation' (Martins, 1986:145).

For Martins, a revised research approach into organisation–environment and inter-organisational relationships would involve a theoretical recognition that organisations are historically constructed through social processes and represent part of a wider social totality whose structures influence and constrain organisational arrangements. Research methodologies would therefore acknowledge that organisations are expressions of underlying social relations, not reducible to their visible dimension and that social relations and contexts are not generally empirically observable and must be abstracted from the concrete and 'real'. Additionally the role and ideology of the analyst cannot be disregarded (Martins, 1986:150).

Writing in relation to regional planning organisations, Martins provides a research framework which incorporates aspects of the perspectives outlined in this paper, that is policy analysis, political geography and organisation theories. Martins proposes a 'context appropriate' methodology for the study of the roles of network

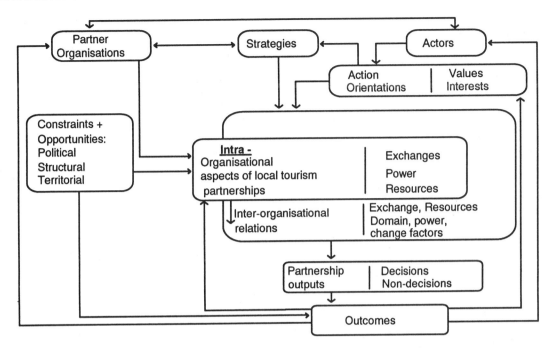

Figure 49.1 *Local tourism partnerships—a framework for analysis*

organisations in regional planning. The context is seen as involving:

- The *institutions* which relate to the activities or policy areas of concern for the partnership and or its sponsors.
- The *issues* bearing on the regional planning (tourism development) exercise, their substantive content and social importance.
- The *policies* or *policy intentions* of relevant institutions.

The researcher may then progress towards methodological choices concerning:

- The form and structure of the regional planning (tourism partnership) team—*corporate organisation*.
- The nature and extent of relationships and linkages with other agencies and planning systems—*intercorporate* organisation.
- The methods and techniques employed—*operational practice*.
- *Products* available for the partnership.
- Dynamics of the partnerships process (Martins, 1986:135).

Martins's research framework has been adapted for the study of local tourism partnerships and is shown in Figure 49.1.

Conclusion

Local tourism partnerships cannot realistically be separated from their local, regional and national contexts. There is therefore a need to develop research methodologies which take account of the political socio-economic, institutional and environmental circumstances within which local tourism partnerships operate.

Perspectives from policy analysis, political geography and aspects of organisation theories can inform the development of such context-appropriate methodologies. The framework adapted from Martins (1986:154) to some extent represents a synthesis of these perspectives and might assist in the analysis of local tourism partnerships taking account of the specific nature of local contexts.

It has only been possible here to briefly outline relevant aspects of policy studies, political geography and organisational analysis. It is hoped that these salient features might contribute to the development of applicable research methodologies.

References and bibliography

Barrett, F. J. and Srivastva, S. (1991) 'History as a mode of inquiry in organisational life: a role for human cosmogony', *Human Relations*, 4(3): 231–254.

Bramwell, W. and Broom, G. (1989) 'Tourism development action programmes—an approach to local tourism initiatives', *Insights*, A6-11–A6-17.

Britton, S. (1991) 'Tourism, capital and place. Towards a critical Geography of tourism', *Environment and Planning: Society and Space*, (9): 451–178.

Burrell, G. and Morgan, G. (1979) *Sociological Paradigms and Organisational Analysis*, Heinemann, London.

Campbell, M. (Ed.) (1990) *Local Economic Policy*, Cassell, London.

Chisholm, M. (1990) *Regions in Recession and Resurgence*, Unwin Hyman, London.

Cochrane, A. (1991) 'The changing state of local government: restructuring for the 1990s', *Public Administration*, 69 (Autumn): 281–302.

Edwards, J. and Deakin, N. (1992) 'Privatism and Partnership in urban regeneration', *Public Administration*, 70 (Autumn): 359–368.

Employment Department, Northern Ireland Office, Welsh Office, Scottish Office (1992) *Tourism in the United Kingdom—Realising the Potential*, HMSO, London.

English Tourist Board (1991) 'Planning for success—a tourism strategy for England 1991–1995', ETB.

Fasenfest, D. (1991) 'Comparative local economic development. A framework for further research', *Policy Studies Review*, 10(2/3): 80–86.

Fitzgerald, J. (1990) 'Partners in urban regeneration', *The Planner*, 76: 79–81.

Gaunt, R. (1991) 'Matching public measures and private sector objectives: the experience of Cardiff, Wales', *Policy Studies Review*, 10(2/3): 138–148.

Hall, R. H., Clark, J. P., Giordano, P. C., Johnson, P. V. and Van Rockel, M. (1977) 'Patterns of inter-organisational relationships', *Administrative Science Quarterly*, 22: 457–474.

Harloe, M., Pickvance, C. and Urry, J. (1990) *Place, Policy and Politics—Do Localities Matter?*, Unwin Hyman, London.

Hassard, J. and Pym, D. (1990) *The Theory and Philosophy of Organisations: Critical Issues and New Perspectives*, Routledge, London.

Hicks, H. G. and Gullett, C. R. (1975) *Organisations: Theory and Behaviour*, McGraw-Hill, New York.

Inskeep, E. (1991) *Tourism Planning—an Integrated and Sustainable Development Approach*, Van Nostrand Reinhold.

Karpik, L. (Ed.) (1978) *Organisation and Environment: Theory, Issues and Reality*, Sage, London.

Knoke, D. (1990) *Political Networks—the Structural Perspective*, Cambridge University Press, Cambridge.

Leach, S. and Stewart, J. (1982) *Approaches in Public Policy*, George Allen & Unwin, London.

Leifer, R. (1989) 'Understanding organisational transformation using a dissipative structure model', *Human Relations*, 42(10): 899–916.

Levine, S. and White, P. E. (1961) 'Exchange as a conceptual framework for the study of inter-organisational relationships', *Administrative Science Quarterly*, 583–601.

Litterer, J. A. (1973) *The Analysis of Organisations*, John Wiley, Chichester.

Litwak, E. and Hylton, L. F. (1962) 'Inter-organisational analysis. A hypothesis on co-ordinating agencies', *Administrative Science Quarterly*, 395–420.

Martins, M. R. (1986) *An Organisational Approach to Regional Planning*, Gower, Aldershot.

Meyer, P. B. (1991) 'Local economic development: what is proposed, what is done and what difference does it make?', *Policy Studies Review*, 10(2/3): 172–179.

Northern Ireland Tourist Board (1992) *Annual Report*, Vol. 44, *1991–1992*, NITB.

O'Toole, L. J. (1983) 'Inter-organisational cooperation and the implementation of local market training policies: Sweden and the Federal Republic of Germany', *Organisation Studies*, 4(2): 129–150.

Paddison, R. (1983) *The Fragmented State—the Political Geography of Power*, Blackwell, Oxford.

Pearce, D. (1992) *Tourist Organisations*, Longman, Harlow.

Raelin, J. A. (1982) 'A policy output model of inter-organisational relations', *Organisation Studies*, 3(3): 243–267.

Reed, M. (1991) 'Scripting scenarios for a new organisation theory and practice', *Work Employment and Society*, 5(1): 119–132.

Scottish Tourist Board (1992) *Twenty-Third Annual Report, 1991–1992*, STB.

Sellgren, J. (1990) 'Local economic development partnerships—an assessment of local authority economic development initiatives', *Local Government Studies*, July/August: 57–78.

Shaw, K. (1992) 'The development of new urban corporatism: the politics of urban regeneration in the north east of England', *Regional Studies*, 27(3): 251–286.

Smallbone, D. (1990) 'Enterprise agencies in London—a public-private sector partnership', *Local Government Studies*, September/October: 17–32.

Smallbone, D. (1991) 'Partnership in economic development: the case of UK local enterprise agencies', *Policy Studies Review*, 10(2/3): 87–98.

Taylor, P. and House, J. (Eds) (1984) *Political Geography: Recent Advances and Future Direction*, Croom Helm.

Turner, G. (1992) 'Public/private sector partnership—panacea or passing phase?', *Insights*, March: A85/A91.

Valler, D. (1991) 'Strategy and partnership in local economic development—a case study in local economic strategy making', *Policy Studies Review*, 10(2/3): 109–116.

Wales Tourist Board (1993) *Annual Report 1992–1993*, WTB.

Warren, R. L. (1967) 'The inter-organisational field as a focus for investigation', *Administrative Science Quarterly*, 12(3): 396–419.

Warriner, C. K. (1984) *Organisations and their Environments: Essays in the Sociology of Organisations*, JA1 Press.

50 Scotland's role in aiding tourism development in Eastern Europe and in the countries of the former USSR

A. S. TRAVIS

Introduction

Historically Scots have been an innovative, hard-working people who have made a massive contribution to the development of other societies when economic and other constraints at home have forced them to migrate abroad. The postwar period has seen a new flowering of Scots innovation in Scotland itself, and the subsequent transfer of this knowledge and entrepreneurial skills abroad. In the field of tourism development as a key sector of economic development, Scotland has been in the forefront of both thinking and action. Scotland has provided a template for others to follow. In the 19th century, Scots innovators were pacesetters throughout the English-speaking world, in a wide range of activities. Today, in the transformed European scene where, since the pulling down of the Berlin Wall, the whole of Eastern Europe and the former USSR have been opened up to trade, development, and investment, Scots and Scottish institutions have become very active. My proposition, in this paper, is that the notable role of Scots and Scottish institutions in aiding tourism development today in the lands of the former Eastern bloc, is a new phase of a continuing historical process of Scottish innovation abroad, but in a field in which the perceptions of Scottish prowess are less developed.

Scots migrations and overseas development contributions

Scotland has tended to view the history of outward migration of its people negatively, as this process has been one of loss both in quantitative as well as in qualitative terms. However, viewed from the point of view of those receiving societies, it is hard to imagine Canadian history, and the history of New Zealand, Australia, and parts of the USA without the contribution of Scots in fields as diverse as agriculture, commerce, banking, investment and development, media, and food industries. Whole regions were themselves the subject of development by Scots, and New Zealand's Otago Province would be inconceivable without its Scots heritage, as would Canada's Nova Scotia. Equally in Africa and India, as well as in the Dominions, the innovative Scots contribution has been a major one.

Postwar innovation within Scotland

Since World War II an extraordinary phase of development and innovation has taken place in Scotland itself, and in many ways it may be viewed as a sort of Scottish second Renaissance. In planning and development Scotland has been a European pacesetter. The work done at the national and regional scales in physical planning by the Scottish Development Department and the regional authorities, in economic development by the former Scottish Development Agency, in conservation by bodies such as the National Trust for Scotland, in the voluntary sector, and agencies like the Countryside Commission for Scotland, in the public sector, provided models which were envied across the world. Special regional development agencies like the former Highlands and Islands Development Board, generated international attention as a test model for problem-solving elsewhere. England, Wales and other countries followed on from test models tried and found to be effective in Scotland. Thus innovation in economic development, planning, conservation and the informal linking of various related interventionist agencies and policies, laid foundations for follow-up initiatives by the private and voluntary sectors. Tourism initiatives grew out of this special environment that related to the period from the 1960s to the 1980s. A voluntary sector Scottish tourist body in the 1960s, laid the foundations for the statutory Scottish Tourist Board that emerged late in that decade, and the creative interactions between that body and not only the commercial sector, but also the public sector agencies, the voluntary sector, as well as the academic sector, was unique, for its period, in Europe.

The fund of practical experience by this orchestrated range of creative agencies in Scotland, went hand-in-hand with a pattern of innovation by the large and important traditional centres of tertiary activity, such as the banking and insurance groups, the lawyers and academics, and the growing and changing tourist industry in Scotland. Without the specific character of this range of experience and set of creative interactions, it is unlikely that Scotland could have positioned itself so well for a new phase of international development and contributions abroad by Scots and Scottish agencies.

In a year of working abroad, in Poland, the author became aware of the notable but surprisingly unrecorded Scottish contribution to this new phase of development in Eastern Europe and the former Soviet Union. Perhaps it takes a non-Scot, who has had the rich experience of working in Scotland in that remarkable period of the 1960s and 1970s, to appreciate Scottish creativity and diligence, both in Scotland and in the new lands of economic opportunity in the East, in this current period.

New development opportunities in the East

The pulling down of the Berlin Wall some three to four years ago, started a period of change which was first to revolutionise the situation in the former Communist states of Eastern and Central Europe, and then in turn lead to the more radical changes within the former USSR itself.

For large and populous countries like Poland, this is the fourth year of momentous changes, wherein nations change from having command economies with centralised controls, and go by stages to market economies, with democratic government, privatised industry, decentralised power, and responsive central government. Such changes are only proving possible, because of the opening up of these countries to foreign investment, as well as to aid programmes from the European Union (the former Commission of the European Communities) on the one hand, via PHARE and TACIS, and a series of bilateral programmes between free countries of the West, and the newly freed Eastern economies. Such aid programmes include those offered by France, Ireland, the USA, Switzerland, Germany, The Netherlands and the UK. Much of UK aid is via the auspices of the UK Know-How Fund. It must be emphasised, however, that this is not a sudden switch of attention by Scots and the British generally from countries in the British Commonwealth, and from English-speaking countries such as the USA, for there have long been trading connections with the Baltic countries especially, and with Poland, Latvia and Estonia in particular. Historic cities such as Gdansk (the former Danzig), long had quarters in which Scots traders and craftsmen settled, from medieval times onwards, whilst in the 19th century migrants from Poland and the Baltic States settled in Scotland, and at the end of World War II, General Ander's (Polish) Army was demobilised

in Scotland, leading to a rapid expansion of the Polish community there.

This environment of sudden change and opportunity for investment, aid and development in the East, is one to which Scots and Scottish agencies have reacted quickly and randomly. The Scottish dimension, as such, is an uncoordinated one, and as yet there is no register or central list of all the Scottish activities ongoing in Eastern Europe and the CIS. In fact it has proved to be a research task in itself to obtain such information, and being based in Poland during this period, has meant that one could only obtain indicative, rather than comprehensive data, for such a paper.

The processes of modernisation and development of tourism as part of emergent market economies has created extensive needs for advice, foreign investment, technical know-how, training and exchanges, for a large group of countries, containing a population far greater than that of the European Union, and on territory which covers an area several times that of the 12 EC countries. To create the transport and infrastructural systems for modern tourism throughout this 'new world', a superstructure of hotels, information and computerised booking services, well-managed attractions, a modern system of marketing, market- and consumer-responsive skills and abilities, market research, and so on, represents a gigantic challenge and opportunity for Western countries in general, for the UK, and especially for Scotland. Here, in a recessionary period is the opportunity to utilise our skills and experience, and to gain economically from enabling a group of countries to do in five years what it has taken many countries five generations to achieve.

What then are the realms of the Scottish contribution to changes in Eastern Europe and beyond?

This special anniversary of the Scottish Tourist Board and of the Scottish Hotel School is a most appropriate frame for reviewing the realms of the Scots contribution in the East, for they relate centrally to them. In order to assess this, the author has had contact with the range of European agencies, UK bodies, some Scottish agencies and some Scottish firms. Whilst the data requested was all supposed to relate directly to tourism, it is clear that in some instances the connection is indirect, and where it is totally unrelated to tourism, the reference has been excluded. The review is indicative, and cannot attempt to be comprehensive. Furthermore, having been done whilst the author was based in Poland, it was difficult to double check on details, and to get them supplemented where it would have been desirable to do so.

Within the tourism field, Scottish action in the East European and ex-USSR areas has related to the whole spectrum of institutional changes, guidance on product development and investment, planning, marketing and market research, management and training/education. Thus, not only governmental and local agencies, but also academic institutions and commercial and professional firms, as well as voluntary sector bodies, have all played their roles. Critical in this context has been the enabling role of the institutions, whether at the world scale (such as the World Bank), at the European scale (such as the Commission of the European Communities and its instruments), or British institutions (such as the UK Know-How Fund). Activities under these institutional frameworks are spelt out in the next section of this paper.

Institutional umbrellas for the delivery of tourism assistance

As only one mention occurred relating to a World Bank initiative linked to a Scottish endeavour, but many relating to European and to British funding, the indicative studies have been limited to these two key scales of activity.

European funding

The largest block of European funding from the European Union (i.e. the former Commission of the European Communities) to the East, relate to PHARE for the East European countries and TACIS for the countries of the former USSR. Of 1000 million ECU allocated to the PHARE Programme, about 200 million ECU are allocated to Poland, and of that some 2.5% of the budget is allocated to the Tourism Development Programme. This point needs to be emphasised, as tourism is a relatively lightly funded field, as compared to agriculture or manufacturing industry.

Scottish involvements in the PHARE and TACIS nations are considerable, and some indicative examples are given to reflect this, especially in the tourism-related spheres. Some eight examples are given:

- Poland—proposals for tourism marketing and market research for the Gdansk region, in association with Gdansk regional bodies, Strathclyde University (Scottish Hotel School) and the Glasgow Caledonian University.
- Poland—Łódź Tourism Development Initiative, by the Łódź Foundation for Promotion of Entrepreneurship, in association with the Edinburgh Consortium and Firn, Crichton & Roberts (Fife).

- Poland—Kraków/Kazimierz District Conservation, Renovation and Tourist Development in association with Edinburgh City (unclear if this was PHARE or UKKNF funding).
- PHARE group of countries—Local Scottish Technical and Further Education colleges are actively developing links throughout these countries, both in relation to training (languages, business studies, etc., which lay good foundations for tourism), and to local technical assistance, e.g. Lauder College in Dunfermline, and the College in Glenrothes).
- PHARE and UKKNF—contracts have been obtained by the universities of St Andrews, Dundee, Glasgow, Heriot-Watt and Paisley, in a wide variety of scientific, technical, and business studies areas, including active commercial development in Central and in Eastern Europe. Detailed replies are still awaited from these universities, and clarification as to how far tourism-related subjects are involved.
- All PHARE countries—East European Enterprises Ltd, Scotland, has set up offices and has representatives in all the PHARE countries, and secured PHARE, UKKNF and other contracts—details are still awaited reanalysis relating to tourism specifically.
- Hungary—Tourism training programmes in Hungary (under PHARE), have had inputs from staff in Strathclyde and Glasgow Caledonian universities.
- TACIS countries—CAROS, the new commercial company set up by Scottish Agricultural Colleges, is running contracts in the TACIS countries, in the agricultural production and development spheres, and it seems that extension of this base into rural tourism and investment has been raised.

CEC Ouverture Programme

This programme, launched in 1991, involves tourism as part of Local Economic Development. It was co-funded by the Commission, under Article 10—the European Regional Development Fund. It involves all regions and cities of the EC countries and their East European partners. The Ouverture Programme was an initiative of the Strathclyde Regional Council, and its East European Headquarters is located in Glasgow. Some 7 million ECU are being spent on this programme in the 1991–1994 period. On each project an East European partner is linked to two CEC regional or city partners. Out of a total 52 projects, some five to date specifically relate to tourism development.

The five tourism projects involve:

—A mountain-tourism project in Bulgaria.
—The Bartok tourist information and development project in Hungary.

—The Baltic Gateways project in Poland.
—The Łódź Business Development Services project in Poland.
—The Promotion of Tourism Project in Gizycko, in Poland.

Of the three Scottish authority involvements in Ouverture to date (two involving Strathclyde Region, and one involving Glasgow City Council), it is the Łódź project which is partly related to tourism, and includes Strathclyde.

Three other relevant Scottish activities in this sphere are the new USTI-II project in the Czech Republic, involving the City of Dundee (details yet to be obtained), and two advice papers from Scottish sources:

—tourism strategy advice (in Slovakia) by J. Fraser, Director of Loch Lomond, Stirling and Trossachs Tourist Board, and
—local economic development advice (in Slovakia) by P. Stott, Head, Partnership Unit, Strathclyde Regional Council.

United Kingdom funding

Most of the UK funding of initiatives in Eastern Europe has been provided from the United Kingdom Know-How Fund (UKKHF). Examples of relevant indicative work from the general funds of the UKKHF, are as follows.

Of the £1 million given from the UKKHF to establish some four regional management centres in Poland, contracts for two of the four were won by Scottish academic groups:

—Łódź: Edinburgh University, in consortium with Edinburgh Chamber of Commerce, and Firn, Crichton & Roberts.
—Gdansk: Strathclyde and Glasgow Caledonian Universities.

The four resultant regional management centres are known as:

(1) The Łódź Foundation for the promotion of Entrepreneurship,
(2) The Gdansk Managers Training Foundation,
(3) The Lublin Business School, and
(4) The Wielkopolska Business School in Poznan.

Three of the centres have already become associated with tourism initiatives, and they include Łódź and Gdansk. Complementing such initiatives is the development in Łódź of Management Accounting Systems by Stirling

University—critical for the newly emerging private sector hotels, attractions and travel companies.

Whilst in the CIS information has been received about the joint initiative of Aberdeen University and Robert Gordons with regard to oil and gas industry technical assistance and training, associated with Grampian Enterprise, no data has yet been received about tourism initiatives there. However, it is known that as far as the TACIS countries (as well as the PHARE nations) are concerned all eight established Scottish universities have multiple involvements in technical assistance, training and/or research activities there, and that many of the newer universities and colleges are also actively developing programmes. Similarly, Scottish local enterprise companies are involved in joint ventures, some with a tourism component.

The environmental tranche of the UK Know-How Fund was developed in its first key phase by S. McKinley from Scotland, and has nurtured matters of environmental protection in relation to the dynamic factor of tourism. Scottish participation has been notable in Bulgaria, where the National Trust for Scotland did a small study on conservation and visitor management at the Rila Monastery. Environmental impact assessment courses in several East European countries have been conducted by the University of Aberdeen's Centre for Environmental Management, and a sustainable tourism project has been undertaken in Mazuria, Poland, where a largely English team included Scottish-trained Dr R. Denman as a consultant.

Enterprise by companies and entrepreneurs

As already mentioned there has been a flowering of commercial links and enterprise by many sorts of Scottish companies in the freed Eastern bloc, including law firms, property companies, insurance firms, manufacturing firms and processing firms.

In TACIS countries, Scottish supermarket development is under exploration, in Russia, by McQuittys; Air Ukraine is involved with Scottish insurers; and Kiev farmers, through McQuittys, are exploring joint venture activities. Many ventures seemingly remote from tourism have tourism dimensions to them. Rydens are this year opening offices in St Petersburg; they already have a Czech office and are also opening a Polish one. The property scene is increasingly relating to hotels, restaurants, and commercial attractions as well as offices, housing and industrial plants.

In the PHARE countries, the heavy interest in Hungary and the Czech Republic is spreading rapidly to Poland, and gradually to the Baltic states, and the more sluggish economies of Romania and Slovakia. Development

Options Ltd is active in Poland and Hungary, as is Firn, Crichton & Roberts from Fife. S. Clark Associates have long-term technical aid contracts in Hungary and Romania, whilst the lively McQuittys have been into a wide range of initiatives in Estonia and Latvia, a few of which have a tourism dimension: the importing of loghouses (also suitable for self-catering lets), insuring and developing an Estonian Airways Company, and so on. Links to a cycling club in Estonia and to tourism training have also arisen.

Regional and local government initiatives have been mentioned. In Russia there have been initiatives by Glasgow Chamber of Commerce (Rostow on Don), and by Lothian and Edinburgh Enterprise. Actors on the Polish scene have included Fife Regional Council, Glasgow Development Agency, and Edinburgh District Council. Wroclaw, Łódź, Gdansk and Kraków have been the action locations. Detailed data on tourism aspects is still awaited.

Evaluation and conclusions

It will be evident from the foregoing paper that Scotland and Scottish firms and institutions are very active in both Eastern Europe and the CIS countries. The data-gathering exercise has proved time-demanding and rather frustrating, for as yet it appears that no Scottish organisation does a listing of Scottish initiatives in one of the boom areas for trading and investment today. If this is true for general investment, trading and aid, it is even more complex and difficult in the tourism sector which needs a very detailed database. I thank my various collaborators, listed in the 'Acknowledgements' section, for at least enabling me to display indicatively the richness of this field. I hope this paper will stimulate one of the Scottish agencies to address more fully the urgent needs for full listing, coordination, and even some sensible orchestration in this field.

Thus the Scottish tourism initiatives appear to be extensive, uncoordinated, but seemingly fruitful. Nowhere are the lessons gained being recorded and pooled; new entrants to the field waste much time and resources getting data and contacts from scratch. Many agencies compete and overlap, firms compete for some market segments and ignore other bigger markets, because of the lack of market research. There is a potential role for Scotland-wide agencies to do ground-clearing work to help firms and organisations in Scotland to trade, develop, invest, and aid the New East. Ground-seed funding is needed for small commercial entrepreneurs in this sector, if they are to reach a stage of viability and profitability.

The UK Know-How Fund and Ouverture appear to be effective, quick and responsive in fulfilling their set briefs. They could well give more attention and greater funding to tourism-related initiatives. PHARE and TACIS funding relates to slower and more complex bureaucratic procedures, and often confused responsibilities. The intentions are excellent, but the delivery mechanisms and arrangements constraining. Tourism is too important to several of these countries to be handled by multiple bilateral and international agencies and programmes, on an uncoordinated basis. Scottish skills, experience, and knowledge within the tourism sector are such that with more coherent feedback and delivery coordination, Scotland could now take a central role in helping and investing in countries of the former Eastern bloc, both for their sake, and for the economic benefit of her own folk through this process.

Acknowledgements

The author would like to express his sincere thanks to the following people and organisations in connection with obtaining data for this paper:

—Dr G. Adams and Dr B. Hay, of the Scottish Tourist Board,
—Professor C. Jenkins of the Scottish Hotel School, Strathclyde University,
—Mr J. Firn of Firn, Crichton & Roberts, in Fife,
—Mr R. Brown, Director, Ouverture Programme, Glasgow,
—Mr G. McQuitty of McQuittys, in Fife,
—Mr J. Reynolds, of EPEUR, at the Department of the Environment (UKKHF) in London,
—Mr J. Henley, of the Edinburgh Consortium, Scotland.

51 The development of Scotland as a tourist destination

A. J. DURIE

Seeing Scotland, Madam, is only seeing a worse England
(Samuel Johnson, 1778)

Though there have been some excellent studies of the growth of tourism in the Highlands (Smout, 1983; Butler, 1985), as yet no general picture has emerged of the rise of tourism in Scotland during the 19th century. This is a surprising lacuna, given that tourism in its many forms had become by the later 19th century an activity of very considerable economic importance in many areas, both coastal and inland. What adds interest to any analysis is that tourism was a genuinely new industry, whereas other leading sectors in the economy, such as textiles, had had a long pedigree in Scotland. In this paper, therefore, I want to focus on the growth of tourism in Scotland over the period *c.* 1770 to 1914. For the purposes of this analysis, the paper is divided into four sections; discovery (1770–1810), development (1810–1840), expansion (1840–1870), consolidation and challenge (1870–1914). As in any chronological categorisation, these are very far from watertight compartments.

The discovery of Scotland (c. 1770–1810)

While intrepid travellers and explorers from England or the Continent had made their way to Scotland for many centuries, it was mostly path-breaking exploration without any notion that others would wish to follow. Yet in the later 18th century things began to alter. Not only did more visitors come, but their accounts were published. There are, for example, those of Johnson and Boswell, and that of Mrs Murray of Kensington. These began to change the outside perception of Scotland, which had been, not without substance, of a strange and hostile land peopled by inhabitants of an uncertain temper. The revised image was of a land of natural beauties, including Fingal's Cave which Sir Joseph Banks called 'the cathedral of the Seas' after his visit in 1772, a country of the picturesque and the historic, of strange but interesting customs and distinct culture. Of course, access was still very difficult, and accommodation uncertain, except for those who had good connections with the Scottish landowning class. A group who in particular were quick to appreciate what Scotland

could offer the visitor were the sporting fraternity who began to make their way north in increasing numbers to fish or shoot, the Colonel Thornton constituency, whose tour of slaughter in 1786 so displeased Scott. His was a safari-type colonial expedition but in his wake were to follow many others; as early as 1797 the laird at Aviemore was instructing the local innkeeper to give preference to travellers rather than southern sportsmen. By 1840, according to Lord Cockburn (1888), 'attracted by grouse, the mansion houses of half of our poor devils of Highland lairds are occupied by rich and titled Southrons'.

Development (1810–1840)

These early tours did much to change the image of Scotland, and prepared the ground for the much more rapid development that was to follow. If there is one starting date for tourism in Scotland, as opposed to the intrepid travelling of the few, an argument can be made for the year 1810 which saw the publication of Walter Scott's *Lady of the Lake*. This became prescribed reading for generations of visitors to the Trossachs. The marriage of verse and scenery seems to have been the formula for success, as the romantic gaze turned to Scotland (Andrews, 1989). Clearly, interest in North Britain had been building ever since 1793 when war had made travel on the Continent difficult or impossible; a review in 1809 of Carr's *Caledonian Sketches* commented that 'since the Continent has been shut against us, Edinburgh is as much visited by every dashing citizen who pretends to fashion as Margate or Tonbridge'.[1] The *Scots Magazine* in 1810 remarked that the 'fame of Scottish scenery is every day spreading wider and wider'. As well as the increasing number of visitors' accounts of Scotland being published, guide books also began to appear: *The Traveller's Guide through Scotland and Its Islands* was in its third edition by 1806. But Scott was to open the floodgates with his romantic and safely sanitised presentation of Scotland. Within months of the publication of the *Lady of the Lake*, the Trossachs had become a much-favoured destination; Mrs Grant of Laggan, for instance, noted in her diary for 17 September 1810 that she had come to Callander 'to meet some English friends and accompany them to these same Trossachs to which all the world are going to disturb the wood nymphs and emulate Walter Scott. How much we owe to Burns and Walter Scott'. Literary tourism, to view the places made famous by verse or prose, remained a feature of 19th century travel, and the visiting of writers' birthplaces or homes was a kind of pilgrimage. Abbotsford and Alloway alike were key stops on many a tourist's itinerary.

The absence of any such person or connection was a serious handicap to the attraction of this kind of monied and educated tourism, as was quickly appreciated. Sir John Sinclair was quite serious when he wrote to Scott in November 1810 to congratulate him on increasing the number of visitors to Loch Katrine 'beyond measure; my carriage was the 297th in the course of this year when there never had been above 100 before in any one season'.[2] The entrepreneurial Sir John went on to urge Scott to write a sequel, called the *Mermaid* or *The Lady of the Sea* to be set in his native Caithness in the hope of inspiring a similar tourist boom there. *The Scottish Tourist* (1852 edition) noted of St Andrews that it 'abounds in the same kind of interesting objects and associations as Melrose and Iona, and had it been written into popular notice by Burns, Byron or Scott, it would probably be drawing far more wealth from the visits of fashionable visitors'. The power of literary association remained strong throughout the 19th century, a late example being the role of Barrie in promoting interest in Kirriemuir, not a locality previously high on many visitors' agenda.

Literary tourism was, therefore, a very important component in the growing number of visitors to Scotland, and was particularly important in drawing the longer-distance traveller. It was a love of Ossian that induced the Prussian architect Karl Friedrich Schinkel to make a trip to Staffa and Iona in July 1826. Others were devotees of Burns. But it seems to have been Scott who was of the greatest significance. Lord Cockburn found in September 1840 that there were an extraordinary number of travellers, 'foreign but chiefly English', in the Oban area, 'attracted by scenery, curiosity, superfluous time and wealth, and the fascination of Scott'.

The attractions of Scotland were many and increasingly known to the outside world through pen, artists' impressions or personal acquaintance. And while Edinburgh and the Highlands were the most popular destinations, tourists used their time in transit to purpose. The mills at New Lanark were much visited and amongst the several hundred signatures in the visitor's book for September 1821 are to be found those of

William Flankland of Wells, Somerset, 'on a tour', and Mr Stalleyblack and family of Surrey, 'returning from a tour to the Highlands'.[3] The Porter family from Worcester called there on 28 March 1823; the family journal noted of Mr Owen that he was said to be 'a deist and a very immoral character, and the people in his establishment are a very bad lot', but the author added judiciously that 'I cannot answer for the truth'.[4]

The picture, therefore, by the 1820s and 1830s is of an ever-increasing number of visitors to Scotland coming both from England and Europe, with even a few Americans making their presence felt—about a hundred a year visiting Abbotsford in the late 1830s (Durie, 1992a). Another aspect of tourism often neglected, however, is the way that during this period Scots themselves began to use their summers to travel and holiday. Thomas Handyside Baxter of Dundee took his first jaunt to the Highlands in August of 1811 and found to his surprise there were places of beauty and order 'where I had always thought that there was nothing but Poverty and Barrenness'.[5] Sea-bathing had long been established as a health-giving activity, and more and more upper-class and professional families from the big cities began to spend time during the summer at a seaside resort, whether on the Ayrshire or the East Lothian coast. The number and significance of Scottish spas began to increase; Moffat had long been established but Bridge of Allan was beginning to develop; it was still (according to a description in 1836) a small watering place, 'a delightful summer weekend retreat which attracts many visitors from Edinburgh and Glasgow' (Durie, 1993).

Underpinning the growth in this period was the improvement of access to and within Scotland—better roads, but above all the coming of the steamship. This new means of transport opened up all sorts of possibilities for travel, as it allowed for much more regular services than had been possible with sail and particularly facilitated tourist travel on the west coast with its more sheltered waters. The artist, William Daniell, sketched a steamboat on the Clyde near Dumbarton in 1818, the deck of which is crowded with a well-dressed company of men and women. Operators were quick to respond to the opportunity of tapping the tourist trade; in 1826 one foreign visitor observed no fewer than 60 to 70 steamboat notices posted in George Square, most of them offering pleasure trips to the Scottish lochs and Staffa. The *Scottish Tourist and Itinerary*, first published in 1825 and significantly dedicated to Sir Walter Scott, carried a list of the principal steamboat tours, referring to the way in which the use of steam-vessels 'had laid open to thousands scenes of uncommon grandeur, which previously had been surveyed only by the enthusiastic traveller'. And while the west coast was the principal beneficiary, sailings on the east coast also flourished; the Quaker industrialist, Edward Pease, had a fine passage by steamer in August 1847 up 'the beautiful Firth of Forth' from Edinburgh to Alloa.[6]

Expansion (1840–1870)

If the coming of the steamboats had done much to open up Scotland, the railways were a further great advance in what one contemporary was to call the 'perfect revolution that has been effected in favour of the tourist'. The opening of cross-border routes was completed by an ever-widening network of trunk and branch lines, some of which had tourist traffic very much in their sights. The promoters of the Dingwall and Skye Railway stressed in their prospectus, which was advertised in the *Railway News and Joint Stock Journal* in the spring of 1864, that 'the countryside which the proposed line will traverse is of a most picturesque character, abounding in the finest scenery and stocked with game so that tourists and sportsmen will both benefit by such a district thrown open to them and the pleasure traffic is likely to form an important ingredient in the success of this scheme'. The problem for many such lines, however, was the lack of traffic outwith the summer months, packed though they might be in July and August.

What does seem clear is that there was both a marked expansion in the number of visitors coming to Scotland from the 1840s onwards, and a change in their social composition. There is, alas, little in the way of hard statistical evidence to corroborate the first assertion, but there are two sources which at least point in the right direction—visitors' books such as those kept at Abbotsford and at the Burns Monument at Ayr, and the visitors' lists published in the local newspapers of the more fashionable resorts, for example, North Berwick, Elie, Strathpeffer, Campbelltown and Moffat (Durie, 1992b). The Abbotsford series of visitors' books, complete from 1833 onwards, is particularly valuable. The numbers calling there rose from 1364 in 1848 to over 5000 in 1858 and were to rise yet further. What study of the addresses given shows is the rise in American visitors, especially after the Civil War, from a few hundred at best pre-1860 to two or three thousand most years thereafter (Durie, 1992a). Little systematic work has yet been done on visitors' lists but a preliminary analysis of those for Moffat shows a doubling of summer visitors between 1858 and 1863.

As to the social composition of the tourist flow, the intriguing development of the post-1840 period is the growth of tourism which was not just monied and upper-class. Of course, following the example of Queen Victoria

herself, who first visited Scotland in 1842, the upper classes continued to come, to shoot or fish, or to cruise in their private yachts on the west coast; but they no longer had exclusive possession of Scotland. Contemporaries noticed the change: one steamship commander was reported in 1861 as saying that he had been on these boats for many years, and had seen a great change in the traffic. 'For a long time, we had few, except the wealthy, many of whom came thousands of miles, from almost all parts of the world to see the wonders of Fingal's Cave, and the interesting island of Iona. But now I see large numbers of the middle and humbler class of society coming out this way, and they will constitute the grounds of future success to the proprietors of these boats.'[7]

Central to this change, and instrumental in it, was the work of Thomas Cook, the Field-Marshal of excursions (Brendon, 1991). There were other excursion promoters, but none in my view as important in the Scottish context. His first sortie across the Border was in 1846 with a party of 350 and he was to be found three or four times in the summer months in Scotland most years for the next thirty or so years. Reviewing his life-work in 1861, he claimed to have personally taken nearly 40 000 visitors by special train to Scotland on his Tartan Tours, about a quarter of whom he took on from Edinburgh and Glasgow to Loch Lomond and the Trossachs. In the same period he had taken 45 parties to Staffa and Iona, the poverty of whose inhabitants aroused his philanthropy. Even the Scottish railway companies who would like to have taken over his business and did temporarily suspend their dealings with him, admired his acumen. The General Manager of the North British Railway Company in 1865 said of Cook that he could speak from personal experience of 'the success that invariably attends his excursions over this railway between Scotland and England over the past eighteen years'.[8]

Many travellers who were not going on a tour conducted by Cook or one of his excursion agents, nevertheless bought their tickets to Scotland through him. Cook claimed in an interview in 1864 that more than a million passengers had been under his charge for excursions between Scotland and England; this figure may well include Scots travelling to England, for the same railways that brought English visitors in could take Scottish travellers out. But the scale and efficiency of his operations is certainly borne out by observers. The *Railways News* reported on 8 September 1866 that Mr Cook had that week brought 3000 excursionists from the Midland towns of England on a visit to Scotland, and commented that 'the Leicester printer is a great man in his own way, and he generally manages things with great success. Looking to the large numbers he has to marshal and provide quarters for, it is wonderful how few hitches occur, how few letters appear in the newspapers'. A lady writer spoke for many of his clients when she praised him in these terms:

Dear Sir, Those who have puzzled over Bradshaw, hoping to make the most of their time in travelling, can appreciate your efforts in the planning of excursions by which they can travel over a large extent of country without losing an hour of time or missing a train. I shall never forget the delightful excursion with you to the Highlands of Scotland, to classic Iona and the world renowned Island of Staffa.[9]

Cook's great contribution to tourism was in the provision of tours costed down to the last penny, and run to a very tight schedule, which could if the client wished be extended. While there were those of means who travelled with Cook for reasons of comfort, Cook opened Scotland to those whose time and money alike were limited, and gave confidence to the many people who had had little or no experience of travel. He issued briefing notes which were clear and persuasive, which made it clear amongst other things that it was entirely safe and proper for unaccompanied ladies to join his Highland tours. There was developed a network of approved Scottish hotels, Cook heartily defending Highland hotels against the oft-made complaint of exorbitant charges, and he ensured that rail, coach and steamship connections were in place as promised.

Not everyone, it has to be said, was enthusiastic about the growing tide of excursionists. Some aristocratic tourists resented the plebeian excursionists. Major Markham and a friend, in Scotland on a walking holiday in 1838, travelled by boat from Edinburgh to Stirling on which two upper-class gentlemen were also taking passage. When they got to the Royal Inn where they were to stay the night, 'we walked into the room we were in before and found our former aristocratic steam-boat companions; they seemed horrified at mingling with commoners, so rang the bell, asked for a private room and toddled off'.[10] John Henry Newman, who was staying at Abbotsford in July 1872 complained bitterly about the intrusiveness of visitors. 'There are these excursionists again—Cooke's—walking past the windows—You can't conceive the state of this place in this point of view. Yesterday men of that kidney were before the windows at 6 o'clock in the morning and they go on all day.'[11]

Accessibility and promotion were important factors in swelling the flow of tourists to Scotland. Guide books, both national and local, appeared in ever-increasing quantities, and were often reprinted at surprisingly short intervals. Black's *Guide to Scotland* averaged a new edition every second year. What dictated this pattern was both demand and the extent of change that every year seemed to bring in the provision of new railway services and routes, reconstructed, renovated or newly opened hotels, hydropathic and other facilities. The provision of more accommodation was particularly needed—there were times that towns such as Inverness or Callander were simply swamped by the summer demand. Mrs Manby and her sister from Worcestershire found themselves in August 1855 unable to get into the Caledonian at Oban, 'the only decent hotel in the place. We were obliged to come to another, a most uncomfortable place, men smoking and [word illegible] all over the place'.[12] Complaints about the quality of accommodation and the prices charged were frequent and this appears to have been not the only problem: one correspondent to the London *Times* (1 September 1869) complained about Scotland that:

throughout the whole country, wherever tourists have penetrated you cannot but feel that a large proportion of the population is pitted against you to cheat you if it can, and this warfare is conducted on the most irritating principles, by means of constant petty charges, for pier dues, porterage and for items in your hotel bill which are specially ordered by strangers. This year the most flagrant overcharge has been in the matter of beer.

But whether his experience was typical is open to question; the Sladden family in 1859 found that the Royal Hotel in Stirling was excellent, 'at least we met with every comfort combined with moderate charges'. Other items of complaint were the weather, the standard of cooking, and the Scottish Sunday which, some visitors, especially from the Continent, found far too strict.

Yet, by and large, the advantages of Scotland outweighed the difficulties of distance and climate. What worked in Scotland's favour was the amalgam of attractions: scenery, sport, antiquities, literary associations and shrines, castles, great houses and ruined abbeys. And the Scottish resorts were not merely passive recipients of tourist visitors; they, and their publicists, worked at enhancing the appeal of their locality, by providing facilities such as bathing stations, bandstands, reading rooms, walks, bowling greens and the like. Great care was taken to highlight any local points of historic interest, real or speculative. One visiting American, the journalist J. M. Bailey, remarked in half-jest after a tour in the Lothians and Borders that there were nearly five hundred castles in the area, and that 'Queen Mary was imprisoned in all of them. That unfortunate must have been in jail about four-fifths of the time. What I now want, what I really pant after, is a ruin that wasn't her prison, that

Sir Walter Scott hasn't written about, and that Queen Victoria didn't visit in 1842. But I don't know where to look for it'.[13]

The width of Scotland's appeal is well caught by Walter Cooper Dendy, a successful London medical practitioner and travel author, whose study, *The Wild Hebrides*, was published in 1859.

> On the Rothesay to Mull steamer there are a mixture of tourists, the mere routine excursionist, slave to his guide book, those who have come for the scenery, others for the fishing, a botanist, a geologist 'come to pummel the sides of Ben Nevis for pebbles', civic magnates, a double-refined gallant, girls and dowagers, and others beside. Most ominously, and this is a problem not peculiar to Scotland or the 19th century, there is the 'desecrating vagrant, whose highest pride is to carve his initials on one of the holy tombs on Iona, chip off a morsel of moulding from the prentice pillar in Roslin and filch one of Macalister's stalactites from the spar cave of Strathaird'.

One of the consequences of the increasing numbers of tourists was a much greater concern for the preservation of historic sites and buildings, as on Iona where there had been complaints about the way in which the curious old inscriptions had been fast disappearing under the 'iron-shod feet of the tourists'.[14] Tourism did have its beneficial side.

Consolidation (1870–1914)

By the later 19th century, Scotland was very well established as a tourist destination. Its resorts, whether coastal or inland, enjoyed large numbers of visitors during the summer. Its portfolio of attractions was strengthened by the growing popularity of golf, which benefited resorts such as Dunbar and North Berwick. And whereas there had been perhaps only 17 courses in Scotland in 1848, including the links at Banchory, as many as 200 new courses were laid out between 1875 and 1914. Demand continued strong for fishing and shooting, and specialist publications such as J. Watson Lyall's *Sportsman's & Tourist's Timetable and Guide to the Rivers, Lochs, Moors and Deer-Forests of Scotland* catered for this constituency. New activities made their appearance: mountaineering and cycling. The Cyclists' Touring Club founded in 1878 issued a handbook for Scotland listing recognised hotels, routes and repairers. The motor-car also made its appearance, though to the detriment of first-class receipts on some Highland lines.

But there were poor years as well as good ones. In 1883 it was alleged in a letter to *The Times* that the travelling English public had apparently been scared away by high prices, with the result that hotels were almost empty. Ten years later, the Chicago Columbian Exposition kept many Americans at home who might otherwise have travelled to Europe—the *Scotsman* newspaper estimated that, whereas in a good season something like 10 000 Americans would pass through Edinburgh, 'this year the number will be about 1,000'. Scotland had achieved popularity as a tourist destination, and on a substantial scale, but then as now, it was a competitive world. There were alternative destinations with different attractions and a better climate, and the appeal of Scott, once so potent, was beginning to lose its allure. As in so many other areas of the economy, Scottish tourism was apparently very healthy in the late 19th century, but there were worrying signs for those who cared to look beneath the surface.

Acknowledgement

Much of the primary research in various English Record Offices was funded by the Transport History Trust, to whom I offer my thanks.

Notes

1. *Quarterly Review*, Vol. 1, February, 1809, pp. 180–183.
2. Sir Walter Scott, *The Letters of; 1808–1811*, Edited by H. J. C. Grierson (1932) London, pp. 418–419.
3. Glasgow University Archives, D 42/31/14 New Lanark Visitor's Book, 1821–24.
4. Hereford and Worcester Record Office. BA 3940/66. Porter Family Journal of a tour in Ireland and Scotland, 1823, pp. 42–54.
5. Dundee University Archives. MS/114/1. Thomas Handyside Baxter Diary, 1810–11.
6. Durham Record Office D/Pe/11/62.
7. T. Cook, *Twenty Years on the Rails* (1861), Leicester, p. 30.
8. Thomas Cook Archives. Notes of Introduction to America and Addresses. James McLaren to Thomas Cook, 23rd October 1865.
9. Thomas Cook Archive. Notes of Introduction, Lydia K. Fowler to Thomas Cook, November 6th 1865.
10. Northamptonshire Record Office. Cam 852. Major C. A. Markham. Diary of a Walking Holiday in Scotland 1838.
11. Ian Ker, *John Henry Newman, A Biography* (1988), Oxford, p. 672.
12. Hereford and Worcester Record Office, BA 3550 2(ii) Mrs Manby. Journal of a holiday in Scotland, 1859.
13. J. M. Bailey, *England from a Back-window* (1879), Boston, p. 284.
14. E. M. Macarthur, *Iona. The Living Memory of a Crofting Community, 1750–1914* (Edinburgh), 1990, p. 96, citing a letter to the *Scotsman* by James Nicol on the 9th of August 1856.

References

Andrews, M. (1989) *The Search for the Picturesque. Landscape, Aesthetics and Tourism in Britain, 1760–1830*, Part 4:

The Highlands Tour and the Ossianic Sublime, Scholar Press, Aldershot.

Brendon, Piers (1991) *Thomas Cook. 150 Years of Popular Tourism*, Secker & Warburg, London.

Butler, R. W. (1985) 'The evolution of tourism in the Scottish Highlands', *Annals of Tourism Research*, 12(30): 371–392.

Cockburn, Lord (1888) *Circuit Journeys* (1983 edn), Byeway, Hawick.

Durie, A. J. (1992a) 'Tourism in Victorian Scotland: the case of Abbotsford', *Scottish Economic and Social History*, 12.

Durie, A. J. (1992b) 'The better-off tourist in Victorian Scotland: the value of visitors' lists', *Scottish Local History*, 26: 17–18.

Durie, A. J. (1993) 'Bridge of Allan, Queen of Scottish spas: its nineteenth century development as a health resort', *Forth Naturalist and Historian*, 16: 91–103.

Smout, T. C. (1983) 'Tours in the Scottish Highlands from the eighteenth to the twentieth centuries', *Northern Scotland*, 5: 99–121.

52 Destined to fail? An investigation of the Hi-Line destination marketing system

S. M. PRINGLE

Introduction

The failure of the Hi-Line system was reported in *The Scotsman* newspaper of 10 October 1992 by Morton (1992:5). The article which accompanied this headline briefly described the scale of the collapse and reported the views of some of the parties involved. This paper investigates the concept behind Hi-Line, the stages in its development and the reasons for its eventual collapse. It also considers the need for such a system and requirements for success and discusses current destination marketing systems to see if lessons have been learned at Hi-Line's expense.

Destination marketing

The aim of destination marketing is to promote an area, whether city, region or country, and to advertise events, amenities and accommodation within the scheme's catchment area. Most destination marketing organisations offer reservation and sales facilities through which visitors can book accommodation and travel, purchase tickets for local events or arrange sundry services such as insurance or equipment hire. These facilities allow visitors versatility through being able to plan a holiday which exactly matches their requirements while removing many of the coordination problems by enabling all accommodation and tickets reservations to be made through one point of contact. An additional benefit for the visitor comes from dealing with an organisation which can offer advice based on local knowledge of the destination area.

The origins of Hi-Line

Perceived need for the system

The Highlands and Islands Development Board (HIDB) was established with the aim of assisting social and economic development of the Scottish Highlands and Islands. Part of its remit was the creation and development of industry, including tourism.

The area which the organisation covered includes a diverse range of visitor attractions, accommodation and related services. These appeared to lend themselves well to inclusion in multi-centred holidays but, in the absence of a mechanism to coordinate bookings, arranging an itinerary could prove to be very time-consuming. In the view of the HIDB, the effective promotion of these properties and facilities to a worldwide market required a centralised, coordinated marketing operation. This would offer a service which freed visitors from the laborious process of identifying and reserving accommodation by providing a tailor-made holiday creation service.

The proposed system

The decision to develop such a facility coincided with the emergence within tourism marketing circles of new ideas about linking properties electronically to a central reservations office. Computer-based hotel reservation systems and holiday sales facilities had been in use since the 1970s. The extension of this to public sector tourism marketing was given serious consideration and three pilot schemes were launched, one of these being Hi-Line, the other two being in England and Wales.

The challenge to Hi-Line's developers was to produce a facility capable of supporting existing marketing operations. The end product had to be able to represent adequately a wide range of individual properties and make information about these available to an international market. The system which was proposed took the form of a central office which acted on behalf of and coordinated the efforts of the fifteen area tourist boards (ATBs) associated with the scheme. Consultants commissioned to conduct a feasibility study indicated that such a scheme was feasible but that detailed assessment of the technical aspects would also be necessary.

A study was undertaken to investigate the possibility of implementing a computer-based facility which could handle the management and communication requirements. The technical consultants reported that it was possible to implement such a system. Their proposal was based on a central minicomputer which would hold and process all records. The system would run software which had already been developed and would need only minor modification to meet the requirements of the specification.

ATBs would access the system through terminals connected by dialling in, using the telephone network, allowing them to perform inventory management on behalf of hotels in their area. They would also act as agents of Hi-Line and promote its use where possible. Members of the public would be able to make bookings by telephone, either through the central reservation office or through intermediaries such as the ATBs or tourist information centres.

The findings and recommendations of the consultants' reports were considered and the decision was made to launch the venture. The start-up and running costs of the venture were to be met initially by public sector funding and through commission charges, although it was proposed that the scheme would eventually be self-financing. Investment came from HIDB and the ATBs situated within its catchment area. Grant assistance was to be available until the company had become self-financing, with this period of growth and stabilisation being expected to last five years.

The system in operation

Launch of the system

Appropriate computer hardware was identified and purchased. Offices were located in Dingwall. Highlands and Islands Tourism, Information and Booking Services Ltd was formed as a private limited company to develop and operate the facility with two staff plus a manager. The company went into business in January 1984, trading as Hi-Line. The original objectives, reiterated by Hill and Wayne (1988:3), were:

> To contribute to the Development of Tourism and the Local Tourism Economy by:
>
> - providing a reservation service to the tourism marketing enterprise of others (mainly in the public sector) by making it easier for potential visitors to fulfil their holiday intentions;
> - offering an excellent holiday planning and booking service to potential holiday makers to the areas covered;
> - operating the service at no cost to the marketing enterprises.

Early problems

Hi-Line experienced a wide variety of problems from the outset. Many of these were technical. The operation of a system which depended on telecommunications to such an extent proved to be fraught with problems. Inadequacies were exposed in the computer program, which spent its entire working life under development. It was never able to perform management information reporting or the accounting functions which had been specified originally.

Organisational and procedural problems compounded the situation. The company's three staff were responsible for training ATB staff *in situ* throughout the region. They also maintained the central system and therefore had little time to market the system. ATBs were left to promote Hi-Line locally and to recruit hoteliers into the scheme.

The company reported a good winter during 1985/86 but the summer of 1986 was poor. Hi-Line's inability to launch active promotions during the downturn caused it problems which were only remedied when HIDB undertook a late-season campaign in the autumn of 1986. Following this mixed year and beset by a wide variety of problems, the future of the company became uncertain. HIDB granted the company a stay of execution by introducing new management and injecting funding for further development work.

Reorganisation and recovery

The company reorganised extensively to overcome its early setbacks. The aims and objectives were revised. The system was redesigned and was used in a more restricted form as a central facility for making and recording bookings. The telecommunications links to ATBs were withdrawn, although the use of an alternative communications method based on Viewdata was immediately considered as a possible replacement. More effort was made to contract directly with hoteliers. The overriding consideration was the provision of quality service to the customer since this was identified as being the source of reward. Hi-Line's role was defined as that of being an adjunct to the marketing activities of other enterprises and its aim was to provide a central facility to assist in the promotion of these. Commission rates charged to hotels were revised from the original 10% to 12.5% for direct bookings or 15% for those received through travel agents.

The following years saw an increase of turnover and a reduction of the grant requirement as Hi-Line established itself. Research into Hi-Line's business by Arthur Young (Consultants) in summer 1987 reported that Hi-Line was succeeding in encouraging new business into its area and that users considered that the service being offered was excellent. The survey involved telephone follow-up interviews with approximately 10% of the visitors who had used Hi-Line to make bookings. Of those interviewed, 40% were found to be on their first visit to the Highlands and Islands and 96% said that they would make use of the system again. Accommodation providers also praised the system's ability to bring them business, guarantee payment and provide adequate representation of their area.

Anticipating the withdrawal of public funding in 1988, the company managed to reach the point where it could meet its own operating costs. However, it could not afford to stand still. The aim was now to restructure in order to reduce the financial burden on HIDB. This involved considerable change to the company and its business plan.

The need for expansion

An important objective was to achieve profitability by the early 1990s. Research indicated that the vast increase in turnover required could only be achieved through considerable growth of the company. This could not be accomplished while Hi-Line confined its activities to the Highlands and Islands area. A plan to extend its coverage was adopted with the eventual aim being to offer a service to accommodation providers throughout all of rural Scotland.

On the basis of this scheme, a business forecast was drawn up in 1988 which indicated that the company could make the transition to profitability during the 1990/91 financial year with predicted profits of almost £60 000. Perth and Stirling were chosen as targets for the first phase of the expansion, scheduled for 1990.

The costs of expansion

The original computer system operated by Hi-Line had never been capable of meeting the demands imposed on it. Extension of Hi-Line's catchment area as outlined in the 1988 business plan required more powerful and reliable data processing. A firm of consultants was hired to specify hardware and software which could meet the new requirements. Their recommendations were acted upon and a new system was procured in 1989, becoming operational in October of that year. The software was still under development at this point but the system took reservations and performed the basic functions required of it.

The acquisition of the new system involved considerable outlay. This was met in part through a grant from HIDB and also through an increase of share capital to £500 000. Following this, the HIDB share holding was 30% with another 30% in the hands of corporate shareholders and the remainder with private individuals.

The restructured company was launched in the private sector in 1989. With the change of name to Tourism Services Scotland Ltd and revised financial status came new responsibilities. Commission-based income was needed to keep the company going. Earning this depended on the company's being able to offer the right products and services to the appropriate market.

The search for a wider market

Increasing its catchment area enlarged the range of properties which Hi-Line represented but it also needed to reach a wider market if it was to increase its turnover. Several possible avenues were explored during the late 1980s and early 1990s.

Hill and Wayne (1988: Appendix E) made mention of a possible collaboration with the BRAVO system. This was a BTA-sponsored scheme which planned to act as a switch between airline computer reservation systems and those such as Hi-Line which were operated at regional or national level. Hi-Line's directors indicated enthusiasm for establishing a link with BRAVO. This could have provided a large market for the services offered through Hi-Line in return for the effort of preparing 'ready-made' packages for sale on-line through the combined systems.

To secure more overseas business, Hi-Line introduced a free fax service for selected travel agents. This provided 24-hour service and the company guaranteed a response to enquiries within 36 hours. It was hoped to offer an interactive service allowing agents direct access to Hi-Line's database from a terminal for on-line bookings.

The USA was seen as an important potential market for Hi-Line. The company made use of the Special Counsellor on Travel to Scotland (SCOTS) promotion to the travel trade in North America and received 'encouraging interest' although little returned in the way of business. By the end of 1991, plans were under way to provide a live link to the Leisure SABRE facility of the SABRE global distribution system which would have made Hi-Line directly accessible to thousands of travel agents in the USA and around the world.

The end of the line

Financial forecasts, facts and figures

Many of the long-term plans mentioned previously were contained in a paper covering the first years of Hi-Line's operation by Wayne (1991). Delivering this at a conference in Assisi in November 1991, the company's managing director Ned Wayne gave a very positive view of prospects and reported that 1991 had been a record year for Hi-Line. This optimism was echoed in the chairman's report for that year. However, less than a year later, the company had gone into receivership.

Despite Hi-Line's apparently successful operations, its financial situation was always precarious. While in receipt of assistance from HIDB, Hi-Line had seen a steady growth of turnover with a general reduction of losses as shown in Tables 52.1 and 52.2. Grants produced an even

Table 52.1 *Hi-Line turnover record*

Turnover	84/85	85/86	86/87	87/88	88/89	89/90	90/91	91/92
Predicted	—	—	—	—	1723	3321	4335	5127
Actual	535	621	912	1087	1182	900	1280	—

Source of figures: Highland and Islands Tourism, Information and Booking Services Ltd (1985, 1986, 1987, 1988) and Tourism Services Scotland Ltd (1990, 1991, 1992).

balance sheet for the first four years of trading. However, turnover for the first years in revised ownership compare badly with predicted figures. Although the accounts for 1991 showed an operating profit, the company's accumulated losses were mounting and had reached more than £73 000 by the end of 1991. The chairman's statement in the company's final published accounts, published in 1992, reported that it was hoped to be able to maintain the company on a going-concern basis and that renegotiation of contracts was under way with HIE, the company's major customer and shareholder. However, the state of Hi-Line's financial affairs worsened until, with debts reported to have reached approximately £300 000, the company could no longer continue trading. It went into receivership in October 1992.

Post mortem

Cause of debt

While the financial figures tell their own story, the reasons for the failure are somewhat recondite.

Hi-Line's collapse indicates that, although the scheme appeared to address a genuine requirement, not all of the factors necessary for success were present.

The company's business forecast was based on the continuation of growth in its original market combined with an increasing volume of business from other parts of Scotland as the service expanded. These figures were based on conservative estimates of growth and the company had undertakings from marketing enterprises to make use of its services as its geographical coverage increased.

Many problems which the company's directors could not possibly have foreseen lay ahead, however, and several factors acted against its success.

1989/90 was, in its chairman's words, always going to be difficult for Hi-Line. A move to new premises and the introduction of the new computer system resulted in considerable disruption and took its toll on the resources and staff time. An attempt to involve the company in the 'SCOTLAND 90' campaign run by the Scottish Tourist Board was unsuccessful owing to problems with the promotional material. The summer of that year saw very poor business and the company was forced to cut its staff and revise its business plan.

During its first four years, between 30% and 40% of Hi-Line's turnover had been generated by winter visitors who had come to ski. The service which Hi-Line offered skiers included the arrangement of travel, insurance, accommodation, ski hire, tuition and lift passes. This combination of products generated considerable commission earnings and contributed significantly to Hi-Line's fortunes. Financial projections were based on the assumption that income from skiing-related business would continue to be regular and reliable. However, the unpredictable weather intervened. The winters of 1988/89 and 1989/90 were very mild with negligible snowfalls. Skiing was extremely limited and visitor numbers were much lower than average. Reduced demand for accommodation and services meant lost business for Hi-Line and contributed to its reported turnover falling far short of the business plan prediction.

The company's problems were compounded by the worsening economic conditions in the UK during the early 1990s. The recession may have increased domestic tourism by reducing the number of people taking holidays abroad, but with USA and European economies also suffering, the number of tourists from these sources was correspondingly reduced. With fewer visitors, Hi-Line's commission-based income again suffered.

The number of US tourists in Europe decreased during the Gulf War of 1991 as concern over the safety of transatlantic flights reduced visitor numbers, resulting in a generally poor year for tourism.

Table 52.2 *Hi-Line after tax profit/(loss) record*

Profit/(loss)	84/85	85/86	86/87	87/88	88/89	89/90	90/91	91/92
Prediction	—	—	—	—	(42 500)	(14 100)	59 700	101 700
Actual	(72 106)	(77 492)	(47 975)	(43 359)	(52 575)	(15 988)	(19 947)	—
Accumulated	Nil	Nil	Nil	Nil	(52 575)	(53 998)[a]	(73 945)	—

[a]Adjusted figure.
Source of figures: Highlands and Islands Tourism, Information and Booking Services Ltd (1985, 1986, 1987, 1988) and Tourism Services Scotland Ltd (1990, 1991, 1992).

Unfulfilled ambitions

Hi-Line had been born with considerable grant assistance from HIDB which also supported the venture throughout its formative years. The company benefited from the marketing of HIDB, and later HIE, which ensured that Hi-Line was closely linked to all promotions for tourism in its area. The planned expansion of coverage to include all of Scotland would have benefited considerably from a similar arrangement with the Scottish Tourist Board (STB) but this was not forthcoming. This reluctance to adopt a central reservation facility to serve all of Scotland tourism had a profound effect on Hi-Line's long-term plans.

The extent to which the company had pinned its hopes on the creation of a single system for Scotland is obvious from the chairman's statement in the company's report for the year 1990/91. The chairman, D. Alistair Gardner, opined:

> Unfortunately the STB continues to fail to grasp the opportunity of including a central reservation office function in their domestic marketing efforts so development of business outwith the Highlands and Islands continues to be limited. (Hi-Line Annual Report, 1991)

Undoubtedly, Hi-Line's directors were hopeful that, should the STB opt for such a scheme, their system would be chosen as the preferred means of destination marketing for Scotland. In the article describing the collapse of the venture, a HIE spokesman indicated that Hi-Line's turnover represented only one-fifth of 1% of all revenue earned in the Highlands through tourism. In the company's best year, turnover amounted to over £1.28 million. This small fraction could have been increased considerably had the various agencies and tourist boards agreed to use the company as their preferred channel.

The STB defended its reluctance to commit to Hi-Line on the grounds that it could not be seen to be favouring only one of a number of potential booking channels for tourism services and products. Both STB and HIE representatives were also adamant that there was no way in which they could give Hi-Line more backing than had already been provided. The STB had awarded Hi-Line a grant of £65 000 to help with its replacement computer system, thus indicating its support for the scheme. HIE had been involved through its share holding and by its use of Hi-Line in joint promotions, but its research in 1992 had shown that Hi-Line was facing insolvency. It was therefore deemed inappropriate to renew contracts with the company.

Information at the mercy of technology

The company's original plan to provide an on-line information and booking service with remote terminals had been arrived at rationally. It appeared to present a solution to the problem of coordinating accommodation reservations over a wide area. Its implementation did not require elaborate technology. However, it suffered because the system could not cope with the variable quality of the phone service and the delays which this caused. The impact which this had on the company's initial credibility is impossible to estimate and although Hi-Line overcame this particular technical problem, this was only achieved by considerably reducing the service offered. The massive investment made by British Telecom in the late 1980s to upgrade communications facilities in the Highlands and Islands would have helped to overcome some of these problems. However, the company had changed its plans and priorities considerably by the time these improvements had taken place so they brought little in the way of benefit.

The proposed link with the BRAVO system was ill-fated. The 1988 business plan had referred to BRAVO as an 'important market place development'. This computer switch facility would give Hi-Line access to international airline computerised reservation systems through which an increasing volume of international travel bookings were being made. BRAVO approached Hi-Line, considering the company to be a leader in the field of regional computer databases. BRAVO initially planned to become operational in the autumn of 1989 but its launch was postponed and the scheme eventually folded when a major backer pulled out. Lack of support from the trade was cited as the reason for withdrawal.

Hi-Line's management recognised that achievement of its long-term plans called for expansion of markets. Hi-Line would perhaps have benefited from the early access to the important US market via BRAVO had it become operational as planned. In the absence of this stepping stone, alternatives were proposed, with the favoured route involving a link with the widely used and well accepted technology of the SABRE system. However, the rewards and greater financial stability resulting from this would still have been offset considerably by the impact which worldwide recession and the Gulf War had on this market.

The replacement computer system acquired in 1989 had been specified with Hi-Line's expanded role in mind. The full capacity of this system was not utilised by Hi-Line and the company found itself with surplus capacity which was not generating return but for which it had increased its deficit. Although this was not a particularly serious problem, the company was nevertheless fortunate to find a user for this in MinoTel Great Britain.

The cost of quality

One aspect of Hi-Line which users remarked upon was the quality of the service which it provided. The company took great pride in this, but the standards which it set were only achieved at considerable cost. The time taken to process a booking could be as long as twenty minutes. For an enterprise which depended exclusively on turnover for its income, this proved to be too long. However, there was no set limit on the time which staff were allowed to convert an enquiry into a booking. This resulted in the company's being unable to cope with demand at what should have been peak trading periods. This in turn led to lost business, reduced turnover and less commission income.

Had the system evolved as originally planned, the on-line access would eventually have extended beyond the area tourist boards and would have included live access to all the properties represented by the system. This would have allowed Hi-Line staff to process bookings more quickly and increase the profitability of the company. However, the inability of technology to handle the demands made by the original system prevented this goal from ever being accomplished.

Hotel reservations

Even if the technology had been capable of delivering the proposed service, the resistance of the accommodation providers to the Hi-Line scheme had to be overcome.

Research carried out in summer 1993 (S. M. Pringle, unpublished work) indicated that hotels of the size and ownership most common in Hi-Line's catchment area are the least likely to adopt computerised reservation systems. Reasons given for this were that the property was too small to justify the use of a computer, the associated costs were too high, freesale of rooms involved a lack of control, the system could not represent the hotel adequately, and the loss of personal touch from using systems could detract from the appeal of the property.

As a rule, hoteliers involved with Hi-Line were complimentary about the quality of its service. The consultants' report commissioned by Hi-Line in 1987 reported favourable reaction, as did original research in 1993. The initial lack of credibility caused by the failure of the ambitious early system appears to have been overcome. However, there were several aspects of the hotel trade which Hi-Line did not or could not accommodate.

Inadequate explanation to hoteliers of the proposed role and potential benefits of the system appears to have caused problems. Hoteliers were reluctant to pay commission to, and provide an allocation of rooms for, a system which they did not understand. Initially the few hotels represented by the system received little business through it and others were reluctant to sign up because the system did not appear to be doing well. One aspect of Hi-Line which did not suit some properties was its use for the arrangement of single-night accommodation with hotels which were used to, and possibly preferred, holidaymakers who stayed for one or two weeks.

The general feeling in the hotel trade appears to be that its members were not adequately consulted about the way in which properties would be represented or sold and that hotels ended up paying for facilities which they did not need.

In the face of these arguments and given the resistance experienced by the company during the operation of Hi-Line, linking up hotels throughout Scotland could have been a slow, painful and ultimately incomplete process.

Commission costs

Another significant factor which deterred hotels from using Hi-Line was the overhead of commission charges. The cost of using Hi-Line was in line with most reservation systems and agencies. Initially the system had charged 10% of the hotel's rate for bookings which it made. This soon proved to be too little since the company was paying 8% of the hotel's rate as commission on bookings received from travel agents. After restructuring in 1989, the charge levied on hotels was increased to 12.5% or 15% if the booking had originated from a travel agent. Travel agents were still authorised to deduct 8% of the rate.

While the use of commission charges proved to be an easily worked way of financing the company, this was unsatisfactory as the sole source of funds in the long term. The proposed expansion of the system was to involve more third parties, all of whom would have levied their own charges. Had BRAVO or a replacement offering access to global systems ever come to fruition, the commission payments could have been prohibitive. A booking originating from an agency and relayed by SABRE, a switch and Hi-Line to the hotel could involve four layers of commission. Either the hotel would have to increase its room rate to pay commission to all of the parties or Hi-Line would have to pay the three layers above it, resulting in a net loss. With many of the hotels represented by Hi-Line being seasonal, their margins would be extremely stretched when faced with such high commission payments. There was no simple way to overcome this problem.

Buyer behaviour

Another research outcome (S. M. Pringle, unpublished work) was an analysis of the source of hotel bookings.

Of 96 respondents, 25% indicated that bookings direct to the hotel from guests accounted for more than 90% of business while 57% indicated that more than 60% of bookings came this way. In general, the smaller the hotel, the higher the percentage of bookings were direct. Travel agency bookings accounted for 5%. Some properties included in this research were located within the Hi-Line catchment area. Although these results were obtained from a small sample, findings indicated that traditional methods generally found favour with small hotels and their clientele.

The price of pioneering

One factor in Hi-Line's favour was that it had arguably the most experienced management in the field of national computer reservation facilities anywhere in the world. This worked in its favour while the business was making progress but once it hit problems there was nobody else with greater experience to whom they could turn. Of the other national systems started in the early 1980s, the English scheme had collapsed and the Welsh scheme had encountered computerisation problems and ended up as a private marketing company.

Other systems and their aims

Investigation of the factors which resulted in Hi-Line's collapse invites comparison with other destination marketing systems in the UK and elsewhere. While there are several to choose from, two are considered to be particularly comparable, namely the Gulliver system which serves Ireland and the SwissLine system which was set up in Switzerland.

Gulliver

The Gulliver system was initiated by Bord Failte (BFE) and the Northern Ireland Tourist Board (NITB) in 1992. There are distinct similarities between Gulliver and Hi-Line: the development of both resulted from the perceived need to develop tourism as an asset to an area with traditional industry in decline. Both services were intended to offer access on a worldwide basis to all necessary information and facilities for planning and booking a holiday.

The most significant difference between the systems is the funding. Although much of the initial cost of both was met by grants from public or European sources, Gulliver is owned and operated by publicly funded agencies. This relieves the obvious commercial pressure which dogged Hi-Line until its demise.

While funding is important, so too is the technology on which the rapid provision of accurate information depends. The software and hardware on which Gulliver is based was developed by a well-established and experienced supplier, namely Digital Equipment. This augurs well for the service since, with a high degree of dependence being placed on the immediate availability of information, problems with the host system could put the service out of commission. Lack of reliability was a problem for Hi-Line which suffered for being an early entrant to its field. With little relevant experience in industry to call on and a restricted number of systems to choose from, it was held back severely at the start and suffered badly during its formative years as a consequence.

Gulliver also benefits from reliable distribution and maintenance of data through its use of the Minitel Viewdata service. This allows on-line access to accommodation providers for receipt and acknowledgement of bookings or to alter rates and allocation. This facility is reported as being in use by properties with as few as three rooms (Bord Failte, 1993:4) which indicates the problem of signing up properties normally perceived as being too small to benefit from on-line access is being overcome. Use of Viewdata gives tourist information centres and travel agents easy access, which helps Gulliver to reach a wider market. Hi-Line worked towards offering wider access but initial problems with telecommunications links forced plans to be curtailed. The possibility of offering Viewdata access to accommodation providers was mentioned in the 1987 company report and again in the 1991 paper, but this did not materialise. Once again, Hi-Line appears to have suffered for its ambitious plans and the inability of technology to help it to deliver its promises.

Gulliver covers the whole of Ireland and it is closely linked to the marketing of all tourism by BFE and NITB. In comparison, Hi-Line's operation was always associated with a part of Scotland which is seen as remote even by natives of the country. The effort and resources required to extend its role to include all of rural Scotland imposed considerable demands on the company at a stage in its development when it would have benefited from a period of consolidation. While Hi-Line may have been unrealistic in its hopes of what the STB might offer it, the tourist trade's perceptions of the company might have been enhanced if it had enjoyed a national role. However, this was neither suggested nor promised by the STB.

In the long term, it is likely that the most significant difference between the systems will be in the combined areas of ownership, support and funding. The involvement of two national tourist organisations with their combined marketing campaigns and vested interest in the success of the system should be sufficient to help Gulliver weather the inevitably unpredictable financial and technical demands made on it as it develops. With tourism being subject to the vagaries of the world's political and economic climates as well as the even less predictable nature of the elements, this is the most likely reason why Gulliver should succeed while the seemingly comparable Hi-Line venture folded.

SwissLine

While the Gulliver system appears to be meeting its objectives, the SwissLine destination marketing facility compares with Hi-Line in one respect: it failed in 1992.

The system was set up as an independent company under the ownership of the Swiss National Tourist Office, the Swiss government, Swiss Federal Railways, Swissair, the Swiss Hoteliers' Association and the country's post and telecommunications operators (Infocentre, 1992). Initial funding amounted to £5 million. The aims were similar to those of Hi-Line with the intention being to offer national, regional and local information as well as a direct reservation system. As with Gulliver and Hi-Line, hotels would have live access for inventory maintenance. Worldwide distribution would involve airline CRS. All of the parties involved were optimistic about the company's plans and prospects. However, a lack of public and private sector support forced the venture into liquidation in 1992 (Vlitos-Rowe, 1992). The significant factor which emerged from the brief report of the enterprise's failure was that 85% of Swiss make their own reservations directly rather than through travel agents or tour operators. This compares with the figures given earlier for UK hotel bookings and again raises the question of the need for hotels to offer on-line access through destination marketing or other computer reservation systems. The lack of commission income resulting from this direct buying may not have been the cause of SwissLine's collapse, but factors reported in the account of the system's failure are very similar to those which overtook Hi-Line.

Lessons to be learned

Ned Wayne made mention of problems facing computer-based destination marketing in his address to a conference in late 1991 (Wayne, 1991):

> If the area [served by the system] and the number of accommodation units is small, then a computerised Central Reservation Office is unlikely to be financially viable, especially if that area is not synonymous with an internationally perceived destination.

> The cost of setting up a Central Reservation Office to support public sector tourism marketing in the first instance is probably not viable for the private sector.

These words turned out to be somewhat prophetic in the light of the next year's events.

In the meantime, the destination marketing system which appears to be most successful is Gulliver. Its role as the destination marketing system for Ireland gives it an identity which eluded Hi-Line. It has continuing financial backing and marketing support from the public sector. Use of existing communications technology allows the system to offer access and distribution facilities to a wide range of users and suppliers without the overheads of a proprietary network. Much of the necessary pioneering work has already been done by schemes such as Hi-Line. Developers of other schemes would do well to observe its progress over the next few years.

In Scotland, the nascent 'TITAN' project (Edinburgh Tourist Board, 1993:1) aims to offer a destination marketing and reservation system with links to similar facilities in other European countries. It is interesting to note that the first stated aim of the scheme is 'To increase the cost effectiveness of tourism destination information and reservation services in Europe'.

Summary

The Hi-Line scheme was founded on a perceived and tested need for a destination marketing system. However, it suffered from several problems:

- it made ambitious use of inadequate technology;
- its successful privatisation required long-term financial stability which demanded rapid early growth;
- the associated expansion required vastly improved facilities which involved high capital costs;
- successive poor skiing seasons resulted in reduced trade and low turnover;
- the low throughput resulted in poor cost-effectiveness, more akin to a public service than a private commercial enterprise;
- links with national marketing did not materialise.

The company had ambitious plans. While some of them were founded on sound predictions, many were the result of wishful thinking or were simply unrealistic. The venture certainly appears to have had more bad luck than good and the widespread recession, public sector spending cutbacks and even the weather dealt blows to its finances.

By the time the company went into receivership its grant funding amounted to £225 000 from HIDB and another

£65 000 from STB. Its turnover had increased from £535 000 to a peak of £1 280 000 in the final year for which accounts are available, but the company's figures were always well below the goals set out in the 1988 plan. Although it showed a trading profit, it was carrying a huge burden of debt.

Its precarious financial position obliged HIE to refuse to renew contracts with the company, effectively dealing the final blow to the scheme. Its final debts were reported to be £300 000 and the loss to local employment totalled 12 jobs.

However, the overall cost of Hi-Line's failure cannot be measured only by reference to these but also in terms of the lost potential for the system as a source of revenue in its own right and as a channel for supporting tourism in Scotland, both in and beyond the Highlands and Islands.

Conclusion

The need for coordinated marketing of accommodation, travel and leisure services was recognised by HIDB in 1984 and this requirement is possibly even greater now with the continuing decline of traditional local industry and growing dependence on the service sector, especially tourism.

The one opinion which has been voiced more than any other by contributors to this paper is that, 'Hi-Line was good in concept'. It was also widely renowned for its excellent service quality. However, this was in part responsible for the company's plight, for, although management was quick to react when trade was slack, it did not set targets to increase throughput and turnover when business was good. Hampered by the inability of computer and communications systems to support the provision of high-speed, high-quality service, the company was forever unable to break out of the circle which linked its turnover, its debt and the technology at its disposal.

The Hi-Line system certainly suffered for its early entry to a market which even now may not be ready for the enterprising use of technology which was proposed. The system appears to have been operated in the most pragmatic way possible. While the process of restructuring was disruptive, when the need arose to alter the company's way of operation or reduce its staff, management was not slow to act. However, the transition from what started as a public service to what needed to be a commercially aware, competitive private sector company was not really accomplished with any degree of success.

The factors which contributed to the final demise of the venture undoubtedly include the economic strictures imposed by the recession, loss of business resulting from the Gulf War and poor winters which caused considerable loss of revenue through the lack of skiing. The service also lacked the sales push which its operators had hoped for from hotels and area tourist boards. The elevation of Hi-Line to the role of a national system to represent Scotland could have increased its turnover sufficiently to save it. Had it enjoyed this status, bodies such as STB would perhaps have been more reluctant to let the company expire. If the company had not suffered these setbacks and had it managed to secure a formally recognised extended role, the system might have flourished. However, the company's eventual dependence on commission-based income had serious consequences for it and the hotels which it represented. The compounding effect which accompanied each layer of expansion only served to worsen the predicament as increased turnover threatened to result in further reductions in profit.

On paper, it would appear that a system can survive in the private sector without assistance. However, given the small margins available from the businesses represented, and in view of the fact that such a service acts as a useful middleman but can be bypassed if its costs to its customers become too high, it appears that the unreliable nature of trade in the harsh commercial world dictates that without guaranteed long-term funding, such a scheme is not viable.

The most likely source of this support is central or local government through enterprise schemes, as in the case of Gulliver. Even recognised national systems are not certain of success, however, and the availability of funding is not sufficient to guarantee survival: SwissLine enjoyed both of these supposed advantages but still collapsed.

The determinants governing success or failure of such a scheme are not simple. Gulliver appears to indicate that destination marketing requires the correct mixture of a number of factors. This is supported by comments made by representatives of STB who identified the availability of finance, management, marketing and technology as being vital factors for the successful operation of such a scheme.

No particular organisation and no single factor can be blamed for Hi-Line's unfortunate end; nor can it be shown that improved financial arrangements or technology alone would have saved the venture. In conclusion, the Hi-Line scheme appears to have suffered throughout its existence for being so ambitious and so pioneering. Its creators should be commended for helping to open up new avenues for tourism marketing.

References

Bord Failte (1993) 'Gulliver update', promotional brochure, Issue 2, Bord Failte, Dublin.

Edinburgh Tourist Board (1993) Tourism Information Technology Access Network (TITAN) proposal document.

Highlands and Islands Tourism, Information and Booking Services Ltd (1985) *Company Annual Report 1984/1985*, pp. 3–6.

Highlands and Islands Tourism, Information and Booking Services Ltd (1986) *Company Annual Report 1985/1986*, pp. 2–6.

Highlands and Islands Tourism, Information and Booking Services Ltd (1987) *Company Annual Report 1986/1987*, pp. 2–5.

Highlands and Islands Tourism, Information annd Booking Services Ltd (1988) *Company Annual Report 1987/1988*, pp. 3–5.

Hill, Martin and Wayne, Edward (1988) 'Hi-Line: forward to 1992', internal planning document obtained by personal communication.

Infocentre Ltd (1992) 'Link Tourism Technology News', promotional brochure, Infocentre Travel Systems Ltd, London.

Morton, Tom (1992) 'Blame for collapse denied by Tourist Board', *The Scotsman*, 10 October.

Tourism Services Scotland Ltd (1990) *Company Annual Report 1988/1989*, pp. 4–7.

Tourism Services Scotland Ltd (1991) *Company Annual Report 1989/1990*, pp. 3–6.

Tourism Services Scotland Ltd (1992) *Company Annual Report 1990/1991*, pp. 4–8.

Vlitos-Rowe, Irene (1992) 'Destination database and management systems', *EIU Travel & Tourism Analyst*, 5: 84–108.

Wayne, Edward (1991) 'Hi-Line: a case study of a working computerised central reservation office in public sector tourism', Proceedings of International Conference on Telecommunications in Public Tourism Organisations, Assisi, Italy.

53 Scotland's newest visitor attractions

R. SMITH

For almost two hundred years Scotland has been thought of as an interesting country to visit. An early 19th-century trickle of highly educated and well-connected European travellers has swollen in the late 20th century to a regular tide of visitors from most parts of the world. The travel motivations of the 1.7 million overseas visitors who came to Scotland in 1992 (STB, 1993a) are likely to have been complex and varied. It is also probable that the satisfactions which they derived from a stay in this peripheral province of northern Europe were diverse. On the basis of additional questions placed in the British Tourist Authority's 1991 'Overseas visitor survey', the Scottish Tourist Board is able to tell us that the aspect of the country most liked by overseas visitors was Scotland's scenery. This scored an 86% approval rating, placing this attribute some way ahead of 'the friendly people' (74%) and 'castles, churches, museums and sites of historic interest' (73%) (STB, 1993b).

Of course these scores reflect what people felt about the country after deciding to come, rather than their pre-existing perceptions of Scotland as a travel destination. A recent market study of Western European residents suggests that Scotland is not seen as offering good value for money, providing good food and drink, or having available much for children to do (Scott, 1994). But there is a good chance that a large part of the satisfaction felt by the respondents to the earlier BTA survey with the scenery, people and—for want of a better word, heritage—of Scotland, was derived from the meeting of long-cherished expectations.

This reminds us that Scotland has an important place in the history of tourism. For Scotland was among the world's first Romantic destinations. Whereas the European Grand Tour took the 18th-century gentleman traveller to continental European cities and great houses mainly in order to study the remains of past civilisations and to experience contemporary cultural life, the pioneering 19th-century visitor to Scotland was typically in search of a feeling, a mood—a Romantic experience. This did not require to be sustained by what actually existed—at least not in the same way as the Grand Tour was sustained by archducal art collections or the ruins of classical civilisation. Instead, it was the mystery of Scotland, the thrilling glimpses of a heroic Celtic otherness as mediated by the works of 'Ossian' and Scott, which drew the enthusiast to the scenes of an imagined historical Caledonia (Womack, 1989). It was not an encounter with a real past that was sought, but a close and emotional engagement with a literary vision. A landscape that had previously seemed merely dreary or horrid now provided ample opportunity to heighten the intensity of the experience by offering the chance of personal indulgence in the new taste for wild places and rugged mountains.

Although the literary antecedents are largely forgotten and certainly unread, the feelings they invented linger with us to this day. Scotland's lochs and hills and glens are now a prime asset in the country's efforts to sell itself in the international marketplace. Scottish tourist agencies, with welcome back-up from the more generous promotional budgets of whisky companies, are relentless in their presentation of images of the Scottish landscape, together with its more colourful denizens.

The later 19th century added some new aesthetic sensibilities. By that time it was usually politically comfortable to feel a certain melancholy at the enforced clearance of much of the native Highland population from the land. The empty straths of the Scottish Highlands were confirmed as the repository of historical regret. And in our own day, as new fashions in sensibility sweep the developed world, extra variations can still be added. As the international media coverage of the 1993 Braer disaster off Shetland seemed to underline, dramatic threats to the environment make our rugged and underexploited landscapes seem all the more unspoilt and precious.

Visitor attractions are often said to be at the heart of tourism. Yet, because of its historical development as a tourist destination, Scotland has perhaps been less dependent on organised visitor facilities than other travel destinations. On an international scale the country has several other enviable tourism assets, including some well-known events. Every year Edinburgh hosts the world's biggest arts festival, although rather astonishingly a recent study has shown that the mawkish and militaristic event known as the Tattoo, a classic example of the theory of 'staged authenticity', produces much greater economic returns for the city than the International Festival or the fringe (STB, 1992). The high international profile of Scotland as the home of golf is undoubtedly a growing asset as the game gains in popularity with the world's business elites, and one which the 'Tourism—the

State of the Art' organisers were happy to cash in on by offering attendance at the Open Championship as an add-on option to delegates. Scotland also has what may be a unique instance of a persistent non-event working as an element of attraction—in the sinuous but evanescent form of the Loch Ness Monster. Local entrepreneurship has, however, seen to it that there are at least two interpretive centres to console and divert the disappointed visitor.

Specific individual attractions, in the sense of organised facilities for visitors, are not an important element in determining the image of Scotland abroad. Edinburgh Castle might register as a 'must see' for most potential first-time visitors, but thereafter one suspects that the 'castles, churches, museums and sites of historic interest' which were enjoyed by 73% of the overseas visitors who actually came here are only dimly glimpsed from abroad, shrouded perhaps in that lingering Romantic mist.

The purpose of this paper is to consider some current issues in visitor attraction development in Scotland. It is desirable at the outset to be clear what the term means. The STB have worked up a useful definition, which is gaining currency in the field (Leisure Consultants, 1990; Yale, 1991) and which it seems reasonable to adopt here. In the STB view a visitor attraction is:

> A permanently established excursion destination, a primary purpose of which is to allow public access for entertainment, interest or education, rather than being principally a retail outlet or a venue for sporting, theatrical or film performances. It must be open to the public without prior booking, for published periods each year, and should be capable of attracting tourists or day visitors as well as local residents. (STB, 1993a)

This definition has the great merit of emphasising that visitor attractions perform a multiple role. As well as catering for a tourist market they also serve a local residential market—and what can often be a substantial day-visitor market. Apart from providing a breakdown by Scottish local government region, the STB's annual voluntary (and therefore incomplete) survey of attractions is presented in terms of 'free' versus 'paid' facilities, and is additionally broken down into the categories set out in Table 53.1.

The dominance of 'museums/art galleries' and 'country parks' is evident. However, it should be borne in mind that 'country parks', which are usually administered by local authorities and do not charge admission, are because of their very openness much more difficult to monitor than other types of attraction, and are much more likely to be visited by locals than tourists. When 'country parks' are excluded from the figures, local authorities still emerge as the key providers in Scotland. In 1992 attractions operated

Table 53.1   *Visitor attractions: 1992 results by category*

Category	Percentage of visits 1992	Total visits 1992
Historic houses	5	1 581 187
Castles	11	3 422 513
Monuments	<0.5	98 305
Churches/abbeys/cathedrals	2	623 214
Gardens	5	1 480 963
Museums & art galleries	27	8 401 269
Wildlife/zoos/safari parks	4	1 292 225
Interpretation/visitor centres	8	2 596 370
Industrial/craft premises	5	1 668 075
Country parks	27	8 545 525
Miscellaneous	6	1 747 26
Total		31 456 912

Source: Scottish Tourist Board, Research Handbook, RH26, 1993.

by them drew 26% of the total visits, those operated by the private sector 24%. While it may be true that this dominant position is sustained by the fact that many municipal attractions do not charge for admission, it is nevertheless clear that local authority museums, galleries etc., in spite of tightening constraints on public spending, continue to be of vital importance to Scotland's tourism offering.

In 1992 those properties of Historic Scotland (the government heritage agency) where a record is kept drew 10% of all visits; those of the National Trust for Scotland (a voluntary, mass membership organisation) a further 8%. In terms of the care and interpretation of Scotland's built heritage, however, the importance of these two bodies is greater than appears from the visitor statistics. Historic Scotland has 330 monuments in its care, together with the royal residence Holyrood House and the Royal Parks. Its flagship property is Edinburgh Castle, which with around one million visitors each year is the most visited 'paid' attraction in Scotland. Historic Scotland is undertaking expensive programmes at both Edinburgh and Stirling castles in order to raise the standard of facilities and to improve the effectiveness of interpretation for the visiting public (see Foley, Chapter 83 in this volume). The National Trust for Scotland, which enjoys the support of some 234 000 paid-up members, makes 114 of its properties accessible to the public. Its lead attraction is Culzean Castle and Country Park in Ayrshire, which in 1992 drew 353 000 visits. A large part of the real significance of the National Trust for Scotland lies, however, in the fact that, like its sister organisation for the rest of the UK, it has led the way in developing services both for its members and for other visitors to its properties.

Although the National Trust for Scotland is proud of its voluntary status, it might be considered to be a quasi-public organisation. Its primary aim is not the generation of profit. It also holds certain legal privileges and derives a significant part of its income from government grants. When the provision of local authorities, Historic Scotland and the NTS is taken together it is clear that there is a substantial public sector factor at work in the operation of Scottish visitor attractions. Together these bodies look after and interpret significant elements of Scotland's built heritage.

Of course, many of the properties which HS and NTS have taken on are redundant relics of ruling class power. These remain with us in the form of castles, fortified houses and—still embodying considerable political potency—the later country houses of the landed elite. All of these properties were built to impose and it is not surprising that they are held to be an important part of the national heritage. The strength of their construction has helped them to survive better than more modest buildings. Also, in spite of some criticism, there appears to be a broad consensus that the cultural capital accumulated by the owners of these properties, whether it be the buildings themselves or their contents, deserves to be protected and is worth making accessible to all. This, it should be pointed out, is an attitude which can vary according to the urgency of historical circumstances, as witness the almost complete destruction of church fitments and furnishings at the time of the Protestant Reformation in Scotland, or the burning of the big houses of the Anglo-Irish ascendancy in the 20th-century struggle for Irish independence. Yet in spite of their bias towards the architectural legacy of the historically dominant classes, there are certain other aspects of the work of HS and NTS which relate to more plebeian aspects of Scottish heritage. One of the author's favourite HS properties is the charming Biggar Gas Works. And the NTS, through its Little Houses Scheme, has made an important contribution to preserving the appearance and vitality of places such as Dunkeld and Culross. With the opening of Robert Smail's print workshop at Innerleithen it has recently diversified into industrial heritage. Local authorities also frequently intervene to support elements of built heritage under threat.

The modern consensus about what is worth preserving and presenting now extends very widely. Throughout the 1970s and 1980s, and often in the teeth of central government indifference, some imaginative pressure groups such as the Dundee Heritage Trust, together with a few supportive councils and other local agencies, have created visitor attractions which relate in a direct and immediate way to Scotland's industrial and agricultural past (see work by Arnold, Brockie and Hill—all in Fladmark (1993)).

New Lanark, an 18th-century industrial village which drew 149 000 visitors to its Visitor Centre in 1992, and a small number of other industrial heritage sites, have managed to establish themselves in a relatively short time as popular attractions. What is particularly striking in such a small—and from the industrial heritage point of view, significant—country is that there is no overall strategic plan to guide the development of industrial heritage attractions or to ensure that disappearing industries are presented to a public audience in any kind of representative way (Ewing, 1989). One of the most obvious examples of the episodic nature of industrial heritage provision is the fact that Glasgow, once the shipbuilding capital of the world, has no popular interpretive facilities for its most famous industry. The body which campaigns to secure a Maritime Heritage Centre for the city has so far failed to secure sufficient public funding to achieve its ends. Any hope of its managing to do so is, it would appear, predicated on a major leisure operator being persuaded to jointly develop the preferred site. Nor is the precariousness of the project a matter which can be explained in terms of museum professionals' disdain for meretricious heritage gimmickry. Certainly, the Scottish Maritime Museum at Irvine and the Scottish Fisheries Museum at Anstruther do present elements of the national maritime heritage, but their displays could not be considered to be a full representation of shipbuilding history. Even plans for housing machinery in a re-erected engine shop at Irvine will not change the situation. The fact is that there is plenty of room for both a museological collection-based approach and an interpretive 'experience'—and so far nothing much of either in the historic heartland of Scottish shipbuilding.

In Scotland a considerable amount of work has been undertaken since the 1970s by public bodies to prepare regional interpretive plans (Fladmark, 1993:125ff). Much of this appears to be of a preliminary nature and remains to be put into effect. It also relates mostly to the countryside rather than town or city centres. Although much restoration and development activity is being undertaken in the historic old town of Stirling through a linked programme supported by several public bodies (The Stirling Initiative, no date), some five years after the publication of comprehensive proposals (KPMG, 1989) for the enhancement of Scotland's prime tourist thoroughfare—Edinburgh's Royal Mile—little visible difference can be seen in the interpretive provision or basic visitor-friendliness of this prominent route. This might be said to be a consequence of having to seek agreement from all parties interested in what is still intended to be a living locality. In both Stirling and Edinburgh improving heritage interpretation has proved to be tied closely to other issues. These include not only encouraging new or improving existing visitor attractions, but also establishing effective partnership organisations, deploying better visitor management techniques and having regard to community priorities.

As throughout the UK, many visitor attractions have been opened or improved in Scotland during recent years. These often have a heritage base. Some of them offer high standards of interpretation (Centre for Environmental Interpretation, 1993). Brown (1988) has drawn attention to the very rapid development of the UK visitor attractions sector during the 1980s, its Cinderella status in the tourism industry overcome by a host of new attractions, many breaking new ground, and by much greater professionalism at all levels. In the UK the rapid pace of development was not being fully sustained even before the full onset of the recession. Writing in 1990, Robinson observed:

> The 1980's were a decade of plenty during which the number of visitor attractions in the United Kingdom nearly doubled; plenty of creative ideas, plenty of sites for new developments, plenty of listed buildings and industrial heritage assets for enhancement, plenty of quaysides and docks, plenty of customers with plenty of money to spend. As the decade drew to a close, there is clear evidence that the tide has turned. Tougher times have arrived.

Although the downturn in new developments has been far from catastrophic, it remains a fact that in Scotland as elsewhere in the UK relatively little has been undertaken in the field of visitor attraction development by the private sector, largely because of the short tourist season and the weakness of the Scottish domestic market. There remain several important commercially conceived developments which have been an unconscionable time gestating, and several others which it is now fairly clear will never be born (Johnstone, 1993). Opening visitor attractions in Scotland as anything other than an add-on activity to some other core business (e.g. the successful visitor centre at the Baxter's food processing plant), or without a substantial element of public funding, is a very risky business indeed.

It is public development funding which has made the difference in terms of getting many projects established. Tourism planners in Scotland have been aware for some time that the range of things for visitors to do in wet weather is too narrow. As a result they have sought to encourage the provision of more and better visitor attractions (Scottish Development Agency, 1988; STB, no date; STB et al., 1989; STB and Scottish Enterprise, no date). In the last years in which it retained a

development function through the allocation of funds under Section 4 of the 1969 Development of Tourism Act, the Scottish Tourist Board explicitly preferred to spend the money on developing visitor attractions rather than on, for example, helping provide new accommodation. Thus the STB Annual Report for 1992–93 (p. 12) states: 'The Board continues to target projects which will give visitors things to do and see and this category attracted 71% of our funds spread over 40 attractions'. The economic development agencies in Scotland have also been proactive in this field, in some cases over a number of years. Latterly there has been felt to be a particular need for attractions which appeal to families and provide a range of different features.

This is more or less in line with the perceived trends for the 1990s in the UK market for commercial attractions and independent museums (Leisure Consultants, 1990; Middleton, 1990). For example, Leisure Consultants point to the projected increase in the child population (8% by the year 2000) and older age groups (ie. 45–54s, the over 65s, and later in the 1990s the 35–44s), and conclude:

> The major implications of these trends are that some of the more traditional, more sedate attractions, such as gardens, museums, historic houses, can expect support from the gradual ageing of the adult population. More physically participative attractions like theme parks, and others like zoos and safari parks, which are supported by the family formers with their children/teenagers, will have to cope with fewer numbers in certain key visitor groups. They will need to consider how they can try to broaden their appeal, and draw more from the expanding older age groups; they will also need to adapt to changes in family structures, and in the composition of the groups who visit.

Middleton expects a rather larger increase in the number of children of school age (+ 17% on the 1991 figure) and sees this as 'the main positive trend for museums over the next decade'. He also considers other factors to be significant such as: the growing importance of older people in the 1990s; the development in the last twenty years of a more affluent society; the increase since 1973 of that section of the population which should be considered 'inner directed'; the greater number of more educated visitors by the year 2000; certain positive changes in personal mobility (although there are some negative ones); growing demand from schools; positive indicators for growth in certain tourism markets. These led him to estimate that between 1989 and 2000 there could be an increase in volume potential for museum visits in Great Britain of 30%.

Surveys conducted for the Leisure Consultants study revealed that the six strongest influences on consumers' decisions to visit an attraction were (in descending order):

- a chance to learn and find out about things
- facilities undercover and protected from weather
- attractive buildings and surroundings
- some place to have a meal or snack
- a chance to have fun
- admission cost.

Leisure Consultants also expect the market for attractions in Great Britain to grow, and to be accompanied by an increased frequency of visit and greater spending on admissions. They speculate that:

> The most significant area of personal values as far as attractions are concerned seems to revolve around the desire for the authentic and genuine, for quality and integrity in what is offered. This will appear in several guises, notably:
>
> - more stress on the meaning and value of activities
> - the influence of green issues
> - a focus on the present and future, at least as much as on the past.

Very little in-depth customer research has been undertaken at Scottish visitor attractions, and still less has been published, but given the presumed dominance at Scottish attractions of the domestic (i.e. UK) holiday visitor and local day-trippers these trends will demand serious attention.

Certainly the 1992–97 Corporate Plan of the National Trust for Scotland shows a keen awareness of the importance of demographic change and other social trends. These are viewed particularly in terms of consolidating (rather than extending) the organisation's current key support by age and social group (i.e. older adults and higher socio-economic groups) and in terms of expanding areas of NTS activity.

The 1993 Corporate Plan of Historic Scotland, with what reads like the zeal of the convert to tourism, propounds:

> It is . . . important to the Scottish tourism economy that Historic Scotland should continue with its investment in improved visitor facilities. We will continue, and increase, our co-operation with local enterprise companies, area tourist boards, and local authorities. We also regard it as central that we are able to continue to market the estate in care vigorously to the travel trade at home and abroad and we have recently appointed a Travel Trade Officer to specialise in this area. (Historic Scotland, 1993:11)

Historic Scotland likewise considers that the anticipated trends towards increased disposable income, longevity, increased leisure time and greater mobility will provide opportunities to increase the number of visitors.

The emphasis on cooperation with other agencies is appropriate, for this is essentially the *modus operandi* of visitor attraction development in Scotland. The opening of new attractions has tended to be episodic and piecemeal, dependent on the painstaking assembly of funding from different sources and subject to delay. For all that, 1993 proved to be a good year, one in which several ambitious new ventures opened their doors. These newcomers, in their different ways, certainly illustrate the heterogeneous nature of development funding, but also the growing recognition of the need to achieve high standards of presentation and facilities.

The St Mungo Museum of Religious Life and Art in Glasgow is a local authority undertaking. The Glasgow Museums and Art Galleries Department rescued the failing project from a voluntary group and transformed the concept into an innovative museum, drawing on material in Glasgow's existing collections and commissioning other objects for the display. The curator claims that this is the 'first museum to explore all religions' (O'Neill, 1993) and, although aspects of the project have provoked an all-too-unholy row with certain religious interests, and equally intemperate criticism from certain museum professionals, it has also generated widespread and occasionally percipient interest in its aims (Arthur, 1993). Part of the significance of the St Mungo Museum, and in this aspect it resembles Edinburgh City Council's recently established People's Story museum, is the way in which working with community interests to present their perspectives and encourage their ongoing participation has been from the outset an integral part of the concept.

Deep-Sea World at North Queensferry is a development of an aquarium concept pioneered in New Zealand. Private sector driven, it nevertheless gathered funding from STB, Scottish Enterprise, Fife Enterprise and Dunfermline District Council. It is certainly a weatherproof attraction, and Deep-Sea World appears at this early stage to have pulled off the difficult trick of drawing leisure, tourist and education group visitors to an untried location. It also appears to have successfully weathered the growing public indifference or downright hostility to wildlife attractions, most clearly exemplified by the struggle of Glasgow Zoo to generate funds for development, and to have succeeded in capitalising on young people's genuine enthusiasm for environmentally aware attractions.

The opening of Discovery Point in Dundee is the culmination of a long-term project initiated by the Dundee Heritage Trust. The project involves the display of the Antarctic explorer vessel RRS *Discovery* which was built in the city in the early part of the century. To that extent it is comparable with several other marine heritage projects up and down the coasts of the British Isles.

The difference lies in the purpose-built visitor centre on the quayside, a landmark building intended as part of a not-fully-realised waterfront development, which comes with a range of facilities and a particularly ambitious high-tech audio-visual interpretation. The project has drawn heavily on public sector funding and the title 'Discovery' has been appropriated by the city as a promotional emblem. Indeed the project is seen as vital to the development of a tourism identity for Dundee.

The fourth major attraction to open in 1993 was a new interpretive display at Edinburgh Castle, called 'The Honours of Scotland'. This is a key component of Historic Scotland's extensive development plan for the site. The exhibition is a themed presentation of the Scottish crown jewels. The jewels are real, but to tell their story the exhibition deploys some of the now perhaps too familiar techniques of the heritage centre. And at a site which attracts such large numbers of non-Scots with little knowledge of Scottish history, the suitability of this particular choice of theme, with its concentration on symbols of royal sovereignty (which are somehow transmuted into symbols of a vanished nationhood—an effect originally contrived by none other than Sir Walter Scott), is also open to question. Nevertheless, the project is symbolic of the determination of Historic Scotland to attempt a more popular presentation of its sites.

These four newly opened attractions are almost emblematic of the forces at work shaping this sector of tourism in Scotland. There may be room for more bold and imaginative private-sector initiatives of the Deep-Sea World type, but the risks seem almost prohibitive. Certainly, although the UK market is still believed to be maturing, there will not be a major theme park development in Scotland. This has nothing to do with the relative failure of EuroDisney, although some might have hoped for a home-grown D. C. Thompson version, but with the small size of the local market.

For those attractions already established in Scotland and seeking to maintain viability, the setting up of the Association of Scottish Visitor Attractions is an important step towards raising operational standards in the industry. Starting out as an initiative of attraction operators, ASVA now features in its publications 126 attractions which have undergone inspection and have met its quality standards. Although enjoying some public funding for its development work, ASVA embodies an essentially industry-led approach to improving the quality of the product. The annual Tourism Oscar award scheme operated by the *Herald* newspaper, Caithness Glass and Grampian Television, in association with the Scottish Tourist Board, is a complementary approach which seeks to raise Scottish public awareness of good practice in the tourism industry, including visitor attractions.

Public sector support will continue to be the enabling factor in the establishment of new visitor attractions. The reallocation of tourism responsibilities among public bodies resulting from the review conducted by the Secretary of State for Scotland in 1993 means that responsibility for tourism development projects now lies with the Enterprise network. It is too early to say how the relatively inexperienced Scottish Enterprise LECs will adapt to this new challenge. A strategic plan for Scotland as a whole should be a priority. It should be a matter of close interest that in 1991 Ireland adopted a strategy to interpret the country's history and culture for tourism (Bord Failte, 1992). This resulted in the establishment of a canon of themes and storylines as, among other objectives, an aid to discrimination between projects seeking public support.

Scotland is of course at a quite different stage in its development and the approach adopted in Ireland would be unlikely to be directly transferable. On the other hand, now that the Highlands and Islands Enterprise area has achieved upgrading (in a sense!) to Objective 1 status for European Union structural funds, the importance of strategic planning for the direction of the available funds becomes all the more crucial. In common with the rest of the United Kingdom, Scotland has already made good use of European Regional Development Funding to support many tourism developments. This, however, has been planned for on a regional basis (Strathclyde Integrated Development Operation, 1990). There is, as always, a danger that a piecemeal approach to visitor attraction development which is based on local and regional priorities could be at the expense of larger-scale opportunities. The welcome publication of a new 'Scottish Tourism Multiplier Study' (Highlands and Islands Enterprise et al., 1993) will provide tourism planners in Scotland with further and persuasive evidence as to the potential economic benefits of visitor attraction development, but does not relieve anyone of the need to take a strategic view.

Visitor attraction projects in Scotland are carried forward for many different motives. Some of them are extrinsic to the economic value of the project. It would be naive to deny that departmental empire-building can be one motivation among others. Our beliefs about culture and history are also important factors. An illustration of the complexities of adjudication between priorities and the interplay of tourism-related and non-tourism considerations is provided by the long-running dispute between the cities of Glasgow and Edinburgh and different factions of the Scottish art establishment as to where—and indeed whether—a new National Gallery of Scottish Art should be established. The fact that at one stage the project was intended to involve the closure of the purpose-built 19th-century National Portrait Gallery is evidence of the confusion of the thinking, at least as far as the tourism aspect of the argument is concerned. To destroy one tourism asset in order to divert potential visitors to another one elsewhere, regardless of where it happens to be built, is indeed fatuous.

The great row about the special exhibition to celebrate Glasgow's 1990 reign as European City of Culture ('Glasgow's Glasgow') was equally splendid and just about as muddled. In Scotland we now seem to be learning to take our visitor attractions seriously. The economic importance of tourism is coming to be better understood. There are worthwhile efforts to devise more varied and interesting visitor attractions which can appeal to both Scots and visitors to Scotland. Our national identity has incorporated much historical nonsense, and we sometimes do not seem to mind parodying ourselves in ways first devised by Victorian gentry and sustained by the political comfort of historical myths. Yet, as long as we continue to have arguments about how we want to see ourselves represented in museums and heritage attractions and about what we want to set before our visitors, we have a society worth living in—and a country worth visiting.

References and bibliography

Arthur, Chris (1993) 'The art of exhibiting the sacred', *The Month*, July: 281ff.

Bord Failte (1992) *Heritage and Tourism* (The Second Conference on the Development of Heritage Attractions in Ireland), Bord Failte (Irish Tourist Board), Dublin.

Brown, John (1988) 'Visitor attractions: a look back and ahead', in *The Tourism Industry 1988/89*, The Tourism Society, London, pp. 29ff.

Centre for Environmental Interpretation (1993) 'Interpretation', September.

Ewing, Robert G. (1989) 'Industrial museums in Scotland: development and prospects', *Scottish Geographical Magazine*, 105(3): 179–181.

Fladmark, J. M. (Ed.) (1993) *Heritage: Conservation, Interpretation and Enterprise* (Papers presented at the Robert Gordon University Heritage Convention 1993), Donhead Publishing, Aberdeen.

Highland and Islands Enterprise, Scottish Enterprise, Scottish Tourist Board, Scottish Office Industry Department (1993) 'Scottish tourism multiplier study 1992', ESU Research Paper No. 31, three volumes.

Historic Scotland (1993) *Corporate Plan—1993*, Historic Scotland, Edinburgh.

Johnstone, Anne (1993) 'The tourism trap', *Herald*, 10 December.

KPMG (1989) 'Edinburgh. The next initiative', Peat Marwick McLintock, London.

Leisure Consultants (1990) *What's the Attraction?*, Vol. 1: *A Guide for Operators*, London.

Middleton, Victor T. C. (1990) 'New visions for independent museums in the UK', Association of Independent Museums, Chichester.

The National Trust for Scotland, 'Corporate plan 1992–97', unpublished.

O'Neill, Mark (1993) 'Keeping the faith', *Museums Journal*, May: 22.

Robinson, Ken (1990) 'Visitor attractions', *The Tourism Industry 1990/91*, The Tourism Society, London, pp. 31ff.

Scott, Kirsty (1994) 'Tourists rate Scotland poor value', *Herald*, 12 January (report of a study by Henley Centre for Forecasting).

Scottish Development Agency for the Scottish Tourism Coordinating Group (1988) 'Finance for tourist attractions and conference facilities', Glasgow.

STB (Scottish Tourist Board) (no date; *c.* 1989) 'Visitor attractions. A development guide', Edinburgh.

STB (Scottish Tourist Board) and Scottish Enterprise (no date; *c.* 1993) 'Close to home. Making Scotland more competitive in the UK holiday market', Edinburgh.

STB (Scottish Tourist Board) et al. (1989) 'A development prospectus for visitor attractions', Edinburgh.

STB (Scottish Tourist Board) (1992) 'Edinburgh Festivals study'.

STB (Scottish Tourist Board) (1993a) 'Overseas visitors' likes and dislikes, 1991', Research Handbook, RH23, Edinburgh.

STB (Scottish Tourist Board) (1993b) *Research Newsletter*, 4 (May): 29, Edinburgh.

The Stirling Initiative (no date; c. 1993) 'Stirling initiative. Planning for prosperity', Stirling.

Strathclyde Integrated Development Operation (1990) 'Tourism development strategy', Glasgow.

Womack, Peter (1989) *Improvement and Romance. Constructing the Myth of the Highlands*, Macmillan, London.

Yale, Pat (1991) *From Tourist Attractions to Heritage Tourism*, Elm Publications, Huntingdon.

54 Industry's contribution to Scottish tourism: the example of malt whisky distilleries

G. McBOYLE

Introduction

The traditional vision of a tourist on vacation does not usually place him or her within the walls of a factory, yet that is exactly where growing numbers of tourists can be found, eager to observe and understand the operations of other people's workplaces, and to shop for the products or mementos of the company. The industry-led formula is a winning one: either free or for a small fee visitors enjoy a corporate welcome and an interesting new experience while the company hopes to gain new converts for its products or preserve its established customer base. The success of Scottish malt whisky distilleries in this type of industry tourism is the subject of this paper.

Objectives

The objectives of the paper are to:

- trace the evolution of Scottish distillery tourism within the context of industry tourism in the UK
- identify the factors responsible for the success of distillery visitor centres
- outline their benefits to parent companies, distillery communities and Scottish tourism
- assess the impact on the centres of the emerging economic realities of the 1990s

Definition

For the purpose of this paper, a *visitor centre* is defined as an area(s) or structure(s) designed by the host company solely for the purpose of providing hospitality to the visiting public along with information about the company's operation, processes and products. Very often, the centre will include a retail outlet and catering facilities. The centre, and the attraction of which it is part, must be open to the public *without prior booking* for published periods each year.

Industry tourism in the UK

Industry tourism or, more broadly, workplace tourism has roots in the UK that go back many years to the tradition of welcoming visitors to view production at such factories as Cadbury's chocolates, Ford motor vehicles, Wedgwood pottery and Baxter's soups. Seeing how an industry operates and, more fascinating still, watching how other people work underpins the appeal to the tourist of spending leisure time in industry (Stevens, 1988; Jackson, 1989; Menzies, 1989; Ryan, 1989; Middleton and Parkin, 1989; Fraser, 1990–91; Wooder, 1992; and ETB [English Tourist Board], 1992).

To meet the demands of tourists seeking such intellectual stimulus, visitor attractions within workplaces grew rapidly in number after 1980 (Johnston, 1989). *See Industry at Work* (ETB, 1988) was a key document in encouraging more industries to become involved in workplace tourism. Subsequent publications include: *Visitor Attractions: a Development Guide* (STB [Scottish Tourist Board], 1989); *Realise the Advantage of Visitor Facilities in Scottish Industry* (STB and The Highland and Islands Development Board, 1990); and *Visit Britain at Work* (BTA [British Tourist Authority], 1990).

The 'win–win' nature of industry tourism was quickly recognised. The visitor enjoys an interesting, informative and pleasurable experience being given a tour of the work site, the opportunity to buy factory products or related memorabilia and often to partake of catering facilities. For coach tours the factory stopover is a boon.

For its part the company gains in both tangible and intangible ways. Direct revenue may be generated from such items as entry fees, shop sales and catering receipts, but perhaps more important are the intangible benefits in terms of:

- enhancing public confidence in the company by projecting an image of quality in both product and the production process
- promoting product awareness, especially to international visitors
- reinforcing customer loyalty to company brands
- stimulating staff morale and company pride (ETB, 1988; Stevens, 1988)

Other than the initial cost of providing special facilities, health and safety considerations for visitors represent the main deterrents for the company.

The growth of distillery visitor centres

Some of the best examples of enterprises that have been quick to seize the opportunities in the growth of tourism over the last 20 or so years are the Scottish malt whisky distilleries. The first distillery visitor centre was established in 1969 at Glenfiddich. By 1993, almost one in three malt distilleries had dedicated visitor centres (Figure 54.1). In addition to these 27 distilleries, Historic Scotland had also

established a visitor centre at Dallas Dhu museum distillery. Between them, they welcome over one million visitors annually (Table 54.1). Indeed, so successful has the tourism function become at Glenturret and Edradour distilleries, that it now represents their predominant function.

Nor are viewing opportunities limited to the visitor centres. A further 19 malt distilleries and one grain distillery publish their willingness to welcome the visiting public when prior arrangements can be made (Figure 54.2). Some use the special facilities normally restricted to company, trade and VIP guests; others may provide the public with a simpler and perhaps more authentic experience of the distillery as a workplace.

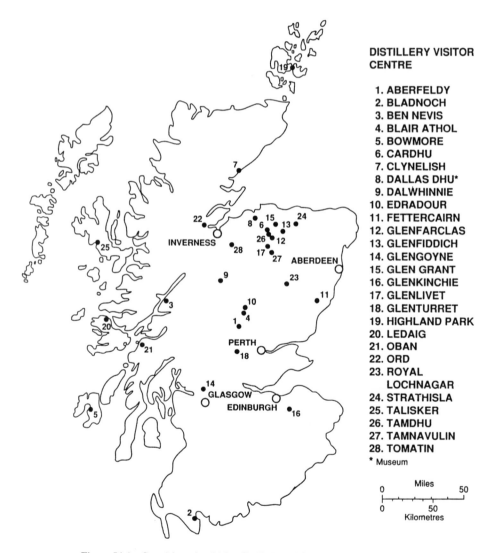

DISTILLERY VISITOR CENTRE

1. ABERFELDY
2. BLADNOCH
3. BEN NEVIS
4. BLAIR ATHOL
5. BOWMORE
6. CARDHU
7. CLYNELISH
8. DALLAS DHU*
9. DALWHINNIE
10. EDRADOUR
11. FETTERCAIRN
12. GLENFARCLAS
13. GLENFIDDICH
14. GLENGOYNE
15. GLEN GRANT
16. GLENKINCHIE
17. GLENLIVET
18. GLENTURRET
19. HIGHLAND PARK
20. LEDAIG
21. OBAN
22. ORD
23. ROYAL LOCHNAGAR
24. STRATHISLA
25. TALISKER
26. TAMDHU
27. TAMNAVULIN
28. TOMATIN
* Museum

Figure 54.1 *Scottish malt whisky distilleries with visitor centres, 1993*

Table 54.1 *Number of visitors (1992) at distillery visitor centres*

Distillery with visitor centre (VC)	Year VC opened	Number of visitors in 1992 ('000s)
Aberfeldy[1]	1987	29.6
Bladnoch[1]	1988	15.9
Ben Nevis[11]	1991	47.5
Blair Athol[1]	1983	77.1
Bowmore[10]	1974	8.2
Cardhu[1]	1988	24
Clynelish[1]	1988	11
Dallas Dhu[a8]	1988	10.4
Dalwhinnie[1]	1991	37.5
Edradour[5]	1986	94
Fettercairn[4]	1989	9
Glenfarclas[6]	1973	67.3
Glenfiddich[7]	1969	121
Glengoyne[9]	1978	32.7
Glen Grant[2]	1978	15.8
Glenkinchie[1]	1986	25.6
Glenlivet[2]	1977	63.3
Glenturret[3]	1980	146
Highland Park[3]	1987	16.7
Ledaig[13]	1990	7.4
Oban[1]	1988	62.3
Ord[1]	1982	43.8
Royal Lochnagar[1]	1986	71.1
Strathisla[2]	1980	10.1
Talisker[1]	1986	40.2
Tamdhu[3]	1977	13.1
Tamnavulin[4]	1985	31.7
Tomatin[12]	1992	7.4
Total numbers in 1992		1139.7

[a]Museum.
Data obtained from distillery company or distillery visitor centre.
1. United Distillers.
2. The Seagram Co. Ltd.
3. The Highland Distilleries Co. plc.
4. Whyte and Mackay Distillers Ltd.
5. Campbell Distillers Ltd.
6. J. and G. Grant International Ltd.
7. William Grant and Sons International Ltd.
8. Historic Scotland.
9. Lang Brothers Ltd.
10. Morrison Bowmore Distillers Ltd.
11. Nikka Distillers.
12. Takara Shuzo and Okura and Co. Ltd.
13. Tobermory Distillers Ltd.

At the time of writing, no visitor centre had been constructed at a grain distillery; all were located at malt whisky distilleries where the spirit is produced from malted barley using the batch (pot still) method. Most whisky sold, however, is blended whisky, i.e. a mix of malt and grain whiskies blended to a lighter, standardised taste.

Lacking a major distillery centre within Edinburgh, the Scottish capital and major tourist destination, several companies joined forces to fund The Scotch Whisky Heritage Centre, located a mere stone's throw from Edinburgh Castle. Opened in 1988, the £2 million centre provides a pseudo-distillery visit by explaining the history and processes in making malt and blended whisky, and offers a well-stocked shop and whisky tasting. In 1992 the Centre recorded over 100 000 visits.

The historical growth of visitor centres is shown in Figure 54.3. After 1973, when Glenfarclas joined Glenfiddich, development of visitor centres continued steadily. By 1980, 11 were in existence. The recessionary years of 1981–84 saw a slowing of growth but in the years between 1986 and 1988 11 centres opened; nine of these were related to the Guinness takeover of Distillers Company plc in 1986.

In contrast to data from other UK workplace attractions (Wooder, 1992), attendance at distilleries is overwhelmingly non-local. Most distilleries report that 40% to 50% of their visitors are overseas tourists. Only 5–10% come from Scotland, with the remainder mainly English.

The number of foreign visitors has been growing steadily. At Glenfiddich distillery, for example, in 1973, 21% of visitors came from overseas; in 1985 the corresponding figure was 42%; and by 1991, 50% were foreign. More than half the overseas visitors at the distillery came from six countries—France, Germany, USA, Australia, Canada and Italy.

Factors of success

There appear to be four main factors responsible for the success of distillery tourism:

- the regional distribution of visitor centres
- the range of centre facilities
- the visitor experience
- the marketing concept of The Malt Whisky Trail

The regional distribution of visitor centres

Figure 54.1 illustrates the distribution of visitor centres at malt whisky distilleries throughout Scotland. The widespread distribution of these distilleries is largely a result of their colourful history. Originally distilled for private use on almost every Scottish farm, Scotch whisky became subject to heavy taxation in the 18th century. The results was innumerable illicit stills, ingenious methods of outwitting excisemen and a vigorous market in smuggled whisky! Many contemporary, and now legal, distilleries stand on the same spot as their illicit forebears, hidden among the solitary Highland glens, secluded lowland valleys or distant islands.

The result is that each of the major tourist areas of Scotland has at least one distillery visitor centre accessible to it. A few miles from Edinburgh and Glasgow lie, respectively, Glenkinchie and Glengoyne visitor centres.

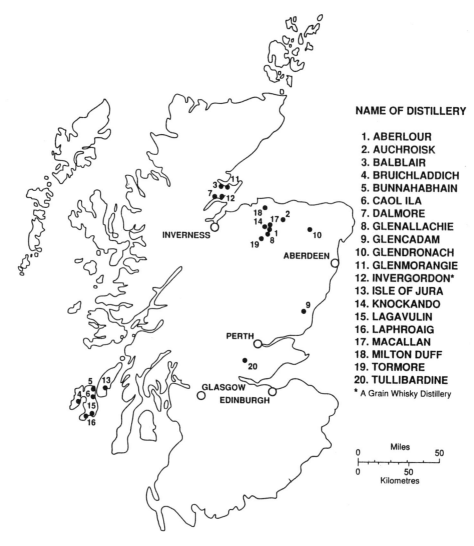

NAME OF DISTILLERY

1. ABERLOUR
2. AUCHROISK
3. BALBLAIR
4. BRUICHLADDICH
5. BUNNAHABHAIN
6. CAOL ILA
7. DALMORE
8. GLENALLACHIE
9. GLENCADAM
10. GLENDRONACH
11. GLENMORANGIE
12. INVERGORDON*
13. ISLE OF JURA
14. KNOCKANDO
15. LAGAVULIN
16. LAPHROAIG
17. MACALLAN
18. MILTON DUFF
19. TORMORE
20. TULLIBARDINE
* A Grain Whisky Distillery

Figure 54.2 *Distilleries open to the public by arrangement, 1993*

Along the major tourist route from Edinburgh to Inverness lie Glenturret, Aberfeldy, Blair Athol and Edradour in the Trossachs, Dalwhinnie half-way along the route, and Tomatin and Ord near Inverness. Royal Deeside, a popular tourist venue, has Royal Lochnagar, while the west coast is served by Oban, and Ben Nevis at Fort William. In addition, most of the major islands host a distillery visitor centre: Bowmore on Islay; Ledaig on Mull; Talisker on Skye; and Highland Park in Orkney.

Almost a third of the visitor centres, however, lie in Speyside, an area known also for its fishing and hunting opportunities. Here The Malt Whisky Trail guides visitors

along a 70-mile scenic route that encompasses eight distillery centres.

The range of centre facilities

The visitor's experience varies according to the nature of the distillery facilities. All distilleries with centres provide a tour and a free dram of whisky. Even the basic level of visitor centres also provide information displays of the production process and often of the characteristics and history of the company and/or the local area. Some use walk-through exhibits, others audio-visual presentations.

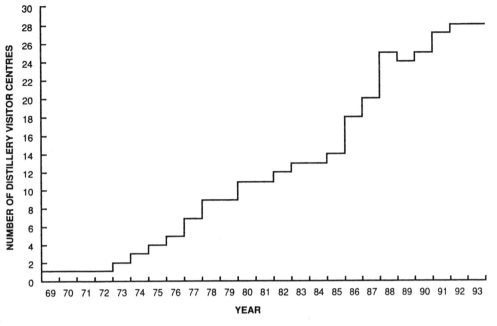

Auchentoshan opened 1975 and closed 1989: Glen Garioch opened 1976
and closed 1989.

Figure 54.3 *Growth of visitor centres at Scottish malt whisky distilleries*

All centres have a shop for their whisky and sometimes other brand souvenirs.

Twenty centres fit this primary level of facility (Table 54.2) yet vary greatly in attendance. Fettercairn distillery, a small production unit off the major tourist routes, hosted about 9000 visitors in 1992, while Edradour, exploiting its uniqueness as the smallest distillery in Scotland and its location in a popular tourist area, drew 94 000 visitors. While Glenturret recorded 146 000 visits and Glenfiddich 121 000, 70% of centres drew fewer than 50 000. About 37% attracted fewer than 20 000 (Table 54.1).

Four distilleries provide, in addition, simple catering facilities such as a coffee shop or small restaurant

Table 54.2 *Range of visitor numbers and centre facilities*

Number of visitors	Level[a]	Distillery
under 20 000	primary	Bladnoch[b]/Bowmore/Clynelish/Fettercairn/Glen Grant/Highland Park/Strathisla
	secondary	Tamdhu/Ledaig/Dallas Dhu
20 000 to 50 000	primary	Aberfeldy/Dalwhinnie/Glengoyne/Glenkinchie/Ord/Talisker/Tamnavulin/Tomatin
	secondary	Ben Nevis/Cardhu
50 000 to 100 000	primary	Edradour/Glenfarclas/Oban
	secondary	Glenlivet/Royal Lochnagar
	tertiary	Blair Athol
over 100 000	secondary	Glenfiddich
	tertiary	Glenturret

[a]primary = tour/dram/whisky shop.
 secondary = primary plus a cafe and/or an extensive gift shop.
 tertiary = secondary plus corporate dining facilities.
[b]the centres underlined are owned by United Distillers and indicate the range in visitor numbers and facilities, and the regional spread of the company's centres.

(Table 54.2) Royal Lochnagar and Glenlivet distilleries exemplify this secondary level of visitor centre. Although currently it has no catering facilities, Glenfiddich has been placed in this category by virtue of its high attendance, extensive shop facilities and foreign language capabilities. During peak periods at this distillery, guides can accommodate visitors in six languages, including Japanese, and brochures are available in seven.

A further two distilleries, Blair Athol and Glenturret, have developed catering and hospitality facilities of a more sophisticated nature. Glenturret will cater silver service meals by arrangement, with guests piped to the sound of bagpipes. Blair Athol woos corporate clientele through its high calibre dining and entertainment facilities.

This range of facilities offers a variety of experiences for the tourist. In the Pitlochry area, for example, tiny Edradour distillery is simplicity itself, with production buildings changed little since 1825. Blair Athol, by comparison, has a sophisticated, well-appointed visitor centre boasting high-tech, audio-visual facilities and an elegant coffee shop. The fact is, there is no one distillery experience and each different niche of the tourist market is provided for.

The visitor experience

Part of the success of the distillery visit lies in its compatibility with the visitor's image of Scotland. To overseas tourists, Scotland is perceived as a land of outstanding scenery and friendly people, a country whose dramatic history is reflected in its ancient buildings and a destination which can offer a welcome solitude amid its natural beauty (STB, 1992a). The rural setting of the distillery, the hospitality extended, the preservation and use of original structures and the quiet, traditional process in which the spirit is produced, all serve to confirm this image.

The setting

The historical necessity of localised production, pure water supply and secluded location has bequeathed to the industry a widespread distribution of distilleries among regional landscapes. Dalwhinnie, for example, is approached along the picturesque valley of Glen Garry or over the windswept moors of the Grampian Mountains. Bowmore enjoys the wildness of the Islay seascape. And Royal Lochnagar is set among the wooded hills of Deeside close to Balmoral Castle.

The architectural heritage of the distillery buildings has been carefully preserved by the whisky companies. Tamnavulin's centre, for example, is housed in a gracious old stone mill set in a small ravine. The ivy-covered, old

stone buildings of Blair Athol and the white-washed neatness of Glenturret distilleries complement the gentle landscapes of Perthshire. The setting and the visual aesthetics of the distillery are thus an integral part of the visitor's experience.

The welcome

Companies have gone to considerable expense to ensure that first impressions are memorable. Though some have created reception areas that aim for the authentic feel of old stone buildings, most have been furnished to a high standard making extensive use of glass, polished wood and stone, and traditional woollen fabrics.

Scottish custom places a high premium on hospitality and great emphasis has been placed on the welcome extended by the personnel. Guides are generally local residents, frequently students in summer months, and usually dressed in tartans. Trained to explain the whisky production process and answer visitors' questions, it is their responsibility to convey a sense of warmth, friendliness and competence in keeping with the image the distillery wishes to present. For many of the smaller visitor centres that have opted for simplicity and authenticity rather than elaborate surroundings, it is upon the welcome and pride of the staff that their continued success relies.

The tour

Once welcomed in the reception area, visitors are usually introduced to the whisky production process by displays or audio-visual presentations. Made in the same way for hundreds of years, only three ingredients are used for malt whisky: water, barley and yeast. No additives are permitted and each step of the process is happily shown to visitors with no sense of secrecy or confidentiality.

History and craftsmanship dictate the process, which is simplicity itself. On the tour, visitors will see ground malted barley mixed with hot water to form a sugary liquid called 'wort'. When cool, the addition of yeast begins a fermentation process and when this subsides the liquid is distilled, usually twice in traditional, onion-shaped, copper pot stills. It is the time-honoured role of the stillman, without any physical contact with the liquid, to divert the spirit at the appropriate moment to begin a lengthy process of maturation, which may be eight, ten, twelve, fifteen or more years, but certainly no less than three.

Scottish frugality ensures that little is wasted in the process: residue from the wort ('draff') and pot ale from the distillation goes to make cattle food; oak casks are used and reused up to three times. Spent lees are periodically removed to waste facilities, but water taken from local sources for the cooling process is clean, though warm, and allowed to return to water bodies. This return flow cools quickly in the Scottish climate and so aquatic life suffers no apparent detrimental effect. With little waste and virtually no pollution, ecological integrity is maintained through the legacy of tradition and thrift.

The plant tour highlights the 'mystical' elements of malt whisky production: the role of peat in drying malted barley to flavour the whisky to the extent dictated by each distillery's own tradition; the intriguing differences in flavour brought about by the shape of the pot stills, unique to each distillery and carefully maintained in their original contours; and the subtle, but significant influence of the oak casks' previous contents on the final flavour of the whisky. Even the long, slow maturation process has its whimsy in the 'angel's share'—the spirit that evaporates from the cask each year. Distilleries will stress that, despite many attempts to produce malt whisky elsewhere in the world, none has been successful in replicating the distinctive flavour of a Scottish malt.

The enigmatic elements of the process are heightened by the quiet, almost sleepy atmosphere of the distillery. Production staff are few, usually only about three to six involved at any one shift. They are frequently outnumbered by tour guides. Glenturret distillery, for example, has usually two production workers per shift, but 22 permanent employees for tourism activities (Ireland, personal communication, 1992). For Glenfiddich, the comparable figures are six workers per shift compared to a summer staff of 44 tour guides (Mair, personal communication, 1992). Distillery tourism, therefore, is based less on 'the theatre of work' (Leishman, 1989) and more on 'the magic of production'.

The distillery tour always includes that more tangible expression of sociability—the offer of a free dram of whisky. Normally held in a special reception area at the culmination of the tour, the group sampling of the distillery's product serves to confirm the hospitality extended by the company and the pride in the quality of its product.

Shopping and refreshments

Fortified by a knowledge of the distillery's operation and a taste of its product, visitors are afforded a further 'freedom of the distillery' by being encouraged to browse in the shop for whisky, related accessories and memorabilia of the company. Quality of furnishing and products is again high, in line with the image of the malt whisky itself. Other than for whisky, most if not all the merchandise is designed solely for that distillery and is not purchasable elsewhere—another expression of a unique experience. Some centres also offer the opportunity to take refreshments, especially of Scottish fare.

Summation

Though the traditional image of Scotland is confirmed, much more emerges during the visit. The product, its mystique and the qualities which the company wishes to portray, all introduce additional themes to the visitor's psyche. Table 54.3 summarises attributes of the visit and the themes they represent. The long-term return to the company in public relations depends on how successfully the distillery conveys these concepts such that a bond is forged between visitor and product. In this context, the product is bought not only for its own intrinsic qualities but also for the wider experience which it symbolises.

For the visitor, being given the privilege of entering and freely observing the internal operations of the distillery, of enjoying the social ambiance of a free drink, all the while being treated as a valued guest and indeed friend of the company, promotes a strong psychological affiliation with the distillery and its brands. The experience is a powerful mechanism for developing new customers and for reinforcing brand loyalty among existing patrons.

The marketing concept of The Malt Whisky Trail

As with all attractions, marketing plays an important role. Stretching along a 70-mile route in Speyside, The Malt

Table 54.3 *Attributes of the malt whisky distillery visit and the conceptual themes they represent*

Attributes of the distillery visit	Themes
● preservation and use of original buildings ● historic exhibits ● use of traditional materials and fabrics ● time-honoured production methods ● tradition of hospitality	Heritage
● personal attention ● freedom to view entire operation ● free dram	Hospitality
● only three natural ingredients used ● billion-pound industry built on traditional craft ● the appeal of the inexplicable	Mystique of whisky
● high standard of facilities ● high calibre of products for sale ● high priority on staff training	Quality
● each malt whisky is unique ● shop products (non-whisky) sold only on site ● each distillery has its own ambiance	Uniqueness
● visitor made to feel part of company 'family' ● logo merchandise	Affiliation

Whisky Trail as it is now called, represents the advertising flagship of distillery tourism. Overseas marketing by the BTA has been highly effective in drawing foreign tourists to the Trail, and by implication, in raising interest in distillery visits generally in Scotland. The more recent Islay and Jura Whisky Tour has adopted the same concept.

The Malt Whisky Trail originated as a marketing concept in the early 1970s as the brainchild of Mr David Illingworth, then working in the Tourist Office of Moray and Nairn Joint County Council. Prior experience elsewhere had convinced him of the value in a rural area of a major attraction, particularly one that offered wet weather respite. Glenfiddich visitor centre, which opened in 1969, and the subsequent interest shown by Strathisla and Glenfarclas distilleries, encouraged him to promote a 15-mile trail for visitors to sample the sights and tastes of the three distilleries.

At first advertised informally through the Tourist Office, the Trail soon required a higher quality marketing tool. With the collective support of Illingworth's colleagues in other tourist offices in the region, the participating distillery companies were cajoled into overcoming their natural rivalry and together provided 50% of the printing costs of new brochures. The good business sense of using economies of scale to provide cost-effective means of marketing their visitor centres, especially overseas, has underpinned the continuing cooperation between the distilleries which now also include Tamdhu, Glenlivet, Glen Grant, Tamnavulin and Cardhu and represent six parent companies. In 1993 Speyside Cooperage joined the venture.

The Malt Whisky Trail's administrative committee operates as a loosely knit organisation of member company representatives and government officials, each with a different mandate, but sharing a common goal in the promotion of the Trail. Tourism members include one representative from each of: The Moray Tourist Board; the Grampian Highlands and Aberdeen Tourism Marketing Company; and Highlands and Islands Enterprise, a regional development body funded through the Scottish Office Industry Department. Their function is to coordinate the activities of the Trail, market it effectively and provide an interface with government in addressing special needs, e.g., signposting improvements. The BTA assists the committee with funding for an annual brochure that includes information in six languages.

Once a comfortably short tour of three distilleries, the present Trail of eight distilleries and one cooperage offers a daunting challenge even to the most determined whisky connoisseur! Its appeal now owes more to the freedom of choice it offers the tourist and tour operator, than to the notion of visiting each and every attraction. The 'critical mass' of eight distilleries in a small area ensures that independent travellers will not only find a distillery with relative ease, but that a flexible schedule is possible given the several options available for them. For coach drivers faced with the requirement of a timed arrival at some centres, the availability of alternatives ensures that a distillery visit is always possible even when tour schedules are upset. It is this combination of flexibility and variety along with a consistently high-quality experience which may best explain the continuing success of The Malt Whisky Trail.

Benefits of distillery tourism

The company

Direct benefits

Direct returns for the company arise mainly from sales of whisky and related souvenirs, and from bar and food services if provided. The average spend per head on all sales is about £4 to £6 with higher amounts being recorded typically among the more isolated distilleries, on Islay for example, where fewer opportunities exist for alternative purchases. Where a distillery has consciously targeted an upscale market, figures of £8 to £10 per head are also claimed. Despite these revenues, however, most of the centres operate at a loss.

Indirect benefits

Returns to the company are largely intangible, long-term and hard to quantify: essentially they are enhanced public relations and wider brand recognition. Visitor centres are the company's opportunity to display the quality of its product and production processes, and to increase market share. Product awareness and promotion is furthered by the on-site sale of the distillery's malt whisky and/or associated blends, as well as souvenir items, from pencils to sweaters, bearing the appropriate logo.

Well-furnished visitor centres active with tourists also present a highly positive image to trade and distribution personnel; visitor facilities may also be used for corporate entertaining.

Additional benefits accrue in terms of enhanced staff morale and loyalty. There is something uplifting about working in a company whose operation attracts thousands of visitors each year from all parts of the world. A strong sense of self-worth and pride in the company makes staff good ambassadors for the firm and its products (ETB, 1988).

Local communities

Locally generated employment is the most direct benefit of distillery tourism. Since most distilleries lie in rural areas, alternative employment sources are often scarce, especially for women. Distilleries can offer flexible hours on a part-time or 'on-call' basis which can accommodate family commitments. Peak demand for guides in summer months also coincides with the availability of local students.

To assess the total employment generated (direct, indirect and induced) in local communities by visitor centre spending, use was made of the employment multipliers developed by the Surrey Research Group (1993). For rural attractions, the multiplier is 0.0578 per £1000 of tourist expenditure and for remote rural attractions the corresponding value is 0.0672.

Twenty-four visitor centres were classed as rural. Assuming their 1.07 million visitors per annum spend a total of £5.35 million (£5 per head) *on-site*, then spending at the rural centres accounts for 309 full-time equivalents (FTEs). About 100 of thse FTEs would be generated along The Malt Whisky Trail since it accounts for about one-third of the total spend at rural visitor centres. Little leakage of employment would occur at distilleries other than at Glenfiddich which looks outside the region for guides with specialised language skills.

For the four distilleries classed as remote rural (Bowmore, Ledaig, Talisker, Highland Park) assuming a total spend on-site of £0.58 million from their 72 500 visitors (£8 per head), then 39 FTEs are created.

Spending at the visitor centre also generates income for the company, for employees and for supplier services. As part of this income is re-spent on further goods and services, additional income is induced within the local communities. Repatriation of income would not be a widespread problem.

The Surrey Research Group (1993) provides total income multipliers (direct, indirect and induced) of 0.3322 per £1 of tourist expenditure for rural centres, with a corresponding figure of 0.5363 for remote rural attractions. Using the same values for visitor centre spending as above, this implies that the 24 rural visitor centres generate income of £1.78 million, of which £0.58 million would occur along The Malt Whisky Trail. The four remote rural distilleries would account for an additional £311 000 of income in local economies.

Given the small size of these predominantly rural communities, the impact of distillery visitor centres is clearly beneficial to local economies. It must be noted, however, that these figures are provided as *indicators* of economic impact only, not as accurate representations. Furthermore, they refer *only* to the effect of visitor spending *on-site* at distillery centres. Visitor expenditures off-site, for example on accommodation, catering outlets, transportation services etc., were not known but would generate additional income and employment opportunities.

Off-site spending, however, is not always as buoyant as local businesses might wish. Many distilleries have become 'en-route' stopovers for touring coaches on restricted schedules allowing limited, if any, discretionary time in local communities. Moreover, even for independent travellers, the distillery centres are usually situated at a distance from their overnight destinations. Many communities are thus unable to capitalise fully on the distillery attractions.

Most distilleries have been sensitive not to undermine the benefits to local businesses. For example, being mindful of the potential loss of trade to local retailers, neither Glenfiddich nor Glenfarclas distilleries have catering facilities despite large numbers of visitors. To assist local businesses, many distilleries allow them to advertise their services in the visitor centres. In many ways, therefore, the centres have carved for themselves a significant role in their local economies.

Scottish tourism

Distillery attractions have also benefited Scottish tourism. The traditional lure of Scotland lay in its scenery and wildlife, its ancient buildings and its friendly people (STB, 1992a). Distillery tourism combines many aspects of these images while providing the visitor with an insight into one of the UK's top five export earning industries: annual export earnings from malt and blended whiskies topped £1.8 billion in 1991 (The Scotch Whisky Association, 1992a; 1992b).

Reception facilities are generally first class, with the costs borne largely by the whisky industry which has also provided the opportunity for tourists to purchase high-quality Scottish-made products. Further, from a purely practical standpoint, distillery centres provide a range of wet weather facilities (Table 54.2) distributed widely throughout Scotland (Figure 54.1) in rural areas where few other indoor attractions exist. This is particularly important in a country where weather is not the most popular aspect of a tourist's stay (STB, 1992a; Hay, 1989).

Distilleries differ from other workplace attractions in that visitors are mainly 'non-local' (Wooder, 1992). Attendance therefore tends to follow the pattern of visitor numbers to Scotland. For example, the 40% increase in trips by foreign visitors to Scotland between 1980 and 1991 (STB, 1992b and 1992c) provided a growing market for visitor centres. Conversely, the drop in tourist numbers in the recession years of 1982 and 1991 was mirrored by falling attendance at the distilleries. Thus, though essentially a private sector initiative, distillery visitor attractions and Scottish tourism are closely interwoven.

The relationship is very evident in Speyside. The Malt Whisky Trail draws a significant number of visitors into a rural area that might otherwise be bypassed by overseas tourists. As high as 20% of visitors to the Moray region claim that the Trail was their prime reason for visiting (Burgess, personal communication, 1992). Indeed, one-third of all distillery visits occur on The Malt Whisky Trail (Table 54.1).

Recognising the value of these industry-led initiatives, the STB helped offset construction costs at several distilleries, particularly during their formative period as tourist attractions. Glengoyne, Glenturret and Royal Lochnagar distilleries all received financial assistance from the STB under Section 4 of the Development of Tourism Act 1969 (STB, 1984–85; 1985–86; 1987–88; 1989–90). The distillery visitor centre is now so clearly established a concept that STB granting policy places a low priority on further funding assistance.

Restructuring of local government in 1991 saw the formation of Local Enterprise Companies whose mandate may include provision of financial assistance for such developments.

Costs

Though companies benefit from visitor centres in a public relations sense, constructing and operating the facilities is a major expense. Capital costs can be as high as £500 000, but average around £250 000. Plant modification may also be necessary to ensure the safety of touring groups. Wages and benefits for what is a labour-intensive operation are partially controlled through the use of temporary and part-time staff. 'Dramming', i.e the provision of a free dram of whisky, is an unusual additional cost.

The figures in the mock income statement in Table 54.4 are all fictitious but have been confirmed as realistic by company sources. The hypothetical centre faces an annual loss of £81 750 unless depreciation and the operating costs of heating, lighting, security, etc. are subsumed under the distillery budget. Net loss would then lie in the region of £26 750. Clearly, the return on investment to the company is likely to be negative on a 'stand-alone' basis. The visitor centre can only be justified as a marketing tool for brand promotion within the wider operating costs of the company as a whole. (It should also be noted that these figures make no provision for capital renewals, rental fees or loan repayments, costs that arise in a true commercial venture. As noted by Middleton (1989), the number of commercially viable visitor attractions in Britain is very small.)

For those companies pursuing a more independent financial footing for their visitor centres, a number of options are available.

Table 54.4 *Mock income statement for a hypothetical distillery visitor centre*

Assumptions:		
● capital costs of centre £250 000		
● annual visitor numbers 50 000		
● average spend per visitor £5		
Gross income (50 000 × £5)	£250 000	
Less: value added tax (VAT), (17.5%)	43 750	
Net profit		£206 250
Cost of goods sold		
(50%) of gross income)		£125 000
Net profit on sales		81 250
Expenses:		
Wages and benefits	£70 000	
Operating	30 000	
Depreciation	25 000	
Dramming	15 000	
Marketing	10 000	
Consumables	7 000	
Repairs and maintenance	6 000	
Total expenses		£163 000
Total income (loss)		(£81 750)

Admittance fees

If, in our hypothetical visitor centre, admission of £2 per person were charged, the net income from admittance might be about £60 000 allowing for VAT (value added tax) and reductions for children and pensioners. As long as the average spend per head remains the same, the additional revenue would bring the centre onto a more profitable basis.

Although many distilleries still adhere to a principle of free hospitality, an increasing number are opting for an admittance charge. Besides providing additional revenue, a fee implies a quality experience and helps, whether intended or not, to target a more upscale market. Against these factors are the fears of a possible dilution of spending in the distillery's retail or catering areas, a reduction in visitor numbers, i.e. potential whisky buyers, and a weakened public relations image.

Current experience seems to invalidate at least two of these concerns. Attendance figures at Glenturret distillery have increased over 50% between 1985 and 1991 (BTA/ETB Research Services, 1987; 1991) despite the fact that the distillery has charged for admittance since 1980. Visitor numbers did drop sharply at Glengoyne distillery for two years following the introduction of an entry fee, but have latterly stabilised around 33 000 (BTA/ETB Research Services, 1991; 1992a; 1992b; Scott, personal communication, 1993). Both distilleries tend to attract an upscale market, perhaps in part related to the screening effect of the charge, and both claim higher spends per person than the industry average, apparently refuting any fears of dilution of retail spending. Both centres, however, enjoy favoured locations in high-traffic tourist areas. Whether more remote centres could charge with impunity is open to question.

In 1993, Glenfarclas introduced an entrance fee and The Highland Distilleries Company extended its policy of charging admittance to include Tamdhu and Highland Park along with Glenturret. That same year, United Distillers, the largest owner of visitor centres, began charging on an experimental basis at Oban and Royal Lochnagar. Entrance costs at the latter two distilleries are offset by a voucher for the purchase of whisky in the centre's retail outlet. The impact of these policy changes remains to be seen.

Season extension

If Glenlivet is typical, 75% of attendance at distilleries occurs during June to September (Campbell, personal communication, 1992). Revenue gains may be possible where visitor numbers could be increased in off-peak seasons. The shoulder months of April, May and October offer the best hope of 'second holiday' tourists. Outside these months, centre operation is likely to be unprofitable though many distilleries choose to maintain a year-round presence.

Market segmentation

Increasing the 'revenue per person ratio' implies targeting the higher socio-economic groupings. Entrance fees may prove to be a screening mechanism for this purpose. Selective marketing practices and representation at upscale trade shows are other options.

Coach tours account for 50% of visitors. Some bring affluent foreign tourists, others touring pensioners. Where several distilleries lie on the tour route, the choice of distillery is often left to the discretion of the coach driver. This allows flexibility in a schedule that may require alteration for unforeseen reasons. It also means that drivers may be encouraged to favour certain distilleries over others. Competition to attract the more select coach lines may be expected and the question of providing incentives to drivers is likely to prove a sensitive issue.

Conclusion

Growing popularity of a distillery visit ensured wider public exposure to distillery brands and prompted many companies to invest in specialised visitor centres, some simple, others 'state-of-the-art' facilities. Participating whisky companies now find themselves in the business of tourism management. United Distillers, for example, has established a separate division in the company to oversee the operation of its 13 distillery attractions, 11 of which have visitor centres. By design or default, distilleries have become a significant part of the tourism map of Scotland.

Some whisky companies have decided against involvement in this tourism market. The Macallan distillery, for example, has declined a mass market role, choosing instead to express an exclusivity by providing hospitality only by special arrangement. Allied Distillers has several distilleries but no dedicated visitor centres. The question facing non-participating companies is whether the lack of representation on the visitor centre network will, in the longer term, result in reduced market share.

For those companies operating visitor centres, the less affluent 1990s may engender changes that affect the character of distillery tourism. Pressure for 'stand-alone' profitability may prompt more centres to charge for admission. Market segmentation may also occur, spurring a differentiation between those centres which vigorously pursue an upscale clientele and those whose welcome is more far-reaching.

Increased emphasis on a tourism function implies a greater need to meet the visitor's expectations and demands. This is especially true where an admittance fee is charged; the tourist is no longer being welcomed as part of the distillery 'family' but invited to participate in a bona fide visitor attraction. Does a paying visitor feel value for money, for example, if the whisky production process is not in operation, a situation that is common in distilleries for several weeks during the summer 'silent season'? To ensure visitor satisfaction, companies will require two types of information: one, of the expectations of their individual client base acquired through surveys of visitor preferences, dislikes etc.; and the other, of the broader context of tourism trends generally.

In the latter respect, much of the tourism literature points to a new trend—'green tourism'—characterised as being small in scale, sensitive to local economies and social norms, finding pleasure in the natural landscape and cultural history of an area, maintaining ecological integrity and delighting in the preservation and reuse of old buildings and structures (Green, 1990). For the 'green tourist', distillery attractions have much to offer. They provide a quality experience, educating the visitor in the many components of this heritage industry which has maintained a compatible relationship with the environment, both physical and social. It may well be these characteristics, of an environmentally and socially friendly industry, that will underpin the future success of the Scottish malt whisky distilleries as visitor attractions—and provide their strongest marketing edge.

For the moment, the whisky companies have achieved a fortuitous combination of informal hospitality, insight into the workings of a billion-pound industry and specialised merchandise for the shopper. But few other workplaces can conjure up such intrigue on the plant floor: the hazy influence of peat and pot still on the final product and the mystifying interaction of cask and spirit during a maturation process that continues untouched for many years. More than anything, perhaps, it is the mystique of the inexplicable that gives distillery tourism its unique cachet.

Acknowledgements

Many people gave of their time to talk about distillery visitor centres. Specifically I would like to thank (in alphabetical order): Anne Burgess, Moray Tourist Board; Silvia Corrieri, Caledonian Malt Whisky Distillers, Ltd; Brian Hay, Scottish Tourist Board; Gordon Henry and David Illingworth, Grampian Highlands and Aberdeen; Mark Lawson, Chivas Brothers Ltd; Jim McColl, Morrison Bowmore Distillers Ltd; Tom Thomson, United Distillers; and Jim Turle, Lang Brothers Ltd.

References

BTA (British Tourist Authority) (1990) *Visit Britain at Work*, Visitor Publications, Croydon, England.

BTA (British Tourist Authority) and ETB (English Tourist Board) Research Services (1987) 'Visits to tourist attractions 1986', British Tourist Authority and English Tourist Board Research Services, Hammersmith, London.

BTA (British Tourist Authority) and ETB (English Tourist Board) Research Services (1991) 'Visits to tourist attractions 1990', British Tourist Authority and English Tourist Board Research Services, Hammersmith, London.

BTA (British Tourist Authority) and ETB (English Tourist Board) Research Services (1992a) 'Visits to tourist attractions 1991', British Tourist Authority and English Tourist Board Research Services, Hammersmith, London.

BTA (British Tourist Authority) and ETB (English Tourist Board) Research Services (1992b) 'Sightseeing in the UK 1991', British Tourist Authority and English Tourist Board Research Services, Hammersmith, London.

Burgess, A. (1992) Personal communication with Director of Tourism, Moray Tourist Board, Elgin, 8 July.

Campbell, A. E. (1992) Personal communication with the Supervisor, The Glenlivet Visitors Centre, Glenlivet Distillery, Glenlivet, 14 July.

ETB (English Tourist Board) (1988) *See Industry at Work*, English Tourist Board, Hammersmith, London.

ETB (English Tourist Board) (1992) 'Industrial tourism', Tourism Development Advisory Sheet 6, English Tourist Board, Hammersmith, London.

Fraser, K. (1990–91) 'People and processes: the diversification of industry into tourism', M.Sc. thesis, Strathclyde University, Glasgow, Scotland.

Green, S. (1990) 'The future for green tourism', *Insights*, D5–D8.

Hay, B. (1989) 'Tourism and the Scottish weather', in *Weather Sensitivity and Services in Scotland*, S. J. Harrison and K. Smith (Eds), Scottish Academic Press, Edinburgh.

Ireland, P. (1992) Personal communication with Tourist Manager, Glenturret Distillery, Crieff, 21 July.

Jackson, K. (1989) 'Industry, image and interpretation', *Interpretation*, 42: 4–15.

Johnston, J. (1989) 'Work fascinates me', *Interpretation*, 42: 15–16.

Leishman, M. (1989) 'One man's workplace is another man's theatre', *Interpretation*, 42: 2–3.

Mair, D. (1992) Personal communication with Chief Guide, Glenfiddich Distillery, Dufftown, 17 July.

Menzies, A. (1989) 'Industrial tourism', *Insights*, A1.1–A1.4.

Middleton, P. and Parkin, I. (1989) 'The suspension of disbelief', *Leisure Management*, 9(5): 46–49.

Middleton, V. T. C. (1989) 'Marketing implications for attractions', *Tourism Management*, 10: 229–232.

Ryan, M. (1989) 'Industry tourism', *Leisure Management*, 9(1): 56–58.

Scott, J. N. (1993) Personal communication with Public Relations Manager, Glengoyne Distillery, 8 April.

STB (Scottish Tourist Board) (1984–85) 'Annual report', Scottish Tourist Board, Edinburgh, Scotland.

STB (Scottish Tourist Board) (1985–86) 'Annual report', Scottish Tourist Board, Edinburgh, Scotland.

STB (Scottish Tourist Board) (1987–88) 'Annual report', Scottish Tourist Board, Edinburgh, Scotland.

STB (Scottish Tourist Board) (1989–90) 'Annual report', Scottish Tourist Board, Edinburgh, Scotland.

STB (Scottish Tourist Board) (1989) *Visitor Attractions: a Development Guide*, Scottish Tourist Board, Edinburgh, Scotland.

STB (Scottish Tourist Board) (1992a) *Tourist in Scotland 1991*, Scottish Tourist Board Pamphlet, Edinburgh, Scotland.

STB (Scottish Tourist Board) (1992b) 'Overseas tourism statistics for the UK and Scotland', *Research Newsletter*, 3: 24–28.

STB (Scottish Tourist Board) (1992c) 'Overseas tourism statistics for the UK and Scotland', *Research Newsletter*, 2: 25–29.

STB (Scottish Tourist Board) and The Highlands and Islands Development Board (1990) *Realise the Advantage of Visitor Facilities in Scottish Industry*, Scottish Tourist Board, Edinburgh, and The Highlands and Islands Development Board, Inverness, Scotland.

Stevens, T. (1988) 'Work watching: the growth of industry tourism', *Leisure Management* 8(12): 40–43.

Surrey Research Group (1993) 'Scottish tourism multiplier study 1992', ESU Research Paper 31, Vols 1, 2 and 3.

The Scotch Whisky Association (1992a) 'Statistical report 1991', The Scotch Whisky Association, Edinburgh, Scotland.

The Scotch Whisky Association (1992b) *Scotch at a Glance*, pamphlet of The Scotch Whisky Association, Edinburgh, Scotland.

Wooder, S. (1992) 'Industrial tourism', *Insights*, B63–B66.

55 'I stood all the way from Corrour': marketing the West Highland Railway in Scotland

D. STEWART-DAVID

For all organisations the only thing that really matters at the end of the day is not the technology, or company policies, or computer systems, or products, or even the employee development programme, but the long term satisfaction of customers.

Piercy (1992)

I stood all the way from Corrour.

Scotrail Passenger, Glasgow Queen Street, May 1993

Transport is a service rarely in demand for its own characteristics. Demand for public transport . . . is usually derived from some other function.

Cole (1987)

Lines proposed for Closure . . . Glasgow–Fort William–Mallaig; Stirling–Oban.

Beeching (1961)

Introduction

This paper offers a consideration of the problem of marketing West Highland line trains in ways which match supply and demand and maximise net revenue yield. The West Highland line is that which runs from Glasgow to Fort William and on to Mallaig (see Appendix 1 for map and distances). It will be well known that the line serves an isolated area where tourism is the largest and fastest-growing industry. It is very evident that tourism is a luxury product with a pronounced seasonality of demand. The demand for rail travel is derived from this seasonality, and this explains why there was in 1993 (and previous years) a very markedly different supply of seat-miles in the high peak from 21 June to 4 September, as is evident from the British Rail timetable (see Appendix 2). The West Highland line from Glasgow to Fort William and Mallaig is the case studied for three reasons. They are, firstly, because it was the source of the quotation which is the proximate cause and the title of the paper, secondly, because of the historical appropriateness of presenting a study of this line in its centenary year at a Scottish conference on tourism, and, thirdly, because the line so well illustrates the dilemmas of the effective supply and demand of an amenity which is not in itself profitable.

The problem

The title of this paper was the exclamation of a disgruntled young woman who had arrived in Glasgow at four o'clock on a Saturday in late May. The diesel multiple unit ('Sprinter') train she travelled on was 16 minutes late, and its four cars were very well-loaded, though observation suggested that there were about 280 passengers disembarking from a train with a nominal seating capacity of 288. Had she stood all the way from Corrour, she would have been on her feet for 95 miles and rather more than three hours. Corrour is a small, little-used station on Rannoch Moor, some 28 miles east of Fort William (see Appendix 1). Its main function is as a passing place for trains, as the West Highland is a single-track railway. There are no houses at Corrour Station, but there is a youth hostel about a mile away at Loch Ossian Pier. It was clearly apparent, not least from the young woman's stentorian comment, that her customer satisfaction was low, though it was equally clear that she had suddenly decided to abandon a youth hostelling holiday and flee, without booking, on the first available service, and that she was demonstrating a common inexperienced consumer characteristic—the transference of personal disappointment to some perceived failure of the operator (Wilkie, 1986).

The answers

So why did she stand all the way from Corrour? There are six answers to the question. They are:

- The nature of the markets
- The seasonality of demand
- The pattern of transport supply
- Customer behaviour on trains

- Train crew behaviour towards standing passengers
- Government policy towards the financing of railways

The market

The first answer to the question lies in the market for the West Highland line. The market segments served by the line are described in the following paragraphs.

The Department of Transport representing the taxpayer is the first market segment. Though the line is operated at very low direct costs, the economics of railway operation relates unit costs to consistent traffic density (Preston, 1994). The West Highland line has—and always has had—a low traffic density in relation to its fixed infrastructure costs, though modern methods of railway operation and maintenance have reduced such costs in real money terms. There is also a marked seasonality of demand, and this does affect direct costs, for the provision of additional train capacity in the short 'high season' peak has proved to be inescapable. It is doubtful whether the line's traffic has covered its total costs in any year since 1945, and it was certainly making substantial losses by the time the Beeching Report was published in 1961. The remit of Richard Beeching as Chairman of British Railways Board was to reshape British Railways to eliminate subsidy costs to the taxpayer. In the event the social and political costs of many proposed closures, including that of the West Highland line, were deemed to be unacceptable. Here it may be noted that the similar route from Stirling to Oban was closed between Stirling and Crianlarich, but that it proved possible to interwork the Crianlarich to Oban service with the West Highland Railway, as the map (Appendix 1) shows. Privatisation of the line may offer scope for the reduction of direct costs, as will be shown.

The second market segment, in terms of financial importance, are 'backpacking' tourists. They are not all young, though it is significant that one of the peak seasonal trains is called 'The Young Explorer'. Characteristically this segment travels on discount price tickets and often uses either rail cards (such as Young Person's or Senior Citizen's cards) or 'Rover' tickets, including BritRail passes for overseas visitors.

Offering some similarities to the backpacker segment are the 'trippers'. Many of the trippers are travelling to view the scenery from the line, or to travel on the steam train from Fort William to Mallaig, or even to travel behind some cult diesel locomotives which are (as we shall see) used in the high season. The time and distances involved means that many trippers are short break travellers, rather than day-out trippers. In May 1985 the British Rail 'normal' discount price ticket, called

'Saver' and 'Super Saver', replaced the 'Cheap Day Return' which precluded an overnight stay. Both the backpackers and the trippers are served by the day-time Regional Railway services, and by the scheduled steam-hauled passenger services between Fort William and Mallaig, which are run by InterCity on a commercial basis.

A third category of user of these services are local residents, making the trip by train either because they do not have access to a car, or because the train is more convenient or more comfortable than alternative modes. This segment is the most constant in size through the year, and is therefore proportionally the least important at peak times.

On the nightly InterCity sleeping car trains from London to Fort William and vice versa, there are completely different segments, as is evidenced by the availability of first-class accommodation and Motorail vehicles permitting the family car to be transported. Though discount packages are offered for Motorail users, the absence of any non-sleeping-car accommodation, and of any journey facilities which are not cross-border, means that the services are inherently expensive to use. The market segments served by these services are all small, and include business travellers (including members of Parliament), the 'hunting, shooting and fishing' leisure sector, and families from the south of England wishing to avoid the long haul with a car to the West Highlands, and using the Motorail facility. It is the writer's judgement, supported by internal BR data, that the economic viability of sleeping car services on most routes in Britain is tenuous, as the difference in operating pattern between the night services and high-intensity day services becomes ever greater.

In addition to these passenger segments, a small but profitable quantity of freight traffic (e.g. alumina) contributes usefully to the cost of the line's infrastructure. However, the total volume is small and in this respect the Scottish line shows a marked contrast to similar routes in Switzerland or Austria, where the environmental advantages of keeping freight off the roads has encouraged regional or central governments to manipulate the market to ensure that rail is used where possible, even though on Alpine routes there is often the additional transshipment cost of loading standard gauge railway wagons onto narrow-gauge transporters. In Britain rail freight is not subsidised, but Whitelegg (1992) has made a powerful case that road freight is, and evidence of road 'improvements' made to cope with delivery lorries is present in many areas of natural beauty, to the detriment of the environment—hence the sceptical view of improvements.

The peak

The demand for travel on the West Highland line is very severely peaked, and observations confirm BR data from 1989, which suggest that the level of demand on a peak August Saturday is five times greater than the mean for the period October to March. In 1993 the southbound train service until 19 June and from 6 September consisted of three day-time trains from Fort William to Glasgow run by Regional Railways (Scotrail), and one sleeping car train from Fort William to London. The trains from Fort William have, since January 1989, almost invariably consisted of a single two- (winter) or three- (summer) car diesel train (henceforth known by the brand name of 'Sprinter') which offered 186 standard class seats as far as Crianlarich, where the train joins to another two- or three-car set from Oban (Fox, 1989). Observations suggest that the train from Fort William usually has a higher load factor than that from Oban, with the result that there are often vacant seats from Crianlarich to Glasgow. The 'Sprinter' trains which operate the service most of the year have replaced the previous generation of trains which comprised a rake of coaches hauled by a diesel locomotive. The seating capacity of a locomotive-hauled train was between 300 and 440 passengers, compared to the 288 capacity of a four-car 'Sprinter', or 432 when a six-car train is provided. It is clear that in the high peak of the summer even six-car 'Sprinter' trains have inadequate capacity to meet the demand and in fact an entirely different timetable operates, with many of the services being operated by rakes of passenger coaches hauled by locomotives normally used for other duties, such as the haulage of engineers' trains. The West Highland line is unusual (in Britain) in that the summer peak timetable operates Monday to Saturday, and not just on Saturdays. The relatively low service provision on Sundays is in marked contrast to similar services in Continental Europe.

Behaviour on trains

Customer behaviour on trains has a marked influence on the phenomenon of standing passengers, especially in the shoulders to the high peak. To accommodate 292 passengers the 'Sprinter' trains have a very much higher seating density, and far less luggage space, than the train coaches hauled by locomotives. The almost inevitable result is that passengers with bulky baggage such as rucksacks habitually place them on seats. It is quite likely that a passenger boarding a train at Corrour on a busy shoulder peak day would find all seats occupied with people or with baggage. At Crianlarich this crowded two-car train will have coupled to the probably less crowded two-car train from Oban, and there is a corridor connection allowing movement down the length of the combined train. Helpful train staff might well have (a) persuaded the owners of seat-occupying baggage to deposit their belongings elsewhere (it should be noted that the luggage racks will not accept rucksacks), or (b) have informed the young woman that there were seats available after Crianlarich. The writer has no way of establishing whether the train crew were helpful on this occasion, though on more than 20 other journeys made in similar circumstances, the writer has observed that train conductors offer guidance to standing passengers according to four circumstantial variables. These are:

1. The age, gender and apparent frailty of those standing.
2. The personality of the train conductor.
3. The extent to which the standing passengers are a nuisance to train crews. For example when there are refreshment trolley services provided, as on most Fort William trains, the attendants often encourage passengers to sit (and place their baggage out of the gangway), in order to allow the trolley to pass.
4. The availability of seats that are unreserved and readily accessible.

A factor which inhibits railway staff from offering seats to young standing passengers is the fact that it is observable that many young people travelling by train choose to stand rather than sit in proximity to other age groups, especially if the choice is to stand with relatively large amounts of space and be adjacent to belongings, or to sit in high-density seats away from possessions.

Strategies to respond to peak disequilibrium

Faced with an excess of demand over supply for a product such as a seat/kilometre, which cannot be stockpiled, the operator can adopt six strategies. They are:

1. To offer increased capacity at busy times.
2. To limit peak demand by compulsory reservation, and turn away those who come too late to book a journey.
3. To switch-sell journeys to less busy times.
4. To manipulate demand through differential pricing, so as to maintain equilibrium between supply and demand.
5. To offer a high standard capacity level and adopt a creative marketing strategy to promote off-peak business to absorb surplus capacity.
6. To maintain a standard (and therefore economical) level of service provision geared to the mode of demand and allow overcrowding to the limits of

physical possibility at peak times—the Malthusian misery solution.

It must first be said that these strategies are not mutually exclusive. It is clear, for example, that differential pricing often generates extra peak revenue which may justify expenditure on increased capacity. The judicious mixture of these approaches is one of the major skills of travel marketing. It is greatly facilitated by the good use of information systems, both of computerised reservations, and as a source of data about demand patterns. On InterCity rail services the fact that British Rail uses sophisticated segmented pricing where Deutsche Bundesbahn (for instance) would apply standard prices and provide additional capacity, explains the much higher British net revenue figures (Steward-David, 1993). If we analyse the ways in which Regional Railways apply the six strategies, we find the following phenomena.

Extra capacity at peak times

The West Highland line timetable (Appendix 2) reveals the increased frequency of trains in the high peak. It understates the additional supply, for, as has been explained, the 'Sprinter' trains are substantially replaced by locomotive-hauled trains with much greater seating and luggage capacity. These trains have a poorer power-to-weight ratio compared to 'Sprinters' and this is one reason why the peak services are very much slower. Though the coaches used are quite old by British standards, they offer a low density of seating and better window views than 'Sprinters', so their passenger acceptability is reasonable, and the fact that the journey time from Mallaig to Glasgow is increased (e.g. on the 10.25 service) from 5 hours 19 minutes to 6 hours 3 minutes may not be that much of a deterrent, given that we are discussing average speeds of the order of 26–30 mph. The problem with the provision of peak capacity is that it increases direct costs of operation substantially, not least because of the lower train/km per crew hour. There is no doubt that the availability of two or three additional 'Sprinter' units to the West Highland service would allow a much greater flexibility of supply, especially at the shoulder peaks, and would meet the high peak demand with lower staff costs. However, the rate of return from units bought to be used in this way would not be acceptable to the British Government, though road schemes in tourist areas often receive Department of Transport funding to cope with substantial congestion on a limited number of peak days, in spite of adverse environmental consequences. The new generation of 'Sprinter' trains built in the late 1980s are widely used on tourist routes within the UK (e.g. the Cambrian Coast line, the Settle and Carlisle route, and services to Stratford on Avon) and in many cases the ability of these trains to deliver a faster and more frequent service most days of the year has been matched by their inability to cope with peak demands on perhaps twenty or thirty days a year; but the operational cost of supplementing the units with trains of a previous generation (when these are available at all) is inordinately high. The penalty for highly efficient utilisation of trains and crews, is the inability to cope with the highest peaks of demand.

Switch-selling and mandatory reservation

The problem of limited capacity at high peaks is common to all forms of public transport, to roads, to hotels and to package tours which combine such operations. A very common commercial approach is to switch-sell potential customers from one departure time or date to another, or to another destination. This approach is indeed used to control demand for the sleeping car trains from London to Fort William and return. However, it cannot be used effectively on the day-time Regional Railways trains for several reasons. The first is that whilst seat reservation is possible on almost all West Highland line trains, it is not mandatory. There are three reasons why not. The first is that the 'walk on' facility is known to be one of the major selling points of rail travel. The second is that the optional travel market segments served by these particular services are inherently spontaneous, and turning away impromptu travellers because they had not made reservations would be commercially unacceptable. The third reason is that it would be impossible to stop passengers without reservations boarding at intermediate stations, so the condition would be unenforceable, in contrast, for instance to air transport operation (except perhaps on Aeroflot). Selling seat reservations with tickets—common on business trains—is impossible when many passengers have some form of 'go as you please' ticket.

Differential pricing

Differential pricing is widely used by British Rail InterCity sector to maximise revenue yield and redistribute demand (Cole, 1987). Typically peak hour business trains are restricted to full-price ticket holders. Travellers with discount price tickets, or having used a railcard to obtain a discount, are prohibited from travelling on such peak trains, and are surcharged if they do. Travellers with deep discount Apex and Super Apex tickets are required to travel on individually specified trains. This is an extremely successful approach to demand management, but it relies on there being three clear segments: price-insensitive business travellers; derived demand travellers for whom journey schedule can be traded for discount; and optional travellers for whom an Apex ticket may be the means of making journeys which would be precluded or would be made by coach.

On Regional Railways the services are run with Public Service Obligation (PSO) subsidy and the market segments are far from clearly differentiated. Two implications are inherent in this. The first is that the prime marketing objective is market share and/or optimum load factors rather than maximum yield. The second is that a wide spread of ticket prices is of less utility. It would be possible to place a peak seasonal surcharge on every train, but this revenue would have to be collected by the conductors, and the surcharging process would be labour-intensive and might well be unpopular, especially with local residents for whom the train is more of a utility than a luxury. The fact is that no such peak pricing is applied to Regional Railway services, though it is an option which could be applied after privatisation, especially if the fragmentation of the railway system leads to a decline in the availability of 'go as you please' tickets. What is more surprising than the absence of a peak period surcharge is the absence of off-peak excursion tickets designed to stimulate demand, though some railway tours are organised which offer off-peak short breaks, usually without accommodation off the train. A major constraint on the promotion of off-peak use of all Regional Railway services is the very small advertising and promotional budget allocated to the services.

The standard service approach

This approach to seasonality of demand establishes a level of service which would meet the demand for seats on the great majority of services operated in a year. If the logic were applied to the West Highland line, then the same timetable would apply (at least on Mondays to Saturdays) throughout the year, and the Scotrail services would be operated by two-car 'Sprinter' trains from Mallaig and from Oban, combining into four-car trains at Crianlarich (and splitting there on down journeys from Glasgow). This would engender load factors of more than 100% for less than 3% of all journeys. The facility to avoid standing is available to all passengers prudent enough to reserve a seat, and Travel Centres would be in a position to advise passengers of the likelihood of the need to reserve a seat to avoid standing. (There are other reasons for making seat reservations, e.g. to obtain a seat in a particular location in the train, or to ensure that a group of people are seated together.) The economy of operation gained from running this kind of service all the year round is very great, and the 'Sprinter' trains have offered the first important improvements in journey times since 1914 (Caplan, 1988). The obstacle to this approach is simple, on the occasions when the services do burst past 100% load factor they may do so dramatically, so that the problem is not merely that of standing passengers, but of trains so full of passengers and their baggage that potential travellers simply cannot board the train. A passenger holding a return ticket from (say) Spean Bridge to Manchester is likely to be less than satisfied if she cannot board the last train of the day because there is not even any standing room. Whilst over 90% of Scotrail passengers on the route travel on discount tickets, it is also true that the vast majority are tourists, and tourism, in spite of experience to the contrary is undertaken in the hope that it will be a pleasure. Frustration of this pleasure is a source of bitter complaint and the erosion of a reputation for quality which has been created for ten months of the year. Faced with this threat, the operator, as we have seen, increases train capacity to cope with the high peak, even though it is highly likely that the extra revenue of the high peak does not cover the additional costs of peak service provision.

Prospects for the West Highland line as a tourist railway

Strengths

The line's passenger traffic has grown by more than 20% since it was modernised in 1988. In marketing terms tourism in the region is growing, and the outdoor pursuits category of tourism has shown itself to be more recession-proof than many other segments. The rail market share of passenger traffic has grown since 1988, and discount travel using Young Persons' and Senior Citizens' Railcards has shown sustained development.

The cost of operating the line has fallen dramatically in real money terms for three reasons. These are: the reduction in infrastructure costs thanks to Radio Electronic Token Block signalling and modern track maintenance methods; the reduction in train costs through the introduction of 'Sprinter' trains, which have, for instance, 50% of the fuel cost of a diesel locomotive (Fox, 1989); staff costs are lower thanks to the closure of signal boxes and the more productive use of train crews. Complementing these financial strengths is the thought that the political cost to the Conservatives of closing a high-profile Scottish railway with improving performance is unthinkable, as was demonstrated when the Ness Railway Bridge was rebuilt on the Far North line.

Weaknesses

The main weakness of the market for travel on the West Highland line is that symbolised by the title—that growth in travel seems to have contributed multiplicative seasonality to the existing additive seasonality (Cooper et al., 1993), with the result that the high season peak already exceeds the capacity of the 'Sprinter' fleet, and there are signs that this problem is spreading to the shoulder peaks, with the ironic result that there is a need to resort to the previous generation of train, with its higher costs and slower running times. The present pricing approach does little to control peak demands, and the example of InterCity's approach suggests that more use could be made of demand management.

Opportunities

Rail privatisation is both an opportunity and a threat. The rail franchise holders (if any bid), will negotiate payments with Railtrack Ltd for use of infrastructure, and also, which may be more important, with leasing companies for the use of trains. Privatisation may mean that the West Highland train operators can obtain the use of additional 'Sprinter' trains in the crucial summer months—at a price. If the privatised bus industry is anything to go by, then national wage agreements for rail staff will start to disappear, and on the West Highland line one might expect to find a cut in the real money value of wages, though it is unlikely that this will cut costs as much as the productivity gains achieved in the past six years. Privatisation may encourage imaginative promotions, such as an increased number of excursions along the full route using preserved steam or diesel locomotives.

Road pricing may start to play a role in the development of sustainable tourism, which could alter the competitive position of rail compared to road.

Threats

The biggest threat to the West Highland line's prosperity lies in rail privatisation, or rather in railway fragmentation, for this may threaten the viability of discount rail cards, and of 'go as you please' Rover tickets, both of which are crucial to the marketing strategy of Regional Railways. Other drawbacks to rail privatisation may be a threat to sleeping car services, where costs are hard to control; but cheap 'coach'-type rail journeys to London may reappear.

Conclusion

The young woman who claimed she had stood all the way from Corrour was in a shoulder peak train that had four cars when it was scheduled to have six. Even so, she could have reserved a seat, and even if she had not, she could quite possibly have found a seat. Clearly she was not a satisfied customer, but the cause of her dissatisfaction was the ability of Scotrail to create the long-term satisfaction of many of its customers, not least the government. Recent broad-brush criticisms of British Rail have tarred the entire management of this nationalised industry with the petulant generalisation of the girl who stood from Corrour. A considered analysis suggests that the West Highland line in 1994 offers a better service at lower cost than at any time in the previous hundred years, and that its biggest problem is the economic handling of a growing summer peak.

Appendix 1

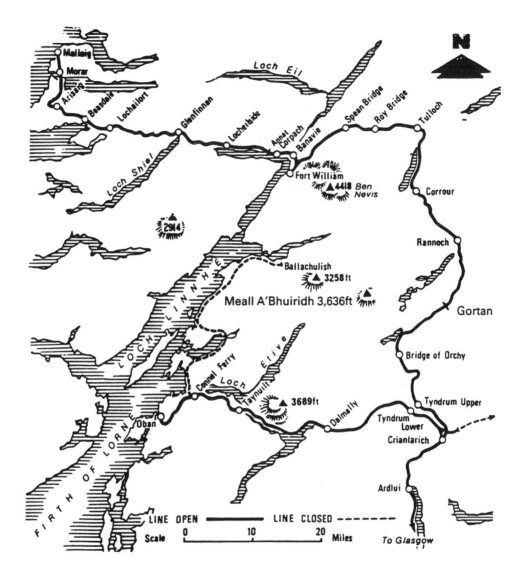

Appendix 2 (The railway timetables shown are reproduced with the kind permission of British Rail)

SCOTRAIL - WEST HIGHLAND LINE

Table 227

Glasgow Queen Street — Oban, Fort William and Mallaig

Mondays to Saturdays | Sundays

Miles	Miles			◇	◇ A C	◇ D	MFSO ◇ E G	MFSX ◇ J K	◇			MFSX ◇ L	◇				◇ N	◇ P	◇ Q	◇ N			◇			
—	—	Edinburgh 10	228 d		07 00	07 30	08 30	08 30	11 30				17 00					08 30	11 30	11 30			16 30			
0	0	**Glasgow Queen Street**	226 d		08 12	08 42	09 50	09 50	12 42				18 12					09 42	12 42	12 42			18 12			
10	10	Dalmuir	226 d		08 27	08 57	10 09	10 09	12 57				18 27					09 57	12 57	12 57			18 27			
16½	16½	Dumbarton Central	226 d		08 36	09 06	10 20	10 20	13 06				18 36					10 06	13 06	13 06			18 36			
25½	25½	Helensburgh Upper	d		08 53	09 23	10 42	10 42	13 23				18 53					10 23	13 23	13 23			18 53			
32¼	32¼	Garelochhead	d		09 04	09 34	10 55	10 55	13 34				19 05					10 34	13 34	13 34			19 05			
43	43	Arrochar & Tarbet	d		09 24	09 58	11 17	11 17	13 55				19 25					10 54	13 55	13 55			19 25			
51	51	Ardlui	d		09 42	10 11	11 32	11 32	14 10				19 47					11 07	14 10	14 10			19 47			
59¾	59¾	**Crianlarich**	a		09 59	10 27	11 50	11 50	14 25				20 02					11 23	14 25	14 25			20 02			
—	—		d		10 06	10 32	11 53	12 03	14 31	14 37		18 25	20 08	20 14				11 26	14 31	14 31	14 37		20 08	20 14		
64¼	—	Tyndrum Lower	d			10 39	12 02		14 38			18 32	20 15					11 33	14 38	14 38			20 15			
76¼	—	Dalmally	d			10 56	12 21		14 55			18 52	20 32					11 50	14 55	14 55			20 32			
79½	—	Loch Awe	d			11 01	12 26		15 00			18 57	20 37					11 55	15 00	15 00			20 37			
83½	—	Falls of Cruachan	d			11x05			15x04			19x02	20x42					12x00	15x04	15x04						
88½	—	Taynuilt	d			11 15	12 43		15 14			19 12	20 52					12 10	15 14	15 14			20 52			
95¼	—	Connel Ferry	d			11 26	12 56		15 25			19 23	21 03					12 21	15 25	15 25			21 03			
101½	—	**Oban**	a			11 38	13 10		15 37			19 35	21 15					12 32	15 37	15 37			21 15			
—	64¼	Upper Tyndrum	d		10 17			12 16		14 48				20 25							14 48			20 25		
—	72¾	Bridge of Orchy	d		10 31			12 35		15 02				20 39							15 02			20 39		
—	87¾	Rannoch	d		10 52			13 07		15 23				21 06							15 23			21 06		
—	95	Corrour	d		11 04			13 22		15 35				21 18							15 35			21 18		
—	105	Tulloch	d		11 20			13 43		15 51				21 34							15 51			21 34		
—	110¾	Roy Bridge	d		11 30			13 53		16 01				21 44							16 01			21 44		
—	114	Spean Bridge	d		11 36			14 01		16 07				21 50							16 07			21 50		
—	122¾	**Fort William**	65 a		11 54			14 15		16 20				22 03							16 20			22 03		
—	—		d	08 45	12 00					16 25				22 10			12 00				16 25			22 10		
—	125	Banavie	d	08 51	12 06					16 31				22 16			12 06				16 31			22 16		
—	126	Corpach	d	08 56	12 11					16 36				22 21			12 11				16 36			22 21		
—	129	Loch Eil Outward Bound	d	09 02	12 17					16 42				22 27			12 17				16 42			22 27		
—	132¾	Locheilside	d	09x07	12x22					16x47				22x32			12x22				16x47			22x32		
—	139¼	Glenfinnan	d	09 17	12 32					17 00				22 42			12 32				17 00			22 42		
—	148½	Lochailort	d	09x33	12x48					17x15				22x58			12x48				17x15			22x58		
—	153¼	Beasdale	d	09x42	12x57					17x24				23x07			12x57				17x24			23x07		
—	156¾	Arisaig	d	09 50	13 06					17 32				23 15			13 06				17 32			23 15		
—	161¼	Morar	d	09 58	13 14					17 40				23 23			13 14				17 40			23 23		
—	164¼	**Mallaig**	a	10 05	13 25					17 47				23 30			13 25				17 47			23 30		

Mondays to Saturdays

Miles	Miles			◇			◇	◇	MFSO ◇ E G	MFSX ◇ L	MFSX ◇ J L	◇ A			◇	
—	0	**Mallaig**	d	06 00			10 30					16 10			18 15	
—	3	Morar	d	06 07			10 37					16 17			18 22	
—	7¼	Arisaig	d	06 16			10 46					16 26			18 31	
—	11	Beasdale	d	06x22			10x52					16x32			18x37	
—	15¼	Lochailort	d	06x31			11x01					16x41			18x46	
—	25	Glenfinnan	d	06 48			11 18					16 59			19 03	
—	31¼	Locheilside	d	06x57			11x27					17x08			19x12	
—	35¼	Loch Eil Outward Bound	d	07 03			11 33					17 14			19 18	
—	38¼	Corpach	d	07 09			11 39					17 20			19 24	
—	39¼	Banavie	d	07 13			11 43					17 24			19 28	
—	41¼	**Fort William** 65	a	07 20			11 53					17 31			19 35	
—	—		d	07 30			12 03				15 52	17 38				
—	50¼	Spean Bridge	d	07 43			12 16				16 12	17 51				
—	53¼	Roy Bridge	d	07 49			12 22				16 19	17 57				
—	59¼	Tulloch	d	08 01			12 33				16 33	18 08				
—	69¼	Corrour	d	08 17			12 49				16 56	18 25				
—	76¼	Rannoch	d	08 29			13 04				17 11	18 36				
—	92	Bridge of Orchy	d	08 49			13 24				17 34	18 55				
—	99¼	Upper Tyndrum	d	09 05			13 40				17 52	19 11				
0	—	**Oban**	d		08 05			13 10	16 00	16 48			18 08			
6¼	—	Connel Ferry	d		08 16			13 26	16 19	16 59			18 19			
13	—	Taynuilt	d		08 27			13 37	16 32	17 10			18 30			
18¼	—	Falls of Cruachan	d		08x35			13x45		17x18			18x38			
22	—	Loch Awe	d		08 41			13 52	16 49	17 25			18 44			
24¼	—	Dalmally	d		08 47			13 58	16 55	17 30			18 51			
36¼	—	Tyndrum Lower	d		09 05			14 16	17 18	17 49			19 09			
42	104¼	**Crianlarich**	a	09 19	09 19		13 48	14 23	17 25	17 56	18 04	19 22	19 22			
—	—		d	09 25			13 53	14 27	17 30		18 08	19 28				
50¼	113¼	Ardlui	d	09 42			14 11	14 44	17 49		18 26	19 46				
58¼	121¼	Arrochar & Tarbet	d	09 57			14 26	14 58	18 04		18 41	20 00				
69¼	132	Garelochhead	d	10 16			14 49	15 17	18 26		19 08	20 19				
76¼	138¼	Helensburgh Upper	d	10 28			15 01	15 29	18 39		19 20	20 31				
85¼	147¼	Dumbarton Central 226	d	10 45			15 15	15 45	18 56		19 44	20 45				
92¼	154¼	Dalmuir 226	d	10 54			15 24	15 54	19 07		19 55	20 54				
101¼	164¼	**Glasgow Queen Street** 226	a	11 14			15 44	16 14	19 30		20 18	21 14				
—	—	Edinburgh 228	a	*12 20*			*16 50*	*17 20*	*20 50*		*21 20*	*22 20*				

Sundays

		◇ N	◇		◇ Q	◇ P	◇	◇		◇ N	
Mallaig	d	10 30					16 10			18 15	
Morar	d	10 37					16 17			18 22	
Arisaig	d	10 46					16 26			18 31	
Beasdale	d	10x52					16x32			18x37	
Lochailort	d	11x01					16x41			18x46	
Glenfinnan	d	11 18					16 59			19 03	
Locheilside	d	11x27					17x08			19x12	
Loch Eil Outward Bound	d	11 33					17 14			19 18	
Corpach	d	11 39					17 20			19 24	
Banavie	d	11 43					17 24			19 28	
Fort William	a	11 53					17 31			19 35	
	d	12 03					17 38				
Spean Bridge	d	12 16					17 51				
Roy Bridge	d	12 22					17 57				
Tulloch	d	12 33					18 08				
Corrour	d	12 49					18 25				
Rannoch	d	13 00					18 36				
Bridge of Orchy	d	13 20					18 55				
Upper Tyndrum	d	13 35					19 11				
Oban	d		12 35		12 35	16 15		18 08			
Connel Ferry	d		12 46		12 46	16 26		18 19			
Taynuilt	d		12 57		12 57	16 37		18 30			
Falls of Cruachan	d		13x04		13x04	16x45		18x38			
Loch Awe	d		13 11		13 11	16 52		18 44			
Dalmally	d		13 16		13 16	16 57		18 51			
Tyndrum Lower	d		13 35		13 35	17 16		19 09			
Crianlarich	a	13 46	13 46		13 46	17 23	19 22	19 22			
	d	13 53			13 53	17 26	19 28				
Ardlui	d	14 11			14 11	17 41	19 46				
Arrochar & Tarbet	d	14 26			14 26	17 55	20 00				
Garelochhead	d	14 49			14 49	18 14	20 19				
Helensburgh Upper	d	15 01			15 01	18 26	20 31				
Dumbarton Central	d	15 15			15 15	18 40	20 45				
Dalmuir	d	15 24			15 24	18 49	20 54				
Glasgow Queen Street	a	15 44			15 44	19 05	21 14				
Edinburgh	a	*16 59*			*16 59*	*20 22*	*22 22*				

For general notes see front of timetable

- **A** **Lord of the Isles**
- **C** Mondays to Fridays from Stirling (Table 230), except Glasgow Public Holiday Mondays 30 May and 19 July
- **D** From Falkirk Grahamston (Table 230)
- **E** **Oban Explorer**
- **G** 4 July to 3 September
- **J** **Centenary Explorer**
- **K** 5 July to 1 September(except 11 August)
- **L** 5 July to 1 September
- **N** From 3 July
- **P** 3 July to 4 September
- **Q** Until 26 June

From time to time it is necessary to undertake extensive engineering work at weekends. This frequently affects services and passengers are advised to look for specific announcements of possible diversions and delays making a final check at stations or telephone enquiry bureaux.

Appendix 2 (*continued*)

Sleeper INTERCITY

Table 404

THE WEST HIGHLANDER

London and Fort William *Sleeping Accommodation only*

		Mon-Fri ⓛ 🚗	Saturday ⓛ 🚗 A	Sunday ⓛ 🚗
Occupy cabins at Euston:		*1955*	*2110*	*1930*
London Euston	dep	2025	2200h	1950
Crewe	dep	2242	0105•	2207
Preston	dep	2349	0153•	2253
Dalmuir	arr	0432b	0726	0432
Helensburgh Upper	arr	0457b	0751	0457
Garelochhead	arr	0512b	0806	0512
Arrochar & Tarbet	arr	0538c	0832	0538
Ardlui	arr	0554c	0848	0554
Crianlarich	arr	0616e	0910	0616
Upper Tyndrum	arr	0631f	0925	0631
Bridge of Orchy	arr	0649g	0943	0649
Rannoch	arr	0719	1013	0719
Corrour	arr	0736	1030	0736
Tulloch	arr	0756	1050	0756
Roy Bridge	arr	0812	1102	0812
Spean Bridge	arr	0818	1108	0818
Fort William	arr	0835	1125	0835
Vacate cabins at Fort William by		*0835*	*1125*	*0835*

		Mon-Fri ⓛ 🚗	Saturday ⓛ 🚗 A	Sunday ⓛ 🚗
Occupy cabins at Fort William:		*1930*	*1840*	*1840*
Fort William	dep	1945	1900	1900
Spean Bridge	dep	2003	1918	1918
Roy Bridge	dep	2010	1924	1924
Tulloch	dep	2024	1939	1939
Corrour	dep	2048	2001	2001
Rannoch	dep	2107	2014	2014
Bridge of Orchy	dep	2132	2043	2043
Upper Tyndrum	dep	2152	2105	2105
Crianlarich	dep	2204	2121	2121
Ardlui	dep	2224	2141	2141
Arrochar & Tarbet	dep	2241	2159	2159
Garelochhead	dep	2306	2226	2226
Helensburgh Upper	dep	2320	2240	2240
Dalmuir	dep	2340	2308	2308
Preston	arr	0414	0422	0414
Crewe	arr	0503	0521	0503
London Euston	arr	0735j	0827	0725
Vacate cabins at Euston by		*0800*	*0830*	*0800*

Notes:

ⓛ   Sleeper Lounge

🚗   Motorail
London to Fort William
and Fort William to London

A   16 July to 3 September

b   Arrives 11 minutes earlier on Saturday mornings

c   Arrives 9 minutes earlier on Saturday mornings

e   Arrives 0609 on Saturdays

f   Arrives 0625 on Saturdays

g   Arrives 0644 on Saturdays

h   Departs 2220 from 23 July

j   Arrives 0725 Tuesday to Friday

•   Following morning

References

Beeching, R. (1961) *The Reshaping of British Railways*, British Railways Board, London.

Caplan, N. (1988) *The West Highland Lines*, Ian Allan, Weybridge.

Cole, S. (1987) *Applied Transport Economics*, Kogan Page, London.

Cooper, C., Fletcher, J., Gilbert, D. and Wanhill, S. (1993) *Tourism Principles and Practice*, Pitman, London.

Fox, A. (1989) 'The sprint to the Isles', *Modern Railways*, August.

Piercy, N. (1992) *Market-Led Strategic Change*, Butterworth–Heinemann, Oxford.

Preston, J. (1994) 'Does size matter—a case study of European railways', Universities Transport Study Group conference paper, Leeds.

Stewart-David, D. (1993) 'Fresh air and standing passengers—a study of InterCity marketing', Paper to the Chartered Institute of Transport, Newcastle.

Whitelegg, J. (1992) 'Rail's contribution to improving the environment', in *Travel Sickness*, Roberts, J., Cleary, J., Hamilton, K. and Hanna, J. (Eds), Lawrence & Wishart, London.

Wilkie, W. (1986) *Consumer Behaviour*, John Wiley, New York.

56 How different are Scottish family holidays from English?

S. K. TAGG AND A. V. SEATON

Introduction

The family holiday is a central institution throughout the developed world and a major market for tourism suppliers. Yet little research exists indicating the respective roles its major participants—children and their parents—play in the choice, experience and satisfaction levels associated with holidays (Seaton and Tagg, 1994). This paper reports on part of a larger study investigating the family holiday in four European countries. The study involves interviews with nearly three thousand families in Belgium, France, the UK and Italy. The survey was the first to gather data from the responses of both children and adults to a common measurement instrument, the Strathclyde Triple Role Family Tourism Inventory (STRFTI), described in more detail under 'Methodology', below.

In this report the responses of children in England and Scotland were disaggregated from the UK sample and examined in order to assess their similarities and differences in family holiday behaviour.

Scotland versus England

No published research exists predicting or reporting on differences in English and Scottish family holiday behaviour or the reasons that may underlie them. However, at an intuitive level, several factors could reasonably be expected to influence the kinds of variations in holiday that might exist between the two countries.

Geography

Differences between the two countries can be seen in terms of weather, in that Scotland is colder and wetter, and in the distance that needs to be travelled to foreign destinations. This means that the English families in this sample are within one day's driving distance of the Channel ports.

Cultural

Scotland differs from England in many cultural and consumer patterns. The Scottish consumer is more associated with saving and self-reliance. Holiday-taking is different in Scotland with a different pattern of official holidays both at the New Year and in terms of local bank holidays.

Economic climate

There were differences in the onset of the early 1990s recession in the two countries. Although Scotland lost jobs, most of its traditional heavy manufacturing industry had already disappeared in the 1970s and 1980s. However in the early 1990s the West Midlands lost more jobs, and suffered more from the drop in house prices. In 1992 the West Midlands was more 'shocked' by the recession than Scotland, and worse off, especially in holiday expenditure. The average weekly disposable income in Scotland was £257.15 and in the West Midlands £252.39. The average weekly expenditure on hotel and holiday expenditures was £9.80 for Scotland and £7.80 for the West Midlands (CSO, 1993).

Family structure

The percentages of households with single adult and one or more child was 5.6% for Scotland and 6.7% for the West Midlands. This difference will include a majority of single mothers, where the father's access may be limited to taking the child on holiday (CSO, 1993).

Methodology

The questionnaire (STRFTI) was developed at the Scottish Hotel School and represents two years of qualitative and quantitative testing. It involves around a hundred items designed to cover the behaviours, attitudes, interests and opinions of respondents towards family holidays. More specifically the Strathclyde Triple Role Family Tourism Inventory covers five areas, as well as some basic socio-demographic characteristics, and characteristics of the holiday itself:

1. Decision patterns
2. Activities and social interactions

3. Satisfactions
4. Future intentions
5. Attitudes and opinions

Responses were directed to the *last main holiday* that the child took with *one or both* of its parents. All responses were pre-coded and formatted as easy-to-answer tick-boxes; the attitudes and opinions were recorded with five-point Likert scales. The coverage of the questionnaire expresses an implicit theory of the involvement of teenagers in family holidays. Teenagers can be involved in deciding where to go, they can vary in terms of what they do while on holiday, and vary in terms of how happy they were on holiday. They will also have consequent and concomitant attitudes, opinions and intentions towards holidays, and family holidays in particular. The attitude and opinion items represent a range of views culled from research of press statements. These aspects of family holidays were recalled by the children at a period between 2 months and, for the majority, two years after the holiday.

Sample

The sample was taken from schools in the Glasgow area of Scotland and in the West Midlands of England. In total there were 334 pupils from Scottish schools and 610 from English Schools. Cooperation was obtained from a convenience sample of schools. The schools were all in major urban conurbations where tourism propensity is high, and they were chosen, as far as possible, to reflect upper and lower socio-demographic extremes, in order to provide a representative social cross-section of families for the whole of the UK. The fieldwork ran from September 1992 to December 1992. Each school agreed to allow the sampling of between 50 and 100 pupils from their school roll. The research proceeded as follows. The

child's questionnaire was administered on a day normally fixed about six weeks in advance, to samples of schoolchildren aged 12–18, in the classroom, under the direction of a briefed researcher. Some schools provided the total respondent sample in one large hall session, others cumulatively by allowing access to several classes during the course of the day. There was a high degree of supervisory control of the questionnaire which was carefully explained to the children, with opportunities for them to seek clarification at any point during the completion session. The questionnaires took about twenty to thirty minutes to complete, and were collected by the researcher at the end of the session.

Because of the convenience sampling of schools it is possible that the sample in Scotland and England may differ in a way not representative of the differences of the two populations. For this reason the differences between the countries are investigated both in the raw form, and in appropriate ways to correct for monitored differences. Some of the differences between the samples may be because of class differences between the countries.

All differences between the measures on the questionnaire are examined and the interesting and statistically significant ones are reported here. Because of the possibilities of reporting spurious significant results in such an exercise, the level of significance used was 1%.

Results

Socio-demographic

Age
The Scottish respondents differed significantly in age profile (see Figure 56.1). There were more under 12, slightly more 13–14, less 15–16 and more 17–18 (chi-square 83.8, df = 4).

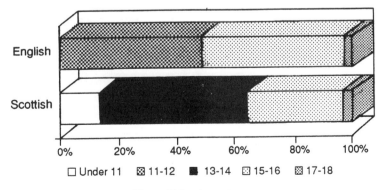

Figure 56.1 *Age category*

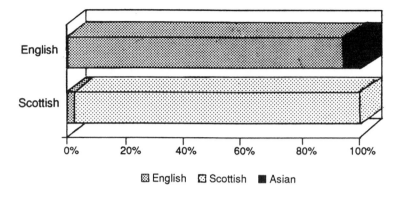

Figure 56.2 *Nationality*

Sex

There was not a significant difference in sex distribution for the samples, although the Scottish respondents were 60% male and the English 56%.

Nationality

Although the obvious difference in nationality between the Scottish and West Midlands schools swamps the graph, it is worth noting that there are more pupils identifying themselves as English in the Scottish schools than vice versa, and more identifying themselves as Asians in the West Midlands schools (see Figure 56.2) (chi-square 871.4, df = 2). If all the citizens in the UK are put together there is no significant difference.

Father's occupation

Scottish respondents' fathers were less frequently coded as professional or working class, and more frequently in the lower middle grouping (see Figure 56.3) (chi-square 11.4, df = 3).

Mother's occupation

Although the differences in mother's occupation class were along the same line, they were not significantly different.

These socio-demographic results suggest that although there are some differences between the two national samples, they are broadly comparable. This means that simple differences in proportion are worth investigating, but that differences in age and class are worth investigating as possible causes of spurious differences.

The holiday itself

The first question asked: 'When did you last take a main summer holiday away from home with one or both of your parents?' A larger number (88%) of Scottish schoolchildren had taken one within the last two years, whereas only 78% of the West Midlands children were in that category. Scottish children included 36% without a holiday in the last year; the West Midlands schools had a figure of 42%. This suggests that the Scottish children

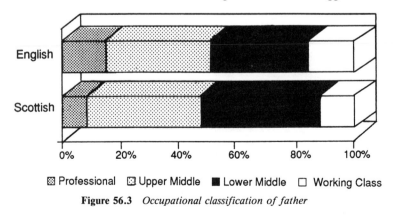

Figure 56.3 *Occupational classification of father*

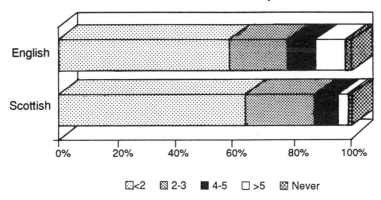

Figure 56.4 *Years since last holiday*

had had a more recent holiday (see Figure 56.4) (chi-square 22.0, df = 4).

Investigation of the relationship of this effect with the socio-demographic variables suggests that age explains most of this effect. Older children are much less likely to be reporting on a holiday in the last two years: for example 68% of 13–14-year-olds are recalling a recent holiday, contrasting with only 54% of 15–16-year-olds, and 39% of 17–18-year-olds. As none of the sub-tables for each age group achieves a significant chi-square, this suggests the difference for Scottish children may be due to the fact that fewer of them are above fifteen. So we can only conclude that there is not a clear difference between the countries in how many years since their last holiday.

When asked 'How often does your family take a main holiday?', the Scottish students were significantly different. They more frequently endorsed the response 'most years' rather than 'some years' which was more the English response (see Figure 56.5) (chi-square 14.4, df = 2). This suggests that the English sample have slightly more children with lower expectation of annual holidays. This

difference only persists within the 17–18 subgroup. This means that the Scottish school pupils have a higher frequency of family holiday, particularly for the 17–18 group. Asked as to ever taking holidays at other times of year, the English responded 15% at Christmas as against the Scots' 9%, with no other differences.

A further question asked was 'Which parent or parents did you go with?' There seems to be a slight tendency for Scottish children to be in a conventional family as in Table 56.1. Note the figures do not add up to 100, as children can report the presence of more than one of the categories. Chi-squares can be calculated only separately for each parent: only one approached significance, that for stepfather (chi-square 5.2, df = 1, significance < 0.05). This indicates that the English children were more likely to have had a stepfather in the family holiday party.

Table 56.7 gives a summary of where the holidays were taken. Again more than one country could have been ticked. The Scots report taking more holidays in England than Scotland, whereas the English report a higher proportion of holidays at home. Scots were significantly

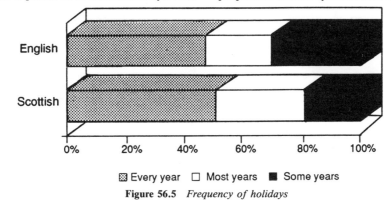

Figure 56.5 *Frequency of holidays*

Table 56.1 *Percentage of schoolchildren holidaying with various classes of adults*

Which parent or parents did you go with?	Scottish	English
Father	84	81
Mother	92	90
Stepfather	2	4
Stepmother	1	2
Other	8	9

Table 56.3 *Percentages travelling abroad for father's occupation class*

Father's occupation class	% Scots abroad	% English abroad	Chi-square (df = 1)
Professional	77	60	2.2
Upper Middle	70	48	15.3
Lower Middle	73	42	27.1
Working	54	32	5.6

more likely to have ticked Scotland (chi-square 81.8, df = 1). However, the English were more frequent travellers to Wales (chi-square 23.3, df = 1) and the Scots to Ireland, among the home countries. The English were as frequent travellers to Italy as they were to Scotland!

The English are more frequent travellers to all of the countries with the exception of North America, probably because of Scottish direct flights to Florida that are cheaper than to many European destinations, and Spain, which is the traditional cheap sun package destination (chi-square 13.3, df = 1). When this question is looked at to investigate the frequency of travelling abroad, the Scots again come off better. A majority (69%) of Scots had their last holiday abroad, whereas only 45% of the English reported that (chi-square 46.5, df = 1). This difference persisted even when examined separately for each sub-class except 'professional' (see Table 56.3). However, there is a suggestion that it is a difference that is not so applicable for the extremes of the class range. The professional class in England was more comparable with the Scottish range. The Scottish working class proportion was lower than the overall Scottish range, although a majority still took holidays abroad.

There were no differences in the reported length of the last recalled holiday.

Table 56.2 *Holiday destinations*

In what country or countries was the holiday taken?	Scottish	English
England	28	35
Scotland	21	3
Wales	4	17
Ireland	3	1
France	12	17
Spain	24	16
Switzerland	3	7
Greece	3	6
Italy	2	3
Portugal	2	2
North America	9	6
Others	6	6

The Scots tend to be more frequent users of package holiday, timeshare, or fly/drive (see Figure 56.6). The English more frequently use independent travel, or stay with friends and relatives. The differences for self-catering, cruise, second home and camping were less than 2% either way. There is much larger use of staying with friends and relatives among the Engish (chi-square 6.9, df = 1), probably because it is a cheaper holiday option.

Table 56.4 suggests that the English family holidays only differ in having parents' friends more frequently (chi-square 6.2, df = 1), and the Scots a non-significant lower frequency of having friends. As to size of party, the English had a non-significant tendency to larger parties. As to payment the English reported more frequently father only paying (chi-square 10.0, df = 1). There were non-significant tendencies for the Scots children to report more cases of father and mother paying for the holiday, and the 'don't know' category. This might be explained by differences in family structure for the English and the younger age of the Scots.

Table 56.5 shows the Scots in our sample were less likely (but not significantly) to have younger brothers and sisters than the English, probably because of their lower age.

Table 56.6 on spending money shows that there was no significant difference in terms of its presence, or source. It is interesting to note that the Scots were more frequent to respond that this came from personal savings or earned from own work (72% versus English 65%), and the English that it was frequently solely pocket money provided by parents (35% versus Scottish 28%), but this was not a significant difference.

Fewer Scottish children's families owned a second home abroad (see Table 56.7) (chi-square 16.3, df = 1), but there were more who owned a fixed site caravan, but not to the level of significance.

Decision patterns

The children were asked, 'Were you asked where you wanted to go before the holiday was finally decided?' The Scottish children reported more frequently that they had been asked (74% as against 63%: chi-square 12.6, df = 1).

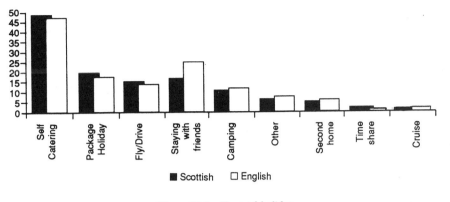

Figure 56.6 *Type of holiday*

This effect was examined for age, and the difference was apparent only for the 16–17 age band, chi-squares not being significant for the other groups.

The difference in rates of being asked was also examined for class effects; it only persisted for the father's occupational group and the mother's housewife group; in all other class categories there were no significant differences between the countries. This could be an indication that the differing employment situation in those class groups between the two countries explains some of this difference.

A further question was asked, 'How big was the part you played in choosing the holiday?' A higher (but not significant) proportion of Scottish children felt that they played an appreciable part in the decision where to go.

When asked 'Who made the final decision?', the Scots were significantly different (chi-square 11.4, df = 3). They were lower in the proportion reporting 'father mainly' decisions (8% as against 16% for the English) and higher for 'mother and father together' decisions (65% as against 57% for the English). This might tie in with differences in family structure.

There were no significant differences in usage of travel agents. There was no difference in terms of how long ahead the holiday was booked, or whether it was the first time to the destination.

Vacation activities

There were no differences in the reported frequency of being with parents, day or night. There was no difference in the reported number of times the family ate out. Scottish children were more likely (65% to 58%), but not significantly, to report that their parents made new friends. Although there was no difference in reports of the children themselves making friends, the nations differed in the sex of the friends made. Scots were more likely to report same sex friends (24% to 14%) and the English to report both sexes (chi-square 9.5, df = 2). This effect was not significant separately for either sex group, 'explaining' the difference is due to the higher proportion of males in the Scottish sample.

The question, 'Did you stay in contact with those friends?', showed no difference between the groups, with less than half maintaining any contact, although 28% were still in touch.

The respondents ticked from a list of holiday activities. The English students were at least 5% more frequent at visiting museums, touring by car (chi-square 11.9, df = 1), making videos (chi-square 7.4, df = 1), reading a book, visiting historic towns (chi-square 8.5, df = 1) and visiting heritage sites. More Scottish students claimed to have taken part in sport, but there was not a significant difference.

Table 56.4 *Party composition*

Party composition	Percentage base	Scottish	English
Anyone else	Total sample	86	83
Brothers/sisters	Number with anyone else	84	82
Other relatives	Number with anyone else	19	21
Friends	Number with anyone else	17	21
Parents' friends	Number with any friends	48	58
Own friends	Number with any friends	59	56
Siblings' friends	Number with any friends	24	26

Table 56.5 *Family composition*

Family composition	Scottish	English
Elder brothers	39.7	38.3
Younger brothers	35.3	40.3
Elder sisters	34.4	36.7
Younger sisters	31.5	34.8

Table 56.6 *Spending money*

If you had your own spending money where had you got it from?	Scottish	English
Personal savings	49.5	44.8
Pocket money provided	64.7	73.8
Earned from own work	31.8	31.2
Other	10.6	9.8

Vacation satisfactions

When asked, 'Was it the holiday you would have chosen?', there was not a significant difference between the countries on this question, although more Scots replied 'yes'.

When asked, 'How much did you enjoy the holiday overall?', the Scots were more frequent in responding 'very much'. The most common English response was 'quite a lot' (see Table 56.8) (chi-square 10.6, df = 3). This difference is only apparent within the 11–12 age subgroup, whereas it is not significant in any other group. The younger Scots used the 'very much enjoy' category almost exclusively.

Future intentions

When asked whether they wanted their children to have holidays like their parents, the Scots were significantly different (chi-square 24.8, df = 3). This difference was maintained within age groups. They more frequently endorsed 'very like' (42% against English 28%), and the English endorsed 'different' or 'very different' (28% against Scottish 16%). The Scots more frequently (but not significantly) wanted to go on holiday again with their parents (74% against English 66%).

Attitudes and opinions

There were no differences between the nations on how old children should be before going on holiday on their own. The questionnaire included 45 Likert scale items, the

Table 56.7 *Family accommodation owned*

Does your family own?	Scottish	English
A timeshare apartment	8.0	7.2
A second home in the UK	15.4	12.1
A second home abroad	12.3	27.7
A mobile home/caravan	13.6	14.3
A fixed site caravan	16.0	8.4
A boat	13.0	9.0
A tent	60.5	61.4

Table 56.8 *Overall enjoyment*

How much did you enjoy the holiday overall?	Scottish	English
Very much	63.1	52.3
Quite a lot	29.9	38.7
Not much	6.0	7.4
Not at all	0.9	1.7

complete list of which is available from the authors. As a data reduction exercise a multiple discriminant analysis was performed to highlight the more distinguishable differences in ratings. The top ten loading scales are interpreted in Table 56.9. All of the interpreted scales had *t*-tests significant at 1% even after adjusting for the linear effects of age, sex and class differences by using regression residuals, and all the differences were in the direction of Scots agreeing more with the statements. The correlation of the items with the discriminant function indicates how much they overlap the content of the best weighted composite of all items for distinguishing Scottish from English attitudes.

The multiple *R* is the correlation between the best weighted composite of age, sex and father's occupation class with an item. High values, such as that for travel book reading, suggest that this item is more strongly related to those variables. The residual from the multiple regression was then saved and analysed by *t*-test. The degrees of freedom are above 800 when the assumption of homogeneous variation can be made, and has a lower value when the variances are heterogeneous. All effects were significant at 1%.

Summary of differences

- The Scottish sample was less old than the English.
- The Scottish sample was more lower middle class.
- The Scottish sample report more frequent holidays, primarily for the 17–18 group.
- The English pupils were more likely to have had a stepfather in the family holiday party.
- Scots were more likely to have holidayed in Scotland.
- The English were more likely to have travelled to Wales.
- The Scots were more likely to have travelled to Spain.
- The Scots were more likely to report having had their last holiday abroad.
- The English were more likely to have been staying with friends and relatives on their last major holiday.
- The English pupils more frequently reported parents' friends with the party.
- The English parties more frequently reported father only paying for the holiday.

Table 56.9 *The ten highest loading items on the discriminant function between Scottish and English attitudes*

Question	Correlation with discriminant function	Multiple R for age, sex and father's occupation	t-test on residual (degrees of freedom)
I like to get a good suntan on holiday	0.38	0.14	4.63 (690)
I like discussing holidays with family and friends before I go	0.31	0.21	2.83 (830)
I read travel articles in newspapers for holiday ideas	0.28	0.18	2.69 (835)
It's important to have new clothes to wear on holiday	0.27	0.16	2.57 (836)
I like reading travel books regardless of whether a holiday is coming up soon	0.26	0.27	3.20 (831)
You don't need to go outside your own country to have a great holiday	0.26	0.11	2.89 (720)
Holidays are the high spot of my year	0.23	0.11	3.03 (634)
I like a travel firm to make all the main arrangements for my holiday	0.22	0.03	3.48 (654)
TV travel programmes help me to choose my holiday	0.21	0.11	2.88 (836)
You have to be careful with foreign food on holiday	0.21	0.15	2.37 (836)

- Fewer Scottish pupils reported owning a second home abroad.
- Scottish children reported more frequently they had been asked where they wanted to go before the holiday was decided, primarily for the 16–17 age band.
- Scottish children differed in their reports of who made the final decision: they were more likely to report mother and father, and lower for the father mainly.
- English pupils reported more frequently touring by car, making videos and visiting historic towns.
- Scottish children more frequently endorsed the 'very much' response to the question, 'How much did you enjoy the holiday overall?': the English endorsed the 'quite a lot' category. This difference is primarily due to the 11–12 age group.
- Scottish pupils more frequently endorsed the 'very like' response to the question, 'Do you want your children to have holidays like your own family holidays?'
- More Scottish pupils agreed with 'I like to get a good suntan on holiday'.
- More Scottish pupils agreed with 'I like discussing holidays with family and friends before I go'.
- More Scottish pupils agreed with 'I read travel articles in newspapers for holiday ideas'.
- More Scottish pupils agreed with 'It's important to have new clothes to wear on holiday'.
- More Scottish pupils agreed with 'I like reading travel books regardless of whether a holiday is coming up soon'.
- More Scottish pupils agreed with 'You don't need to go outside your own country to have a great holiday'.
- More Scottish pupils agreed with 'Holidays are the high spot of my year'.
- More Scottish pupils agreed with 'I like a travel firm to make all the main arrangements for my holiday'.
- More Scottish pupils agreed with 'TV travel programmes help me to choose my holiday'.

Discussion

Scots appeared to have been more recently on holiday, because they were a younger sample. They go more frequently on holiday, although this difference exists only in the eldest group. So although the sample is of a lower class, the Scots market does seem to have been more persistent and less subject to the recession.

The Scottish children seem to have been on holiday in a more conventional grouping with both mother and father, whereas the English may be more likely to take friends (perhaps because of more second homes), particularly parents' friends. Perhaps the English have a higher number of divorced fathers taking them on holiday. This is corroborated by the final decision maker in Scotland being more likely to be mother and father, and the father alone in England.

The geographical differences show particular effect in terms of where the holidays are taken. The Scots generally moved south, including to England. They took significantly more holidays abroad, probably because of less recession and worse weather! This geographical distance effect is associated with less independent travel and more package holidays, timeshare and fly/drive. The English showed noticeably more staying with friends or relatives, an indicator of holidays in times of tight family budgets. The Scots had fewer owners of second homes abroad, more owners of second homes in the UK, caravans and boats. Such capital investment in holidays is associated with geographical position. The English can drive in a day to a second home abroad in France: an equivalent drive by Scots leaves them in England. Perhaps the English second home abroad could be a result of the spectacular gains in property values by some families in the 1980s.

The spending money questions showed a tendency for Scottish children to use personal savings and for more English to be provided with pocket money. Perhaps the Scottish reputation for thrift is carrying through to another generation.

The proportion of Scots reporting being asked about the holiday was higher, especially for 15–16-year-olds, lower middle and mother as housewife categories. This is perhaps attributable to the common usage of package holidays in these groups by Scots. There were remarkably few differences in what was done on holiday, although the English students were more frequent visitors to museums, tourers by car, makers of videos, visitors to historic towns and heritage sites and readers of books. The Scots were more likely to have taken part in sport. There were no differences in swimming or sunbathing.

Scots appeared to have enjoyed their holiday more, although this is largely concentrated in the 11–12 group. They were more likely to want to have holidays like their parents in all age categories, and showed a tendency to want to go again with their parents.

Some differences in opinion were related to decision making. Scots reported more frequent discussing with their family and friends. They were agreed more strongly that 'Television travel programmes help me to choose my holiday', and reported more frequently that they read travel articles in newspapers for holiday ideas. The Scots agreed more strongly that they like reading travel books regardless of whether a holiday is coming up soon. The Scots agreed more frequently that they like a travel firm to make all the main arrangements, although there were no reported differences in usage.

In one way Scots' attitudes were contradictory: Scots were more definite than the English in endorsing the statement that you don't need to go outside your own country to get a great holiday, and were more frequent travellers abroad.

The Scots express real enjoyment with their holiday: Scots more frequently agreed that 'holidays are the high spot of my year'. Also they agree more strongly that 'It's important to have new clothes to wear on holiday'.

In some ways the Scots were more conservative in attitude to holidays: they were more frequent to endorse that you have to be careful with foreign food. They more strongly agreed with 'I like to get a good suntan on holiday'. They also were more in agreement that the weather can make or break a holiday. These last two may relate to meteorological differences between the nations!

This study shows that the Scottish sample is more positive towards the family holiday, and more involved in the decision, and even want to repeat the experience! Some of these differences are due to the age of the sample; but there are some national differences that persist.

Scots may be a little more conservative, and stay on the beach while on holiday. The English get up and tour! More Scots use the package, fly/drive and timeshare type of holiday. This is possibly as a consequence of the distance they have to travel. Perhaps their children's involvement in the decision is only a function of the types of holidays they more frequently use. Perhaps some of the more conservative attitudes flow from this.

This study would suggest the Scottish market is one more inclined to organised holidays abroad, and was probably less depressed than the English holiday market at the time of the survey. The English show more inclination to visit friends and relatives and to indulge in tourist activities.

The answer to the question how different are Scottish family holidays from English, would suggest that the Scots may involve their children more in decision making, are less active tourists, have worse weather to escape, and further to travel, go on holiday more often, and more frequently abroad, and the children may be more happy.

However, the differences are marginal rather than substantial and may be consequent on the economic cicumstances that may average out at £2 more per week (or £100 a year) spending on holidays.

References

Seaton, A. V. and Tagg, S. K. (1994) 'The family vacation in Europe: paedonomic aspects of choices and satisfactions', *Journal of Travel and Tourism Marketing*, 3(4) (in press).

CSO (Central Statistical Office) (1993) 'Family spending: a report on the 1992 Family Expenditure Survey', Her Majesty's Stationery Office, London.

Part 5

TOURISM AND HUMAN RESOURCE MANAGEMENT

Labour, employment and human resource management issues are among the most crucial facing the international tourism and hospitality industry in the 1990s. Growth in demand for tourism products and services will probably continue to generate substantial employment opportunities, but responses to these opportunities, real or perceived, will differ between countries, distinct industry sectors, public and governmental or quasi-governmental agencies with a tourism remit, and even different corporations and companies involved in the tourism and hospitality sectors.

Tourism employment in the private sector is generally characterised by low pay and relatively poor conditions of employment. In the hotel industry, for example, low wage policies are often a part of competitive strategy. The increasing internationalisation of the hotel industry has generated concern that Western hotel firms can, will, and do 'export' such policies, especially in respect of new projects in developing countries. However, the competitive strategies and concomitant policies of firms in the private sector (whether in hotels or some other tourism industry) are to a large degree both constrained and enabled by the employment policies of government, which vary from the highly regulated to the hardly regulated at all; for example, the countries of the European Union who are parties to the Social Chapter of the Maastricht Treaty have far greater regulation of employment than does the UK (which opted out of this aspect of the Treaty) and many other countries where rates of pay are left more to market mechanisms.

Government, then, is an important consideration when analysing likely patterns of labour demand and utilisation in the international tourism industry. However, the labour and human resource management practices of individual firms and corporations cannot be ignored. Not all firms in the private sector of the tourism industry pursue low wage strategies and those that do not, together with many of those that do, still exhibit excellence in other aspects of their employment practice. There is limited but growing evidence to suggest that in certain industries, and some sections of particular industries, greater attention to the human resource function is forthcoming than has hitherto been the case, because of corporations' realisation that training, development and labour retention can help attain competitive advantage. There are, however, a number of problematic human resource issues facing commercial organisations in the 1990s, issues that arise from the growth of the international tourism industry.

The first concerns cultural adaptation. There is considerable evidence to suggest that in sectors such as hotels, insufficient willingness has been shown by companies to adapt to local cultural conventions. Organisational culture cannot be imposed on societies where that culture is at odds with local values. Failure to adapt to local culture can, secondly, mean that tourism organisations end up employing an overall quality of labour which is not the best and, further, which is more difficult and expensive to train. This leads, finally, to the consideration of the relationships that the private sector has with the public, whether the latter is in the form of one or more ministries of tourism, national tourism organisations or more localised and regionalised agencies that include tourism among their responsibilities.

In order to change, contain or influence tourism development, governments have formally (or sometimes informally) offered explicit or implicit aid to the private sector. In the UK context, it has been pointed out that the overseas marketing activities of national tourism organisations acts as massive subsidy to the commercial sectors of the tourism industry. Also in the UK, as elsewhere, various agencies have been charged with offering assistance to the private sector with employment and other forms of training and human resource planning. For the foreseeable future, it is in the area of employment training and human resources that the bond between the public and the private sector is likely to be strongest. The reasons for the strengthening of this bond will vary. In some cases it will be because governments, having invested in tourism, will seek to ensure that a quantity and quality of human resources is developed and delivered. In other instances, the availability of support for training will appeal to cost-conscious firms anxious to defray the risks entailed by providing such training themselves.

Whatever the case, human resources will be a key tourism issue in the 1990s and beyond. It is gratifying that within the tourism and hospitality fields there is a developed and developing literature on human resources and a quality of research which is, on the whole, high. In this section, we present some of this research and commentary which demonstrates, if demonstration were required, the rich diversity of interests, opinions and prognostications for the future. The section includes a paper by Eddie Brogan of Scottish Enterprise, one of the conference's major sponsors, which offers a timely and insightful study of tourism and human resource policy in Scotland.

Inskeep offers practitioner insights into the training and development of human resources at national and international level. His work is supported by Tom Baum's examination of policy development for tourism at national level. Vera, Pedreño and Ivars provide useful insights into human resource planning within a defined geographical area and labour market. At the level of specific issues in training and education, Cameron and Harvey explore important issues in academic and vocational strategies for mentoring, and Olesen and Schettini exemplify the application of specific training practices in the case of 'adventure tourism'. Lucas and Perrin deal in a highly original way with the issue of training and education for foreign languages in the hotel industry. Continuing with the question of human resource management in hospitality, McMahon examines productivity issues while Jones, Nickson and Taylor explore what is fast becoming one of the most interesting areas of human resource management practice in hospitality, namely the creation and maintenance of an organisational culture.

Eddie Brogan
Scottish Enterprise
Roy C. Wood
The Scottish Hotel School

57 Human resource development in tourism: the Scottish perspective

E. BROGAN

Introduction

The purpose of this paper is to report on the progress of recent efforts to improve the standard of human resource development in tourism businesses in Scotland. These efforts, initiated by the various government agencies with an interest in tourism and training in Scotland, are now being taken forward jointly by the government agencies and the industry on the basis of an agreed national strategy and building on the new integrated economic development and training agencies: Scottish Enterprise (SE) and Highlands and Islands Enterprise (HIE). These efforts are felt to be essential if the tourism industry in Scotland is to realise its potential by offering high standards of facilities and services in an increasingly competitive and sophisticated international tourism marketplace.

The industry context

Tourism is vitally important to the Scottish economy. In 1992 it is estimated that over 10 million tourists spent over £1.7 billion in Scotland (UKTS, 1992; IPS, 1992). This represents around 4% of Scottish GDP, allowing for multiplier effects. Around £1.4 billion of the total represents 'export' sales, being expenditure by visitors from the rest of the UK and overseas. In employment terms current estimates suggest that some 160 000 people are employed in tourism-related activities in Scotland with around 25 000 self-employed bringing the total to 185 000 or 8% of the labour force. Tourism will, if anything, increase in importance to the Scottish economy as jobs in other sectors, particularly manufacturing and agriculture, continue to decline. Importantly, at a local level, tourism is often the mainstay of the whole economy, particularly in rural areas of Scotland.

Recent performance has been mixed. Visitors from Scotland itself and the rest of the UK account for around 70% of total earnings but there has been a long-term decline in spending, in real terms, by UK visitors as they have increasingly taken their main holidays overseas. The decline in the number of Scots holidaying at home has been particularly evident as improved communications and increased levels of car ownership bring traditional holiday destinations within day-trip distance. The figures for 1991 and 1992 (UKTS, 1991, 1992; IPS, 1992), however, show some 'bottoming out' in terms of the domestic market, though whether this is an end to the decline or a temporary blip due to the recession remains to be seen. The number of overseas visitors to Scotland, on the other hand, has risen steadily over the last 10 years. Scotland has particularly strong links with the USA, Canada and Australia, but it is mainly to Europe that Scotland will look for growth over the next 5–10 years.

Overall, Scotland's tourism prospects are good. The industry is growing worldwide at a steady rate of around 5% p.a. and Scotland has very significant basic tourism strengths in its landscape and relatively unspoilt environment, in its colourful history, in its rich built heritage, in the wide range of opportunities which it offers for sport and recreation and in its distinctive national identity. All these strengths are relevant to a market which is increasingly environmentally sensitive, sophisticated and interested in holidays built around activities and special interests.

Market trends, however, also present major challenges to the tourism industry in Scotland. To compete effectively with countries such as Ireland, England and France, Scottish tourism businesses must be skilled in identifying and meeting the needs of an increasingly segmented and sophisticated market, delivering quality facilities and high standards of service, effectively promoted and at competitive prices. Scottish Enterprise's own tourism strategy (Scottish Enterprise, 1992) recommends adopting a market-driven approach involving strategies, projects and programmes aimed at developing new products and securing improvements to existing products in key areas such as the accommodation sector, visitor attractions, sport and recreational facilities etc. *Sustained* improvement, however, will require a major commitment to the recruitment and development of skilled people at all levels in the industry. This drive for effective human resource development in the industry is, therefore, fundamental to all other efforts to develop the tourism industry in Scotland and to realising Scottish Enterprise's ambition of an industry where the quality of facilities and standards of service are sufficiently high to generate repeat visits and favourable recommendations, and to offer secure and worthwhile rewards to owners and staff.

Identifying the issues—'Training for advantage'

The current effort to promote more effective human resource development in the Scottish tourism industry has its roots in the Scottish Tourism Co-ordinating Group (STCG) set up to promote effective joint working on the part of the main national government agencies involved in tourism and chaired by the Scottish Office minister with responsibility for tourism. With a remit from STCG, PA Consulting Group was commissioned in 1989 to review the current situation and bring forward recommendations as to how training and career development in the industry might be improved. The PA review, 'Training for advantage' (PA Consulting Group, 1989), was overseen by a steering group which included the Scottish Development Agency (SDA) and the Training Agency (TA) in Scotland (the predecessors of Scottish Enterprise), Highlands and Islands Development Board (HIDB) (the predecessor of Highlands and Islands Enterprise) the Scottish Tourist Board (STB), the Scottish Office and the Managing Director of The Gleneagles Hotel, the latter to bring an industry perspective to the review process.

In the course of the work PA consulted widely with employers, employees, prospective employees, training providers and staff in the relevant government agencies. The key findings were as follows.

The employer's view

Although some differences in views were found, depending on the location, size or type of establishment, there was broad consensus amongst most industry representatives who participated in the study that:

- the sector did perceive that people issues *are* the key to business advantage, especially concerning improving standards and attracting the right calibre and quantity of entrants.
- despite this perception, there was a very low willingness to invest in people, especially in the owner-proprietor and small business area
- this was combined with the view that training should be low cost, and preferably subsidised
- there was a low regard for 'academic' training, which was often seen as being irrelevant, and delivered by individuals with little experience of 'the real world'
- much available provision was not delivered in a suitable

way. In particular, the sector was unwilling to buy classroom training, delivered during college term times, rather than where and when it suited the industry.
- employers had very little information on what training provision was available.

The training provider's view

Providers of training from both the public sector and the private sector agreed that provision had in the past been supply-driven and unresponsive: providers tended to deliver courses in areas where they had skills, rather than in what the market required. The main reason expressed for this was lack of demand from employers. Other main findings from interviewers with training providers included:

- marketing of training courses had been very poor: providers had equated marketing with advertising, and taken the view that 'the course markets itself'
- providers believed that employers paid lip-service to training and distrusted both formal courses and formal qualifications
- providers believed that employers had poor regard for training
- few providers had effective ways of understanding the industry's needs. Private providers tended to concentrate on service offerings such as customer care, and try to find a market for it. Most public sector providers had formal industry advisory groups, or course committees; however, few were truly effective
- in general, progress towards improved provision was slow, uncoordinated and dependent more on individual initiative than agreed direction

The employee's view

The analysis of the view of employees in the tourism industry, covered both those currently employed in the industry and also potential entrants, contacted through job centres. The main findings from the interviews were:

- tourism jobs in general, and hotel and catering jobs in particular, were not perceived as attractive
- the perceived drawbacks of tourism jobs included:

  —poor conditions
  —unsocial hours
  —low pay
  —seasonal employment

- the image of a job was often dependent on the establishment; for example, high-profile hotels or visitor attractions were considered more favourably

- employees had a low opinion of the employers, especially with regard to 'exploitation' and lack of respect shown to staff
- many employers were perceived to have little knowledge or experience of the industry
- for many actual and potential employees, the concept of a career was not relevant
- few potential entrants believed that they would receive any training for jobs in tourism. Existing employees were content to leave training to the employers
- there was, however, a general understanding of the importance of customer care training for tourism jobs, and a growing awareness of the value to an individual of good people handling skills in, for example, sales roles

General conclusion

PA concluded that employers did not see the business benefit of investing in their employees who were often part-time, temporary and viewed as low-calibre. Employers and entrants perceived tourism jobs as having little status, low pay and poor conditions. Training providers perceived tourism businesses as being apathetic about training and provided what they could rather than what really was actually required. These problems were linked in a vicious circle and PA set out a range of recommendations to address the key issues of stimulating employer demand for training, improving the supply of, and access to, training, and enhancing the status of careers in tourism. There was a view at the time that of the three the first was the most important. If employer interest in human resource development could be stimulated, addressing the other two areas would be relatively much easier.

There was to be a focus on local delivery to meet local needs and improve availability. This was particularly significant in view of the then proposed merger of SDA, HIDB and TA to form Scottish Enterprise (SE), and Highlands and Islands Enterprise (HIE) in the HIDB area, with their networks of Local Enterprise Companies (LECs). PA also proposed a National Implementation Group to act as a focus for a new effort in tourism training and for the development and promotion of the various initiatives which PA were recommending.

The way forward—the Tourism Training Initiative

The PA review, therefore, had identified the scope of the problem and had recommended a way forward based on stimulating demand for training on the part of businesses, improving the supply of training and enhancing career prospects in the industry. Emphasis had been placed on local efforts but with the need for a national coordinating and developmental mechanism.

The PA review was followed up by the Tourism Training Initiative (TTI) which was launched in November 1990 by Mr Ian Lang, then Minister of State at the Scottish Office. A 'Task Office' of the relevant government agencies was charged with taking forward the Initiative, the primary objectives of which were:

- to stimulate the uptake of training by working with individual business at a local level
- to improve the supply of training
- to create local networks to improve communications between the industry, training providers and public sector agencies such as the emergent Local Enterprise Companies and the Area Tourist Boards (ATBs).

The key feature was to be the appointment of a dedicated 'Tourism Training Executive' to undertake this work in each area. The approach was piloted over a year (1991) in three areas: Ayrshire; Moray, Badenoch and Strathspey; and the Western Isles.

The intention was that the lessons learned during the course of the pilots would be applicable to the new LEC networks as a whole, and would help shape their programmes and projects in this area of work.

At the beginning of the Initiative a baseline report was prepared providing information on factors such as the take-up of training, the use of external training provision, the availability of training information and the general awareness on the part of tourism businesses of the benefits of training to business performance. The Executives were each set targets and the impact of the Initiative in each area was then monitored.

Initially, the Executives ran a campaign to raise awareness of training issues. This included roadshows, talks to business groups, newsletters, media activities etc. In addition, training directories were produced and local coordinating groups established. The main thrust of the Initiative, however, was to be a company visitation programme to encourage businesses to undertake training through existing or newly developed courses.

The monitoring work (The Host Consultancy, 1991) showed that, in general terms, at the end of the year the Executives had met the targets set for them and that they had been most successful in:

- increasing the take-up of training in the three pilot areas
- raising satisfaction levels with external training provision
- creating a focal point for the dissemination of training information

- raising general awareness of training on the part of operators

However, the most significant finding was that the Executives had not been successful in the critical area of making operators aware of the benefits of training to their own business performance.

A number of important lessons were learned if this was to be achieved:

- training had to be seen in its widest sense, i.e. in terms of covering the full range of human resource development issues such as recruitment and retention, career development etc.
- human resource development, in turn, had to be seen in the context of the overall development of the business, and training or human resource development support needed to be delivered in a broader business development context if it was to be effective
- standards, quality standards such as the Scottish Tourist Board Grading and Classification scheme, and training standards, such as Scottish Vocational Qualifications (SVQs) for employees, and 'Investors in People' for companies, were important tools in stimulating improved human resource development in tourism business
- there needed to be a major effort to create a 'training culture' in tourism businesses where effective human resource development was regarded as an essential and continuing component of the successful operation of the business
- only a limited amount could be achieved in one year. A long-term commitment was required if the fundamental problem of changing attitudes to human resource development in the tourism industry was to be tackled effectively

Various recommendations as to how LECs could benefit from the experience gained in the course of the pilots were drawn together in the form of guidelines and promoted to the LECs at a series of seminars in February 1992. These guidelines covered the need for a clear understanding of the business development/training needs of the industry in each area, setting goals and objectives, delivering support to tourism businesses in an integrated manner and ensuring that staff working tourism businesses themselves had the necessary skills for the job.

Having concluded the TTI area pilots and disseminated the findings generally across the LECs, and to other interested parties it was recognised that there was still a need to drive the whole tourism training effort forward,

in particular, to build on the valuable lessons learned during the course of the TTI area pilots themselves. It was recognised that what was required was a long-term, sustained effort. The TTI pilots had confirmed that there was to be no 'quick fix'!

By this time also the LECs were becoming very active in the tourism industry. Almost all the LECs had identified tourism as a strategic priority in their first round of business plans and were actively seeking ways to help develop the tourism industry in their areas. The LECs are particularly well geared to meeting the needs of the tourism industry in terms of their local area focus, their comprehensive coverage of Scotland, and their business development and training powers and resources. The tourism industry, however, comprising such a large number of, generally, small businesses is a fairly resource intensive industry to work with and a carefully planned and strategic approach was required, particularly if the core problem of stimulating companies to adopt a 'training culture' was to be tackled.

Developing and implementing a national strategy— Tourism Training Scotland

In addition to managing the Tourism Training Initiative area pilots, the Task Force set up an industry consultative Forum to work with the Task Force members to help shape and take forward the overall tourism training effort. In order to achieve a more effective effort at a national level the public sector Task Force and the industry Forum merged during 1992 to form Tourism Training Scotland (TTS).

TTS draws its membership from a wide range of organisations who have an interest in the tourism training field: SE, HIE and STB, the central government agencies with responsibility for training and tourism, SCOTVEC with its role in validating and promoting vocational qualifications, the training providers who work with the industry and a wide range of representatives of different sectors of the industry itself—hotels, visitor attractions, self-catering operators, museums, countryside facilities etc. TTS is chaired by Mr Peter Lederer, Managing Director of The Gleneagles Hotel.

TTS sees its role in overall terms, as developing and promoting a national strategy for human resource development and training in the tourism industry. In addition to developing and publishing strategy itself (Tourism Training Scotland, 1993), TTS has given considerable thought as to what its unique contribution should be *vis-à-vis* others involved in the field, and the LEC networks in particular, and has decided to focus on:

- developing approaches to Scotland-wide issues
- promotion of a coordinated approach at both the national and local level
- promotion of best practice, generally, in human resource development in the industry

TTS also sees itself as having an important role in monitoring progress in improvements to human resource development and training in the tourism industry particularly in respect of Scotland-wide issues such as the uptake of vocational qualifications, Investors in People, the availability of quality training, and standards generally in training in the industry.

TTS's mission reflects the importance which is attached to seeing training in the context of achieving a competitive and world-class tourism industry for Scotland: 'To transform Scotland's competitive position in tourism, through promoting quality training and career development for all who work in the industry, to ensure that a world class quality of service is enjoyed by all visitors in

Scotland'. The starting point in developing the TTS strategy was an identification of the needs and characteristics of the tourism industry itself. As noted earlier, the tourism industry in Scotland has to become much more focused on the needs of the market and to offer quality facilities, high standards of service and value for money in what is becoming an increasingly competitive international marketplace. The tourism industry represents a particularly difficult challenge for a number of reasons:

- It is a fragmented industry, dominated by a very large number of small businesses. This makes it a difficult industry to reach and influence, and a resource-intensive industry to work with in business development and training.
- It is the visitor that is the common theme and in business terms the industry is, in fact, a whole series of different sectors: accommodation, visitor attractions, catering and retail outlets, sports facilities, transport operations etc., all with their own characteristics and needs.

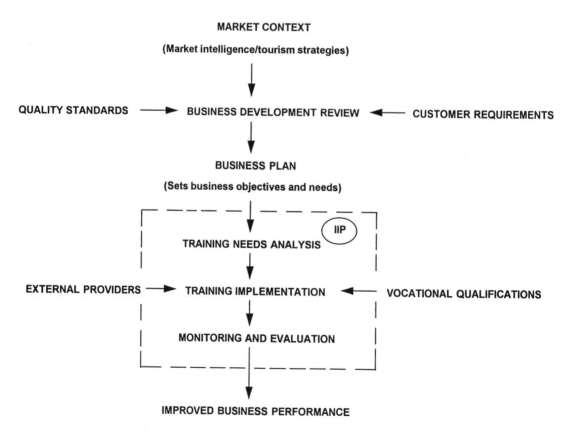

Figure 57.1 *Integrated training and business development*

● It is an industry that is relatively easy to enter and many businesses are operated by managers with little relevant previous experience.

● Previous research work by the Host Consultancy, in particular, showed that it is an industry characterised by low levels of skills generally.

● Seasonality of employment acts as a further impediment to a sustained effort in staff development and training.

● The PA review showed that it is an industry which, rightly or wrongly, has a poor image as an employer, often being associated, in the minds of potential recruits, with low pay, unsocial hours and lack of a proper career structure.

How then, in practical terms, does TTS propose to meet this challenge?

TTS has, drawing on the previous research work by PA and Host Consultancy, and on the knowledge and practical experience of its own members, identified three strategic priorities.

(1) 'Creating a training culture within tourism businesses'

There is a need to establish within individual tourism businesses a 'training culture' whereby an ongoing commitment to the development of the human resources of the business is seen as an essential and integral part of the business as a whole (Figure 57.1). If such a commitment on the part of individual businesses to human resource development and training is to be achieved, it is essential that these activities are seen as bringing benefits to the business in terms of enhanced profitability. The operators of tourism businesses need to have a clear idea of who their customers are, and of the overall development needs of the business so that the skills of the managers and staff can be seen in their proper place as central to the successful operation of the business. This is essential if the training which is done by businesses is to be relevant and properly targeted at improving business performance.

Customer-focused quality standards, for example the STB Grading and Classification and the Association of Scottish Visitor Attractions (ASVA) inspection schemes, have tremendous potential to act as a yardstick to help businesses to identify where they fall short of customer requirements, and to act as an incentive to encourage businesses to address shortcomings which may be identified.

Case studies and other methods of promoting best practice are of considerable value in demonstrating to businesses the practicalities of staff development and training, and in demonstrating the benefits which can be obtained.

Changing attitudes and persuading tourism businesses to adopt a training culture requires a commitment from the top in each business, and an understanding on the part of managers of human resource development and training issues. Managemant development, therefore, is a theme which underpins much of the work of TTS.

Lastly, much effort, and much industry expertise, has gone into the development of Investors in People as the national standard for effective investment in human resource development. The standard has five key requirements for companies.

● defining business objectives

● making a public commitment from the top to develop all employees to achieve those objectives

● reviewing regularly the training and development needs of all employees

● taking action to train and develop individuals on recruitment and throughout their employment

● evaluating the investment in training and development to assess achievement and improve future effectiveness.

Investors in People acts as a yardstick against which businesses can assess their human resource development activities, and as a lever and framework for implementing improvements with a particular emphasis on in-house development of staff.

(2) 'Enhancing professional standards and the status of jobs in the industry'

Despite the current recession, looking to the longer-term, labour supply is anticipated to be one of the major challenges facing the industry worldwide. TTS believes that it is important *now* to encourage the industry to adopt positive and effective recruitment and retention policies which will help address staff and skills shortages, and assist in reducing the horrific costs associated with staff turnover in the industry.

Related to the ability of tourism businesses to recruit and retain suitably trained staff is the need to take steps to ensure that businesses address career development issues with their staff, and to find ways of presenting the career opportunities which do exist in the industry in an effective and attractive way to potential new recruits from schools and colleges and from other industries.

Scottish Vocational Qualifications (SVQs) can act as an incentive to staff to improve their skills and can also assist in promoting career development within the industry.

(3) *'Improving access to quality training by enhancing communications and mutual understanding between the tourism and training industries'*

Whilst an extensive range of external training provision already exists, there is a need to ensure that gaps, for example in the visitor attractions sector, can be filled and to improve communications between training providers and the industry to promote a better understanding of the industry's requirements.

There is a need to take steps to assist tourism businesses to identify and access training that is appropriate to their own individual needs.

There is a need to provide quality assurance to businesses buying external training to build confidence in seeking outside support and to promote high standards on the part of providers themselves.

TTS believes that, if anything, the emphasis should be on helping businesses themselves to develop skills to provide in-house training using their own managers and supervisors. This will allow both effective, targeted training to be delivered by the staff of the business itself, and also appropriate external training to be brought in as required.

The strategy is summarised in Figure 57.2. It has been widely promoted and has in itself been very valuable in promoting a common understanding of the issues facing the industry in the field of staff development and how these might be addressed.

How then does TTS propose to take the strategy forward to implementation?

It has to be stressed that TTS is seeking to achieve its objectives primarily by supporting and influencing the efforts of others who have direct contact with the operators and managers of tourism businesses themselves. In this context we have in mind, particularly, the network of Local Enterprise Companies as the prime agency for the delivery of business development and training support to industry, the Area Tourist Boards who represent an important channel of communication with the 15 000 or so businesses that make up their membership, training providers working with businesses, and the various industry associations and organisations who can use their membership structures and support mechanisms to promote the enhancement of skills in the industry.

Figure 57.2 *Strategy summary*

In line with its role in developing approaches to Scotland-wide issues, in promoting a coordinated effort on tourism training, and in disseminating best practice, TTS has developed a number of specific initiatives which together represent the first phase of work in taking the strategy forward to implementation.

Quality standards

As the result of a study to investigate opportunities for promoting staff development and training through the STB and ASVA inspection schemes, a set of 'Service Quality Guides' has been developed for the serviced accommodation, self-catering and visitor attraction sectors. The guides, which make more explicit the service criteria taken into account at the inspection, have been field-tested and will be launched early in 1994. They will be targeted at the 5000+ businesses which are members of the STB and ASVA schemes and have tremendous potential to stimulate demand for training in these two priority sectors. Work is currently underway with the LECs to ensure that local support and follow-up is available to maximise the impact of the guides. The criteria in the guides are drawn from the relevant SVQs and this will help promote the uptake of SVQs in the longer term.

Investors in People

Scottish Enterprise has appointed a full-time IIP adviser who promotes the uptake of IIP by tourism businesses generally across Scotland, drawing on practical experience gained by working with a number of individual businesses and on experience across the SE and HIE networks. This will lead to better intelligence about overall progress with IIP throughout the industry in Scotland and will form the basis for more effective promotion of IIP to tourism businesses in Scotland.

Training of trainers

To address the specific needs of owners, managers and supervisors, in small to medium businesses, a training skills package has been produced which will introduce and develop in-house training and coaching skills. The package will draw on, and promote, existing courses and materials thus encouraging increased involvement in training and a greater uptake of qualifications in the longer term. The package will be launched in January 1994 and has an important role in supporting the 'Service Quality Guides' referred to above.

'Staff Development Guide'

A 'Staff Development Guide' is being produced for tourism businesses which draws together various elements of TTS work, e.g., recruitment and retention guidance, advice on SVQs, how to buy external training support etc., in a single publication. The objective is to introduce, to smaller tourism businesses in particular, the range of human resource development issues to be considered and how they relate to each other. In a sense, therefore, this will be an introduction to the principles which underpin IIP.

Career development

A comprehensive review of careers material available to both prospective and current employees has been undertaken. The review has identified existing material, target audiences and distribution mechanisms, together with possible gaps in provision and methods of addressing such gaps. A strategy for the effective dissemination and promotion of tourism careers information to a wider audience is being produced and will involve interfacing with the activities of a range of other organisations, such as the educational sector, at a national level and through the LECs.

Scottish hospitality careers fair

Scottish Enterprise is working in partnership with a number of the major hotel companies in Scotland (Mount Charlotte Thistle Hotels, Scottish Highlands Hotels, Moat House International Hotels and Jarvis Hotels) to mount a national hospitality careers fair in five locations across Scotland in March 1994.

Promotion of best practice

PR Consultants Scotland Ltd have been commissioned to implement a strategy to promote best practice in human resource development throughout the tourism industry in Scotland. This will be done through the trade press, national and local media, the promotion of case studies etc. Implementation of the strategy is the responsibility of a dedicated tourism executive (based in PR Consultants Scotland Ltd) working closely with LECs, ATBs, and the industry itself.

Importance has been attached to the development of a series of initiatives which are comprehensive in terms of addressing the range of staff development issues faced by the industry. This is essential if the vicious circle identified by PA is to be reversed. The various initiatives are also designed to be mutually reinforcing thus the 'training of trainers' short course and the staff development guide will help businesses address training needs highlighted by the 'Service Quality Guides'. The 'Service Quality Guides' will promote the uptake of SVQs in the longer term and the 'Staff Development Guide' will introduce the principles which underpin IIP.

As at a national level, TTS is of the view that local efforts require to be driven by the needs of the industry and effectively coordinated. TTS has proposed, therefore, that at a local level across Scotland LECs should take the lead in the setting up of training groups bringing together the LECs themselves, ATBs, training providers and the industry. The purpose of these groups would be:

● to improve communications between the various players at a local level
● as a result to enhance understanding of the needs and priorities of the industry
● to evolve a strategy to address needs and opportunities
● to mobilise and coordinate efforts to take the strategy forward to implementation.

In addition such local groups represent the basis for a two-way communication with TTS:

● to enable TTS to communicate its strategy and the results of its work to those working with businesses on the ground
● to enable TTS to draw on the experience gained at a local level through contact with the industry

TTS and local tourism training groups, would together represent a powerful network for development work and for the dissemination of good practice. Such groups have already been established in some areas, such as Glasgow, but it is TTS's view that they would bring benefits to other areas where tourism is recognised as a key sector.

Figure 57.3 shows the overall structure of the current effort, highlighting the importance of co-ordination at a national and a local level and the need for strong national–local linkages. It is in this latter respect that the SE, and HIE, organisational structures are a particular strength.

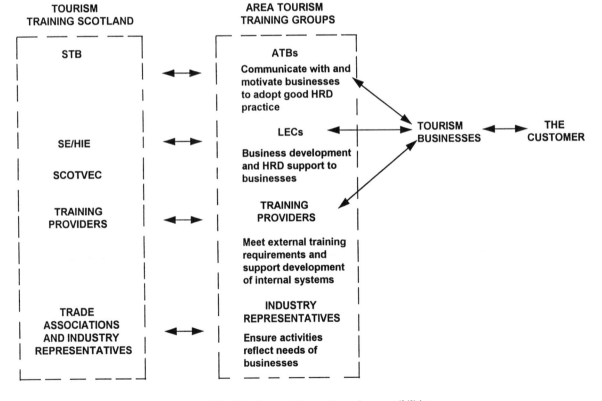

Figure 57.3 *Tourism training: roles and responsibilities*

The role of Scottish Enterprise

Scottish Enterprise, through the Tourism Team in Scottish Enterprise National, has coordinated the work of Tourism Training Scotland to date, in terms of the production of its strategy and responsibility, in partnership with HIE and STB in some cases, for implementation of the various initiatives which are now underway.

Critical to the progress made by TTS to date, however, has been the active involvement of all the public agencies and of the various industry members who, through the various working groups of TTS, have made a major contribution to the development of the strategy and the various initiatives designed to take it forward to implementation. This division of responsibilities has made for an effective partnership between the industry representatives and the public agencies in TTS.

The TTS strategy recognises that, with such a diverse and fragmented industry, taking the strategy forward to implementation requires the active support and involvement of those organisations working directly with individual tourism businesses. This will primarily be the LECs but other organisations—the ATBs, Enterprise Trusts, training providers, trade associations etc.—also have a contribution to make.

All the various national initiatives require the active support of the LECs. For example, the 'Service Quality Guides' will be targeted at over 5000 businesses which are members of the STB and ASVA inspection schemes and could generate substantial demand for support from LECs to help businesses address training needs. The support of the LECs is needed to deliver the 'training of trainers' short courses/seminars and the proposed staff development guide is intended not as a stand-alone, but as a flexible tool for LEC staff and counsellors to use when working with tourism businesses. In addition, SEN will also be looking to the LECs to participate in and support the initiatives in the areas of IIP, the promotion of best practice, and career development.

It is obviously important that local tourism business development and training activities also reflect the broader tourism development objectives for the area and are planned, targeted, and integrated, both internally within the LEC and with the activities of other local organisations with a contribution to make. It is with respect to the latter that the TTS strategy recommends the establishment by LECs of local tourism training fora to ensure effective collaboration at a local level.

The overall objective of the TTS strategy is therefore a concerted effort to enhance skills in the tourism industry based on a common understanding of industry needs and how these might be addressed. This requires effective planning and coordination at both a national and a local level and good two-way communications, especially between SEN and LECs, so that national initiatives have local support and reflect local needs. The relationship between SEN and the LECs is therefore critical to the whole effort in terms of providing the link between the overall national strategy and programmes and the key delivery mechanism at a local level.

The whole effort, therefore, builds on the resources available centrally within Scottish Enterprise to evolve strategy and develop national initiatives, together with the resources which exist in the LECs to deliver direct business development and training support, on a Scotland-wide basis, to what is a fragmented and diverse industry.

There is, however, still a long way to go and arrangements are now being put in place to monitor the impact of the various initiatives and progress overall in improving human resource development in tourism businesses in Scotland. The process also needs to be developmental, with new initiatives and approaches being required to meet new challenges, or to build on progress which has been made.

Conclusion

In terms of taking forward a national effort to improve the standard of human resource development in the tourism industry, the Scottish experience has thrown up a number of valuable lessons.

Firstly, it is essential to gain a clear understanding of the characteristics and needs of the industry. As at the individual business level the overall human resource development effort must be directed at developing an industry which meets the requirements of target markets in terms of quality of facilities, standards of service, and effective marketing and promotion.

Secondly, in such a fragmented industry there is a need for a framework or strategy that ensures that the whole range of issues is addressed in a coherent manner, and that there is common understanding and coordinated action as a result.

Thirdly, there is much to be gained from an effective industry/public sector partnership which uses the expertise of the industry to shape how the resources within the various government agencies can most effectively be used to address the needs of the industry.

Fourthly, the real challenge lies in taking the strategy forward to implementation. In Scotland the SE/HIE networks provide a real opportunity to achieve this, over a period of time, with the overall strategy and national initiatives providing a framework for and supporting local delivery.

References

IPS (The International Passenger Survey) (1992).
PA Consulting Group (1989) 'Training for advantage'.
Scottish Enterprise (1992) 'Towards a tourism strategy'.

The Host Consultancy (1991) 'The Scottish Tourism Training Initiative report'.
UKTS (The United Kingdom Tourism Survey) (1991, 1992).
Tourism Training Scotland (1993) 'Annual report and strategy'.

58 Training for tourism in developing countries

E. INSKEEP

Introduction

The importance of education and training for tourism is becoming well-recognized by developing countries and international assistance agencies. Many countries and the international agencies now realize that tourism can be an important means for socio-economic development and, of course, in many places tourism already is a significant sector. They are also realizing that tourism can bring problems as well as benefits and is highly competitive with other destinations. They are commencing to understand that the overall benefits of tourism accrue to places that offer quality-level facilities and services and do not damage the environment or create serious problems for the local societies and cultural traditions. These countries and international agencies understand that an essential element of achieving successful tourism development is formulating and implementing integrated education and training programmes.

In addition to the need for overall professionalization of tourism operations and management, some countries where many expatriates work, or may in the future work, in tourism have policies of indigenizing tourism employment as rapidly as possible. This is seen as being important in order to increase the local benefits of tourism and reduce possible resentment of foreign workers by local employees. Indigenization policies also require emphasis on all levels of training of local persons.

The types of tourism training programmes in developing countries are not all that different from those applied in more developed places. However, formulation and implementation of the training programme must be tailored to the particular characteristics of the local situation. Considerable experience has been accumulated in preparing and implementing tourism education and training programmes in developing countries, and some observations and conclusions can be drawn from this experience. At the same time, training approaches are continuing to evolve, based on evaluation of experience and new developments in the tourism field.

As used in this paper, the term 'developing countries' refers to all those places which are receiving some form of international assistance in their development programmes. This includes both lower and middle income countries located in all the major regions of the world.

Some of these countries already possess substantially developed tourism sectors and have well-established tourism education and training programmes, while others are just commencing to develop tourism and organize training for this sector. Still other countries need to improve and expand present training programmes. This paper is addressed especially to training approaches that are being, or need to be, applied in places that do not currently have adequate training programmes.

The importance of manpower planning

As the basis for formulating comprehensive and integrated training programmes, manpower planning must be carried out at the national and sometimes regional levels. When international agencies are involved in the country, they will often provide assistance in preparing the manpower planning study. It is not the subject of this paper to review techniques of tourism manpower planning in detail, except to note that the standard four-step approach is typically applied:

1. Evaluating the present utilization of manpower in tourism and identifying any existing problems and training needs. This will require a detailed survey of the employment patterns of tourism-related private enterprises and public sector tourism agencies, including interviews with employers about their personnel training needs.
2. Projecting the future manpower needed by number of personnel required in each category of employment and determining the qualifications for each category of job. The manpower projection is based on the projected or targeted future development of tourism and application of employee ratios appropriate to the area and type of proposed tourism development.
3. Evaluating the human resources available in the future. This evaluation will include the numbers and characteristics of persons who will be available for employment in the future and also the expected education levels of future trainees, often a significant factor in developing countries where general education levels may be low. The location of where potential trainees will be living relative to the location of tourism employment may be an important consideration.

4. Formulating the education and training programme required to provide the requisite qualified manpower. This formulation will include review and evaluation of the present public and private sector training resources within the country, often a critical factor in less-developed countries.

In newly developing tourism areas, the manpower planning study is often conducted as part of a comprehensive national or regional tourism planning project. If this is the case, manpower needs can be based on the overall plan recommendations, such as the number and type of accommodation units targeted. This approach provides for maximum integration of manpower planning into the tourism development process.

Usually, tourism is being developed in a country in large part for its economic benefits, including employment generation in job-deficient areas. Therefore, the gross number of persons available for employment will not typically be a constraining factor on development. However, the capability to provide adequate training programmes to produce the required number of qualified persons to work in tourism may be a constraint, at least during the early years of development. Consequently, the pace of development will need to be related closely to the capacity for training personnel. Otherwise, the desired quality level of tourism services will not be achieved and tourism will eventually suffer from this problem.

The manpower plan must be carefully monitored, based on actual experience of providing the qualified persons needed to work in tourism, and updated as necessary. Because situations can be difficult to predict in newly developing tourism areas, and may turn out to be rather different than anticipated, it is especially important to monitor and periodically update the manpower plan.

Some special considerations in training

An important consideration in formulating training programmes can be the need for upgrading existing inadequately trained personnel in tourism. It is often the case that personnel, particularly those who work in the public sector of tourism and in smaller private tourism enterprises, have received little or no training because of lack of resources, or their training may have been limited only to basic skills and not higher technical, supervisory and managerial skills which are needed in the country. Larger hotels and tour and travel agencies, especially those associated with international chain companies, will have their in-house training programmes and bring in expatriates for the higher-level positions. However, these companies will not nearly satisfy all the training needs

of the country and, over the longer term, it is likely that the country will have adopted policies to phase out expatriate personnel and to require employment of nationals. Thus, all levels of upgrading training for present tourism personnel may need to be emphasized during the early stages of the training programme, as well as being integrated into the long-term programme.

Another major consideration in some areas is the need to incorporate very basic subjects in the beginning level of training in hotel, catering and tour and travel operations. Although the country may well have an overall adequate number of persons with the basic educational qualifications to enter tourism training schools or otherwise receive training, there may be a very justifiable policy of giving priority to employment of persons living in the local areas where tourist facilities are being developed. The persons available for employment in those areas, such as those living in traditional villages, may have very limited educational backgrounds and outside exposure. They will need to be taught basic subjects including concepts of personal hygiene and grooming and the social skills necessary to deal with foreign or more sophisticated domestic tourists. Also basic training in mathematics and improvement in reading and writing may be necessary.

In such situations, special remedial pre-training programmes should be organized to give personnel the basis for subsequently learning technical skills. Such a remedial programme was organized, for example, for young persons living in traditional villages located near the Nusa Dua resort in Bali, Indonesia, in order to prepare them to take the regular training courses required to obtain employment in the resort. This programme was very successful and many of the present resort employees are from these villages, thus bringing benefits of tourism directly to local people.

There is often the need to take a very broad-scoped view of tourism training needs. In addition to training of personnel working in directly related tourism occupations, such as hotels, restaurants, tour and travel operations and public sector tourism management, persons indirectly employed in the 'supplying sectors' may require specialized training that is not available from other sources. These indirect employees that require training may include performing artistes, handicraft artisans, retail shop personnel, taxi and tour bus drivers, farmers providing food items used in tourism, interior decorators, furniture designers and manufacturers, and others.

In Fiji, for example, a special training programme was organized for retailers who sold duty-free and handicraft goods to tourists on how to better display and merchandise their wares. Also in Fiji, a special handicraft improvement programme was implemented over a period of time to train artisans to produce higher-quality and more authentic craft items and a craft store outlet was established to sell these items to tourists. A handicraft improvement programme was also recently implemented in Ethiopia as one component of a tourism project there. In Bali, as part of its planned approach to developing tourism, traditional farmers were advised and trained on how to produce higher and more uniform quality of local food items to be sold to hotels and restaurants, in order to reduce the importation of food items. This programme included streamlining the marketing and transportation of these food items to hotels and restaurants.

There are other interesting examples of advice and training provided for tourism-related activities. In Myanmar (Burma), the internationally assisted tourism training school organized a demonstration project on how locally produced furniture and decor could be designed and produced for furnishing hotel rooms. As part of a regional tourism training programme for South Asia, a special course was organized for training of scuba-diving instructors working in resorts in the Maldives. In several places, special programmes have been organized for training local persons to produce high-quality and authentic traditional dance, music and drama performances for tourists. Such training can also greatly help in maintaining and even revitalizing the traditional arts in places where they might otherwise be greatly modified or lost completely.

Often very important is 'sensitivity' training of officials who have contact with tourists to ensure that they are treated courteously and respectfully. This type of training is particularly being applied in many countries in Africa, Asia and elsewhere for customs and immigration officials in order to educate the officials about using proper public relations techniques in dealing with tourists while still applying the necessary legal requirements and procedures.

Training in the foreign languages of the predominant tourist groups can be a critically important aspect of the training programme. If the local language is different from that of most or all foreign tourists, virtually everyone working directly in tourism must know at least some foreign language for basic communication with tourists, and many personnel, such as tour guides and hotel receptionists, must be fluent in foreign languages. Therefore, foreign languages are typically incorporated into regular tourism training programmes and also often offered as separate courses that employees can take as they have time available.

Sometimes overlooked in training programmes, and particularly important where the 'host and guest' cultures are very different, is the need to include explanations about the behavioural patterns and expectations of different types of tourists. Although there is always some danger in over-generalization and stereotyping, exposure of tourism personnel to the typical profiles of tourists of different national and cultural backgrounds and of various age, interest and socio-economic groups is essential. If the tourists' behavioural patterns and expectations are not well understood, misunderstandings can arise, resulting in dissatisfied tourists and confused employees.

Highly specialized types of training are sometimes needed in developing countries. For example, many countries are having an influx of tourism-related transnational companies of hotel management chains, tour and travel agencies, restaurants and even retail shops. These countries may wish to attract such companies but on terms that are mutually favourable. Because of their inexperience in negotiating contracts with transnationals, however, they are concerned that they will be taken advantage of and not receive their fair share of benefits. So, they request advice and training on dealing with transnationals. In fact, such advice and training are available from the United Nations and other international assistance programmes. Related to the type of training is how to negotiate mutually equitable contracts with international tour operators on handling of ground tour operations of tour groups being brought in by the international operators.

Other areas of specialized training include establishment and application of tourist facility standards such as for licensing of accommodation, restaurants, tour and travel agencies, tour guides and classification of hotels. There is often great need for this type of training in newly developing countries whose facilities and services may not meet international standards and where licensing requirements are non-existent or inadequate. Also often essential in developing countries is training in the establishment and operation of tourism information systems, including collection of data, conducting of special surveys, analysis of data and data reporting techniques.

Incorporating new concepts and trends in training

Tourism is changing rapidly and many new concepts and trends have emerged in recent years that affect this sector. While these may be familiar to many persons in more developed countries, they may be little known in developing countries and need to be emphasized in the content of training programmes. Fundamental is introducing countries to the carefully planned and managed approach to developing tourism, and maintaining viability of the tourism product.

A basic concept that must be incorporated in training programmes is that of sustainable tourism development, and how tourism can be planned and managed so that its resources are perpetually conserved. Related to sustainable tourism is the concept of establishing carrying capacities for specific tourism development sites and, more generally, for tourism regions. Often the essential need for provision of adequate infrastructure for most types of tourism must be emphasized. Training in developing heritage tourism including techniques of interpretation, environmental, historic and archaeological conservation, cultural maintenance and management of visitor use of heritage sites is very important. Techniques for applying environmental and socio-cultural protection measures and monitoring techniques in development planning must be included in tourism management training programmes. A basic concept to be emphasized is that of developing and maintaining 'quality' tourism in all aspects of facilities and services, and how to offer 'good value for money' which tourists now expect.

Concepts, principles and techniques of community-based tourism should be included in tourism management courses. Specialized forms of tourism, such as ecotourism, village tourism, cultural tourism and the many forms of special-interest tourism, now have important tourist markets and are particularly suitable for certain types of developing country environments and societies. The concepts of these forms of tourism, and their principles and techniques of development and management, need to be explained.

In the area of marketing and promotion, the concept of matching tourist markets with the tourism product often must be impressed on tourism officials. Approaches to 'niche' and selective marketing should be explained, along with the more conventional marketing approaches. Specific techniques of marketing of specialized forms of tourism such as ecotourism and cultural tourism often need to be emphasized. In the increasing number of countries that are developing conference and convention facilities, there must be training in formulating and applying convention marketing strategies and promotion techniques. Often training is required in how to effectively participate in international tourism trade fairs and conduct overseas trade seminars.

In the area of food production, for example, there may be a need to include preparation of national and regional cuisine. This has often been neglected in the past, because preference was given to various international cuisines; but now more attention is being given to introducing tourists to local foods as part of their cultural experience. Also, encouragement of national and regional cuisines has the advantage of using locally produced food items and indigenous skills.

Approaches to formulating training programmes

The basic approach to formulating training programmes is designing them to be comprehensive and integrated. This is important whether it is the first programme for a newly developing destination or is updating an existing programme in a country that already has a considerably developed tourism sector. A combination of training approaches is virtually always required.

A fundamental question is whether to establish a tourism training school, centre or institute in the country if one does not already exist. Tourism training institutions require substantial human and financial resources to establish and maintain properly. However, they are often justified in places where a reasonably sized tourism sector is anticipated. In addition to the manpower planning study, a feasibility analysis is needed for the proposed institution to ensure that it is justified, determine its size and development staging, the type and level of training to be offered, its location, financial support and other considerations.

Tourism training institutions typically include at least basic and intermediate skills training in all the hotel and catering departments and usually in tour and travel operations, including training for tour guides. They usually offer both upgrading and regular programme courses at the certificate level. Some of these training centres have expanded over time to include advanced skills training and supervisory and management diploma or degree level programmes. In larger countries, the centres may also eventually offer programmes in tourism management designed for public sector tourism officials. Hotel and tourism management programmes at the bachelor's or master's degree levels may also be established in existing universities. In some places, tourism training has been attached to vocational schools or polytechnic colleges. In larger countries, there may be more than one tourism training centre, some of which may be public and others private. For the private schools, government needs to establish minimum quality standards and an accreditation procedure.

Many developing countries have established tourism training centres, usually with some form of international agency technical and financial assistance to get them started. Some of these centres have been quite successful, and even acquired regional and international reputations, such as Utalii College in Kenya. Others have languished for various reasons—premature termination of international assistance, lack of adequate government support, difficulty of retaining competent faculty because of low salary levels, provision of inadequate physical facilities, and other reasons. In some cases, the institutions seem to be perpetually at the 'take-off stage' but, because of the reasons mentioned, have never quite taken off and made a substantial contribution to tourism training in their countries.

The World Tourism Organization (WTO) has a programme of designating existing tourism education institutions throughout the world in both the more and less developed countries as international centres. This designation is based on the institutions meeting certain standards and criteria and making formal application to the WTO. Several international centres have already been designated by the WTO in Europe, North America, Africa and Asia, and applications are pending from other institutions.

The WTO has recently produced a directory of tourism education institutions located throughout the world (*World Directory of Tourism Education and Training Institutions*). This is available from the WTO office in Madrid.

In addition to establishing training institutions, and often supplementing the programmes of these training centres, there are several types of training techniques which are typically considered and applied in internationally assisted training programmes of developing countries. These include the following:

- On-the-job training provided in the places of employment such as hotels and restaurants. For the lower-skilled level of employees, on-the-job training may be sufficient; but it may not be adequate if the enterprises themselves do not possess suitable knowledge and skills.
- Short in-country courses on various aspects of tourism—hotel and catering specializations and tourism management subjects such as planning and marketing. The usual approach is for each course to have one or two international core lecturers supplemented by local lecturers. These courses are organized to be highly intensive and include lectures, case studies, exercises and local field trips. In-country courses are often considered more cost-effective than overseas fellowships because they can reach a larger number of persons per unit cost expenditure.
- Fellowships for participation in overseas training programmes, which can range from short workshops and seminars and short- to medium-length training courses, to one- or two-year graduate-level university education, usually at the master's degree level, in tourism or hotel management. The longer-term fellowship programmes often include a combination of academic training, on-the-job attachments and study tours.

- Fellowships for overseas study tours to observe examples of various types of tourism development, marketing approaches, organization of national tourism administrations and other topics. Study tours must be carefully organized to be fully effective.
- Fellowships for overseas on-the-job attachments in the areas of training needs, such as attachments to well-managed tourism offices, hotels and tour and travel agencies.
- Correspondence courses which are available on all aspects of hotel, catering, tour operations and tourism management. Such courses have the advantage of being relatively inexpensive and can be taken while the participants continue their work activities.
- Counterparting by local staff of international experts (or national consultants) working on tourism projects in the country. Counterparts of the same professions to the international experts are officially appointed to work with the experts and thereby expand their knowledge. They are also involved in the particular project activities which they may need to follow through when the experts leave. It is common for a counterpart to understudy an expert in a particular position and then assume full responsibility for that position when the expert leaves.

On United Nations assisted projects, the present policy is to maximize use of qualified national consultants and reduce the number and time input of international experts/consultants. This approach makes more effective use of limited financial resources, and gives national consultants more experience in their professions. Also national consultants tend to know more about the local situation than do the international consultants, although they may lack the international perspective that is needed in such areas as product development and marketing. However, qualified national consultants are not always available in the country.

In newly developing tourism areas, it is common for all these types of training to be combined into an integrated programme specifically designed to fit the country's needs. An approach that is being increasingly used is that of arranging for training that is interspersed with practical experience in a programme of intermittent training and work. This provides the opportunity for the participants to apply their knowledge as they learn it, thus reinforcing the training and making it more realistic.

Regional training programmes may also be designed. For example, the WTO and UNDP financial support, has organized long-term regional training programmes in south Asia (involving ten countries) and eastern and southern Africa (involving 20 countries) during the past several years. Regional programmes offer the advantage of exposing more persons to specialized subjects for which training could not be justified in each country. Regional programmes also provide the opportunity for tourism personnel to meet and exchange ideas with their counterparts in other countries in the region, and be able to visit examples of tourism development and management in these countries. Some participants in regional programmes have established long-term communication links with their colleagues in neighbouring countries as a result of these regional training programmes.

In UNDP-sponsored tourism training projects, increasing emphasis is being placed on encouraging cooperation among developing countries. This involves tourism personnel from one country visiting other developing countries which have better developed tourism sectors to observe how tourism is developed and managed in those countries and sometimes to take training courses in the institutions in those countries. This form of learning experience can be more relevant, because of somewhat comparable situations in the countries, than the personnel taking their training only in the developed and often culturally different countries, and it is also usually more cost-effective.

Selection of participants for training programmes must be carefully made, especially for overseas fellowships. Proper selection is both the responsibility of the government and any international agencies providing the fellowships. The participants should have suitable backgrounds and motivation to benefit from the programme. Experience has demonstrated that some participants have been selected for overseas training based on political considerations rather than professional ones, and these participants may view the overseas experience as more of a vacation than a learning experience. Training participants must also be given the opportunity to apply their knowledge upon returning from their training, and be placed in positions where they can use what they have learned. For counterpart-type training, suitably qualified and motivated counterparts should be appointed to work with international experts on tourism projects, so there is maximum transfer of knowledge and enhancement of local capabilities.

For public tourism management training, some fellowship recipients may change jobs after returning to their home countries, especially leaving government to earn higher salaries in the private sector, unless a bonding procedure is applied. (Such persons, however, are still bringing skills to the country's private sector development.) On long-term overseas fellowship programmes, there have been cases of the fellowship recipients remaining in the country where they did training and

taking jobs there. Thus, the investment in their training has been lost by the developing country. There must be safeguards built into the system to ensure that maximum benefit accrues to the country from the training programmes.

The present United Nations approach on tourism projects (as well as other types of projects) in developing countries is to place increasing emphasis on local 'capacity-building'. This policy implies that a substantial proportion of the project budget should be devoted to training, whether this is in-country or overseas training, of local staff in order to give them greater capabilities to carry out the work themselves. Through local capacity-building, the countries do not need to rely on international technical assistance in the future.

Providing sufficient local financial resources to carry out adequate training programmes, and especially to support a tourism training centre, is a continual struggle for developing countries with limited government budget resources. International assistance may be available to commence the initial training programme but eventually the country itself must support the programme. Even when international assistance is available, the government must often make a substantial contribution, such as providing the physical facilities and local staff for establishing and maintaining a permanent training centre.

In addition to use of general government funds, various techniques have been successfully applied to provide these financial resources for training. The most common and successful one is to establish a training levy, in the form of a tax on tourists' hotel expenditures—usually of the order of about one per cent—which can only be used for tourism training purposes. Sri Lanka, for example, applies a training levy on tourist hotel expenditures. Also, arrangements can be made to involve private tourism sector enterprises in making a financial contribution to the tourism training programme.

Public and tourist education programmes

An essential element of the training programme is public education about tourism, commonly termed a tourism awareness programme. In newly developing tourism areas, there is often very little knowledge and understanding about tourism by the general public. Tourism awareness programmes include explanations about the concept of tourism, its socio-economic and environmental benefits, possible problems that can arise, and the tourism development objectives and plans that have been prepared for the area. The programme can include descriptions of the different behavioural patterns of foreign tourists and how local people can cope with these. The programme should also indicate ways in which local residents can benefit from tourism through direct or indirect employment and other means. If training for tourism is being organized, the programme should explain how persons can apply to participate in this training. As tourism develops in the area, the programme can be continued on a regular basis and include current events taking place in tourism.

Tourism awareness programmes can also help overcome any traditional resistance that may exist to working in tourism. Some years ago in a southeast Asian country, the first major tourism training institution was called a 'servants' school' by local young people, until they learned more about tourism and how it can offer a satisfying and rewarding career.

Tourism awareness programmes can use local media: television, radio, newspaper and magazine articles and meetings. In remote areas, often the radio is the primary means of mass communication. In some traditional areas, imaginative techniques can be used, such as conveying tourism messages in traditional puppet shows and drama. In the immediate area of proposed tourism development, it is very useful to hold meetings with local villagers to describe the tourism project being developed, discuss how the villagers can handle situations that will arise with tourists, and explain how they can support tourism and benefit from it. These meetings often need to be followed through with assistance to the villagers on ways to benefit from tourism. This may include training of some villagers to work in tourism and providing small business loans to establish tourism enterprises and technical advice on operating the enterprises.

Tourism awareness programmes can be aimed at specific objectives. In some eastern and southern African countries, there has been a serious problem of village farmers encroaching into game park habitats and seriously poaching animals in the parks, often as a result of economic necessity. Through discussions with these villagers, and applying techniques of revenue-sharing with the villages of tourist admission fees to the game parks and training of villagers to work in the game parks and associated tourism enterprises, they have learned the importance of game conservation to tourism and to their own best welfare. The villagers are now being much more cooperative, and even self-policing, in the conservation of wildlife and wildlife habitats.

Often the government, even at the ministerial level, also needs to be educated about the benefits and pitfalls of tourism. Especially important is for government officials to understand the importance of coordination among public agencies and between government and the private sector on tourism development and management. A common educational approach when tourism is being planned in a country is to organize a national tourism seminar aimed at higher-level government officials, private sector representatives and community leaders. This seminar will focus on presentations and discussions about concepts of tourism, its international and regional development patterns, and how best to plan for tourism in the country. The seminar should be well-publicized so the general public is aware of its conclusions and recommendations. These seminars may become regularly scheduled annual or biannual events.

Even in countries where tourism is already substantially developed, there may be many misconceptions about tourism that require public education to overcome. For example, tourism is a major component of the economy in Jamaica but was suffering serious marketing problems in the 1980s because of internationally publicized acts of violence by local Jamaicans against tourists, as well as a general dislike of tourism by some Jamaicans. Through a carefully planned public education campaign, the government was able to impress on residents the economic importance of tourism to the country, and the need to provide a safe and friendly environment for tourists. As a result of this and other efforts, tourism became better-accepted by Jamaicans and violent acts against tourists decreased—tourism regained its good international reputation and substantially revived in the country.

Equally important is educating tourists about the destination they are visiting and how best to handle themselves so that they show respect for that environment and society. Tourists should be informed about the salient characteristics of the local society and environment and especially local customs that should be observed. Local policies and laws relative to tourism, such as tipping policies and drug laws, should also be explained to tourists. If crime is a problem in parts of the tourism area, tourists should be warned to take precautions. This information can be conveyed in attractively designed brochures and tactfully expressed signs, as well as being included in tour guide books. Well-trained tour guides can perform an important role in informing tourists about local customs. If necessary, penalties can be assigned for serious infractions of local customs and laws.

It has been found that most tourists will observe local customs and laws if informed about them. An example of this is in the Maldives, which is an orthodox Islamic country where beach and marine tourism has been well developed. Nude bathing is strictly prohibited by custom and regulation, and both the resort management and tourists involved are fined if nude bathing is seen to take place. The tourists are informed of this regulation and there have been very few infractions of it, even though most tourists are from cultures where nude bathing is commonly accepted and they are in an environment conducive to this activity.

Conclusions

The importance of training for tourism in developing countries is generally well recognized, although adequate funding and sometimes technical capabilities to carry out the necessary training can be major limiting factors. It is crucial to satisfy training needs on a systematic, comprehensive, integrated and programmed basis, applying techniques of manpower planning. This planning, however, should be flexible, with adjustments made to the programme based on monitoring of actual training results, continuing training needs and changing circumstances in the tourism sector.

The formulation of tourism training programmes observes some general principles but often must give special consideration to immediate needs for upgrading present employees, must include basic remedial pre-training, must be broad-scoped and include training in other sectors, must emphasize foreign languages and typical tourist profiles, and may need to include highly specialized forms of training. It is important that new concepts and emerging trends in tourism development and marketing be part of the training content.

Effective training approaches must consider a combination of in-country and overseas types of academic and practical training, with emphasis placed on cost-effective approaches. Training participants must be carefully selected and their training properly utilized. A major question to be considered with respect to the best use of limited resources is whether to develop a permanent training institution in the country and what form this should take. Each training programme must be specifically tailored to the needs of the country, and take into account local cultural traditions and attitudes. Nevertheless, the experience gained elsewhere in implementing training programmes can provide useful models and often can be adapted to local situations.

Important components of tourism training in developing countries are public education about tourism and informing tourists about local customs, policies and laws. In addition to general public education, tourism awareness programmes can be specifically targeted to suit local situations. Imaginative techniques should be applied in implementing public and tourist education programmes.

The amount of international assistance being made available for tourism training is substantial, but there is never enough assistance to satisfy global needs. Present indications are that UNDP assistance is somewhat decreasing, because of limited funds. Fortunately, the European Union has become heavily involved in assisting tourism projects. Also, the World Bank is again assisting on tourism development, after having neglected this sector for several years. Some bilateral aid agencies fund tourism projects, including tourism training.

In any case, the developing countries themselves must assume considerable responsibility for tourism training. In some places, the countries need to give higher priority to tourism training with respect to providing adequate facilities, funding and technical inputs. Other countries have already made much progress in developing self-sustaining in-country tourism training institutions and programmes.

Note

The content of this paper is drawn from the experience of the author in formulating and implementing internationally assisted tourism training programmes in developing countries.

59 Managing the development and implementation of national human resource policies for tourism

T. BAUM

Introduction

Comprehensive human resource development for tourism, is widely recognised as a vital component in sustainable tourism development. The case for this has been made increasingly effectively at both academic and professional levels. Recent examples where this issue is specifically addressed, in the literature, include Conlin and Baum (1993) and Burns (1994); these contributions add the dimension of sustainability to a debate which has tended to focus on the need to invest in human resource development in support of increased productivity or enhanced service quality (for example, Baum (1993a), Enz and Fulford (1993) and Goffe (1993)). These approaches, in turn, build on analysis, drawing on work from the late 1970s and the 1980s, which had moved the discussion of human resource concerns, within tourism, from what might be described as the micro, company- and job-specific level, on to the wider macro labour market plane, with the focus placed in the context of broader employment and social policy issues (for example, Bagguley (1987), Byrne (1986), Gabriel (1988), Guerrier and Lockwood (1989), Riley (1991) and Wood (1992)).

Adding the concept of sustainability to the human resource agenda, within international tourism, is of considerable importance as a complementary dimension to the ground which much of the literature, such as that noted above, has addressed to date. Sustainability leads to a concept of human resource development which seeks to counter traditional short-term, operationally oriented approaches to human resource planning and development in tourism, within which labour has been seen as a necessary support resource to the physical and economic development of products and markets. One of the underpinning themes in this paper is the need for tourism planning to give recognition to the impact of development on the character and balance of the labour market within local economies (Conlin and Baum, 1993). At the same time, there is a need to recognise the strengths and deficiencies of that local labour market and the

consequences of these for the formulation of tourism development policies. In all its other dimensions, sustainable tourism development draws its strength from a synergetic relationship with its local environment, reflected especially in product development and marketing. The human resource field has not benefited from this link in any significant way, with a general failure to acknowledge the association between sustainability and the labour environment. Lane (1992) touches on this issue by contrasting 'no career structure' and 'employees imported' as features of non-sustainable tourism with those of 'career structure' and 'employment according to local potential' in sustainable tourism development. Development from this human resource perspective is 'of' the local community and not simply 'in' the communities as is frequently the case within the traditional tourism development paradigm.

In many ways, however, this concentration on the human resource agenda as central to wider discussion of tourism development issues represents a formal recognition of what has been tacitly acknowledged, through investment by both the public and private sectors, for many years. A model has evolved, without clear rationalisation or, indeed, specific articulation, whereby the human resource needs of tourism are deemed to be successfully met by way of a two-pronged approach. Firstly, there is intensive initial training, through public sector schools, colleges, universities and apprenticeship schemes. This is complemented by on-going investment in upgrading and updating skills by employers, assisted in some countries by the state through agencies such as the former Hotel and Catering Training Board (UK) and CERT (Ireland). The model is, generally, crude in its operation in that few links are made between provision, by way of education and training, and either the quantitative or qualitative needs of the industry. This model has been transposed, without critical evaluation of its impact or suitability, to much of the developing world through a diversity of aid programmes under the auspices of agencies such as the European Union (EU), the International Labour Office (ILO), the United Nations Development Programme

(UNDP) and the World Tourism Organisation (WTO).

Despite the almost universal application of this public–private sector model of human resource development for tourism, the actual impact it has made on the industry, worldwide, must be questioned. Notwithstanding the excellent work of colleges and universities in the tourism and hospitality field in the UK, it is salutary to note that under 10% of the two-million-plus employees in the largest sector of the industry, that of hotel and catering, have formal training and qualifications for the work that they are undertaking (Battersby, 1990). While the introduction of National Vocational Qualifications (NVQ) and, in particular, the Accreditation of Prior Learning (APL) will go some way to altering this situation, this deficit of trained personnel certainly represents an indictment of public and private sector investment in the education and training of tourism employees. Similar conclusions can be drawn from studies which look at the attrition rate of those who do enter the tourism industry after formal training (for example, CERT (1986)) and point to very high levels of dropout or movement to other career areas within relatively short periods after graduation. A frequent response to high levels of early career attrition is to question the relevance of the education provided and, in particular, the 'realism' of expectations which young people have on graduation. This coin may be turned around, of course, and the complex issue of the conditions and rewards that some sectors of the industry offer can be advanced as an alternative response to the high level of dropout.

The concern for the lack of impact of education and training extends beyond the failure of the industry to retain its qualified personnel and also relates to the limited effect that investment in training and in support infrastructure has on the actual delivery of the tourism product. In the context of the Caribbean, for example, two leading figures within the region's tourism environment can be quoted in illustration of this point. Jean Holder, Secretary-General of the Caribbean Tourism Organization, writing about the region's tourism product in 1993, noted that 'we have failed to deliver it, pleasantly, courteously and professionally—everytime . . . everywhere'. John Bell (1991) of the Caribbean Hotel Association, in discussing the state of the region's tourism and hospitality schools after two decades of national and donor investment, wrote:

> Despite the labor intensive nature of the hotel and tourism sector, and many technical and practical skills involved, those hotel training schools, invariably government owned, that do exist within the region are horribly underfunded, under-established and in general treated like low grade technical schools for students who cannot make it into other careers.

Critical issues

A considerable proportion of discussion relating to the human resource domain in tourism, within the literature, focuses on the identification of what are deemed to be the critical problems (for example, Go (1990) and Worsfold and Jameson (1991)). Consideration of these issues in the literature is presented in a way which, as I have said elsewhere (Baum, 1993b), is characterised by reiteration and repetition. The same themes emerge, albeit with some local or cultural modification, worldwide and within both developed and developing economies. These interrelated concerns include areas such as: the impact of changing demographics; skills shortages; labour turnover; failure to attract quality school- and college-leavers; the poor image of the tourism industry as an employer; uncompetitive rewards and poor working conditions; religious and cultural taboos to employment in tourism; failure of education providers to meet industry's needs; and failures to recognise long-term human resource benefits in the face of short-term priorities. These issues also emerge in the context of an empirical study of the human resource issues within tourism at a national level (Baum, 1994).

At a national or transnational level, the last issue, that of what might be called 'short-termism' in the human resource field is arguably the most serious and yet it is a concern which is not widely addressed in the literature. Its manifestation is quite frequent, at both national and corporate levels. Elsewhere, I use an example from Singapore to illustrate this issue (Baum, 1993b) and it is one that is worth repeating here. The national tourism 'Product Development Plan' (STPB, 1988) is a complex and multi-faceted programme for tourism development, considering issues such as: urban regeneration; infrastructural requirements in terms of transportation, accommodation and utilities; and theme park and resort development, as well as cultural, artistic and events programmes. The plan provides a sophisticated link between the international marketplace, in terms of demand, product development and the needs and rights of the local community. Nowhere, in the plan, however, is reference made to the inevitable human resource implications of such ambitious development plans within an already tight labour market, or to the consequences on the human resource environment of growth projections for tourism, at that time running at 15% per annum. It is as if the labour market implications of development were totally forgotten in the preparation of the plan. This problem is by no means unique to this example. Other cases can be drawn upon, at a national, local or, indeed, individual project level, from around the world, although counter-examples of careful lead-time planning can also be found (for example, EuroDisney). The impact time, in the human resource area, is, arguably, longer than that required in any of the other tourism development activities. However, the planning of human resource requirements is frequently neglected until the last minute at the corporate level as a means of saving on payroll costs and at the national level because, ultimately, it is difficult to identify any single body with unitary responsibility for this area.

This last point focuses on what this paper argues is the most significant single deficiency in the human resource environment within international tourism and that is one of the ownership and coordination of the area. In most countries, responsibility for aspects of human resource development, in the tourism-related environment, is fragmented and diffuse and can be found, in part, within both the public and private sector. Typically, this responsibility may lie with a diversity of bodies, accountable to different national or regional government departments, with transnational agencies, and with private sector companies and associations. Examples of bodies whose brief may include a significant human resource component may include:

- national and regional tourism organisations;
- ministries with specific responsibility for tourism;
- other ministries and agencies responsible for the delivery of aspects of the tourism product (the environment, agriculture, culture etc.);
- security and home affairs ministries with responsibility for police, immigration, customs and related officials;
- national or regional education ministries, perhaps with a divide between responsibility for tertiary, vocational and higher educational provision;
- labour/employment/manpower ministries;
- transnational governmental agencies, such as those in the EU, the Caribbean (the Caribbean Tourism Organization) or ASEAN;
- schools, colleges and universities (public and private sector);
- specialist agencies responsible for education, training, certification and related areas (for example, CERT in Ireland);
- quasi-governmental funding agencies for education and training (for example, FEFC, HEFC, SHEFC, and TECs in the UK);
- national statistical collection agencies;
- private and public sector tourism companies;
- industry representative associations and their education/ training arms (for example, SHATEC in Singapore and, at a transnational level, the Caribbean Hospitality Training Institute); and

- a diversity of private sector consultancies, working on behalf of individual companies or within donor aid projects and at national or transnational level.

Beyond these bodies, the impact of other areas of general, non-tourism-specific policy development and implementation (such as education, training, social legislation, the environment etc.) on the human resource environment, cannot be ignored.

Within this complex environment, responsibilities and structures have evolved through history, tradition and bureaucratic convenience rather than in response to the needs of the tourism industry and its employees. It is not surprising, therefore, to find the lack of oversight and policy management that exists in most countries with respect to the area under discussion. In an attempt to unravel the management of the human resource environment, within tourism, at a national level, a study of the allocation of responsibilities, with particular focus on the role of national tourism organisations (NTOs) was undertaken during 1991/92.

Study methodology

This study, which formed part of a broader research project into human resource issues in the context of wider tourism policy formulation (Baum, 1992a), was based on a mailed questionnaire survey, addressed to the Chief Officers of 108 NTOs. Completed questionnaires were received from 66 of the population (a 61% response rate), with a reasonably representative spread from all major geographical regions. The responses also included the NTOs of countries with varying levels of economic development. In 1987 data from OECD and the UN were used in order to categorise respondents into three groups according to per capita income. Although somewhat arbitrary, this segmentation provides a useful classification of respondents into three groups:

Per capita income less than US$1000 (Group A)	29 (44%)
Per capita income between US$1000 and US$8000 (Group B)	16 (24%)
Per capita income greater than US$8000 (Group C)	21 (32%)

Responsibilities for policy development and the management of human resources in tourism

The main outcome of the study was to confirm the original hypothesis that there is little by way of overarching coordination of the complex human resource environment within tourism at a national level. Despite the diversity of agencies which input into the area, to a greater or lesser extent, there are few national attempts, at either a policy or implementation level, to ensure that necessary linkages are made between the work of the various bodies and that they are working towards common goals and targets. One partial exception is the model provided by CERT in Ireland, where real attempts are made to link the policy priorities of government in all areas that affect tourism with labour market and education concerns. This role is strongly supported by empirical research and is well described by Walsh (1993).

The study identified that responsibility for managing responses to human resource issues in tourism, at a national level, can be attributed to three areas—the private sector of the tourism industry (48%), NTOs (41%) and the ministry responsible for tourism (36%). Interestingly, education and training authorities do not feature as agencies with any significant role in dealing with issues of this kind. Thus, NTOs were identified as significant but not pre-eminent agencies in taking responsibility for dealing with human resource concerns in tourism. The study looked in some detail at the human resource functions of NTOs on the basis that these agencies are

Table 59.1 *NTO functions—a comparison between 1975 and 1991/92 research studies*

Function	Number and percentage reporting function	
	1975 WTO study	1991/92 study
Determination of manpower and training needs for tourism	61 (64%)	45 (68%)
Formulation/design of training programmes	56 (59%)	37 (56%)
Organisation of vocational training programmes	56 (59%)	47 (71%)
Establishment of hotel and tourism schools	40 (42%)	23 (35%)
Granting of fellowships	45 (47%)	27 (41%)
Reception of trainees	46 (48%)	28 (43%)
Conduct of manpower/training needs research	n.a.	34 (52%)
Coordination of national vocational training standards/certification schemes	n.a.	19 (29%)
Operation of hotel and tourism schools/training centres	n.a.	16 (24%)
Provision of financial support for education/training		
—to schools/training centres	n.a.	14 (21%)
—to trainees	n.a.	8 (12%)
No human resource functions	9 (9%)	8 (12%)

n.a., information not sought.

reasonably comparable between countries. A further incentive for this analysis was the availability of comparable data from a 1975 World Tourism Organisation Study (WTO, 1975), which is the only published source of its kind to address aspects of the same field as this study. The extent of NTO involvement in eleven human resource areas was sought, six of which had also been considered by the 1975 WTO research. Table 59.1 presents the results of these studies.

It is interesting to note the relatively limited changes that occurred over the 15-year period between the two studies, notwithstanding some variation between responding samples. The most significant change relates to the increase in NTOs organising vocational training courses. This represents an interesting development and may reflect a number of influences and organisational/ environmental changes in the intervening period. These may include the growing recognition of the importance of skills development, especially in the area of service/ customer care, within all tourism sectors. It may also signify the increasing need for in-service and updating training for many personnel in the industry, within a working environment faced with constant change in terms of its markets, the expectations of its customers and the use of support technology. At the same time, as the preceding quotation from Bell illustrates, the traditional providers of education and training for tourism, where they are in existence, have not received resourcing at a level which permits them to respond to these changes in the needs and levels of demand within the tourism industry.

The growing importance of the organisation of vocational training, as an NTO function, is reflected within each of the three subgroups but is most significant among the more affluent nations. This increase appears to indicate a significant change in the perceived importance of specific skills development and training issues within the tourism industries of developed countries, possibly driven by changes in the labour market and the education and training environment in particular.

The most frequently identified function, in 1975, was that of determining manpower and training requirements, checked by almost two-thirds of the respondents. This function remained very significant in the study reported here and, indeed, showed a marginal increase in the level of response. It is reasonable to speculate, however, that the nature of this function has changed, significantly, in the period between the studies and that the activity, today, represents a somewhat more sophisticated and comprehensive activity than it did in 1975.

When this function is considered in relation to the three subgroups identified within this study (which were also applied to the 1975 data), considerable variation is evident. The two less affluent groups of countries were much more likely to identify this function than was the case with the wealthiest group of countries and this pattern remained consistent between the two studies. In all three cases, the proportion increased significantly between 1975 and 1991/92.

The above two functions showed an increase in activity, within NTOs, between 1975 and 1991/92. The remaining functions saw a significant decrease in the proportion of NTOs identifying the particular function over the same period, although in no case was this fall dramatic.

The figures in Table 59.1 disguise some variation with respect to the three subgroups. In particular, three of the functions were identified by the same or a higher proportion of the poorest group in 1991/92 when compared to 1975, demonstrating the increasing sophistication and range of responsibilities within the NTOs of developing countries. The only area of decline was that of granting fellowships. By contrast, decreases were almost universal, with respect to the functions of NTOs from the middle subgroup, between the two studies. This picture may point to a sharpening of purpose and definition of functions in some NTOs, reflecting a greater emphasis on marketing and related activities. Finally, with respect to the most affluent group, the pattern is not so clear-cut. Two of the functions show a significant decrease. These are the establishment of hotel and tourism schools and the reception of trainees. By contrast, the granting of fellowships increased by some measure and the formulation/design of training programmes remained constant.

The study also looked beyond the NTO role in human resource initiatives and identified other agencies with responsibilities in the area. What emerged was consistent with the argument regarding fragmentation. With regard to some of the functions, clear alternatives to NTOs emerged. For example, education ministries feature strongly with respect to a number of functions, notably the provision of financial support for training (82%), the operation of training schools (71%, but with stronger emphasis here in less affluent countries), the formulation/ design of training programmes (47% of the total sample and 67% of the most affluent group), and the establishment of hotel and tourism schools (74% of the full sample, 79% of the lowest income group and 67% of the highest income group). The level of education ministry involvement in other areas was somewhat lower but education-related agencies also feature, notably schools and colleges which take responsibility with respect to the formulation and design of training programmes (26%), the organisation of vocational training programmes

(29%), and the establishment of hotel and tourism schools (20% within the public sector and 11% in the private sector).

Ministries of tourism do not take active responsibility with respect to many of the identified functions. An exception is that of determining manpower and training requirements, where the ministry was identified by 39% of the sample. Likewise, human resource/labour/ manpower ministries also feature in limited roles with respect to determining manpower and training requirements (21%) and the granting of fellowships (12%). Some limited roles were also identified with respect to other public and private sector agencies, such as those previously listed, and in many instances responsibility is clearly shared between two or more bodies.

Thus, while a diversity of agencies contribute to the development and implementation of human resource policies within tourism, at a national level, this research study affirms the overall fragmentation of the management of this area. What is clear is a fairly general lack of overview of policy development and implementation in relation to human resources, within tourism. This must be to the overall detriment of what is recognised as a critical area for the future development and sustainability of tourism in both developed and developing countries.

Responses to the human resource environment at national and transnational levels

Mechanisms to overcome the significant deficiency discussed above have been proposed (Baum, 1993c) through the application of a conceptual framework or model which seeks to bring together all the diverse concerns and interests that impact on the area so that human resources can be considered, from all perspectives, in the context of a developing national tourism economy. The model is designed to provide a pragmatic response to fragmentation, allowing tourism policy makers and planners, at a national level, to incorporate the heterogeneity of concerns which impact on the area within a single policy development framework. The approach goes beyond consideration of the institutional arrangements for the management of human resource issues in tourism, which was the focus of the research discussed in this paper, and attempts to incorporate a much wider environmental scan of areas such as tourism markets, physical and socio-cultural product, the wider labour market, and the traditions and history of the institutions and organisations which are addressed. The model is, above all, flexible and is designed to be community-responsive, linked closely to the needs and aspirations of the local tourism economy and all its constituent parts. It is, thus, supportive of sustainability of human resources in tourism.

The focus of this discussion, heretofore, has been on the human resource environment, within tourism, at a national level. Similar concerns may be identified in relation to more local tourism industries, ranging from specific communities or resorts to much larger units, such as states within a federal political structure. At a relatively localised level, Bird (1989) pinpoints the lack of sensitivity and sustainability, within tourism planning, to be found in the Malaysian island of Langkawi and gives particular attention to a failure to consider human resource concerns within the overall planning process. Clearly, application of the planning model could have assisted in this environment. At a provincial level, in Canada, Dowler (1993) discusses how Ontario's tourism industry is recognising the need for an integrated approach to the management of education and training and demonstrates the validity of the model at this level.

There is a further context in which consideration of these issues is valid and that is the transnational. For a variety of reasons, there are situations where consideration of human resource concerns, at a purely national level, is inadequate. For example, in the Caribbean and the South Pacific, the number of very small states means that it is often unrealistic to make provision for the full range of education and training requirements of tourism, either in vertical (reflecting the industry's sectoral breadth) or horizontal (referring to the range of skills levels) terms. Thus models of cooperation provide the preferred response and this approach has been strongly encouraged by international funding agencies, notably the European Union. Outcomes of this process include the establishment of the transnational Caribbean Hospitality Training Institute, as the educational arm of the Caribbean Hotel Association. In the same region, another example is the institution of the recently launched Hospitality Occupational Standards for Training (HOST) initiative, which is to provide formal certified recognition of the in-company and prior learning of tourism employees throughout the diverse countries of the Caribbean. Projects in southeast Asia have similar objectives and this model of interregional cooperation will soon be applied in the South Pacific and south Asia, although the latter initiative incorporates countries ranging in size from Bhutan to India and, thus, does not result from the same country size concerns as that in some other regions. Implicit in approaches of this kind is the need to take an overview of the whole human resource environment of a region, in the context of tourism, as a starting point. The initiatives attempt to overcome institutional and political barriers to cooperation, within and between

countries. However, the extent to which such projects will continue beyond donor funding periods remains to be seen.

A somewhat different transnational issue, in this broad context, is exemplified by the situation in European Union countries. While the twelve states all exhibit major differences in the nature and value of their respective tourism industries and their labour markets have evolved on the basis of diverse traditions, there are growing pressures for Union-wide homogenisation of labour policies and the application of common regulations covering a number of areas within the tourism industry. Rules governing free movement of labour, in particular, have emphasised what has long been a feature of the tourism industries in a number of European countries, that of seasonal mobility from countries such as Ireland, Italy, Portugal and Spain to the industrial centre of Europe for off-season work. This process is considered in more detail elsewhere (Baum, 1992b). The porous nature of European borders, combined with pressures towards transnational uniformity in areas such as education and training, will contribute to creating a need for the development of human resource policies for tourism at a level which reflects Union needs. An initial move in this direction was provided by the Community Action Plan (Commission of the European Communities, 1991) but the document is by no means comprehensive in its approach to the human resource area, concentrating almost exclusively on vocational training provision.

Conclusions

This paper looks at the management of human resources and related policy development, within tourism, at a national level and focuses on the fragmentation that generally exists, in an institutional context, in this area. Research is considered which reinforces the identified deficiencies. However, this discussion and the empirical information that is used in its support, represents an initial investigation that merits consideration in much greater detail, both on the basis of case studies of individual national structures and through further comparative transnational research. The need is also clearly identified for consideration of policy development that reflects the growing internationalisation of human resource policy development and implementation.

This discussion commenced by addressing the issue of sustainability within tourism and its relationship to the human resource domain. This remains a central concern. Sustainability will only become fully recognised as an item on the human resource agenda when fragmentation of human resource management is overcome and policy-makers are able to take an integrated overview of the multiplicity of concerns which impact on the implementation of human resource priorities in tourism.

References

Bagguley, Paul (1987) 'Flexibility, restructuring and gender: changing employment in Britain's hotels', Working Paper 24, Lancaster Regionalism Group, Lancaster.

Battersby, David (1990) 'Lifting the barriers: employment and training in tourism and leisure', *Insights*.

Baum, Tom (1992a) 'Human resources in tourism: a study of the position of human resource issues in national tourism policy development and implementation', unpublished Ph.D. thesis, University of Strathclyde.

Baum, Tom (1992b) 'Human resource concerns in European tourism: strategic response and the EC', *International Journal of Hospitality Management*, 12(1): 77–88.

Baum, Tom (1993a) 'Human resources: the unsung price–value issue', in Hawkins, Don and Ritchie, J. R. (Eds), *Brent World Travel and Tourism Review*, Vol. 3, CAB International, Wallingford.

Baum, Tom (1993b) 'Human resources in tourism: an introduction', in Baum, Tom (Ed.), *Human Resource Issues in International Tourism*, Butterworth-Heinemann, Oxford.

Baum, Tom (1993c) 'Creating an integrated human resource environment for tourism', in Baum, Tom (Ed.), *Human Resource Issues in International Tourism*, Butterworth-Heinemann, Oxford.

Baum, Tom (1994) 'The development and implementation of national tourism policies', *Tourism Management*, August (in press).

Bell, John (1991) 'Caribbean tourism realities', in Hawkins, D. and Ritchie, J. R. (Eds), *Brent World Travel and Tourism Review*, Vol. 1, CAB International, Wallingford.

Bird, Bella (1989) 'Langkawi from Mahsuri to Mahathir: tourism for whom?', INSAN, Kuala Lumpur.

Burns, Peter (1994) 'Sustaining tourism's workforce: cultural and social-values perspectives with special reference to the role of expatriates', *Journal of Sustainable Tourism* (in press).

Byrne, Dominic (1986) 'Waiting for change? Working in hotels and catering', Low Pay Unit, London.

CERT (1986) 'Where are they now?' CERT, Dublin.

Commission of the European Communities (1991) 'Community action plan to assist tourism', Com(91) 97 final, CEC, Brussels.

Conlin, Michael and Baum, Tom (1993) 'Comprehensive human resource planning: an essential key to sustainable tourism in island settings', Paper to Conference on Sustainable Tourism Development for Islands and Small States, University of Malta, Malta.

Dowler, Susan (1993) 'Competency based hospitality and tourism training', *Proceedings of the Second Island International Forum*, Bermuda College, Bermuda.

Enz, Cathy and Fulford, Mark (1993) 'The impact of human resource management on organizational success: suggestions for hospitality educators', *Hospitality and Tourism Educator*, 5(2): 17–24.

Gabriel, Yiannis (1988) *Working Lives in Catering*, Routledge & Kegan Paul, London.

Go, Frank (1990) 'Tourism and hospitality management: new horizons', *Journal of European Industrial Training*, 14(3): 45–53.

Goffe, Peter (1993) 'Managing for excellence in Caribbean hotels', in Gayle, Dennis and Goodrich, Jonathan (Eds), *Tourism Marketing and Management in the Caribbean*, Routledge, London.

Guerrier, Yvonne and Lockwood, Andrew (1989) 'Core and peripheral employees in hotel operations', *Personnel Review*, 18(1): 9–15.

Holder, Jean (1993) 'Island tourism and price and value relationship: a global perspective', in Hawkins, Don and Ritchie, J. R. (Eds), *Brent World Travel and Tourism Review*, Vol. 3, CAB International, Wallingford.

Lane, Bernard (1992) 'Sustainable tourism: a philosophy', a publication of the Rural Tourism Unit, Department of Continuing Education, University of Bristol.

Riley, Michael (1991) 'Human resource management: a guide to personnel practice in the hotel and catering industries', Butterworth-Heinemann, Oxford.

STPB (Singapore Tourist Promotion Board) (1988) 'Product development plan', STPB, Singapore.

Walsh, Mary Ena (1993) 'Republic of Ireland', in Baum, Tom (Ed.), *Human Resource Issues in International Tourism*, Butterworth-Heinemann, Oxford.

Wood, Roy (1992) *Working in Hotels and Catering*, Routledge, London.

WTO (World Tourism Organisation) (1975) 'Aims, activities and fields of competence of national tourism organizations', WTO, Madrid.

Worsfold, Philip and Jameson, Stephanie (1991) 'Human resource management: a response to change in the 1990s', in Teare, Richard and Boer, Andrew (Eds), *Strategic Hospitality Management: Theory and Practice for the 1990s*, Cassell, London.

60 A Spanish Mediterranean tourism model: the tourist labour market in the Province of Alicante (within the Valencian Region)

F. VERA, A. PEDREÑO AND J. IVARS

The tourist labour market in the Province of Alicante

The unique characteristics of the model presented by the introduction of tourism in the Valencian Region, as in other places in the Mediterranean which have almost spontaneously become specialized in offering tourism services (Aguiló, 1990; Aguiló and Torres, 1990; Vera and Marchena, 1990; among others), are reflected in the notable deficiencies inherent in training and professionalization within the tourism industry.

This situation contrasts with the evolution of tourism in this area and, uniquely, in the Province of Alicante. In this province, which constitutes our model in this paper, the service industry has shown itself to be dynamic, as illustrated by the level of the tertiary boom which surpasses the regional and national average (Fuentes and Sagarribay, 1993) (see Table 60.1). However it is only when we make a breakdown study, sub-sector by sub-sector, given the heterogeneous branches of the services industry, that we can begin to properly comprehend the more specific evolution of tourism activity. Thus, in the case of hospitality and catering and trade, closely related in Alicante to the development of tourism, the dynamics were positive between 1979 and 1989. Indeed, this contrasted development puts hospitality in the most advantageous position (see Table 60.2). It is worth pointing out that since 1989 the recession and structural problems have been felt, and as such a close analysis of figures, not yet available, of the years 1989–1992 would certainly present a less positive picture.

As far as jobs dynamics are concerned, the province of Alicante has shown itself to be more dynamic (see Table 60.1) in all branches of the service industry than the whole of the Valencian Region, and much more so than Spain as a whole (Fuentes and Sagarribay, 1993). It is mostly branches such as hospitality where the greatest rate of growth has been registered in the tourism industry itself, although it is also true that profits spread to other sub-sectors such as trade. Indeed the development of trade is related to the boom in tourism (see Tables 60.2, 60.3 and 60.4). Therefore, the contribution of tourism to the 'gross added value' of the service industry, and to the dynamism of employment gives us reason to pay special attention to the structural problems evident in the tourism sector and, among them, the professionalization and training of a workforce faced with preconceptions from past years during which improvization was so often applied.

Evidently, the fact that our model has been a leading tourist destination since the early 1960s has not led to the development of a suitably coherent education and training policy, even when faced with changes both in supply and demand which have been foreseeable and forthcoming since the 1980s. Such changes mark the new scenario of tourism as a qualified activity in the regional development process.

We should bear in mind here the fact that the employment structure within services offered by tourism is profoundly marked by the conditions under which the model has developed. In our case, this started with the beginnings of mass tourism, driven to the Mediterranean

Table 60.1 *Province of Alicante: gross added value and employment by sectors 1981–1989*

Sectors	G.A.V.				Employment			
	1981	%	1989	%	1981	%	1989	%
Fish	3.174	0.6	6.802	0.4	4.418	1.2	2.036	0.5
Industry	151.866	23.9	385.900	25.3	128.978	38.8	123.158	23.0
Construction	36.994	7.3	148.202	9.4	36.801	8.4	42.422	0.6
Services	295.065	68.0	932.751	61.2	165.056	43.4	231.033	62.4

Source: 'Renta Nacional de España y su Distribución Provincial', Banco Bilbao–Vizcaya.   Million G.A.V.

Table 60.2 *Province of Alicante: gross added value and employment development in the services industry*

	G.A.V.		Employment	
Years	Trade and services	Hospitality and restaurant	Trade and services	Hospitality and restaurant
1979	100	100	100	100
1983	117	140	115	123
1985	151	229	135	165
1989	172	234	153	170

1979 = 100.
Source: 'Renta Nacional de España y su Distribución Provincial', Banco Bilbao, Vizcaya.

coasts by the international agencies, and evolved to the present-day situation characterized by the model's depletion due to the maturing of the sun–sea–sand product and its inability to compete in the international context. The following features are basic if we are to understand these coordinates in the context of employment and training.

1. Temporary employment, as a direct consequence of the prevalence and specialization of a mass demand motivated by the enjoyment of sun and beaches and, given the lack of alternative formulas, totally dependent on the weather. This temporary nature of tourism-linked employment explains both the lack of interest given to upgrading qualifications or professionalizing the different levels of the employment structure, and the failure of the private sector to invest in training. It should be remembered that the negative policy of closing down establishments has been considered an effective way of helping business to survive in the sector for quite a few years.

2. The concept of tourism as an unexpected phenomenon— an intrinsically momentary opportunity which draws agents, entrepreneurs and workers away from other industries. The former, in our model, were attracted by the prospect of doing quick business, whereas the workforce was attracted to this new sector, motivated by the hope of finding better economic conditions than

those being experienced in the more 'traditional' industries (mainly fishing and crop farming). Thus the secretarial 'pouring-in' of assets was accompanied by strong migratory movements channelled towards the coast from backward areas, forming an outline of asymmetric flows between dynamic areas, dedicated to tourist activity, and areas which had entered into continual decline. Thus real peripheries were created in the division of labour imposed by the new phenomenon of industrialized leisure and recreation. It is not strange then that the municipal areas most affected by the growth in tourism differed from other areas in that the number of inhabitants who had migrated in exceeded the native population and formed the workforce of the tourism industry. This phenomenon will not repeat itself in our model since the tourist spaces have now been constructed and their workforce fixed. What could happen instead are pendular movements between neighbouring areas or a restructuring of the jobs market within the regional territory itself.

3. Bearing these conditions in mind, it follows to some extent that there is no existing tradition of proper education or training in our sector. This has led to any training being largely carried out in the company itself through work experience with all the risks this involves. Certainly it is true that in recent years some hotel companies, largely the big hotel chains, have concerned themselves with continuous professional training (computerization, languages), albeit to a limited extent with the exception of the most important chains and with the support of regional governments.

4. The crisis presented by this model, influenced in turn both by external factors (especially the new competitor destinations, alternative products and changes in demand trends) and internal ones (price and salary increases, the inflexible nature of the traditional offer and obsolete destinations) raises the need for a reorientation towards guaranteeing future competitiveness. This necessity implies quality service, product diversification and, in short, professionalization—weighty topics at a

Table 60.3 *Province of Alicante: hospitality and restaurants—percentage of participation in the regional G.A.V. and employment*

	G.A.V.			Employment		
Years	Total	Services	Hospitality and restaurants	Total	Services	Hospitality and restaurants
1979	29.83	28.91	43.82	30.17	27.86	40.74
1983	31.42	30.79	46.50	32.40	29.97	45.76
1985	31.63	32.15	52.58	31.77	30.76	50.54
1989	31.67	32.50	49.94	32.01	31.27	48.51

Source: 'Renta Nacional de España y su Distribución Provincial', Banco Bilbao, Vizcaya.

Table 60.4 *Province of Alicante: hospitality and restaurants—percentage of the total of the services industries*

	G.A.V.	Employment
Years	Hospitality and restaurant services	Hospitality and restaurant services
1979	11.10	13.00
1983	13.34	13.94
1985	16.93	15.97
1989	15.11	14.50

Source: 'Renta Nacional de España y su Distribución Provincial', Banco Bilbao, Vizcaya.

time when the current recession (in terms of affluence) is being hidden behind the appearance of competitivity derived from the latest devaluations in our currency. Given this current situation, entrepreneurs and governments seem to be prepared to push to one side the serious structural problems of the tourist industry.

In this sense it is worrying that the preferred response of the acting agents in tourism to the trends being observed in the industry is one limited to actions taken on prices, by way of maintaining or even cheapening the costs of services, without a parallel increase in productivity. This generates company decapitalization and is detrimental to product quality, having a consequent negative impact on demand (Torres Bernier, 1993). Therefore, the lack of qualified training, although characteristic of the early life of a tourist destination, has been maintained, contrary to the requirements of an activity that ought no longer to be considered as an essentially ephemeral industry meant to adjust the trade balance, if it is to guarantee its position as a real strategic activity in the economic future of the Mediterranean coastal regions.

Evidently current recognition of the importance of qualified training is a direct consequence of a tourist destination first maturing and consolidating its position during the creation and growth stage, and only then moving towards offering a quality product. Thus, the Valencian Region, now that the overwhelming growth period is over and given the new nature of demand, in its necessary reconversion away from the image of a traditional destination and in this transit process towards quality of tourist services, must take on new assumptions as far as professionalization is concerned. This should be done throughout all the different levels of employment in the industry, and should be supported by education and training programmes hampered until now by negative features (insufficient, incomplete, non-integral and obsolete, according to Torres Bernier (1993)).

Repercussions of current trends in the tourist industry on the labour market

The transformations undergone by the tourist industry, summed up by the notion of cyclic changes, condition, among other things, employment and training. On the one hand, given the new products (new destinations, diversified products, promotion techniques) it is possible to detect balances and imbalances between supply and demand within the industry. It is essentially possible to evaluate the activities and occupations that will have greatest specific importance.

On the demand side, all the changing circumstances (or new motivations) are essentially related to, and point towards, the quality requirement. In a services activity, quality is based on personal contact and service; this implies firstly that educational and training elements are fundamental factors for results to be achieved, and secondly that professionalization and proper workforce preparation must replace the aforementioned precarious situation of self-training.

In this sense, positive changes in employment and training could be pinned down to redefining posts whose responsibility it is to serve the public, recognizing the need for qualifications in the area of customer service, a decrease in temporary employment (favoured by the increase in alternative tourism and staggered holidays), and new technologies aimed at increasing productivity (Monfort and Amor, 1994).

Nevertheless priority must first be given to elaborating and developing an integral plan that should tackle everything from the beginnings of basic professional training to postgraduate university degrees, without forgetting occupational training and the upgrading of skills (Torres Bernier, 1993).

Structure of the tourist labour market in the Province of Alicante

The importance of the human factor in offering tourist services should never be underestimated either for those in managerial posts who design the services or for baseline employees whose job it is to carry them out. In contrast to tangible production, tourist services produce a set of experiences which, once lived through, will determine the customer's degree of satisfaction and the degree of quality. Obviously then the human component plays a vital role.

The fact that human resources in tourism are being studied more and more is a direct consequence of the growth of competition and the diversification of offers at all levels. Quality of service (affecting largely, though not exclusively, the human factor) has been converted into a key competitivity factor, achieving greater differentiation

Table 60.5 *Gross production (G.A.V.) hospitality and restaurants—Provinces of Alicante, Valencia and Castellón (1988)*

	Number of jobs	%	In millions (ptas)	%
Alicante	33 500	7.6	140 988	9.3
Valencia	27 543	3.6	114 138	4.2
Castellón	8 008	4.5	27 147	4.7

Source: 'Renta Nacional de España y su Distribución Provincial', Banco Bilbao, Vizcaya.

among tourist firms (the opposite strategy would be that of reducing prices, often applied in our model, with a consequent fall in standards).

In synthesis then, a significant part of quality strategies is necessarily based on a greater 'personalization of the service', increasing contact, in terms of time, quality and disposition, between the person offering the service and the customer (Horovitz, 1991).

Such questions are a direct response to the growing requirement of the tourist demand market for higher standards of quality having direct implications on the human factor in terms of volume and qualifications. The importance of this factor is recognized in the basic aims of current tourist policies, as shown by the emphasis laid on training in local and state government studies published in recent years.

The tourist labour market in Alicante: size and complexity

The tourist labour market derives from the important participation tourism has in the local GDP. Fayos (1991) quotes it as 19.5%, whereas in the other two provinces in the Valencian Region it is slightly less: 8.0% in Valencia and 6.5% in Castellón.

Determining the exact volume of employment created by tourism is a highly complicated exercise, especially if we consider direct employment and indirect employment stemming from the interrelated areas of tourism and other sectors and sub-sectors (accommodation, transport, construction etc.). Even when we concentrate on those sub-sectors traditionally considered to be clearly tourist ones, such as hospitality and catering, we have to differentiate the figures in terms of tourists and local consumers or non-tourists. This must be borne in mind in order for the figures available to be indicative and useful.

Figures of the Spanish Tourism Department, the SGT, for 1990 put the number of jobs generated by tourism at 1 421 000 (11.2% of the working population) of which 838 000 were directly related (56% of the total) and 585 000 indirectly so (42.17%).

In the case of Alicante, the most important employment creation has been that linked to the construction industry owing to the introduction of a tourism model characterized in part by the residential and self-catering centres along the coast, and based on an expanding demand characterized by foreign investment in property.

As earlier mentioned, this rapid growth in tourism resulted in human asset migratory flows and was characterized by the creation of an important non-hotel offer (usually rented accommodation) which, in turn, lent certain unique characteristics to its labour market, i.e. less direct human participation than is usual in business-run hotel establishments, and more job creation in other areas such as management and maintenance of properties. The greatest impact the self-catering and residential offer had on the jobs market was produced in the construction industry and, to a lesser extent, in property promotion and selling.

From 1990 onwards, with a fall in demand and excess supply, the jobs market has witnessed an increase in unemployment and migratory flows have ceased to move towards coastal areas.

A significant part of the non-hotel offer is illegal (something which the Valencian Government sought to correct with the Decree 30/1993 which aims to register and classify the said offer) with the result that, apart from being seen as illegal competition by lawful competitors, levels of clandestine practices being carried out in the job market are on the increase (in property maintenance and promotion especially).

Segmentation of the jobs market: duality of the tourist labour market in the tourism industry

Various writers divide the labour market into two groups—primary labour and secondary labour (Shaw and Williams (1994) and Benitez and Rohles (1993)). The 'primary labour group', or 'core group', is made up of full-time workers who enjoy good working conditions, a relatively high income, promotion prospects and stability. They constitute the managerial and professional stratum. The 'secondary labour group' or 'peripheral group' suffer lower wages, little or no prospect of promotion and job instability. These tend to be temporary or casual workers who are poorly qualified and largely dependent on the amount of activity and business offers. This group can be divided into a 'first peripheral group' with relatively better conditions, and a 'second peripheral group' made up by those workers who suffer the worst conditions.

While to consider the Alicante tourist labour market model along these lines would be to oversimplify it, nevertheless the above description does serve to illustrate the weaknesses of the tourist labour market as a whole, faced with the importance tourism has for our local economy. Many of the peculiarities of our particular tourist labour market are due to the acute seasonality of the 'sun, sea and sand' product. Such concentrated seasonality causes certain contractual circumstances (temporary contracts), making it difficult to manage fixed assets, damaging professionalization and favouring illegal employment.

The 'yearly holiday programmes for old age pensioners' promoted by the Spanish National Institute of Social Services represent an attempt to mitigate the impact seasonality has on our coastal tourist areas. As far as employment is concerned, the said programmes aim to create a constant level of tourist demand in order to make it possible to maintain (if not generate) the highest number of jobs possible in the tourist industry (INSERSO, 1990). The main sub-sectors involved in these programmes are hotels, travel agencies, transport, insurance companies, health and advertising. The campaigns affect notably the Benidorm area, because of its hotel capacity, yet its estimated profitability should not be exaggerated, bearing in mind that the profit margins are reduced and serious problems are experienced in the public sector payments to hotels.

The 'scattering' and structure of the tourist companies have direct implications on the work market. Business 'scattering' is a result both of the predominance of one-establishment companies and of a reduced number of waged workers. Management of such companies is often made up of the proprietors themselves who often lack specific training. The consequent activity of the entre-preneur and the absence of fixed technical standards and intermediate managerial posts make promotion difficult which, in turn, means that baseline employees find it difficult to improve their professional category. During the years in which demand was growing, this phenomenon led to a proliferation of small firms (most notably restaurant establishments or small construction companies) being created by workers with experience who saw this as the only way open for them to improve their work situation.

If the freezing of professional categories tends to favour a bipolar tourist labour market, hidden or clandestine jobs help to maintain and boost, in terms of volume, a 'secondary labour group'. This fundamentally affects, as would be expected, the least qualified groups of workers, and the effect is at its greatest during the high season period. In the province of Alicante, 19.3%, 13.7% and 14.2% of inspections carried out in 1991, 1992 and 1993 respectively in the hospitality sector found the law was

being broken (in a total of 2391 cases), affecting 6476 workers altogether, and resulting in fines of a total of 274.6 million pesetas. In most cases the crime was failing to pay workers' National Insurance payments, although there were also many cases of illegally employing under-age or immigrant workers, as well as irregularities in contracts and unemployment benefit.

The need for a more highly qualified workforce in the tourist industry

As has been indicated, the economic relevance of tourism to our local economy together with the transformations which have come about as the product has matured has raised the need for a better qualified workforce. As far as managerial positions are concerned, the traditional mentality, influenced by growing demand in the past, lacking in outside and inside information, and reticent to change in general, must be changed in the face of substantial changes in tourism itself. It is baseline employees who are the least qualified and yet who tend to have most contact with the customers and for this reason have the most direct responsibility for the quality of service offered. Thus any attempt to improve quality must necessarily include as a priority a better-trained workforce. This fact was understood and included in the Institut Turistic Valencia's plan for competitivity, *Initiatives '93*, in which one of the main aims of tourism policy was identified as improving the quality of the tourist services by way of improved training of entre-preneurs, professionals and workers in the sector, either through continued education or professional upgrading. Three lines of action were outlined:

- Specialization grants for professionals
- Training programmes aimed at all levels and areas of the tourist industry
- Development of an educational infrastructure destined to fill the gaps in the existing education and occupational training system (including the creation of restaurant and/or hotel schools and the creation of three centres, one per province, in charge of further education and upgrading programmes in hospitality and tourism)

Conclusion

The analysis of the tourist labour market in the Province of Alicante is clearly related to the characteristics of the introduction and development of tourism in the regions of the Spanish Mediterranean Arc. The important impact it has on the gross added value and employment should be sufficient reason in itself to dedicate more attention to human resource training and education, in a real attempt to increase competitivity and overcome current deficiencies.

References

Aguiló, E. (1990) 'Crisis turística. ¿Hacia un nuevo modelo de crecimiento?', *Cuadernos de Información Económica*, no. 41–41.

Aguiló, E. and Torres, E. (1990) 'Realidad y perspectivas del sector turístico', *Papeles de Economía Española*, no. 42, 292–305.

Benitez, J. and Robles, A. (1993) 'Segmentación del mercado de trabajo turístico', Estudios Turísticos, no. 115, Dirección General de Política Turística, Secretaría General de Turismo, Madrid.

Cuadrado, J. R. and Rio, C. del (1993) *Los Servicios en España*, Pirámide, Madrid.

Fayos, E. (1991) 'Turística Valenciana 90', Papers de Turisme, no. 4, Institut Turistic Valencià, Valencia.

Fuentes Pascual, R. and Sagarribay Solana, S. (1993) 'El sector servicios en la provincia de Alicante', Estructura Económica de la Provincia de Alicante, Excma. Diputación Provincial y Universidad de Alicante, Alicante.

Horovitz, J. (1991) *La Calidad del Servicio*, McGraw-Hill, Madrid.

INEM (1991–92) *Estudio Sectorial. Servicios de Naturaleza Turística*. 2 vols, 623 pp., Las Palmas de Gran Canaria.

INSERSO (1990) 'Impacto económico del Programa de Vacaciones de la Tercera Edad', INSERSO, Madrid.

Monfort Mir, V. and Amor, F. (1994) 'Análisis del mercado turístico', Documentación del Curso Master en Turismo (2º ciclo), Universidad de Alicante.

Shaw, G. and Williams, A. (1994) *Critical Issues in Tourism*, Blackwell, Oxford.

Torres Bernier, E. (1993) 'Capacitación y formación turística en España. Especialización y cualificación', *¿Crisis del Turismo? Las perspectivas en el nuevo escenario internacional*, Instituto de Desarrollo Regional de la Universidad de Sevilla y Secretariado de Publicaciónes de la Universidad de Málaga, Seville, pp. 93–104.

Vera Rebollo, J. F. and Marchena, M. (1990) 'Turismo y desarrollo: un planteamiento actual', Papers de Turisme, no. 3, Institut Turistic Vallencià, Valencia.

VVAA (1992) *Les Cahiers d'Espaces*, no. 28, Editions Touristiques Européennes, Paris.

61 Formal mentoring: the 'state-of-the-art' in tourism education?

L. C. CAMERON AND D. HARVEY

Rapidly increasing demand has led to the advancement and sophistication of all areas of Australia's tourism and hospitality industries since the mid-1970s. This has been fortuitous, not only for the Australian economy but also for those seeking employment. However, such rapid changes have led to increasing demands for more highly qualified, sophisticated and entrepreneurial employees.

Along with the changing demands upon the tourism and hospitality industry have come changes in the educational requirements of employees serving in these industries. As a consequence educational institutions are being asked to provide employees with the necessary qualifications to meet the needs of a rapidly changing industry.

Questions remain as to whether our educational institutions are meeting these requirements. As is, the question remains as to whether our educational institutions should be providing for all the changing requirements of the industry or whether some of the responsibility should fall upon the industry associations and employers to provide appropriate employee training.

While such debates have been progressing other external forces have had considerable impact on the training and educational environments in not only the tourism and hospitality industry but in industry as a whole. The Australian system of higher education has been restructured from a three-level system of Colleges of Technical and Further Education (TAFE), Colleges of Advanced Education (CAE) and Universities, to a two-level system, which has evolved from the combining of Colleges of Advanced Education and Universities. The second major influence has been the introduction of the training guarantee levy. This levy was introduced by the government to encourage employers to invest money in the training and development of employees. Employers are required to invest 1½% of gross salaries into the training and development of employees (Tamsitt and Chalmers, 1991). Another area of influence was the Charmichael Report which urges new entry-level training and presses for competency-based training in Australia (Smith, 1992).

Educational institutions must now meet not only the changing demands of a rapidly evolving tourism industry, but also the demand for additional short courses which have increased since the introduction of the training guarantee levy. All this must be done within the confines of a rapidly transforming educational environment and short courses must meet competency standards.

Workplace demands on the tourism environment

Australian tourism and hospitality employers have, in the past, tended to rely on short-term casual employees who had no desire to develop careers within their particular industry. Edgell (1990) suggests that as the environment changes we must recognise the need for a highly educated and trained professional workforce that is well-motivated and well-paid. This has not necessarily been the case, as the Australian taxation system, in the early 1970s, supported people holding more than one job. This meant that employees within the tourism and hospitality industry tended to be employees with no long-term commitment to the industry.

The lack of clearly defined career paths for employees in the tourism and hospitality industry has contributed to the disproportionate number of semi-skilled jobs. Department of Employment, Education and Training (DEET) (1988) statistics, show that 59% of jobs within the tourism and hospitality industry fall into the category of either semi-skilled or trade skills jobs. The statistics point out that almost half, or 42%, of all workers in the tourism and hospitality industry are employed in the semi-skilled sector, for example, waiting, housekeeping, bar and clerical workers, while 17% were employed in trade areas such as silver service or chef positions.

Of the education that has been provided for these semi-skilled employees much has been on-the-job training and very few, if any, of the employees that fall into this category would have had post-secondary education. Vocationally skilled employees have normally received some post-secondary education through Colleges of Technical and Further Education (TAFE). Government pressure for investment in further education evolving from the Finn Committee suggests a more general education in TAFE training and development of employees (Smith, 1992). This leaves the way open for employers to link with education providers to supply the tourism and hospitality industry with a more highly skilled workforce. The benefits of investing in higher levels of education are twofold: individuals who are more highly educated can be more easily trained to meet the needs of their employer, and employees are enabled to meet their own intrinsic needs through increased career opportunity (Gamble, 1992).

The TAFE sector has been the traditional provider of training for employees within the tourism and hospitality industry. Employees have been provided with traditional vocational training such as apprentice-chef and bar-attendant skills, while a more recent trend within Australian TAFE Colleges has been to skill employees for more sophisticated levels such as silver service training. Andrew Smith (1992) suggests that such TAFE courses now be linked to Competency Based Training (CBT) based on the Australian Standards Framework (ASF) and form a focus for career development. Stone (1991:206) suggests that through this form of career development various benefits emerge for employees: they are more promotable; it reduces turnover of employees; it taps employee potential; it satisfies employees' needs; it assists affirmative action plans and reduces managers' hoarding of key subordinates.

The College of Advanced Education (CAE) sector of the Australian education system, which has now been combined into the Australian University system has traditionally provided a niche for potential management employees in the tourism and hospitality industry. Traditionally a small number of these institutions provided their tourism and hospitality students with block release thus enabling trainees to gain some hands-on experience within the particular industry. Block-release required that the student be placed as an employee for one semester in specific tourism or hospitality areas to facilitate the transfer of the students' learning of theory to the workplace. However this system appears to expose a real weakness. No clearly defined links have been made between the needs of the individual and that of the organisation within which the work practice is being gained, other than that of the student gaining 'a bit of practical experience' while the links to the organisational needs are even more imprecise.

The opportunities gained through such work-experience programmes do contribute to the learning process, especially for those students who come straight from high school. These programmes expose often under-age student/employees to work experience in areas such as alcohol and gambling within the constraints of an academically based course.

The ability to confirm that learning has actually taken place and that transfer of knowledge has occurred through hands-on work experience and that this knowledge and experience is meeting the needs of both individual and employer alike is imperative. What processes can be put in place to facilitate the transfer of learning and the utilisation of classroom skills in the workplace and the reverse?

Transfer of educational training to the workplace

As noted above, the Australian government has placed a new and increasing emphasis upon the training and development of employees. Employers must spend 1.5% of gross wages and salaries on training (Tamsitt and Chalmers, 1991). For many larger employers that is much less than they had traditionally spent on training. In the area of tourism and hospitality this has frequently been the case, as employers, owing to the low levels of education of their semi-skilled employees, have traditionally had to spend an inordinate amount of money on the training of lower-skilled employees, thus enabling them to meet the organisation's established work skills requirements. Notwithstanding this point, it is critical that any monies invested in education and training is transferred with learning to increased workplace activities and gains.

Learning by doing, or on-the-job training (sometimes known as 'sitting with Nelly') methods of training transfer have been adequate in meeting the training needs of the tourism and hospitality industry in times gone by. Notwithstanding this, employees not only need the traditional theory of educational institutional training, but they also need something that makes their particular competencies stand out from others graduating with similar qualifications. The hands-on practical experience that is provided by traditional 'sitting with Nelly' work experience programmes does have its benefits, but the student or new graduate needs to be seen to have more. Wexley and Latham (1991) confirm this when they suggest that on-the-job training should be conducted in conjunction with other training.

Academic programmes and those integrating block work release are of benefit to students and organisations alike. However, in order to ensure that the benefits of both traditional academic programmes and work experience support the transfer of theory into work practices, formal mentoring is recommended. This has been confirmed by Austin (1977, 1984) in concluding that students that are involved in their own educational processes are more likely to have increased levels of growth and achievement.

Evolving from this is the question which forms the focus for this paper. Should a formal mentoring programme be introduced to integrate and facilitate the transfer of traditional theory-based learning to the workplace? How can mentoring assist students and new graduates to combine study and work experience to achieve increasing levels of growth and satisfaction?

The increasing demand for more highly qualified employees within the tourism and hospitality industry often means that employees graduate with tertiary qualifications and enter the industry without any practical experience prior to employment. The rapid growth of fast-food chains such as McDonald's and KFC have been extremely beneficial in the hands-on educational experiences of many secondary and tertiary students. Students who are studying at tertiary institutions and have had the benefit of having worked for one of the international food chains have had the opportunity of obtaining additional experience to offer to any potential employer. The benefits of having worked part-time in this or similar type organisations prior to or in conjunction with academic study can only continue to contribute to a more effective and efficient workforce.

Hands-on work experience cannot be surpassed as a means to a more rapid transfer of knowledge as well as contributing to the student's own investment in the learning process. It is in this area that the answer to the question asked in the title of the paper begins to emerge. Is formal mentoring the 'state-of-the-art' method through which employees can gain the competitive edge educationally by more effectively combining traditional processes with work experience under the guidance of a mentor and, in doing so, transferring their theoretical knowledge into workplace productivity?

What is mentoring? Is it 'state-of-the-art'?

The art of informal mentoring is certainly not 'state-of-the-art', in terms of educational processes. Informal mentoring has been utilised as a teaching tool for centuries. Mentor was identified as a teacher, trusted adviser and friend by Homer in his poem *The Odyssey*. Homer identified through Greek myth the story of Telemachus, son of Odysseus, who was left in Mentor's care, while his father went to the Trojan War. This relationship was that of a caring person who offered more than just friendship and support for a young person's future. The relationship between Mentor and Telemachus was an informal relationship in which Mentor provided an affiliation similar to that of a father and guardian. Kram (1985) identified such informal mentors as primary mentors. That is, the mentor is an individual who is unselfish, caring and altruistic and extends a one-on-one relationship beyond that of a normal caring work relationship (Kram, 1985).

While the informal mentoring relationships discussed above are not 'state-of-the-art', formal mentoring, which has been utilised as a staff development tool since the middle of the 1970s, can be identified as being 'state-of-the-art'. Mentoring can not only assist in developing employees but also contribute to the students' ability to actively participate in their own education as the mentor assists in the transfer of knowledge from educational institution to workplace. Mentors in formal relationships established for the purpose of facilitating training transfer from educational institution to workplace are known as secondary mentors. Kram (1985) suggests that secondary mentors are much more formal. These mentors offer their protégés an exchange of ideas on a business-like basis, and encourage and challenge the students to engage in their own educational development. This role has been equated to that of the master in an apprenticeship (Clutterbuck, 1986).

Mentoring is much more than a relationship similar to an apprenticeship. Kram (1985:2) defined it as 'a relationship between a young adult and an older, more experienced adult that helps the younger individual learn to navigate in the adult work and the work world' while Bowen (1985:31) defined mentoring as 'the process which occurs when a senior person in terms of age and experience (the mentor) undertakes to provide information, advice and support to a junior person (the protégé) in a relationship lasting over an extended period of time, and marked by substantial emotional commitment on the part of both parties'. For the purpose of this paper, mentoring is a means by which a senior and more experienced individual acts as a facilitator of self-education and learning to a more junior member of staff. The paper takes this definition one step further and suggests that senior members of staff in the tourism and hospitality industries should be appointed as formal mentors to students perusing tertiary studies in the area to encourage their participation in their own education and development. This 'state-of-the-art' process of formal mentoring is recommended in situations where students obtain the benefits of hands-on work experience at the same time as they are pursuing their tertiary studies. The mentoring process establishes a support system in which the student (protégé) is matched with and supported by a senior employee (mentor) who has extensive organisational knowledge and a high level of aptitude and work-related skills, as well as the personality and motivation to assist the trainee not only to attain the greatest possible benefit from their university or college study but also to utilise this in their own desire to learn through work experience.

Since the mid-1970s, trainers and educators in the United States of America, Canada and the United Kingdom have been translating the benefits gained from informal mentoring to meet the educational and training needs of both students and employees. Mentoring has been used as a staff development tool in nursing, in business management development, and in multicultural and multinational work environments, as well as being used in education at primary, secondary and tertiary levels and to facilitate corporate mergers. However, Rutherford and Wiegenstein (1985) found little evidence of formal mentoring in the hospitality industry in the USA, and our research has confirmed this is the case in Australia as well. Educational requirements and staff skills required to meet the needs of the tourism and hospitality industry frequently overlap many of the areas identified as being assisted by traditional formal mentoring programmes. Frequently staff in the tourism and hospitality industry have to work in multicultural environments as well as in countries which are not their countries of birth. Both these situations create difficulties that can be overcome through effective mentoring situations.

Mentoring has been used in numerous areas of education: Wenn (1986) demonstrated the benefits of mentoring for preschool children; Silrum and Pullen (1984) utilised mentoring in high school teaching and their programme is suggestive of the recommendations put forward in this paper. Monash University's Centre for Retail Management is integrating mentoring programmes to support distance education students who are studying for the Bachelor of Business (Retail Management). Students, while working in the retail sector and studying their bachelor's degree by distance education are appointed to a mentor within their work environment. The mentor ensures that the student has the opportunity to put what they are learning in theory into practice in the work environment. The APM Training Institute which is training marketing diploma students in Sydney has a similar process where students are linked to a mentor in an organisation where they obtain work experience one day each week under the guidance and support of their workplace mentor (*HR Monthly*, 1993).

Workplace mentors are appointed to encourage and motivate students to take control of their own educational and developmental outcomes while they are still participating in their high school (Davis, 1986) or tertiary study (Erkut and Mokros, 1984). Mentoring can also be utilised for short developmental courses or in transitional situations where it is necessary for the transfer of theoretical knowledge in moving from student and tertiary institution to employee and workplace utilisation. Formal mentoring programmes at this stage can facilitate development and reduce the potential of becoming student or workplace dropouts (Ringuet, 1992). Cosgrove (1986) confirms the contribution of mentoring by suggesting that

students who participate in mentoring programmes are more satisfied with their university environment and show greater developmental gains than those not involved in mentoring programmes. Similarly this process can be adopted for tertiary students in either the university or college of TAFE system participating in tourism and hospitality study. Formal mentoring is also recommended for facilitating learning where courses already include block-release work experience—thus integrating more senior management into the teaching process and exposing them to the problems and difficulties experienced in the transition process from university to tourism and hospitality workplace.

How is mentoring 'state-of-the-art'?

Formal mentoring has many benefits that can be utilised, not only by the mentor and protégé but also by the organisation as a whole. Mentoring is in fact the product of high achievement (Erkut and Mokros, 1984). However, high achievement cannot be attained without the dedication of the person wishing to learn, grow and develop (the protégé) and the person that is willing to contribute unselfishly to the development (the mentor). Of this person Hurley (1988:42) suggests that the 'mentor [is] to success what feathers are to flying'.

Without such a relationship the organisation would not continue to benefit from the outcomes of the affiliation. Benefits to the organisation come in the form of reduced turnover of staff (Ringuet, 1992), an area in which the tourism and hospitality industry have an extreme record. Mentoring can also provide the organisation with a pool of 'upwardly mobile' young employees from which to develop their strategic human resource needs. The mentoring process also adds to the organisation's stability as mentors impart the norms of the organisation to new individuals, thus promoting a cooperative rather than competitive relationship. Although research has not yet been able to offer definite balance-sheet gains to the organisation, socialisation and cultural gains are significant even if it is difficult to put a price on socially desirable outcomes.

Kram (1983) suggests the mentoring relationship consists of two specific functions. The first career function group consists of sponsorship, exposure-and-visibility, coaching, protection and challenging assignments. The second area she identified as contributing to protégé development is that of psychosocial functions and these consist of role modelling, acceptance and confirmation, counselling and friendship (1983:614) (see Figure 61.1). Both career and psychosocial functions can be present in the mentoring support process established

Career Functions[a]	Psychosocial Functions[b]
Sponsorship Exposure-and-visibility Coaching Protection Challenging assignments	Role modelling Acceptance-and-confirmation Counselling Friendship

[a]Career functions are those aspects of the relationship that primarily enhance career advancement.

[b]Psychosocial functions are those aspects of the relationship that primarily enhance sense of competence, clarity of identity, and effectiveness in the managerial role.

Figure 61.1 *Mentoring functions (from Kram (1983))*

to encourage students and new graduates to take control of their own growth and achievement through their educational experiences. Students participating in tourism and hospitality education courses which integrate mentoring into their work experience activities would be more inclined to initially experience Kram's (1985) psychosocial functions; however, as their contribution to their own learning experience increases, the career functions will expand. The mentoring process and the individual's contribution to their own desire for a satisfying educational experience will not continue if the match between mentor and protégé characteristics are not complementary and if the protégé does not possess internal 'locus of control', that is does not have control of their personal situation and career outcomes (refer to Figure 61.2).

Mentor and protégé must have certain characteristics in order that the mentoring relationship contributes to outcomes which encourage the protégé to contribute to their own achievement and growth. It is imperative that mentor and protégé characteristics are compatibly matched in order to receive successful mentoring outcomes that encourage protégés to invest in their own development as well as the opportunity to transfer skills learned and utilise them effectively. Cameron and Jesser (1992), basing their study on work done by Hunt and Michael (1983:487), examined some of the factors that mentoring offers as a contributory factor in the transfer of training to the workplace. Figure 61.2 identifies the fact that the mentor and the protégé must be matched effectively in order not only to attain successful mentoring outcomes for the organisation but also to encourage the

individuals to seek their own satisfaction, growth and development.

Without the correct match between mentor and protégé characteristics the mentoring relationship will not promote the protégé to achieve his or her own educational outcomes within the confines of the protégé's locus of control. This will reduce the mentor's ability to act as a facilitator by assisting the protégé to transfer theoretical skills learned in academic courses, such as, tourism and hospitality courses to workplace environments. Formal mentoring programmes ensure that money spent on training is put to the best possible benefit of the individual and the organisation. But, as with any form of training, support must also come from top-level management. Mentoring programmes that integrate senior-level management staff into the mentoring of junior employees or undergraduate students, assist in developing the level of support contributed by management. Clutterbuck (1991) suggests that mentoring provides the opportunity for senior management to take some responsibility for staff development.

Research by Buonocore (1987) suggests that employees in the tourism and hospitality industry often experience feelings of abandonment, confusion, fear and helplessness. Pavesic and Brymer (1990) confirm these findings when identifying stress, demanding supervisors, routine jobs, lack of career paths for advancement, company politics and low motivation as significant contributors to poor worker attitudes and lack of fulfilment.

Our research makes a contribution to a better understanding of how employees feel about their mentor's or

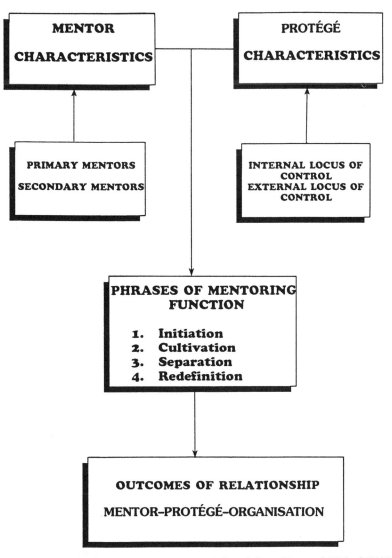

Figure 61.2 *Formal/informal mentoring process (adapted from Hunt and Michael (1983))*

protégé's characteristics and how appropriate orientation training of mentors and protégés if matched correctly can give rise to a desire for exceptional educational growth and achievement and the successful transfer of theoretical skills to the workplace.

Research support/indicators from case studies

This paper is informed by the examination of three different mentoring systems that have been established to support new graduates entering the workplace. The three organisational cases have evolved from research into employee development, with the core of the research aimed at improving the transfer of theoretical training to meet the needs of the Australian workplace. The three diverse industry areas examined were communications, petroleum and the tourism and hospitality industry. The examination is of developmental tools utilised by Telecom Australia, Esso Petroleum and the tourism and hospitality industry based on an analysis of five-star hotels in Australia.

The research instruments varied and took the form of either telephone or mail surveys, observation, or structured interviews based on pre-established questionnaires. Opinions were sought not only from the training and development managers or the human resource managers but also from the mentors and protégés themselves. Various areas in relation to employee investment in learning, self-development and mentoring were examined; however, for the purpose of this paper, only selected areas of our research will be discussed.

The three organisational areas of our research were clear in identifying that mentoring is not a stand-alone developmental tool. Notwithstanding this, formal mentoring programmes will provide support to the protégé's desire for self-development, the mentor's desire for intrinsic rewards and positive organisational outcomes alike when integrated with other forms of tertiary training and education.

This paper examines only two areas of our research which we feel can offer an immediate contribution to tourism and hospitality industry educators wishing to implement this new 'state-of-the-art' method of development along with other more traditional forms of education and training. The first area to be covered are the methods we have identified which may facilitate the introduction of formal mentoring in encouraging undergraduate students and new employees to participate in their own educational process and assist the transfer of their formal training to the organisation. Both Merrill and Reid (1981) and Byrd and Moore (1982) suggest methods that demonstrate appropriate workplace behaviours and provide confirmation that learning transfer has taken place. The paper will go on to show how formal mentoring processes, as outlined in the decriptive models, can be introduced to best support those tourism and hospitality organisations aiming for state-of-the-art developmental processes in the education of new graduates and students and in encouraging them to participate in developing their own ability to transfer theoretical skills to the workplace. While these are minuscule in terms of the mentoring process, they are offered as a means of introducing a new 'state-of-the-art' model of learning transfer to an area that seems certain to benefit from it.

The first of the areas are the characteristics that mentors must possess in order to make a positive contribution to the career development of their protégés. It is evident that the characteristics of mentor and protégé must be matched in order to obtain successful mentoring outcomes. These characteristics fall into four specific areas, as outlined in Figure 61.3. It is suggested therefore that organisations within the tourism and hospitality industry should be aware of these characteristics if they

wish to introduce mentoring programmes to assist in the development of employees that are willing to take control, or at least contribute to, their own growth and achievement by the transfer of training from educational institution to workplace environment. Mentors, to contribute to a successful mentoring relationship, must, for the most part, be selected on the basis of the characteristics demonstrated in Figure 61.3.

Characteristics that contribute to learning and development

Our research into the three respective organisational areas revealed strong ideas held by both mentor and protégé as to how they felt formal mentoring could contribute to an individual's desire to learn, succeed and transfer knowledge. Characteristics such as age and gender have been identified previously by other authors such as Hurley (1988), who suggests that a successful mentoring relationship normally has a mentor who is 8 to 15 years older than their protégé, and Levinson et al. (1978) who recommend that same-gender mentoring leads to more successful mentoring relationships. The characteristics identified by participants in our various research areas as having the ability to make successful contributions to mentoring and learning outcomes have been summarised in Figures 61.3 and 61.4. The major point for the reader to note is the fact that these characteristics contribute to the encouragement of the protégé to take control of their own desire to learn and be successful in line with the role model established by their mentor.

Firstly, the characteristics governed by the organisation need to be addressed. The mentor should be allowed to volunteer and in doing so this person must be made aware of the time commitment that is to be made to facilitating the learning processes of the new protégé (Kram, 1985). This is the case whether the protégé is an undergraduate student undertaking a work experience programme or a new graduate going through a workplace orientation programme. The mentor must also encourage the protégé to take responsibility for their own mentoring outcomes. Tourism and hospitality industries wishing to develop mentoring programmes or support educational institutions introducing mentoring can do so in this area by ensuring roster systems facilitate mentor availability.

Secondly, not only must mentors be selected on their aptitude to perform their respective work requirements but their selection must also be based on knowledge developed over years of experience. Such aptitude and knowledge skills fall in line with Kram's (1983) career functions of formal mentoring in which she suggests the mentor provides sponsorship, exposure and visibility,

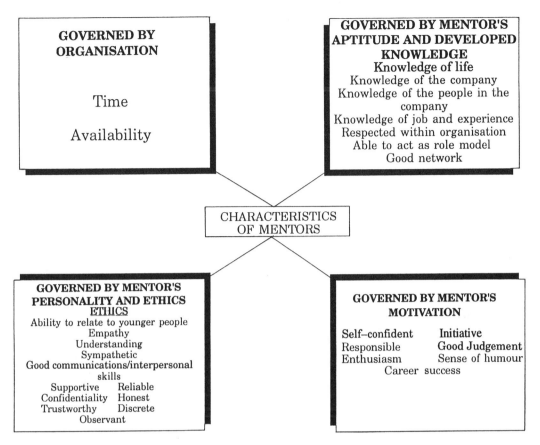

GOVERNED BY ORGANISATION

Time

Availability

GOVERNED BY MENTOR'S APTITUDE AND DEVELOPED KNOWLEDGE
Knowledge of life
Knowledge of the company
Knowledge of the people in the company
Knowledge of job and experience
Respected within organisation
Able to act as role model
Good network

CHARACTERISTICS OF MENTORS

GOVERNED BY MENTOR'S PERSONALITY AND ETHICS
ETHICS
Ability to relate to younger people
Empathy
Understanding
Sympathetic
Good communications/interpersonal skills
Supportive   Reliable
Confidentiality   Honest
Trustworthy   Discrete
Observant

GOVERNED BY MENTOR'S MOTIVATION

Self–confident   Initiative
Responsible   Good Judgement
Enthusiasm   Sense of humour
Career success

Figure 61.3 *Characteristics of mentors*

coaching and protection, and challenging assignments for their protégé. It is through the industry or through educators identifying mentors with skills similar to those in Figure 61.3 that the career functions can be integrated into the transfer of learning and students or new graduates challenged by their mentor-driven assignments to seek their own growth and achievements.

Thirdly, the mentor's personality and ethical standards will have enormous influence upon the behaviour of the junior protégé in the transfer of learning. The mentor must possess a people-oriented leadership style. This should expose the psychosocial functions identified by Kram (1983) and outlined in Figure 61.1. A people-orientated mentor will provide the protégé with a role model of people-orientated behaviour that encourages the undergraduate or new employee to grow and develop in the image of their mentor. It is imperative that the organisation or educator introduce role models that develop protégés who are keen to invest time and effort in their own development with the support of their mentor.

Finally, the mentor's motivation toward their work organisation, toward their job and especially toward their protégé must be high. The protégés should also be motivated toward their job, their workplace and their own educational outcomes if their mentor exhibits high levels of motivation.

It is evident from Figure 61.3 that there are many contributory factors to the successful matching of mentor and protégé characteristics. It is imperative, however, that these factors be taken into account when encouraging new employees and students to take control of their own career outcomes with the help of mentoring, this 'state-of-the-art' learning tool.

The disabilities in Figure 61.3 suggest that the characteristics of successful mentoring fall into four specific categories. First there are those things governed by the organisation and over which the mentor has little or no control, but without which the transfer of learning from theory to workplace would not take place. However, from the protégé's perspective, and as listed in Figure 61.4, the mentor can assist the protégé to understand the organisational factors governed by the organisation. Secondly there are those characteristics related to the mentor's aptitude and knowledge of the organisation and his or her job. It is imperative that the mentor has not only sound knowledge of the organisation's norms and protocol but also sound technical competencies in order to ensure that the protégé has the opportunity to utilise their theoretical skills within the workplace under the guidance of the mentor.

However, Figure 61.4 also suggests that the protégé should be equally intelligent in order that these mentoring characteristics are matched. Thirdly there are those characteristics related to the mentor's personality and upbringing; they would be present in the mentor's attitude to any protégé and they should conversely be present in the protégé; as demonstrated in Figure 61.4, such matching will facilitate the process of self control of learning in any organisational environment. A mentor who demonstrates people-oriented leadership skills will provide a

learning environment that encourages their protégé to utilise their theoretical skills and encourages them toward growth and achievement. Finally there are those characteristics that are directly related to the mentor's personal motivation. When the mentor's motivation is matched by the enthusiasm and ambition of their protégé the opportunity for successful transfer of learning is expedited.

The most appropriate matching of the mentor and protégé characteristics identified in Figures 61.3 and 61.4 has been recognised as being instrumental in the rapid transfer of theoretical knowledge between mentor and protégé. However, Kram (1983) suggests that the protégé is normally the major benefactor in the mentoring process. Mentors must be senior personnel who have personal maturity, who possess sound knowledge of the company and who also have a high level of technical skill and aptitude in performing their particular job. The mentor must also have people-oriented rather than task-oriented leadership skills, as leadership and role modelling are key factors in successful mentoring outcomes. It is

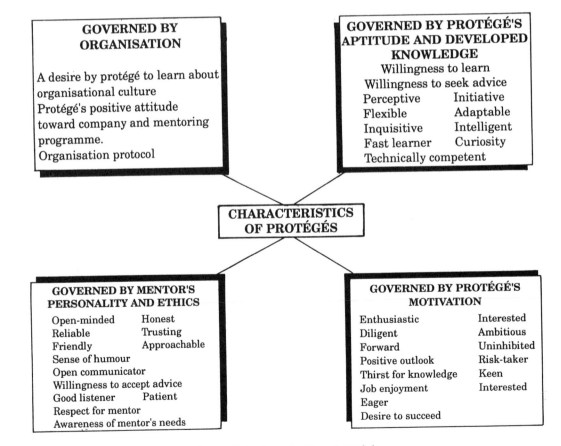

Figure 61.4 *Characteristics of protégés*

imperative that protégés secure a mentor who can control but not dominate each of the four areas identified in order to expedite the protégé's abilities to take partial control of their own learning process. As the protégé is introduced to new work experiences they can utilise the mentor's characteristics identified in each of the mentoring roles.

Protégés must also be selected to suit their particular mentor's characteristics. Protégés who were either interviewed (in structured interviews) or whose opinions were sought through survey questionnaires expressed opinions along similar lines to those of their mentor in relation to what skills they felt that they should possess in order to fully utilise their mentoring experience. As discussed in previous paragraphs, when matched successfully these characteristics contribute to productive mentoring outcomes.

Figure 61.4 identifies how protégés, like their mentors, have four similar characteristic areas in which students with tertiary training in the tourism and hospitality industry can be encouraged to develop their own desires to learn while also being assisted to transfer tertiary training to the workplace. By matching mentor/protégé pairs with characteristics high in the four characteristic categories outlined in Figure 61.3 this can contribute to successful mentoring outcomes in the transfer of theoretical knowledge to the workplace. In dealing with these one by one, the coordinator of mentoring programmes can ensure the maximum benefit to the organisation, student or new employee as these characteristics simplify the transfer of learning.

Notwithstanding this, a major mentoring difficulty that was exposed in our examination of formal mentoring cases was the fact that, even though formal mentoring programmes can be described as 'state-of-the-art' in the transfer of theoretical learning from educational institution to workplace, at least one of the three mentoring programmes examined appeared to receive inadequate basic orientation training. Figure 61.5 identifies some of the processes in the relationship that were recommended by training and development managers, by human resource managers and by mentors and protégés. Such processes not only encourage protégés to take responsibility for their own educational development and growth under the guidance of their mentor, but also encourage the transfer of academic theory learned into workplace training by utilising the mentoring function.

Orientation to mentoring as a facilitator of learning transfer

In our research into the use of formal mentoring programmes in Australia it became evident that one of the

1. Discussions to clearly define mentoring

2. Discussions to clearly define roles of mentor and protégé

3. Training to identify the benefits of mentoring

4. Training in communication skills

5. Training in counselling skills

6. Training in leadership skills

7. Training in time-management skills

8. Training must identify company structure, salary and promotion systems

9. Training must combine mentors, protégés and mentoring programme coordinators

10. Follow-up training must ensure the process is occurring

Figure 61.5 *Ten training tools to facilitate orientation to formal mentoring programmes*

major problems that had occurred was that the mentors and protégés had received induction into the organisations but had not received adequate orientation to the mentoring processes. These difficulties were expressed by both mentor and protégé alike, and such failure to understand the basic principles of the mentoring process can discourage protégés from taking control of their own desire for education and growth as well as slowing the training transfer process.

The training programmes recommended as part of mentor orientation in Figure 61.5 form the core of training necessary to ensure the rapid introduction of both mentor and protégé to the process. Training sessions can be introduced either at the same time as the matching process or following on from the mentor pairs being selected. One of the difficulties experienced by mentor and protégé participants in our research was that training sessions for mentors and protégés were not conducted concurrently. In order that the relationship between mentor and protégé is given every opportunity to grow and develop, training programmes should be introduced as joint training, so as to enable each party to develop similar interpretations and understanding of the processes involved. In this way protégés are encouraged to take responsibility for their own learning while at the same time mentors are encouraged to enable the protégé to support but not dominate the protégé's development within the guidelines identified. Training which assists participants to define the process, roles and benefits of mentoring should be participated in together. Details of company structure, salary and promotional prospects should be covered in the organisation's orientation training; however, because of the time differences between orientation of mentor and protégé, it is possible that this can be reinforced in a mentoring training session.

Counselling and leadership training should be orientated toward mentors, but can also benefit both parties, as can training in time management.

A deficiency that appeared in the training of individuals participating in the programmes that were covered by our research was that no follow-up occurred to ensure that any weaknesses that may have appeared could be corrected through further training or in the redesign of new mentor orientation programmes.

Conclusions

Our paper has argued that formal mentoring can be a facilitator in the transfer of academic knowledge to the workplace, but that it can only do so if the characteristics of the mentor and protégé are correctly matched and are supported with the most appropriate training. While our research was drawn from three diverse areas, the need for further implementation and development of the model suggested for the transfer of theory into practice in the tourism and hospitality industry still remains 'state-of-the-art'.

References

Austin, A. W. (1977) *Four Critical Years: Effects of College on Beliefs, Attitudes and Knowledge*, Jossey-Bass, San Francisco.
Austin, A. W. (1984) 'Student involvement: a developmental theory for higher education', *Journal of College Student Personnel*, 25, 287–300.
Bowen, D. D. (1985) 'Were men meant to mentor women', *Training and Development Journal*, February: 30–34.
Buonocore, Anthony J. (1987) 'Reducing turnover of new hires', *Management Solutions*, June: 4–10.

Byrd, J. and Moore, L. T. (1982) 'Decision models for management', in D. G. Long (Ed.), *Learner Managed Learning: The Key to Lifelong Learning and Development*, Kogan Page, London, 1990.
Cameron, L. C. and Jesser, P. (1992) 'Mentoring can add extra value to the training dollar', *HR Monthly*, April, 14–15.
Clutterbuck, D. (1986) 'Mentoring', *Industrial & Commercial Training*, 18(6): 13–15.
Clutterbuck, D. (1991) *Everyone Needs a Mentor: Fostering Talent at Work*, 1st edn, Institute of Personnel Management Press, London.
Cosgrove, T. J. (1986) 'The effects of participation in a mentoring—transcript program on freshmen', *Journal of College Student Personnel*, 27: 119–124.
Davis, D. R. (1986) 'Mentoring for High School Students', cited in *Mentoring: Aid to Excellence in Education, the Family and the Community*, Proceedings of the First International Conference on Mentoring, Vols I & II, Gray, W. E. and Gray, M. M. (Eds), International Association for Mentoring, Vancouver, pp. 16–19.
Department of Employment Education and Training (1988) Statistics.
Edgell, David L. (1990) 'The challenges for tourism education for the future', *Journal of Tourism Research*, 29(2): 51–52.
Erkut, S. and Mokros, J. R. (1984) 'Professors and models and mentors for college students', *American Educational Research Journal*, 21: 399–417.
Gamble, P. R. (1992) 'The educational challenge for hospitality and tourism studies', *Tourism Management*, March: 6–10.
HR Monthly (1993) Advertising article; author unknown.
Hunt, D. M. and Michael, C. (1983) 'Mentorship: a career training and development tool', *Academy of Management Review*, 8: 473–485.
Hurley, D. (1988) 'The mentor mystique', *Psychology Today*, May: 41–43.
Jacobi, Maryann (1991) 'Mentoring and undergraduate academic success: a literature review', *Review of Educational Research*, 61(4): 505–532.
Kram, K. (1983) 'Phases of the mentor relationship', *Academy of Management Journal*, 26: 608–625.
Kram, K. E. (1985) *Mentoring at Work: Developmental Relationships in Organizational Life*, Scott, Foresman, Glenview, IL.
Levinson, D., Darrow, C. N., Klein, E. B., Levinson, M. H. and McKee, B. (1978) *Seasons of a Man's Life*, Knopf, New York.
Merrill, D. W. and Reid, H. (1981) 'Personal styles and effective performance', in D. G. Long (Ed.), *Learner Managed Learning: The key to lifelong learning and development*, Kogan Page, London, 1990.
Pavesic, D. and Brymer, R. (1990) 'Job satisfaction: what's happening to young managers?', *The Cornell HRA Quarterly*, 30(4): 90–96.
Ringuet, Ray (1992) 'Improving retention using mentors', *Managers Magazine*, 67(6): 26–27.
Rutherford, D. G. and Wiegenstein, J. (1985) 'The mentoring process in hotel general managers' careers', *The Cornell HRA Quarterly*, 25(4): 16–23.
Silrum, L. and Pullen, J. (1984) 'Mentoring connection: an advanced course offering for high school students', *Mentoring: Aid to Excellence in Education, the Family and Community*, Proceedings of the First International Conference on Mentoring, Vol. 1, pp. 159–160.
Smith, Andrew (1992) 'Australian training and development in 1992', *Asia Pacific Journal of Human Resources*, 31(2): 65–73.

Stone, Raymond J. (1991) *Human Resource Management*, John Wiley, Brisbane.

Tamsitt, G. and Chalmers, M. (1991) *Training Guarantee Handbook,* CCH Australia Ltd, Sydney.

Wenn, Ross (1986) 'Starting from scratch: The Victorian (Australia) mentoring experience, 1982–1986', cited in William A. Gray and Marilynne Miles Gray (Eds), *Mentoring: Aid to Excellence in Education, the Family and the Community*, Proceedings of the First International Conference on Mentoring, Vol. 1.

Wexley, Kenneth N. and Latham, Gary P. (1991) *Developing and Training Human Resources in Organisations*, 2nd edn, HarperCollins, Artarmon.

62 From classroom to cornice: training the adventure tourism professional

R. M. OLESEN AND P. SCHETTINI

Introduction

Adventure tourism continues to be one of the fastest-growing sectors of the tourism industry in British Columbia. Sectoral growth rates of at least 15% per year are expected through the 1990s (Mitchell, 1992). However, the supply of qualified guides and operations managers has failed to keep pace with the expansion in demand, thus constraining output growth. Most guides have gained experience in related adventure activities as a consequence of lifestyle decisions rather than via clearly defined career development programs. In turn, they usually are supervised by managers who began in similar circumstances and worked their way up via seniority to their current positions. They generally bring to their roles specific technical skills and possible certification by a professional adventure body such as the Canadian Mountain Guides. However, they rarely have completed an educational program designed to bring together the more general business, service and environmental skills essential to an operational philosophy embodying the procedures and standards of 'professionalism'.

This problem in a broader context has been recognized by the tourism industry (Mitchell, 1992). However, while operators acknowledge the importance and desirability to the industry of enhanced educational qualifications and the contributions these can make to the level of professionalism, internally generated solutions have not been forthcoming.

In fact, the problem of developing a better-trained, more professional labour force in adventure tourism is not a consequence of the industry's unwillingness to recognize or address the problem. Nor is it even primarily a result of the rapid growth it has experienced in recent years. Rather, we argue that it follows from what economists describe as market failure: a case in which individual actors making rational decisions produce aggregate outcomes that are sub-optimal.

The first part of the paper provides a brief overview of the adventure tourism industries in British Columbia and identifies key human resource issues. A human capital approach, emphasizing the contrast between general and firm-specific skills, is used to explain failure of the private marketplace to generate adequate numbers of appropriately qualified personnel. In light of that failure, a case is made for intervention by government and public educators, in cooperation with professional associations and institutes within the industry, in supporting the development of a more highly trained adventure tourism labor force.

The second part describes the process of curriculum and program development undertaken in establishing the Adventure Travel Guide Diploma program at the University College of the Cariboo (UCC) in Kamloops, British Columbia. Particular attention is paid to the role played by the industry during the developmental process and to special problems encountered in mounting the program.

Adventure tourism

The growth of adventure tourism has been accompanied by a trend toward specialization and differentiation of the adventure travel product. Key components of adventure tourism in British Columbia are: heli-skiing; winter touring—cross-country and ski touring; mountaineering; backpacking; trail riding; nature observation; scuba diving; river rafting; kayaking; canoeing; sailing tours; and boating tours. Other adventure activities include para-sailing, hot-air ballooning, bicycling, dog-sledding, heli-hiking and heli-biking. Activities such as fishing and hunting and the associated guiding and outfitting industries, as well as downhill skiing and snowmobiling, could also be included under a broader definition of adventure tourism. However, they are normally (if somewhat arbitrarily) excluded from the list because of their consumptive use of the resource base.

An economic profile of the key adventure tourism industries in British Columbia is presented in Table 62.1. The inventory of operators in each industry ('Operator class') was estimated from information published by the Provincial government in the form of either an adventure travel guide, a travel planner or an accommodation directory containing adventure-related information. It is worth noting that the published sources of information

Table 62.1 *Economic profile of the BC adventure travel industry, 1986*

			Economic activity measures			
Operator class	Number of operators	Employment (person-years)[a]	Revenue (million)	Investment (million)	Wages (million)	Purchases (million)[b]
Heli-ski	8	125	17.8	9.7	3.5	9.1
Cross-country/ski	55	185	3.9	3.1	1.4	1.9
Mountaineer/backpack	47	260	5.9	2.1	2.3	2.5
Horse/trail	59	265	6.4	30.1	1.4	2.7
Nature observation	25	80	2.8	5.8	0.7	1.4
Scuba diving	30	70	2.3	5.7	0.7	2.3
Rafting	46	140	4.4	4.4	1.3	0.7
Kayak/canoe	34	65	1.7	1.3	0.6	0.7
Sailing tours	38	315	7.0	10.7	2.0	4.9
Boat tours	21	65	1.9	2.7	0.7	1.1
Other	33	.0	1.6	0.8	0.3	1.0
Total	396	1610	55.7	76.4	14.9	29.0

[a] Person-year equivalents.
[b] Purchases from, value added, wage income, and employment accruing to BC residents only.
Source: Outdoor Recreation Council (1988a).

frequently provide differing estimates of the number of operators in each class. Such discrepancies clearly point to problems in attempting to estimate the size and evaluate the performance of these young and growing industries.

Table 62.1 shows that total industry revenues for 1986 were esimated at $55.7 million. Other findings in the Outdoor Recreation Council study (1986) included the following:

- The industry is characterized by a wide distribution of income. In 1986, while the average revenue was $141 000 per operation, the median was much lower—closer to $30 000.
- The number of businesses offering adventure travel packages tripled over the 1976–86 period.
- If hunting ($21 million) and fishing ($57 million) activity is included, total industry revenue equals $133.7 million.
- Many adventure travel operations are family-run businesses offering activities close to home with the owners having other employment through much of the year. The average year-round employment level was 4.1 people per operation.
- The industry directly generated an estimated 1610 person-years of employment in 1986. Operations are seasonal, with August employment levels double those in winter. An estimated 30–40% of employment was made up of part-time or casual workers.

A more recent status report on tourism (Pollock, 1992) observed that, while the North American adventure travel sector is reputed to be growing at an average annual rate

of 10–20%, many individually run enterprises in British Columbia are currently doubling their business each year. In 1977, only a single river raft company operated in the province; in 1992, there were 50. (In 1992, a twelve-day river rafting trip sold for C$2225 while generating additional spending on pre/post airfares, accommodations and retail purchases.) In 1965, Canadian Mountain Holidays took a total of 13 guests heli-skiing in the Bugaboos. In 1991, the same firm catered to 5000 guests who paid an average of C$3500 per week to go heli-skiing in one of nine British Columbia heli-ski resorts.

Human resource issues

The demand for trained and experienced staff in the adventure and outdoor recreation sectors of the tourism industry has been projected to grow at an annual compound rate of 3.6%. Since this figure is over twice the anticipated 1.6% per year growth of the overall BC labor force, a net increase of 4400 trained people will be required by these sectors of the tourism industry alone by the year 2001 (Mitchell, 1992).

The production and delivery of the adventure travel products by the industries that make up the adventure tourism sector typically is labor-intensive, with the elasticity of substitution of labor for capital being low. The quality of the products is highly dependent upon the capabilities, training and experience of first-line employees such as guides, as well as upon the level of professionalism they demonstrate.

In general, the adventure travel industries have been able to provide industry-specific technical training and certification through the relevant adventure associations. For example, the Canadian Association of Nordic Ski Instructors trains and examines candidates for certification as Level I Instructor; Level II Instructor and Telemark Instructor. The Canadian Institute of Safety, Search and Rescue trains and examines candidates for certification in Wilderness Emergency Response and Advanced Wilderness Emergency Response. However, there is a need for acquisition of broader skills and knowledge in addition to the more specific skills that have characterized the adventure tourism labor force (Pollock, 1988).

General versus specific skills

Economists draw an important distinction in the theory of human capital between two broad skill categories: general and specific. The key distinction is that general skills are readily transferable from one employer to another. The wider the range of potential employers who value a skill, the more general it is. At the other end of the continuum, specific skills are valued by fewer employers and have a much narrower range of transferability. (The terminology is potentially confusing because the category into which a particular technical competency falls will depend upon the demand conditions.)

The implications of this distinction between general versus firm-specific skills are far-reaching for both employers and employees. When a person acquires general skills, it raises their productivity not only in their current job but also for a wider range of other potential employers. The employee thus becomes more valuable to the current employer and more marketable to others at the same time. In contrast, acquisition of a specific skill enhances the productive value of a worker for a single employer (in the limiting case) or a narrower range of potential employers.

Implications for education and training

Employers will find it in their self-interest to provide (that is, pay for) training for their employees whenever they can reasonably expect to recapture this investment in 'human capital'. The value of the employees' enhanced productivity benefits the employer through additional profits, and the employees through higher earnings. If the training of an employee yields benefits greater than costs, it will be undertaken. Then, since firms will take all costs and benefits into account in the case of specific skills, they will carry out the socially ideal amounts of investment in their employees. As a result there is no necessity for government intervention because the market functions effectively.

In the case of general skills, the proposition that firms will find it in their self-interest to provide the socially optimal amount of training does not hold. This is not because the costs outweigh the benefits. Indeed, the benefits may exceed the costs in exactly the same amount as in the specific skills case of the previous paragraph. The difficulty arises because once the employer has made the investment in the employee's human capital by providing the general skills training, the employee's enhanced skills set and productivity are worth more to a wide range of other employees. These others will have an incentive to bid the newly trained employee away from the firm that financed the training. Then, athough individual workers may offset some of the difference by investing in themselves, and while firms may attempt to offset their risks through some form of employee repayment obligation should they choose to leave the firm, such arrangements themselves are costly and leave the final result (viewed from a social perspective) an underinvestment in general skills.

In short, a purely private tourism labor market will under-supply general skills training because employers who would benefit from providing it do not have a reasonable assurance that they will be able to capture the return on investment in their employee's human capital. (A more extensive application of human capital theory to tourism can be found in Ellis et al. (1991).)

A role for government and public educators

The present and future development of adventure tourism requires a labor force that demonstrates both technical skills in the relevant adventure fields and effective skills relating to business operations, leadership and problem solving, service and the environment. The more specific technical skills training, along with the examination and certification process, are appropriately delivered by the professional adventure associations. The typical professional association's training operations tend to be small, partly because there are few if any economies of scale in their production, partly because the absolute numbers of trainees are relatively small and the competencies are characterized by limited transferability between activities as diverse as mountaineering and scuba diving. (A list of specific industry bodies relevant to UCC's program is presented in Appendix 1.)

We have argued that because of market failure, private industry will support only sub-optimal levels of general skills training. On the other hand, publicly funded postsecondary institutions such as community colleges and universities have the capacity to bridge the gap through their broader perspective and ability to exploit economies of scale in the development and delivery of general education and skills training. With a growing industry and increased demand for trained professionals, higher enrolments bring lower costs per graduate. At the same time, that form of education and training fits their mandates. Because these skills are more widely transferable, there is a broader range of employment opportunities for graduates, including positions in areas outside adventure tourism.

A further problem faced by employees in the adventure tourism industries is the seasonal nature of employment. Publicly funded post-secondary educational institutions are in a position to work with many of the professional adventure associations to build training in multiple technical skills into their programs and thus to enhance the potential for more continuous employment throughout the year. That is, they are able to take advantages of economies of scope as well as economies of scale.

The following section provides a brief description of the Adventure Travel Guide program developed and offered at UCC to meet the demands for a broader range of specific technical and general skills in the British Columbia adventure travel labor force.

The UCC Adventure Travel Guide program

In 1992, after four years of planning and consultation with representatives of government and the many professional adventure associations that certify skill levels in their respective adventure fields, the University College of the Cariboo launched an Adventure Travel Guide Diploma program. The two-year program of study brings together various elements of guide training for a broad range of outdoor adventure activities. It combines general education and theoretical training in the classroom with practical skills training in the natural environment. Topics such as wilderness travel, first aid, leadership, search and rescue, marketing, accounting, business and computer applications are included in the program. A key objective is to provide students with the interpersonal, hospitality, technical, business, and organizational skills necessary to secure long-term employment in the adventure travel industry. Activities, including national level certification courses in canoeing, kayaking, nordic and backcountry skiing, rock and ice climbing, and mountaineering, are used as a platform upon which to mount the delivery of general skills education. For a description of the program course requirements see Appendices 2 and 3.

Curriculum and program development

The Adventure Travel Guide Diploma program was originally designed to have two key components: the first

was a mix of technical guiding skills in the broad areas of paddling, climbing and skiing; the second, the business skills required for success in a fast-growing competitive industry. However, as the program went through successive stages of development with extensive input from industry and government, including the provincial ministries of Advanced Education and Tourism, the following five fundamental areas (see Figure 62.1) emerged in the current program design:

1. *Technical skills*: wilderness guiding skills in canoeing, kayaking, rock-climbing, mountaineering, nordic, tour and telemark skiing, river rafting, ice climbing; functional skills in wilderness emergency response, rope handling and rope rescue, wilderness first aid, emergency situation and SAR management, and avalanche control.
2. *Business skills*: accounting and cost controls, marketing and promotion, computer applications, operations management, legal liability and risk management.
3. *Hospitality and service skills*: communication and human relations skills, leadership skills, problem-solving skills.
4. *Environmental skills*: working knowledge of the wilderness environment, the natural resource base, geography, mountain geomorphology, fluviology and meteorology.
5. *Intimate involvement in industry associations*: essential for technical skills certifications; facilitates communication of changes in practices and philosophies; reinforces industry commitment to and support of the program; provides opportunities for students to network with potential employers.

One of the philosophies underlying this program is the pursuit of an integrative approach to the education and training of students. The key program areas identified above are important individually but are also linked where appropriate and feasible at the level of each course, both in the classroom and in the field. For example, when students prepare for and carry out advanced mountain trips, each must take on leadership roles and apply the knowledge they have learned in order to plan, carry out and complete the trip. Requisite business skills are brought into focus before each trip.

Students approach trip planning in the context of an adventure product design task, identifying potential markets and promotional strategies, detailing requirements and costs as well as other factors including contingencies that come to play in operations management. Computer applications skills enhance this process

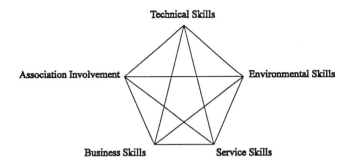

Figure 62.1 *The five fundamental areas in the UCC Adventure Travel Guide program*

and in addition are particularly useful in maintaining financial control and keeping track of equipment. When students are in the field, they must demonstrate a knowledge of and concern for the environment and must display the service skills necessary to create a professional environment for their clients (the other students and instructors). Students are taught (and practice) technical activity skills not only by UCC's own instructors, but also by professionals from various professional adventure organizations such as the Association of Canadian Mountain Guides.

In order for the program to establish credibility within the various associations in Canada and throughout North America, it was important to maintain a student-to-instructor ratio that met the standards of the relevant associations. For instance, rock-climbing and mountaineering courses have one instructor for every four students. Consequently, there will be four or five instructors in a field class with 16–20 students. In contrast, conventional classroom courses, such as in human resource management, are delivered in a more traditional ratio of one instructor to 20–25 students.

The high ratio in technical skill courses makes the program expensive to run. However, it has several beneficial aspects. It decreases the probability of accidents. It also allows Association Guides to work alongside full-time UCC instructors in the training of our students. In this way, the associations appropriate a measure of ownership of our technical skills courses without taking complete control.

One advantage for students is that they can be examined and may qualify for certification directly from the relevant association while receiving credit toward completion of the UCC diploma. At the completion of the program, a student could end up with a diploma from UCC supplemented by sixteen or even more certificates issued by the associations in a variety of specialty fields. (The exact number depends upon the electives that a student

chooses in the second year of the program, as well as upon student aptitudes.)

A list of courses that constitute the Adventure Travel Guide Diploma program is included in Appendix 2. A flow chart showing the progress from one level of technical skill training to the next is included in Appendix 3.

Industry involvement

UCC invited industry input from the early stages of development of the program. One of the first meetings was coordinated by the Pacific Rim Institute of Tourism (PRIT), an agency of the BC Ministry of Tourism with a mandate to coordinate efforts between government, industry and education. Fifty people, representing tourism and adventure associations and agencies as well as federal and provincial government ministries, were present. Topics discussed included: the need for common ground among participants (particularly the adventure associations!); the feasibility of establishing core (that is, general) education requirements and management skills training for outdoor guides; and means of meeting the growing labor force training needs of the industry. Program drafts were circulated to industry for feedback during the development stages.

In some cases, there exists more than one potentially relevant association for a particular skill area. Decisions had to be made about which associations were best-suited to coordinate with the UCC program. For example, should the Association of Canadian Mountain Guides be chosen over the Federation of Mountain Clubs of BC? Would the BC Recreational Canoeing Association or the Canadian Recreational Canoe Association be the most valuable contact? Consideration was even given to distancing the program from the associations and certifying bodies to avoid the politics that could be anticipated with industry involvement. However, the final decision recognized the many benefits the program and our students would enjoy from associations' involvement in the design and delivery of the technical skills components of the program.

Instructor attributes

The degree of industry involvement associated with the Adventure Travel Guide Diploma meant that a number of staffing considerations had to be taken into account. Not only was it necessary to recruit staff with the necessary educational qualifications, experience and technical expertise, but it was also vital that they have credibility and a good working relationship with the adventure associations. UCC has successfully recruited instructors with experience in a variety of adventure operations in many parts of the world. They are qualified to industry and association standards in their various technical specialties, while also possessing the business skills, teaching experience and educational qualifications required to meet the academic and professional standards of the program.

Student recruitment and selection

When the Adventure Travel Guide Diploma program was first advertised, UCC received over 800 requests for information and over 350 applications for 22 positions. Taking into account the demanding nature of the program and its anticipated popularity, a selection and admission process was adopted involving the following elements:

- *Educational standing.* A minimum of high school completion with at least a C+ in English and Mathematics at the grade 11 level (the same requirements as for admission to first-year university degree study).
- *Orientation session.* A compulsory orientation session for applicants where the program and its requirements are explained in detail. (Many potential students decide that they are not ready for the program after attending this session.)
- *Resumé.* A detailed description of education and work experience. (Required to assess background in guiding and/or adventure fields.)
- *Information form.* A statement setting out the mix and level of outdoor skills a potential student might have.
- *Program interview.* An interview with program instructors serving to verify and amplify the information contained in documentation received.
- *Upon acceptance.* Students are required to supply:
  1. Medical Examination Form, signed by the student's doctor.

2. UCC Assumption of Risk and Indemnifying Release Waver, signed by the student.

Successful applicants must possess well-developed skills in at least one of the three broad areas of paddling, skiing or climbing. Students wishing to enter the program but lacking certifiable outdoor experience are required to seek some form of introductory training from organizations such as Outward Bound or the Adventure Associations. This increases their chances of being accepted into the program in the following year. (The average age of our students is 26 years with 30% female and 70% male.)

Institutional liability

The program is physically and mentally demanding. The dangerous nature of many of the field activity courses requires a strong emphasis in the curriculum on safety and high standards of professional performance, both by students and by instructors. UCC developed a 'Release of All Claims and Waiver of Liability' form to provide a measure of legal protection for the College in the event of an accident. The release cannot, of course, exempt UCC from the responsibility to take due care in order to avoid either direct or vicarious liability. However, it does serve to document the risks assumed by students and hence to clarify the duty of care owed by UCC.

The need for supplemental funding

Delivery of the Adventure Travel Guide curriculum requires a considerable inventory of capital equipment ranging from cross-country skis to kayaks. It also involves the use of mountain huts, camp sites, vans and trailers for transporting students and equipment, and the use of helicopters. There are also certification fees and supplemental contracts for additional instructors from the specific adventure associations to achieve the required student–instructor ratios in field-based activity courses. These factors contribute significantly to costs.

Funding provided under conventional public education funding formulas in British Columbia was not sufficient to cover the total cost of the program. This problem was solved by adding a designated activity fee component to the tuition charges for field courses. Total student fees are currently C$5500 (approximately £2750) per year. This amount covers approximately one-third of the costs of the program.

Problem areas

Many of the courses offered in the Adventure Travel Guide program do not fit conventional course schedule formats. The Activity courses (those with the TRIP acronym) must for both practical and pedagogical reasons be delivered in block format rather than being semesterized. They also are subject to periodic rescheduling owing to weather conditions and the availability of Adventure Association personnel. These contingencies present challenges that require regular meetings with staff in Administration and the Registrar's office.

Facilities pose another problem. The block format of the program requires dedicated instructional space, but that space is needed only during certain periods of the year. In addition, some classrooms are used as labs for first aid courses or equipment evaluation and maintenance, and therefore need more space than would normally be required. Considerable storage space is required for the extensive equipment inventory, but it also must be relatively accessible to the classroom. In order to provide the unique space requirements it has been necessary to locate the program in facilities off campus.

As anticipated, there have been bureaucratic complications both within the College and in working with the large number of adventure associations. One important example arises in granting advanced credit for a specific skill course when a student has prior certification by the relevant Association. College policy allows for the granting of credit for work undertaken elsewhere when the institution is recognized by the Association of Universities and Colleges in Canada (AUCC). However, the adventure associations have not been recognized—and, owing to the non-traditional nature of their activities from the perspective of Canada's post-secondary educational institutions, are not likely to be recognized—by the AUCC. Therefore, it has been necessary to modify College guidelines to allow the granting of appropriate credit.

In a program where components of the curriculum are frequently delivered away from Kamloops, at times out of Province and even out of country, it has been necessary, with the anticipated resistance of the bureaucracy, to modify institutional practice and issue credit cards and telephone calling cards to program instructors. This practice in turn gives rise to the need for additional financial controls.

Since hospital and medical costs in other countries may exceed the levels covered by British Columbia's health services commission, students are required to purchase additional medical insurance whenever they leave Canada on a program expedition. Emergency protocols in the case of an accident also have been established. (Fortunately, all problems to date have been of a relatively minor nature and have been handled by the instructors on site.)

In order to make the program work, given the student/instructor contact hours on field courses and expeditions, a degree of flexibility has been required in applying the contract between the Faculty Association and the College to adventure guide instructors. For example, if an instructor is on an expedition with a group of students over a ten-day period, how much of each twenty-four hour day should be deemed to be with the students for the purposes of calculating instructional hours?

Finally, the popularity of the program combined with the wish to admit applicants with the greatest prospects for success has resulted in the scheduling of orientation sessions in Calgary, Montreal, and Toronto in addition to Kamloops. This procedure increases overall program costs and in addition raises the question of establishing quotas for students from within and outside British Columbia.

Despite these and other difficulties, problem areas have been minor obstacles to the development and operation of what to date has been a highly successful program.

Conclusion

This paper has focused on a key problem facing the rapidly growing adventure tourism industry. It is widely acknowledged that there is a shortage of labor with both the general educational qualifications in business, service and the environment, and the specific technical skills required to deliver the adventure tourism product with the standard of quality and professionalism demanded by the industry. Our analysis, based on a human capital approach, suggests that, although the private marketplace can be effective in providing the specific technical skills training required by the industry, this is not the case when it comes to general business operations, communication, service and environmental skills that are more broadly transferable. The primary reason for this is that there is a wider range of employment opportunities for employees equipped with these general skills. An employer supporting this training faces the risk of losing the newly trained employee (and the investment) to a competitor who has not incurred the cost of training. Under these circumstances, the private market will under-supply training.

Therefore, an opportunity exists for public educators and governments to play an important role in providing at least a partial solution to the problem. The UCC Adventure Travel Guide Diploma program is an innovative example of college educators working closely with industry and government to meet the special labor force training requirements in a specific sector of the tourism industry. The working relationships that have been developed between the various sectors of the industry and the University College have resulted in a program that combines state-of-the-art technical skills training with the general educational preparation needed to meet the high standards of product quality and professionalism demanded by the industry.

Acknowledgement

The authors wish to thank James Seldon for his valuable comments and suggestions.

References

Ellis, D., Kostiuk, B., Schettini, P. and Seldon, J. (1991) 'Toward professionalism: educators, government and industry in the tourism labor market', New Horizons Conference Proceedings, World Tourism Education and Research Centre, Calgary, pp. 571–580.

Mitchell, Barbara (1992) 'Tourism the professional challenge: a framework for action', Pacific Rim Institute of Tourism, Vancouver, pp. 10–11.

Outdoor Recreation Council (1988a) 'Adventure travel in British Columbia, 1', Outdoor Recreation Council of British Columbia, Vancouver.

Outdoor Recreation Council (1988b) 'Adventure travel in British Columbia, 2', Outdoor Recreation Council of British Columbia, Vancouver.

Pollock, Ann (1988) 'Adventure travel in western Canada', Tourism Canada, Ottawa, pp. 11–17.

Pollock, Ann (1992) 'Tourism in British Columbia', Open Learning Agency, Burnaby, pp. 47–48.

Appendix 1:
Adventure travel industry certification

Students in the UCC Adventure Travel Guide Diploma program are provided with an opportunity to be examined for the following existing industry certificates:

Canadian Association of Nordic Ski Instructors: Level I Instructor
Canadian Association of Nordic Ski Instructors: Level II Instructor
Canadian Association of Nordic Ski Instructors: Telemark Instructor
Whitewater Kayak Association of BC: Flatwater Instructor
Whitewater Kayak Association of BC: Assistant River Instructor
Whitewater Kayak Association of BC: Senior River Instructor
Nordic Ski Guides Association: Guide
Association of Canadian Mountain Guides: Ski Tour Guide
Association of Canadian Mountain Guides: Climbing Instructor
Red Cross Flatwater Canoe Instructor
Canadian Recreational Canoe Association: Moving Water Instructor
Canadian Recreational Canoe Association: Trip Instructor
BC Government: River Rafting Guide
BC Government: River Rafting II
BC Provincial Emergency Program: Search and Rescue Management
BC Provincial Emergency Program: Rope Rescue Team Member
BC Provincial Emergency Program: Rope Rescue Team Leader
Canadian Avalanche Association: Level I
Swiftwater Rescue Association: Swiftwater Rescue Technician I
Swiftwater Rescue Association: Swiftwater Rescue II
Swiftwater Rescue Association: Swiftwater Rescue Instructor
Canadian Institute of Safety, Search and Rescue: Wilderness Emergency Response
Canadian Institute of Safety, Search and Rescue: Advanced Wilderness Emergency Response
BC Parks: Public Safety and Park Security Certificate
National Association of Scuba Diving: Open Water
National Association of Scuba Diving: Advanced Open Water
National Association of Scuba Diving: Master Diver
National Association of Scuba Diving: Diver Supervisor

Note. Additional industry association certification will continue to be added.

Appendix 2:
UCC Adventure Travel Guide Diploma program outline

YEAR 1			
REQUIRED THEORY COURSES		**REQUIRED ACTIVITY COURSES**	
Course	**Course Title**	**Course**	**Course Title**
ADVG 101-1	The Adventure Tourism Industry	TRIP 150-3	Wilderness Travel
ADVG 102-1	Wilderness Travel	TRIP 151-3	Flatwater Canoe Instructor
ADVG 103-2	Wilderness Emergency Response	TRIP 153-3	Kayak I
ADVG 105-2	Guiding Leadership I	TRIP 155-3	Nordic Ski Instructor Level I
ADVG 110-2	Natural History I	TRIP 156-3	Ski Tour I
ADVG 111-2	Emergency Situation & SAR Mgt.	TRIP 157-3	Rock Climbing I
ADVG 112-2	Food Preparation	TRIP 158-3	Mountaineering I
TMGT 111-3	Tourism: An Industry Perspective	TRIP 159-3	Avalanche I
COMP 191-3	Computer Applications	TRIP 160-2	Swiftwater Rescue I
		EXPD 150-1	Expedition I
		PRAC 150-1	Work Experience Practicum
Total Required Credits	**18**	**Total Required Credits**	**28**

YEAR 2			
REQUIRED THEORY COURSES		**ELECTIVE ACTIVITY COURSES** **Continued**	
Course	**Course Title**	**Course**	**Course Title**
ACCT 121-3	Accounting I	TRIP 260-3	General Mountaineering
TMKT 115-3	Tourism Marketing	TRIP 261-3	Climbing Instructor
ADVG 201-2	The Wilderness Environment	TRIP 262-3	Rope Rescue
ADVG 202-2	The Cultural Environment	TRIP 263-3	Rope Rescue Team Leader
ADVG 203-2	Adv. Wild. Emergency Response	TRIP 264-3	Sea Kayaking I
ADVG 204-2	The Business of Adventure Tourism	TRIP 265-3	Sea Kayaking II
ADVG 205-3	Guiding Leadership II	TRIP 266-3	River Rafting I
ADVG 206-2	Legal Liability & Risk Management	TRIP 267-3	Natural History II
Total Required Credits	**19**	TRIP 268-3	Natural History III
		TRIP 269-3	Elective Activity Course
		TRIP 270-3	Open Water Diver
		TRIP 271-3	Advanced/Master Diver
ELECTIVE ACTIVITY COURSES		TRIP 272-3	Dive Supervisor
		TRIP 273-3	Swiftwater Rescue II
Students must successfully complete **8** of these elective activity courses in conjunction with Required courses to be eligible for a Diploma.		TRIP 274-3	Swiftwater Rescue Instr.
		TRIP 275-3	River Rafting II
		TRIP 276-3	Ice Climbing
TRIP 242-3	Canoe II	ADVG 240-3	Backcountry Ranger
TRIP 244-3	Kayak II		
TRIP 251-3	Moving Water Canoe Instructor	**Total Required Credits**	**24**
TRIP 252-3	Canoe Trip Leader	**More electives are available.**	
TRIP 253-3	Ass. River Kayak Instructor		
TRIP 254-3	Senior River Kayak Instructor		
TRIP 255-3	Telemark Instructor	**REQUIRED 2ND YEAR ACTIVITY COURSES**	
TRIP 256-3	Nordic Ski Instructor Level II	EXPD 200-1	Expedition II
TRIP 257-3	Ski Tour II	PRAC 200-1	Activity Log Practicum
TRIP 258-3	Ski Tour Guiding		
TRIP 259-3	Rope Handling		

Appendix 3: Adventure Travel Guide Diploma—activity course flowchart

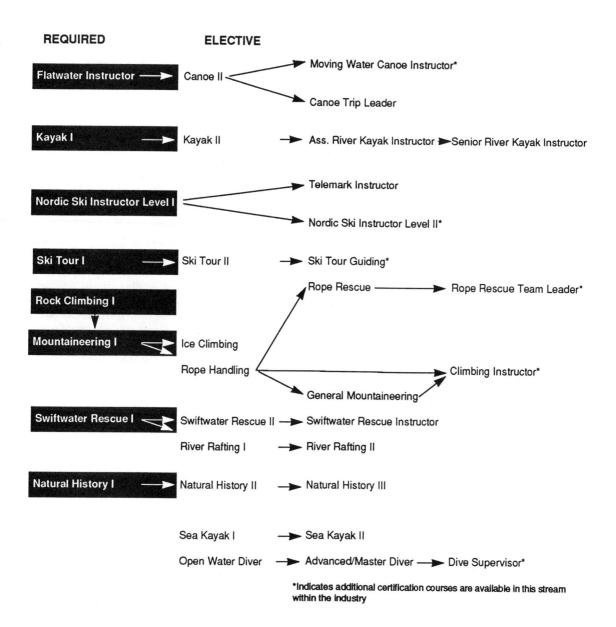

*Indicates additional certification courses are available in this stream within the industry

63 The importance of languages to foreign tourism: a comparative study of Britain and France, with particular reference to hotels

R. LUCAS AND A. PERRIN

Introduction

The creation of the single European market and increasing globalisation have placed the issue of language skills firmly on the policy agenda of governments and organisations. The main reasons for this relate to the need to secure 'competitive advantage': increasing foreign tourism and expanding business opportunities are vital activities for generating more revenue to the economy. Whilst the acquisition of different language skills among a broader section of the population may be a longer-term national objective, in tourism, the onus to develop such skills is more immediate and selective. Here the language need is presumed to focus more closely on the 'hosting activity' than on the tourist. The sectors of tourism activity that are compared and contrasted in this paper are the hotel industries in France and Britain.

The first part of the paper considers the implications of current and predicted tourism trends in France and Britain, and identifies regional differences in foreign tourism patterns between the two countries in order to identify the language needs of their hotel industries. National differences in language education and training are then discussed. The second part presents and discusses the results of a survey among 202 British and 128 French hotels about language policy and practice. Issues addressed include: the differing language needs of hotels, which relate to foreign visitors' occupancy rates and the geographical location of hotels; 'gaps' in the level and extent of language skills among relevant staff and in other areas where foreign languages could be utilised in the form of literature; how hotels approach language training and what their future language plans, if any, entail. The paper concludes with some recommendations that are directed both at governments and organisations.

The state of the art

The British Tourist Authority (BTA) is one of a number of voices that has maintained that the provision of language facilities for foreign visitors to Britain is wholly inadequate (BTA, 1989, 1991). Only an estimated 20% of the British population can speak a foreign language (Tarpey, 1991). English is not the native language of almost half Britain's overseas visitors, and of the 320 million people in the European Union, 53% do not speak English (Pearce, 1991). English may be the world's accepted official business language, but if Britain is to maintain its position as a leading tourist destination against strong competition, tourist providers must operate in the language of their customers (BTA, 1991:3–4). The first HOTREC white paper sees the diversity of culture, language and nature as a unique selling point of the European tourism product (HOTREC, 1992).

In short, action is required to develop language skills in order to:

- increase foreign visits and foreign spending;
- improve business communications;
- provide a high-quality service in order to gain competitive advantage;
- provide an efficient service and make foreign visitors welcome;
- promote return visits.

Given this apparently poor state of language development in Britain, the broad aims of this study were to:

- consider language needs in terms of foreign tourism patterns;
- identify the language policies and practices of hotels;
- compare British 'practice' with that of France, Europe's leading foreign tourist destination.

Tourism trends and language implications

France and Britain are both leading players in terms of European and world tourism. There are, however, significant differences between their tourist products and in the language mix of their foreign tourists. This section outlines these broad national differences in order to identify the potential language needs of each country. It should be noted that some of the figures discussed in this section relate to the UK as separate British figures are not given in the source material.

France

France is Europe's leading tourist destination and was the top tourism earner during the 1980s. Between 1980 and 1990, tourism earnings rose by over US$13 000 million to reach US$21 651 million in 1990 (Euromonitor, 1992:41). France's popularity is based on a wealth of natural resources including mountains, coastlines and good climate, and other features such as cuisine, wine and architectural sites. The country is easily accessed by air, sea, road and rail. France shares borders with six major European countries and is now linked to Britain by the Channel Tunnel.

Tourism has been at the forefront of the national economic agenda since 1980, when an action plan was launched to:

● understand and monitor tourism's contribution to the French economy;

● promote France;
● encourage investment in tourist facilities;
● increase the role of tourism in regional development;
● update tourism management and training (Boniface and Cooper, 1987:88).

Foreign tourism in France showed a dramatic increase between 1986 and 1991. The outlook thereafter was considered to be good, owing to factors that include the opening of EuroDisney, the hosting of the winter Olympic Games in Albertville and the opening of European frontiers. The main clutch of foreign visitors (1989) have come from near-neighbouring European countries—former West Germany (9.1 million), the UK and Ireland (6.2 million) and The Netherlands (3.7 million) (see Figure 63.1) (Euromonitor, 1992:109). The Benelux countries, Italy and America each provide at or around 3 million visitors per annum. The primary language needs would thus appear to be English and German.

A closer estimation of language needs can be gauged from a regional analysis of foreign tourism. Of France's 22 Provinces, Île de France, including Paris, generates the most foreign visits, shown in Table 63.1. The Côte d'Azur and the Rhône-Alpes contain the major beach and skiing facilities.

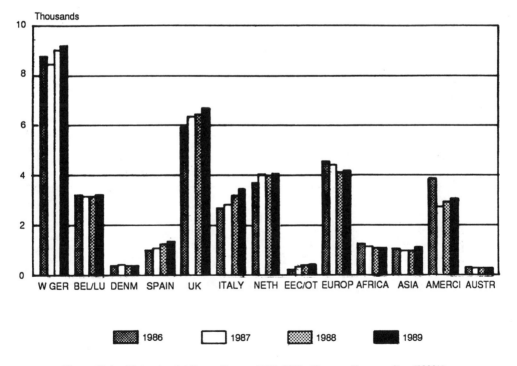

Figure 63.1 *Major tourist flows: France 1986–1989. (Source: Euromonitor (1992))*

Table 63.1 *Destinations of foreign visitors to France (1989)*

Region	'000 visitors	Per cent
Île de France	7421	38.3
Côte d'Azur	2180	11.3
Rhône-Alpes	1637	8.5
Bourgogne	1109	5.7
Alsace	904	4.7
Bretagne	516	2.7
Centre	894	4.6
Midi-Pyrénées	855	4.4
Aquitaine	512	2.6
Champagne-Ardennes	423	2.2
Nord–Pas-de-Calais	382	2.0
Basse Normandie	378	1.9
Lorraine	291	1.5
Haute Normandie	272	1.4
Picardie	270	1.4
Franche Comté	203	1.0
Poitou-Charentes	136	0.7
Auvergne	142	0.7
Limousin	114	0.6
Pays de la Loire	na	na
Languedoc-Roussillon	na	na

Source: Euromonitor (1992).

Predictions to the year 2000 (these relate to the Île de France only) shown in Figure 63.2 indicate that increased visits will continue to come mainly from France's close European neighbours. Although this points to a continuing need to develop English and German, increased knowledge of Italian looks likely to become a more pressing need in the late 1990s. The small, but growing, number of Japanese visitors would also appear to pose something of a language challenge.

The United Kingdom

The UK is fourth in the league of European tourism earners (Euromonitor, 1992:41), and the fifth world tourism earner (BTA, 1992). Tourism earnings increased from US$6893 million in 1980 to US$14 998 million in 1990; this represents a slightly lower growth rate in earnings than for France. British tourism is based upon its culture, countryside, attractive coastline and British Heritage. At present, 60% of foreign tourists arrive by air and 40% by ferry, although the Channel Tunnel should make for easier access from Europe.

Since 1990, UK tourism has suffered adverse effects resulting from the Gulf War, recession and fluctuating exchange rates, and, overall, foreign arrivals dropped in 1990. The UK's main foreign visitors (1990) came from the USA (3 million), France (2.3 million), Germany (1.8 million) and the Irish Republic (1.5 million) (Euromonitor, 1992:135). Although a sizeable base of foreign visitors come from English-speaking countries, French and German would appear to be the languages for which some

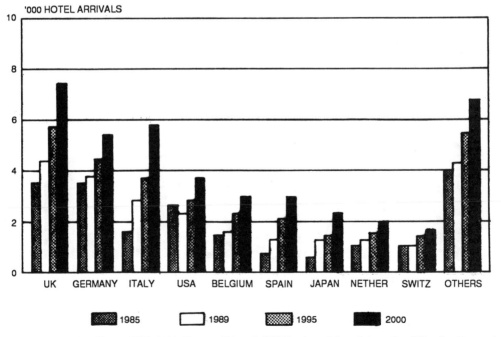

Figure 63.2 *Foreign tourism: France 1985–2000. (Source: Edwards (1992), adapted from* International Tourism Forecasts to 2005, *Economist Intelligence Unit Special Report No. 2454)*

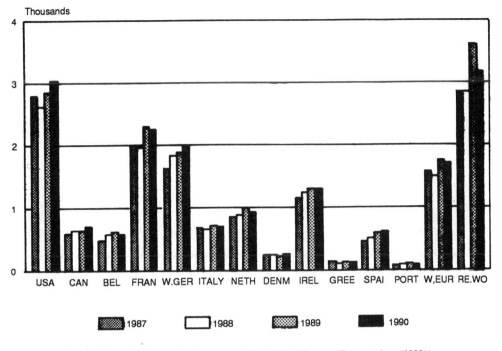

Thousands

1987 | 1988 | 1989 | 1990

Figure 63.3 *Major tourist flows: UK 1987–1990. (Source: Euromonitor (1992))*

Table 63.2 *Destinations of overseas visitors to Britain (1990)*

Region	Percentage visits	Percentage nights
London	57.2	39.1
South East	10.9	9.3
Heart of England	6.9	4.7
West Country	7.4	6.0
Thames & Chilterns	7.4	5.9
North West	5.5	4.4
East Anglia	5.3	4.8
Yorkshire & Humberside	5.0	4.0
Southern	5.3	4.9
East Midlands	3.5	2.8
Northumbria	1.8	1.4
Cumbria	1.4	0.8
Wales	3.8	2.8
Scotland	8.9	8.1

Source: Department of Employment: International Passenger Survey.

level of knowledge and skill is required. However, as Figure 63.3 shows, there is a broader mix of foreign tourists from across the world coming to the UK compared to France (see Figure 63.1). This suggests that there may be a greater need for attention to be paid to a number of minority languages in the UK, whereas the emphasis in France falls more on mainstream European languages.

As in France, language needs in Britain can be further refined by examining regional tourism patterns, shown in Table 63.2. Britain's capital, London, seemingly has more foreign tourist 'pulling power' than Paris, and foreign tourism is more evenly 'spread about' British regions than is generally the case among the French Provinces. Therefore the major language need in Britain is more specifically concentrated in a particular part of the country.

Euromonitor forecasts suggest that Europe will continue to be the continent most visited by tourists from across the world (Edwards, 1992:200–201). As Figure 63.4 shows, the extent to which British tourism growth is more heavily reliant on the USA and the rest of the world is greater than in France (see Figure 63.2). This suggests not only that the potential language needs in Britain are more diverse but also that the requirements for language use exist on smaller, more specific scales than in France.

The language base

The foundation of the body of language skills in any country derives largely from the priority that the education system affords it. This may be less easy to effect in Britain whose domestic business needs focus on customers from a wide variety of nations with a diverse

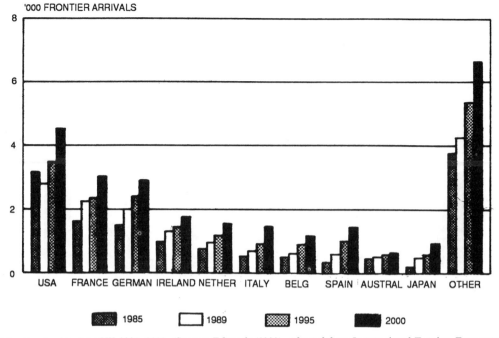

'000 FRONTIER ARRIVALS

Figure 63.4 *Foreign tourism: UK 1985–2000. (Source: Edwards (1992), adapted from* International Tourism Forecasts to 2005, *Economist Intelligence Unit Special Report No. 2454)*

language base. Nevertheless, in terms of tourism, France's primary needs have been identified as German and English, and Britain's as French and German, all of which are mainstream European languages. This section considers how the education systems of both nations have dealt with language teaching (see Eurydice: European Unit, 1988).

Schools

In France, the teaching of one foreign language from among English, German, Italian or Spanish may be available at primary level in the Écoles Élémentaires. In the first year of secondary school (Collège), the vast majority (87%) of pupils study English. Beyond this, two-thirds of secondary school children learn at least two or more languages (English, German, Italian, Spanish, Portuguese, Russian). Foreign languages are a compulsory part of the curriculum to age 18.

In Britain, language teaching is not afforded such priority, with the consequential effect that, as a general rule, pupils study fewer languages for a shorter period to a lower level of attainment (Holschen, 1989). Some of the problems relate to a lack of qualified teachers, poor resources and inadequate funding. In general, at secondary schools up to two languages can be learnt, mainly French,

German and Spanish. Changes in national education policy during the 1980s meant that before 1988, pupils could drop languages by the end of the third year (age 14). The National Curriculum (1988) includes one foreign language, and in Scotland all pupils between ages 12 to 16 must learn at least one foreign language. After age 16 languages are no longer compulsory—only 10% of British pupils continue with formal education in languages after age 16.

Hospitality education

Ostensibly the education system in France gives the French a 'grass roots' competitive advantage over the British in terms of language skills. Even so, skills need maintenance and development, and as the evidence from French curricula in hospitality education shows, the French seem more prepared to persist with developing language skills than are the British (see Rutter and Teare (1992)).

Hospitality and catering education in France and Britain is not directly comparable. In France there is more emphasis on technical skills than on management skills, and there are no courses really equivalent to a British degree. Hospitality education in France takes place on three levels. There are three types of craft courses.

Table 63.3 *Language provision in French hospitality education*

Course[a]	Number of languages	Year 1	Year 2	Year 3
BTS	2	2 hours	2 hours	na
BTH	2	3 hours	3 hours	3–4 hours
BAC PRO	1 or 2	3 and 1 hours	3 and 1 hours	na
BEP	1 or 2	3 and 2 hours	3 and 2 hours	na
CAP	1	2 hours	2 hours	na

[a] For complete titles, see section headed 'Hospitality education'.
Source: Rutter and Teare (1992).

The Certificat d'Aptitude Professionnelle (CAP) is a basic craft course, the Brevet d'Étude Professionnelle (BEP) is a full-time craft programme and the Baccalauréat Professionnelle Restauration (BAC PRO) includes a work placement. The Brevet de Technicien Hôtellerie (BTH) is equivalent to a BTEC National Diploma and the Brevet de Technicien Superieur (BTS) is equivalent to an HND. A significant language element is a compulsory element in all courses, as shown in Table 63.3.

In Britain, where languages are available on BTEC National Diplomas, HNDs or degrees, it is usually as an option in the curriculum. The opportunity to learn and/or develop language skills may also come from a placement abroad. Nevertheless, there are some courses which include two languages in the curriculum and a one-year placement abroad, of which the BA (Hons) in International Hotel Management at the Manchester Metropolitan University is an example. Even so, language provision in British hospitality education is poor compared to that of France.

Other means

A number of different language schemes have developed in Europe, such as the 'Lingua' programme designed to support the teaching of Danish, German, Greek, English, French, Irish, Italian, Letzeburgesch, Dutch and Portuguese among the Member States. In France, the Groupement d'Establissements des Métiers de l'Hôtellerie (GRETA) is a consultancy which provides language courses for adults, and in Britain the BTA's 'Winning Words' scheme gives awards for a commitment to meeting the needs of overseas visitors.

Hotel companies may also offer language training, but not usually at hotel level. The 'Académie Accor' in Paris, where most of Accor's management training takes place, offers only a limited number of places on language courses. Forte pay a £100 bonus to customer-contact staff who speak French, German, Italian or Spanish and they

can be identified by wearing a flag badge (BTA, 1989). Gaps can also be filled by employing foreign staff, and perhaps more importantly, through the provision of literature which has been translated into various foreign languages.

This part has identified that there are differing foreign tourism patterns in France and Britain that lead to different language needs. A superior language education would appear to give France potential competitive advantage over Britain. The second part presents empirical evidence on the 'state of the art' of languages in hotels.

Survey evidence: language policy and practice

Survey method and response

Two broadly similar post questionnaires, distributed to 200 French and 245 British hotels in French and English respectively, sought information on:

- the present usage of languages;
- language training;
- predictions of anticipated future changes.

More specifically, the questionnaires sought details about the location, rating and size (by number of bedrooms) of hotels. Respondents were asked to specify the average percentage occupancy rate of foreign visitors, to estimate the average percentage occupancy rates of return visits by foreign guests and to speculate about possible increases in the numbers of foreign guests in the future. They were then asked to specify the languages used currently in the hotel, and those which might need to be used in the future. Questions were asked about the number and types of languages spoken at front desk, and in which other areas of the hotel it was important to have someone speaking two or more languages. Information was also sought on other means of welcoming foreign guests, such as using brochures in various languages. Respondents were asked to place various factors in order of importance in relation to the recruitment of front desk staff: these included language skills, appearance and past experience. Respondents were also asked to specify details of their staff language training arrangements and to identify where languages should be taught within the education system. Finally respondents were asked if there was anything that could be changed within the hotel so that foreign guests could be dealt with in a better way, and to add any 'other comments'.

Hotels were selected randomly from the major guide books, such as Michelin, the Logis de France and hotel chain directories. Questionnaires were distributed according to the proportion of hotels in each area.

The response rates of 202 hotels in Britain (73%) and 128 hotels in France (64%) are considered to be very high, although the geographical pattern of respondents did not quite correspond to the proportional representation of hotels on an area basis. Although all classifications of hotel were represented in the responding sample, those with a rating of one star or less were under-represented. This relates mainly to the sampling method (hotels in guide books are generally 'better' quality). The responding British hotels were larger on average (by number of rooms) than the French hotels.

Language usage and need

French hotels had higher percentage occupancy rates of foreign visitors than British hotels. The French hotels also had a higher percentage of return visits from foreign guests but the reasons for these differed between the two countries, seemingly related to type of customer. In Britain over 40% of return visits related to a business trip, but only 10% of return visits in France fell into this category. Location of the hotel was a significant reason for return visits in both countries (around 25% of cases).

Language usage among staff in British hotels was more diverse across a wider range of languages. In France, English was used in 95% of hotels, German in 65%, Spanish in 38% and Italian in 37%. In Britain, French was used in 80% of hotels, German in 50%, Italian in 27% and Spanish in 21%. Although the language stock of the major European languages was lower in the British sample, the language stock of minority languages (Dutch, Japanese, Arabic, Welsh, Russian, Portuguese, Danish and Swedish) was higher.

When the availability of language skills is considered on a regional basis, some interesting refinements become apparent. In Britain, French, German, Italian and Spanish were widely available in London, which attracts

57% of foreign tourists. French was spoken widely in most areas with the exception of the North East and the East Midlands. German was most widely spoken in East Anglia, the North East and the South. Italian was not offered to any significant extent outside London. In France, language needs are also related to the proximity of its borders with other countries as well as foreign tourist arrivals. Thus in Alsace and Lorraine, German is widely available but Italian and Spanish are not, whereas in Languedoc-Roussillon, Aquitaine and Midi-Pyrénées, Spanish is widely on offer, but German and Italian are not. As noted above, English is spoken almost everywhere in France.

The first area of customer contact—reception—is probably the main area where language skills need to be deployed. Here the average number of staff speaking one or more languages was higher in France (3.4 persons) than in Britain (1.48 persons). Over 25% of British hotels did not employ a single member of staff who could speak a foreign language. The British hotels were larger on average than those in the French sample, and would probably employ more staff. In other words, even if smaller French hotels employed no other linguists, they nevertheless enjoy a disproportionate benefit of having more skilled language staff than their British counterparts.

Although the main language provision in hotels mirrors the language needs of foreign tourists identified in the first part of the paper, skill levels are undoubtedly higher in French hotels than in British hotels. This is particularly interesting because the responding hotels in both samples were not concentrated in the areas which receive the highest numbers of foreign visitors. In other words, it can be said that French hotels are 'better prepared' in terms of language skills, even though there may not be a significant requirement for them.

In terms of expected future needs, all French hotels which did not currently use English expected to need it

Table 63.4 *Importance of language skills by department*

Areas	France			Britain		
	Number	%	Rank	Number	%	Rank
Reception	124	96.9	1	192	95.0	1
Restaurant	106	82.8	2	163	80.7	2
Management	97	75.8	3	145	71.8	3
Sales	77	60.2	4	92	45.5	4
Bar	70	54.7	5	65	32.2	5
Concierge	54	42.2	6	58	28.7	6
Housekeeping	43	33.6	7	28	13.9	8
Room service	25	19.5	8	34	16.8	7
Banqueting	25	19.5	8	17	8.4	9
Kitchen	8	6.3	10	13	6.4	10

Source: Survey, 1992.

Table 63.5 *Other language facilities to welcome guests*

Facilities in foreign language	France			Britain		
	Number	%	Rank	Number	%	Rank
Brochures	104	81.3	1	60	29.7	2
Letters/fax	90	70.0	2	34	16.8	4
Staff encouraged to speak	87	68.0	3	70	34.7	1
Room facilities	74	57.8	4	54	26.7	3
Menus	65	50.8	5	32	15.8	5
Computer service	9	7.0	6	6	3.0	6

Source: Survey, 1992.

in the future. A growing need for all the major European languages, and significantly, Japanese, was expected in both countries. In other words, a language gap can be said to exist.

Reception staff are not the only occupational group that need to speak foreign languages, although hotels identified them as being the most important. As Table 63.4 shows, French hotels attached more importance to having someone who could speak more than one language across all departments than was the case among British hotels. An element of British complacency can be gleaned from one respondent's perception that 'most foreigners speak some English'.

In terms of welcoming foreign guests, personal contact, though important, is not the only means at hoteliers' disposal. French hotels offered a much bigger range of other facilities in foreign languages than British hotels, shown in Table 63.5. Hotels which had high percentage occupancy rates of foreign visitors and a high level of return visits provided more translated literature. Although it cannot be stated with certainty that a more extensive provision of literature in different languages has generated more foreign customers who are more likely to return, literature provision of this kind would appear to be a useful marketing tool. The provision of translated literature serves as an additional aid to, and perhaps substitute for, spoken language skills.

Acquiring language skills

The French respondents claimed to give considerably more encouragement to their staff to learn different languages (64%) than their counterparts in Britain (33%). Even so, language training or sending staff on foreign placements was a minority practice, although it was carried out more frequently by French hotels (36%) than by British hotels (20%). In both countries, training was most likely to be found in hotels with a four- or five-star classification, but was absent from hotels with a one-star classification or less. The methods used to encourage

staff differed between the two countries. In Britain nearly a quarter of respondents used some form of bonus or higher rates of pay, whereas in France, practical assistance from the Chamber of Commerce was used in 20% of cases.

If hotels cannot, or do not, train staff in languages, they can 'buy' them in through recruitment. For front office staff the French hotels placed more emphasis on language skills and appearance than British hotels which considered attitude and social skills to be most important attributes. This difference may go some way towards explaining why French hotels employ more receptionists with language skills than British hotels.

The majority of respondents in both countries placed the onus of learning languages on the education system, particularly at primary level.

When asked to predict future guest patterns, more French hotels (89%) than British hotels (76%) expected to see an increase in foreign visitors in the future. A greater proportion of British hotels foresaw the need to make changes to deal with future developments, the main ones being to speak at least two foreign languages and to have more foreign literature. To a lesser extent the French also believed that language improvements of some kind would become necessary. These findings point to positive intentions and suggest that some British hoteliers are aware of their relatively modest language skills achievements.

Conclusions and recommendations

A comparison between two sizeable samples of French and British hotels has identified that in France, there is a generally higher level of language skills provision, through the spoken word and in literature, and a perception that language skills are needed across a broader number of departments than in Britain. The French education system and hospitality education offer significantly better language provision in terms of numbers of languages to be studied and the period of time over which pupils are required to study languages. Additionally French

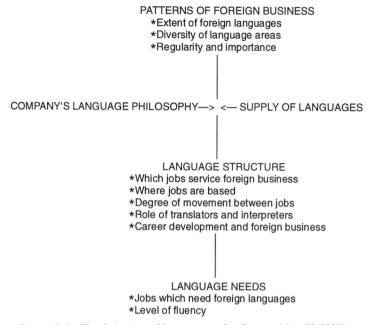

PATTERNS OF FOREIGN BUSINESS
*Extent of foreign languages
*Diversity of language areas
*Regularity and importance

COMPANY'S LANGUAGE PHILOSOPHY—> <— SUPPLY OF LANGUAGES

LANGUAGE STRUCTURE
*Which jobs service foreign business
*Where jobs are based
*Degree of movement between jobs
*Role of translators and interpreters
*Career development and foreign business

LANGUAGE NEEDS
*Jobs which need foreign languages
*Level of fluency

Figure 63.5 *The derivation of language needs. (Source: Metcalf (1991))*

tourism language needs may be more easy to develop since they focus more closely on the main European languages, whereas British tourism language needs are more diverse among a greater number of world languages.

Governments, particularly the British government, could effect improvements to the stock of language skills through education policy within schools and higher education (Pearce, 1991). Government language-training schemes in Britain have been more temporary and short-term than long-term, seemingly hampered by a lack of resources. Tax relief to individuals who are prepared to finance their own language training is another possible consideration (Pearce, 1991).

Language training could be more widely promoted within the hotel industries themselves, particularly the minority languages, including Japanese, for which there will be an increased need in the future. This could be effected on a regional basis to reflect the differing regional language needs of each country. Where the language gap cannot be filled entirely with staff who have a reasonable command of languages, hotels could go some way to compensate for the gap by providing a wider range of literature in appropriate languages.

Information technology is becoming increasingly utilised in language teaching, both in the classroom and in business (Rushby, 1990). The National Council for Educational Technology (NCET) exists to promote and support the improvement of teaching and learning

through the appropriate use of new and existing technologies, including satellite television (NCET, 1992a), electronic mail (NCET, 1991) and Minitel and Télétel (NCET, 1992b).

Essentially each business can, and should, identify its own particular needs through a simple audit procedure shown in Figure 63.5. It may well be the case that the relatively poor level of language provision in British hotels owes something to lack of systematic analysis of needs, although it was also clear that there was rather more complacency among British respondents than among French respondents.

Increased levels of fluency in languages may come over time, but the need to offer increasingly higher standards of service in a highly competitive field is more short-term and pressing. It remains to be seen whether competitive advantage in British tourism is damaged by a seemingly less positive approach to providing and developing language skills than is the case in France, or whether other factors of the tourism product are sufficiently strong to keep attracting foreign tourists to Britain.

References

Boniface, B. G. and Cooper, C. P. (1987) *The Geography of Travel and Tourism*, Heinemann, London, pp. 47–61 and 85–93.

BTA (British Tourist Authority) (1989) 'Lost for words', BTA, London.

BTA (1991) 'Winning Words', BTA, London.

BTA (1992) 'Guidelines for tourism in Britain—key points', BTA, London.

Edwards, A. (1992) 'International tourism forecasts to 2005', Special Report 2454, the Economist Intelligence Unit, London.

Euromonitor (1992) 'European tourism 1992', Euromonitor, London.

Eurydice: European Unit (1988) 'The teaching of languages in the European Community', Eurydice, Brussels.

Holschen, M. C. (1989) 'Foreign languages in secondary education', Ministry of Education and Science, Special March, p. 26.

HOTREC (1992) '1992 challenges: for Europe's hospitality industry', *British Hotelier and Restaurateur*, June: 12–13.

Metcalf, H. (1991) 'Foreign language needs of a business', Report No. 215, Institute of Manpower Studies, Brighton.

NCET (National Council for Educational Technology) (1991) 'Electronic mail and modern languages', Modern languages Information File No. 15, June, NCET, Coventry.

NCET (1992a) 'Modern languages and satellite television', Modern Languages Information File No. 17, January, NCET, Coventry.

NCET (1992b) 'Minitel and Télétel—on-line information from France', Modern Languages Information File No. 18, January NCET, Coventry.

Pearce, G. (1991) 'Languages and the British manager', Bonjour Europe, British Institute of Management, London, pp. 1–7.

Rushby, N. (1990) 'Beyond the language lab', *Personnel Management*, February: 71.

Rutter, D. and Teare, M. (1992) 'Catering education and training in France—a comparative study', Occasional Paper No. 8, Institute of Education, University of London.

Tarpey, D. (1991) 'Mind your languages', *Caterer and Hotelkeeper*, 12 September: 40–42.

64 Productivity in the hotel industry

F. McMAHON

Introduction

Productivity in the hotel industry is becoming increasingly significant as labour costs rise. Since the hotel industry is labour-intensive, its profitability depends on the success achieved in making good, productive use of its workforce. One might expect that the importance of maximising labour productivity would be reflected in how jobs are designed, how productivity is measured, and how staff are trained to meet rigorously set performance standards. In fact, the reality has been quite different for most hotel companies to date.

Significance of productivity

Productivity is the relationship between the inputs and the outputs of a productive system. This is sometimes represented in a formula:

$$\text{Productivity} = \frac{\text{Wealth produced}}{\text{Resources consumed}}$$

It has long been recognised by economists that productivity is a crucial factor in determining the standard of living of the citizens of any country. If changes in the productive system can lead to continually growing output of goods and services, without corresponding increases in the use of resources being consumed to produce those goods and services, then a rising standard of living may be expected.

This simple approach to national economics runs into problems when one starts to measure inputs and outputs. This national output is extremely heterogeneous since it includes physical consumer goods, buildings, and government services such as education. This difficulty is overcome by reducing all products to a common denominator—namely money. Similarly all the inputs in terms of the labour of workers can be reduced to a sum of money and can be combined with use of productive services such as capital.

However, a measure of productivity which combines labour costs and capital costs is not all that useful. Accordingly, it is more common to separate labour productivity from capital productivity. This is done by dividing total output by the cost of labour to give labour productivity, and by dividing total output by the cost of capital to give the productivity of capital.

Countries which have been successful in continually raising productivity, such as Japan which averaged 6% per annum over an 18-year period from the 1960s, or West Germany which averaged 4% per annum over a similar period, have been the envy of other countries with much more modest rates of increase. Not only do the successful countries enjoy the immediate fruits of their success; they also attract investment from other countries, thereby assisting the further development of their economies.

Productivity of the firm

The benefits of increasing productivity at national levels are mirrored at the level of the individual firm. A firm enjoying increasing productivity is in a position to pay higher wages, invest in new equipment, sell its output at competitive prices and still make a handsome profit.

Manufacturing industry has long recognised the benefits of increasing productivity and, since the end of the 19th century, much effort has been devoted to increasing the productive capacity of the firm. Many thinkers, starting with F. W. Taylor, have sought ways of mechanising and automating processes, of reducing or eliminating unnecessary handling and revolutionising the recruitment, training and motivation of workers to increase productivity. This sustained approach has enabled a reduced labour force in the manufacturing sector to produce more and more goods each year. If one ignores arguments about the quality of life and damage to the environment (only because they are outside the scope of this paper) then it must be conceded that the increases in productivity in the manufacturing sector have been very impressive.

Productivity in the hotel sector

There are compelling reasons why productivity increases are crucial to the hotel industry. Firstly, the service sector of which the hotel industry is part, is an increasingly important sector of the economy. As fewer and fewer workers in the manufacturing sector can produce all the physical goods we need, then more and more workers are concentrated in the services sector. In developed Western economies such as the USA, more than 70% of workers are in the service sector. Secondly, the services sector has traditionally been labour-intensive. If the workers in that sector are to enjoy parity of wages with workers in the manufacturing sector, then productivity in the services sector must rise in line with increases in the manufacturing sector. Many authors have pointed to the failure of the service sector to match the manufacturing sector in this regard. Shiffler and Coye (1988) state that productivity in service industries in the United States rose at an annual rate of only 1.7% compared to 2.7% in manufacturing for the period 1960 to 1985.

Since hotels are generally labour-intensive (though individual hotels and hotel groups have taken steps to reduce their need for labour) they are particularly vulnerable to pressure from staff for increased wages. In several countries, including Ireland, wage increases are negotiated nationally while in other countries the norm is established nationally and individual firms negotiate around that norm. Such practices can put pressure on hotel companies to increase wages where no increase in productivity has occurred. It has been argued by Blois (1984) that labour costs increasing more steeply than prices, caused by a lack of productivity, are a contributory factor in causing inflation.

The importance of labour costs in the hotel industry can most readily be illustrated by the dominance of labour costs in the profit and loss accounts of hotel companies. Simpson Xavier Horwath, in their 'Irish hotel industry review' (1992) calculated that the total cost of labour amounted to 28.9% of revenue in 1991. Horwath and Horwath International (1988) have published data on the labour productivity ratio (i.e. units of gross profit generated by one unit of labour) for hotel companies in different continents. All the ratios were between 2.52 and 3.09 which would indicate that the cost of labour is between 25% and 32%.

Labour intensity in the hotel industry

Evidence offered above on the extent of labour cost in the hotel industry—generally around 30%—points to the classification of the hotel industry as a labour-intensive industry.

Other evidence of this fact can be seen in the ratio of staff to guest bedrooms in hotels. This ratio varies enormously from a low of 0.3 staff per room in some Scandinavian countries to 1.5 and even 2 per room in some underdeveloped countries. Generally, the ratio is high in low-wage countries and much lower

in countries where wages and related payroll costs are high. The latter point is important—it is not just the wage cost that is important, but also the costs associated with payroll such as employers' social security costs, employers' pension contributions and so forth.

But one should also remember that hotels are increasingly becoming capital-intensive as well as labour-intensive, partly because of escalating site costs, especially in major cities. Partly because of rising guest expectations and partly because of the desire of hotel operators to install mechanical objects to replace personal services (shoe polishing machines, tea-makers, etc.), the cost of constructing modern hotels has risen sharply. A cost of 100 000 US dollars per room is now quite normal and is often exceeded. The cost of construction makes it imperative that the property is run efficiently if the project is to be viable.

Hotel industry as an employer

Given the importance of labour in the hotel industry, one might expect that the industry would pride itself on the way it nurtured this vital resource. Yet, in reality, the hotel industry has had a very poor reputation as an employer. The image of employment in the industry is one of long hours, poor pay, poor working conditions, high labour turnover, heavy reliance on casual and part-time labour, low levels of trade union organisation and a low level of commitment to staff training by employers. To justify this characterisation of the hotel industry point by point would require more space than this paper permits. But one may cite, in overall support of the negative image, the fact that in many Western countries, there is widespread unemployment existing alongside many vacancies in the hotel and catering industry. It seems that many unemployed people prefer to live off welfare state payments rather than work in the hotel industry. Worland and Wilson (1988) cite the extent to which the hospitality industry in Australia has come to rely on part-time labour and that the most important age groups are the under-25-year-olds and the over-60 age group. Many UK authors have identified the demographic time-bomb which threatens the hospitality industry in the UK because of a drastic shortage in the age group 18 years to 25 years, upon which the UK industry has come to rely. Innovative schemes being developed by major hotel companies to attract retired and semi-retired people to take jobs in the hotel industry may well be successful. But they beg the question of why such schemes should be necessary in an era of mass unemployment.

Difficulties in measuring productivity in the hotel industry

The characteristics of service industries affect the process of measuring productivity. These characteristics have been well summarised by Teare (1989) and include:

- The sale, production and consumption of a service take place almost simultaneously
- A service cannot be centrally produced, inspected, stockpiled and is delivered where the customer is, by people out of the immediate supervision of management
- Delivery of service usually requires some degree of human contact
- The consumer's expectations of the service are integral to his or her satisfaction. Quality of service is largely a subjective matter

In manufacturing industry, outputs may consist of standardised products that can be easily measured in terms of quantity, volume or weight. In service industries, however, there is a great diversity of output and so physical measures of output cannot readily be used. Instead, money is used as the measure. An immediate drawback of measuring output in money rather than physical terms is that any price increase is shown as a productivity increase.

The quality aspect of service poses a particularly knotty problem for those seeking to measure productivity. Staff in hotels may serve their customers in a convivial manner, striking exactly the right balance between friendliness and obtrusiveness, meeting all the expectations of the guest in terms of conviviality, timing and assistance. Or they may serve in a surly, unfriendly, patronising or obtrusive manner which leaves guests thoroughly dissatisfied. In the short term, there will be no differences in the productivity of the waiter, as measured in money terms, but in the longer term there is a great difference. How does one design a productivity measurement system which takes account of these differences?

A further difficulty in measuring productivity in hotels is posed by the possibility of substitution of materials for labour. For example, a chef can reduce his payroll by reducing his staff and purchasing ready-made desserts. If one is using a partial productivity measure such as payroll as a percentage of revenue, then this substitution of bought-in desserts for those made on the premises will show up as an increase in productivity. But is it a real increase in productivity?

The opposite problem/solution also arises. A head chef, under pressure from his manager to increase gross profit, can do so by deciding to make all desserts on the premises, even though this may mean hiring extra staff.

Boella (1992) supplies a number of different productivity measures for different hotel or catering activities, for example, the number of employees per room in a hotel, or the labour to materials ratio in a school meals service, or the number of meals served for each member of staff in a staff canteen. All of these are useful measures but all are partial measures and could be manipulated to look good. Very often, such ratios are most meaningful when used to compare units of an organisation which have similar operating procedures (such as branches of the McDonald's restaurant chain) or to compare results of one time period with results of another time period in a single unit (such as employees per room in a hotel in July 1994 with July 1993). Different partial measures, used in combination, can provide a better picture than any one composite measure. It may be fashionable to say 'just give me the bottom line' but such information rarely gives a true picture of the success/failure of a business enterprise. Ball et al. (1986) concluded that few yardsticks exist for the evaluation of hotel performance and that we are still some way from producing a productivity framework for the management of hotels. More recently, Ball and Johnson (1989) concluded that the failure of a fast-food chain to incorporate quality within its concept of productivity would be particularly short-sighted, given the presence of customers on site in fast-food restaurants and their involvement in the service process.

This involvement of the customer in the service process and the fact that the customer's perception of service quality is often more important than the actual output reality, was focused upon by Blumberg (1991). He gave particular weight to the service-time dimension. As the actual service-time delivered closely approximates this target parameter, customer satisfaction levels will rise. But as the level of service performance crosses the threshold of the time requirement, the level of customer satisfaction and perceived service quality delivery no longer rises. In fact, it plateaus. In some cases, the level of customer satisfaction may actually drop as the service performance levels apparently improve the customer often views too much service as badly as too little service.

Productivity levels in the hotel industry

Bearing in mind all the difficulties there are in measuring output in the hotel industry, one nevertheless may wish to know whether the hotel industry rates highly or lowly in the productivity stakes.

Medlik (1989) estimated that output per head in the UK hotel and catering industry was £5900 in 1985. This compared with £10 000 per head in the economy as a whole. This indicates a performance well below average for the hotel and catering industry. But perhaps even more damning was his conclusion that output per head in the hotel and catering sector had actually fallen by 0.7% over the period 1979 to 1985. In the same period output per head for the economy as a whole had risen by 2.3%. In computing these figures Medlik had defined output as value added at factor cost (constant prices).

US authors have similarly characterised hotel productivity as being well below that of manufacturing industry.

Reasons advanced by Heizer and Render (1988) for poor productivity in the services sector are that such work is:

- Typically labour-intensive
- Frequently individually processed
- Often an intellectual task performed by professionals
- Often difficult to mechanise and automate

Witt and Witt (1989) concluded that these reasons apply to the hotel industry and felt that Guerrier and Lockwood (1988) may have summed up one of the major problems facing hotels: traditionally the development of hotel managers encourages a 'being there' style and discourages reflection and planning. Their 'hands-on' bias may make them reluctant to spend time on, and even afraid of, paperwork and figurework. Witt and Witt go on to support this view by quoting the findings of Martin and Clark that hotel managers make very little use of management techniques which have been successfully used in the manufacturing sector.

The validity of the points made by these authors is accepted. But do they give the full explanation? Surely there are some jobs in the services sector which suffer all the characteristics mentioned above but are not regarded as low in productivity. For example, dentistry is labour-intensive, involves individual processing and is difficult to mechanise or automate. Yet in many societies dentistry is among the best paid of professions. The key to their success is not the number of patients they can process but the value put on the work they do. Why is filling the belly rewarded at a much lower level than filling a tooth? The answer must lie in the availability of many competing means of filling the belly but very few substitutes for filling the tooth.

The technology of many catering enterprises is not far removed from the technology of the home. Therefore, it is comparatively cheap for competitors to enter the catering industry. Hotels in many countries experience competition from bed and breakfast establishments which are also family homes. If the hotel industry is to command a greater reward for its services, it will have to develop its use of technology to give it a greater advantage *vis-à-vis* home-based competitors.

Productivity levels and staff

Many authors have identified aspects of staffing as being a key to productivity improvement. Jones (1990) saw an important role for a productivity committee to involve staff in the process and concluded that, with labour costs being such an important element, it is clear that the potential for improvement may stem largely from the workforce's ability and willingness to decrease their input or increase their output. Witt and Witt (1989) cited the benefits of flexible working in hotels to increase productivity. Merricks and Jones (1986) suggested two approaches to improve labour productivity: firstly by increasing the performance of individual members of staff after work study and related techniques, and secondly by combining staff into teams more efficiently through scheduling. An essential feature of either approach is the need to ensure high levels of staff motivation. Jones and Lockwood (1989) stressed the need for reward systems designed to facilitate and encourage productivity. A climate must be created so that employees of the organisation are made aware that productivity is important. Among the ways this can be achieved they recommend that it be part of the induction process and of on-the-job training programmes. The concept of human engineering (the adaptation of the work environment and facilities to the psychological and physical needs of the worker as it affects productivity) is seen as an important factor in productivity by Keiser (1989).

Productivity and staff training

Perhaps the most important study of hotel productivity was published by Prais et al. (1989). This study was one of a series of studies comparing industries in the UK and Germany. The hotel study found evidence of significant differences in productivity between German and UK hotels. For the British hotels, there was an average of 2.06 guest nights per employee, taking all full-time equivalent persons engaged in the hotel reckoned on the basis of hours worked by each person; in the German sample the average was 4.01 guest nights per person. Thus the German hotels apparently required only about half (51%) of the labour per guest night that the British hotels of the same quality grading did. More detailed studies were carried out on two departments—housekeeping and reception—and in each case the German hotels were found to be more productive by a large margin. The labour requirements in Germany as a percentage of the requirement in Britain was 59% in housekeeping and 63% in reception. Since every effort had been made to compare hotels of similar quality and allowances had been made for differences in approach, the differences in productivity were very much greater than could have been anticipated. Thus the scope for economies in labour usage in UK hotels is considerable. Perhaps as a result of the greater labour productivity, prices of hotel rooms in major towns in Germany were 20% lower than in Britain.

An analysis of the differences in physical capital in German and UK hotels concluded that the German hotels had probably spent more on equipment and refurbishment but the additional investment was small both in relation to the total capital cost of the building and in relation to the considerably more efficient usage of labour in Germany.

There is a major difference in approach to vocational training between the two countries. The authors found that the number of people qualifying for hotel occupations each year was 11 000 in Germany and 5500 in the UK. The difference is mainly at the craft level: 8000 in Germany as against 2000 in the UK. In the hotels they sampled, 35% of German staff had relevant qualifications while only 14% of UK staff were qualified.

An analysis of the syllabuses for housekeeping and reception courses in the two countries concluded that the German courses are significantly broader in scope than in Britain, and that this greater breadth had not required any reduction in depth. The German examination system relies on formal written and oral examinations and a practical examination conducted in a hotel (not the one in which the candidate served his apprenticeship) in front of three examiners who do not know the candidate. These examiners are appointed, respectively, by employers, the education authorities and the relevant trade union.

The German employers were found to be much clearer on the reliability and content of qualifications. The degree of responsibility assumed by housekeepers and receptionists in German hotels was considerably higher than in British hotels, freeing the general manager to spend more time to plan longer-term marketing strategies.

It is difficult to escape the conclusion that the greater investment in people in the German industry results in major benefits in productivity for the hotel industry in that country.

There are hotel groups in the UK which show an admirable commitment to greater productivity. In the course of her research for her dissertation on 'labour productivity in the Irish hotel industry', Juliet Ryan (1993) assessed the approach of the De Vere hotel group. This company has 26 hotels, all classified as three-star or better. In their mission statement, corporate objectives,

hotel objectives and departmental objectives, the emphasis on productivity is clearly to be seen. When staff are recruited it is a condition of their employment that they may be requested to work in departments other than their own. Performance standards are set and included in the contract of employment. Training policies have been adopted to encourage staff to continue their education and gain National Vocational Qualifications. Employee performance is appraised formally once a year (twice a year for management staff). Utilisation of staff is measured on a weekly basis and productivity is assessed every four weeks.

Productivity and design

Some hotel companies have sought greater productivity by improving the design of hotels. Examples of this approach include:

- Kitchens which are placed to service two or more restaurants
- Bar service areas located between the cocktail bar and the lounge bar allowing one staff member to serve both during slack periods
- Hotel reception units which include the hotel telephone unit
- Design of hotel bedrooms and bathrooms to minimise cleaning time

A striking example of the latter has been the design of the Formule One hotels in South Africa which have reduced labour content to a minimum (no restaurant, no bar, moulded plastic bathroom unit, minimalist self-service breakfast provision). Whether such a hotel is ultimately profitable depends on the reaction of the customers—reducing the cost of inputs to a business does not ensure productivity or profitability unless the value of the outputs can be maintained.

Airline catering shows how productive a catering operation can be, measured in terms of output of meals per staff member, per hour. Great thought and planning have gone into the design of equipment and choice of menu items to ensure the speed of service and standardisation of quality. The limited time available on many air routes—effectively no more than half an hour between London and Dublin to serve a four-course meal and choice of beverage—pushes the airline caterers into careful planning of every aspect of the operation.

Hoteliers may protest that their style of catering bears little resemblance to airline catering. But good design of equipment, minimisation of storage requirements, matching or cooking requirements of menu items and equipment, reduction of choice—all features of airline catering—can provide an example for the hotel and catering industry.

UK survey

The National Economic and Development Office published the results of a postal survey of productivity in UK hotels in 1992 (NEDC, 1992). They received 144 responses from hotels, representative of all size categories from under 10 rooms to more than 200 rooms. Thirty-five per cent of the hotels belonged to a larger group, the remaining 65% being independent hotels.

The questionnaire sought to establish the extent to which hoteliers used or did not use various techniques of operational management and productivity measurement. The results of the survey would seem to indicate a fairly low level of usage of many management techniques which have been virtually standard practice in manufacturing industry for very many years.

For example, in regard to estimating labour requirements, hotels were asked about their use of forecasting of business. Table 64.1 gives their responses in respect of both the 'Rooms' division and the 'Food & beverage' division. There is clearly no agreement on the optimum period for forecasting the volume of business to estimate staff requirements. Since most hotel staff are employed on a weekly wage basis, one could see the logic of using such a forecasting period. But it found favour with only just over half the respondents. Of those who responded positively to this question on forecasting, only 45% said they used one or more of the ratios to plan staffing. So what do the other 55% use to estimate their need for staff?

Perhaps the answer lies in the use of detailed productivity measurement after the event. This is not, in theory, a very effective way of estimating staffing requirements but would, at least, be better than no method. So, do UK hotels measure productivity after the event? In response to a question on the use of various ratios to measure productivity, the percentage who answered 'yes' were as set out in Table 64.2.

Table 64.1 *Use of forecasting of business*

	Rooms	Food & beverage
Next day's business	36	33
Few days ahead	41	40
Weekly forecast	58	52
Monthly forecast	55	45
Annual forecast	51	43

All figures are given in percentages.

Table 64.2 *Use of ratios by UK hoteliers*

Ratio	Used by (%)
Value added/no. of employees	8.3
Revenue/wage cost	48
Total cost/wage cost	26
No. of customers/no. of employees	26
Wage cost/no. of employees	13
Gross profit/revenue	33
Wage cost/revenue	46
Bed nights/employees	15
Other ratios	4

Approximately four-fifths of respondents ticked at least one ratio. This would indicate that there is some desire on behalf of hoteliers to measure some aspect of productivity. But productivity in a service organisation is a complex concept and cannot be adequately measured by a single ratio. If the UK hotel industry was seriously concerned about productivity measurement, there would be a far greater use of various ratios.

Performance standards

One way of achieving greater productivity is to set performance standards for as many tasks as possible. These standards seek to define the amount of work expected from a unit of worker's time. For example, one could set a standard of fourteen bedrooms to be cleaned by each house assistant, each day. When UK hoteliers were surveyed on their use of such performance standards, only half made any response. Out of a range of jobs to which performance standards might be applied (chamber maid, receptionist, breakfast waiter/ess, bar staff, cooks, etc.), the only job which attracted a significant response was that of chambermaid.

Flexibility of staff

One way of achieving greater productivity of labour in the hotel industry is to have a labour force which is highly flexible. In this way staff can move from department to department to meet the demands which customers are creating. Typically, different departments have their peak activity at different times of the day and while some of this is predictable—dining room at breakfast time, reception check-out immediately after breakfast—much of it is not always predictable. If a hotel staff has been trained to do many or, ultimately, all jobs with equal skill, then it can respond to shifting demand by moving the staff to meet that demand.

Hoteliers were asked what steps they had taken to ensure that staff could be moved from one job to another.

Table 64.3 *Steps to ensure staff flexibility*

None	9%
Recruit flexible staff	60%
Train to extend skill range	62%
Switch them when necessary and hope they can cope	9%

Their responses are shown in Table 64.3. There are degrees of flexibility. At the lower levels one can train each staff member to do one other job; at a slightly higher level one can train each staff member to do two other jobs and so on until, at the highest level of flexibility, every staff member can do every job in the hotel. In the UK survey most hoteliers who claimed their staff had some flexibility were making the claim at the lowest level, i.e. they claimed that there was one category of staff which could successfully undertake duties in a different department.

There is further evidence to suggest that hotel staff are not very flexible. When managers were asked how they coped with the need to increase labour supply at very short notice, their response indicated a range of activities—but moving staff from another department was not among the most popular. Table 64.4 shows that the first preference of managers in dealing with the shortages in the 'Rooms' division is to re-arrange rotas, with employment of casuals and paying overtime as the second and third choices. The responses in regard to the 'Food & beverage' division are the same as regards the first and second choices but in third place was the option of the manager standing in. Transfer of staff from other departments came sixth for the 'Rooms' division and even lower for the 'Food & beverage' division.

Apart from commenting on the small part that transfer of staff from other departments plays, one may also comment on the extent to which managers or heads of departments may stand in, to make up for the shortage

Table 64.4 *How to increase labour supply at very short notice—first choices of respondents*

	Rooms division	Food & beverage division
Pay overtime	19	12
Offer time off in lieu	14	17
Pay bonus incentive	1	0
Bring in casuals	20	22
Transfer employees from other departments	12	7
Recruit quickly	3	4
Rearrange rota quickly	34	27
Managers stand in	15	18
Heads of departments stand in	10	10

Table 64.5 *Use of operational management techniques*

	Not familiar	Not used	Occasional	Regular
Method study	19%	34%	16%	6%
Work study	13%	39%	18%	6%
Work measurement	13%	37%	15%	13%

of labour. Since neither managers nor heads of departments are paid overtime, this may appear to be an inexpensive solution. However, the diversion of senior staff from their duties can have a very dramatic impact on the long-term viability and success of the hotel.

Use of operational management techniques

The NEDO survey sought to establish the extent to which hoteliers used, or did not use, operational management techniques which are commonplace in the manufacturing industry sector. The results (see Table 64.5) indicate that very few hotels make use of method study, work study or work measurement techniques. These results indicate a very low level of usage of techniques which have the potential to raise labour productivity levels in the hotel industry. Similar results were found by Martin and Clark (quoted by Witt and Witt) when they reported that 76% of UK hoteliers seldom or never used a range of operation management techniques.

Quality management in hotels

One reason advanced as to why hotels do not use quantification techniques to improve productivity is that there must be a strong emphasis on quality in hotels, especially four- and five-star hotels. With some justification it is claimed that steps to increase productivity will often lead to a decrease in the quality of the service being offered. For example, one may increase productivity by requiring each waiter to serve twenty rather than fifteen customers during each lunchtime shift. But there may well be a decrease in the quality of service experienced by customers when the waiter is under greater pressure.

So, to what extent do hoteliers emphasise quality in their staff training and use quality management techniques in their hotels? The results of the UK survey, shown in Table 64.6, would suggest that very little attention is paid to formal techniques of quality management in hotels.

What are the opinions of UK hoteliers in regard to the factors which may contribute to higher productivity

Table 64.6 *Use of quality management techniques*

	Not familiar	Not used	Occasional	Regular
BS 5750	33%	40%	8%	1%
Total quality management	35%	40%	3%	4%
Quality circles	33%	38%	4%	8%

in the hotel industry? When asked to state their agreement or disagreement with some statements, they showed strong agreement with the following two statements:

- That productivity would be higher if employees were better trained
- That high labour turnover in UK hotels results in lower job efficiency

Interestingly, most hoteliers did not feel that labour turnover in their own hotel was high but obviously felt that high labour turnover is damaging efficiency in the industry in general. A survey of four major London hotels by Denvir and McMahon (1992) found labour turnover rates in the range of 58% to 112%, which is well above rates generally found in the manufacturing sector.

How do management practices in Ireland compare with practices in the UK, in regard to productivity management? This was one of the questions which Juliet Ryan, a postgraduate student at the Dublin Institute of Technology, Cathal Brugha Street, set out to establish, working under the supervision of this author. Questions which had been asked of UK hotels were included in a questionnaire to Irish hotels in the period November 1992 to March 1993. Comparisons may be made in respect of four areas:

- Extent to which hoteliers use forecasting to assess the need for staff
- Extent to which ratios are used to measure productivity
- Techniques used to adjust the labour supply to meet a short-term peak in demand
- Extent to which performance standards have been set for various job categories

Use of forecasting to plan staffing

The majority of hotels in Ireland and the UK use forecasting of business to assist in the planning of staff needs. Weekly forecasts are the most popular period in both countries and for both room sales and food and beverage sales. But this tendency to prefer weekly forecasts rather than monthly or other periods is very much stronger in Ireland than in the UK, as Table 64.7 shows.

Table 64.7 *Use of weekly forecasting in UK and Ireland*

	UK hotels	Irish hotels
Rooms division	58%	73%
Food & beverage	52%	79%

Table 64.8 *Use of ratios to measure productivity*

Ratio	Use in UK	Use in Ireland
Revenue/wage cost	48%	69%
Total cost/wage cost	26%	59%
No. of customers/no. of employees	26%	36%
Wage cost/no. of employees	13%	40%
Gross profit/revenue	33%	70%
Net profit/revenue	33%	67%
Wage cost/revenue	46%	49%
Bed-nights/employee	15%	31%
Value added/no. of employees	8%	9%

Use of ratios

Both surveys asked hotels to indicate whether they used certain ratios to measure productivity. The responses (see Table 64.8) have indicated that Irish hotels make much greater use of ratios than their UK counterparts. No one measure enjoys universal popularity but ratios which are revenue-based are relatively more popular—in each country the three most popular ratios involve revenue compared with something else.

Adjusting labour supply to meet demand

What hotel managers say about how they adjust their labour supply to meet a short-term demand is also of interest. The two surveys asked managers to rank in order of preference the options used in their hotel to increase labour supply at very short notice. Since their actions may vary as between different divisions, they were asked to answer in respect of 'Rooms' division and 'Food & beverage' division separately. Table 64.9 sets out the three most popular options in respect of 'Rooms' division for UK and for Ireland.

Table 64.9 *Increasing short-term labour supply for the 'Rooms' division*

	UK	Ireland
Rearrange rota quickly	27%	16%
Bring in casuals	16%	40%
Pay overtime	15%	
Offer time off in lieu of overtime	—	30%

As noted earlier in respect of the UK, the response of using staff from other departments (labour flexibility) did not find great favour with Irish hoteliers.

Use of performance standards

In both the UK and Ireland just over half the hotels surveyed indicated that they made some use of performance standards. By far the most frequent use of such standards was in respect of chambermaid work. The UK survey indicated that the next most popular area for use of performance standards was in respect of food service personnel. All other categories of work scored less than 20%.

The Irish survey found that large hotels made greater use of performance standards than medium or small hotels and that five-star and four-star hotels were more likely to use them than lower-graded hotels.

Conclusions

Productivity in the hotel industry is generally regarded as low compared with manufacturing industry and the gap is not closing. As a result, wages and other conditions of employment in the hotel industry are unfavourable, compared with other industries.

The hotel industry in Ireland and the UK makes comparatively little use of operations management techniques, such as work study techniques, to improve productivity.

The approach of the German hotel industry and education system in putting emphasis on the training of hotel staff to predetermined standards has borne fruit in that German hotels can achieve the same quality standards as UK hotels with substantially less labour.

Hotel companies which wish to break out of the 'low productivity, low wages' trap need to initiate a different approach at many levels. At the highest organisational level, this will involve re-stating their mission, their objectives and departmental objectives. At lower levels it will involve the introduction of performance standards, productivity measurement and control, and a revised staffing policy in respect of recruitment, training, flexibility and reward system.

A model for productivity improvement

Whilst there is no general agreement on a framework model for productivity improvement, the experiences quoted above have suggested measures which can contribute to the process. The following ten steps could be combined and adopted to suit a particular hotel enterprise.

1. Identify the key tasks which determine the success or failure of the enterprise.
2. Use operational management techniques, including work study, to improve the efficiency with which those tasks are completed.
3. Develop performance standards for those key tasks.
4. Implement a staffing policy which treats people as the principal resource to ensure productivity, and which would seek to retain the best staff, train them to do their jobs in the defined way and train them to be flexible to undertake other tasks when necessary.
5. Communicate to all staff the importance of the key tasks and their performance standards.
6. Implement a system of monitoring and control for the key tasks based on measurement criteria which have been agreed with the staff concerned.
7. Design a reward system which encourages productivity for individuals and for groups.
8. Harness the benefits which technology can bring, especially information technology. These benefits can include fewer staff, better matching of the supply of staff and demands for staff, and better information on the costs and benefits of various hotel activities.
9. Implement a Quality Management Programme.
10. Initiate an on-going research programme and an ethos which constantly seeks improvement in all aspects of the business.

Hotel companies which successfully adopt this approach will accrue benefits in terms of increased profitability and will be in a position to improve the pay levels and other conditions of employment of their workers. Such a dual benefit is surely worthy of the best efforts of all concerned.

References

Ball, S. and Johnson, K. (1989) 'Productivity management within fast food chains—a case study of Wimpy International', *International Journal of Hospitality Management*, 8(4): 265–269.

Ball, S., Johnson, K. and Slattery, P. (1986) 'Labour productivity in hotels: an empirical analysis', *International Journal of Hospitality Management*, 5(3): 141–147.

Blois, K. (1984) 'Productivity and effectiveness in service firms', *Service Industries Journal*, November: 49–59.

Blumberg, D. (1991) 'Improving productivity in service operations on an international basis', *National Productivity Review*, Spring: 167–179.

Boella, M. (1992) *Human Resource Management in the Hospitality Industry*, 5th edn, Stanley Thornes, London.

Denvir, A. and McMahon, F. (1992) 'Labour turnover in London hotels', *International Journal of Hospitality Management*, 11(2): 143–154.

Guerrier, Y. and Lockwood, A. J. (1988) 'Work flexibility in hotels', *Proceedings of the Annual International Conference of the Operations Management Association*, University of Warwick, January, pp. 160–175.

Heizer, J. and Render, B. (1988) *Production and Operations Management*, Allyn & Bacon, Boston, MA.

Horwath and Horwath International (1988) 'Worldwide hotel industry', London.

Jones, P. (1990) 'Managing food service productivity in the long term: strategy structure and performance', *International Journal of Hospitality Management*, 9(2): 143–154.

Jones, P. and Lockwood, A. (1989) *The Management of Hotel Operations*, Cassell, London, p. 141.

Keiser, J. R. (1989) *Principles and Practices of Management in the Hospitality Industry*, 2nd edn, Van Nostrand Reinhold, New York, pp. 207–211.

Medlik, S. (1989) 'Profit from productivity in tourism', *Tourism*, 61: 14–15.

Merricks, P. and Jones, P. (1986) *The Management of Catering Operations*, Holt, Reinhart & Winston, London, pp. 127–128.

NEDC (1992) 'Costs and manpower productivity in UK hotels', NEDC, London.

Prais, S. J., Jarvis, V. and Wagner, K. (1989) 'Productivity and vocational skills in services in Britain and Germany: hotels', *National Institute Economic Review*, November: 52–74.

Ryan, J. (1993) 'An evaluation of labour productivity in the Irish hotel industry', unpublished dissertation, Dublin Institute of Technology.

Shiffler, R. E. and Coye, R. W. (1988) 'Monitoring employee performance in service operations', *International Journal of Operations and Production Management*, 8(2): 5–13.

Simpson Xavier Howarth (1992) 'Irish hotel industry review', Dublin.

Teare, R. (1989) 'The hospitality industry in the 1990s; some critical developments', *Marketing Intelligence and Planning (UK)*, 7(9,10): 48–49.

Witt, C. A. and Witt, S. F. (1989) 'Why productivity in the hotel sector is low', *International Journal of Contemporary Hospitality Management*, 1(2): 28–33.

Worland, D. and Wilson, K. (1988) 'Employment and labour costs in the hospitality industry: evidence from Victoria, Australia', *International Journal of Hospitality Management*, 7(4): 363–377.

65 'Ways' of the world: managing culture in international hotel chains

C. JONES, D. NICKSON AND G. TAYLOR

Introduction

Until recently the international hotel industry has been dominated by American hotel chains (Littlejohn and Roper, 1991), enjoying high, stable growth with little real competition in this market (Barge, 1993). By the 1970s the emphasis was on the development of a standardised product which could effectively be exported outside the country of origin (Teare, 1991:56). The Americans also provided an influential 'best practice' model for hotel management, emphasising efficiency and management systems as mechanisms to ensure consistency of experience for guests (Barge, 1993; Guerrier, 1993).

The 1980s saw a 'significant growth in the international nature of the hotel industry' (Littlejohn and Roper, 1991:200), with newer, non-American arrivals on the scene (Barge, 1993). As a consequence the American influence is in decline (Littlejohn and Roper, 1991:201). In the face of growing competition and increasingly saturated markets it has become clear that standardisation and efficiency alone are considered to be insufficient to ensure survival. Barge (1993) concludes, 'The management *systems* which were so successful in providing consistency of experience and efficiency all over the world have contributed as much as they will be able'. He goes on to ask, 'What management *philosophy* will be necessary to succeed into the next century?' (emphasis added). The almost imperceptible way in which the debate has shifted from *systems* to *philosophy* is, we will seek to demonstrate, significant since it reflects the increasing importance of the rhetoric of 'corporate culturism' (Wilmott, 1993) embedded within models of human resource management.

We have noted above how the American dominance of the international hotel industry was premised upon high levels of standardisation and efficiency as essential ingredients for success. More recently the corporate culture literature, fuelled by an interest in the so-called 'excellent companies' (Peters and Waterman, 1982), has shifted attention from the quantifiable hard 'S's of systems and strategy to the more intangible soft 'S's of style and shared values (Thompson and McHugh, 1990:22). This emphasises communication, openness,

autonomy, flexibility, commitment, motivation and trust, circulated via the rhetoric of human resource management as a welcome departure from more traditional, bureaucratic approaches (Armstrong, 1993; Storey, 1992a). A significant part of this process has been to focus attention upon making the most effective use of culture, both organisationally, nationally and locally, to enhance corporate profitability. Culture is portrayed as the glue that binds hitherto diverse groupings within organisations into 'families' (Barham and Rassam, 1989). Viewed from this unitarist perspective, senior managers are perceived to have an important role to play in creating, promoting and sustaining the corporate culture across the organisation (Legge, 1989). In decentralised internationally based corporations, corporate culture is seen as a device not merely through which to integrate employees into the organisation, but via which to produce cohesion and consistency (at management level at least) across structures which are dispersed geographically. Indeed, the creation of a global corporate culture is seen by some as an essential element of a 'globalisation agenda' (Rhinesmith, 1991:43).

Much of the corporate culture literature directed at practitioners tends to take an unproblematic view of the notion of corporate culture (Van Meek, 1992). In particular it fails to recognise the possibilities of different, clashing or competing cultures both within organisations and external to them. Where this is highlighted it tends to be in relation to companies becoming international, in that a dimension to this process is the question of how to transport a corporate culture across national boundaries. Of particular concern to companies are the difficulties which large decentralised organisations might face when corporate cultures, removed from the specific national contexts in which they were developed, fail to mesh with local or ethnic culture of the host country (Hofstede, 1980)—or alternatively of corporate headquarters losing control when local managers identify too strongly with local needs at the expense of corporate objectives (Korbin (1988) cited in Scullion (1992)). In this context the training and development of managers who can act in the role of 'culture brokers' achieves a new significance as large organisations are faced with choices about from where to draw their managerial staff.

The aim of this paper is to explore the way in which two of the newer players on the international hotel scene—a Swedish-based group which we have called Swedco hotels and a French-based group which we have called Frenco—utilise the corporate culture motif. The focus of the paper is upon hotel managers (both general managers and functionally specific managers such as Front-of-House, Food and Beverage, Personnel and Training), and their perceptions of the management philosophy and style of the companies for whom they work. We will explore the extent to which the two companies draw upon the national culture in which they originated and, if so, whether this facilitates or impedes the cohesion they seek to develop. The paper will also discuss the degree to which expatriate managers, albeit unwittingly, act as carriers of the parent country culture. Finally we will explore the extent to which it is possible to identify the beginnings of a standardised 'best practice' approach to management in international hotels centred around the ideas of human resource management.

Corporate culture, culture brokers and internationalisation

The truly transnational corporation is held to be a company 'with the ability to manage across national boundaries, retaining local flexibility while achieving global integration' (Scullion, 1992:68). Bartlett and Ghoshal (1989) (cited in Storey (1992b)) note that 'the transnational is not a specific strategic posture or particular organisational form. In essence, the transnational is a new management mentality'. Here Bartlett and Ghoshal are indicating that in their view it is the way in which companies utilise and develop their managerial expertise in order to achieve a global perspective that distinguishes an international from a multinational organisation (see also Barham and Rassam, 1989). Much of the literature regarding internationalisation is less optimistic than Bartlett and Ghoshal appear to be about the possibility of organisational solutions to the problems of management and work organisation transcending national boundaries.

In the literature on convergence and divergence, national and local cultures are held to be powerful forces halting any trend towards globalisation (see Rose (1985) for a review of this debate). Drawing upon the idea of layers of culture (national, industry, occupational, corporate, organisational, managerial, work group), Pizam (1993:206, 222–223) concludes that while culture has little impact upon the physical product (the international

hotel room, menu, management and operational systems), the national and ethnic dimensions of individual behaviour will make the transfer of management style, communication, motivational tools, etc., more problematic—a point of departure from the assumptions which underpin the excellence literature. Thus, to follow Pizam's line of thought, we might expect standardisation in international hotels to end with the hardware. This view accords with that of Hofstede (1980, 1990), namely, that the nationally specific nature of management education and training will limit the ability of organisations to develop a standardised style or philosophy of management even at a corporate level and thus '[t]he convergence of management will never come' (1990:405). We will return to this theme in considering our case study evidence. First it is necessary to consider the approaches to managing across national boundaries which companies have in practice been identified as taking.

Early accounts of corporate culture have tended to portray the phenomenon as both imperialist and protectionist; multinational corporations carrying forward company values and expectations and devising strategies to ensure that these were not contaminated by outside influences. In this 'ethnocentric' approach, parent country nationals occupy positions as expatriate managers. Their 'expertise' is in the area of the corporate culture and other cultures appear to be regarded as both alien and suspect.

More recently writers have suggested a variety of approaches which might be more responsive to inputs from local or national cultures encountered outside the country of origin. For example, Watson and Littlejohn (1992) amongst others, have identified 'polycentric' and 'geocentric' approaches as developments upon this theme. In the 'polycentric' approach decentralisation allows for greater sensitivity to local environments, mediated by host country managers. Here managers are primarily regarded as 'experts' in the local culture, although they are thoroughly socialised into corporate culture norms as well. In the 'geocentric' approach, which is suggested to be the most developed model, the organisation is truly global, with the best people (irrespective of nationality) being developed as managers, and the perspective taken is of the organisation as a global entity. General managers are valued for their ability to interpret local environments in the more uncertain, more changeable and more complex context of the international corporation (Duenas, 1993:11). Being responsive and reflective is regarded as significant to the continued success and health of the company. The most developed form, according to Duenas (1993:13) is the organisation that is willing to listen, learn and utilise cultural difference to its advantage. Organisations become 'cultural melting pots' (Schneider, cited in Kidger (1991:153)) and in this final form corporate culture is portrayed as permeable but strong enough to withstand and accommodate cultural difference.

In both multinational and transnational companies 'cultural expertise' is firmly identified with manageral staff. In some cases this expertise is located in internationally mobile, often expatriate, managers (Van Maanen and Laurent, 1993:282–283; Forster, 1992). In more developed forms there is less emphasis on moving manageral staff than in ensuring that all managers are equipped to operate from a global perspective. The emphasis in all cases appears to be on management style as a carrier, and to some extent mediator, of the corporate philosophy—managers, as we suggested earlier, acting in the role of culture brokers, translating and interpreting between parent national, corporate and host or local cultures.

Although companies may articulate a particular approach to the role of managers as 'culture brokers' we know less of how this operates in practice, nor of the way managers view, understand and experience the process or are prepared for it. Drawing upon case study evidence we will now go on to consider the reality of the cultural milieu inside the international hotel chains which we visited and the extent to which managers are equipped to act as culture experts.

The international hotel industry: case study evidence

Swedco

The Swedco Hotels Group, now part of a conglomerate which has interests in forestry and engineering as well as hotels and restaurants, was formed in 1983. Swedco has recently undertaken a phase of rapid expansion that has taken it beyond its traditional Scandinavian base and into nine European countries. The company operates two brands; the three-star hotels 'originally conceived for the Swedish, Volvo-driving, frequent business traveller' (Satchwell, 1991), are found mainly in Sweden; and the four-star Swedco Star hotels (the company's export product), with their extensive conference and leisure facilities, which are located in the central areas of major cities. The first Swedco Star outside Scandinavia was opened in Germany in 1986 and has recently become the centre for Swedco Europe, part of a programme of re-organisation which reflects a shifting of corporate interest to take account of European integration.

In the United Kingdom the first Swedco Star was opened in 1988 in central London. The company now have three sites in the London area, and one in Edinburgh. The in-house magazine for Swedco employees (December 1991) describes the three important cornerstones of the Swedco business concept as 'philosophy, pricing and the Scandinavian/Swedish profile'. The core philosophy of the Swedco Hotel Group is 'doing things the Swedco Way', a way that encompasses the physical product (design, decor, etc.) as well as elements of presentation, service and style. The Swedco concept is described by managers in terms of hardware and software components. The former are concerned with the physical product, and the latter with the human resources and with the need to create 'well trained and service minded people' (Manager, Austria).

Duenas (1993) argues that companies that attempt to build a strong corporate culture do so 'by attending the basic human needs' that 'transcend any national cultural differences'. A British personnel manager described Swedco as having 'more than a corporate identity' and suggested that 'the Swedco Way is being part of the Swedco family'. This apparent paternalism is echoed by a general manager who felt it involved 'taking an holistic view of family, home/private affairs of the people. We try to look after our staff in every aspect we can do'. The Swedco aim is 'to be the most sought after employer' and they appear to treat staff, especially management staff, better than is the average for the industry (Maxwell, 1992:7). Although Maxwell (1992:7) suggests that this draws upon the 'Swedish family oriented culture', the influence of the Swedish model of industrial relations cannot be ignored. Indeed the Swedco Way booklet which staff receive is basically a staff handbook such as might be found in many British companies with well-developed personnel policies. Interesting to note, trade union representation has not survived Swedco's move into Britain.

To the British staff the open and informal approach at Swedco appears to be something very different from what many have experienced in other hotel chains (particularly national as opposed to international chains). For one British Food and Beverage Manager the experience of working for Swedco was 'like leaving home every morning and going to work in another country'. In another hotel the British Personnel Manager described the difference in working for Swedco as opposed to a UK hotel group as 'amazing, coming to this place is a knock to the system'. It was felt by several managers that the decentralisation and the flatter organisational structure that were perceived to be part of the 'Swedco Way' allowed for greater autonomy and faster decision making. Managers were committed to the ideas of team working and of allowing staff to demonstrate initiative—particularly in dealing with issues affecting the customer. One British

Sales Coordinator noted 'They do like you to use your initiative which is something I have not found much at all in other hotels'. A Front-of-House Manager commented, 'They let you make mistakes as long as they don't recur'.

Swedco operate a management training centre (the Swedco Business School) at their corporate headquarters in Stockholm where 'our non-Nordic colleagues' receive the appropriate cultural training. Its purpose is the 'describe Sweden, Swedishness, Swedish service philosophy and service management' (Annual Report, 1990). Interestingly, unlike IKEA where managers are believed to need to understand Swedish to appreciate fully the culture of the country and the company (Duenas, 1993), the company language of Swedco is English. A number of managers were convinced by the Swedishness of the management style, as they were by the Swedishness of the hotels' internal fabric: 'The structure of the building is very open, light and refreshing—it reflects the style of management' (Food and Beverage Manager, British), or 'Swedishness is something staff pick up' (Quality and Training Manager, British). Views as to the degree of authenticity of the Scandinavian atmosphere range from the belief that 'the actual hotel is very Scandinavian' (Personnel Manager, British) to 'there is nothing typically Swedish about the hotel, it is an international hotel with a Swedish touch'. Others echoed this last view, arguing that the corporate message, 'was nothing unique, nothing that Sheraton aren't doing or Hyatt or anybody else'. Another respondent commented, 'If people have been through other courses with other hotels, it does become a case of teaching your grandmother how to suck eggs'. There is thus some evidence to suggest that the management philosophy and style integral to the corporate culture initiatives being developed by newer players such as Swedco draws upon an approach established by the American chains. They also continue to rely heavily upon the business and financial systems developed by the Americans.

Swedco hotels operate as profit centres and in attempting to control their business operations Swedco employ established international systems. Manuals have been produced to cover operational aspects of front-of-house, restaurants and conference facilities (a key area for Swedco). 'The concept manuals will tell you how rooms should be laid up, what should be in the bedroom and all that sort of stuff' (Assistant General Manager, British). There is regular contact (often weekly) between the hotel units and corporate headquarters in Sweden, and this facilitates information gathering. Swedco managers appear to be business and marketing managers first and hoteliers second (*Caterer and Hotelkeeper*, August 1991). They are expected to adopt an open

management style and to be willing to lead by example in taking on any task that needs to be done. Indeed staff are expected to be functionally flexible. 'Costs in housekeeping are cut due to careful planning of structures and furnishings' (*Hotels*, June 1991:59), allowing for greater efficiency in these areas, and contracting out housekeeping and portering also achieves cost savings.

While the influence of American management systems and standardisation around the key elements of the international hotel room continue to be apparent, Swedco do attempt to go beyond this and add a Swedish feel to the product itself. In Edinburgh a Danish designer helped to create a Scandinavian atmosphere in the hotel. Managers see 'the Swedco Way' reflected in the light and spacious rooms, the use of open spaces and the purchase of Scandinavian furniture and fittings (some from IKEA). This attempt to add a Swedish element to an otherwise standardised product is also reflected in the inclusion of the ubiquitous smorgasbord as a key part of the menu. A Swedish General Manager felt that among the Swedish elements in the hotel it was the smorgasbord that 'makes us stand out a bit' and that helped to provide 'an edge' in a highly competitive market. This certainly seems to be successful in the case of the Austrian operation we visited where non-residents book up to three weeks in advance to dine at the hotel on a Sunday. However, it should be noted that 'our smorgasbord is the easiest thing for us to prepare . . . ', it represents 'the best of both worlds—a very good product and very little input'. Although many managers felt that it was important that 'we always try to keep at least one Scandinavian in the kitchen' to add authenticity to the menu, the fact remains that smorgasbord is a cold buffet and customers serve themselves.

Swedco are operating in a sphere of economic activity whose very nature, it could be argued, is a function of the instantaneous consumption of the hospitality product (Sparks and Callan, 1992). The majority of international hotel users are experienced travellers who value both standardisation and stability (Barham and Rassam, 1989:180). With regard to these 'accidental tourists' repeat business is generated from certainty. The Swedco managers we interviewed have considerable experience of the international market. It is important, however, to understand the role of Swedishness in differentiating the Swedco product from that of other international hotels and to set this in the context of corporate culture on the one hand and operational pragmatism on the other.

The majority of the general managers (with the exception of one Englishman) are, as we have noted, Scandinavian or (for example) 'completely Swedenised Germans who have all worked in Sweden for ten years'

(Swedish General Manager). Functional managers, on the other hand, tended to be host country nationals. The importance of Scandinavian general managers in the process of acculturation cannot be overstated. It is no coincidence that employees appear to be much more convinced by the Swedco Way in hotels where the general manager is Scandinavian. From a corporate perspective such general managers act as culture brokers translating Swedishness into the common language of international hotels. They take 'the management style' and mix it with the accepted wisdom of the hotel milieu. It was suggested that 'as long as you put the Swedco concept into your unit there is little interference from head office' (General Manager).

If it is true that international managers need to understand 'how their own culture affects their own style' (Barham and Rassam, 1989), it is interesting to consider this fact in light of comments made by Scandinavian (non-Swedish) managers working in the UK. A general manager described a time when there were 'a lot of Swedish managers in the hotel. They all used to speak Swedish, nobody could understand them'. Such overt Swedishness, it was suggested, 'had a negative effect'. Another general manager was convinced that it was wrong to be 'overdoing the Swedish feel so that it offends the local market. There should be just enough that the local market gets a little tempted by it'. These comments suggest that national culture needs to be drawn upon sparingly if staff and customers are not to be alienated by it.

The words Scandinavian, Swedish and even Nordic appear to be used interchangeably in literature produced by Swedco. Studies of the nature of national cultures (Hofstede, 1980) have claimed to identify a 'Nordic' group that includes both Sweden and Denmark, but a Danish General Manager of one of Swedco's UK hotels argued that the two countries have significant cultural differences. In Denmark he felt a 'Swedish image would be negative'. When asked whether the company image was Swedish or Scandinavian or a mixture of both he commented, 'I don't know to be honest but we talk about Swedish', adding that in his view Swedco 'would have a bigger market if we said we were Scandinavian'. One Swedish General Manager talked of the Swedco Star concept as being more Scandinavianised because of the company's export product it had to represent Swedishness in a variety of European settings. Another General Manager added, 'it is important for the image to have a strong Scandinavian influence in the units'. This degree of cultural ambiguity highlights at least one of the difficulties of demonstrating the relationship between corporate culture and competitive advantage.

At Swedco the corporate culture is premised on an ethnocentric approach. It is utilised both as a unifying device in terms of some aspects of the hardware (rooms, layout, menu) and software (management style, customer service) and simultaneously as a device used to endow these standardised features with an element that was distinctly Swedco, thus, in theory at least, providing the purchaser with the opportunity to enjoy palatable bites of Swedishness without jeopardising the standards expected in international four-star hotels. The evidence highlights the complex and dynamic relationship between layers of culture and the challenge which this can present to companies like Swedco in balancing any positive benefits to be gained from integrating elements of Sweden or Scandinavia into the product against the potentially negative effects that concentrations of Swedish managerial staff can have upon non-Swedish managers.

We will now consider the case of Frenco to determine the extent to which their approach mirrors or is different from that taken by Swedco.

Frenco

The emergence of new players on the international hotel scene is perhaps best illustrated by the rapid expansion of the French-owned, hospitality-oriented, Frenco group. In the space of twenty-five years the company has grown from a single hotel in France to the biggest hotel group in the world. Frenco now operates 'over 2000 hotels on all continents and is present in all segments of the market' (Frenco Company Report, 1993). Such a rapid expansion has a number of consequences, not least the shift in emphasis from being a French company to being a global organisation. A corollary is an attempt to engender a truly international outlook in the company, which has obvious implications in terms of the mix of corporate and national cultures. Before considering this in detail, it is necessary to outline the Frenco corporate philosophy.

The most specific articulation of the Frenco philosophy and the values and principles upon which it is based is contained in the 'little blue book' on *Frenco Ethics and Management*. The Frenco philosophy is explicitly influenced by the 'excellence literature' and current human resource management thinking which suggests the organisation's most valued assets are its people (Barham and Rassam, 1989:183). This influence is further reflected in the 'values' such as quality, profit, growth, innovation, training, participation, decentralisation and communication which are held to symbolise the Frenco philosophy. The notion of decentralisation finds expression in the ideas of autonomy, openness and responsibility which are held to characterise the Frenco management style and in the Frenco concept of 'intrapreneur' or in-house entrepreneur (Barham and Rassam, 1989:179) in which managers are expected to identify improvements themselves. Employees are encouraged to take responsibility for decisions (*Caterer and Hotelkeeper*, 19–25 August 1993) within the context of 'le droit d'erruer'—the right to be wrong, with the proviso that people learn from their mistakes in making decisions.

Virtually all the managers to whom we spoke (both British and French) affirmed this approach was the norm within Frenco. On the question of openness, all the managers argued that it was something which was inherent within the company. This is evident in open structures like the 'open table': 'where I have eighteen people [employees] around the table, with no management around . . . I have dinner with them for four hours, and explain to them about the company for half an hour, and for three and a half hours they ask questions. . . . It's very open' (Managing Director). General managers run similar systems within individual units and the company also practise an open-door policy: 'My door is always open, you are first to close it'. The influence of human resource management thinking is thus very strong in Frenco and it is also possible to see here many similarities with the corporate philosophy and style of Swedco.

The Frenco management style appears to be standardised across the company. The transfer of managers between brands could be said to facilitate the spread of the Frenco culture as a unifying mechanism across the organisation. Frenco also appear to be recognising the difference between utilising international managers (expatriates moved around the company) and developing, at company level at least, a form of international management (an attempt to manage the company globally) (Bartlett and Ghoshal, 1992; Thompson et al., 1993; Barham and Rassam, 1989:147–167). This is illustrated by an 'ideal' Frenco career path of an individual who can communicate in at least two languages, who has worked in at least two different brands, and has experience of two professional areas, with the intention of creating a truly rounded 'international manager' who sees the company from a global perspective.

As Barham and Rassam (1989:162) note, 'there is no point trying to develop international managers if the organisation's culture remains ethnocentric'. Any attempt to chart the growth and internationalisation of Frenco and the cultural implications for the company of such a process, must recognise the centrality of the role played by the company's training centre near Paris, established in 1985 in response to the rapid expansion of the Group.

Frenco have recognised that this is the 'cornerstone of our corporate culture' (quoted in Barham and Rassam (1989:182)). It has evolved into a 'corporate university of service' concerned with training managers, both at a technical level and, in a less tangible sense, in the culture and philosophy of the company.

The intention of the training centre is to generate some degree of learning, interaction and networking by bringing together managers from the whole Group. It is described in a Frenco training centre document as 'the melting pot, showcase and broadcaster of the Frenco culture' and as 'the international crossroads for communication, exchange and the sharing of experience . . . a forum for ideas, debate and conferences, where management trends are discussed'. The rationale behind this echoes the need to equip managers to act effectively in a culture broker role: 'we have a lot of people that want to broaden and enlarge what they do and they don't know how to behave with other people. If you take people from here to Moscow or to Sweden try to imagine how people behave from here to China' (interview with MD Hospitality Studies and Training). This is achieved through mechanisms such as team-building games, for example, the 'Planet Frenco' which encourages participants to understand and participate in the corporate culture, and through the showpiece Summer University, which brings together senior managers to generate ideas for future strategy (Training Centre Document).

Frenco managers were enthusiastic about attending the training centre, and appeared to enjoy the opportunity to meet people from other countries. A UK Managing Director noted, 'If you recruit a new manager and let him [*sic*] work with us for three or four months in the UK and then you let him go to the [training centre] for a management course, he is completely changed'. However, it is not simply the course, 'the course is no different from so many. I think in the course he learns something technically, but he also learns the philosophy and that is very important'. Within Frenco line managers are responsible for training their own staff and attend 'Training the Trainer' courses to equip them for this task (Barham and Rassam, 1989:182). In such a process, it was suggested, the managers 'change for the world' (Managing Director) and pass the corporate philosophy down the chain.

Prima facie then, Frenco appear to be able to transfer an internationally acceptable corporate culture across national boundaries, as it attempts to become a genuinely geocentric company. The Frenco culture, described as a 'mariage en famille' (Barham and Rassam, 1989:91), is held to 'expresses the common objectives and spirit of togetherness which creates a Group unified in spite of its diversity and its originalities' (*Frenco Ethnics and Management* booklet). A Frenco executive is reported as saying (Barham and Rassam, 1989:44), 'We do have a Frenco way of doing things, in finance, in marketing and in our philosophy of management. But this must be adapted to the local culture. . . . We are not imperialist'. In this recognition of and respect for the complexities of differing cultures it is possible to see Frenco grappling here with becoming the learning organisation which Duenas (1993) describes as being the most developed form of international company. It is clearly Frenco's intention to shift the emphasis away from being a French company operating internationally and towards being an international organisation which happens to be based in France. Thus at company level Frenco do not appear to draw upon corporate culture to spread the idea of 'Frenchness' in the way that the Swedco Way is said to represent Swedishness. In practice 'changing for the world' may not be as straightforward as this would suggest.

Large corporations tend to be somewhat pragmatic in the approach which they take when selecting managers based on an assessment of the reliability and expertise of managers in host countries (Korbin, 1988) (cited in Scullion (1992)). Several of the French general managers who had managed overseas (outside Europe) made the point that in places like Asia-Pacific and the Middle East there always seemed to be a French general manager, because the locals might not understand what Frenco was all about. In the UK there is a 50/50 split between French and English general managers, which senior managers concede is not ideal. For a number of the French managers there have been some problems in terms of utilising a French approach alongside the 'international' Frenco approach. One French manager commented, 'it is difficult because we are trained Europeans, our company is French and on top of that we speak French . . . Frenco has French roots, we live in France'.

The recognition that change would not occur instantly was also articulated by a number of managers in the brands. In the words of one senior French manager, 'I would be hypocritical if I was telling you there wasn't some French to it because Frenco is French. Okay we may be international, or at least we think we are, but we are French'. Thus, although there is a strongly expressed desire at corporate level to move towards an approach to management that stressed the international spread of the organisation and de-emphasised the French origins of the company, the continued reliance on expatriate managers is making this difficult. Another French manager felt that the French style of management was 'very, very honest . . . which can be hard to take', while

another felt that the French may be perceived as 'hot-tempered . . . always making quick decisions and always late'. It was suggested that there might be a tendency by host country managers to be culturally deterministic and to generalise French managers in this way.

Indeed this was something that English managers had picked up on. Typical of this view was the following comment: 'We have got a lot of French general managers here and their whole working style is different from the English culture. They are much more aggressive and forthright and outright and they will say what they think. And sometimes that can be damaging to the English culture'. These statements appear to reflect a possible tension between an espoused corporate management style and a residue of French management training and education which has traditionally been characterised by high levels of formality, hierarchy and centralisation (Torrington and Holden, 1992). The danger for British managers is in being unable to distinguish between the national and corporately specific elements of this and receiving contradictory messages as a result. An example of this can be seen in the reaction to the openness policy. As with Swedco, this openness was well received by British staff: 'There are some methods of management which are French, I think the openness of the company is very French. [. . .]. Whereas, having worked in British companies, to see a general manager you normally have to make an appointment three weeks beforehand and you hardly know their name'. The notion of 'openness' appears to be one so alien to many British managers that they believe it reflects the approach of the nationality owning the hotel in which they work. Thus in Swedco openness is associated with Swedish styles of management, in Frenco with French styles! In fact, evidence suggests the openness would probably be quite novel to French employees and has more to do with the move towards an approach which draws upon models of international human resource management rather than on nationally specific management styles.

Fulfilling corporate objectives while being sensitive to local requirements is therefore a delicate balancing act. This is equally true of balancing the continued need for standardisation and control with giving managers greater autonomy and responsibility. The degree of autonomy which managers have is clearly delineated:

> There are only a few things with us that are rigid, that is the product. The hardware of the bedrooms, that the manager can't touch, the uniforms, the branding, the logo, the headed paper and all that sort of business. And obviously we like to know what is going on and we keep an eye. But it's up to him [*sic*] and if he can do something that is a better system than elsewhere then we will learn from that and use it. (Senior Manager, British)

As with Swedco, Frenco continue to base their operations around established business systems but have overlaid this with current human resource management practices which encourage autonomy and delegated responsibility within a framework of centralised financial and reporting mechanisms.

As part of this process of moving towards being a truly international organisation there is an increased willingness to recruit general managers from outside the industry: 'Well yes, we say now we would recruit a general manager that hadn't any hotel experience. Obviously it would be better if they did but what we would be looking at much more is their people management skills, regardless of the industry, their budget management skills, their control of a business, their profitability' (Senior Manager, British). There is here a reflection of the concerns expressed by Guerrier (1993) about the increasing inability to define a 'corpus of knowledge' that can be defined as central to hotel management, and there appears to be some evidence in both case studies we have considered for a shift towards general hospitality management skills as further standardisation occurs. A French General Manager noted, 'I think tomorrow people don't want to be bothered with choice, that is why [the mid-market brand] is so great, in terms of bedrooms you have no choice. . . . And what I see in the future is a no-choice menu . . . with more friendly service'.

Clearly there had not been a massive change overnight from an ethnocentric to a geocentric approach at Frenco. Such a change is likely to be gradual and evolutionary, and to a large extent may be facilitated by Frenco's presence in all market segments, and of course, via the training centre(s). This discrepancy between the rhetoric of internationalisation and the reality of national specificity was echoed by managers from South America who complained that the training centre was too Eurocentric and who now have a training centre of their own in São Paulo, Brazil. As the strategy progresses it may be that any residual Frenchness is most likely to be found in the company's luxury brand, where it might be used as a source of competitive advantage in the four-star market in a way similar to that identified in Swedco. All the other brands appeal to the customer on the basis of a standardised international product with requisite level of service in which utilising the national identity of the parent company is perhaps of less significance.

Conclusions

Clearly organisations are faced with more choice as to the exact mix of local and expatriate managers which they use. In the two case study companies, both had a continued reliance on expatriate managers, although Frenco were attempting to move away from this. Breaking down the national identity which these managers bring with them is proving more difficult than the rhetoric of corporate culture would suggest. The evidence demonstrates that, however unintentionally, Frenchness and Swedishness have been experienced negatively by other managers.

A further confusion is the extent to which organisations are drawing upon the increasingly standardised rhetoric of human resource management (Storey, 1992a) within the international hotel sector and the confusion of this with nationally specific management styles. Thus managers who had had experience of working in other international hotels recognised this as part of a common language ('nothing that Hyatt or Sheraton are not doing'), while other managers found this more novel and felt it was unique to the company and reflected that particular corporate culture which was in turn drawing upon a national orientation to management and work organisation. As we suggested in the case of Frenchness and openness there was no necessary link. While ethnocentric and geocentric approaches recognise the problems that can be generated by a lack of fit with host country management cultures, these do not take account of the fact that, as emerged from our evidence, parent country managers can bring with them a high level of national cultural identity which can prove to mesh somewhat uneasily with and confuse the corporate message.

In relation to this, where organisations are utilising the services of host country nationals as managers, they need to be aware of the extent to which these might be anyway 'marginal men' (Smith, 1989). That is, rather than bringing to the organisation the local culture, their training as hotel managers (particularly where this is in the international hotel arena) may mean they are more carriers of a standardised 'best practice' and thus in reality increasingly marginalised in terms of the local or national culture in which they are thought to be 'experts'.

The desire to encourage the development of an international perspective to management, as opposed to giving managerial staff international postings, may also be driven as much by pragmatic financial considerations as by a recognition of the benefits accruing from a global perspective. The well-publicised examples of the failure of the expatriate approach, and the increasing reluctance of managers to take postings abroad (Forster, 1992; Scullion, 1992) may be making this too expensive and too risky an option to pursue. It seems likely that, for the foreseeable future at least, large international organisations may resemble 'cultural mosaics' rather than 'cultural melting pots' (Schneider, 1988) (cited in Kidger (1991:153)). In addition, standardisation continues to be an important element of business strategy in international hotels and there is some evidence that developments in international human resource management may in the longer term lead to the emergence of a common philosophy and management style in this sector.

References

Armstrong, Michael (1993) *Human Resource Management: Strategy and Action*, Kogan Page, London.

Barge, Peter (1993) 'International management contracts', in P. Jones and A. Pizam (Eds), *The International Hospitality Industry: Operational Issues*, Pitman, London.

Barham, Kevin and Rassam, Clive (Eds) (1989) *Shaping the Corporate Future—Leading Executives Share Their Vision and Strategies*, Unwin Hyman, London.

Bartlett, Christopher and Ghoshal, Sumantra (1990) 'The Multinational Corporation as an International Network', *Academy of Management Review*, 4.

Bartlett, Christopher and Ghoshal, Sumantra (1989) *Managing Across Borders: The Transnational Solution*, Hutchinson Business Books, London.

Bartlett, Christopher and Ghoshal, Sumantra (1992) 'What is a global manager', *Harvard Business Review*, September–October: 124–132.

Duenas, Guillermo (1993) 'The importance of intercultural learning in the international transfer of managerial and organisational knowledge', Paper presented at 11th EGOS Colloquium, Paris, July.

Forster, Nick (1992) 'International managers and mobile families', Paper presented at Employment Research Unit Annual Conference, Cardiff Business School, University of Wales, September.

Guerrier, Yvonne (1993) 'The development of a "corpus of knowledge" for hotel and catering managers', Paper presented to 11th EGOS Colloquium, Paris, July.

Hofstede, Geert (1980) *Cultural Consequences: International Differences in Work Related Values*, Sage, London.

Hofstede, Geert (1990) 'The cultural relativity of organisational practices and theories', in D. C. Wilson and R. H. Rosenfeld (Eds), *Managing Organisations: Texts, Readings and Cases*, McGraw-Hill, Maidenhead.

Kidger, Peter (1991) 'The emergence of international human resource management', *International Journal of Human Resource Management*, 2(2): 149–163.

Korbin, S. J. (1988) 'Expatriate control and strategic control in American multinationals', *Human Resource Management*, 25: 63–75.

Legge, Karen (1989) 'Human resource management: a critical analysis', in J. Storey (Ed.), *New Perspectives on Human Resource Management*, Routledge, London.

Littlejohn, David and Roper, Angela (1991) 'Changes in international hotel companies' strategies', in Richard Teare and Andrew Boer (Eds), *Strategic Hospitality Management: Theory and Practice*, Cassell, London.

Maxwell, Gill (1992) 'HRM and quality in the UK hospitality industry: where is the strategy?', Paper presented to the 2nd Annual Conference on Human Resource Management in the Hospitality Industry.

Peters, Tom and Waterman, R. H. (1982) *In Search of Excellence: Lessons from America's Best-Run Companies*, Harper & Row, New York.

Pizam, Abraham (1993) 'Managing cross-cultural hospitality enterprises', in Peter Jones and Abraham Pizam (Eds), *The International Hospitality Industry: Operational Issues*, Pitman, London.

Rhinesmith, Steven (1991) 'Going global from the inside out', *Training and Development*, 45: 42–47.

Rose, Michael (1985) 'Universalism, culturalism and the Aix Group: promise and problems of the societal approach to economic institutions', *European Sociological Review*, 1(1): 65–83.

Satchwell, M. S. (1991) 'Scandic's aim: mid market', *Hotels*, June, p. 59.

Schneider, S. (1988) 'National vs corporate culture: implications for human resource management', *Human Resource Management*, 27(2): 231–246.

Scullion, Hugh (1992) 'Strategic recruitment and development of the "international manager": some European considerations', *Human Resource Management Journal*, 3(1): 57–69.

Smith, V. L. (1989) 'Eskimo tourism: micro models and marginal men', in V. L. Smith (Ed.), *Hosts and Guests: The Anthropology of Tourism*, 2nd edn, University of Pennsylvania Press, PA.

Sparks, Beverley and Callan, Victor (1992) 'Communication and the service encounter: the value of convergence', *International Journal of Hospitality Management*, 3(11): 213–224.

Storey, John (1992a) *Developments in the Management of Human Resources*, Blackwell, Oxford.

Storey, John (1992b) 'Making European managers: an overview', *Human Resource Management Journal*, 3(1): 1–11.

Teare, Richard (1991) 'Developing hotels in Europe: some reflections on progress and prospects', *International Journal of Contemporary Hospitality Management*, 3(4): 55–59.

Thompson, Paul and McHugh, Dave (1990) *Work Organisations: a Critical Introduction*, Macmillan, London.

Thompson, Paul, Jones, Carol, Nickson, Dennis, Wallace, Terry and Kewell, Beth (1993) 'Transnationals, globalisation and transfer of knowledge', Paper presented to 11th EGOS Colloquium, Paris, July.

Torrington, David, and Holden, Nigel (1992) 'Human resource management and the international challenge of change', *Personnel Review*, 21(2): 19–30.

Van Maanen, John and Laurent, André (1993) 'Some notes on globalisation and the multinational corporation', in Sumantra Ghoshal and D. Eleanor Westney (Eds), *Organisational Theory and Corporation*, Macmillan, London.

Van Meek, Lynn (1992) 'Organisational culture: origins and weaknesses', in Graeme Salaman, Sheila Cameron, Heather Hamblin, Paul Iles, Christopher Mabey and Kenneth Thompson (Eds), *Human Resource Strategies*, Sage, London.

Watson, Sandra and Littlejohn, David (1992) 'Multi- and transnational firms: the impact of expansion on corporate structures', in Richard Teare and Michael Olsen (Eds), *International Hospitality Management*, Pitman, London.

Wilmott, Hugh (1993) 'Strength is ignorance; slavery is freedom: managing culture in modern organisations', *Journal of Management Studies*, 30(4): 515–552.

Part 6

TOURISM AND THE ENVIRONMENT

Tourism is now one of the world's major industries and all forecasts predict continued expansion. This growth has led to increasing concerns over the impact on destinations, in particular where the attraction is based on fragile and remote environments. The natural environmental resource base, essential for many tourism activities and high on the list of motivations for visiting areas worldwide, has in recent years been given more recognition as developers no longer consider tourism a non-consumptive use of resources (Butler, 1991). Attitudes towards the relationship between tourism and the environment have gradually changed, from (sometimes reluctant) initial recognition of adverse environmental impacts to more recent acceptance of their mutual dependence. The examination of this relationship has now blossomed into an expansive field of study, involving a wide range of academic disciplines, including pure sciences, social sciences and business-related subjects.

However, the debate is confused as the terms 'tourism' and 'environment' remain nebulous, open to a variety of interpretations. This is reflected in the literature on this topic and the high incidence of contradictory evidence. The focus of research has shifted and diversified at a number of levels. Where previously work concentrated on the environmental impact at tourism destinations, the contribution to global environmental change through transport services is now included. Rather than concentrating only on the extremes, such as fragile, 'natural' wilderness areas, or mass concentrations at seaside resorts, the less obvious or spectacular impacts are examined along with associated areas, for example urban and rural man-made environments. The tourism–environment debate has progressed to the extent that the field of study now appears to be forming discrete sub-sections, concentrating on specific sectors or issues.

These emerging specialisms are reflected in the papers presented here from industry responses to public sector policy guidelines, from social and cultural links to environmental conservation designations. Key issues include:

- management of the built heritage—conservation and interpretation;
- exploitation of natural landscapes in National Parks;
- the inclusion of local community and cultural factors in decision-making;
- tourist types or holiday products—mass versus alternative markets with the associated fashionable terminology (green, eco, soft, progressive tourism);
- industry responses—environmental policies, audits, training and public relations;

- public sector policy statements from global (WTO, 1993) to national agency level (ETB, 1991; SNH, 1993), and the value of voluntary codes of conduct, principles and guidelines.

Adding to or, some believe, confusing the debate is the concept of sustainability and sustainable tourism development. Although attractive in its simplicity and widely endorsed, the WCED definition of the term sustainable development is vague and inoperative. Sustainability is characterised by contradictions, paradoxes and conflicts which go far beyond the tourism environment debate (Dovers, 1993). The initial euphoric reception and adoption (at least in guidelines) by both public agencies and industry has been followed by more sceptical critiques and a closer examination of detailed considerations in the implementation of these policies. The *Journal of Sustainable Tourism*, first published in 1993, is a welcome addition which offers a focus for detailed discussion and in-depth analysis of this evolving approach to tourism. It seems clear that what is needed now is research on practical implementation rather than the production of further codes of conduct, principles and public relations exercises.

The papers here reflect some of the variety noted above: from theoretical to pragmatic, from optimistic to alarmist, from platitudes to hard decision-making.

The papers in this section begin with an overview of key environmental concerns, placing the debate in the context of tourism industry growth and in particular the airlines sector (Somerville, British Airways). It provides a succinct, yet detailed account of five specific concerns of the aviation industry, suggesting clear, imaginative yet practical responses to each.

The second paper (Wheeller) presents an individual, irreverent critique of the current state of the debate, which although informal and anecdotal in style is nevertheless important as it presents some of the key issues and reservations on the tourism/environment debate in a readily accessible form.

This broadly theoretical overview is followed by three papers which represent the growing literature on industry responses to environmental matters. Specific methodologies are analysed and the range of company practices reviewed. These include a focus on specific methodologies, such as best practice in environmental auditing (Goodall) which is complemented by the same topic viewed from a different prospective (Brown), and international comparisons where the economic rationale for 'greening the hospitality industry' in North America (Wight) provides some excellent examples to compare with the experience of British firms (Goodall). Some interesting contradictions are apparent, for example the identification of resistance to environmentally friendly policies where Brown finds opposition in upper management and (Wight) points to the corporate level leading the way.

The role of public sector agencies is well exemplified in the case study on Dartmoor, England (Greenwood), which draws together the difficulties of reconciling tourism and conservation policies in a National Park through an innovative multiple agency initiative. The findings from this three-year programme includes some typical examples of the practical difficulties that can be encountered. Some of the findings of this case study have echoes in Wight's lessons from industry (for example, the need for partnership, cooperation, corporate commitment integrating environmental and economic decision-making) which perhaps suggests the need to avoid over subdivision of environmental issues into sectoral categories. The case study on tourism in Sagarmatha National Park, Nepal (Robinson), provides an interesting comparative study to Dartmoor, not only in the exotic geographical sense but also in its emphasis on some key issues relating to fragile environments and cultures and the debate surrounding alternative tourism strategies. The need for local community involvement is emphasised in another contrasting location, Sub-Arctic Norway (Sletvold), who considers sustainable strategies and the concept of consuming cultural landscapes and seascapes. The overlap with cultural and man-made heritage issues, in particular values, interpretation and exploitation is inevitable,

further illustrated in the paper examining tourism and historic buildings management (Berry). This review highlights issues related to tourism and conservation of built heritage, for example ownership, conflicting agency objectives, balancing capacity with cashflows and interpretive policies, all of which are equally relevant to natural environmental attractions.

The range of interrelated but distinct specialisms within the umbrella heading 'tourism and the environment' have only been touched on in this introduction. On the wider debate it seems we are over the identification/recognition stage and have only glimpsed the enormous size of the implementation task ahead.

Hugh Somerville
Rory MacLellan

References

Butler, R. W. (1991) 'Tourism, environment and sustainable development', *Environmental Conservation*, 18(3).

Dovers, S. R. (1993) 'Contradictions in sustainability', *Environmental Conservation*, 20(3).

ETB (English Tourist Board) (1991) 'The green light. A guide to sustainable tourism', ETB, London.

Journal of Sustainable Tourism, Editors: Dr W. Bramwell, Sheffield Hallam University and B. Lane, University of Bristol, Vol. 1, No. 1, July 1993.

SNH (Scottish Natural Heritage) (1993) 'Sustainable development and the natural heritage. The SNH approach', SNH, Edinburgh.

WTO (World Tourism Organisation) (1993) 'Sustainable tourism developments: guide for local planners', WTO, Madrid.

66 Airlines, tourism and environment

H. SOMERVILLE

Objectives

This brief paper is designed to:

(1) Give some background relating British Airways to tourism.
(2) Review the major environmental concerns related to civil aviation.
(3) Outline the response of British Airways and the aviation industry to this environmental challenge.
(4) Speculate on the implications for those involved more directly in tourism.

Environmental responsibility and British Airways

British Airways has an established record of involvement in environmental matters, including many aspects of the airline's engineering operations, recycling of materials such as tyres and waste oils, and the 'Assisting Nature Conservation' programme which has worked with a number of wildlife organisations to contribute to the preservation of threatened species around the world.

The growing importance of the environment as a focus for management was recognised in 1989 by the appointment of David Hyde as Director of Safety, Security and Environment, followed shortly afterwards by the appointment of Hugh Somerville as Head of Environment. These appointments have led to a drive over the last two years for the integration of environmental considerations into every relevant decision and procedure. Although British Airways is primarily concerned with improving its own environmental performance the challenge for everyone involved with tourism, whether it be 'green, alternative, eco-, sustainable' or just 'tourism' is to examine their existing operations against environmental standards and attitudes, identify the main areas of concern and take management action as appropriate.

It is not, and will never be, the objective to paint a bright green image of British Airways. We are well aware that to attempt this is to attempt a contradiction in terms because of the very nature of our business. It is, however, our objective to go about our business in a genuinely responsible manner and to attempt to illustrate that we are doing so.

- Generation of more than $3 trillion in gross output in 1992
- Employment of 130 million people in 1992
- Employment Growth of 5.2%
- Annual average capital investment growth of over 7%

Figure 66.1 *Tourism—the world's largest industry (Source: World Travel and Tourism Council (1991))*

Background

Tourism has been called 'the world's biggest industry'. In 1992 it is expected to employ about 1 in 14 people worldwide. Tourism generates considerable global prosperity and Figure 66.1 illustrates this point. Figure 66.2 illustrates the rapid growth in tourist arrivals in a recent decade.

The industry has many components including travel agents, tour operators, and airlines and other transport modes, as well as the widely varying nature of tourist destinations, attractions and facilities. The human desire to travel and tour ranks high as an aspiration which can be increasingly satisfied with increasing standards of living and greater freedoms as repressive regimes are toppled.

Airlines provide an essential part of modern-day tourism through carrying people quickly and safely to the locations they wish to visit. Figure 66.3 illustrates the growth in commercial air travel in the last decade.

British Airways operates a scheduled airline, a charter company and a leisure company. In 1990, British Airways carried more international passengers than any other airline, over 19.5 million. Figure 66.4 shows the importance of leisure traffic to British Airways. In fact over 60% of revenue passenger kilometres (RPKs) are derived from leisure travellers.

Main impacts of aviation

Within British Airways, we have identified five main areas of technical concern that relate to the impact of the airline on the environment:

- Noise
- Emissions to the atmosphere
- Congestion, in the air and on the ground
- Waste minimisation and disposal
- Tourism

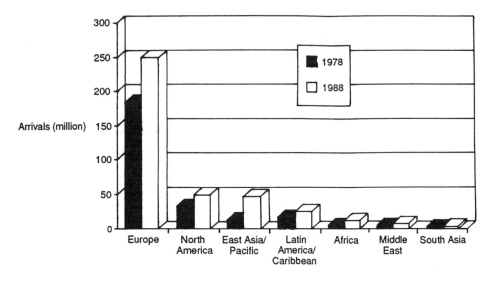

Figure 66.2 *Growth in international tourist arrivals, 1978–1988 (Sources: WTO (1980, 1990) and Beekhuis (1989))*

While this paper is directed at the relationship of airlines to the environmental impact of tourism, this can only be discussed in the context of the overall impact under all of these headings.

Why are these problems for aviation?

Noise

For noise, the answer is obvious—noise has historically been considered the only environmental impact of aircraft. It remains a problem for the industry despite the major advances in control of engine noise which have led to a decrease of 75% in the number of people around Heathrow affected by the 'threshold of noise nuisance' as measured by the historically accepted measure of noise nuisance and as shown in Figure 66.5. This overall reduction in the integrated measure of noise impact has been achieved despite a very marked increase in the number of aircraft movements and an even greater proportional rise in the number of passengers. Figure 66.6 shows the worldwide improvements in exposure to aircraft noise.

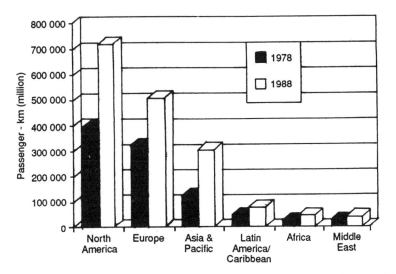

Figure 66.3 *Growth in commercial air travel, in passenger-kilometres flown, 1978–1988 (Source: ICAO (1988, 1989))*

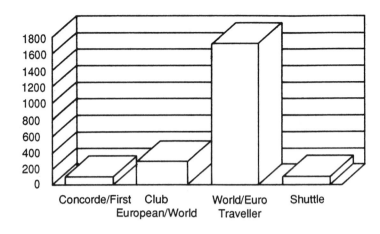

Figure 66.4 *Leisure traffic and British Airways (Source British Airways internal data)*

This situation is going to continue to improve further over the next ten years for a number of reasons. The major contribution will come from the phase-out of the older, noisier Chapter 2 aircraft through implementation of the ICAO (International Civil Aviation Organisation) resolution in Europe and of similar regulations in the USA and elsewhere. The increased proportion of twin-engined aircraft will also be important through their more rapid climb-out because of the greater power per engine needed as a result of safety requirements in case of engine failure.

At some time in the future, however, increased movements and the larger size of aircraft could decrease or even reverse this improving trend. Current engine configurations do not offer much potential for improvement, thus making it important that airport developers give careful consideration to developing stringent land-use controls in the vicinity of airports. Within this, the encroachment of housing towards airports will increase the number of potential noise protesters. The nuisance

of noise results from the proximity of a significant noise source to people; the aviation industry has made large improvements in source control which should perhaps be rewarded by greater flexibility of number and times of movements at airports and matched by measures to control land use.

Gaseous emissions

Noise is being overtaken by gaseous emissions as the most serious environmental concern of aviation. This is despite the major improvements in aircraft fuel efficiency shown in Figure 66.7.

Carbon dioxide, the principal 'greenhouse gas', is of obvious interest, although emissions from aviation are small compared to other sources such as ground transport and power stations. Figure 66.8 illustrates the 'greenhouse effect'. Emissions of carbon dioxide are directly related to fuel consumption. Consequently the improvements

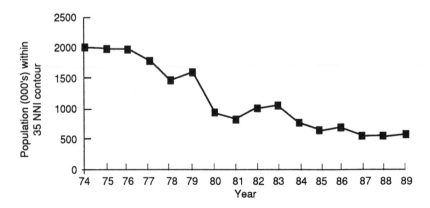

Figure 66.5 *Noise exposure within the London Heathrow area (Source: UK Department of Transport (1991))*

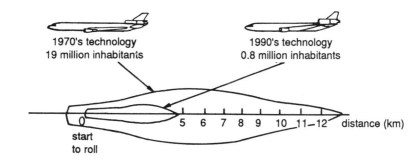

Figure 66.6   *Worldwide exposure to aircraft noise (Source: adapted from Airbus Industrie (1991))*

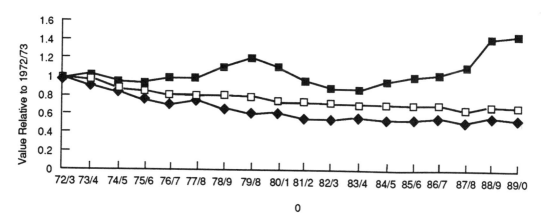

Figure 66.7   *British Airways trends in fuel consumption and efficiency;* ■ *, total fuel;* □ *fuel per tonne km;* ◆ *, fuel per pax km (Source: British Airways internal data)*

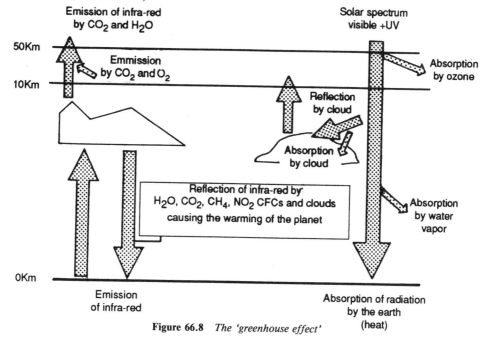

Figure 66.8   *The 'greenhouse effect'*

	UK	Global
Civil aviation	5–10(1)	500–600
All fossil fuels	575 (2)	20 000 (3)

Figure 66.9 *Emissions of carbon dioxide (approximate annual total (1988) in millions of tonnes) (Sources: (1) British Airways estimate; (2) UK Department of the Environment (1990); (3) UNEP (no date))*

in fuel efficiency have been paralleled by improvements in 'emission efficiency'. Aviation contributes 2–3% of global CO_2 emissions from fossil fuels worldwide. Figure 66.9 illustrates this.

Genuine questions are also being asked about the effects of condensation trails but the most immediate concern is to quantify the emissions of nitrogen oxides (NOx) at cruising altitudes and to determine their fate and possible effects with particular respect to the potential for input to ozone formation. During the internal British Airways Review we found that we were unable to calculate NOx emissions at cruising altitudes, an inhibition which has clearly not been felt by others with less access to operational information. After discussions with Rolls-Royce we are now working with Warren Spring Laboratory to calculate these emissions, and we will be promoting work to interpret their fate and effects. The area of interest is the potential contribution of ozone, generated as a result of NOx emissions at cruise altitudes, to global warming. Aircraft emissions also contribute to ground-level atmospheric contamination, although here the contribution is believed to be much less than other major sources.

Congestion

Congestion is a critical problem because of the immediate threat that it poses to air travel and the gross economic penalties that result from holdups in the air and around airports. In environmental terms, each and every consequence of congestion leads to unnecessary consumption of energy and materials with resulting increases in emissions and waste. For example, our calculations indicate that we burn, unnecessarily, some 63 000 tonnes of fuel per year because of the air traffic delays over Heathrow and Gatwick alone, and half of that is burned to carry the fuel that is carried in case we need it! Figure 66.10 illustrates the economic losses that could arise from inaction in this area.

Waste

Waste provides one of the most obvious dilemmas in the airline business through the conflict between providing the high standard of service that airline passengers desire and the creation and disposal of unnecessary waste. However, in-flight catering is not the only source of waste. Engineering and maintenance activities generate large quantities of waste, some of which require special procedures for disposal. Substantial savings can be identified both in quantity and cost. This is important as it is anticipated that in the next decade the costs of waste disposal will rise at a rate well above inflation. Figure 66.11 illustrates the main departments responsible for British Airways' waste bill.

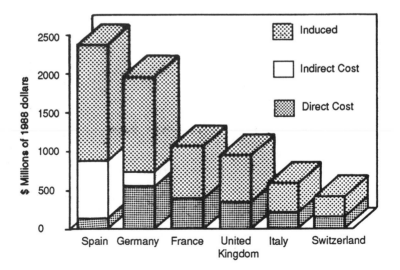

Figure 66.10 *Projected annual economic losses from inaction over congestion, year 2000 (Source: ATAG (1991))*

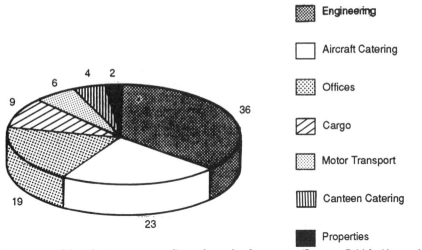

Figure 66.11 *Percentage of British Airways waste disposal cost by department (Sources: British Airways internal data)*

Tourism

Airlines are also involved in the tourism and environment debate. It is essential for airlines to be committed to resolving any tourism and environment conflicts because their very existence depends on it. Airlines, despite their heavily pushed business images, are actually dependent on leisure travellers. In fact some routes are dominated by leisure travellers. Passengers travelling for holiday purposes provide the major market for many of the routes of an international scheduled airline. Figure 66.12 shows a selection of important leisure routes for British Airways.

Therefore airlines cannot hide behind their business image, nor claim that they are only involved in transporting people from A to B. All airlines are involved in transporting passengers for leisure purposes. The natural

and inherited environment is one of the major resources of the tourism industry and the quest for attractive environments is one of the main reasons for travel. Thus airlines, like their fellow tourist industry members, have a responsibility in maintaining the balance between tourism and the environment. There is not room in this paper for a full discussion of the positive and negative impacts of tourism, but they are in the main related to congestion, inappropriate activities or behaviour and poorly planned development. The consequences of degraded tourism environments will affect airlines as it will other members of the tourism industry.

These five areas of environmental concern pose a significant challenge to the aviation industry and demand a response from individual airlines.

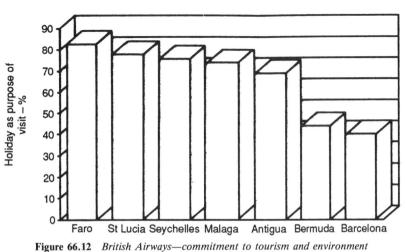

Figure 66.12 *British Airways—commitment to tourism and environment*

The response of British Airways

One of the most fundamental moves any organisation, however small, can make is to develop a corporate environmental goal or objective. BA has a corporate 'Good Neighbour' goal—'to be a good neighbour, concerned for the community and the environment'. This is supported by a Company Environmental Policy Statement. We have recently completed a review of the environmental aspects of our facilities at Heathrow and the 'Worldwide flying operations', copies of which are available separately.

Figure 66.13 shows that the airline has developed two main supporting limbs to our environmental programme. The technical limb comprises a rolling series of reviews or 'audits' of our main locations (LHR, MAN, LGW) as well as specific studies: quantifying our emissions, studying our waste generation and disposal, analysing our aqueous effluents and drainage, and reviewing our engineering procedures. The 'light green' limb also has a number of components such as: 'Greenwaves', our Environmental Suggestion Scheme; Greenseal, our Environmental Award for Excellence; and a number of recycling initiatives. Perhaps the most important of a large number of activities is 'Assisting Nature Conservation', a long-established scheme for promoting the reintroduction of threatened species to their natural habitats and for training individuals in habitat management. This scheme has already contributed to the conservation of over 50 species, through establishment of partnerships with a group of leading conservation organisations.

Between these two limbs is the torso or body corporate of management of environmental matters and the arms

which the body feeds—communication. Examples of initiatives include establishment of an 'Environment Council' of those Executive Directors most directly concerned with the environment and the complementary development of a network of some 150 Environmental Champions throughout the company. Communication has been both internal, through staff briefing videos, seminars and extensive cooperation from in-house publications such as *BA News*, and external, by selected briefing of industry, 'Green' and other press. Communication will be on-going and in the next six months will include an internal environmental awareness campaign to management and staff to reinforce the 'environment is good for business' message. Our first 'Annual environmental report' which will document BA's environmental performance is being compiled and will be used to set objectives for the future.

The aviation industry has also responded

British Airways is not alone in responding to the environmental challenge. Others such as Swissair, Lufthansa and SAS have developed environmental policies and taken a critical look at their own operations. We are also aware that charter airlines such as Britannia are looking at these issues. In support of these individual airline efforts, the industry associations have in the past year established their own environmental groups. These complement the long-standing groups concerned with the technical aspects of noise and emissions. These groups are aimed at addressing the need for coordination and communication on 'enviropolitical' matters. IATA has in addition, with BA taking the lead through Sir Colin Marshall, established a specific Infrastructure Action

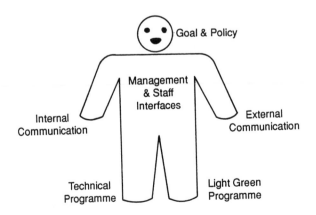

Figure 66.13 *Implementing the environmental action plan*

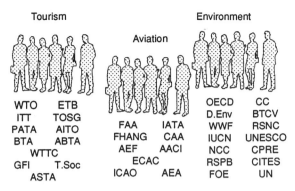

Figure 66.14 *Many players and organisations*

Group, led by John Meredith on assignment from British Airways, to address the problems of congestion. British Airways is involved in a joint initiative between that group and a federation of pressure groups, the Airfields Environment Federation, to develop acceptable ways of determining the environmental constraints to airport growth.

What is the message for the tourism industry?

To approach an understanding of the interactions of tourism with the environment it is first necessary to appreciate the complexity of the interactions between the groups involved. Quite apart from the tourist, there are many different groups involved who will often not have similar viewpoints on environmental questions (see Figure 66.14).

There are a wide range of ways in which negative environmental impacts can be inflicted on the vast ranges of geographical locations visited by tourists. This is a popular subject with the media who are not always scrupulous in exercising objectivity. What is at stake is the future of the world's largest industry and perhaps even the fundamental right of the individual to travel. We have to learn to manage the environmental impacts constructively if the world is not going to lose the benefits of tourism of which there are many, for example:

● Generating health and prosperity
● Bringing people and cultures together
● Helping the world to communicate
● Satisfying the desire to enjoy the experience of different environments

The economic consequences of failure would be vast and the possibility of serious indirect political consequences

should not be dismissed. While it is tempting to dismiss concerns which cannot be defined in monetary terms, recent history is full of incidents—Bhopal, Valdez, Love Canal etc.—where environmental costs have proved enormous. Tourism has had its own share of problems, with whole areas becoming blighted because of a shortsighted approach to profit maximisation.

All of this generates a goose and golden egg image of the industry. It should be remembered that geese do not lay eggs without feeding adequately. The tourism goose is feeding on the natural and inherited environment whether it is the Costa Brava, the National Park or Stonehenge. Thus not only the goose but also its feeding grounds must be nurtured. This calls for a series of measures to be considered by all tourism operators and the suggestions shown in Figure 66.15 are offered in the knowledge that we still have a long way to go.

British Airways recognises the lack of research and practical advice in this area and are addressing this problem, for example through our involvement in the World Travel and Tourism Council (WTTC) Tourism and Environment Research Centre in Oxford. WTTC is a recent initiative that involves Sir Colin Marshall and the new tourism centre will serve initially to assemble and evaluate information relating to the environmental impact of tourism. We are also working with our own tour

---

- Put our own house in order—take a good environmental look at your operation, including what goes on in your offices as well as your destinations.
- Remember the maxim *"Good Environmental Management is Good for Business"*, saving materials and energy is almost always good for both.
- Accept that you are indirectly and in part responsible for some of the more direct impacts, for example noise and emissions, of those that carry your customers, ie the airlines.
- Consider introducing new, more "environmentally friendly" tour products or adapt your existing ones.
- Respect other cultures and do not dominate them.
- Educate travellers with respect to the locations they are visiting wherever these are—we must also educate ourselves about the destinations and cultures to which we transport people.
- Form partnerships with conservation organisations.
- Invade new locations with caution, think of the environmental impact at the very beginning. Seek to "Leave places As You Find Them"—in cooperation with Local Government, Tourist Authorities, and Environmental organisations.
- Ask the "What if" question, that is, "what if we do not consider the environment?"
- Above all, work with others in the industry to achieve a high standard of environmental compatibility.

Figure 66.15 *Some suggestions*

operator, British Airways Holidays, on a programme of environmental education and awareness which includes advice in the main 'Worldwide' brochure and a planned series of destination guides.

These arguments and initiatives are important because we all share the responsibility for the long-term future of the environment. There may be arguments about how close we are to the precipice and as to how deep and harmful the fall into the chasm may be. These arguments are no excuse for inaction.

References

Airbus Industrie (1991) *Environmental Protection*, Airbus Industrie, Toulouse.

ATAG (1991) *The Economic Benefits of Air Transport*, Air Transport Action Group, IATA, Geneva.

Beekhuis, J. (1989) *Travel and Leisure: World Travel Overview 1988–89*, AMEX Publishing Corporation, New York.

ICAO (1988) *Statistical Yearbook: Civil Aviation Statistics of the World 1987*, International Civil Aviation Organisation, Montreal.

ICAO (1989) *Statistical Yearbook: Civil Aviation Statistics of the World 1988*. International Civil Aviation Organisation, Montreal.

UK Department of Environment (1990) *Digest of Environmental Statistics*, HMSO, London.

UK Department of Transport (1991) 'British Airways internal environmental review'.

UNEP (no date) *Environment Data Report*, United Nations Environmental Program, Geneva.

WTO (World Tourist Organisation) (1980) *Yearbook of Tourism Statistics*, WTO, Madrid.

WTO (World Tourist Organisation) (1990) *Yearbook of Tourism Statistics*, WTO, Madrid.

WTTC (World Travel and Tourism Council) (1991) 'The WTTC report', World Travel and Tourism Council, Brussels, Belgium.

67 Egotourism, sustainable tourism and the environment—a symbiotic, symbolic or shambolic relationship

B. WHEELLER

A recent *Financial Times* 'Survey' claims that 'Broadly environmental management means managing a business with an eye to its impact on the environment' (Maddox, 1993). This does not seem a very broad interpretation to me. Not surprisingly the underlying assumption, not only of Maddox's article but of the entire feature on 'environmental management', appears to be that the environment should be viewed, and treated, solely from a business perspective. Furthermore, though no definition is given, the distinct impression is that the environment is strictly physical in dimension and scope. I would suggest that in most situations this is too narrow, too blinkered a perspective. Certainly in the present context of the relationship between tourism and the environment I am convinced that this is so.

A provocative slant on environmental issues is provided by *The Economist*'s brief on 'Aid and the environment. The greening of giving'. The main thrust of the argument is that while everyone appears to agree there is a need for sustainable development, just what this actually entails, and the means of achieving it, remain somewhat vague. 'In principle, this idea is clear enough: development, not merely economic growth should be the target and it should lead to enduring improvements in welfare' (*The Economist*, 1993). Easier said than done. And a statement all-too-familiar to those, who over the last few years, have been following the ecotourism debate/debacle.

For this paper, initially, I too was inclined to emulate the *Financial Times* example and avoid a definition of the environment. However, aware of the title of this conference I was drawn to the definition given by the rather grandly named World Travel and Tourism Environment Research Centre (WTTERC) (no shrinking violet this). Their second annual review presents 'the current "State of the Art" of specifying and achieving environmentally compatible growth through commercial operations in worldwide Travel and Tourism' (WTTERC, 1993). Again the commercial perspective, again not surprising given the centre's high-profile sponsorship.

They state 'we interpret environment in the broad sense as "earth's resources" and in a narrower context of Travel and Tourism as "natural and built resources" (in places where visitors are received, accommodated, transported or organised by tourism business)' (WTTERC, 1993).

Since being a lad I have had great difficulty differentiating between natural and man-made environments. Middle age hasn't provided the answer to this (or any other problems). If we believe in Darwinism then through the evolutionary process man is part of nature and therefore anything that man does, creates or destroys is surely also part of the evolutionary process and therefore part of nature as well.

So where's the distinction? Too simplistic? Semantics? We don't talk of mammal-made environments, fish-made environments or animal-made environments. Yet presumably to some extent these exist. But nature and man are somehow separated, hence man-made environments. In the evaluation stakes nature becomes the paradigm of virtue, man vilified for desecrating the environment (shades of the 'traveller good/tourist bad' syndrome here).

Gunn, in his worthy text *Tourism Planning*, explains how Sargent had argued that mankind is dramatically different from other organisms, how people have control of their own and other organisms' destiny—'In organisms other than man, the natural ecosystem's organismic detritus is fed back into the environment and recycled (Sargent, 1974). But this is not so with mankind' (Gunn, 1994).

Unesco, however, to some extent recognise the fusion between nature and man. In 1972 it adopted the Convention concerning the Protection of the World Cultural and Natural Heritage. According to the Director-General, 'The Convention covers the cultural and the natural heritage, which have traditionally been considered as separate entities, and makes the bold assumption that there are monuments and sites that belong to the whole of humanity' (Mayor, 1991). Unesco's emblem apparently symbolises the interdependence of cultural and natural properties: the central square is a form created by man and the circle represents nature, the two, according to Unesco, being intimately linked.

The environment in a tourism context, in addition to the traditional natural/physical perspective, must have a cultural and social dimension. Sofield (1991) develops this argument in his search for principles of sustainable ethnic tourism. (Anyway, if we are to believe the current promotion campaign for Sicily, 'Tourism is Culture'.) It is everything that affects, or is affected by tourism. Providing an actual working definition is a somewhat daunting task and it is, therefore, hardly surprising that the relationships between the environment and tourism appear so shambolic. This is further compounded when one acknowledges that, despite an excess of definitions, nobody is certain what tourism itself actually is. Whilst many profess individually to know, no two perceptions will be precisely the same.

Over the years, Middleton has expressed strong views that the tourism industry has become 'misrepresented and crudely caricatured as a major environmental predator' (Middleton, 1993). Not surprisingly this echoes 'Too often, around the world, Travel and Tourism is misunderstood as an activity mainly concerned with the mass movement of packaged tourism to fragile environment a periphery of pleasure. This review stresses that the world's largest industry is based on visits for all purposes including business travel, visits to friends and relatives, holidays and other social, cultural and leisure travel' (WTTERC, 1992). There can be no doubt that Middleton's views are valid and should be respected.

This confusion of definitions is not of course restricted to tourism, but vagueness and liberal interpretations have always accompanied tourism development debates. Ecotourism is no exception. I am always perplexed by the term 'ecotourist'. My doubts were fuelled a couple of years ago when our guide on a trip to Mongolia described Genghis Khan as the original 'green-man, the first ecotourist'. I couldn't determine whether this was because, again according to our guide, Genghis had apparently established the first National Park (for hunting) outside Ulan Bator or because he 'lived off the land while travelling'. Either way it seems an interesting interpretation. Dirks, in 'A new breed of traveler', believes 'anyone can be an eco-traveller. All eco-travel takes is sensitivity, respect and an innate sense of curiosity about other cultures and environments' (Dirks, 1993). To an extent, any desire for a definitive definition of ecotourism, or of sustainable tourism is redundant. People will interpret the notion as they will, as best suits them and their circumstances. No international decree will

disperse the convenient clouds of confusion that have enveloped eco/sustainable tourism.

The popular argument is that we are destroying our environment and that this is not natural. Tourism is of course seen as part of this destruction. I suggest that this process does seem perfectly natural—human, if inhumane. There does not seem anything inconsistent in destroying our environment because to many 'our environment' is, or at least is perceived to be, synonymous with someone else's environment. Western society is inextricably linked with the growth mentality.

Amazingly (or understandably depending on one's perspective), other societies seem to want to ape our 'success'. All growth has costs and benefits. We are out for ourselves. It is a question of what is best for me and if someone, or somewhere, else pays the cost, then too bad as long as I get the benefits. Doesn't this 'devil take the hindmost' mentality realistically reflect mainstream consciousness? And isn't this Darwin's survival of the fittest?

So, despite agreeing with many aspects of Middleton's arguments, I nevertheless feel that, however broad, however sweeping one's compass of 'tourism', tourism will always include an element of 'exploitation'. This isn't meant as a criticism of tourism *per se*, more an emotive threnody on human behaviour. This observation seems appropriate since we are continually being told tourism is a human activity. Let us theoretically attempt (I know it's simplistic, even naive) to split tourism into three sectors—the commercial provider, the tourists and the 'host' population (not included in the providers). The commercial sector is profit-orientated and inevitably, it seems to me, there will be 'exploitation' in some form here. So too, with the tourists—while not motivated by profit they are by self-interest, the 'what's in it for me attitude'. Similarly, the host community wants to extract something from the tourist. Assuming it's not money, it might be an opportunity to learn a foreign language, a gift, a sexual conquest—whatever. It's often a matter of 'taking'. Too cynical? Dream on. Unfortunately, this seems a far more realistic view of how things are, and will continue to be, than the wishful, wistful, whimsical, Goody-two-shoes, green approach.

The notion of a 'global village', of 'think global, act local' belongs in the same realms of fantasy as Major's 'classless society'. Maybe some in the 'first' world are moving towards a supposedly more environmentally sensitive, sustainable consumption pattern. This generally seems to be one of substitution rather then reduction. We are not actively giving up anything. But if globally our overall consumption rate is increasing, as surely it is, I wonder just what the net benefits of our marginal shenanigans actually are. It's a classic case of the 'haves' and the 'have nots', the image conscious 'haves' fine-tuning their/our privileged lifestyle for status (not breadline self-preservation) purposes, while the 'have-nots' strive by any means, fair or foul, to catch up or simply survive.

Recent developments in tourism seem to mirror this general pattern of consumption.

> The growing popularity and, in certain sectors of society, the . . . acceptance of sustainability, of green awareness, of ecotourism are based not so much on philanthropic concern for the environment, or for the good of mankind, but on vested interest—and immediate vested interest at that. It's a little like giving to charity: it makes us feel better. We rarely sacrifice so much as to cause any adverse effect on ourselves. The utility derived (by us) usually outweighs the cost of that sacrifice. So too . . . with expressed support for sustainable tourism. (Wheeller 1993a)

Most of the ideological roots of new aware tourism have been around for years. However, though the concept of sustainability has long been associated with development economics, it has only recently been in vogue in tourism (Seaton, 1991). Seminal works by Murphy (1985) and Krippendorf (1987) raised awareness and these were followed by a deluge of material endorsing green tourism and its 'sophisticated spin-off' ecotourism. Sober warnings contained in first-rate articles by, for example, Cohen (1989), Cazes (1989), Butler (1990) and Pigram (1990) were to all intents and purposes ignored, swamped in an excess of green rhetoric. De Kadt too pointed out that alternative tourism has meant many things, all of which run counter to mainstream development in western civilisation (Nash and Butler, 1990).

There are journals on sustainability, a specialist journal on sustainable tourism, a journal for the eco-traveller, editions of established journals dedicated to ecotourism, a wide range of related articles in these and other journals, magazines and newspapers, together with a welter of government and official publications. There are books, books in press, chapters in books, and book reviews; conference proceedings and conference reports; television documentaries on ecotourism, slots in the TV travel shows and programmes on the wireless. Sustainable tourism has stimulated a flood of student dissertations, from undergraduate through to doctorate. Existing tourism consultants take on a green hue, while new ecotourism specialists enter the consultancy market. Organisations concerned with tourism impact have spawned and multiplied.

The *Journal of Sustainable Tourism* was launched last year and on the evidence of the first two editions is proving a useful addition to the relevant literature. In the inaugural article, the editors (Bramwell and Lane, 1993), provide a succinct overview of the evolution of sustainable tourism plus a somewhat up-beat brief of the journal's objectives. Most of the subsequent articles have good references and these, together with the conference reports (e.g. Godfrey, 1993) and book reviews provide excellent source material. The editors too have, by allowing the Jonahs and Doubting Thomases an opportunity to fully air their views, elevated the journal to a forum for debate.

The first-class *Tourism Management* has increasingly given considerable space to tourism and environmental issues. Recently there was a special issue on ecotourism (*Tourism Management*, 1993) and there have been numerous relevant articles and reviews (see, for example, May (1991), Cooper and Ozdil (1992), Owen et al. (1993)). The last article, in particular, adopts a positive approach to sustainable tourism, arguing, and through case studies 'proving', that sustainable tourism can be achieved in practice. While personally I would question some of their conclusions—for example, regarding the Conwy Project (it relies on 'upgrading' and 'spreading the load' which I believe are not necessarily sustainable prerequisites (Wheeller, 1993a))—articles such as this are part of the important growing trend citing examples of 'successful' sustainable/ecotourism projects. The bullish confidence evident in this development cannot be ignored and reflects the belief that many academics and practitioners have in the concept of sustainable tourism—'Success in achieving sustainable tourism development can be realised' (Owen et al., 1993).

Tourism in Focus from Tourism Concern is an excellent source of material for those interested in impacts of tourism. Given its shoestring budget this publication is, I believe, a great credit to its editor, Tricia Barnett. Issue No. 9 (Tourism Concern, 1993) is specifically on eco-tourism, though all editions contain useful information, as does its predecessor, *The Newsletter*.

The same cannot be said of Tourism Concern's publication *Beyond the Green Horizon* (1992): a discussion paper on 'principles for sustainable tourism' produced in conjunction with the World-Wide Fund for Nature. Though a committee member of Tourism Concern I always had strong reservations about any attempts to provide a code of ethics or principles and was particularly reticent about supporting this document. My views are best summed up by Ashcroft's stinging review:

> Reading each principle in turn I found myself increasingly asking the questions, Why? How? When? With what? It soon became very tiresome ploughing through so many platitudinous points, which sounded like a converted and over-virtuous boy scout promise. Indeed it is questionable just how much effort should be put into definition of

principles for sustainable tourism when so little effort seems to be put into practical action to achieve them. (Ashcroft, 1993)

To be fair to Tourism Concern this was meant as a first step.

According to Bramwell and Lane (1993) it was noted by Waldstein (1991) that all politicians and all large corporations claim to be pursuing pro-environmental policies. He warns of the 'limousine environmentalism' where lip-service masks a lack of positive actions. 'It is easy to discuss sustainability—implementation is the problem. . . . The time has come 'to walk the talk' (Bramwell and Lane, 1993). As Bramwell and Lane somewhat understatingly observe, 'It will be no easy walk'. But just how many first steps are required before one can in reality 'walk the talk'?

A plethora of articles have appeared in the other main tourism journals (see, for example, Stevens (1990), Green (1990), Bramwell (1991) and Wight (1993)) and in a variety of other journals/magazines/newspapers etc. (see Lane (1989), Anscombe (1991), Platt (1991), M. Wheeler (1992) and Hutchings (1993)).

Tourism planning texts that set the current debate on eco/sustainable tourism in a wider context include Pearce (1989), Inskeep (1991), Smith and Eadington (1992) and Gunn (1994).

The above is a selected review of some of the conventional sources of the relationship between tourism management, the environment and ecotourism. I apologise for any omissions. Brevity precludes an analysis of wider source material. I would, however, like to make a couple of exceptions and draw attention to a superb novel—*Day Trips to the Desert* (Nicholson, 1993) 'a sort of travel book'. In addition to some interesting reflections, and contradictions, in the traveller/tourist relationships, he writes evocatively of the impact of the environment on himself, and a spiritualism similarly referred to by Ryan (1994). Also, I strongly recommend a short story, 'American dreams' (Carey, 1988)—a quirky parable of tourism impact on a small, rural town(ship).

Most people in the world don't 'go on holiday'. All tourism and not just the notion of eco-sustainable tourism is, in a sense, elitist. However, global tourist numbers will continue to rise as countries industrialise. 'But it seems inconceivable that tourists from these emerging economies will behave in the pseudo-sophisticated manner that some tourism commentators are suggesting should be the new mode of travel/tourist behaviour. It is naive and unrealistic to expect otherwise' (Wheeler, 1992). These tourists will want as much as possible and at the least cost (to them) as possible—a philosophy (despite a smug

smokescreen of self-righteousness) not a million miles away from that of our contemporary caring traveller.

Hypocrisy is probably one of our finest qualities, allowing a multitude of sins to pass by undetected and unpunished. It is a gilt-edged, guilt-free passport to inconsistent behaviour. Let me use a couple of examples to illustrate our hypocrisy towards the 'environment'. A boy is on holiday, fishing off a pier, say at Blackpool. All morning he has had no luck—piscatorial-wise (though the fish are counting their blessings). Tired of the jovial 'caught anything yet?' enquiries of the strolling day-trippers, he decides to have his dinner—sandwiches. Whilst munching, it occurs to him to change his bait and, discarding the worm, he pinches some bread, from the sandwich, onto his hook. Again no luck—but still the friendly queries. He then decides on a significantly different tack, to keep the same bait but to change quarry. Rather than cast into the sea he allows his line to settle on the pier. Instant success—he hooks a seagull and reels it in. Pandemonium ensues amongst the 'pier-group' onlooking deck-chair crew who, in disgust, run off instead for the police/RSPCA with a view to immediate retribution.

Now was the boy an ecotourist when he was fishing for fish? Yes, because he wasn't catching any? But what about the worm? (Incidentally the flippant advice to tourists to take only photographs, leave only footprints doesn't seem too eco-friendly if you happen to be a worm up for a little fresh air.) If he had caught fish would he have been eco-friendly? Does it depend on the species he caught, whether they are rare or plentiful, or whether his catch is eaten to sustain his family, thrown back (often, damaged, to die), given to his cat—which then dies—or what? Why don't the same criteria apply to catching the seagull as to fish and why the public outcry? Why does the Labour Party tacitly support angling but not 'blood sports'? We eat cows but not horses. Other nationalities eat dogs etc. etc. I don't know what the answers are but there are glaring inconsistencies in attitude and behaviour.

You decide to visit friends in the country. Driving at night a rabbit or hedgehog jumps out into the headlights (not that too many hedgehogs jump). If safe, you take evasive, 'eco'-action—you slow down to avoid the animal. In such circumstances few would deliberately kill. You continue your journey. Everyone is happy. And yet, take off the radiator grill or, even more apparent, simply check the windscreen and you see the thousand spattered insects that you have killed. You know you are doing this but have the capacity to ignore it; you don't take evasive 'eco'-action with this species, you don't slow down or cancel your journey. You modify your behaviour only when it suits, but not sufficiently to seriously inconvenience yourselves (or in this case your friends, assuming they are looking forward to seeing you in the first place).

Even if you did your friends a favour, cancelled your journey and stayed at home, no doubt you would be causing some sort of environmental problem as you used up resources in one form or another. (This seems a reasonable argument against those who believe that people should no longer go on holiday but stay at home. See also Wheeler (1993a).)

Imagine that, in the 1920s, dreams of the sun, the sea and the beach had not become *de rigueur* and that the subsequent coastline craze had not evolved. Instead it was the wilderness rather than the seashore that had caught the imagination, that was subsequently to become 'the popular'. Imagine that tourist communications and facilities had developed rapidly in these areas we (still) regard as inaccessible and inhospitable—say the jungle, the tundra, the desert. Improbable, but just imagine. What would the situation and debate be now if the masses had avoided the coastline and the beach but gone instead to these other far-flung destinations? Would mass tourism have destroyed the pristine environment there just as we are told it has destroyed wherever it has gone? Presumably. What would the ecotourism lobby be suggesting in these circumstances? Wouldn't it be advocating the same notions of sustainable tourism that are being espoused now? Tourism at one with nature; non-consumption, non-exploitative, avoiding degradation and destruction of the 'environment', but rather tourism in harmony, in balance with nature? Presumably it would be suggesting an alternative, more aware, more acceptable, more politically correct behaviour to the 'contemporary' destructive norm.

Under the imaginary prevailing circumstances what could this back to nature solution be? What could be more eco-friendly than lying on an undeveloped beach, taking the occasional dip in the sea? You guessed it—the beach holiday, the ultimate in minimum interference with nature. Wouldn't this be the perfect paradigm of eco-virtue?

But isn't that what many have now? Why then isn't the current holiday pattern of the 'masses', the beach holiday, considered eco-friendly? The main reason seems to be simply because it is the 'mass'. It's the absolute numbers involved and the infrastructures and super-structures 'needed' to service this volume that's the problem.

There has been growing awareness, interest, debate and, I believe, subsequent confusion rather than clarification over eco/sustainable tourism. But, amongst all this, are there any answers? I think not. Just a never-ending series of laughable codes of ethics: codes of ethics for travellers; codes of ethics for tourists, for government, and for tourism businesses. Codes for all—or, more likely, codeine for all. Codes and 'advice' have emanated from almost every conceivable source—from religious zealots, from professional and commercial organisations, from government bodies (see, for example, O'Grady (1981), Tourism Society (1991), WTTERC (1993), Tourism Concern (1991, 1992), Ecotourism Society (1993) and Center for Responsible Tourism (1993) etc.). But who really believes these codes are effective? I am pretty wary of platitudinous phrases like 'we are monitoring progress'. Has there been any progress—indeed, has there been any monitoring? Perhaps I am missing it and the answer itself is actually in code. Maybe, in appropriate parlance, I can't see the wood for the trees. The futility of these codes was best summed up by a friend's recent visit to Las Vegas—city of ten million lights. There was a sign in his brightly lit hotel bathroom that read, 'In the interests of energy conservation please switch off the light before leaving'.

Maybe my cynicism is misplaced. At the Tourism and the Environment Conference (1992, London) luminaries of the calibre of Krippendorf evidently felt that codes of practice were an essential, functional element in tourism management. His embracing of the codes of practice and recommendations given in recent UK official documentation—*Tourism in the National Parks. A Guide to Good Practice* (ETB, 1990), *The Green Light* (ETB, 1991a), *Tourism and the Environment—Maintaining the Balance* (ETB, 1991b)—was little short of euphoric. He strongly advocated their adoption worldwide (Krippendorf, 1993).

The belief seems to be that doing something in terms of furthering the ecotourism cause is better than doing nothing, that if we each do our bit then things will be better. 'Every step, no matter how small, adds to the sum of the overall responsible tourism effect' (Wood and House, 1991). I do not necessarily hold with this argument. It assumes, of course, that the step is in the right direction—that 'responsible' tourism effort is indeed the current way forward). Also, the trouble is that while, in our tourism activities, we are doing our little 'bit', in a supposedly correct direction, we are simultaneously (and it would appear inevitably) doing a 'lot' not quite so correctly—witness the rabbit/insect example.

A number of the supposedly eco-friendly holidays seem to be two-centre destinations with, in the case of photo-safaris one week being eco-friendly in the bush then one week recovering afterwards in pampered luxury on the beach—a sort of 'let us spoil you in unspoilt Africa' (*The Times*, 1994) attitude. No doubt, for image purposes, the package as a whole would be deemed eco-friendly and statistically categorised under nature tourism (always a safe bet, politically). But is this a fair reflection of the visitors' experience? In getting to the airport/ the flight/transfers etc., speed and convenience take precedence. And the second week?

I see nothing (in terms of practical application) in ecotourism that requires us to seriously question or change our pseudo-respectable, middle-class, educated values. Yet it seems to me that these are a critical element of the tourist/traveller problem which in itself is fundamental to the current appeal of ecotourism—the very reason why travellers wish to distance themselves physically and culturally as far as possible from the tourist (see Boorstin (1962), Cohen (1972), Rivers (1974) and Fussell (1982, 1990)). Travel, not tourism, has always been regarded as a symbol of suave sophistication. Marry this with another pillar of respectability—ostentatious concern for the precious environment—and we have the perfect symbol of respectability: ecotourism/ego-traveller (Wheeller, 1991).

Maybe, in the example earlier, we should have killed the rabbit/hedgehog. This might have shaken us out of our lethargy perhaps sufficiently to really question whether minor modifications of our behaviour really make any difference whatsoever—apart from enabling us to smugly hide behind the respectable façade of ecotourism. It seems merely to serve as an excuse to allow us to behave much as before but from a higher moral platform.

Certainly, though, we should kill the old golden-goose cliché. I don't believe that tourism nurtures the goose that lays the golden egg, or that there is a symbiotic relationship between tourism and the 'environment'. If anything, tourism 'gooses' the environment. The cuckoo is a far more appropriate symbol (Wheeller, 1993a). There is also the danger of plunging into the eco-trap—the myth being perpetrated that the continual up-grading of the tourism product (to provide 'quality') somehow automatically, and simultaneously, enhances the tourism environment in an eco-friendly, harmonious and sustainable way (Wheeller, 1993a).

Perhaps it is my own interpretation of the situation that is chaotic but, despite a multitude of best intentions and considerable effort on the part of individuals and organisations, the relationship between sustainability, ecotourism and the environment remains a complete shambles. Then again, isn't The Shambles itself one of York's top tourist attractions.

It is suggested that nature's resources should be 'employed' for tourism in a non-exploitative manner— for example, whale-watching might replace the old traditional forms of this extractive industry. Are we seriously to believe that (economically?) this new form of mammal voyeurism is going to replace the traditional industry? (I suppose if we are to believe that urban tourism is the answer to urban unemployment then we just might.) Isn't there a real danger that too many ecotourists eager to witness the whales off New Zealand, Chile or wherever are disrupting the mammals mating behaviour? Presumably this form of tourism must be 'managed correctly'—but then shouldn't all tourism be 'managed correctly'? Perhaps it should be; but I don't think it can be. Given the imbalance in world economies the ideals of sustainable principles (and of sustainable tourism) in a global arena are impossible to achieve.

Realistically I'm afraid it's more likely to be a case of 'we'll manage', as in 'we'll make do' rather than in the conventional management sense of 'managing', a pragmatic, ad hoc approach for what is essentially a fragmented ad hoc industry. I really don't see how we can have a tourism policy for such a diverse phenomenon as tourism—apart from, as I've suggested before, something along the lines of 'all those involved in tourism should behave nicely'.

The WTTERC differentiated between ecotourism and sustainable tourism potential, seeing, it would appear, ecotourism as a (possible) form of sustainable tourism. They argue though that ecotourism is not the only logical, sustainable response to the environmental impacts of travel and tourism. 'In fact ecotourism can only make a marginal, though important, contribution because of the limited nature of its market' (WTTERC, 1993). They believe that 'without careful management it is no more sustainable than other forms of tourism development and may cause more problems than it solves' (1993:11). With this I agree, though I have reservations about the concept of 'careful management'. Quite rightly they argue that the 'true target for better performance and a globally relevant contribution must be the core 95% of the world's Travel and Tourism' (1993:11). I am, however, amazed by their assertion that 'the hackneyed and insulting concept of mass tourism, as used in the 1960s and 1970s, has no relevance for growth in the next decade' (1993:10). To me it has every relevance as we move towards, not away from, megamass tourism.

Changing fashion in tanning terms and fears of melanoma may have a significant impact on patterns of tourism, but not I suspect on the volume. Similarly with anti-tourist terrorism: rather than forgo their holiday, tourists will just go to more friendly, more suitable places. Anyway isn't this pattern of dispersal reminiscent of spreading the tourist load that we have (mistakenly) been told is the answer to honeypot tourism?

I do not see why the onslaught of virtual reality should have the devastating effects on demand and tourism destinations that some predict (Gerken, 1993). The argument seems to be that, as a result of virtual reality, people will not bother going to places any more. Supposedly they will have 'experienced it' and therefore satisfied that element of the seen it/done it mentality without ever, physically, being in the destination. To me in the early 1950s the images of the *National Geographic Magazine* were the (then) equivalent of virtual reality. Later *Zoo Quest*, *The Komodo Dragon*, Hans and Lotte Hass, Armand and Michaela Dennis and Cousteau's exploits in the *Calypso* were virtually virtual reality. Cinemascope, Surroundasound etc. were further stages in this continuum, as indeed, I suppose, are the current television travel programmes. But doesn't each of these advances, as it reaches a wider and wider audience, further stimulate and encourage travel to these destinations rather than satisfying a desire from a 'sedentary stance'. As far as I can see, without my head-set on, virtual reality will heighten the desire to travel rather than temper it.

Aren't numbers of all tourist set to escalate—business, VFR, holiday, whatever? Ecotourism is not immune from this explosion, though, of course, estimates vary. On the contrary, according to Ryan, reporting on the paradoxical effects of green tourism in County Clare, Ireland 'tourism is expected to double in size by the year 2000 and ecotourism is the fastest growing sector' (Ryan, 1994). Spectacular growth is also predicted by Dirks in the new journal, *Eco-Traveler*, '8 million people have subscribed to this mode of travel (i.e. eco-travel) and an additional 35 million are expected to do so in the next three years' (Dirks, 1993).

There are no indications of where Dirks's figures are from and how they were derived. Even so, they raise one of the conundrums of ecotourism. On the one hand, if, as the WTTERC suggest, ecotourism is a peripheral, marginal phenomenon, then what is all the fuss about? Against this, if it does have sufficient substance and volume to make a significant contribution to 'tourism planning and management' then how on earth (and where on earth?) is it to avoid the inherent problems associated with volume?

Actually to refer to this apparent dilemma as a conundrum is misleading as the 'solution' seems pretty straightforward. The fuss, the attention ecotourism is receiving is, in my opinion, totally out of proportion to its effectiveness as a salutary management tool. This, of course, is the precise reason for that attention—ecotourism's impotence is its main attraction. The perfect political fob, it soothes consciences, demands no sacrifices and allows extended holiday choice while providing an ideal shield, doubling as a marketing ploy, for the tourism industry. Lurking behind a 'management' façade, green

ecotourism is simply a policy of growth: witness 'more people than ever before are beating a path to the Burren as green tourism takes a hold in the West of Ireland' (*Independent on Sunday*, 18-9-1991).

Currently ecotourism seems to be neatly, and conveniently, sidestepping the critical issues of volume, of mass. As projections for increased participation in tourism, including ecotourism, are realised then the futility of eco/sustainable tourism will, I believe, become painfully apparent.

References

Anscombe, J. (1991) 'The gentle traveller', *New Woman*, June: 51–53.

Ashcroft, P. (1993) 'One hundred and one dull machinations', *Journal of Sustainable Tourism*, 1(2): 346.

Boorstin, D. (1962) *The Image. What Happened to the American Dream*, Weidenfeld & Nicolson, London.

Bramwell, B. (1991) 'Shades of green tourism', *Leisure Management*, February: 40–41.

Bramwell, B. and Lane, B. (1993) 'Sustainable tourism: an evolving global approach', *Journal of Sustainable Tourism*, 1(1): 1–5.

Butler, R. (1990) 'Alternative tourism: pious hope or Trojan horse?', *Journal of Travel Research*, Winter: 40–45.

Carey, P. (1988) 'American dreams', in *Contemporary Australian Short Stories*, Bail, M. (Ed.), Faber, London, pp. 331–342.

Cazes, G. (1989) 'Alternative tourism: reflections of an ambiguous concept', in *Towards Appropriate Tourism*, Singh, T., Theuns, L. and Go, F. (Eds), Lang, Frankfurt, pp. 117–126.

Center for Responsible Tourism (1993) 'Codes of ethics for tourists', Center for Responsible Tourism, Box 827, San Anselmo, CA 94979, USA.

Cohen, E. (1972) 'Towards a sociology of international tourism', *Social Research*, 39: 1.

Cohen, E. (1988) 'Traditions in the qualitative sociology of tourism', *Annals of Tourism Research*, 15: 29–46.

Cohen, E. (1989) 'Alternative tourism—a critique', in *Towards Appropriate Tourism*, Singh, T., Theuns, L. and Go, F. (Eds) Lang, Frankfurt, pp. 127–142.

Cooper, C. and Ozdil, I. (1992) 'From mass to responsible tourism: the Turkish 1992 experience', *Tourism Management*, 13(4): 377–387.

Dirks, B. (1993) 'A new breed of traveler', *Eco-Traveler*, No. 12, Special section: 'World Traveler', North West Airlines.

The Economist (1993) 'Aid and the environment. The greening of giving', *The Economist*, 25 December: 54–56.

Ecotourism Society (1993) 'A guide for planners and managers', Ecotourism Society, PO Box 755, North Bennington, VT 05257, USA.

ETB (English Tourist Board) (1990) *Tourism in National Parks. A Guide to Good Practice*, ETB, London.

ETB (English Tourist Board) (1991a) *The Green Light. A Guide to Sustainable Tourism*, ETB, London.

ETB (English Tourist Board) (1991b) *Tourism and the Environment—Maintaining the Balance*, ETB, London.

Fussell, P. (1982) *Abroad. British Literary Travelling between the Wars*, Oxford University Press, New York.

Fussell, P. (1990) 'The quest for reality', *The Guardian*, 18 October.

Gerken, G. (1993) *Das Grosse Nagual Wiener*, Bauer Spezialzeitschriftenverlag K. G., Munich, pp. 68–72.

Godfrey, K. (1993) 'Tourism alternatives', *Journal of Sustainable Tourism*, 1(1): 66–70.

Green, S. (1990) 'The future for green tourism', *Tourism Insights*, September: D5–12.

Gunn, C. (1994) *Tourism Planning*, Taylor & Francis, London, p. 82.

Hutchings, V. (1993) 'Green gauge', *New Statesman and Society*, 19 November: p. 93.

Inskeep, E. (1991) *Tourism Planning*, Van Nostrand Reinhold, New York.

Krippendorf, J. (1987) *The Holidaymaker*, Heinemann, London.

Krippendorf, J. (1993) In Tourism and the Environment Conference Proceedings, ETB, London.

Lane, B. (1989) 'Modern mass tourism: a critique', *The Independent*, 13 May.

Maddox, B. (1993) 'Eyes open wider to the green scene', *Financial Times* survey, 22 December, p. 1.

May, V. (1991) 'Tourism, environment and development—values, sustainability and stewardship', *Tourism Management*, June: 112–118.

Mayor, F. (1991) 'Message' in *Anatolia: a World Heritage*, Ministry of Culture, Ankara.

Middleton, V. (1993) *Tourism*, Issue 78, Tourism Society, London.

Murphy, P. (1985) *Tourism. A Community Approach*, Routledge, London.

Nash, D. and Butler, R. (1990) 'Towards sustainable tourism', *Tourism Management*, 11(3): 263.

Nicholson, G. (1993) *Day Trips to the Desert*, Sceptre, London.

O'Grady, R. (1981) *Third World Stopover: the Tourism Debate*, World Council of Churches, Bangkok.

Owen, E., Witt, S. and Gammon, S. (1993) 'From theory to practice', *Tourism Management*, December: 463–474.

Pearce, D. (1989) *Tourist Development*, Longman, Harlow.

Pigram, J. (1990) 'Sustainable tourism, policy consideration', *Journal of Tourism Studies*, 2(November): 2–9.

Platt, S. (1991) 'The tender tax', *New Statesman and Society*, 9 August: 19–20.

Rivers, P. (1974) *The Restless Generation. A Crisis in Mobility*, David Pointer, London.

Royal Bank of Canada (1990) 'The treasures of travel', *Royal Bank Letter*, 71(2).

Ryan, S. (1994) 'The battle of the Burren', *Sunday Times* 2 January: 28.

Sargent, F. (1974) *Human Ecology*, American Elsevier, New York, p. 16.

Seaton, A. (1991) 'Quality tourism sustained! A small island case from the Shetlands', in 'Quality Tourism—Concept of a Sustainable Development', *AIEST Annual*, **33**: 209–237, St. Gallen, Switzerland.

Smith, V. and Eadington, W. (1992) *Tourism Alternatives*, University of Pennsylvania Press, Philadelphia, PA.

Sofield, T. (1991) 'Sustainable ethnic tourism in the South Pacific. Some principles', *Journal of Tourism Studies*, 2(1): 56–72.

Stevens, T. (1990) 'Greener than green', *Leisure Management*, September: 64–66.

The Times (1994) Zimbabwe Airways Advertisement, *Times Magazine*, 8 January.

Tourism Concern (1991) 'Himalayan code', Tourism Concern, Roehampton Institute, London.

Tourism Concern (1992) *Beyond the Green Horizon*, Tourism Concern and WWT, London.

Tourism Concern (1993) *Tourism in Focus*, No. 9, Tourism Concern, London.

Tourism Society (1991) 'Sustainable tourism. Development in balance with the environment', Tourist Society, London.

Waldstein, E. A. (1991) 'Environmental policy and politics' in *Political Issues in America*, Davies, P. J. and Waldstein, E. A. (Eds), Manchester University Press, Manchester and New York.

Wheeler, M. (1992) 'Applying ethics to the tourism industry', *European Review*, 1(4): 227–235.

Wheeller, B. (1991) 'Tourism troubled times', *Tourism Management*, June: 91–96.

Wheeller, B. (1992) 'Is progressive tourism appropriate?', *Tourism Management*, March.

Wheeller, B. (1993a) 'Sustaining the ego', *Journal of Sustainable Tourism*, 1(2): 128.

Wheeller, B. (1993b) 'Willing victims of ego-trap', in *Focus*, No. 9: 14, Tourism Concern, London.

Wickers, D. (1992) 'Whither green', *Sunday Times*, 5 January.

Wight, P. (1993) 'Eco-tourism: ethics or eco-shell', *Journal of Travel Research*, 31(3): 3–9.

Wood, K. and House, S. (1991) *The Good Tourist*, Mandarin, London.

WTTERC (World Travel and Tourism Environment Research Centre) (1992, 1993) 'Report on environment and development', *Annual Reports*, WTTERC, Oxford.

68 Environmental auditing: current best practice (with special reference to British tourism firms)

B. GOODALL

A duty of care—the tourism industry's environmental responsibility

Tourism products and tourist experiences depend on the quality of destination environments. This dependence is on primary resources: the destination's physical environment (both natural and built heritage). Used within certain limits, destination environments are a sustainable resource, in the sense that present use does not compromise the ability of future generations to meet their needs, even though all components of the destination environment are not naturally renewable. Exploitation of the primary resource base for tourism requires development of secondary tourism resources such as accommodation and infrastructure in destinations and of the means of transport to reach destinations. Tourism, like any other industry or service, consumes resources, produces wastes and has potential to damage the environment, the very resource base which supports its existence. Compared to heavy industry, tourism is a relatively benign use of the environment, but there is increasing evidence that its present and past resource-use practices have resulted in significant environmental problems (Mathieson and Wall, 1982; Pearce, 1985; Farrell and McLellan, 1987; Romeril, 1989; Cater and Goodall, 1992). Mass tourism, in particular, is a fairly throughput-intensive activity and its continued operation at current levels (ignoring predicted growth), transporting large numbers of holiday-makers over long distances to concentrated destinations where high consumption is encouraged, implies further environmental damage. Given this dependence on environment the tourism industry, tourist destinations, and the tourists themselves might be expected to share a common interest in caring for the environment. Not only is there a destination dimension to consider, relating to overuse of primary resource sites, resource demands for accommodation and infrastructure and pollution from local emissions and waste disposal, but also a wider global one, involving issues such as stratospheric ozone depletion, tropical deforestation and acid rain to which tourist travel and secondary resource provision contribute.

Even though the overwhelming volume of environmental and resource threats come from economic sectors other than tourism, this is no reason for ignoring tourism's relevance to environmental quality. Some erosion and pollution is the result of inappropriate tourism development or of excessive visitor numbers in certain destinations, reflecting both the domination of promotional efforts over destination approaches to tourism and an earlier lack of understanding of the tourism–environment relationship. Increasing societal awareness of environmental and development issues at both global and national scales (World Commission on Environment and Development, 1987; Department of the Environment, 1990), placing emphasis on concepts such as sustainable development, accompanied by environmental legislation requiring evaluation of proposed developments, and allied to the green consumer phenomenon, is changing the general operational milieu of business. Business thinking on the environment is being realigned, adopting more ethical and responsible attitudes and switching from reactive to anticipatory modes of behaviour (Lloyd, 1990). Tourism firms have not been in the vanguard of such change but they can no longer afford to be spectators.

The need for action is clear; the general business milieu is increasingly receptive—how is the tourism industry reacting? Tourism, in the United Kingdom, is seen as a private sector activity and responsibility therefore rests with existing tourism firms to grasp the environmental initiative. The industry at large, and firms individually, can be expected to adopt additional objectives concerning the maintenance and enhancement of the environment and resources. Environmental quality becomes an integral component of total quality management (Welford and Gouldson, 1993:77–79) for tourism firms, given tourism's dependence on environment. This implies sustainability of tourism's physical resource base and the practice of environment-sustainable tourism, that is, prioritising the duty of care for the environment. If this is over-ambitious, at the very least, tourism firms can review their existing operations to make them environmentally more friendly. Since it is present tourism use that damages the environment, techniques are needed which measure and monitor current environmental performance of tourism firms and which evaluate alternative ways of improving that performance. Environmental auditing provides the basis for such business practice and is consistent with the view of management as a controlled cyclic process based on continuous monitoring of impacts and change, the development of knowledge and the feeding back of these into decision-making by formalised processes. The adoption of environmental auditing by tourism firms is, however, a means to an end—sustaining the viability of the tourism industry!

Implementing environmental auditing in tourism— principles and procedures

Environmental auditing, originally developed as a management tool in manufacturing industry to assess compliance with environmental legislation and regulations, provides tourism firms with the means to evaluate operationally their current environmental performance, identifying any negative impacts and evaluating opportunities for change. Defined as 'a management tool comprising a systematic, documented, periodic and objective evaluation of how well organizations, management and equipment are performing with the aim of safeguarding the environment by facilitating management control of environmental practices, and assessing compliance with organizational policies, which would include regulatory equipments and standards applicable' (European Commission, 1991), environmental auditing is one component of an environment management system for tourism firms acting to reduce the negative environmental impact of their activities. It is an effective means of implementing and assessing, through regular and comprehensive review, a tourism firm's environmental policies and a flexible tool, applicable at both company and establishment levels, e.g. the hotel chain and the individual hotel, as well as to tourist destinations (Stabler and Goodall, 1993). Use of environmental auditing can bring commercial benefits ranging from cost reductions from waste minimization, marketing advantages, improved company image, raising loan capital, facilitation of insurance cover, better employee motivation and recruitment, to the identification of environmental problems before they become liabilities incurring litigation and clean-up costs and the development of benchmarks of good environmental practice (Welford and Gouldson, 1993: 101–102; Goodall, 1994a, 1994b). No tourism product or service can be perfectly environmentally sustainable since fossil fuel is consumed in transporting tourists to and from destinations, but even here environmental auditing can be the catalyst for making the product more environmentally friendly, e.g. reduced fuel consumption and emissions resulting from better routeing or improved engine efficency.

What progress has the British tourism industry made in evaluating environmental performance? Before answering this question guidelines need to be established as to what might be expected of tourism firms: these cover both the principles underpinning action to improve practices demonstrated to have negative environmental impacts and the management procedures necessary to monitor environmental performance.

There are three dimensions—technical, legislative, and business—bearing on these principles. Certain improvements involving equipment and materials, depend upon technological knowledge. Consider, for example, further reduction in noise nuisance from aircraft. Over the past two decades, many airlines have achieved significant reductions in noise disturbance from aircraft, at and around airports, as they modernised their fleets, replacing older, noisy aircraft by quieter, new ones, e.g. the take-off noise footprint, at the 85 dB(A) contour, of a Boeing 767-300 (with RB 211-424H engines) has an area some 3.5 times smaller than that of the older Boeing 747-100 (with JT9D-7/7A engines). However, technical limits appear to be restricting any future dramatic progress in cutting aircraft noise at source (British Airways, 1993). Improved environmental performance in one area may transfer environmental problems elsewhere. The increased efficiency of modern jet aircraft engines reduces fuel consumption and carbon dioxide (CO_2) emissions. However, the technology promoting better fuel efficiency—increased combustion temperature—leads to greater nitrogen oxides (NO_x) emissions (which are also thought to contribute to global warming) (British Airways, 1993). Airlines, seeking safer chemicals to use in aircraft chemical toilets, switched away from formaldehyde (thought to be carcinogenic) but still rely on ammonium salts (a potential skin irritant) (Elkington and Hailes, 1992). Where technological knowledge constrains practical action, tourism firms proceed with 'business as usual', although, if the environmental damage is so great then, in the absence of any technological fix, prohibition of the activity in question may be the only course of action. The latter requires national legislation and, frequently, international agreement.

The legislative framework set by governments is part of the operational milieu of tourism firms. Increasingly firms' activities which interact with the environment are subject to legislative regulation. Not only are health and safety of employees and consumer protection targeted areas but also minimum legal standards for air and water quality and the control of waste disposal are set. Such legislation is consistent with the 'polluter pays' principle. Where business is subject to environmental legislation the very minimum required of tourism firms is that they comply with all legislation relevant to their environmental performance. Legislative regulations may be of international origin. For example, under the Law of the Sea (UNEP, 1991), environmental protection is a duty and there are rules covering pollution from ships, for example, companies operating cruise liners in the Baltic, North, Mediterranean and Red Seas must compact and bring ashore all glass, metal and plastic rubbish, although food waste can be discharged more than 20 km from the nearest shore. The International Civil Aviation Organisation exercises responsibility for the development of environmental standards for aircraft, e.g. aircraft noise certification, which are confirmed in national legislation. Tourism firms must comply with a wide range of national environmental legislation, including pollution control and land-use planning. Foremost is legislation dealing with air and water quality and waste disposal. In the United Kingdom standards controlling road vehicle emissions and noise in use are set and updated via regulations made under the 1972 and 1974 Road Traffic Acts; all public places for music and dancing are licensed under the 1982 Local Government (Miscellaneous) Provisions Act by the local authority with nuisance from entertainment noise being covered by the 1990 Environment Protection Act; the latter act also deals with disposal of all 'controlled waste' (including commercial waste from tourism premises), placing a duty of care on producers of waste to ensure that waste on their premises, e.g. a hotel, is safely contained in appropriate waste containers and that it is transferred to a registered carrier or licensed waste disposal operator; consents for the discharge of aqueous trade effluents, for example, from activities such as vehicle washing and catering, are required under the 1989 Water Act. It must be emphasised that compliance with such legislation only ensures a safe minimum environmental standard, leaving room for further improvement in the environmental performance of tourism firms.

The decision to modify practices, over and above compliance with legal requirements, is clearly a business one. Action will depend upon the consequences for a firm's costs and revenues, the incidence varying through time (Goodall, 1992). Consider the introduction of energy conservation measures into a hotel. 'Good housekeeping practices' which match source to load in respect to heating, ventilation and air-conditioning equipment can bring immediate savings at low cost. Other options, such as heat recovery systems (e.g. installation of heat exchangers) or alternative energy sources (e.g. installation of solar panels) incur capital costs in anticipation of lower future energy costs and are likely to have a long payback period. If there is any associated price increase, average occupancy may fall and revenues decline. The timing of any change will also reflect unexpended economic lives of current equipment and buildings, but sooner or later opportunities arise to replace equipment and refurbish buildings. Thus the adoption of improved environmental practices depends on the trade-off between the costs and benefits of such actions. This is recognised in that fundamental criterion of regulatory pollution control, *best practicable means* (BPM), under which changes in practice are evaluated in terms of what is reasonable taking into account costs of modification and effect on the firm's viability. In the European Union this concept now appears as *best available technology not entailing excessive cost* (BATNEEC): BAT normally applies but the presumption may be modified where the costs of applying BAT are excessive in relation to the environmental protection or improvement achieved. It is also consistent with *best practicable environmental option* (BPEO) which, emphasising integrated pollution control, recognises that a firm could release emissions into more than one environmental medium and identifies the preferred option as that most beneficial or least damaging to the environment as a whole. The cost–benefit equation underpinning any firm's adoption of environmentally sound practices has to be viewed as a value-maximising strategy for its shareholders (Campbell, 1990). The most enlightened firms act according to the *precautionary principle*, modifying their business practices even before clear causal links to environmental damage have been established by scientific evidence.

The World Travel and Tourism Council (1991) recommends the tourism industry adopts a systematic and comprehensive approach to the environment which involves the use of environmental auditing and impact assessment procedures at individual company level. Any tourism firm formally adopting environmental auditing will have previously agreed a corporate policy embracing environmental objectives as part of that firm's mission statement. Thus, one of British Airway's (1993) seven goals is stated as being 'a good neighbour, concerned for the community and the environment'. This implies that a scoping exercise has been undertaken to identify the principal environmental issues facing the firm, i.e. an understanding established of the nature of the interaction between its operations and the environment; it also implies that an environmental review has been completed to determine the baseline against which future performance can be measured. A formal environmental policy follows in which the tourism firm sets itself objectives covering:

(1) compliance with relevant environmental legislation and indication of a willingness to develop reasonable and workable regulations;
(2) reduction or elimination of any negative environmental impacts of current activities and avoidance of any negative impacts from proposed developments;
(3) development of environmentally friendly products;
(4) sustainable use of resources, which includes increasing the efficiency of resource use, minimisation of waste and reduction of overconsumption (especially where resources are non-renewable and non-recyclable), the substitution of environmentally benign inputs and equipment wherever possible, and the safe disposal of wastes where the latter are unavoidable;
(5) the fostering amongst employees, and also customers and communities in which it functions, an understanding of environmental issues.

The policy statement provides the basis for formulating an action plan setting specific targets for improved environmental performance. Corporate policies and plans are implemented and assessed through management techniques such as environmental auditing and a formal environmental management system is required within the tourism firm, with appropriate recognition of responsibility at senior management level. In this context, BS 7750, the British Standards Institution's standard on environmental management systems (British Standards Institution, 1991) provides a generic model to help firms establish, develop and maintain their own purpose-built environmental management system. It is fully compatible with the European Community's voluntary eco-management and audit scheme (Commission of the European Community, 1992) introduced by Council regulation in 1993.

Environmental auditing must be undertaken regularly to assess whether a tourism firm's environmental management system is functioning effectively and to measure the extent of improvement in the firm's environmental performance relative to its stated objectives. A methodological examination of the firm, its facilities and operations is involved, including analysis and testing to verify that legal requirements and internal policies are being met. Judgements are based on evidence gathered during audit concerning the measurement of environmental performance (from inspection of company records, examination of maintenance programmes, site inspections of buildings and operational processes, etc.) and the effectiveness of management control systems (including chains of responsibility, competence of personnel, and authorisation procedures). Wherever possible, comparison is made with industry averages to establish appropriate benchmarking. In summary the key purposes of an environmental audit are:

(1) to judge whether the tourism firm's environmental management system is performing satisfactorily;
(2) to verify compliance with relevant environmental legislation;
(3) to verify compliance with the firm's stated policy;
(4) to minimize human exposure to risk from the environment and to ensure appropriate health and safety provision;
(5) to identify and assess the firm's risk resulting from environmental failure of its activities;
(6) to assess the impact on the environment, both local and global, of its plant, processes and products;
(7) to advise the firm on any environmental improvements it could make;
(8) to review the firm's internal procedures needed to achieve its environmental objectives (after Welford and Gouldson (1993)).

The audit report provides the firm's management with information about compliance status, detailing any consequences of not correcting deficiencies (especially if litigation against the firm is likely), and includes recommendations for appropriate improvements, prioritised in relation to the firm's environmental policy. The regular practice of auditing monitors improvement in the firm's environmental performance over time, bringing a more consistent approach to evaluation of the firm's environmental impact and leading to further development of integrated environmental management systems. This reinforces the World Travel and Tourism Council's (1991) view that annual environmental audits of all on-going tourism activities are an integral management tool of a tourism firm with a proactive commitment to environmentally responsible tourism. Various forms of environmental audit can be undertaken by tourism firms, ranging from full corporate and site audits to partial ones highlighting particular environmental issues or concentrating upon compliance or individual products (Goodall, 1992, 1994b), some of which are more apposite at the firm scale and others at the establishment level (Stabler and Goodall, 1993). The results are given added credence where audits are conducted independently (or at least subject to external validation) and are publicly available (Pearce, 1992). Coupled with environmental impact assessment of proposed tourism development (Green and Hunter, 1992; Butler, 1993), the management techniques exist, therefore, for tourism firms to improve their overall environmental performance—always assuming that management is willing.

Best British environmental practice

The 'model' firm has a formal, written environmental policy agreed at board level, with a management structure and full environmental auditing procedures to implement it, and publishes at least an annual report evaluating its current environmental performance. How do British tourism firms measure up? To date, on most counts, generally not that well! Since the adoption of eco-management and audit is voluntary, the onus is upon the individual firm and the nature of the tourism industry—a fragmented, competitive, high-risk industry, dominated by many, small, family-operated firms in tourist destinations—militates against such innovation. This remains so even where there is encouragement and advice available from trade organizations—for example, the Hotel Catering and Institutional Management Association (1991) urges member companies to formulate a policy embracing commitment to the concept of sustainable development and to taking practical action to protect the environment—as well as from other non-profit organizations, for example Green Flag International, established by a group of conservationists to work with tourism firms to improve the environmental quality of holidays. Many tourism firms are sympathetic towards the general environmental concern but this is not always translated into action, even less frequently into an agreed, written environmental policy: this is especially so in the case of tour operators (Elkington and Hailes, 1992). The lead comes from large firms, especially in the air transport and hospitality sectors. British Airways, for example, has environmental objectives as an agreed goal of corporate policy, has produced a 'health, safety and environment manual' for internal use, and is developing environmental performance indicators to measure progress. They also have an exemplary management structure under which the Head of the Environment Branch draws on an internal advisory Environment Council and reports through the Director of Safety, Security and Environment to the Chairman and the Board. The International Hotels Environment Initiative (1993), involving eleven trans-national hotel chains, has also produced an environmental practice guide (based largely on Inter-Continental Hotels' in-house manual) which pools experience and is available to the whole of the hospitality sector.

Systematic information on the use of environmental auditing by British tourism firms is lacking. It is highly unlikely, however, that tourism firms outperform British industry in general where less than half of all companies have formal environmental policies and less than a quarter carry out any environmental auditing procedure (Coe, 1991); moreover, performance in the small firm sector is particularly poor as only one in ten firms undertakes any auditing (Barrow and Barnett, 1990). The response in the tourism industry, primarily from transnational and multi-establishment firms, reflects the complexity of environmental auditing and the demands it makes on company resources. Auditing can be expensive in its own right and may entail employment of external consultants (for small firms the 'in-house' option is rarely practicable). Examples are to be found of tourism firms using particular types of audit but few firms are aware of, and none use, the full range.

Results from a targeted sample of tourism firms, i.e. which had publicly declared their interest in environmental issues, carried out by the Tourism Research and Policy Unit at Reading revealed less than half of these committed firms carried out formal audits: individual responses frequently emphasised that many sensitive issues were involved and, therefore, the firm did not wish its position to be identified. Where auditing was undertaken, partial audits were most common with hotel chains most likely to use site audits at establishment (hotel) level whilst product and associate (supplier) audits were most commonly used by tour operators. Compliance audits were considered irrelevant by tour operators but used by a quarter of the hotel chains responding and also regularly practised by airlines. Compliance audits have been completed for British Airways by external consultants of the firm's special waste storage facilities at both Gatwick and Heathrow airports and environmental reviews have been undertaken in collaboration with consultants, of such diverse activities as British Airways Holidays and aqueous effluents from its activities at Heathrow (British Airways, 1993). Eurocamp had Green Flag International carry out an independent environmental audit of their activities and do undertake associate audits of their equipment suppliers' environmental practices relating to production methods, packaging and waste disposal. ARA Catering have also made suppliers responsible for reducing packaging, although not requiring formal audits.

Most audit reports remain internal company documents, understandable if incriminating information will be revealed or information is considered commercially sensitive. Information made public in company environmental reports is often difficult to interpret because the environmental parameters quoted, e.g. emission or waste quantities, lack perspective in relation to total inputs or outputs, industrial averages or company targets (Pearce, 1992). Allowing for limited disclosure, it must be concluded that, at present, environmental auditing is a minority business management practice within the British tourism industry, confined in the main to a few large firms. The latter can bring smaller firms acting as their suppliers into the net by demanding evidence of environmental probity of those suppliers (but they are not necessarily part of the tourism industry). Furthermore where environmental auditing is used it appears to be on a 'one-off' basis in many cases and the ideal of regular repeat remains to be achieved.

Limited use of environmental auditing does not preclude improvement of British tourism firms' environmental performance, but improvements that have taken place are those bringing obvious benefits to profitability. These improvements can be illustrated under headings pertinent to environment-sustainable tourism.

Source reduction of inputs

Where current tourism levels can be met using fewer inputs resource demands will be reduced: this is especially important where resources, e.g. fossil fuels, are non-renewable and non-recyclable. Foremost amongst current best practice are energy-conservation measures, particularly in the transport and hospitality sectors. Actions target either operator efficiency in terms of 'good housekeeping practices' which can be introduced immediately by adapting current work practices or building, equipment and system efficiency requiring capital investment (the timing of which reflects the firm's replacement policy and the unexpended economic lives of current buildings and equipment). In the former case, airlines have improved aircraft fuel efficiency as a result of better estimation of safe fuel load and reduced tankering (fuel carried to a destination to avoid picking up fuel there at high cost), as well as in-cabin measures to reduce weight such as stocking duty-free spirits bottled in lightweight plastic. In hotels, reduced energy consumption is achieved by shutting off equipment when not needed (e.g. radiators in unoccupied bedrooms) and matching operation to load (e.g. night setback on refrigeration plant). Better forecasting of food demands in hotels and restaurants minimises overproduction and plate waste whilst certain caterers have reduced road hours in distribution activities by delivering outside congested periods. Some hotels and caterers are adapting their product purchasing policy via 'pre-cycling' which aims to reduce packaging (e.g. doing away with individual pre-packed portions) and considers the advantages of local and bulk buying in reducing transport consumption. Improved environmental performance deriving from capital investment includes better building insulation, heating ventilation and air-conditioning systems, lighting systems, etc. in all types of buildings. Environmental benefits from reduced resource use, especially energy consumption, are primarily global in impact, although there may be some, e.g.

water conservation, which are of value to a particular destination.

'End-of-pipe' technologies to reduce wastes and pollution

Production generates wastes and, since disposal is increasingly controlled by legislation and charged, cost savings for tourism firms follow from reductions in the amounts needing disposal. Source reduction of inputs helps reduce waste generated but more direct methods involve reuse, for example, an airline switching to reusable cutlery and crockery for in-flight meals, a restaurant determining the optimum number of times cooking oil can be re-used, or British Airways' retreading of tyres up to six times (British Airways, 1993). Recovery from waste, involving the sorting, storage and collection/ delivery of materials for recycling, is now practised by tourism firms for many wastes, e.g. paper, cardboard, glass, metals, plastics, laser cartridges, kitchen oils, wood pallets, etc. Although not a major source of pollutants, tourism should seek to minimize emission discharges to the environment wherever possible; however, there are limits to what can be done in the short term, because, for instance, the composition of existing fleets of airlines, coach operators and car hire firms is fixed. In the longer term, fleet replacement policy provides an opportunity to introduce less-polluting vehicles, for example, by switching to diesel or unleaded petrol-driven vehicles for airline ground services, by hotels and organizations like the National Trust, as well as for hire cars included in package holiday deals. Such improved environmental performance is technology-dependent, for example, the new Boeing 777, powered by GE 90 engines incorporating a dual annular combustor, due in service with British Airways towards the end of 1995, is expected to reduce NO_x emissions by some 40% (British Airways, 1993). There will always be some wastes which need to be disposed of in a responsible manner, with special care being exercised in the case of any hazardous wastes (which do arise from airlines' maintenance and servicing programmes for example). Improvements in disposal practices are possible, for example, the National Trust, following an internal environmental audit and consultation with the National Rivers Authority, has introduced a septic tank husbandry guide (Jarman, 1992), whilst airlines now collect in-flight sewage in sealed containers for discharge into sewers on arrival at airports. Both global and destination environments benefit from such end-of-pipe technologies, the latter where pollution was localised.

Control of environmentally unfriendly/substitution of environmentally benign inputs

Current tourism activity continues to use a range of toxic, corrosive, infectious, explosive or flammable materials. International agreement may have been reached on phasing out the production of such materials, but their use can persist for some considerable time. The production of PCBs (polychlorinated biphenyls), used for their 'cooling' properties in electrical equipment but acknowledged as carcinogenic and toxic at low levels of concentration in the environment, ceased some ten years ago, but equipment is still in use in hotels, etc. and its disposal will need to be carefully controlled when replacement takes place. The production of halons was banned from the end of 1993, but essential uses will still be permitted, e.g. in portable fire extinguishers on board aircraft (British Airways, 1993). In other cases, tourism firms have been able to substitute environmentally benign inputs, for example, hotel chains now insist on toiletries and cleaning materials which are CFC (chlorofluorocarbon)-free and phosphate-free and increasingly use environmentally responsible paper products, i.e. non-chlorine gas bleached toilet tissues, unbleached coffee filter papers, minimum bleached tea-bags. Airlines are using less harmful chemicals to clean aircraft and, when preparing aircraft for repainting, may now use an aquastrip (high pressure water) system in place of the toxic dichloromethane and phenol mixture previously used. Whilst a non-polluting potassium acetate solution is now used to clear runways at Gatwick and Heathrow airports of ice and snow, there is no alternative to the use of (polluting) glycol in aircraft de-icing treatment (O'Connor and Douglas, 1993). Stationery, tour operator brochures and other paper products made from recycled paper or increasingly from pulp supplied from sustainable yield managed forests are commonly used. The environmental benefit is realised primarily at the global scale, except, again, where pollution was localised in a destination.

Noise reduction

Tourism can expose tourists, employees and third parties to noise (i.e. unwanted sound), especially as a consequence of its use of air transport, as well as putting them at risk from non-tourism sources of noise. Noise control can provide tourists with a better environment, help improve employees' productivity and limit annoyance to third parties. Aircraft noise is a source of nuisance to people living near airports, with sleep disturbance from night flights being particularly controversial. Measured in terms of the number of people affected by aircraft noise above the accepted threshold level for integrated noise exposure there has been a considerable improvement over the last 20 years at London Heathrow where the number has dropped by 75% (from 2 million in 1974) as aircraft noise has been reduced and flight-paths have been designated to minimise the numbers of persons overflown (British Airways, 1993). Hotels aim to maintain reasonably low sound levels throughout guest areas and especially a low level of sound transmission between adjoining guest rooms to ensure an appropriate degree of privacy. In new hotels much is achieved at the design stage by separating noisy plant rooms from guest areas and building to high standards of insulation. In existing hotels maximum sound levels in guest rooms can be established for telephone ring, television sound, etc. and the equipment set accordingly but there may be a need to relocate, even eliminate, noise sources such as discos. Where the noise source is outside the control or influence of the tourism firm some 'barrier' has to be considered, e.g. better windows and sound insulation. Since sound attenuates rapidly in the atmosphere, benefits from noise reduction are spatially highly localised.

Development of environmentally friendly products

So far, best practice has emphasised resource consumption and waste/pollution minimisation, but environmentally damaging effects to primary tourism resources may also follow from:

(1) the nature of the tourism activity, e.g. piste preparation in skiing areas. In the Cairngorms, Scotland, it is acknowledged that damage caused by winter tourism reduces the area's attractiveness to summer visitors;
(2) the volume of tourists, for example, the delicate tomb frescoes in the Valley of the Kings, Upper Egypt, are suffering from increased humidity due to body moisture from tourists and progressive fading from use of camera flashes (now banned);
(3) the behaviour of the tourists, for example, even a photographic safari can disturb the breeding and feeding of wildlife.

Much therefore depends on the holiday product. Both large and small tour operators have been innovative in creating new products, ranging from cycling tours to ecotours, and in modifying existing products, e.g. the type of accommodation used, as part of their drive to make holidays more environmentally responsible. Saga Holidays discuss environmental policy in general with destination authorities. Pure Crete encourage the restoration of derelict, vernacular properties for use as tourist accommodation. Many small tour operators use local accommodation (sometimes people's homes) and public transport. Moswin Tours has, for over a decade, ruled that company coaches should not drive into areas of medieval buildings. Tourist numbers may also be restricted, at least in terms of group size, e.g. Zoe Holidays restricts numbers participating in its wildlife and natural history tours whilst Explore Worldwide's small-group tours are designed to minimise demands on destination infrastructure.

Clearly the destination environment benefits in the above cases, but environmentally friendly products need careful interpretation. For example, the 'environmentally friendly' rooms of certain international hotel chains have air and water purification systems (highly desirable for guest comfort in tropical/subtropical destinations)—in reality these are *environmentally controlled* rooms consuming more energy. A 'transfer' problem arises where British tour operators offering Himalayan treks substitute kerosene for local woodfuel at campsites: this reduces deforestation rates in the destination but a non-renewable resource is being substituted for a potentially renewable one and extra energy is consumed transporting kerosene to the area. The balance or trade-off may not be clear-cut, an idea extendable to holiday complexes such as the Center Parcs developments. These are located and designed to high environmental standards, avoid areas of environmental value and incorporate the latest energy-conservation measures. However, such 'indoor' tropical paradises consume more energy than if located in a tropical destination although there will be transport savings if tourists are diverted from long-haul destinations.

Staff environmental training

The tourism firm's environmental commitment must be communicated to its workforce; hence, its environmental management system should include training on environmental issues for all staff to ensure they understand the firm's environmental objectives and implement plans accordingly. Tour operators, such as Allegro Holidays and Eurocamp, provide environmental training for staff, including their destination representatives and agents. British Airways features environmental issues throughout its corporate training programmes, runs awareness campaigns when appropriate, e.g. regarding the duty of care for waste disposal under the Environment Protection Act, and involves the workforce in identifying environmentally responsible ideas (British Airways, 1993).

Environmental education of customers

Tourists vary in their environmental awareness and, especially where visiting fragile destinations, may need advice on what is acceptable behaviour, even where the product is supposedly environmentally friendly. Tour operators can help educate tourists about the customs, culture and environmental issues of the destinations visited. Some include advice in their brochures, e.g. Arctic Experience, Thomsons; others issue advice amongst information distributed to their tourists, e.g. Allegro Holidays, Bales Tours, CV Travel, EcoSafaris, Eurocamp, Headwater Holidays, Moswin Tours, and Saga Holidays. Such tour operator-issued codes of conduct for behaviour are a first step in consumer education, but there is a need to standardise coverage and advice, as, for example, in the skiers' code currently under consideration by the Association of Independent Tour Operators. The benefits of such consumer education are noted first and foremost in destinations; but even tourists' home environments may benefit in the long term from their residents' greater environmental awareness.

Support for environmental organisations and projects

Many tourism firms, especially tour operators, translate their awareness of environmental issues into practical action or support, financial or in kind, for environmental organizations and conservation. Examples of practical action include: CV Travel advising communities on waste disposal and promoting local crafts; Greek Islands Club beach 'clean-ups' on certain Ionian islands; and Sunvil Travel assisting with staff time in the creation of Cyprus's first national park. Tour operators often target financial support for destination conservation activities, e.g. Naturetrek to the Annapurna Conservation Area Project, Nepal, and Turkish Delight to the foundation attempting to save the Dalyan Delta from development (because it is important for loggerhead turtles). Most popular is general support for conservation organisations, either through direct membership, e.g. Flamingo Tours and Grassroots Travel of the East African Wildlife Society, or through financial donations, e.g. Alternative Travel Group to the World Wildlife Fund and the Royal Society for the Protection of Birds, Arctic Experience to the Wildlife Trust and the Whale and Dolphin Conservation Society, and Explore Worldwide to Friends of the Earth. However, the level of support may be linked to the numbers purchasing particular package holidays, e.g. Citalia (England) to the Venice in Peril Fund, Thomsons to Friends of the Ionian, Marriott Hotels to a local dolphin conservation project for every guest in their

Turks and Caicos Islands hotel, whilst all profits from Bird Holidays go to the Royal Society for the Protection of Birds and Cox and Kings offer a week's sponsorship for a researcher from the Whale and Dolphin Conservation Society for each tourist on their whale-watching holidays. Large firms appear particularly active in this context; thus British Airways made donations to over thirty environmental organizations in the 1992–93 financial year, including international ones, e.g. World Rainforest Survival Trust, national ones, e.g. Council for Preservation of Rural England, and local ones, e.g. Berks Bucks and Oxon Naturalists Trust, as well as giving assistance in kind via British Airways Assisting Nature Conservation for wildlife species protection and sponsoring the 1992/93 Tourism for Tomorrow Awards (British Airways, 1993).

Such actions are testimony to the positive attitude of tourism firms, even where associated with volume of business, but they are an easy way to demonstrate the firm's 'greenness' to the market. Support for particular projects benefits certain destinations, but the overall pattern is haphazard and does not necessarily bring relief in the most pressing cases; nor does it address wider global issues.

The state of play and future directions

Although British tourism firms are increasingly aware of their environmental responsibility positive action remains limited. Very few tourism firms have formal environmental policies and internal environmental management systems. This response pattern reflects the structure of the tourism industry, the nature of the tourism product and the fact that action is voluntary, a response to market forces.

Obstacles to tourism firms adopting formal environmental management procedures will remain significant. The industry's structure militates against the rapid diffusion of environmental auditing practices, given its highly competitive nature and the domination of many sectors by small firms operating on low profit margins. Unless required to by law, such firms will only adopt best environmental practice where there is an incontrovertible commercial advantage, i.e. the primary objective remains sustainability of profitability and viability of the tourism industry, but without detriment to the environment (Romeril, 1989).

Current patterns of adoption reflect company resources since environmental management involves firms in costs. The small size of most tourism firms rules out an environmental specialist within their overall management structure, whilst external consultants can be both expensive and disruptive. Moreover such firms may face

'diseconomies' of small scale, for example, small firms, such as independent hotels, need to sort, store and arrange either collection or delivery of recyclable materials whereas large firms may enjoy in-house opportunities, based on scale economies, to benefit from recycling. This is demonstrated in an American example: Disney World, Florida, has its sewage works linked to an organic composting factory converting sewage sludge into fertiliser for use on the theme park's landscaped areas (Woolf, 1991). Similarly the nature of the 'total' tourism product (a combination of transport, accommodation, catering and visitor attraction/activity components) raises problems: each component may be supplied by a separate firm and the same level of environmental commitment by all firms contributing to the supply of a given package cannot be guaranteed.

Will there be an early improvement in the situation? Acquisition and merger, leading to greater concentration, i.e. formulation and dominance of large firms, especially tour operation and travel agency, will help, as also will greater vertical integration between sectors, because larger firms, on the above evidence, are more able and willing to undertake environmental auditing. However, as long as auditing remains voluntary its adoption will be slow and piecemeal. Environmental auditing will not become mandatory in the near future. The European Community's eco-management and audit scheme for manufacturing firms was watered down to a voluntary scheme; likewise the BS 7750 environmental management standard is voluntary. Moreover, in the United Kingdom the dominant government attitude is that 'the market' can cope and relaxation of certain legislative pollution standards is under consideration. There could be spin-off from other legislation, for example, consumer protection where EC Directive 990/314/EEC on Package Travel, Package Holidays and Package Tours clearly imposes certain responsibilities on tour operators regarding their products and may encourage such firms generally to behave more responsibly. In due course environmental auditing will become the norm, part of best environmental practice of firms, but this position is still a long way off. As companies become more committed to environmental management, the balance of actions undertaken by tourism firms can be expected to switch from the current emphasis on 'end-of-pipe' technologies, largely aimed at pollution control and waste reduction, to source reduction of inputs and the formulation of environmentally more friendly products.

Will the adoption of best environmental practices by tourism firms bring environmental improvement and lead to environment-sustainable tourism? More tourism firms will review the environmental consequences of their operations. Particular destinations, heavily dependent on primary natural resources, will benefit. But tourism is a growth industry and expansion may lead to greater environmental damage even where future operations are environmentally more efficient than current ones, e.g. standardised environmental performance indicators such as emission amounts per available seat-kilometre showed a clear improvement in British Airways' flying operations for 1992–93 over 1991–92, but total CO_2 and NO_x emissions increased by over 6% because of increased volume of business (British Airways, 1993). From an economic viewpoint the cost–benefit trade-off means that the elimination of all pollution and environmentally damaging business practices is not feasible since there will always be cases where the cost of prevention is excessive. Furthermore, whilst tourism activities in certain destinations may become environmentally sustainable in relation to the actual primary resources used, e.g. ecotours to tropical rainforest, such activities can damage environment through their requirements for secondary resources, especially long-haul transport. Tourism cannot achieve full global and local environmental sustainability in the foreseeable future—it is therefore even more imperative that environmental auditing and best environmental practices are widely diffused to ensure tourism operations and activities become as environmentally compatible as possible.

References

Barrow, C. and Barnett, A. (1990) 'How green are small companies?', Cranfield School of Management, Cranfield Institute of Technology, Cranfield.

British Airways (1993) 'Annual environmental report', British Airways, London.

British Standards Institution (1991) *Environmental Management Systems: Parts I–III*, British Standards Institution, London.

Butler, R. W. (1993) 'Pre- and post-impact assessment of tourism development', in D. G. Pearce and R. W. Butler (Eds), *Tourism Research: Critiques and Challenges*, Routledge, London, pp. 135–155.

Campbell, A. (1990) *A Sense of Mission*, Hutchinson, London.

Cater, E. and Goodall, B. (1992) 'Must tourism destroy its resource base?', in A. M. Mannion and S. R. Bowlby (Eds), *Environmental Issues in the 1990s*, John Wiley, Chichester, pp. 309–323.

Coe, T. (1991) *Managing the Environment*, British Institute of Management Foundation, Corby.

Commission of the European Community (1992) 'Proposal for a Council Regulation allowing voluntary participation by companies in the industrial sector in a Community Eco-audit Scheme', Working Document COM (91) 459, Commission of the European Community, Brussels.

Department of the Environment (1990) *This Common Inheritance—Britain's Environmental Strategy*, HMSO, London.

Elkington, J. and Hailes, J. (1992) *Holidays that Don't Cost the Earth*, Victor Gollancz, London.

European Commission (1991) 'Draft proposal for a Council Regulation establishing a Community scheme for the evaluation and improvement of environmental performance in certain activities and the provision of relevant information to the public (Eco-Audit)', Document XI/83/93, Revision 4, European Commission, Brussels.

Evans, M. (1990) 'Green tourism—a hotelier's view', *Insights*, September: D9-11, English Tourist Board.

Farrell, B. H. and McLellan, R. W. (1987) 'Tourism and physical environment research', *Annals of Tourism Research*, 14(1): 1–16.

Goodall, B. (1992) 'Environmental auditing for tourism', in C. P. Cooper and A. Lockwood (Eds), *Progress in Tourism, Recreation and Hospitality Management*, Vol. 4, Belhaven, London, pp. 60–74.

Goodall, B. (1994a) 'Environmental auditing', in S. F. Witt and L. Moutinho (Eds), *Tourism Marketing and Management Handbook*, 2nd edn, Prentice Hall, Hemel Hempstead, pp. 113–119.

Goodall, B. (1994b) 'Environmental auditing: an emerging tool for tourism firms', *The Geographical Journal* (in press).

Green, H. and Hunter, C. (1992) 'The environmental impact assessment of tourism development', in P. Johnson and B. Thomas (Eds), *Perspectives on Tourism Policy*, Mansell, London.

Hotel Catering and Institutional Management Association (1991) 'Environmental issues', Technical Brief No. 13, HCIMA, London.

International Hotels Environment Initiative (1993) *Environmental Management for Hotels: the Industry Guide to Best Practice*, Butterworth-Heinemann, Oxford.

Jarman, R. (1992) 'Trust audit shows benefits', in B. Johnson (Ed.) *Environmental Assessment and Audit: a User's Guide, 1992–1993*, Ambit Publications, Gloucester, pp. 41–42.

Lloyd, T. (1990) *The 'Nice' Company*, Bloomsbury, London.

Mathieson, A. and Wall, G. (1982) *Tourism: Economic, Physical and Social Impacts*, Longman, Harlow, pp. 93–132.

O'Connor, R. and Douglas, K. (1993) 'Cleaning up after the big chill', *New Scientist*, 16 January: 22–23.

Pearce, D. (1985) 'Tourism and environmental research: a review', *International Journal of Environmental Studies*, 25(4): 247–255.

Pearce, F. (1992) 'Corporate shades of green', *New Scientist*, 3 October: 21–22.

Romeril, M. (1989) 'Tourism: the environmental dimension', in C. P. Cooper (Ed.), *Progress in Tourism, Recreation and Hospitality Management*, Vol. 1, Belhaven, London, pp. 103–113.

Stabler, M. J. and Goodall, B. (1993) 'Environmental auditing in planning for sustainable island tourism', Paper given at the International Conference on Sustainable Tourism in Islands and Small States, 18–20 November 1993, Foundation for International Studies, University of Malta, Valletta, Malta.

UNEP (United Nations Environment Program) (1991) *The Oceans the Convention and You*, UNEP, Geneva.

Welford, R. and Gouldson, A. (1993) *Environmental Management and Business Strategy*, Pitman, London.

Woolf, J. (1991) 'The greening of Mickey Mouse', *The Observer*, 10 February: 57.

World Commission on Environment and Development (1987) *Our Common Future* (The Brundtland Report), Oxford University Press, Oxford.

World Travel and Tourism Council (1991) 'WTTC policy: environmental principles', World Travel and Tourism Council, Brussels (mimeographed).

69 The greening of the hospitality industry: economic and environmental good sense

P. WIGHT

Introduction

Tourism both depends upon, and affects the quality of, the natural and cultural environment. The tourism industry has awakened to some new realities. Like other businesses whose operations affect the environment, it is being held to close scrutiny and accountability for the effect of its activities on the environment. The paradox is that for many years it has proclaimed its awareness and sensitivity to the environment, but actions have not always corresponded to those assertions. Environmental issues are not fading, and we will continue to live with them as we move past the 1990s and into the new millennium. Tourism represents a potentially valuable instrument for sustainable development, and the industry has much to gain from promoting and applying this concept—combining economic opportunities with environmental conservation and enhancement activities.

The hospitality industry, comprising commercial food and accommodation services, is an enabler, rather than a primary motivator, for tourists. However, it can play a major role in assisting consumer awareness as well as contributing to resource conservation, while at the same time deriving specific economic benefits from these activities. The greening of the hospitality industry and of tourism—positioning the industry to respond to the environmental challenge—represents a pivotal issue for the 1990s and beyond.

The thoughtful, green consumer

A number of trends have emerged which have begun to influence lifestyles and leisure and tourism choices. One of the most evident of these is the growth of the 'green' movement and general concern about the impact of modern industry, including tourism development, on the physical and social environment. Public and tourist concern over the environment is not just a passing fad (Cook et al., 1992; Wight, 1993).

More and more, tourists are demanding environmentally friendly products and services. Environment is becoming a competitive issue, for the whole industry. A survey

conducted by the WTO confirms that not only are tourists becoming more environmentally conscious, but the behaviour of the travel trade has also been affected (Economist Intelligence Unit, 1992).

Which environment?

In tourism, many of the concerns related to the environment have dealt with the relationship of the tourism industry to the 'external' environment (both natural and cultural). For example, special reports on tourism and the environment by the Economist Intelligence Unit in 1989 and 1992 dealt virtually exclusively with the external environment, as did the 'World Travel and Tourism Review' (Smith and Jenner, 1989; Hawkins et al., 1991; Jenner and Smith, 1992).

However, the 'internal' environment of any tourism operation also plays a part in conservation. The hospitality industry is a microcosm of the external environment, in terms of attitudes to, and use of, resources. An establishment's organizational, management and operational system should reflect a holistic approach to the environment and to sustainability.

Industry response: business environmental positioning

The hospitality industry is a major generator of solid wastes, and is an inefficient consumer of water and fossil fuels. It uses large quantities of paper, not to mention environmentally unfriendly products such as disposable plastics, non-recyclable containers, cleaning fluids and other supplies. The new generation of conservation-conscious traveller is increasingly sensitive to the onslaught of advertising flyers in hotel rooms, the use of unrecyclable and biodegradable products, and other wasteful practices.

In Italy, hoteliers in the Veneto region are discovering that 'going green' may be a way to lure back dissatisfied customers. The region makes up 10% of Italy's hospitality industry, yet it saw a slowdown of demand in 1992 despite an excellent year in 1991. Its Northern European guests were dissatisfied with the region's attitude to the environment. The region created a consortium which provides free environmental consultation, to demonstrate the important coexistence between hotels and their habitat, and to send a strong positive message to tourists (Morton, 1993). The first hotel to apply this approach, the Hotel Ariston in Milan, increased its occupancy by 15%, while the Milan hotel occupancy is down 25%.

The greening of the hospitality industry makes good business sense and is applauded by guests, who are willing to accept changes to better the environment. At the Boston Park Plaza Hotel, which established a four-star conservation programme, business increased $750 000 in 1992 from groups that want to align themselves with a hotel that is committed to the environment (Marshall, 1992).

The Swedish Hotels and Restaurants Association (SHR) is involved in comprehensive initiatives, which range from focusing on environmental matters at conferences to information sharing, contracting research, and developing networks. 'Hotel and restaurant enterprises, like most of us, have come to realise how they themselves affect the environment' (Nyren, 1992).

The International Hotels Environment Initiative (IHEI) has an operational manual which guides individual hotel managers in what changes to make, whether to the laundry or to the lighting system. It enlisted the support of 11 of the world's leading chains, which between them control more than one million hotel rooms worldwide. This initiative smashes the myth that sound environmental awareness is at odds with hotel profitability, and is aimed at promoting and supporting good environmental practice within the hotel industry.

Internal environmental programmes

Waste management

Almost one-half of the waste generated in North America may be recyclable. Leaders in the hospitality industry have discovered that the benefits of recycling are too great to ignore. These include reduced landfill fees, increased local legislation requiring recycling, and public demand for recycling. However, other benefits can include a sense of team spirit among employees, as well as the contribution to conservation of the environment. In some hotels, savings are going back to the hotel operation, in others, they are going to local charities.

The hotel chain that initiated the first comprehensive 'green' programme, was Canadian Pacific Hotels & Resorts (CP). According to their research, the average guest generates a pound of solid waste a day, and two pounds on check-out day (Jesitus, 1992). With 20 000 checkouts a day, the waste is considerable.

Reduce

The Canadian Restaurant and Foodservices Association (CRFA) mainly comprises small, independently owned outlets. Because of relatively narrow profit margins, members are most likely to undertake only those environmental initiatives which lead to reduced costs and/or increased sales, thus the CRFA has focused its efforts on waste reduction and reuse. As part of a members' education and action programme, the CRFA has published a booklet 'Going green without seeing red'. This is causing an 'environmental ripple' across the entire food services industry.

Reduction of garbage can be achieved in numerous areas: rejecting over-wrapped produce such as bananas or oranges; buying beverages in returnable containers; eliminating throwaway cups or cutlery; and not buying or selling 'tetrapack' containers or blister-plastic packaging. The purchase of bathroom amenities without elaborate packaging can reduce costs by up to 10%. At the Walt Disney World Dolphin, guests stay an average of four nights, so the hotel's goal is one 2-oz. container of each product per stay. With more than 400 000 room-nights per year, this can add up to a significant saving. The Saunders Hotel Group's Boston Park Plaza is part of a property-wide conservation programme. It has introduced a 24-oz. pump dispenser for liquid soap, mouthwash, shampoo and hair conditioner. These replace the more than two million individual packages annually which previously became garbage (Selwitz, 1993).

Reuse

A number of organizations routinely reuse everything possible, from storing food in reusable plastic containers (not cling-wrap) to sending surplus foods to food banks or soup kitchens, and selling organic kitchen scraps for animal feed, or composting kitchen and yard wastes.

In Thailand, the Amari Hotels in Pattaya offer guests the option of having their sheets changed every other day instead of every day, thus saving water, cutting detergent use, and reducing operating costs. About 40% of guests accept this option (Goodno, 1993). This is similar to CP's practice, as well as that of hotels in Sweden and Germany. The Swiss Hotel Association, too, asks members to encourage guests to reuse bathroom linen.

Recycle

The Marriott has had properties involved in recycling since at least 1988. One property, when first starting, reduced 35% of its garbage going to the dump in just one month. By simply removing glass from its waste stream, the Marriott in Schumburg, Illinois, has cut its tonnage by almost 30% (Hasek, 1990).

The Hyatt Regency, Chicago, has a recycling programme run by a subsidiary company. The hotel produces an average of 70 000 pounds of trash each month. This includes almost 500 pounds of glass nightly, and 10 tons of cardboard every 6 days. The recycling centre on the premises had a capital cost of $25 000, but that cost was recovered in less than a year. The hotel was recycling 40% to 50% of its waste within a year, with over 50% reduction in its waste bill—about $60 000 savings in 1990.

The IHEI suggests that companies list every product they use, and for each product, check whether it should be reduced, reused, recycled or replaced, as a means of evaluating impact and determining proper disposal methods.

Conservation of energy and water

To many people, saving energy or water means some sacrifice of personal comfort, to others, it is a way to cut costs. In the hospitality industry, it has appeared contradictory to think of maintaining guest comfort, while increasing conservation. However, by applying energy-efficient management and low-energy design techniques, not only to new-built projects, but also to existing schemes, a huge annual savings may be realized. Some facilities can consume up to 10 times more energy than others. This variation is due to building design, design of services, and occupant's behaviour. Oreszczyn (1993) estimates that improvements in any of these can result in halving a building's energy consumption, and that, of these, 20% of energy is wasted through inefficient management.

Lighting

In the last few years there has been a revolution in lighting technology, which has provided many choices for retrofits and new installations. The potential for savings in energy use and cost is significant. Some existing lighting systems can be retrofitted to provide the same amount of light with only 20% of the electricity previously used. Also, the new lamps will operate up to 10 times longer than the equipment being replaced.

In Ontario, Kenora's Inn of the Woods Lakeside Hotel has achieved an annual $14 000 energy cost savings, by converting 278 incandescent bulbs to compact fluorescents (Senett, 1992). The savings were exactly as originally projected, and the $11 000 conversion was paid back in about eight months. The planning of the retrofit involved Ontario Hydro, so qualifies for a $4200 rebate under their Energy Efficient Lighting Program. An additional advantage is that the new equipment needs far less maintenance.

At the Royal Connaught Hotel in Hamilton, more than 1000 lights were replaced with compact fluorescents. The total cost of the project was just over $35 000 and saved 63 kilowatts of power. This represents a saving of $33 113 on the hotel's annual hydro bill. In addition, Ontario Hydro provided a $16 875 incentive (Menzies, 1992).

Heating, ventilation and air conditioning

The biggest user of energy in hotels is the heating, ventilation and air conditioning (HVAC) system (22%), followed by the guest rooms (19%) and the kitchens (12%) (IHEI, 1993). Energy cost for HVAC can range from 25% to 50% of the total energy cost—the lower figure related to smaller, unsophisticated hotels in moderate climes, and the higher figure to luxury hotels in subtropical and tropical countries. Opportunities for energy efficiency is very high.

CP's Prince Edward Hotel in Charlottetown, PEI, has reduced consumption of 97 000 litres of fuel in one year through the use of a water source heat pump. This transfers heat from an overhot room into a water loop which traverses the building, and heats cool rooms. The more balanced the load, the more efficiently it runs (Watson, 1992). The extra heat is used to pre-heat hot water, and to heat the swimming pool. This has meant that the hotel, which used to run two 75 h.p. boilers now needs only one, thus cutting electrical, maintenance, and chemical costs.

The Ritz Hotel, London, has recently upgraded its energy management system. The three large boilers installed 20 years ago were replaced with four high-efficiency gas-fired units. A cooling system was installed in the hotel restaurant and a computer-controlled energy management system (EMS) was implemented to control and monitor energy consumption. Also, when the old boilers were removed, 7000 sq. ft were freed and converted to more bedrooms (Oreszczyn, 1993).

Water

Water savings alone may contribute considerable dollar savings. Companies now offer electronic sensors to control water flow (for toilets, urinals, showers and sinks) which not only reduces water consumption but also reduces vandalism because there are no knobs or handles to break, and water cannot be left running.

In Boston, the Saunders Hotel Company was faced with stiff increases in water and sewer bills so it refitted its Lenox Hotel. Showers had flow resistors and heads, reducing flow to from 6–7 to 3 g.p.m. (at a cost of only $20 per head). Water faucet aerators reduced flow from

4 to 1.5 g.p.m. and there was no noticeable flow difference to guests. Similarly, 1.6 gal/flush toilets replaced the 6–7 gal/flush toilets. The results were dramatic: for the first quarter of 1989 the sewer and water use was 1.88 million gallons, down almost 75% from the previous year. Total payback was less than two years (Marshall, 1990).

Water and energy use are often linked. The food-services industry is examining the efficiency of its operations and cutting wasteful practices. According to Ontario Hydro, sanitizing and dishwashing account for 18% of costs of an establishment, requiring considerable water, power, labour and detergent, also service and maintenance. Waste heat recovery saves on both water and power by recycling rinse water (at 180°F) to the next load's wash. Other features are being built into new machines: reuse of machine-generated steam; gas-heated machines for use in northern locations where power costs are high; water-saving machines using up to 59% less water; and greater insulation of machines. 'The incentive to choose a high-efficiency dishwasher is going to be the bottom line: to save money. The bonus is energy is saved through efficiency' (Conroy, 1992).

Certain retrofits may be costly, but effective. The Sheraton purchased two laundry-water reuse systems for hotels in Seattle and Long Beach, at $71 000 each. However, the systems, which treat and rinse the final rinse water of the preceding wash for the next wash cycle, save about $39 000 a year. The net effect of this is that the system pays for itself in less than two years.

Quality of air and water

Air emissions from the hospitality industry contribute to pollution from CFCs, burning of fossil fuels, exhausts, etc. The industry should aim to reduce emissions at source, reduce consumption, and switch to less harmful products. There have been great improvements in maintenance products: sprays without ozone-destroying materials, odour-free products, and biodegradable or refillable containers. Now manufacturers of air conditioners and heating units are offering products which save money and eliminate the need for chemical deodorizers.

Near Vail, Colorado, Beaver Creek ski resort has no above-ground parking, and the amount of dust and other airborne particles is measured continuously. Each commercial and residential fireplace in the resort has an attached red light. If the air is polluted by vehicles or chimneys, fires must be doused immediately, benefiting both internal and external air quality (Wilson, 1990).

While non-smoking rooms are common in the hotel business, 'green rooms' which contain water and air filtration systems are the newest element in amenities for the industry. These rooms are designed to appeal to those with allergies, health-and-fitness enthusiasts and environmentally conscious travellers. More and more hotels are buying their own equipment as the demand for these rooms increases. The cost of converting to 'green rooms' is about $500 per room for the Sheraton Grand at Dallas/Fort Worth, with a surcharge of $5 to the guest, this is a payback period of only 100 occupied nights (Bond, 1992). These rooms achieve higher than average occupancy rates, and have directly related repeat business.

Product purchase

Purchasing decisions can make a great contribution to environmental protection, and are a key element of environmental protection in the hospitality industry. At the worldwide level, the hospitality industry may have a significant impact on supply industries. At the local level, it can benefit the economy if products are bought locally, which also reduces transportation costs. A key concept is 'precycling', where purchase decisions support responsible products and packaging, assist recycling, and reduce waste. This becomes very significant where landfills are scarce or costly.

Most companies that are committed to the principles of recycling and waste reduction have not paid higher prices only to support the public interest. Rather, they have instituted new purchase policies that offer additional business benefits. The Westin's company policy is to use recycled paper products for its stationery, paper towels and toilet paper. By using recycled paper, for the Westin letterhead alone, they saved $10 000. In addition, certain Westin hotels (such as the Bayshore Hotel in Vancouver) discourage suppliers from overpackaging. The Bayshore refuses to discard items such as waxed box containers, and insists that suppliers pick them up for reuse themselves (Baragon, 1991).

At the Hotel Inter-Continental, LA, liquid amenities are packaged in 100% PET-G resin recycled from soft-drink bottles; soap ingredients are vegetable-based; tinting and colouring agents are food-grade suitable; animal testing is avoided; only recycled fibres are used in packaging; and all papers are acid-free and water-based with vegetable-based inks used in printing (Selwitz, 1993).

The Sheraton Senggigi Beach Resort in Lombok, Indonesia, had a very limited supply and variety of local vegetables. Instead of importing, the chef and the local farmers experimented with a wide range of vegetable seeds to determine what crops grow well locally. Now the farmers have a new source of income which is more profitable than the traditional rice crop, the hotel has a regular supply of fresh vegetables, and the Sheraton Group has an enhanced image through developing an alternative, mutually beneficial approach (IHEI, 1993).

The SHR provides its members and associates with educational information to influence product purchase, and is networking with all others in the industry, from farmers to suppliers. All companies should be using their positions as purchasers to work with suppliers to improve environmental performance. Implementing a product purchase plan involves: auditing all products and services, and assessing their environmental impact; determining availability of environmentally friendly alternatives; prioritizing actions; and educating suppliers about better alternatives.

External environmental programmes

The environmental activities of the hotel sector, as demonstrated in such leadership documents as CP's 'Green partnership guide' or in the IHEI's *Environmental Management for Hotels*, are focused on *internal* operations related to resource use and conservation. A number of ad hoc initiatives do exist, which recognize the relationship of the hospitality industry to the external environment; however, a systematic approach is needed.

Relationship with local community and wider society

Marshall (1991) advocates that the hospitality industry provide hospitality to the nation's hungry. Apparently, fear of lawsuits is commonly cited as justification for food dumping. But Good Samaritan Food Donor Acts can protect from legal liability for good-faith donations of prepared food. An increasing number of convention managers are requesting that excess food be donated to a charity (Hasek, 1990).

At the Days Inn in Baltimore, goods that would have otherwise been thrown away (e.g. sheets, bedspreads, soap and food) are given to a local ministry that assists the homeless (Hasek, 1990). CP's 1992 audit showed that 90% of all soap, 76% of shampoo and conditioner, and 80% of body lotion remaining after checkout was redirected to local and third-world charities. The Renaissance Hotel in Edmonton, Alberta, is donating partially used soap and shampoo containers to local youth shelters. In Seattle, the Stouffer Madison Hotel donates partially used containers of conditioners, shampoos and lotions, and partial toilet-tissue rolls to an organization that channels supplies to homeless shelters (Selwitz, 1993). Thus the hotel cuts down its waste while saving the

external organizations part of their cost of buying products.

In 1989, Best Western hotels joined with the American Society of Interior Designers (ASID) to launch a national community service project to aid homeless shelters. The hotels are encouraged to contribute furniture, fixtures and equipment to designated shelters, and ASID members work with the shelters to develop and implement design plans using the donations. Within a year, four projects had been completed, and it was typical for Best Western to donate 25 rooms of furniture and equipment (H&MM, 1990b).

In the UK, Forte Plc has programmes oriented toward the communities in which it operates. In association with the Conservation Foundation, it launched a 'Community Chest' scheme in the 1980s to provide monthly grants to aid local environmental programmes. This has helped create school gardens, plant trees and reseed village greens. It also has Colonel Sanders Environmental Awards aimed at encouraging community tidiness and litter reduction (IHEI, 1993).

In his inaugural address, the president of the American Hotel and Motel Association asked the lodging industry to take steps against illiteracy, pointing out that educational deficiencies cost businesses about $30 billion annually. Best Western International donated 50 000 surplus road atlases and hotel travel guides to Chicago's public schools for use in classrooms (Nozar, 1990). It is also getting on board city-wide traffic-reduction efforts in Phoenix, where the company is based. To encourage car-pooling, Best Western offers its corporate employees preferential parking and other considerations, which may include flexible work hours (Jesitus, 1992).

Relationships with external natural and cultural resources

As the Indonesian Minister of tourism recently commented, 'people don't come to certain places for their hotels, but for their natural beauty, attractive culture and interesting tourist objects' (Campbell, 1993). But the hospitality industry has been slow to recognize this fact.

The Ramada International not only has significant *internal* conservation programmes, but has an especially high profile with respect to *external* environmental conservation. It offers a joint programme with American Express, where Ramada automatically contributes to The Nature Conservancy when guests pay by American Express. Its 'Hotels of the New Wave' programme is a grassroots effort, in which the company allows each property's staff to initiate and implement its own ideas. Ramada encourages individual hotels to work with local environmental groups to promote community causes and contribute to major environmental groups.

The Jupiter Beach Hilton in Florida developed a 'Turtle Watch' programme. It organizes evening lectures and has established an incubation pen if eggs are laid too close to the heavy beach traffic. Resort naturalists monitor the nests and guide guests along the beach to watch turtles lay eggs in June and July. This has proved to be a successful conservation and awareness programme. It had the additional benefit of earning wide recognition when presented with a special Judges Award by the Travel Industry Association of America.

In Asia, Hong Kong's major hotels use the twin concerns of environmental preservation and heritage conservation as part of their marketing programmes. Initially, they introduced menus on recycled paper, as a small contribution to conservation. However, early in the 1980s Singapore launched a multimillion dollar restoration programme and repositioned itself as a 'Green Dream' destination. Hong Kong has now become a catalyst for the regional hotel industry to clean up the environment in order to sustain tourism over the long term (Knipp, 1993). Major hotel chains have joined this effort: the Hilton, in conjunction with the World Wildlife Fund, is emphasizing a 'Healthy Oceans Campaign' focusing on city children; the Shangri-La Group, with Asian resorts, has strict guidelines related to building heights, lighting systems and sewage-treatment plants; and the Mandarin Oriental Group has introduced a glass-recycling programme for Hong Kong properties, and managed clean-up campaigns for local beaches.

Lessons learned

Partnerships

Partnerships, or strategic alliances (with government, public institutions, or other companies) may help split initial high costs of some conservation measures. A number of utilities have programmes where incentives are directed toward energy savings. Ontario Hydro's Savings By Design programme is intended to promote any project that reduces electrical demand (kW) or energy (kW.h) through improved electrical efficiency, whether new projects or retrofits. Funding assistance of $500/kW of demand reduced is available. The Royal York Hotel in Toronto replaced some older motors in its main air supply, make-up and exhaust air fans. It saved more than 708 000 kW.h, representing $42 500 annually. In addition, the $40 000 grant from Ontario Hydro meant that the project paid for itself in a year.

There are a number of programmes through which operators may obtain advice about energy efficiencies. In the UK, the Energy Efficiency Office helps managers assess if their buildings are using excessive energy, and provides grants to help organizations with such consultancy costs (Oreszczyn, 1993).

The US Water Alliances for Voluntary Energy Efficiency (WAVE) is a non-regulatory programme that offers mostly technology-based solutions. Hotels and motels are encouraged to install and implement water-saving techniques and equipment. Owing to the fact that laundries can be significant water-users, a hotel or motel can reduce its water use by 15% to 30% or more by changing to water-efficient equipment, with payback periods of one to four years. WAVE has served as a stimulator to intensify energy-conserving laundry practices (Shaw, 1993).

Industry partnerships can assist where costs are high. For example, recycling can present problems of inadequate space for storage of materials to be recycled. However, in Vancouver, a group of maintenance and housekeeping management personnel from downtown properties have discussed sharing the cost of the daily pickup service to make that option more economical (Baragon, 1991). Strategic alliances and partnerships make good economic and environmental sense.

Corporate commitment

Much of CP's Green Plan success is due to its senior personnel. CP's president and CEO launched the green programme, and said, 'either protect the environment that is the basis of your industry, or have no industry to worry about' (Jesitus, 1992). A top-down approach can provide vision. While employees are enthusiastic about recycling in theory, in practice they may not be systematic unless recycling is brought in as an official policy initiative (Baragon, 1991).

Corporate commitment may also attract and keep workers. In initial surveys, more than 80% of CP's employees said they would feel better about working for a company with an environmental policy (Jesitus, 1992).

Employee involvement

One of the surest ways to enlist the cooperation of employees is to make them a part of the solution. When the Opryland Hotel in Morgantown, West Virginia, began looking into recycling in late 1989, one of its first tasks was finding out how workers at all levels felt about the idea. Surveys found high enthusiasm and uncovered ideas that management had not even considered (e.g. recycling office and computer paper, motor oil, batteries, and kitchen fats and oils). This employee input also increased programme acceptance (Jesitus, 1992).

CP, in beginning its greening activities, surveyed each of the company's 10 000 employees. More than 90% of respondents favoured the programme. It conducted a detailed environmental audit of its hotels, and its 12-step Green Plan is directly based on staff input. This approach is comprehensive, produces support, and improves corporate image. Idealism and enthusiasm alone are not enough to make green programmes a way of life in the hospitality industry. CP admit that their biggest problems are their managers at the individual property level, in terms of implementing the plan. However, the firm which assisted CP in its green plan, warned that any audit and subsequent environmental education must stress cooperative benefits as opposed to a 'policing' approach. This is particularly important in the context of existing infrastructures, and established procedures (Jaquette, 1991).

Inter-Continental Hotels & Resorts tackle the problem at various levels and have a quarterly eco-newsletter, *The Daily Planet*, geared toward sharing success stories, and fostering consistency among hotels (Jesitus, 1992). They developed a 200-page environmental manual which mandates the 3 Rs, and at each hotel, the manager's bonus depends on compliance and accomplishment. They are producing their manual in a number of languages, to assist in meeting targets.

Guest and industry education

At the Star Hotel, Sollentuna, Sweden, all personnel are given information on the hotel's environmental programme, and there are regular meetings of an environmental group representing all departments to increase staff awareness and provide information. It has a similar education programme for guests. There is information on the Star's environmental programme in each room, with an invitation for guests to participate, for example, by turning out lights, or by using towels several times.

Guests like a company that is environmentally sensitive. CP's programme already has lured some business the hotel may not otherwise have booked (Jesitus, 1992). Similarly, the Hyatt Regency in Chicago's recycling programme has been used as a marketing tool to attract conventions (Hasek, 1990).

Education of staff at all levels has proved to be invaluable at Inter-Continental and CP. Similarly, guests need and welcome education. Radisson Hotels International has had occasional guest complaints about in-room occupancy sensors which control the HVAC.

Guests feel they should be able to leave the air conditioning on full blast when they're not in the room, unlike their attitudes when they leave their own homes (H&MM, 1990a). Although they seem to have a double standard regarding their hotel room, one wonders what is being done to *educate* guests about this device, and its benefits.

Today's hotel guests do seem willing to accept conservation measures such as bulk amenity dispensers, water-saving devices, and the replacement of non-recyclable items with recyclable ones, *if* they know the benefits. At the Holiday Inn in Leicester, UK, a letter is left in each room, explaining environmental programmes to guests, and requesting comments. In the three years of the programme, no adverse comments have ever been received (IHEI, 1993).

One of the biggest challenges in the hospitality industry is to implement conservation measures, while still meeting guest perception. Guests need to be educated *and* asked for their opinion. To increase acceptance of a hotel's environmental programme, guests should feel like they are doing a good deed. Translate savings into meaningful language (e.g. reinterpret paper reduction in terms of trees saved), and promote the hotel's good environmental record. Encourage guests to feel that they are participants in a programme that is morally and ethically right. If they don't know the problems, they are unlikely to want to be part of the solutions.

Recognition and awards

At the employee level, recognition assists in maintaining enthusiasm and generating ideas. Ramada evaluates the best ideas from each property and the best earn a Chairman's Award at the annual convention, and cash incentives. Any incentive helps, even publicity in a staff newsletter.

At the industry-wide level, there are a now numerous environmental awards given by local, national and international organisations. These all assist in promoting environmental stewardship.

The Thai Wah Group has won the International Hotel Association's 1992 Environmental Award. It rescued a polluted and unreclaimed mining property, and turned it into a resort. It was their thorough commitment to the environment which gave their Laguna Beach Resort the edge. They considered all aspects, from construction materials, aesthetics, and xeriscaping (landscaping using species of plants and trees, often indigenous, which require little watering), to water and energy efficient designs and programmes, traditional craftsmanship, minimal impact on local way of life, and incorporation of traditional economic activities (IHA

Report, 1993). Celebration of success is a vital role, and can be expanded to the local community.

Marketing

The dean of Florida International University's Hospitality Management School rather overstates the case for green marketing: 'It is time for hotels to hop on the environmental bandwagon. It saves money and planet Earth, too. . . . Taking steps to save energy and reuse waste saves money while saving the Earth. So don't turn red at the suggestion for making your hotels more environmentally sensitive; turn green—all the way to the bank. Conservation pays' (Marshall, 1992). Yet Knipp (1993) maintains that most tourism representatives discount possible short-term gains in occupancy levels from environmental action, stressing that it strengthens ties with the local community and eventually improves the image of a hotel company, in the eyes of both guests and staff. However, sincere environmental action can be a useful tool in a marketing programme. It is the strong green sell of a business with no equivalent environmental actions which is not legitimate or sustainable (Wight, 1993).

In a WTO survey, one-third of all travel trade respondents claimed to have already taken environmentally friendly action or initiatives in marketing and promotions, and a further 22% said they intended to do so. These actions ranged from using recycled paper in brochures, to making contributions to environmental charities, to giving clients environmental guidelines or codes of conduct (Economist Intelligence Unit, 1992). It is conceivable that in the near future, companies will list their environmental activities in an official green 'report card' which will detail the energy a company has saved, the pollution it has reduced through buying recycled products and developing new manufacturing technologies, etc.

Future directions

New technologies

Solar power is a possible application in the hospitality industry (e.g. to heat shower water in guestrooms or heat dishwashers in hotel restaurants) but has a longer pay-back period. Cogeneration produces savings from the simultaneous production of electricity and use of free heat energy which would otherwise have been lost. The Hotel del Coronado in San Diego has used a solar gas turbine engine for cogeneration since 1983. This 800-kW engine provides 35% of the hotel's electrical need; the steam from its waste heat provides up to 95% of the hotel's heat in summer and 70% in winter (Seal, 1991).

Heating problems often relate to the high cost of heating, and draughts. A Canadian system provides an alternative to conventional heating systems which expend most energy by blowing hot air throughout a given room or lobby. Co-Ray-Vac uses its energy to heat objects in that room (e.g. carpets, appliances). The advantages are that it eliminates draughts and chills because the system creates no air currents, and in saving the energy of blowing air, it cuts heating costs by as much as 50%. It is ideal for hotel lobbies, back rooms, open-air restaurants and pubs (Brunet, 1991/92). New technologies are continually evolving to address problems, and their costs are decreasing.

Adoption of codes of ethics and practice

Many companies are establishing internal 'codes of conduct' as a means for encouraging ethical behaviour for their organizations. The tourism industry is seeing this in the realm of environmental codes. A number of tourism organizations (ministries, associations and operators) have recently developed codes of ethics, or guidelines, but these vary in usefulness. Many codes of practice do not provide the specific guidance expected in a code of practice (e.g. in New Zealand or Australia).

Canada has developed a comprehensive 'Code of Ethics and Guidelines for Sustainable Tourism'. Specific practices are recommended for each tourism sub-sector, such as: energy conservation related to all areas, including heating, air conditioning and lighting; waste minimization through reduction, reuse and recycling; water conservation; minimizing pollution; selection of energy-conserving modes of transportation; purchase policies related to 'green' products and packaging, and environmentally sensitive suppliers; and periodic audits.

We can no longer place the responsibility for the environment elsewhere. At both personal and professional levels, we have to take responsibility for actions. Our notions of ethics must consider impact beyond our immediate horizons. However, good environmental management is fully compatible with good business practice. These should be viewed as the 'double bottom line' (balancing ecological and fiscal considerations) and in the long term are essential for business survival. Ethical codes and practical guidelines are an excellent step in achieving this.

Standards: integrating environmental and economic decisions

Thailand has actual pollution problems (air, water, litter, and loud traffic) exacerbated by high visibility (on beaches and commercial areas). This presents an image problem and occupancy rates recently plummeted to 20%–30%, with better hotels struggling to keep rates above 50%. The Thai Hotel Association launched an environmental code, which calls for improved waste management, developing recycling programmes, offering information, raising environmental consciousness of guests, staff and the community, improved hotel facilities and equipment, and monitoring environmental quality. In 1994, a green leaves symbol will designate hotels which have qualified to the environmental standards. Although there are only 27 members of this group so far, they represent 7000 of the 27 000-plus rooms (Goodno, 1993).

The Danish Hotels and Restaurants Organization has a similar programme. Although environmental initiatives are at a preliminary stage, there is now increasing realization that guests are more environmentally aware, and that a number of environmental investments are actually profitable. A working group has been set up to develop standards and minimum environmental criteria required for the right to use their 'Green Key Sign' (Eller, 1993).

In 1989, Inter-Continental Hotels mandated the greening of the hotel chain. They also penalize managers who fail to meet environmental standards. For example, in 1991, the company released an environmental manual to its 103 hotels in 48 countries around the world. It includes a checklist of more than 130 targets, and general managers must meet 95% of the company's goals or their bonus pay suffers. The company has twice-yearly internal audits which prevent 'faking it'. So far, Inter-Continental's North American properties lead in meeting their goals. Corporations may increasingly take such a standards-oriented approach.

One of the most compelling reasons to become more environmentally responsible, is the threat of government regulation. If the lodging industry doesn't clean up its own act, regulators will. Thus, environmental efforts at the corporate or association level may spare business regulatory burdens (Jesitus, 1992).

Comprehensive environmental audit

At present, there is little or no comprehensive environmental auditing in the hospitality industry. The IHEI Industry Guide mentions only energy audits. However, a comprehensive environmental audit is desirable, and can yield financial as well as environmental and other benefits. These are being undertaken by only a few leaders in the hospitality industry. Advantages are that staff can contribute, they provide a database for preliminary decisions, and can be used for performance measurement and monitoring.

Beyond compliance to competitive advantage

Around the world, business is recognizing that it must increasingly move 'beyond compliance'. In the field of corporate accounting and reporting, this means that companies must ensure they comply with fiscal reporting and begin to report on a growing range of environmental performance indicators.

Agenda 21, the 1992 UNCED report, calls on business and industry to 'report annually on their environmental records, as well as on their use of energy and natural resources. Companies will likely move from zero environmental performance reports, to incorporating environmental reporting in annual reports, to free-standing environmental reports' (IISD, 1993). This will be driven by corporate citizenship, but competitive advantage will be the main motivator.

Conclusions

While it is clear that the combined forces of consumer opinion and government regulation will make it increasingly necessary for all business to become environmentally sensitive, leaders in the hospitality industry have already recognized the need to join the environmental movement. The emerging culture of corporate environmentalism is driven by bottom line concerns. It is about positioning a firm to capitalize on market opportunities and responding to new demands. The challenge in the future will be to: consider long-term financial payback periods; increase the hospitality industry's awareness of the linkages between their internal and external environments; understand that protecting *both* is necessary for their long run wellbeing; and translate this into an integrated and comprehensive approach, rather than ad hoc measures at the individual business level.

References

Baragon, Ellen (1991) 'Recycling: cleaning up', *B.C. & Yukon INNFOCUS*, October/November: 68.
Bond, Helen (1992) '"Green rooms" growing roots in industry', *Hotel and Motel Management*, 207 (17 August): 46–47.
Brunet, Robin (1991/92) 'Breathing easier', *B.C. & Yukon INNFOCUS* December/January: 17–19.
Campbell, Delse (1993) 'Tourism minister calls for building moratorium', *Hotel and Motel Management*, 208 (7 June): 8.
Conroy, Christine (1992) 'In search of an environmentally-friendly dishwasher', *Foodservice and Hospitality*, 25(2): 79–84.
Cook, Suzanne D., Stewart, Elizabeth, Repass, Kelly and US Travel Data Center (1992) 'Discover America: tourism and the environment', Travel Industry Association of America, Washington, DC.

Economist Intelligence Unit (1992) 'Markets: environmental concern makes business sense', *Travel Industry Monitor*, 29 (August): 2–3.

Eller, Paul B. (1993) Marketing Director, HO-RE-CON, Personal communication, 25 October.

Goodno, James B. (1993) 'Leaves rate Thai hotels on ecology', *Hotel and Motel Management*, 208 (26 April): 8, 52.

Hasek, Glenn (1990) 'Hotels keeping watch on waste', *Hotel and Motel Management*, 205 (10 September): 3, 81.

Hawkins, Donald E. and Ritchie, Brent J. R. (Eds) (1991) 'World travel and tourism review: indicators, trends and forecasts', CAB International, Wallingford, Oxon.

H&MM (Hotel & Motel Management) (1990a) 'Technology report: enermetrix addresses energy management', *Hotel and Motel Management*, 205 (11 June): 76.

H&MM (Hotel & Motel Management) (1990b) 'Hotels assist homeless shelters', *Hotel and Hotel Management*, 205 (24 September): BW3, 26.

IHA Report (1993) 'Thai resort wins 1992 environmental award', *Hotels* 27(2): 57–58.

IHEI (International Hotels Environment Initiative) (1993) *Environmental Management for Hotels*: the Industry Guide to Best Practice, Butterworth-Heinemann, Oxford.

IISD (International Institute for Sustainable Development) et al. (1993) 'Coming clean: corporate environmental reporting, opening up for sustainable development', Deloitte Touche Tomatsu International, London.

Jaquette, Leslee (1991) 'Canadian Pacific hotels creates "green plan"', *Hotel and Motel Management* 206 (4 February): 54–58.

Jenner, Paul and Smith, Christine (1992) 'The tourism industry and the environment', Special Report No. 2453, Economist Intelligence Unit, London.

Jesitus, John (1992) 'Ecoviews: green business is now everybody's business', *Hotel and Motel Management*, 207 (2 November): 133–134.

Jesitus, John (1993) 'Pushing the planet', *Hotel and Motel Management*, 208 (26 July): 35–36.

Knipp, Steve (1993) 'Asian hotel chains emphasise "green"', *Hotel and Motel Magazine*, 208 (26 July): 35–36.

Marshall, Anthony (1990) 'Hotel discovers it pays to be stingy with water', *Hotel and Motel Management*, 205 (24 September): 12.

Marshall, Anthony (1991) 'Be hospitable to guests, workers, environment', *Hotel and Motel Management*, 206 (25 February): 18–20.

Marshall, Anthony (1992) 'Conservation can save the earth—and money, too', *Hotel and Motel Management*, 207 (21 September): 13.

Menzies, David (1992) 'Cohen's Midas touch at the golden arches', *Canadian Hotel and Restaurant*, 70(7): 22–24.

Morton, Tracy (1993) 'Veneto hoteliers heed environment's call', *Hotel and Motel Management*, 208 (22 March): 8, 44.

Nozar, Robert (1990) 'Best Western maps out battle against illiteracy', *Hotel and Motel Management*, 205 (30 July): 6.

Nyren, Allan (Ed.) (1992) 'Environment temperature 92', Report 1992:5 from the Swedish Hotels and Restaurants Association, Stockholm.

Oreszczyn, Tadj (1993) 'Energy efficient', *Leisure Management*, 13(5): 58–60.

Seal, Kathy (1991) 'Energy-saving programs can zap utility bills', *Hotel and Motel Management*, 206 (25 March): 52.

Selwitz, Robert (1993) 'Hotels look to recycle, reduce waste with amenities', *Hotel and Motel Management*, 208 (26 July): 33.

Senett, Jack (1992) 'Envirowatch', *Canadian Hotel and Restaurant*, 70(10): 19.

Shaw, Russell (1993) 'Ecoviews: turning off water waste', *Hotel and Motel Management*, 208 (5 April): 17–18.

Smith, Christine and Jenner, Paul (1989) 'Tourism and the environment', *Travel & Tourism Analyst*, 5: 68–86.

Watson, Julie (1992) 'Envirowatch', *Canadian Hotel and Restaurant*, 70(2): 20.

Wight, Pamela (1993) 'Improved business positioning: environmentally responsible marketing of tourism', Paper presented at the 24th Annual TTRA International Conference, Whistler, BC 14 June.

Wilson, Janet (1990) 'Luxury-friendly resort pampers environment too', *Hawaii Citizen*, 15 December.

70 Environmental auditing and the hotel industry: an accountant's perspective

M. BROWN

Introduction

As we approach the end of the twentieth century we are faced with one of our most important challenges—that of reducing the effect we are having on the environment. A number of major environmental (and human) disasters[1] have served to highlight the problems we are inflicting on our environment. Environmental concern is no longer the preserve of a few dedicated environmentalists. There is growing public awareness of the damage the environment is suffering and will continue to endure unless action is taken (Rouse, 1991).

Initially the main focus of the attention of environmentalists was on the chemical and manufacturing companies. However, environmental interest is now extending to the service industries (Elkington, 1990; Elkington et al., 1991). Companies are finding themselves under pressure from investors who are now looking for those companies which show a responsible attitude to the environment. Consumers are now looking for 'environmentally friendly' products in their supermarket (Elkington and Hailes, 1988) and may be willing to pay a premium for environmentally friendly products (Rouse, 1991). Green consumerism has extended to tourism and the tourist is now looking for 'greener holidays' (Wood and House, 1991, 1992; Elkington and Hailes, 1992).

In this paper an attempt is made to link the actions of the general manager as regards the hotel's environmental impact and the control system operated by his head office. It is hypothesised that the nature of reporting requirements placed on the manager and the performance appraisal system used by the organisation does not encourage the manager to introduce environmental initiatives within the hotel. Conclusions are drawn from the results of a questionnaire survey of general managers which was made during 1993.

Environmental auditing

It is becoming evident that the organisation which becomes environmentally responsible in its operations will benefit in a number of ways. There is increasing demand for environmentally friendly products and services (Rouse, 1991). This should result in increasing turnover and profits and long-term sustainability of the industry (STB, 1993). Cost savings can be achieved through energy efficiency schemes, for example (STB, 1993). Legislation regarding the environment is also going to affect organisations. New hotels will require assessment on their environmental impact, and those hotels which include a leisure complex will find themselves responsible for any water pollution they may cause (Barnard, 1992).

As organisations recognise that they will have to respond to pressure to become environmentally responsible in their actions, management will be faced with the dilemma of how to start this 'greening' process. Elkington and Burke's (1991) 'ten steps to environmental excellence' form a good reference point for those organisations unsure of how to proceed. Although not every step may be appropriate to every organisation, it is a useful checklist for those organisations starting on the road to environmental excellence.

The first step identified by Elkington and Burke (1991) is the formation of an environmental policy. From this starting point the remaining steps detail the way the company should go about achieving the objectives and aims of the environmental policy. The organisation may decide to formulate its own environmental policy or, alternatively, may decide to adopt one of the public charters such as the Valdez Principles.[2] The advantage to the company of forming its own environmental policy is that it can be designed to suit the particular circumstances of the organisation. However it may be viewed less seriously than if it were developed independently of the organisation (Gray et al., 1993). Whichever option is chosen, it is important that the adoption of the environmental policy is published, as this signifies the seriousness with which the company views its environmental responsibility. If the adoption of the policy is not made known publicly then the sincerity of the management and its commitment to the environmental policy must be in doubt. Organisations which have adopted an environmental policy and subsequently ignored its objectives have found themselves the subject of adverse publicity and public backlash (Elkington et al., 1991). It is important therefore that the formation and publication of the environmental policy is viewed as an important step by the organisation. To lend credence to the environmental policy it is important that it should have the backing of the most senior members of management (CBI, 1990). This can be demonstrated by entrusting a senior member of management with the task of overseeing the achievement of the aims of the policy. Without this commitment by the most senior members of management, the policy is in danger of being viewed merely as a public relations exercise. In other words the greening of the organisation should come from the top down, as 'without board representation . . . the organisation is only playing at going green' (Gray et al., 1993:49).

Although Elkington and Burke (1991) have identified the development of an environmental policy as the first step towards 'environmental excellence' some organisations may find the task of forming an environmental policy too daunting. The publication of the environmental policy indicates to the public (and environmental bodies) a strong commitment by the organisation to environmental improvement. Failure can have dire consequences for the company as they will face public humiliation if found out.

The alternative is to start with an 'environmental survey', which is 'the simplest type of environmental audit' (Gray et al., 1993:83) or an environmental audit. There is not a universally accepted definition of exactly what an environmental audit is (Gray and Collison, 1991), but one definition which may be used is that of the Confederation of British Industry (CBI) where the task is seen as:

> the systematic examination of the interactions between any business operation and its surroundings. This includes all emissions to air, land and water; legal constraints; the effects on the neighbouring community, landscape and ecology; and the public's perception of the operating company in the local area . . . its main purpose is a management system for providing information on environmental performance against predetermined targets. (CBI, 1990:6)

The definition is useful in describing the principle behind the environmental audit, but it does not explain the procedures involved. A useful checklist is provided by Gray and Collison (1991) who identify 12 major elements in an environmental audit. This checklist is useful because it not only considers the environmental procedures but integrates them into the whole monitoring and control process of the organisation.

The twelve elements identified by Gray and Collison (1991) are:

(1) to identify the most important of the organisation's environmental interactions;
(2) to assess the degree of environmental impact;
(3) to learn about how to deal with and reduce or improve the organisation's impact;
(4) to identify a priority list of interactions to be dealt with;
(5) to establish standards and policies;
(6) to identify responsibilities;
(7) to train staff;
(8) to change practices and put policies into action;
(9) to develop environmental information systems;
(10) to monitor performance and performance appraisal;
(11) to assess performance against standards;
(12) to reappraise this list, starting from the top, on a systematic and continuing process.

It is important that the organisation recognises that to become truly environmentally responsible they must both introduce information systems of environmental data and monitor achievement of environmental standards and targets. Gray and Collison (1991) go even further in that they suggest that the environmental audit should be integrated with the performance appraisal system of the organisation. The company should initiate monitoring of environmental performance as part of the greening process and take this process one stage further. If managers and employees are to be monitored, then environmental standards or targets should be set at the outset. This will then allow achievement of environmental targets to form part of the performance appraisal system of the business (Gray and Collison, 1991).

As industries are increasingly forced to accept their responsibilities with regard to the impact they have on the environment, they will be looking for ways to implement more environmentally responsible methods of operating. This has resulted in an increase in the number of environmental consultancies and an increase in the number of environmental audits being carried out (Elkington, 1990). However, as it is suggested that only 20% of companies have undertaken an environmental audit (Gray et al., 1993), there is certainly a long way to go.

The environmental audit is an integral part of greening the organisation and should not pose insurmountable difficulties for the organisation which genuinely wishes to make a start (albeit tentatively) on the road to 'environmental excellence'.

Accounting and the environment

The role of accounting is seen by many as simply the provision of financial data. This financial information can be used for a number of purposes such as comparison of trading results with budgeted results, controlling expenditure levels, monitoring performance etc. However, Gray (1990) argues that accounting is not restricted to those areas requiring financial description but should be viewed in a wider capacity—that of providing management information. In fact he goes further in his argument by stating that the accountant's greatest expertise lies not in the provision of financial data but in 'the design of, recognition of, assessment of and control of the information systems in an organisation' (Gray, 1990:65).

If the role of accountancy is viewed as being much wider than the provision of financial data then it can be extended to providing not only financial information but also environmental information (Gray et al., 1993; Gray and Collison, 1991). Therefore, when it is accepted that the accountant is not excluded from the environmental management process within the organisation, he will become involved in the development of environmental information systems, and the monitoring process and assessment of environmental performance. Monitoring and assessment against standards have already been identified as one of the components of an environmental audit (Gray and Collison, 1991).

For an organisation to be successful it will form corporate goals and objectives at senior management level which are then transmitted to its managers. For ultimate success these managers must be encouraged to adhere to the plans as laid down by the senior management, thereby achieving the company's objectives. As discussed by Salter the 'task of all chief executives is encouraging their policy-level managers to take action that reinforces efforts to achieve corporate goals' (Salter, 1973:94). This will involve some form of control and monitoring of the managers. The control system used by the organisation is a matter for the senior management to decide.

Hopwood (1974) identified budget reports and performance evaluation as the two components within the control system of an organisation. The control system need not necessarily be confined to these two areas but can also include supervision, enforcement of standardised policies, review and approval of plans and the culture of the organisation (Merchant, 1985).

Hopwood (1974) identifies three ways of using accounting information to evaluate the performance of the manager. They are, firstly, 'budget constrained'. This is a short-term form of appraisal because the manager has to achieve his budget even if this may be 'at the expense of other valued and important criteria' (Hopwood, 1974:110). The second basis of evaluation is 'profit conscious'. This allows the manager to take a more long-term view. He will have to achieve the required profit target but is relieved of the short-term pressures of the 'budget constrained' manager. The third basis of evaluation is 'non-accounting'. This style allows budgetary information to play a 'relatively unimportant part' in the evaluation process. The basis of evaluation may take the form of initiatives, innovative ideas etc. Both the 'budget constrained' and 'profit conscious' styles of evaluation involve the manager with close monitoring of costs, whereas the 'non-accounting' style involves a low monitoring of costs.

The second component of the control system is that of performance appraisal. The form of performance appraisal should be designed to encourage the manager to take actions to further the goals of the organisation.

As identified by Hopwood 'one of the principal means by which senior managers attempt to motivate their managers . . . towards effective performance is by linking organisational rewards to the level of their performance' (Hopwood, 1974:95). Therefore if the general manager is to be effective in achieving the environmental goals of the organisation the control system must be designed to monitor, appraise and reward him.

The hotel industry

The focus of attention by environmentalists has widened from the heavy manufacturing and extractive industries to the tourism industry. There are now not only 'green consumers' but also 'green tourists'. In response to the 'greening' of the tourism industry guides have been published for the 'green tourist' (Elkington and Hailes, 1992; Wood and House, 1991, 1992). The guides focus on the tourism industry (Wood and House, 1991, 1992) and the tour operator (Elkington and Hailes, 1992) as opposed to the hotel industry. However, the hotel industry cannot ignore the green issue, as it will increasingly have to respond to environmental pressure from the tour operators, who are in turn responding to pressure from the green tourist.[3] The effect this will have on the hotel industry is that the tour operator will scrutinise the accommodation to ensure that it meets certain environmental criteria such as energy efficiency and recycling (Elkington and Hailes, 1992). Elkington and Hailes (1992) also suggest that the accommodation should be subject to environmental audits. Pressure will also come from other areas—growing public awareness and concern (Smith, 1993), sustainability of the industry (IHEI, 1993), and market forces (IHEI, 1993).

As the hotel industry awakens to its responsibility for its environmental impact there should be an increase in initiatives both at an individual hotel level and at group level. The management may decide to become fully environmentally responsible from the outset. They can follow Elkington and Burke's (1991) 'ten steps to environmental excellence' by developing an environmental policy and implementing this throughout the hotel. Alternatively they may decide to be less ambitious and start by carrying out an environmental survey of the hotel. The advantage of the environmental survey is that it can be done by the manager (or another competent member of staff). However, management should be aware that an environmental survey is not a substitute for a complete environmental audit (Gray et al., 1993), as there will obviously be some areas where expert knowledge is required, for example, in the area of energy efficiency schemes or impending legislation.

The environmental impacts of an hotel will vary depending on the size, location and standard of the hotel, but the following broad categories are those which should initially be considered by the manager of the hotel when carrying out an environmental audit or survey. He should detail the 'inputs', 'leakages' and 'outputs' of the hotel (Gray et al., 1993) and review each in turn. The 'inputs' identified by Gray et al. (1993) include energy, food, laundry etc. 'Leakages' are waste, packaging, heat etc. 'Outputs' include such intangibles as comfort and service. The manager should consider the opportunities to reduce, recycle or reuse each of the inputs and leakages. When considering any environmental savings on the inputs and leakages the manager will also consider the impact this will have on the output of the hotel, i.e. on how the guest is affected.

Carrying out an environmental audit or survey is a useful first step in the greening process as it identifies potential areas for improvement. However, two problems are encountered before any environmental improvements (Gray et al., 1993) can be implemented. The first constraint is that of cost. Any major environmental improvements will usually involve the hotel in additional costs at the outset. This will be a problem for hotels which do not have the funds available (even though the long-term savings may outweigh the initial investment). Energy-saving measures which have been introduced in a number of hotels are giving a payback of between one and two years (IHEI, 1993). The second constraint to introducing some environmental improvements has been identified as the effect on the guest's comfort or service provided (Gray et al., 1993). For example, an opportunity to reduce the laundry's environmental impact may be identified by reducing the volume of laundry processed. This would result in a saving of water, energy and reduce the amount of detergents used. However, this may be achieved by not changing bedding on a daily basis for stay-over guests. Although environmentally preferable

it may prove to be unacceptable from the service perspective. One possible way of reducing any unfavourable reaction from the guest is to communicate the reasons for the change to the guest (Barnard, 1992).

In 1993 the greening of the hotel industry was given a major boost by the publication of an environmental manual aimed specifically at the hotel industry. The manual, entitled *Environmental Management for Hotels: the Industry Guide to Best Practice*, was published by the International Hotels Environment Initiative (IHEI). The IHEI was formed in 1991 by the Prince of Wales Business Leaders Forum and now consists of eleven members from the major hotel groups (IHEI, 1993). The main driving force for the initiative was John van Praag, formerly of the Inter-Continental hotel group, who, having seen the success of his company's environmental manual, felt that it should be made available to all hotels. The publication of the manual is an attempt to make the knowledge gained, not only by the Inter-Continental group but by all the large hotel chains, more widely available throughout the industry.

The manual gives a more comprehensive analysis of 'inputs' for the hotel than those identified by Gray et al. (1993). For example, there are eleven sections in total covering areas such as indoor air quality, external air emissions, noise etc. What is perhaps of most use is that it gives practical examples of initiatives and savings achieved by the hotels contributing. The hotel manager therefore has the opportunity of looking at sections individually, having identified particular problem areas within his hotel.

Survey of general managers

A questionnaire survey of 297 general managers throughout the UK was carried out in late-1993. The sample consisted of general managers from large and medium-sized hotel groups and from independent hotels. Usable replies (response rate of 35.7%) were received from 89 general managers and 17 general managers who were also the owner of the hotel. The questionnaire attempted to ascertain the extent of what is currently being done by the hotel industry and the manager's response to the environmental issue.

A number of typical environmental measures were given and the manager asked to report the main reason for implementing them. The six reasons offered were cost, environment, customer pressure, regulatory requirement, competitor action or not applicable in the hotel. The replies are summarised in Table 70.1. Out of 17 possible initiatives the most-cited reason for implementation was on the basis of cost. This was the main reason for each

Table 70.1 *Main reason for environmental initiatives*

Environmental initiatives	Environmental (%)	Cost (%)	Customer (%)	Not applicable (%)	No. of responses
Vegetarian options on the menu	3.85	0.00	90.38	1.92	104
No smoking areas	9.62	0.00	73.08	12.50	104
Energy-efficiency schemes	11.54	70.19	0.00	14.42	104
Energy usage monitored	8.65	75.96	0.00	11.54	104
Recycling of glass	45.28	7.55	0.00	39.62	106
Recycling of aluminium cans	23.58	1.89	0.94	71.70	106
Recycling of paper	24.53	6.60	0.00	66.98	106
Recycling of cooking oil	36.19	22.86	0.00	31.43	105
Recycling of food	15.24	12.38	0.00	66.67	105
Water use restrictors	12.62	23.30	0.00	62.14	103
Bedlinen and towels changed less often	5.66	24.53	1.89	67.92	106
Reduced level of toiletries	3.77	28.30	1.89	65.09	106
Purchasing dept. policy of only buying 'environment friendly' products	19.05	5.71	7.62	65.71	105
Reduced level of packaging	10.38	16.04	1.89	69.81	106
Employee awareness schemes	21.90	19.05	2.86	55.24	105
Environmental bedrooms	6.60	7.55	3.77	81.13	106
Buy local produce	7.62	28.57	18.10	43.81	105

of the following measures: water use restrictors, energy efficiency schemes and monitoring, bedlinen and towels changed less often, reduced level of toiletries, reduced level of packaging, environmental bedrooms, buying local produce. The environment was given as the main reason for implementation of the following measures: recycling of glass, aluminium cans, paper, cooking oil and other food waste, purchasing department policy of buying environmentally friendly goods, and employee awareness schemes. The customer was cited as the main reason in the following cases: vegetarian options on the menu and no smoking areas. Although all the initiatives could be viewed as being environmental, it is perhaps not surprising that the main reason for introducing the majority was on the basis of cost savings rather than environmental.

From an environmental viewpoint the fact that these measures are being operated at all in the hotel industry is encouraging. However, there are a high number of instances when over 65% of the respondents are not carrying out any of the initiatives at all, for example, recycling of aluminium cans, paper and food, bedlinen and towels changed less frequently, reduced level of toiletries, purchasing department policy, reduced level of packaging and environmental bedrooms.

The managers were asked to identify the importance they placed on a number of criteria for environmental change. The results are summarised in Table 70.2. Care of the environment was not regarded to be as important as health and safety, quality, cost or customer care and demand. This was not an unexpected response. However, what was unexpected was the response that competitors' actions were viewed as the least important of all the

Table 70.2 *Criteria for environmental change*

	Mean	Standard deviation	No. of responses
Cost	4.50	0.83	105
Care for the environment	4.05	0.87	105
Customer care	4.43	0.67	105
Quality	4.51	0.72	104
Customer demand	4.19	0.81	105
Potential legislation	3.78	1.18	103
Personal beliefs	3.68	1.16	105
Industry standards	3.41	0.99	104
Competitors' actions	2.98	1.14	105
Health and safety	4.53	0.77	105

5, very important; 1, not at all important.

criteria for environmental change. One possible reason for this may be that the manager does not view a competitor who claims to be environmentally friendly as a threat to his business.

Table 70.3 summarises a number of comments which could be made when considering the hotel industry and the environmental issue. The manager was asked to indicate his agreement or otherwise. From the responses there is strong agreement that the hotel industry does have an impact on the environment. However, the managers feel that hotels which claim to be environmentally friendly are using it as a marketing exercise.

The final section considered if the form of control helps or hinders the manager in improving the environmental performance of his hotel. It was hypothesised that perhaps a lack of action in the hotel industry may be linked to the control system operated by the hotel and an attempt was made to determine the extent of control

Table 70.3 *General managers' attitudes to the environmental issue*

	Mean	Standard deviation	No. of responses
The hotel industry has an impact on the environment	3.93	0.93	103
The hotel industry does not affect the environment to the same extent as manufacturing industries	3.70	1.23	105
Hotels which claim to be 'green' are using it as a marketing ploy	3.79	1.02	105
Most hotel managers do not have time to worry about the environment	3.07	1.15	104
It is not possible to function profitably and become environmentally friendly	2.39	1.10	104
Customers would consider any environmental improvements as simply a cost-cutting exercise by the hotel	2.94	1.23	105
Customers need to be educated to accept environmental improvements within the hotel industry	3.87	1.07	104
Environmental change is fine so long as the customer is not affected	3.64	1.15	105

5, strongly agree; 1, strongly disagree.

exercised over the general manager. The replies (as shown in Table 70.4) suggest that the hotel manager is controlled both by his budget and achievement of profits. Environmental reporting and achievement of environmental targets are both viewed as being unimportant to his head office (or equivalent). This is emphasised by the apparent agreement that head office emphasises regular reporting of financial data and that this form of reporting is more important than non-accounting data (see Table 70.5).

Using the distinctions drawn by Hopwood (1974) it would appear that the hotel industry is very much involved in control through budgets and achievement of profits rather than more informal forms of control. The top three reports from the manager's perspective were achievement of budget, maintenance/improvement in profitability and report on customer complaints. This would suggest that the manager will be judged primarily

Table 70.4 *General managers' perceptions of importance placed on control criteria*

	Mean	Standard deviation	No. of responses
Achievement of budget	4.64	0.61	88
Maintenance/improvement in profitability	4.71	0.50	87
Report on customer complaints	4.25	0.87	88
Adherence to operations manual	3.39	1.07	85
Report on staff turnover	2.80	1.06	88
Report on external factors affecting the business	3.26	1.06	87
Report on internal initiatives being taken	3.86	0.90	87
Environmental reporting	2.85	1.13	87
Achieving environmental targets	2.62	1.24	86

5, very important; 1, not at all important.

Table 70.5 *General managers' views of reporting requirements*

	Mean	Standard deviation	No. of responses
Head office emphasises regular reporting of accounting information	4.57	0.72	87
Non-accounting data is very important to head office	3.30	1.06	86
Head office operate an informal style of control	3.00	1.36	87

5, strongly agree; 1, strongly disagree.

on financial performance. The report of customer complaints appears to be the only form of non-accounting information on which head office places any importance. The reports viewed as the least important were staff turnover, environmental reporting, and achievement of environmental targets. As environmental initiatives do not appear to be recognised as part of the appraisal system, the manager is not encouraged to introduce environmentally friendly measures. This is disappointing, as the manager does appear to accept that the hotel industry does have an impact on the environment, but his head office has not as yet recognised this or has not introduced environmental monitoring into the performance appraisal system. When asked if environmental improvements would be recognised as part of the reward system, 63 (70.79%) of the managers gave a negative reply. Therefore the majority of managers do not have the incentive to introduce any initiatives based on purely environmental criteria. Of those 23 managers who replied that any environmental improvements would be recognised, only 4 stated that the recognition would be financial, 13 that the recognition would be prestige and 6 said that recognition would be both.

Where an environmental initiative happens to reduce costs as well as reducing the environmental impact of the hotel then the manager would presumably be willing to implement the measure as this would have a favourable impact on his financial reporting.

Conclusion

Despite the acceptance that the hotel industry does have an impact on the environment and the introduction of a number of environmental initiatives, the hotel industry does have a long way to go to achieve environmental excellence. It would appear that the form of control operated by the manager's head office (or equivalent) does not facilitate or encourage the introduction of environmental initiatives. The manager appears to be constrained by the financial requirements, i.e. achievement of both budget and profits. This is not unexpected, as it is normally assumed that improvement in the environment is at the expense of profits (Elkington and Burke, 1991). Unless the environmental issue is recognised more fully by the senior management within the hotel, the general manager will not be able to introduce measures based purely on environmental criteria.

If the greening of the hotel is to be achieved the lead must come from the hotel's head office. This will involve the publication of an environmental policy, or at the very least carrying out an environmental audit. Environmental targets and initiatives should be recognised in the performance appraisal system operated by the hotel and non-accounting information such as environmental reporting should become part of the appraisal system. The greening of the hotel industry will then have started.

Notes

1. Bhopal disaster, Chernobyl nuclear disaster, Exxon Valdez oil spill, the discovery of holes in the ozone layer.
2. The Valdez Principles were developed by the Social Investment Forum in the USA. They were developed after the Exxon Valdez oil spill by a group of investors who were concerned about the incidence of such environmental disasters.
3. Green tourists may be defined as travellers who wish to minimise their impact on the local environment.

References

Barnard, L. (1992) 'A growing concern', *Inside Hotels*, June/July: 28–33.
CBI (1990) 'Narrowing the gap: environmental auditing guidelines for business', Confederation of British Industry, London.
Elkington, J. (1990) 'The environmental audit: a green filter for company policies', *Plants, Processes and Products*, Sustainability/WWF, London.
Elkington, J. and Burke, T. (1991) *The Green Capitalists: How to Make Money—and Protect the Environment*, Victor Gollancz, London.
Elkington, J. and Hailes, J. (1988) *The Green Consumer Guide: High Street Shopping for a Better Environment*, Victor Gollancz, London.
Elkington, J. and Hailes, J. (1992) *Holidays that Don't Cost the Earth*, Victor Gollancz, London.
Elkington, J. and Knight, P. with Hailes, J. (1991) *The Green Business Guide*, Victor Gollancz, London.
Gray, R. (1990) *The Greening of Accountancy: the Profession after Pearce*, ACCA, London.
Gray, R. and Collison, D. (1991) 'Environmental audit: green gauge or whitewash?', *Managerial Auditing*, 6(5): 17–25.
Gray, R. with Bebbington, J. and Walters, D. (1993) *Accounting for the Environment*, Paul Chapman, London.
Hopwood, A. (1974) *Accounting and Human Behaviour*, Haymarket Publishing, London.
IHEI (International Hotels Environment Initiative) (1993) *Environmental Management for Hotels: the Industry Guide to Best Practice*, Butterworth-Heinemann, Oxford.
Merchant, K. (1985) 'Organisational controls and discretionary program decision making: a field study', *Accounting, Organizations and Society*, 10(1): 67–85.
Rouse, B. (1991) 'Green audits make business sense', *British Hotelier & Restauranteur*, December: 20–21.
Salter, M. (1973) 'Tailor incentive compensation to strategy', *Harvard Business Review*, March–April: 94–102.
Smith, D. (1993) 'Business and the environment: towards a paradigm shift?', in D. Smith (Ed.), *Business and the Environment: Implications of the New Environmentalism*, Paul Chapman, London.
STB (1993) 'Going green: guidelines for the Scottish tourism industry', Scottish Tourist Board.
Wood, K. and House, S. (1991) *The Good Tourist*, Mandarin, London.
Wood, K. and House, S. (1992) *The Good Tourist in the UK*, Mandarin, London.

71 Dartmoor Area Tourism Initiative— a case study of visitor management in and around a National Park

J. GREENWOOD

It is estimated that 103 000 000 visitor days are spent in the 11 National Parks of England and Wales each year, contributing £550 to £900 million to the local economy annually (FNNPE, 1993). Within these figures is hidden a major conflict: enormous visitor pressure on some of our most sensitive landscapes and the communities and wildlife that live within them; and a vital source of income and employment without which many of these areas would suffer both economically and socially. Effective visitor management of such areas is seen increasingly as a crucial mechanism for minimising visitor pressure and maximising economic benefit to provide a sustainable future for our National Parks. This paper is a summary of the first major visitor management project involving a National Park in the UK, where the adoption of a wider area and its promotion and development is being seen as a very real solution.

The Dartmoor Area Tourism Initiative (DATI) was a public and private sector partnership cooperating to develop sustainable tourism in the Dartmoor National Park and its surrounding areas. DATI began in April 1991 with a lifespan of 3 years. This paper outlines its progress from April 1991 to January 1994.

DATI built upon the success of a previous two-year Tourism Action Programme (TAP). This had been marketing led with very limited resources but provided a firm basis for further targeted and appropriate marketing to be progressed. During the TAP's operation a comprehensive 'Interpretation Strategy' was produced for the Dartmoor area and became the basis of DATI's project development work.

The overall aim of the Initiative was visitor management through appropriate marketing and project implementation of the wider Dartmoor area—over 700 square miles, including the whole of the Dartmoor National Park (368 square miles) and West Devon Borough Council, and significant tracts of Teignbridge and South Hams. The National Park itself receives in the region of 10 000 000 visits per year, and research suggests 70% of these are by people living locally. The pressure from visitors causes difficulties within the Park including litter pollution, traffic congestion, the demise of wildlife habitats, and anti-tourism feeling among some sectors of the local community. DATI was envisaged very much as a preventative measure, to ensure existing problems did not escalate. Primarily, we sought to open up new recreational opportunities, particularly in the areas surrounding the Park, to improve the benefits tourism makes to the local economy and to inform all involved of their role in the long-term future of the area.

Ten sponsors provided core funding of approximately £73 000 per annum and a commitment to achieve a comprehensive work programme. These were the English Tourist Board (ETB), West Country Tourist Board (WCTB), Countryside Commission, Dartmoor National Park Authority (DNPA), Devon County Council (DCC), West Devon Borough Council (WDBC), South Hams District Council (SHDC), Teignbridge District Council (TDC), the Dartmoor Tourist Association (DTA) and the Duchy of Cornwall. In addition DATI worked alongside many other agencies in order to achieve its aims and objectives.

Three full-time members of staff, a Project Manager, Project Officer and Secretary, based in offices in Princetown, were largely responsible for the implementation of the work programme. It is worth noting that in its first year DATI was only fully staffed for 6 weeks. Inevitably this delayed the implementation of some projects. In addition, following the resignation of the original Project Manager, many projects had to be reorganised and upgraded, again causing significant delay. Unfortunately, such difficulties are not uncommon among short-term projects of this nature. Work was guided by Project and Marketing Groups with representatives from each of the sponsors, who met quarterly. A Steering Group also met at regular intervals to monitor progress and make strategic and policy decisions. When necessary, smaller working groups were formed to progress certain projects.

In April 1992, DATI received confirmation of £81 223 grant assistance over three years from the European

Commission Devon and Cornwall Multi-Fund Operational Programme. This was available for local authorities implementing capital tourism projects in the Plymouth Travel to Work Area within the life of DATI, on a matching funding basis. Although this represented an important funding boost for the Initiative, the claim process proved complicated and time-consuming and by December 1993 no actual EC monies had yet been received.

An extensive work programme combined appropriate marketing (continued from the previous TAP) and a wide range of interpretive projects—nine main areas of work, each having as many as 10 individual areas within its remit. The nine main areas were marketing, development of public transport potential, farm diversification, sustainable tourism, public relations, advisory and informational role, elements of the interpretation strategy, management of pressure, and monitoring. The remainder of this paper considers examples of DATI's work in each of these nine areas.

As the Initiative drew to a close in January 1994 much of this programme had been achieved. Those elements of it outlined here are primarily those of the DATI core staff, but it must not be forgotten that sponsor agencies made a significant contribution to its implementation under DATI's strategic overview.

Marketing

The aim here was the use of marketing as a tool for visitor management by: incorporation of the previous TAP marketing projects to enable effective integration of marketing and interpretation work; 'selling' the right areas and sites to visitors; and implementing a principle of 'reciprocity of information'.

Continuing the marketing advances achieved by the previous TAP, DATI's marketing activities were carefully targeted to achieve visitor management on a local level. Consequently, *local* media coverage was particularly important, to reach local residents, the main users of the moor for recreation. DATI was particularly successful in gaining regular local press coverage, varying from straight printing of press releases to half-page features on particular initiatives. All new publications and initiatives received widespread local promotion which was, for this area, more cost-effective than a glossy, high-profile and expensive campaign.

DATI also operated an extensive information service, primarily on accommodation, but also covering attraction details, weather information, events, student and media enquiries, visitor complaints and general information, totalling between two and three thousand enquiries per year.

Approximately half of these were accommodation enquiries as the DATI office serviced requests for information generated by the local tourist association's advertising for its brochure 'Guide to Dartmoor'. Linked to this was a computerised accommodation and information booking service using the Tourist Information Management (TIM) system. By the end of year 2, up to three pages of detailed information on every inspected accommodation outlet had been fed into the computer, providing the most extensive accommodation base available for the area. This proved extremely popular with visitors requiring detailed accommodation information, though very few bookings were made by the office, visitors preferring to do this themselves. Working with the tourist association, DATI widened the distribution of their guide, mailing out copies to 350 targeted TICs. This resulted in requests for further copies (totalling 2000) from TICs throughout the South and Midlands regions each year and represents a major advance in the guide's distribution.

DATI also established two annual awards to encourage higher standards within the tourism industry—the Winning Warmest Welcome Award, to encourage excellence in customer care, and the Moor Care award, to encourage environmentally friendly operation amongst local tourism businesses. Both of these awards were initiated by the previous TAP but in two years DATI increased the number of entries to both awards by over 50%, and ensured worthwhile publicity for the winners.

Recruitment campaigns for membership of the local tourist association also formed part of DATIs remit. In year 1, a DATI-led recruitment campaign resulted in a 25% membership increase, thus significantly widening the scope of the association. During 1993, the Association employed a part-time temporary recruitment officer, resulting in an overall doubling of members during the life of the Initiative.

Initially it was felt that DATI need not lead familiarisation trips to the area as other agencies were already doing this (similarly with advertising). Instead DATI acted as 'host for a day' in partnership with lead agencies, on approximately a dozen 'fam' trips. In response to concerns amongst local businesses about the drop in visitor numbers and spend during 1991/92, in its final year DATI increased its destination marketing and successfully hosted a film trip by the *Holiday* programme. In all marketing activities the areas surrounding the moor featured strongly, reinforcing DATI's visitor management objectives.

The provision of training/awareness seminars and a business advice service also formed part of DATI's marketing remit. In two and a half years DATI became an important training provider in the area, particularly in specialist areas such as farm tourism. The training provided was in direct response to expressed local need, for example, a business/management one-day seminar held in year 1 as a result of a survey of local tourist association member needs. The quality of provision and this direct response to expressed training needs ensured DATI became an important on-the- doorstep source of training.

In 1991, DATI was highly commended in the ETB's England for Excellence award, 'Tourism destination' category, in recognition of its specialist approach in using marketing as a tool for visitor management.

Development of public transport potential

Here, DATI led two major new initiatives—a 'Coach Drivers' Handbook' and a public transport guide, both covering the wider Dartmoor area.

For a number of years the National Park Authority has promoted a recommended coach route network to coach drivers and companies, to encourage them to use suitable routes when visiting the moor. DATI's role was to expand this further and make it more persuasive. In consultation with the DNPA, County Transport Co-ordination Centre, the Bus and Coach Council and The Coach Drivers' Club a comprehensive 'Coach Drivers' Handbook' for the Dartmoor Area was produced. This not only provides a detailed map and listings of attractions and refreshment stops but also suggested tours (with interpretation), providing ready-made half- and full-day tours for drivers. The Handbook was genuinely welcomed by drivers and a local company adopted two routes outside the Park—an important step forward for DATI's management objectives. A French/German translation was also produced but effective distribution of this proved difficult on DATI's limited budget.

Wherever possible in its publications and promotions, DATI encouraged visitors to use public transport during their visit to the moor, for example, in the children's pack and viewpoints leaflets we will hear about later. This was formalised in a major new publication 'Next Stop Please' designed to demonstrate recreational opportunities in the area that can be reached by bus or train. Ten thousand copies of this were printed in January 1994 and its use by visitors is being watched closely by the National Park Authority.

Farm diversification

In order to prioritise and guide DATI's work in this specialist area, a sub-group of sponsoring agencies was

formed. It was agreed that DATI aim to complete and monitor four pilot diversification schemes on working farms—one in each District and one high moorland Duchy of Cornwall farm. By the end of year 2, the following schemes were developed (with funding assistance by the Devon Rural Development Programme).

Duchy of Cornwall

A typical high moorland farm with limited camping and B&B involvement, this farm was ideal for a trail to inform visitors of traditional Dartmoor farming methods. Working closely with the farmer and Duchy of Cornwall officer, a route for a trail and several points of interest were quickly identified and researched. By June 1992, 1000 copies of a leaflet guide to the trail had been produced and a series of monthly evening walks around the trail, guided by the farmer, promoted. These proved very successful, attracting up to 20 people per walk and in addition the farmer began giving tours to organised groups who had booked in advance. In 1993, the farmer used the trail to promote his accommodation (now extended to include a camping barn) and targeted all local schools offering an ideal educational visit destination. This was successful and the farmer is continuing the work, focusing on group visits.

Teignbridge District

A small dairy farm on the outskirts of the Moor had been running a traditional cream tea operation during the summer months for several years. This represented an important source of income for the farmer but owing to a lack of marketing, visitor numbers had plateaued. Again, working closely with the farmer's wife, and Devon County Council (the owners) a ruined folly was identified as an excellent viewpoint only a short walk from the farmhouse. Using this as an 'added extra', 1000 copies of a promotional leaflet were produced and distributed throughout the District, and advice provided on local advertising. In 1993 the farm reprinted the leaflet and visitor levels were such that they did not anticipate needing to reprint again in 1994.

South Hams District

This farm outside the National Park had no prior involvement in tourism but had indicated an interest to the Council's Environment Service, both as an educational resource and as a means of generating income. Having no previous involvement, the farmer wished to 'test the water' before fully committing himself to a project such as those outlined above. A potential trail route and points of interest were identified with the farmer and a guided walk (in September 1992) promoted through the South Hams Environment Service events programme and posters around the area. Approximately 35 people attended the walk, many purchasing cream teas afterwards in the farm house. Following this success, the farmer felt confident about a larger involvement and a self-guided trail leaflet was produced in 1993 and a number of open days held throughout the summer.

West Devon District

Surprisingly, a suitable working farm was most difficult to find in West Devon, the most rural of the three districts in the Dartmoor area. After many site visits, a lowland dairy farm, its only visitor involvement small-scale clay-pigeon shooting and fishing facilities, was eventually found. The farmer was keen to develop a trail to improve business and explain to his visitors the landscape and wildlife of the farm. Working with the farmer and an officer from West Devon Borough Council a trail was agreed and researched, to be printed and monitored in summer 1993. However, by that time there was some doubt as to the future of the farm and this project was put on hold.

Following the success of the three pilot projects completed in year 2, it was felt important to make the information and lessons learnt as widely available to farmers in the area as possible. For this purpose, an awareness day was programmed for November 1992, to include presentations by DATI, Agricultural Development Advisory Service (ADAS) and farmers involved in the above pilot projects. With the help of ADAS, an invitation to attend was mailed to every working farm in the DATI area (1500). To cope with the response, another two awareness days were held in January 1993. Over 150 farmers attended these events. Assessment sheets completed on the day revealed a need for farm tourism marketing training and this was provided in October 1993. In addition, approximately 15 advisory site visits were made to interested farms following the awareness days.

In addition to these pilot projects, DATI also looked at accommodation barns, local produce and activity-break initiatives. Building on general support amongst sponsors, and the possibility of a 'Bunk Barns Development Project' being developed in the area with the Youth Hostels Association, DATI hosted an Accommodation Barns Awareness Day in June 1992. Over 60 people attended, representing 10 interested farms and nearly 30 separate agencies. DATI, with several other

agencies who attended the day, committed monies to the funding of a dedicated Barns Officer and this post began in May 1993 with the Dartmoor area a priority in the first year. By December 1993 a small network of potential barns in the Dartmoor area had been identified and works begun.

The promotion of locally produced goods to visitors and tourism businesses is important for a number of reasons:

- they represent an important part of local identity;
- they perpetuate specialist skills in an area;
- money spent on local goods reduces leakages, keeping more visitor spend in the area, helping to maintain a stable and diverse local economy.

Working in partnership with the National Park Authority, and following research and discussions with a range of local agencies, an extensive new database of nearly 200 small-scale producers was collated in 1992/93, including food, drink, craft and plant producers. These were invited to an open meeting held in Okehampton in January 1993. Approximately 70 people attended and after a wide-ranging and positive discussion a small number of volunteers agreed to form a Steering Group to pursue the priorities identified at the meeting. This core group, working with a number of local agencies, raised £3000 sponsorship and organised promotional and retail events during 1993, including the production of a new Food, Drink and Craft guide in which nearly 50 local producers are featured. This proved popular with producers and local residents alike and it is hoped it will be extended during 1994 as a priority for a new loose cooperative known as 'Dartmoor Area Producers' formed following a second open meeting in November 1993.

DATI also worked closely with the local branch of the Farm Holiday Bureau, Devon Farms, to pilot an activity-breaks promotion for autumn 1992. However, although a useful networking exercise for both the Initiative and the farms, it was very limited in funding and generated few enquiries.

Sustainable tourism

Aims here included: marketing of 'green tourism' to all involved and cultivation of best practice; establishing a project to assess the ways and means for the tourist industry to make a direct contribution to the care and management of the surrounding environment on which it depends; and encouraging community-led tourism initiatives and development of a 'Green Charter' for the Dartmoor area.

With the proliferation of 'green charters' it was agreed that DATI should take this step further, providing more than just general aims. After much research, 2000 copies of the 'Green business guide for the Dartmoor area' were produced in May 1992. Aimed at tourism businesses, and adopted by the local tourist association, the guide outlined a policy for going green, offered practical suggestions on how to achieve it and local contacts, who could help them do so.

A joint launch with the Devon Wildlife Trust received regional television, radio and newspaper coverage. Copies were mailed to all inspected accommodation and attractions in the area during June 1992. A questionnaire the following October revealed that whilst some action had been taken by businesses since receiving the guide, work was needed to encourage them further. A step towards this was a Green Tourism Awareness day held jointly with the South Devon Green Tourism Initiative in October 1993. The Guide was generally accepted as being the most comprehensive of its type at that time and generated much interest from other tourism projects and local government around the UK.

Following the 'Green Business Guide', the next priority was getting the 'green' message across to visitors to the area. Following research of existing messages (for example in the *Dartmoor Visitor* free newspaper) 10 000 copies of the 'Green visitor guide for the Dartmoor area' were printed in March 1993. Produced in attractive A6 'handy size' and illustrated with cartoons, the Guide includes messages on litter, wildlife and livestock, using public transport and driving with care, supporting local businesses, and generally caring for the area during a visit. This is a popular publication with visitors, but it remains to be seen if it has any practical impact on behaviour.

The encouragement of community-led tourism projects was tackled through three approaches:

(1) provision of in-kind support, including advice and contacts;
(2) provision of small amounts of pump-priming funding;
(3) active network membership of the Devon Rural Action Programme.

By adopting this flexible approach, DATI supported schemes as diverse as village trails, arts projects and town signing, and became an important source of local support for such initiatives.

The importance and need for a sustainable tourism industry and environment in which it operates is a thread which runs throughout the work of the Initiative. DATI tried to reach as many sectors of those involved as possible, from tourism businesses to visitors, councillors to communities. The latter have perhaps been the most difficult to target, but all parish councils were mailed information on DATI, local tourism and how to get more involved. In 1992 DATI was highly commended for its approach in Devon County Council's 'Keep Devon Shipshape' awards.

Tourism contribution research was put on hold until year 2 whilst the green business and visitor guides were being developed. In that time, two projects involved with developing ways and means by which the tourism industry might make a direct contribution to the care and management of the surrounding environment began. These were the WCTB 'Celebrate the Countryside' campaign, and the South Devon Green Tourism Initiative, a national pilot project. Owing to the limited resources and timescale of DATI, involvement in both of these initiatives was identified as the most effective way for DATI to pursue this issue.

Public relations

The aim here was to use local and national media to stimulate interest in DATI to encourage a favourable image for both the project and the tourism industry within the area.

DATI's concentration on local media and the resulting wide coverage has been mentioned above. However, DATI also received good coverage nationally for its approach and visitor management, particularly in specialist tourism publications. For example, DATI was cited as an example of good practice in both *The Green Light* (ETB, 1991) and *Tourism in National Parks. A Guide to Good Practice* (ETB, 1992), and has been similarly featured in *Tourism Enterprise* (ETB, 1993) and the Countryside Commission newsletter (Countryside Commission, 1992). DATI press releases appeared regularly in the ETB's monthly *Anglofile* magazine, furthering the message that there was much of interest in the wider Dartmoor area.

In an attempt to ensure that local tourism businesses and local people were aware of DATI's aims and role in the area, an information leaflet was produced in July 1992 and mailed to over 300 businesses, over 100 parish councils and generally through information centres etc. In addition, a quarterly newsletter sent to over 300 tourism businesses every quarter informed them of DATI's progress and invited them to get involved. After a slow start in 1991, by November 1992 these newsletters produced positive feedback from businesses and raised awareness of DATI's work and how they could benefit from it.

Advisory and informational role

One of DATI's greatest achievements was its coordinating role, through both its work and its management groups. DATI as a concept provides a strategic overview for appropriate tourism development and marketing throughout the area, and few of its achievements would have been as successful without this wider view. DATI has been instrumental in getting agencies around the table to swap ideas, offer mutual support and, crucially, avoid duplication of effort and funding wherever possible.

Some examples of DATI's coordinating role include the introduction of twice-yearly Project Officer days, the provision of cycling and special needs information packs, and guided walks provision. The Project Officer days provided a much-needed forum for 15–20 Project Officers involved in tourism and countryside projects on the ground in and around the DATI area to discuss the issues affecting them all. Run on a loosely structured and informal basis to allow as much discussion as possible, and offered at cost price, these proved popular and affordable forums. This initiative was welcomed at both county and regional level and as a result DATI hosted a Devon-wide event in November 1993 when 50 tourism and countryside officers attended.

The Dartmoor area offers many cycling opportunities for visitors and is a popular destination for this activity. A number of agencies in the Dartmoor area produced free cycling information, including route guides, codes of conduct, maps and cycle hire opportunities. However, these were available from different places, requiring several telephone calls, visits or letters to obtain them. DATI simply pooled copies of all the information into the office and promoted it as a one-stop source through local papers and specialist magazines. The response demonstrated the need for such a simple, low-cost but effective coordinating approach, and in 1994 this is being progressed further by local agencies. A similar approach was adopted for a special needs information pack as the area has a wide range of suitable accommodation and some good recreational provision.

Using monies carried over from year 1, and building on the project achievements throughout 1991 and 1992, a specialist tourism consultancy was appointed in December 1992 to produce an interpretive map of the Dartmoor area for the 1993 season. Development of the map was guided by a small sub-group and 12 000 copies were produced in spring 1993. The map was fundamental to achieving DATI's objectives as it was the first time such a detailed recreational and interpretive map was available for the wider area. Incidentally, unlike many other Local Area Initiatives, this is the only occasion on which DATI used consultants, all other work being done by the core staff or local officers. Despite reservations by some sponsors, the map has sold well, particularly in National Park information centres.

The Dartmoor area is fortunate to have a number of agencies who provide excellent guided walks and events programmes. Some are well-established and promoted, others are not. Such events are popular with visitors and local people alike and provide an informative and enjoyable visitor experience. Although many of these events programmes contained similar provision, the organisers were not meeting regularly to swap ideas, share problems or coordinate promotion. For this purpose, in November 1991, DATI organised an events coordination sub-group who have since met regularly. Their priority was identified as producing a central leaflet, which would promote each agency and the range of events on offer. 10 000 copies of this leaflet were produced in March 1991 and distributed throughout the area. A reprint was provided for the 1993 season. Despite the interest generated by the leaflet, the sub-group felt there was a need to further centralise events information. A telephone Events Hotline was operated from the DATI office during 1993 as a pilot scheme. Unfortunately only a limited number of calls were received, but limited promotion due to lack of funds probably explains this, as those who did enquire found the service very useful and often called again.

Effective distribution of publications is essential if any project's aims are to be realised. Out of necessity, DATI utilised existing distribution networks of its sponsoring agencies, particularly the National Park Authority and local Districts. However, this did not prove entirely effective, being limited to information centres and information points, services which local people tend not to use. Discussions in March 1993 identified distribution strategy and implementation as a priority for consideration at the end of the Initiative and a working group was formed to take this issue forward during 1994.

Interpretation strategy

A significant part of DATI's work programme was to make a major contribution to the implementation of the Interpretation Strategy, concentrating on areas outside the National Park. DATI's main contributions to this were village projects, countryside viewpoints, the Plym Valley Cycle Way and a children's activity pack. Whilst some of the 'honeypot' villages in the National Park receive visitor numbers out of all proportion to their size and population and suffer the associated congestion, pollution, erosion and anti-tourism feeling, there are many other villages in the area of similar interest which would welcome more visitors as a source of support for local businesses and services. With this in mind, and as a tool for encouraging visitors off the moor, in 1991 DATI produced and promoted a leaflet entitled 'The secret villages of the Dartmoor area'. This promoted nine small and as yet 'undiscovered' villages spread around the edge of the National Park. The leaflet proved popular with visitors and was actively adopted by a number of the villages involved, and surrounding accommodation providers. To extend this approach further, towards the end of year 1, DATI targeted four town/village projects in the three Districts to be pursued as pilots for the area.

South Hams

A small and picturesque village on DATI's southern border, Ermington, was chosen as it had previously been a 'secret village', as it is situated on the newly formed Erme Valley trail, and as local interest in tourism already existed.

Working closely with SHDC and the local community (mainly the school), a trail around the village on local footpaths was identified and research undertaken. A guided walk generated much interest, and a local resident produced artwork for a self-guided trail leaflet produced and promoted in summer 1993. The school has since adopted the trail and carries out regular litter picks, flora surveys and other projects.

West Devon

North Tawton is a small town of great architectural interest in the north of the DATI area and the Tarka Trail passes close by. A town trail leaflet had been produced in 1975 but was never updated and many of its points of interest no longer existed having been demolished, removed or built on! Working closely with the Town Council and a local historian, a series of short walks were researched and agreed to provide an up-to-date publication. With support from WDBC and the Tarka Project, a trails leaflet was produced at the end of year 2, for distribution and promotion during spring 1993.

The very north of the Dartmoor area is home to many small villages with much of interest to offer the visitor— walks, history, folklore, local produce etc. Yet in visitor terms it is a largely unexplored area, apart from the market town of Hatherleigh. With so much to offer the visitor, and many rural businesses in need of support, it was seen as an important key to DATI's visitor dispersal aims. In 1992, 12 parishes were invited to get involved in a small promotional project. (Three of the parishes were just outside the DATI boundary, in the Torridge

district.) Of the 12, 7 actively supported the project. Building on this initial interest and consulting with the parish councils at regular intervals, an identity for the area was developed and a promotional leaflet featuring 10 villages produced for the 1993 season. This was produced with support from WDBC, Torridge DC, the Tarka Project, individual parishes and the Devon Rural Development Programme. Initial reports after the main 1993 season suggest visitors *have* used these new leaflets and visited the villages. It is hoped that this trend will continue in future years.

Teignbridge

Situated on the eastern border of the National Park, Buckfastleigh was targeted as a pilot town for a number of reasons. Many local shops and other businesses had closed down during 1990/91, the town is particularly rich in industrial and architectural history, and, despite having three large attractions on its doorstep (attracting over 500 000 visitors per annum) very few visitors actually visit the town. A local organisation had already produced a basic promotional booklet and it was agreed with local representatives that the most effective use of DATI input would be to improve the booklet and ensure more effective distribution. Unfortunately, a change in local personalities nine months into the project, resulted in DATI's offer of support being rejected. However, a group of local businesses continued to work regularly with a DATI representative and a range of local tourism issues were targeted for action. In December 1993 a consultant's report recommended all groups in the town work together to produce a town strategy focusing on tourism as a mechanism for regeneration and discussions are currently taking place.

Whilst the funding for these projects has come primarily from DATI and its sponsors, the in-kind support from a range of organisations and local communities must not be forgotten, nor underestimated. Without such support, these projects would never have been achieved on a sustainable basis, i.e. with local support for their success, hopefully ensuring a long-term future. It is intended that the results of these developments will be monitored over coming years to assess their effectiveness at drawing visitors to settlements outside the National Park. In addition to the above projects, in-kind or pump-priming support has been offered to similar interpretation projects where appropriate. For example, DATI input into leaflets, trails or events in Bridestowe (West Devon), Tavistock (West Devon), Moretonhampstead (Teignbridge) and Chudleigh (Teignbridge).

The brief for the countryside viewpoints element of the Interpretation Strategy was 'to develop access and interpretation at notable viewpoints throughout the area'. Following a feasibility study in January 1992, nine potential viewpoints were identified around the DATI and National Park boundaries. Each offered superb views of the moor, and opportunities for interpretation on a theme linking each site to the moorland landscape—for example, agriculture, forestry, mineral extraction, geology, river landscapes and so on. On this basis, and working closely with councils, landowners, rangers and local communities, 6000 copies of two free leaflets promoting the viewpoints were produced in November 1992—Dartmoor Horizons: 'Eastern' and 'Western'. These proved to be two of the most popular leaflets DATI produced, but it is not known whether visitors used the viewpoints as a series, to be visited one after another, or just for one visit. The two local councils most heavily involved have adopted these leaflets to ensure they are updated and reprinted for a long-term future. At two of the viewpoint sites, on-site interpretation has been provided in the form of panorama boards. A board was placed on site at Blackingstone Rock in March 1992, and similarly at Hatherleigh Monument in spring 1993. These expand on the linking theme and also promote other viewpoint sites. It is hoped that a third will be placed on site during 1994 at Lee Moor.

The Plym Valley Cycle Way connects Plymouth with the edge of the moor and is a heavily used off-road access route. Although little progress had been made on interpretation or capital works along the cycle way for some time, an earlier management study provided direction. Working with an existing management group, DATI assisted in prioritisation and implementation by:

● providing on-site information boards at eight access points along the cycle way. These provided opportunities for management as some parking opportunities were purposely unmarked and a cyclists' code encouraging less speed and more quiet enjoyment of the surrounding area was included;
● financially supporting capital works, including seating provision and the creation of 'glades' for important local butterfly populations;
● producing an interpretive guide for the cycle way, which includes the cyclists' code and historical and wildlife information. This fulfilled a large local demand and has been reprinted to extend its management role.

As is the case in many areas, there is very little interpretation available for children visiting the National Park, let alone the wider Dartmoor area. For this reason,

and because children are the visitors of the future, it was felt important for DATI to produce a fun activity pack for children which promoted the wider area and a caring visitor attitude. Many months' research resulted in the Dartmoor Area Back Pack, including a game, puzzles, postcards, a map, colouring-in, and quizzes. The game 'Dartmoor Journey', is about crossing the area in the most sensitive manner and is full of messages about using public transport, not feeding the ponies, visiting the wider area, buying local produce and not parking in people's gateways! These messages are reinforced in the puzzles and quizzes and hopefully will go some way to ensuring both current and future visitors to the area will carry a greater awareness of their role in its future. The National Park Authority took on the production and distribution of the pack to ensure its future post-DATI.

Management of pressure

A practical visitor management project was grant-aided by DATI each year as a demonstration site for visitors to the Moor. For example, the first scheme in 1991 tackled the problems caused by walkers in the Birch Tor area—very heavily used, visible from the road and important archaeologically and ecologically. Walkers were redirected onto a new path which contoured up to the tor and avoided sensitive gullies where erosion of the banks was increasing at a rate that caused concern. Information on site explained the works and was felt to be successful in redirecting pressure and creating awareness. Walkers are now invited to use the original route because wooden ladders installed on the gully sides have been successful in stabilising the soil and vegetation.

A second project, undertaken during 1992, was a path from Princetown to Nuns Cross, heavily used by walkers, horseriders and cyclists. This combined pressure over a number of years caused major erosion of the bridlepath which was widening at an alarming rate. Creation of a durable path using local materials is proving successful to contain the erosion, and vegetation is now regenerating on the sides of the path.

Monitoring

A simple aim to set up efficient monitoring controls to highlight areas of achievement and future development potential proved difficult to implement. DATI was used as a rural initiative pilot for the current LAI monitoring scheme. This required a 'baseline statement' of tourism and leisure opportunities in the area prior to DATI produced with the WCTB. Also, each DATI-led project had a monitoring sheet which included a timetable of events, costings, officer time and pointers for future action. These proved almost impossible to fill in in any great detail, or predict with accuracy, as so many projects were being dealt with simultaneously.

In addition to this on-going monitoring and in an attempt to overcome the difficulties of the monitoring sheets, DATI established a comprehensive spreadsheet system to provide a single monitoring document which could be easily updated, and would be readily available to sponsors when required. This proved more useful and practicable and became a regular feature at management meetings and indispensable when considering DATI's achievements and future direction past March 1994. Indeed a three-year action plan post-DATI is now being implemented and monitored using a spreadsheet.

In addition, where practicable, and budget allowing, DATI completed surveys of its work, in partnership with the WCTB. In the first two years, two surveys were completed—the Green Business Guide survey mentioned above and a visitor survey. In December 1992 a questionnaire was sent to 970 potential visitors to the area, using names and addresses of people who had contacted the DATI office for information. The questionnaire achieved an excellent 54% response rate, providing a range of useful information. This was repeated in December 1993, achieving a similar response rate, and it is hoped that over the years a shift in visits to the area surrounding the Moor will be able to be demonstrated through these and other survey work.

For example, in addition to ETB/DATI monitoring systems a DNPA/DCC visitor survey in 1991 included sites outside the National Park for the first time, to reflect the DATI area, for example, Abbeyford Woods, Ugborough, Trusham, Lydford Forest. An all-parks visitor survey in 1994 using the wider DATI area will hopefully indicate any first signs of an increase in visitation to the areas surrounding the Moor.

The way forward

As mentioned earlier in this paper, DATI was a three-year project and effectively ended in January 1993 when its core staff moved on to pastures new. However, its work and ethos continues through a working group made up of the Project and Marketing groups, with smaller groups looking at specific issues such as marketing, information distribution, cycling etc. It is hoped that through this mechanism and the combined continuing commitment of local agencies, the achievements of DATI will remain in place and further develop for years to come.

To conclude, obviously, adoption of a wider area is not going to be the solution for every national park, though it is being seen as a major part of the answer for Dartmoor. However, whether appropriate or not, there are many lessons to be learnt from the Dartmoor area experience. A truly strategic overview to which those responsible for its implementation are wholly committed is fundamental, as is the acceptance of a practical role in the sustainable future of National Parks by all those involved, ourselves included.

References

Countryside Commission (1992) *Enjoying the Countryside*, Spring: p. 3.
ETB (1991) *The Green Light. A Guide to Sustainable Tourism*, English Tourist Board, London, p. 37.
ETB (1992) *Tourism in National Parks. A Guide to Good Practice*, English Tourist Board, London, p. 31.
ETB (1993) *Tourism Enterprise*, January: 22–23.
FNNPE (1993) *Loving Them to Death? Sustainable Tourism in Europe's Nature and National Parks*, Federation of Nature and National Parks of Europe, p. 13, Grafenau, Germany.

72 Strategies for alternative tourism: the case of tourism in Sagarmatha (Everest) National Park, Nepal

D. W. ROBINSON

The past decade has witnessed the appearance of alternative tourism designs that both recognize tourism's negative impacts and portray a more positive role for tourism linked to sustainable development. Often grouped under the title of alternative or appropriate tourism (Smith and Eadington, 1992), these forms of tourism include ecotourism (Boo, 1990), nature travel (Durst and Ingram, 1988), ethnic tourism (McKean, 1989), and adventure travel (Kutay, 1990; Zurick, 1992). Common to all of these is the tourist's desire for a participatory experience in a distinctive and often remote natural and/or cultural environment.

With a combined annual growth rate estimated at 20% to 27%, these alternative models of tourism are the fastest-growing segment of the world travel market (Passoff, 1991). Much of this growth has been associated with third world destinations, such as the Himalaya regions of Tibet, Nepal and Bhutan, the coastal and rainforest regions of Central and South America, and the savannah regions of Africa. Currently, however, conflicting opinions abound on the role of alternative tourism in third world development. Those who champion its core principle of sustainability argue that alternative tourism can be of assistance in solving difficult third world dilemmas about conservation and economic development, as well as promoting a more equitable distribution of tourism earnings (Adams, 1992; Gonsalves, 1987; Harrison, 1992; Healy, 1992). Others suggest that the discussion on alternative tourism may be distorted, and argue that it may merely be an initial phase in an evolving system of conventional tourism which is more likely to be the ruin of ecologically and culturally sensitive areas of the third world (Butler, 1990; Cohen, 1987; Greenwood, 1989; Machlis and Bacci, 1992; McKercher, 1993; Wight, 1993).

A destination which has come to typify the intense debate over the role of tourism in conservation and economic development is that of Sagarmatha (Everest) National Park in Nepal. While adventure travellers continue to be graciously welcomed to this area, and

massive increases in visitors have generated a variety of economic and social benefits at both the local and national levels (Robinson, 1992), there has also been increasing international concern expressed about tourism's negative impacts on this fragile mountain environment and its indigenous Sherpa population. Although a large body of literature exists that has portrayed Sagarmatha National Park as both a cultural and ecological catastrophe in the making, more recent reports (e.g. Fisher, 1990; Stevens and Sherpa, 1992a, 1992b, 1992c) suggest that these criticisms are premature and have ignored the adaptive strategies which have been developed to reconcile the stresses of tourism with local capabilities and needs.

The purpose of this paper is to describe and reappraise the economic, socio-cultural, and environmental changes that have been associated with the rapid growth of adventure travel in Sagarmatha National Park. In this context, the paper examines both the benefits and contradictions that tourism poses for sustainable development in Sagarmatha National Park, and outlines adaptive strategies that have been formulated to limit negative impacts on the local culture and environment. In seeking to further the discussion on the role of tourism in third world development, the case study of Sagarmatha National Park serves to illuminate the processes that underlie the expansion of tourism into frontier regions of the world (Zurich, 1992) that would not otherwise be expected to develop mass tourism, and offers lessons to guide the development of policies to promote locally directed rural development and natural resource protection in other remote and sensitive tourism destinations.

The information presented in this paper draws on the author's research experiences during two periods (five months in total) of fieldwork in Sagarmatha National Park and Kathmandu, Nepal, in the fall of 1990 and the spring of 1992. This fieldwork involved meetings with Ministry of Tourism officials in Kathmandu, general field observations in both the popular and less frequented trekking districts of the national park, discussions with the national park wardens, and interviews with Sherpas residing in the national park. This information is set against recent reports of change in the region from the tourism research literature.

Background on adventure tourism in Nepal

In a manner similar to many other third world countries that have large external debts, poverty, and scarce natural resources, Nepal has increasingly embraced tourism as a source of easily generated revenue. Having experienced unprecedented tourism growth in the past 25 years, Nepal is now among the more popular of the international tourism destinations. Today, tourism is Nepal's foremost source of foreign income and its major industry (Robinson, 1992). Nepal's fame lies primarily in trekking and mountaineering, and it was here in the 1960s, that the world's first commercial treks took place. Trekking and mountaineering visits to the Himalaya region of Nepal (which includes the protected national parks of Sagarmatha, Langtang, Shey Phksumdo and Rara, and the Annapurna Conservation Area) currently account for approximately 25% of all tourist visits to this country. This represents an increase from a mere 650 trekkers and mountaineers in 1966 to over 46 000 in 1989 (although this number fell to 35 750 in 1990 owing to major political uprisings in Nepal during 1990 and the impact of the Gulf War on international travel). Hoping to maintain the growth of high mountain visitation, the Nepal Ministry of Tourism is planning infrastructure development in existing mountain parks, and plans to open up new trekking areas (such as Mustang, opened in March 1992) where they hope to divert some of the growing number of adventure travellers.

The most renowned tourist destination in Nepal is Sagarmatha National Park. Established in 1976 and declared a World Heritage Site in 1980, the park is famous for both its towering mountains, including Mount Everest, and the culture of its Sherpa people. The park is home to approximately 3000 Sherpas who live within its 1243 km^2 borders and is associated with the Sherpa culture more than any other Nepalese park. Migrating from Tibet in the early 16th century, the lives of the Sherpa are interwoven with teachings of Buddhism, and their communities have traditionally been based on agropastoralism and trade with Tibet. The main trekking area in the park consists of four valleys near Mount Everest which are known as Khumbu region (Figure 72.1). Within Khumbu are eight Sherpa villages and over 100 seasonal herding and secondary crop sites. These villages and secondary settlements are not part of the park

proper, although all Sherpa grazing and forest lands are administered by the national park (Stevens and Sherpa, 1992a).

Tourism-related changes in Sagarmatha National Park

Since Nepal opened its borders to foreigners in 1951, Sagarmatha National Park has experienced a rapid increase in visitor numbers. The opening of the region's only commercial airstrip at Lukla (9000 feet) in 1964 reduced the travel time from Kathmandu to 40 minutes (as opposed to a walk in of one week from Jiri or two weeks from Kathmandu) and significantly boosted visitor numbers to the park. This region annually hosts mountaineering and trekking tourists numbering approximately twice the local population: in 1988 11 366 individual trekking permits were issued for the park, although the Ministry of Tourism's most recently available statistics indicate a decline to 5144 in 1990 (which was associated with domestic political problems and the impact of the Gulf War on international travel).

The changing economy

With tourism as the driving force during the past 20 years, the Khumbu has undergone a rapid transition from a subsistence to a cash economy and has experienced a rapid expansion of its local economy. An increasing dependency on tourism-generated income has brought considerable local economic benefits, and the Sherpas now enjoy a standard of living which is as high as any of the country's ethnic minorities.

Although Sherpas have a reputation for mountaineering skill, mountain-climbing was not a traditional Sherpa occupation. Sherpa involvement with mountaineering began inauspiciously in the 1920s when the British hired Sherpas for the servile work of portering (load-carrying) and guiding in the pioneering explorations to Everest as well as Himalayan expeditions in North India. When trade between Khumbu and Tibet was severely impacted by the Chinese annexation of Tibet in 1959, trekking and mountaineering emerged as a new and lucrative financial opportunity. When commercial trekking began in Khumbu in the 1960s, entire Sherpa households were able to get involved in the industry. Sherpas were hired as high-status guides and later as office personnel in charge of hiring in foreign-owned trekking agencies in Kathmandu. These Sherpas, in turn, ensured high employment rates for their family and friends in Khumbu villages as porters, cook staff, and camping staff (Adams, 1992).

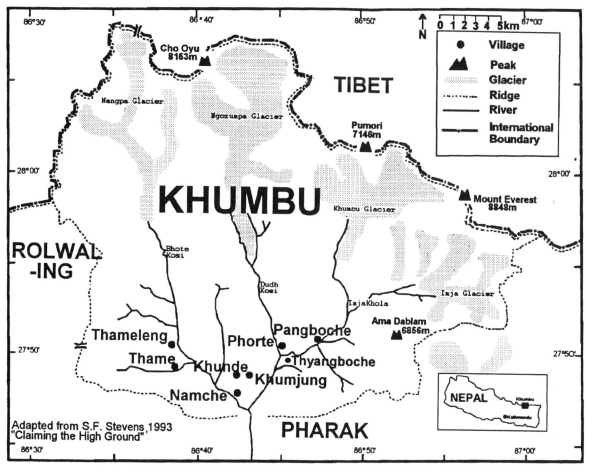

Figure 72.1 *Khumbu Region*

In the 1970s, many young Sherpa men and families began to move to Kathmandu where greater employment opportunities existed in the trekking and mountaineering industry. Those with enough capital opened their own trekking agencies and hired villagers to work for them. Sherpa entrepreneurship has continued, and of the 100 trekking and travel agencies in Kathmandu in 1989, 26 of the 56 larger agencies registered with the Nepal Trekking Agent Association were controlled by Sherpas. Five of these larger agencies employed a total of 94 permanent salaried staff, 70 employees during part of the year, and 670 at peak season (Adams, 1992; Kunwar, cited in Fisher, 1990:115).

Employment in the mountaineering and trekking industry in Khumbu itself has flourished at a wide range of levels. In the villages, many Sherpas have converted their homes into teashops and lodges to accommodate the growing number of foreign visitors, and today most households earn income from providing food, lodging, clothing, equipment or handicrafts. Khumbu Sherpas control most of the region's highly profitable tourist lodges, inns and teahouses, and have virtually monopolized tourism employment in the region. Young men and boys often gain low-paying jobs as porters, kitchen assistants or mail-runners on treks or expeditions. Those with more experience tend to gain salaried positions with an established trekking agency as cook or *sherpa* (a kind of general assistant to a trekking party). The most experienced Sherpas who possess leadership abilities may secure positions as trek or expedition leader (*sirdar*), which enables them to hire other villagers for daily wage work on a trek or expedition. Overall, the economic benefits appear to have been spread quite extensively throughout Khumbu; Adams (1992) reports that 80% of the 141 village households and 92% of the urban Sherpa households from Khumbu currently earn income from tourism.

It is typical for Sherpas to earn cash wages only during the high tourism seasons of autumn and spring, and although this is only four or five months per year, their incomes are nevertheless high by Nepalese standards. The owner of a popular lodge may gross over US$10 000 a year, and many are now among the wealthiest families in the region. In 1992, even a kitchen boy could earn more than 1500 rupees (US$50) per month, which is the equivalent to the salary of many office workers in Kathmandu. *Sirdars* may earn more than five times as much, for besides their base-salary they often make considerable extra money by making use of their own family members, servants, and packstock on treks and by over-reporting porter costs and other trail charges to their companies (Stevens and Sherpa, 1992a). Since young Sherpas contribute to their parents' household until they marry in their mid- to late-twenties and establish their own households, several members of a Sherpa household will often earn income from trekking. While women from poor households have often earned some income from portering, trekking employment to date has been male-dominated, and it is only recently that women have begun to work as members of kitchen and camp crews. There are today only one or two examples of women *sirdars* in the Khumbu (Stevens and Sherpa, 1992a).

A frequent criticism of tourism in third world areas, and one that has been applied to this region, is the often exploitative nature of the tourist–host financial labour relationship. Although Sherpas have been involved in tourism through traditional wage relationships, Adams's (1992) examination of the Sherpa economy indicates that the Sherpas have become neither 'commoditized' nor 'domesticated' as part of a subordinate local economy serving a Western-dominated tourism industry. Rather, increasing Sherpa ownership of trekking companies and unique tourist–Sherpa relationships have provided the Sherpas with opportunities to reconstitute their traditional social relationships, which were mixtures of both reciprocity and wage labour based upon the Sherpa ideals of individualism and independence.

Today, tourism is extremely popular with the Khumbu Sherpas. Although some disaffection with tourism does exist, the Sherpas know that most of the region's inhabitants have gained substantially in financial terms, in standard of living, and through improved medical and educational facilities. Sherpa ownership of a substantial proportion of tourism businesses means that 'financial leakage' has undoubtedly been less than in many other third world tourism areas. Primarily through tourism, this somewhat remote and poor rural society has rapidly become comparatively affluent—a situation which Stevens and Sherpa (1992a) and Adams (1992) have characterized

as representing one of the world's foremost examples of successful local economic development through tourism.

However, notwithstanding the Khumbu's current positive economic situation, the course of subsequent events will require careful attention. Not all Sherpa families have benefited equally from tourism, and neither have all Khumbu villages benefited from tourism. Related to the increasing demands from trekking and mountaineering groups, the inflation of the price of food and supplies in Khumbu has financially burdened those poorer families not involved in tourism. Also, while the region's tourism centre of Namche (11 000 feet) has experienced massive economic benefits, those villages remote from the main trekking routes, such as Thame, have changed very little.

Despite the aims of the Nepal government, there would appear to be little scope for further growth of tourism in Khumbu. This is primarily because the two airlines that fly into Lukla are severely limited in the number of tourists they can transport. Lukla's rudimentary landing strip, as well as the frequently turbulent flying conditions between Kathmandu and Lukla, have generated—for better or worse—a significant transportation bottleneck. Trekkers, however, will always have the option of a one- to two-week walk in, and helicopter charters from Kathmandu are becoming popular. Yet, even though the number of tourists is likely to remain fairly constant, new lodges continue to be built in Namche and along the lower Khumbu trekking route leading to Namche. As Fisher (1990) has noted, should the number of lodges proliferate too rapidly in this region, then earnings will be divided into an increasing number of shares, with average incomes diminishing or some businesses prospering at the expense of others. Khumbu Sherpas are also facing increased competition for trekking and mountaineering employment from neighbouring Solu Sherpas and other ethnic groups, such as Rais, Gurungs and Tamangs, who migrate seasonally into Khumbu in increasing numbers to seek primarily portering employment. A new trend of foreign ownership of accommodation facilities, such as the newly reopened Japanese-owned luxury Everest View Hotel near Namche, also threatens Sherpa domination of the lodge industry.

The greatest apparent risk for large-scale tourism employment in the region is that tourism itself is susceptible to many events that can cause a major decline in the industry. The ramifications of such events as domestic political problems (as occurred in Nepal in both 1990 and the spring of 1992), a change in the government's tourism policy (Nepal establishes new tourism goals and policies every five years), economic recession, or another international oil crisis could be financially catastrophic to the region's newly monetarized economy. However, given that many 'tourist Sherpa' still return to their traditional lifestyles in the summer monsoon and winter seasons, most Sherpas do not as yet appear to have severed either their traditional economic or psychological ties to customary village life. As both Adams (1992) and Fisher (1990) have suggested, unlike inhabitants of other parts of the world who are heavily involved in tourism, most Sherpas would still be capable of returning to their customary ecological niche, and those who have been sufficiently educated would have the option of obtaining office jobs in Kathmandu and elsewhere.

Socio-cultural change

Acculturation of indigenous peoples, where entrepreneurs transform remote destinations into tourist places, has become an important issue for a growing number of scholars (Din, 1988; Greenwood, 1989; Nunez, 1989; Zurick, 1992). While acculturation is difficult to determine or measure because it hinges on the resiliency of the culture, a number of anthropological, geographical and general impact studies (Fisher, 1990; Furer-Haimendorf, 1975, 1984; Pawson et al., 1984; Robinson, 1992; Singh and Kaur, 1986; Stevens and Sherpa, 1992a; Zurick, 1992) indicate that the region's economic transformation has not been achieved without some social and cultural cost to the Sherpas.

Since the advent of tourism in this region in 1950, a profound change in patterns of livelihood has occurred, with many local occupations having declined in importance. For many young people, particularly men, trekking employment is more attractive and certainly more lucrative than both traditional village-based agricultural work or work in the more skilled professions such as local schoolteacher or carpenter (Fisher, 1990; Stevens and Sherpa, 1992a). Moreover, although there are exceptions, even young Sherpas from wealthier families tend to prefer the short-term financial rewards of trekking employment to the delayed benefits of higher education. Although these changes could eventually rob the region of an important facet of its traditional culture, this seems unlikely to occur given that the Sherpas still value (and indeed are required to retain) the traditional village-based skills essential to their 'off-season' agropastoral subsistence lifestyle. However, these changes in livelihood patterns have contributed to a variety of changes in both the social structure and cultural fabric of the Khumbu.

For example, while land and animal ownership was the traditional source of local social status, nascent class differences have now developed based on cash income

from tourism and the overtly different lifestyle associated with it. Those families with high earnings from tourism businesses, large numbers of pack animals, and *sirdar* positions have become both increasingly more affluent than neighbouring villagers and increasingly more influential than local religious leaders and regional elders. Owing to their involvement in the tourism industry, many of the new Sherpa elite also spend more time out of Khumbu than at home, with many spending 10 months a year away from their villages (Adams, 1992). This social restructuring has in some instances adversely affected Khumbu political institutions. To serve effectively in a *panchayat* (village government) it is necessary to live in the area, but given the large seasonal outflow of the region's most capable young men, *panchayat* members are often either capable but absentee leaders or are villagers with minimal interest in local affairs. According to Fisher (1990), this has fragmented village interests, with different individuals or groups promoting often disparate goals, and a lack of consensus occurring on important issues, such as management of common pasture lands or the development of new hotel facilities.

Social restructuring associated with tourism has also impacted the region's demographic make-up. For example, seasonal migration among the Sherpas has contributed to a decrease in the birth rate and a concentration of births nine months after the summer monsoon (Pawson et al., 1984). While the family-planning service now available through the Khunde Hospital has contributed to the lower birth rate, this decline has been generated in part by the lesser economic importance of children in a tourism-dominated economy than in the formerly agropastoralism-dominated economy. A further demographic change wrought by Sherpa involvement in the high-altitude mountaineering industry is the region's notably high mortality rate among its young male population: Fisher (1990) indicates that from 1950 through to the middle of 1989 (not including the period between the two World Wars), 84 Sherpas died on mountaineering expeditions in Nepal, the majority of whom were Khumbu Sherpa.

While the impact of tourism on social structure has often been quite explicit, the Westernization of the Sherpa culture is a much more difficult and value-laden issue to address, with much depending on how one perceives the dynamics of culture (Greenwood, 1989). Sherpas certainly admire the West because their association with it to date has been financially very lucrative and has opened up new avenues of social mobility and wealth (Fisher, 1990). Because of this, the Sherpas have inevitably adopted some facets of Western culture, lifestyle, and values. Thus, other than for ceremonial occasions, traditional robes (chubas) are rarely worn by many Sherpas; rather, both young and old Sherpas now prefer Western-style dress (often garments given to them by foreign visitors) and some flaunt Western accoutrements such as a Walkman and headphones. In the new cash economy, many Sherpas also purchase more readily available manufactured items, such as cooking utensils or cloth, from Asia. Foreign sponsorship (in the form of monetary or material gifts, business partnerships, and trips to a sponsor's home) is also currently provided to over one-third of Khumbu families (Adams, 1992), and has contributed to many Sherpas having travelled extensively in foreign lands and to an increasing number having gained university training abroad. Through contact with tourists, as well as their own international travel, Sherpas have certainly gained a broader understanding of modern hygiene, Western languages, and material culture generally.

As the foregoing passage indicates, certain facets of cultural change related to tourism are now quite apparent in Khumbu; yet if the essence of culture, as Greenwood (1989) has defined it, is something that people believe in implicitly and something that gives them the very meanings by which they organize their lives, then the Sherpa culture is both intact and strong. Buddhism has always been the centralizing agent of Sherpa culture, and recent studies by both Fisher (1990) and Stevens and Sherpa (1992b) concur that there seems to have been no lessening of the Buddhist faith or weakening of its core values among the Sherpas. Indeed, local interest and involvement in many Buddhist rituals, such as the annual Mani Rimdu festival at Thyangboche Monastery, appear to be as strong as ever. Moreover, unlike in some third world tourism places, tourism has not fostered any sense of cultural inferiority among the Sherpa people. Indeed, rather than becoming overly Westernized, Sherpas tend to think of themselves primarily and uncompromisingly as Sherpa (Fisher, 1990), and have come to value some of their traditions even more strongly than they did prior to the advent of tourism (Stevens and Sherpa, 1992a).

The resiliency of the Sherpa identity has been supported by Western respect and admiration for Sherpa culture and by the unique nature of the social relationships which often develop between Sherpas and Western visitors during a mountain adventure. The image that Westerners have developed of the Sherpa—that of an egalitarian, peaceful, industrious, independent, and compassionate people—in many ways represents a dramatic realization of what Westerners would like to be themselves (Fisher, 1990). Mountaineering and trekking also afford a great deal of personal interaction between tourists and hosts, with the foreign visitor often feeling what Adams (1992) has termed an 'unfulfilled gratitude' toward their Sherpa companions at the close of an arduous trip. Fisher

contends that, because of a very positive Western perception of the Sherpa culture, coupled with distinctive host–client interactions, the Sherpa have been massively reinforced by Westerners for being Sherpa and have every reason to value and maintain their Sherpahood.

Tourism, however, is still recent to this region; it is only since the late-1970s that visitors have begun to outnumber the local Sherpa population and Sherpa involvement in tourism has become widespread. While the Sherpa have to date effectively embraced tourism within the confines of their own culture, one is drawn to ponder the nature and extent of change that further development will inevitably bring. Given the 'independent explorer' type of tourist (Cohen, 1987) who is most commonly attracted to destinations such as Sagarmatha, further socio-cultural change may prove to be minimal: independent explorers tend to be culturally sympathetic toward host communities and to travel in small numbers, and therefore tend to have less impact on a host culture than does mass tourism. Such optimism, however, may prove to be unfounded for a number of reasons. For example, in a given trekking group the average Sherpa-to-tourist ratio is two-to-one and often greater, the trek usually extends from two to four weeks (Robinson, 1992), and most tourists trek toward Mount Everest through a narrow corridor that is inhabited by fewer than 1000 Sherpas (Stevens, 1993). Consequently, contact with local Sherpas is extensive and penetrates deeply into the personal lives of the Sherpas, and the potential for change is therefore greater than in mass tourism (Butler, 1990). Moreover, research (Robinson, 1992) suggests that Khumbu tourists are typically more concerned with environmental rather than cultural degradation and many arrive in Khumbu quite naive of local customs and manners and often display inappropriate tourist behaviour. (In an effort to educate tourists about Sherpa customs Stevens and Sherpa (1992a) have recently posted guidelines for 'Responsible Tourism in Sagarmatha National Park' in all Khumbu lodges.)

While tourism has helped to finance the rebuilding of the Thyangboche Monastery and other religious places in the region, the fear exists amongst some Sherpas and scholars that while preserving the artefacts of Buddhism, tourism may eventually destroy the spirit needed to maintain it (Fisher, 1990; Robinson, 1992; Zurick, 1992). To thrive, the Buddhism religion requires knowledgeable specialists and the commitment of local people, but the prolonged absence of Sherpas from the villages may result in many Sherpas having little experience of Buddhist rituals. Moreover, as more young Sherpas are attracted to tourism, the possibility of a dwindling number of monks in the monasteries (as did occur at Thyangboche in 1978) could ultimately result in an insufficient critical mass of clergy for Buddhism to flourish (Fisher, 1990; Furer-Haimendorf, 1984).

Ultimately, the extent of future change will depend upon the Sherpas' continuing ability to absorb tourist demands in creative and conservative ways that do not detract from their core cultural values and beliefs. Essential to this is the Sherpas' wilful reconstitution of their own culture (Adams, 1992). Given that the Sherpas have successfully adapted to tourism thus far with little direction from the national park or the Nepal government, the future may be similarly positive if they are permitted themselves to grapple with the issues of how much inter-action with outsiders is desirable, and where and when this interaction should occur.

The changing environment

The major contradiction of a rapid increase in Khumbu tourists has been the region's conspicuous lack of a substantive tourism development plan, which is necessary to safeguard the region's ecological integrity from the resource-based demands of trekking and mountaineering. The threat of tourism exceeding the region's natural carrying capacity has been extensively documented, and the Khumbu has long been cited as a representative model of contemporary environmental degradation where tourism developments have frequently operated ahead of the region's ability to provide infrastructure and sound management (Ives and Messerli, 1989; Sharma, 1989; Shrestha, 1989; Thompson and Warburton, 1985). Many of the region's resources (forests, woodlands and grazing lands, trekking pathways, and water) possess 'common pool' attributes, for which it is difficult to implement easily effected controls. Consequently, overuse of resources and lack of incentives to increase or protect the region's resource base have all become serious regional issues. The region's most pressing environmental problems that have been associated with tourism include forest degradation, competing land uses on fragile land surfaces, and waste disposal.

Forest degradation

Conflicting reports exist on the extent of deforestation in Khumbu. Some sources have claimed that owing to increased fuelwood demands generated by the rapid growth of tourism, more deforestation has occurred in Khumbu during the past two decades than in the preceding 200 years (Coburn, 1984; Tseten, 1990). Other studies (Brower, 1990; Byers, 1987; Ives and Messerli, 1989; Stevens and Sherpa, 1992a) suggest that reports of widespread deforestation are exaggerated, with old change associated with traditional Sherpa land-use practices often

being mistaken for recent change attributed to the impacts of outsiders. Considerable deforestation has occurred just south of the park boundaries, with much of the timber being imported into the park for increased construction of new tourist lodges and larger homes for newly wealthy Sherpa families.

The increased use of subalpine forest and woodlands for fuelwood caused the national park authorities to ban the use of fuelwood by trekking and mountaineering camping groups in 1979. While this ban has worked effectively with camping groups, the net effect has been inconsequential because, as tourist numbers increased, so did their preference for staying at the local lodges which were unaffected by the park's fuelwood regulations. By 1984, it was estimated that fuelwood use by lodges may have increased regional fuelwood requirements by as much as 10% (Pawson et al., 1984). Today, owing to the local lodges' continued use of wood as their predominant source of fuel, it is estimated that more fuelwood is burned on behalf of tourists than was before the introduction of the ban (Stevens and Sherpa, 1992b). As the number of lodges continues to grow, the use of fuelwood will constitute an even greater threat of forest degradation in many parts of the region's subalpine area. A problem of even more pressing concern, however, is occurring in some of the region's higher alpine elevations where juniper shrub species are harvested for fuelwood. This very slow-growing shrub affords important ground cover, and its rapid loss has been associated with high rates of soil erosion (Byers, 1987). Although Sherpas are now forbidden by park regulations to use anything but dead wood from currently protected forest areas, these regulations are neither strictly enforced nor commonly adhered to when it comes to the juniper shrubs.

In recent years, steps have been taken both to reduce further degradation and to regenerate the region's forest cover. International concern has led to the implementation of foreign-sponsored reforestation programmes, such as the tree nursery project at Phorte that is funded by the Himalayan Trust and the Edmund Hillary Canada Foundation. As Sherpa understanding of forest degra-dation has increased, so too has their fear of an impending fuelwood crisis. As a result, new park strategies have been introduced and local community initiatives have been spawned. The park now requires that local people obtain a permit to cut trees for construction timber for lodges or housing, and Sherpa concern has led to the re-implementation of the forest guardian (shinggi nawa) system which operated prior to the creation of the national park. Reintroduced in 1980, the village-appointed forest guardians have the power to impose fines for the breaking of regulations, with the monies generated being used for community development. The national park, however, has not given the guardian system legal standing, and the system is currently supported by the Himalayan Trust which provides each guardian with an honorarium which is distributed through the park warden (Steven and Sherpa, 1992a).

Despite the efforts of both regeneration projects and local initiatives, the region still faces the possibility of a major fuel crisis at some point in the future. Given the fuel demands of the massive seasonal influx of tourists, as well as the demands of both local Sherpas and seasonal migrants seeking employment, the region's greatest long-term need is for a readily available alternative source of fuel to that of wood. The national park and Nepal government are urgently required to take more initiative in introducing alternative energy resources, such as mini-hydro projects (as currently exist in Namche and Thame) or the use of kerosene stoves for high-altitude lodges. These energy sources are, however, very expensive for local people, and would require subsidizing if they were to be widely adopted in the region. Given that Nepal's major parks (Sagarmatha, Langtang, and Annapurna Conservation Area, and including Royal Chitwan) currently generate in excess of US$800 000 in entry fees, US$230 000 for trekking permits, and US$300 000 for mountaineering fees (Wells, 1992), the government would be wise to substantially increase its expenditures on maintaining the parks. A fuel subsidy would have ample economic justification given that severe impacts related to deforestation could lead to an economically disastrous decline in visitor numbers (Robinson, 1992).

Land-use management

Forest degradation and loss of ground-cover have been aggravated by pastoral land-use changes associated with tourism. Recent reports (Brower, 1990; Stevens and Sherpa, 1992c) suggest that the increasing importance of packstock (yak or yak crossbreeds), rather than porters to transport trekking and mountaineering goods, has contributed to the collapse of some communal pastures and has substantially increased grazing pressure in some neighbouring woodlands and grasslands. The loss of herbaceous ground-cover in the higher alpine elevations has also exacerbated the problem of soil loss associated with increased harvesting of juniper shrub. These changes may have long-term impacts on forest regeneration, as well as on grassland productivity and soil erosion (Byers, 1987).

While tourism has also increased regional demands for food, most of this demand has been satisfied by increased imports of food generated by agricultural restructuring in the area to the south of the park. The state of agricultural production in Khumbu itself is subject to conflicting reports. Fisher (1990) reports that in 1974 Khumbu Sherpas began hiring Solu Sherpas in large numbers to work their fields while they pursued more lucrative trekking jobs. However, as the Solu Sherpas increased their involvement as load carriers in the tourism industry, the marginal fields were increasingly abandoned for lack of workers to cultivate them. Stevens and Sherpa (1992c) dispute this, and report that long-abandoned marginal land has often been mistaken for recently abandoned land, and that during recent years the area of crop production has actually expanded such that regional production is now at an all-time high.

Waste disposal and sanitation

An increasing problem in this area, and one that has been extensively documented, is that of waste-disposal. The indiscriminate disposal of human waste, and the dangerous threat to health associated with it, remain serious problems in the more popular trekking areas. Reckless surface disposal and water-course disposal have led to widespread water contamination in the region, and increased construction of sanitation facilities by the national park is urgently required. The more popular trekking routes and mountain base camps are also infamous for the quantities of refuse left by an increasing number of travellers. In recent years, the importation of plastic and glass bottles, and other non-biodegradable products such as alkaline batteries and tin cans, have conspicuously heightened the problem. The situation has also been exacerbated by the Sherpa concept of pollution (called *tip* (Ortner, cited in Fisher, 1990:131)), which concerns only the self, or human creations and artefacts, and is unrelated to Western-style perceptions of litter. Ironically, Sherpas themselves are responsible for the bulk of litter along the trekking routes.

In recent years, the refuse problem has been compounded by the Ministry of Tourism removing the traditional limit to the number of mountaineering expeditions which are allowed on major peaks in any given climbing season. This ruling, as well as a recent massive increase in the growth of commercial (client-funded) mountaineering expeditions to the region, resulted, for example, in over 350 climbers residing at the Everest base camp during the spring of 1992. Everest base camp sites are littered with the detritus of scores of expeditions, and Byers et al. (1992) estimate that since 1963 over 500 empty oxygen bottles have been dumped above base camp at the South Col. Unfortunately, the Nepal government ignored recent remonstrations in 1992 from the international climbing community to restore the mountain's sanctity by imposing drastic limits on the number and size of future expeditions (Gillian, 1993). Instead, the Ministry of Tourism chose to increase the fee per climber from US$1100 to US$10 000 and to reintroduce laws and a deposit system requiring all expeditions to pack out their litter and discarded mountaineering equipment. How strictly this system will be enforced remains to be seen.

Hampered by a lack of funding and shortage of staff, the national park has been unable to implement clean-up projects of trekking routes and mountaineering base camps. Rather, clean-up expeditions continue to be conducted by concerned environmental groups from abroad, as well as by trekking agencies who frequent the region. More recently, Sherpa concern has led them to initiate their own clean-up campaigns, such as the Sagarmatha Club of Namche project, and Stevens and Sherpa (1992c) report that the newly formed Sherpa Pollution Control Committee, supported by an endowment from the World Wildlife Fund, will work with the national park to coordinate future clean-up projects in the region.

Lessons for alternative tourism

The foregoing reappraisal of the nature and extent of tourism-related change in Sagarmatha National Park suggests that while the region is not without notable detrimental impacts, its characterization as an ecological and cultural catastrophe in the making has been premature. Some reports of adverse environmental impacts appear to have been overstated, and many of the worst impacts are being alleviated through both local and international efforts. Sherpas have also become highly affluent by Nepalese standards and, despite a changing economy and some social restructuring, their culture is strong and in many ways appears to have been intensified rather than adulterated by the presence of tourism. Other impacts, however, especially those of forest degradation and loss of ground-cover, remain serious problems, despite efforts to address them.

Many remote alternative tourism destinations in the third world operate in tourism development contexts that are not dissimilar to that of Sagarmatha National Park: most have a sizeable indigenous population that possesses strong cultural ties with past traditions and evolving ties to a land and renewable resource base; the indigenous population recognizes that their region, traditions and culture are of interest to the modern tourist; and, most have a limited but evolving infrastructure to cope with increasing tourist numbers. So the Sagarmatha National Park case study offers the following lessons to guide the successful development of alternative forms of tourism in other remote, ecologically and culturally sensitive areas of the world.

The need for regional tourism planning

Having lacked a tourism development plan, Sagarmatha National Park is now responding in ad hoc fashion to counter the undesirable impacts of uncontrolled tourism development. The Sagarmatha experience indicates the necessity of establishing *a priori* a regional tourism development plan which considers the region's natural and social carrying capacities, and which encompasses a clear vision of what constitutes development that is *appropriate* to maintaining an area as a viable alternative tourism destination. Further environmental and cultural change, or the overdevelopment of services and facilities, could sufficiently change the tourism product provided by this region to cause the park to be abandoned as a destination for the true adventure traveller (Zurick, 1992). The growth of adventure tourism in Sagarmatha has in many respects paralleled the stages of Butler's (1980) tourist area cycle model. Having passed quickly through the early stages of 'exploration' (few visitors and meagre facilities) and 'involvement' (residents provide services to increasing numbers of visitors), the region appears to be in the stage of 'development' (commercial and national agencies become involved in developing the area, the destination is advertised internationally, and visitor numbers peak). However, should tourism planning (or a lack of it) take the region beyond the 'development' stage, into 'consolidation' (development focuses almost exclusively on tourist services) and 'stagnation' (serious and long-term impacts occur), then Sagarmatha National Park may lose its niche in the international adventure travel market.

The measure of appropriate tourism development ultimately rests in the measure of its sustainability (Zurick, 1992), which is determined by how successfully it protects the region's natural resources and environmental quality, minimizes adverse cultural impacts, and preserves the kind of experience which is important to its visitors. In seeking to achieve these outcomes, a regional tourism plan may regulate visitor ceilings and visitor user fees, set visitor quotas where necessary, authorize tourist access to given areas and guide tourist behaviours/activities, direct the development of infrastructure and services, generate taxation policies to equitably distribute tourism income, and regulate the utilization of the region's natural resources. Management planning must also be an ongoing process involving periodic reviews to allow for changing regional objectives and adjustment to existing regulations (Robinson, 1992).

For example, given that volume of tourists is closely tied to regional change (Butler, 1990), a strong case can be made for reducing tourist numbers in Sagarmatha National Park while increasing their per capita expenditures. The park entry fee (about US$10) and trekking permits (about US$5/week) are currently so low as to be inconsequential to the majority of park visitors. Reducing visitors would not necessarily hurt the local economy if trekking fees were increased and the revenues put toward park improvement, or used for local subsidies (for alternative fuels for example) or local community development programmes. Gurung (cited in Wells (1992:5)) has further suggested that, in order to spread tourists more evenly through Nepal's parks, trekking or park entry fees could be set at different levels with relatively high fees for overcrowded areas and low fees for rarely visited areas. From this perspective, alternative tourism development would preferably be selective and small in scale, which, while generating only modest economic returns, would better safeguard the local culture and protect natural resources (Wallace, 1992).

Protected area management

Essential to the coordination of regional tourism planning is a protected area authority that has real decision- and policy-making clout and adequate funding to service its programmes. Sagarmatha National Park managers have been criticized for focusing their efforts on forest protection at the expense of providing a lack of direction for tourism development, especially with regard to regulating visitor numbers, the proliferation of lodges, overgrazing by packstock, and dealing with waste disposal (Stevens and Sherpa, 1992b). In reality, however, the park authorities have been in the difficult position of having quite limited political power and insufficient funding to effectively run conservation or development projects. The park authority is required to run its programmes on whatever budget it is allocated by the government, it has no legal authority to intervene in village affairs, and it has at present minimal jurisdiction over visitors. For example, while the park authorities regard excessive visitations as contributing to substantial environmental degradation, a complex system beyond their influence dictates the level of visitation, with the Department of Immigration issuing all visas and trekking permits, the Nepal Mountaineering Association issuing trekking peak (below 6000 m) permits, and the Ministry of Tourism authorizing expeditions to the higher peaks.

Successful tourism planning requires the expertise of individuals who are familiar with the region's social, cultural and ecological underpinnings, and who share a commitment to maintaining the region's long-term vitality. Protected area managers in the third world are often native to the area or have resided for long periods in the area, and therefore tend to be knowledgeable of the area's successes and problems. Furthermore, since they can also provide the security of long-term planning, park managers should have real decision-making influence when it comes to where, when and what kind of tourism should be permitted when the principal attraction is a protected area (Boo, 1990; Wallace, 1992).

Local involvement

The experience at Sagarmatha National Park demonstrates that local people can benefit economically from tourism development while maintaining their cultural integrity and major control of their local land and resource base. Although some of the processes that have shaped this balance may be unique to the region, others have wider applicability. The seasonality of tourism has allowed the Sherpas to maintain subsistence agriculture as a major part of their lifestyle and to not become entirely dependent on tourism revenues. Their close-knit society and strong culture have also been helped by distinctly supportive host–client relations. Perhaps of most significance, tourism development in Khumbu has been shaped first and foremost by the Sherpa themselves, with relatively little direction from the national park or local governments. Through their entrepreneurial efforts and support by foreign loans, the Sherpa have been able to dominate lodge ownership and regional tourism employment. The integration of *panchayat* (village government) in Khumbu has also enhanced community involvement in directing aspects of tourism development, and the reintroduction of the traditional forest guardian system has seemingly led the local people to see the forests again as their resource and responsibility, and has increased their concern for forest protection (Stevens and Sherpa, 1992c). Although Sherpa access to forest and grazing resources has been restricted by park regulations, these costs appear relatively minor in comparison to their economic gains from tourism.

While the accomplishments in Sagarmatha National Park may be difficult to realize in other tourism places of the third world, there are valuable lessons to be learned on the involvement of local communities. Since local people must live with the long-term consequences of tourism development, local communities must at the outset be educated to develop an understanding of what tourism means as a concept (Wray, 1989), and be made aware not only of its potential economic benefits but also of both the positive and negative changes that tourism may bring to their lifestyles and social structures. Tourism must also be developed within the traditions of existing communities, essential to which is the involvement of local communities in decision-making processes that directly influence their lifestyles, affect their community development, or use the locality's natural resources. The more aware local people are made of the potential rewards and pitfalls of tourism, and the more they are involved in and benefit from tourism development, then the greater the likelihood that they will accept the tourism industry and commit to preserve the natural and cultural values upon which tourism is based (Robinson, 1992).

Conclusions

In conclusion, the experience of Sagarmatha National Park demonstrates that the longevity and prosperity of tourism in culturally and ecologically fragile areas depends not only on the tourism industry's ability to identify and develop tourism opportunities, but also on the industry's ability to conserve a region's natural and cultural assets (Val, 1990). Although the region is not without outstanding environmental and socio-cultural issues, the new approaches which are at present being implemented in the park offer optimism for its long-term prospects as a viable adventure tourism destination. Alternative tourism brings with it the potential to inflict both beneficial and detrimental impacts, and for other remote tourism destinations in the third world which offer exciting opportunities for the development of alternative forms of tourism, Sagarmatha National Park offers encouragement that alternative tourism designs can exist that effectively balance local economic development with ecological and cultural conservation.

References

Adams, V. (1992) 'Tourism and Sherpas, Nepal: reconstruction and reciprocity', *Annals of Tourism Research*, 19: 534–554.

Boo, E. (1990) *Ecotourism: the Potentials and Pitfalls*, Vols 1 and 2, World Wildlife Fund, Washington, DC.

Brower, B. (1990) 'Range conservation and Sherpa livestock in Khumbu, Nepal', *Mountain Research and Development*, 10: 34–42.

Butler, R. W. (1980) 'The concept of the tourist area cycle of evolution: implications for managers of resources', *Canadian Geographer*, 14: 5–12.

Butler, R. W. (1990) 'Alternative tourism: pious hope or Trojan horse?', *Journal of Travel Research*, 28: 40–45.

Byers, A. (1987) 'Landscape change and man-accelerated soil loss: the case study of the Sagarmatha (Mt. Everest) National Park, Khumbu, Nepal', *Mountain Research and Development*, 7: 209–216.

Byers, A., Banshota, K. and McCue, G. (1992) 'Environmental impacts of back country tourism on three sides of Everest', Paper presented at the IVth World Congress on National Parks and Protected Areas, February 1992, Caracas, Venezuala.

Coburn, B. A. (1984) 'Sagarmatha: managing a Himalayan World Heritage Site', *Parks*, 9: 10–13.

Cohen, E. (1987) 'Tourism—a critique', *Tourism Recreation Research*, 12: 13–18.

Din, K. H. (1988) 'Social and cultural impacts of tourism', *Annals of Tourism Research*, 15: 563–566.

Durst, P. B. and Ingram, C. D. (1988) 'Nature oriented tourism promotion by developing countries', *Tourism Management*, March: 39–43.

Fisher, J. (1990) *The Sherpas: Reflections on Change in Himalayan Nepal*, University of California Press, Berkeley, CA.

Furer-Haimendorf, C. von (1975) *Himalayan Traders: Life in Highland Nepal*, John Murray, London.

Furer-Haimendorf, C. von (1984) *The Sherpas Transformed*, Sterling Publishers, New Delhi.

Gillian, P. (1993) 'Last one to the top buys the drinks', *Sunday Times* 10 April: 42–46.

Gonsalves, P. S. (1987) 'Alternative tourism—the evolution of a concept and establishment of a network', *Tourism Recreation Research*, 12: 9–12.

Greenwood, D. J. (1989) 'Culture by the pound: an anthropological perspective on tourism as cultural commoditization', in Smith, V. (Ed.), *Hosts and Guests: The Anthropology of Tourism*. University of Pennsylvania Press, Philadelphia, PA, pp. 171–186.

Harrison, D. (Ed.) (1992) *Tourism and the Less Developed Countries*. Halsted Press, New York.

Healy, R. G. (1992) 'The role of tourism in sustainable development', Paper presented at the IVth World Congress on National Parks and Protected Areas, February 1992, Caracas, Venezuela.

Ives, J. D. and Messerli, B. (1989) *The Himalayan Dilemma: Reconciling Development and Conservation*, Routledge, New York.

Kutay, K. (1990) 'The new ethic in adventure travel', *Buzzworm: The Environmental Journal*, 1: 31–36.

Machlis, G. E. and Bacci, M. E. (1992) 'Is ecotourism ideologically biased, elitist, short-sighted, anti-democratic and unsustainable?', Paper presented at the IVth World Congress on National Parks and Protected Areas, February 1992, Caracas, Venezuela.

McKean, P. F. (1989) 'Towards a theoretical analysis of tourism: economic dualism and cultural involution', in Smith, V. (Ed.), *Hosts and Guests: The Anthropology of Tourism*, University of Pennsylvania Press, Philadelphia, PA, pp. 119–138.

McKercher, B. (1993) 'Some fundamental truths about tourism: understanding tourism's social and environmental impacts', *The Journal of Sustainable Tourism*, 1: 6–16.

Nunez, T. (1989) 'Touristic studies in anthropological perspective', in Smith, V. (Ed.), *Hosts and Guests: The Anthropology of Tourism*, University of Pennsylvania Press, Philadelphia, PA, pp. 265–274.

Passoff, M. (1991) 'Ecotourism re-examined', *Earth Island Journal*, Spring: 28–29.

Pawson, I. G., Stanford, D. D., Adams, V. A. and Norbu, M. (1984) 'The growth of tourism in Nepal's Everest region: impact on the physical environment and structure of human settlements', *Mountain Research and Development*, 4: 237–246.

Robinson, D. W. (1992) 'Socio-cultural impacts of mountain tourism in Nepal's Sagarmatha (Everest) National Park: implications for sustainable tourism', in J. Thorsell (Ed.),

World Heritage Twenty Years Later: IVth World Congress on National Parks and Protected Areas, IUCN, Gland, Switzerland, pp. 123–131.

Sharma, L. P. (1989) 'Mountain tourism in Nepal: how compatible is it with the fragile Himalayan environment?', in S. C. Singh (Ed.), *Impact of Tourism on Mountain Environment*, Research India Publications, Meerut, India.

Shrestha, T. K. (1989) 'Impact of tourism on the Himalayan ecosystem of Nepal', In S. C. Singh (Ed.), *Impact of Tourism on Mountain Environment*, Research India Publications, Meerut, India.

Singh, T. V. and Kaur, J. (1986) 'The paradox of mountain tourism: case references from the Himalaya', *Indu*, 9: 21–26.

Smith, V. L. and Eadington, W.R. (1992) *Tourism alternatives*, University of Pennsylvania Press, Philadelphia, PA.

Stevens, S. F. (1993) *Claiming the High Ground*, University of California Press, Berkeley, CA.

Stevens, S. F. and Sherpa, M. Norbu (1992a) 'Tourism development in Sagarmatha (Mount Everest) National Park, Nepal', Paper presented at the IVth World Congress on National Parks and Protected Areas, February 1992, Caracas, Venezuela.

Stevens, S. F. and Sherpa, M. Norbu (1992b) 'Tourism impacts and protected area management in highland Nepal: lessons from Sagarmatha National Park and Annapurna Conservation Area', Paper presented at the IVth World Congress on National Parks and Protected Areas, February 1992, Caracas, Venezuela.

Stevens, S. F. and Sherpa, M. Norbu (1992c) 'Indigenous peoples and protected area management: new approaches to conservation in Highland Nepal', Paper presented at the IVth World Congress on National Parks and Protected Areas, February 1992, Caracas, Venezuela.

Thompson, M. and Warburton, M. (1985) 'Uncertainty on a Himalayan scale', *Mountain Research and Development*, 5: 114–135.

Tseten, K. (1990) 'Conservation and adventure travel', *Himal*, 3: 27.

Val, E. (1990) 'Parks, aboriginal peoples, and sustainable tourism in developing regions: the international experience and Canada's Northwest Territories', in J. Vinning (Ed.), *Social Science and Natural Resource Recreation Management*, Westview, San Francisco, CA.

Wallace, G. N. (1992) 'Real ecotourism: assisting protected area managers and getting benefits to local people', Paper presented at the IVth World Congress on National Parks and Protected Areas, February 1992, Caracas, Venezuela.

Wells, M. P. (1992) 'Economic benefits and costs of protected areas in Nepal', Paper presented at the IVth World Congress on National Parks and Protected Areas, February 1992, Caracas, Venezuela.

Wight, P. (1993) 'Ecotourism: ethics or eco-sell?', *Journal of Travel Research*, 31: 3–9.

Wray, G. W. (1989) 'Tourism initiatives in Canada's Northwest Territories: the Pangnirtung experience—a partnership for sustainable development', Paper presented at the World Conference on the Environment, October 1989, Canary Islands, Spain.

Zurick, D. N. (1992) 'Adventure travel and sustainable tourism in the peripheral economy of Nepal', *Annals of the Association of American Geographers*, 8: 608–628.

73 Northern coastal tourism. Concepts, resource basis and sustainability strategy

O. SLETVOLD

Introduction

Norway has for centuries attracted individual travellers and tourists interested in spectacular nature and quaint culture. With the greening of tourism and a general touristic interest in peripheries, Norwegian authorities see a bright future for the tourist industry (NOE, 1993; NORTRA, 1993). The country scores comparatively highest in Europe on the dimension of natural beauty (Haahti, 1986). It is profiled mainly through three natural assets: the fjords, the mountains and the midnight sun. However, only along the northern, Arctic[1] coast can these three features be experienced at the same time and place.[2]

Modern tourism in North Norway is dominated by inland traffic to the North Cape. For most international tourists a visit to the coastal areas is merely a part of a more extensive round-trip of 2–3 weeks' duration, where Northern Scandinavia is conceived of as one destination (Viken, 1991). The summer tourism in this area is estimated at roughly half a million visitors. The typical tourist is an experienced traveller from continental Europe with education and income well above average. Travelling in Norway has been considered expensive, but less expensive group tourism is growing.

Lately regional authorities have focused on strategies for developing coastal tourism by spreading tourism in Northern Norway towards the coast (Sletvold et al., 1992). Statistical categorizations and delimitation problems hinder good estimates for the size of the coastal part of the traffic. A recent tourist survey (Jacobsen, 1992a) found that the landscapes of fjords and mountains were important motivators for visitors to the Lofoten Islands. Little research has concentrated on studying contents and meanings of coastal tourism *per se* in these regions, or on the resource basis and capacities of such tourism.

This paper aims at contributing theoretically to the understanding of the resource basis of northern coastal tourism and to the discussion of the aspects mentioned. It is concerned with this tourism seen as the experiencing of landscapes (Sletvold, 1993), and with touristic consumption here within the framework of local community viability.

Coastal tourism

Judging from Pearce (1989:58ff) 'coastal tourism' is a well-established term for 'one of the most significant forms of tourism'. The history of seaside resorts represents well-known examples of coastal tourist development (Urry, 1990:16ff). Much coastal tourism should be regarded as urban tourism, because of the concentration of accommodation, consumption and the behavioral pattern of tourists in hotels, entertainment and shopping areas along the beaches of the world. Pearce's examples (1989:58ff, 87ff) show that such coastal tourism is predominantly southbound, going from the cool regions of the north towards the sunny and sandy beaches of more temperate or tropical areas.

Another important form of coastal tourism is the cruise traffic. Cruise ships in the western fjords, along the coast or on their way to the North Cape and the Svalbard Islands are frequently seen in Norway. No research has been undertaken to find out how these tourists experience the sights the ships pass by or the ports of call, although one presupposes that life inside the ships is of great importance.

Tourism by car or bus along the coasts of Northern Norway is a different coastal tourism in several respects from these more frequent forms. Firstly it is non-urban. It is a kind of rural tourism, as delimited by Pigram (1993), mainly 'travel through a nonurban area' and/or 'centered around nonurban way of life' (Messerli, 1990). Secondly, a desire for sunbathing and swimming cannot explain coastal tourism here. People occasionally swim in fjord inlets and sunbathe above the 70th parallel during the summer, but not as a regular activity. Thirdly, traditionally it is not a resort-based tourism, but rather takes the form of round-trips (Flognfeldt, 1992), with short-stop enjoyment of particular features of these coastal landscapes and ways of life (Jacobsen, 1992a).

Landscapes

Nature denoted as sceneries or landscapes implies several things. First, such terms point to the distinction made by

Lévi-Strauss (1979) between 'nature' and 'the natural'. Nature should be seen as pre-social, existing before man put any meaning to it and thereby made nature natural. The naturalness of nature is a cultural or social construct. Consequently, experiencing the natural is a learnt experience. Locals and tourists establish differing configurations between societies and environments (Urry, 1992:2), and one such configurational set is 'the landscape'. It denotes the continuous surface we see all around us, the unity of impressions on our senses (Walmsley and Lewis, 1984), but interpreted by our consciousness. It includes both the human and the natural (Meinig, 1979), and it is less loaded with aesthetic connotations than 'scenery', more inclusive and ubiquitous. To further stress these nuances we will often use the term 'cultural landscapes'.

Secondly, landscape implies a value component. Jones (1988) examined the use of 'cultural landscape' as a term in Norwegian research. The use ranges from a functional–utilitarian or areal planning point of view, through an historical–archeological view of the landscape as a palimpsest, via a heritage and conservationist usage, to a more general interpretationist view of the landscape as the sum of the elements around us that carry meaning for man. Because cultural landscapes are inescapably related to the physical world, interpretations of it also involve knowledge of that physical landscape (Lewis, 1979) and of its environmental properties (Meinig, 1979). This becomes obvious in connection with sustainability perspectives and the values therein.

Urry (1992) also discussed briefly aspects of the relationship between man and the natural, making a clear distinction between a touristic appropriation of the landscape through visual consumption, and other views of the natural as a resource basis, production arena or inheritance of which we are stewards. In this view landscape and scenery partly overlap: it is nature 'embellished for aesthetic appropriation' (1992:3). Such an understanding of the landscape is urban or suburban, a result of city life, where rural areas become gardens, or vistas to enjoy from the car (Pigram, 1993:158).

Impressions of landscapes are taken in through all our senses, but primarily through the eyes. Therefore theories of reading the landscape and seeing the world as texts (Fiske, 1989) are particularly interesting for the understanding of the relations between the tourist and the landscape. This implies different, parallel readings of the same landscape or social setting between tourist segments and between tourists and locals, and these interpretations change as part of changing cultures. Using semiotic theory one can also identify several levels of readings of a landscape (Viken, 1993). The iconic level

of meaning is associated with the immediate recognition of pictorial aspects of a view. The indexical reading couples the sensorial impressions to reflection and knowledge of causalities, and the symbolic reading concerns the emotional, perhaps more unconscious experience, and even philosophical reflection.

How locals arrange interpretations of their environments for tourists represent examples of the processes of attraction marking and development (Lyngnes, 1990). To produce touristic presentations of valuable ways of life and balanced ways of natural resource management are relevant aspects of this. The underlying assumption of intersubjectivity points towards questions of tourists' willingness or potential as hermeneuticists (Jacobsen, 1992b).

The landscape also has a function as upholding identity (Svedin, 1982). Schancke (1987) showed how the indigenous Sami people as hunters/gatherers and reindeer-herders have looked upon the landscape used for the reindeer. Their understanding is quite different from what only a few years ago was the understanding of the regional tourism organization, or the tourist expectations they try to build on: the area was profiled as 'Europe's last wilderness' (Finnmarkopplevelser, 1990). The slogan is still alive in the market. For the Sami, details of nature have been carrying meanings as offering places, and the whole landscape is an arena for performing the profession of reindeer herding. Landscapes that to a touristic gaze (Urry, 1990) seem to be almost completely untouched parts of nature, 'really' contains both meaningful memories and traces of human activity. According to Tuan (1979), a culture's most cherished places are not necessarily visible to the eye—we may add: at least not to the tourist gaze.

We will consider the northern coastline as cultural landscapes in the same way. Their topographical basis is the island-strewn, fjordic, craggy but ice-free and mild shores, and the subsistence basis is the fish resources, always within rowing distance. The fjords, the fishing grounds, the sounds and the islands carry meanings for the inhabitants, meanings that are found in their names, in their histories in the minds of the local population, in the practices of fishing, in the physical, industrial constructions, in the surviving remnants of earlier living, and in the institutions of small fishing communities (R. Jacobsen, 1992:1–24). These meanings are not necessarily the ones that are accessible to tourists. Landscapes are read most immediately on the iconic level (Viken, 1993), and it is a question as to what extent meanings of indexical character appeal to what tourists, and whether such meanings should be made accessible at all. The main point here is that we need to incorporate the sea into our concept of coastal landscapes (or seascapes) to be experienced.

Natural elements

The touristic experience of the coast is a sum of both micro details and macro panoramas. The term 'coast' itself mainly gives macro connotations. As an areal category it roughly refers to the stretches from the outer skerries to the points inland where you no longer see or smell salt water. This delimitation must be related to the topographical shape of the coast. There is a difference, especially for the macro experience, between a straight and flat beachline and a steep and twisting fjordline. To Theroux (1984:135) the irregularity of a coast gives long and wide views, emphasizing the panoramic landscape character, as if overviewing land and sea from some vantage point. This perspective is also prominent in the motivation for summer tourists in Lofoten: they say they come there to see special and magnificent landscapes (Jacobsen, 1992a:67).

The coast also contains momentary and micro pictures: the single wave splashing a stone, profiles of cormorants resting on a cliff, playful seals, the tail fin of a whale, majestic eagles, or sand between your toes. These are experiences on a more human scale, partly of a closeness which makes use also of the hearing and tactile senses. The distinction between the macro and the micro can be said to correspond to two types of using nature, the aesthetic and the recreational (MacCannell, 1989:80). The aesthetic is one of sightseeing, which again is a question of the scenery as a total, or of particular landmarks, or of both. It may also be labelled 'gazing' (Urry, 1990), although the term is more generic for superficial touristic consumption behavior. The recreational usage is more appropriating. One has to leave the car or the road and risk the direct touch or the smell or the roar. It is also a matter of activity and sweat, or even of harvesting from nature. The magnificence of touristic recreation in Norway seems to be that it gives tourists opportunities for a constant variation between these forms of using nature.

The sea is a dominant element in the picture of the coast. The fascination of the sea has loaded it heavily with meanings. As a symbol the sea is probably an archetype, independent of cultural differences (Haikola, 1982): pure and primeval nature in a way that land is not, largely untamed and untamable, uncivilized and uncivilizable (Fiske, 1989). One can plough the land or reshape its surface and contours according to one's wishes. One cannot change the plasticity and smoothness of the sea surface. The sea is ever changing, yet unchangeable,

contained in itself, omnipresent. It is at the same time terrifying and friendly. It yields food, but its stretches cannot be cultivated. Apart from minor human scratches along its shores it evades our control. This likens the sea to other overwhelming masses, and to some the sea is a powerful crowd symbol (Canetti, 1973). As something not fully controllable it might be better watched from some distance.

Even though some of these features are the same along all shores, there are significant differences in the sightseeing or the gazing at the seascapes between the North Cape and Waikiki Beach. Other natural elements influence the experience, as do the particular social and situational characteristics, i.e. individual backgrounds and the loneliness/crowdedness of the moment. The sea is always seen in interplay with the dry land, with light and climate, and with elements of culture.

The most unique touristic feature of the northern coasts is the midnight sun, or more generally the day-and-night-light during the periods of no darkness. The light conditions, and the coloring given to the landscapes by the changing light, is reported to be the highest-rated natural feature (Viken, 1991). In addition there is the fact that the Norwegian Arctic coast faces westward and north, towards the sun. On clear days and nights it can give an unhindered view towards the non-setting sun. There are no equally accessible Arctic coastlines in the world with this natural advantage. The travelling Lévi-Strauss experienced the sunset/twilight time of the tropics as a time for summing up and coming to terms with the day that had passed (1973:77). If this divide between day and night is more or less wiped out, time structure becomes more floating, and the feeling of out-of-time-and-place becomes more predominant (Jafari, 1987).

Another important element of the coast is the shore. Physically the shore is the stretch of land bordering immediately on the sea. It is a zone where the land that man can cultivate meets nature, and where natural elements on both sides may be seen to mingle (Theroux, 1984:135). Along beaches the regularly retreating sea makes temporary playing grounds where people can invade nature safety. Instead of nature being an enemy, it becomes a source of thrills (MacCannell, 1989). The work of the tides and the touristic appropriation of the shore can be coupled, both literally and on a symbolic level. The moon causes the variations in the height of the tide. At the same time it is a great mythical feature and symbol of romance, inspiring longing but also lunacy. Walking an Arctic shore as the tide ebbs may then be shaped into a meeting with great symbols of nature, combining the moon and the sea and the sun. The shore as a meeting place also couples male and female principles, in the sensual contrasts between smooth water and the rough land (MacCannell, 1992:114).

There is a variety of shores. Many of these are looked upon as natural: the mainly sandy beach, the polished cliffs and bare slopes, beaches of pebbles and boulders, the skerries. Along the northern coasts of Norway they are all represented in great variation and seemingly endless numbers. There is another group of shores more evidently cultural, manipulated for fishing and agricultural use, which we will discuss below. The kind of shore that seems to constitute the most powerful image of these regions is hardly a 'shore' at all, given the size and steepness of its elements. It is the image of mountains rising vertically from the horizontal carpet of sea: 'the Alps by the ocean'. Again we notice the combined effect of more basic elements of nature in a joint picture. The most well-known of such shores are found along the Lofoten Islands and at the cliff of the North Cape.

The northern shores are not particularly inviting as beaches for swimming and sunbathing. They represent what Fiske calls 'the wild beach', an anti-suburban beach representing 'a potentially subversive challenge that nature mounts against culture' (1989:57). For tourists who come to these shores they may be arenas for the opposite of the controlled collectivism of leisurely life on local or touristic beaches. The arenas open for non-regulated behavior, contrasting with everyday life (Iso-Ahola, 1982), but still in accordance with 'the call of the wild'. It is an arena where the stage props and wings are unspoilt nature, clean air and unpolluted water. The thrill lies in lack of litter and the absence of a feeling of haste, and in the possibility of making the first footprints in the sand. It is 'pre-social and pre-human' (Rojek, 1993). There is non-restricted access for everyone almost everywhere, and the opportunities for having a stretch of shore to oneself are better than anywhere else in Europe. The flexible motor home is an important instrument for the furthering of touristic invasion of these shores. Tourism in most of the region has not reached a level where there is a scarcity of space, something that enhances the possibility of romantic gaze. Enjoying this freedom in an unpolluted environment is important for tourists in Lofoten (Jacobsen, 1992a:68).

That the northern coasts are landscapes for the romantic gaze is strengthened by the criteria for a classical landscape summed up by Cosgrove (1984): the subjectivity of the lonely eye, the removal of traits of toil and technology. The beauty lies in the lack of dominant signs of modern life, and the lack of evidence of nature being exploited. The final important touch to the scenery is given by the appearance (or non-disappearance) of the midnight sun. The experience of this can be highly emotional. Both the

erasure of the divide between day and night, which might give a feeling of timelessness, and the slowly changing coloring of the skies and the details of the landscape support the possible emotional elevation of such moments.

The romantic image of the coast as something beautiful also goes back to the emergence of artistic representations of northern coastal landscapes and coastal life, both in painting and writing. Norwegian and foreign painters have for the last century shown an ever-growing interest in the Lofoten area, where the landscapes are perceived as particularly dramatic. Therefore they have been worthy of the paint and brush. The importance of light conditions to painting also strengthens the points above about the Arctic light. There are today several galleries for nationally famous painters and an artists' school in Lofoten, something which further shows that the shaping of what nature is like, and what is natural, is a cultural process. It has been institutionalized. What current tastes have found beautiful enough to be hung on bourgeois walls is also something to be visited. That writers contribute to the shaping of mental pictures of natural and cultural landscapes which later can be confirmed by sightseeing is for Northern Norway best known through the case of Knut Hamsun's novels and the films based on them.

The expression 'tourism *towards* the sea' has been used (Sletvold et al., 1992). Unless one has an amphibious vehicle, the trip to the coast has its ultimate destination on the shore (although in Norway there are rows of islands that make the mainland shore only the antepenultimate one). It represents a kind of limit to where motoring man on vacation can go. When one comes to the shoreline and does not intend to stay, one either has to go back from it or to proceed along it. In this way a trip along a coast is a way of finding the contours of a territory or of circumscribing man's natural habitat. The sea is an element for immersion (Haikola, 1982). One may see a symbolic act in the movement towards the element from where life is presumed once to have crept ashore, or a contemplation of where it all might end. There seems to be established evidence that experienced tourists expand their horizons both literally and figuratively, through going to new places and changing motivation. Pearce (1993) models tourist motivation as a 'travel career tapestry'. Seeking the peripheries of the solid land and the northern rim of European nature and culture may be examples of weft and warp in such a tapestry.

Cultural elements

There are cultivated, conquered, constructed and controlled shores. They are not only the beaches of tourist resorts or suburban beaches in general, but also appear as fishing settlements, harbors, dikes, jetties and piers. Some of these are more cultured than others, more imbued with meaning. Fiske (1989:41) talks of the beach as an arena with too much meaning. With its double character of land and sea, it becomes an anomalous category. The beach of a seaside town or a resort becomes a text with a variety of meanings to be interpreted, giving reasons for unformalized but accepted zoning. Most shores of the Arctic belong to the least regulated end of such a scale. But of course they are not empty of meaning, either to the tourists or to the locals.

Some cultural elements are visible and accessible to the tourist, and the gaze most easily discovers the physical structures. Other aspects of the coastal culture depend upon a context of local interpreters and means of access. An anonymous green slope on a small island may be the site of a 17th century church now removed, and this indication of former institutionalized religious life can only be experienced through local management, by means of a boat and a local interpreter.

Man-made physical structures are important cultural elements in the landscapes, for the dominance of nature. The pier is an example of cultivated coast (Urry, 1990), representing man's attempts to dominate and conquer nature, with the Brighton piers as the symbol of coastal tourism. Another aspect of this is the double role of such symbols as towers, as markers for their respective cityscapes (MacCannell, 1989): the Eiffel tower is a synonym for Paris and vice versa. On the Arctic coast the attempts to control and cultivate nature have left other, less imposing constructions. A parallel to city towers are the lighthouses, both because of their shape and size and through their function as watch-towers for human traffic along the coast. One may look upon the traditional fishermen's cabins (*rorbu*) as a marker for Lofoten. The simple constructions of fish racks (to hang fish on during the process of drying) are seen everywhere along the shores and may also be a symbol of the fishermen's way of life. Their unpretentious size and pure functionality fits the total picture of life in the area.

A long but oversimplifying list of local cultural landscapes can be mentioned. There are the different kinds of fishing villages, the old trading sites, the coastal agricultural landscapes, the archeological details, the dwellings left behind by modernization, and the technological landscape elements of bridges and tunnels and modern fishing harbors; and there are shores resulting from road construction (Sletvold et al., 1992:30ff). The sea as an important element for the understanding of the cultural elements of the coastal zone cannot be over-estimated. The examples mentioned all have their closeness to the sea in common: you can see it, hear it and smell it—or even spit in it—all along. And considering the natural forces at work in a winter storm, some of the physical monuments that coastal communities have built for communication or a minimum of shelter, represent equally evident symbols of mastery of the sea as southern piers do. The lighthouses have been an important element in a number of paintings that mainly show roaring and raging seas. Furthermore the sea is a complementary element for any indexical reading of coastal culture, even when you cannot see it. As a food chamber it is the primary reason for existence along these otherwise rather inhospitable shores. This meaning is part of the contextual knowledge that broadens the experience of attractions otherwise out of reach of the sea, for example, galleries or museums.

It is a question for further research what role such manifest cultural elements of the northern coast play for the tourists. Jacobsen in his Lofoten survey (1992a) found that the wish to experience local culture and settlements was an important motive, and more so than anticipated by local tourist authorities. At the same time there is very little resort tourism in the region. The tourists are constantly on the move. Therefore it is a question whether contact with culture and society in such tourism is basically different from the superficial one we are used to in more industrialized tourism. If travelling is the dominant behavior in these areas of natural beauty, we are close to the romatic gaze (Urry, 1990:45). Tourism towards the coast is still predominantly individual traffic, and the romantic gaze has implications of solitude and privacy. The tourist is a single observer, having the advantage of a subjective point of view to the scenery. The existence of other tourists seems to disturb the romancing of the landscapes and its details of culture. Our analysis above of the natural elements of the northern coasts also shows further evidence of such a romantic tendency.

The population density of these regions is very low. Therefore analysing tourism along or out to these coasts may also imply a question of whether the cultural elements become too diminutive to be noticed, in a way that ridicules our discussion of them as important for the tourist experience and in the end for the concept of cultural landscapes. Compared to the wide stretches of the sea and the dominant verticality of much of the land, the farms and villages and other physical cultivated elements could be felt to disappear in the macro landscapes. This experience will be strengthened if societal forms and settlements along the coast cannot be sustained in the future.

The result of this would be twofold. It could turn out as an experience of what is conceived as wilderness.

'Wilderness' is nature not planned, arranged or surrounded by legislation or prohibition, not territorialized, even unconquerable (Shields, 1991). A wilderness is a landscape not marked or designed in the ways that a natural park in many countries would be. By labelling an area as Nature to preserve it as such, one incorporates it into the socially controlled environment and makes it conform to social ideals of what nature should be like (Rojek, 1993). However, this removes the more mythical features of the image of wilderness. Along the Arctic coastline a number of areas are defined as nature reservations, otherwise behavior is relatively unrestricted. Access is in principle free, and one doesn't have to walk or drive far from a main road to see 'the freedom and independence of the land' that, according to Wright (1975), are important mythical features of the wilderness. The image of wilderness has been used to promote the northernmost county of Norway, but then primarily the inland plateau. With growing tourist traffic this image will weaken, also because of the necessity for more regulation.

The often modest proofs of physical cultivation along the coast could also result in a visual impression of a landscape which is so desolate, severe, cold and depressing that its meaning becomes one of nature suppressing culture. People inhabiting these shores might be looked upon as tough and self-determined recluses. Theroux clearly gets such an impression of quaintness from travelling the western coast of Scotland (1984:325), an area in some respects comparable to the Norwegian coastline.

Lofoten tourists do not experience this archipelago as a desolate area (Jacobsen, 1992a). Neither do they seem to confirm an impression of it as wilderness, although this descriptor was not presented as an alternative in the survey. One obvious reason for a fairly balanced, harmonious impression of the natural and cultural is the fact that the kind of tourism which Jacobsen surveyed is dependent upon the infrastructure of a modern society: roads, ferries, shops. One is never far from civilization. This, of course, structures tourism spatially too (Sletvold et al., 1992:62ff). Because of the rather narrow shape of the country there are only a couple of main roads or thoroughfares spanning North Norway south–north, but there are many dead-end roads leading out to the coastal villages. Unlike much rural tourism, the possibility of round-trips is limited, giving well defined corridors of movement between destination points (Pigram, 1993; Viken, 1991).

To find other reasons for the apparent satisfaction with the experiential mixture of nature and culture more research is needed. One possible reason for satisfaction lies in the esthetic relationship between the man-made

constructions and the elements of nature as to size, location, materials, colors etc. The houses on the coast are mostly detached, wooden constructions, often single small farms, probably perceived as modest, painted in clear and fresh colors, and thus seen as adjusting well to the natural side of the landscape, having a 'natural' location around the inlet or between knolls. The dominant tourist opinion seems to be that this is authentic, and for this kind of cultural element there is little chance of staging authenticity. There are, however, many exceptions, mainly in the service centers which have expanded rapidly to meet the demands of commerce, communication, education and municipal administration. Several of these, and in particular their architecture, are perceived as out-of-character, not accepted as vernacular and localized culture.

Contrasting with these modern elements are the abandoned single houses or villages, rapidly deteriorating. They may be looked upon as picturesque, belonging in the landscape, and therefore exotic and authentic. As such they represent possibilities of developing tourist attractions. Other examples in the same category would be the jetty that was too weak, the harbor that became too small, fishing boats that are left on the shore to rot, the grazing fields and outhouses on the outer skerries. These all contribute to the story of the modernization of a peripheral way of life. They also pose a well-known heritage-as-tourism problem: what elements of the past are to be kept—conserved or frozen—in what way and for whom?

All these elements, the surviving and the newly built environment, may be sights seen and read as parts of the landscapes. Together they convey pictures of how inhabitants along the coast have been adjusting to the demands of modernization. Still they may fit nicely into an image of the authentic periphery, where life is considered to be harsh, but simple, healthy and natural, and where nature is controlled but not conquered, harvested more than exploited.

Sustainability and local community viability

Northern coastal tourism may be related to the perspective of sustainability in two ways, of which the second has most to do with the above understanding of such tourism as experiencing particular landscapes.

Sustainability and connoted concepts belong to a somewhat different paradigm from the ones we have made use of so far. They are used mainly within policy formulation and for a strategic perspective (Brundtland, 1987; de Kadt 1992). The three main issues are those of managing resources renewably, of finding the balanced scale, and of distributing benefits in an equitable way. This perspective, therefore, has more to do with the physical basis of the landscape and its environmental properties, than with the landscape as an experiential resource. But there is no denying that physical changes in the nature, or at least the knowledge of such changes, will affect attitudes towards landscapes and the way they are experienced and interpreted. The concern is with what has become familiar environmental problems of tourism development (Mathieson and Wall, 1982). Such problems, and negative social and cultural impacts, in the heavily developed tourism areas in the world explain much of the search for alternative or similarly labelled tourism (Butler, 1992; Valentine, 1992).

Although most tourism in Norway is small-scale and probably even 'alternative' in a world context, environmental problems from tourism can be seen in the most popular destinations along the northern coasts: traffic congestion along narrow roads and in small villages, ferry queues of 12–15 hours, popular mountain paths suffering erosion, too low a waste handing capacity, disturbance of birds' and animals' mating grounds etc. The examples illustrate the problems of scale in areas of very limited physical space in latitudes with vulnerable nature, and how delicate and difficult the balance is—'the thin end of the wedge' (Butler, 1992). Furthermore, problems like these in the long run represent profiling and market communication problems, if one considers a 'green' image to be part of the sustainability concept, as Norway wants to. People travel to northern coasts expecting a kind of anti-urban landscape with plenty of space and fresh air and the distant natural sounds of the ocean and the seagulls in pleasant villages. Instead they might come to a Lofoten where roads are overcrowded with mobile homes and tightly scheduled coaches, where loud French or German voices are more prominent than the cries of the seagulls. Then sustaining a green image can be problematic. Another important factor for the sustainability of this kind of long-distance, round-trip tourism is its dependency upon costly and polluting transport (Flognfeldt, 1993). Touristic airborne pollution and road traffic, with heavy energy consumption and carbon dioxide emission may become the target of criticism.

The second and main connection between sustainability and experiencing coastal landscapes follows a different line of reasoning. We replace the overexposed term 'sustainability' with the concept of 'local community viability'. This takes into consideration the particular characteristics of the northern coastal villages (Thuen and Wadel, 1981), with respect to industrial and employment systems and professional and social community networks. The typical coastal village in Northern Norway has been

predominantly dependent upon fisheries. The fishing boats, land-based industry and single households often constitute tightly coupled systems (Jentoft, 1991). These societies have for generations been characterized by strong social integration and local identity, but lately also by vulnerability and industrial inflexibility, because of the technological development of the fisheries and the dramatic fluctuations of the fish resources.

As we have seen, northern coastal tourism can be understood in the experiential interplay between what is considered as natural elements in the landscape and the more consciously interpreted cultural and social elements; and these elements are conceived of as constituting a whole. One main focus is upon the ways that human living has made and will continue to make its imprints on the spectacular natural landscapes. Tourism then depends upon living societies and not upon resorts with heavy touristic infrastructures. Therefore the tourism future of these regions does not merely depend upon the development of isolated tourism strategies and their success. It will depend more upon, for example, the success of fish resources management regimes of the seasonal coastal fisheries and the year-round activities in the Norwegian and Barents Seas (Hardin, 1968; Jentoft, 1991), and upon the national and European policy towards the regions and peripheries in general (Brox, 1984, 1989; Selstad 1993).

There is a scenario where fisheries are managed in a more industrial-efficient way which makes people and communities along the coast superfluous (Selstad, 1993). Then people living on the coast cannot sustain an understanding and presentation of themselves as communities with a future based upon the resources of the seas. If the strong and positive identity so far formed from centuries of culturing this hard nature cannot be upheld, then the landscapes that tourists come to experience will also have other messages and present other readings than those presented above, at least with reference to indexical interpretations. There may very well be markets for products where the harbors and villages are merely kept alive as arenas for the staging of a life forgone. We have mentioned some examples of whether and how to conserve former coastal culture. There are ghost fishing villages that today can be presented as a contrast to other, thriving harbors. But the experiences of the coast that one wants to present are based in the sustained development of coastal culture rooted in local practices and local knowledge. The alternative is that without living societies, fishing villages, coastal farms and activities on the sea, these landscapes may return to some kind of ghost wilderness. The strategy of tourism development in these regions therefore should be one of reaching traffic levels and finding products and production forms that will function as a complementary industrial activity, supporting the viability of local community development (Sletvold et al., 1992).

Conclusion

This paper has attempted to clarify the attraction core in the coastal tourism by contrasting travelling along the Norwegian Arctic coast with tourism along other shores. Based on a culturally determined understanding of landscapes, it is tourism in landscapes where the natural elements are most impressive, but where elements of culture convey man's struggle with the dominating nature. The attractivity of the coastline is shaped especially by the variety of shores seen in interplay with the sea and given a particular tint through the bright nights of Arctic light. Easy access to relative loneliness may determine it as an example of the romatic gaze. To the degree that tourists immerse themselves in the villages and ways of life on the coast, they may also uncover less exposed meanings of the coastal landscapes. Such more contextual interpretations may deepen the esthetic and recreational pleasure of experiencing the Arctic coast.

A sound and balanced tourism development is a difficult task. There are the dynamics of the tourism industry itself and other growth factors that tend to escape local control to consider (Butler, 1992). The discussion of these topics in relation to Norwegian Arctic coastal tourism has only just started. Development here will be heavily influenced by factors external to tourism, such as the management of fish resources. The viability of the local communities will determine to what extent the understanding of the cultural landscapes can be sustained, reflecting upon the character of the tourist experiences.

Notes

1. Based on a criterion of latitude, the region is part of the Arctic, stretching above the Arctic circle. If climate is the criterion, the area is temperate or sub-arctic. In any case it must be differentiated from the High Arctic. In the paper both 'northern' and 'arctic' are used, although 'northern' might give wrong connotations, often being used about European countries such as Great Britain or Germany.
2. This coastline stretches for 2000 km north/northeast to the Russian border, characterized by thousands of inhabited and uninhabited islands. Known history here goes back 10 000 years. The settlements on the coast are mainly small fishing villages around natural harbors and single small farms in rural landscapes. The fisheries along the coast and in the Norwegian and Barents Seas form the industrial basis for living. There are no towns of more than 50 000 inhabitants. Two-thirds of the population of 400 000 live in densely populated areas, leaving the rest to be even more spread out, with a population density of four per square kilometre. In the northernmost county there is 75 metres of shoreline per inhabitant.

References

Brox, Ottar (1984) *Nord-Norge—fra allmenning til koloni*, Universitetsforlaget, Oslo.

Brox, Ottar (1989) *Kan bygdenæringene bli lønnsomme?* Gyldendal, Oslo.

Brundtland, G. H. (1987) *Our Common Future*, Oxford University Press, Oxford.

Butler, Richard (1992) 'The thin end of the wedge', in V. Smith and W. R. Eadington (Eds), *Tourism Alternatives*, University of Pennsylvania Press, Philadelphia, PA.

Canetti, Elias (1973) *Crowds and Power*, Penguin, Harmondsworth.

Cosgrove, D. (1984) *Social Formation and Symbolic Landscape*, Croom Helm, London.

Finnmarkopplevelser (1990) Brochures, FO A/S, Alta.

Fiske, John (1989) *Reading the Popular*, Unwin Hyman, London.

Flognfeldt Jr, Thor (1992) 'Areal, sted, reiserute', ODH-rapport, Lillehammer.

Flognfeldt Jr, Thor (1993) 'Green tourism—the whole route, or just a make-up?', Paper for the Northern Forum Conference Symposium on Arctic Tourism and Ecotourism, Tromsø, September.

Haahti, Antti J. (1986) 'Finland's competitive position as a destination', *Annals of Tourism Research*, 13: 11–35.

Haikola, Lars (1982) 'Om symboler', in Allwood, J., Frängsmyr, T. and Svedin, V. (Eds), *Naturen som symbol*, Liberförlag, Stockholm.

Hardin, Garret (1968) 'The tragedy of the commons', *Science*, 162: 1243–8.

Iso-Ahola, Seppo E. (1982) 'Towards a social psychology of tourism motivations—a rejoinder', *Annals of Tourism Research*, 9: 256–261.

Jacobsen, Jens K. (1992a) 'Ferieliv i Lofoten og Vesterålen', *Gjesteundersøkelse 1991*, Nordland Fylkeskommune, Bodø.

Jacobsen, Jens K. (1992b) 'Tourism as hermeneutics', Paper for the 3rd National Norwegian Congress of Sociology.

Jacobsen, Roy (1992) *Seierherrene*, Gyldendal, Oslo.

Jafari, Jafar (1987) 'Tourism models: the sociocultural aspects', *Tourism Management*, June, pp. 151–159.

Jentoft, Svein (1991) 'Hengende snøre. Fiskerikrisen og framtiden på kysten', Ad Notam, Oslo.

Jones, Michael (1988) 'Progress in Norwegian cultural landscape studies', *Norsk Geografisk Tidsskrift*, 43: 153–169.

de Kadt, Emanuel (1992) 'Making the alternative sustainable: lessons from development for tourism', in V. Smith and W. R. Eadington (Eds), *Tourism Alternatives*, University of Pennsylvania Press, Philadelphia, PA.

Lévi-Strauss, Claude (1973) *Tristes Tropiques*, Picador, London.

Lévi-Strauss, Claude (1979) *Myth and Meaning*, Schocken, New York.

Lewis, G. J. (1979) *Rural Communities: a Social Geography*, David & Charles, Newton Abbot.

Lyngnes, Sølvi (1990) 'Kultur for reiseliv', FDH-rapport, Alta.

MacCannell, Dean (1989) *The Tourist*. Schocken, New York.

MacCannell, Dean (1992) *Empty Meeting Grounds. The Tourist Papers*, Routledge, London.

Mathieson, A. and Wall, G. (1982) *Tourism: Economic, Physical and Social Impacts*, Longman, Harlow.

Meinig, Donald, W. (Ed.) (1979) *The Interpretation of Ordinary Landscapes*, Oxford University Press, New York.

Messerli, H. (1990) 'Enterprise zones and rural tourism development', unpublished MA thesis, George Washington University, Washington, DC.

NOE Nærings- og energidepartementet (Royal Norwegian Ministry of Industries and Energy) (1993) 'Sats på reiseliv!', Internt notat, Oslo.

NORTRA (Norwegian Travel Marketing) (1993) 'Markedsplan', Oslo.

Pearce, Douglas (1989) *Tourism Development*, 2nd edn, Longman, Harlow.

Pearce, Philip (1993) 'Fundamentals of tourist motivation', in D. G. Pearce and R. Butler (Eds), *Tourism Research*, Routledge, London.

Pigram, John (1993) 'Planning for tourism in rural areas', in D. G. Pearce and R. Butler (Eds), *Tourism Research*, Routledge, London.

Rojek, Chris (1993) *Ways of Escape: Modern Transformations in Leisure and Travel*, Macmillan, London.

Schancke, Audhild (1987) 'Det samiske landskap', *Fortidsvern*, 3: 17–19.

Selstad, Tor (1993) 'Norden som nytt tilreiseområde', *Nordrevy*, 5(November): 25–38.

Shields, Rob (1991) *Places on the Margin: Alternative Geographies of Modernity*, Routledge, London.

Sletvold, Ola (1993) 'The Norwegian Arctic coastline as a landscape for tourism', Paper for the Northern Forum Conference Symposium on Arctic Tourism and Ecotourism, Tromsø, September.

Sletvold, O., Viken, A. and Svensson, K. H. (1992) 'Ut mot havet. Kystturisme i nord', FDH-rapport, Alta.

Svedin, Uno (1982) 'Naturen som symbol och materiell verklighet', in Allwood, J., Frängsmyr, T. and Svedin, U. (Eds), *Naturen som symbol*, Liberförlag, Stockholm.

Theroux, Paul (1984) *The Kingdom by the Sea: a Journey around Great Britain*, Washington Square Press, New York.

Tuan, Yi-Fu (1979) 'Thought and landscape: the eye and the mind's eye', in D. W. Meinig (Ed.), *The Interpretation of Ordinary Landscapes*, Oxford University Press, New York.

Thuen, T. and Wadel, C. (1981) *Lokalsamfunn og offentlig planlegging*, Universitetsforlaget, Oslo/Tromsø.

Urry, John (1990) *The Tourist Gaze*, Sage, London.

Urry, John (1992) 'The tourist gaze and the "environment"', *Theory, Culture & Society*, 9: 1–26.

Valentine, Peter S. (1992) 'Nature-based tourism', in B. Weiler and C. M. Hall (Eds), *Special Interest Tourism*, Belhaven Press, London.

Viken, Arvid (1991) 'Destinasjon Nordkalotten', FDH-rapport, Alta.

Viken, Arvid (1993) 'Den turistiske opplevelses mystikk', *ARR Idehistorisk Tidsskrift*, 3: 10–19.

Walmsley, D. J. and Lewis, G. J. (1984) *Human Geography: Behavioural Approaches*, Longman, Harlow.

Wright, W. (1975) *Six-guns and Society: a Structural Study of the Western*, California University Press, Berkeley, CA.

74 Conservation, capacity and cashflows— tourism and historic building management

S. BERRY

Introduction—conservation of what?

Owners of historic buildings are faced with reconciling the protection and preservation of the property with the need to encourage visitors and profit from their access. They have to balance the survival of the building against the potential threat which income generation from tourism might pose for it. Ironically, the justification for the building's survival is likely to have been its potential as a tourism asset and a vehicle for educating visitors about what it symbolises. Although the retention of old buildings of merit or with special associations, such as being the home of someone of national or international interest, is accepted as a very respectable and valid action there is a question which needs to be addressed: *Exactly what is it that we seek to keep and attract visitors to*?

The wide-ranging and often discursive debate about the conservation of artefacts of the past has raged long enough to be so familiar that recapitulation of it is unnecessary (Hewison, 1987; Rumble, 1988a). However, there are important issues which many organisations do not address clearly and therefore their policy towards what they are conserving and how they seek to do it may be poorly articulated. Many buildings have layers of history, some of which is easy to see and other, significant, phases of which may now be lost, either because they are hidden behind more recent additions or because they have been demolished. Sometimes the only evidence of a phase may be a document or a picture, because even the foundations have gone. Faced with a hotchpotch of a building or group of buildings which symbolise different phases of the history, then the issue remains the same— conservation of what? In a world where, rightly, priorities have to be identified and costs are one of the factors which constrain choice, the lack of a clear focus can result in poorly thought-through conservation policies.

From the policy towards conservation derives the business policy within which income generation from tourism must be fitted. Failure to start with a realistic appraisal of the basic overview of how the buildings are to be cared for will result in a strategic overview which has very weak foundations indeed. Altruism and emotive reactions are not appropriate starting points for the survival of any historic building because buildings are expensive to maintain and, in a world where so many are accessible to the public, no one can reasonably expect that the generation of funds to protect old buildings will be easy to obtain, no matter how committed the individual or group might be to it. Indeed the future of the building may suffer because of the failure to be pragmatic about financial expectations and constraints. No longer may an owner of a historic building expect an amorphous body called 'the state', but in fact the taxpayer, to support his or her chosen commitment, especially if there are no clear objectives for the building's care or plans for income generation to protect its future. The public increasingly expects owners of buildings to put them to work to earn some of their keep, especially if they are contributing to its upkeep in some way in the form of grants and fund raising. Thus becoming part of the tourism business is a necessity for many.

Plans for the future of any building may generate controversy because many experts on conservation seem unable to agree on what they are interpreting and on the best way of conserving what they are so know-ledgeable about. There is still an unresolved debate about what we mean by an authentically historic building and whether conservation is now more acceptable than restoration. This helps to cloud the issues and raises doubts in the mind of many of the better-informed lay public, who support the retention of historic buildings as to what they are actually trying to keep (Rumble, 1988b).

Different views on any subject have their validity up to a point, but when they threaten to undermine the development of realistic plans to assist with the financing of the survival of historic buildings they become in many senses destructive. Even more confusing for many clients is that, although experts often have clear views as to what the current best practice is, they are often unable or unwilling to recognise that their ever-rising expectations about the quality of current 'best practice' may impose costs which the site cannot recoup. A compromise on conservation standards may be necessary and owners and managers must have some degree of pragmatism in order to balance the survival of the site against desires to maintain some or all at exemplary high standards. Such attitudes may earn them criticism from the experts but can result in the building's survival. It is fascinating to note too how the experts' own view of what should be done alters anyway, and so there is some validity in weighing up whether what they regard as the best action or interpretation will be the case in a few years' time and whether or not what has been done on the advice of conservation experts will stand the test of time. Given the ever-rising costs of much conservation work, that is a very real issue. Constrained by cost, owners have to distinguish between taking action to maintain their buildings and restoring them.

Thus, arguably, the care of buildings may be divided between conservation and restoration—the former in the more literal sense meaning taking action if required in order to ensure that a building and its setting is kept in good repair and the latter returning some, or part of it, to how it may have looked at a given date in time. Both are contentious but the latter more so—as reaction to the restoration work on the Queen's House at Greenwich showed (Amery, 1990). Both require careful attention to the logic and scholarliness of the research upon which actions are based and a sound understanding of the methodology that is then applied—not least because of the way in which opinions change.

The issue of choice, between approaches to the care of a building, should be debated, not only in order to ensure that the options for the site are well rehearsed and understood but also to check the impact upon the capital and recurrent costs. They will also influence the interpretation of the building and its context and the public should be party to the debates which underlie the decisions made and the rationale for the options taken. Any organisation which feels that it cannot explain its decisions to the people from whom it is expecting to raise cash and other forms of support (such as time), will find the public more wary and more critical than in the past, not least because there is so much competition within the historic building sector and beyond, for public support.

Thus the way in which buildings are interpreted and the quality of the communication about the choices which have been made must continue to improve if the public is to be attracted. The display by the National Trust at Ightham Mote in Kent (UK) shows not only why the Trust is seeking to raise £10 million to spend on the conservation of this medieval moated manor house but also the problems the Trust faces when undertaking work of this sort. Implicitly, the Trust recognises that more explanation, on why the public should support the high costs of running and opening a historic building, is now required. Precisely what is being conserved is one of the questions which had to be asked. Decisions, made have had to be placed in the context of both the need to undertake the work in order to save the building and the extent to which any part of the building should be changed from when the Trust acquired it, to reveal earlier structures. The broader issue then faced is whether any changes in one part of a building should be matched by changes in another and, if so, what and for what reason. At what point does the exercise evolve from conservation into restoration and, if it does, can anyone be sure the results are indeed accurate? Should more recent layers of a building be removed?

As more historic buildings are opened to the public all over the world, so the marketing concept of the USP (unique selling point) becomes more important and good interpretation serves an important role in attaining not only a reasoned rationale for the care of the building but also a basis for effective marketing. The dual use of interpretation is important because it is an expensive process which requires a very detailed physical and documentary survey, not only of the site but also of its vicinity, to understand its evolution. The building must also be set in its ever-changing context; for example, the reasons why an industrial building falls into disuse may be far more wide-ranging than local factors or poor management; many country houses were funded by incomes from a landed gentry with enormous investments overseas and in many businesses (an issue which in many countries raises interesting issues about exactly what they did symbolise, other than the self-indulgence of the owner). Many buildings were designed as symbols of assertion—not only the obvious ones such as castles but also churches, some mills and other industrial buildings, and that helps to explain facets of their design which a purely functional role cannot (Girouard, 1980). The austere and regular rhythm sought by the architects of the famous terraces of early Georgian Bath were using the site and the design to attain a sense of dignity and showmanship where the interior design of any part of the house played a secondary role. Buildings which are hard to run as attractions now, have always been impractical because their symbolic importance depended heavily on their visual impact rather than their practical role.

That a considerable proportion of the world's most famous historic buildings have always been white elephants must be accepted as a fact of life which their owners, on the whole, recognised. It is a pity that so little of the interpretation of these places gets that crucial message over to the public who are being asked to support them. The sense of style and theatre which they were there to convey is one of their more striking facets and often why they survived in the first place—that role should be made more explicit to their visitors. Alienating the visitor by simply not offering a sense of the place is one of the issues which those who wish to keep their support must consider seriously.

Explanation of the role of a building should also include its contents but rarely is an overview of these offered, either in management plans or to the public, so that there is a context within which individual items may be set. The issue of how the content of a building should be regarded raises the issue of whether buildings which have lost their original contents be refurbished with purchases which are intended to give more interest, as at Chiswick, Burlington's villa in London. Is it right to move beam engines and put them into mills or pumping stations from which the originals have gone? The furniture, no matter how carefully chosen may not be in the taste of the owner, even if appropriate in style and period. Perhaps the moving of equipment to refurbish industrial buildings is more questionable if one is to be a purist because the work, once done is more permanent.

Not only are many buildings overlaid with a long history of changes in role and status but, even now, when treated in effect as monuments to our cultural and economic pasts, they are often expected both to interest the public in their own right and to house collections. Some of the collections, such as the 16th- and 17th-century portraits which are on display at the vast late-16th century Montacute in Somerset and the industrial artefacts which will be displayed in the Rahmi H Koc Museum of Industry[1] which is being housed in an ancient warehouse in Istanbul, are complementary to the building, but many collections have little relevance to their host structure and play a secondary role to the degree that the anomaly looks curious to the public. For example, a collection of old musical instruments at Michelham Priory in East Sussex is often a source of puzzlement to visitors, as are the ceramics and other items from Asia and China which are housed in the Upper Belvedere in Vienna.

The generation of income from tourism—capacity, communication and cash flows

Communication, capacity and commercial ventures are interlinked but the strong association between the three is often not clearly recognised and therefore is not developed. Thus the management overview of the site may lack cohesion. Interpretation is not only about communication but also about capacity and commercial success. Effective interpretation will play an important role in the attraction and the management of visitors and thus help to determine how capacity limits might be set, managed and monitored. These in turn help to determine what commercial activities on the site might be viable.

Communication

Communication is best understood if it is divided into two parts: (a) making the place accessible and welcoming and (b) interpretation.

Access and welcome

There are still many sites which leave visitors puzzled from the entrance to the exit. Attention should be paid to making the visitor feel wanted in unfamiliar surroundings in which they need to get their bearings at two levels—to function and to absorb the sense of the place. Even today, some managers do not make clear the entrance to their site on a public road and that, when access is so often by car, is extremely thoughtless. Visitors are tolerated, not welcomed. The lack of a brief indication of what is there is another indication of a lack of thought about the need to convince visitors that the place is worth parting with their cash for.

Investment in making a site seem accessible and welcoming is possible without great expense and intrusion. Clear information about the site can include the more traditional approaches, such as signs, but also well-designed and simple maps or plans which are given to visitors as part of the admission price in lieu of the traditional ticket. If a visitor is made aware of what is available and where to find it then the site may be better used, and its capacity increased without endangering it, because visitors are flowing through it in an effective manner, owing to good route-planning. Visitors normally stay longer and are more likely to spend when a site is well-managed. Research suggests that unless a site can absorb people's interest for about 2 hours, there is little point in providing facilities such as shops and restaurants because the scale of the attraction will not retain sufficient people to make them economic.

The layout of buildings frequently determines where the entrance, the restaurant and the shop will be. In the Royal Pavilion (Brighton) the restaurant is on the first floor and not on the route of the visitors, therefore clear signs and an attractive entrance are of great importance, especially as visitors may not be sure how long their tour will take and the facility has to attract as many visitors as it can from its potential market. As the Pavilion is in the town centre where there are quite a lot of small cafes, it is faced with competition which more isolated sites such as country houses do not have.

Interpretation

'The public's' interest in access to and learning about historic buildings is part of the well-rehearsed argument in favour of keeping them. However, the validity of this part of the argument is increasingly difficult to sustain because of the wide range of buildings which are now accessible internationally.

Historic sites and museums often communicate poorly to their visitors and that affects their survival because the public are left feeling that the encounter has been unsatisfactory, even uncomfortable. They leave with an uneasy feeling that they have gained little but that it was expected that they should have done—as if they were born with a microchip on which were imprinted all of the cultural and other signposts they would have needed in order to do so (Durrant, 1992).

Market research frequently identifies the lack of site interpretation as something which affects the enjoyment of a visit. A recent report on the properties which are managed by English Heritage assessed several of their most prestigious properties as having strikingly poor interpretation (e.g. Stonehenge, Battle Abbey) a problem which the organisation is seeking to remedy (NAO, 1992).

The debate about meretricious and misleading interpretation and the allegations that much interpretation conveys a simplistic view of whatever the subject might be has been well aired. Inevitably any interpretation of anything will be selective and that is partly a consequence of the state of knowledge of most places and their contexts, but careful research and a clear and sensibly developed structure to the interpretation of a building can only enhance the quality of a visit. To asume that the visitor cannot distinguish between a well-intended and researched display and a poor one, which has no clear objectives, has no flow and is based on inadequate research, is unreasonable. To simply expect only those who are *aficionados* of the historical periods in which the building flourished to enjoy the visit is also to make some surprising assumptions about their reasons for visiting, for they too can enjoy looking at an interpretation which may offer a different view. Thus interpretation may offer a challenge to visitors with a wide range of backgrounds, even within a clearly targeted age and socio-economic grouping (Berry and Standeven, 1992; Waterson, 1992).

Interpretation for many does not require ornate and expensive projects which run the risk of becoming outdated before they have paid their way, the calculation of which should also include any interest which is charged or forgone, depending on the source of the capital.

Many historic sites still depend on guide books, and yet they have a very limited role for most visitors because they are of little use on site and because the pace of research and of redisplay quickly overtakes them. Most people visit historic sites with at least one other person and guidebooks cannot easily be shared. The simpler leaflets which many attractions are now turning to offer a cheaper, more easily used and up-to-date alternative. They are also economic at long print runs, which means that copies can be produced for visitors from the major overseas generating countries such as France and Germany. By contrast, guide books are often expensive to produce and then become out of date before the print run is sold—especially for smaller properties. Most visitors do not wish to absorb the detail which they may offer and the writing style can be off-putting (National Trust and English Heritage are among organisations that are reviewing their role).

Research into how visitors use museums suggests that most exhibits and exhibitions command only a cursory and intermittent span of attention and that the message must be clearly and straightforwardly presented (Durrant, 1992).

The majority of sites have buildings in which a simple and clearly laid out guide to the site and its context may be put, thus giving groups a chance to learn about the place before they go in. Such an approach is employed at Sissinghurst in Kent where an oasthouse on the path between the garden and the ticket booth houses an exhibition which explains the garden's evolution and the world of the Nicolsons who developed it as it is today. This exhibition can easily be altered to include new information and does not include anything more hi-tech than a back-projected slide projector. Anything which generated noise would have been too intrusive in a display of this type, which lacks the space to house anything which could be distracting. The exhibition is effective without being expensive in the context of the capacity of the place which is its subject.[2]

One of the best sources for interpretation is people, well-briefed staff and volunteers at reception points, in the car park, looking after rooms. Contact with people who are interested in and knowledgeable about a site is highly valued.

Capacity

Capacity management has recently become a fashionable concern of managers of historic buildings, partly because of research on the impact of visitors on buildings. However, the art of capacity management is still in its infancy and only a few attractions, such as Beamish, have really looked at its implications for site management. The National Trust in the UK is also doing so. Many issues have to be addressed, not only the issue of what the site can tolerate without being irrecoverably damaged—which is one extreme—but also the viability of investment in any facilities such as restaurants and shops. When sites are quite complex and vary in their ability to cope with people, as an open air museum or a complex of buildings or a large country house does, then on what assumptions should the calculations be based?

The capacity of a building is normally constrained by the fact that alterations to increase its ability to absorb more people will change its character and undermine the case for keeping it. However, there may be areas where minor modifications might be acceptable, for example in basements and in outhouses. Not only must the capacity of the areas which need protecting be considered, but also forecasts as to the level of demand, otherwise investments in changes may be made which are not justified.

Thus, capacity management will affect income and expenditure and requires careful handling. The increase in visitors to Sissinghurst Garden in Kent after a television series about the Sackville-Wests who designed and lived on the site meant that timed tickets had to be introduced. Estimates of the impact of the decision had to include a projection of the impact of any decrease in income from admissions, the restaurant and the shop. The problem with the management of a garden is that estimating how long people will take to go round it is harder than for a house. Therefore issuing tickets has to be done with careful attention to the numbers which are already present, based on counting them in and out with a laser counter. By contrast, timed tickets for a house can normally be issued on the simple assumption of so many at set times because visitors flow through it on a predetermined route and this tends to ensure that most take about the same time. If there is a waiting period before visitors can go into a house then there have to be activities which fill their time, for example an exhibition, a shop, a restaurant.

More typical management techniques include opening earlier to prevent crushes after lunch and designing flows so that culs-de-sac and awkward corners are eliminated.

Cash flows

Historic buildings are now an interdependent part of the tourism and leisure industry, particularly now that cultural tourism is reasserting itself as the growth sector of that industry. In the UK about 40% of the population visit at least one historic house during the peak holiday period between July and September. If they are prestigious or welcoming, some houses are also a major attraction for inbound visitors because the information offered helps visitors who might otherwise lack the cultural knowledge to enjoy them.

Owners of historic buildings have to accept that the taxpayer cannot and will not be able to support them; there are simply too many of them. Business planning is an integral part of the management of historic buildings now: grant-giving bodies, sponsors, banks and any other potential backers now expect to see a business plan when any money is sought, to convince them that the management has a clear and realistic view of its objectives for the long-term survival of the building and a clear grasp of relevant management techniques. Operations which cannot provide business plans with realistic objectives and well managed accounts, or which fail to show respect for their legal responsibilities such as the payment of VAT and PAYE and other normal business overheads, are likely to encounter major difficulties with fund-raising, because they will be regarded as failing to observe good and ethical business practices and their competence to care for the property in their care will be questioned.

In response to the need to review the use of resources carefully, many organisations now set income and commercial performance targets. In the UK, English Heritage and the National Trust are well-known examples of organisations which do so. The National Trust looks at the profit which is generated by the tourist-related activities, and not just the turnover, because that does not indicate whether an activity is actually generating a profit which can be ploughed back into the enterprise; and more managers are following the same necessary practice and are as a result looking at activities and cost and income centres. Amongst the techniques which are becoming more widely applied are: sensitivity analysis (measuring the extent to which different changes in expected costs of revenues will affect the expected viability of products and identifying projects offering the best financial returns); payback; and net present value (NAO, 1992:28ff).

Such management tools are all the more essential as historic buildings become either the centre of or an adjunct to a range of commercial activities. Not all owners of historic buildings depend solely on visitors. Consultancy (Beaulieu in Hampshire) and consultancy combined with restoration and conservation (British Engineerium, Hove, East Sussex), conference trade, membership organisations (National Trust, Historic Williamsburg—Virginia), letting property (National Trust), franchising designs (Royal Pavilion, Brighton, East Sussex) are but some of the other activities, and their respective opportunity costs have to be weighed up.

The tourist, the sponsors, the grant bodies all have expectations and interests in the operation, which might create conflicts of interest that managers have to reconcile in the best interests of the business. That is harder for historic houses than for purely commercial operations because the objective of developing a business is to ensure that the building or buildings survive—conservation may impose limitations on maximising efficiency as a business operation. Thus the application of performance indicators, though worthwhile, has to be done in an appropriate manner. That visitors should receive value for money is a sensible objective, but the definition of value is going to include an assessment of the quality of the visit in terms of enjoyment.

Although the quality of management of historic buildings as tourist attractions is improving, and in spite of the fact that in most countries with a reasonable tourism infrastructure a lot is known about visitors to attractions, a substantial proportion of site managers lack a clear view of their public. They spend a considerable amount of money on marketing methods which are no longer regarded as effective, such as large numbers of leaflets and little generalised advertisements in the local press. Some still attempt to meet the needs of all comers rather than accept that they should be more specific, for example, investing in the education market. But this is a competitive and expensive sector unless a high volume is attained, as at Fishbourne Roman Palace (West Sussex, England). In some cases the building might be better suited to a well-targeted middle-class, middle-aged market. Most historic buildings and sites share one key characteristic with any other category of product: they simply cannot be marketed to everyone. The most successful target a specific market and then identify its perceptions of itself and work within them, adapting to meet changes in those perceptions where necessary or moving out of that market and into another if that is required. Research has also clearly shown that the majority of historic sites have very limited catchment areas, and yet some managers still advertise far too widely (Berry and Standeven, 1992).

Historic buildings now share with many operations the need to control costs, both fixed and variable, and they do not command the support of the public or of other potential backers if they do not. The increase in paid staff has made staff costs a major issue for many historic sites. As historic sites move to more explicitly generating income from tourism, so in some cases, such as the Sussex Archaeological Society in East and West Sussex (England), their staff costs have risen faster than the income. Unless the investment in staffing then results in a rapid rise in income, the bill for permanent staff, which is part of the fixed costs of running the operation, should be cut and, where necessary, seasonal and short-term contract staff should be used, for both are variable costs. However, both have to be costed into the overheads of the operation and therefore into the pricing strategy. One implication may be that buildings should have their opening hours extended in order to use these people more effectively. Additional part-time staff are a small additional overhead per visitor when compared to the wage bill for permanent staff, and the additional income will normally be at marginal cost. The publication by the ETB and the regional tourist boards in England, 'Places to visit in winter', features more historic buildings than in the past as the message about the need to recoup more of the staff costs hits home. For many operations, the payback on investment in the salaries of some full-time staff should be carefully monitored.

In the interest of effectively saving costs on staff and hence freeing more income for the care of the building, it is a pity that there is ambivalence towards volunteers on sites (as used at St Louisburg, Canada), because using well-trained and highly appreciated volunteers, can make superb use of the growing retired population. The National Trust is now greatly dependent upon them and the need to control staff costs has become part of the strategy of many organisations. Volunteers should be used as more than fundraisers. In a world where more and more people live by themselves, contact with others on visits to attractions has a value and the volunteers can act as the communicators, freeing the paid staff to work on their respective responsibilities (Iley, 1993).

The operating costs of historic buildings as tourism enterprises tends to make small buildings uneconomic. There is an argument that 'the public' expects a full range of facilities on any historic site and organisations which own small buildings are finding that their operating costs per visitor tend to be higher than those for middle to larger size properties; economies of scale apply to the effective management of buildings as tourist attractions. Many smaller ones will probably close and be used in other ways. The great interest internationally in historic buildings now means that there are more people who are willing to live in and care for the smaller ones, and they may well survive better than they would as tourist attractions.

Conclusion

The management of historic buildings and their settings as tourism operations must always be constrained by the key objective—the needs of the building. However, that requirement does not mean that clear objectives and a well-planned and efficient tourism operation which maximises income generation without jeopardising the building cannot be attained. Visiting historic buildings is a popular tourism and leisure activity from which the public can gain enjoyment and learn about their own, or another society's, past. That so many people do visit means that a well-managed tourism operation should be able to contribute effectively to maintaining the building—which is what the public would hope that their visit would do.

Notes

1. Information about the R. H. Koc museum from Mr J. Minns, British Engineerium, Hove, who is the designer.

2. Information from knowledge gained as a member of the Regional Committee for the Kent and East Sussex region of the National Trust, who are well briefed on issues—also well covered in press releases from the Regional Public Affairs Office.

References

Amery, C. (1990) 'Little house of horrors', *Financial Times*, 30 April.

Berry, S. and Standeven, J. (1992) 'East Sussex tourism survey attractions report', Leisure Research Unit, University of Brighton.

Durrant, J. (Ed.) (1992) *Museums and the Public Understanding of Science*, Science Museum, London, pp. 7–9.

Girouard, M. (1980) *Life in the English Country House*, Penguin, Harmondsworth, pp. 2–3.

Hewison, R. (1987) *The Heritage Industry*, Methuen, London.

Iley, S. J. E. (1993) 'Befriending museums', *Recreation Museums*, **51**(3): 27–39.

NAO (1992) *Protecting and Managing England's Heritage Property*, National Audit Office, p. 40.

Rumble, P. (1988a) 'Dwelling in a false past?', *Conservation Bulletin*, June: 3.

Rumble, P. (1988b) 'Conservation, good or bad', *Conservation Bulletin*, February: 4.

Tait, S. (1980) 'National finders and keepers', *The Times*, 18 December: 17.

Waterson, M. (1992) 'Opening doors on the past', in D. Uzzell (Ed.), *Heritage Interpretation*, Belhaven, London, pp. 48–56.

Part 7

TOURISM AND SOCIETY

As well as constituting an area of economic activity tourism is a major social force in both its destination and originating regions. Though social and societal critiques of tourism had been prominent elements in early popular analyses of tourism (e.g. Young, 1973; Turner and Ash, 1975), it is only in the last 10–15 years that they have been taken on board in managerial analyses, particularly through the currency of 'community tourism' first advocated by Murphy (1985). Even today there is still something of a divide between practitioners and managerial writers primarily interested in tourism's economic potential, and social scientists more concerned about its social impacts. The two orientations need to be seen as complementary in tourism practice and education if future tourism development is not to be experienced as a blight as much as a blessing (Seaton, 1991).

This part brings together papers examining tourism demand and supply as social and societal phenomena, drawing on theoretical perspectives derived from anthropology, sociology, urban analysis, semiotics and history.

The subjects of the papers comprise: a critical historiography of tourism as a historical phenomenon (Towner); appraisals of the development of tourism anthropology (Selwyn) and the sociology of hospitality (Wood); an overview on cross-cultural encounters in tourism (Reisinger's paper, which develops rather ambitious prescriptions in the wake of earlier work by Bochner and his associates (1984)); an exploration of host coping strategies in tourism-receiving areas (Brown and Giles); studies in tourism representation of destinations and travel (Wilson, Dann); an assessment of the relationship between tourism and traditional crafts (Evans); an examination of managerial practices at a major tourist attraction in Edinburgh in relation to postmodernist formulations of 'the tourist gaze' (Foley); and research into what seems likely to become a fast-developing area, tourism and health (Page, Clift and Clark). There are five socio-cultural case studies which include an engagingly fresh typology of Greek tourists (Wickens), a rigorously conducted study of tourism impacts in York (Snaith and Haley), a look at the impacts of tourism development in Mexico and in Malaysia (Evans, Holden) and an unusual attempt at comparative analysis of conflict in Chinese tourism, using both Western and Chinese theoretical perspectives (Li and Sofield).

The contributions that focus on specific regions represent a bias that deserves comment—a preoccupation with the effects of Western tourism demand upon less-developed nations of tourism supply (Evans's two papers, Holden, Reisinger, Li and Sofield, Wilson). This was also evident in two seminal collections on tourism's socio-cultural impacts (Smith, 1979; Smith and Eadington, 1992). The bias, which parallels anthropology's long, but changing, preoccupation with 'primitive' societies rather than more 'modern' ones, reflects a principled prioritising of regions where unequal power balances within the tourism development process put at risk vulnerable host communities and environments. However, long-haul tourism is a small proportion of total international tourism flows and, for the future, it is important that socio-cultural analysis should not lose sight of mass tourism-receiving regions in Europe, if the field is not to appear structured by a particular kind of romanticism preoccupied with cultural transformations in faraway places which excite less interest at home. Blackpool, Butlins, city tourism (viz. the Snaith and Haley paper) and other developed tourism forms are as worthy of serious, socio-cultural examination as exotic embodiments of the 'other' in Fiji, Java and Mexico. It is to be hoped that in the future writers will produce more cultural studies of mass tourism supply and demand closer to home, and perhaps make more explicit the relationship between their own value systems and their subjects. This will lessen the impression that, behind the cultivated Olympian impartiality of the commentator, lurks a long-haul travel freak, driven by a tacit, romantic conservatism, seeking to preserve the primitive/natural from the commercial/industrial—while enjoying the benefits of both. Papers on the research-funded anthropologist as elite, super-tourist have still to be written.

A. V. Seaton, University of Strathclyde

References

Bochner, Stephen (1984) *Cultures in Contact*, Pergamon, Oxford.

Murphy, Peter E. (1985) *Tourism: a Community Approach*, Routledge, London.

Seaton, A. V. (1991) 'Tourism education in the 1990s: business, science or humanity', in Bratton, R. D., Go, F. M. and Brent Ritchie, J. R. (Eds), *New Horizons in Tourism and Hospitality Education, Training and Research*, University of Calgary, Calgary, pp. 427–438.

Smith, Valene L. (1979, revised 1989) *Hosts and Guests: the Anthropology of Tourism*, University of Pennsylvania Press, Pennsylvania.

Smith, Valene L. and Eadington, William R. (1992) *Tourism Alternatives*, University of Pennsylvania, Pennsylvania.

Turner, Louis and Ash, John (1975) *The Golden Hordes*, Constable, London.

Young, George (1973) *Tourism: Blessing or Blight?*, Penguin, Harmondsworth.

75 Tourism history: past, present and future

J. TOWNER

Tourism has a long history. We know of its existence in ancient Egypt (Casson, 1974) and it seems reasonable to assume that travel for pleasure would have been a feature of many past societies where levels of productivity were sufficient to sustain forms of leisure (Nash, 1978). And yet, our knowledge is highly biased towards Western and Classical societies and we remain remarkably ignorant about tourism in other past worlds. How, for instance, did tourism evolve in China or parts of India? It seems highly unlikely that tourism was a purely Western invention.

This fundamental bias in the historical record is perhaps the most noticeable feature of tourism's past but, even within Western societies, our understanding is highly selective. Much of what we know and think is important about the evolution of tourism is conditioned by particular historical perspectives. The focus of this paper is, therefore, on the historiography of tourism history, as it developed in the past, its present state and its future prospects.

Research into tourism's history has consisted of two main characteristics. The first concerns the distinct themes which have attracted attention. These themes include the tourism activities of particular groups of people, generally the wealthy, and a concern with the development of particular tourism places such as spas and seaside resorts. This is partly, but not entirely, due to the nature of historical source material which tends to favour the powerful in society. In most cases the dramatic and prestigious episodes have triumphed over the ordinary and regular.

The second characteristic of research relates to the groups undertaking the work. This includes not only professional historians but also social science tourism specialists. In addition, these two distinct camps have been joined by a considerable number of popular writers attracted by the apparent éclat of the subject matter and its nostalgic appeal to modern readers (e.g. Gregory, 1991; Wechsberg, 1979). Each group has brought its own distinctive perspective to tourism's history.

The past

Research into tourism history before the 1970s helped to illuminate three broad areas: travel and tourism in the ancient worlds, Grand Touring in the 17th and 18th centuries and the growth of spas and seaside resorts (Towner and Wall, 1991). A further, closely related field, was the study of changing tastes and fashions for landscape and the arts, which clearly had an influence on tourists' choice and evaluation of destinations.

Some of the earliest research into tourism history was done at the beginning of this century. Ludwig Friedländer (1907), in his study of life and manners in ancient Rome, wrote extensively on travel and the emergence of second-home villas for wealthy Romans on the Bay of Naples. This pioneering effort was not really supplemented until the 1960s and early 1970s when Balsdon (1969) wrote his major study of life and leisure in Rome, and Lindsay (1965) and D'Arms (1976) wrote of leisure and pleasure in Egypt and the Bay of Naples. Tourism in the ancient world received its most recent authoritative summary with the work of Lionel Casson (1974) who considered its significance in Egypt, Greece and Rome. Classical sources have provided a rich quarry for historians ranging from literary records, inscriptions and graffiti to archaeological remains. The latter have enabled researchers to investigate the size and layout of villas, hotels and restaurants in ancient Rome (D'Arms, 1976; Kleberg, 1957), whilst the writings of Horace, Virgil, Pliny the Younger and others, provide a vivid evocation of villa life for the rich and powerful (Ackerman, 1990).

Most of the research on tourism in the ancient world has been undertaken by classical scholars and has been characterised by a thorough command of source materials and a meticulous approach to the subject. Past research in this particular area means that we know more about forms of tourism in, for instance, ancient Rome, than we do for many later periods of history.

The prestigious Grand Tours of Europe which developed in the 16th, 17th and 18th centuries, were also the subject of early research. Bates (1911) and Mead (1914) produced detailed studies of British continental travel in the 17th and 18th centuries making use of diaries, letters and journals of the aristocracy and gentry as well as contemporary guidebooks. Continental travel was not confined to the British, however, but it was not until Schudt's (1959) work that other nationalities were included in a major review. The role of the Grand Tour in developing aesthetic tastes and creating art collections in Britain has received exhaustive attention from art historians (for instance, Bowron, 1982; Burgess and Haskell, 1967; Ford, 1981; Haskell, 1959; Sutton, 1982), perhaps reinforcing the image of past tourism as an exclusively upper-class and essentially cultural experience.

Scholarly work on the Grand Tour has always been supplemented by a vast array of popular works. Amusing anecdotes, extensive illustrative material and the nostalgic appeal of a 'golden age of travel', help explain this enthusiasm. These popular books have been of variable quality (although always aesthetically pleasing), though Hibbert's (1969) was a good account of some aspects of the tour itself. Scholarly and popular works all shared one characteristic, however. They focused exclusively on the attitudes and activities of the tourists themselves. The tour has rarely been placed in a wider social context and the views of the host society remain largely unknown (Towner, 1985). Even more recent research on the Grand Tour has tended to follow a well-worn path (Black, 1992).

Another major theme for past research has been the development of specific tourist locations, especially spas and seaside resorts. These are large-scale tourist forms which have created their own source material and contemporary commentary. A stimulating early work on English watering places was undertaken by Reginald Lennard (1931) in the early 1930s based on a close analysis of primary data. The same theme was explored by Carl Bridenbaugh's (1946) pioneering research into the spas of colonial America. Broader themes of general tourism were explored by Moir (1964) for England and Dulles (1940) for the United States. Seaside resort development in England was studied at an early date by the historical geographer E. W. Gilbert (1939, 1954), who was notable in considering the wider implications of resorts beyond the comings and goings of the rich and influential. During the 1960s, French historians produced a number of papers relating to activities of the English upper classes at French seaside and mountain resorts (Boyer, 1962, 1963; Duloum, 1963, 1970; Joly, 1963). As with the Grand Tour, a preoccupation with the lives of the rich, together with entertaining anecdotal material, resulted in a host of popular works on spas and seaside resorts which Walton (1983) characterised as 'journalistic in tone and of little scholarly merit'.

Standing in complete contrast, however, was the classic work of J. A. R. Pimlott (1947). He produced an outstanding survey of the Englishman's holiday from Elizabethan times to the 20th century. He ranged from spas and seaside resorts to continental touring, from the activities of the rich to those of the poor. He was particularly ingenious in his search for primary data, trawling not only diaries, letters, journals and guide books, but also newspapers, periodicals, official reports, novels and illustrations. For breadth of coverage and research, his book remains unsurpassed.

One other theme that past research has illuminated is that of the aesthetics of tourism; the changing tastes and fashions of the tourists, especially their evaluations of landscapes. Hussey (1927) provided an early examination of the rise of picturesque taste and a scholarly analysis of 18th-century aesthetic theories was developed by Hipple (1957). A literary analysis of travel by Parks (1964) related changing tastes, especially the rise of romantic conceptions, to tourism activity and this was but one of many studies which included the aesthetics of travel (for instance, Burke, 1968; Brand, 1957; Manwaring, 1925; Nicolson, 1955).

Three major works moved beyond the aesthetics of tourism to embrace the links with philosophical and scientific movements. Frantz (1934) showed how 17th-century travellers in Europe, in their tireless accumulation of lists and measurements of all they saw, reflected the scientific inductive philosophies of Bacon and Descartes. Fussell (1965) related the 'empirical tourism' of 18th-century travellers to the humanist outlook of the Augustan age where the quest was for evidence of enduring, human reason. Marjorie Hope Nicolson (1959), sought to explain the developing taste for mountain and wild scenery in the late 17th and early 18th centuries by the rise of scientific thought. She argued that this new taste, which was to have a profound influence on changing tourist itineraries and landscape evaluations, was due to science changing people's awe for God to an awe for an expanded cosmos which included mountains and other remote areas. Recent work which continues this strong tradition of landscape taste and tourism include Andrews (1989), Lowenthal and Prince (1965) and Newby (1981).

Past research into tourism history has thus developed a number of particular themes. Despite evident strengths in ancient tourism, Grand Touring, spas, seaside resorts and aesthetics, a distorted picture of the past was, nevertheless, produced. Studies tended to focus on the activities of a social elite, especially when they engaged in dramatic and prestigious events. The importance of particular forms of tourism tended to become equated with quantifiable measures such as length of time spent on holiday and the amount of money expended. Thus, the *significance* of tourism in people's lives was generally overlooked. A short holiday, once a year, could be more important for some people than a lengthy winter season in Nice or Cannes for others. The attitudes of host societies and the wider social, economic and political contexts of tourism also received scant attention. Wealthy tourists, and their activities in particular destination areas, created the dominant picture of tourism's history.

The present

There are two notable developments in tourism history research today. The first is the growing interest of social historians in leisure. Historians subsume tourism within the wider arena of leisure and they avoid the awkward and rather artificial breakdown of the subject into either leisure, or recreation, or tourism. Not only has the field been empirically expanded, but historians have introduced a much-needed theoretical and ideological debate into the evolution of leisure. Without engaging in this debate, tourism history would be in danger of becoming merely a superficial preface to contemporary tourism research.

The second major development in tourism history research has been the attempt by some tourism social science researchers to provide an historical perspective on models and concepts evolved for present-day tourism. If these models and concepts were to acquire an acceptable 'depth' of explanation, then relating them to past circumstances would strengthen their claim to validity.

Walton and Walvin (1983) and Bailey (1989) have provided valuable summaries of the developments in leisure history in Britain since the 1970s and they both identify certain important characteristics. A major focus of historical research has been into the leisure experience of the working class and its transformation in the late 18th and early 19th centuries (Bailey, 1979; Malcolmson, 1973; Rule 1986). From seeing leisure closely integrated with the world of work, historians have debated the extent to which leisure was broken down or transformed under the pressures of urbanisation and industrialisation. Leisure emerged in new ways in the later 19th century—ways which included tourism (Walton, 1981; Walton and Walvin, 1983).

As well as emphasising that the working classes also had forms of tourism, social historians have argued the underlying causes of change. Leisure (and hence tourism) was not just a consequence of the industrial revolution, technological change and class structures. Nor were leisure activities simply passed down from one social class to another. Both Cunningham (1980) and Thompson (1963) argue that working-class culture had its own momentum and was not simply a passive recipient of ideas from above. Similarly, Thompson (1988) has recently shown that 19th-century middle-class leisure practices were not just derived from the upper classes, but evolved in a much more intricate manner that did not adhere to simple class stereotypes. Not only were these social divisions complex, but as Walton (1981) Walton and Walvin (1983) and Cunningham (1990) emphasise, there were significant regional and local differences in leisure habits in Britain. These important variations in demand areas deserve further exploration (see below).

There has also been a useful debate over the role of transport technology in tourism development. A simplistic view of railways 'creating' seaside resorts is debated by Walton (1983) and Simmons (1986). Railways created certain *patterns* of tourism but growth may have occurred in different ways without them.

These ideas have clear implications for tourism history. So often, a picture is presented of tourism's evolution being driven by changes in transport (Burkart and Medlik, 1990) or the mechanistic process of successive class intrusion (Cosgrove and Jackson, 1972; Pearce, 1982). Bailey's (1989) view on the evolution of leisure as 'a process that has been erratic, complex and contentious' is a useful corrective to simplistic notions of the evolution of tourism.

Certain social history works have made a major contribution to our understanding of tourism. John Walton's (1981) research on working-class tourism in 19th-century Lancashire is notable because he explored conditions in the destination areas (the resorts) but balanced this with the particular circumstances evolving in the generating areas (the Lancashire mill towns). This even balance is also found in his work on the English seaside resort (Walton, 1983). Together with McGloin, Walton has also provided a useful critique of historical research techniques (Walton and McGloin, 1979, 1981). Urban historians have also produced stimulating work related to tourism. Neale's (1981) Marxist perspective on the growth of Bath is a refreshing change to the usual catalogue of famous visitors to the spa, and he includes a consideration of the wider impacts of tourism including local labour demands. Elsewhere, Borsay (1989) and McInnes (1988) have debated the emergence of provincial 'leisure' towns in England outside the world of the spas and seaside resorts. This richer and more balanced view of leisure and tourism can also be seen in Haug's (1982) study of the effect of tourism on Nice in the 19th century. Using census data, he isolates the main tourist, local middle-class and local working-class areas of the city and considers the unequal provision of services between the wealthy and the poor. For Haug, the rich visitors, so intriguing to others (Graves, 1957) are 'not very interesting individually' but provided the force that caused important changes elsewhere in the area.

The rising interest of social science researchers in tourism history is probably most clearly marked by the collection of writings on the evolution of recreation and tourism in Canada edited by Wall and Marsh (1982), and a special issue of the *Annals of Tourism Research* edited by Butler and Wall (1985). In the former, historical analyses are provided mainly by geographers who are interested in tracing the relationship between people and environments as revealed by recreation and tourism. In the latter, most of the articles are written by social scientists and a dominant feature of the papers is the attempt to use models and conceptual frameworks to organise and inform research. Thus, Meyer-Arendt uses Butler's (1980) cycle of tourist area evolution to study the development of Grand Isle, Louisiana, as does Hugill for examining early 20th-century automobile touring in the USA. Wightman and Wall link spa development in the Canadian Rockies to Nelson's (1974) framework for studying national parks and Towner relates the Grand Tour to Leiper's (1979) conceptualisation of the overall tourism system.

One of the major problems inherent in these attempts is the lack of historical data which enables models to be rigorously tested. For example, Butler's model has been used extensively (e.g. Cooper and Jackson, 1989) but the absence of consistent and accurate data raises questions about the degree of *post hoc* reasoning involved. The general conceptual frameworks evolved by social scientists are, however, of value in identifying and structuring the complex interrelationships arising from leisure, recreation and tourism and ensuring that an holistic view is taken of processes and outcomes (Pearce, 1989; Thurot, 1980).

What is particularly noticeable about the present state of tourism history research is that, despite being an interdisciplinary field of interest, there are few substantive links between historians and social scientists (Towner, 1988; Towner and Wall, 1991). There seem to be no methodological barriers to closer cooperation as both history and the social issues increasingly share a whole range of approaches. And yet, few historians publish papers in tourism journals, and few tourism researchers seem aware of the substantial body of research developed in leisure history. This is a major weakness, because it is often at the frontiers between different disciplines that the most interesting and useful research occurs.

The future

The future of tourism history research will be influenced by a whole range of issues. There are, however, a number of ideas that can be explored. These include: (1) the need for closer interdisciplinary links, (2) the integration of tourism within the wider leisure field, (3) the value of a lifestyle/life cycle approach, (4) the use of an holistic systems approach, (5) the development of non-Western perspectives on tourism's evolution, and (6) the use of a wider range of source material in research.

The need for closer interdisciplinary links has been argued for above and does not need further amplification. Integrating tourism history within the wider field of leisure, recreation and tourism is part of this process. The absence of sub-divisions within leisure has enabled historians to research the whole interconnected world of leisure without becoming preoccupied with classifying activities as leisure or recreation or tourism. In North America much relevant research appears under the heading of 'recreation' and communication between disciplines is frustrated by this seemingly trivial difference (Towner and Wall, 1991; Wall, 1989). Furthermore, as Hughes (1991) recently points out, the creation of a separate 'discipline' of tourism owes more to the demands of the 'industry' than to scholarly endeavour.

Tourism history could profitably explore the lifestyle/life cycle approach to leisure (Glyptis, 1981). So often, research focuses on particular tourism episodes—going to spas, going to the seaside, going on the Grand Tour—rather than considering how these episodes related to other aspects of people's leisure lifestyles. Furthermore, these leisure lifestyles need to be incorporated into the life cycle. How did patterns of tourism change for individuals through their lives? The availability of suitable primary data presents a problem here, but there is a body of information in the form of long-term diaries that enable some research to be undertaken. The episodic approach to tourism history has tended to ignore the longer-term, almost routine practices. The rhythms and structures of usual life and the role of leisure and tourism within this framework can easily be distorted by a focus on intermittent events. So, we find the Grand Tour taking precedence over the regular migration of Venetian merchants to their country villas (Muraro, 1986). The annual cycle of informal hospitality amongst the gentry of England (Heal, 1990) can be overshadowed by the visits to spas and seaside resorts. The self-help creation of holiday-homes by the relatively poor (Hardy and Ward, 1984) or the development of a weekend cottage zone around Paris (Green, 1990; Herbert, 1988) becomes obscured by a focus on Thomas Cook's tours abroad.

Tourism history can be usefully viewed within an holistic systems framework which is related to wider social, economic, political and technological worlds. Research needs not only to consider tourist destination areas and transport routes but also to explore processes in the tourist-generating areas (Lieper, 1979; Pearce, 1989). Understanding the development of Blackpool, Coney Island, Nice or Cannes requires research into conditions in the centres of demand as much as activities at destinations. As discussed above, historians have pointed to important local and regional variations in leisure cultures (Abrams, 1992; Crump, 1986; Cunningham, 1990; Davies, 1992; King, 1987; Walton and Walvin, 1983). Generating areas cannot, therefore, be considered as uniform regions. Leisure varied not just with social strata but from place to place.

In tourist destination areas, more attention needs to be given to the effects of tourism in creating centres of consumption. Thus, food, fuel and a whole range of direct and indirect services are involved (Haug, 1982; Hembry, 1990; Neale, 1981). Tourism history has tended to be preoccupied with the activities of the holiday-makers at the expense of impacts on the host society. Leisure historians have already highlighted issues of power and control of resources and development (Cannadine, 1980; Neale, 1981; Roberts, 1983; Walton, 1983) which can often be usefully related to the balance between core and periphery areas (Britton, 1982).

The tourism system is dynamic. As well as considering the processes which created particular systems, examining change and continuity in those systems is an important area of research (Cunningham, 1990). Were some changes a reflection of technological shifts in transport or due to more deep-seated cultural change? The pace of change also needs consideration. Some systems showed remarkable long-term endurance, such as the allure of southern Europe for north Europeans. Other systems experienced rapid rise and fall. Distinguishing between the more profound influences on change and continuity and the more superficial veneer of fashion remains a major task for research.

Tourism history needs to become more ideologically aware. Many commonly held views derived from past writings are laden with unstated value-judgements. Spas 'declined' when the upper classes forsook them for more exclusive destinations, seaside resorts 'waned' when their social tone altered. No matter that the actual numbers of visitors increased; they were the wrong sort of visitors. This view permeates the idea of the 'golden age of the traveller' before vulgar tourism began and can be traced in modern critiques of tourism (Boorstin, 1964).

The lack of attention paid to gender is also a reflection of these unstated biases. Women have generally remained hidden from tourism history, whether as tourists (Mains, 1966; Meyer, 1978; Pemble, 1987) or as workers (Bouquet, 1985; Neale, 1981), yet their significance was clearly very great. The rapid expansion of research in this area of leisure history is uncovering a major omission in the historical record (Davies, 1992).

A further major bias in research was highlighted at the beginning of this paper. The history of tourism is primarily the history of west European (especially British) and North American tourism. As well as dominating empirical research, Western concepts of leisure and tourism dominate the picture. How they have been manifested in other societies in the past remains virtually unknown. It can be argued that correcting this one-sided view of history is, in fact, the main task for future tourism history research.

Finally, some observations can be made about the range of source material used in research. Until now, much of our knowledge has been derived from a fairly limited range of information. The letters, diaries and journals of a restricted group of tourists together with guide books have generally formed the basis for much research in the pre-19th-century era. After that, census data becomes available, and this is supplemented from the 1920s by a growing volume of official tourist statistics. These sources have been reviewed in detail by Pimlott (1947), Walton and McGloin (1979) and Towner (1988) and so will not be discussed at length here. Rather, three potentially fruitful and under-used sources will be outlined.

For the very recent historical past, the possibilities of oral history are especially attractive. This approach has been used in important studies of leisure in Manchester and Salford by Davies (1992) and has also been used in a Scottish context by Blair (1985) and Smout and Wood (1990). Particularly important here is the opportunity to explore the leisure and tourism experiences of a wide range of people and to place these experiences within their everyday lives. Recent work by Cross (1990) shows how the mass observation surveys of the late 1930s, despite their methodological weaknesses, can give a vivid insight into attitudes towards leisure in the near past.

Works of fiction, especially novels, can provide valuable insights into the mentalities of a culture and their potential for tourism history was briefly noted by Pimlott in 1947. Nevertheless, no systematic review has been made of the vast amount of material that could be used. Herbert (1991) has shown how novels like Jane Austen's can be used to capture the sense of place as experienced by people in the past—a valuable context for understanding their leisure. Jane Austen's books are full of direct references to leisure and tourism in polite society in early 19th-century England, as are the earlier works of Smollett, Fielding and Sterne. In later periods, the social novels of Dickens, Trollope and Henry James provide a rich vein of information as do those of H. G. Wells and Arnold Bennett. Bennett's *Anna of the Five Towns* (1902) for instance, has a marvellous portrayal of the anticipation and excitement of a first holiday away from home—a visit to the Isle of Man from the Potteries. No statistics can capture that significant event in someone's life. Thomas Mann's *Buddenbrooks* (1901) gives us an understanding of the role played by the seaside at Travemunde for the wealthy merchant classes of Lubeck on the north German coast. Further examples are boundless. However, in addition to cataloguing these works, methods of analysis and interpretation have to be devised. Their potential is to provide not only factual details but an appreciation of the role of leisure and tourism in past cultures.

The visual arts are a further source of information that have been little used. A major review of visual images in historical interpretation has recently been produced by Haskell (1993) which forms a useful starting point for explorations of this kind. For the world of pleasure, visual images may simply be ways of piecing together past activities, whether in paintings, cartoons or photographs. More subtle interpretation is possible, however. Ludolf de Jonghe's *Farewells Before a Country House* for instance, portrays a whole world of 17th-century Dutch leisure culture (Schama, 1987). For mid-19th-century France, the social art historian Robert Herbert (1988) links Impressionist art, leisure and Parisian society together and demonstrates the potential of fusing picture analysis with socio-historical material in exploring ideas of leisure and tourism in past societies. Thus, literary works of fiction and the visual arts should not be seen as merely surrogates for the lack of tourism statistics in the past. They can, if used with sensitivity, be a way of gaining insight into the world of leisure and tourism in the lives of people in other ages.

Conclusion

This paper has reviewed work on the history of tourism as it has developed since the early years of this century. As well as referring to some of the main works in the field, the paper has indicated the strengths and weaknesses in our knowledge about tourism's past. It has also suggested some possible research developments for the future.

There are, perhaps, two outstanding tasks that need repeating. The first concerns developing closer links between historians and their research on leisure history and the mainstream tourism research of social scientists. If our knowledge of tourism is to acquire 'depth', then tourism history should not simply be an uncritical but diverting introduction to tourism textbooks but a substantial area of research in its own right. The second task is the development of historical research in non-Western societies. A modern tourism 'industry' may be the creation of western Europe and North America but that is not the only model which may be valid. Other societies in other periods could have had their own versions of tourism.

We are constantly told that tourism is set to be the world's largest industry. If that is so, a greater appreciation of its origins and diversity would seem well justified.

References

Abrams, L. (1992) *Workers' Culture in Imperial Germany*, Routledge, London.

Ackerman, J. S. (1990) *The Villa: Form and Ideology of Country Houses*, Thames & Hudson, London.

Andrews, M. (1989) *The Search for the Picturesque: Landscape Aesthetics and Tourism in Britain, 1760–1800*, Scholar Press, Aldershot.

Bailey, P. (1979) *Leisure and Class in Victorian England*, Methuen, London.

Bailey, P. (1989) 'Leisure, culture and the historian: reviewing the first generation of leisure historiography in Britain', *Leisure Studies*, 8: 107–127.

Balsdon, J. P. V. D. (1969) *Life and Leisure in Ancient Rome*, The Bodley Head, London.

Bates, E. S. (1911) *Touring in 1600*, Constable, London.

Black, J. (1992) *The British Abroad: The Grand Tour in the Eighteenth Century*, St Martin's Press, New York.

Blair, A. (1985) *Tea at Miss Cranston's*, Shepheard-Walwyn, London.

Boorstin, D. (1964) *The Image: A Guide to Pseudo-events in America*, Harper, New York.

Borsay, P. (1989) *The English Urban Renaissance*, Clarendon, Oxford.

Bouquet, M. (1985) *Family Servants and Visitors: The Farm Household in Nineteenth and Twentieth Century Devon*, Geo Books, Norwich.

Bowron, E. P. (1982) *Pompeo Batoni and his British Patrons*, Greater London Council, London.

Boyer, M. (1962) 'Hyères, station d'hivernants au XIXe siecle', *Provence Historique*, 12: 139–165.

Boyer, M. (1963) Le caractère saisonnier du phénomène touristique à l'époque aristocratique et ses conséquences économiques, *Université Aix-Marseille: Annales de la Faculté de Droit et des Sciences Economiques*, 53: 27–51.

Brand, C. P. (1957) 'A bibliography of travel books describing Italy published in England 1800–1850', *Italian Studies*, 11: 108–117.

Bridenbaugh, C. (1946) 'Baths and watering places of colonial America', *William and Mary Quarterly* (third series), 3(2): 151–181.

Britton, S. G. (1982) 'The political economy of tourism in the third world', *Annals of Tourism Research*, 9(3): 331–358.

Burgess, A. and Haskell, F. (1967) *The Age of the Grand Tour*, Crown, New York.

Burkart, A. J. and Medlik, S. (1990) 'Historical development of tourism', Centre des Hautes Etudes Touristique, Aix-en-Provence.

Burke, J. (1968) 'The Grand Tour and the role of taste', in R. F. Brissenden (Ed.), *Studies in the Eighteenth Century*, Australian National University, Canberra, pp. 231–250.

Butler, R. W. (1980) 'The concept of a tourism area cycle of evolution: implications for management of resources', *Canadian Geographer*, 24: 5–12.

Butler, R. W. and Wall, G. (Eds) (1985) 'The evolution of tourism: historical and contemporary perspectives', special issue, *Annals of Tourism Research*, 12(3).

Cannadine, D. (1980) *Lords and Landlords: the Aristocracy and the Towns 1774–1967*, Leicester University Press, Leicester.

Casson, L. (1974) *Travel in the Ancient World*, Allen & Unwin, London.

Cooper, C. and Jackson, S. (1989) 'Destination life cycle: the Isle of Man case study', *Annals of Tourism Research*, 16: 377–398.

Cosgrove, I. and Jackson, R. (1972) *The Geography of Recreation and Tourism*, Hutchinson, London.

Cross, G. (1990) *Worktowners at Blackpool: Mass-Observation and Popular Leisure in the 1930s*, Routledge, London.

Crump, J. (1986) 'Recreation in Coventry between the wars', in W. Lancaster and A. Mason (Eds), *Life and Labour in a Twentieth Century City: the Experience of Coventry*, Cryfield Press, London.

Cunningham, H. (1980) *Leisure in the Industrial Revolution: 1780–1880*, Croom Helm, London.

Cunningham, H. (1990) 'Leisure and culture', in F. M. L. Thompson (Ed.), *The Cambridge Social History of Britain 1750–1950*, Vol. 2, *People and their Environment*, Cambridge University Press, Cambridge.

D'Arms, J. (1976) *Romans on the Bay of Naples*, Harvard University Press, Cambridge, MA.

Davies, A. (1992) *Leisure, Gender and Poverty. Working Class Culture in Salford and Manchester, 1900–1939*, Open University Press, Buckingham.

Dulles, F. R. (1940) *A History of Recreation: America Learns to Play*, Appleton-Century, New York.

Duloum, J. (1963) 'Naissance, dévelopement et déclin de la colonie anglaise de Pau (1814–1914)', *Université Aix-Marseille, Annales de la Faculté de Droit et des Sciences Economiques*, 53: 65–77.

Duloum, J. (1970) *Les Anglais dans les Pyrénés 1739–1896*, Les Amis du Musée Pyrénéen, Lourdes.

Ford, B. (1981) 'The Grand Tour', *Appoll*, 114: 390–400.

Frantz, R. W. (1934) *The English Traveller and the Movement of Ideas, 1660–1732* (reprint edition, 1968), Octagon, New York.

Friedländer, L. (1907) *Roman Life and Manners under the Early Empire*, transl. by L. A. Magnus (reprint edition, 1965), Routledge & Kegan Paul, London.

Fussell, P. (1965) *The Rhetorical World of Augustan Humanism*, Clarendon Press, Oxford.

Gilbert, E. W. (1939) 'The growth of inland and seaside health resorts in England', *Scottish Geographical Magazine*, 5: 116–135.

Gilbert, E. W. (1954) *Brighton: Old Ocean's Bauble*, Methuen, London.

Glyptis, S. A. (1981) 'Leisure life styles', *Regional Studies*, 311–326.

Graves, C. (1957) *Royal Riviera*, Heinemann, London.

Green, N. (1990) *The Spectacle of Nature: Landscape and Bourgeois Culture in Nineteenth Century France*, Manchester University Press, Manchester.

Gregory, A. (1991) *The Golden Age of Travel, 1880–1939*, Cassell, London.

Hardy, D. and Ward, C. (1984) *Arcadia for All: the Legacy of a Makeshift Landscape*, Mansell, London.

Haskell, F. (1959) 'The market for Italian art in the seventeenth century', *Past and Present*, 15: 48–59.

Haskell, F. (1993) *History and its Images: Art and the Interpretation of the Past*, Yale University Press, New Haven, CT.

Haug, C. J. (1982) *Leisure and Urbanism in Nineteenth Century Nice*, Regents Press, Lawrence, KS.

Heal, F. (1990) *Hospitality in Early Modern England*, Clarendon Press, Oxford.

Hembry, P. M. (1900) *The English Spa 1560–1815: a Social History*, Athlone Press, London.

Herbert, D. (1991) 'Place and society in Jane Austen's England', *Geography*, 193–208.

Herbert, R. L. (1988) *Impressionism: Art, Leisure and Parisian Society*, Yale University Press, New York.

Hibbert, C. (1969) *The Grand Tour*, Putnam, London.

Hipple, W. J. (1957) The beautiful, the sublime, and the picturesque in eighteenth century British aesthetic theory, Southern Illinois University, Illinois.

Hughes, G. (1991) 'Conceiving of tourism', *Area*, 23(3): 263–267.

Hussey, C. (1927) *The Picturesque* (reprint edition, 1967), Cass, London.

Joly, J. (1963) 'Le tourisme britanique en Savoie et en Dauphiné', *Revue de Geographie Alpine*, 51: 43–107.

King, E. (1987) 'Popular culture in Glasgow', in R. A. Cage (Ed.), *The Working Class in Glasgow 1750–1914*, Croom Helm, London.

Kleberg, T. (1957) *Hotels, Restaurants et Cabarets dans l'Antiquité Romaine*, Bibliotheca Ekmaniana 61, Uppsala.

Lennard, R. (1931) *Englishmen at Rest and Play: Some Phases of English Leisure, 1558–1714*, Clarendon Press, London.

Lieper, N. (1979) 'The framework of tourism: towards a definition of tourism, tourist, and the tourist industry', *Annals of Tourism Research*, 6(4): 390–407.

Lindsay, J. (1965) *Leisure and Pleasure in Roman Egypt*, Muller, London.

Lowenthal, D. and Prince, H. (1965) 'English landscape tastes', *Geographical Review*, 55: 186–222.

McInnes, A. (1988) 'The emergence of a leisure town: Shrewsbury 1660–1760', *Past and Present*, 120: 53–87.

Mains, J. A. (1966) 'British travellers in Switzerland, with special reference to some women travellers between 1750 and 1850', University of Edinburgh doctoral dissertation.

Malcolmson, R. W. (1973) *Popular Recreations in English Society, 1700–1850*, Cambridge University Press, Cambridge.

Manwaring, E. (1925) *Italian Landscape in Eighteenth Century England*, Oxford University Press, Oxford.

Mead, W. E. (1914) *The Grand Tour in the Eighteenth Century*, Houghton Mifflin, New York.

Meyer, P. J. B. (1978) 'No land too remote: women travellers in the Georgian age', University of Massachusetts doctoral dissertation.

Moir, E. (1964) *The Discovery of Britain: the English Tourists, 1540–1840*, Routledge & Kegan Paul, London.

Muraro, M. (1986) *Venetian Villas: the History and Culture*, Rizzoli, New York.

Nash, D. (1978) 'Tourism as a form of imperialism', in V. L. Smith (Ed.), *Hosts and Guests*, Blackwell, Oxford.

Neale, R. S. (1981) *Bath: a Social History, 1680–1850*, Routledge & Kegan Paul, London.

Nelson, J. G. (1974) 'Canadian national parks and related reserves: research needs and management', in J. G. Nelson, R. C. Scace and R. Kauri (Eds), *Canadian Public Land Use in Perspective*, Social Science Research Council of Canada, Ottawa.

Newby, P. T. (1981) 'Literature and the fashioning of tourist taste', in D. C. D. Pocock (Ed)., *Humanistic Geography and Literature*, Croom Helm, London.

Nicolson, M. H. (1959) *Mountain Gloom and Mountain Glory*, Cornell University Press, Ithaca, NY.

Nicolson, N. (1955) *The Lakers: the First Tourists*, Hale, London.

Parks, G. B. (1964) 'The turn to the romantic in the travel literature of the eighteenth century', *Modern Language Quarterly*, 25: 22–33.

Pearce, D. (1989) *Tourist Development*, Longman, Harlow.

Pearce, P. L. (1982) *The Social Psychology of Tourist Behaviour*, Pergamon Press, Oxford.

Pemble, J. (1987) *The Mediterranean Passion: Victorians and Edwardians in the South*, Oxford Univerity Press, Oxford.

Pimlott, J. A. R. (1947) *The Englishman's Holiday*, Faber & Faber, London.

Roberts, R. (1983) 'The corporation as impresario: The municipal provision of entertainment in Victorian and Edwardian Bournemouth', in J. K. Walton and J. Walvin (Eds), *Leisure in Britain 1780–1939*, Manchester University Press, Manchester.

Rule, J. (1986) *The Labouring Classes in Early Industrial England, 1750–1850*, Longman, London.

Schama, S. (1987) *The Embarrassment of Riches: an Interpretation of Dutch Culture in the Golden Age*, Fontana Press, London.

Schudt, L. (1959) *Italianreisen im 17. und 18. Jahrhundert*, Schroll-Verlag, Munich.

Simmons, J. (1986) *The Railway in Town and Country 1830–1914*, David & Charles, Newton Abbot.

Smout, T. C. and Wood, S. (1990) *Scottish Voices, 1745–1960*, Collins, London.

Sutton, D. (1982) *Souvenirs of the Grand Tour*, Wildenstein, London.

Thompson, E. P. (1963) *The Making of the English Working Class*, Gollancz, London.

Thompson, F. M. L. (1988) *The Rise of Respectable Society: a Social History of Victorian Britain, 1830–1900*, Fontana, London.

Thurot, J. M. (1980) 'Capacité de charge et production touristique', Études et Memoires 43, Centre des Hautes Études Touristique, Aix-en-Provence.

Towner, J. (1985) 'The grand tour: a key phase in the history of tourism', *Annals of Tourism Research*, 12(3): 297–333.

Towner, J. (1988) 'Approaches to tourism history', *Annals of Tourism Research*, 15(1): 47–62.

Towner, J. and Wall, G. (1991) 'History and tourism', *Annals of Tourism Research*, 18(1): 71–84.

Wall, G. (1989) 'Perspectives on temporal change and the history of recreation', *Progress in Tourism, Recreation and Hospitality Management*, 1: 154–160.

Wall, G. and Marsh, J. (Eds) (1982) *Recreational Land Use: Perspectives on its Evolution in Canada*, Carleton University Press, Ottawa.

Walton, J. K. (1981) 'The demand for working class seaside holidays in Victorian England', *Economic History Review*, 34(2): 249–265.

Walton, J. K. (1983) *The English Seaside Resort, 1750–1914*, Leicester University Press, Leicester.

Walton, J. K. and McGloin, P. R. (1979) 'Holiday resorts and their visitors: some sources for the local historian', *Local Historian*, 13(6): 323–331.

Walton, J. K. and McGloin, P. R. (1981) 'The tourist trade in Victorian Lakeland', *Northern History*, 17: 153–182.

Walton, J. K. and Walvin, J. (1983) *Leisure in Britain, 1780–1939*, Manchester University Press, Manchester.

Wechsberg, J. (1979) *The Lost World of the Great Spas*, Weidenfeld & Nicolson, London.

76 The anthropology of tourism: reflections on the state of the art

T. SELWYN

Introduction

The purpose of this paper is to trace the outline of the (perhaps, more properly, an) anthropology of tourism as it has developed so far and how it may develop in the future. Accordingly it begins by looking back at some of the main influences behind the construction of the subject, at some of the issues raised by its present practitioners, and, finally, at possible directions in which it may be going.

In his comprehensive account of the study of tourism in the social sciences (1988), Crick argued that the social scientific treatment of tourism might conveniently be grouped into three categories—the study of the semiology of tourism, the study of its political economy, and the study of tourism and social change. The present paper seeks to build upon this broad canvas, taking it as axiomatic that the complex nature of tourism itself demands a response from anthropologists that is similarly broad and wide-ranging. Indeed, one of the stimulating features of the anthropological study of tourism is that it requires the anthropologist to make cross-border raids across disciplinary boundaries—which, some would argue, is just as it should be in an intellectually plural and cosmopolitan world.

Templates and benchmarks

For the present purposes of tracing the contours of the anthropology of tourism as it has developed up to the present, the work of six authors is given special prominence; MacCannell (1976, 1992), Cohen (1972, 1979a, 1979b, 1988), Smith (1977, revised in 1989), de Kadt (1979, 1990), Crick himself (1985, 1988) and Urry (1990). MacCannell informs us that his book *The Tourist* (1976) was written partly in response to Lévi-Strauss's view that modernity had 'smashed up' structures and, hence, that structuralist interpretations of the modern world were impossible. MacCannell's response was to argue that there was at least one category of modern person—the tourist—whose aims and motivations included the recovery of those senses of wholeness and structure absent from everyday contemporary life.

MacCannell pursued this theme of cognitive fragmentation and placed it within a wider compass in *Empty Meeting Grounds* (1992), 'the starting point' of which was 'the non-controversial assumption that the cultures of the world have been radically displaced and fundamentally and forever altered by the movements of peoples' (1992:3). This displacement and movement (of migrants, refugees, tourists and others) has given rise, MacCannell argues, to two quite different kinds of 'displaced thought'. On the one hand there is the cultural 'bricolage' associated with those who use the signs, symbols and artefacts of the different cultures through which they pass creatively to formulate and reformulate the new hybrid cultural structures of the postmodern world. On the other hand there are styles of thought grounded in forms of consumerism in which culture and cultural artefacts appear primarily as saleable commodities. One of the most interesting aspects of this latter style is that it often seems to depend on the mythological reconstruction of those senses of 'rooted' tradition which the processes of 'globalisation' have appeared to demolish.

These few remarks are already enough to reveal several of the themes which occupy spaces in the anthropology of tourism: questions about the nature of the highly mobile global world inhabited by tourists and other travellers; questions about the cognitive orientations and dispositions of such travellers; implicit questions about the symbols and representations used to service those dispositions; questions about the relation between postmodern, modern and even (or perhaps especially) pre-modern forms of expression (for MacCannell is making a big claim in linking the mythologies of tourists and the tourist industry with the kind of myths discussed by Lévi-Strauss); questions about the relationship between the postmodern tourist and the 'Other' who lives in the tropical 'destinations' to which tourists go; and so on. But we need to take more soundings.

Cohen has objected to MacCannell's main formulation—that *all*, or even most, tourists seek 'structures', even if make-believe ones—by arguing that there is no such person as *the* tourist, but a whole variety of types of tourist. This objection derives from one of the main theoretical concerns present throughout Cohen's very considerable body of work in the anthropology of tourism. In various ways, Cohen has been concerned to devise classifications of tourists (from the 'organised mass tourist' of the package tour industry to the 'drifter tourist' associated with independent travel, for example). One of the aims of such classification systems is to discuss (and to some extent explain) the motivations and dispositions of the different types of tourists with reference to their place in the social and cultural milieu from which they come. Hence, for example, Cohen argues that *because* of his or her social and cultural 'alienation', a 'drifter' tourist may well be interested in locating and experiencing those senses of wholeness, tradition, structure and authenticity (of which contentious term more later) of which MacCannell, after Barthes (1984) and others, speaks. On the other hand the 'organised mass tourist', assumed by Cohen *not* to be socially or culturally 'alienated' is likely to be interested in nothing more than the 'mere recreation' which sun, sea and sand can provide (1988, for example).

Cohen also objects to what he sees as a general assumption in the sociological and anthropological literature on tourism, propagated by MacCannell and many others— that tourism is necessarily associated with processes of cultural 'commoditisation', which he himself links closely to the issue of what MacCannell terms 'staged authenticity' (1976). This refers to the idea that tourists are systematically 'cheated' by those who stage cultural productions for financial reward. The 'authentic' cannot be bought, the argument runs. Thus, while tourists may well be in search of the 'authentic', it is to be found 'back stage', so to speak, rather than on it, and in a domain in which cultural productions are not exchanged as commodities.

One of Cohen's other criticisms, made together with a more general plea which anthropologists would find hard to resist, is that anthropological studies of tourism need to be grounded in the 'emic'. We need, he argues, to hear from tourists themselves while grounding such evidence in closely observed social settings.

This is a point at which Smith's well-known *Hosts and Guests* (1977, 1989) enters the discussion. Not only did her collection of essays shift the focus away from the tourist to those living in tourist 'destinations', but it placed the subject in a domain defined by traditional modes of field research in locations familiar to a mainstream of anthropological work (islands, villages and other settlements in the Arctic, Mediterranean, Africa and Pacific, for example).

At least two important theoretical observations were made in Smith's book, pursued elsewhere by the authors who made them as well as others. While Graburn traced the structural similarities between tourist and sacred experiences (1977), Nash pointed up the way in which tourism was in some cases and in some senses a form of imperialism (1977).

If the greatest value of Smith's book lay in the careful ethnographic research of her contributors, the main drawback arguably lay in the very terms of its title. 'Host' and 'guest' may be useful in some limited situations but are, ultimately, too simple in a complex world in which 'hosts' no longer meet 'guests' in some latter day Maussian paradigm but in which 'hosts' are also 'guests' and 'guests' 'hosts'. In her work on the Greek Cycladean island of Nisos (Anafi), for example, Kenna shows that a sizeable proportion of tourist developments are financed from abroad by expatriate emigrants (1993)—a familiar pattern in other parts of the world too. But a Greek or Albanian American is hardly a 'host' in Smith's sense. Furthermore if 'hosts' can also be 'guests', and vice versa, both may simultaneously be investors in, and consumers of, tourist services; and both belong to worlds which are at once traditional, modern and postmodern. In other words the real world is greatly more complex than Smith's elegant title might imply.

So far we have identified not only certain questions which are raised by the anthropology of tourism but also certain distinctive styles of analysis. These range from the imaginative intellectual bricolage of MacCannell (which follows a tradition occupied by Lévi-Strauss, Barthes and French structuralism) to the more careful analytical style of Cohen (who, for much of the time occupies, the distinctively Mertonian ground of 'theories of the middle range') to a style of ethnographic reporting characteristic of American followers of a basically rather traditional and functionalist sort of British anthropology.

Although not within the terms of any narrowly conceived definition of an 'anthropologist', de Kadt's two main contributions to the anthropology of tourism are, in the opinion of the present writer, seminal. de Kadt's *Tourism: Passport to Development?* (1979), commissioned by the World Bank, contained a series of essays by social scientists—some of them fully paid-up members of anthropology departments (Boissevain, as in Boissevain and Inglott (1979) and Wilson (1979), for example)— concerned with the opportunities presented by the development of tourism to the people of tourist 'destinations'. The questions posed were taken up again, over ten years later, in a discussion paper in which notions associated with so-called 'alternative tourism' (AT) were examined for what they had to contribute to debates taking place (in a post-Brandt and Brundtland world, with Rio just over the horizon) about 'alternative' and, particularly, 'sustainable' development (de Kadt, 1990).

Part of de Kadt's argument was that the term development was almost exclusively associated with *economic* development, and that such economic development was generally conceived of in terms of, and indeed was defined by, a mainstream of Western capitalist nostrums about development which had not changed a great deal from the days of works such as Rostow's *The Stages of Economic Growth* (1960). The challenge from AT, however, lay in its concern with 'authenticity' and forms of 'authentic development' which placed environmental, cultural and social questions at the heart, rather than on the periphery, of development debates. Indeed, de Kadt argued that there was a growing 'sense of outrage' at those ideas about development which disregarded the social, natural and cultural consequences involved, and which based development strategies on what he called the 'hegemony of materialism'.

It is clear from these observations that de Kadt's concerns intersect with those of MacCannell. Coming at it from quite different directions, both are concerned with 'authenticity' and with processes, including (yet not exclusively) 'development processes' which, driven by materialism and commodification, leave, in de Kadt's terms, 'nature, culture and community' out of focus, except, of course (which is MacCannell's argument), in the mind of 'The Tourist'—who is, apparently, increasingly preoccupied precisely with their *rediscovery*! Furthermore the industry's growing promotion of such types of specialist tourism as 'nature tourism', and 'cultural tourism' seems to confirm that de Kadt's and MacCannell's complementary insights about contemporary states of deracination has some degree of foundation in the 'real world' of consumer choices.

Up to now we have identified several actors, or arenas, whose practices and interrelationships have been the concern of anthropological students of tourism: tourists, persons living in tourist 'destinations', governments and other politico-economic agencies at levels from the local to the international, and (just coming into focus from the last observations of the previous paragraph) the tourist industry itself. Turning back to Crick we may add another actor to this list. This is the *observer* of tourism—for us, the anthropologist him- or herself.

In an important article on the close kinship between tourists and anthropologists (1985), Crick argued that the anthropological study of tourism raised a basic epistemological issue: what (if anything) was the *difference* between the 'scientific' knowledge of the anthropologist and the knowledge acquired by the tourist? As we all (really) know, he argued, scientific, including anthropological, research involves behaviour and procedures which are at least 'ludic' and at most 'anarchistic'. As Crick rightly insists, anthropologists play all sorts of 'games' in their research—but these are not only justified but form part of the reality of scientific processes. Anthropologists and other scientists, like tourists, go in for quite a lot of 'clowning' (such as, we could well suggest, juggling and playing with ideas). According to Crick, such a 'Derridadaistic' approach to anthropological field research 'boils science down to human dimensions' and 'returns us to the company . . . (i.e. tourists) . . . of our classificatory kin'.

This line of thought was taken up, pursued and elaborated by Urry, who argued that in an age of the 'end of certainty', we can no longer look towards one overarching model of scientific explanation, no one scientific meta-narrative, but instead a plurality of models and narratives. This sort of argument has recently become fashionable and widely broadcast. As the postmodernist clerisy remind us, we live in a world where knowledge is not 'one but many'. Urry expresses the idea by arguing that in the postmodern age of the 'end of certainty'— 'Some degree of accommodation is being reached between the ''scientific knowledge'' (of historians, museum curators, et al.) and the ''tourist knowledge'' of the high street'. For Urry, therefore, Hewison (1987) and his followers are mistaken in making 'an absolute distinction between authentic history and heritage' (1990:110). History and truth are not 'out there' but are 'assimilated into ourselves and resurrected into an ever-changing present' (1990:110).

Urry's insistence that 'heritage' is not so much 'bogus history', as Hewison has it, but (potentially at least) 'democratised history' is, on the face of it, attractive. The 'heritage industry' has provided ordinary people—rather than museum curators and/or professors of history or sociology—with opportunities to represent their own history. On reflection, however, this position, occupying as it does a now-familiar postmodern, post-structuralist, anti-enlightenment, post-Marxist territory is difficult to sustain for long (cf. Norris (1993) for a philosophical discussion of the general issues). The implications for the anthropology of tourism are that Crick's epistemological issues remain.

How then might we represent the present state of play in the development of the anthropology of tourism? One suggestion would be to say that anthropologists have been interested (a) in the immediate realms of the six principal actors, or arenas, in the tourism process: tourists; the 'industry'; anthropologists, or more generally 'participant observers' themselves, i.e. all those interested either in analysing and commenting on the nature of tourism or more directly in participating in one or other branch of the tourism industry (museums, writing guide books, guiding, and so on); 'hosts' or (because that is an unsatisfactory term) people living in tourist 'destinations'; government at regional, national levels, including non-governmental bodies; and international agencies; and (b) in the relations and interrelationships between these arenas (Figure 76.1).

Some strategic arenas and issues for the anthropology of tourism

One way of checking whether the above brief exercise in tracing a lineage and a framework of the subject has any merit is to survey, equally briefly, a sample of the work both within the arenas suggested and in the relationships between them, attempting, at the same time, to identify some of the principal theoretical issues raised. However, in the same spirit as we made the point earlier, we would do well to record Dann's observation, made over a decade ago in response to Nash's attempt to define a narrowly bounded arena for the subject (1981), that the anthropology of tourism is unlikely to bear much fruit unless anthropologists are prepared to work from a multidisciplinary perspective (1981). We may thus

conveniently (if approximately) work our way around Figure 76.1.

Apart from those raised by MacCannell and his followers there are several related issues which have arisen from anthropological work on tourists themselves. One of these concerns the cognitive disposition of tourists. While Graburn, as mentioned above, following Turner and others, has drawn attention to the similarity of the tourist to the pilgrim (Graburn, 1977, 1983; Turner, 1974), Dann has focused on the tourist as a child (1986). Seemingly contradictory claims such as these provide much of the steam behind Cohen's request for more careful classifications of tourists. Cohen's own suggestion (which is, it must be said, theoretically and ethnographically highly problematic) is that while some tourists ('alienated intellectuals', for example) may be fuelled by a pilgrim-like search for the authentic, others ('organised mass tourists', for example) may more often be driven by more childlike and hedonistic motives.

Another whole field which is to be found in this general arena of study of tourists, which is possibly one of the richest seams of actual and potential work in the anthropology of tourism, is to be found in the semiology

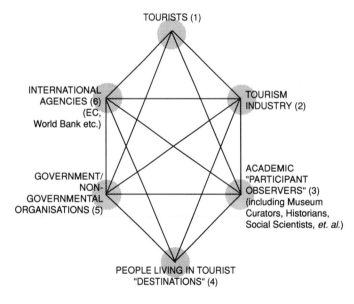

(1) cf MacCannell 1976, 1992 et al.
(2) cf Mars 1984, Dann 1988 et al.
(3) cf Crick 1985; Cohen 1988, Urry 1991 et al.
(4) cf Smith 1989; Cohen 1989 et al.
(5) cf Richter 1993; Picard 1993 et al.
(6) cf de Kadt 1976, 1990 et al.

Figure 76.1 *The field of the anthropology of tourism: arenas and relationships*

of tourism. This has included analyses of tourist representations. Following such illustrious exemplars as Barthes' 'Guide Bleu' (in *Mythologies*, 1984) and, be they found in brochures (Dann, 1988; Selwyn, 1993), museums and memorials (Golden, 1994; Handleman and Shamgar, 1991), photographic representations (Edwards, 1992) or in the variegated imagery and promotional material employed by government departments or agencies (Picard, 1992; Wilson, Chapter 80, this volume), or elsewhere, work on tourist representations is proceeding apace.

Closely intertwined with both of the above are considerations of the relation between tourist dispositions, religion (in the widest sense), and mythology. One of the most intriguing early pieces in this genre was Dufour's 'Myths du week-end' (1977) in which he explores the extent to which tourism in general, the 'week-end' in particular, contributes to the modern's sense of alienation and/or liberation. He comprehensively traces the relation of tourist myths, concerned as these are with such things as physical beauty, excessive eating and drinking, love, games of chance, contact with an 'earth mother', freedom, magic, and so on, to Greek mythology (myths of Aphrodite, Bacchus, Eros, Fortuna, Oedipus, Prometheus, Sorcier, and so on). Whatever else it does, the study must give those who would draw thick boundaries between states and stages of pre-modernity and postmodernity cause for thought.

Issues concerned with the extent to which tourists engage in behaviour which is, in some senses, 'like' religion and/or religious ritual has been addressed by Graburn (1977), Jafari (1983) and others.

Moving to the second arena in Figure 76.1, the tourism industry, we encounter Mars's sociology and anthropology of the hotel industry (1973; Mars et al., 1979) and restaurants (1984) together with work on tourist guides and guided tours (Schmidt, 1979; Katz, 1985; Cohen, 1989; for example). More recent work on museums (Golden, 1994; for example) might also fall into this category as well (assuredly) as into the next.

Some of the issues concerned with the relation between travel, tourism and knowledge have already been discussed and fit into a set of concerns which emanate from work in the third of our arenas in which are to be found, at least, the following theoretical issues.

First, following Said (1985), there is the issue of the political economy of knowledge associated with travel. Part of the problem goes back at least to Bacon (see Adler (1989), for example) and concerns the extent to which, and the conditions under which, travel can be part of 'scientific' projects and/or the extent to which travel-derived knowledge is, and always has been, inevitably linked to global power relations.

Second, there is the related heady and postmodern issue of whether the knowledge of the modern tourist is *really* different from that of a scientific observer (such as an anthropologist).

The third issue to be found in this arena revolves around the question of authenticity. There has been, it may be said, a great deal of confusion surrounding this term. Much of this confusion derives from the writings of both MacCannell and Cohen—as both use the term indiscriminately in two quite different senses. On the one hand there is MacCannell's assertion that the tourist, like a pilgrim, is searching for a sense of the authentically social (which is an essentially totemic feeling in, very precisely, a Durkheimian sense)—in order to reclaim that which has been lost in the isolation and fractured state of postmodern life. The same sense is picked up by Cohen—for example in his assertion that *because* 'educated drifters' and intellectuals share senses of alienation they are drawn to the authentic: 'the greater the alienation of the tourist, the greater the search for authenticity' (1988). Which is to say, more colloquially, that the postmodern intellectual, made miserable by the erosion of community, proceeds periodically, as a tourist, to the tropics, Corfu, St Tropez or Brighton in order to find it.

But both writers use the term authenticity in another, quite different, sense. Whether in MacCannell's discussion of 'staged authenticity', or in Cohen's discussion of the imagined (i.e. imagined by tourists) 'primitive and remote' northern Thai mountain villagers—who are *actually* politically and economically integrated into the Thai Lowlands—the two writers use authenticity to refer to the *quality of knowledge associated with tourist experiences*.

I have discussed this semantic confusion at greater length elsewhere (Selwyn, forthcoming) and suggest that one solution is to make a clear distinction between two different senses of the term. In a first sense tourists may be said to be seeking 'authentic' experiences by pursuing, on holiday, senses of social solidarity (which might be found on the beach or in the disco as well as in confrontation with the 'primitive Other'). In a second sense the 'authentic' may be used to refer to statements which are open to what we may describe as 'Popperian' processes of confirmation, refutation and so forth.

Moving into the fourth arena is to move into familiar anthropological territory: the ethnography of social settings influenced by tourism, including tourist resorts and 'destinations'. Apart from Smith herself, one of the pioneers of this genre is Boissevain who has been working on issues associated with the ethnography of Maltese tourism for twenty years or more. An early work concerned the nature of the dependency of the small island of Gozo upon Malta itself (Boissevain and Inglott, 1979). Boissevain's work reminds us yet again (in case we felt in need of reminding) that the anthropology of tourism has always been embedded in concerns with development and dependency.

More recent ethnographic accounts which focus on social or cultural questions related to tourism are to be found in work by Bouquet and Winter (1987), Cohen (1989), Black (1990), Brown (1992), Bowman (1991), Meethan (1990), Ireland (1992), in several contributions in Hitchcock, King and Parnwell (1993), as well as in one of the very best ethnographic movies available, O'Rourke's *Cannibal Tours* (1987). This work has addressed, among other matters, issues associated with sex and gender (shifts in gender roles in tourist-influenced economies, tourist-related sexual relations, and so on), questions concerning the relation between (long-established resident) 'insiders' and (newly arrived tourist/second home occupant) 'outsiders', disjunctures between 'official' (tourist-related) and 'unofficial'/'local' rhetorics of place, various kinds of effects of tourism on villages and communities, questions concerned with the nature of 'tourist culture' and (or in relation to) 'local culture', and so on.

In the fifth and sixth of our arenas there is considerably less strictly anthropological work to be found. Richter is not an anthropologist in the narrow sense and yet her work (1993, for example) seems indispensable to any anthropologist concerned with tourism-related issues working in the geographical fields covered by her work. Picard's work on Bali (1992), however, which concerns the way that the Indonesian government 'sells' Bali and the way in which the Balinese themselves are responding to government tourism policies is deeply challenging and suggestive for a mainstream of anthropological concerns. This brings us round to the sixth and final arena, where, presently, de Kadt's work (1979, 1990) is not only pioneering but exemplary, using, as the latter of these works does, such texts as *The Brundtland Report* (1987). Perhaps the point about the importance of the study of international agencies may be made with an example. It is clear, for example, that any future anthropological work on economy and society in contemporary rural France—which might well contain sizeable sections not only on agriculture but also tourism—would need to discuss the influence and significance of the EU and (even more crucially) the recently completed GATT agreements.

To sum up. Anthropologists of tourism are at present to be found working in a number of arenas which may be distinguished in a way suggested by Figure 76.1. Many of the theoretical and ethnographic concerns suggest the importance not only of distinguishing one arena of interest from another but also of examining issues which

derive, precisely, from the relations and interrelationships between them.

Some possible future directions

Wilson has traced the development of the anthropology of tourism through several stages until the present one, which he identifies as 'an emergent critique of post-modernism'. As others have done, he further emphasises the need for an interdisciplinary approach to the subject, and we have followed that path here. He also makes a plea for longitudinal ethnographies of tourist fields which will allow anthropologists to identify, in a detailed way, social processes as they develop over time: the period when anthropologists made very general statements (about 'commoditisation' or 'authenticity', for example) has passed (1993:35).

Following these comments, we might suggest that the anthropology of tourism might become at once more rigorously ethnographic and more theoretical. Several specific ethnographic topics (some of them being presently the subject of anthropological work) come to mind as being candidates for future study: we need, first of all, as Cohen has so frequently pointed out, much more detailed 'emic' studies of tourists. It seems wholly surprising that, with the single and magnificent exception of O'Rourke in *Cannibal Tours*, so little work has actually been done with tourists themselves. Secondly, there are surprisingly few detailed ethnographic studies of the various organisations and institutions which make up the tourist 'industry'. Thirdly, present moves to bring tourism and migration studies closer together (Kenna, 1993, for example) suggests a greater degree of ethnography 'on the move', so to speak. Fourthly, it is clear that, as international agencies (often in company with universities) move increasingly into the field of 'cultural policy'—which will frequently entail tourism policy—the agencies themselves need urgently to be subject to critical ethnographic scrutiny (see Shore, 1993).

The theoretical issues posed by the anthropology of tourism arise partly out of a growing interest in the relations between the arenas in which, as we have seen, anthropologists have tended to concentrate their ethnographic efforts up to now. To the extent that these relations and interrelationships are embedded in complex global systems and processes which provide the widest imaginable economic, political, social and cultural context in which the subject needs to operate, it is possible to suggest that some of the issues to which the anthropology of tourism may make its own distinctive contribution may include the following. First, there are the issues associated with *displacement*—in a world of an increasing number not only of tourists but also of migrants and refugees. Second, there are the very closely linked issues associated with movements to *re-establish* senses of place, which may go together with nostalgic feelings for lost 'communities', and so forth, and play a central role in nationalist and ethnic movements: sociologists and anthropologists of tourism have a considerable amount to offer to debates about nationalism and ethnicity as workshops in anthropology departments at the universities of Oxford and London, in the spring of 1994, have suggested. Third, at a time when tourists have become (and not only in Egypt) the occasional victims of fundamental challenges to assumptions about aspects of economic and social management in the modern world, issues associated with the relation between the pre-modern, the modern and the postmodern (linked closely as this is with the relation between 'tourist knowledge', 'scientific knowledge' and 'religious knowledge') will remain a live topic for further investigation and analysis. Finally, at a time when tourists, migrants and refugees stand at the heart of debates about the interpretation of history, the authenticity of memory, and the political economy of culture, it may be appropriate to suggest that the anthropology of tourism is no longer to be found on any sort of periphery.

References and bibliography

Adler, J. (1989) 'Origins of sightseeing', *Annals of Tourism Research*, 16: 7–29.

Barthes, R. (1984) *Mythologies*, Paladin, London.

Bender, B. (1993) Exhibition on Stonehenge prepared by staff and students of Anthropology Department of UCL, University of London.

Black, A. (1990) 'In the eyes of the beholder? The cultural effects of tourism in Malta', *Problems of Tourism*, University of Warsaw, 13(3/4).

Boissevain, J. (1991) 'Ritual play and identity: changing patterns of celebration in Maltese villages', *Journal of Mediterranean Studies*, 1:87–100.

Boissevain, J. and Inglott, P. S. (1979) 'Tourism in Malta', in de Kadt, E. (Ed.), *Tourism: Passport to Development?*, Oxford University Press, Oxford, pp. 265–284.

Bouquet, M. and Winter, M. (Eds) (1987) *Who from their Labours Rest? Conflict and Practice in Rural Tourism*, Avebury, Aldershot.

Bowman, G. (1991) 'Fucking tourists: sexual relations and tourism in Jerusalem's Old City', *Critique of Anthropology*, 9(2): 77–93.

Britton, S. (1983) *Tourism and Underdevelopment in Fiji*, ANU Press, Canberra.

Brown, N. (1992) 'Beachboys as culture brokers in Bakau Town, The Gambia', *Community Development Journal*, 27(4): 361–370.

Brundtland, G. (1987): see World Commission on Environment and Development (1987).

Cohen, E. (1972) 'Towards a sociology of international tourism', *Social Research*, 39(1).

Cohen, E. (1979a) 'A phenomenology of tourist experiences', *Sociology*, 13(2).

Cohen, E. (1979b) 'Rethinking the sociology of tourism', *Annals of Tourism Research*, 6(1): 18–35.

Cohen, E. (1988) 'Authenticity and commoditisation in tourism', *Annals of Tourism Research*, 15(3).

Cohen, E. (1989) 'Primitive and remote: hill tribe trekking in Thailand', *Annals of Tourism Research*, 16: 30–61.

Crick, M. (1985) ' "Tracing" the anthropological self: quizzical reflections on field work, tourism and the ludic', *Social Analysis*, 17: 71–92.

Crick, M. (1988) 'Sun, sex, sights, savings and servility: representations of international tourism in the social sciences', *Criticism, Heresy and Interpretation (CHI)*, 1(1): 37–76; republished (1989) in *Annual Review of Anthropology*, 18: 307–344.

Dann, G. (1981) 'Comment on Nash, D. "Tourism as an anthropological subject" ', *Current Anthropology*, 22: 5.

Dann, G. (1986) 'The tourist as a child', paper presented to the Research Committee on Leisure of the International Sociological Association, New Delhi.

Dann, G. (1988) 'Images of Cyprus', *Problems of Tourism*, University of Warsaw, 3/4.

Dufour, R. (1977) 'Les myths du week-end: alienation ou liberations', Ph.D. thesis, Centre des Hautes Etudes Touristiques, University of Aix-en-Marseille.

Edwards, E. (1992) *Anthropology and Photography 1860–1920*, New Haven, CT, Yale University Press.

Fees, C. (1988) 'Christmas mumming in a north Cotswold town: with special reference to tourism, urbanisation and immigration-related social change', Ph.D. thesis, Institute of Dialect and Folk Life Studies, University of Leeds.

Golden, D. (1994) 'The Museum of the Diaspora tells a story', Selwyn, T. (Ed.), *Chasing Myths* (in press).

Graburn, N. (1977) 'Tourism: the sacred journey', in Smith, V. (Ed.), *Hosts and Guests: The Anthropology of Tourism*, Blackwell, Oxford, pp. 17–32.

Graburn, N. (1983) 'The anthropology of tourism', *Annals of Tourism Research*, 10: 9–33.

Handleman, D. and Shamgar, L. (1991) 'The presence of the dead: memorials of national death in Israel', *Suomen Antropologi*, 4: 3–17.

Hewison, R. (1987) *The Heritage Industry: Britain in a Climate of Decline*, Methuen, London.

Hitchcock, M., King, V. T. and Parnwell, M. (Eds) (1993) *Tourism in South-East Asia*, Routledge, London.

Ireland, M. (1992) 'Come to Cornwall, come to Land's End: a study of visitor experience at a touristic site', *Problems of Tourism*, University of Warsaw, 15.

Jafari, J. (1983) 'Understanding the structure of tourism', in Nebell, E. C. III (Ed.), *Tourism and Culture: a Comparative Perspective*, University of New Orleans Press, New Orleans.

de Kadt, E. (Ed.) (1979) *Tourism: Passport to Development?*, Oxford University Press, Oxford.

de Kadt, E. (1990) 'Making the alternative sustainable: lessons for development from tourism', IDS Discussion Paper, 272, Institute of Development Studies, University of Sussex.

Katz, S. (1985) 'The Israeli teacher guide', *Annals of Tourism Research*, 12: 49–72.

Kenna, M. (1993) 'Return migrants and tourist development: an example from the Cyclades', *Journal of Modern Greek Studies*, 11: 75–95.

Kent, N. (1983) *Hawaii: Islands under the Influence*, Monthly Review Press, New York.

MacCannell, D. (1976) *The Tourist: A New Theory of the Leisure Class*, Schocken, New York.

MacCannell, D. (1989) 'Introduction' to special edition on semiotics of tourism, *Annals of Tourism Research*, 16: 1.

MacCannell, D. (1992) *Empty Meeting Grounds*, Routledge, London.

McDonald, M. (1987) 'Tourism: chasing culture and tradition in Britanny', in Bouquet, M. and Winter, M. (Eds), *Who from their Labours Rest? Conflict and Practice in Rural Tourism*, Avebury, Aldershot, pp. 120–134.

Mars, G. (1973) 'Hotel pilferage: a case study in occupational theft', in Warner, M. (Ed.), *The Sociology of the Workplace*, George Allen & Unwin, London, pp. 200–210.

Mars, G. (1984) *The World of Waiters*, George Allen & Unwin, London.

Mars, G., Mitchell, P. and Bryant, D. (1979) *Management Problems in the Hotel and Catering Industry*, Saxon House, Farnborough.

Meethan, K. (1990) 'Voluntary action in Brighton neighbourhood associations', Ph.D. thesis, University of Sussex.

Nash, D. (1977) 'Tourism as a form of imperialism', in Smith, V. (Ed.), *Hosts and Guests, The Anthropology of Tourism*, Basil Blackwell, Oxford, pp. 33–47.

Nash, D. (1981) 'Tourism as an anthropological subject', *Current Anthropology*, 22(5): 461–481.

Norris, C. (1993) *The Truth about Post-Modernism*, Blackwell, Oxford.

O'Rourke, D. (1987) *Cannibal Tours* (film: available from O'Rourke and Associates, Canberra, Australia).

Picard, M. (1992) 'Cultural tourism in Bali: national integration and regional differentiation', in Hitchcock, M., King, V. T. and Parnwell, M. (Eds), *Tourism in South-East Asia*, Routledge, London, pp. 71–98.

Richter, L. (1993) 'Tourism policy-making in South-East Asia', in Hitchcock, M., King, V. T. and Parnwell, M. (Eds), *Tourism in South-East Asia*, Routledge, London, pp. 179–199.

Rostow, W. (1960) *The Stages of Economic Growth*, Cambridge University Press, Cambridge.

Said, E. (1985) *Orientalism*, Penguin, Harmondsworth.

Schmidt, C. J. (1979) 'The guided tour: insulated adventure', *Urban Life*, 7(4): 441–467.

Selwyn, T. (1993) 'Peter Pan in South-East Asia: views from the brochures', in Hitchcock, M., King, V. T. and Parnwell, M. (Eds), *Tourism in South-East Asia*, Routledge, London, pp. 117–137.

Selwyn, T. (Ed.) (forthcoming) *Chasing Myths: Essays in the Anthropology of Tourism*.

Shore, C. (1993) 'Inventing the ''People's Europe'': critical approaches to EC ''cultural policy'' ', *Man*, 28: 4.

Smith, V. L. (Ed.) (1977, revised 1989) *Hosts and Guests*, University of Pennsylvania Press, Philadelphia, PA.

Turner, V. (1974) *Dramas, Fields and Metaphors: Symbolic Action in Human Society*, Cornell University Press, Ithaca, NY.

Urry, J. (1990) *The Tourist Gaze: Leisure and Travel in Contemporary Societies*, Sage, London.

Wilson, D. (1979) 'The early effects on tourism in the Seychelles', in de Kadt, E. (Ed.), *Tourism: Passport to Development?*, Oxford University Press, Oxford.

Wilson, D. (1993) 'Time and tides in the anthropology of tourism', in Hitchcock, M., King, V. T. and Parnwell, M. (Eds) *Tourism in South-East Asia*, Routledge, London, 32–47.

World Commission of Environment and Development (1987) *Our Common Future* ('The Brundtland Report'), Oxford University Press, Oxford.

Wright, P. (1985) *On Living in an Old Country: The National Past in Contemporary Britain*, Verso, London.

77 Some theoretical perspectives on hospitality

R. C. WOOD

Introduction

The term 'hospitality management' now enjoys wide circulation as a label for describing business activities and an area of academic study encompassing hotel, catering and restaurant operations. Indeed, so accepted is the term that there exists little elaboration of its meaning (though see Christian (1979), Nailon (1982), Wood (1983) and Hepple et al. (1990)) and, more significantly, no systematic attempt at comprehending what is implied conceptually by the word 'hospitality'.

According to Ambrose Bierce's *Devil's Dictionary* (1967), hospitality is 'The virtue which induces us to feed and lodge certain persons who are not in need of food and lodging'. Eschewing this comic view (and there are many others), recourse to the more conventional undergraduate tactic of reference to a standard dictionary yields: 'friendly and liberal reception of guests or strangers' (*The Little Oxford Dictionary of Current English* (4th edn), 1969); 'friendly and generous entertainment of guests' (*The Oxford Minidictionary* (3rd edn), 1991); and 'hospitable treatment or reception'. In the latter case, that of the *Longman Concise English Dictionary* (1985), reference is drawn back to the root 'hospitable' which in addition to the definition 'offering a generous and cordial welcome (to guests and strangers)' also lists 'offering a pleasant or sustaining environment'. At one level then it seems that 'hospitality' is a very simple and precise term in so far as the last of these attempts to clarify meaning alerts us to the possibility of disassociating the personal aspects of hospitality (generosity, cordiality) from the impersonal (the provision of a hospitable environment).

It is such a distinction that in fact points to a certain elusiveness in a more considered use of the term, particularly in conjunction with the word 'management' the resulting compound of which may be regarded as an oxymoron. The objective of this paper is to dissect the concept of hospitality and to draw out some implications of the term for an understanding of hospitality management. The assumption underlying this exercise is that both concepts are problematic, not only in a definitional sense but also in the sense that there is genuine uncertainty as to what constitutes hospitality management as a distinct activity and field of study.

Two conceptions of hospitality

In order to demonstrate the problematic nature of hospitality as a concept it is necessary to point to the distinction between 'ancient' and 'modern' hospitality common to historical accounts of the phenomenon. In what is in any case a limited literature, the distinction is explored here by reference to two commentaries, published some sixty years apart, of the origins and historical development of hospitality. The necessary artificiality of this approach is more than compensated for by the clarity with which each account outlines the conceptual difficulties attendant on discussions of hospitality.

Muhlmann (1932) in his contribution on 'hospitality' to the *Encyclopaedia of the Social Sciences* concentrates primarily on primitive and archaic societies. Hospitality is seen as essentially organic, as a vital and integral part of such societies revealing much about their cultural values and beliefs. According to Muhlmann, the factors which promote hospitality in these contexts are (a) the fear of strangers, (b) religious rules governing hospitality, (c) the need for trade, (d) the desire to display personal wealth and largesse, and (e) the desire to exchange news. Strangers are feared because they appear as bearers of magical and/or mystical powers. Hospitality 'represents a kind of guarantee of reciprocity—one protects the stranger in order to be protected from him' (1932:463). In religious terms, Muhlmann notes that amongst Greeks and Romans hospitality was religiously sanctioned, certain gods watching over strangers and religious convention requiring the entertainment and care of those so protected. In the Middle Ages, monasteries performed hospitable functions by taking in travellers and others, often providing specially built accommodation in the form of hospices. Gift exchange between guest and host represents, for Muhlmann, an early form of trade in which the proper behaviour of people in exchanging gifts served as a lubricant to the development of closer trade links predicated on more rational means of exchange. The display function in hospitality is not new: it is particularly associated with the proffering of food and indeed, the excess of such hospitality is neatly parodied as early as Petronius' account of Trimalchio's feast in *The Satyricon* written in the first century AD. In the desire (and need) to receive and exchange news are found the seeds of the nation state and diplomacy as understood in the modern sense, needs that remained simple for only a short time before requiring a degree of institutionalisation that entailed greater formality in hospitality.

This last point is important for it leads Muhlmann to argue that the hospitality of ancient and primitive societies bear little resemblance to that of the modern world (1932:464):

> The germ of the decay of hospitality is inherent in the institution itself, in that it inevitably extends frontiers and the domain of peace and promotes trade; as a result there arise public legal principles, which go beyond the personal and the familiar and take the place of hospitality. . . . Primitive hospitality was addressed to the public enemy; in the modern world the distinction between friend and enemy in the political sense is irrelevant. The old hospitality was a social or religious obligation; that of modern times rests with the discretion of the individual. The old hospitality was an integral part of the culture, often a junction of law, custom, religion and trade; that of modern times is incidental and casts little light on cultural life.

At first sight this can be adjudged a somewhat jaundiced and pessimistic view. Fear of the stranger is still an important element of host–guest relationships, albeit in modified form, as contemporary analyses of tourism have shown. Magical and mystical powers are not the problem of modern hospitality. Rather, strangers, in the form of tourists, bring with them the threat of social and environmental damage and the erosion of the values and traditions of host communities (Ryan, 1991). At the same time, for many tourist destinations, the dependency on tourism as *trade* is very clearly marked in terms of (at least) the economic exchange which in many cases fosters the dependency of hosts upon guests.

However, Muhlmann's complaint is that, in essence, the organic and spiritual qualities of hospitality have disappeared, replaced in the public sphere by a formally rational system of (usually monetary) exchange whereby hospitality is provided in particular institutional forms (hotels, restaurants) that are essentially impersonal. For the most part, hospitality is no longer about the personal giving of the host's own food and accommodation but a matter of impersonal financial exchange. To use the jargon of contemporary leisure and tourism studies, hospitality has been commoditised (Rojek, 1985).

Similar views to those proposed by Muhlmann are advanced by Heal (1990) in her study of hospitality in early modern England (c. 1400–1700). She argues that hospitality in modern society lacks centrality in our value systems (1990:1):

For modern Western man hospitality is preponderantly a private form of behaviour, exercised as a matter of personal preference within a limited circle of friendship and connection. As such it is also considered a social luxury, to be pursued when circumstances are favourable, but abandoned without serious loss of status when they prove adverse.

In early modern England Heal argues, hospitality was both a form of social duty and social control: open hospitality was accepted as part of the social system but at the same time there was a need to regulate both the potential disorder it could create and the burdensome costs that could be generated by the provision of hospitality. This was achieved in an abstract sense by stressing the boundaries of duty. A man's first duty was to his family and household and then other kin, neighbours, friends and finally strangers and enemies.

The view of hospitality that derives from the work of Muhlmann, Heal and others (see especially Pitt-Rivers (1977)) is one that sees hospitality as radiating from the household, developing, as societies develop, into a more institutionalised phenomenon that nevertheless retains its characteristic as a highly personal form of social behaviour. As Heal (1990:19) states in the context of her study of early modern England, the concept of hospitality was: 'bound to that of reciprocity, of the exchange of gifts and rewards to which value not simply articulated in money terms attaches . . . when Englishmen wrote of hospitality, they used a language of exchange in which reciprocities were not assigned a monetary value'. The arguments advanced by Muhlmann and Heal could be construed as verging on the highly romanticised, seemingly suggesting that hospitality has been 'polluted' since, in the public sphere, its provision became a form of rational economic exchange rather than a social duty. There is some evidence to support this view. A number of other studies suggest either directly or more implicitly that until the beginnings of the modern hotel industry, the provision of impersonal forms of hospitality was never regarded as more than a necessary evil, as subordinate to (or sometimes incorporated in) the personal hospitality of the powerful host whether in individual or corporate form (Stone, 1932: Hayner, 1964).

Having said this, there is no *logical* reason to suppose that the privatisation and rationalisation of social relationships attendant on industrialisation makes the provision of commercial hospitality in all respects a form of exchange calculated solely in monetary terms, it is equally possible that the quality of hospitality has changed little but the mode of exchange—the mechanisms of giving and receiving—has. This is clearly not the view of Muhlmann and Heal but it is one that in their preoccupation with the historical they do little to refute. The view of both authors is, seemingly, that the mode of exchange invariably dictates the quality of an economic and social experience. Put crudely, once hospitality is paid for it is no longer hospitality, and forms of hospitality untainted by monetary exchange are assumed to be in some way superior. This view *is* highly romanticised and nostalgic and, more significantly, produced without detailed reference to analysis of the commercial provision of hospitality. As a result, attention is directed to the earlier point concerning modes of exchange and processes of giving and receiving.

Gifts, exchanges and hospitality

Such issues are traditionally and most explicitly dealt with by 'exchange theory' which has its roots in Mauss's classic work *The Gift* (1967, first published in 1925) a book retaining its influence despite alternative contemporary reformulations of the nature of reciprocity and exchange associated with American writers such as Blau (1964) and Homans (1961). The latter view social exchange and economic and market exchange as very similar: individuals behave in a hedonistic and utilitarian fashion, engaging in social interaction on the basis that such interaction will yield returns. Mutual reciprocity exists but the basis of exchange is calculative and involves little trust or shared values.

This view has been criticised as making unfounded psychological assumptions about individuals, particularly in respect of the extent to which people are self-seeking and calculative (Abercrombie et al., 1984; Turner, 1974). Also questioned is the extent to which it is possible to posit a distinction between social and economic forms of exchange. Social exchange may occur without economic exchange (though not necessarily without the expectation of future economic exchange), but whether the reverse is true is more doubtful. Many forms of socio-economic exchange are regulated by third parties, often the state via the medium of law, such that any absence of trust in reciprocity and the failure of exchange to meet the expectations of the parties to it is catered for by the provision of bureaucratic mechanisms of recourse that offer one or both parties the prospect of restitution.

Plainly put, it is not sensible to conceive of economic exchange without social exchange, a view recognised in point of fact by some recent defenders of modern exchange theory (e.g. Bredemeier, 1978) as well as its critics. In the tradition of exchange theory still firmly rooted in Mauss's anthropological commentary, the interrelationship between social and economic exchange is taken to involve shared values and trust. Models of

exchange may vary and will have varied consequences for the nature of reciprocity but the social dimensions to reciprocity are not dependent on the mode of economic exchange. The phenomenon of hospitality, like many other cultural phenomena, retains vestiges of its pre-industrial form as defined by Muhlmann and Heal.

This and many of the other issues discussed above are analysed at length in a paper by Burgess (1982) which, incomprehensively, has attracted little attention, given the fundamental issues with which it deals. It is possible to concentrate on only a small part of Burgess's work here, but his principal arguments derive from the proposition that gift exchange is a valuable metaphor for studying hospitality and hospitable behaviour. His views may be usefully summarised as follows.

- Though any gift may have symbolic and/or utility value, those who give seek to enhance the value of their gifts by transferring some part of the self to the recipient, the object of such behaviour being to establish symbolic bonds between the parties which may communicate *inter alia*, degrees of formality, warmth and sincerity in a relationship.
- Gifts convey information about, and confer identity upon, those who give, just as the nature of the hospitality on offer in a particular context establishes the commitment and involvement of the host in the provision of hospitality.
- Gift exchange, like hospitality, entails an assessment of the needs and desires of the recipient by the giver and this is often directed to achieving the best possible outcome in terms of establishing bonds of trust.
- Gift exchange, like hospitality, is directed towards establishing an interaction order whereby the nature of the exchange entails certain implicit rules guiding the behaviour of parties to it.
- The reciprocity involved in social exchange is such that parties to the act assume a *shared* responsibility for its outcome.

The interesting implication of Burgess's arguments is—as suggested in the previous section—that whilst the economic dimensions to reciprocity are not unimportant, the social aspects of the process of exchange enjoy priority in interactional relationships. Further, the use of gift exchange as a metaphor for hospitality and hospitable behaviour highlights the extent to which modern hospitality continues to evidence features of pre- and non-industrial societies. Burgess himself provides some interesting insights on the latter, but is less direct in exemplifying his major themes in a contemporary context. However, it is easy enough to provide a selection of brief illustrations of the five themes listed above.

- As Burgess notes, many providers of hospitality impress their own personal stamp upon hospitality services. They may adopt a 'host role' working within their own organisation and interacting with guests in an effort to convey something of the 'self' and imprint their own personality upon the operation. In corporate organisations, similar functions are performed by the proprietors' representatives, specifically managers.
- Irrespective of the economic dimension to exchange, it is often the case that elements of the hospitality package remain uncertain or ill-defined. For example, Stringer (1981:364) in his study of the British bed-and-breakfast business notes that many tourists experience difficulties in staying in another person's home and there was 'occasional sensitivity as to whether guests were genuinely welcome'. Successful reciprocity in a hospitality organisation is predicated on the willingness of the host to clearly define the parameters of the act of exchange and to respond to guests' uncertainties in this area.
- Modern marketing theory has at its heart the (perhaps idealised) notion that satisfying the wants and needs of consumers is paramount. This applies no less to the provision of hospitality where, however, hosts may be required to be more immediately responsive to the often mercurial demands of guests, since it is the immediate response, the solution of an individual guest's particular problem that is both expected and serves to establish personal bonds between parties to the exchange. A hotelier may have many guests but a crucial and tacit dimension of the hospitality relationships is that service is rendered to each individual.
- To say that social interaction is rule-bound is to articulate a truism. Several studies of behaviour in hospitality organisations have concerned themselves with rules that govern the behaviour of parties to acts of exchange (see Mars and Nicod (1984) for a competent review). These rules, which are more or less flexible depending on context, are primarily concerned with *how* to both give and receive, and circumscribe acceptable and unacceptable behaviour, serving to ensure that exchange and reciprocity are kept within acceptable boundaries. Examples would include mutual respect for public and private areas of the organisation (Goffman, 1959), participation in the rituals of the organisation by the guest (Burgess, 1982), and the maintenance of prevailing standards of decorum (Wood, 1994).

- The intention to give (whether or not in return for economic consideration) is premissed on certain assumptions concerning the shared role of giver and recipient in ensuring that an act of exchange is successful. In purchasing a good—a tangible item—it is often the case as noted earlier that third party regulation of exchange—via the medium of the law—exists to support the exchange. Thus the recipient is expected to treat the item purchased in an appropriate way in return for which the provider offers a guarantee of the item's functional integrity. In many instances, providers of goods offer guarantees beyond statutory rights of the 'If this product fails to satisfy . . .' type. Similar legal guarantees exist in respect of the purchase of services. However, with hospitality services, where functional aspects of the object of exchange are more difficult to define, both negative and positive feedback is more immediate and providers often have mechanisms to redress grievances in a more rapid and direct way. In the case of both goods and services therefore, elements of trust are built into a relationship that transcend legal obligations. The point is an important one. Muhlmann's view, reported in the first section above, that 'public legal principles' replace hospitality in modern societies overstates the issue. Public legal principles are an adjunct to exchange utilised as a last resort. Many of those who supply goods and services attempt to offer a personal guarantee of their products and restitution of grievances is sought at an early stage of the post-exchange event where this breaks down. However, just as providers seek to offer repair mechanisms for acts of reciprocity that break down then so do recipients face obligations to ensure such acts are successful in their outcome, by not using products for purposes for which they were not intended. Translated to the provision of hospitality, the obligations of the guest include forbearance from unreasonable claims and complaints against the host and the services the latter provides, and practical engagement with the rules and conventions of the hospitality unit in such a manner as to ensure its smooth running.

Hospitality and hospitality management: a final note

Any discussion of the concept of hospitality, is, in the absence of an academic literary tradition of any substance necessarily abstract in its conception. However, from the foregoing discussion, two principal points emerge.

- The differences between industrial and pre-industrial hospitality are not so great as would be apparent from the accounts of those who view rational economic exchange as in some way diluting the nature of hospitality. Indeed, the economic dimension to reciprocity in modern economies could be viewed as a formalisation of that which was always implicit in such acts.

- Modern commercial hospitality is defined relative to at least two reference points: the historical conventions of public and commercial hospitality, and private hospitable behaviour. Commercial hospitality embraces elements of both and the inherently social nature of hospitality in a symbolic sense is preserved even within a system of reciprocity characterised by rational economic exchange.

If this analysis is broadly correct, then hospitality management is about the management of reciprocity and exchange. This does not mean that such management has to be successful, though it will almost certainly be directed towards successful outcomes. The rosy view of archaic and pre-industrial hospitality explored earlier in the paper emphasises the importance of highly personalised forms of hospitality to the lubrication of anything from inter-familial to inter-state diplomacy. What it ignores in its preoccupation with attitudes to the nature of hospitality is the manner in which hospitality is delivered, the actions of those physically engaged in the planning, coordination and execution of hospitality services. There is also a convenient failure to explore failures in hospitality, historically speaking, and the consequences of such failures.

Failures to address the mechanisms by which hospitality is delivered is a major weakness of those views that regard contemporary hospitality offered commercially as being depersonalised and lacking social significance. The contemporary provision of commercial hospitality continues to exhibit highly personalised qualities. Indeed, modern commercial hospitality is no less organic in form and delivery than that of the pre-commercial age. Mystique direction towards cushioning (if not overwhelming) the recipients of hospitality is a feature of the commercial hospitality organisation. Such mystique, represented by attempts at the tailoring of service to each individual guest's needs within essentially impersonal organisational structures may be regarded as serving to deliberately obfuscate the economic basis of exchange. The fact that hospitality is purchased is far less significant than the fact that *what* is purchased remains undefined beyond a specification of essential terms—for example, bed-and-breakfast, full board and so on.

Within set parameters, hospitality managers are allowed a great deal of latitude and flexibility in providing

hospitality, precisely because the economic basis to exchange is only a minor part of the total hospitality package. As Nailon (1982) argues, the hospitality manager is engaged in the manipulation of a variety of resources—those in the external environment and those that form part of the management, technical and human resource infrastructure of the organisation. Nailon's account serves to remind us that the modern hospitality organisation is directed ideologically to the satisfaction of what are perceived as individual needs and wants in a social setting. This is reflected in the extensive body of evidence that outlines the nature of the hospitality manager's role set as essentially social, as 'meeter and greeter' of guests, as peripatetic controllers of their units, as flexible operators in terms of their labour management practices.

Hospitality management training and practice retains strong attachments to 'ideal' forms of delivery of hospitality services that emphasise the social dimension to reciprocity. At the same time, as Burgess (1982) notes, a difficulty for commercial hospitality is the extent to which these ideals are distorted (or at least mediated) by cultural conventions that in the UK at least have required a certain distance between host and guest. This is an important point yet its significance should not be exaggerated. Barriers and boundaries are defining features of acts of reciprocity and exchange. In the case of hospitality, attention to the abstract features of the phenomenon, though important, should not blind us to the extent to which the management of other forms of exchange is directed however haphazardly or successfully to achieving highly personalised social transactions.

In this context, a meaning for hospitality management beyond the merely mechanistic begins to emerge. Both outside and within the hospitality management research community the term has generated some unease. Heal (1990) sees the term 'hospitality management' as constituting a paradox, as exhibiting a tension between generosity and exploitation in the marketplace, as perhaps verging on the oxymoronic. Close scrutiny of the nature of exchange and reciprocity in social relations makes this view appear superficial. In this paper an attempt has been made to explore a little more deeply the validity of the concept of 'hospitality management' relative to the phenomenon of hospitality more generally. Burgess (1982) ended his exploration of the issue by implying a need for more detailed analysis of the concept at the abstract, theoretical level. This is a sensible prescription and one, furthermore, that might yield sufficiently valuable insights that can be put to good use in advancing research in the field more generally as well as repelling criticisms—both real and those arising from academic snobbery—directed at the legitimacy of hospitality *management* as an independent field of enquiry.

References

Abercrombie, N., Hills, S. and Turner, B. (1984) *The Penguin Dictionary of Sociology*, Penguin, Harmondsworth.

Bierce, A. (1967) *The Enlarged Devil's Dictionary*, Gollancz, London.

Blau, P. (1964) *Exchange and Power in Social Life*, John Wiley, New York.

Bredemeier, H. C. (1978) 'Exchange Theory', in T. B. Bottomore and R. Nisbet (Eds), *A History of Sociological Analysis*, Basic Books, New York.

Burgess, J. (1982) 'Perspectives on gift exchange and hospitable behaviour', *International Journal of Hospitality Management*, 1: 49–57.

Christian, V. A. (1979) 'The concept of hospitality'. Paper presented at the International Jubilee Conference, Hague Hotel School.

Goffman, E. (1959) *The Presentation of Self in Everyday Life*, Penguin, Harmondsworth.

Hayner, N. S. (1964) 'Hotel life: physical proximity and social distance', in E. W. Burgess and D. J. Bogue (Eds), *Contributions to Urban Sociology*, University of Chicago Press, Chicago.

Heal, F. (1990) *Hospitality in Early Modern England*, Clarendon Press, Oxford.

Hepple, J., Kipps, M. and Thomson, J. (1990) 'The concept of hospitality and an evaluation of its applicability to the experience of hospital patients', *International Journal of Hospitality Management*, 9: 305–318.

Homans, G. (1961) *Social Behaviour: Its Elementary Forms*, Harcourt Brace, New York.

Mars, G. and Nicod, M. (1984) *The World of Waiters*, George Allen & Unwin, London.

Mauss, M. (1967) *The Gift*, Routledge, London.

Muhlmann, W. E. (1932) 'Hospitality', in E. R. A. Seligman (Ed.), *Encyclopaedia of the Social Sciences*, Macmillan, New York.

Nailon, P. (1982) 'Theory in hospitality management', *International Journal of Hospitality Management*, 1: 135–143.

Petronius (1986) *The Satyricon*, Penguin, Harmondsworth.

Pitt-Rivers, J. (1977) *The Fate of Shechem*, Cambridge University Press, Cambridge.

Rojek, C. (1985) *Capitalism and Leisure Theory*, Tavistock, London.

Ryan, C. (1991) *Recreational Tourism: a Social Science Perspective*, Routledge, London.

Stone, U. B. (1932) 'Hotels', in E. R. A. Seligman (Ed.), *Encyclopaedia of the Social Sciences*, Macmillan, New York.

Stringer, P. F. (1981) 'Hosts and guests: the bed-and-breakfast phenomenon', *Annals of Tourism Research*, 8: 357–376.

Turner, J. H. (1974) *The Structure of Social Theory*, Dorsey Press, Homewood, IL.

Wood, R. C. (1983) 'Theory, management and hospitality: a response to Philip Nailon', *International Journal of Hospitality Management*, 1: 135.

Wood, R. C. (1994) 'Hotels and social control', *Annals of Tourism Research*, 21: 65–80.

78 Social contact between tourists and hosts of different cultural backgrounds

Y. REISINGER

Introduction

Today many tourism industry officials are concerned in determining what can be done to increase the number of international tourist arrivals that contribute to the improvement in the country's economic situation. One of the important criteria that determines which tourist destination is most likely to be chosen by tourists for their holidays is the quality of tourist–host contact. It is important to know how to develop positive tourist–host contact. The only way to achieve it is to understand that success depends on the recognition of cultural differences between tourists' and hosts' backgrounds.

The large increase in the number of international travellers in the South Pacific region and other parts of the world, particularly the non-English-speaking travellers from Asia and Japan and more lately China, has created opportunity for intense interactions of tourists and hosts from diverse cultures and heavy demand for sensitivity to the cultural differences and needs of others. This indicates that an understanding of cultural differences in tourist–host contact will become an increasingly important factor contributing to future successful tourism business operations.

The purpose of this paper is to summarise findings of the existing literature on the concept of social contact and to show its relevance and importance to the cross-cultural tourist–host contact.

Social contact

Social contact refers to the 'personal association taking place under certain circumstances, or to the interaction which covers a wide range of behaviours from observation of members of the other group without any communication, to prolonged intimate association' (Cook and Sellitz, 1955: 52–53). Social contact is characterised by two common elements. Firstly, it is always between a minimum of two people (Bochner, 1982), and secondly, it has potential to be positive, negative or superficial (Fridgen, 1991).

There are of course many kinds of social contact. Each contact can take place in a 'multitude of different situations' and can refer to a 'multitude of different experiences' (Cook and Sellitz, 1955:52). For instance, social contact can develop between children, college students, or factory workers. It can take place in recreation camps, within the work environment or residential neighbourhood. It can be referred to as short-term interpersonal encounters or long-term friendships.

Tourist–host social contact

The tourist–host contact refers to the personal association or interaction between tourists and hosts. Tourists are temporary visitors staying at least 24 hours in the country visited for the purpose of leisure, recreation and holiday (McIntosh and Goeldner, 1990). Hosts are people of the visited country who are directly and indirectly employed in the tourism industry and provide service to tourists. Nettekoven (1979) refers to these people as 'professional hosts', in contrast to the local residents who can also be referred to as hosts.

The tourist–host contact occurs in a wide variety of situations as tourists travel in planes, stay in hotels, dine in restaurants, visit tourist attractions, shop at local news agencies, and so on. This contact may consist of business transactions at stores as well as enquiries at the front office, or polite greetings. It may take different forms; for example it may occur between tourists and hosts who are members of different cultural groups.

Contact hypothesis

The contact hypothesis was developed in the United States after World War II, in the study of social contact between two different racial or ethnic groups. The contact hypothesis states that social contact between two different ethnic groups results in changing the attitudes and relations of the interacting members. Further, this change in attitudes and relations, in most cases, is a favourable one. According to Amir and Ben-Ari (1988), Allport (1954) and Cook (1962) the contact among individuals from diverse groups creates opportunity for mutual acquaintance, enhances understanding and acceptance among the interaction group members, and consequently reduces intergroup prejudice, conflict and tension. Fulbright (1976) and Bochner (1982) reported that social contact between individuals from different cultural groups results in mutual appreciation, understanding, respect, tolerance and liking. It helps to bridge gaps between people; it lessens social prejudices and racial tension (Mann, 1959; Robinson and Preston, 1976). It encourages positive attitudes among contact participants, thus reducing ethnic prejudices and negative stereotypes; it improves interaction between the individuals; it contributes to the cultural enrichment and learning about others (Nunez, 1963; Li and Yu, 1974; Unesco, 1976; Vogt, 1977).

Contact hypothesis as applied to tourist–host contact

The contact hypothesis can be applied to tourist–host contact. It was proposed that social contact between tourists and hosts from different cultural groups leads to enhancement of tourists' and hosts' attitudes toward each other; it gives them an opportunity to learn about each other's culture (Bochner, 1982). For instance, there is empirical evidence to suggest that tourist–host contact results in a positive attitudinal change towards their hosts (Pearce, 1982b). Amir and Ben-Ari (1985) reported that Israelis' negative pre-holiday attitudes towards Egyptians changed after holidaying in Egypt. It was also suggested that the longer the social contact exists, the more positive attitudes of tourists become towards the host country (Li and Yu, 1974). Positive attitudes often lead to the forming of cross-cultural friendships (Gudykunst, 1979). Many studies have found that tourists develop friendships with hosts and take pride in the hosts' countries (e.g. Boissevain, 1979). Cohen (1971) reported that tourist–host contact increases the hosts' self-esteem. Some studies found that tourist–host contact results in psychological satisfaction with mutual interaction (Stringer, 1981). Table 78.1 demonstrates positive effects of cross-cultural tourist–host contact.

The contact hypothesis was, however, questioned. Amir (1969: 337–338) reported that 'it would be naive to assume that any . . . contact will produce the same

Table 78.1 *Cross-cultural tourist–host contact—positive effects*

Developing positive attitudes towards each other
Learning about each other's culture and customs
Reducing negative perceptions and stereotypes
Developing friendships
Developing pride, appreciation, understanding, respect and tolerance for each other's culture
Increasing self-esteem of hosts and tourists
Psychological satisfaction with interaction

results'. Milman et al. (1990) noted that tourist–host contact does not automatically contribute to positive attitudinal changes nor to the reduction of perceived cultural differences. For instance, the attitudes of Israeli tourists visiting Egypt either remained unchanged or deteriorated as a result of the trip to Egypt. In the case of US students visiting the former USSR, the students' attitudes towards the host country improved only marginally (Pizam et al., 1991). It was argued that tourists can only modify their attitudes and be more confident in their beliefs (Pearce, 1977, 1988), regardless of whether these beliefs are positive or negative. For instance, Americans viewed Greeks more negatively, while Greeks viewed Americans more positively as a result of mutual cross-cultural contact (Triandis, 1972; Triandis and Vassiliou, 1967).

It was also reported that contact between people from diverse cultures may result in negative attitudes, perceptions, stereotypes and prejudices. It may increase tension, hostility, suspicion, and often violent attacks (Bochner, 1982; Bloom, 1971; Tajfel and Dawson, 1965). Differences in language, national origin, identity and cultural values (Feather, 1976, 1980b) generate tension, misunderstanding (Bochner, 1982; Sutton, 1967); tourist isolation, separation, segregation from the host community (Bochner, 1982); clashes of values, conflict (Biddlecomb, 1981; Boissevain, 1979; Choy, 1984; Pi-Sunnyer, 1982; Petit-Skinner, 1977), exclusion from mutual activities, social barriers, difficulty in forming personal friendships (Peterson and Neumeyer, 1948; Schmoker, 1954; Asar, 1952; Rathore, 1958); feelings of inferiority, self-rejection (Bettelheim, 1943; Lewing, 1941); jealousy, xenophobia, disinterest, rudeness, hostility (Pearce, J. A., 1980); communication problems (Argyle et al., 1981; Klineberg, 1980; Porter, 1972); ethnocentrism (Triandis and Vassiliou, 1967); culture shock (Bochner, 1982). For instance, Brewer (1984), studying American tourists in a Mexican town, concluded that the interaction between natives and tourists may result in lesser rather than greater understanding owing to lack of communication between the two groups. Anastasopoulos (1992) reported that travel to Turkey had a negative impact on Greek tourists' perceptions of the host population. When there are differences in cultural backgrounds, social contact between tourists and hosts may turn into a negative experience. This type of experience creates only disappointment, discouragement and dissatisfaction (Pearce, 1982b). Such negative feelings inhibit social contact (Kamal and Maruyama, 1990). Also, the more frequent the contact, the more likely negative feelings and attitudes will develop (Anant, 1971). Table 78.2 demonstrates negative effects of cross-cultural tourist–host contact.

Table 78.2 *Cross-cultural tourist–host contact—negative effects*

Developing negative attitudes towards each other
Tension, hostility, suspicion and misunderstanding
Isolation, segregation and separation
Clashes of values
Difficulties in forming friendships
Feelings of inferiority and superiority
Communication problems
Ethnocentrism
Culture shock
Dissatisfaction with mutual interaction

Factors influencing social contact

The question arises, 'what factors determine the positive and negative effects of social contact?'

Firstly, it has been argued that different opportunities for social contact (Amir, 1969), defined as the opportunities 'provided by the situation for the participants to get to know and understand one another' (Cook, 1962:75), provide different chances for interaction (Schild, 1962) and produce different experiences. If opportunities for contact are provided, the contact may produce positive experiences and encourage future interaction. Otherwise it may create negative experiences (Kelman, 1962) and discourage further interaction. However, although the opportunities for contact exist, people from different ethnic backgrounds may not establish even minimal contact with each other. They may interact with their own nationals, who are not their friends but speak the same language and have a similar background, rather than with foreigners. Therefore, it seems that the provision of opportunities for contact is not sufficient for the development of cross-cultural interaction.

Secondly, a number of researchers have pointed out that social contact depends on the interactants' attitudes to each other (Amir, 1969; Guttman and Foa, 1951; Smith, H., 1955, 1957) and sociability (Williams, 1964). Those with positive attitudes tend to be more active in social relations, and those with less positive attitudes tend to be less active (Festinger and Kelly, 1951). Also, the more prejudiced a person is, the less likely it will be for that person to be involved in interactional contact (Williams, 1964). Since attitudes influence perceptions (Bochner, 1982), social contact also depends on the interactants' perceptions of each other.

Thirdly, it was found that social contact is positively related to social motivators such as the desire to interact with people (Cohen, 1972; Schul and Crompton, 1983). Those who want to socialise with other people are more likely to get involved in social contact.

Fourthly, it was also reported that there are special conditions under which contact takes place (Amir, 1969; Amir and Ben-Ari, 1988). The degree to which the participants are cooperative or competitive in their social contact (Allport, 1954; Williams, 1947), mutual interests, common goals, shared activities (Sellitz and Cook, 1962) and equal status (Kelman, 1962; Sellitz and Cook, 1962; Triandis and Vassiliou, 1967) determines the social contact. Factors which create favourable conditions for the development of social contact are as follows:

1. equal status between the contact participants
2. contact between members of majority groups and higher status members of minority groups
3. a favourable social climate and/or an authority that promotes interaction
4. intimate rather than casual or superficial contact
5. pleasant, mutually rewarding rather than stressful contact
6. common activities, interests, goals of higher importance to the group rather than the individuals
7. cooperation rather than competition between contact participants
8. functional importance of contact and similar philosophies (Amir, 1969; Amir and Ben-Ari, 1988; Bochner, 1982; Robinson and Preston, 1976).

It was argued that only under these conditions is social contact effective and does it bring positive and rewarding experiences. The above conditions tend to reduce the negative attitudes, prejudices and tension (Amir, 1969, 1976; Triandis and Vassiliou, 1967). Positive attitudes between participants develop, friendships form, and the potential for future interaction is increased. The opposite applies to the unfavourable conditions for the development of social contact. However, the perceived status, goals, interests, activities, willingness to cooperate or compete are determined by the cultural backgrounds of the contact participants: their values, beliefs, norms, etc. The differences in cultural background create different expectations, generate different experiences, contribute to development of different attitudes and perceptions. The differences in cultural background may create differences in the perceptions of whether the status is equal, whether the goals and interests are mutual, whether the contact participants can get involved in mutual activities or engage in conversation. Consequently, different cultural backgrounds determine willingness to engage in mutual interaction. Amir (1969) suggested that the cultural factors are very important in explaining the social contact. The social contact is determined by the cultural differences in values that, in turn, determine the perceived status and common goals.

Factors influencing cross-cultural tourist–host contact

There are several factors that determine cross-cultural tourist–host contact. Firstly, the provision of opportunities for contact may encourage tourist–host interaction. However, tourists and hosts from different cultural backgrounds may prefer to interact with their own tourists—nationals who speak the same language, have similar backgrounds, travel motivations and interests rather than with foreign hosts. Therefore, cultural background and language spoken determine whether tourist–host contact will be established.

Secondly, tourist–host contact is positively related to the development of positive attitudes (Fisher and Price, 1991). Fisher and Price (1991) also reported that positive attitudes among tourists and hosts develop because tourist–host contact represents voluntary contact. The positive attitude may form cross-cultural friendships (Gudykunst, 1979) or develop intense personal relationships that last for many years (Smith, H., 1957).

Thirdly, positive attitudes result when contact is undertaken for the purpose of social interaction with new people (Robinson and Preston, 1976). Fisher and Price (1991) and Ho (1978) argued that interpersonal motivators, and specifically 'new people' motivators, do result in the development of positive attitudes towards the host community and a high level of social interaction.

Fourthly, it was argued that the cross-cultural tourist–host contact depends primarily on the nature of the tourist–host contact. Tourist–host contact is characterised as: brief (Fridgen, 1991); temporary and non-repetitive (Sutton, 1967); asymmetric in terms of its different meanings for contact participants (Hoivik and Heiberg, 1980), different roles played by participants (Sutton, 1967), their different situational status (Van den Berghe and Keyes, 1984), different motivations, access to wealth and information (Van den Berghe and Keyes, 1984), and different socio-economic and cultural identity (Din, 1989; Jafari, 1989). Tourist–host contact is superficial (Krippendorf, 1987); formal (de Kadt, 1979); lacking spontaneity, limited to business transactions (Fridgen, 1991; Cohen and Cooper, 1986; Jafari, 1989); competitive (Din, 1989); demanding constantly new experiences on behalf of tourists (Sutton, 1967); and its outcomes are ambiguous (Hoivik and Heiberg, 1980). According to MacCannell (1984:384–388), 'any contact which is transitory, superficial, unequal is a primary ground for deceit, exploitation, mistrust, dishonesty and stereotype formation'. These unfavourable conditions provide little opportunity for intensive and long-lasting tourist–host interaction. If a more intensive interaction occurs, it is more likely to be tourist-to-tourist rather than tourist-to-local resident. It is even less likely to develop between tourists and service providers who are profit-motivated (Cohen and Cooper, 1986) and tend to accommodate the tourists' needs only for the purpose of financial gain (Jafari, 1989). However, it can be argued that since tourists are highly concentrated in the places of tourist attractions and isolated by the 'environmental bubble', most tourist encounters are primarily with service providers whom Nettekoven (1979) referred to as 'professional hosts'.

Fifthly, the cultural background of tourists and hosts determines the level of the cross-cultural tourist–host contact. Since tourists and hosts have often different cultural identities, the differences in their cultural backgrounds, whether they are regional or national, additionally affect the intensity and duration of contact. Sutton (1967) and Taft (1977) argued that the influence of cultural background of tourists and hosts is very important in explaining their social contact. The influence of cultural background is particularly strong when tourists and hosts speak different languages, have different values, life philosophies and totally different perceptions of the world (Bochner, 1982; Sutton, 1967).

Sutton (1967) distinguished three types of tourist–host contact based on cultural background. In the first type, tourists and hosts have similar backgrounds and their social contact is most effective. According to Feather (1980a) those with a similar cultural background are likely to interact socially because they perceive themselves more positively (Obot, 1988). The similarity in the cultural background increases mutual attraction and liking, and decreases social distance (Brewer and Campbell, 1976). In the second type, tourists and hosts have different cultural backgrounds but the differences are small. Therefore, tourists and hosts are likely to interact socially. For instance, the differences in cultural background of German tourists and Austrian hosts are very small. German tourists and Austrian hosts speak the same language, have very similar traditions, customs and lifestyle. Therefore, German tourists and Austrian hosts are likely to understand each other and interact socially. In the third type, tourists and hosts have completely different cultural backgrounds. The dissimilarities in cultural background inhibit social interaction (Feather, 1980a,b) and the probability that tourist–host encounters will lead to friction and misunderstanding is high (Sutton, 1967). For instance, Japanese tourists and French hosts have different cultural backgrounds. They speak different languages, have distinct histories and traditions, and they even eat different food. Therefore, they are not likely to understand each other and interact socially. Similarly, Japanese tourists and Australian hosts have different cultural backgrounds. In order to facilitate the Japanese tourists' stay in Australia and eliminate the interaction difficulties, many Japanese tourists are taken care of by Japanese hosts.

The analysis of cultural backgrounds of tourists and hosts provides important information about the possible reasons for misunderstandings between tourists and hosts. The differences in their cultural background may inhibit interaction, reduce it or even eliminate the opportunity of future contact. Table 78.3 demonstrates factors that affect cross-cultural tourist–host contact.

It is important to note that the influence of cultural background on tourist–host contact varies with: different types of tourists, different types of travel arrangements, the role of a tour guide, the stage of tourism development and the ratio of tourists to hosts, the amount of information tourists and hosts have about each other, and the mode of tourist–host interaction.

Cohen's (1972, 1974) institutionalised mass and individual tourist, who is surrounded by the environmental bubble and taken care of by tour companies and tour guides can escape the influence of foreign culture in the contact with foreign hosts. It has been argued that the mass tourist has little opportunity for direct tourist–host contact and the influence of differences in the cultural background of host on tourist is reduced. However, this depends on, for example, the individual tourists, their interests and the experiences they seek, the type of tours they want to participate in, the country they want to visit, etc. For instance, the mass sex tours organised for German and Japanese tourists provide maximum opportunity for direct tourist–host contact.

The individual and non-institutionalised tourist, such as the explorer and drifter who seeks more authentic cultural experiences and desires more interaction with foreign natives, has more opportunity to interact with native hosts and is exposed more to foreign culture. For instance, German backpackers who travel individually around Australia have numerous opportunities to interact with Aboriginal people, to get familiar with their lifestyle, to appreciate their music, dance and art, and

Table 78.3 *Factors that affect cross-cultural tourist–host contact*

Opportunity for contact
Attitudes to each other
Social motivators/purpose of travel
Nature of tourist–host contact
Cultural background

consequently, to better understand the Australian history and culture.

Organised, guided and all-inclusive tours protect tourists from direct contact with foreign hosts and from different cultures, stresses and anxieties. Therefore, they reduce the impact that cultural differences have on the tourist–host contact. Anastasopoulos (1992) reported that in the case of travel to a country perceived as 'unfriendly', contact with the host population may even be resisted by tourists. Tourists may develop intimate relations with the tour participants rather than with foreign hosts.

The tour guide who speaks the tourist's language, and understands the tourist's culture and customs can facilitate tourist contact with foreign hosts and enable tourists to feel secure and less alienated in the host community. The tour guide's role is to develop a positive tourist–host contact by helping the tourist to overcome the cross-cultural interaction difficulties. Schmidt (1979) reported that by emphasising the educational aspects of sightseeing, tour guides quickly remove many of the tourists' interaction difficulties and anxieties. However, the tour guides can also isolate tourists from contact with native hosts. For instance, in some political and economic systems (e.g. the former USSR or China), the tour guide's role is to present the host community in the best light and to hide 'uncomfortable' information from tourists. In such systems the tour guide's role is to reduce the chances for direct tourist–host contact and to isolate tourists from the influence of the host culture on tourist–host contact.

In the early stage of tourism development, when cultural differences between tourists and hosts are noticeable and hosts are not prepared for large numbers of tourists who have different lifestyles, habits and needs, and who converse in different languages, the influence of the cultural background of tourists and hosts on their mutual contact may be negative and limit their interaction. In the later stage of tourism development, as the number of tourists increases, the differences between tourists and hosts may become even more noticeable. However, it can be argued that, as hosts become more involved in tourism development and acquire more professional, interpersonal and intercultural skills, the negative influences of different cultural backgrounds on tourist–host contact diminish, thus creating the opportunity for future tourist–host interaction. Better knowledge and understanding of the cultural background of the other party may bring pleasure instead of frustration when interacting with foreigners, speaking new languages and learning about the culture of others.

The amount and the quality of information tourists and hosts have about each other determines whether they perceive themselves positively or negatively and whether they are willing to interact with each other. The vague information in travel brochures does not provide tourists with information on the foreign hosts' culture. The quality of the information provided by tour guides can also be questioned. V. Smith (1978) has argued that local guides may provide a distorted view of the host culture to visitors. For instance, in countries such as the former USSR or China, tour guides may distort information in order to reply to tourists' enquiries with 'party line' answers. Tour guides may also refuse to answer certain questions on economic, political and social problems. This often creates false experiences and expectations of tourists. This can further disrupt the cross-cultural interactions between tourists and hosts.

Marsh and Henshall (1987) identified four distinct modes of tourist–host interaction, namely: 'separatism', 'involuntary', 'voluntary' and 'integration'. The 'separatism' mode protects tourists from the influence of the host culture. Tourists are taken care of by tour companies and they do not have the chance to interact frequently with native hosts. The 'involuntary' mode provides tourists with more opportunities to contact foreign hosts. Tourists on semi-independent packages, have more independence and, therefore, are more vulnerable to cultural differences. In the 'voluntary' mode, tourists use services independently, are actively involved in daily life and culture of the hosts, especially in smaller tourism centres 'off the beaten track' and, therefore, they are under greater influence of the foreign culture than tourists who are involved in the 'involuntary' mode of interaction. In the 'integration' mode, which involves visiting friends and relatives (VFR), tourists have the greatest opportunities to interact with hosts through their friends and relatives. They experience a lifestyle similar to that of the hosts. They are under the influence of the host culture. Since the holiday is normally of long duration (6–12 months), tourists become integrated into the foreign lifestyle. It can be argued that the easy and quick access to the friends of the family and to the information network of the hosts enables tourists to learn quickly about the foreign culture and adapt to it. However, this also depends on the individual differences, interests, motivations, etc.

The influence of tourists' and hosts' cultural background on their social contact varies depending on numerous other factors; for example, the level of mixing between tourists and hosts, the extent to which tourists and hosts participate in mutual activities, and their satisfaction with each other's presence (Husbands, 1986). Table 78.4 demonstrates factors that determine the influence of cultural background in tourist–host contact.

It was argued that regardless of the many factors that determine the cross-cultural tourist–host contact tourists

Table 78.4 *Factors that determine the influence of cultural background on tourist–host contact*

Type of tourist	institutionalised mass v. non-institutionalised individual
Type of travel arrangements	organised v. non-organised
Role of tour guide	facilitating v. isolating
Stage of tourism development	early v. later
Amount and quality of information	vague v. adequate
Mode of tourist–host interaction	'separatism', 'involuntary', 'voluntary', 'integration'

will always be influenced by their cultural background and experience interaction difficulties with their hosts (Pearce, 1982b).

Interaction difficulties in cross-cultural tourist–host contact

The major interaction difficulties in the tourist–host contact due to cultural differences were found in interpersonal communication (e.g. polite language usage, expressing feelings and emotions, reactions to criticism, complaining, apologising); non-verbal signals (e.g. physical contact such as touching, spatial behaviour, facial expressions, gestures, posture, eye contact); patterns of interpersonal interaction (e.g. greetings, self-disclosure, self-presentation, self-restraint, managing conflict) (Bochner, 1982). These differences make the interaction very difficult. The same verbal or non-verbal signals and patterns of interaction have different meanings in various cultures and are likely to be misunderstood. For instance, referring to someone by the first name to show friendliness and a lack of formality in interpersonal relations may be regarded by Australian hosts as polite but may be considered as impolite by Asian tourists. Openly disagreeing or saying 'no' may be considered by Japanese and other Asian tourists as rude; however, Australian hosts may regard it as an acceptable way of behaviour. Touching and slapping on the back may be regarded by Australian hosts as expression of friendliness but may be considered as lack of respect and dignity by Chinese tourists. Gift-giving may be regarded by Japanese tourists as an appreciation of time and effort spent with them; however, Australian hosts may consider it as bribery. Tipping may be regarded by European tourists as a reward for being well served but may be considered as an insult by Australian hosts. Expressing an interest in family matters may be regarded as polite in India and Pakistan but may be considered as rude in Australia. The 'OK' gesture in America may be confused with the

Japanese gesture to refer to money (Morsbach, 1973). The continuous escort of tourists by hosts everywhere may be viewed by the Chinese hosts as a courtesy. However, American tourists may consider it as an intrusion, lack of freedom in choice of activities, privacy and lack of trust (Wei et al., 1989). The Japanese hosts' willingness to take care of the affairs of their guests in advance and fulfil their needs immediately (Zimmerman, 1985; Befu, 1971) may be frustrating for American and Australian tourists who know best what their needs are and may regard the Japanese hosts' hospitality with discomfort. The examples of cultural differences in the tourists' and hosts' backgrounds are endless. Stringer (1981) reported that even a different custom of handling cutlery and eating habits may create interaction difficulties between tourists and hosts.

The reasons for interaction difficulties is that when tourists and hosts interact socially in their own culture they know which behaviour is proper and which is wrong. They behave in a way accepted by their respective cultures. They accept proper and reject wrong behaviour. Those who are engaged in socially unacceptable behaviour are considered as ill-mannered. Those who are engaged in socially acceptable behaviour are considered as well-mannered. But when tourists and hosts interact with someone from another culture, they do not know what behaviour is proper and what is wrong. The behaviour which is seen as proper in one culture is not always seen the same way in another culture. Since tourists and hosts are confronted with a culture different from their own, many situations are unfamiliar to them. It is difficult for them to engage in interaction with someone who has different standards of behaviour, a different way of thinking, communicating, doing things, etc. The differences in cultural values, lifestyles, traditions, etc. decide how the behaviour of others is interpreted and perceived, whether it is regarded as proper or irritating or even insulting. If the behaviour of others is perceived as proper, it is likely that tourists and hosts will engage in mutual interaction. However, a common reaction to different behaviour of culturally different people is dislike, and one which leads to prejudices. The necessity to adapt to a new culture within a short period of time can cause additional frustration, leading to even more negative feelings about members of the other culture.

Brislin et al. (1986) indicated that the major reasons for interactional difficulties are cultural differences in categorisation, differentiation, in-group and out-group distinction, and attribution processes. According to the theory of Brislin et al. (1986), conflicts arise in cross-cultural tourist–host interaction because there are major differences in the way tourists and hosts categorise the same set of behaviours. Stereotypes develop because tourists and hosts are unable to acquire and categorise appropriately much information about the other culture in a short period of time. Tourists and hosts who have not been exposed to a particular culture's standards or categorisation, are more likely to impose their own culture's categories on others' categories and use unfamiliar categories wrongly. Tourists and hosts also differentiate between various concepts in a distinct way. For instance, the concept of 'friendship' may have different meanings to American tourists and Chinese hosts. Americans regard friendship as superficial, without obligations. Chinese assume mutual obligations and expect reciprocation (Wei et al., 1989). This often creates false expectations and frustration due to unconfirmed expectations. Tourists and hosts also have different ways of judging others and themselves, according to their own standards.

Insensitivity to cultural differences may cause numerous problems between tourists and hosts. The major cultural problems identified by Wei et al. (1989) are: ethnocentrism (belief in the superiority of own culture), communication problems (insufficient fluency in a foreign language, problems related to interpretations and lack of information), dissatisfaction with poor quality service (lack of concern for visitors, lack of tradition of hospitality, lack of interpersonal skills of the hosts), and differences in lifestyle (customs, food, etiquette, developing friendships).

The perception of service quality by tourists is particularly important for the assessment of their hosts. Interacting with service providers is the primary way in which tourists form their perceptions of service and make judgements about their hosts/service providers. Cultural differences influence the interaction processes between service providers and tourists. Service providers may be perceived differently by tourists and hosts. The tourists' and hosts' perceptions of service providers may have different implications for the assessment of service quality. Qualities such as being friendly, prompt, helpful may have different meanings in different cultures. Being open, informal, relaxed may be admired in many Western cultures. In other cultures (e.g. in Asia) these qualities may be viewed as a lack of good manners, grace or efficiency and create unpleasant encounters between tourists and hosts. Therefore, there is a great scope for the development of negative perceptions of service quality by tourists when tourists and hosts have different cultural backgrounds. The ability to recognise different service expectations of tourists and the need to cater to those expectations, according to the tourists' definitions of service quality, is important. Since tourists' expectations are shaped by their culture, their culture is the basis for

the service standards acceptable by tourists. It can be argued that the tourists' expectations are also shaped by other factors, e.g. media, intermediaries, etc. However, although the other factors exist, the influence of culture on individuals is the most important (Porter and Samovar, 1988).

Culture shock

The differences in cultural background of tourists and hosts may also create a sense of culture shock (Bochner, 1986; Furnham and Bochner, 1986) described as 'the reaction of . . . to problems encountered in . . . dealings with host members' (Bochner, 1982:172). Culture shock was also described as a 'state of stress and anxiety that results from disturbing impressions' (Craig, 1979:159) or 'the loss of equilibrium they (tourists) feel when they lose familiar signs and symbols of social intercourse and when they encounter . . . differences in an alien culture'. Oberg (1960) defined culture shock as shock that takes place when people lack familiar cues about how to behave in a new culture. Lundstedt (1963) referred to culture shock as a reaction to an unsuccessful attempt to adjust to new surroundings and people. Culture shock appears because of the rejection of the host community, confusion of values, feelings of incompetence (Taft, 1977).

Tourists may face culture shock when they travel to unknown cultures since many encounters with taxi drivers, hotel staff, receptionists, shop assistants and custom officials are stressful for them owing to the differences in tourists' and hosts' culture and languages. Many contact situations are confusing. The inability to adjust to a new culture and new standards within a short period of time makes tourists feel inadequate and hopeless. Many symptoms of culture shock have been reported, such as strain, sense of loss, feelings of being rejected, embarrassed, frustrated or confused about own identity and values, anxiety, fatigue at constant adaptation, negative feelings toward hosts, refusing to learn the new language, increase in irritation, criticism, decline in initiative and spontaneity, preoccupation with worries (Bochner, 1982; Oberg, 1960; Taft, 1977; Textor, 1966). In such circumstances the tourist–host contact creates conflict between tourists and hosts, increases the 'irritation level' (Doxey, 1976) and generates stress (Pearce, 1982b; Holmes and Rahe, 1967). This reduces or even eliminates the opportunity for future tourist–host contact.

There are many stages of culture shock ranging from excitement, confusion and rejection of a new culture, to understanding the host culture and becoming more culturally aware and sensitive (Adler, 1975). Brein and

David's (1971) U-shaped pattern of discomfort of living in a new cultural environment refers to: the optimistic stage; difficulties in coping with the new culture stage; feelings of frustration and confusion stage; learning to cope and feelings of satisfaction stage; looking forward to return home stage. Gullahorn and Gullahorn's (1963) W-shaped model of adjustment process refers to: honeymoon stage; hostility stage; humour stage; at home stage; reverse culture shock stage; and readjustment stage. The W-shaped model is, however, inaccurate, given the complexity of tourist types, individual differences and experiences. Also, at present more tourists are better informed about the foreign countries they intend to visit and the difficulties they may encounter. Tourists can get more professional advice before travelling abroad and may not experience culture shock at all. It was also argued that the environmental bubble protects tourists from culture shock and a mass tourist does not experience culture shock to the same degree as individual and non-institutionalised tourists. Furthermore, the length of the tourist stay in a foreign country determines whether or not the tourist will experience the influence of foreign culture. The tourist whose stay in a foreign country is shorter is less exposed to the influence of foreign culture than the tourist whose stay is longer. However, Taft (1977) argued that tourists who visit a large number of cultures in a short time can be in a constant shock because they have little chance to adapt to each new culture. Also, tourists may experience culture shock limited only to the initial stage (Gullahorn and Gullahorn, 1963; Taft, 1977). Some tourists may never leave the 'honeymoon stage' (Gullahorn and Gullahorn, 1963) or 'enthusiasm and excitement' stage (Brein and David, 1971), particularly when their stay in a foreign country is very short. Instead of being frustrated, visitors may feel excited about new experiences in the foreign culture (Mehrabian and Russell, 1974), meeting new people and speaking new languages.

Culture shock plays an important role in the cross-cultural tourist–host contact. Its duration depends on the extent of cultural differences between tourists and hosts and the level of the tourist–host contact.

Many theorists reported that the differences in cultural background affect tourists and hosts more in developing countries than in developed countries (Biddlecomb, 1981; Boissevain, 1979; de Kadt, 1979). Pearce (1982a) argued that in technologically developed countries the differences between tourists and hosts are not significant, therefore, the chances for tourist–host contact are great. In less advanced societies, the contrasts between tourists and locals are significant (Biddlecomb, 1981; Boissevain, 1979; de Kadt, 1979) and the opportunities for tourist–host contact are small. Krippendorf (1987:60) stated that a 'true meeting is possible only when people have something in common'. Visitors to the third world and natives belong not only to different cultures but also to different social classes. Since tourists and hosts share nothing, have different roles to play, no meaningful dialogue can take place. Misunderstanding instead of understanding and confrontation instead of meeting takes place. However, caution must be exercised in making such generalisations. There is still insufficient information available on the underdeveloped areas.

It is important to note that, although both tourists and hosts are highly skilled socially in their own culture, they may not be socially skilled in a foreign culture. They do not have both verbal and non-verbal skills to interact smoothly. Therefore, they may feel even more inadequate, frustrated and embarrassed (Bochner, 1982) by their inability to cope in a foreign culture. However, those who have vast travel experience and are trained in foreign cultures, languages and international relations, are better prepared to interact socially in foreign cultures, and instead of experiencing negative feelings they may even enjoy dealing with foreign people.

Conclusion

Cultural differences, together with asymmetry of the frequent and transitory tourist–host contact, are the most important factors which influence interaction difficulties between tourists and hosts (Pearce, 1982b; Sutton, 1967). Therefore, understanding of cross-cultural tourist–host contact and the influence of the cultural background of tourists and hosts is the key feature for identification of the future potential for tourist–host interaction and the effects of this interaction on the overall tourist holiday satisfaction.

Recommendations for the development of positive cross-cultural tourist–host contact

The following recommendations highlight the need for the improvement of tourist–host contact by better training of personnel in the tourism and hospitality industry in the area of cultural awareness and human relations.

The development of positive cross-cultural tourist–host contact depends mainly on understanding the specific nature of the tourist–host contact together with the role cultural differences play in the tourist–host interactions. The following recommendations for the development of positive cross-cultural tourist–host contact are suggested.

1. The provision is recommended of an effective educational programme and a better appreciation and understanding of foreign cultures, languages and international relations, for all those involved in international tourism, travel and hospitality at national and regional levels. The psychological study of tourists and their cultural backgrounds should be introduced. Such training would facilitate the communcation between tourists and hosts and provide more relaxed conditions for tourist–host interaction, thus establishing positive tourist–host contact.

2. The range of possible culturally contrasting behaviour in tourist–host contact between different cultural groups should be analysed. Cultural differences that lead to negative perceptions should be identified and isolated from the tourists' experiences. The development of tourist–host contact should be based on shared and internationally accepted standards of behaviour.

3. Specific attention should be given to the attributes of professional hosts who are in direct contact with tourists and provide services to tourists. The service providers' concern for tourists, welcoming attitude towards tourists, effort to understand tourists' needs, hosts' tolerance and generosity are universally expected by all international tourists. These service attributes should be emphasised in every educational and training programme.

4. The provision of well-skilled hosts is imperative. Only those employees who are suitable to the job, are interaction-oriented, and have strong interpersonal skills, should be hired.

5. The establishment of licensing or certificating requirements is needed to train all those working with international tourists. Special training for tour guides and interpreters in the tourist's language and culture is required in order to interpret, explain and respond quickly and appropriately to the cross-cultural interaction difficulties which determine the outcome of the tourist–host contact. For example, many European countries (including those in Eastern Europe), and Japan and the USA have national examinations for international tour guides in several foreign languages and examinations which test applicants' knowledge of national and foreign politics, history, geography and cultures. Aptitude, organisational skills and financial management skills tests are also common.

6. More attention should be directed towards informing tourists about host cultures through media and travel intermediaries. The tourists' respect and willingness to understand the host culture and pride in their own cultural background may result in positive tourist–host contact.

7. Raising standards of general education for local residents of tourist destinations should also be considered. For instance, short courses on international politics, world geography, history, foreign languages and cultures, and socio-cultural and economic impacts of international

tourism should be offered to the general public. Free access to museums, national and international exhibitions and festivals to host communities should also be provided. Developing more links with international universities, opening new courses specialising in international relations and emphasising the importance of coexistence with other cultural systems, supporting cross-cultural research, appointing more foreigners in academia and the public service, organising more international student exchange programmes and youth holiday camps are also examples of improving the general education level of local hosts. This can be done via both governmental and non-governmental organisations. As a result, knowledge of different cultures and people would be improved and the ability to understand tourists with different cultural backgrounds would be enhanced. The negative experiences of tourists and hosts are caused mostly by the lack of exposure to other cultures. They can be overcome if both parties are able to appreciate and respect each other's cultural background, learn to be proud of it, and eliminate feelings of their own cultural superiority and ethnocentrism.

A number of benefits would follow for all those attending educational and training programmes:

1. greater understanding of own and others' cultures
2. the development of appreciation, respect and pride in own and others' cultures
3. an increase in self-esteem and self-worth
4. a decrease in negative attitudes, perceptions, stereotypes, prejudices and racial discrimination
5. a decrease in tension, hostility and suspicion resulting from cultural misunderstandings
6. improved communication levels and reduced culture shock
7. an increase in enjoyment from cross-cultural interaction
8. greater opportunities for developing cross-cultural friendships
9. better understanding of the everyday difficulties encountered in social relations with other cultures
10. better job performance of those who have direct contact with international tourists
11. greater satisfaction with job performance
12. the development of the positive perceptions of hosts by tourists and vice versa
13. an increase in positive economic, and socio-cultural impacts of cross-cultural interaction
14. improvement in the international tourists' cultural experiences

The responsibility for developing the educational programmes may differ depending on destinations and the importance of tourism development for the host community. The internationalisation of tourism education should be considered by recognising the important role and involvement of international tourism organisations such as World Tourism Organisation (WTO) or Pacific Asia Travel Association (PATA) that could set priorities and guidelines for the educational programmes.

8. The ratio of tourists to hosts at the destination of tourism development should be monitored.

9. Less rigid travel arrangements that would give tourists more discretionary time and opportunity to interact with native hosts, group activities that would assist in reducing cultural distance between tourists and hosts, and smaller size tour groups that would give them more independence should be offered to tourists.

10. Priority should be given to surveys of international tourists, their expectations, their satisfaction levels and the types of social interactions with hosts that would create positive experiences for tourists and hosts. Questions related to service shortcomings and suggestions for the improvement of tourist–host contact in the delivery of service should be incorporated in surveys. Service quality should be constantly monitored.

In today's competitive environment no business can survive without satisfied customers. The growth in international travel provides big markets for international tourism exports. A major obstacle that could stand in the way of potential tourist destinations fully benefiting from the increase in international travel, is lack of understanding of the importance of cultural differences. There is a need to devote efforts to understanding the tourists' cultural backgrounds and improving interaction with international tourists.

References

Adler, P. (1975) 'The transition experience: an alternative view of culture shock', *Journal of Humanistic Psychology*, 15(4): 13–23.

Allport, G. (1954) *The Nature of Prejudice*, Addison-Wesley, Reading, MA.

Amir, Y. (1969) 'Contact hypothesis in ethnic relations', *Psychological Bulletin*, 71(5): 319–342.

Amir, Y. (1976) 'The role of intergroup contact in change of prejudice and ethnic relations', in Katz, P. (Ed.), *Towards the Elimination of Racism*, Pergamon Press, New York, pp. 245–308.

Amir, Y. and Ben-Ari, R. (1985) 'International tourism, ethnic contact, and attitude change', *Journal of Social Issues*, 41(3): 105–115.

Amir, Y. and Ben-Ari, R. (1988) 'Enhancing intergroup relations in Israel: a differential approach', in Barkai, D., et al. (Eds), *Stereotyping and Prejudices: Changing Perceptions*, Springer Verlag, Berlin.

Anant, S. (1971) 'Ethnic stereotypes of educated North Indians', *Journal of Social Psychology*, 85: 137–138.

Anastasopoulos, P. (1992) 'Tourism and attitude change: Greek tourists visiting Turkey', *Annals of Tourism Research*, 19(4): 629–642.

Argyle, M., Furnham, A. and Graham, J. (1981) *Social Situations*, Cambridge University Press, Cambridge.

Asar, P. (1952) 'Images of India and America held by students from India at MSU', Department of Sociology and Anthropology, Michigan State College.

Befu, H. (1971) *Japan: an Anthropological Introduction*, Harper & Row, New York.

Bettelheim, B. (1943) 'Individual and mass behaviour in extreme situations', *Journal of Abnormal and Social Psychology*, 38: 417–452.

Biddlecomb, C. (1981) *Pacific Tourism: Contrasts in Values and Expectations*, Pacific Conference Churches, Lota Pacifica Productions, Suva, Fiji.

Bloom, L. (1971) *The Social Psychology of Race Relations*, George Allen & Unwin, London.

Bochner, S. (1982) *Cultures in Contact: Studies in Cross-Cultural Interaction*, Pergamon Press, New York.

Bochner, S. (1986) 'Training in intercultural skills', in Hollin, C. and Tower, P. (Eds), *Handbook of Social Skills*, Pergamon Press, New York.

Boissevain, J. (1979) 'The impact of tourism on a dependent island: Gozo, Malta', *Annals of Tourism Research*, 6(1): 76–90.

Brein, M. and David, K. (1971) 'Intercultural communication and the adjustment of the sojourner', *Psychological Bulletin*, 76: 215–230.

Brewer, J. (1984) 'Tourism and ethnic stereotypes: variations in a Mexican town', *Annals of Tourism Research*, 11(3): 487–501.

Brewer, M. and Campbell, D. (1976) *Ethnocentrism and Intergroup Attitudes: East African Evidence*, John Wiley, New York.

Brislin, R., Cushner, K., Craig, C. and Yong, M. (1986) *Intercultural Interactions: a Practical Guide*, Sage Publications, USA.

Choy, D. (1984) 'Tourism development: the case of American Samoa', *Annals of Tourism Research*, 11(4): 573–590.

Cohen, E. (1971) 'Arab boys and tourist girls in a mixed Jewish–Arab community', *International Journal of Comparative Sociology*, 12(4): 217–233.

Cohen, E. (1972) 'Towards a sociology of international tourism', *Social Research*, 39(1): 164–182.

Cohen, E. (1974) 'Who is a tourist? A conceptual clarification', *Sociological Review*, 22(4): 527–555.

Cohen, E. and Cooper, R. (1986) 'Language and tourism', *Annals of Tourism Research*, 13(4): 533–563.

Cook, S. (1962) 'The systematic analysis of socially significant events: a strategy for social research', *Journal of Social Issues*, 18(2): 66–84.

Cook, S. and Sellitz, C. (1955) 'Some factors which influence the attitudinal outcomes of personal contact', *International Sociological Bulletin*, 7: 51–58.

Craig, J. (1979) *Culture Shock!: What not to do in Malaysia and Singapore, How and Why not to do it*, Times Books International, Singapore.

Din, K. (1989) 'Islam and tourism: patterns, issues, and options', *Annals of Tourism Research*, 16(4): 542–563.

Doxey, G. (1976) 'A causation theory of visitor–resident irritants, methodology and research inferences. The impact of tourism', *Sixth Annual Conference Proceedings of the Travel Research Association*, San Diego, pp. 195–198.

Feather, N. (1976) 'Value systems of self and Australian expatriates as perceived by indigenous students in Papua New Guinea', *International Journal of Psychology*, 11: 101–110.

Feather, N. (1980a) 'Similarity of values systems within the same nation: evidence from Australia and Papua New Guinea', *Australian Journal of Psychology*, 32(1): 17–30.

Feather, N. (1980b) 'Value systems and social interaction: a field study in a newly independent nation', *Journal of Applied Social Psychology*, 10: 1–19.

Festinger, L. and Kelly, H. (1951) *Changing Attitudes through Social Contact*, University of Michigan, Institute for Social Research, Ann Arbor, MI.

Fisher, R. and Price, L. (1991) 'International pleasure travel motivations and post-vacation cultural attitude change', *Journal of Leisure Research*, 23(3): 193–208.

Fridgen, J. (1991) *Dimensions of Tourism*, The Educational Institute of the American Hotel and Motel Association, USA.

Fulbright, F. (1976) 'The most significant and important activity I have been privileged to engage in during my year in the senate', *The Annals of the American Academy of Political and Social Science*, 424: 1–5.

Furnham, A. and Bochner, S. (1986) *Culture Shock: Psychological Reactions to Unfamiliar Environments*, Routledge, New York.

Gudykunst, W. (1979) 'The effects of an intercultural communication workshop on cross-cultural attitudes and interaction', *Communication—Education*, 28(3): 179–187.

Gullahorn, J. and Gullahorn, J. (1963) 'An extension of the U-curve hypothesis', *Journal of Social Issues*, 19(3): 33–47.

Guttman, L. and Foa, U. (1951) 'Social attitude and an intergroup attitude', *Public Opinion Quarterly*, 15: 43–53.

Ho, D. (1978) 'The concept of man in Mao Tse-Tung's thought', *Psychiatry*, 41: 391–402.

Hoivik, T. and Heiberg, T. (1980) 'Centre–periphery tourism and self-reliance', *International Social Science Journal*, 32(1): 69–98.

Holmes, T. and Rahe, R. (1967) 'The social readjustment rating scale', *Journal of Psychosomatic Research*, 11: 213–218.

Husbands, W. (1986) 'Periphery resort tourism and tourist–resident stress: an example from Barbados', *Leisure Studies*, 5(2): 175–188.

Jafari, J. (1989) 'Sociocultural dimensions of tourism: an English literature review', in Bystrzanowski, J. (Ed.), *Tourism as a Factor of Change: a Sociocultural Study*, European Coordination Centre for Research and Documentation in Social Sciences, Vienna.

de Kadt, E. (1979) *Tourism: Passport to Development?*, Oxford University Press, London.

Kamal, A. and Maruyama, G. (1990) 'Cross-cultural contact and attitudes of Qatari students in the United States', *International Journal of Intercultural Relations*, 14: 123–134.

Kelman, H. (1962) 'Changing attitudes through international activities', *Journal of Social Issues*, 18: 68–87.

Klineberg, O. (1980) 'Stressful experience of foreign students at various stages of sojourn: counselling and policy implications', in Colho, G. and Ahmed, P. (Eds), *Uprooting and Development*, Plenum Press, New York, pp. 271–294.

Krippendorf, J. (1987) *The Holiday Makers: Understanding the Impact of Leisure and Travel*, Heinemann, London.

Lewing, K. (1941) 'Self-hatred among Jews', *Contemporary Jewish Record*, 4: 219–232.

Li, W. and Yu, L. (1974) 'Interpersonal contact and racial prejudice: a comparative study of American and Chinese students', *The Sociological Quarterly*, 15: 559–566.

Lundstedt, S. (1963) 'An introduction to some evolving problems in cross-cultural research', *Journal of Social Issues*, 19(3): 1–9.

MacCannell, D. (1984) 'Reconstructed ethnicity: tourism and cultural identity in Third World communities', *Annals of Tourism Research*, 11(3): 375–391.

Mann, J. (1959) 'The effect of inter-racial contact on sociometric choices and perceptions', *The Journal of Social Psychology*, 50: 143–152.

Marsh, N. and Henshall, B. (1987) 'Planning better tourism: the strategic importance of tourist–resident expectations and interactions', *Tourism Recreation Research*, 12(2): 47–54.

McIntosh, R. and Goeldner, Ch. (1990) *Tourism: Principles, Practices and Philosophies*, John Wiley, New York.

Mehrabian, A. and Russell, J. (1974) 'An approach to environmental psychology', in Bochner, S. (Ed.), *Cultures in Contact: Studies in Cross-Cultural Interaction*, Pergamon Press, New York.

Milman, A., Reichel, A. and Pizam, A. (1990) 'The impact of tourism on ethnic attitudes: the Israeli–Egyptian case', *Journal of Travel Research*, 29(2): 45–49.

Morsbach, H. (1973) 'Aspects of non-verbal communication in Japan', *Journal of Nervous and Mental Disease*, 157: 262–277.

Nettekoven, L. (1979) 'Mechanisms of intercultural interaction', in de Kadt, E. (Ed.), *Tourism: Passport to Development?*, Oxford University Press, London, pp. 135–145.

Nunez, T. (1963) 'Tourism, tradition and acculturation: weekendismo in a Mexican village', *Ethnology*, 2(3): 347–352.

Oberg, K. (1960) 'Cultural shock: adjustment to new cultural environments', *Practical Anthropology*, 7: 170–179.

Obot, I. (1988) 'Value systems and cross-cultural contact: the effect of perceived similarity and stability on social evaluations', *International Journal of Intercultural Relations*, 12: 363–379.

Pearce, J. A. (1980) 'Host community acceptance of foreign tourists: strategic considerations', *Annals of Tourism Research*, 7(2): 224–233.

Pearce, P. (1977) 'The social and environmental perceptions of overseas tourists', in P. Pearce (1988), p. 151.

Pearce, P. (1982a) 'Tourists and their hosts: some social and psychological effects of inter-cultural contact', in Bochner (1982).

Pearce, P. (1982b) *The Social Psychology of Tourist Behaviour*, International Series in Experimental Social Psychology 3, Pergamon Press, Oxford.

Pearce, P. (1988) *The Ulysses Factor: Evaluating Visitors in Tourist Settings*, Springer Verlag, New York.

Peterson, J. and Neumeyer, M. (1948) 'Problems of foreign students', *Sociology and Social Research*, 32: 787–797.

Petit-Skinner, S. (1977) 'Tourism and acculturation in Tahiti', in Farrell, B. (Ed.), *The Social and Economic Impact of Tourism on Pacific Communities*, Center for South Pacific Studies, University of California, Santa Cruz, CA.

Pi-Sunnyer, O. (1982) 'The cultural costs of tourism', *Cultural Survival Quarterly*, 6(3): 7.

Pizam, A., Milman, A. and Jafari, A. (1991) 'Influence of tourism on attitudes: US students visiting USSR', *Tourism Management*, 12(1): 47–54.

Porter, R. (1972) 'An overview of intercultural communication', in Samovar, L. and Porter, R. (Eds), *Intercultural Communication: a Reader*, Wadsworth Publishing, Belmont, CA.

Porter, R. and Samovar, L. (1988) 'Approaching intercultural communication', in Samovar and Porter (1988).

Rathore, N. (1958) *The Pakistan Student, American Friends of the Middle East*, Incorporated, New York.

Robinson, J. and Preston, J. (1976) 'Equal status contact and modification of racial prejudice: a reexamination of the contact hypothesis', *Social Forces*, 54(4): 911–924.

Schild, E. (1962) 'The foreign student as stranger, learning the norm of the host culture', *Journal of Social Issues*, 18: 41–54.

Schmidt, C. (1979) 'The guided tour', *Urban Life*, 7(4): 441–467.

Schmoker, J. (1954) 'Our unofficial ambassadors', *Phi Delta Kappan*, 35: 312–314.

Schul, P. and Crompton, J. (1983) 'Search behavior of international vacationers: travel specific lifestyle and sociodemographic variables', *Journal of Travel Research*, 22: 25–31.

Sellitz, C. and Cook, S. (1962) 'Factors influencing attitudes of foreign students toward the host country', *Journal of Social Issues*, 18(1): 7–23.

Smith, H. (1955) 'Do intercultural experiences affect attitudes', *Journal of Abnormal and Social Psychology*, 51: 469–477.

Smith, H. (1957) 'The effects of intercultural experience: a follow-up investigation', *Journal of Abnormal and Social Psychology*, 54: 266–269.

Smith, V. (1978) *Hosts and Guests: the Anthropology of Tourism*, Blackwell, Oxford.

Stringer, P. (1981) 'Hosts and guests: the bed and breakfast phenomenon', *Annals of Tourism Research*, 8(3): 357–376.

Sutton, W. (1967) 'Travel and understanding notes on the social structure of touring', *International Journal of Comparative Sociology*, 8(2): 218–223.

Taft, R. (1977) 'Coping with unfamiliar cultures', in Warren, N. (Ed.), *Studies in Cross-Cultural Psychology 1*, Academic Press, London.

Tajfel, H. and Dawson, J. (1965) *Disappointed Guests*, Oxford University Press, London.

Textor, R. (1966) *Cultural Frontiers of the Peace Corps*, MIT Press, Cambridge, MA.

Triandis, H. (1972) *The Analysis of Subjective Culture*, Wiley–Interscience, New York.

Triandis, H. and Vassiliou, V. (1967) 'A frequency of contact and stereotyping', *Journal of Personality and Social Psychology*, 7: 316–328.

Unesco (1976) 'The effects of tourism on sociocultural values', *Annals of Tourism Research*, 4(2): 74–105.

Van den Berghe, P. and Keyes, C. (1984) 'Introduction: tourism and re-created ethnicity', *Annals of Tourism Research*, 11(3): 343–352.

Vogt, J. (1977) 'Wandering: youth and travel behavior', *Annals of Tourism Research*, 4(1): 25–41.

Wei, L., Crompton, J. and Reid, L. (1989) 'Cultural conflicts: experiences of US visitors to China', *Tourism Management*, 10(4): 322–332.

Williams, R. (1947) *The Reduction of Intergroup Tensions*, Social Science Research Council, New York.

Williams, R. (1964) *Strangers Next Door*, Prentice Hall, Englewood Cliffs, NJ.

Zimmerman, M. (1985) *How to do Business with the Japanese*, Random House, New York.

79 Coping with tourism: an examination of resident responses to the social impact of tourism

G. BROWN AND R. GILES

Introduction

A need to understand the nature of tourism impact is well recognised and a pragmatic approach toward development has been accompanied by a desire to maximise economic benefits while minimising any negative social consequences. Research to identify community attitudes toward development applications is becoming a common part of the planning process; however, very little interest has been demonstrated in post-development studies which seek to examine the way communities adapt to the social effects of tourism.

According to Krippendorf (1987:68), the social effects of tourism are so significant that they 'should have been studied before everything else'. It has also been suggested that 'investigations of the consequences of tourism in tourist areas ought to begin from an analysis of the individual and collective adaptations made by a host people ... such adaptations may be considered the primary consequences of tourism' (Nash, 1989:48). Despite these pronouncements, the academic literature includes very few studies which have focused on host adaptations to tourism.

This paper will discuss the type of modifications to their daily lifestyle made by members of a host community in response to the social impact of tourism. Craik (1991:105) has suggested that 'in contrast to the dissipation of economic impacts and imbalances across a whole economy or region, social and cultural impacts have immediate consequences ... on the everyday lives of residents'. These consequences are unlikely to be evenly distributed throughout the year; they will be most pronounced during the peak tourist season. As Dogan (1989:220) has noted, 'local inhabitants who appear to change their behaviour in the presence of tourists are observed to return to their customary lifestyle after the tourists have left'.

The paper will include the results of an exploratory study which was based on the proposition that residents develop ways of coping during peak periods of tourism activity. Coping strategies would entail temporary changes in behaviour, when residents do things differently to how they would be done in 'normal', non-peak periods. They could be categorised, using McConnell's (1986) definitions, as being 'defensive' or 'direct'. Defensive coping involves 'protecting self by getting away from threatening inputs and either mental or physical escape from the traumatic situation. One either flees from the problem and in future avoids going near the stress-inducing situation, or blocks out the threatening inputs and denies the inputs are stressful' (1986:331). Direct coping involves taking stock of a situation, identifying an ultimate goal or adjustment, and coming up with a new approach.

After reviewing the relevant literature and discussing the study, models of coping strategies will be developed. The implications for further research will be considered.

The social impact of tourism

In their seminal work on tourism impact, Mathieson and Wall (1982:157) contended that 'social impacts of tourism were, until recently, a neglected area of study'. They noted that early studies, such as those by Young (1973), Jafari (1974), and Turner and Ash (1975), had been very broad in coverage, providing lists of impacts. The 1970s had also seen a spate of studies of host attitudes to tourists (and their impacts), such as those undertaken by Knox (1978), Thomason et al. (1979), and Pearce (1980) (Mathieson and Wall, 1982:157).

Other early studies examined the social impacts of tourism in a specific location, including East Africa (Ouma, 1970), Spain (Greenwood, 1972), the Caribbean (Bryden, 1973; Lundberg, 1974; Perez, 1975), Bali (Francillon, 1975; McKean, 1976), and the Pacific Islands (Farrell, 1977; Finney and Watson, 1977) (cited by Mathieson and Wall, 1982). More recent studies, in a similar vein, have been those by Boissevain (1979) on Malta, Sethna (1980) on selected Caribbean countries,

Belisle and Hoy (1980) on Santa Marta, Colombia, Liu and Var (1986) on Hawaii, Milman and Pizam (1988) on Central Florida, Brayley and Var (1989) on Canada, and Ross (1992) on the Australian city of Cairns.

When categorising the nature of tourism impact, Kendall and Var (1984) found that the social impacts of tourism may include congestion, crowding, noise, litter, property destruction, pollution, environmental degradation, ad hoc development, loss of wildlife, more and better leisure facilities and parks and gardens, and an increase in employment and business opportunities. Allen et al. (1988) added that the consequences of tourism, as found by impact studies by Pizam (1978), Rothman (1978), Cooke (1982), Loukissas (1983), and Getz (1986), include increases in prices, congestion, noise, and crime; disruption of family relationships and structure; and resentment by local residents.

These impacts should not be considered universal (Ap, 1990), and certain impacts will be felt more readily than others. Long-term, slow-developing impacts are less likely to directly affect individuals in their everyday activities and are less likely to generate an accompanying resident-coping response. Pigram's (1987) study on attitudes, perceptions, and implications regarding tourism in the NSW resort of Coffs Harbour, devoted one of its six sections to the social impact of tourism. He found that the seasonal nature of tourism had broad implications for Coffs Harbour, with short-term effects including 'interference with the daily activities of local residents' (1987:53). In the study, residents were asked to indicate 'the perceived degree of tourist interference on such daily activities as driving in town, shopping, and a range of recreational and leisure activities. They were also asked to indicate any perceived change in the levels of enjoyment associated with these activities'.

Pigram found that 'the greatest perceived hindrances created by tourists were on driving in town (76% of residents), shopping (60%), use of the beach (25%), and dining in restaurants (21%)'; however, he did not examine how residents change their behaviour in response to these impacts as the study reported in this paper proposed to do.

An emerging area of tourism social impact research has consisted of attempts to ascertain how residents differ in their perceptions of, and attitudes toward, tourism impacts. Research has sought to identify the extent to which differences in these perceptions and attitudes can be attributed to variables such as demographic characteristics or the level of tourism development in the community.

According to Long et al. (1990:3) many social impacts studies have 'focused on identifying differences in attitudes toward tourism among different types of local residents'. They state that the types of local residents have been identified on a number of bases:

(1) Pizam (1978), Belisle and Hoy (1980), Liu and Var (1986), Milman and Pizam (1988), Husbands (1989), and Brayley and Var (1989) segmented residents on the basis of socio-demographic characteristics, such as socio-economic status (Belisle and Hoy, 1980) and culture (Brayley and Var, 1989), and generally found that such characteristics do not to any significant degree explain variations in resident attitudes.

(2) Belisle and Hoy (1980) and Sheldon and Var (1984) found, when they segmented residents on the basis of place of residence, that generally 'the perception of tourism impact varies with the distance a person [the resident] lives from the tourist zone' (Belisle and Hoy, 1980:95). More specifically, 'the perceived impact of tourism decreases as the distance between the individual's home and the tourism sector of the community increases' (Long et al., 1990:3).

(3) Another basis on which residents have been segmented is that of economic dependence on tourism. Pizam (1978), Milman and Pizam (1988), Thomason et al. (1979), and Murphy (1983) used this basis and generally found that the favourability of attitudes toward tourism increases with the individual's economic dependence on tourism (Long et al., 1990).

Allen et al. (1988:16) and Long et al. (1990) suggested that differences in socio-demographic characteristics, place of residence, and level of economic dependence on tourism 'provide little explanation, apart from economic dependency, of the variations among residential groups [and individuals]' perceptions of tourism's impacts. They therefore proposed (as had Doxey (1975), Williams (1979), Butler (1980), Cooke (1982), Getz (1983), and Haywood (1986) before them) 'levels of tourism development in the community' as a better basis for explaining differences in residents' perceptions. They therefore sought to determine the relationships between levels of tourism development and residents' general satisfaction with community life. Their findings were that 'the perception of tourism impacts would increase with increasing levels of tourism development' (Long et al., 1990:9). These findings were supported in a study by Ross (1992), who investigated 'the relationships between specific impacts on community facilities, global judgements of tourism's impacts on a community, and overall satisfaction with community life' (1992:14).

The most recent studies of social impacts have criticised the nature of the research which has been conducted.

Ap (1992:666) states that this research 'has provided a knowledge base that is exploratory in nature and primarily descriptive'. Birtles (1992:72) goes so far as to say, 'I am, as a scholar, profoundly dissatisfied with this material. It is going nowhere in an epistemological sense . . .', and Mathieson and Wall (1982) noted that 'most of these [social impacts] works have a poorly developed conceptual basis'. Possibly as a result of this, 'there is limited understanding of why residents respond to the impacts of tourism as they do, and under what conditions residents react to these impacts' (Ap, 1992:666).

With this in mind, these recent studies have attempted to develop acceptable and useful theoretical bases for examining and understanding residents' perceptions of tourism's social impacts. In attempting to answer questions such as, 'Do residents oppose tourism developments in a select or all-or-none fashion?' and 'What kinds of residents oppose or support tourism and how can we explain this opposition or support?', Pearce et al. (1991:147) and Birtles (1992) proposed the use of an equity-social representational perspective, while Ap (1992) proposed a social exchange process model.

Resident adjustment studies

Doxey (1975) theorised that a destination community regressed in their reaction to tourism from initial euphoria through apathy and irritation to antagonism as the adverse impacts of tourism increased. He termed this the 'Index of Tourist Irritation'. This was a unidirectional model which represented an aggregate approach, focusing on attitudes at the community level.

Another unidirectional, community-wide conceptualisation was proposed by Butler (1980) in the form of the tourist-area life cycle model. Butler contended that residents' attitudes to tourism go from approval to opposition as a destination grows and the adverse impacts of tourism become more perceptible.

In contrast to these contributions, Butler (1975) recognised that it is more likely that a range of attitudes toward tourism and its impacts, and a corresponding range of strategies for coping with these impacts, could coexist in a given destination. He thus developed a framework to attempt to cover the whole range of attitudes and resultant behaviour (strategies) likely to occur in a region. This framework consisted of a four-cell typology encompassing:

- Attitude: favourable
  Behaviour: aggressive promotion and support of tourism activity;

- Attitude: favourable
  Behaviour: slight acceptance of and support for tourism activity;
- Attitude: unfavourable
  Behaviour: silent acceptance of but opposition to tourism activity;
- Attitude: unfavourable
  Behaviour: aggressive opposition to tourism activity.

Dogan (1989:225) also recognised that 'combinations of strategies may exist simultaneously' in host reactions to the impacts of tourism. Dogan's research was quite extensive, first reviewing the major socio-cultural consequences of international tourism, then identifying the primary kinds of strategies which have been developed by hosts affected by these impacts.

Dogan found that on a macro-level (that is, across whole communities) there are several possible reactions on the part of residents to adjust themselves to the socio-cultural changes resulting from tourism. Which reaction is adopted depends on residents' perceptions: 'To the extent that the impacts of tourism are perceived as positive, their [the residents'] reaction takes the form of acceptance of the change; to the extent that it is perceived as negative, their reaction becomes more of a resistance' (Dogan, 1989:220). Thus, five types of response to tourism were identified: *resistance, retreatism, boundary maintenance, revitalisation*, and *adoption*.

Resistance was suggested to occur in places where, as a result of numerous intense and broad negative tourism impacts, 'widespread enmity and aggression against tourists and touristic facilities' occurs. *Retreatism* involves the community 'closing into itself, avoiding contact with the foreigners, revival of old traditions, and increasing cultural and ethnic consciousness'. *Boundary maintenance* 'involves establishing a well-defined boundary between the foreign and the local cultures'. *Revitalisation* was identified by Dogan as the community adopting a strategy whereby they preserve, display, adorn, and boast of their cultural resources to tourists, thus accepting some forms of tourism. *Adoption* as a strategy entails 'an active effort for the demolishment [*sic*] of the traditional social structure and for the adoption of Western culture symbolised by tourism' (Dogan, 1989:224).

As Ap and Crompton (1993) noted in their investigation of resident response strategies in a small Texan community, Dogan's was a study of international tourism to third world countries, and as such its applicability to their study was limited. The 'clash of cultures in the Texan communities was much less pronounced than in the international context in which Dogan formulated his framework' (Ap and Crompton, 1993:48), and because 'the strategies reported here are more a function of residents' reactions to tourism numbers and the behaviour of individual tourists than of the existence of a cultural gap which underpinned Dogan's conceptualization' (Ap and Crompton, 1993:50). Thus, the relevance of Dogan's study is limited to the idea that residents may adopt forms of individual adjustment equating to those found for whole communities, and to the observation by Dogan that those affected by tourism would make their attempts at coping based on their values, interests, and cultures (Dogan, 1989).

Ap and Crompton's (1993) research was that most closely related to the present study. They derived a continuum of strategies based on empirical observation. This continuum consisted of four broad resident response strategies. The first was *embracement*, which Ap and Crompton described as enthusiastic and effusive welcoming and praise of tourism. They suggested that this strategy mirrored the 'favourable, aggressive promotion' strategy in Butler's (1975) framework. The second strategy Ap and Crompton termed *tolerance*, which embodied 'residents internalizing inconveniences or costs and being sufficiently cognizant of [tourism's] benefits to accept it "warts and all", without changing manifest behaviour to adjust to it' (1993:49). This strategy was compared with Butler's favourable, slight acceptance description. The third strategy on the continuum was *adjustment*, which was cited as consisting of rescheduling activities to escape crowds or using local knowledge to avoid inconveniences caused by visitors. Interestingly, Ap and Crompton suggested that those who adopted the strategy of adjustment were apparently uninterested in tourism, and merely accepted it as a part of resort-town life and accommodated it, 'without expressing any feelings towards it' (Ap and Crompton, 1993:49). The fourth strategy proposed was that of *withdrawal*, which could be either physical (moving out of town) or psychological (keep quiet and don't get involved with tourists). Ap and Crompton placed their withdrawal strategy between Butler's two 'unfavourable' categories ('silent acceptance of, but opposition to, tourist activity' and 'aggressive opposition to tourism activity').

The present study differs from the work of Doxey (1975), Butler (1975, 1980), and Dogan (1989) which proposed models of resident *attitudes* to tourism and conceptualisations which were concerned with host communities on a macro-level, rather than with individual residents and their adaptations and adjustments. Ap and Crompton's (1993) study differed less in these respects because it had a more individual orientation; however, their continuum of resident responses included both attitudinal and behavioural elements. The following study was concerned with behavioural adaptations. It addressed attitudes toward these modifications to everyday behaviour not toward the tourism impact which stimulated it.

Coping with tourism in Byron Bay

An exploratory study was conducted which took the form of a focus group discussion with six female residents of Byron Bay in northern NSW. Byron Bay is the most easterly point on the mainland of Australia and is a popular tourist resort. It has a pattern of visitation which exhibits seasonal peaks during the Christmas–New Year and Easter school holiday periods.

It was decided to adopt an approach to the discussion which incorporated elements of a 'nominal group technique' (NGT), in which sessions offer a degree of structure with interaction only occurring after individuals have spent time writing down responses to a moderator's question. It has been claimed that the NGT technique is 'superior to unstructured focus groups in balancing participation and affording an equal status to all participants. Hence, NGT groups impose no restrictions on the number, heterogeneity, or previous acquaintanceship of the participants' (Katrichis, 1987:563).

The group members ranged between 30 and 50 years of age. They all lived in Byron Bay and the meeting was held in the home of one of the participants. It was thought that this venue would provide a comfortable, supportive environment which would encourage informality with participants openly discussing issues in their own language of everyday experience. It is important to emphasise that the objective was to identify types of responsive behaviour, not to determine the significance of possible causal factors such as place of residence in relation to the focus of tourism activity or the extent to which the resident is economically dependent on tourism.

The focus group was conducted in May 1993, at a time when residents would have 'returned to normal' after the busy Easter holiday, but when any modifications to their behaviour during this period should have been easy to recall. A brief explanation of the study was provided and then each participant was asked to write a list of any changes in the way they had behaved during the peak tourist season. The moderator asked each participant, in turn, to describe the first item on her list and provided an opportunity for group discussion. The process continued until the items on each list had been discussed, without duplication. At this point, each participant was asked to describe her attitude toward the behaviours she had described. The discussion, which lasted about three hours, was recorded using an unobtrusive, miniature audio recorder.

Table 79.1 *Coping strategies employed by residents in Byron Bay*

Shopping behaviour	Travel behaviour
Avoid regular supermarket	Take alternative route
Use corner stores more	Walk rather than drive
Plan ahead by bulk-buying	Leave home earlier
Early-morning/late-night grocery shopping	Avoid certain roads
Buying the 'bare minimum'	Travel south but not north
Stocking up (before Xmas) when prices lower	Don't travel, if I can get out of it
Shopping at times when shelves are fully stocked	Avoid particular places
Get to the bakery early	Don't travel out of town
Become more organised with shopping	Avoid cycling in main streets

Recreation behaviour	Other behaviours
Consciously choose times to go to the beach	Discourage friends from visiting town
Go to different beaches	Work longer hours
Stop eating out	More conscious of locking house, shed etc.
Dine out in another town	Stay inside house
Change fishing spot	Avoid town
Walk in streets to see tourists	Collect mail at different time

The results of the discussion revealed that each individual made a number of changes to her behaviour. No difficulty was experienced in being able to recall these changes and there was a high degree of similarity in the way residents coped. The nature of the discussion indicated that many of the coping strategies comprised a language of common experience within the group.

The impact of tourism forced changes to shopping behaviour, leisure activities and in terms of an ability to move, at will, in the area (Table 79.1). It was apparent from both the placing on respondents' lists and from the discussion that coping with domestic activities, particularly grocery shopping, was considered to be the most significant.

It would seem that coping takes three forms: reorganisation, retreat and reaffirmation. The main strategy employed by local residents during peak periods of tourist activity involved a *reorganisation* of daily activities. However some people temporarily *retreated* from normal life and there was some evidence of a need to *reaffirm* one's identity as a resident of the host community.

The stimulus for most of the responses was a desire to avoid congestion and crowding at locations such as supermarkets and car parks, on certain roads and at recreational sites such as favourite beaches. It was apparent that people are made *more conscious of their*

everday behaviour as any reorganisation involves actively *planning* changes in timing and locations. There appears to be a reduced opportunity for spontaneity as behaviour becomes more deliberate and rational.

People cope by leaving home earlier, taking an alternative route or using a different mode of transport. These actions seem to be consistent with McConnell's (1986) 'direct' forms of coping. Prerequisites for the success of these strategies are local knowledge and an understanding of tourist behaviour. A predictability in the latter means that residents are not taken by surprise; they are able to take a small road, to a car park which they know will not be used by tourists at a particular time. Although the majority of this behaviour involved attempts to avoid the crowds, there was some support for Ap and Crompton's (1993) concept of 'embracement'. The discussion revealed agreement that, on occasions, it was enjoyable to walk in the streets and go to locations where tourists create a sense of vitality and an invigorating environment.

The most extreme type of reaction was when residents felt unable to continue their normal activities. They were not reorganised, they ceased during the peak season and residents retreated to their homes. These were 'defensive' forms of coping (McConnell, 1986). A sense of 'imprisonment' was expressed with a suggestion that there were 'no escape routes' at the height of the season. The nature of the 'invasion' seemed to be at its worst when the residents were unable to relate to the behaviour of the tourists. The extent of this reaction seemed to be proportional to the difference between the residents' self-image and their perception of the type of tourists.

An interesting finding was the desire to be recognised as a local resident. For instance, people did not want to be confused with the tourists when shopping. This is an indirect impact of the host–guest relationship but involves communication between local residents. It concerns a desire to be acknowledged as a permanent member of the community and clearly, there is scope for frustration with this problem to be at its greatest when temporary shop assistants, employed during the peak season, are unable to recognise *regulars* who have a *usual* order. Residents wish their identity to be confirmed when interacting with other local people and a suggestion of the need for a *locals only* queue seemed to be more of an example of Dogan's (1989) 'boundary maintenance' than of a desire for preferential treatment.

The attitude of participants to the changes in their behaviour was not as negative as one might have expected them to be based on the nature and scale of the changes. Overall, there was a high degree of tolerance, possibly associated with an expressed recognition that there is a

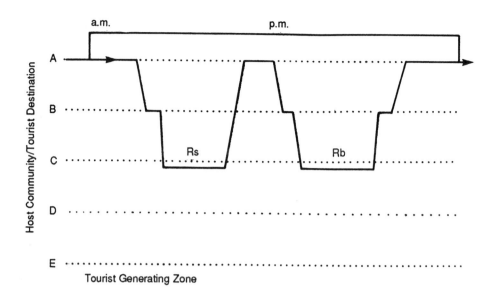

Figure 79.1 *'Normal' pattern of resident behaviour. A, home of local resident; B, community facilities and services, mainly used by host community; C, facilities and services used by local residents and tourists; main zone of interaction; D, tourist facilities and services; E, home environment of tourists; Rs, shopping by residents; Rb, visit to the beach by residents*

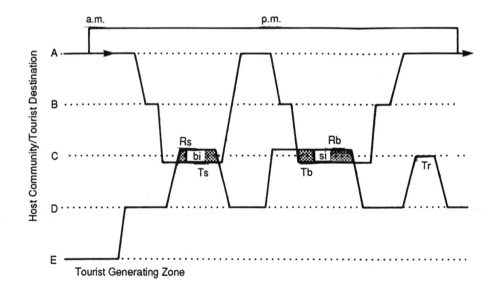

Figure 79.2 *Pattern of tourist impact. A, home of local resident; B, community facilities and services, mainly used by host community; C, facilities and services used by local residents and tourists; main zone of interaction; D, tourist facilities and services; E, home environment of tourists; Rs, shopping by residents; Rb, visit to the beach by residents; Ts, shopping by tourists; Tb, visit to the beach by tourists; Tr, visit to the restaurant by tourists; si, interaction between residents and tourists when shopping; bi, interaction between residents and tourists at the beach*

price to pay for living in a pleasant environment which inevitably attracts large numbers of tourists at particular times of the year. It was also suggested that it is good to be shaken out of one's routine and to be more organised. However, there was considerable resentment and anger expressed by those who felt forced to adopt 'anti-social' behaviour as a 'prisoner' in their own homes, especially if it was necessary to adopt this 'siege mentality' for longer than had been expected.

It could be suggested that residents appear to be prepared to modify their behaviour during the peak tourism season if the timing, duration and intensity of the impact is as expected. There was evidence that residents were finding it harder to cope because the peak season was lasting longer than used to be the case. This created a greater degree of uncertainty, making it harder to predict when life would return to normal.

Expectations and attitudes toward coping seemed to be based on a combination of specific and general prior experience—of the nature of the impact of tourism in Byron Bay and a predisposition toward tourist behaviour which may have been gained elsewhere. For instance, it was found that a perceived increase in the intensity of tourism was more readily accepted by residents who had previously lived in Sydney. They interpreted their local experience within a different framework and an understanding of the personal context which shapes

reactions to the impact of tourism is clearly very important.

Figures 79.1 to 79.5 are presented as ideographic representations of coping strategies. They are based on the results of the Byron study and illustrate potential implications of the findings.

A simplified pattern of daily activities in the host community suggests that residents may shop in the morning and go to the beach in the afternoon (Figure 79.1). During the peak tourist season, interaction between host and guest will occur when both choose to use the same shops and beaches, at the same time (Figure 79.2). The degree of tourism impact may be a product of the perceived distance between the residents' self-image, within the context of their normal way of life, in zone A–B, and their beliefs about the tourists and their culture in zone E, as manifested by the behaviour of the tourists in zone C–D. The movement of the tourists from their home area to the destination (E to D) equates to the stage of 'emancipation' and their behaviour at the destination (T in zone D–C) to that of 'animation' in Jafari's (1987) tourism model.

Some residents may dramatically change their normal behaviour by retreating to their homes during the peak period of tourism activity (Figure 79.3). A shopping trip may be used to stock-up on grocery items in order to extend the period of time they are able to stay at home. Figure 79.3 suggests that this solitary outing from home

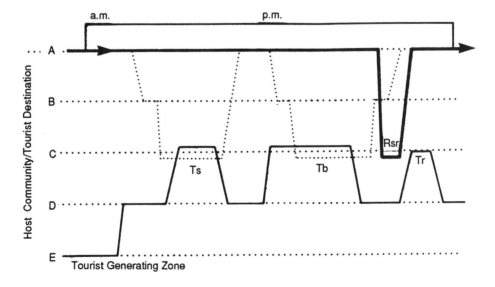

Figure 79.3 *Resident strategy of retreat. A, home of local resident; B, community facilities and services, mainly used by host community; C, facilities and services used by local residents and tourists; main zone of interaction; D, tourist facilities and services; E, home environment of tourists; Ts, shopping by tourists; Tb, visit to the beach by tourists; Tr, visit to the restaurant by tourists; Rsr, reorganised shopping trip by resident*

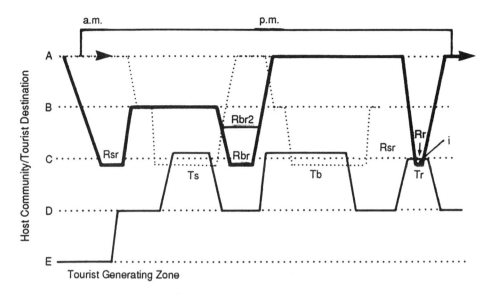

Figure 79.4 *Resident reorganisation strategy. A, home of local resident; B, community facilities and services, mainly used by host community; C, facilities and services used by local residents and tourists; main zone of interaction; D, tourist facilities and services; E, home environment of tourists; Ts, shopping by tourists; Tb, visit to the beach by tourists; Tr, visit to the restaurant by tourists; Rsr, reorganised shopping trip by resident; Rbr, reorganised visit to the beach by residents; Rbr2, reorganised visit to the beach by residents (alternative location); Rr, visit to the restaurant by residents; Ri, interaction between residents and tourists at the restaurant*

is of a shorter duration than normal and occurs at a later time, to ensure that no tourists will be encountered. The shopping trip may be conducted in such a way to reaffirm one's identity as a local resident.

Figure 79.4 illustrates that residents may reorganise the timing of their activities in order to avoid congestion caused by tourists. It also suggests that some residents may employ a form of 'embracement' by consciously choosing to go to a restaurant which is used by tourists. The figure implies that the success of a coping strategy depends on the predictability of tourist behaviour (T), which may be viewed as incursions into resident space, and the existence of temporal gaps (X), into which resident activities can be moved. If it is not possible to find a free time, residents seeking to avoid tourists would need to find alternative locations which are not used by tourists.

The perceived need to adapt one's behaviour during the peak season would be a function of a wide range of contact situations occurring throughout the destination. Thus, the social impact of tourism would comprise a composite variable which reflects the degree to which residents perceive their space to have been invaded (Figure 79.5).

A cumulative model which portrays resident behaviour over an extended period would indicate that residents have maximum scope to freely determine their behaviour

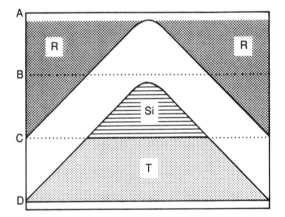

Figure 79.5 *Resident response to the social impact of tourism. A, home of local resident; B, community facilities and services, mainly used by host community; C, facilities and services used by local residents and tourists; main zone of interaction; D, tourist facilities and services; T, tourist activities; Si, social impact of tourism; R, resident (adaptive) behaviour*

before the arrival and after the departure of tourists. It would show that coping strategies may be only employed during a part of the season, when tourism impact is at its greatest. It would also suggest that the duration between the expected end of the peak season and when it actually ends may affect residents' ability to cope. This may subsequently have a negative affect on resident attitudes toward tourism.

An alternative model could illustrate a different end to the period of coping in which a sense of inertia is exhibited. This would occur when residents continue in a pattern of reorganised activities longer than is necessary to avoid contact with tourists. An example of support for this proposition would be if residents are sufficiently happy with any new shopping venues that another type of stimulus is required before they will return to the shops which they normally use. In this case, there would be a time lag between the end of the peak tourist season and reversion to routine.

Discussion

This paper has discussed the concept of coping in the context of resident behaviours stimulated by the impact of tourism. It is an area which has received very little attention from tourism researchers and a preliminary exploration of the subject in Byron Bay has revealed considerable scope to empirically examine the validity of a number of propositions.

In the focus group, people were asked to describe examples of how they had changed their behaviour during the peak tourism season. No attempt was made to determine the proportion of behaviour which had been modified relative to that which continued as usual. The focus group comprised female residents and it would be valuable to compare these results with any coping strategies adopted by male residents and their respective attitudes toward the strategies.

Ap and Crompton (1993) have advocated the need for an instrument to measure 'dimensions of the (residents') strategies continuum'. This view is supported as it would assist attempts to quantify many of the relationships discussed in this paper. It would be possible to measure the extent and nature of coping strategies adopted in different types of communities and to determine the role of factors which may influence any differences. Thresholds of behaviour, such as the point at which people may choose to retreat after having reorganised their activities, could be examined. Relationships could be illustrated by showing the level of resident response in proportion to the degree of tourism impact.

The figures provided in this paper indicate that the social impact of tourism may be a function of the extent to which resident space is perceived to have been invaded at a particular time. However, they also show that it may be determined by the scope which exists for residents to reorganise their activities, thereby minimising the points of contact. An examination of the relative importance of these factors would make a valuable contribution to our level of knowledge about the relationship between tourism and resident responses.

The Byron Bay study has also shown that there is a need to further develop our understanding of the dynamics of tourism impact by examining the significance of variables such as the number and type of tourists with whom residents interact, the duration of the impact, the location where the impact occurs and the contextual framework of the interaction in terms of the personal history of residents. It would seem that despite an extensive literature devoted to the social impact of tourism, this remains a subject with many unanswered questions.

References

Allen, L., Long, P., Perdue, R. and Kieselbach, S. (1988) 'The impact of tourism development on residents' perceptions of community life', *Journal of Travel Research*, 27(1): 16.

Ap, J. (1990) 'Residents' perceptions research on the social impacts of tourism', *Annals of Tourism Research*, 17: 610.

Ap, J. (1992) 'Residents' perceptions on tourism impacts', *Annals of Tourism Research*, 19: 665.

Ap, J. L. and Crampton, J. L. (1993), 'Residents' strategies for responding to tourism impacts', *Journal of Travel Research*, Summer.

Belisle, F. and Hoy, D. (1980) 'The perceived impact of tourism by residents: a case study in Santa Marta, Colombia', *Annals of Tourism Research*, 7(1): 83.

Birtles, A. (1992) 'Impacts of tourism: environmental impacts', in *Australian Tourism Outlook Forum: Contributed papers*, Bureau of Tourism Research, Canberra.

Boissevain, J. (1979) 'The impact of tourism on a dependent island: Gozo, Malta', *Annals of Tourism Research*, 6: 76–90.

Brayley, R. and Var, T. (1989) 'Canadian perceptions of tourism's influence on economic and social conditions', *Annals of Tourism Research*, 16(4): 578.

Brown, G. (1992) 'Community attitudes toward tourism in Byron Shire', UNENR, Lismore.

Bryden, J. (1973) *Tourism and Development: A Case Study of the Commonwealth Caribbean*, Cambridge University Press.

Butler, R. W. (1975) 'Tourism as an agent of social change', in F. Helleiner (Ed.), *Tourism as a Factor of National and Regional Development*, Occasional Paper No. 4 Department of Geography, Trent University, Peterborough, Ontario.

Butler, R. W. (1980) 'The concept of a tourist area cycle of evolution: implications for management of resources', *Canadian Geographer*, 24: 5–12.

Cooke, K. (1982) 'Guidelines for socially appropriate tourism development in British Columbia', *Journal of Travel Research*, 21(1): 22–28.

Craik, J. (1991) *Resorting to Tourism*, Allen & Unwin, North Sydney.

Dogan, H. (1989) 'Forms of adjustment: sociocultural impacts of tourism', *Annals of Tourism Research*, 16: 216.

Doxey, G. V. (1975) 'A causation theory of visitor–resident irritants: methodology and research inferences', *Proceedings of the Travel Research Association, 6th Annual Conference*, San Diego, California, 195–198.

Farrell, B. H. (1977) *The Social and Economic Impact of Tourism on Pacific Communities*, Center for South Pacific Studies, University of California, Santa Cruz.

Finney, B. R. and Watson, A. (Eds), (1977) *A New Kind of Sugar: Tourism in the Pacific*, East–West Technology and Development Institute, East–West Center, Honolulu.

Francillon, G. (1975) 'Tourism in Bali—its economic and socio-cultural impact: three points of view', *International Social Science Journal*, 27: 723–752.

Getz, D. (1986) 'Models in tourism planning: towards integration of theory and practice', *Tourism Management*, 7: 21–32.

Greenwood, D. (1972) 'Tourism as an agent of change: a Spanish Basque case study', *Ethnology*, 11: 80–91.

Hunter Valley Research Foundation (1991) 'Tweed tourism strategy', The Foundation, Maryville.

Husbands, W. (1989) 'Social status and perceptions of tourism in Zambia', *Annals of Tourism Research*, 16(2): 237–253.

Jafari, J. (1974) 'The socio-economic costs of tourism to developing countries', *Annals of Tourism*, 1: 227–259.

Jafari, Jafar (1987) 'Tourism models: the sociocultural aspects', *Tourism Management*, (June): 151–159.

Katrichis, Jerome (1987) 'The nominal group technique as an alternative to the unstructured focus group as a qualitative research tool in marketing', in M. Wallendorf and P. Anderson (Eds), *Advances in Consumer Research, 14*, Association for Consumer Research, Provo, UT., p. 237.

Kendall, K. and Var, T. (1984) 'The perceived impact of tourism: the state of the art', Simon Fraser University, Vancouver.

Knox, J. (1978) *Classification of Hawaii Residents' Attitudes Toward Tourists and Tourism*, Tourism Research Project Occasional Paper No. 1 University of Hawaii at Manoa, Honolulu.

Krippendorf, J. (1987) *The Holiday Makers: Understanding the Impact of Leisure and Travel*, Heinemann Professional, Oxford.

Lefrancois, G. (1983) *Psychology*, 2nd edn, Wadsworth, Belmont, CA.

Liu, J. and Var, T. (1986) 'Resident attitudes toward tourism impacts in Hawaii', *Annals of Tourism Research*, 13: 193.

Long, P., Perdue, R. and Allen, L. (1990) 'Rural resident tourism perceptions and attitudes by community level of tourism', *Journal of Travel Research*, 28(3): 3.

Loukissas, P. (1983) 'Public participation in community tourism planning: a gaming simulation approach', *Journal of Travel Research*, 2: 18–23.

Lundberg, D. E. (1974) 'Caribbean tourism: social and racial tensions', *Cornell Hotel and Restaurant Administration Quarterly*, 15(1): 82–87.

Mathieson, A. and Wall, G. (1982) *Tourism: Economic, Physical, and Social Impacts*, Longman Scientific, New York.

McConnell, J. (1986) *Understanding Human Behaviour*, 5th edn, CBS Publishing, New York.

McKean, P. F. (1976) 'Tourism, culture change and culture conservation in Bali', in D. J. Banks (Ed.), *Changing Identities in Modern S. E. Asia and World Anthropology*, Mouton, The Hague.

Milman, A. and Pizam, A. (1988) 'Social impacts of tourism on Central Florida', *Annals of Tourism Research*, 15(2): 191.

Murphy, P. (1983) 'Perceptions and attitudes of decision making groups in tourism centres', *Journal of Travel Research*, 21: 8–12.

Nash, D. (1989) 'Tourism as a form of imperialism', in *Guests and Hosts: the Anthropology of Tourism*, 2nd edn, V. Smith (Ed.), University of Pennsylvania Press, Philadelphia, PA, p. 37.

Ouma, J. P. B. (1970) *Evolution of Tourism in East Africa*, East African Literature Bureau, Nairobi.

Pearce, J. A. (1980) 'Host community acceptance of foreign tourists: strategic considerations', *Annals of Tourism Research*, 7: 224–233.

Pearce, P., Moscardo, G. and Ross, G. (1991) 'Tourism impact and community perception: an equity-social representational perspective', *Australian Psychologist*, 26(3): 147.

Perez, L. A. (1975) 'Tourism in the West Indies', *Journal of Communication*, 25: 136–143.

Pigram, J. (1987) 'Tourism in Coffs Harbour: attitudes, perceptions, and implications', Coffs Harbour City Council, Coffs Harbour.

Pizam, A. (1978) 'Tourism's impacts: the social costs to the destination as perceived by its residents', *Journal of Travel Research*, 16(4): 8–12.

Reider, L. (1988) 'Byron Shire tourism plan', Report commissioned by Byron Shire Council.

Ross, G. (1992) 'Resident perceptions of the impact of tourism on an Australian city', *Journal of Travel Research*, 30(3): 13.

Rothman, R. A. (1978) 'Residents and transients: community reaction to seasonal visitors', *Journal of Travel Research*, 16(3): 8–13.

Sheldon, P. and Var, T. (1984) 'Resident attitudes toward tourism in North Wales', *Tourism Management*, 5: 40–47.

Thomason, P., Crompton, J. L. and Van Kamp, B. (1979) 'A study of the attitudes of impacted groups within a host community toward prolonged staying tourist visitors', *Journal of Tourism Research*, 18(3): 2–7.

Turner, L. and Ash, J. (1975) *The Golden Hordes: International Tourism and the Pleasure Periphery*, Constable, London.

Young, G. (1973) *Tourism: Blessing or Blight?* Penguin, Harmondsworth.

80 Probably as close as you can get to paradise: tourism and the changing image of Seychelles

D. WILSON

Introduction

References to paradise occur with monotonous frequency in tourist brochures advertising holidays in the Seychelles Islands. The following description is typical:

> The islands of the Seychelles are probably as close as you can get to Paradise! No high rise hotels, bars and discos, instead, crystal clear turquoise waters, bordered by perfect snow white beaches and shaded by palm trees. Bring mask and snorkel or learn to scuba dive and discover a spectacular coral and fish life. Explore dense rain forests or just relax on virtually deserted beaches. At night enjoy an excellent dinner in one of the many restaurants offering seafood and local specialities. Its undisputed scenic beauty, tropical climate and friendly people are the ingredients for, without doubt, a perfect holiday in Paradise. (Ingrams World Travelplan, 1993–94:20)

The Seychelles Tourist Office also endorses this paradise image in its official promotional advertising:

> Nature's Own Paradise . . . The Seychelles. Uncrowded. Unspoilt. Its sun kissed islands in the middle of the Indian Ocean, fringed by silver sands, are sanctuaries for exotic flora and fauna that simply cannot be found anywhere else. Explore the fascinating marine life. (Seychelles Tourist Office advertisement in *Country Living*, November 1993:164, quoted in its entirety)

Both these passages are accompanied by pictures of beaches fringed with coconut palms, one completely deserted, the other featuring a solitary couple carrying masks and flippers towards the sea. What is especially interesting about the image of the islands which emerges from these pictures and texts is their focus on the natural history and natural beauty of the islands. This 'paradise' is essentially one without people. There are passing references to the 'friendly people' and the 'specialities' of the local cuisine, but apart from this the origin and culture of the inhabitants of Seychelles remains a total mystery to the would-be visitor.

There is a growing academic interest in the construction and manipulation of such tourist images. For example, in a recent review of the literature Echtner and Ritchie

(1991) discuss the methodological problems of accurately measuring destination images, and emphasise no fewer than four key components of such images: those that are attribute based as opposed to those which are holistic, and those which are functional as opposed to those which are more psychological and intangible. Using this terminology, much the 'paradise' imagery of Seychelles resides at the holistic and metaphysical end of the image spectrum. They also state that one objective of improved image measurement is 'the creation and management of a distinctive and appealing perception, or image, of the destination' (1991:2).

However, a number of writers including Adams (1984), Weightman (1987), Garcia (1988), and Selwyn (1993) have considered the way in which tourist brochures can distort and misrepresent such images. Adams argues that the most striking images are singled out, 'simplified', and 'packaged' for the brochures and that these 'provide a framework or mental grid through which the traveller will filter his perceptions while abroad' (1984:469–471). Adams is in fact considering images of local culture rather than landscape, and he concludes that the ethnic stereotypes in the tourist literature about Toralja in Indonesia are 'generally based on a reworking of existing, indigenous ethnic markers—although at times it may be permuted almost beyond recognition' (1984:481–482). Garcia is more negative in his conclusions, arguing that a tourist can visit a country and return 'without noticing any of its important realities' (1988:93) because of a conspiracy between the local economic elite and the international tourist industry to generate and perpetuate myths about the destination in order to increase their own financial gains. The myths generated often pre-date the tourist literature as such and are found embedded in books, films and romantic fiction, etc. He suggests that Sri Lanka has long been considered an exotic and mythical country. To the Greeks it was a 'marvellous island', to the 16th-century Portuguese it became the 'island of spices', and the 19th-century British transformed it into a 'lost Eden', writing accounts 'which filled the island with terrible demons, idyllic landscapes, fantastic beasts, etc. making its halo of exoticism yet more tangible'. Finally, with the arrival of tourism the image is brought up to date with the introduction of two new elements— cultural exoticism and relaxing beaches (1988:99–100)— both of which now assist the marketing and selling of the island by the tourist industry. Information about the social, economic and racial problems facing the country, some of which are a consequence of tourism development, is rarely provided by the tour operators, and the actual visit often takes place in an 'environmental bubble' which cocoons the tourist against too much intrusive contact with the realities of Sri Lankan life.

Weightman considers how 'the tour brochure directs expectations, influences perceptions, and thereby provides a preconceived landscape for the tourist to "discover"' (1987:230), and especially how the structure of such tours in India presents a false image of the country in which the Aryan North predominates over the Dravidian South and in which the urban predominates over the rural. Finally, Selwyn analyses tourist brochures advertising holidays in southeast Asia, and shows how it is possible to 'read' such brochures from two theoretical positions. First, they can be seen as embodying a 'structuralist' orientation in which the tourist 'goes on holiday in order to recreate, frequently with representations from the imagined pre-modern world, the structures which life in the postmodern world has appeared to demolish' (1993:18). Thus brochures encourage tourists to make a 'sacred' journey to a tropical paradise in which they will be free from the constraints of the everyday world and from which they will return refreshed and rejuvenated. Secondly, Selwyn discerns a more recent 'post-structuralist' trend where 'the dominant theme in the material . . . is that of "commoditisation", the gathering together of everything, from sites to emotions to persons, into a cash nexus' (1993:127). Tourists have become voracious consumers of the tourism product, and the language of the brochures now 'seems to rule out the possibility of tourism being part of any larger project associated with other, and possibly more sober, spheres of his or her own life, work and thought' (1993:129). From either viewpoint, however, tourism brochures are becoming increasingly removed from the everyday world and more obsessed with manipulating their 'own promotional lexicon and repertoire of myths'.

The present paper builds on a number of these ideas, especially that images can have a long history, that they can seriously misrepresent reality, that they can be manipulated for financial gain, and that they can carry potent messages for the tourist consumer. This paper also extends the analysis by attempting to relate the paradise image of Seychelles to other aspects of the socio-economic and political development of the islands, and draws upon a much wider range of source material in order to reconstruct a series of images of the island as seen from abroad. It examines the writings of a diverse group of commentators which includes explorers, colonial administrators and churchmen, more recent journalists, researchers and travel writers, and finally the anonymous writers of the ubiquitous tourist brochures. Without doubt the images and stereotypes which emerge from these accounts reveal more about the social, economic and political values and objectives of their white European authors rather than about the culture of the local inhabitants. For, in a very real sense, our knowledge of the Seychelles and their inhabitants resides primarily in the writings of these outside observers, rather than in anything the Seychellois people themselves have actually said or done. From this perspective, tourist brochures provide merely the latest in a long line of images of the islands, and it is argued that a number of fundamental transformations in the image of Seychelles have taken place over the last 150 years. Furthermore, it will be shown that the paradise image of the tourist brochures is not only of relatively recent origin but has itself just undergone a remarkable metamorphosis.

Paradise lost

The uninhabited islands, a mere 112 square miles in total area, were first settled by the French in 1770, accompanied by their African slaves. Ceded to Britain after the Napoleonic War, Seychelles remained a remote and isolated British colony until the opening of an international airport in 1971 and the subsequent development of tourism. The Islands gained their independence in 1976. The colonial experience of Seychelles parallels that of other islands in the Indian Ocean such as Mauritius and Reunion, as well as that of the Caribbean. Broadly speaking, this consisted of intense colonisation, slavery, plantation agriculture, indentured labour, and the emergence of a multiracial society with a cultural focus on a distant European metropolitan country. Contemporary Seychelles thus contains a complex legacy of French, English, African and Asian traditions introduced by the various settlers, although the Seychellois now share in common the Creole language, the Catholic religion, and a cash economy. But from the very beginning, the economic viability of Seychelles, although remote in location and tiny producers in terms of quantity, has depended on their ability to supply competitively priced agricultural exports for an international market. A shortage of labour after emancipation forced a change from cotton and sugar to the production of copra, and tourism was initiated by the British in the late 1960s in an attempt to provide an additional source of foreign exchange for the islands in the face of a rapidly declining coconut industry (Benedict and Benedict (1982) provide a good historical review in their anthropological study of Seychelles, and Wilson (1979, 1994) considers the development of tourism).

So far this has been a basically factual and descriptive account. But how was the island and its growing population of non-white Seychellois—the Creoles—being described by Europeans? The first reports appear in the mid-19th century, and it is significant that they focus not so much on the place as on the people who lived and worked there, especially the attitude of the emancipated slaves towards work on the plantations upon which the livelihood of the European settlers depended: 'it is impossible for Europeans who ... have never had to depend upon their labour for support to form a just notion of the misery and torment they frequently occasion' (Holman (1835:91), on a voyage round the world); 'lazy at all times' (Belcher (1843:273), during his own circumnavigation of the globe aboard HMS *Sulphur*); 'they (the slaves) had already made the fatal discovery that in these islands life was sustainable almost without the necessity for exertion' (Keate (1850:283), a Civil Commissioner visiting the islands from Mauritius). Thus begins to emerge one of the most recurrent themes in early writing and reports about the Islands—that they were inhabited by an extremely idle population of ex-slaves.

Other images were also beginning to emerge in the mid-19th century. For example: 'this disposition to take advantage of those who are too good natured to treat them with rigour, added to their laziness, and a constant desire to pilfer, form the worst features of their character' (Holman, 1835:91); 'reputedly indolent and good natured, addicted to drink, especially rum, of easy morals and long lived' (Pelly (1865:233), a British colonel briefly visiting the islands); 'proprietors had little prospect of reaping where they had sowed', such as the extent of the 'constant nocturnal depredations' (Ward (1865:126), the Civil Commissioner at the time). So alongside the image of the lazy black the attributes of untrustworthy, alcoholic and promiscuous are also to be found emerging.

Over a hundred years later the same sort of stereotypes are still to be found, although Ommanney, who spent two years in the area engaged in marine research, at least attempts to find an explanation for the behaviour of the Creole population in their poor living conditions:

The ordinary standards by means of which most of us try to regulate our lives seem simply not to exist. Lying and petty thieving, swindling and cheating, on a greater or lesser scale, are all part of the game of life, which, in a community where poverty is so widespread, is a game to be played with all available weapons. (Ommanney, 1952:155)

What becomes ideologically interesting are the interpretations placed on these alleged propensities, especially with regard to the 'immorality' of the Seychellois women. For nearly a century their behaviour is seen as quite deplorable, and indicative of the paradise lost that existed in the islands:

The climate is healthy ... but the morality of the place is frightful. The marriage ceremony is a dead letter. Incest is too common to be taken notice of ... melancholy to relate there are few virtuous girls left on the island ... if only the islands had been a little more anglicised, how different would have been the result. French morals are lax enough, but here they run wild, having all the grossness, without a particle of French polish, and making it a paradise lost. Compare the English settlement at Tristan d'Acunha [*sic*], a little island in mid-Atlantic, and populated by about 43 English who for virtue, industry and social happiness are immensely superior to the inhabitants of Seychelles. (Devereax (1869:144), who spent 18 months in the Indian Ocean aboard HMS *Gorgon* suppressing the slave trade)

Another commentator who deplored the moral laxity he observed was Oxanne, the Anglican Archdeacon in Seychelles during the 1930s, who invokes a remarkable racial theory to help explain the behaviour of the Seychellois woman:

It is not that the Seychelles girl is immoral. She is not, but she is absolutely and completely amoral. In other words, morals, to her mind, do not enter into matters relating to sex. It does not occur to her that she is sinning in obeying the sex impulse. ... It is hard for us to judge these girls. They start life with a crushing handicap. What European blood they have comes from the latin race that has a reputation for being notoriously erotic. That latin blood is mixed with the naturally hot blood of the African girl who is already 80% animal. Add to this the effect of a tropical climate on the one hand, and a constant diet of fish on the other, and you get a girl who, from the sex point of view, is the acme of eroticism. (Oxanne, 1936:139–140)

So why should white Europeans have chosen to emphasise an image of the Creole population as uncultured, idle, drunk, lying, promiscuous, thieving, and superstitious? It can be suggested that such a stereotype is particularly convenient if, at the same time, the writer also wishes to support the continuing economic exploitation, colonial domination and political emasculation of the non-white population of the islands. It is surely more than mere coincidence that these alleged propensities of the black population were often seen as part of the natural (i.e. racial) character of the African (e.g. Oxanne's 'animality of the African girl', Holman's 'dispositions of the Negro', etc.). Such explanations serve to reinforce the notion of white racial superiority and justify the continuing imposition of colonial 'government' and 'education' upon the as yet 'uncivilised' Creole descendants of the African slaves.

Garden of Eden

Evidence that these stereotypes were more than simply naive and innocent misconceptions emerges when we consider the way in which this same set of 'facts' about the behaviour of the Seychellois have been reinterpreted in more recent years. Coinciding with the rise of tourism in the late 1960s and early 1970s, a completely opposite image of Seychelles emerges in the literature, this time as a 'Garden of Eden' with all its attendant connotations of carnal knowledge and sexual indulgence. The first signs of this transformation appeared some 40 years ago, and Ommanney provides an early example of the new genre:

> Not many people work really hard in the Seychelles and fewer still are ambitious or efficient. In a country where the climate is gentle and enervating and where, at a pinch, life can be supported on some fish caught in a trap, and bread-fruit or bananas from the trees outside the door, there is no need to make a feverish struggle out of life. One's needs are few and the accumulation of money for its own sake can be left to a small, greedy minority. (Ommanney, 1952:150)

Out of nowhere the Seychellois have suddenly been turned into exemplars of Marshall Sahlins' 'zen road to affluence' whereby affluence is measured by limiting needs and desires rather than increasing production and consumption (Sahlins, 1972). This new image was actively promoted by President Mancham himself, who told the following story to a journalist:

> A Seychellois fisherman was quietly netting fish from his pirogue and was approached by an inquisitive tourist. The fisherman explained that he caught enough fish for his and his family's needs, and then he went home to attend his garden for an hour, and then he sat on the beach and looked at the sea. The tourist was horrified. He patiently explained that if the fisherman caught more fish than he needed he could sell them, buy another boat and have a man working for him, then another and another—and then he would be rich and would hardly have to work

at all. He could sit and look out at the sea for most of the day which, of course, the fisherman was quick to point out was precisely what he did already! (quoted in Wilson (1979:221)

Wollacott, writing in the mid-1970s, perceptively describes this changing interpretation as follows:

> Of course, the history of the Seychelles can be re-read as luck and the supposed vices of the inhabitants as virtues. British neglect can be seen as contributing to the islands' greatest assets, their unspoilt beauty and the racial mixing consequent on the different groups' isolation from their home countries. And indolence, promiscuity and drunkenness can be glossed as a refreshing indifference to material wealth, a healthy uninhibited sexuality, and a carefree enjoyment of liquor. (Martin Wollacott in *The Guardian*, 17 October 1975)

Devereax's 'frightful morality' thus becomes transformed into an image of a sexual paradise, and by the early 1970s tourists were being lured to the Seychelles by a steady stream of glowing reports about the 'Islands of Love' to be found there:

> They call these the love islands. I'm not surprised. Never in the field of sexual relations have so many had so much so often . . . A virtually unspoilt paradise, with breathtaking beaches, the Seychelles have also acquired a reputation for having rejuvenating qualities. Many wealthy business tycoons have given up the 20th century rat race to settle down with lovely native girls . . . At dinner last night I sat opposite a stunning Creole girl. When the time came for dancing she was led on to the floor for a wobbly waltz by a grey-haired gentleman . . . 'They are married', whispered the guest on my left. 'He is 40 years older than she is, but they have just had a baby'. He looked out beyond the reef to the moonlit sea. 'Ah, that Seychelles magic'. (John Smith, 'The Passion Patrol', in *The Sunday People*, January 1975)

An extreme example of this new genre, perhaps, but not an isolated one as the following newspaper article headlines from the same period indicate: 'Forgotten Eden' (Martin Wollacott in *The Guardian*, 17 October 1975); 'Lotus life in love-nut land' (Jean Robertson in *The Sunday Times*, 4 July 1976); 'Bold-eyed girls and indelicate plants in a paradise made for eccentrics' (Macdonald Hastings in *The Times*, 26 June 1976); 'Where everything is spotless and indolence is no sin' (Alan Bailey in *The Times*, 24 June 1976); 'Islands of Love' (C.I. in *The Financial Times*, 11 November 1978, although the title is in parentheses).

The mysterious botanical references are to the *coco-de-mer*, a species of palm unique to the archipelago, and embodying a bizarre and exotic history. The nuts, with their unmistakable callipygian shape and weighing up to

30 pounds, were known in Asia and Europe long before the Seychelles were discovered, and were believed to be the product of a large submarine tree, hence the name *coco-de-mer* or sea coconut. Perhaps because of their rarity as well as their uncanny resemblance to the female human pelvis, the nuts were also believed to possess incredible aphrodisiacal properties. Lionnet (1986) recounts how the nuts were considered the property of kings when washed ashore in the Maldives, and that ordinary persons retaining them had their hands cut off or were put to death. Rudolf the Second, a 17th-century Hapsburg monarch offered 4000 gold florins for one which was on the market in Belgium at the time. General Gordon (later of Khartoum fame), who visited the islands in 1881 while Governor of Mauritius, became convinced that Praslin (the nut is only found on this island and its satellites) was the original Garden of Eden and that the *coco-de-mer* was the actual tree of knowledge of good and evil. Enterprising French sailors, after discovering the nut on Praslin, made their fortunes by flooding the Indian market with them. Nowadays the *Vallee-de-Mai*, the principal reserve, is a leading tourist attraction.

So by the mid-1970s the Seychellois were no longer being seen as inferior because they lacked European cultural values, but were being presented as superior because they have avoided contamination by those very same values! It can be argued that both stereotypes are equally false although the new trend represented an ideologically appropriate shift as the islands began to compete for business in the international tourist market. This new image also reflected currently fashionable ideas about sexual liberation as well as other themes of the 1960s counter-culture such as those which devalued the traditional Protestant work ethic in favour of a more laid-back 'zen' approach to life. Finally, it was actively propagated by Sir James Mancham, the first president of Seychelles after independence in 1976, with his international playboy lifestyle and his personal campaign to attract tourist investment to the islands. In Mancham's Seychelles the 'love-nut' became a particularly potent symbol of the sexually emancipated islands that he was trying to sell to the rest of the world as the latest jet-set resort.

Trouble in paradise

However, only a year after leading the Seychelles to independence, President Mancham was deposed in a *coup d'état* in 1977, and replaced by Albert René. René turned the islands away from the pro-Western, pro-capitalist democracy of Mancham, and introduced instead his own brand of one-party revolutionary socialism, based on the example of countries like Tanzania and Cuba.

As might be imagined, this dramatic shift to the political left in Seychelles was not welcomed by the Western media and seemed to produce a collective anxiety which can be seen clearly in the newspaper reports of the period. Articles ceased to focus on tourism and become obsessed instead with these ominous political developments, as the following headlines indicate: 'Paranoia in paradise' (Gregory Jaynes in the *New York Times*, 23 December 1979); 'The day they took me for a spy in paradise' (Leslie Thomas in the *Daily Mail*, 28 January 1982); 'Why the guns are out in this unhappy paradise' (Nicholas Fairbairn in *The Times*, 18 August 1982); 'Everything not quite lovely in the Garden of Eden' (Barrie Penrose in *The Sunday Times*, 3 January 1985); 'Shadow over paradise' (James Mancham in *The Economist*, 13 April 1991). Note the difficulty they seem to have in escaping from the image of Seychelles as 'paradise', even though the social and political 'reality' now clearly contradicts, even denies, the paradise image.

The attempt of René's government to involve all the Seychellois people in the establishment of revolutionary socialism also comes in for comment in the Western press, and again there is a thinly disguised ideological slant to the headlines: 'Austerity in the sun' (Special Correspondent in *The Economist*, 11 June 1977); 'Seychelles finding lethargy an enemy' and 'Traditional happy-go-lucky view of life said to hinder progress' (Gregory Jaynes in the *New York Times*, 23 December 1979). Finally, books about Seychelles written during this period also reek of ideological positioning; for example *Political Castaways* (Lee, 1976), *The Unquiet Islands* (Franda, 1982), and *Paradise Raped* (Mancham, 1983).

Needless to say, all this revolutionary ferment took its toll on the numbers of tourists prepared to visit Seychelles, and numbers slumped dramatically by nearly 50% between 1979 and 1982 (from 78 852 to 42 280 respectively), and were not to regain their 1979 level for another decade. Franda discusses the reasons for this catastrophic decline in tourism and includes the following: increased cost of air travel following the rise in oil prices; decline in real incomes in the developed countries; poor advertising after René came to power, reflecting the lack of interest shown by the new government towards tourism; bad publicity (further coup attempts, internal repression of the population, the enforced exile of many Seychellois, etc.); the identification of Seychelles with revolutionary socialism; the deteriorating image of Seychelles with curfews and military presence on the streets well publicised in the European press; the decreasing 'value for money' of a holiday in the Seychelles; and the more austere image of the islands as the revolutionary government tried to 'clean up' the previous image of Seychelles as the 'Islands of Love' so assiduously fostered by the deposed President Mancham (Franda, 1982:76–79). Carroll gives the following explanation for the sharp reduction in tourist numbers:

> General world recession, high local prices (partly caused by the revaluation of the rupee in March 1981), increased air fares and the ban on landings by South African Airways since September 1980. An agreement with Swaziland's national airline allowed the important South African trade to resume, but in November 1981 the entry by this route of a group of mercenaries, seeking to oust the government, had a very damaging effect on tourism. These factors (which kept many would-be visitors away for the rest of the 1982/83 season) meant a further fall in arrivals. (Carroll, 1991:871)

These two accounts are quoted in some detail in order to show that a country's 'image' is a multifaceted concept which can embody a whole range of components (as suggested by Echtner and Ritchie above) reflecting specific socio-economic and political factors as well as the dreams and fantasies manipulated by the tourist marketing machine, a point largely overlooked by the writers reviewed in the introduction to this paper. So, what sort of overall image of Seychelles emerges in the 1980s? It would appear to have reverted once again to that of a paradise lost (although this time because of Marx rather than immorality), of a country suffering under the strictures of totalitarian government, military repression and economic collapse, and of a people toiling to fulfil the alien patterns of work demanded by revolutionary socialism. But not only is Seychelles mourned for its lost innocence, there is also a thinly disguised imputation of Western cultural superiority, that this sort of situation is almost inevitable if ideological identification with the West is abandoned. In sum, this new image can be seen as 'appropriate' for a country which had clearly refused to play the capitalist game and which had gone over to the Evil Empire at the height of the cold war confrontation between East and West.

Nature's own paradise

However, René's government did a *volte face* on tourism in the mid-1980s when they decided that the islands were unable to survive economically without tourist revenues. Following a massive reinvestment programme and advertising campaign, tourist numbers had by 1989 regained their high point of a decade previously. The Seychelles are once again considered a desirable holiday location. But what attracts tourists to go there in the 1990s? Many, if not most, of the tourists now going to Seychelles are unfamiliar with the sexual paradise images

of the 1970s, and they are certainly not found in newspaper headlines or travel writers' reports any more. In fact, the suggestion of sex as a reason for visiting Seychelles has completely disappeared, and it must be asked if this provides a unique example in third world tourism of a resort which has successfully escaped from such an image? Even the image of the famous 'love-nut', the *coco-de-mer*, has been expurgated and its more lurid sexual overtones removed, as can be seen from Figure 80.1. The postcard showing two scantily clad young women, the one on the right holding the phallic-looking catkin from the male palm (the *coco-de-mer* is a dioecious species), has no date although its imagery is typical of the Mancham era. In the more recent pictures this male stamen (which in fact hangs down rather flaccidly from the palm and does not stand erect as in the postcard) has disappeared, the setting has been removed from the beach (another symbol of hedonistic pleasure) and replaced with the less sexually suggestive forest and garden background, and the young women are wearing more clothes and are more modestly poised. In the final picture, taken from the British Airways brochure for 1994, women have disappeared entirely, and the *coco-de-mer* is simply presented as a 'double coconut'. It can even be suggested that the featured nuts get progressively less erotic in appearance as the present day is approached. This last suggestion of course represents the opinion of the author who was in fact accused of male bias during a presentation of an earlier draft of this paper when 'a female graduate student in the audience rose to express indignation about the parallel that was uncritically drawn between symbol and reality' (Stewart, 1993:45) and who argued that the nuts were getting more feminine-looking rather than less. However, whilst the point that women may see the symbolisation differently is both a valid and interesting observation, the fact that the sexual paradise imagery of Seychelles has clearly always been directed at men lends legitimacy to a male interpretation, even if it remains one-sided.

Tourists are now drawn to the islands by a different set of images—the Creole cuisine, for example, is given a lot of publicity today but was unmentioned throughout the 1970s. Unfortunately the author's files contain relatively few newspaper cuttings for recent years (which itself might indicate the eclipse of Seychelles by newer, even more exotic long-haul destinations), but perhaps the following headlines give some indication of the extent of the transformation: 'Where Crusoe would have been content' (Robin Young in *The Times*, 17 December 1980—an early example); 'Innocence in Eden' (Michael Watkins in *The Sunday Times*, 22 May 1988); 'Fresh fish and fruit-bat: a feast of Creole cuisine' and 'A melting-pot of

Postcard with typical 1970s-style imagery

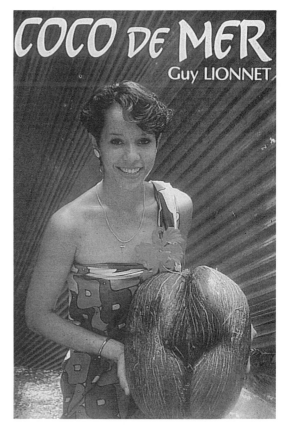

Book Cover 1986

Seychelles Government Tourist Information Brochure 1992

Holiday Brochure 1993

Figure 80.1

flavours in the islands of the Seychelles' (*The Financial Times*, 10 August 1991); 'Small is beautiful in the Seychelles' (Eric Jacobs in *The Sunday Times*, 15 March 1992); and 'Stamp of Approval . . . the Seychelles really are a paradise of palmy beaches and turquoise seas' (Frederic Raphael in *The Sunday Times*, 16 May 1993). This new image is also the one found in the quotations with which this paper commenced and where the islands are presented as 'Nature's Own Paradise' by the Seychelles Tourist Office themselves.

Looking more closely at the most recent selection of holiday brochures available also reveals a lot about the images of present-day Seychelles being marketed to tourists. As can be seen from Table 80.1, the photographs they contain focus almost exclusively on the hotels, swimming pools and beaches. Wining and dining are given little emphasis, there are no pictures of night-clubs and dancing, the wildlife of the islands advertised so strongly in the Seychelles government's promotional literature gets scant attention, even water-sports get virtually no publicity, and there is not one single picture of game-fishing. There are only two photographs specifically showing local people (solitary individuals at that, rather than groups which might threaten the desert island image), and none at all of other local places of interest, nor of cultural activities such as camptole and sega music and dancing, nor of local arts and crafts, let alone agriculture or industry. Finally, there are no views

Table 80.1 *Analysis of 1993–94 tourist brochure photographs*

	British Airways	Inghams	Kuoni	Sunset
Beach deserted	0	4	7	1
Beach + single tourist	0	2	0	0
Beach + tourist couple	2	2	0	0
Beach + several tourists	0	1	0	0
Hotel seen from air	1	2	3	8
Hotel + adjacent beach	1	2	2	5
Hotel + swimming pool	1	0	2	3
Hotel + pool + beach	3	6	4	1
Hotel in grounds	2	4	3	8
Bedrooms	0	1	0	4
Cuisine	0	1—couple dining alone	0	0
Drinks	0	1—cocktails, no people	0	0
Weddings/honeymoon	0	1—couple in pirogue	0	0
Sunsets	1	2	0	0
Coral islands seen from air	0	1	1	1
Birds	0	1—terns	1—terns	0
Marine life	0	1—diver in shoal of fish	0	0
Coco-de-mer	1	0	0	0
Giant tortoises	0	1	0	0
Snorkelling	0	0	0	1
Scuba diving	0	0	0	1
Tennis	0	1	0	0
Yachts	0	0	0	2
Parascending	0	0	0	1
Transport	0	2—an oxcart and a hirecar	0	0
Local markets	0	1—fruit in Victoria market	0	0
Local people	2—young girl with parasol and fisherman	0	0	0
Other places, buildings, people, arts, crafts, agriculture, industry or indicators of modernity	0	0	0	0
Totals	14	37	23	36

of Victoria, the nation's capital, nor of the harbour or international airport which are the lifeblood of the Seychelles' communications with the outside world. Not only have the Seychellois people and their culture become invisible in their own country, any sign of modernity and development which indicates that Seychelles is a relatively prosperous, middle-income country (with a per capita income of around $6000) has also been conveniently ignored in the pursuit of this new tourist paradise image.

A similar impression is given in the texts accompanying these pictures. Not one of these four brochures gives any information at all about the culture, languages, history, economy or politics of the islands! The focus is on the natural beauty of the place and the relaxing experience the holidaymaker can anticipate: 'A tapestry of tropical forest, exotic flowers, tea and cinnamon plantations, from where cascading waterfalls tumble down to secluded, palm-fringed coves . . . visit too the peaceful beauty of other Seychelles Islands—for a taste of life at an even more relaxed pace' (British Airways Worldwide, 1993–94:39); 'Lush tropical islands lapped by the gleaming turquoise waters of the Indian Ocean, combine this with powdery white sand beaches shaded by Casuarina trees and Coconut palms and you have the hallmark of these unique islands' (Kuoni Worldwide, 1993–94:178):

> Mahe has many secluded beaches and coves . . . The capital is the sleepy town of Victoria which one should not miss . . . [Praslin] is similar to the mainland with equally beautiful beaches where life moves at a leisurely pace. Praslin is the home of the unique and famous double coconut 'coco-de-mer' only to be found in the protected 'Vallee-de-mai' and also the rare black parrot . . . [La Digue] is the most secluded of the inner islands. It has an extensive palm grove with a few old type planters' dwellings still in existence. Unusual cliff formations can be seen along much of the coastline. The underwater seascape is astounding and ideal for snorkelling and scuba diving. Life runs at a slow pace and the main means of transport is by ox cart. (Sunset Travel Holidays, 1994:25)

And so it goes on. Time and again it is the natural beauty, the natural history, and above all else the peace and tranquillity which are the dominant brochure motifs today—paradise is alive and well again, except that the Seychellois people have disappeared from it! It is as if the local people themselves no longer have a part to play in the image of their own country—apart, that is, from the occasional smiling waitress or receptionist, and even these are few and far between. And this disappearance of references to those aspects of the Creole culture which so obsessed our earlier writers makes perfect sense when the nature of Seychelles new tourist industry is considered.

It is clearly assumed by the anonymous writers of the travel brochures today that the prime motivation of their tourists is to 'escape', to 'get away from it all', to find a 'desert island paradise' remote from the pressures of daily life at home. The intrusion of local people clearly interferes with and disrupts these images and so have been eliminated from them.

In terms of Selwyn's analysis reviewed earlier, evidence is to be found here which supports several of his main contentions: that these brochures manipulate a powerful set of 'paradise' myths and symbols as part of their promotional repertoire; that the tourist is being encouraged to undertake a 'pilgrimage' to this paradise although this journey is becoming a highly 'commoditised' experience which seems increasingly divorced from any connections to the real world; and where:

> the sites are no longer signifiers which, linked together, form coherent structures within which individual tourists find historical and biographical meaning, but instead they are centres of physical and emotional sensation from which temporal and spatial continuities have been abolished. (Selwyn, 1993:120–121)

Paradise in transition

There is one final, newly emergent image of Seychelles to be considered, as the political situation in the islands undergoes yet another revolution, although a remarkably peaceful one this time. René, under considerable pressure from aid-giving Western countries following the withdrawal of the Soviet Union from the Indian Ocean area, suddenly announced the reintroduction of multi-party politics with democratic elections. The bias of our press reporters can once again be seen at work in their headline comments on the political transformation now taking place: 'Nation awakes to future of free enterprise and multi-party democracy' (Liz Thurgood in *The Guardian*, 20 January 1992); and 'Seeking a soft landing away from the old balancing act' (Vahe Petrossian in *The Guardian*, 20 January 1992); 'Playboy's return to a battle for paradise' (Richard Dowden in *The Independent*, 7 June 1992), following Mancham's return; and 'Fighting for paradise lost' (Tom Rowland in *The Daily Telegraph*, 4 August 1993), although the fight referred to here concerns the owners of land and houses appropriated by René's government who are now demanding them back.

In the first multi-party general election for 17 years, held in July 1993, the ex-dictator René unexpectedly won and Mancham, who returned after 15 years in exile, is now installed as Leader of the Opposition. In the author's opinion this victory reflects René's popularity at the grass-roots level where many people believe that, in spite of all the accusations of corruption against his government in recent years, he nevertheless better represents their interests than the new democratic and more capitalist opposition parties. Mancham, when asked by a reporter shortly after his return whether the Seychelles were now a paradise lost, replied: 'Well, at the moment, I would like to say Paradise in transition . . . I think in the long term the Seychellois will get their joie de vivre back' (*The Courier*, no. 134, July–August, 1992:38). However, his playboy image probably went against him as Seychelles, a far more sophisticated society today than the one he was exiled from, are now committed to advertising their islands' natural rather than human resources to a respectable up-market clientele.

Conclusion

This paper has suggested that particular historical periods in Seychelles have certain dominant images associated with them. Understanding these images involves placing the islands firmly within the historical context in which they were first discovered, colonised and subsequently developed economically. Furthermore, these various stereotypes of the islands and their inhabitants are ideological products which reflect the interests and objectives of white Europeans in Seychelles and have little to do with the actualities of Seychellois belief or behaviour. The recent metamorphosis of the paradise myth in Seychelles provides an illuminating example of image manipulation at work. As this paper started with a quotation it seems appropriate to end with another, and Crick's words seem particularly appropriate:

> The places in the glossy brochures of the travel industry do not exist: the destinations are not real places, and the people pictured are false . . . One cannot sell poverty, but one can sell paradise. Those on the receiving end have not always been impressed with how their country's image has been manipulated by overseas commercial interests. (1989:329)

References

Details of newspaper articles, advertisements and travel brochures have been included in the text above.

Adams, K. M. (1984) 'Come to Tana Toraja, "Land of the Heavenly Kings"': travel agents as brokers in ethnicity', *Annals of Tourism Research*, **11**: 469–485.

Belcher, E. (1843) *Narrative of a Voyage Round the World, Performed in H.M.S. Sulphur During the Years 1836–42*, 2 vols, Colburn, London.

Benedict, M. and Benedict, B. (1982) *Men, Women and Money in Seychelles*, University of California Press.

Carroll, J. (1991) 'Seychelles', in *Africa South of the Sahara Yearbook for 1991*, Europa Publications, London, pp. 868–877.

Crick, M. (1989) 'Representations of international tourism in the social sciences: sun, sex, sights, savings and servility', *Annual Review of Anthropology*, 18: 307–344.

Devereax, W. C. (1869) *Cruise on the Gorgon; or 18 Month's on H.M.S. Gorgon, Engaged in the Suppression of the Slave Trade on the East Coast of Africa*, Bell & Daldy, London.

Echtner, C. M. and Ritchie, J. R. Brent (1991) 'The meaning and measurement of destination image', *Journal of Tourism Studies*, 2: 2–12.

Franda, M. (1982) *The Seychelles: Unquiet Islands*, Westview Press, Boulder, CO.

Garcia, A. (1988) 'And why don't you go to the Seychelles?', in P. Rossel (Ed.), *Manufacturing the Exotic*, IWGIA, Copenhagen.

Holman, J. (1835) *A Voyage around the World*, 3 vols, Smith Elder & Co, London.

Lee, C. (1976) *Seychelles: Political Castaways*, Elm Tree Books, London.

Lionnet, G. (1986) *The Romance of a Palm*, L'Ile Aux Images, Mauritius.

Mancham, J. (1983) *Paradise Raped: Life, Love and Power in the Seychelles*, Methuen, London.

Ommanney, F. D. (1952) *The Shoals of Capricorn*, Longmans Green, London.

Oxanne, J. A. F. (1936) *Coconuts and Creoles*, Philip Allen, London.

Pelly, L. (1865) 'On the island of Mahe, Seychelles', *Journal of the Royal Geographical Society*, 35: 233–237.

Sahlins, M. (1972) 'The original affluent society', in M. Sahlins, *Stone Age Economics*, Tavistock, London, pp. 1–39.

Selwyn, T. (1993) 'Peter Pan in South-East Asia: views from the brochures', in M. Hitchcock, V. T. King and M. J. G. Parnwell (Eds), *Tourism in South-East Asia*, Routledge, London, pp. 117–137.

Stewart, Y. (1993) 'Are female speakers taboo?', *Anthropology Ireland*, 3(2): 43–46.

Ward, S. (1865) 'The past and present state of Her Majesty's colonial possessions, 1863', British Parliamentary Papers, 1865, xxxvii.

Weightman, B. A. (1987) 'Third world tour landscapes', *Annals of Tourism Research*, 14: 227–239.

Wilson, D. (1979) 'The early effects of tourism in the Seychelles', in *Tourism—Passport to Development?*, E. de Kadt (Ed.), Oxford University Press, Oxford, pp. 205–236.

Wilson, D. (1994) 'Unique by a thousand miles: Seychelles tourism revisited', *Annals of Tourism Research*, 21(1): in press.

81 Travel by train: keeping nostalgia on track

G. M. S. DANN

Introduction

There are some recent indications that travel by train is becoming increasingly significant for a select group of affluent tourists. Apparently, some are prepared to pay large sums of money in order to transform an activity originally associated with the industrial working class (Boorstin, 1987; Coltman, 1989; Urry, 1991a) into a more highly stratified pursuit. At the same time, there seems to be a growing emphasis on nostalgia in tourism (Dann, 1992b, 1993; Graburn, 1993), as evidenced for example in heritage tourism (Davis, 1992; Urry, 1991a).

This paper attempts to explore the connection between nostalgia and the re-emergence of rail travel by examining some contemporary promotional material. With a primary focus on travelogues (Dann, 1992a), content analysis of qualitative data reveals five inter-associated themes which are briefly investigated under the following headings:

- Land of hope and glory: the imperial quest
- Travelling first class: living above one's station
- The pain of the train: travail by rail
- Tracking back to childhood: playing at trains
- Window gazing: the voyage of voyeurism

Land of hope and glory: the imperial quest

According to Davis (1992:21), the main reason why Britain, 'a relatively small nation was able to build an empire which far exceeded anything that monarchs like Henry VIII and Elizabeth I could have contemplated' was that it was the world's first industrial nation. Among the various associated 'firsts', now captured and paraded in the Ironbridge Gorge museums was the manufacture of the 'first iron rails, the first iron wheels, iron boat, cast iron bridge, and even the first high-pressure steam locomotive' (Davis, 1992:23). Those who visit this World Heritage site are thus able to appreciate the connection between the train and former imperial glory. They can relive those days of majesty and Empire by immersing themselves in a glorious past that somehow manages temporarily to obliterate the inglorious present and uncertain future.

A similar, though less vicarious, experience can be achieved in evoking nostalgia by actually travelling on famous trains with historic associations (Page, 1975). The *Royal Scotsman*, for instance, which runs tours through the Highlands for the affluent has been described by an *aficionado* as follows:

> Everywhere you go you will meet places consecrated by history, places with all the charm of lost causes, tragic queens, and castles long ago, and marked with names that are familiar from old ballads, from Shakespeare's Macbeth, from Walter Scott and the poems of Burns. (Stegner, 1992:74)

Then there is China's *Orient Express*, whose faithfully restored coaches traverse the Silk Road, once the ancient trading route that Marco Polo trod and chronicled over 700 years ago. This route of caravans for fourteen centuries was:

> The world's oldest and longest highway ... Opened in 139 BC ... over the eras (it) brought in Buddhism, Christianity and the armies of Islam—as well as jade, garlic, glass, tea and horses. (King, 1991)

In Zimbabwe, *The African Queen*, complete with 1929 rolling stock for its 24 regal passengers:

> evokes a deep sense of nostalgia for those days when Europe's pampered élite left their luxury liners at the Cape of Good Hope and travelled 3200 kms by rail to see the world's greatest waterfall. It's an old time romance that is gratefully experienced today in the five or six day champagne tours organised by Rail Safaris on the tracks originally laid to advance Cecil Rhodes' vision of 'painting the continent red' for the British Empire. (Gardiner, 1991)

In India, the *Desert Queen*, 'which pulls a column of polished mahogany carriages that belonged to past maharajahs and viceroys' is 'no normal train', since 'even Victoria in her prime would have paled against the imperial resplendency of the *Desert Queen*'. The travel writer continues his account with a description of the imperial train prior to its departure for Jaipur:

She stood aloofly at the head of her palace on wheels while her subjects fussily polished her brass. As lesser locomotives puffed and blowed in the station, the Queen almost condescendingly exuded a discreet column of steam from beneath her boiler. (Wilkie, 1992:15)

Of course India is *par excellence* evocative of empire and colonialism, and travelogues are replete with such imagery. The same Wilkie (1992:14), for example, refers to a group of retired British military gentlemen at Delhi's Imperial Hotel 'with trim toothbrush moustaches who were murmuring together on the marble verandah' before partaking of a buffet luncheon, or what they still referred to as 'a spot of tiffin'. He describes the lounge of the old Windamere Hotel in Darjeeling (end of the line for the *Queen of the Hills*) with its 'leather chairs, bookcase containing *Who's Who 1947*, the Waverley novels and Mrs Beeton's *Household Management*, a log fire and a Welsh grandfather clock' (Wilkie, 1992:20). There is also the *Nilgris Queen* bound for Ootacamund, 'a summer place for the stiff upper lips of the Raj' where 'gentlemen needed a place to consort with those of like breeding'. Even today, the club of 'Snooty Ooty', complete with musty volumes, sepia photographs and the stuffed heads of tigers, leopards and elephants, is 'one of the few establishments in all India where men without jackets and ties are invited to leave' (Ferguson, 1991).

However, the connection between the glorious past and travel by rail is not limited to the great civilisations of the Old World. It may also be found in the New, as can be seen for instance, in the following list of trains extracted from Amtrak's (1976) timetable:

Abraham Lincoln	(Chicago–St. Louis)
Colonial	(New York/Boston–Newport News)
Connecticut Yankee	(Springfield–Philadelphia–Washington)
Empire Builder	(Chicago–Seattle)
Henry Hudson	(Albany–New York)
James Whitcomb Riley	(Washington–Chicago)
North Coast Hiawatha	(Chicago–Minneapolis–Seattle)
Pilgrim	(New York–Boston)

The association between trains and empire of a more sinister variety can be discovered in Field Marshal Goering's alleged passion for trains. According to Lambert (1984:37, 38, 41), Adolf Hitler's right-hand man, often used to simulate plans for Nazi expansionism on the 26-metre model railway installed in the attic of his palatial Berlin home.

Travelling first class: living above one's station

Many of the trains highlighted so far have a royal or imperial connection, one which is associated with luxurious travel for the rich in their nostalgic quest for the historically famous. Thus, being a 'king' or a 'queen' for a day (Gottlieb, 1982) becomes possible only when one has the ability to pay. The average daily cost on board the previously mentioned Royal Scotsman tours, for example, is in the region of US$1000 per day (Stegner, 1992:112), while a one-week trip on China's *Orient Express* runs to approximately 5800 Canadian dollars (King, 1991). Other high-priced tours include a four-day round trip from Madrid on the *Al-Andalus Express* at 152 000 pesetas double (single supplement 66 500) (Pullmantur, 1990:16), a seven day excursion on the same train from Seville to Malaga and back from £1055 (Mundi Color—Iberia, 1989:47), and 23 hours on board the *Ghan Train* from Alice Springs to Adelaide for Australian $395 (McArthur, 1992).

The sheer opulence of such first-class travel is thus commensurate with its affordability and exclusivity. The *Royal Scotsman*, for instance, is described as a 'moving Paradise Hotel with attendant angels' (Stegner, 1992:75). Catering to just 21 passengers:

There it stands, maroon cars with gold lettering, a kilted piper marching the platform playing a pibroch, a pair of young men with trays of champagne waiting to welcome us aboard. They usher us into the club car—velvety paneling, gleaming brass, flowers in cut-glass vases, hunting prints on the walls, picture windows, easy chairs, [and an] observation platform like the old Santa Fe Chief. (Stegner, 1992:81)

The bar contains over 100 varieties of single-malt whisky, dinners are black tie affairs, side trips include a visit to a stately home with entertainment provided by the local aristocracy, and chefs, servants, stewardesses and maids are all there to cater to the least whim and fancy of those under their care. The writer, while admitting that it is all very expensive, believes that he has fully merited the trip. Interestingly he adds 'our mood is resigned and nostalgic' (Stegner, 1992:126).

Similarly, Zimbabwe's *African Queen* caters to only a minuscule but affluent clientele. In the reported words of the operator:

We are much more laid back and exclusive than other trains. . . . We look after every passenger as our personal guest and invite him and her to enjoy a home on wheels. There's always something to celebrate with champagne for breakfast on every departure. Twenty-four passengers, in fact, is a very small number for a rail-based operation. When you consider our coaches weigh 120 tons then you realize that we are running 5 tons of coaching stock for each guest. (Gardiner, 1991)

On board the *Legendary Ghan Train* first-class passengers have access to a lounge car, bar car, restaurant car and entertainment car. They dine with tablecloths, china, printed menus and wine glasses, and receive Legendary Ghan after-dinner mints. However, the historic naming of the Ghan is derived from the Afghans 'who once carried people and supplies into Australia's "red centre" by camel train' (McArthur, 1992), thereby reinforcing the connection between luxury rail travel and the exotic past.

On China's *Orient Express*, described as a 'trek of sheer luxury' (for just 49 people), champagne flows and the band plays at Urumqi station, there is a feast of shish kebab outside a Kazak village, at Dunhuang 'we sit beside an oasis and sip champagne', and going across the Gobi desert passengers are served a seven-course banquet. Moreover, all these gastronomic delights are woven into a nostalgic backdrop of Hang Dynasty tombs, Mingsha sand dunes, Magao grottoes and Yellow River pagodas, which transform the tour into a trip through history to places inaccessible to less affluent mortals.

A less sophisticated variant of first-class nostalgia travel can be found in the 'dinner trains' of the United States. The *Blue Diamond Train*, for instance, takes passengers on a 4-hour trip along the New York and Lake Erie Railroad. It has 'classic dining cars . . . attractive window drapes, red carpeting, crisp linen and fresh-cut flowers'. The train has living connections with two old movies, *Planes, Trains and Automobiles* and *The Natural*. It also permits a stopover for the purchase of antiques and hand-crafted items from a local Amish community (Kribs, 1992).

Then there is *The Napa Valley Wine Train* which takes patrons for a 3-hour, 57-km trip through the vineyards of northern California. They 'ride in restored 1915 Pullman cars with interiors decked in mahogany paneling, brass and etched glass accents' and dine off 'sea food pasta, salmon and prime rib' (Finnegan, 1992:36b). There is also the *Crooked River Dinner Train*, where 'a diesel engine of The City of Prineville Railway pulls two restored 1940s dining cars with wood paneling' with an optional stop at a cattle ranch for a 'western hoedown'; the *Cascadian Dinner Train*, where either a 1924 Porter or a 1930 Heisler pulls an assortment of 1920s rolling stock against the scenic backdrop of Mount Rainier; the *Lewis River Dinner Train* (1926 Illinois Central suburban carriages) which runs north of Portland; and the *Spirit of Washington Dinner Train* which transports passengers in 1937 deco-style stainless steel cars, has dome diners from Santa Fe's Super Chief Line, and which stops at the Château Ste Michelle winery for a tasting session (Finnegan, 1992:36c). The same edition of *Sunset*

Magazine (1992a) additionally promotes rides on the *Verde River Canyon Train*, the Grand Canyon Railway (established in 1901; with cowboy gunfights, an historic depot and museum), the Roaring Camp and Big Trees Railroad (with chuckwagon barbecue, country music and general store) and the *Skunk Train* which promises 'relaxation and great family fun in the heart of the redwoods'.

However, the *pièce de résistance* must surely be the *Orient Express*, which in the *New York Times* travel supplement (1984:117) was advertised as '1883–1983 and still the train of the century'. According to the accompanying commentary:

> The Orient Express was founded one hundred years ago, and quickly established itself as a favorite of the rich, the famous and the powerful. Now the Venice Simplon Orient Express has created its own legend, offering luxurious sleeping cars and superb cuisine and service.

The picture shows the famous blue carriages edged in gold and bearing the name 'Compagnie Internationale des Wagons Lits'. The porters and train stewards are in smart but ancient uniform, and there is a passenger leaning out of the first-class compartment attired in coat and tails. With an added air of mystery, and hidden allusions to international spies (generated by authors such as Agatha Christie), the *Orient Express* supremely manages to combine nostalgia with first-class travel by rail. More recently, however, *Condé Nast Traveler* (Anonymous, 1993) refers to the launching of the new *Eastern and Oriental Express*. Even though it is promoted by the same owners, it promises a more luxurious experience than the original. Passages aboard trial runs along the 1920-km journey from Singapore to Bangkok cost US$1130 for the 41-hour trip. However, the British Broadcasting Corporation (1993) notes that regular services commencing in September 1993 have suites with bodyguards for which the asking price is upwards of £3000. According to this source, much of the multi-million pound investment in up-market nostalgia has already been recovered and advanced ticket sales are said to be booming.

The pain of the train: travail by rail

One is reliably informed by Boorstin (1987:85) that:

> The old English noun 'travel' (in the sense of a journey) was originally the same word as 'travail', (meaning 'trouble', 'work' or 'torment') and the word 'travail', in turn, seems to have been derived, through the French, from a popular Latin or common Romanic word

trepalium, which meant a three-staked instrument of torture. To journey—to 'travail', or (later) to travel—then was to do something laborious or troublesome.

Travel is thus something to be actively worked at—the endurance of pain for gain—in contrast to being a mere tourist, a passive recipient of pleasure.

When the former connotation is applied to rail travel, accounts of journeys undertaken tend to stress adventure through suffering and encounters with the seamier side of reality. A good example of this sort of travel writing is an article appropriately entitled 'Turning sweat into steam' (Jenkins, 1992). The travelogue describes the harsh conditions experienced on a journey from Ahmedabad to Udaipur aboard the *Mewar Fast Passenger Train*. Here there are two classes of travel—'second class which is foul, and first, which is merely filthy'. Engine 2470 is reckoned to be 'a beast: big, black, unesthetic and ungainly, leaking water, oil, grease, goo and scalding steam'. The cab of the locomotive, in which the author rides, is said to be the 'worst place to be on the train'. Descriptions include various assaults on the senses: 'the prolonged and exceedingly painful steam whistle', 'flying soot, sparks and scorching heat', 'scorched vegetable patties crunchy with a coating of cinders', 'the heavy bucket used as a toilet by the engine crew'. And yet, on reflection, the genuine traveller emerges victorious from the ordeal, with a smile on his face, sorry that it is all over. As a fitting endpiece, he nostalgically observes:

> Sadly, the era of steam engines is coming to an end. India's railway minister recently announced in his budget that all of the current 2815 steam engines will be phased out by the year 2000.

Another instance of travail by rail is Trebay's (1990) account of a journey from Chihuahua to Los Mochis in northern Mexico. First comes the pain: 'Much of the journey I spent inhaling flying ash in the vestibule between cars', and

> The track plunged through a long tunnel and then launched us, mole blind, over a train bridge no wider than our wheels. The tracks swung down until the line circled over itself and made a complete loop, a feat attempted in only three other places in this hemisphere.

and eventually: 'I wobbled back to my seat—with the feeling that I'd spent hours in a paint mixer' (Trebay, 1990:238). But was it worth all the discomfort? Apparently so, for this is the train that passes through the world famous Copper Canyon:

> I took in the spectacle of canyon walls fanned in enormous pleats, of notched accordion ridges, and of cyclopean phallic outcrops polished by erosion and wind, and made a simple resolution to return. (Trebay, 1990:238)

Interestingly, one has come across two other versions of the same journey. The first is by a woman, Kaye (1991) and the emphasis is on the canyon and its native people (Tarahumaran Indians). While there is virtual absence of pain, the nostalgia is omnipresent, as for example: 'Deep within the Sierra Madre's mountains, the past few centuries have almost slipped by unnoticed', and, 'this time-warped village', and, 'tiptoeing through a veil of clouds and glimpsing Shangri-La'.

The second journey is undertaken by a male travel writer (Sylvain, 1992) some three months later. Here the awesomeness of the canyon, described in the accompanying purple passages, is certainly the reward for some pain (the 6 a.m. start, the bleary-eyed passengers, the endless climbing, the nosing through jagged rock walls). However, more germane to the present argument is the author's distancing himself from the tourist role. The idea of a tourist train is said to be the furthest thing from the investors' minds when they began researching a coastal link back in 1872, and, unlike the Grand Canyon in Arizona, here there are no 'crowded overlooks or buzzing helicopters filled with sightseers'. When the writer finally confesses that 'what I like about Copper Canyon is what it lacks: people', one senses a complete identification with Boorstin's lost art of travel.

Another example of the pain of the train is taken from Paul Theroux's (1984) classic essay on the New York subway. Sometimes his descriptions of the 'Doomsday Express' become quite horrific, especially when he refers to suicides (one a week), 'man under' (one a day), 'space cases' (jammed between the train and platform), murders (six in 9 months), 'window kickers', 'lushworkers' (persons who rob drunken or sleeping passengers), or members of the 'flop squad' (decoys who pretend to be asleep in order to attract 'lushworkers'). Yet, for all the danger, dirt, noise and graffiti, Theroux survives. Furthermore, he emerges as a strong supporter of the rapid transit system. It is cheap, convenient, quick and hassle-free. Without it New York would come to a standstill and end up looking like old Calcutta.

Finally, the link between travail and nostalgia is epitomised in Thailand's 'death railway' intended by the Japanese to link Bangkok with Rangoon. For the Thai tourism authorities (Anonymous, 1986) it is the burial site of the 16 000 Allied prisoners of war who died constructing the line that constitutes the sombre focal point for families who come to pay their last respects, since most of the railway was either dismantled by the British or of deliberate poor construction. In order to alleviate the suffering associated with this memory, tourists can now visit nearby natural attractions (waterfalls and caves), rent a raft on the river, or even stay at the more distant and jungle-surrounded River Kwai village hotels. In the eyes of the travel writer (Bragg, 1991a), however, it is the famous 'bridge on the River Kwai' that is the most evocative feature of the place since it conjures up the memorable 1957 David Lean film starring Alec Guinness (even though the actual location of the movie was a river valley in Sri Lanka). One is thus able to recall the patriotic 'Colonel Bogey March' and the clipped military tones of the character Nicholson 'who became obsessed with creating a bridge that would stand forever as a monument to the unconquerable spirit, integrity and superiority of the British army'. Thus, even in the absence of a train, the spirit of the railway can, via pain, symbolically call to mind the land of hope and glory.

Tracking back to childhood: playing at trains

As previously noted, travel by train is not simply a journey between two points. It is full of symbolism which evokes a glorious, aristocratic and adventurous past. Contributing still further to these sentiments of collective nostalgia is the concomitant desire to return to a personal past, more specifically to one's own childhood.

Thus, even in modern Japan, with its high-speed 'bullet train', efficient inter-city network and accent on punctuality, one still finds 'a very important emotional attachment to trains and what they represent: separations, journeys, nostalgic yearnings for the faraway, etc.' (Graburn, 1983:6). According to Graburn (1983:7), trains become sources of social solidarity, symbols of local identity and national unity. They are connected with such rites of passage as going to university, obtaining a job or going to war, and these associations are further reinforced in novels and films. Consequently, it is not surprising that trains also become vehicles of learning, agents of socialisation through which cultural knowledge is imparted about the nation's geography, history, technology, etc., wherein the values relating to social cohesion are instilled. No small wonder either that model trains, train puzzles and trains in picture books assume such importance, at least as far as Japanese boys are concerned (Graburn, 1983:6).

A similar evocation of childhood can be found elsewhere, particularly in those accounts which reminisce about the imperial glory of yesteryear. Wilkie (1992:14), for example, whose journey across India allows him to relieve the days of the Raj, prior to departure from Delhi reflects as follows:

> The beckoning whistle of a steam train pierced the balmy afternoon air, tapered away and dissolved into the distance. The last time I had heard the whistle of a steam engine was as a child, standing on the platform of Edinburgh's Waverley Station, dwarfed by huge wheels in a hissing cloud of steam, asking my father why the engine needed a policeman's helmet as well as a funnel.

Perhaps the recall of childhood also accounts for the urge experienced by a number of male travel writers (no doubt spurred on by the associated pain) to join the engine driver on the footplate (Jenkins, 1992) and why 'the return to the train feels each time more like a homecoming' (Stegner, 1992:123). It may further explain why even a high-tech train, such as the Euro Disney line from Saint-Germain-en-Large to Marne-la-Vallée, is referred to as the 'train to nostalgia' and the station hotel as 'evoking golden days and railroad barons' (Champin, 1992).

Trains of childhood and playing trains can additionally be transported to the present by the very existence and labelling of locomotives as 'toy trains'. In India, for instance, the trip from Kalka to Simla, described as a 'six hour vision of paradise' and 'the most scenically beautiful train route in the world' is by narrow-gauge 'toy train' (Bragg, 1991b). So too is the 5-hour run from Mettuppalayam to Ootacamund (a.k.a. Ooty) on 'the world's greatest little train ride', immortalised in David Lean's *Passage to India* (Ferguson, 1991). Interestingly, Miller (1992), who undertakes the same 45-km, 5-hour journey in the state of Tamil Nadu, establishes the connection with childhood as follows: 'Climbing aboard, Panbian pulls the whistle's cord and just for a moment looks like every kid in the world who ever wanted to do that'. Meanwhile, over in the West, such children's stories as 'Thomas the Tank Engine' and 'The Little Engine that Could' are said to be enjoying renewed and rediscovered popularity.

Finally, adults can further immerse themselves in childhood fantasy by taking rail trips where the accent is entirely on pleasure, and where, in Meadian (1934) terms, the 'I' of the Self counter-defines the 'safety first' messages of the 'Me'. An example of such hedonistic travel can be found in Jamaica's *Appleton Express*, described as a 'rollicking adventure' (MacDonald, 1992). Here participants begin with a breakfast at Montego Bay station and are handed a rum punch as soon as they step on board. Thereafter they have a stopover at a crafts market, take a buffet lunch at a distillery, and imbibe increasing quantities of rum as the day wears on. In fact: 'The rum stays flowing for the entire ride, and the train's conductor joins the dancing in the aisles'. The bar coach becomes the party centre, the PA system belts out reggae, conversations flow along with the alcohol, and friendships become duly cemented. All in all, it is reckoned to be a fun way to experience the back country without being troubled by its surrounding poverty.

Window gazing: the voyage of voyeurism

The last example highlights a protectionist attitude towards pain, i.e. while the train can and does transport people into the past, it nevertheless somehow manages to safeguard individuals from encountering the harsher aspects of reality. This travelling capsule can thus carry out a function analogous to the 'environmental bubble' of recreational tourism, where the cocoon-like structure provides cover for its protégés from the externalised strange and unfamiliar (Cohen, 1979). On the *Appleton Express*, for instance, inebriated passengers gaze upon the shanties of rural Jamaica, consoling themselves with the observation that these pitiful abodes are 'certainly cleaner and more attractive than the hovels in Montego Bay' (MacDonald, 1992). Of course, they actually experience neither object of comparison, except perhaps vicariously.

Similarly, those on board the *Ghan Train* crossing the hostile Australian wilderness are only once permitted to go for a stroll (at 7 a.m. in Port Augusta), sufficient 'to convey the sense of isolation'. At all other stops the doors remain locked. In the words of the conductor, 'If we let people out to wander around, they would die' (McArthur, 1992).

Passengers travelling on Zimbabwe's *African Queen* can view from the carriage window 'a mosaic of wildlife from elephant to giraffe, impala and zebra, and sometimes the elusive black rhino'. Yet through the course of 15 daylight hours traversing game areas 'where every type of wildlife can be *viewed*', there is no hint or suggestion of disembarking for closer contact with the objects of their vision (Gardiner, 1991).

That voyages are often voyeuristic may also be appreciated in reference to the 448-km journey from Guayaquil to Quito. Here the train crosses jungles and other tropical regions of Ecuador, climbs up and down the Nariz del Diablo (with a gradient of 45°!) and passes Cotopaxi, the highest *active* volcano in the world. According to the publicity, these are 'colorful *things* and people which will remain in his [the traveller's] *memory* forever' (Dirección Nacional de Turismo (1976:10)—emphasis added). Moreover, specially chartered autoferros, with adjustable seats and bar/snack service on board, allow tourists to stop for a few minutes to take

pictures. The taking of the photograph thus appropriates reality and reinforces the act of sightseeing as vicarious experience.

Advertising, too, sometimes places the accent on window gazing. In this connection, Williamson (1983:78) provides a picture of an instantly recognisable railway carriage. Inside are all the luxuries associated with the *Orient Express*. Outside, and leading out of the photograph, lie the promise and enchantment of mysterious Istanbul. Since there is no person in the picture (the invisible man strategy), the viewer steps into and identifies with the scene. In the doing he ultimately consumes himself as both subject and object.

Urry (1991b:87) further elaborates on this theme by suggesting that 'the modern subject is a subject on the move, especially since the development of the railway', and that 'it is not the pedestrian flaneur who is emblematic of modernity but rather the train passenger'. Moreover, he maintains:

> The rapid forces of mobility have radical effects (on) how people *experience* the modern world . . . (including) how landscapes and townscapes have come to be typically viewed as through a frame. (Urry, 1991b:90)

However, it is left to Boorstin (1987:86–87) to establish the historical connection between gazing and nostalgia since, according to him, the very first organised rail tour:

> was arranged in 1838 to take the people of Wadebridge by special train to the nearby town of Bodmin. There they witnessed the hanging of two murderers. Since the Bodmin gallows were in clear sight of the uncovered station, excursionists had their fun without even leaving the open railway carriages.

The irony of the situation (referred to elsewhere as 'milking the macabre'—Dann (1994)), is heightened with the realisation that for such a memorable experience the burghers of Wadebridge had only to travel a distance of some 11 km.

Conclusion: resurrecting the railway in a postmodern era

In spite of the working-class origins of early rail travel, by 1869, when the first coast-to-coast service was introduced in the United States, it was clear that a certain amount of creature comfort was expected by a more upwardly mobile clientele, since, as Coltman (1989:126) observes, the carriages were decorated with paintings, and there were libraries, barbers and even manicurists on board. Some fourteen years later in Europe, when the *Orient Express* commenced operations between Paris and

Istanbul, the de luxe train was described as having 'silk walled carriages, turkish carpeted drawing rooms, mosaic tiled bathrooms complete with hot showers, and tapestried dining cars with waiters dressed in 18th-century style silk breeches and powdered wigs' (Coltman, 1989:126). During the period between the first and second world wars it was also quite fashionable for well-heeled Americans to take the *Golden Arrow* from Victoria to Dover, the *Flèche d'Or* from Calais to Paris and the *Train Bleu* from Paris to the Riviera (Coltman, 1989:126). Even the names of the trains conjured up notions of opulence. Moreover, it should not be forgotten that some very well known five-star hotels, such as Banff Springs in Canada, owed their fame and fortune to the railroads (Coltman, 1989:127).

However, with the advent of the motorway and jet transportation, much of this luxury rail travel declined as space became gobbled up by time and the accent came to be placed on speed rather than on comfort. That the train did not entirely disappear may be attributed to the force of collective memory and the apparent continuing need for the affluent to seek a means both conveniently to forget the humble origins of rail travel and to distinguish themselves from the proletariat by accentuating the discrimination associated with such travel. By selectively turning to their own self-defined past as a pleasant status-enhancing alternative to the present or future (Davis, 1979:vii–ix), the upwardly mobile thus created the linkage between themselves and trains through the medium of nostalgia.

The tourism industry has quickly learned to appeal to this 'yearning for yesterday' (Davis, 1979). After all, the *Orient Express* was not in continuous operation. It only recommenced its high-priced routes in 1982 (Coltman, 1989:126). Similarly, China's *Orient Express*, with its elegant carriages constructed in the 1950s for the sole use of top party officials, which since 1983 had lain idle in Beijing, was only recently resurrected as a luxury tour vehicle for wealthy Canadians (King, 1991). Again, it was not until 1986 that the full possibility of exploiting Zimbabwe's *African Queen* for up-market tours became a reality.

Others have taken similar, though perhaps less class-conscious, initiatives. For example, one can now take a steam train from Williams, Arizona, to the breathtaking Grand Canyon. Included in the ride are free 'wild west' entertainment and free snacks (*Sunset Magazine*, 1992b:165). Then, a decade ago, as part of its Heritage '84 campaign, the British Tourist Authority ran an advertisement in the *New York Times* (1984:63) encouraging Americans to view Britain's cathedrals in combination with a BritRail pass. They could now witness the tallest cathedral (Salisbury) and that with the most stained glass (York Minster), contemplate the hallowed spot where Thomas à Becket was slain (Canterbury), and even celebrate the 900th anniversary of another (Worcester) by attendance at a 'three choirs festival'.

Opportunities seem limitless, even if enthusiastic market segmentation experts occasionally target less affluent groups, as for instance in the *Murder Mystery Dinner Trains* of the New York and Lake Erie Railroad (Kribs, 1992). And if people become bored with trains, they can always turn to the stations (MacKenzie and Richards (1986) in Urry (1991b)). *New York Magazine* (O'Hara, 1992:123), for example, announces a weekly tour of Grand Central organised by the Municipal Arts Society, during which participants can learn about the station's architecture, history and future; and similar trips can be taken around Washington's Union Station.

All of this and more comes under the rapidly expanding umbrella of 'heritage tourism'. As William Davis (1992:21), chairman of the British Tourist Authority and the English Tourist Board, is quick to recognise: 'Many people tend to see Britain as some kind of medieval Disneyland. This is good for the tourist trade'. Citing the Great Little Trains of Wales (Davis, 1992:28) as just one example of many which has turned industrial heritage into a tourist attraction, he sums up the success of such ventures as follows:

> Britain has retained a stunning array of visual evidence of the skill and inventiveness, the spirit of adventure, the energy and the dogged determination of those bold pioneers. (Davis, 1992:21)

As has been argued, the train, perhaps more than any other means of transport, through its various associations, manages to capture all that is wholesome from the past— it calls to mind former imperial glory, the noble arts of travel and sightseeing, the quality of endurance and the roots of childhood. Certainly those were the good old days, but they can become even better when the nostalgia they evoke becomes financially rewarding. Yet, as Urry (1991b:91) relatedly observes:

> The present fascination with history (the heritage industry) is not solely the product of capitalist commodification of history, but is an element of reflexive modernization.

Acknowledgement

Gratitude is expressed to Paul Wilkinson of York University, Ontario, for supplying the travelogue material on which this paper is based.

References

Amtrak (1976) *National Train Timetables*, Dittler Bros, Atlanta, GA.

Anonymous (1986) 'Death railway revisited', *Saen Sanuk*, 6(8): 16.

Anonymous (1993) 'Word of mouth', *Condé Nast Traveler*, July: 45.

Boorstin, D. (1987) *The Image. A Guide to Pseudo Events in America*, 25th anniv. edn, Atheneum, New York.

Bragg, R. (1991a) 'The bridge on the River Kwai', *Toronto Star*, 30 March.

Bragg, R. (1991b) 'India aboard the Rajdhani Express', *Toronto Star*, 27 April.

British Broadcasting Corporation (1993) BBC World Service Television (Asia), news item, 4 July.

Champin, F. (1992) 'Disney conquers Europe', *House Beautiful*, November: 42–44.

Cohen, E. (1979) 'A phenomenology of tourist experiences', *Sociology*, 13: 179–201.

Coltman, M. (1989) *Introduction to Travel and Tourism. An International Approach*, Van Nostrand Reinhold, New York.

Dann, G. (1992a) 'Travelogs and the management of unfamiliarity', *Journal of Travel Research*, 30(4): 59–63.

Dann, G. (1992b) 'Tourism and nostalgia: looking forward to going back', Paper presented to the international congress 'le tourisme international entre tradition et modernité', Carrefour Universitaire Méditerranéen, Nice, 19–21 November.

Dann, G. (1994) 'Tourism: the nostalgia industry of the future', in W. Theobald (Ed.), *Global Tourism: The Next Decade*, Butterworth-Heinemann, London, pp. 55–67.

Davis, F. (1979) *Yearning for yesterday. A Sociology of Nostalgia*, Free Press, New York.

Davis, W. (1992) 'History at work', *Highlife*, May: 20–29.

Dirección Nacional de Turismo (Ecuador) (1976) *This is Ecuador*, 8: 83.

Ferguson, J. (1991) 'Where the Raj kept cool', *Globe and Mail*, 23 November.

Finnegan, L. (1992) 'All aboard, bon appetit. The dinner trains are rolling', *Sunset Magazine*, June: 36b–c.

Gardiner, C. (1991) 'Zimbabwe's African Queen', *Toronto Star*, 16 February.

Gottlieb, A. (1982) 'Americans' vacations', *Annals of Tourism Research*, 9: 165–187.

Graburn, N. (1983) 'To pray, pay and play. The cultural structure of Japanese domestic tourism', *Cahiers du Tourisme*, série B, no. 26.

Graburn, N. (1993) 'The past in the present in Japan: nostalgia and traditionalism in contemporary Japanese tourism', Paper presented to the International Academy for the Study of Tourism, Seoul, July.

Jenkins, T. (1992) 'Turning sweat into steam', *Globe and Mail*, 7 March.

Kaye, S. (1991) 'The grandest: Copper Canyon', *Globe and Mail*, 19 October.

King, P. (1991) 'Following the Silk Road on China's Orient Express', *Toronto Star*, 1 June.

Kribs, M. (1992) 'Wining, dining and riding the rails', *Globe and Mail*, 10 October.

Lambert, D. (1984) *The Golden Express*, Hamish Hamilton, London.

MacDonald, J. (1992) 'A rum way to see Jamaica's back country', *Toronto Star*, 18 January.

MacKenzie, J. and Richards, J. (1986) *The Railway Station: a Social History*, Oxford University Press, Oxford.

McArthur, D. (1992) 'Luxury rides wilderness rails', *Globe and Mail*, 8 February.

Mead, G. (1934) 'Mind, self and society', Chicago University Press, Chicago.

Miller, J. (1992) 'India's ancient train keeps chugging along', *Toronto Star*, 1 February.

Mundi Color—Iberia (1989) 'España for discerning travellers, summer 1990', Artigraf, London.

New York Times (1984) 'The sophisticated traveler', Part 2, 18 March.

O'Hara, R. (1992) 'Tours', *New York Magazine*, 25 May: 123.

Page, M. (1975) *The Lost Pleasures of the Great Trains*, Weidenfeld & Nicolson, London.

Pullmantur (1990) 'Circuitos terrestres y aereos, Abril-Octubre '90', Pullmantur, Madrid.

Stegner, W. (1992) 'Sailing the Royal Scotsman', *American Way*, November: 74–81, 110–118, 123–126.

Sunset Magazine (1992a) 'Sunset travel directory', June: 164c–d.

Sunset Magazine (1992b) 'Sunset travel directory', September: 165.

Sylvain, R. (1992) 'Mexico's Copper Canyon an awesome rail journey', *Toronto Star*, 18 January.

Theroux, P. (1984) 'Subterranean gothic', in B. Burford (Ed.), *Granta 10: Travel Writing*, Granta, Cambridge, pp. 213–230.

Trebay, G. (1990) 'Treasures of the Sierra Madre', *Condé Nast Traveler*, November: 224–231, 236–258.

Urry, J. (1991a) *The Tourist Gaze*, Sage, London.

Urry, J. (1991b) 'Tourism, travel and the modern subject', *Vrijetijd en Samenleving*, 9(3/4): 87–98.

Wilkie, K. (1992) 'Lifelines of India', *Holland Herald*, October: 12–23.

Williamson, J. (1983) *Decoding Advertisements*, Marion Boyars, London.

82 Fair trade: cultural tourism and craft production in the third world

G. EVANS

Introduction

The development of an international craft market and industry, reviving lost or declining practices and styles, now renders the label *tourist arts* (Graburn, 1976; Cohen, 1993) inadequate, or at best misleading. The explosion in demand for original craftpieces—functional and decorative—has reached beyond the tourist-exposure which has fuelled ethnic art trade: 'Handcrafts are the second largest source of income, after agriculture in the developing world' (Pye, 1986).

Outlets for contemporary and 'authentic' replicas are found in European cities, through mail-order networks (including via Aid and Fair Trade Agencies) and through direct commissioning activity between entrepreneurs (gallery, shop owners) and indigenous artist-producers and studios. These dealings take place in trade and art centres, alongside tourist-trade in third world tourist locations from Indo-America to Africa and the Far East, and at places of production, at 'source' in studios and workshops in villages and towns (Popelka and Litrell, 1991). They do not presuppose tourism or tourist interaction, but in the absence of local or even national promotional and distribution agencies and 'owing to the geographical and cultural hiatus that often separates the producers from the consumers . . . their production is significantly influenced by intermediaries' (Cohen, 1993).

The range and, importantly, the development and quality control of aboriginal and 'ethnic' art (*sic*) and crafts, are increasingly influenced by these factors; tourists, unwittingly, are the beneficiaries of this cultural interaction and trade. The growth of ethnic art shops and retailing in museums and galleries in 'generator' countries (as well as in urban and regional cities and 'hubs' in receiving countries themselves) provides the 'leisure-shopping' experience:

> The immediate gratification felt by the department store customer in the act of purchase, and the experience of handling objects and learning more about them, which was the joy of the fair-goer, are united in the museum store, and seal the museum-going experience for many visitors. Appropriately enough in our culture, it is the commercial setting which legitimizes as aesthetic setting. (Harris, 1990)

The role of marketplaces is fundamental in tourist management. They are often the prime source of souvenir and artefact, the closest many get to local interaction, beyond the hospitality industry. They do offer a compromise, a meeting ground between both tourist and local people, that is both authentic *and* staged, since they can be located and housed in strategic sites, away from sensitive and private areas. Natural markets, which occur regularly in towns and rural areas, also provide a genuine experience of local produce and cultural interaction. Their exploitation would, however, destroy a local amenity and exchange that would not easily be recreated (akin to your local shops turning into Oxford Street or Times Square!).

This paper assesses the role and relationship between crafts and cultural tourism, based on original research from Central America (Mexico: Teotitlan del Valle, Oaxaca; San Miguel d'Allende, Guanajato; San Cristobal, Chiapas; and New Mexico: pueblos; Santa Fe; Taos; Albuquerque) and the Indonesian island of Lombok, the 'other Bali' (Sasak Women of Lombok—three villages), as examples and models of local cultural, crafts and tourism management.

Heritage sites, public and private museum and gallery collections and trading posts were visited and observation made at live ('staged') performances and at crafts villages/studio centres. Interviews ('folk data'—Gottlieb, 1982), with craft artists and intermediaries were based upon the development of commissions and purchase of contemporary art and craftworks for import to England, and included repeat liaison with artist-producers in Mexico and Lombok between 1990 and 1993.[1]

Primitive art

Few anthropologists investigated the role of aesthetic ideas in the tribal world at a time (18th–19th centuries), when this could have still been the subject of fieldwork among the native populations of developing countries. With acculturation progressing at an ever-increasing pace, many of the traditional functions performed by certain objects vanished, or were served by industrially manufactured products. A large proportion of the now 'meaningless' artefacts ended up in museums, and with this final harvest the traditional collecting activity more or less came to an end.

While only a limited number of objects continued to be produced for tribal use, the production of crafts for an outside market grew in importance. These 'ethnic' arts, which employed native technologies to satisfy foreign tastes, have a history almost as long as the history of the encounter of Western civilisation with the tribal world.

Depending on the structure of the market, there was a tremendous variation in the quality of what was offered for sale. Neither producers nor buyers considered these wares works of art; for their makers they were a source of cash income on the basis of traditional skills; for the tourists they were curios and mementoes.

Typologies

Feest (1992) lists four kinds of 'art', differing in terms of the artists' self-evaluation, their producer–consumer relationship and their function and meaning.

- *Tribal art*—as produced by members of tribal societies primarily for their own use. As a rule there was no professional specialisation beyond the gender division of labour (van den Berghe, 1992). Functionality was the overriding criterion for a product: the aesthetic component was not seen in isolation from the whole (much as religion in these societies was not separable from the total way of life—Native American and other aboriginal cultures have no equivalent word for 'religion', or for art and individual art-forms such as dance, drama).
- *Ethnic art*—as produced by members of tribal societies primarily for the use of members of *other* groups—in the case of Mexico/New Mexico, for the use of White Americans and Ladinos (mixed Spanish and 'white' blood) and in Lombok, for other racial groups and recently for white tourists and traders. These artefacts are not thought of as 'art' by their makers. The technology of production is largely traditional, although new materials and treatments are introduced from buyers/intermediaries, in some cases substantially changing the form the art takes. Specialisation is increasingly encouraged, although Indian craftsmen often do not know why their products are bought— for producer they are a source of income, but in the long run may become a symbol of the makers' ethnic (but not necessarily *tribal*) identity.

- *Pan-Indian art*—as produced by indigenous Natives, who feel themselves no longer exclusively bound to the values and customs of their *original* tribal societies. They work for the art market of the dominant White society and consequently regard themselves as *artists*. While still drawing on the experience of their specific cultural background, their style is no longer unique to the tribe, but is largely shaped by White expectations about 'Indian style'. The first government-funded Indian Art School (The Studio) was opened in Sante Fe in 1932, following the 1931 Exposition of Indian Tribal Art in New York. In other aboriginal societies, such as Maori, North Australian (Aratjara) and Javanese, contemporary artists straddle both 'pan-Indian' and 'ethnic' art categories.
- *Indian mainstream art*—is produced by artists who happen to be Indians. They have their individual influences, which may or may not find expression in their art. The subject matter of their art may be related to their ancestry or ethnic heritage, their style is not:

> My artistic energy has been devoted to exploring the social and psychological facets of the North American Indian's relationship with European settlers. As an artist, I see a mutual strength in the marriage I have with the land, flora, fauna and the ways of the native culture. My personal struggle is to maintain my native identity and heritage while drawing from the best of all other cultures. (Plains Cree, Native Indian artist, Indigena Fine Art Publishers, Arizona, 1992)

These typologies can also be applied to other forms of socio-cultural expression, notably performance (encompassing, in Western terms, dance, drama, music, costume etc.). The significance of craft/artefact production (including the most significant, textile and ceramics) is their object-nature and commodification potential (Litrell, 1990). This separation and 'reification' in the West has made the commodification of artworks possible; the unique nature of works of art and museum pieces ('treasures') is the basis of our art trade and collections; and this exchange and rarity value has encompassed primitive and ethnic arts, from commissions to acquisitions.

Markets for such products are not limited to tourist exposure, although clearly tourist-art is particularly adapted to the transient visitor (by size/weight/price). Another example of cultural production for international markets is folk-music ('world music') an even more replicable 'tourist memento' relying on Western distribution and commercial exploitation, but one with potential for local/national (including producer) development and control. Best-known examples from the

Table 82.1 *Aesthetic–formal sources and traditions*

	Minority society	Novel/synthetic	Dominant society
Minority fourth world	Functional traditional, e.g. Lega, Maori, Pueblo/Lombok pottery	Reintegrated, e.g. Kuna *molas*, pueblo *kachinas*	Popular, e.g. Navajo jewellery
External	Commercial fine, e.g. Maori wood-carving	Souvenir/novelty, e.g. Seri, Makonde carving, Xalitla *amate*	Assimilated fine, e.g. Santa Fe Indian painting, Namatjira watercolours, Navajo rugs

areas discussed here are the Gamelan (Bali and Lombok) and Mariachi (Spanish/Flamenco–Mexican fusion) musics and the ancient Mexican fisherman's song which was adapted to 'La Bamba', the source for the Beatles' hit cover version of 'Twist and Shout', via black American singers, now covered again by a Jamaican reggae band—postmodernism in action?—or just culture constantly borrowing and adapting itself?

In terms of tourist interaction and trade, 'ethnic' and 'pan-Indian' art are now the established forms for Amerindians; and in the case of Lombok, 'tribal' crafts have recently evolved, with the help of intermediaries, to the 'ethnic' art stage. Whilst the demise of tribal 'art' may be regretted, as such societies were destroyed and alternative materials and technologies superseded functional objects (e.g. metal for clay, wool for cotton), the development of a tourist and art and craft market has effectively revitalised indigenous art, albeit in Western terms and tastes (Popelka and Litrell, 1991).

Graburn (1976) (adapted here for Table 82.1) analyses art and craft forms for intended audiences within minority 'fourth world' communities and external civilisations (consumers—tourists and home-imports).

The traditional art-souvenir cycle often ends in imported mass-production, and tourism can revive lost or fading craft skills, for example, among the Aaraya women of Kuna, Panama, 'who had to be taught to make the traditional mola blouse' (Christie Mill, 1990). The *mola* was also used as symbol of ethnic reassertion by this group (Swain, 1993). Native Mexican replicas can be found in British craft shops, manufactured in *Indonesia*—post-Fordism has arrived as one indigenous group undercuts another, to the benefit of Western buyers. The 'delegation' of production can be seen in the rug weavers from Zapotec/Mixtec tribes, who work in the Navajo style; the authentic versions are too highly priced, having been adopted by the US art market. The impact of transport and tourism was also evident in the

first wave of Mexican tourism. Up until the 1950s, *sarapes* were produced for indigenous use and trade in Oaxaca and Chiapas; however, following the arrival of the Pan-American Highway and tourism development, tourists were targeted for the *sarapes*, produced by weavers in Teotitlan del Valle. Initially the *sarapes* had functional, poncho-like neck-slits. By the late 1950s, this had disappeared, and the *sarapes* were designed for use as interior decoration, as wall-hangings—functionality transformed into tourist art (Popelka and Litrell, 1991).

To put it another way, as colonial and post-colonial intervention has removed tribal society and culture from its roots, from land-use to sacred ritual, another form of economic development—tourist and export culture—has stimulated creativity and acculturation, not in an artificial way (notwithstanding museum/ancient 'fakes'), but in a pragmatic form of cultural change. As with all 'culture', perpetual ownership is not an option, given a dynamic society only varying by the rate, degree and violence of change:

> Cultural cross-pollination is healthily creative, and works organically to find its own way. The danger is that fashionability can . . . create a consumer society in which ethnic phenomena are drained of their meaning, and reasserted as little more than infinitely transferable badges of a wholly superficial allegiance to different cultures. (Bracewell, 1994)

Whilst the fate of the Native Indian and Sasak has been both violent and continuing, 'there has been both continuity and change in the history of the native arts under White influence . . . the changes seem to outweigh the continuity, but they must be regarded as the price paid for the survival of the arts' (Feest, 1992).

As an economic development option and value-added aspect (and in certain circumstances, an alternative) to tourism development, indigenous production, of which artefacts and cultural production are growth areas, warrants greater attention and investigation of successful models of producer-control:

> The study of Fourth World arts is, *par excellence*, the study of *changing* arts—of emerging ethnicities, modifying identities, and commercial and colonial stimuli and repressive actions. (Graburn, 1976)

Intermediaries

The role of intermediaries in the development and management of tourism in developing countries, particularly the impact on indigenous communities, has been at best, paternalistic, and at worst, exploitation (in some cases genocidal for societies concerned), whether led by dominant societies represented by state governments, or Western agencies and industry (Goodland, 1982). In most cases, the need for skills-exchange and, in some instances, protection from short-term profit maximisation is pivotal to local economic and sustainable development. The case of village studio-based craft production by indigenous communities in Mexico and Lombok provide examples of both fair trade, and the sensitive use of intermediaries, as well as a degree of self-management by artist-producers themselves.

An atypical example of ethnic art and craft tourism is described by van den Berghe (1992; van den Berghe and Colby, 1991), from successive study in San Cristobal, a Mayan Indian city and ex-colonial town in the highlands of Chiapas in the South-Eastern border region with Guatemala (see also Vogt (1978, 1990)). Here Ladinos act as middlemen between participating Indian groups and effectively as buffers between tourists and Indians. They 'mediate, facilitate and benefit from the tourist–touree interaction, occupy all the niches of the hospitality industry, but they also use their knowledge of the local situation to bring tourists and tourees together' (van den Berghe, 1992). This internal colonial role is confirmed by their 'membership of the dominant ethnic group in the polity and economy of the country . . . They are at ease in the market place and are firmly planted in the "modern" sector of the local economy. In effect they exploit their position at the intersection of modernity and authenticity' (van den Berghe, 1992).

Intervention in Indian affairs is not confined to Ladinos; the Instituto Nacional Indigenista (INI) run cooperatives to display and sell Indian crafts to tourists and organise 100–300 Indian women weavers and piece-rate workers. The institutionalisation (and commodification) of crafts production also serves to separate producer from consumer, and with the role of

Ladino middlemen 'many tourists do not even go to the Indian villages. As thousands of Indians come to the San Cristobal market daily, tourees are widely available for viewing without leaving town' (van den Berghe, 1992).

The reaction and impact on local communities is varied, however, beyond the unavoidable points of contact (road, town periphery), because between the two Indian communities, Zinacantecos and Chamulas, the former have little interest and do not welcome tourists, seeing this as undignified—photography is not accepted and there is little direct craft trade. Their neighbouring tribe have 'embraced' tourism and are the active craft seller-producers, despite the fact that the Zinacantecos designs are more attractive to many tourists.

Ladinos or Chamulas Indians in fact sell the Zinacantecos' handicrafts. Craft production has also adapted to the market segments. Tourist art, smaller pieces and items made of cheaper materials and more quickly produced, are sold alongside higher-quality and higher-priced ethnic art, for more discerning (and well-off) tourists and traders—cases, respectively, of 'encroaching' and 'complementary commercialisation' in tourist arts (Cohen, 1988).

In New Mexico, these dealings take place in trade and art centres, alongside tourist attractions, in Sante Fe, Taos (Kemper, 1978, 1979) and Albuquerque, NM, and in Mexico at places of production, such as Teotitlan del Valle, Oaxaca (hand-dyed/woven textiles) (Popelka and Litrell, 1991), Tonala (recycled glassware), San Miguel d'Allende (recycled aluminium) and Tlaquepaque (a Sante Fe-style art gallery 'suburb' of Guadalajara).

In fact, cultural quarters, such as Sante Fe and Taos are the focus for intense tourist art and craft business (Sante Fe, $134 million turnover: Eichztaedt (1988)) and craft *production* takes place elsewhere; studio and housing rents also create a 'gentrification effect' and a non-indigenous, professional art gallery 'class'. In Mexico, Tlaquepaque outside Guadalajara, has followed these New Mexican models and is dominated by US art trade and gallery-owners, although some local production and ownership continues, mostly family-based, such as at Tonala nearby (coloured glass, volcanic stone and recycled tin products).

Pueblo crafts have incorporated imported and imposed technology. Their influences include the Spanish, such as silver-making, wool-weaving and looms, as well as modern and traditional farming, oil and mineral production and forestry and, more recently, tourism development and management, from skiing to gambling. An example of modern materials and treatment in ethnic art is the distinctive black pottery produced in Teotitlan, Mexico, which is worked with car aerials to produce a burnished finish, and the use of recycled glass (coke bottles) and aluminium, from cans and wheel hubs, melted down and recast into bowls, cups and cutlery— ethnic, pan-Indian(?) or sustainable pan-American art!

The home purchase of ethnic art may respond to a former tourist visit, 'among their most valued possessions' (Wallendorf and Arnould, 1988) (perhaps restricted by carrying capacity, available cash etc.) and in practice will present a wider range and quality of products, without the hassle. The price of Western import mark-up may be worth it. Such availability may also stimulate a first visit at a later date, and serve as a source of information on ethnic art forms. It may just serve as part of an eclectic goods market which we take for granted (eating in a Curry House does not lead to a holiday in India . . .). A developed craft market does, however, present a positive opportunity for indigenous production, beyond the constraints, culture-clash and other deleterious effects of tourist trade. Three models of producer exhibition, commission and distribution can be extracted:

- *Artist—broker—outlets (national and for export)*. Direct commissioning from *source*, producer guaranteed sale, buyer influences style and quantities, subject to market (consumer) demand/assessment and feedback.
- *Artist—market/exhibition—consumer (trade and tourist)*. Specialist art and craft markets (e.g. Oaxaca), located in central and destination locations. Range of products from basic to quality, possibly fake-authentic (Messenger, 1989).
- *Artist(s)—cooperative—controlled retail/exhibitions*. Collective production (village or studio-based) is sold via special trade centres in regional towns and resorts. A wide range and 'best quality/examples' stocked.

These are obviously not exclusive and could be complementary. They do offer a degree of control and where desired, distance between producer and consumer, as well as greater opportunity for economic development. As experience and confidence is gained, the brokers' role may be taken over by national and potentially indigenous representatives, thus cutting out the middleman and reducing monetary leakage. In Mexico this would require support in the form of capital and greater recognition for indigenous production.

For a growing minority of tourists, however, and one increasingly sought and encouraged by independent tour operators, only the *real thing* will suffice those for whom their travel is a 'sacred journey' (Graburn, 1976) and where 'crafts . . . can serve as tangible evidence of having found the authentic or having participated in the

indigenous life of a community' (Briggs, 1980; MacCannell, 1976):

> I spent three vacations out there on the Navajo reservation which is a real interesting experience to go out . . . and be the minority [*sic*] person. We could watch some of the people make the rugs . . . and to buy one and talk with them. I've got the name of the woman who made it on the back of the piece. (Litrell, 1990)

The Navajos clearly tolerated the authentic-seeking, rug-watcher, but when original artefacts are in question, tribal ownership and views have to be asserted, with no guarantee that they will be heeded. An example was the Museum of Modern Art (MoMA), New York, who wished to borrow a Zuni statue of a tribal war god. This could not be countenanced by the Zuni tribe, since this sacred 'art' was not a collection-piece, this god was dangerous, the statue was to them still *live* (Clifford, 1990).

Note that the MoMA viewed the piece as *modern*; 'functioning tribal arts are rarely classifiable as "antiquities" because even if they are very old, they represent living, not dead cultures' (Evans-Pritchard, 1993).

Museums have also intervened to revive and protect styles and precious objects. In the early 1900s the Museum of New Mexico encouraged Pueblo artists to copy early Native American designs kept in the Museum in order to revive a dying artform and stimulate Pueblo pottery industry for tourist and 'authentic recreation' (Brody, 1976). In the 1960s the Mexican tourism ministry helped artisans to produce fake Olmex axes and exhibit these, the objective being to stem the flow of authentic antiquities from ancient sites and to 'reclassify fakes as modern traditional art that draw on ancient heritage' (Evans-Pritchard, 1993).

Lombok

The island of Lombok is due east of Bali, with a population of two million and an intact Balinese culture, left over from Balinese rule from the 1600s to the mid-19th century, from when it was a neglected Dutch colony until 1940. 80% of the population are Sasaks, the remainder Balinese and Chinese; however, this majority are the poorest group, effectively 'fourth world minorities' as with the actual minority Indian communities of Mexico. The Sasaks are Muslim, converted from the indigenous religion of *Wektu telu* (the native language) which derived from animism (ancestor and spirit worship). Like Mexican Indians who were converted to Catholicism by invaders, the Sasaks have adapted the new religion with symbols and traditions from the past, mixing Hindu-Buddhism with Islam.

Tourism in Lombok is relatively undeveloped, and is comparable to Bali 25 years ago. Luxury hotel and apartment developments on the north-west coast (Sengigi) feature in long-haul package tours, and as 'overspill' for Australian and New Zealand tourists. The south coast is still unspoilt; however, tourist development is planned, and pressure will intensify as Bali reaches saturation point and destination-fatigue sets in. Indeed, twin island holidays are already promoted (20-minute plane journey), with Lombok as the 'unspoilt haven' that ten years ago was the epithet afforded Bali. Lombok's proximity to Bali's tourist market has created specialist craft communities in villages such as Gunung Sari, Beleka, Senanti and Sukaraja. Gamelan ceremonies and staged performances can be seen here, but away from Bali's 'madding crowds'.

The host Sasak community, outside of the few hotel areas, has yet to 'act' for the tourist: 'Westerners are such a rarity that children run away in fear, an *orang bulan* (moon person) is a sensation, with people crowding round to touch the pale skin' (Wheeler et al., 1992).

Sasak women potters

Throughout Indonesia, earthenware pottery ('tembikar') is produced by village potters for local domestic use. The Sasak's craft stands out from all other groups, for its rich variety and beauty. The pots are from three major pottery-producing villages of Lombok, Benyumulek, Penujak and Masbagijik Timur, which formerly supplied most of the island's population with their cooking, storage and serving vessels ('tribal' and 'ethnic' art). These traditional pots have specific functions in domestic and ritual life. They are handmade, using simple home-made tools of wood, bamboo, metal blades, shell and stone, and even discarded obsidian river pebbles that have been handed down through generations. Firing is carried out in hollow mounds and more recently in hand-made kilns.

The Sasak women potters are recognised within their communities as 'masters' of their craft and are looked up to as teachers, yet they see their work primarily as the only means of making a living available to them, and with encroaching tourist development, a viable alternative to servile hospitality work away from their homes. Starting at an early age, the skills of the potters are passed from generation to generation, from mother to daughter (van den Berghe, 1992). It is a folk art tradition that dates back thousands of years and provides the main source of income for over 1500 potter families in the three villages. Although the women are the actual potters, the overall

production is a family enterprise. Most potters are assisted by their husbands, children and other relatives in the various tasks involved, including clay-gathering, processing, finishing and decorating, gathering fuel, firing and childcare. Lombok's landscape is dominated by Indonesia's second-highest volcano, Gunung Rinjani, surrounded by hills of greyish-brown clay, the source material.

Living on one of the most densely populated islands of Indonesia, the Sasak are one of the poorest, least-educated cultural groups in the country. Potter families are mostly landless, or own land that is less than sufficient to meet their food needs (the island's climate provides only one rice crop a year). Wage labour in the villages is limited to share-cropping and day-labour at planting, and weeding at harvest times; many villagers run small businesses and increasingly seek work outside the village. The production and sale of pottery in local markets is therefore of vital importance to survival; but where the majority of customers are equally poor, prices are inevitably low.

Since 1988 the Lombok Crafts Project has been assisting the women potters of three villages to improve the standard of living through technical and marketing assistance. A bilateral agreement between Indonesian and New Zealand governments, has funded the building of work shelters and showrooms. Technical, quality and design skills have been improved through advice on marketing, finance and distribution, and export of pottery is now developing with independent trade organisations ('ethnic' art).

One of the most important technical changes introduced by the Project is the open-topped kiln now used in Penujak village. In choosing this kind of kiln over more advanced designs, the potters have met the needs of greater fuel efficiency and productivity, as well as satisfying their wish to work together as they always have. Through this bilateral assistance programme, quality, durability and marketability of the pottery has improved significantly, without loss of integrity or intrinsic values of the creative process and ritual experience. This has helped to increase the income of the potters substantially, and all surplus profits from sales are used by the potters to improve living and working conditions in the villages. It is likely, however, that a two-tier production may develop, ensuring protection of tribal quality and significance, similar to the San Cristobal and Oaxaca (Mexico) and Pueblo (New Mexico) experience.

Fair trade?

In the shadow of NAFTA and the Uruguay-round of the General Agreement on Tariffs and Trade (GATT), control and regulation by third world countries of investment, ownership, and intervention to protect indigenous industry and culture will be sacrificed in the name of free trade. In fact, protectionism by the USA and European powers will ensure that financial and other key services remain out of reach of developing countries, whilst technology, brands and intellectual property rights will be forced on countries, such as Mexico and Indonesia, both of whom are likely to lose as a result of full free trade, despite the fatal attraction of post-Fordist industrial development exploiting cheap labour and infrastructure costs (Goldin et al., 1993).

Tourism development can take one of either of these routes, the one of time-limited economic maximisation—destructive of fragile socio-cultures—or the one of sustainable (eco, crafts and cultural-based) development, that is genuinely participatory and, of necessity, planned and controlled.

Fair trading is a complex and problematic issue; however, companies which attempt to trade fairly do have a number of similar features. All are committed to the support of their producers as well as the promotion of their products. They also endeavour to include consumers in this process by providing them with information about the origin and culture of the goods so that they may make informed choices (similar to environmentally friendly/green product information, now familiar in supermarkets). A recent collaborative project (Oxfam, Traidcraft, Twin Trading) involves the import of coffee under the 'Cafedirect' brand, from cooperative farmers in Peru and Guatemala, which guarantees price stability. A premium of 25p is paid by consumers of this product, which is the first to be sold in major supermarkets, and with greater local processing ('value-added') and reduced distribution ('middlemen') costs, growers receive more than four times the normal income from other brands (Jones, 1993).

Fair traders are also questioning and reassessing ways of production at every level, this involves exploring mutually supportive trading relationships and encouraging environmentally sustainable production, as demonstrated in Mexico and Lombok, which will not damage the physical environment or the local economy. It also involves empowering the workforce so that the trade relationship is not an exploitative one, but is of mutual benefit.

Apart from the financial and practical aspects of trading, there are cultural issues of fairness which require consideration, for instance, the problem of turning individual artistry into mass production, so that what was once a pleasurable combination of work and craft, merely becomes 'cash-crop' employment. This has, so far, been resisted in the above case studies. Also, there is the problem of different socio-cultural perspectives: what may seem hierarchical and feudal to Western eyes, may sometimes be part of an equally valid working system.

The environmental impact of production is an important aspect of fair trading. An obvious facet of this is the use of recycled raw materials (glass, aluminium, natural dyes in Mexico and natural tools and fuel in Lombok). Perhaps less well acknowledged are the ways in which third world trading can affect the actual structure of a community. Small businesses and workshops run by families, such as in Lombok and Teotitlan, Oaxaca, provide work for members of isolated villages. Their ability to maintain a sustainable trade may often continue the life of these communities, arresting the drift of people towards the cities and resorts, and help to keep vital craft skills and cultural expression alive, for the benefit of those people, and as an externality, for the public good.

Christie Mill (1990) poses the conundrum: 'Does tourism force people to remain artisans at the expense of attempts to achieve economic growth and independence?' The encouragement of cultural *involution* through staged authenticity (Graburn, 1976) and tourists seeking the 'old ways' and customs, may be valid where control and choice is effectively absent from local communities. Other issues include control over land-ownership and land-use, protection from economic 'dumping' from first world producers and dominant cultural invasion. Note that the block to the recent GATT agreement was culture, not just trade: France's subsidy of French-language film production, against Hollywood and an anglo, globalised media industry):

> multi-national financial domination, which swamps many countries with pictures and music from abroad . . . where standardised, stereo-typed productions whittle away at national cultures and attempt to impose a uniform lifestyle on the whole planet. (Jack Lang, World Conference of Ministers of Culture, Unesco, Mexico, 1982)

In the pueblos, Lombok and the craft-based villages reviewed here, the attachment to traditional lifestyles and beliefs, which are bound up with crafts and food production, and with the physical environment itself, are fundamental choices, rather than 'least worst' alternatives to economic survival. Given the fourth world minority status of these communities, it is naive to think of an open labour market in new industries, such as tourism, where free trade is in conflict with fair trade, and racial and sex discrimination in employment and wage rates is widespread.

In fact, the role of women (Bronstein, 1982; van den Berghe, 1992; Swain, 1993) and control over the destiny of these indigenous communities, from the local production presented here, is the only viable alternative, whilst discrimination by dominant societies remains the norm. The frustration of the Mayan Indians in Chiapas, following imposition of 'free markets' on their lands (from 'ejidos'—usage, not ownership rights; communal farming system, dating back to pre-Columbian times and enshrined in the Mexican Constitution), pre-NAFTA, has led to insurgency and bloodshed, as bemused tourists lose a few days' heritage touring and gain a novel holiday tale. For the indigenous community there are no alternatives.

Conclusion

The opportunities for cultural production and producer-control are evident from the New Mexico Pueblo art markets, and also from cooperative distribution initiatives in Mexico. These act, not only as buffer and quality-control, but as an alternative to the commercialisation by the American art and gallery trade and super-profits of some intermediaries (lessons from the Taos and Sante Fe (New Mexico) and Bali experiences).

In Lombok, the prospect of tourist-led development and influx threatens the social fabric, and acculturation may be inescapable, unless development and transport routes are restricted (the 'closed' Pueblo model may offer an alternative). The established craft industry will also continue to offer an alternative to village communities, and an opportunity for tourist trade at staged markets and resort sites. As a diversification strategy and value-added element of tourism (Barratt Brown, 1993), craft demand and management is a major opportunity for indigenous communities and artists:

> Crafts may well gain competitive advantage as Western countries develop post-modern economies ... the so-called 'narrow cast market' should stimulate demand ... homogeneity in tastes are now being reversed with increasing fragmentation within the mass market. (Hillman-Chartrand, 1988)

> Oh Penan—jungle warriors of the Tree
> What would the future hold for Thee?
> Would you choose to carry on with Primitive Traditions
> Or cast that aside and join our Civilisation?

(James Wong, Third Volume of Poetry—'Sarawak environment and tourism minister, timber concessionaire and golfer', in 'Money for Old Hope', Vidal, J., *The Guardian*, 7 January 1994, pp. 7–8)

Note

1. With thanks and acknowledgement to: Dr Tom Bloom, Milagros-Folk Art, Bristol; Katy Aston and Sarah Coop, Intan Crafts, London and Jakarta; and Rob Baker, Economic Development of Diverse Communities, San Francisco

References and bibliography

Barratt Brown, M. (1993) *Fair Trade: Reform and Realities in the International Trading System*, Zed Books, London.

van den Berghe, P. L. (1992) 'Tourism and the ethnic division of labour', *Annals of Tourism Research*, 19(1): 234–249.

van den Berghe, P. L. and Colby, B. N. (1991) 'Ladino–Indian relations in the highlands of Chiapas, Mexico', *Social Forces*, 40(1): 63–71.

Boniface, P. and Fowler, P. J. (1993) *Heritage and Tourism in the 'Global Village'*, Routledge, London.

Bracewell, M. (1994) 'A Question of Ethnics', *The Guardian*, 8 January: 14–15.

Briggs, C. L. (1980) *The Wood Carvers of Cordova, New Mexico*, University of Tennessee Press, Knoxville, TN.

Brody, J. J. (1976) 'The creative consumer: survival, revival and intervention in South-West Indian arts', in Graburn (1976).

Bronstein, A. (1982) *A Triple Struggle Latin American Peasant Women*, Inter-Action Inprint/War on Want, London.

Caruna, W. (1993) *Aboriginal Art*, Thames & Hudson, London.

Christie Mill, R. (1990) *Tourism: the International Business*, Prentice Hall, Englewood Cliffs, NJ.

Clifford, J. (1990) 'On collecting arts and culture', in *Out There: Marginalisation and Contemporary Culture*, Vol. 4, Ferguson, R. (Ed.), MIT Press Cambridge, MA.

Cohen, E. (1988) 'Authenticity and commoditization in tourism', *Annals of Tourism Research*, 15: 371–386.

Cohen, E. (1993) 'Introduction: investigating tourist arts', *Annals of Tourism Research*, 20(1): 1–8.

Coote, J. and Shelton, A. (1992) *Anthropology, Art and Aesthetics*, Clarendon Press, Oxford.

Daly, H. E. and Cobb, J. B. (1989) *For the Common Good: Redirecting the Economy towards Community, the Environment and a Sustainable Future*, Merlin Press, London.

Eichztaedt, P. (1988) 'India arts: heritage affects legal standing', *The New Mexican Newspaper*, Alberquerque, August 21, p. 131.

Evans-Pritchard, D. (1993) 'Ancient art in modern context', *Annals of Tourism Research*, 20(1): 9–31.

Feest, C. F. (1992) *Native Arts of North America*, Thames & Hudson, London.

Goldin, I., Knudsen, O. and van den Mensbrugghe, D. (1993) *Trade Liberalisation: Global Economic Implications*, OECD, Paris/World Bank, Washington, DC (HMSO, London).

Goodland, R. (1982) *Tribal Peoples and Economic Development—Human Ecological Considerations*, World Bank, Washington, DC.

Gottlieb, A. (1982) 'American's vacations', *Annals of Tourism Research*, 9(1): 165–187.

Graburn, N. H. (1976) *Ethnic and Tourist Arts: Cultural Expressions from the Fourth World*, University of California Press, Berkeley, CA.

Harris, N. (1990) *Cultural Expressions: Marketing Appetites and Cultural Tastes in Modern America*, University of Chicago Press, Chicago, IL, p. 80.

Hersey, I. (1991) *Indonesian Primitive Art*, Singapore.

Hillman-Chartrand, H. (1988) 'Crafts in the post-modern economy', *Journal of Cultural Economics*, 12: 2.

Jones, J. (1993) 'Fair trade', *Green Magazine*, West Sussex, pp. 12–15.

Kemper, R. V. (1978) 'Tourism and regional development in Taos', *Studies in Third World Societies*, No. 6, pp. 89–103.

Kemper, R. V. (1979) 'Tourism in Taos and Patzcuaro', *Annals of Tourism Research*, 6(1): 91–110.

van der Kraan, A. (1980) *Lombok: Conquest, Colonization and Underdevelopment 1870–1940*, Heinemann, London.

Krulfeld, R. (1961) 'The village economies of the Sasak of Lombok: a comparison of three Indonesian peasant communities', in Richter (1993).

Leong, W.-T. (1989) 'Culture and the state: manufacturing traditions for tourism', *Critical Studies in Mass Communication*, No. 6, pp. 355–375, in Evans-Pritchard (1993).

Litrell, M. A. (1990) 'Symbolic significance of textile crafts for tourists', *Annals of Tourism Research*, 17: 228–245.

Litrell, M. A., Anderson, L. F. and Brown, P. J. (1993) 'What makes a craft souvenir authentic?', *Annals of Tourism Research*, 11: 197–215.

MacCannell, D. (1976) *The Tourist: A New Theory of the Leisure Class*, Schaker Books, New York.

MacCannell, D. (1984) 'Reconstructed ethnicity: tourism and cultural identity in third world communities', *Annals of Tourism Research*, 11(1): 375–391.

MacCannell, D. (1991) *Empty Meeting Grounds: the Tourist Papers*, Routledge, London.

Messenger, P. (1989) *The Ethics of Collecting Cultural Property: Whose Culture? Whose Property?*, University of New Mexico Press, Albuquerque, NM.

Muller, K. (1991) *East of Bali: from Lombok to Timor*, Singapore.

Popelka, C. A. and Litrell, M. A. (1991) 'Influence of tourism on handcraft evolution, *Annals of Tourism Research*, 18: 392–413.

Pye, E. (1986) 'Crafting the future', *Craft International*, 4(1): 27–35.

Richter, A. (1993) *Arts and Crafts of Indonesia*, Thames & Hudson, London.

Sayer, A. (1992) *The Arts and Crafts of Mexico*, Thames & Hudson, London.

Swain, M. B. (1993) 'Women producers of ethnic arts', *Annals of Tourism Research*, 20(1): 32–51.

Tadmore, M. (1984) 'Developing crafts in developing countries', *Craft International*, 1(4).

Traidcraft (1993) *Social audit*, Traidcraft plc, Gateshead.

Vogt, E. Z. (1978) *Bibliography of the Harvard Chiapas Project, the First Twenty Years, 1957–1977*, Peabody Museum of Archaeology and Ethnology, Harvard University, Cambridge, MA.

Vogt, E. Z. (1990) *The Zincantecos of Mexico, a Modern Maya of Life*, Holt, Rinehart & Winston, Fort Worth, TX.

Wallendorf, M. and Arnould, E. (1988) ' "My favourite things": a cross-cultural inquiry into object attachments, possessiveness, and social linkage', *Journal of Consumer Research*, 14: 531–547.

Wheeler, T., Stoney, R., Spitzer, D., Nebesky, R. and Lyon, J. (1992) *Indonesia: Travel Survival Kit*, Lonely Planet Publications, Hawthorn, Australia.

83 Managing the tourist gaze: visitor services at Edinburgh Castle

M. FOLEY

This paper presents a case study of a popular tourist attraction within the framework of 'the tourist gaze' offered by John Urry (1990). It is not intended to present this as the definitive analytical approach in tourism studies. Rather, it is meant to give practitioners an opportunity to evaluate a theoretical perspective in terms of its usefulness as an informant for management action. The purpose, then, is to stimulate discussion on the role of theoretical developments in the working practices of those whose jobs are in the tourism industries. Additionally, it is intended to encourage re-evaluation of empirical work in the field which could be said (more correctly) to be empiricist. There is benefit for practitioners in possessing an understanding of the theoretical and ideological bases of change in their internal and external environments. These benefits include the ability to interpret data and events arising outwith and within their organisations from a critical standpoint and the opportunity to assimilate a broader agenda in policy formulation. Moreover, if such analyses can be made accessible to practitioners, there is a greater possibility of meaningful dialogue between those who study tourism and those who work in the field.

The case study of Edinburgh Castle was conducted within a specification devised by the European Cultural Tourism Project by Dr Greg Richards. The work was undertaken alongside separate research carried out by Fred Coalter at the Centre for Leisure Research at Heriot-Watt University, Edinburgh.

The tourist gaze in a postmodern world

The 'modern' idea that rational approaches can lend themselves to understanding natural and social phenomena is a product of the 'Enlightenment' of the 17th and 18th centuries. This conception of the 'modern' as progressive, developmental and coherent implies that there is a pattern which underpins social life—even if the pattern itself is incomprehensible. It suggests that there is a 'big picture' or a single, all-embracing explanation for the way things are. On these terms, concepts of tourism, as a differentiated social and cultural phenomenon, have developed in ways that both emanate from, and reinforce, these perspectives. Theoretical developments (e.g. Foucault (1971, 1979) and Derrida (1978, 1987)) throughout the 20th century have indicated disillusion and scepticism with the possibility of grand explanations. These have suggested that more meaningful understandings of social life can be derived when adopting a stance described as 'postmodern'. The term 'postmodern' is, itself, a matter of debate and exploration. It is by no means certain that two users of the term will share an agreed definition of its meaning. This paper is not intended as a piece of theoretical writing, so it is proposed to explore the term only briefly to facilitate a working understanding that will inform and enlighten discussion of the case-study below.

A central idea of postmodernism is challenge and denial of any separation between high and low culture. Attention is drawn to the impact and immediacy of cultural forms and to an instrumental consumption of these based upon pleasure (as opposed to contemplation). Audience participation and the reduction of differences between that which might have been considered aesthetic and the commercial sphere are implicit in these ideas. A particularly important issue is that of the 'spectacle' where reality itself draws (and is drawn) closer to representations of itself. This leads to the consumption of media where these signs and representations of the 'real' can be accorded greater credence than the reality. It can be seen as a cultural 'melting pot' of contrasting and, often, contradictory ingredients with the products being gratification and illusion.

According to Urry (1990) a distinctive tourist gaze is produced when the following criteria are satisfied. Firstly, the place to be visited must be *differentiated* in some aspects from experiences conventionally assumed in the daily life of tourists. One way of distinguishing from the ordinary is in the *uniqueness and/or celebrity* of the object. Another dimension of the extraordinary may be the *recognition and interpretation of signs* which form part of an established context of tourism-related objects. Aspects of that which might be expected to be *familiar are seen to be unfamiliar* in cross-cultural contrast.

Conversely, the *ordinary may provoke interest when presented in unfamiliar contexts*, such as the conduct of household chores in the 18th century. Ordinary tasks such as eating or drinking, when offered against *a distinctive background* may be rendered extraordinary. Lastly, an apparently ordinary object can be given singularity because of *local signage authenticating its distinctiveness*.

Visitor services at Edinburgh Castle

Edinburgh Castle is the most popular visitor attraction in Scotland. The site has been fortified since the 6th century AD and the physical features suggest even earlier occupation.

The castle sits on a volcanic 'plug' called the Castle Rock. This is the core of an extinct volcano, shaped by glacial erosion to near-vertical on the north and south sides and to a more gradual slope on the west. The gentle descent to the east is a result of a 'tail' fashioned upon the hard plug as glaciers moved across the landscape from the west. This came to be the principal thoroughfare of Edinburgh old town, linking the castle with the Palace of Holyroodhouse. Until the Jacobite rebellion was quelled in 1745, much of Scottish political and institutional history was enacted in and around here.

The prominence of the castle allows easy merchandising to visitors. It dominates the main shopping streets lying between the 'old' and 'new' towns. The main railway station and embarkation points for airport buses are close by. Every public service bus touches Princes Street, giving a full view of the castle. Princes Street has buildings on one (the north) side only. The south side is a park garden disguising the railway which lies directly below the castle. The largest hotels are nearby. At twilight the castle is floodlit and visible across the city. The silhouette of the castle on its rock has become a powerful symbol in the marketing of tourism and of Scottish produce.

The castle belongs to the Crown and is managed on its behalf by the Historic Scotland agency. Historic Scotland was created out of the Historic Buildings and Monuments division in 1991. Although the division had called itself Historic Scotland since 1985 for marketing purposes, the formal change was more than the ratification of a user-friendly title. Executive agencies are established within the government's Next Steps programme, intended to devolve ministerial responsibility for achieving objectives to managers. Ministers determine overall policy, resources and performance targets. Agencies have freedom to organise work to produce the results desired. The effect is to shift operations onto a quasi-commercial basis. Staff remain civil servants, but their responsibilities for effective, efficient and economical conduct of their duties is more apparent than before. Moreover, corporate management begins to include concepts such as strategic planning, quality management and internal markets. This is not to say that these activities and ideas were ignored in the past. Rather, it emphasises the changes expected by ministers in the ethos of senior management and the outlook of all staff.

Historic Scotland exercises a role in the conservation and interpretation of the nation's heritage through its listing, scheduling, grant-awarding and excavation powers. Some historic properties remain in private ownership, some may belong to bodies in the voluntary sector (such as those managed by the National Trust for Scotland) and some are owned by local government. Edinburgh Castle is one of 330 properties being looked after and presented to the public by Historic Scotland itself. A large part of the strategic management and marketing responsibilities for the castle cannot be disaggregated from the Scotland-wide programmes of the agency. Similarly, it is both impossible and (apparently seen as) undesirable to apportion expenditure to a specific cost centre such as the castle. There is a recognition of the attraction and importance of the castle. However, there is a powerful, internal belief in managing, financing and marketing it as part of a wider package.

A further complication is that the castle is not a single, homogeneous entity but a package of cultural attractions. The castle comprises several buildings that have evolved since the 11th century. Many are in use as exhibits (e.g. the Great Hall). Others house collections of artefacts (e.g. the Scottish Crown Jewels) or belong to third parties (e.g. regimental museums). Lastly, some buildings are used as part of the military garrison. The continued location of a military garrison within the castle is said to be an attraction to tourists. For example, visitors expressed disappointment over the suspension of sentry patrols at the gates during the 'off' season. These economies had been a result of expenditure restrictions on the army.

During 1985 a study of visitor facilities concluded that in reception, attractions and presentation, the castle had not kept pace with visitor demands. Commissioned by the Ancient Buildings and Monuments Directorate, the consultants' remit had been to address problems of traffic and visitor flows, inadequate services and lack of interpretation. The report proposed massive public works, especially around the Esplanade which was to be levelled and redeveloped into a permanent arena. This particular suggestion provoked an outcry and failed to secure public support or government resources. Another significant proposal was to tunnel below the Castle Rock to provide a service and military access.

Announcing a £6 million development scheme in 1988, the Secretary of State identified a new shop (opened 1990), a vehicle tunnel (opened in 1990), improved historical interpretation and provision for school parties. In 1991 a second phase of improvements incorporating a new restaurant (completed 1992) and a major exhibition (completed 1993) of the Honours of Scotland (the Crown Jewels) was announced.

The approach to presentation and interpretation of the castle is based upon the warders who act as tour guides for parties who form themselves within the gates. These are complemented by guide booklets and buildings. Attempts have been made in some places to tell a 'story' using real incidents which took place in the castle. These range from the dalliances of monarchs to the misdemeanours of soldiers. In latter case, dummy figures are shown incarcerated in gaol wearing authentic uniforms and lit to maximise impact of the squalor, while simultaneously ensuring maximum visitor vision. All artefacts on show are the genuine article. Particular care is taken to authenticate objects and decor. Of the attractions outdoors, the ramparts and their cannons are popular.

Management at Edinburgh Castle

Managers identify two issues in local site services for visitors. These are quality of staff with customer contact roles and development of the product without compromising the integrity of the castle. Both are aimed at increasing satisfaction, throughput and expenditure by visitors.

Staffing

The title of 'warder' at the castle is historically significant and, like the organisational structure, is based upon its military past. Attempts have been made to identify alternatives to the title warder, which, it is recognised, may have negative connotations. No viable alternative has been identified that describes accurately the tasks undertaken. Staff are not referred to as 'warders' within public areas of the castle.

Those with direct responsibility for the quality of visitors' experiences are warders on grades MSG 4 and 5. Other staff will come into contact with visitors (e.g. shop and ticket assistants) but their remit does not extend to personal intervention in the visit. Investigation of these issues suggested a shifting nature to the warders' jobs and that these have been affected by changing organisational ethos.

Warders on the MSG 5 grade are usually seasonal appointments and are in static posts throughout the castle.

This means adopting both a security and an informational role. Warders are rotated around various points to enrich their experiences and improve their product knowledge. Although static, they are not statues: they are expected to deal with visitor enquiries about all aspects of the castle, not only the part where they are situated. In addition, they are expected to intervene in the process of a visit where behaviour may be detrimental to general enjoyment or if they can improve the experiences of visitors. MSG 4 grade warder job descriptions are identical to MSG 5, except for an additional responsibility to lead tours. Staff on the MSG 4 grade are chosen according to experience, product knowledge, communication and customer-care skills. Staff on both of these grades wear identical and unique uniforms. By involving customers in the service-delivery using information points and tours, the intention is to associate the uniform with help. It would be divisive, then, to differentiate artificially between grades who may be perceived as, or feel judged as, offering lower quality help. The uniforms have been redesigned recently away from the forbidding aspect of a police-style serge and towards something similar to a countryside ranger.

As well as the desire to make staff seem more approachable, a three-year training programme developed the interaction skills needed to match customers' expectations of warders. The main feature of this programme has been customer-care training. Staff are expected to improve their product knowledge by reading texts made available by management. Some staff have been supported in foreign-language tuition. In accordance with the new ethos, trainers strive to change both the style and content of information imparted. Previously, delivery was felt to be unpalatable, dry and deadpan, reflecting a curatorial orientation and an assumption of visitor knowledge of architecture or history. Information was given freely, but often without regard for context or understanding of its significance. Now, warders are encouraged to develop a more individual style—while ensuring that the basic information and itinerary are covered. This allows opportunities for personal anecdotes and tailoring of delivery to suit the audience. Warders are encouraged to participate in shaping their work-environment by communicating with management. This has involved regular meetings to exchange information and a suggestions scheme for improvements to visitor services. The intention is to foster a culture in which staff feel valued and recognise the importance of internal markets.

The onset of agency-status gave managers freedom to negotiate local conditions of service and (to an extent) reward systems reflecting their organisational objectives.

Perhaps the most significant change wrought by these powers has affected warders' job conditions. The effect for visitors has been the opening of the castle on Sunday mornings. Until 1991, opening hours were 09.30 hours to 18.00 hours Monday to Saturday, and 11.30 hours to 18.00 hours on Sundays. Now, the castle is open on Sundays from 09.30 hours. Warders' contracts were amended, by agreement, to a 5-day specification rather than Monday to Friday. Under the 'old' arrangements, weekend work was paid at the overtime rate. Now, overtime is paid outwith individuals' 5-day contracts. These five days may include Saturday or Sunday. Overtime has been minimised further by judicious use of casual staff to cover peaks, lunch-breaks and periods of absenteeism. Managers believe that the principle behind the changes was a matter of consensus but concede that warders are financially worse off.

Nowhere is greater customer-orientation more apparent than in the recruitment policy for warders. Often, in an established organisation, there is a residue of long-serving staff appointed to address contemporary needs whose skills may be only incidentally related to current requirements. These difficulties are addressed in training programmes and staff development reviews. Nevertheless, it is unlikely that the aggregate skills of a staff complement reflect exactly management's requirements in the job. This perspective is more likely to be demonstrated by the skills and experience demanded of the most recent recruits. Currently, advertisements seek warders with good, applied foreign-language skills. In addition, past experience in a customer-related or retail field is emphasised and if this is in tourism, then so much the better.

Product development

For most visitors, the tour is a significant part of the product. That managers want this to prevail is evidenced by the continuation of entry fees which include the price of a tour. It is not possible to pay entry excluding the tour—although it is not compulsory to join one. Managers view the style and delivery of the tour as indivisible from the experience of the castle. Product development, where this extends beyond maintenance, ensures that the tour can be enjoyed and that further expenditure will be encouraged. Tours start every 15 minutes at peak times. It is common to have 50 visitors in a tour party. Visitors are not committed to one guide, but may drift away at a point of interest and join another when ready to continue. This flexibility led to difficulties before the construction of the service tunnel. Movements of vehicles and troops through the narrow entrance and cobbled lanes had necessitated pressing oneself against walls to avoid injury or incident. In parties of 50, this was hazardous and, inevitably, interrupted the flow of information. So the major public works undertaken at the castle in the last 60 years—the tunnel—while not intended solely, or even primarily, for the comfort of visitors has had a significant effect on the development of a tourism product.

Reconstruction of the shop to double shelf-space while franchising an area to a quality retailer has increased revenue. The cafeteria has reopened recently after bomb damage. Its success has not yet been measured, but the design has been a matter of public and media comment, recalling reactions to 19th-century proposals. Although the Crown is not subject to Planning Regulations, staff were keen to emphasise that the process of seeking and receiving local authority approval was conducted on an 'as if' basis.

In developing the product, commodification of the castle's offerings is avoided. Modern technologies are evaluated and used in the interpretation of exhibits when considered appropriate. Thus video and simulations are both deployed. However, there is a marked differentiation by marketing management between the presentation of 'real' events that took place in the castle, verifiable by documentary sources, and the construction of stories and tales that do not attempt to represent 'actual' events. The latter type of presentation would be regarded as entirely inappropriate and unacceptable by managers.

Income from admissions is a function of pricing policies and the number of visitors attracted. Clearly, there is a direct relationship between visits and income. Trading income comprises expenditure by visitors in the cafeteria and in the shop. Although there is a connection between the number of visits and trading income, it is possible to secure growth in the latter without increasing the former—e.g. by increasing the opportunities for expenditure and by attracting visitors with a high propensity to spend or with a higher daily expenditure rate.

Table 83.1 gives the recorded number of visitors since 1983. Although the effect of inflation will affect interpretation of figures shown in Table 83.1, it is apparent that the doubling of total income per visitor has been achieved with a disproportionately high increase in the trading income per visitor compared to admissions income. Broadly, this is commensurate with the management policy of improving opportunity and quality of trading outlets.

Aims and objectives

The mission of Historic Scotland as stated in the Corporate Plan (1992–1995) is to 'safeguard the nation's

Table 83.1 *Visitor numbers and income in pounds sterling (1983–1991)*

Year	Total income per visit (net of VAT)	No. of visits	Admission income per visit	Trading income per visit
1983	1.51	818 100	1.09	0.42
1984	1.79	847 069	1.26	0.53
1985	1.85	923 256	1.31	0.54
1986	1.98	832 485	1.39	0.59
1987	2.03	967 424	1.38	0.65
1988	2.53	957 584	1.79	0.74
1989	2.37	1 033 697	1.70	0.67
1990	2.59	1 078 120	1.78	0.81
1991	3.26	973 620	2.25	1.01

Source: Historic Scotland.

built heritage and promote its understanding and enjoyment making the best use of resources available'. In the White Paper, 'This Common Inheritance' (cm 1200, 1990), five strands identified to the government's approach, of which two relate directly to the castle. These are looking after properties in government care and promoting enjoyment and understanding of heritage. Paraphrasing the main functions of Historic Scotland, these can be divided into the following:

- protecting monuments in care and ensuring their sound conservation and maintenance;
- encouraging visitors to monuments in care, and ensuring that they enjoy and benefit from their visits;
- increasing public access to grant-aided historic buildings and monuments;
- encouraging knowledge about Scotland's built heritage.

The development strategy being pursued assumes modest growth in central government contribution and expects generation of income to offset the shortfall between expenditure and exchequer funds. As far as the castle is concerned, this will allow the Scottish Honours project to proceed, together with essential maintenance projects. The decision to adopt a strategy that involves expenditure of about £9.7 million over 'baseline' reflects the level of public interest in heritage, the need to maximise value for money by tackling maintenance problems early and the importance of seizing current opportunities.

The function of promoting and preserving has been attributed a number of performance indicators that will affect the castle. These are:

- increase by 4.5% the number of visitors to monuments where an admission charge is made;
- improve presentation to visitors, in keeping with status of the monuments;
- improve quality and variety of goods for sale to visitors;
- increase revenue from admissions, trading and functions.

Marketing

Data on visitor profiles is confined to a study carried out in 1985. These data indicate that visitors were:

- predominantly aged between 20 and 50;
- evenly divided between men and women;
- predominantly professional and managerial occupations;
- tended to have experienced higher education;
- coming with friends and/or family;
- mostly on holiday;
- Americans (29%), English (22%) and Scots (19%);
- two-thirds were on a first visit, while one-third were repeat visits;
- most wanted a general look rather than to see something specific;
- parking and weather were the least satisfactory aspects of most trips;
- mostly wanted more information about what to see.

Target markets being developed are based upon the type of visitors to Edinburgh. Eighty per cent of visitors to the city come to the castle. The profile of these visitors will affect future income. Broadly, two strategies have been adopted to reach different groups. Firstly, there is a need to attract those with disproportionately high per diem spend rates to boost trading income. This group is likely to contain a high proportion of foreign holidaymakers and business tourists. These are reached through marketing at travel trade exhibitions throughout the world (especially in Japan). The focus of activity on these trips is the quality travel market. In countries like Japan, where holidays are relatively alien to the indigenous culture, there is little to be gained from direct, personal marketing. Rather, in product life-cycle terms, the approach is to reach the 'early adopters'. Similar exhibitions in Europe are used to reach tour (especially coach) operators and a package ticket is offered for entry to a number of the properties. In all cases, managers concede that the castle is used as the flagship with which it is possible to increase interest in other, less well-known properties.

At home, the need to increase visitation levels and to broaden visitor profiles towards a representative spread of the Scottish population drives marketing efforts. Advertisements in the *Daily Record*, a newspaper with a mainly manual-occupation readership have led to a substantial amount of free publicity. This has taken the form of colour, 'pull-out' sections featuring Historic Scotland's properties combined with an offer of free entry. Such 'free' promotion is an active part of the marketing strategy. Travel journalists are given tours of properties and provided with ready-written copy. Historic Scotland commissioned a television advertisement to highlight their properties to Scots only. Again, the objective has been to broaden the socio-economic base and to increase throughput.

Management issues

Given the information presented above, the following issues are identified for management:

A. Public policy issues
(1) reconciliation of objectives implying the attraction of large numbers with a stake in Scotland's heritage with the need to develop overseas markets;
(2) the ties of public funding and the extent to which these inhibit development;
(3) the future role of the 'agency status' and changes to bodies such as English Heritage;

B. Strategy issues
(1) possible demands for increased commodification;
(2) the extent to which better value for money might be achieved by contracting out and/or franchising some visitor services;
(3) the relationship with other occupiers of the castle in the face of changing roles for the armed forces;
(4) the relationship with bodies responsible for Edinburgh's tourism development;
(5) reconciliation of curatorial orientations with increased access;

C. Financial issues
(1) how to increase average spend per visitor in real terms;
(2) gearing of future funding and implications for activity/development;

D. Marketing issues
(1) how to increase throughput while minimising negative impacts (especially overcrowding at peak times);

(2) quality assurance and the Citizen's Charter;
(3) the possibility of using the castle's image for the licensing and endorsement of 'quality' products and services.

Visitor services and the tourist gaze

Edinburgh Castle and its exhibits could be seen as a high culture experience. They contain much of architectural, cultural and social interest and would reward a contemplative approach by visitors competent to address them in this way. Yet, some features of the castle are presented to maximise immediacy and impact upon visitors. It would be impossible to interpret the historical context of the castle in ways that could be assimilated within an afternoon's visit. The marketing-based approach taken is based upon a need to maximise expenditure by creating opportunities within the castle for spending. At the same time, quality-led initiatives demand user-friendly services which have rejected assumptions of aesthetic and cultural analysis on the part of visitors. Both competitive pressures and internal throughput requirements dictate that 'pleasure' is an objective worth achieving and that it can be produced by anecdotal interventions by staff, audio-visual material and information boards. It has been suggested (Foley, 1993) that use of tour-guides to interpret attractions within the castle can lead to significant visitor participation in the shaping of their own experiences and those of others. These reductions of differences between the aesthetic nature of a visit to a historic site and the commercial considerations inherent in government initiatives designed to introduce quasi-market values and practices are key issues for those with curatorial orientations who wish to minimise commodification. The use, in particular of audio-visual material as 'interpretation' of the historical context of the castle has implications for the construction of visits as 'spectacle' and for merging of perceptions of reality and representation (e.g. the reality and representation of the military tattoo in the Esplanade at the front of the castle).

Within this analysis, contrasting and contradictory ingredients are evident. Examples of these are: the tension between expectations of contemplative behaviour on the part of visitors in letting the exhibits speak for themselves and interpretive techniques aimed at impact and based on mass media; the shifting orientations between curatorial/scientific and recreational/pleasure ideologies underpinning strategy; the presence of a working military garrison alongside the most-visited chargeable attraction in Scotland and in the roles of primary visitor services staff in both regressive and customer-oriented tasks. Yet, it would be incorrect to call this a 'melting pot'. That would require a synthesis of these and other elements which had eliminated the obvious contrasts between ingredients into a coherent whole. It is apparent from the above that such a synthesis has not occurred. Rather, the castle is a mosaic of contradictory approaches to delivering a tourism product. This lack of integration should not be interpreted as undermining the nature of the product—it is reasonable to harness contrast and contradiction as elements in achieving satisfaction and impact. However, the implication of an approach like this is that a rationale for it exists and is unified in marketing strategy.

Elements of differentiation from daily life are easy to discern in the experience of the castle, as are its uniqueness and celebrity, together with the singularity of some specific exhibits (e.g. the Scottish Crown Jewels) and the spectacle of the military tattoo. The power of Edinburgh Castle as a sign of 'Scottishness' and of its 'typicality' as a type of garrison in Scotland have been mentioned above. Partly, this is achieved through the dominance of Edinburgh's skyline by the castle and the inability of visitors to escape its silhouette anywhere in the central area of the city (day or night). The same effect is achieved in the use of images of the castle and its military tattoo in merchandising Edinburgh and Scotland through brochures and guide books. In both cases, a process of recognition of a tourism-specific image has been fostered and engendered. While many items in the castle are extraordinary, there are some which derive their distinctiveness to the tourist from local 'markers'. Examples include the cannon 'Mons Meg' and the chapel of St Margaret which might otherwise be unremarkable.

The presentation of the familiar is achieved, in part at least, in the presentation of aspects of the working life of the castle in the past, including domestic and military arrangements. These are reinforced by the current use of the castle by the military and the, obviously popular, manifestations of this in the presence of soldiers conducting both ceremonial and functional duties (e.g. sentry duty, the firing of a field-gun from the ramparts at 13.00 hours every day). Lastly, the commonplace activities of eating, shopping and personal hygiene are offered in singular visual environments, all of which have been the subject of considerable, recent investment.

In addressing the issues identified for management outlined above, the notion of the tourist gaze and the reconciliation of contradictions in the delivery of the services will need to be addressed. In themselves, these should not be taken as an agenda for further planning, strategy or investment. These issues are more usefully contributors to development when construed as a framework for encouraging critical reflection upon the role of the castle in Scottish cultural life and in the images of Scotland being offered to visitors. They demand that the ideological basis of policy and strategy are explicit and evaluated as part of development rather than taken as implicit and beyond contention as axiomatic or matters of widespread consensus.

References

Derrida, J. (1978) *Writing and Difference*, Routledge, London.
Derrida, J. (1987) *The Post Card*, University of Chicago Press, Chicago, IL.
Foley, M. (1993) 'Using participant observation in the evaluation of environmental interpretation', Paper presented at the CEI/SIBH International conference 'Weighed in the Balance—Research and Evaluation in Interpretation', Edinburgh, July.
Foucault, M. (1971) *Madness and Civilization*, Tavistock, London.
Foucault, M. (1979) *The History of Sexuality*, Allen Lane, London.
Urry, J. (1990) *The Tourist Gaze*, Sage, London.

84 Tourist health: the precautions, behaviour and health problems of British tourists in Malta

S. J. PAGE, S. CLIFT AND N. CLARK

Introduction

It is widely acknowledged that tourist-travel has positive benefits when combined with a holiday (Page, 1994). Yet there is a growing body of literature which questions the message, images and promotion of these positive benefits for those who take a holiday, since there are hidden health risks associated with tourist-travel and potential health problems associated with certain forms of risk-behaviours, particularly among package holidaymakers (Cossar et al., 1990). The recent *British Medical Bulletin* (Behrens and McAdam, 1993) review of 'Travel medicine' provides a concise insight into the difficulties associated with tourist health abroad, including the epidemiology of travel health (Reid and Cossar, 1993), jet lag and motion sickness (Nicolson et al., 1993) specific forms of illness (e.g. malaria, diarrhoea, venomous bites and stings, hepatitis and skin diseases), and accidents (Bewes, 1993). It also emphasises the need for preventive measures (Dawood, 1993) and the necessity of screening returning visitors (Churchill et al., 1993). In addition to this wider range of potential health risks, one has to consider the HIV/AIDS pandemic and the risks associated with the sexual behaviour of tourists abroad.

This paper reports the results of a survey of tourist health among 785 British tourists in Malta in March 1993 as part of the Travel, Lifestyles and Health Research Project funded by the South-East Thames Regional Health Authority and the Higher Education Funding Council (see Clift and Page (1994) for further details of the wider remit for the project). The paper commences with a brief review of the literature on tourist health and is followed by discussion of the tourism context of the study. The aims and objectives of the study are then considered together with the methodology and some of the main findings. The implications of the survey are then critically analysed and the significance for tourist health is examined.

Research on the health problems of UK travellers/tourists

Tourist health is a neglected, almost hidden aspect of tourism and tourism behaviours although there is a growing literature on the health problems experienced by UK holidaymakers abroad (e.g. Cossar et al., 1990; Cartwright, 1992). For this reason, it is pertinent to outline some of the main findings of these studies which are not widely known outside of a small group of medical and health researchers with an interest in tourist-travel medicine. Cossar et al. (1990) report a review of travel-related illnesses experienced by travellers returning to Scotland. Data were collected by means of self-completion questionnaires from a total of 13 816 travellers between 1977 and 1985. Most questionnaires were distributed to travellers at their return airport (Glasgow and Edinburgh) for return by prepaid envelope. Response rates from different sample groups varied between 20% and 77% with a mean of 32%. This must be regarded as a low rate of return and consequently estimates obtained of illness rates have to be treated with caution. It is reasonable to assume that returning travellers who experience illness during or shortly after their trip abroad would be more likely to return questionnaires thereby inflating estimates of illness.

Overall, Cossar et al. found that 36% of travellers reported illness. In 18% of cases alimentary symptoms (diarrhoea and/or vomiting) were reported; a further 10% reported alimentary symptoms and other problems and 2% reported respiratory problems. Age also emerged as a significant factor associated with reported illness, with the 20–29 age group having the highest attack rate of 48%. This then declined as age increased, with the lowest attack rate among those aged 60 and above (20%). No sex differences in illness rates were found and 37% of smokers reported illness—a significantly higher rate than among non-smokers (32%). As might be anticipated, illness rates varied markedly according to country visited. The most visited countries in Cossar et al.'s sample were Spain (52%), Greece (9%) and Yugoslavia (6%) (prior to the current conflict). Malta attracted 5% of the sample and was one of four locations visited during both summer and winter. Attack rates in Malta were higher in summer (32%) than in the winter months (21%) but this difference was not statistically significant.

Data on the use of pre-travel health advice were available from a sample of 645 travellers. Surprisingly, attack rates were higher among those who sought advice prior to travel (37%) compared with those who did not seek advice (26%). This may reflect the fact that those travellers who anticipate problems are more likely to seek advice than those who do not expect problems. No further details are given on the characteristics of those seeking and not seeking advice (e.g. age and destination) which might throw further light on this difference.

It is evident from Cossar et al. that 'alimentary' problems (especially diarrhoea) are the most common health problems experienced by travellers. By far the most extensive data available on the epidemiology of such problems are reported by Cartwright (1992). Working in association with Thomson Tour Operators Limited, Cartwright analysed data on illness reported by Thomson clients aged 16 and above on self-completion questionnaires completed during their return flights home to the UK (part of this questionnaire is reproduced in Page (1994)). Specified illnesses were coded as 'stomach upsets', 'respiratory symptoms', 'combination of stomach upsets and respiratory symptoms' and 'other'. For the summer seasons from 1984 to 1991 data from no fewer than 2 756 321 questionnaires were analysed. Data for the winter seasons from 1988 to 1991 have also been processed. The main results obtained can be summarised as follows:

- During the summer seasons the incidence of travellers' diarrhoea rose from April to a peak in August–September, falling again in October. The peak incidence in the years 1984 to 1986 was approximately 15% whereas from 1989 the peak incidence had fallen to around 6%
- Incidence rates varied by country visited in a similar way for each year studied. In 1991 the lowest incidence levels were obtained from Italy and Florida (with attack rates of below 5% throughout the season). At the other end of the scale the peak incidence rates rose to 23% in Turkey, 34% in Tunisia and no less than 40% in the Dominican Republic
- Data for Malta is of particular interest in relation to the present study, and for May to October 1991 attack rates for diarrhoea remained below 10%

Cartwright cautions that the information available is totally subjective and is not capable of verification on a case to case basis. Furthermore, the data cannot be correlated with any causative organisms.

Conway et al. (1990) report findings from a survey of the behaviour and health problems of a moderately sized

sample of UK travellers/tourists abroad. Some 978 16–40-year-olds drawn from the register of an urban general practice in Nottingham were sent a detailed questionnaire to complete. The main aim of the study was to assess the extent of risk behaviours for HIV transmission amongst a sample of adults from Nottingham who travelled abroad, but questions were included on a variety of other health issues. A total of 545 analysable questionnaires were returned giving a response rate of 56%, although response rate varied by age, with the lowest response rate among 21–28-year-olds and the highest from 31–40-year-olds. Women were more likely to respond compared with men. A total of 354 respondents (65%) had been abroad during 1989 and/or 1988, whereas 191 respondents (35%) had not been abroad during the previous two years. In addition, 90% described their last visit abroad as a holiday and 56% of trips were to Spain, France or Greece. Visits beyond Europe were reported by 7% of travellers. 61% travelled with their partners, 35% with children and 16% with parents. Travelling companions varied significantly with age.

The survey included a variety of questions about behaviour and health problems. Although 82% had taken suncreams abroad, 59% reported some degree of sunburn. In fact, 25% reported being very or fairly burned and 5% experienced pain for two or more days due to burning. Men were less likely to take suncreams, less inclined to use them and reported more severe sunburn. Younger people were also less likely than older people to take precautions against the sun (e.g. avoiding the midday sun, keeping well covered up, staying in the shade and using suncream). Only 59% of 16–20-year-olds always or almost always used suncreams compared with 74% of 21–40-year-olds. Among the sample, 12% of travellers reported vomiting and 26% reported diarrhoea during their last trip. In terms of the causes of vomiting, 54% believed it was due to alcohol, and 44% attributed the problem to food. Diarrhoea was attributed to food by 79% of those reporting it, 32% suggested that water was the cause and 20% alcohol. Two travellers received medical treatment for vomiting and three for diarrhoea. Some 12% of travellers reported insect bites/stings, 5% cuts/bruises and 2% reported blisters. Only four travellers received medical treatment at a hospital or by a doctor for injuries suffered abroad.

The main focus of the Conway et al. survey was the sexual behaviour of travellers. Their findings will be summarised briefly as the present study did not address sexual behaviour (see Clark and Clift (1994) for a fuller review of this issue). In total, 8% of the sample had formed what Conway et al. describe as a new romantic or sexual relationship on their last trip abroad and 5% of travellers ($n = 17$) reported a relationship which included sexual intercourse. 12 out of the 17 people reporting sexual intercourse were carrying condoms, but only 5 of these reporting using them on all occasions. 8 out of 17 had not used condoms at all. Both sex and age differences in sexual behaviour were found. 8% of men compared with 2% of women had sexual intercourse abroad, and younger people were more likely to report having intercourse (e.g. 11% of 16–20-year-olds compared with 1% of 36–40-year-olds). As might be expected, single people and travellers not accompanied by a partner were more likely to report sexual intercourse than married and 'accompanied' travellers. A number of 'risk factors' predicting sexual activity abroad were also identified. Having sexual intercourse with a new partner was 'significantly associated with getting drunk whilst abroad, with general risk behaviour such as having experimented with cannabis and other non-prescribed drugs, and with the number of partners individuals had had in the last 2 years' (Conway et al., 1990).

Finally, a limited amount of information is available on mortality among British tourists in Malta (Licari, 1992). In July 1981 a 61-year-old man died of typhoid fever shortly after returning from Malta. Other tourists who had stayed in the same hotel were followed up ($n = 182$) and 35% reported alimentary symptoms. During 1992, 143 deaths were recorded among foreign visitors of which 83 were of British visitors. More deaths were recorded for males and the frequency of deaths clearly increased with increased age. 56 of the deaths occurred in people aged 65 and above. Heart attacks or some form of heart disease were the major cause of death (45 cases). Accidents accounted for five deaths.

Having examined the principal research on the health problems experienced by British package holidaymakers abroad, attention now turns to the tourism context of the study.

Recent research on tourism in Malta

As a tourist destination, Malta is strategically located in the heart of the Mediterranean, comprising the main island of Malta and the sister islands of Gozo and Comino with a resident population of over 350 000 and a land area of 313 km². Despite the range of tourism research which has emerged on small islands (Pearce, 1987; Wilkinson, 1989), Malta has attracted comparatively little recent research. Much of the published tourism research deals with the 1960s, 1970s and early 1980s and is focused on a limited number of themes. The general development of tourism in Malta since 1945 is discussed by Ogelthorpe

(1984), who emphasises the government's decision to pursue tourism growth in the aftermath of colonial rule in the 1960s. Ogelthorpe (1985) also discussed the wider implications of tourism development for the island's economy and population in relation to planning problems, pressures posed for infrastructure provision and the costs and benefits of tourism for the island. More generalised studies of trends in tourism in Malta describe some of the salient patterns and identify the processes shaping visitor arrivals (e.g. Lockart and Ashton, 1991). More specialised studies of specific aspects of tourism have also been published which emphasise the economic impact of tourism in Malta (PA Cambridge Economic Consultants, 1988) and the technical aspects of calculating tourism multipliers in the Maltese economy (Braguglio, 1992) as well as the implications for tourism planning (e.g. Inskeep, 1991). Furthermore, a number of studies have examined ethnographic aspects of the socio-cultural impact of tourism on Maltese society (e.g. Boissevain, 1977; Boissevain and Inglott, 1979). However, no studies have attempted to examine the activity patterns of tourists (aside from Lockart and Ashton's (1991) study). Therefore, existing research has failed to consider the relationship between tourist activities, the scope of risk-taking behaviour and the consequences for tourist health among its visitor population. To establish the scale and nature of British holidaymaking in Malta it is useful to outline the recent trends in Maltese tourism.

The 1960s marked the effective introduction of package holidays and Table 84.1 highlights the effect of this new form of tourism for the island after 1965. In fact as Lockart and Ashton (1991) point out, Table 84.1 represents an above-average performance for Malta's tourism industry as arrivals expanded at 17% per annum after 1965, in excess of the 6.5% world average recorded by the World Tourism Organisation.

Yet such statistics obscure the impact of a high volume of tourists on the local economy, society and culture which has not been without its critics. One school of thought suggest that tourism has assisted the local population in improving their average earnings, thereby providing a much higher average standard of living. The critics, however, argue that this has not been without major social, economic, cultural and ethical costs to Maltese society. In their view, mass tourism has exploited Malta's limited tourism resources and left the island with a legacy of environmental problems and a niche market based on cheap package holidays largely controlled by UK, German, Italian and other European tour operators. It is the UK package holiday market which is the focus of this research.

Table 84.1 *Trends in Maltese tourism since 1960*

Year	Number of hotels	Employees in hotels	Employees in catering	Tourist arrivals (000s)	Gross income from tourism (LM million)
1960	26	503	—	19.7	1.0
1965	38	819	—	47.8	1.9
1970	110	2723	—	170.8	9.8
1975	91	3672	—	334.5	28.1
1980	100	5159	1583	728.7	111.9
1981	111	5614	1817	705.5	105.0
1982	117	4712	1350	510.9	76.6
1983	116	4630	1359	490.8	67.8
1984	116	4537	1543	479.7	63.1
1985	116	4283	1485	517.8	69.8
1986	115	4354	1554	574.2	79.3
1987	122	4926	1598	745.9	113.0
1988	124	[a]	[a]	783.8	130.0

[a] In 1988, the number of employees in hotel and catering was 6874.
Source: Lockart and Ashton (1991).

Survey of tourist behaviour and health issues in Malta

As a small island, Malta is also a good site for a survey of tourist behaviours and its effect on their health, since it is small enough to allow sampling of tourists across a wide range of sites on the island. Furthermore it attracts a considerable number of UK tourists throughout the year. Malta received one million visitors in 1992 and at least 60% of visitors in a given year are from the UK. The survey had four principal aims:

- to establish a detailed profile of the type of British visitors holidaying in Malta
- to understand the nature and extent of health problems which British holidaymakers encountered during their visit
- to investigate the relationships between tourist behaviour prior to and during their visit to Malta and their health on holiday
- to assess the range of preventive measures tourists take when holidaying in Malta in terms of vaccinations, medication and other forms of treatment

Methodology

Data were collected from British tourists by structured face-to-face interviews in 14 different sites on Malta. A team of 36 undergraduate tourism studies students undertook interviews. A total of 3 hours was devoted to training to ensure that interviewers were familiar with the questionnaire and the data required. Interviewers worked in small teams for mutual support and were located at 13 different sites across the island. These were chosen as

sites likely to have a high concentration of British tourists and included tourist attractions such as Mosta Cathedral, areas with tourist complexes (e.g. Buggiba) and transport terminals (e.g. Gozo ferry) and Malta International Airport. With the exception of the airport, where surveying times were tailored to UK flight times, the fieldworkers worked from approximately 9.30 a.m. until 4.00 p.m. Interviewing was principally carried out on Monday 29 March 1993, with some further interviews on Thursday 1 April. As Table 84.2 shows, the sample was drawn from a wide range of sites, reflecting the more popular locations in coastal, inland and urban areas, on a similar basis to the surveys carried out by Lockart and Ashton (1991).

Table 84.2 *Interview locations*

Location	Number of tourists interviewed	Percentage
Tal 'Qali	48	6.1
Valletta	134	17.1
Zurrieq	15	1.9
Sliema Harbour	108	13.8
Mdina	69	8.8
Gozo Ferry	159	20.3
Luqa Airport	86	11.0
Mosta	50	6.4
Bahar Ic-Caghaq	2	0.3
Qawra	20	2.5
St George's Bay	31	3.9
Golden Bay	2	0.3
Bugibba	45	5.7
No location recorded	16	2.0
Total	785	100

Sampling

Given the context of the interviews and the fact that individuals approached were at liberty to refuse to participate in the survey, it is not possible to guarantee a perfectly random sample of the British tourist population on the island. However, it was considered important to obtain, as far as possible, equal numbers of men and women and an even distribution of individuals across the age range from the upper teenage years to the sixties and above. The reason for selecting a sample on these criteria is based on evidence from Cartwright (personal communication) who found that the age distribution of British package holidaymakers returning from Malta in March 1992 was strongly skewed with a large representation of tourists in the 50–65 age group, with fewer in the 18–30 age group. Research by Cossar et al. also demonstrated higher illness rates among younger age groups, and for this reason efforts were made to ensure a good representation of tourists in the 18–30 age group. In addition, a more even spread of age groups would be more representative of British tourists visiting the Mediterranean rather than just Malta. Interviewers were asked to attempt to interview at least two men and two women in each of six age groups corresponding with decades giving a total of 24 interviews per interviewer. This was considered a reasonable target to achieve in the one and a half days available for interviewing. Interviewers were given a table on which to record the age of respondents they had questioned. The only other criterion employed was that tourists should have been on the island for at least 3 days, since it is widely recognised that 'tourist health' problems often have a 3-day incubation period.

The questionnaire

It was considered essential to keep the questionnaire short and easy to administer so as not to cause tourists too much inconvenience. In addition, the simpler the questionnaire, the fewer the potential errors on the interviewers' part in completing it. The questionnaire used by Cossar and his associates at the Communicable Diseases (Scotland) Unit and that used by Byrant et al. (1991) in Calgary were taken as a model in constructing the survey instrument. Inclusion of the same questions would have the advantage of allowing comparisons to be drawn with previously collected data. The questionnaire addressed four main issues. The first set of questions concerned details of the holiday (e.g. length, when booked, type of accommodation and companions). The second section asked about pre-travel advice about health matters, health precautions and

medications/preparations taken on holiday. The third section asked tourists about food and drink consumed while on holiday and swimming in the sea and swimming pools. The fourth set of questions concerned health problems and symptoms experienced while on holiday, subjective attributions regarding the cause of the problems and the actions taken in response to them. Information was also collected on smoking habits, alcohol consumption while on holiday, age, sex and home town in the UK.

Results

Sample interviewed

In total, 785 people participated in the survey and information on sex and age group was recorded for 774 individuals (47.8% male, 52.2% female). The age distribution achieved was fairly even with 21.4% under 29; 16.5% 30–39; 16.3% 40–49; 20.7% 50–59 and 25.1% 60 and over. No significant sex difference in age distribution was apparent (see Table 84.3).

The sample age distribution is not representative of the age distribution of UK tourists in Malta which undoubtedly has a higher percentage of people in the age ranges 50–59 and 60+. The younger age groups are over-represented and the older age groups under-represented. This has the advantage, however, of allowing comparisons across fairly evenly sized samples for each age group.

Length of stay at time of interview

Just over a third of respondents (34.1%) had been on Malta between 3 and 5 days, 38.1% 6 or 7 days, and the remainder (27.7%) for 8 days or longer (up to 30 days). Most people interviewed had been on the island for no more than 14 days (98.1%). Information on length of stay is clearly important to consider in relation to holiday health since it is likely that over a period of one or two weeks, the longer a person's stay the greater the incidence of health problems. Length of stay was strongly related to

Table 84.3 *Sex and age group composition of the survey sample (n = 774)*

Age group	Males		Females		Total	
	n	%	n	%	n	%
29 and under	78	21.1	88	21.8	166	21.4
30–39	62	16.8	66	16.3	128	16.5
40–49	51	13.8	75	18.6	126	16.3
50–59	74	20.0	86	21.3	160	20.7
60 and above	105	28.4	89	22.0	194	25.1

Table 84.4 *Percentage of the total sample travelling alone or with companions*

Companions	Percentages
Alone	6.1
Parents	4.2
Friends	28.9
Boyfriend/girlfriend	8.2
Husband/wife	58.5
Children	8.0

Table 84.5 *Percentage of the total sample seeking health advice prior to travel*

Advice sought from	Percentages
General practitioner	13.2
Practice nurse	1.8
Chemist	6.0
Travel agent	14.1
Relatives	7.3
Friends	9.9
Other sources	1.8

age of respondent. Younger people were significantly more likely to have been on the island for a shorter period than the older respondents ($\chi^2 = 23.06$, df $= 8$, $p < 0.005$). Among the group aged 29 or under, for instance, 13.8% had been in Malta for more than a week. This compares with 36.6% of people aged 60 and over.

Type of holiday, time of booking and previous visits

An overwhelming majority of respondents (89.4%), were on package holidays and 10.6% had booked a flight only, making their own accommodation arrangements. This is reflected in the fact that 81.8% were staying in a hotel. A majority (64.0%) had booked their holiday between January and March 1993 (20.1% in January, 21.8% in February and 22.1% in March). 36.0% had booked sometime in 1992—few people made bookings more than six months in advance of their holiday. Some 69.6% of holidaymakers were visiting Malta for the first time and 30.4% had visited the island previously. Of these, 43.5% had visited once before, 19.6% twice, 13.0% three times and 23.9% four or more times (range 4–50). A small proportion of visitors questioned had lived, worked or been stationed in Malta and so were very familiar with the island.

Holiday companions

Table 84.4 reports the percentages of people visiting the island alone or with partners, family or friends. As might be expected, the extent to which respondents were travelling with certain categories of companions was influenced by age. Sex differences were also present. The findings can be summarised as follows:

● Visitors travelling alone were significantly more likely to be male ($\chi^2 = 8.01$, df $= 1$, $p < 0.005$)
● Visitors travelling with parents were significantly younger than those not with parents ($\chi^2 = 34.95$, df $= 4$, $p < 0.0001$)
● Visitors travelling with friends were more likely to be in their teens and twenties or 60 and older than aged between 30 and 59 ($\chi^2 = 18.05$, df $= 4$, $p < 0.05$)

● Women were more likely to be travelling with friends than were men ($\chi^2 = 6.72$, df $= 1$, $p < 0.01$)
● Visitors in their teens and twenties were much more likely to be travelling with boy/girlfriends than those in older age groups ($\chi^2 = 91.27$, df $= 4$, $p < 0.001$)
● The youngest age group was also much less likely to be travelling with a spouse than the remaining age groups ($\chi^2 = 166.33$, df $= 4$, $p < 0.001$)
● Men were more likely to be with spouses than were women ($\chi^2 = 4.66$, df $= 1$, $p < 0.05$)
● Visitors with children were more likely to be in their 30s and 40s than in either younger or older age groups compared with those without children ($\chi^2 = 28.53$, df $= 4$, $p < 0.0001$)

Advice and precautions taken prior to travel

Table 84.5 reports the percentages of tourists seeking health-related advice prior to travel. Sex and age group had no significant bearing on any of these categories of advice seeking. In general only a small minority of tourists visiting Malta seek health advice from medical, paramedical or non-medical sources prior to travel. Interestingly, the most commonly consulted source is the travel agent rather than the GP. There is also some evidence of lay referral to friends and relatives but this is on a limited scale. No sex or age differences were apparent for any of these forms of advice seeking. Some 22.6% of visitors claimed to have read something on health issues prior to travel and 14.8% had read the

Table 84.6 *Percentage of the total sample taking preparations and medicines on holiday*

Preparation/medicine	Percentages
Travel sickness tablets	24.2
Insect repellent	29.4
Pain-killers	61.0
Anti-diarrhoea tablets	29.9
Water purification tablets	5.1
Suncream	75.9
Prescribed medicines	28.5

Table 84.7 *Percentage in each age group taking preparations/medicines on holiday (df = 4)*

Preparations/medicines	Teens/ 20s	30s	40s	50s	60s and above	χ^2	p
Travel sickness tablets	16.8	32.0	28.3	25.3	21.5	11.38	<0.05
Insect repellent	28.7	32.0	36.2	29.6	23.6	6.48	ns
Pain-killers	49.1	64.1	68.5	63.0	64.6	14.77	<0.01
Anti-diarrhoea tablets	18.6	26.6	37.8	37.7	30.3	19.35	<0.001
Water purification tables	4.2	3.1	6.3	6.2	5.6	2.18	ns
Suncream	80.8	84.4	76.4	77.8	65.1	20.06	<0.0005
Prescribed medicines	13.8	16.4	22.8	36.4	46.2	63.76	<0.0001

Department of Health booklet on travel health. Sex and age group again had no bearing on the incidence of such active information seeking. Furthermore 7.8% of respondents claimed to have had vaccinations prior to travel despite the fact that none are mandatory nor recommended for Malta. No sex or age differences were apparent. 97.0% reported having travel insurance.

Medication and protection taken on holiday

Of much greater interest than the advice and precautions taken prior to travel are the data on medications and preparations taken on holiday. Table 84.6 reports the percentages of visitors taking a wide range of preparations to prevent or treat health problems. The most common preparations/medicines taken were suncream and pain-killers. A substantial minority had also taken travel sickness tablets, insect repellent and anti-diarrhoea tablets. Well over a quarter of visitors also had prescribed medicines with them. The likelihood of taking preparations/medicines was a function of age and sex. The following significant associations were found (see Table 84.7):

- Travel sickness tablets—visitors in their teens and twenties were least likely to have travel sickness tablets and those in their 30s most likely ($\chi^2 = 11.38$, df = 4, $p < 0.05$)
- Pain-killers—visitors in their teens and twenties were less likely to have pain-killers than all other age groups ($\chi^2 = 9.30$, df = 1, $p < 0.05$)
- Anti-diarrhoea tablets—visitors in their teens and twenties and in the thirties were less likely to have anti-diarrhoea tablets compared with other age groups ($\chi^2 = 19.35$, df = 4, $p < 0.001$)
- Suncream—visitors in their teens and twenties and those in their thirties were more likely to have suncream, and visitors sixty and above were less likely to have suncream compared to those in their forties and fifties ($\chi^2 = 20.06$, df = 4, $p < 0.0005$)

- Prescribed medicines—a very strong age trend emerged in the extent to which visitors reported having prescribed medicines. Visitors in their teens and twenties were least likely to have prescribed medicines and those aged 60 and above most likely to have them ($\chi^2 = 63.76$, df = 4, $p < 0.001$).

Behaviour of British tourists on holiday

Respondents were asked to indicate the frequency with which they had engaged in a wide variety of activities on the scale: 'often', 'sometimes' and 'never'. Table 84.8 reports the responses to these items for the total sample. It is clear from these results that:

- A majority of visitors reported eating in hotels 'often' rather than catering for themselves, although a large majority 'sometimes' or 'often' ate in restaurants
- Eating from street vendors are reported by just over 40% of visitors but a majority appeared to avoid this altogether
- Over a quarter reported eating raw fruit 'often' and almost a half 'sometimes'

Table 84.8 *Frequencies of selected behaviours while on holiday (total sample* n *varies between 765 and 784)*

Behaviour	Often	Sometimes	Never
Ate in hotels	78.6	9.2	12.2
Catered for self	11.7	20.3	68.0
Ate in restaurants	33.0	57.4	9.6
Ate from street vendors	6.5	34.9	58.6
Ate raw fruit	25.4	48.4	26.2
Took ice in drinks	29.5	27.1	43.4
Drank unpasteurised milk	3.0	10.8	86.1
Ate local cheeses	12.3	38.2	49.6
Ate ice cream	16.8	43.2	39.9
Swam in the sea	4.1	15.6	80.3
Swam in the swimming pool	18.6	28.1	53.3
Drank tap water	11.1	19.4	69.5
Drank still bottle water	63.0	20.7	16.2
Drank carbonated water	19.5	22.0	58.5

- Drinking unpasteurised milk was avoided by a large majority of visitors but over half reported eating local cheeses 'often' or 'sometimes'
- Eating ice cream at least 'sometimes' was commonly reported. Just under 40%, however, had 'never' eaten ice cream
- Water consumption shows an interesting pattern with a majority drinking *still* bottle water 'often' while avoiding tap water and bottled carbonated water. It appears, however, that just over 30% drank tap water at least 'sometimes'. Over a quarter reported taking ice in drinks 'often' but over 40% never had ice
- Swimming in the sea was not a popular activity (the sea temperature was quite cold) but 46.7% of tourists reported swimming in pools at least 'sometimes'

The incidence of several of these aspects of behaviour showed marked age variations. These were as follows:

- Older age groups were more likely to eat in hotels than the younger age groups. Thus, 87.7% of the 60+ group 'often' ate in hotels compared with 71.9% of the youngest group. Similarly 5.6% of the oldest age group 'never' ate in hotels compared with between 13–16% in other age groups ($\chi^2 = 23.28$, df = 8, $p < 0.005$)
- Older age groups were less likely to self-cater than younger age groups ($\chi^2 = 31.1$, df = 8, $p < 0.0001$)
- Younger age groups were much more likely than older age groups to eat from street vendors at least 'sometimes'. Thus, 45.8% of teens/twenties 'sometimes' ate from vendors compared with only 19.0% of those aged 60 and over ($\chi^2 = 47.29$, df = 8, $p < 0.0001$)
- A clear age trend emerged for taking ice in drinks with this being increasingly less likely as age increased. Thus 28.3% of teens/twenties 'never' took ice compared with more than half of those aged 60 and over (57.4%) ($\chi^2 = 38.01$, df = 8, $p < 0.0001$)
- The oldest age group was less likely to eat ice cream than the younger groups ($\chi^2 = 33.83$, df = 8, $p < 0.0001$). Thus, 52.3% of those aged 60 and above never ate ice cream compared with 33.5% of the youngest group
- Swimming in the sea was not particularly common, but clear age differences emerged with the two younger age groups being more likely to swim in the sea than the older age groups. Among the oldest age group, 91.8% reported never swimming in the sea ($\chi^2 = 46.25$, df = 8, $p < 0.0001$)
- Swimming in swimming pools was reported more frequently but in the total sample only 18.6% of respondents had 'often' been swimming in pools. Again, a distinct age trend was apparent with increasing

age associated with an increasing proportion of visitors 'never' swimming in pools ($\chi^2 = 42.16$, df = 8, $p < 0.001$)
- Drinking still bottle water was a common activity and certainly more common than drinking tap water. Such consumption was clearly age-related. In moving from the youngest group to the oldest the percentage who reported never drinking still bottle water increased steadily from 9.6% of teens/twenties to 24.2% of those aged 60 and above ($\chi^2 = 35.74$, df = 8, $p < 0.001$). A sex difference also emerged with women more likely to drink still bottle water 'often' compared with men ($\chi^2 = 8.60$, df = 2, $p < 0.05$). Drinking carbonated water was much less commonly reported and no significant age trends emerged.

Smoking and alcohol consumption

Some 32.1% of the total sample reported being smokers and both age and sex differences were apparent. The two younger age groups were more likely to smoke than the three older groups (e.g. 40.6% of visitors in their teens/twenties smoked compared with 28.4% in their sixties and above) ($\chi^2 = 9.74$, df = 4, $p < 0.05$). 37.1% of men smoked compared with 27.3% of women ($\chi^2 = 8.01$, df = 1, $p < 0.05$).

88.2% of the total sample reported drinking while on holiday with a tendency for levels of consumption to fall slightly with increasing age. 91.0% of teens/twenties consumed alcohol compared with 80.8% of those 60 and over ($\chi^2 = 16.96$, df = 4, $p < 0.005$). Of greater interest are the data on levels of consumption. Visitors were asked how their level of drinking compared with their usual levels at home. In the total sample answering this question ($n = 708$), 48.6% reported that their consumption was higher than usual but a marked age trend was apparent. 64.1% of those in their teens and twenties reported higher consumption compared with 39.1% in the 60s and above. Intermediate percentages were obtained for the intervening age groups ($\chi^2 = 26.62$, df = 8, $p < 0.001$).

Health problems encountered

Table 84.9 reports the reported frequency of health problems and symptoms experienced by five age groups in the sample. No sex differences were apparent and the data are not broken down by sex. The severity of the health problem/symptoms and certainly their nuisance level is reflected in the number of days visitors reported being affected. 292 visitors (37.2%) in total were affected by some problem. The modal period was one day (48.3% of those reporting a problem). Just under a third reported

Table 84.9 *Percentage of the total sample and five age groups reporting health problems and symptoms (df = 4)*

Health problem/symptoms	Total sample	Teens/ 20s	30s	40s	50s	60s and above	χ^2	p
Diarrhoea	7.0	9.0	10.2	8.7	4.3	4.6	6.93	ns
Headache	19.9	32.3	18.8	18.9	17.3	13.3	22.24	<0.005
Breathlessness	2.8	3.6	0.0	0.8	3.1	5.1	9.81	<0.05
Vomiting	2.3	4.8	2.3	1.6	0.6	2.1	6.97	ns
Temperature	1.8	3.0	0.0	2.4	1.2	2.1	4.29	ns
Chest pain	1.8	2.4	0.0	0.8	2.5	2.6	4.48	ns
Sunburn	16.1	23.4	18.0	15.7	14.2	10.3	12.24	<0.05
Sore throat	8.8	14.4	9.4	7.9	6.2	6.7	9.09	ns
Accident	1.1	1.8	0.0	1.6	1.2	1.0	2.33	ns

being affected for two days (32.2%) and 11.6% for three days. Given that 72.3% of the sample had been on Malta for seven days or less, being affected for even a day could cast a shadow over the holiday experience. 16 people in the entire sample (5.5% of those with symptoms) were affected for between 4 and 7 days. For some unfortunate tourists this meant that they were affected for the whole period of their holiday.

The breakdown of problems by age group revealed the following patterns:

● Headaches were most common among the youngest age group and the incidence declined as age increased. Respondents in their teens and twenties reported headaches at over twice the rate of those in the oldest age category
● Breathlessness was more common in the two oldest age group and the youngest age group than in the thirties and forties group
● Sunburn showed a clear age trend, being most common in the youngest age group and declining with age. Visitors in their teens and twenties were more than twice as likely to have experienced sunburn than those aged 60 and over.

Actions taken in response to health problems

Table 84.10 reports the percentage of the total sample who had taken a range of different actions in response to health problems and who intended to consult their GP on return home. It is clear that the most common response to health problems while in Malta was to self-medicate. Interestingly, just over 4% of people questioned said they intended to consult their GP on return to the UK. If this is an accurate estimate of the proportion of British holidaymakers who go abroad each year who intend to see their own GP, it points to a potentially enormous number of consultations on travel-related issues.

Table 84.10 *Actions taken in response to health problems (frequency and percentage of total sample)*

Action	n	%
Changed plans	45	5.7
Consulted holiday rep	4	0.5
Took medication	78	9.9
Saw a doctor	11	1.4
Stayed in bed	35	4.5
Went to hospital	3	0.4
Will consult own GP	32	4.1

Preparations/medicines taken and health problems experienced

It is obviously of interest to use the data available to explore the relationship between the preparations/ medicines taken on holiday to Malta and the health problems/symptoms experienced while there. It might be expected that those people who show more cautiousness and forethought prior to travel would be less likely to succumb to health problems. An alternative view, however, is that those people who anticipate problems may be more likely to take preparations/medicines to deal with them when they arise.

The relationship between the preparations and medicines taken and health problems experienced were explored initially by cross-tabulating responses to each preparation/medicine with the health problems listed in the questionnaire. Table 8.11 summarises the significant results obtained from this procedure. Given that a large number of cross-tabulations are involved here and that some of the variables are strongly skewed, the results of this analysis have to be treated cautiously. It is also the case that some of these cross-tabulations bring together precautions and health problems which have no obvious bearing on one another (e.g. insect-repellents and the incidence of accidents). In such cases there would appear to be no clear grounds for expecting any relationship to emerge. In other cases, however, strong associations are

Table 84.11 *Preparations/medicine available and the incidence of health problems (summary of significant associations/in all cases df = 1)*

Health problem/ symptoms	Travel sickness tablets		Insect repellent		Pain-killers		Anti-diarrhoea tablets		Suncream		Prescribed medicines	
	χ^2	p	χ^2	p	χ^2	p	χ^2	p	χ^2	p	χ^2	p
Diarrhoea			8.17	<0.005			7.61	<0.01	10.15	<0.005		
Headache	4.14	<0.05	13.32	<0.0005	4.30	<0.05	5.31	<0.05			10.02	<0.005
Temperature			4.00	<0.05								
Sunburn	16.70	<0.001	5.94	<0.05								
Sore throat			11.38	<0.001					8.89	<0.005		

Table 84.12 *Percentage of visitors with or without the preparation/medicine listed who report selected health problems*

Health problem/ symptoms	Travel sickness tablets		Insect repellent		Pain-killers		Anti-diarrhoea tablets		Suncream		Prescribed medicines	
	with ($n=190$)	without ($n=595$)	with ($n=231$)	without ($n=554$)	with ($n=479$)	without ($n=306$)	with ($n=235$)	without ($n=550$)	with ($n=596$)	without ($n=189$)	with ($n=234$)	without ($n=561$)
Diarrhoea			11.3	5.2			11.1	5.3	8.7	1.6		
Headache	25.3	18.2	28.1	16.4	22.3	16.0	25.1	17.6			27.2	16.9
Temperature			3.5	1.1								
Sunburn	25.8	12.9	21.2	13.9								
Sore throat			14.3	6.5					10.6	3.2		

to be expected. Anticipation of diarrhoeal problems, for instance, would be reflected in having anti-diarrhoeal tablets available and this is likely to have a bearing on reported rates of diarrhoea.

No significant associations appeared for breathlessness, vomiting, chest pain or accidents and no significant associations appeared for water purification tablets. This may well be accounted for by the fact that the incidence of these problems/measures is very low in the sample as a whole. The two problems most closely associated with precautions are headache (with five preparations significantly associated) and diarrhoea (with three). Sunburn and sore throat have two. Interestingly, the preparation which appears most 'predictive' of health problems while in Malta is insect-repellent. This is associated with no fewer than five health problems. Table 84.12 reports the incidence of selected health problems among those with preparations/medicines and those without them. The results in Table 84.12 show clearly and consistently that a higher proportion of people with a given preparation/medicine reported health problems/symptoms than those without a preparation/medicine. For example, individuals with suncream available were over five times more likely to report diarrhoea than those without suncream.

Tourist behaviour and health problems

By far the most interesting question which can be addressed using the data available is whether reported behaviour has a bearing on health problems/symptoms experienced. Table 84.13 summarises the significant associations which emerged. Table 84.13 suggests that sunburn, headaches and sore throats may be predictable from behaviour while on holiday. Caution is required, however, since some of the associations in Table 84.13 may reflect age differences in both the behaviour and the health problem rather than any direct connection between the variables concerned. For example, not drinking carbonated water is associated with a significantly higher incidence of chest pain, but this is almost certainly due to the fact that chest pain is more common among elderly tourists and the level of consumption of carbonated water is very low in the older age groups. The strongest associations in Table 84.13 are present between swimming in the sea and swimming in swimming pools and a constellation of headache, sunburn and sore throat. Table 84.14 reports the data in greater detail in a comparison of the incidence of these health problems in relation to reported level of swimming. Table 84.14 reveals that swimming in the sea or pools was associated with a higher

Table 84.13 *Behaviours while on holiday and experience of health problems/symptoms (summary of significant associations/in all cases df = 2)*

| | Health problems/symptoms | | | | | | | | | |
| | Diarrhoea | | Headache | | Chest pain | | Sunburn | | Sore throat | |
Behaviour on holiday	χ^2	p	χ^2	p	χ^2	p	χ^2	p	χ^2	p
Catered for self							6.39	<0.05		
Ate in restaurants							6.44	<0.05		
Ate from street vendors	10.34	<0.01	6.31	<0.05						
Ate raw fruit	5.85	=0.05					8.20	<0.05		
Ate ice cream			13.80	=0.001			7.04	<0.05		
Swam in sea			11.75	<0.005			7.93	<0.05	8.13	<0.05
Swam in swimming pool	8.39	<0.05	15.76	<0.0005			22.30	<0.0001	13.17	<0.005
Drank carbonated water					7.08	<0.05	10.94	<0.005		

Table 84.14 *Health problems associated with swimming in the sea and in pools (percentage reporting a problem at each level of behaviour)*

| | Swimming in the sea | | | | | |
Health problems/symptoms	Often	Sometimes	Never	χ^2	df	p
Headache	21.9	31.1	17.6	11.75	2	<0.005
Sunburn	25.0	23.0	14.1	7.93	2	<0.05
Sore throat	21.9	10.7	7.8	8.13	2	<0.05

| | Swimming in pools | | | | | |
Health problems/symptoms	Often	Sometimes	Never	χ^2	df	p
Headache	26.7	25.5	14.6	15.76	2	<0.0005
Sunburn	32.0	17.7	11.0	22.30	2	<0.0001
Sore throat	16.4	7.7	6.7	13.17	2	<0.005

incidence of headache, sunburn and sore throat. These associations are consistently stronger for swimming in pools than for swimming in the sea.

In order to test for the possibility that these associations are an artefact due to age variations in both activities and health problems, further analyses were conducted controlling for age. Table 84.15 reports the numbers of respondents at each age level who swam in the sea and in pools 'often' or 'sometimes' and those who 'never' swam in the sea and in pools. Also reported are the percentages of people in each group who experienced headache, sunburn and sore throat. 'Often' and 'sometimes' responses are collapsed to reduce the occurrence of expected cell frequencies below five. The results in Table 84.15 show the following:

- There is some evidence of significant associations between swimming and headache, sunburn and sore throat, but in general the results are not significant
- In 23 out of 30 cases, however, the incidence of these health problems is greater among those swimming 'often' or 'sometimes' than among those never swimming

Smoking, alcohol and health problems

Smoking was found to have significant associations with: headache (27.7% who smoke reported headaches compared with 16.3% who did not smoke; $\chi^2 = 13.12$, df = 1, $p < 0.0005$); vomiting (4.4% of smokers reported vomiting compared with 1.3% of non-smokers; $\chi^2 = 5.85$, df = 1, $p < 0.05$) and sunburn (20.9% of smokers were sunburnt compared with 13.8% of non-smokers; $\chi^2 = 5.73$, df = 1, $p < 0.05$).

Alcohol consumption *per se* had no bearing on reported health problems. Amount consumed compared with usual was significantly associated with vomiting, however. Out of 713 respondents providing data of alcohol consumption, only 2.1% reported vomiting. Among those consuming more, the same and less alcohol the percentages were 1.7%, 1.2% and 12.2% respectively ($\chi^2 = 21.72$, df = 2, $p < 0.0001$). It may be that vomiting, for what ever reason, results in reduced alcohol consumption. The reverse seems rather implausible!

Predicting health problems

Attempts have already been made in the last three sections to explore interrelationships between precautions taken,

Table 84.15 *Percentage of tourists swimming or not swimming who developed health problems by age group (in all cases df = 1)*

| | Swimming in the sea | | | | | | Swimming in pools | | | | | |
| | Often/ sometimes | | Never | | | | Often/ sometimes | | Never | | | |
Health problems	n	%	n	%	χ^2	p	n	%	n	%	χ^2	p
Headache												
Teens/20s	51	29.4	116	33.6	0.17	ns	102	35.3	65	27.7	0.73	ns
30s	40	35.0	88	11.4	8.59	<0.005	67	28.4	61	8.2	7.25	<0.01
40s	18	27.8	109	17.4	0.51	ns	58	22.4	69	15.9	0.49	ns
50s	27	25.9	134	15.7	1.01	ns	73	19.2	88	15.9	0.11	ns
60 +	16	25.0	178	12.4	1.08	ns	64	20.3	130	10.0	3.09	ns
Sunburn												
Teens/20s	51	21.6	116	24.1	0.03	ns	102	28.4	65	15.4	3.08	ns
30s	40	32.5	88	11.4	6.96	<0.01	67	17.9	61	18.0	0.00	ns
40s	18	27.8	109	13.8	1.35	ns	58	27.6	69	5.8	9.69	<0.005
50s	27	18.5	134	12.7	0.25	ns	73	16.4	88	11.4	0.49	ns
60 +	16	6.3	178	10.7	0.02	ns	64	14.1	130	8.5	0.91	ns
Sore throat												
Teens/20s	51	15.7	116	13.8	0.01	ns	102	11.8	65	18.5	0.95	ns
30s	40	15.0	80	6.8	1.31	ns	67	13.4	61	4.9	1.81	ns
40s	18	22.2	109	5.5	3.87	<0.05	58	13.8	69	2.9	3.76	ns
50s	27	3.7	134	6.7	0.02	ns	73	8.2	88	4.5	0.40	ns
60 +	16	6.3	178	6.7	0.00	ns	64	9.4	130	5.4	0.55	ns

Table 84.16 *Summed indices constructed from items included in the questionnaire*

Scales	Items	Range of scores
Advice		
Total advice	GP, practice nurse, chemist, travel agent, relatives, friends, other, read material, read government leaflet	0–9
Lay advice	relatives, friends	0–2
Professional advice	GP, practice nurse, chemist, travel agent	0–4
Written advice	read material, read government leaflet	0–2
Precautions		
Total precautions taken	vaccinations, travel sickness, insect repellent, pain-killers, anti-diarrhoea, water purification, suncream, prescribed medicines, travel insurance	0–9
Non-prescribed preparations	travel sickness, insect repellent, pain-killers, anti-diarrhoea, water purification, suncream	0–6
Behaviour		
Behaviour factor 1	swimming in pool, swimming in sea, eating from street vendors, ice cream	4–12
Behaviour factor 2	raw fruit, local cheese, restaurants, ice in drinks	4–12
Health problems		
Total health problems	diarrhoea, headache, breathlessness, vomiting, temperature, chest pain, sunburn, sore throat, accident	0–9
Health problem factor 1	chest pain, breathlessness	0–2
Health problem factor 2	diarrhoea, vomiting, temperature	0–3
Health problem factor 3	headache, sunburn, sore throat	0–3

N.B. Higher scores indicate more advice, more precautions, higher frequency of behaviour and more health problems. Table 84.17 reports significant Pearson correlations between the four behaviour problem scales and a range of possible predictors of health problems. It is clear that the correlations reported (while statistically significant) are consistently very low—the highest correlation being no greater than 0.23. The fact that such low correlations are significant at or beyond the 1% level is due entirely to the large sample size.

behaviour while on the island and health problems experienced. Attempting to identify patterns in the data is made difficult by a number of factors:

- sex and age group differences in the measures obtained
- the reduction in sample size when sub-groups are investigated
- the statistical problems raised by applying statistical tests repeatedly in a large number of comparisons
- the skewed distributions of many of the variables, e.g. low frequencies of certain health problems
- the unsophisticated level of measurement involved (nominal in most cases or nominal–ordinal)

It should also be noted that the χ^2 test is strictly used to test the hypothesis of no-association between two variables and the χ^2 statistic is not a direct measure of the strength of association between the variables. While a number of interesting significant results have been reported, the relationships and trends detected are generally quite weak. In order to meet some of the difficulties noted above, items included in different sections of the questionnaire were combined in order to create scales with broader meaning and a wider range of values. This was guided in part by exploratory factor analyses applied to sections of the questionnaire (not reported here) and by consideration of the data itself. With respect to consultations and advice sought prior to travel, for instance, scales were constructed based on the total number of sources consulted, professional sources consulted, lay sources consulted and written material

consulted (see Table 84.16 for details of the scales developed).

The relationships which appear in Table 84.17 are of interest as:

- No relationships with sex are apparent
- The younger groups reported more health problems overall and gained higher scores on the headache, sunburn and sore throat measure
- Smokers reported more health problems overall and gained higher scores on the headache etc. measure
- Whether visitors drank alcohol or not had no bearing on health problems
- Length of stay on Malta at time of interview had no bearing on health problems
- The advice measures show positive correlations with the health problem measures. In other words people who sought advice tended to report more problems with health
- Similarly, the precautions measures are positively correlated with reported health problems. Interestingly, having non-prescribed preparations is associated with health problem factors 2 (diarrhoea etc.) and 3 (headache etc.), whereas prescribed medicines is associated with health problem factor 1 (chest pain/breathlessness)
- Behaviour factor 1 (swimming/street food) is significantly associated with total health problems and the third health problem factor. Thus, visitors who swam in the sea/pools etc. were more likely to report headache, sunburn and sore throat

Table 84.17 *Correlations between predictor variables and health problem measures (all values significant at or beyond 1% level, two-tailed)*

Predictor variables	Total problems	Chest pain	Diarrhoea	Headache
Sex[a]	—	—	—	—
Age group[b]	−0.16	—	—	−0.19
Smoker/non-smoker[c]	−0.13	—	—	−0.14
Alcohol[d]	—	—	—	—
Time on island[e]	—	—	—	—
Total advice	0.20	0.11	0.14	0.15
Lay advice	0.15	—	—	0.18
Professional advice	0.19	0.12	0.12	0.14
Read advice	—	—	—	—
Total precautions	0.23	—	0.15	0.21
Preparations	0.19	—	0.13	0.18
Prescribed medicine	0.11	0.09	—	—
Swimming/street food	0.18	—	—	0.21
Fruit, local cheese etc.	—	—	—	—

[a]Male = 1, female = 2.
[b]Higher age group = higher score.
[c]Smoker = 1, non-smoker = 2.
[d]Alcohol drank = 1, no alcohol = 2.
[e]3–5 days = 1, 6–7 days = 2, more than a week = 3.

Table 84.18 *Predicting health problems: results of forward stepwise regression analyses (*n = 731*)*

Predictors in order of inclusion in the stepwise regression analysis	Beta	Predicted health problems	Multiple R	F	p
1. Professional advice	0.04	Chest pain/	0.08	4.95	<0.05
Constant	0.03	breathlessness			
1. Non-prescribed medications/preparations	0.11	Diarrhoea/	0.16	6.54	<0.0005
2. Age group	−0.10	sickness/vomiting			
3. Prescribed medicines	0.08				
Constant	0.13				
1. Swimming/street food	0.13	Headache/	0.38	28.82	<0.0001
2. Non-prescribed medications/preparations	0.13	sunburn			
3. Lay advice	0.12	sore throat			
4. Age group	−0.16				
5. Prescribed medicines	0.13				
6. Smoker/non-smoker	−0.10				
7. Professional advice	0.08				
8. Read advice	−0.08				
Constant	0.47				

Forward stepwise regression analysis was employed to predict the three specific health measures from the predictor variables in Table 84.17 (excluding 'total advice' and 'total precautions' which are not independent of other variables in the list). Table 84.18 reports the results of this procedure. The patterns revealed are as follows:

- Professional advice is the only variable which predicts chest pain/breathlessness. It is likely that those visitors who have a tendency to experience such symptoms were more likely to visit their GP or consult other sources of advice prior to travel
- Experience of diarrhoea etc. is more common among people taking non-prescribed preparations and prescribed medicines and among younger visitors
- Headache, sunburn and sore throat is predicted by a combination of no fewer than eight variables. Interestingly, the behavioural factor of swimming (in sea/in pools) and eating street food is the strongest predictor. In addition, this group of problems is more likely among those with non-prescribed preparations (which includes suncream), who sought lay advice, who are younger, have prescribed medicines, who smoke, who sought professional advice but who did not read literature on health.

Discussion

It is evident from this survey of tourist behaviour on Malta that small islands provide a useful context in which to examine the range and complexity of health-related problems among British holidaymakers. Previous research on Maltese tourism has emphasised the more

visible and identifiable physical effects—the social, economic and environmental problems associated with tourism—while the research by Lockart and Ashton (1991) was the first systematic attempt to assess the activity patterns of tourists on the island. Their survey provided a useful context for this study since it identified many of the major areas and tourist zones in which British holidaymakers spend their leisure time when visiting the island. Even so, existing knowledge of tourist behaviour and its effect on their health has been based on a number of post-travel studies. The advantage of undertaking a detailed investigation of British holidaymakers for one particular destination is that it yielded a number of results in common with other large-scale studies which remain the main source of data on tourist health (e.g. Cossar et al., 1990; Cartwright, 1992). In many respects, this type of survey addresses the hidden aspects and effects of tourist behaviour since it is widely argued that tourism has a rest, relaxation and recuperation function which is promoted by tour operators. Yet there are serious consequences of marketing tourism in this way, since, as this study shows, tourism can also adversely affect the health of certain holidaymakers contingent upon their risk-taking behaviour. In this section, the major findings from the survey are discussed in relation to previous research before addressing their tourist implications.

Health advice and precautions

Few holidaymakers actively sought health advice prior to travel but the groups referred to most often were travel agents (14.1%) and GPs (13.2%). However, 22.6% read something on health issues before travel and 14.8%

reported reading the Department of Health leaflet. A substantial majority reported taking suncream (75.9%) and pain-killers (61.0%) and smaller numbers of holidaymakers reported taking travel sickness tablets (24.2%), insect repellent (29.4%) and anti-diarrhoea tablets (29.9%). Well over a quarter of tourists (28.5%) also had prescribed medicines with them. Significant age differences emerged in the extent to which preparations/medication were taken on holiday. Visitors in their teens/twenties were less likely to have travel sickness tablets, pain-killers and anti-diarrhoea tablets than older groups but more likely to have suncreams. Having prescribed medicines showed a clear age trend with the incidence increasing with age (e.g. 1.8% of tourists in their teens/twenties compared with 46.2% in their 60s and above).

Conway et al. (1990) reported that 82% of travellers had taken suncreams abroad—a figure close to that found here—but the sex difference they found with men less likely to take suncreams was not replicated. They also report that young people were less likely to take precautions against the sun. Data are not available in the present survey on actual use of suncreams—but it is interesting that younger people were more likely to report having suncreams than were the older age groups. It may be significant that the present survey covers a considerably wider age range than the Conway et al. survey which targeted 16–40-year-olds.

Behaviour on holiday

Visitors were given a list of 14 behaviours and asked to indicate how often they had engaged in them. These were primarily concerned with patterns of eating and drinking. Eating in hotels and drinking bottled water were frequent activities for a majority of visitors, whereas over half the sample 'never' catered for themselves, ate from street vendors, drank unpasteurised milk, swam in the sea, swam in swimming pools, drank tap water or drank carbonated water. One reason for not drinking tap water is the promotion of bottled water by the tour operator's representatives, even though in most locations Maltese drinking water is viewed as 'safe to drink', although slightly salty.

In general, older age groups compared with the younger ones were more likely to eat in hotels, less likely to self-cater, less likely to eat from street vendors, less likely to take ice in drinks, less likely to eat ice cream, less likely to swim in the sea or pools and less likely to drink bottled water. It is clear, therefore, that older visitors were more likely to avoid potential infection risks associated with consuming 'street food' and coming into contact with

sea/pool water. Whether this was motivated by a concern about health or reflected different motivations and attitudes is not known. Drinking alcohol was commonly reported (88.2%). In the total sample, 48.6% reported that their consumption was higher than usual. The youngest age group in particular, reported higher levels of alcohol consumption than usual (64.1% of those in their teens/twenties). This pattern of increased alcohol consumption, especially among younger tourists, replicates the earlier findings of Conway et al. (1990).

Health problems experienced

Tourists were questioned about nine health problems/symptoms and generally the incidence of these problems was low. Nevertheless, 19.9% reported headache, 16.1% sunburn (even in March), 8.8% sore throat and 7.0% diarrhoea. Headache and sunburn showed significant age trends being more prevalent in the youngest age group than the older groups. Almost a third of visitors in their teens/twenties reported a headache (32.3%) and almost a quarter (23.4%) experienced sunburn.

37.2% of visitors reported some problem. Of these 48.3% were affected for a day or less, 32.2% for 2 days, 11.6% for 3 days and 5.5% for between 4 and 7 days.

The incidence of sunburn in this study (16.1%) contrasts markedly with the figure reported by Conway et al. (1990) of 59% of travellers reporting some degree of sunburn. Unfortunately, no information is given by Conway et al. on the times of year their respondents took their last holiday/trip abroad, but it can be reasonably assumed that a majority of holidays would have been taken during the summer season. Even at the end of March it was hot in Malta, with temperatures in the high 20s Celsius, but it might be expected that the rates of sunburn would be higher later in the season when temperatures rise still further well into the 30s. Interestingly, Conway et al. found that the younger group in their sample (16–20-year-olds) were less likely to take precautions against the sun, but they did not report a higher incidence of sunburn among the younger group. As the present survey covers a much wider age range of tourists (from teens to eighties) this may be a factor accounting both for the lower overall sunburn rate and for the emergence of significant age differences in reported sunburn.

Cossar et al. (1990) report that 28% of their sample experienced 'alimentary symptoms' and Conway et al. report that 26% of their sample suffered from diarrhoea. The diarrhoea rate found in the present study (7%) is very close to Cartwright's (1992) estimates of Maltese rates of stomach upset below 10% between May to October for

1991. The higher figures in the Cossar et al. and Conway et al. studies probably reflect the more diverse patterns of travel involved and the times of year tourists were taking their holidays. It is well established that diarrhoea attack rates vary by holiday location and show a seasonal cycle with higher rates during the summer months. It is also possible that low response rates in these studies and a greater tendency for those experiencing health problems to return a questionnaire, may have produced inflated estimates.

Actions taken in response to health problems

The most common responses to health problems were to take medication (9.9% of total sample), change plans (5.7% of total sample) and stay in bed (4.5% of total sample). Out of the entire sample, 11 tourists consulted a local doctor (1.4%) and only 3 visited the island hospital (0.4%). However, 32 visitors reported that they would consult their doctor on returning home about the problem experienced. In the Conway et al. (1990) study, 3 travellers received medical treatment for diarrhoea and 2 for vomiting, and 4 travellers required treatment at a hospital or by a doctor for injuries (i.e. 2.5% of the sample). Cossar et al. (1990) report actions in response to health problems as a proportion of those reporting illness (36% of the sample). Of these 24% were confined to bed, 9% saw a doctor abroad and 1% were admitted to hospital. For their total sample, this represents estimates of 8.6% confined to bed, 3.3% seeing a doctor and 0.4% admitted to hospital. Differences between the present survey and previous research make comparisons quite difficult, but the estimates for medical treatment appear to be lower for the present study. While the percentages consulting a doctor and visiting the hospital on Malta were low, it should be noted that self-referral at these rates among the total annual tourist population would represent a considerable number of consultations. Thus if 1.4% of the one million overseas tourists who visit Malta annually wished to see a doctor, this would represent 14 000 consultations in the course of a year. A hospital attendance rate of 0.4% would represent 4000 hospital visits by tourists during 1993. Similarly, if 60% of Malta's one million tourists per year come from the UK, and 4.1% of visitors intend to consult their GP on return from holiday, this suggests that as many as 24 000 British visitors to Malta each year may consider consulting their GP on return as a result of some health problem experienced on holiday.

Can health problems be predicted among tourists?

A number of significant associations between the availability of medicines/preparations and reported health problems were identified. For instance, availability of travel sickness tablets, insect repellent, pain-killers, anti-diarrhoea tablets and prescribed medicines, were all significantly associated with experience of headaches. Interestingly, in *every* case in which a significant association emerged, the percentage incidence of health problems was higher among those *with* a given medicine/preparation than those *without* it. For example, 11.1% of those with anti-diarrhoea tablets reported diarrhoea compared with 5.3% of those without them. These findings are consistent with the earlier finding of Cossar et al. (1990) that travellers who consult a doctor prior to travel are more likely to report health problems than those who do not.

A number of significant associations also emerged between measures of holiday behaviour and health problems. Sunburn, in particular, was significantly linked with seven aspects of behaviour, especially swimming in swimming pools. In general, the associations identified made sense although in some cases it seemed likely that an aspect of behaviour and a health problem were associated on account of significant age differences in both, rather than there being any intrinsic or causal linkage between the behaviour and the health problem (e.g. the association between drinking carbonated water and the experience of sunburn). Of particular interest is the constellation of associations between swimming in the sea, swimming in pools and headache, sunburn and sore throat. The results showed quite clearly that the incidence of all three of these problems was *less* prevalent among those 'never' swam in either the sea or pools, than in those who swam 'sometimes' or 'often'. Sunburn, for instance, was almost three times more prevalent among those 'often' swimming in pools than among those who 'never' swam in pools. Associations were stronger for swimming in pools than swimming in the sea. This may reflect the fact that sea swimming was less common. The water temperature was quite cold and respondents who reported 'swimming' in the sea may have actually 'paddled' rather than fully immersed themselves in the water.

Since significant age group differences were apparent in both swimming behaviour and the incidence of headache and sunburn (all more common in the younger age groups) it was necessary to control for age in assessing the association between swimming and health. Unfortunately, when this was done, only five significant results out of 30 emerged. Nevertheless, in 23 out of 30 comparisons, with age controlled, the incidence of these health problems was more common among swimmers than non-swimmers. This evidence must be treated with caution, but it does indicate that swimming, sunburn, headache and sore throat represent a cluster of behaviour–health problems variables which are dynamically interrelated. This would be consistent with the findings from large-scale and well-controlled experimental studies of health and sea bathing conducted by Kay and his colleagues (see Kay and Jones, 1992). It has also to be remembered that the youngest age groups were also more likely to be smokers, to drink on holiday and to drink more than usual. These associations with age may well account for the fact that smoking was significantly associated with both headaches and sunburn. The fact that a number of health problems were more common among smokers than non-smokers replicates the earlier findings of Cossar et al. (1990). Increased alcohol consumption in contrast, appeared to have no bearing on health problems in the total sample, with the exception of vomiting. It might be expected that over-indulgence would be associated with vomiting, but in fact the reverse pattern is revealed in the data. This suggests that those tourists who had experienced vomiting, for whatever reason, tended to reduce their alcohol consumption below their usual level.

Predicting the incidence of reported health problems among tourists is fraught with difficulties, owing to the crudeness and simplicity of the data available, the low level of measurement, the low frequency of health problems, and the lack of information regarding the causal factors involved (for example, while most cases of diarrhoea are probably due to an infective agent (Farthing, 1993) no information is available on whether this was so for cases of diarrhoea reported in the survey). It is also the case that factors of sex and particularly age have a significant bearing on behaviour and health problems reported and these factors need to be controlled either statistically or by analyses conducted within age groups. While the total number of tourists interviewed was fairly substantial, sample sizes are rapidly reduced when analyses are attempted for specified age groups. This may be why the attempt to find associations between swimming and health problems with age controlled was largely unsuccessful. Alternatively, it may mean that the association between swimming and such problems as headache and sore throat in the total sample is an artefact due to age differences in behaviour and health. To explore these issues further an attempt was made to condense the data available on pre-travel advice, precautions/medications taken on holiday and behaviour patterns while in Malta, and produce a smaller number of scales which could be used to 'predict' health problems reported. Four measures of health problems were also constructed—the first was simply the number of health problems experienced in total, and the remaining three

brought together specific problems which were associated with one another.

With respect to the total number of reported problems, the pattern of correlations with predictor variables shows clearly that a higher level of problems were associated with: younger age, smoking, more advice taken prior to travel, more preparations/medications taken on holiday and a pattern of behaviour involving swimming and consumption of 'street food'. Virtually the same pattern of associations also emerged for a specific health problem cluster involving sunburn, headache and sore throat. The diarrhoea, temperature and vomiting cluster was associated only with the total and professional advice measures and the total precautions and non-prescribed preparations measures. For chest pain/breathlessness, in contrast, reported incidence was associated with total and professional advice and the availability of prescribed medicines. It has to be acknowledged, however, that the associations revealed are extremely weak. Multiple regression analysis was employed to determine whether prediction of health problems could be improved. The highest multiple correlation emerging was 0.38 for predicting scores on the headache/sunburn/sore throat cluster from eight variables, including the swimming/street food pattern of behaviour, the availability of non-prescribed preparations, younger age, smoking and three categories of pre-travel advice. While the correlation is statistically significant it indicates that less than 16% of the variance in the headache etc. measure could be accounted for by the predictor variables available. It is interesting, however, that the pattern of associations observed is consistent with the results reported by Cossar et al. (1990) in showing that reported health problems are more common among younger tourists, those who seek advice prior to travel and smokers.

Conclusion

A significant proportion of British holidaymakers to Malta in March 1993 were 'late bookers', often booking within two weeks of departure. The consequences for tourist preparation for their holiday are significant if health advice and pre-holiday planning were constrained by a lack of time. This late booking situation at Easter was partly induced by the Maltese National Tourist Organisation's pursuit of market share to fill spare capacity at marginal cost. Such strategies may increase the probability of health problems among the more 'at risk' groups of visitors due to inadequate preparation time and poor advice from commercial tourism sources. The age distribution of tourists questioned in this survey was deliberately intended to be evenly spread across a wide age range so the study was more representative of British tourists visiting the Mediterranean rather than just Malta. As a result, the results do provide scope for a similar study in another Mediterranean destination where one would expect results of the same order of magnitude, perhaps with the exception of destinations specialising in activity holidays for young people (e.g. those provided by 'The Club').

The survey highlighted the role of travel agents as sources of health advice for holidaymakers when purchasing a holiday. This assumes an even more important role now that the EC Directive on Package Holidays is operational (see Downes, 1993). Yet holidaymakers consulted only a limited range of sources of health advice prior to travel, with the GP also emerging as an important point of reference. Yet it is evident from earlier studies (Reid et al., 1986) that accurate, up-to-date information and consistent advice from non-medically trained personnel (e.g. travel agents) is essential if holidaymakers are to be able to recognise potential health risks and to take the necessary action to address such issues. Without the necessary briefing from travel agents or holiday representatives in the resort, holidaymaker behaviour will remain unchanged as there is little evidence to suggest that printed literature (e.g. the Government's leaflet 'Health Advice to Travellers') is sufficiently targeted to potential holidaymakers (see Stears (1993) for a discussion of travel health promotion strategies pursued locally in the UK).

Holidays are often sold to tourists on their positive benefits for health, and their experience and educational role. Yet if nearly 37% of tourists questioned, in what is widely acknowledged as a 'safe destination' from a personal safety and health perspective, experienced some form of health problem, then the holiday may not be fulfilling its social and psychological role for these holidaymakers. In some cases this may lead to customer dissatisfaction, a feature neglected by many of the smaller tour operators and the destination area. For example, the younger age groups have a greater propensity to experience headache and sunburn and in some cases this leads to lost days whilst on holiday. Furthermore, there maybe a general reluctance among holidaymakers to consult a local GP in the resort, with self-medication a preferred option in some cases. This is a worrying feature for the tourist destination where GP services to holidaymakers often lack the responsiveness of the holidaymaker's own health service. Also, the fear of an unknown GP examining and diagnosing holidaymakers may form a cultural barrier towards addressing minor ailments, which are referred to the host country's GP on return. Thus, the results of the survey emphasise the need to provide adequate warnings to holidaymakers (possibly

in the resort) of the risk-taking behaviour which could adversely affect their intrinsic enjoyment of the destination and possibly impair their health. This is not an easy task for many reasons, not least because some holidaymakers appear to feel less inhibited and more willing to take significant risks once on holiday.

References

Behrens, R. H. and McAdam, K. P. (Eds) (1993) 'Travel medicine', *British Medical Bulletin*, 49: 2.

Bewes, P. C. (1993) 'Traumas and accidents', *British Medical Bulletin*, 49(2): 440–449.

Boissevain, J. (1977) 'Tourism and development in Malta', *Development and Change*, 8: 523–38.

Boissevain, J. and Inglott, P. S. (1979) 'Tourism in Malta', in de Kadt (Ed.), *Tourism—A Passport to Development?*, Oxford University Press, Oxford.

Britton, S. G. (1980) 'Spatial organisation of tourism in a neo-colonial economy', *Pacific Viewpoint*, 21(2): 144–165.

Braguglio, L. (1992) 'Tourism multipliers in the Maltese economy', in Johnson, P. and Thomas, B. (Eds), *Perspectives on Tourism Policy*, Mansell, London.

Bryant, H. E., Csokonay, W. M., Love, M. and Love, E. J. (1991) 'Self-reported illness and risk behaviours amongst Canadian travellers while abroad', *Canadian Journal of Public Health*, 82: 316–319.

Cartwright, R. Y. (1992) 'The epidemiology of travellers' diarrhoea in British package holiday tourists', *PHLS Microbiology Digest*, 9(3): 121–124.

Churchill, D. R., Chiodini, P. L. and McAdam, K. P. W. (1993) 'Screening the returned traveller', *British Medical Bulletin*, 49(2): 465–474.

Clark, N. and Clift, S. (1994) 'Young people, health and holidays abroad', Travel, Lifestyles and Health Working Paper No. 3, Christ Church College, Canterbury.

Clark, N., Clift, S. and Page, S. J. (1993) 'A safe place in the sun? A survey of health precautions, behaviours and health problems among British Tourists in Malta', Travel, Lifestyles and Health Working Paper No. 1, Christ Church College, Canterbury.

Clift, S. and Page, S. J. (1994) 'Travel, lifestyles and health', *Tourism Management* (in press).

Conway, S., Gillies, P. and Slack, R. (1990) 'The health of travellers', Department of Public Health Medicine and Epidemiology, University of Nottingham and Nottingham Health Authority.

Cossar, J. H., Reid, D., Falcon, R. J., Bell, E. J., Riding, M. H., Follett, E. A. C., Dow, B. C., Mitchell, S. and Grist, N. R. (1990) 'A cumulative review of studies on travellers, their experience of illness and the implication of their findings', *Journal of Infection*, 21: 27–42.

Dawood, R. M. (1993) 'Preparation for travel', *British Medical Bulletin*, 49(2): 269–284.

Downes, J. J. (1993) 'Legal liabilities and the travel trade: the EC package travel directive part II', *Travel and Tourism Analyst*, 2: 69–87.

Farthing, M. J. G. (1993) 'Travellers' diarrhoea', *British Medical Journal*, 306(6890): 1425.

Inskeep, E. (1991) *Tourism Planning*, Van Nostrand, Reinhold, New York.

Kay, D. and Jones, F. (1992) 'Recreational water quality', *PHLS Microbiology Digest*, 9(3): 125–128.

Licari, L. (1992) 'Deaths in British visitors to Malta', Unpublished paper, Health Information Systems Unit, Malta.

Lockart, D. G. and Ashton, S. E. (1991) 'Tourism in Malta', *Scottish Geographical Magazine*, 107(1): 22–32.

Nicolson, A. M., Pascoe, P. A., Spencer, M. B. and Benson, A. J. (1993) 'Jetlag and motion sickness', *British Medical Bulletin*, 49(2): 285–304.

Ogelthorpe, M. (1984) 'Tourism in Malta: a crisis of dependence', *Leisure Studies*, 3: 147–161.

Ogelthorpe, M. (1985) 'Tourism in a small island economy: the case of Malta', *Tourism Management*, 6: 23–31.

PA Cambridge Economic Consultants (1988) 'The economic impact of tourism in Malta', PA Cambridge Economic Consultants, Cambridge.

Page, S. J. (1994) *Transport for Tourism*, Routledge, London.

Pearce, D. G. (1987) *Tourism Today: a Geographical Analysis*, Longman, Harlow.

Reid, D. and Cossar, J. (1993) 'Epidemiology of travel', *British Medical Bulletin*, 49(2): 257–268.

Reid, D., Cossar, J. H., Ako, T. I. and Dewar, R. D. (1986) 'Do travel brochures give adequate advice on avoiding illness?', *British Medical Journal*, 293: 1472.

Stears, D. (1993) 'Travel health promotion: a survey of the work of distinctive health promotion units in the UK', 'Travel, Lifestyles and Health', Working Paper No. 2, Christ Church College, Canterbury.

Wilkinson, P. F. (1989) 'Strategies for tourism in island microstates', *Annals of Tourism Research*, 16(2): 153–177.

85 Consumption of the authentic: the hedonistic tourist in Greece

E. WICKENS

Introduction: tourism in Greece

Greece has a long history of tourism, traditionally attracting visitors fascinated by the art, history and philosophy of classical times. In terms of historic sites, Greece is undoubtedly one of the richest in the world, with a plethora of ancient and Byzantine monuments and artistic treasures. However, over the last two decades, the natural beauties of Greece, particularly its sunny beaches, have been preferred to its historical monuments. A survey carried out by the National Tourist Organisation of Greece shows that during the period 1984–85, 46% of tourists chose Greece as a holiday destination because of its hot sunny climate and its blue sea, while 9% chose it because of its antiquities. With its 9000 miles of coastline, 2000 islands and mild climate throughout the year, Greece is very attractive to foreign visitors seeking a relatively inexpensive holiday.

According to the same survey, 65% of visitors were skilled workers, clerical staff or students and 70% were between the age of 16 and 40. The average length of stay was 14 days and the average expenditure was US$22 per day. More than half of all arrivals occurred in the summer months of June, July and August. Approximately 90% of foreign visitors to Greece originate from Europe, with the UK, West Germany, France and Italy as the 'major tourist-generating countries'.

Having capitalised on her natural resources in pursuit of economic progress, Greece is now faced with a number of environmental problems (e.g. traffic congestion, water shortages and air pollution). The traditional landscapes of the coastal regions of mainland Greece, as well as her islands, have been transformed in order to house the modern tourist. Although attempts are being made by the Greek authorities to change Greece's image away from that of a land of sun, sea and sand, Greek seaside resorts such as Pefkochori, in Chalkidiki, Northern Greece, still remain a magnet for millions of sun-seekers.

Drawing on observational evidence collected during two periods of field work (1991–1993) in Pefkochori, I firstly discuss some preliminary findings concerning the tourist's experience of Pefkochori and then briefly explore some aspects of the socio-cultural impact of tourism on this host community.

Tourism in Pefkochori

In the last twenty years, the inhabitants of Pefkochori have experienced its transformation from a village into a resort. Pefkochori has metamorphosed from a small tranquil fishing and farming village into a bustling cosmopolitan seaside resort. This transformation is a direct consequence of the increased demand for small, affordable accommodation units close to the beach. The 'unique selling point' of Greece as a holiday destination, which is exploited by tour operators to market their package holidays, is of course the sun. Pefkochori, to borrow a phrase from Urry, can 'guarantee to produce the ideal tanned body' a fashion ideal pursued by Northern European tourists (Urry, 1990:38).

According to the 1991 census, the total resident population of Pefkochori is 1150 inhabitants. The resort lies towards the foot of Kassandra, the western 'finger' of the peninsula of Chalkidiki, in Northern Greece. This thickly wooded peninsula consists of three such 'fingers', Kassandra, Sithonia, and Mount Athos (also known as the 'Holy Mountain'). The region of Chalkidiki is a fast-developing tourist area and is evolving into one of the largest tourist centres in Northern Greece. Both Kassandra and Sithonia have extensive modern tourist accommodation, while Mount Athos is a monastic republic. Chalkidiki, like other holiday regions in Greece, becomes congested during the summer months with both domestic and foreign visitors who are attracted there more by its sunny beaches than by historic monuments.

The development of tourism in Pefkochori has been encouraged by the village authorities since the 1970s. The 'quiet revolution' brought about by tourism was initially triggered by the commercialisation of domestic tourism and was accelerated by the coming of international tourists in the late 1970s. Today, in Pefkochori there are small hotels, self-catering apartments and other rented accommodation providing around 3200 beds. The vast majority of the locals are either self-employed or employees in tourist-related services. In many cases, tourist-orientated enterprises are operated by families, i.e. husband, wife, children and grandparents. In this way overheads are kept to a minimum and profits maximised. There are over 250 of these tourist enterprises in the village, operated either by the indigenous population or by Thessalonikious.

Promoting the village as a tourist attraction involved the adoption of a new commercial name. Seventeen years ago, the village was called Kapsochora, meaning a 'burning place'. According to legend, Aigis (this was its ancient name) was the object of many pirate assaults, being burnt regularly by these 'marauding fiends', and so the village became known as a 'burning place', and subsequently was called Kapsochora. With the advent of international tourism, the village, was renamed Pefkochori (meaning pinewoods), a name thought to be more appropriate to its scenic location and therefore more attractive to tourists. The President of the village told me that the need to give the village a new name was due partly to onomatophobia. The locals believed that Kapsochora was rather an unattractive-sounding name for a holiday resort. Furthermore, the decision to 'ennoble the village name' was part of a marketing strategy, designed to project a distinctive image as a 'greener paradise'. Thus the metamorphosis of a small fishing/farming village into a cosmopolitan holiday resort is symbolised by the adoption of a new name, designed to convey a new identity.

Defining the 'tourist'

> The tourist is a voluntary and temporary traveller, travelling in the expectation of pleasure from the novelty and change experienced on a relatively long and non-recurrent round trip. (Cohen, 1974:533)

By this definition, a tourist seeks the pleasurable experiences which arise from the novelty of 'cultures different from his own'. Cohen's definition, although helpful, is written at too high a level of generality to do justice to the variety of tourists found in Pefkochori during the summer months. For example, he does not define what he means by the term 'pleasure' and so fails to recognise the wide variety of sources of pleasure which motivate individual tourists. Nor does this definition recognise the type of tourist who persistently returns to the same holiday resort.

One of the objectives of my fieldwork in the summer of 1993 was to attempt to identify the various 'expectations of pleasure' which motivate a tourist's holiday behaviour. It was hoped that these motives might provide the basis for a subdivision of Cohen's 'institutionalised tourists'.

Cohen has developed a fourfold tourist typology—the drifter, the explorer, the individual mass tourist and the organised mass tourist. This typology is based on the 'degree of institutionalisation of the tourist'. His first two types comprise 'the non-institutionalised' and his second two types the 'institutionalised' tourists. Institutionalised tourists use the facilities offered by tour operators. They visit popular destinations which cater specifically for this type of consumer. Individual mass tourists, unlike the organised mass tourist, have some control over their holiday itinerary.

My preliminary fieldwork indicates that institutionalised tourists may usefully be subdivided fivefold. Somewhat playfully, I have labelled these subdivisions: the 'Cultural Heritage', the 'Raver', the 'Shirley Valentine', the 'Heliolatrous' and the 'Lord Byron'. This subdivision is based on analytically separate motivation/behaviour patterns which reflect the primary characteristics of a particular tourist-type. In reality, tourists tend to exhibit a mixture of two or more such behaviour patterns but, nonetheless, this subdivision has proved useful as an analytical tool in giving structure to my observations. Hence, in my discussions about travel motives with respondents, the weather and the beach were common themes amongst them all and on their own cannot be used to distinguish between the various types. Future fieldwork will aim to validate, develop and refine this subdivision of the institutionalised tourist.

The 'Cultural Heritage' type is interested in the natural beauties of Greece as well as its culture and history. The promise often found in glossy tourist brochures of an experience of a 'traditional Greek village life' influences the Cultural Heritage tourists' selection of Pefkochori as a holiday resort. Pefkochori is used by this type of tourist as a 'base' to explore the rest of Chalkidiki. The Cultural Heritage tourist often escapes the 'hubbub' of a busy holiday resort, by taking daily excursions to the historical monuments of Thessaloniki or by visiting other parts of Chalkidiki—for example, traditional Greek villages such as Aghia Paraskevi which is located away from the coast. The 'quest for authentic experiences' (incorrectly, in my view) which has been identified by MacCannell (1973) as the primary motive of all tourists, plus the escape from the grey skies, were constant in this type of respondent theme. However, even this type of tourist does not want to experience the physical hardships of a traditional village, but demands the comforts of the tourist's own culture. Cultural heritage tourists mainly comprise family groups or older holidaymakers.

'Ravers' are attracted by the 'cheapness of the resort', particularly the cheapness and availability of alcohol, as well as the sun, beach and nightlife. Their experience of

Pefkochori is mainly confined to swimming/sunbathing during the day and clubbing at night. This type of tourist is an active and willing consumer of the sensual pleasures made accessible by a two-week, packaged celebration of the 'here-and-now'. In contrast, to the Cultural Heritage, the Raver's experience of the 'real flavour' of a Greek village is just incidental. This tourist type comprises young people, with males being in the majority.

The 'Shirley Valentines' are women on a mono-gender holiday who hope for romance and sexual adventure with a 'Greek God'. This particular 'expectation of pleasure' is based on the Greek male stereotype which has been perpetuated by newspapers and the film *Shirley Valentine*. These 'seekers of sexual adventures' often date with Greek waiters or other local men. Escape 'from domesticity', 'from family life' plus a 'break in the sun' were identified by this type of tourist as contributory factors in their selection of this holiday resort. This type of tourist has also been observed in other Greek holiday regions, including Rhodes and Crete (see Kousis, 1989).

The 'Heliolatrous' tourists are sun-worshippers who try indefatigably to change their colour. Suntan for them is seen as a fashion accessory and Pefkochori is seen as 'home plus sunshine'. Their experience of a Greek holiday is confined primarily to the beach, and occasionally to the open-air restaurants serving Greek and international cuisine found along the seafront. Often they may venture to a Greek taverna in search of a 'typical village evening entertainment'.

The defining characteristic of the 'Lord Byron' tourists is the annual ritual return to the same destination, often to the same place and sometimes to the same hotel or rented accommodation unit. This type of tourist has a kind of 'love affair' with Greece, with its relaxed, 'laid back' and 'outdoors' way of life. A Lord Byron told me:

> I go back to the same place, because this place has got inside my soul . . . I find the people friendly and welcoming. . . . I've made some friends and they are always pleased to see me. I feel I am no longer a statistic.

Being treated as a guest and not a tourist was a common theme amongst the Lord Byron respondents. This type of tourist is more likely to experience 'the real flavour' of Greek hospitality, often being invited by locals for a meal either in their homes or in a taverna. In discussions about travel motives with this type of tourist, it was evident that Pefkochori was seen by them as a place which provided them with security and familiarity as well as comfortable facilities. A sense of 'nostalgia' was also detectable in their conversations. Although they expressed some concern about the changes that have been taking place in Pefkochori as a result of mass tourism, in common with the other tourist types, the Lord Byron demands that services and facilities be provided to 'Western standards'.

Hedonism and tourism

> The world of hedonism is the world of fashion, photography, advertising, television, travel. It is a world of make-believe in which one lives for expectations, for what will come rather than what is. (Bell, 1976:70)

During the summer months, Pefkochori is a paradigm-case of a miniature world of hedonism, a world of 'instant joy, relaxing and letting go' which is governed by the 'ethic of hedonism, of pleasure and play—in short, a consumption ethic' (Bell, 1976:63). Lundberg (1985:130) says of pleasure that it:

> depends partly upon . . . the anticipation of good things to come. Pleasure may come from the relief of pain, respite from boredom, escape from the routine of life. It may be the feelings that come with sensuous gratification—a warm bath, basking in the sun, eating, drinking, sex, or even the thought of it. Change in itself may bring pleasure. Play is generally thought to be exciting and associated with pleasure.

My fieldwork clearly indicates that the search for pleasure in its various dimensions—aesthetic, physical, emotional, sensual and sexual—is the primary motivation of the tourist: e.g. sightseeing, being looked after by others, drinking and eating outdoors in a taverna, strolling along the waterfront, dancing, flirting with waiters, roasting in the sun, parading topless on the beach, and casual sexual encounters. As a Lord Byron put it: 'dining outdoors in a taverna on a hot summer's night is one of my holiday's great pleasures, drinking ouzo and enjoying good company'.

Pefkochori is perceived by many respondents as a 'low key' destination, a 'romantic place' which provides the tourist with the opportunities to relax, to feel less constrained, to please oneself, to be able to 'relate in a less formal manner', 'to let down one's hair' and to 'have one's fling'. In this respect, tourism represents a kind of a 'separate life' for the tourist. Tourists, to borrow a phrase from Berger (1963:160) 'temporarily leave behind their "serious" identities and move into a transitory world of make-believe', that is they enter into 'a world of play'. Play has been defined as 'a free activity quite consciously outside ordinary life, as being not serious but at the same time absorbing the player' (Huizinga, 1950:13). According to the same source, one of the functions of play is to set free subjectivity. Tourists in Pefkochori seek opportunities to live albeit temporarily, without the inhibitions and restraints of their everyday life, and to enter into a game of 'metamorphosis' which frees their impulses and feelings.

The concept of play which has been deployed by a number of scholars (e.g., Norbeck, 1971; Turner, 1974; Lett, 1983) in their analysis of the 'non-ordinary touristic world' constitutes an important explanatory factor in 'the rites of reversal'—the occasions (for example, during fairs and festivals) when 'customary rules of moral conduct are suspended' (Norbeck, 1971:51). Holiday resorts are said to provide 'liminal' spaces in which everyday life is turned upside-down, and the rules of 'ordinary' life are forgotten (Turner, 1974). Significantly, Pefkochori is a liminal 'touristic space' where, to borrow a phrase from Bauman (1992:xxiii) 'morality has been privatised' and 'like everything else that shared this fate, ethics has become a matter of individual discretion'. Indeed, the anonymity and freedom that tourists enjoy in this resort facilitates this inversion and encourages the privatisation of 'fun' morality. As one Shirley Valentine expressed it:

You are here to please yourself. . . . As far as I can, I leave my everyday life behind. When I'm in England, I'm fitting into an appointed role of somebody's wife, somebody's secretary. Here, you can relax, and rub off some of the sharp corners. You are not restricted. Greeks are very tolerant of us. . . . If you give yourself a chance, you can find out things about yourself that you did not know about before. . . . I am less age-conscious here. . . . I like sex but not with my husband . . . I come to Greece for a bit of fun.

For many tourists, including the Ravers, the Shirley Valentines, and to some extent the Heliolatrous, a package holiday is seen as providing a licence to practise hedonism and Pefkochori is perceived as a space structured to facilitate hedonistic attitudes. As Sinclair (in Bell, 1976) has observed, young people would drive twenty miles away from their 'familiar' place, where it was impossible to escape from the 'consequences of misbehaviour', to a place where anonymity was assured making it possible for them to 'shed their sexual inhibitions'. Distance then, seems also to facilitate the 'fun' morality which is practised in this resort.

Pefkochori is perceived as a world of freedom 'to transcend social-structural limitations, freedom to play— with ideas, with fantasies, with words, and with social relationships' (Turner, 1974:68). Typical hedonistic behaviours witnessed in Pefkochori include excessive consumption of alcohol, parading topless on the beach, wearing provocative clothes 'to please oneself', getting involved in sexual liaisons with the 'charming' stranger, and indulging in sexual activities on the beach. Such

behaviour is epitomised by the British couple which was 'arrested for making love in the main street of a Greek village at mid-day'. When the couple was asked 'if they would do the same thing back in Lancashire' the reply was 'Good heavens, no. . . . What do you think we are?' (quoted in Moynahan (1985)). As Krippendorf (1987:33) expresses it:

Tourists are free of all constraints. . . . Do as one pleases: dress, eat, spend money, celebrate and feast. . . . The have-a-good-time ideology and the tomorrow-we-shall-be-gone-again attitude set the tone.

Staged authenticity

Although it is individuals who travel, a considerable part of a tourist's experience of a place and its people is shared with other visitors (Lundberg, 1985). They collectively consume the same product, i.e. Pefkochori and its 'culture'. For example, all tourists use similar facilities and consume more or less similar food and drink. Although, as Cohen points out, some tourists derive 'pleasure from the novelty and change experienced', nonetheless they do not entirely leave their everyday life behind. My fieldwork supports the view that many tourists have 'deep-rooted habits and needs which cannot be shaken off' (Krippendorf, 1987:32).

According to some local entrepreneurs, Western European tourists expect services and facilities to be provided to Western European standards. In order to accommodate this type of tourist, Pefkochori has created artificial attractions and events for them. Tourists, and in particular the Lord Byron, the Cultural Heritage and, to some extent the Heliolatrous, seek Greek authenticity, that is an experience of the 'real atmosphere' of a Greek village, of a Greek taverna, etc. This, they find, to borrow a phrase from MacCannell (1973), in 'areas decorated to look like back regions', in attractions such as the pseudo taverna evening. The taverna evening is packaged to satisfy the tourist who wants to experience a traditional evening of 'Greek style' entertainment.

Intended mainly for foreign consumption, the taverna evening is transformed from a mundane social event into a spectacle, designed to make the evening exciting and memorable for the tourist. The taverna serves a hybrid cuisine—the traditional *mezedes* (a variety of salads and appetisers) being structured into a Western-style three-course meal with everyone having the same. The meal itself is a combination of Greek and Western European dishes. The rationale for the standardisation of the content of these meals is that it allows for the efficient processing of large numbers of coach parties, i.e. a taverna can predict the number of meals it needs to prepare and so maximise its profit.

In addition, it offers staged performances of Greek traditional dances, which have been hybridised, i.e. simplified and modernised, especially for tourists. For example the *khasapiko* (a butcher's dance), and its popularized version the *syrtaki*, and the *zembetico* (a man's solo dance expressing a mood of melancholy and suffering) are mass-produced, to be consumed by the tourists, just like any other product. These hybrid Greek dances are performed by a small group of men and women, dressed in traditional native costumes. These groups are instructed to encourage tourists to participate in these dances, which end with the traditional smashing of plaster plates. The sound of bouzouki music played in the taverna has also been modified, in order to appeal to the tastes of Western European visitors. Tourists then consume what I call a 'hybrid playful experience' of a traditional evening entertainment which has been modified to appeal to the international consumer.

What is quite apparent about these type of pseudo-events is that they appeal to foreign cash-customers. The 'expectation of pleasure' from a game of 'going native' seems to motivate particularly 'the touristic consciousness' of the Cultural Heritage, the Lord Byron and the Heliolatrous visitors. They are willing to play this game of being a tourist by day and a native by night, because it is and exciting. At the same time, they are aware that these sites and performances are staged, and that what they are consuming is not authentic but rather, a hybrid product.

Staged modernity

Mirroring the staging of authenticity, is the phenomenon of staged modernity. Marshall Berman defines modernity as a mode of common cultural experience. He writes:

> To be modern is to find ourselves in an environment that promises us adventure, power, joy, growth, transformation of ourselves and the world—and at the same time, that threatens to destroy everything we have, everything we know, everything we are. Modern environments and experiences cut across all boundaries of geography and ethnicity, of class and nationality, of religion and ideology; in this sense, modernity can be said to unite all mankind. (Berman, 1991:14)

An instance of the staging of modernity in Pefkochori is the conversion of a *kafeneio* (a traditional place where men gather to drink Greek coffee and play cards or *tavli*) into a bar. Here, the sound of bouzouki has been replaced by the sound of Western European pop music and modern Greek songs with an international flavour to them. Similarly, an *ouzeri* (a men's traditional drinking place) has been converted into a restaurant serving international cuisine. According to some local entrepreneurs, many tourists and, to some degree, the Lord Byron tourists demand the familiar—for example, food like roast beef and Yorkshire pudding, schnitzel or the traditional English breakfast served with fried eggs, bacon and baked beans. Tourists also demand drinks that they are accustomed to at home, for example, whisky, German beer, English bitter, English coffee, tea with milk. It is significant that in tourist resorts, Nescafé has nearly replaced the Greek word for coffee, and is used by many Greeks as well as by tourists. Tourists also demand the same comforts that they have at home (e.g. good plumbing). This demand for the 'familiar' has necessitated the 'simulation' of Western-style attractions, which are to be found along the waterfront. Pefkochori, with its open-air dining and entertainment facilities—pubs, bars, discos, restaurants, tavernas, arcades, and boutiques—are an example of what Baudrillard (1989) calls a 'simulacrum of the world', since these facilities are reproductions of Western models. They also serve to satisfy the 'hedonistic spirit' of the Ravers, and the Shirley Valentines.

The tourist quest for hybrid playful experiences induces hosts to stage Greek authenticity which is actually an amalgam of traditional and the familiar objects and comforts of the tourist's own European cultures, e.g. language, food, drink, and music. This act of simulating a 'microcosm of the West' (Baudrillard, 1988) is an attempt to create a modern atmosphere similar to, yet different from, the one that the tourist can find at home.

Modernity and change

The staging of modernity serves two purposes. Not only is it seen as a tourist attraction and therefore a cash earner, but it also satisfies Greek xenomania. This craving by Greeks, particularly among young people, for modern cultural experiences arises partly from feelings of inferiority. Greeks no longer want to be perceived or even labelled as 'backward', and thus they embrace a version of modernity with enthusiasm.

What is particularly interesting about such cosmopolitan places of entertainment as bars and discos, is that they are not only popular with tourists but also with locals and in particular with young Greeks. Moreover, some Greek youths have acquired a taste for international brands of alcohol such as whisky, as a fashion accessory. The desire to imitate the drinking habits of tourists as well as their leisure pursuits is perhaps one of the most obvious consequences of the 'demonstration effect' of the tourist on the locals. Young people envy what they see as the 'pleasure-oriented' lifestyles of tourists and try to copy them, not realising that the way the hedonistic tourists behave in Pefkochori is not normally the way they behave at home.

Norms governing dress have drastically changed to the extent that young Greek women, even some middle-aged women, feel free from any traditional constraints on dress. They copy the dress (or lack of it) of young female tourists, and thereby, to borrow a phrase from Baudrillard, break the 'traditional patterns of social regulation, which link lifestyles closely to age' (Baudrillard, 1991).

Fieldwork shows that, despite the hybridisation of cultural values which is at work in Pefkochori, nudity and some types of tourist dress give offence to some Greeks, particularly to the older generations, who still seek to place restrictions on the sexual behaviour of young women. The older generation is concerned that the promiscuity of female tourists has been provoking 'undesirable' demonstration effects in young Greek girls, leading them to abandon their traditional moral values. Twenty years ago, young girls were not even allowed to talk to men without the presence of their parents. Nowadays, these strict moral codes have been all but abandoned by young local women. These changes have also been observed by Kousis (1989) in her study of family life in a village in Crete.

Modernisation and change from a rural community to one based on tourism brings changes in 'people's attitudes, beliefs, their values' (Ryan, 1991). This is certainly the case in Pefkochori. As Ryan points out, in the absence of a 'tourist bubble', the impact of tourism on host cultures is much more profound. Culture, after all, is also about people and their 'patterns of everyday life as well as about buildings, monuments and souvenirs' (Williams, 1963).

The emergence of a hybrid culture in Pefkochori

What has emerged in Pefkochori is a hybrid culture which neither reflects the normal culture of tourists, nor the traditional culture of a Greek village. It is a cross between a heritage museum and a pleasure-seeker's paradise. To borrow a phrase from Ryan (1991:145) 'it reflects the non-permanent relationships that occur within tourism'. Ryan describes the culture that emerges in a well-established resort populated by 'institutionalised' and domestic tourists, as a 'hybrid culture'.

In Pefkochori the concentrated presence of tourists over a 20-year period has led to the assimilation of the hedonistic consumer-orientated behaviour of tourists into the behaviour and value system of the local inhabitants. Pefkochori is a paradigm-case of a farming/fishing community which has been undergoing a process of cultural hybridisation, of loss of traditional cultural identity. This hybridisation has led to changes in the attitudes, values and the behaviour of the indigenous population, particularly that of the younger generation. It is in effect, a process of 'acculturation'.

'Acculturation theory' is based on the notion that when two cultures come into contact, as they do in this case via tourism, an 'exchange of ideas and products' will take place (Nunez, 1984). A dominant, strong culture, in this case, Western European culture, will gradually change the weaker culture, i.e. the traditional culture of this peasant community. The results of acculturation are clearly visible in Pefkochori. Tourism has led to Western lifestyles being exported to Pefkochori and hence a raising of the expectations of local inhabitants has stimulated Western consumerism.

The creation of an indigenous 'consumer culture' (Featherstone, 1991) is largely attributable to the economic gains derived from the growth of tourism. An indication of the economic benefits of tourism is the improved living standards of the indigenous population. In Pefkochori, possessing a Mercedes or a BMW signifies not just social advancement, wealth and prestige, but confers an elite status on the owner. In this respect, consumption has become, to borrow a phrase from McKendrick et al. (1982) 'a weapon in battles for status'. The display of luxury electrical appliances such as television sets, videos and stereo sets is envied by others as a simulation of a modern lifestyle, a modern identity. The reconstruction of identity in Pefkochori involves the 'conspicuous' accumulation of modern 'signs of status'. 'Identity' is here used as a 'common denominator of patterns of life and activity' (Featherstone, 1990). Perceived economic benefits and the recently acquired tastes for modern lifestyles motivate the locals and shape their belief that tourism is something good and desirable.

Tourism as 'progress'

Pefkochori provides an example of tourism being the route to socio-economic development and hence a general improvement in the standards and conditions of living of a community which until very recently existed at subsistence level. In the eyes of the residents, tourism is the 'economic saviour of Pefkochori', because it has generated material prosperity and wealth. Looked at purely in economic terms, they perceive tourism as progress, a means of advancing from an inferior to a superior socio-economic position. To quote the President of the village: 'tourism for us means progress. It has liberated us from poverty, and has improved significantly our personal financial positions, our living standards'.

The erosion of the traditional social fabric, i.e. the disruption of traditional patterns of life, customs, and traditions, was perhaps an inevitable consequence of the single-minded pursuit of economic prosperity, via which locals strive to achieve true eudaemonia. The President of the village told me: 'we recognise some erosion of our traditional way of life, but we are prepared to accept it in the name of progress'. Perhaps, it is for this reason that the residents have succumbed so willingly to the temptation to abandon the old way of life and have embraced a version of modernity with such enthusiasm. Yet, it is true that cultures are neither static nor monolithic in reality. But in this case, it is more likely that tourism was not only the trigger but also one of the major contributing factors in speeding up the rate of socio-cultural change. However, tourism alone cannot carry the sole responsibility for the socio-cultural changes observed. I have argued that an interplay of factors including ideological (e.g. xenomania), economic (e.g. the profit motive), cultural (e.g. belief in progress) and psychological (e.g. feelings of backwardness) provide the causal matrix within which the socio-cultural changes in Pefkochori have taken place. In addition the media are contributory agents in reinforcing these socio-cultural changes.

Conclusion

> The right to travel has become a marker of citizenship . . . people are citizens by virtue of their ability to purchase goods and services. . . . Citizenship rights increasingly involve claims to consume other cultures and places throughout the world. (Urry, 1992:4)

Consuming different cultures and places may be considered a right of citizenship by the Western tourist, but this consumption has led to hybridisation of the physical and social character of Pefkochori, i.e. to its transformation beyond recognition in a relatively short period of time. The paradox is that some of the features, both physical (i.e. its rich vegetation) and social (i.e. traditional village life) that make it attractive are rapidly disappearing.

The locals are aware of the power of the tourist industry to hybridise their traditional way of life, but they have accepted it in the name of 'progress'. Yet the locals are not passive but rather proactive, albeit as selective participants in the process of change. A clear illustration of this is the continuing habit amongst locals, including young people, of going to church on Sundays to light a candle and to say a prayer, a clear, sign of the continuing strength of the community's expectation of an at least surface expression of religious convictions. There is of course no reason to believe that the hope in Pandora's box is the Greek Orthodox religion.

References and bibliography

Baudrillard, J. (1983) *Simulations*, Semiotext, New York.
Baudrillard, J. (1988) *America*, Verso, London.
Baudrillard, J. (1989) 'Media, simulations, and the end of the social', in Kellner, D. and Baudrillard, J. *From Marxism to Postmodernism and Beyond*, Polity Press, London.
Baudrillard, J. (1991) in Featherstone (1991).
Bauman, Z. (1992) *Intimations of Postmodernity*, Routledge, London.
Bell, D. (Ed.) (1976) *The Cultural Contradictions of Capitalism*, Heinemann, London.
Berger, P. (1963) *Invitation to Sociology*, Doubleday, New York.
Berman, M. (1991) 'All that is solid melts into air: the experience of modernity', in Tomlinson, J. (Ed.), *Cultural Imperialism*, Pinter, London.
Cohen, E. (1972) 'Towards a sociology of international tourism', *Social Research*, 39: 164–182.
Cohen, E. (1974) 'Who is a tourist? A conceptual clarification', *Sociological Review*, 22: 527–555.
EOT (Greek National Tourism Organisation) (1985) 'Foreign tourist survey 1984–1985', EOT, Athens.
EOT (1989) 'Tourism in Greece', EOT, Athens.
EOT (1990) 'Statistical year book of Greece', EOT, Athens.
Featherstone, M. (Ed.) (1990) *Global Culture, Nationalism, Globalization and Modernity*, Sage, London.
Featherstone, M. (Ed.) (1991) *Consumer Culture and Postmodernism*, Sage, London.
Huizinga, J. (1950) *Homo Ludens: a Study of the Play Element in Culture*, Beacon Press, Boston, MA.
Kousis, M. (1989) 'Tourism and the family in a rural Cretan community', *Annals of Tourism Research*, 16: 318–332.
Krippendorf, J. (1987) *The Holiday Makers: Understanding the Impact of Leisure and Travel*, Butterworth-Heinemann, London.
Lett, J. (1983) 'Ludic and liminoid aspects of charter yacht tourism in the Caribbean', *Annals of Tourism*, 10: 35–56.
Lundberg, D. (1985) *The Tourist Business*, Van Nostrand Reinhold, New York.
MacCannell, D. (1973) 'Staged authenticity: arrangements of social space in tourist settings', *American Journal of Sociology*, 79: 589–602.
Mathieson, A. and Wall, G. (Eds) (1984) *Tourism: Economic, Physical and Social Impacts*, Longman, Harlow.
McKendrick, N., Brewer, J. and Plumb, J. H. (1982) *The Birth of a Consumer Society*, Europa, London.
Moynahan, B. (1985) *The Tourist Trap*, Pan Books, London.
Norbeck, E. (1971) 'Man at play', *Natural History Special Supplement*, 48–53.
Norbeck, E. (1974) 'The anthropological study of human play', *Rice University Studies*, 60: 1–8.
Nunez, T. (1963) 'Tourism, tradition and acculturation: weekendsmo in a Mexican Village', *Ethnology*, 2: 347–352.
Ryan, C. (1991) *Recreational Tourism: a Social Science Perspective*, Routledge, London.
Sinclair, A. (1976) cited in Bell, D. (1976), *The Cultural Contradictions of Capitalism*, Heinemann, London, p. 67.

Tomlinson, J. (Ed.) (1991) *Cultural Imperialism*, Pinter, London.

Turner, V. (1974) 'Liminal to liminoid, in play, flow, and ritual: an essay in comparative symbology', *Rice University Studies*, 60:53–92.

Urry, J. (1990) *The Tourist Gaze*, Sage, London.

Urry, J. (1992) 'Global tourism and European places', Department of Sociology, Lancaster University, a paper given at the BSA.

Williams, R. (1963) *Culture and Society 1780–1950*, Penguin Books, Harmondsworth.

86 Tourism's impact on host lifestyle realities

T. SNAITH AND A. J. HALEY

According to Shaw et al. (1991:173), the significance of tourism to the economy of the United Kingdom is, 'considerable and takes a variety of forms ranging from its contribution to the balance of payments through to its role in the creation of jobs'. The economic and political importance of tourism is recognised through the development of ministerial guidelines and tourism growth projects. Interested parties tend to stress tourism's role in terms of the country's balance of payments, its potential as a stimulatory factor, and as an aid to the promotion of regional development (Heeley, 1981).

Because of its economic potential, tourism has traditionally been studied in terms of its economic impact on a region or nation. However, in the late 1970s an increasing awareness developed regarding the potential social, cultural, and environmental impacts of tourism. Studies conducted in the United States (Milman and Pizam, 1988; Long et al., 1990), Europe (Kariel, 1989; Var et al., 1985) and the United Kingdom (Brougham and Butler, 1981; Duffield and Long, 1981; Sheldon and Var, 1984) focused on residents' perceptions of the impact of tourism on their community. This line of research focused on the notion that the continued support of residents was vital to regional tourism's success.

Although inconclusive, the results of early studies suggested the existence of several relationships. Pizam (1978) reported that heavy tourism concentration leads to negative attitudes towards tourism development. Studies conducted by Rothman (1978), and Var et al. (1985) found that residents who were employed in the tourism industry saw tourism development more favourably than those who were not. In Santa Marta, Columbia, Belisle and Hoy (1980) found that the distance of residence from the central tourist zone was a significant predictor of residents' perceptions of tourism development. It has been suggested that residents' perceptions of tourism's impact are unrelated to resident characteristics (Gergely, 1989; Perdue et al., 1990). Studies have shown that residents perceive the positive impact of tourism to be related to its potential as an employment generator (Kariel, 1989; Var et al., 1985). Residents of various communities have also been found to associate certain negative impacts with tourism development. These include increased congestion, crowding and noise (Gergely, 1989; Rothman, 1978; Var

et al., 1985). It has also been suggested by Sheldon and Var (1984), that length of residence affects residents' sensitivity to the impact of tourism.

Many of the early studies were exploratory in nature and limited their attention to particular environments (e.g. small, developing, rural or resort communities). Inskeep (1991:145) suggested that attention should be paid to existing tourism destinations 'which are beginning to suffer some environmental or social problems of overdevelopment or unsuitable development'. Most of this research, although interesting at a descriptive level, lacked a theoretical framework to explain residents' perceptions (Ap, 1990). Recently, the biological concept of carrying capacity has been extended to include social issues. This concept has been recognised as useful in the assessment of the social impacts of tourism (Cooke, 1982; Getz, 1983, 1986; Long et al., 1990; Murphy, 1985; O'Reilly, 1986). According to Murphy (1985), the measurement of social carrying capacity has proved difficult, but recognition of the concept as a means to explain residents' perceptions may have great potential. D'Amore (1983:144) defined social carrying capacity as 'that point in the growth of tourism where local residents perceive on balance an unacceptable level of social disbenefits from tourism development'.

York as a tourist destination

York is a leading destination in the United Kingdom with an estimated 2 610 000 tourists in 1984 (Marketing and Communications Group, 1989). The income received from these visits, excluding accommodation, was estimated at 14.4 million pounds sterling or the US equivalent, 25.5 million dollars (Marketing and Communications Group, 1989).

At a time when the average length of stay in Britain has fallen to an all-time low of 10.8 days (BTA, 1990) there is a great deal of competition between cities attempting to increase visitor levels.

As shown in Figure 86.1, visitor levels have increased from 1 154 000 in 1970, to 2 610 000 in 1984 (Marketing and Communications Group, 1989). In order to cope with the number of tourists, the number of visitor beds has increased from 1900 in 1970 to 5848 in 1988 (Marketing and Communications Group, 1989). Feinstein (1981:119)

Visitors millions

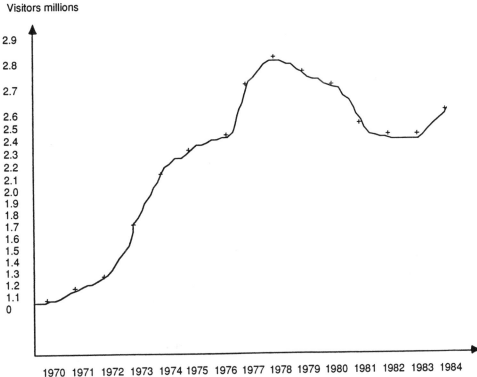

Figure 86.1 *Visitors to York (1970–1984). (Source: Marketing and Communications Group (1989))*

stated that 'tourism has made a vital contribution to the recent prosperity of the city, and that one of the best prospects for the future must lie in its further growth'. This statement concerning the economic potential of tourism development is a constant and dominant feature within local government tourism development policies, a feature compounded by the authority vested in local government to establish tourism development policies (Bouquet and Winter, 1987).

Significance of the study

Interest in the social aspects of tourism are comparatively recent. According to Cleverdon and Edwards (1983), academic recognition of the importance of tourism's impact on a society and culture dates from the early 1970s. More recently, Ap (1990) conducted a review of four studies (Belisle and Hoy, 1980; Liu and Var, 1986; Milman and Pizam, 1988; Pizam, 1978), and found that a variety of approaches had been used to gain insight into residents' perceptions of tourism development. Ap (1990) suggested five possible strategies to improve the measurement of the social aspects of tourism development. These can be summarised as follows:

1. Research should be based within a conceptual and theoretical framework.
2. More attention should be given to the significant findings to date.
3. More emphasis should be placed on longitudinal research.
4. Reliability and validity measures should be reported and identified.
5. Sampling methodology should be accurately reported and described.

The majority of studies on residents' perceptions of tourism development have taken place in small rural or resort-type destinations. In contrast, the urban environment has been largely ignored. This study attempts to extend the work of Perdue et al. (1990) into a large urban area (see Figure 86.2). The authors attempted to develop a greater conceptual and theoretical understanding of residents' perceptions of tourism's impact on their community. With respect to the strategies proposed (Ap, 1990) their model may prove pivotal in establishing a conceptual framework of residents' perceptions of tourism development in relation to their

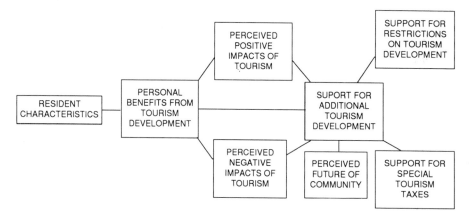

Figure 86.2 *Perdue et al.'s (1990) model of residents' tourism perceptions*

characteristics, perceptions and support for specific policies.

Research questions

1. To what extent do residents' characteristics (home ownership, age, whether or not they were born in York, income, length of residence in York, and distance of residence from the central tourist zone) and economic reliance on the tourism industry (employment in the tourism industry, and the importance of tourism to their occupation) predict positive perceptions of tourism development?
2. To what extent do residents' characteristics and economic reliance on the tourism industry predict negative perceptions of tourism development?
3. To what extent do residents' characteristics, economic reliance on the tourism industry, and positive and negative perceptions of tourism development, predict support for local government control of tourism development?
4. To what extent do residents' characteristics, economic reliance on the tourism industry, and positive and negative perceptions of tourism development, predict support for local tax levies for tourism development?

Hypotheses

1. No differences will be found among the independent variables (residents' characteristics and economic reliance) regarding their ability to predict residents' perceptions of the positive aspects of tourism development.

2. No differences will be found among the independent variables (residents' characteristics and economic reliance) regarding their ability to predict residents' perceptions of the negative aspects of tourism development.
3. No differences will be found among the independent variables (residents' characteristics, economic reliance, and positive and negative perceptions of tourism development) regarding their ability to predict residents' support for local government control of tourism development.
4. No differences will be found among the independent variables (residents' characteristics, economic reliance, and positive and negative perceptions of tourism development) regarding their ability to predict residents' support for local tax levies for tourism development.

The study sample

The city of York is unlike most other English cities in that the city centre is surrounded by walls, and therefore physically demarcated from its suburbs. In order to ensure that each household within the York area possessed an equal chance of being selected for the study, a circle, with a radius of four miles was placed on the map of York and surrounding area. The location on which the centre of the circle was positioned, was called Parliament Street. This street was selected following discussions with the Chief Executive of the York visitor and Conference Bureau, Paul Wells. Conversation at this meeting centred on the question of, 'How could one define the central tourist zone in the city of York?' It was the opinion of Mr Wells that the central tourist zone was fairly well outlined by the new paving works around the city centre

(Paul Wells, personal communication, 7 June 1991). These works were intended to remove vehicles from the central city. Parliament Street is the centremost street in this area and has been selected for redevelopment at a cost of three million pounds sterling (US: 5.3 million dollars), scheduled for completion in early December 1992. Each grid-referenced square on the map which lay on the peripheral boundary of the circle was included if at least 50% of its total area fell within the outer boundary.

Each grid square which fulfilled the above criterion, was enumerated. With this completed, the total sample area was seen to consist of 131 grid squares. From this sample area, 10 grid squares were selected using a random numbers table. The sampling frame consisted of all residential addresses within the 10 grid squares chosen. The completion of this task was facilitated by the use of the Royal Mail's Postal Address File on Compact Disc. The computer then performed a grid search that produced a list of all the streets and residential addresses, including their post codes, contained within those areas. A booklet was compiled from this information which consisted of 7728 residential addresses. Each address was subsequently enumerated.

According to Di Grino (1986), the required number of responses to achieve a representative sample from a population of 25 000 or more individuals is 348. This figure allows for 95% confidence within ±2.5% margin of error. In order to account for non-response, 545 questionnaires were mailed in July 1991. The questionnaires were sent to households selected at random from the residential address file.

Data collection method

After 15 years of research interest in this area, results, on which many recommendations have been made, still appear inconclusive. Low sample response rates, 20% (Liu and Var, 1986), 21% (Davis et al., 1988), 25% (Sheldon and Var, 1984), and a fragmented approach to research methodologies (telephone survey, mail questionnaire, personal interviews, hand-delivered and -collected questionnaires), while highlighting some important perspectives have only served to raise more questions.

Murphy (1981) obtained 283 usable responses, 68 from Windsor, 89 from Torquay, and 126 from York. Again one must wonder about the level of representation achieved by so few responses given the size of the respective populations.

Dillman's (1978) Total Design Method was adopted in an attempt to improve the effectiveness of data collection. Dillman (1978) recommends the use of three separate mailings. The first includes a letter of introducton and the research instrument. The second takes the form of a postcard reminder, and the third is a follow-up letter to non-respondents with a replacement questionnaire.

A total of 315 usable questionnaires was returned. The final response rate was 58%.

The survey instrument used in this study comprised a subset of items from the Lankford Tourism Impact Assessment Model (1991) and a scale developed by Perdue et al. (1990). The instrument consisted of two sections. The first section included 19 closed-style items and required respondents to rate their level of agreement with each item, through indicating their response on a five-point Likert scale which ranged from strongly disagree (1) to strongly agree (5). Each of the items were related to specific aspects of tourism development. Several of them shared an interest in a particular aspect, therefore enabling the creation of subscales. Two scales were developed. The first contained nine items related to positive aspects of tourism development (see Table 86.1), while the second contained eight items pertaining to negative aspects of tourism development (see Table 86.2).

An additional two items were also included in the first section. The first concerned residents' support for local government control of tourism development, while the second regarded residents' support for a local tax levy for tourism development (see Table 86.3).

The second section sought demographic information and is summarised below.

The majority of respondents (32%) were between 31 and 45 years of age. The overall mean age for the sample was 44.4 years ($SD = 0.94$). The actual mean age of adult residents in York was 46 years at the time of the last census in 1981 (Her Majesty' Stationery Office, 1982). Nearly 54% of the sample were born in York, and 68% reported owning their own home. The number of females responding accounted for 53% of the sample. This figure is representative of the actual number of females living in the York area, which according to the latest census was 52.4% (Her Majesty's Stationery Office, 1982). A large proportion of respondents (71%) had lived in York for over 20 years ($M = 33.3$, $SD = 1.15$). Nearly 61% of the sample had an annual household income of less than 14 999 pounds sterling. Nine per cent of the sample reported that a member of their family was currently employed in the tourism industry. In addition, 15% felt that the tourism industry was either important, or very important to their occupation.

The independent variables were entered into the equation on the basis of past research and in accordance with Ap's (1990) recommendations. Further to this the

Table 86.1 *Percentage distributions for the perceived positive tourism impacts scale (*n = 315*)*

			Percentage distribution[a]				
Statements	Mean	SD	1	2	3	4	5
Positive tourism impact perceptions							
More tourism improves the economy	3.58	1.05	2.2	19.4	14.0	47.3	17.1
Tourism should play a vital role in the future	3.38	1.04	3.5	20.3	22.2	42.2	11.7
Benefits of tourism outweigh its negative impacts	3.33	1.07	3.8	21.2	26.0	35.9	13.1
Tourism provides good jobs for residents	3.20	1.14	8.9	21.9	18.1	42.9	8.3
Tourism improves the appearance of York	3.04	1.16	8.4	30.4	18.8	33.0	9.4
Tourism increases recreational opportunities	2.98	1.16	8.6	34.5	15.7	32.9	8.3
York should *not* try to attract more tourists[c]	2.95	1.25	12.4	30.6	19.7	24.5	12.7
York should become more of a tourist destination	2.80	1.14	11.7	33.3	26.3	20.3	8.3
Tourism development improves quality of life	2.59	1.12	15.9	39.4	19.0	21.6	4.1
Mean and standard deviation for the scale[b]	27.8	7.43					
Reliability coefficient (alpha score = 0.89)							

[a]1 = strongly disagree, 2 = disagree, 3 = neutral, 4 = agree, 5 = strongly agree.
[b]Scale range = 9–45.
[c]Reversed coded item.

order of variable entry was such that Perdue et al.'s (1990) model could be tested (see Figure 86.2).

Summary of results

In the process of testing the research questions, several items from within the blocks of independent variables proved significant in their ability to predict the dependent variable. There was a significant relationship between the importance of tourism to the respondent's occupation and the positive perception of tourism development (Beta = 0.21, $p < 0.01$). Similarly, those employed in the tourism industry (Beta = 0.16, $p < 0.05$) were more likely

to perceive the positive aspects of tourism development than those who were not similarly employed. Residents' negative perceptions of tourism development (Beta = 0.18, $p < 0.05$), were found to be significant predictors of respondents' support for local government control of tourism. The most significant findings of the study appeared during the testing of research question four. Those who owned their home (Beta = 0.16, $p < 0.01$) were less supportive of local tax levies to support tourism development than those who rented their home. As the respondents' age increased, so too did their support for local tax levies (Beta = 0.13, $p < 0.05$). The greater the annual household income (Beta = 0.17, $p < 0.01$), the

Table 86.2 *Percentage distributions for perceived negative tourism impacts scale (*n = 315*)*

			Percentage distribution[a]				
Statements	Mean	SD	1	2	3	4	5
Negative tourism impact perceptions							
Tourism increases traffic	4.16	0.84	0.3	5.7	9.5	47.0	37.5
Tourism leads to more litter	4.02	0.89	0.6	7.6	11.8	48.7	31.2
Tourism unfairly increases property prices	3.40	1.09	3.2	21.6	24.8	34.6	15.9
Tourism businesses are too influential politically	3.30	0.95	2.2	17.1	40.3	29.8	10.5
Tourism development increases the poll tax	3.30	1.12	5.4	21.5	28.2	30.1	14.7
Tourism increases the amount of crime	3.07	1.08	4.5	31.7	25.3	29.2	9.3
Tourism negatively affects the environment	2.99	0.95	4.5	27.7	36.3	27.1	4.5
Tourism reduces quality of outdoor recreation	2.78	0.99	5.4	41.5	27.5	20.4	5.1
Mean and standard deviation for the scale[b]	27.0	4.83					
Reliability coefficient (alpha score = 0.75)							

[a]1 = strongly disagree, 2 = disagree, 3 = neutral, 4 = agree, 5 = strongly agree.
[b]Scale range = 8–40.

Table 86.3 *Percentage distributions of residents' support for special tourism taxes, and restrictive tourism development policies* (n = 315)

Statements	Mean	Percentage distribution[a]				
		1	2	3	4	5
Support for restrictive tourism development policies						
Local government should control tourism development	3.53	4.1	14.0	20.4	47.1	14.3
Support for special tourism taxes						
I would support local tax levies for tourism development	2.08	35.1	33.5	21.4	7.7	2.2

[a] 1 = strongly disagree, 2 = disagree, 3 = neutral, 4 = agree, 5 = strongly agree.

more agreeable residents were to a local tax levy for tourism development. Finally, the greatest significance was found to exist between respondents' positive perceptions of tourism development (Beta = 36, $p < 0.001$) and their support for a local tax levy for tourism development. This suggests that the more positively respondents perceived the impact of tourism development, the more supportive they were of a local tax levy for tourism development.

The results of the hierarchical regressions rejected all four null hypotheses. The hierarchical regression models used to test research questions one and four were found to be particularly strong (see Tables 86.4 and 86.7). They explained 17% and 30% of the variance in positive perceptions and support for local tax levies for tourism development respectively. In contrast, the hierarchical regression models used to test research questions two and three (see Tables 86.5 and 86.6) were more modest in their ability to explain the total variance in the dependent variables. The second regression using residents' negative perceptions of tourism development as the dependent variable explained 10% of the variance. The third

regression using residents' support for local government control of tourism development as the dependent variable explained only 8% of the variance.

The four main findings resulting from the data analysis are summarised. First residents' characteristics were able to predict a significant amount of the explained variance in residents' positive perceptions of tourism development. Secondly, residents' characteristics also contributed significantly to residents' support for a local tax levy for tourism development. Third, residents' economic reliance on the tourism industry made a significant contribution to the explained variance in residents' positive perceptions of tourism development. Finally, residents' positive perceptions of tourism development was a significant predictor of residents' support for local tax levy for tourism development.

The finding that residents' characteristics predicted both residents' positive perceptions of tourism development and their support for a local tax levy contradicts earlier research (Belisle and Hoy, 1980; Davis et al., 1988; Gergely, 1989; Milman and Pizam, 1988; Perdue et al.,

Table 86.4 *Hierarchical regression of positive perceptions of tourism development on resident characteristics and economic reliance on the tourism industry* (n = 245)

Independent variables	Beta	R	R^2	R^2 change	F
Resident characteristics					
Home ownership[1]	0.01				
Age	−0.07				
Born in York[2]	−0.06				
Income	0.15*				
Length of residence	−0.11				
Distance from C.T.Z.	0.00	0.28	0.08 (adj = 0.05)		3.30**
Economic reliance					
Importance of tourism to occupation	0.21**				
Employed in tourism industry[3]	0.16*	0.41	0.17 (adj = 0.14)	0.09[c]	6.00***

Significant beta: [+]$p < 0.10$, *$p < 0.05$, **$p < 0.01$, ***$p < 0.001$.
Significance of R^2 change: [a]$p < 0.05$, [b]$p < 0.01$, [c]$p < 0.001$.
[1] Home ownership: rent = 0, ownership = 1.
[2] Born in York: yes = 1, no = 0.
[3] Employed in tourism industry: yes = 1, no = 0.

Table 86.5 *Hierarchical regression of negative perceptions of tourism development on resident characteristics and economic reliance on the tourism industry* (n = 245)

Independent variables	Beta	R	R^2	R^2 change	F
Resident characteristics					
Home ownership[1]	−0.04				
Age	0.05				
Born in York[2]	0.10				
Income	−0.10				
Length of residence	0.11				
Distance from C.T.Z.	−0.08	0.25	0.06 (adj = 0.04)		2.60*
Economic reliance					
Importance of tourism to occupation	−0.13 +				
Employed in tourism industry[3]	−0.09	0.31	0.10 (adj = 0.07)	0.04^b	3.12**

Significant beta: $^+p<0.10$, $^*p<0.05$, $^{**}p<0.01$, $^{***}p<0.001$.
Significance of R^2 change: $^ap<0.05$, $^bp<0.01$, $^cp<0.001$.
[1]Home ownership: ownership = 1, rent = 0.
[2]Born in York: yes = 1, no = 0.
[3]Employed in tourism industry: yes = 1, no = 0.

1990) which suggested that residents' characteristics had little effect on residents' perceptions and attitudes concerning tourism development. The implication that emerges from these findings is that researchers and planners alike should not ignore the potential of residents' characteristics to predict a community's positive perceptions of tourism development and their support for specific tourism policies in large, relatively stable urban populations.

A positive relationship was found to exist between residents' positive perceptions of tourism development and their economic reliance on the tourism industry. This

finding is consistent with the results reported in earlier research (Perdue et al., 1990; Pizam, 1978; Rothman, 1978; Thomason et al., 1979).

Finally, residents' positive perceptions of tourism development were found to predict their support for a local tax levy which would be used to assist additional tourism development. Inasmuch as this represents their support for additional development, this finding agrees with that of Perdue et al. (1990), that support for additional development was positively related to residents' positive perceptions of tourism development. This finding

Table 86.6 *Hierarchical regression of support for local government control of tourism development on resident characteristics, their economic reliance on the tourism industry, and positive and negative perceptions of tourism development* (n = 244)

Independent variables	Beta	R	R^2	R^2 change	F
Resident characteristics					
Home ownership[1]	−0.09				
Age	0.09				
Born in York[2]	0.06				
Income	0.03				
Length of residence	−0.08				
Distance from C.T.Z.	−0.08	0.16	0.02 (adj = 0.00)		0.99
Economic reliance					
Importance of tourism to occupation	−0.09				
Employed in tourism industry[3]	0.08	0.19	0.04 (adj = 0.01)	0.01	1.16
Positive perceptions of tourism development	−0.07	0.26	0.07 (adj = 0.03)	0.03^b	1.83
Negative perceptions of tourism development	0.18*	0.29	0.08 (adj = 0.04)	0.02^a	2.12*

Significant beta: $^+p<0.10$, $^*p<0.05$, $^{**}p<0.01$, $^{***}p<0.001$.
Significance of R^2 change: $^ap<0.05$, $^bp<0.01$, $^cp<0.001$.
[1]Home ownership: ownership = 1, rent = 0.
[2]Born in York: yes = 1, no = 0.
[3]Employed in tourism industry: yes = 1, no = 0.

Table 86.7 *Hierarchical regression of support for local tax levies for tourism development on resident characteristics, their economic reliance on the tourism industry, and positive and negative perceptions of tourism development* (n = 244)

Independent variables	Beta	R	R^2	R^2 change	F
Resident characteristics					
Home ownership[1]	−0.16**				
Age	0.13*				
Born in York[2]	0.11				
Income	0.17*				
Length of residence	−0.09				
Distance from C.T.Z.	−0.07	0.27	0.08 (adj = 0.05)		3.23**
Economic reliance					
Importance of tourism to occupation	0.12+				
Employed in tourism industry[3]	−0.05	0.35	0.12 (adj = 0.09)	0.05^b	4.08***
Positive perceptions of tourism development	0.36***	0.54	0.29 (adj = 0.26)	0.17^c	10.61***
Negative perceptions of tourism development	−0.14+	0.55	0.30 (adj = 0.27)	0.01	9.98***

Significant beta: $^+p < 0.10$, $*p < 0.05$, $**p < 0.01$, $***p < 0.001$.
Significance of R^2 change: $^ap < 0.05$, $^bp < 0.01$, $^cp < 0.001$.
[1]Home ownership: ownership = 1, rent = 0.
[2]Born in York: yes = 1, no = 0.
[3]Employed in tourism industry: yes = 1, no = 0.

is especially interesting because it suggests that educating the local community to recognise the potential benefits of tourism development will increase the likelihood of their supporting additional tourism development. This, according to Murphy (1981), is essential to the development of destinations in countries with strong traditions of local politics and public participation.

Recommendations

This research was somewhat exploratory in that it examined residents of a large urban community in which tourism has been present for an extended period of time. Further research is required in other large urban areas to validate and improve the results of this study. Further to this it is noted that no research has appeared in the literature suggesting that researchers have returned to the original communities on which they based their study. Without such follow-up or longitudinal research, how can we truly appreciate the perceived changes which may occur as a result of tourism's impact on the host community.

Future studies should improve the measurement of residents' support for local government control and support for additional taxes by creating multi-item scales.

This study examined residents' perceptions of tourism development within the theoretical framework of social capacity. Previous research (Sheldon and Var, 1984) suggested that the seasonal nature of tourism may be responsible for varying levels of friction between residents and tourists. In order to address this question, further

research into residents' perceptions of tourism development is required during the shoulder, or quiet tourist season. In York, this is between November and February (Marketing and Communications Group, 1989) based on bed occupancy levels. In addition to this, the suggestion that residents adopt coping strategies in response to tourism's impact may add a further dimension to the nature of resident perception research (Ap and Crompton, 1993; Dogan, 1989).

Similarly to those of Perdue et al. (1990), and the research conclusions of Keogh (1990), the results of this study suggested that public relations programmes aimed at improving tourism's image with the local residents could offer a viable means of increasing local support for tourism. It was Keogh's (1990) belief that a major reason for residents' lack of appreciation of tourism is their lack of knowledge regarding the benefits of tourism to the community. People who are not economically reliant on the tourism industry, and therefore do not perceive any direct benefit from tourism development, should be among the groups targeted. By identifying the interest groups, the information needs of residents can be assessed and public participation programmes developed to assist in the effective and sensitive development of tourism in York. Prentice (1993) has noted that contentious matters in tourism development should be expected to cause a divide within the community according to whether or not its members perceive themselves as benefiting from developments. This was seen as offering an opportunity to pre-identify potential conflicts of interest as well as creating a potential weakness, for there is no guarantee that differences of opinion can be resolved.

It has been said that 'resident responsive tourism is the watchword for tomorrow: community demands for active participation in the setting of the tourism agenda and its priorities for tourism development and management cannot be ignored' (Brent-Ritchie, 1991).

It becomes increasingly difficult to merely pay lip-service to the need for public relations exercises and tourism education programmes. As Mathieson and Wall (1982:4) have noted, 'The consequences of tourism have become increasingly complex and contradictory . . . (and) are manifested in subtle and often unexpected ways'. It may be suggested therefore that we must continue to expand our understanding of residents' perceptions of tourism development if we are to fulfil our task, which in the present context 'is to establish a framework and a process by which to provide leadership to a community, a region or a country in its efforts to formulate a vision as to what it can or should seek to become as a tourism destination' (Brent-Richie, 1993).

References

Ap, J. (1990) 'Residents' perceptions: research on the social impacts of tourism', *Annals of Tourism Research*, 17: 610–616.

Ap, J. L. and Crompton, J. L. (1993) 'Residents' strategies for responding to tourism impacts', *Journal of Travel Research*, Summer.

Belisle, F. and Hoy, D. (1980) 'The perceived impact of tourism on residents: a case study in Santa Marta, Columbia', *Annals of Tourism Research*, 12: 83–101.

Bouquet, M. and Winter, L. (1987) 'Introduction: tourism politics and practice', in *Who from their Labours Rest: Conflict and Practice in Rural Tourism*, M. Bouquet and L. M. Winters (Eds), Gower, Aldershot, pp. 1–8.

Brent-Ritchie, J. R. (1991) 'Global tourism policy issues: an agenda for the 1990's', *World Travel and Tourism Review*, 1: 149–158.

Brent-Ritchie, J. R. (1993) 'Crafting a destination vision. Putting the concept of resident-responsive tourism into practice', *Tourism Management*, October.

Brougham, J. and Butler, R. (1981) 'A segmentation analysis of resident attitudes to the social impacts of tourism', *Annals of Tourism Research*, 8: 569–590.

BTA (1990) 'Digest of tourist statistics', (14) British Tourist Authority, London.

Cleverdon, R. and Edwards, A. (1983) *International Tourism to 1990*, ABT Books, Cambridge, MA.

Cooke, K. (1982) 'Guidelines for socially appropriate tourism development in British Columbia', *Journal of Travel Research*, 21(1): 22–28.

D'Amore, L. (1983) 'Guidelines to planning harmony with the host community', in *Tourism in Canada: Selected Issues and Options*, Murphy, P. E. (Ed.), Western Geographical Series 21, University of Victoria, Victoria, BC, pp. 135–159.

Davis, D., Allen, J. and Cosenza, R. (1988) 'Segmenting local residents by their attitudes, interests and opinions toward tourism', *Journal of Travel Research*, 27(2): 2–8.

Di Grino, B. (1986) 'Community surveys: purchasing confidence and accuracy', *Journal of Park and Recreation Administration*, 4(1): 61–69.

Dillman, D. (1978) *Mail and Telephone Survey: the Total Design Method*, Wiley–Interscience, New York.

Dogan, H. (1989) 'Forms of adjustment: socio-cultural impacts of tourism', *Annals of Tourism Research*, 16(2): 216–236.

Duffield, B. S. and Long, J. (1981) 'Tourism in the Highlands and Islands of Scotland: rewards and conflicts', *Annals of Tourism Research*, 8(3): 403–427.

Feinstein, C. H. (1981) *York 1831–1981: 150 Years of Scientific Endeavour and Social Change*, The Ebor Press, York.

Gergely, R. (1989) 'Tourism as a factor of change: Hungary', European Coordination Centre for research and documentation in social sciences, Warsaw, Poland.

Getz, D. (1983) 'Capacity to absorb tourism: concepts and implications for strategic planning', *Annals of Tourism Research*, 10: 239–263.

Getz, D. (1986) 'Models in tourism planning: towards integration of theory and practice', *Tourism Management*, 7: 21–32.

Heeley, J. (1981) 'Planning for tourism in Britain: an historical perspective', *Tourism Planning Review*, 52: 61–79.

Her Majesty's Stationery Office (1982) 'Census 1981 County Report: North Yorks (Part One)', HMSO, London.

Inskeep, E. (1991) *Tourism Planning: an Integrated and Sustainable Development Approach*, New York: Van Nostrand Reinhold.

Kariel, H. G. (1989) 'Tourism and development: perplexity or panacea?', *Journal of Travel Research*, Summer: 2–6.

Keogh, B. (1990) 'Public participation in community tourism planning', *Annals of Tourism Research*, 17(3): 449–464.

Liu, J. and Var, T. (1986) 'Resident attitudes toward tourism impacts in Hawaii', *Annals of Tourism Research*, 13: 193–214.

Long, P., Perdue, R. and Allen, L. (1990) 'Rural resident tourism: perception and attitudes by community level of tourism', *Journal of Travel Research*, 28(3): 3–9.

Marketing and Communications Group (1989) 'Statistics: tourism in York', York.

Mathieson, A. and Wall, G. (1982). *Tourism: Economic, Physical and Social Impacts*, Longman, New York.

Millman, A. and Pizam, A. (1988) 'Social impacts of tourism on central Florida', *Annals of Tourism Research*, 15: 191–204.

Murphy, P. (1981) 'Community attitudes to tourism', *International Journal of Tourism*, 2(3): 189–195.

Murphy, P. (1985) *Tourism: a Community Approach*, Methuen, New York.

O'Reilly, A. (1986) 'Tourism carrying capacity', *Tourism Management*, 7(4): 254–258.

Perdue, R., Long, P. and Allen, L. (1990) 'Resident support for tourism development', *Annals of Tourism Research*, 17: 586–599.

Pizam, A. (1978) 'Tourism's impacts: the social cost of the destination community as perceived by its residents', *Journal of Travel Research*, 16(4): 8–12.

Prentice, R. (1993) 'Community driven tourism planning and residents' preferences', *Tourism Management*, June, pp. 218–226.

Rothman, R. (1978), 'Residents and transients: community reaction to seasonal visitors', *Journal of Travel Research*, 16(3): 8–13.

Shaw, G., Greenwood, J. and Williams, A. M. (1991) *Tourism and Economic Development: Western European Experiences*, 2nd edn, Belhaven, London.

Sheldon, P. and Var, T. (1984) 'Resident attitudes to tourism in North Wales', *Tourist Management*, 5(1): 40–48.

Thomason, P., Crompton, J. L. and Dan Kamp, B. (1979) 'A study of the attitudes of impacted groups within a host community toward prolonged stay tourist visitors', *Journal of Travel Research*, 17(3): 2–6.

Var, T., Kendall, K. and Tarakcioglu, E. (1985) 'Resident attitudes towards tourists in a Turkish resort town', *Annals of Tourism Research*, 12: 652–658.

87 Whose culture is it anyway? Tourism in Greater Mexico and the Indigena

G. EVANS

Introduction

A study of minorites, their 'culture' and the impact and relationship with Western-style tourism immediately raises issues of definition, domination and 'dead-culture'. What is a minority and what is culture (and can it be 'owned')?—these are often emotive and politicised, and, in the context of developing countries, laden with the cry of cultural imperialism. Indeed, tourism and the tourists' pursuit of authenticity in ancient minority situations could be seen as the ultimate David v. Goliath culture clash, with the outcome inevitably not of the Hollywood-biblical happy-ending variety.

The extent to which academic research and analysis can deal with these issues does therefore require not only a multidisciplinary approach (anthropology, geography, economics, politics, culture, art/history etc.), avoiding 'misplaced concreteness' (Daly and Cobb, 1989), but also an acknowledgement of the limitations of Western thinking and assumptions in applying value-judgements and explaining observed behaviour in 'other' socio-cultures.

An obvious example, relevant to the study of cultural heritage, is the fact that native languages of indigenous Indians (Indigenas) do not contain a word that can be regarded as synonymous with the Western concept of art or heritage, which is usually seen as something separable from the rest of everyday life. The role of culture is therefore inextricably bound up in everyday living and beliefs in non-Western cultures, from Africa, Asia, Australasia, to the Americas. The oral tradition also separates these societies from our reliance on the written word. The Mexican–Indian traditions and the continuity between life and the afterlife (epitomised in the 'Day of the Dead' celebrations) also offer a different view of living culture and 'heritage'. This European disregard for oral history and expression is reflected in the Western academic and curator's line drawn between prehistory and history, the latter signifying the first stage of civilisation (sic), the written (European) word: 'My culture, the Lakota culture, has an oral tradition, so I ordinarily reject writing. It is one of the white world's ways of destroying the culture of non-European peoples' (Means, 1980). In Mexico, prehistory 'ended' with the Spanish conquests in the 16th century. The modalities of white v. 'other' value systems can be epitomised in tourism interaction and impacts on host communities:

> the white cultural framework attempts to universalize *exchange-value* to the exclusion of all other . . . formulas for the translation of speech into writing, of time into money, labor into a commodity, language into language, land into property—into money, versus 'non-White' cultural emphasis on *use value*: stewardship of the land . . . on the home as a place to live (*rather than visit*), not to sell . . . work that is satisfying in itself. (MacCannell, 1984)

Basis of study

This comparative research in Greater Mexico (Meso-america) based upon separate study tours, in 1990, of New Mexico, Southwest USA (Taos, Santa Fe, Albuquerque), including accessible Pueblo villages and cultural festivals, and in 1992, of Mexico—the Independencia region (San Miguel d'Allende, Guanajuato, Hidalgo) and Tlaquepaque/Guadalajara in Central Mexico, and the Oaxaca region in the south, including Oaxaca City (a recent Unesco-designated World Heritage Site), Puerto Angel, Puerto Escondido and Bahias de Huatalco (see Figure 87.1). These three resorts on a coastal stretch of 103 km, respectively represent differing stages of commercial tourism development, from the *limited* (e.g. owner-occupied hotels) to the *expanding* (local/national-owned, sensitive-scale, but foreign investment proposed) and the *over-built* (large-scale, international five-star beach–hotel complexes).

The study offers a comparison of heritage tourism management and impact on Native Indian socio-cultures between New and 'Old' Mexico and thus at national/state policy levels, between the USA and Mexico. Both are epitomised as 'tricultural', meaning Indian, Spanish ('Hispanic') and Anglo; and, until the separation in 1846, New Mexico formed part of greater Mexico—both, therefore, were under Spanish rule for 200–250 years. Tourism, 'fourth world' arts and culture (Graburn, 1976) are viewed in the broader context of the political and economic development affecting Indian communities, and

Figure 87.1 *Location of study sites in Greater Mexico*

the socio-cultural continuity and change they experience—through the gap between 'primitive and modern' (MacCannell, 1984), for which tourism, arguably, provides a special bridge.

The context and political economy relevant to the timing of this research, are the 500th anniversary celebrations of Columbus's 'discovery' of the Americas, and disputed state elections in Mexico during 1992, and the progression towards the North American Free Trade Agreement (NAFTA), between the USA, Mexico and Canada, which came into force on 1 January 1994. 1993 was the United Nations International Year of Indigenous People and, shortly before the end of the year, the UN launched the 'International *Decade* of the World's Indigenous People'.

Minorities

Minorities of all kinds—cultural, religious, linguistic, ethnic and racial—are ubiquitous today; few nation-states do not have one or more minority group within their national territories and minorities are frequently divided by state borders (Ashworth, 1980). Tribal people typically have stable, low energy, sustained-yield economic systems, based more dependently on their specific environment. Whilst leadership and internal democratic systems exist, Indigenas generally lack national representation, and few, if any, political rights. The treatment and relationship between dominant and minority groups presents both a moral and political problem, with national and international implications, not least for tourism and other forms of economic development. These have been recognised by external agencies in project evaluation criteria (Goodland, 1982; WTTERC, 1992).

This is no more so, than in the case of Native Indians of the Americas, whose place in history is rooted in European myth and imperialism. In Mexico, native Indigenas are numerically and geographically in the minority, with less protection and land-reserves than Southwestern (USA) contemporaries, whilst in neighbouring Guatemala, Indians as a whole occupy the majority (c. 55%), but are made up of over 20 tribal groups, receiving even more effective domination and discrimination than in Mexico. Numerical size is therefore only *one* measure of socio-economic minority status and institutional racism is often concentrated in post-colonialist style power (e.g. Afrikaners).

A history of the population and conquest of Native America is beyond the scope of this paper, but the briefest of summaries is given in the Appendix.

From a peak of 57 million Native Americans in 1492, there are estimated to be only 33 million today. In Mexico the Indian population has fallen over 60% from 21 + million in 1492 to 8 million in 1992 (8% of the population). Indian communities are concentrated in poorer, less developed regions of Mexico, including tourist trail, heritage sites and potential tourist resort areas.

The Columbus quincentenary anniversary focused attention on past and present conflicts: '(which) exemplified *par excellence*, heritage and tourism in the global village today—with the raw flesh showing' (Boniface and Fowler, 1993). These 'celebrations' were partially muted by demonstrations in Central and South America, as well as the USA, and used by indigenous populations to protest against miserable living conditions, discrimination and land expropriation, as well as the re-enactment and re-writing of the history of 'Old and New Worlds': 'a sterile argument between triumphalism and political correctness' (Hilton, 1993).

Against this backdrop, tourism development and operations sit uncomfortably between continuing repression and exploitation, and this dreadful inheritance. In Mexico, this is masked by a continuity of a benign form of democracy ('perfect-dictatorship', Mario Vargas Llosa) since independence, the relative success of its tourism industry in economic and product terms and paradoxically, the adoption of Indian cultural heritage as the image and expression of what is Mexico:

> since the 1910 Revolution in Mexico, archaeology has been officially encouraged in order to promote national unity (*sic*) by celebrating a pre-Hispanic past (and thus including the large indigenous population) and to claim Mexico's uniqueness . . . sites that double as museums and tourist sites. (Trigger, 1984)

> The preservation of the past now serves political and economic ends: nationalism and tourism. (Leong, 1989)

One could be forgiven, when the social, environmental and economic impacts on Indigenas are examined (including tourism development), for feeling that such a 'celebration' represents at best, tokenism, and at worst, continued 'internal colonisation' (Graburn, 1976), and cultural imperialism by the Mexican State.

Images of ancient sites and ruins, museum collections and ethnic art, provide not only the unique selling point for domestic and international tourism, but the cultural

emblems and identifications in Mexican society itself, including government communications and media; 'it has become a standard photo-opportunity for PRI (Institutional Revolutionary Party-PRI, more Institutional than Revolutionary) candidates, to appear in the brightly coloured Indian poncho' (Golden, 1994). The image of the Indian, artefact and heritage site is equivalent to the British Beefeater, or American Cowboy; the difference here is that this 'heritage' is still 'living', but has little control over its own culture, or its exploitation. National and Regional Museums contain renowned collections of pre-Columbian 'art', but located in major cities, these all charge entry. Effective access to their living ancestors is limited and this heritage is clearly directed at the majority colonial inheritors and as cultural attractions for the new conquistador–tourist.

> What hurts Indians most is that our costumes are considered beautiful, but it's as if the person wearing it didn't exist. (Menchu, 1984)

Tourism development in Mexico

International tourism development in Mexico originated in the 1950s. In 1961 a National Tourism Council was established, made up of five members appointed by the President. The national Fund for the Promotion of Tourism, FONATAUR, provides state funding and credit finance for government-approved tourism projects, and the Secretariat for Tourism also funds agencies responsible for control and regulation of hotels and travel organisations. Mexico has a highly centralised tourism development system, emphasising its national economic importance.

Unlike other less developed countries (Turkey, Spain) embarking on rapid development subsequently, Mexico was seen as a relatively successful example in economic development terms (Ball, 1971; Jud, 1976). This was due to the mix of its destination offer and experience, from ancient heritage sites, colonial towns and cities, to beach resorts in both Pacific (Acapulco, Puerto Vallarta), and Caribbean (Cancun, Cozumel) coasts. These complementary attractions and seasonal periods combine with Mexico's proximity to the USA and Canada, which provide over 85% of overseas tourists, predominantly on short breaks. The high level of nationalisation, from oil to airlines, and a proportionately high unskilled labour requirement, also reduced the degree of leakage; by the 1970s net foreign exchange earnings were over 80% of gross.

By the late 1970s and early 1980s, Mexico's expansion, consequent public debt (increased by 475% between

1970–1981), trade deficit (increased by 366%) and over-reliance on oil sales in the volatile international oil market, led to rapidly increasing inflation and public debt. At a time of low US dollar rates, growing competition from other destinations, Mexico became more expensive to its prime market and tourism numbers and spend suffered. Its market position and concentrated economy were also its Achilles' heel.

The government's main response was to devalue the peso successively, in 1976 by 37.5%, in 1977 by 14%, against the dollar. The effect of devaluation on international tourism was short-term; in fact net foreign exchange earnings from tourism and its proportion of GDP did not improve between 1975 and 1982, when the peso was floated and exchange controls imposed (Fish and Dickinson Gibbons, 1985).

The overriding determinant was world and North American recession, exacerbated by high domestic inflation/non-competitive prices and airfares. The tourism account began its recovery after 1982 and tourism has increased its positive balance—$1136 million, or 20% of exports by 1986 (WTO, 1990). Tourism is the second-highest foreign currency earner, with receipts of $5324 million (World Bank, 1992). Mexico's regained competitive position combined with the North American upturn resulted in spectacular visitor increases. As a destination, however, Mexico was 'mature' in terms of its prime source-markets and tourists now had lower per capita expenditures; mass charter-based packages increased. Domestic inflation also fuelled imports, border transactions and the benefits from tourism growth were diminished.

The Mexican government has continued to pursue a policy of growth in international tourism and border transactions—hence the keen interest in the adoption of the North American Free Trade Agreement. The latter will require an even more open economy, open to foreign investment (inward and outward); import licences have been removed and trade tariffs reduced. One manifestation of this is a privatisation regime prior to the NAFTA, including State Airlines, banks and the most politically sensitive, the national oil corporation (Pemex), as well as diminishing manufacturing sector (10% reduction between 1990 and 1993 and a further 20% estimated to 1995). Mexico is moving towards a service and satellite economy, of which tourism is a prime sector. Ironically, this may accelerate as a result of both NAFTA and the recent GATT agreement (1993).

Despite increased border manufacturing activity, leakage will be high (value-added goods and services will be retained by the USA) and agricultural products will be increasingly uncompetitive against mass grain imports from the USA. This will directly impact on indigenous production and land use. Full Free Trade (NAFTA and GATT) is forecast to reduce Mexico's income in real terms over the next ten years (Goldin et al., 1993), despite short-term annual growth (3% in 1994—one of the world's highest). The urgency to capitalise on the momentum from these trade agreements and footloose investment, ahead of Presidential elections in 1994, promises a headlong development regime, which is likely to have scant consideration for social, cultural, or environmental impacts.

Foreign involvement in tourism development, with state incentives, promises a second wave of mass tourism development in undeveloped areas, many on existing and expropriated Indian lands. The 1993 government target of 50 000 extra hotel rooms and a 20% increase in tourist arrivals therefore promise a post-Fordist scenario of state-encouraged private-sector tourism development and related infrastructure expansion, dominated by US, Japanese and Mexi-American corporations, targeted at these markets, European and nouveaux riches Mexican tourists. This may be 'optimum' for the private sector, but not for the Mexican economy, environment and community (Bodlender and Ward, 1988). Power (1988) criticises such 'self-defeating' strategies of growth and offers a list of goals for local development: (1) the availability of satisfying and useful work for members of the community; (2) security of access to biological and social necessities; (3) stability; (4) access to the qualities that make life varied, stimulating and satisfying; (5) a thriving, vital community.

The political and macro-economic issues are noted here, not merely for the potential impact on host communities, but to put tourism economic development into its broadest context. The opportunity costs of alternative investment strategies, impacts from other economic activities and improved efficiency—in Mexico this includes oil, manufacturing (notably in US border areas), agriculture—all have produced the effects of acculturation (social, cultural and religious), mechanisation and loss of land. In fact, without the socio-economic policies pursued by third world nations playing a first world 'growth' game, international tourism would not seriously feature in a country such as Mexico. (Perhaps only in smaller, island communities could tourism be said to have the leading dominating influence, the prime agents of change.)

Demonstration effects cannot easily, or solely be traced to tourism; Mexican national TV mixes Anglo images and forms, from game shows to blonde bimbos, with national (ethnic) pride in Indian heritage (more emphasis on the dead-inanimate than the living): 'Faces on the murals may be copper, but those on television are white' (Wright, 1992). However, per capita tourist spending by *Mexicans* reached $62 in 1990 (compared with $154 in the USA) and Mexican tourists in Britain were, remarkably, the highest spenders in 1992 (£4312 for a family of four—higher than tourists from the Middle East, Japan and the USA). The imbalance of wealth in Mexico is extreme; one-third live below the official (i.e. understated) poverty line, and just 35 of the richest families (Mexico has one of the highest numbers of dollar billionaires in the world), earn more than 15 million of the poorest Mexicans, of which over 50% are Indigenas (OECD, 1992).

With only 10% of the population able to afford foreign travel, a status symbol (mostly to the USA and South America, but increasingly to Europe), domestic travel, predominantly visiting friends and relatives, is strong, based on a network of cheap and often hair-raising bus routes, and a growing internal air transport system, as a result of partial air privatisation and deregulation. The latter is under pressure, not only from debt financing and free trade requirements, but also in order to finance upgraded fleets, which will be required to meet US environmental standards.

Post-revolution Mexico continues discrimination and expropriation of Indian land and livelihoods. In the 1970s, the Institute Nacional de Indigenas (INI) followed a policy of modernisation of Indian farming, forcing the introduction of fertilisers, intensive farming and centralisation. Recent appropriation and forced sale of Indian lands for intensive ranching in Chiapas has fuelled ethnic unrest. Again this was in the context of a Western-economic drive for growth, which had little consideration for the interests of this fourth world community. Urbanisation has increased from 42% in 1950 to over 70% today (Barry, 1992). The system of land ownership and control therefore lies at the heart of fourth world conflicts, of which resort and ethnic tourism are a special case: 'Unjust land tenure systems and the political, economic and social policies which enable them to prevail are the chief causes of hunger and poverty in the Third World' (Whittemore, 1981).

Indian communities have often been driven into subsistence agriculture in less fertile areas. Their remoteness, ironically, has served to make their pursuit worthy of several 'experiential' tourist types: 'explorer'; 'elite and unusual' (Smith, 1989)—in independent tours, these often coincide and present a clear destination market segment in Indo-(Latin) America.

New Mexico

In contrast to Mexico, the Native Indians in the southwest of the USA, although also suffering from the cycle of exploitation–separation–integration, have achieved a greater degree of control and acceptance in reservation systems and Pueblo settlements, covering over 17 million acres. Many reservations are now self-governing, with similar powers to those of states, and in 1978 the First Amendment extended protection to native religions (Wright, 1992). The Navajo 'Nation' of over 250 000, covering an area twice the size of Israel, may be the first 'Indian state' (Thornton, 1987). As unlikely as it may seem, this would be the first 'return' to indigenous control of a part of the Americas, which are unique, continuing 'colonies' in a post-colonial world.

In New Mexico, 'pre-tourism' developed in the late 1800s and was well-established by 1920. The encroaching railroad was the main factor of change and promotion of settler immigration and relocation. Natives were allowed to ride for free on trains as romantic exotica and the Sante Fe railway company used Indian symbols in their promotional literature and encouraged Indians to set up craft stalls outside stations. An enterprising 'tour operator', Fred Harvey Corporation, even devised 'Indian Detours' which offered passengers a few days off the train and excursions to Indian villages and sites. During this period, Indian groups began to see tourists as sources of income (Sweet, 1989).

The Indian communities also reflect tribal change within these societies (in Western, paternalistic terms, an 'Indian' is at best a generic, just as an 'African' is—though containing many distinct tribal and ethnic groups): 'How I loathe the term "Indian" . . . a term used to sell things—souvenirs, cigars, gasoline, cars . . . "Indian" is a figment of the white man's imagination' (Lenore Keeshig Tobias, Ojibway, in Wright, 1993). The present-day Indian societies are made up of agrarian-based Pueblo and nomadic Navajos and Apaches who raided Pueblo farms from the 16th century, and descendents are drawn from these various Indian cultures: 'Cultures of the world have been radically displaced and fundamentally and forever altered by the movements of peoples' (MacCannell, 1991).

In fact, some tribes, such as the Mescaleros (Apache), promote tourism more than other groups. This includes the management of a luxury ski-resort ('Ski Apache', 'Inn of the Mountain of the Gods', 'Apache Haven Motel') and game-hunting tours. More recently, exploiting state legislation, reservations have opened popular gambling centres, much to chagrin of non-Indian Americans, some of whom are claiming spurious Indian ancestry, in order to receive reservation status!

Amongst Pueblo settlements, some are more open than others; over two-thirds do not allow cameras or recorders (Laxson, 1991)—a degree of choice and destiny-control is evident, therefore, unlike for their equivalents in Mexico.

The effective access to political power has been one key to this degree of self-determination; Indian communities in New Mexico have exercised a block vote and the US-federal system perhaps provides a more representative form of democracy for minority groups and greater devolved power of land use and economic development, including tourism, and consequently over cultural affairs. These 'rights' were not of course *given* (nor could they be), but have been fought for, increasingly through the politicisation of Indian communities and the rising profile of leaders in the political and campaigning struggles. Indian consciousness and a modern 'movement' had arrived in the southwest states and elsewhere in North America, not just an assertive and self-determining force, but as a rejection of the domination and assimilation of minorities by majority-rulers and of the related social-anthropological processes:

> No European can ever teach a Lakota to be a Lakota, a Hopi to be a Hopi. A master's degree in Indian studies . . . cannot make a person into a human being, or provide knowledge into traditional ways. It can only make you a mental European, an outsider. (Means, 1980)

These oppositional movements are gaining force throughout aboriginal societies and situations worldwide and present parallels with black power movements—the natural desire for rediscovering both their roots ('enculturation'—Laxson, 1991) and recognition of the present-day situation as functions of colonial and post-colonial domination: 'There is no longer any excuse for ignoring the viewpoint of the "discovered", the vanquished, the colonized' (Wright, 1992:9). MacCannell's notion of 'constructed authenticity' can be observed in the degree of control, acceptance and rejection of tourism amongst Pueblo and other Indian communities on the one hand, and their collaboration through pan-Indian and ethnic art trade and tourism with the White society (Evans, Chapter 82 in this volume).

The extent to which Mexican Indian communities have emulated their US counterparts is harder to assess. As part of the political process their powers and numbers are limited and issues of land use, expropriation and development control are often subsumed into regional economic disputes arising from agrarian reform, privatisation

and political corruption. They share common complaints with subsistence farmers and oil workers—a working-class struggle against an urban elite, perhaps, but given the continued discrimination, their special needs and threats are not fully recognised. Unlike in the US southwest, Indian-based tourism promotion is managed by the national/international tour industry and at a local level by intermediaries (Ladinos—Spanish/White—and Mestizos—mixed Indian/Spanish blood), who are therefore almost always non-Indians.

The overriding distinguishing factor is tourism's role and relationship to a third-world developing economy, compared to a diversified and developed economy such as the USA. It is likely, therefore, that where development opportunities present themselves, public or private-led, minority heritage and communities will continue to lose, as Mexico strives for first world status. Indeed an almost surgical approach to the first wave of resort development created Cancun on the Caribbean coast: 'Once virtually uninhabited, the area was computer-selected because of its near-perfect climate, peerless white-sand beaches, proximity to major populations (the USA and Canada) and its pre-Columbian archaeological sites' (*Tourist and Industrial Guide to South/Eastern Mexico-Mexicana*, No. 2, 1992).

Virtually uninhabited?—the previously developed island of Cozumel, has 'despite considerable development, managed to retain much of its charm from years gone by' (op. cit.). Once a sacred place for the Maya and for their descendants, a pilgrimage location for centuries, there are in fact several archaeological sites on this Caribbean island.

The aggressive approach to tourism development was seen more recently in the Pacific area of Bahias de Huatalco. This area in the Oaxaca State contains the highest proportion of remaining Indian population in Mexico and was settled in pre-Hispanic times by Zapotec and Mixtec tribes. In 1984, locals heard rumours of large-scale tourist development of their coastline. Without consultation it was subsequently announced that, by the year 2000, Huatalco was due to have 9000 hotel rooms, 800 000 visitors a year and a permanent population of 100 000 (then only 500).

1300 rooms and 146 000 visitors were planned for 1989. State-funding of infrastructure (airstrips, roads and generous incentives), led to the construction of a 550-room Club Med', five-star Sheraton and El Presidente beach complexes, which target 'one-stop-tour' experiences and discourage visitors from straying from the hotel zone, especially not to the re-sited local village five kilometres behind the beach resort. Local people initially resisted and complained of exploitation and insufficient compensation for their lands; military 'presence' was felt and complaints were soon silenced, and subsequent participation in this enforced development was constrained.

This development cycle now threatens Puerto Escondido, further north along this coastline, following the construction of an international airstrip. Now an off-beat surf-centre, with smaller-scale accommodation, US and Japanese developers plan major hotel developments and the expansion of existing facilities is likely to kill off the local fishing industry and small firms, and widen the 'ring-fence' area from which indigenous populations are expelled and are self-excluded.

The third of these resorts, Puerto Angel, reflects the first wave of tourist development, and a few fading hotels remain, several family-owned and occupied. One of these, the Posada 'Canon de Vata' (Green Canyon), has been developed over 20 years by a North American university-educated Indian, who has reclaimed an arid valley through tropical tree-planting. This has created a micro-climate, and a source of self-generating pumped water and shade, in a subtropical environment. Meals are taken with the family and staff, and this early model of ecotourism might have thought to have attracted interest from state and private organisations; however,to date no assistance or cooperation has been forthcoming from either. The attitude of private and public developers to environmental impacts and alternatives (solar, low energy, recycled), both here, in the environmentally sensitive Baja peninsula, and in tribal lands generally, shows little consideration of sustainable development, environmental standards, or lessons from the past. This is at odds with the lip-service and fancy brochures on sustainable and environmental policies issued by international airlines and hotel operators who are active in Mexico. These are exclusively directed at the physical, not human, environ-ment (International Hotels Environment Initiative; British Airways Annual Environmental Report, 1990).

Huatalco is modelled on the Acapulco example, and represents one of the worst kinds of tourism development, with maximum benefits for international operators and minimum opportunity or consideration for local economy or communities. This approach ignores the prime beneficiaries of local economic development—the local population (Krippendorf, 1987): a complete lack of 'Pareto gain'—in favour of questionable national economic maximisation (Pearce, 1991). Beach tourism represents nearly 90% of Mexican tourism; the remaining 10% is represented by cultural tourists. Resort development does, however, increasingly take place in remoter areas, which in Mexico are unsafe havens for indigenous populations. The impact on these socio-cultures comes not only from the site development and worker-support areas themselves,

but also from the transport infrastructure (Pan-American highway, airstrips), which precedes them. Resorts also serve as 'hubs' for explorer-tourists going into sensitive tribal areas themselves.

Heritage—sites of tourist interaction

The greater control by New Mexico Indians in tourism development, from accommodation, sightseeing and craft sales to staged performance in tourist areas, is a model to which Mexican Indigenas may aspire. For some communities, however, the business of tourism will remain undignified and threatening, and further encroachment and relocation will be resisted. This will require not only a more accountable tourism policy and equitable land use, but also, if sustainable tourism and environmental protection are to be effective, the recognition that minority ethnic communities require protection and consideration at least to the same degree as the built and natural heritage sites—that 'live culture' is given the same recognition as 'dead-culture': 'mass tourism can result in *loving something to death*' (B. Von Droste, Director of the World Heritage Centre, Unesco, quoted in Molstad (1994)).

The various environmental and sustainable tourism initiatives, from industry-sponsored research centres (WTTERC, 1992) to the UN's World Heritage Sites, are biased towards the latter. The protection of ruins is clearly less sensitive than that of indigenous populations, whose inheritance is of such 'concern'. Questions of ownership, access and management of heritage sites and collections, although increasingly raised by indigenous groups and their vocal leaders, seldom feature in tourism promotion and planning.

In sacred sites around Mexico, including regional museums and—the-jewel-in-the-crown—the National Museum of Anthropology in Mexico City, their access and exploitation has been institutionalised along Western lines. Entry is charged and controlled, by state bodies who are staffed largely by non-Indians. The economic benefits from their inherited culture is effectively denied. Local Indians can be found in ruins such as Mitla or Monte Alban and operate as informal guides; they are tolerated, but are outside the museum system itself.

As an area of cultural and tourism investigation, the southwestern USA and Mexican Indian communities are rich in both history and material and, given their proximity to the USA, anthropologists, art historians and 'socio-tourist' investigations are many and wide-ranging. Given the predominance of the White-American tourist, the dominance of the US academic and art trader are also evident. A study of impacts on minority ethnic groups could easily fall into the trap of investigating the 'other' and disregarding and projecting the views of the tourees themselves: 'Reifying culture is fundamental to cultural tourism and fits well with the general sense in Indian folklore that the whiteman is a slave to consumerism' (Evans-Pritchard, 1989).

Studies of 'How "We" see "Them"' provide useful insights into the rationales and reactions of tourists and can demonstrate the cultural gaps that exist:

> I never really feel that I'm welcome in any of the pueblos ... I don't know how I would feel about tourists coming and looking at me either ... I get the feeling they're disgruntled but they'll do it. On the other hand when we go to Europe ... nobody seems to worry about it there. Why is it all right to wander around a Dutch town and take pictures and not okay to wander around Acoma and take pictures? (Laxson, 1991)

Members of the majority culture are socialised to value intellectual curiosity and to ask questions, but the Pueblo people feel that when outsiders learn their religious secrets, the spiritual power of the ceremony is lost. Given the degree of knowledge and experience of these socio-cultural differences that has been built up among travel firms (agents, operators and airlines: Adams, 1984; Silver, 1993), and through frequent American visitor-experience, it seems that the travel industry and those information sources are failing to provide even basic ground rules, and even guide books present a negative image: 'frankly an unfriendly pueblo ... a visit cannot be recommended' (Mays, 1985). This even extends to criticism of the extent of tourist development itself:

> Indians should capitalise on tourist curiosity by creating pueblo hotels, restaurants serving Indian food, or even a pueblo theme park ... You don't see them exploiting in a sense, their own best qualities and heritage. So it doesn't seem like they take advantage of their own traditions. (Laxson, 1991)

The 'worldview' and adaptation of Native Indians to tourist situations, has been less studied from *their* standpoint: 'the attention of social scientists has been elsewhere focused on cultural relativism, ethnic identity and symbolic systems. This leaves the impression that cultural enclaves are all inward-looking populations, disinterested in the world outside' (Evans-Pritchard, 1989).

Academics do not escape this ethnocentrism: 'field-workers are tourists and the two share characteristics that become the butt of Indian jokes and stories that ridicule them' (Freilich, 1970). Deirdre Evans-Pritchard's (1989) study of host group attitudes to guests, paints a universal and sanguine Indian-view, with jokes and humour a key

reaction, and one means of dealing with tourist contact and their often gullible and pathetic behaviour. This is no less so in the tourists' misconceptions of authenticity and inner-meanings, which Indian artists and guides choose to ignore, or 'they respond to tourists' needs for cultural significance by telling them just what they want to hear' (Freilich, 1970).

In 'Burlesquing the "Other" in Pueblo peformance' (Sweet, 1989), the Pueblo people 'for the most part regard tourists as fools' and categorise tourists based on origin or interest:

1. tourists from back-east (the most 'ignorant', Hollywood images . . .);
2. tourists from Texas (*tejanos*—'loud, pushy . . .');
3. hippie-tourists ('a nuisance—joined in when not appropriate . . .');
4. save the whale tourists (backpackers, 'right-on . . .')

All of these are generally derogatory; however, frequent visitors are invited to share more genuine celebrations, epitomised as 'White, or Anglo friend'. Art-trade brokers also develop, over time, a degree of trust and mutual respect, which is effectively earned.

Burlesquing as a phenomenon can be seen as another example, not of acculturation, but of cultural interaction, keeping separate those aspects of white-consumerist society by mocking them, adapting to those cultural forms and emblems (e.g. fashion), which they choose to integrate into performance. This can include contemporary and political issues and therefore follows a tradition of *realpolitik* in art, as a form of social comment, demonstration. The resistance to and then absorption of the Catholic religion into Indian beliefs and ceremonies can be seen throughout Latin America. The banning of traditional/national performance can have the effect of ensuring survival of cultural forms and practices, as well as fusion between religious cultures themselves (also evident in Africa, e.g. Ghanaian choral-singing).

The organisers of the Mas carnival recently held in Rio, Brazil, had made strenuous efforts to separate tourists from the dangers of the 'mass' itself, by erecting staged viewing points, and played down past attacks and muggings of tourists. A reaction to this was a giant float in the parade depicting a tourist (complete with Bermuda shorts, camera) being robbed at gun-point (and compare the *Kachina*-doll tourist in Evans-Pritchard (1989:101)). Tourism inevitably is absorbed into current folklore and expression, despite attempts to censor and 'clean-up'.

After the 1930s, when Indian performances were no longer banned in the southwest USA (Indians gained voting rights in 1924), different Indian tribes developed the group 'pow-wow', a multi-tribal celebration of ritual performances, not just for internal participation, but for cross-cultural, socialisation and educative purposes, including for the White community and tourists. The 'Apache mountain spirit dance', a sacred performance, is 'staged' for White audiences outside reservations, shared by all, as a 'gift' to other communities:

> There are no 'others', when they appear, they are just a furtherance of the same reality, and therefore finding others is a cause for celebration . . . for Europeans the 'other' is a threat. Pagan rites were feared as war dances and all religious dances were banned'. (P. Apodaca, Curator, Native American Art, Bower Museum)

Photography and disrespect

The imposition and encroachment of Western recording devices—audio-visual methods from cameras/video and tape—are not only alien to native cultures and communications, but also clearly threaten to extinguish oral, performance and sacred experience and skills.

Whilst education and warnings to tourists to desist from taking pictures may deter some, the pressure from foreign visitors who may view their holiday as 'once-in-a-lifetime' or just, 'I've paid to be here—I *must* have photographs', is unlikely to diminish, least of all from the explorer-type whose efforts to seek out remote or 'untouched' scenes and inhabitants must be rewarded with evidence ('proof of authenticity') of their trip (anthropologists cannot be exempted from such criticism). The desire for memento-images runs deep, part of our visual-information culture and stimulated by tour brochures and media-coverage:

> The camera is a kind of passport that annihilates moral boundaries and social inhibitions, freeing the photographer from any responsibilities toward the people photographed . . . allowing us to participate, while confirming alienation. (Sontag, 1977)

From observation, the impact on Mexican Indians is one of three: *reaction against the tourist* (where assertion is a realistic option); *resignation* (where tourist contact is frequent and dependent, e.g. markets) and *exchange-value*, i.e. monetary (often by younger members and where no other trade is undertaken, e.g. village, and as part of a visitor 'fee'):

> Modernity and heritage, heritage and tourism confront each other in discordant proximity if and when the world comes to look . . . not wanting to know too much about the realities behind the 'interesting' facades . . . Horwell (1992) purchased food from an Indian (in Taos), 'her poncho'd mother explained they were living in the pueblo,

though most didn't no more, 'cept at festival times when the craft business prospered, but you didn't get no artists paying you $30 fee this weather'. (Boniface and Fowler, 1993)

Some conclusions

'Sustainable Tourism—the World Travel and Tourism Centre's environmental guidelines' (WTTERC, 1992) stresses the physical environment, energy and 'green' issues; one of twelve 'Aims' refers to the 'Exercise of due regard for the interests of local populations, including their history, traditions and culture and future development'. *How* this may be achieved, in terms of the locational and infrastructural implications of tourism development, is not clear. An industry-led initiative, whilst encouraging, can only succeed if national tourism policy is influenced, particularly at a local level, if investment decisions are reconciled with such guidelines and externalities, and, most importantly, if host community involvement and empowerment in planning and development is secured. In the case of Mexican Indian populations, land reservation and development controls will be required for minority living heritage to be assured. The yawning gap between the policy and practice of the international tourism industry and, at the supra-national level, trade agreement signatories remains the prime obstacle to any external counter-weight to Mexican state development policy.

The World Bank, as the prime international financing agency, has recognised the need to consider tribal and indigenous impacts, particularly on land use and cultural traditions (Goodland, 1982). However, the next wave of tourism development in Mexico is likely to be national–privately financed, and limited cost–benefit analysis cannot adequately value or compensate for short- and long-term impacts on host communities (Nebel, 1983). The frailty of cultural tourism and heritage-sites risks a further shift towards 'dead-culture' as indigenous communities and owners of cultural resources are removed as 'obstacles' to development and Westernisation: 'Living Aztecs suffer discrimination, while dead ones are eulogised' (Wright, 1992:252). Ironically, Oaxaca City's designation as a World Heritage Site ('cultural equivalent of the Michelin guide' (Molstad, 1994)), is likely to increase tourist activity, whilst suppression continues in these regions.

The 'quality alternative' is stressed by Independent Tour Operators (AITO) to South America, but these codes are *customer*-led. Tour leaders and travel guides are qualified in language, even culture (*sic*) and many have majored in Latin American Studies (at Western universities (Means, 1980)), but few, if any, are indigenous, and despite the sensitive nature of the environments visited, little or no information is given in brochures and guides, to the habits, do's and don't's of visits to Indian lands and communities.

Consumer and educational guidelines are, however, increasingly available ('Good Tourist's Charter', CART; *Beyond the Green Horizon* (World Wildlife Fund for Nature, 1992); Elkington and Hailes (1992); and see Cleverdon in Rughani (1993) and Stancliffe (1993)).

The holistic interpretation of cultural tourism presented here attempts to highlight the interrelationships with the factors which, at each turn, both create and react to the impacts on minority cultures and which drive growth, assimilation and exploitation of these 'internal colonies'. A multidisciplinary approach also attempts to break out from the academic constraints and preciousness of 'disciplinolatry' (Daly and Cobb, 1989).

Case studies of tourism and ethnic minority societies can present some models, if not *ideals*, of pragmatic solutions to the host–guest meeting ground, that has no need to be 'empty' (MacCannell, 1991), but which requires tourism policy and development that does not ignore local socio-economic needs and living heritage.

The Pueblo Indians of the southwest USA, with a 50-year 'advantage', have reached a compromise and degree of control over tourism and trade, which if their Mexican tribal counterparts are to secure, will require the land and development control largely denied, and the political structures to underpin resource allocation decisions. An early 20th-century 'consociational democratic' model is provided by the Law of Cultural Self-Government for national Minorities adopted in Estonia in 1925. It gave any minority larger than 3000 the right to claim cultural autonomy . . . to set up elected councils, with the right to legislate in the educational and cultural fields (schools, libraries, 'heritage', etc.) and to raise taxes (Lipjhart, 1977). The *choice* to participate in tourism should be available and where intermediaries are still desirable, economic benefits must be retained, not just locally, but by the generators ('owners') of ethnic tourism, whether led by craft, performance or other visitor experience.

As a corollary, tour promotion by national and international operators can ensure greater pre-tour information and guide-training (especially of indigenous representatives), consistently throughout the tour-hospitality system.

The political and economic forces that will require both resistance and change, are substantial in the case of Mexico. Indigenous populations risk being overridden by economic imperatives and resource-exploitation, including mass and invasive tourism. The adaptation and survival of the Indian socio-cultures to date is all the more remarkable for this, and therefore tourism must learn from and mitigate these effects, and render meeting grounds places of mutual respect and experience. The continuity and change, so evident in Native American societies, may in time reverse not only the 'ethnic labeling, which can be devastating: majority stereotyping of minorities generally oppresses', but also the converse, the 'minority stereotyping of majorities [which] often seems to empower' (Evans-Pritchard, 1989).

> Life in general is a mystery. In these ceremonies as in life's journey, there is a mystery beyond every door. We request the outsider to sit and watch and just experience the event, and in time they may come to understand it. (Hopi Indian, Sante Fe, quoted in Evans-Pritchard (1989))

Appendix: Brief history and political economy of Mexico and the Indigena

- *c.50 000–20 000 BC*—People from Asia begin to settle in 'North America' after crossing the Bering Strait (during the last ice age)
- *c.20 000 BC*—Peoples begin to populate 'South America'
- *9000 BC*—Indian communities found as far south as Tierra del Fuego
- *AD 300*—Valley of Mexico developed (now Mexico City), first urban society
- *AD 900–1345*—Chichemec, Toltec and Aztec tribal empires (Mixtecs in Southern, Oaxaca region)
- *1492*—Columbus, 'discovery' (*sic*) begins the European colonisation of the 'New World' and subsequent Spanish conquest of Central and Southern America . . .
- *1519*—Cortes, begins Spanish conquest/colonisation
- *1500 to 1880s*—Mass slave trade ships millions of Africans to the Americas
- *1808 to 1828*—American-born Spaniards (mestizos) lead independence movements across Latin America. New Republics treat Indians as 'obstacles to modernisation' and continue confiscation of lands
- *1848*—USA invades Mexico City; pays $15 million for most of Texas, New Mexico, Arizona, California
- *1876*—Porfirio Diaz, military general, takes power; effective dictatorship until 1911, policy of ruthless modernisation, controlled by foreign investors
- *1890*—Wounded Knee massacre of 200 Sioux Indians marks end of armed Indian resistance to White domination in North America
- *1917*—Following revolutionary movements (Zapata: 'Land and Liberty'), new constitution established; basis of Mexican Constitution
- *1928*—Institutional Revolutionary Party (PRI) comes to power: model of corporatist intervention and nationalisation. Uninterrupted control to present day. National economy collapses under a mountain of debt in 1982
- *1991*—State elections: PRI narrowly re-elected, on NAFTA/growth and privatisation platform
- *1992*—500th anniversary celebrations in Spain, Italy, Portugal, USA and 'Latin' America; special tours, much press-coverage and several major feature-films of Columbus's 'discovery'. President Salinas (PRI) re-elected in questionable vote ('computer failure' at the PRI-led electoral commission . . .)

- *1993*—North American Free Trade Agreement (NAFTA) finally accepted by US Congress; GATT 'free trade' terms finally agreed
- *1 January 1994*—Indigenous peasants in San Cristobal, Chiapas region, rise up, occupy town, on the inauguration of NAFTA, whilst oblivious tourists 'party'. Heritage tours temporarily suspended.

References and bibliography

Adams, K. M. (1984) 'Come to Tana Toraja, "Land of Heavenly Kings": travel agents as brokers of ethnicity', *Annals of Tourism Research*, 11(1): 469–485.

Ashworth, G. (1980) 'World minorities in the eighties', Minority Rights Group, London.

Ball, D. A. (1971) 'Permanent tourism: a new export diversification for less developed countries', *International Development Review*.

Barry, T. (1992) 'Mexico, a country guide', Inter-Hemispheric Education Resource Center, Albuquerque, NM.

Bernal, I. (1977) *The Mexican National Museum of Anthropology*, Thames & Hudson, London.

Bodlender, J. and Ward, T. (1988) *An Examination of Tourism Investment Incentives*, Howarth & Howarth, London.

Bond, M. E. and Ladman, J. (1972) 'Tourism: a strategy for development', *Nebraska Journal of Economics and Business*.

Boniface, P. and Fowler, P. J. (1993) *Heritage and Tourism in the 'Global Village'*, Routledge, London.

Bronstein, A. (1982) *A Triple Struggle: Latin American Peasant Women*, Inter-Action Inprint/War on Want, London.

Bugnicourt, J. (1977) 'A new colonialism', *Development Forum*, (July–August).

Chant, S. (1992) 'Tourism in Latin America: perspectives from Mexico and Costa Rica', in Harrison, D. (Ed.), *Tourism and the Less Developed Countries*, Belhaven, London.

Christie Mill, R. (1990) *Tourism: the International Business*, Prentice Hall, Englewood Cliffs, NJ.

Daly, H. E. and Cobb, J. B. (1989) *For the Common Good: Redirecting the Economy towards Community, the Environment and a Sustainable Future*, Merlin Press, London.

Economist Intelligence Unit (1992) *The World in 1993*, Economist Publications, London, p. 97.

Elkington, J. and Hailes, J. (1992) *Holidays that don't Cost the Earth*, Gollancz, London.

Evans-Pritchard, D. (1989) 'How "they" see "us": Native American images of tourists', *Annals of Tourism Research*, 16(1): 89–105.

Evans-Pritchard, D. (1993) 'Ancient art in a modern context', *Annals of Tourism Research*, 20(1): 9–31.

Fish, M. and Dickinson Gibbons, J. (1985) 'Mexico's balance of payments 1970–1983: contributions of international tourism and border transactions', *Tourism Management*, 6: 106–112.

Frasier, D. (1992) 'That Mexican revolution', in *The World in 1992*, Economist Publications, London, p. 71.

Freilich, M. (1970) *Marginal Natives: Anthropologists at Work*, Harper & Row, New York.

Galeano, E. (1981) 'The open veins of Latin America', in Bronstein, A. (Ed.), *The Triple Struggle*, Inter-Action Inprint, London.

Golden, T. (1994) 'Heirs of Maya make their stand', *The Guardian*, 5 January: 11.

Goldin, I., Knudsen, O. and van den Mensbrugghe, D. (1993) *Trade Liberalisation: Global Economic Implications*, OECD, Paris/World Bank, Washington, DC (HMSO, London).

Goodland, R. (1982) *Tribal Peoples and Economic Development—Human Ecological Considerations*, World Bank, Washington, DC.

Gottlieb, A. (1982) 'Americans' vacations', *Annals of Tourism Research*, 9(1): 165–187.

Goulet, D. (1983) *Mexico, Development Strategies for the Future*, University of Notre Dame Press, Illinois.

Graburn, N. M. M. (1976) *Ethnic Tourist Arts: Cultural Expressions from the Fourth World*, University of California Press.

Hilton, I. (1993) 'Savage reassessments', Review of European encounters with the New World, Pagden, A. Yale, *The Independent on Sunday*, 7 March: 33.

Horwell, V. (1992) 'Truckin down to Taos', *The Weekend Guardian*, 16 March: 31.

In Focus (1992) 'Discovering the Americas', Tourism Concern, Roehampton, London, pp. 12–13.

Jud, G. D. (1976) 'Tourism and economic growth in Mexico since 1950', *Inter-American Economic Affairs*.

Krippendorf, J. (1987) *The Holiday-Makers*, Redwood-Burn, London.

Laxson, J. D. (1991) 'How "we" see "them": tourism and Native Americans', *Annals of Tourism Research*, 18(1): 365–391.

Lea, J. (1988) *Tourism and Development in the Third World*, Routledge, London.

Leong, W.-T. (1989) 'Culture and the state: manufacturing traditions for tourism', *Critical Studies in Mass Communications* 6, pp. 355–375.

Lipjhart, A. (1977) *Democracy in Plural Societies: a Comparative Exploration*, Yale University Press, New Haven, CT.

MacCannell, D. (1984) 'Reconstructed ethnicity: tourism and cultural identity in third world communities', *Annals of Tourism Research*, 11: 375–391.

MacCannell, D. (1991) *Empty Meeting Grounds: the Tourist Papers*, Routledge, London.

Mays, B. (1985) *Indian Villages in the South-West: a Practical Guide to Pueblo Indian Villages of New Mexico and Arizona*, Chronicle Books, San Francisco.

McClure, J. S. (1991) 'Spain: Western Europe's last frontier', *Time Magazine*, No. 4.

Means, R. (1980) 'For the world to live', "Europe" must die', in MacCannell (1991).

Menchu, R. (1984) *An Indian Woman in Guatemala*, Verso, London.

Mexicana (1992) 'Reprivatisation of Mexicana Complete', September, Mexico.

Molstad, A. (1994) 'The great monuments which belong to all humanity', in *The European*, 31 December 1993–6 January 1994: 6.

Moody, R. (Ed.) (1988) *Indigenous Voices: Visions and Realities*, Zed Books, London.

Morris, B. (1993) 'Free trade in the balance', *The Independent on Sunday*, 21 February: 6.

Nebel, E. C. (Ed.) (1983) *Tourism and Culture: a Comparative Perspective*, University of New Orleans, New Orleans.

Nunez, T. A. (1963) 'Tourism, tradition and acculturation: weekendismo in a Mexican village', *Ethnology*.

OECD (1992) 'Mexico—special survey of a non-member country', OECD Economic Surveys, Paris.

Pearce, D. (1991) *Tourist Development*, 3rd edn, Longman, Harlow.

Power, T. M. (1988) *The Economic Pursuit of Quality*, Armonk, Sharp, New York.

Ransom, D. (Ed.) (1994) 'Mexico—through the tortilla curtain', *The New Internationalist*, January: 4–28.

Raynoso y Valle and De Regt, J. P. (1979) 'Growing pains: planned tourism development in Ixtapa-Zihuatanejo', in De Kadt, E. (Ed.), *Tourism—Passport to Development?*, Oxford University Press, New York.

Right, R. (1983) 'Worlds in reverse: Indian response to the Spanish conquest', Radio Series, CBS, Toronto.

Rughani, P. (1993) 'Wish you were here?: tourism, the final brochure', *New Internationalist*, July: 30.

Said, E. W. (1991) *Orientalism*, Penguin, Harmondsworth.

Silver, I. (1993) 'Marketing authenticity in third world countries', *Annals of Tourism Research*, 20(2): 312–318.

Smith, V. (Ed.) (1989) *Hosts and Guests: the Anthropology of Tourism*, University of Pennsylvania, Philadelphia, PA.

Sontag, S. (1977) *On Photography*, Dell Publishing, New York.

Stancliffe, A. (1993) *Be My Guest: an Introduction to Tourism's Impact*, Tourism Concern, London.

Sweet, J. D. (1985) *Dances of the Tewa Pueblo Indians*, Santa Fe School of American Research Press, Santa Fe, NM.

Sweet, J. D. (1989) 'Burlesquing "the other" in Pueblo performance', *Annals of Tourism Research*, 16(1): 62–75.

Thornton, R. (1987) *American Indian Holocaust and Survival*, Norman, University of Oklahoma Press.

Trigger, B. G. (1984) 'Alternative archaeologies: nationalist, colonialist, imperialist', *Man*, 19: 355–370.

Whittemore, C. (1981) *Land for People*, Oxfam Public Affairs Unit, Oxford.

World Bank (1992) *World Development Report*, World Bank, Washington, DC.

World Wildlife Fund for Nature (1992) *Beyond the Green Horizon*, Tourism Concern, London.

WTO (1990) *Yearbook of Tourism Statistics, 1989*, World Tourist Organisation, Madrid.

Wright, R. (1992) *Stolen Continents: the Indian Story*, Pimlico, London.

WTTERC (1992) *World Travel and Tourism Environment Review*, Oxford.

88 Tourism: a commodity of opportunity for change?

A. HOLDEN

Introduction

The advent of the post-industrial society has led to increasing opportunity for travel within service-dominated post-industrial economies. To accommodate this increased opportunity and demand for travel, the travel industry continues to become more sophisticated in its operations, more global, and more vertically integrated. Set within a limited time framework of between one to two weeks it is important for the potential tourist to have ease of access to purchase his or her holiday product with maximum convenience and choice.

The Chambers (1981) dictionary defines 'commodity' as 'convenience: profit, expediency, advantage, privilege: an article of traffic: goods, produce'. For many countries in the developing world the advent of mass participation in an international tourism system, which displays many of the characteristics attributed to this definition of a commodity, offers an opportunity for economic and social change. Gunn (1988) states, 'Worldwide, tourism is looked upon as a smokeless industry with strong and stable economic impacts on host areas. . . . Tourism is viewed as the new wave of economic opportunity and is promoted heavily for this reason alone'. For many countries the post-1950 growth in international tourism demand and development certainly has offered economic and social opportunities.

The main aim of this paper is to give consideration to the interpretation of tourism as a commodity and the implications of this view for lesser developed countries interested in developing tourism in a sustainable manner in the future.

A brief history of touristic commodification

That the tourist may be interpreted as an 'article of traffic' may upset many economists and caring tour operators reading this paper. However, when the adjectives attributed to a commodity in the Chambers definition, i.e. convenience, profit, expediency, privilege and advantage are applied, tourism defined as a commodity in its widest sense is more applicable. It is the purpose of this section to use a historical perspective to assess the nature of tourism and the characteristics of commodification associated with it. It is not the intention, nor is it within the scope of this paper, to give a full account of the history of tourism development.

Holloway (1985) notes that the Greeks hosted visitors during the first Olympic Games in 776 BC and that the wealthy Romans travelled to the coast and as far as Egypt for holiday purposes. Mill and Morrison (1992) also suggest that the Egyptians, Greeks, and Romans travelled for pleasure purposes and identify the growth of a middle class with money from trading, combined with good communications, a single currency, and common languages of Latin and Greek, as reasons for an expansion of travel in Roman times. 'A final development was that of second homes and vacations associated with them. Villas spread south to Naples, near the sea, the mountains, or mineral spas.'

For wealthier Romans the opportunity of the chance to escape from the summer heat of Rome to the coast of the Adriatic and Mediterranean depended upon a servile class freeing wealthier Romans from the more mundane tasks of everyday life. Wealth was needed to buy servants, for capital investment in the summer villa, to free oneself from the necessity to work, and to pay for transportation between the origin and the destination. A system was constructed based on privilege, articles of traffic, i.e. the tourist, advantage, and expediency. The characteristics of the contemporary international tourism system, it could therefore be argued, has its origins in events that were occurring 2000 years ago.

The commodification process was to continue through development of hostelry and accommodation units and a servile class of worker serving a limited elite who could travel, e.g. on the Grand Tour. However, the major event influencing the development of tourism into the major business or industry many choose to interpret it as today, did not take place until the 19th century. It was the Industrial Revolution.

This period represented a shift in emphasis from a more holistic and symbiotic existence with the environment to one of increased time differentiation and spatial separation of home life, work life, and leisure time. Society was transformed from one of being primarily task-orientated to one of being primarily time-orientated. Clarke and Critcher (1991), commenting upon leisure provision, discuss how the urban area was progressively divided into specialised spatial areas. Leisure was forced into defined physical areas, through legislation such as the 1835 Cruelty to Animals Act, which barred traditional land workers' sports such as cock-fighting, dog-fighting and pugilism (interestingly not fox-hunting), and the 1835 Highways Act forbidding the playing of games in the street. Increasing commercialisation of leisure meant that stadia were developed for sports such as football, cricket and rugby, and also music halls, and later the cinema, were developed. A 'spatial mental map' was implanted in the subconscious of the new urban man, where work, home, and leisure were interpreted as having separate spatial and time zones. Combined with technological advancement in transport, i.e. the railways, the spatial boundaries of leisure were expanded out of the urban areas to the seaside, and early mass tourism was born.

The spatial and time zoning of life in the urban areas in industrialising countries were essential elements to allow the development of a contemporary mass tourism industry, where tourism could be sold and exchanged in the international marketplace. Krippendorf (1990) interprets mass tourism as being partly driven by the escape motivation from modern-day urban life. From a functional perspective the holiday is offered as compensation for acceptance of a mundane and alienating system. The release of time from the productive system and the acceptance of different behavioural norms on holiday act as a form of repressive tolerance, necessary to safeguard the structure of established society.

There is no doubt that by definition, tourism must take place in a different spatial area from the home environment, being reliant upon transport to take the tourist there. It is conducted within a specific, limited time period which is predetermined by holiday allowance from work. Therefore tourists require ease of travel, quickness, and convenience to satisfy their diversity of needs which are perceived as potentially being fulfilled through tourism.

A society that transformed itself into an increasingly organised society timewise and spatially, and continues to do so, brought increased opportunities to commodify what people choose to do in their leisure time. Tourism is one of those potential activities. Increasing legislation aimed at increasing leisure, such as the Holidays with Pay Act (1938), increased disposable income, improved post-World War II technology, such as the jet engine, heightened awareness of other countries through the television and the media have all been major factors in contributing to increased demand for travel. As we are aware an industry has developed in response to this growth in demand to make the purchase of travel and associated services accessible to an increasingly widening social spectrum of Western society. In the sense of this perspective of tourism outlined above, a commodity exchange has been developed, around the movement of people and a servile provision to facilitate this movement. This interpretation implicitly constructs the tourist as the article of traffic, searching for a product offering convenience, and maintaining a privileged position of being able to purchase an experience. To accommodate these needs an industry has developed which is expedient and is driven by profit motivation. The ethos of profit motivation is encouraged by continuing worldwide adoption of the capitalist system and embracing of free market liberal economics sanitised of protectionism. An industry has developed offering products for consumption within a tourist system that includes host communities and a variety of physical environments.

The commodity of tourism in the international system

The evidence from the EIU (1989) forecasting growth in demand for tourism until 1999 is impressive. In 1980 just over 300 million international visits to neighbouring countries were recorded. In 1999 this is expected to have risen to 650 million. In 1980, the demand for short–medium haul travel was 90 million arrivals, in 1999 this is predicted to rise to just below 200 million arrivals. In 1980, long-haul arrivals were recorded at 30 million, in 1999 they are expected to rise to approximately 75 million.

Unsurprisingly these figures make attractive reading for any developing country faced with an economic problem of needing to diversify its economic base, earn hard currencies to repay debts or re-invest, and provide employment opportunities, and demographic problems of increasing population numbers and a very young population structure. It is of course many of the lesser developed countries that have the natural physical and cultural attractions that are currently in most demand by tourists from Western countries.

Burns and Holden (in press) comment that the motives of involvement of a third world government in tourism development are primarily economic. The aim is not to provide a holiday destination in the sun where exhausted workers from the industrialised North can recharge their batteries, or by exposure to pre-industrialised conditions, alleviate their cynicism with the postmodern condition. It is the destination that is being put into the marketplace as a form of commodity for consumption by incoming Western tourists.

The importance of tourism to a growing number of developing economies is highlighted by Sinclair (1991).

Commenting upon Kenya in 1988, travel receipts contributed 20% of the total export earnings and exceeded the receipts that were gained from the sale of tea and coffee crops.

Timberlake and Thomas (1990) outline the problems faced by many developing countries in attempting to diversify their economies while faced with large debts. The collapse in the traditional commodity market in 1986 meant that prices plummeted to their lowest levels this century at a time when many developing nations had taken large loans from Western banks, given against the security of high commodity prices in the late 1970s and early 1980s. Timberlake and Thomas also drew attention to the fact that most African debt is owed to Northern governments and international agencies such as the World Bank, whilst the major part of the much larger Latin America debt is owed to private northern banks.

There are dangers of placing a destination into the international market for the purposes of tourism development and economic benefits. The first is that, for many countries lacking the internal resources for tourism development, a heavy dependence will be placed upon inward investment and overseas multinationals for tourism development. Secondly, reliance will also be placed on foreign intermediaries such as foreign airlines and tour operators to supply the tourists and market the destination. This inherently means a loss of control over destination development and image for the recipient country. Thirdly, the more control is exerted over development and markets by outside organisations the greater the economic leakage. Development schemes are likely to reflect a wish to maximise financial benefits to overseas investors as opposed to maximising the positive, economic, environmental, and social impacts of development for the host community. Bull (1991) refers to leakages as 'the reason only a proportion of extra income [i.e. referring to initial tourist expenditure] is spent in the local economy is that other calls are made on that income, which remove part of the flow from being spent on local transactions'.

Wheatcroft (1993) found that in the small island economies of Fiji, the Cook Islands, St Lucia, Aruba, Jamaica and the US Virgin Islands, the cost of imports consumed between 36% and 56% of gross tourism receipts. Sinclair (1991) differentiated foreign exchange leakages by holiday type in Kenya. For beach holidays where the tourist travelled with a foreign airline the foreign exchange leakage was estimated to be between 62% and 78%. Sinclair found that leakages were greater the more that tourists arrived having purchased package holidays. Fourthly, just as primary commodity markets are subject to external influences beyond the control of

producing countries, tourism demand is also responsive to factors such as world recession, increased oil prices, terrorism, and changing consumer tastes in Western countries.

A dependency can therefore be too easily created on Western countries, both for tourism development and for providing tourism markets. *The Guardian* (1991) outlines the reliance of Sierra Leone upon Western aid for the development of its tourism industry. In 1989 tourism made a contribution of only 2% to the gross national product and Sierra Leone had just eight hotels. Even with a restricted market of only 25 000 tourists per annum, the majority came from France, North America and the United Kingdom. In 1991 the government passed a Tourism Development Bill which offered incentives for foreign investment in tourism. Meanwhile with funding received from the European Union the government hopes to improve the infrastructure of the country.

There exists a strong possibility that many countries may choose to interpret tourism as having the same or even better economic potential as more traditional primary commodities. It has proved that for many countries it does have the potential to earn large quantities of foreign currency and can create employment. However, the decision to place any destination into the international tourism market based on the principle of it having similar or enhanced economic potential as traditional commodities is potentially catastrophic if development is formulated in the wrong manner.

It is certain that any development decision will lead to change. It is likely to lead to economic, environmental and social changes. Although similarities have been drawn between primary commodities and tourism, a key difference is that the market travels to consume the destination commodity, as opposed to the primary commodity being transported to the market to be consumed. This means that tourists impact directly upon the physical and cultural destination environment. Evidence of tourism demand increases pressure for development which will impact upon the environment. Tourist behaviour will impact upon the local community. In an unfortunately increasing number of destinations, commodity consumption now also includes directly the host community, in the form of prostitution.

Careless consumption of the environment through inappropriate development derived for short-term financial gain for investors and shareholders also brings unwelcome change. Morgan (1991) describes the re-active planning policies which are being introduced to stop declining numbers of visitors to Majorca attributed to a poor-quality environment in popular destination areas. Bywater (1990) identifies retrospective measures to address the decline in tourist numbers and occupancy rates along the

Italian Adriatic Riviera following the algae scare. Commodity prices under free market conditions are determined by demand and supply factors. There will be winners and losers in economic terms. In tourism the stakes are higher. Not only will there be winners economically but also socially and environmentally. Fukuyama (1992) states that the world is being homogenised into one of liberal democracies encompassing liberal trading policies and free market ideology. If this is so (and the decline of totalitarian states, increasing deregulation of markets in Europe by European Commission directives and worldwide markets through GATT would support this assertion), the opportunities for more countries to enter into the international tourism market will probably present themselves. The success of these destinations in managing change from tourism to maximise the positive impacts and reduce the negative will be closely determined by adopting the correct development policy. Economic, cultural, and physical factors are strongly interlinked and must all be given equal consideration in tourism development to ensure future sustainability.

How sustainable is the tourism commodity?

The extent to which this commodity opportunity is translated into a sustainable development policy for destinations will depend upon the adopted planning approach by destinations. By the use of case studies in Malaysia and Indonesia, the 'top-heavy' planning approach to tourism development will be exemplified. An alternative approach, with a greater emphasis on community planning will be illustrated through the Fiji case study. The benefits and costs of both approaches will be discussed. The importance of adopting the right strategy, especially for lesser developed countries, cannot be overemphasised. Without it, many countries operating in the international tourism market will be as vulnerable as those countries heavily reliant on the cash crop and raw material markets were to falls in commodity prices in the 1980s.

The theme of this paper has been the interpretation of tourism as a commodity to be used by developing countries to earn foreign exchange and bring other economic and associated social benefits. For tourism development to provide these benefits for future generations it should be conducted in a fashion that recognises tourism as a system with associated environmental and social impacts, as opposed to an overriding emphasis being placed on the economic and financial benefits of development. This emphasis shift has begun in the ETB (1991) *Tourism and the Environment* publication and is represented in the model taken from that document (Figure 88.1).

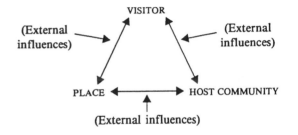

Figure 88.1 *Model of the tourism system*

The following summarised case studies illustrate approaches to tourism development. The first two based on tourism development in Indonesia and Malaysia highlight more traditional approaches to tourism development with economic and financial considerations overriding environmental and social concerns. The third case study based on Fiji presents an alternative approach to tourism development. The first two case studies illustrate the adoption of a 'top-heavy' approach, i.e. heavy investment in plant, with an expected trickle down of economic benefits to local people. Bird (1989) gives an excellent and very detailed account of the tourism development policy and its impacts upon the island of Langkawi off the western coastline of Malaysia. The main development aim of the Malaysian government was to develop the island into a major named resort area to provide the central focus for the development of a mass tourism industry to Malaysia. The second case study describes a tourism development scheme on the island of Java. The schemes have similarities in their objectives and style of development and are reminiscent of many tourism development schemes worldwide. Both rely heavily on overseas investment to develop five-star accommodation and facilities aimed at attracting Western tourists, are supported by government and ignore local consultation and participation, whilst having serious economic, environmental, and social implications for the communities inhabiting the land areas proposed for development.

Bird referring to the development of Langkawi explains how development plans for the island had been forged by the end of the 1970s by federal government without consultation with local people or even local leaders. Bird states, 'giving increasing attention to the tourist industry as an option for development the government was conscious that Malaysia did not have any particular destination or attraction that could serve as a major drawing point for tourists. It was felt that Langkawi had the potential to fulfil this role'. One of the most ambitious parts of the overall development planned for the island was a decision to build a $3 billion Langkawi resort to be situated on 3500 acres of land around a beautiful bay known as Tajung Rhu. Bird states 'this area was known for its numerous casuarina trees, its beach front "carpeted with white flowers", its crystal clear lagoon and waterways, and its magnificent limestone hills'.

Although most of the land required for the project was state-owned a large proportion belonged to local villagers. This land was compulsorily reclaimed by the state government. This resulted in the 'splitting up of a long established community, damage to the anchovy industry and loss of livelihood for many villagers'.

The development company was a public limited company known as Promet with its largest shareholder being Singaporean. The federal and state governments would give direct financial support to the project by providing necessary infrastructure for its development, including an international airport, roads and water and electricity supply.

Initial construction work began on the project in 1984. However, by 1985 Promet was put into receivership and the 400 construction workers on the site had either lost their jobs or walked out over pay disputes. Today Tanjung Rhu is an area of devastation. To describe it as a wasteland or moonscape, an area reminiscent of china clay mining, is the closest visual discription of what is left. Jungle and mangrove swamps have been completely cleared, the sand has disappeared from the beach to be used in construction and the water is silty and unclear. The full ecological cost is unknown without money being made available for research and evaluation.

In 1989 a feasibility study for the proposed development of a 600-hectare site for touristic purposes on the island of Java was undertaken. The development was to be financed by a Japanese developer who already owned 400 hectares of the site. The area had approximately 50 families living on it who gained their livelihoods from fish-farming in the lake, banana plantations, rice and rubber cultivation, and a roadside café serving domestic tourists. The proposed scheme from the consultants, to maximise the financial return to the investor recommended, 'Our market research and knowledge of the tourism, golf and hotel markets in Indonesia indicate there is a major leisure development and investment opportunity at the Bogor Lido Site centred around a major golf facility'. The consultants' report also stated that 'Villages are mainly linear settlements along the adjacent roads. The Consultants understand that the proposed development will mean the resettlement of a number of families'.

Consultation with central and local political figures fully supported the development as they interpreted it as a step forward for modernisation and development,

bringing economic benefits at a national, regional, and local level.

As in the case of Langkawi the plan had been established without any consultation with the families already inhabiting the land. Already the host community most affected by the development had been placed in a reactive position of having to negotiate the best possible deal for themselves in response to a development scheme which was formulated without any prior consultation or participation and was designed to maximise financial return to the overseas investors.

The two case studies illustrate environmental, social, and ethical issues associated with tourism development which is heavily reliant upon inward investment and seeks to maximise financial benefit solely to shareholders. Although governments may interpret tourism as a type of commodity bringing economic benefits, on a macro and micro scale, most development schemes are planned to maximise the financial return to the investor. As the study earlier referred to from Wheatcroft demonstrated this can mean heavy economic leakages from the local community. As with any development decision, tourism carries economic and social implications. Also grandiose developmental projects may never be realised with the government being left with potentially costly and irreversible environmental and social problems. Development may also mean a denial or ignorance of local democracy and land-ownership rights.

An alternative approach to tourism development was developed by the World Tourism Organisation (1988) in a report analysing secondary tourism activity in Fiji. The term secondary tourism activity (STA) is defined as 'all activities in which tourists (and recreating Fijians) may engage (and for which facilities may be provided on a commercial basis) which are not "mainstream" resort accommodation or transport operations, either in respect of their style, or location/area of operations'.

The report points out that STAs usually take place in rural regions where there is no or little tourism development. These activities are operated and controlled by Fijians. The report highlights issues of land ownership and the cultural attribute of holding land sacred and that all land is owned. The report asks key social questions:

- Is close interaction between tourists and local residents a desired goal?
- Should the cultural exchange be an equal learning experience on both parts?
- Which are the aspects of Western culture to be discouraged, and which are to be promoted?
- What negative social patterns do locals have that should be discouraged?

- How do we educate both the local residents and the tourists?
- Should that education of the tourists take place inside Fiji or prior to arrival?

The report establishes a critical link between social involvement and economic success and sustainability of the industry into the future. In consultation with local village representatives it was found that most villages did want involvement in tourism as a means of attaining economic benefit and to create understanding and respect between tourists and local residents. From an image point of view it is important to have this cooperation to make sure that host countries are seen to be giving value for money and to make tourism an economically sustainable activity for those communities that depend upon it.

Tourism: a commodity of opportunity for change?

This paper has raised issues concerning how we interpret tourism, whether as primarily an economic, environmental, or social activity, and how this influences our choice of developmental policy. It has also highlighted similarities between tourism and the primary commodity market in terms of what can be hoped to be achieved economically in developing economies through tourism development. The extent of reliance on Western countries to develop this commodity and provide the markets for its consumption will be critical to the sustainability of the industry in the destination. Wheatcroft demonstrates the greater the dependence upon the West for development the greater the leakages and loss of benefits to the host countries. Sinclair illustrates that the greater the reliance upon foreign intermediaries to supply the demand to the destination the greater the economic leakage. Where development is attempted in a 'top-heavy' manner, unfortunately too typical in many countries, there are economic risks of the development never being realised because of the huge financial requirements. The aim of projects to maximise financial returns to outside investors, as opposed to indigenous local communities, will have serious environmental and social consequences for host communities. This may also include a possible denial of democratic and human rights. Local people will be placed into a reactive mode in any planning approach which is centrally directed. Such large schemes are also likely to create an imbalance in the economic profile on a localised scale by removing sustainable livelihoods, such as farming and fishing, through resource removal, and forcing dependence on outside markets from developed countries. The opportunity cost of development may therefore be very high.

To develop tourism in a sustainable form to be enjoyed by future generations means finding an acceptable balance to host communities between economic, social, and environmental impacts. Critically this will involve consultation with local people and participation of local peoples in formulating and operating of any developmental policy.

The commodification of tourism in an internationally operating tourism system, progressively becoming more liberalised and encouraging freer and increased trade to stimulate economic growth, means that opportunities for change through tourism will exist for many countries. The key issue to sustainability and success in economic, environmental, and social terms will be how this change is managed and, critically, what control over development is established by the host community.

References

Bird, Bella (1989) 'Langkawi—from Mahsuri to Mahathir: tourism for whom?', INSAN (the Institute of Social Analysis), Petaling Jaya, Malaysia, pp. 12–19.

Bull, A. (1991) The Economics of Travel and Tourism, Pitman, London, pp. 139–140.

Burns, Peter and Holden, Andrew (in press) Tourism: Towards the 21st Century, Prentice Hall, Hemel Hempstead.

Bywater, Marion (1991) 'Prospects for Mediterranean beach resorts—an Italian case study', EIU Travel and Tourism Analyst, No. 5: 75–89.

Chambers (1981) Twentieth Century Dictionary, Chambers, Edinburgh, p. 262.

Clarke, John and Critcher, Chas (1991) The Devil Makes Work, Macmillan, London, pp. 51–60.

EIU (1989) 'International tourism forecasts to 1999', Special Report No. 1142, Economist Intelligence Unit, London, p. 13.

ETB (1991) Tourism and the Environment: Maintaining the Balance, English Tourist Board, London, p. 10.

Fukuyama, Francis (1992) The End of History and The Last Man, Penguin, Harmondsworth, pp. 39–51.

The Guardian (1991) 'When the world is your playground'.

Gunn, Claire (1988) Tourism Planning, Taylor & Francis, New York, p. 3.

Holloway, Christopher (1985) The Business of Tourism, Macdonald & Evans, Plymouth, p. 22.

Krippendorf, Jost (1990) The Holiday Makers, Heinemann, Oxford, pp. 22–29.

Mills, R. and Morrison, A. (1992) The Tourism System: an Introductory Text, Prentice Hall, Englewood Cliffs, NJ, pp. 2–3.

Morgan, Michael (1991) 'Dressing up to survive: marketing Majorca anew', Tourism Management, March, pp. 15–20.

Sinclair, T. (1991) The Tourism Industry: an International Analysis, CAB International, Wallingford, p. 192.

Timberlake, Lloyd and Thomas, Laura (1990) When the Bough Breaks, Earthscan Publications, London, pp. 33–36.

Wheatcroft, S. (1993) 'Profits drain away', The Times, 25 November, p. 26.

World Tourism Organisation (1988) Secondary Tourism Activity Development in Fiji, WTO, pp. 81–88.

89 Tourism development and socio-cultural change in rural China

F. M. S. LI AND H. B. SOFIELD

Introduction

Tourism development in China has not been excluded from the tensions created by the pace of economic and social change in that country in recent years. Increasingly, the impact of tourism on host communities requires greater understanding if negative impacts are to be minimized and positive impacts maximized (Britton and Clarke, 1987). Where conservative rural communities are confronted with tourism development, the processes of acculturation, westernization, modernization and sometimes urbanization may be accelerated. Conflicts often arise, some of which may be functional and some dysfunctional (Hoogveldt, 1986). In this context the socio-cultural impacts of tourism are among the least understood phenomena of the tourism industry. This paper examines the impact of tourism on two rural communities in Guangdong Province, southern China, where conflict has arisen over a tourism development centred on the limestone caves of Ling Xiao on the boundary of Yang Chun and Wan Fau counties.

250 kilometres southwest from the capital, Guangzhou (Canton), is a 100-square-kilometre area of karst (isolated limestone) hills where some of China's largest and most spectacular caves are found (Figure 89.1). The surrounding area of calcareous soils is agriculturally poor and sugar cane is the main crop grown by the village communities. Paddy (rice) fields are confined to narrow river valley bottoms where the soil is a little more fertile and not quite so porous. Farming incomes at 700 yuan per annum are among the lowest in Guangdong.

Ling Xiao consists of a huge cave 90 metres high with thousands of geological formations and a river running through the mountain which is accessible from both the north and south sides of the karst (Figure 89.2). Yu Xi (Figure 89.3) consists of the Jade River which takes the tourist through three different karst caverns over a two-kilometre stretch. The boundary of Yang Chun and Wan Fau Counties runs along the bank of the Jade River and over the top of Ling Xiao cave mountain.

Tourism to Ling Xiao began in 1974 in a very small way with one or two thousand visitors a year. After 1978, as tourism began to expand, Yu Leung Hang village in

Yang Chun County and Lam Po village in Wan Fau County (both communities are situated on opposite sides at the base of the Ling Xiao caves mountain) began to organize tours in competition with each other, with both sides claiming territorial rights to do so. Conflict ensued. The Guangdong Province government mediated in the dispute and in 1984 Yang Chun County was given responsibility for developing Ling Xiao and Yu Xi sites under an agreement termed 'The Four Centralizations' (centralized control, planning, development and management). The decision was based on the fact that the county boundaries placed the Yu Xi caves and the southern entrance to Ling Xiao in Yang Chun, and on the fact that Wan Fau was relatively rich because of extensive marble deposits (the county is called 'the Italy of the East') while Yan Chun had only an impoverished agricultural economic base.

Yang Chun County established the 'Ling Xiao Caves Scenic Region Management Company' (LXMC) in the vicinity of Yu Leung Hang village, and in 1984 invested more than 6.5 million yuan (US$1.6 million) in infrastructure (restaurant, powerhouse for internal lighting, recreation area, stairs and paths inside the cave, boats for river trips through the caves, facilities for tour coaches, management office, bridges over the river, a landing, public toilets, etc.) and visitation grew dramatically. In 1992 and 1993 more than two million tourists visited the sites, making them the third most popular destination in Guangdong Province. Total revenue of more than 4 million yuan (US$0.5 million) each year was generated for the company. An estimated 1.5 million additional yuan (US$150 000) per year was earned by the local Yang Chun peasants with sideline industries—souvenir stalls, pony rides, refreshment booths, and calligraphy (interview with the company manager).

The people of Ling Xiao and Yang Chun County officials used the 1984 decision to block entry from the Wan Fau side by sealing the three northern cave entrances with reinforced concrete. However, the Lam Po people still gained entry via the river. But the river being narrow, the boats were 'always crashing into each other and causing arguments' (*Sing Tao Daily*, 9/2/93). Competition for the economic benefits of tourism continued when Wan Fau County built a road from Lam Po village to

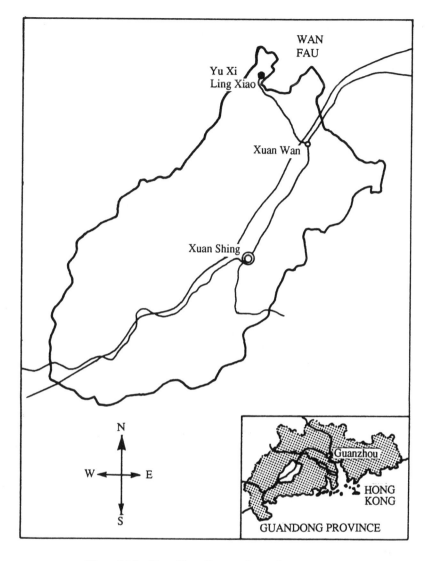

Figure 89.1 *Yang Chun County, Guangdong Province*

the northern bank of the Jade River in 1991/1992 and began to organize rival boat trips through the three caves.

After a series of incidents between both sides in which guides were beaten, tourists harassed and boats destroyed, the Provincial Government issued an edict in October 1992 which reiterated that management of the sites rested with Yang Chun and that both counties were to:

> counsel the locals (clans) not to cause trouble, nor to destroy any scenic resources or tourist facilities in order to protect the stability of the scenic region and the normal operations of tourist activities. (Guangdong Province, 1992)

The LXMC immediately moved to shut Wan Fau County and Lam Po village out of the operation altogether by blocking the Wan Fau river entrance and entry to the Jade River caves with boulders. Tension between the two communities rose and, after several confrontations, violence erupted on 26 January 1993, the fourth day of the Chinese Lunar New Year, when several hundred Lam Po villagers invaded the Ling Xiao cave and fired shots at an estimated 1000 tourists. Over the next three days the villagers systematically blew up the facilities with more than 700 gunpowder bombs, before a contingent

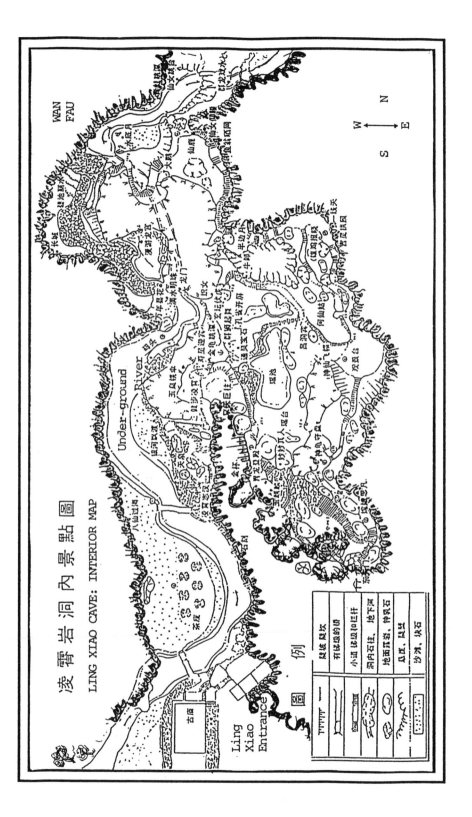

Figure 89.2 *Ling Xiao cave, Yang Chun County*

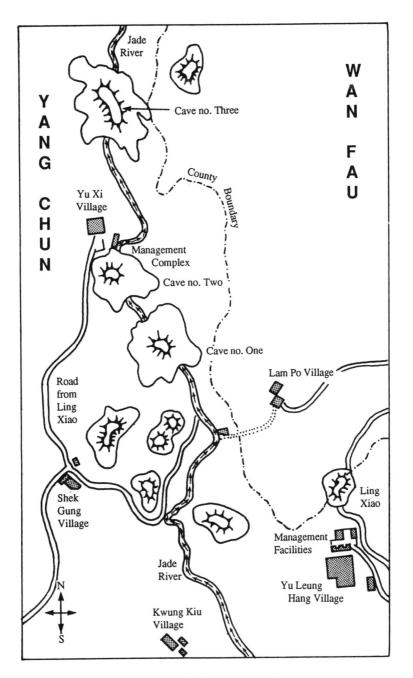

Figure 89.3 *Yu Xi and Ling Xiao*

of Yang Chun police reasserted control. The villagers also seized a boatload of 50 tourists and their Yang Chun guide on the Jade River and held them hostage for several hours. Total direct damage was estimated at more than 4.4 million yuan (US$0.6 million) (*Sing Pao Daily News*, 8/2/93; *Sing Tao Daily*, 8/2/93, 9/2/93, 10/2/93; *Wah Kiu Yat Po*, 9/2/93; *Ming Pao*, 9/2/93, 11/2/93; *South China Morning Post* (*SCMP*), 9/2/93). All tourism ceased.

The provincial government subsequently established an Investigation Working Party with representatives of both communities and counties' officials in an attempt to determine the cause of the attack, apprehend those guilty of breaking the law, settle the conflict once and for all and consider the question of claims for compensation. Evidence indicated that the situation had its origins in a clan boundary dispute reaching back several decades, but that until the advent of tourism and the relatively huge amounts of wealth it was generating, the resources of the caves were not directly coveted.

Chinese versus Western interpretations of issues

The problem of defining the issues involved in the Ling Xiao situation confronts the Western observer with Chinese and socialist perspectives and values. 'Facts' as defined by Chinese socialist bureaucrats may not be 'facts' as defined by Western scholars. Indeed, Western scholars have frequently been accused of 'intellectual imperialism' in their use of Western values and standards to analyse issues that are both Chinese and communist. As Ogden (1992:2) wrote:

> Which values are used is a subjective determination . . . and profoundly affects the conclusions reached. The real question is, do students of China really understand the Chinese situation better when Western . . . values, concepts and models with which they are familiar form the analytical framework? Or does their use simply distort understanding, since different values, concepts, ideals and objectives motivate the Chinese communists?

Pye (1992) considers that in practice the application of contemporary Western social science theories (to tourism developments) in China can be 'a tricky business'. This is not because of the 'grossly over-exaggerated dangers of ethnocentrism and intellectual imperialism', but because the concepts and theories of the Western disciplines were developed out of assumptions about systems which operate quite differently from their Chinese counterparts (Pye, 1992:1162). According to Pye, the very notion of 'system', that is, of a set of interacting variables with a close fit between cause and effect, has to be modified in the case of China where:

> social and economic changes may have only marginal consequences for politics and even such dramatic developments in parts of the economy as those in southern China may be limited and the effects on the national government hard to predict. (Pye, 1992:1162)

Scholars sympathetic to the goals of the Chinese communist revolution, in rejecting Western evaluative standards have by inclination been ready to accept the Chinese leadership's definition of the situation. According to this viewpoint, 'what really matters are Chinese and communist values, ideals, models and objectives and whether or not they have been realized' (Ogden, 1992:2). Harding (1982) has attributed much of the United States's uncritical academic writings of the 1970s about China to a too-willing embrace of Chinese values and the suspension of Western models, standards and perspectives, with consequent loss of objective appraisal. This he argued was because, in the past, American academics had been influenced by the prejudices of the Cold War and had largely ignored China's achievements while exaggerating its shortcomings. Their writings had more to do with American politics than with Chinese reality and Chinese politics. As Rose (1990:55) noted: 'What we do not command at this point is a mode of discourse that is culture- or value-free. When we write about other cultures that is itself a political act'. Uberoi (1978:15) commented that: 'By way of permanent solution, I think that there is nothing for it but to lift our false limitation and admit all theories, native and Western, new and old, classical and vernacular, to fresh scrutiny and independent judgement, for or against, in the light of the relevant facts'. This has begun to happen in contemporary Western ethnography/ethnology/anthropology/sociology, where Western ideas are used to elicit but not to dominate the ideas and practices of the peoples Westerners study.

This paper postulates that a cross-cultural and multidisciplinary approach is necessary for building up a comprehensive understanding of the dynamics of tourism development in China because the complexities of Chinese society and culture do not always lend themselves easily to Western concepts. The social sciences, as practised in both China and the West, are reviewed to assess their applicability to the conflict at Ling Xiao since: 'The impacts of tourism are the most fundamental and of particular concern to anthropologists and other social scientists because established (anthropological) scholarship stresses the validity of maintaining group cohesion as a bulwark against disruption with its accompanying internal conflict and stress' (Smith, 1977:6). The paper draws upon a range of social science disciplines as it attempts to take account of Chinese approaches and definitions to the issues as well as utilizing paradigms from Western research.

Tourism development in China

The CCP regimes in China from 1949 until 1978/79 were ambivalent about tourism as an appropriate form of economic activity. Both domestic and international tourism were almost non-existent (Chow, 1988; Hudman and Hawkins, 1989). Entry was strictly controlled, as indicated by the euphemism: 'the Bamboo Curtain'. Tourism activity was held tightly in the hands of the state machinery and reflected the pattern common to other communist states. That is, what little foreign tourism that existed was sanctioned on the grounds that the successes of communism could be paraded before a selected international audience. From 1954 to 1978 the China International Travel Service (set up to arrange visits by 'foreign friends') played host to only 125 000 overseas visitors (Richter, 1989). Access was restricted to 'showcase' attractions and destinations and contact between tourists and locals was strictly regulated. Guides accompanied foreign tourists at all times and were able to 'quickly and proficiently report the great strides society and the economy had made under socialism' (Hudman and Hawkins, 1989:178). However, Hong Kong Chinese, although required to register with the authorities prior to 1978, were able when visiting friends and relatives to interact freely with the local people (Chow, 1988). Segregation in hotels into the categories of foreign tourists, overseas Chinese, Hong Kong and Macau Chinese, and locals, was rigidly enforced.

Mao died in 1976 and in 1978 the Bamboo Curtain was pulled aside as Deng Xiaoping introduced his 'open door' policies, also referred to as 'socialism with a Chinese face'. Deng overturned three decades of repression of intellectuals, acknowledging that the creative energies of educated specialists were essential for implementing the 'Four Modernizations' (Meissner, 1986). This is a four-pronged effort to marshal national resources to modernize agriculture, industry, the defence forces, and science and technology. To the extent that some market forces of supply and demand had to be accepted to accomplish modernization, socialist values were compromised in a limited way (the supply and price of some 800 basic commodities remained under government control, for example).

Intellectuals who had been banished to the countryside for manual labour were rehabilitated, and universities were encouraged to reopen disciplines, faculties and research institutes. The social sciences, which had been banned since the 1950s after Mao's 'Let one hundred flowers bloom' (1952) campaign and his 'Anti-Rightist Campaign' (1957) re-emerged. The 'twenty bad years' (as they are called in China) of these two campaigns, the 'Great Leap Forward' (1958–1962) and the 'Cultural Revolution' (1966–1969) whose repression of intellectuals had continued until 1976, were quietly put aside.

As part of Deng's modernization programme the Chinese door opened to world tourism. The first national conference on tourism was held in 1978 to formulate guidelines and organizational structures for its development (Gao and Zhang, 1982). Politically, tourism as an acceptable industry was justified in socialist ideology on the grounds that it would advance economic reforms and the policy of opening to the outside world, it would further friendship and mutual understanding between the Chinese proletariat and other peoples of the world, and it would contribute to world peace. In three different speeches in 1979 Deng Xiaoping stated the need for swift growth and development of tourism (National Tourism Administration of the PRC, 1992; He, 1992).

The decision to embrace the industry was not reached lightly because international tourism was recognized by the Chinese government as a major vehicle for modernization which inevitably promoted the penetration of Western values and Western culture. According to Ogden (1991:6):

> The Chinese leadership developed a far greater tolerance for market forces of supply and demand which challenge socialism, than for Western values that might pollute Chinese culture: the government was more willing to sacrifice socialist values than Chinese cultural values in the pursuit of economic development.

In this context, tourism, a valuable new industry and a potentially large generator of foreign exchange earnings, was to be developed around Chinese culture and tradition. Funds were provided for the restoration of cultural sites such as the Ming Tombs, the Xi'an 'terra cotta army' of warriors and horses, and repairs to the Great Wall. Access to a wide range of Chinese cultural heritage sites was approved. In the early 1970s fewer than 12 cities were open to foreign tourists; by 1979, 60 destinations were open; by 1984 there were 200; and by 1987, 469 cities and destinations were approved for foreign visitation (Richter, 1989).

Nunez's (1977:209) observation about the development of tourism in third world countries in general is pertinent in the case of China:

> the situation indicates an interesting irony: in order to survive and perpetuate their cultural identity and integrity, emerging new nations . . . caught up in a competitive world economy encourage and invite the most successful agents of change (short of political or military agents) active in the contemporary world.

Recognizing the danger, and in order to mitigate such impacts, the Chinese leadership determined to keep planning and development firmly under its control. Tourism authorities were established at the national, provincial and county levels, with responsibility for the development of attractions and associated infrastructure. The national government initially assumed responsibility for international promotion and marketing and the provision of travel agency services, although in the last few years provinces and counties have been permitted to engage in their own marketing and set up their own travel agencies.

The growth of China's tourism industry following the 'open door' policy was nothing short of spectacular. In 1978, a total of 1.8092 million tourists visited China. In 1979 that figure expanded to 4.2039 million, an increase of 232%. By 1985 the figure had grown to 17.833 million, an increase of 986%. By 1988, prior to the June 1989 Tiananmen Square incident, the total had swelled to 31.695 million. Tourism receipts grew from US$263 million in 1978 to more than US$2.25 billion by 1988 (source: National Tourism Administration (NTA) of the PRC: *The Yearbook of China Tourism Statistics 1989*).

In 1989, however, there was a drastic decline in response to the bloody suppression of the Tiananmen Square democracy demonstrations. Only 24.5 million foreign visitors were recorded and international tourism receipts fell to US$1.86 billion as general travel, package tours and cruise-line schedules were cancelled worldwide. In 1990 the figure was 27.462 million. By 1991, however, the figure had risen to 33.345 million and tourism receipts to US$2.845 billion. In 1992, tourist arrivals reached 38.115 million and international tourism receipts totalled US$3.947 billion, almost 40% more than the previous year (source: National Tourism Administration of the PRC: *The Yearbook of China Tourism Statistics 1990, 1991, 1992, 1993*).

The fluctuations in tourism visitation mirrored the political changes in China. In the early 1990s in the aftermath of the Tiananmen Square demonstrations, and in the wake of the collapse of communist regimes throughout Eastern Europe and the USSR, China's more conservative leaders gained control of the helm. The legitimacy of communist regimes worldwide had been undermined. Ideology in China gained ascendancy over pragmatism and the 'open door' policy, because it provided a crutch to support the principle of party 'infallibility' based on socialist 'purity'—and that could be used to justify the right of the CCP to govern.

However, in response to the PRC's violent suppression of student protesters, foreign economic sanctions were imposed. The drying up of foreign investment, the halting of all World Bank loans (except those for humanitarian purposes), and the 25% reduction in tourism receipts exacerbated economic problems. The period of rigidity, austerity and recentralization tried by the conservatives contributed to bringing China's economic growth to a virtual halt.

By the end of 1991 their policies were discredited and Deng was able to re-establish his leadership in 1992 on the catch-cry of the need to develop China and speed up the pace of economic reform. It should be stressed that Deng's apparent embrace of capitalist market forces was not acceptance of capitalism *per se* but in fact a close and logical 'fit' with Lenin's philosophy of political evolution. This stated that capitalism had to precede socialism because only the wealth created by capitalist market forces could build the base needed for socialism. Deng postulated that China had moved too quickly in the 1950s to dismantle an embryonic capitalism which was only just beginning to challenge feudalism—that in effect China had tried to leapfrog over the capitalist stage of evolutionary development. The result had been to delay the eventual succession to socialism. However, feudalism was still rampant and responsible for China's 'backwardness'. It had to be countered by capitalist techniques and structures as an intermediary step necessary to achieve the ultimate goal of socialism at some undefined time in the future (Meissner, 1986).

Socialism as redefined by 'Deng's Thought' permitted China to develop by whatever means would be successful: 'It does not matter if the cat is black or white. If it can catch rats it is a good cat' (Deng Xiaoping, 1987). Market values were reasserted, the importance of tourism was reiterated and tourism numbers expanded.

Tourism development in rural China

The development of a major tourist attraction at Ling Xiao only became possible after 1978 in the context of the emergence of the policies of 'socialism with Chinese characteristics' which gradually moved China away from a centrally administered economy to a more decentralized, market-oriented system. Over the next 15 years some 20 million village-run and town-run enterprises were created which led to the 'rural urbanization' of much of China. Hundreds of tourism sites were developed by local interests. The Ling Xiao Nyam Scenic Region Management Company is one of them.

There were two specific policies which permitted this. The first was 'the responsibility system of contracted production' authorized by the Third Plenum of the Eleventh Central Committee in 1978. The second was the decision by the government in 1984 to allow peasants to settle in cities and towns and to engage in business and service industries on condition that they provided for their own grain provisions.

The first policy in effect replaced the village brigades and production teams by devolving responsibility for production down to individual households. This was accomplished by 'de-collectivization'—returning traditionally owned lands to the peasants who were 'assigned' the land for up to thirty years. In this way Chinese socialism was maintained by the continued legal ownership of the land remaining with the state; thus, it was argued, a new landed upper class was not being created. But households were awarded freedom of usury rights and the right to pass on land to descendants, as if ownership resided with the peasants. Wealth that might accumulate under this system was acceptable, provided the rich did not trample on the socialist principle of non-exploitation of labour (Xu and Ye, 1988–89).

Since then households in the countryside have found that from the limited farmland they have been contracted to work 'a massive workforce can be released for other lucrative propositions' (Fei, 1989). In a study of four municipalities covering twenty counties, Fei (1989) found that one-third of the workforce in the countryside would belong to the category of surplus labour if calculated on the basis of one farmhand taking care of four *mu* (about one hectare) of land. Chen Ximen, Director of the Department of Rural Development (State Council Development Research Centre), said at a conference on rural reform in December 1993 that of China's total rural workforce of 440 million, 110 million worked in factories and service industries. The remaining 330 million worked on the country's 100 million hectares of farmland but had work for only one-third of the year (*South China Morning Post*, 4 December 1993).

> This surplus rural labour, who used to be submerged by the practice of 'everyone dipping into the common pot', becomes a new workforce in the countryside once they are given the opportunity to work in enterprises they set up on their own. In consequence, village and town-run enterprises have blossomed everywhere in the countryside. It can be said that village and town industry is the offspring of the combination of surplus labour and new means of production and objects of labour. (Fei, 1989:46)

The second policy was fundamental to the 'rural urbanization' of China, which freed more resources for non-agricultural pursuits. For example, in the four counties in Guangdong surveyed by Xu and Zhang (1988–89) there were only nine towns in the four counties in 1978. By the end of 1984, however, there were 64. In 1978, town populations totalled 275 303 (10.27% of the total population of the four counties); by 1984, town populations had risen to 434 508—15.78% of the total population of the counties.

In 1992, the State Bureau of Statistics recorded that township enterprises registered a gross output of 1.76 trillion yuan, accounting for 31.6% of the country's total non-agricultural output. In 1993, the gross output of township enterprises was estimated to total 2.7 trillion yuan. 'Having the peasants leave the land without leaving the village' to participate in village-run and town-run enterprises has been acknowledged as a guiding principle of national strategic importance (Fei, 1989).

Conflict at Ling Xiao

If we have accounted for the development of a thriving tourist enterprise such as Ling Xiao in the depths of rural China, how do we account for the violence that erupted there in January 1993? The answers to this question are complex and require further investigation. This paper reflects initial fieldwork and attempts to examine the situation from two different perspectives—the first using a Chinese sociological construction to analyse the dynamics of Ling Xiao; and the second using more orthodox Western social anthropological paradigms.

A Chinese paradigm

The re-emergence of the social sciences in China in 1978 as legitimate disciplines following their banning in the 1950s by Mao saw them develop four main features over the next decade (Ming Yan, 1989):

1. *They were 'China-centred'.* This meant that Chinese sociology and the other social sciences had as their major concern the study of Chinese society and they borrowed useful elements from sociological enquiry in other countries for this purpose. They had undergone a 'sinification process', that is, after 1979 Chinese social sciences emphasized their own distinct style. The Chinese-centred nature of Chinese social sciences mirrored 40 years of largely independent and isolated development in China.
2. *Pragmatism.* In this context, it was not necessary to establish academic hypotheses or any theoretical framework. The policy orientation of pragmatism was 'an extremely distinctive trait' in contemporary Chinese social sciences. The government relied increasingly on social scientists to conduct policy-oriented surveys and research. In this context see point (3) below.
3. *Collectivism.* Sociology in China was 'a combined, collective activity', often involving teams of more than twenty or thirty people. Social workers and party officials would be teamed together to carry out surveys and the writing of the report would be a collective effort by the team and academics. For example, in 1989 the Chinese Academy of Social Sciences was appointed by the central government to carry out a

project to compare the social development of the different administrative units of China, for which it used a team of more than fifty workers and academics ('Project on Social Development and Social Indicators. Social Development of the Provinces, Municipalities and Autonomous Regions of China: Comparison and Assessment. 1989').

4. *Openness*. After their re-establishment (in 1979) the Chinese social sciences were compatible and cooperative with those of other countries.

Despite the openness referred to by Ming Yan, the social sciences in China remain in a relative strait-jacket where intellectual creativity, conceptualization, thinking and analysis (except Marxist analysis) are given little attention. Permissible subject matter is still limited and pedagogically rote learning rather than the encouragement of enquiry remains the central strategy for learning. Independent research and study is not encouraged and most research continues to be assigned by government ministries and the CCP, with researchers assuming the role of servants of government and party policy. Communication with the international community of scholars remains restricted. And because the foreign language of most senior academics is Russian, the former influence of Soviet academic approaches and structure of the 1950s remains strong (Guldin, 1992).

The result is a truncated approach to social sciences enquiry, where 'Chinese-ness' and pragmatism reign, which finds little echo in the Western academic environment. It is important nevertheless for showing the way in which Chinese scholars themselves analyse and interpret events, and for providing additional data to be reviewed. The construction of a leading Chinese sociologist, Wu Wenjun (1989), will be utilized to dissect Ling Xiao from a Chinese perspective.

Wu developed an analytical framework to examine social problems in rural China. He identified 'nine trends, seven evils, six scourges and five diseases' based on 'six sources of all ills'. His model may be likened to 'cheung nga kau', or the Chinese ivory artefact in which a series of concentric ivory balls are carved one inside the other (the trends encircling the evils which in turn encircle the scourges which themselves encircle the diseases), resting on a carved wooden base (the sources). His analytical framework, while unorthodox to the Western mind, exemplifies the qualities of 'Chinese centred-ness' and pragmatism identified by Ming Yan, with the sociologist dedicated to serving government policies.

In the context of the violence at the Ling Xiao caves complex, a selected few of the concepts of Wu are set out to indicate the tenor of a Chinese analysis of the situation.

Trends

Trend no. 4. 'Feeling it is right to rebel'
. . . the peasants often raise excessive demands. When they cannot get what they want, they stage sit-down demonstrations, tear down the walls of government offices or factories, loot the factory products, or seize food from the factory mess halls. (Wu, 1989:73–74)

In the case of Ling Xiao, to air their grievances the peasants from Lam Po resorted to violence to achieve their ends and blew up tourist facilities.

Evils

Evil no. 5. Peasants' ethics.
If they see others getting rich they become jealous. They destroy farms, loot orchards, destroy factories and enterprises, they make things difficult for these enterprises or try to extort money from them. (Wu, 1989:77)

In the context of Ling Xiao, the Lam Po clan carried out systematic harassment of Ling Xiao guides and villagers. They created problems inside the caves on the rivers, staircases and paths. They constantly created a management headache for Yang Chun because they could not be controlled.

Evil no. 6. Officials' ethics and abuse of power.
Many officials abuse their power for personal gain or for friends and family.

In the case of Ling Xiao, the Wan Fau police were accused by the Manager of the Ling Xiao complex of providing support for the attempted takeover, especially with the supply of guns and ammunition, and Wan Fau officials were accused of supporting the Lam Po villagers in their violence. He cited the funding by the Wan Fau County of the road from Lam Po village to the Jade River in 1991/92 and the fact that the Lam Po villagers had access to tonnes of gunpowder and to guns, which could only be issued under licence by the police. The Wan Fau police chief denied the accusations, vilified his counterparts in Yang Chun County for beating up Lam Po villagers on false charges of 'spying' and laid the blame for the destruction on the provocative actions of Ling Xiao villagers (*Sing Tao Daily*, 10/2/93).

Scourges

Scourge no. 5. Fights.
All around the country there are thugs who are eager for a fight and ready to use arms, to take advantage of a situation of tension and escalate it, a hazard for some enterprises. Thugs can be manipulated by those wanting to hide their own involvement, hiring them to do their dirty work. (Wu, 1989:80)

Counter-claims by both sides mention 'bullies' descending upon the villagers. For example, the Wan Fau police chief claimed that on 20 January 1993 Ling Xiao sent 'ten bully men to catch people and chickens from Lam Po and threatened the wife of the Secretary of the Lam Po Management that they would kill her husband' (*Sing Tao Daily*, 10/2/93). The Manager of the Ling Xiao complex claimed that Lam Po bullies had blocked the path on top of the mountain, cursed Yang Chun's village people and thrown gunpowder bombs down on them (*Ming Pao*, 11/2/93).

Diseases

Disease no. 2. Jealousy.
In rural areas, destruction frequently occurs—extortion, burning-down of ten-thousand *yuan* households, felling trees and orchards. It is even more common in government circles and must be eliminated. (Wu, 1989:81)

In the case of Ling Xiao, the jealousy of Wan Fau for the wealth earned from tourism for Yang Chun drove the villagers of Lam Po and County officials to try and destroy the tourist facilities.

The prescriptive tone of Wu's model with its exhortations to government to take action continues with his identification of six 'Sources of ills' which needed to be counteracted. His first two take outmoded adherence to communism to task:

1. The ossified old system of communism (created) paper-work, inefficient bureaucracy, endless meetings, unjustified evening-out of qualified/unqualified, lazy/hard working, rich/poor citizens, and promoted centralized decision-making which was irrelevant or inappropriate to local conditions. (Wu, 1989:83)

2. Backward productivity. Communism sent things backwards with uproductive meetings and too many political cadres doing political things instead of producing things. (Wu, 1989:83)

Government at all levels had a responsibility to ensure that these attitudes and practices were abolished.

Wu's next two sources decried the backward serf mentality and the incompetence of the general population. (His comments on both appear to carry elements of the reaction of an academic wronged during the Cultural Revolution):

3. The serf mentality is extremely destructive. Isn't it the jealousy and the mentality of evening-out the rich and the poor at work when destruction occurs? Examples are

everywhere of serfs using the excuse: Capitalism has staged a come-back. Tear it down! Thus they defeat development and progress. (Wu, 1989:84).

4. Over-all, the population is incompetent. Many people have inadequate training. Laymen flood all walks of life, especially in the leadership circles. The ignorance of cadres who have neither learning nor skill and lack the ability to do creative work, hold back progress. (Wu, 1989:85)

Wu's fifth 'Source' identifies the influence of the 'feudal ideology of power'. This is held to be:

autocratic, corrupt, and used to obstruct progress and suppress skilled individuals and developments. Out-dated clan values, akin to the feudal days, channel a village's resources into the hands of an elite few regardless of merit. Bribery rears its head: it sometimes appears to be the only way to get the attention of the clan elders and to gain their approval to get a job done. So corruption goes round in an endless circle, feeding on itself. (Wu, 1989:85)

Wu's final 'Source', 'Diseases from abroad', would be termed 'the demonstration effect' in Western sociology:

Decadent ideas can be introduced from abroad, undermining Chinese values and attitudes. The younger generation is especially vulnerable and leaders must be on guard to root out such evils and immoral practices. (Wu, 1989:85)

In examining Wu's concepts of conflict as a Chinese perspective on Ling Xiao, it must be borne in mind that a danger lies in accepting Chinese statements about identifying and resolving problems because of an insistence upon 'correct presentation' before 'correct fact'. As Lu Xun, China's foremost literary figure of the 1930s succinctly stated: the Chinese take the statement as fact, as if stating that something is true really makes it true. This itself then creates a 'new reality'.

This phenomenon is in fact central to one strand of modern psychology which holds that 'matters treated as problems often become problems'. In this sense, Chinese definitions of problems must be taken seriously. A standard tactic by the Chinese leadership has been to use government control of the media to ensure that the entire country has received the same message about what the issues are. At a later date policies are pronounced which are intended to rectify whatever the leadership has said the problems are. As a number of political commentators have stated, e.g. Burns and Rosen (1986), Cohen (1992), Ogden (1991), Oi (1989), Pye (1981), and Terrill (1980), in China more than in most countries, saying it makes it so, or at least policies respond *as if* it is so. If the leadership states that 'bourgeois attitudes' are an issue that must be dealt with, policies will be formulated to eradicate those attitudes, the bulk of the people will start searching for bourgeois attitudes in others, conceal their own, and generally become concerned . . . over who and what is 'bourgeois'. (Ogden, 1991:3)

If those dealing with the Ling Xiao conflict identify 'bullies' as the cause of the destruction, then policies will be formulated to root out bullies; and the real issues (boundary disputes? clan rivalry?) may go unresolved. It is essential, therefore, that a cross-cultural approach be taken to the analysis of a given situation in China if the complexities of that situation are to be understood.

Western analysis

Distinctions in the Western world between the social sciences as applied to tourism analysis have begun to blur (Dann and Cohen, 1991; Graburn and Jafari, 1991; Nash and Smith, 1991). Anthropology, for example, has traditionally been seen as a 'four fields' discipline encompassing cultural anthropology (also called ethnology/ethnography), archaeology, physical anthropology and linguistics, and many Western scholars move in and out of these four fields freely. Increasingly, more radical thought in Western academic circles challenges the 'ownership' of bodies of knowledge claimed by different disciplines and expounds the need to adopt a multidisciplinary and 'polyphonic' or 'multi-genre' construction if there is to be a future for the social sciences. Writers such as Rose (1990:59), claim that the past decade has witnessed:

the dissolution of boundaries between literature, sociology, anthropology, critical theory, philosophy, cinematography, computer science, and so on: and an ultimate transparency and probable liquidation of that series of sacred centers . . . that now constitute, somewhat precariously, each of the academic disciplines in the human sciences.

This is in marked contrast to the social sciences in China where the Soviet model of the 1950s resulted in very narrow definitions of disciplinary boundaries and very clear distinctions being drawn between the different disciplines. For example, anthropology was (and still is) defined as 'physical anthropology', involved in the study of biological types; and ethnology was (and still is) restricted to the study of China's ethnic minorities with the pragmatic task of 'uplifting them' (Guldin, 1992).

In examining the dynamics of events at Ling Xiao, Western social sciences offer a richness of analytical models. These might include attribution theory (Pearce, 1989), social exchange theory (Ap, 1992), conflict theory

(Kraus, 1981), the concept of 'new-want formation' (Hoogveldt, 1986), dependency theory (Priester, 1989), compensation theory (Bystrzanowski, 1989), the concept of empowerment (Emerson, 1971), deviance and social control (Wilson et al., 1977), modernization theory (Levy, 1966), development theory (Mabogunje, 1980) and others, which would all appear able to make a contribution to understanding the events. Constraints of space prevent a synthesis of those being utilized in this paper. Instead, the Weberian concept of patrimonial authority will form a central but not the only analytical tool for taking a Western academic-oriented view of Ling Xiao. In this context it is postulated that the violence at Ling Xiao can be related in part to the re-emergence of clan structures in rural China since 1978.

When the Communist Party came to power in 1949 it set about establishing a monolithic centralized power structure. It reached out into a majority of villages throughout the country with its grass roots councils of party members wielding authority and with responsibility to implement policies and ensure conformity with central dictates. In part this system was designed to eradicate the last vestiges of the feudal, patriarchal clan structures which had traditionally dominated the Chinese countryside for several thousand years. In many villages, clan elders were removed from power and the communist system of local government set up.

Despite three decades of communism accompanied by massive rural upheaval, including the imposition of the death penalty for thousands of 'capitalist' clan leaders and their families purged during the revolution, the clan system never disappeared completely. Utilizing the Weberian concept of patrimonial rulership, McCormick (1990) has advanced a telling three-point argument for the enduring nature of clan structure in China:

1. it fits long-standing Chinese cultural traditions; many thousands of villages are 'single name' clan-based virilocal communities;
2. it is, with its accompanying forms of corruption (i.e. institutionalized payments to officialdom), 'a rational response' to China's 'rigid and inefficient bureaucracy'; and
3. patrimonial relationships are an integral part of elite relations in China's Leninist system, where 'connections' are vital for getting anything done.

Judd (1992:352) has described this 'patrilineal, effectively androcentric social organization' as 'a living element in contemporary rural China'. Cohen (1990) describes the role of patriliny in rural China as 'a fixed genealogical orientation which provides one set of referents for the assertion and negotiation' of community wants and needs. It constitutes what Pye (1992) has called 'Confucian Leninism' and what Walder (1986) has termed 'organized dependency'.

With Deng's rural reform programme of 1978, old ideas began to make a comeback. The contract responsibility system returned the land to individual households and villages, with the inevitable result that the control structure established by the party and government began to weaken. 'De-collectivization' during the 1980s meant the demise of the former brigades and teams whose leaders were the linchpins in state control and authority as they imposed community quotas and implemented state policies (Oi, 1989).

'Ownership' of the land empowered the clans as it had empowered their ancestors (and subsequently the Communist Party). The traditional system of clan structure, which had been based on land ownership, gradually began to re-emerge and descendants of clan elders began to re-assert clan values and authority. Judd (1992) noted that to the extent to which informal, lineage-based organizations (clan structures and 'old' forms of authority) were efficacious in the rural political economy in competition with official structures, they were a major concern for the government. This was highlighted in a government report (Integrated Task Force of the Development Research Institute, 1987) which identified 'spontaneous organizations' based on ties of kinship, neighbourhoods and 'networking connections' as common in the countryside following de-collectivization and as 'problematic' for the bureaucracy.

According to a survey carried out in Hunan Province in 1989 by the official communist newspaper *Legal Daily* (8/8/89), by the late 1980s the reappearance of clan structures had become 'endemic'. Nearly one-third of all the villages in the north of the province had set up clan organizations, with that figure rising to nearly 80% in some counties. 'There appears to be a striking phenomenon of replacing administrative power with clan power and replacing laws and regulations with clan rules', the newspaper reported.

With the re-emergence of clan power came the subsequent revival of age-old clan disputes. The *Legal Daily* noted that there had been more than 600 clan battles between 1988 and 1989, accounting for 60% of all rural disputes in Yueyang. More than 500 people had been killed or injured. The disputes between rival clans and between clans and government officials often turned into 'pitched battles with peasants using explosives and home-made weapons to settle old scores'. The *SCMP* (30/10/93) quoting Chinese official sources reported that: 'Although the official media has tended to play down the clan problem, there is considerable evidence that clan

organizations and clan disputes are still very much a part of rural China'. It reported a pitched battle in September 1993 between 5000 peasants from two rival clans in southern Hunan which left five dead and 12 seriously wounded before it was finally broken up by a battalion of 200 paramilitary police.

In Ling Xiao, much of the available evidence points to a clan dispute over territorial claims which go back many years. 'Wan Fau' means 'floating cloud' and historically, Lam Po village and the County have claimed and occupied land 'wherever the cloud rises to' despite boundary demarcations to the contrary, according to Ling Xiao residents who dispute those claims. Guangong Province officials assert that the dispute was settled by the CCP in 1949 with a survey of the boundary. However, conflicts over rights to exploit the trees on the hillslopes produced a Province-negotiated settlement in 1964 which gave the southern slopes of the Ling Xiao caves hill to Lam Po village 'in order to meet their need for wood for cooking and daily life'. The boundary was sited along the top of the hill. For the next two decades there appears to have been only very minor disagreements between the clans on either side of the boundary.

Only in 1984 when tourism began to increase and generated a level of income far in excess of normal levels for Yang Chun did conflict again break out into the open. Competition for the tourist dollar resulted in continuing violence between the two communities.

Part of the problem lay in the application by the provincial government of the philosophy of 'Everyone dipping into the common pot' to justify its decision to grant development rights of Ling Xiao to Yang Chun rather than Wan Fau. Under this Maoist edict, the wealth derived for Wan Fau County from its marble deposits was expected to provide for the needs of all. But it disregarded the reality that, with the re-emergence of clans, redistribution of wealth was not occurring, that Lam Po had no marble deposits, and that Lam Po village was as poor a farming community as its counterpart village on the other side of the Ling Xiao caves hill. The clan members, supported by Wan Fau County officials, therefore established their own tourist enterprise to access the benefits from tourism in defiance of the provincial government and in opposition to Ling Xiao.

The situation was one of an imbalance of power between the actors. In our variation of Emerson's (1971) power–dependence relation framework, it can be stated that Ling Xiao had become dependent upon the income derived from tourism, was in control of the resources and therefore perceived the host–guest relationship in a positive light. It had the political support of the provincial government, a legal agreement verifying its rights to manage the tourism resources of Ling Xiao and Yu Xi, and a territorial presence manifested by the infrastructure the Yuang Chun County had developed at both sites, and the residence of villagers there. Lam Po, on the other hand, desired access to the tourist-generated income, derived some benefits from the limited access it had achieved informally, but lacking control over the resources, found itself in an inferior position with little capacity to change the situation. When its access to even a limited amount of income was denied by the actions of Yang Chun, as the disadvantaged actor Lam Po developed negative perceptions and attempted to redress the situation through violence in a vain attempt to gain control of the resources.

Conclusion

A Western analysis will draw upon theoretical models (in this case limited use was made of Weber's patrimonial rulership model and a variation of Emerson's power–dependence concept), as tools to assess the situation in Ling Xiao, whereas the Chinese sociologist will use a descriptive framework (the 'evil' of peasant ethics, the 'disease' of jealousy of peasants, and the 'source of ills' in corrupt, outmoded, feudal, clan values). It is the latter explanation which will be understood in the Chinese social, academic and political environments and will be applied to the task of seeking a solution. To that extent it is bureaucratically sound and culturally valid.

The Ling Xiao situation points in microcosm to the dilemma that confronts the Chinese leadership as it pursues national tourism development—how to achieve the right combination of traditional Chinese culture with socialist culture and modern culture, the latter necessarily incorporating Western values and systems which do not sit easily with the other two, to ensure political stability and the continuation of tourism. The bloodshed of Tiananmen Square demonstrated what can happen at a national level to tourism numbers. The violence at Ling Xiao demonstrated the impacts at the local level. As an industry, tourism has in numerous instances proved itself vulnerable to the shifting winds of political instability and unrest: China's experience is no exception.

References and bibliography

Ap, John (1992) 'Residents' perceptions on tourism impacts', *Annals of Tourism Research*, 19(4): 665–691.

Britton, S. G. and Clarke, W. C. (Eds) (1987) 'Ambiguous alternative. Tourism in small developing states', University of the South Pacific, Suva.

Burns, J. P. and Rosen, S. (Eds) *Policy Conflicts in Post-Mao China*, Armant, New York.

Bystrzanowski, J. (Ed.) (1989), 'Tourism a factor of change: a socio-cultural study', European Coordination Center for Research and Documentation in Social Sciences, Vienna.

Chinese Academy of Social Sciences (1989–90) 'Project on social development and social indicators. Social development of the provinces, municipalities and autonomous regions of China: comparison and assessment', *China Sociology and Anthropology*, 22(2): 64–71.

Chow, W. S. (1988) 'Open policy and tourism between Guangdong and Hong Kong', *Annals of Tourism Research*, 15(2): 205–218.

Choy, Dexter J. L. and Gee, Chuck Y. (1983) 'Tourism in the PRC—five years after China opens its gates', *International Journal of Tourism Management*, 4(2): 116–119.

Cohen, Myron L. (1990) 'Lineage organization in northern China', *Journal of Asian Studies*, 4(3): 509–534.

Cohen, Myron L. (1992) 'Family management and family division in contemporary rural China', *The Chinese Quarterly*, 130: 357–377.

Dann, Graham and Cohen, Erik (1991) 'Sociology and tourism', *Annals of Tourism Research*, 18(1): 155–169.

Deng Xiaoping (1987) *The Selected Works of Deng Xiaoping 1975–1986*, Foreign Language Press, Beijing.

Emerson, R. (1971) 'Power–dependence relations', *American Sociological Review*, 27(1): 31–41.

Fei Xiatong (1989) 'Small towns: a re-exploration', *Chinese Sociology and Anthropology*, 22(1): 42–58.

Gao Di-chen and Zhang Guang-ri (1982) 'China's tourism: policy and practice', *International Journal of Tourism Management*, 4(2): 75–84.

Gee, Chuck Y. and Choy, Dexter J. L. (1982) 'The first China international travel conference', *Annals of Tourism Research*, 9(2): 267–269.

Graburn, Nelson N. H. and Jafari, Jafar (1991) 'Tourism social science', *Annals of Tourism Research*, 18(1): 1–11.

Guangdong Province Government (1964) 'Agreement between the Counties of Yang Chun and Wan Fau for the resources of Ling Xiao hill'.

Gaundong Province Government (1984) 'The Four Centralizations Agreement between the Counties of Yang Chun and Wan Fau on tourism development of Ling Xiao and Yu Xi scenic sites'.

Guangdong Province Government (1992) 'Edict on the management of the Ling Xiao and Yu Xi scenic sites'.

Guldin, Greg (1992) 'Anthropology by other names: the impact of Sino-Soviet friendship on the anthropological sciences in China', *Australian Journal of Chinese Affairs*, no. 27: 133–149.

Harding, Harry (1982) 'From China with disdain: new trends in the study of China', *Asian Survey*, 10: 934–958.

He Guangwei (1992) 'To further study Deng Xiaoping's theory on building socialism with Chinese character, in order to speed up tourism development', *Tourism Tribune*, 7(6): 3–4.

Hollander, Paul (1981) *Political Pilgrims*, Oxford University Press, New York.

Hoogveldt, A. M. H. (1986) *The Sociology of Developing Societies*, Macmillan Education, London.

Huan Shu-ping (1988) 'Developing ethnology in our country and what the construction of socialism needs', *China Sociology and Anthropology*, 21(1): 56–67.

Hudman, Lloyd E. and Hawkins, Donald, E. (1989) *Tourism in Contemporary Society*, Prentice Hall, Englewood Cliffs, NJ.

Judd, Ellen R. (1992) 'Land divided land united', *The China Quarterly*, no. 130: 338–356.

Kraus, Richard C. (1981) *Class Conflict in Chinese Society*, Columbia University Press, New York.

Levy, Marion (1966) *Modernization and the Structure of Societies*, Princeton University Press, Princeton, NJ.

Liang Heng and Shapiro, Helen (1985) 'Intellectual freedom in China: an update', a report of Asia Watch Committee, New York.

Mabogunje, A. L. (1980) *The Development Process: a Spatial Perspective*, Hutchinson, London.

McCormick, B. L. (1990) *Political Reform in Post-Mao China: Democracy and Bureaucracy in a Leninist State*, University of California Press, Berkeley, CA.

Meissner, Maurice (1986) *Mao's China and After. A History of the People's Republic*, Collier Macmillan, London.

Ming Yan (1989) 'New Chinese sociology 1979–1989', *Chinese Sociology and Anthropology*, 22(1): 3–29.

Nash, Dennison and Smith, Valene L. (1991) 'Anthropology and tourism', *Annals of Tourism Research*, 18(1): 12–25.

National Tourism Administration of the PRC, *The Yearbook of China Tourism Statistics 1986–1993*.

National Tourism Administration of the PRC (1992) 'China must speed up tourism development: Deng Xiaoping', *Tourism Tribune*, 7(6): 1–2.

Nunez, Theron (1977) 'Touristic studies in anthropological perspective', in Valene L. Smith (Ed.), *Hosts and Guests. The Anthropology of Tourism*, University of Pennsylvania Press, Pittsburg, PA, pp. 207–216.

Ogden, Suzanne (1982) 'China's social sciences: prospects for teaching and research in the 1980's', *Asian Survey*, 22(7): 581–608.

Ogden, Suzanne (1992) 'China's unresolved issues: politics, development and culture', Prentice Hall, Englewood Cliffs, NJ.

Oi, Jean (1989) *State and Peasant in Contemporary China: the Political Economy of Village Government*, University of California Press, Berkeley, CA.

Pang Shuqi and Qu Li Ping (1989–90) 'Preliminary study of the current structure of social classes and strata in China', *China Sociology and Anthropology*, 22(2): 5–20.

Pearce, Philip (1989) 'Social impacts of tourism', in *The Social, Cultural and Environmental Impacts of Tourism*, New South Wales Tourism Commission, Sydney.

People's Republic of China Government Integrated Task Force of the Development Research Institute (1987) 'Peasants, markets and the system innovate', *China Economic Research*, 1: 3–16.

People's Republic of China State Bureau of Statistics (1992) *Statistical Yearbook of China 1992*, Beijing.

Priester, K. (1989) 'The theory and management of tourism impacts', *Tourism Recreation Research*, 15: 15–22.

Pye, Lucian W. (1981) *The Dynamics of Chinese Politics*, Oelgeschlager, Gunn & Hain, Cambridge.

Pye, L. W. (1992) 'Social science theories in search of Chinese realities', *The China Quarterly*, 1161–1170.

Richter, Linda K. (1983) 'The political implications of Chinese tourism policy', *Annals of Tourism Research*, 10(4): 395–413.

Richter, Linda K. (1989) *The Politics of Tourism in Asia*, University of Hawaii Press, Honolulu.

Rose, Dan (1990) 'Living the ethnographic life', *Qualitative Research Methods*, Vol. 23, Sage Publications, Newbury Park.

Smith, Valene L. (Ed.) (1977) *Hosts and Guests: the Anthropology of Tourism*, University of Pennsylvania Press, Pittsburg, PA.

Terrill, Ross (1980) *Mao: a Biography*, Harper & Row, New York.

Uberoi, J. P. S. (1978) *Science and Culture*, Oxford University Press, Delhi.

Walder, A. (1986) *Communist Neo-traditionalism: Work and Authority in Chinese Industry*, University of California Press, Berkeley, CA.

Wilson, Amy A., Greenblatt, Sidney L. and Wilson, Richard W. (Eds) (1977) *Deviance and Social Control in Chinese Society*, Praeger, New York.

Wu Wenjun (1989) 'Social ills in China and their roots', *Chinese Sociology and Anthropology*, 22(1): 72–85.

Xu Tianqi and Ye Zhendong (1988–89) 'The inevitable trends and main channels of the transfer of China's agricultural labour', *China Sociology and Anthropology*, 21(2): 25–34.

Xu Xuequiang and Zhang Wenxian (1988–89) 'A preliminary study of the driving force behind rural urbanization in areas open to the outside world. A case study of four Guangdong counties', *Chinese Sociology and Anthropology*, 21(2): 35–51.

Yang Chun County Tourist Authority (1993) 'Tourist Map of Yang Chun'.

Yang Chun County Government (1992) 'Guide to Yang Chun'.

Newspaper articles

Legal Daily
8/8/89
—Clan conflict in Hunan Province is reprehensibly against rural social order

Ming Pao
9/2/93
—Hong Kong temporarily stops organizing tours to Ling Xiao
11/2/93
—The conflict at Ling Xiao due to Lam Po boundary being interlocked with Yung Chan's boundary

Sing Pao Daily News
8/2/93
—Because of a boundary dispute a tourist attraction was damaged
—Guns were fired, hand grenades were thrown, tourists were attacked
—Luckily nobody was hurt but Hong Kong tourists fainted

Sing Tao Daily
8/2/93
—Ling Xiao and Wan Fau fight for benefits. Hong Kong tourists in near miss
—Ling Xiao cave was blown up—looks like a deserted town
9/2/93
—Ling Xiao cave was 'robbed'. Allegation that plain clothes policemen were involved
10/2/93
—Wan Fau police provide assurance that no police involved in the explosions

South China Morning Post (SCMP)
9/2/93
—Guangdong tourist attraction destroyed
30/10/93
—Clan unrest in Hunan Province
4/12/93
—Agricultural reform in China
20/12/93
—Chen, K. The Pearl River Delta

Wah Kiu Yat Po
9/2/93
—Chu Sam Lam announces that the Province will investigate the Ling Xiao explosions incident